M|P|

Mander Portman Woodward

CW01668288

HEAP 2026

UNIVERSITY DEGREE COURSE OFFERS

The essential guide to winning your place at university

Brian Heap

56th edition

3303942974

HEAP 2026: UNIVERSITY DEGREE COURSE OFFERS

In order to ensure that *Heap 2026: University Degree Course Offers* retains its reputation as the definitive guide for students wishing to study at UK universities and other higher education institutions, dozens of questionnaires are distributed, months of research and analysis are undertaken, and painstaking data checking and proofing are carried out.

Every effort has been made to maintain absolute accuracy in providing course information and to ensure that the entire book is as up to date as possible. However, changes are constantly taking place in higher education, so it is important for readers to check carefully with prospectuses and websites before submitting their applications. The author, compilers and publishers cannot be held responsible for any inaccuracies in information supplied to them by third parties or contained in resources and websites listed in the book.

We hope you find this 56th edition useful, and would welcome your feedback as to how we can ensure the 57th edition is even better.

Author Brian Heap

This 56th edition published in 2025 by Trotman an imprint of Trotman Indigo Publishing Ltd,
18e Charles Street, Bath BA1 1HX
www.trotman.co.uk

A CIP record for this book is available from the British Library

ISBN 978 1 911724 50 6

The authorised representative in the EEA is Easy Access System Europe Oü (EAS), Mustamäe tee 50, 10621 Tallinn, Estonia.

Printed and bound in the UK by 4edge Ltd, Hockley, Essex.

To keep up to date with the latest news and updates and to access the online resources that accompany this book, use this QR code or visit **www.trotman.co.uk/pages/heap-online-resources**

QUOTES

'Trying to find a university with the right course? This is by far the best way to guide you. Who would think it's easier to find the right course in a book than it is online?'
Amazon reviewer

'The only book I buy annually. An essential and vital resource for anyone working in post-sixteen [education]. Provides everything you need to support students in their higher education choices as a careers adviser or leader.'
Vicky Woodings, Careers Leader, The Bourne Academy

'Our first stop for students sourcing university information and the courses they are interested in.'
Lorraine Durrands, Careers Co-ordinator, Kesteven & Grantham Girls' School

'An invaluable guide to UK degree entry requirements. My "go to" handbook when kick-starting the UCAS process.'
Susan Gower, Head of Year 9 and Careers, Croydon High School

'HEAP University Degree Course Offers *is simply "The Bible" for careers advisors and students alike.'*
Stephen King, MA (Lib), School Librarian and Careers Coordinator, The Duke of York's Royal Military School

'Degree Course Offers *is probably the UK's longest running and best known reference work on the subject.'*
Education Advisers Limited

'Invaluable – HEAP is my "go to" resource.'
Wendy Kerley, Freelance Careers Adviser

'A very useful starting point for exploration of degree courses. Supplements our UCAS programme and careers advice very effectively.'
Paul Meadway, Head of Careers, Hymers College

'If I only had the budget to buy one careers book, it would be HEAP. *Doing my job would be much harder without it!'*
Celia Golding, Careers Guidance Manager, Langley Grammar School

'Degree Course Offers *by Brian Heap – not to be missed. Invaluable.'*
Maidstone Grammar School

'Degree Course Offers *remains an essential component of our careers library, providing a quick reference to entry requirements and course specific tips for university applications.'*
Mid Kent College

'An excellent, inclusive and thorough guide which ALL careers libraries should include, not just schools with sixth forms and colleges. If I were forced to narrow down my choices of higher education materials to one resource, it would be this one.'
Ray Le Tarouilly, Careers Adviser, The Midlands Academies Trust

'There will always be many changes within the world of careers guidance, but one staple is that HEAP *will remain an essential part of my bookcase for years to come.'*
Kelly Spence, Group Careers and Employability Lead, Outcomes First Group

'An excellent one-stop shop for finding out information on different universities and courses.'
Oswestry School

'HEAP helps you make informed choices about university course offers.'
Angie Stone, Librarian, Pate's Grammar School

'We buy this book every year and use it all the time, it offers essential careers and higher education advice.'
Dr Beth Linklater, Director of Student Support, Queen Mary's College

'The students find it an invaluable resource.'
Rebecca Mockridge, Sixth Form Administrator, Queen's College Taunton

'Degree Course Offers *is my bible and I couldn't be without it ... it gives students focus and saves them time.'*
South Thames College

'A fantastic and invaluable resource for UCAS advisers, university applicants and their parents.'
Mark Collins, Head of Economics/Business & Careers, St Teresa's School

'Degree Course Offers ... *a really good resource.'*
www.sueatkinsparentingcoach.com

'The definitive guide to university degree course offers ... clearly laid out and remarkably easy to navigate ... should be stocked in every sixth form library.'
Teach Secondary, October

'Degree Course Offers ... *will keep aspirations realistic.'*
www.tes.com/new-teachers

'I would like to take this opportunity to congratulate you in maintaining the quality and currency of the information in your guide. We are aware of its wide range and its reputation for impartiality.'
University Senior Assistant Registrar

'The HEAP *guide is my most used careers tool in all of my 1:1 personal guidance interviews in years 9, 10, 11, 12 and 13. It's so easy for students to look at the university course listings and become inspired and curious; they then take photos of the pages listing the universities and courses they are interested in to do their own further research. It's also very useful for the older students in years 12 and 13 to easily create a list of universities that they can apply to around their A-level predicted grades. I use it so much that my copy that was new this academic year is already looking old and battered. I refer to it as my magic book and I couldn't do without it.'*
Tasha Walker, Careers Leader, Wilmington Grammar School for Boys

'An extremely useful guide ....'
Woodhouse Grove School

'I've been a UCAS adviser for most of the past 25 years and I've come to rely on HEAP *for clear guidance and up to date info.'*
Gabe Crisp, Aspire Co-ordinator, Worthing College

'It's a really quick way of getting an overview of the standard offer for a particular course or course type ... and is helpful in terms of advising both on offer conditions, but also when choosing A-level subjects for particular interests.'
Etta Searle, Careers Co-ordinator, Wyke 6th Form College

'Up-to-date information, easy to use and accurate.'
Kenneth Nolan, Careers adviser, Xaverian College

CONTENTS

About the author *ix*
About this book *x*

1 YOUR FIRST DECISIONS **1**
Section A: Choosing your course by school subjects 1
Section B: Choosing your course by career interests 4
Course Types and Differences 8
Sandwich Courses and Professional Placements 9
Degree Apprenticeship Courses 11
Mature Applicants 11
Modular Courses and Credit Accumulation and Transfer Schemes (CATS) 11
Foundation Degrees and Foundation Courses 12
Next Steps 12
Taking a Gap Year 13
Graduate Outcomes 13

2 UNIVERSITY CHOICE AND FINANCE **16**
Choosing Your University or College 16
Action Points 16
Finance: What Will It Cost and What Help Is There? 17
Information Sources 18

3 UNIVERSITIES AND ADMISSIONS **19**
Universities, Colleges and their Courses 19
Admissions Policies 19
Course and Admissions Profiles 20

4 APPLICATIONS **54**
Entry Requirements 54
Applications for University and College Courses through UCAS 54
Applications for Music Courses at Conservatoires 56
Applications for Teacher Training Courses 56
Applications for Degree Apprenticeship Courses 56
The UCAS Application 57
Applications to Oxbridge 59
Applications to the Russell Group 61
Applications to Irish Universities 61
Applications to Commonwealth Universities 62
Applications to American Universities 62
The Turing Scheme 62
And Finally ... Before You Send in Your Application 62
What to Do on Results Day ... and After 63

5 ADMISSIONS TESTS, SELECTION OF APPLICANTS AND INTERVIEWS 65
Admissions Tests 65
Degree Subject Examples of Universities and Colleges using Tests and Assessments 67
Selection of Applicants 84
Interviews 85
Multiple Mini Interviews (MMIs) 86

6 HOW TO USE THE SUBJECT TABLES 87
Course Offers Information 87
Degree Apprenticeships 91
Examples of Colleges Offering Courses in this Subject Field 91
Choosing Your Course 91
Admissions Information 92
Graduate Destinations and Employment 92
Other Degree Subjects for Consideration 92
Institution Abbreviations 93
Course Abbreviations 94

7 SUBJECT TABLES 106

8 INFORMATION FOR INTERNATIONAL STUDENTS 430
Applications and the Points-based Immigration System 430
Selection, Admission and Finance 430
University Information and Fees for International Undergraduates 431
British Overseas Territories Students 445

9 DIRECTORY OF UNIVERSITIES AND OTHER INSTITUTIONS OFFERING HIGHER EDUCATION COURSES 446
Section 1: Universities and University Colleges 446
Section 2: Specialist Colleges of Agriculture and Horticulture, Art, Dance, Drama, Fashion, Music and Health Sciences 449
Section 3: Further Education and Other Colleges Offering Higher Education Courses 451

APPENDICES
Appendix 1: UCAS 2026 Entry Tariff Points Tables 458
Appendix 2: International Qualifications 462
Appendix 3: Professional Associations 466
Appendix 4: Booklist and Useful Websites 473

Course Index 474

ABOUT THE AUTHOR

Brian Heap (1929–2024), was a prolific author and leading higher education expert. Brian's books and articles have helped countless students and careers advisors for more than half a century. We at Trotman were honoured to be his publisher, and are confident that his legacy will live on through his publications for many years to come.

Brian wrote, broadcast and advised on courses for much of his adult life. Dubbed 'the guru of university choice', Brian was the best-selling author of several key higher education publications and had extensive experience in guidance work in the fields of careers, degree courses and entry into higher education.

Brian also lectured and advised in many leading schools in the UK and in international schools throughout Europe, the Far and Middle East, and the USA. He was a founding member of the National Association of Careers and Guidance Teachers.

Deemed 'the most outstanding expert in his field' by commentators and writers alike, Brian Heap's commitment to higher education was unparalleled.

ABOUT THIS BOOK

For 56 years, ***University Degree Course Offers (Heap 2026)*** has been a first-stop reference for university and college applicants choosing their courses in higher education by providing information from official sources about how to choose courses and how admissions tutors select students.

University Degree Course Offers aims to provide the latest possible information from universities to help equip applicants to obtain a degree course place in a fiercely competitive applications process. This level of competition will make it essential for every applicant to research carefully courses and institutions.

Schools, colleges and students quite rightly focus on getting through examinations, particularly when employers and, more so, universities, require specific exam grades in a variety of subjects. But once out of the exam room, where to next? There are many students who restrict their applications to a small number of well-known universities. They must realise that in doing so they are very likely to receive rejections from all of them. Applicants must spread their choices across a wide range of institutions. There are also many students who limit their choice to their best subject, but in doing so miss out on some good alternatives.

How do applicants decide on a strategy to find a place on a degree course? There are more than 1,200 separate degree subjects and over 50,000 Joint and Combined Honours courses so how can applicants choose a course that is right for their futures? What can applicants do to find a course place and a university or college that is right for them, when there are so many of both? For the past 56 years, for hundreds of students, the answers have been in the next (nearly) 500 pages of this book.

University Degree Course Offers is again intended to help applicants find their way through these problems by providing the latest possible information about university course offers from official sources, and by giving guidance and information about:

- **Degree courses** – what Honours level courses involve, the range and differences between them, and what applicants need to consider when choosing and deciding on subjects and courses
- **Degree apprenticeships** – what courses are available in different subject areas
- **Universities and higher education colleges** – the range and differences between universities and colleges, and the questions applicants might ask when deciding where to study
- **Admissions information** for every university (listed in **Chapter 3**)
- **Target A-level grades/UCAS points offers** (listed in points order in the subject tables in **Chapter 7**) for 2026 entry to Honours degree courses in universities and colleges, with additional Appendix data for applicants with T-levels, Scottish Highers/Advanced Highers, the Advanced Welsh Baccalaureate – Skills Challenge Certificate, the International Baccalaureate Diploma, BTEC Level 3 National Extended Diploma, the Extended Project, Music examinations and Art and Design Foundation Studies qualifications
- **The UCAS application process** – what to do, when to do it and how to prepare the personal statement in the UCAS application
- **Your course** – how to choose by school subjects or career interests
- **Universities' and colleges' admissions policies** – how admissions tutors select students
- **Which universities, colleges and courses use admissions tests for entry**
- **Finance, fees and sources of help**

- **Graduate destinations data for each subject area**
- **Action after results day** – and what to do if your grades don't match your offer
- **Entry to UK universities and higher education colleges for international students**

University Degree Course Offers provides essential information for all students preparing to go into higher education in 2026, covering all stages of researching, planning, deciding and applying to courses and universities. To provide the latest possible information the book is compiled each year between October and March for publication in May and includes important data from the many universities and colleges.

Every effort is made to ensure the book is as up to date as possible. Nevertheless, the increased demand for places is expected to lead to offer changes during the 2025/26 application cycle, and after prospectuses have been published some institutions may also discontinue courses as a result of government cuts and the changes in tuition fees. It will be essential for applicants to check institutions' websites **frequently** to find out any changes in offers, course availability and requirements. If you have any queries, contact admissions staff without delay to find out the latest information as institutions, for many courses, will be looking for a very close, if not precise, match between their requirements and what you offer in your application, qualifications and grades.

University Degree Course Offers is your starting point for moving on into higher education and planning ahead. It will take you through all the stages in choosing the course and place of study that is right for you. Now go for it!

Trotman
February 2025

Every effort has been made to maintain absolute accuracy in providing course information and to ensure that the entire book is as up to date as possible. However, changes are constantly taking place in higher education, so it is important for readers to check carefully with prospectuses and websites before submitting their applications.

1 YOUR FIRST DECISIONS

The problem You and around 750,000 students (including over 150,000 from the EU and overseas) are applying for some 50,000 degree courses in the UK this year. You have a choice of about 150 main subject areas (most of which are listed in **Chapter 7**), as well as single, joint or combined courses, from over 300 universities and colleges.

The Choice It depends what you want. There are three types of degrees. 1. Academic courses, eg History, Anthropology, Geography and Philosophy. Don't worry about graduate employment yet; many occupations are open to you when you graduate and commence specialist training, eg law, accountancy, business. 2. Vocational courses, eg medical careers, engineering and hospitality management. Some courses have opportunities to spend part of your degree course in full-time employment with pay as part of the course. 3. Practical courses, eg Art and Design, Drama, Music and Sports Studies.

There are two possible options for choosing your degree course:

Many students want to follow a degree course by way of their favourite and best subject. See **Section A**. School subjects are listed along with other degree courses which have some similarities.

Section B lists careers that may appeal to you and the degree courses that are linked to them.

SECTION A

Choosing your course by school subjects

Accounting Accountancy, Accounting, Actuarial Mathematics, Banking and Finance, Business Studies (Finance), Economics, Finance Investment and Risk, Financial Mathematics, Financial Software Engineering, Management Sciences, Mathematics. See also **Section B**.

Ancient History Archaeology, Biblical Studies, Classical Greek, Classics and Classical Civilisation, Latin, Middle and Near Eastern Studies.

Arabic Arabic. See also **Languages** below.

Art and Design Art, Fine Art, Furniture Design, Graphic Design, Photography, Textile Design, Theatre Design, Three-Dimensional Design, Typography and Graphic Communication. See also **Section B**.

Bengali Bengali. See also **Languages** below.

Biblical Hebrew Hebrew, Religious Studies, Theology.

Biology Agricultural Sciences, Animal Behaviour, Animal Nursing, Audiology, Bioinformatics, Biological Sciences, Biology, Biomedical Sciences, Biotechnology, Dental Hygiene, Ecology and Conservation, Environmental Sciences, Genetics, Human Embryology, Infection and Immunity, Life Sciences, Medicine, Microbiology, Molecular Sciences, Natural Sciences, Operation Department Practice, Physiology, Plant Biology, Plant Science, Veterinary Science, Zoology. See also **Section B**.

Business Accounting, Banking, Business Management, Business Statistics, Computing, Economics, Entrepreneurship, Finance, Hospitality Management, Human Resource Management, Information Systems, Logistics, Management Sciences, Marketing, Mathematics, Publishing, Retail Management, Transport Management, Web Design and Development. See also **Section B**.

Chemistry Biochemistry, Cancer Biology, Chemical Engineering, Chemical Physics, Chemistry, Dentistry, Environmental Sciences, Fire Engineering, Forensic Sciences, Medicinal Chemistry, Medicine, Microbiology, Natural Sciences, Nutritional Biochemistry, Pharmacology, Pharmacy, Veterinary Science, Virology and Immunology. See also **Section B**.

Chinese Chinese. See also **Languages** below.

Classics and Classical Civilisation Ancient History, Archaeology, Classical Studies, Classics, Greek (Classical), Latin.

Computer Science Artificial Intelligence, Business Information Systems, Computer Engineering, Computer Science, Computing, Cybernetics, E-Commerce, Electronic Engineering, Games Technology, Intelligent Product Design, Multimedia Systems Engineering, Network Management and Security, Robotics, Software Engineering. See also **Section B**.

Dance Arts Management, Ballet Education, Choreography, Dance, Drama, Education, Music, Musical Theatre, Performance Management, Performing Arts, Sport and Exercise, Street Arts, Theatre and Performance, Theatre Arts, Writing Directing and Performance. See also **Section B**.

Design Technology Food Technology, Manufacturing Engineering, Product Design, Sport Equipment Design, Systems and Control. See also **Section B**.

Drama and Theatre Studies Acting, Community Drama, Costume Production, Creative Writing, Dance, Drama, Education Studies, English Comedy: Writing and Performance, International Theatre, Music, Performing Arts, Scenic Arts, Scriptwriting, Set Design, Stage Management, Theatre Arts, Theatre Practice. See also **Section B**.

Economics Accountancy, Banking, Business Administration, Business Economics, Business Studies, Development Studies, Economics, Estate Management, Finance, Management Science, Mathematics, Political Economy, Politics, Quantity Surveying, Sociology, Statistics.

Electronics Computing, Electronics, Engineering (Aeronautical, Aerospace, Communication, Computer, Software, Systems), Mechatronics, Medical Electronics, Multimedia Technology, Technology. See also **Section B**.

English Language and Literature Communication Studies, Comparative Literature, Creative Writing, Drama, Education, English Language, English Literature, Information and Library Studies/Management, Journalism, Linguistics, Media Writing, Philosophy, Publishing, Scottish Literature, Scriptwriting, Theatre Studies.

Environmental Sciences Biological Sciences, Biology, Earth Sciences, Ecology, Environment and Planning, Environmental Management, Environmental Sciences, Forestry, Geography, Geology, Land Management, Marine Biology, Meteorology, Oceanography, Outdoor Education, Plant Sciences, Sustainable Development, Wastes Management, Water Science, Wildlife Biology, Wildlife Conservation, Zoology.

French French, International Business Studies, International Hospitality Management, Law with French Law. See also **Languages** below.

Geography Development Studies, Earth Sciences, Environmental Policy, Environmental Sciences, Estate Management, Forestry, Geographical Information Science, Geography, Geology, Land Economy, Meteorology, Oceanography, Surveying, Town and Country Planning, Urban Studies, Water Science.

Geology Earth Sciences, Geography, Geology, Geophysical Sciences, Geosciences, Meteorology, Mining Engineering, Natural Sciences, Oceanography, Palaeontology and Evolution, Planetary Sciences, Water and Environmental Management. See also **Section B**.

German German, International Business Studies, International Hospitality Management, Law with German Law. See also **Languages** below.

Government/Politics Development Studies, Economics, Global Politics, Government, History, Human Rights, Industrial Relations, International Politics, Law, Peace Studies, Politics, Public Administration, Social and Political Science, Social Policy, Sociology, Strategic Studies, War Studies.

Gujarati Gujarati. See also **Languages** below.

History African Studies, American Studies, Ancient History, Archaeology, Art History, Classical Civilisations, Classical Studies, Education, Egyptology, Fashion and Dress History, History, International Relations, Law, Literature, Medieval Studies, Museum and Heritage Studies, Philosophy, Politics, Russian Studies, Scandinavian Studies, Scottish History, Social and Economic History, Theology and Religious Studies, Victorian Studies.

Italian Italian. See also **Languages** below.

Japanese Japanese. See also **Languages** below.

Languages Languages, Modern Languages, Translating and Interpreting. **NB** Apart from French and German – and Spanish for some universities – it is not usually necessary to have completed an A-level language course before studying the many languages (over 60) offered at degree level. Many universities provide opportunities to study a language in a wide range of degree courses. See also **The Turing Scheme** details in **Chapter 4**.

Law Criminal Justice, Criminology, European Business Law, Human Rights, International Business, International Relations, Law, Legal Studies, Police Sciences, Social Sciences, Sociology, Youth Justice. See also **Section B**.

Mathematics Accountancy, Actuarial Mathematics, Aeronautical Engineering, Astrophysics, Business Management, Chemical Engineering, Civil Engineering, Computational Science, Computer Systems Engineering, Control Systems Engineering, Cybernetics, Economics, Engineering Science, Ergonomics, Financial Mathematics, Further and Additional Mathematics, Geophysics, Management Science, Materials Science and Technology, Mechanical Engineering, Meteorology, Naval Architecture, Physics, Quantity Surveying, Statistics, Systems Analysis, Telecommunications.

Media Studies Advertising, Animation, Broadcasting, Communication Studies, Creative Writing, English, Film and Television Studies, Journalism, Mass Communication, Media courses, Media Culture and Society, Media Production, Media Technology, Multimedia, Photography, Publishing, Radio Production and Communication, Society Culture and Media, Translation Media and French/Spanish, Web and Broadcasting. See also **Section B**.

Modern Greek Greek. See also **Languages** above.

Modern Hebrew Hebrew. See also **Languages** above.

Music Audio and Music Production, Creative Music Technology, Education, Music, Music Broadcasting, Music Informatics, Music Management, Music Systems Engineering, Musical Theatre, Musician, Performance Arts, Popular and World Musics, Sonic Arts. See also **Section B**.

Persian Persian. See also **Languages** above.

Philosophy Classical Studies, Cultural Studies, Divinity, Educational Studies, Ethics, History of Ideas, History of Science, Law, Mathematics, Natural Sciences, Philosophy, Politics Philosophy and Economics, Psychology, Religious Studies, Social Sciences, Theology.

Physics Aeronautical Engineering, Architecture, Astronomy, Astrophysics, Automotive Engineering, Biomedical Engineering, Biophysics, Chemical Physics, Civil Engineering, Communications Engineering, Computer Science, Cybernetics, Education, Electrical/Electronic Engineering, Engineering Science, Ergonomics, Geophysics, Materials Science and Technology, Mechanical Engineering, Medical Physics, Meteorology, Nanotechnology, Naval Architecture, Oceanography, Optometry, Photonics, Planetary Science, Quantum Informatics, Radiography, Renewable Energy, Telecommunications Engineering.

Polish Polish. See also **Languages** above.

Portuguese Portuguese. See also **Languages** above.

Psychology Advertising, Animal Behaviour, Anthropology, Artificial Intelligence, Behavioural Science, Childhood Studies, Cognitive Science, Counselling Studies, Criminology, Education, Human Resource Management, Marketing, Neuroscience, Nursing, Politics, Psychology, Social Sciences, Sociology, Speech and Language Therapy. See also **Section B**.

Punjabi Punjabi. See also **Languages** above.

Religious Studies Abrahamic Religions (Christianity, Islam and Judaism), Anthropology, Archaeology, Biblical Studies, Christian Youth Work, Comparative Religion, Divinity, Education, Ethics, History of Art, International Relations, Islamic Studies, Jewish Studies, Philosophy, Psychology, Religious Studies, Social Policy, Theology.

Russian Russian. See also **Languages** above.

Spanish International Business Studies, International Hospitality Management, Latin American Studies, Spanish, Portuguese. See also **Languages** above.

Sport and Physical Education Chiropractic, Coaching Science, Community Sport Development, Dance Studies, Exercise and Health, Exercise Science, Fitness Science, Football Studies, Golf Studies, Osteopathy, Outdoor Pursuits, Physical Education, Physiotherapy, Sport and Exercise Science, Sport and Health, Sport Coaching, Sport Equipment Design, Sport Management, Sport Marketing, Teaching (Primary) (Secondary).

Statistics Actuarial Studies, Business Analysis, Business Studies, Informatics, Management Sciences, Statistics. See also **Mathematics** above and **Section B** Mathematics-related careers.

Turkish Turkish. See also **Languages** above.

Urdu Urdu. See also **Languages** above.

SECTION B

Choosing your course by career interests

Accountancy Accountancy, Accounting, Actuarial Science, Banking, Business Studies, Economics, Finance and Business, Finance and Investment, Financial Services, Management Science, Real Estate Management, Risk Management.

Actuarial Work Actuarial Mathematics, Actuarial Science, Actuarial Studies, Financial Mathematics, Risk Analysis and Insurance.

Agriculture Agri-Business, Agricultural Engineering, Agriculture, Animal Sciences, Aquaculture and Fishery Sciences, Conservation and Habitat Management, Countryside Management, Crop Science, Ecology, Environmental Science, Estate Management, Forestry, Horticulture, Landscape Management, Plant Sciences, Rural Resource Management, Soil Science, Wildlife Management.

Animal-related Careers Agricultural Sciences, Animal Behaviour and Welfare, Biological Sciences, Bioveterinary Science, Equine Management/Science/Studies, Veterinary Nursing, Veterinary Practice Management, Veterinary Science, Zoology.

Archaeology Ancient History, Anthropology, Archaeology, Bioarchaeology, Classical Civilisation and Classics, Egyptology, Geography, History, History of Art and Architecture, Viking Studies.

Architecture Architectural Design, Architectural Technology, Architecture, Building, Building Conservation, City and Regional Planning, Civil Engineering, Conservation and Restoration, Construction Engineering and Management, Interior Architecture, Stained Glass Restoration and Conservation, Structural Engineering.

Art and Design Advertising, Animation, Architecture, Art, Design, Digital Media Design, Education (Art), Fashion and Textiles, Fine Art, Games Art and Design, Glassware, Graphic Design, Illustration, Industrial Design, Jewellery, Landscape Architecture, Photography, Stained Glass, Three-Dimensional Design.

Astronomy Astronomy, Astrophysics, Mathematics, Natural Sciences, Planetary Geology, Physics, Quantum and Cosmological Physics, Space Science, Space Technology and Planetary Exploration.

Audiology Audiology, Education of the Deaf, Human Communication, Nursing, Speech and Language Therapy.

Banking/Insurance Accountancy, Actuarial Sciences, Banking, Business Studies, Economics, Financial Services, Insurance, Real Estate Management, Risk Management.

Biology Agricultural Sciences, Animal Sciences, Biochemistry, Biological Sciences, Biology, Biomedical Sciences, Biotechnology, Cell Biology, Ecology, Education, Environmental Biology, Environmental Sciences, Freshwater Science, Genetics, Immunology, Life Sciences, Marine Biology, Medical Biochemistry, Medicine, Microbiology, Molecular Biology, Natural Sciences, Oceanography, Pharmacy, Plant Science, Physiology, Wildlife Conservation, Zoology.

Book Publishing Advertising, Business Studies, Communications, Creative Writing, English Literature, Illustration, Journalism, Media Communication, Photography, Printing, Publishing, Science Communication, Web and Multimedia.

Brewing and Distilling Biochemistry, Brewing and Distilling, Chemistry, Food Science and Technology, Viticulture and Oenology.

Broadcasting Audio Video and Digital Broadcast Engineering, Broadcast Documentary, Broadcast Media, Broadcast Technology and Production, Digital Media, Electronic Engineering (Broadcast Systems), Film and TV Broadcasting, Media and Communications Studies, Media Production, Multimedia, Music Broadcasting, Outside Broadcast Technology, Radio Journalism, Television Studio Production, TV Production, Video and Broadcasting.

Business Accountancy, Advertising, Banking, Business Administration, Business Analysis, Business Studies, Business Systems, E-Commerce, Economics, Estate Management, European Business, Hospitality Management, Housing Management, Human Resource Management, Industrial Relations, Insurance, Logistics, Management Sciences, Marketing, Property Development, Public Relations, Publishing, Supply Chain Management, Transport Management, Tourism.

Cartography Geographic Information Systems, Geographical Information Science, Geography, Land Surveying.

Catering Consumer Studies, Culinary Arts Management, Dietetics, Food Science, Hospitality Management, International and Hospitality Business Management, Nutrition.

Chemistry Agricultural Science, Biochemistry, Botany, Ceramics, Chemical Engineering, Chemistry, Colour Chemistry, Education, Environmental Sciences, Geochemistry, Materials Science and Technology, Medical Chemistry, Nanotechnology, Natural Sciences, Pharmacology, Pharmacy, Physiology, Technologies (for example Food, Plastics).

Computing Artificial Intelligence, Bioinformatics, Business Computing, Business Studies, Computer Engineering, Computer Games Development, Computer Science, Computers, Electronics and Communications, Digital Forensics and System Security, Electronic Engineering, Games Design, Information and Communication Technology, Internet Computing, Mathematics, Multimedia Computing, Physics, Software Systems, Telecommunications, Virtual Reality Design.

Construction Architectural Technology, Architecture, Building Conservation, Building Services Engineering, Building Studies, Building Surveying, Civil Engineering, Construction Management, Fire Risk Engineering, Estate Management, General Practice Surveying, Land Surveying, Landscape Architecture, Quantity Surveying, Surveying, Town and Country Planning.

Dance Ballet Education, Choreography, Dance, Drama, Movement Studies, Performance/Performing Arts, Physical Education, Theatre Studies.

Dentistry Biochemistry, Dental Materials, Dental Technician, Dentistry, Equine Dentistry, Medicine, Nursing, Oral Health Sciences, Pharmacy.

Drama Dance, Drama, Education, Movement Studies, Musical Theatre, Scenic Arts, Teaching, Theatre Management.

Education Ballet Education, British Sign Language, Childhood Studies, Coach Education, Deaf Studies, Early Years Education, Education Studies, Education with QTS, Education without QTS, Music Education, Physical Education, Primary Education, Psychology, Secondary Education, Social Work, Special Educational Needs, Speech and Language Therapy, Sport and Exercise, Teaching, Technology for Teaching and Learning, Youth Studies.

Electronics Automotive Electronics, Avionics, Computer Systems, Computer Technology, Computing, Digital Electronics, Digital Media Technology, Electronic Design, Electronic Engineering, Electronics, Information Systems, Internet Engineering, Mechatronics, Medical Electronics, Motorsport Electronic Systems, Multimedia Computing, Software Development, Sound Engineering.

Engineering Engineering (including Aeronautical, Aerospace, Chemical, Civil, Computing, Control, Electrical, Electronic, Energy, Environmental, Food Process, Manufacturing, Mechanical, Motorsport, Nuclear, Product Design, Software, Telecommunications), Geology and Geotechnics, Horology, Mathematics, Physics.

Estate Management Architecture, Building, Civil Engineering, Economics, Estate Management, Forestry, Housing Studies, Landscape Architecture, Property Development, Real Estate Management, Town and Country Planning.

Food Science and Technology Biochemistry, Brewing and Distilling, Chemistry, Culinary Arts, Dietetics, Food and Consumer Studies, Food Safety Management, Food Science and Technology, Food Supply Chain Management, Fresh Produce Management, Hospitality and Food Management, Nutrition, Public Health Nutrition, Viticulture and Oenology.

Forestry Arboriculture, Biological Sciences, Countryside Management, Ecology, Environmental Science, Forestry, Horticulture, Plant Sciences, Rural Resource Management, Tropical Forestry, Urban Forestry.

Furniture Design Furniture Design, Furniture Production, History of Art and Design, Three-Dimensional Design, Timber Technology.

Geology Chemistry, Earth Sciences, Engineering (Civil, Minerals), Environmental Sciences, Geochemistry, Geography, Geology, Land Surveying, Oceanography, Soil Science.

Graphic Design Advertising, Graphic Design, Photography, Printing, Web Design.

Health and Safety Biomedical Informatics, Biomedical Sciences, Community and Health Studies, Environmental Health, Exercise and Health Science, Fire Science Engineering, Health and Social Care, Health Management, Health Promotion, Health Psychology, Health Sciences, Holistic Therapy, Nursing, Occupational Safety and Health, Paramedic Science, Public Health, Public Services Management. (See also **Medicine**.)

Horticulture Agriculture, Crop Science, Horticulture, Landscape Architecture, Plant Science, Soil Science.

Hospitality Business and Management, Culinary Arts Management, Events and Facilities Management, Food Science, Food Technology, Heritage Management, Hospitality Management, Human Resource Management, International Hospitality Management, Leisure Services Management, Licensed Retail Management, Spa Management, Travel and Tourism Management.

Housing Architecture, Estate Management, General Practice Surveying, Housing, Social Administration, Town and Country Planning.

Law Business Law, Commercial Law, Consumer Law, Criminal Justice, Criminology, European Law, Government and Politics, International History, Land Management, Law, Legal Studies, Politics, Sociology.

Leisure and Recreation Adventure Tourism, Airline and Airport Management, Business Travel and Tourism, Community Arts, Countryside Management, Dance, Drama, Event Management, Fitness Science, Hospitality Management, International Tourism Management, Leisure Management, Movement Studies, Music, Physical Education, Sport and Leisure Management, Sport Development, Sports Management, Theatre Studies, Travel and Tourism.

Library and Information Management Administration, Business Information Systems, Digital Media, Education Studies, Information and Communication Studies, Information and Library Studies, Information Management, Information Sciences and Technology, Management and Marketing, Media and Cultural Studies, Media Communications, Museum and Galleries Studies, Publishing.

Marketing Advertising, Business Studies, Consumer Science, E-Marketing, Health Promotion, International Business, Marketing, Psychology, Public Relations, Retail Management, Sports Development, Travel and Tourism.

Materials Science/Metallurgy Automotive Materials, Chemistry, Engineering, Glass Science and Technology, Materials Science and Technology, Mineral Surveying, Physics, Polymer Science, Sports Materials, Textile Science.

Mathematics Accountancy, Actuarial Science, Astronomy, Banking, Business Decision Mathematics, Business Studies, Computer Studies, Economics, Education, Engineering, Financial Mathematics, Mathematical Physics, Mathematics, Physics, Quantity Surveying, Statistics.

Media Advertising, Broadcasting, Communications, Computer Graphics, Creative Writing, Film/Video Production, Journalism, Media, Multimedia, Photography, Public Relations, Psychology, Visual Communication.

Medicine Anatomy, Biochemistry, Biological Sciences, Biomedical Sciences, Chiropractic, Dentistry, Genetics, Human Physiology, Immunology, Medical Engineering, Medical Sciences/Medicine, Nursing, Occupational Therapy, Orthoptics, Osteopathy, Pathology and Microbiology, Pharmacology, Pharmacy, Physiotherapy, Psychology, Radiography, Speech and Language Therapy, Sports Biomedicine, Virology.

Music Commercial Music, Creative Music Technology, Digital Music, Drama, Folk and Traditional Music, Music, Music Composition, Music Education, Music Industry Management, Music Performance, Music Production, Music Studies, Musical Theatre, Performance/Performing Arts, Popular Music, Sonic Arts, Sound and Multimedia Technology, Theatre Studies.

Nautical careers Marine Engineering, Marine Studies, Nautical Studies, Naval Architecture, Oceanography, Offshore Engineering, Ship Science.

Naval Architecture Boat Design, Marine Engineering, Marine Studies, Naval Architecture, Offshore Engineering, Ship Science, Yacht and Powercraft Design, Yacht Production.

Nursing Anatomy, Applied Biology, Biochemistry, Biological Sciences, Biology, Dentistry, Education, Environmental Health and Community Studies, Health Studies, Human Biology, Medicine, Midwifery, Nursing, Occupational Therapy, Orthoptics, Physiotherapy, Podiatry, Psychology, Radiography, Social Administration, Speech and Language Therapy, Veterinary Nursing. (See also **Medicine**.)

Nutrition Dietetics, Food Science and Technology, Health Promotion, Human Nutrition, Nursing, Nutrition, Sport and Fitness.

Occupational Therapy Art, General and Mental Nursing, Occupational Therapy, Orthoptics, Physiotherapy, Psychology, Social Sciences, Speech and Language Therapy.

Optometry Applied Physics, Optometry, Orthoptics, Physics.

Photography/Film/TV Animation, Communication Studies (some courses), Digital Video Design, Documentary Communications, Film and Media, Graphic Art, Media Studies, Moving Image, Multimedia, Photography.

Physics Applied Physics, Astronomy, Astrophysics, Avionics and Space Systems, Education, Electronics, Engineering (Civil, Electrical, Mechanical), Laser Physics, Mathematical Physics, Medical Instrumentation, Molecular Physics, Nanotechnology, Natural Sciences, Optometry, Physics, Planetary and Space Physics, Quantum and Cosmological Physics, Theoretical Physics.

Physiotherapy Chiropractic, Exercise Science, Nursing, Orthoptics, Osteopathy, Physical Education, Physiotherapy, Sport and Exercise, Sports Rehabilitation.

Production Technology Engineering (Manufacturing, Mechanical), Materials Science.

Property and Valuation Management Architecture, Building Surveying, Estate Agency, Property Investment and Finance, Property Management and Valuation, Quantity Surveying, Real Estate Management, Residential Property, Urban Land Economics.

Psychology Advertising, Animal Sciences, Anthropology, Applied Social Studies, Behavioural Science, Business, Cognitive Science, Criminology, Early Childhood Studies, Education, Human Resource Management, Human Sciences, Linguistics, Marketing, Neuroscience, Occupational Therapy, Psychology (Clinical, Developmental, Educational, Experimental, Forensic, Health, Occupational, Social, Sports), Psychosocial Sciences, Public Relations, Social Sciences, Sociology.

Public Administration Applied Social Studies, Business Studies, Public Administration, Public Policy Investment and Management, Public Services, Social Administration, Social Policy, Youth Studies.

Quantity Surveying Architecture, Building, Civil Engineering, Construction and Commercial Management, Environmental Construction Surveying, Surveying (Building, Land and Valuation), Surveying Technology.

Radiography Anatomy, Audiology, Biological Sciences, Clinical Photography, Diagnostic Imaging, Diagnostic Radiography, Digital Imaging, Imaging Science and Technology, Medical Imaging, Moving Image, Nursing, Orthoptics, Photography, Physics, Physiology, Physiotherapy, Radiography, Radiotherapy, Therapeutic Radiography.

Silversmithing/Jewellery Design Silversmithing and Jewellery, Silversmithing Goldsmithing and Jewellery, Silversmithing Metalwork and Jewellery, Three-Dimensional Design.

Social Work Abuse Studies, Applied Social Science, Community Work, Counselling Studies, Early Childhood Studies, Education, Health and Social Care, Human Rights, Journalism, Law, Nursing, Playwork, Politics and Government, Psychology, Public Administration, Religious Studies, Social Administration, Social Policy, Social Work, Sociology, Town and Country Planning, Youth Studies.

Speech and Language Therapy Audiology, Education (Special Education), Linguistics, Nursing, Occupational Therapy, Psychology, Radiography, Speech and Language Therapy.

Sport and Physical Education Coaching Sciences, Exercise Sciences, Fitness Science, Health and Fitness Management, Leisure and Recreation Management, Physical Education, Sport and Recreational Studies, Sport Journalism, Sports Psychology, Sports Science, Sports Studies.

Statistics Business Studies, Economics, Informatics, Mathematics, Operational Research, Population Sciences, Statistics.

Surveying Building Surveying, General Practice Surveying, Property Development, Quantity Surveying, Real Estate Management.

Technology Audio Technology, Dental Technology, Design Technology, Food Science and Technology, Football Technology, Logistics Technology, Medical Technology, Music Studio Technology, Paper Science, Polymer Science, Product Design Technology, Sports Technology, Technology for Teaching and Learning, Timber Technology.

Textile Design Applied Art and Design, Art, Clothing Studies, Fashion Design, Interior Design, Textile Design (Embroidery, Constructive Textiles, Printed Textiles), Textile Management.

Theatre Design Drama, Interior Design, Leisure and Recreational Studies, Theatre Design, Theatre Management, Theatre Studies.

Three-Dimensional Design Architecture, Industrial Design, Interior Design, Theatre Design, Three-Dimensional Design.

Town and Regional Planning Architecture, Architecture and Planning, City and Regional Planning, Environmental Planning, Estate Management, Geography, Housing, Land Economy, Planning and Development, Population Sciences, Property Planning and Development, Spatial Planning, Statistics, Sustainable Development, Town and Regional Planning, Transport Management, Urban and Regional Planning.

Transport Air Transport Engineering, Air Transport Operations, Air Transport with Pilot Training, Business Studies, Civil and Transportation Engineering, Cruise Operations Management, Industrial Design (Transport), Logistics, Planning with Transport, Supply Chain Management, Sustainable Transport Design, Town and Regional Planning, Urban Planning Design and Management.

Typography and Graphic Communication Design (Graphic and Typographic Design), Digital Graphics, Fine Art (Print and Digital Media), Graphic Communication and Typography, Graphic Design, Illustration, Illustration and Print, Printmaking, Publication Design, Publishing, Visual Communication.

Veterinary Agricultural Sciences, Agriculture, Anatomical Science, Animal Behaviour and Welfare, Animal Sciences, Bioveterinary Sciences, Equine Dentistry, Equine Science, Medicine, Pharmacology, Pharmacy, Veterinary Medicine, Veterinary Nursing, Veterinary Practice Management, Zoology.

COURSE TYPES AND DIFFERENCES

The options

You will then need to decide on the type of course you want to follow. The way in which Honours degree courses are arranged differs between institutions. For example, a subject might be offered as a single subject course (a Single Honours degree), or as a two-subject course (a Joint Honours degree), or as one of two, three or four subjects (a Combined Honours degree) or a Major/Minor degree (75% and 25% of each subject respectively).

A Bachelor of Arts (BA) does not necessarily indicate an arts or humanities course, likewise a Bachelor of Science degree (BSc) does not necessarily have a solely scientific or technical focus. Instead, there is much variation; for example, some Management or Marketing courses are BScs, and some Architecture courses are BAs while others are BScs.

Entry requirements

Courses in the same subject at different universities and colleges can have different subject requirements so it is important to check the acceptability of your GCE A-levels and GCSE subjects (or equivalent) for all your preferred courses. Specific GCE A-levels, and in some cases, GCSE subjects, may be stipulated. (See also **Chapter 6** and **Appendix 1** for information on T-levels, Scottish Highers/Advanced Highers, the Advanced Welsh Baccalaureate – Skills Challenge Certificate, the International Baccalaureate Diploma, BTEC Level 3 National Extended Diploma, the Extended Project, Music examinations and Art and Design Foundation Studies, and **Appendix 2** for international qualifications.)

SANDWICH COURSES AND PROFESSIONAL PLACEMENTS

The benefits

Media coverage on student debt and tuition fees highlights the importance of sandwich courses. Many vocational courses offer sandwich periods and placements of 6 or 12 months in which students spend time away from their university or college in industry, commerce or in the public sector as part of a four-year degree course. The advantages of these courses can be quite considerable. Not only may students receive an income from the company, but contacts made can lead to permanent employment on graduation.

Work-based learning (WBL) programmes

Some colleges also offer work-based learning programmes in which placements last a few weeks when students can gain experience of different careers.

Students report ...

'I was able to earn £15,000 during my year out and £4,000 during my three-month vacation with the same firm.' (**Bath** Engineering)

'There's really no other better way to find out what you want to do for your future career than having tried it for a year.' (**Aston** Human Resources Management)

'It was a welcome break in formal university education: I met some great people including students from other universities.' (**Kingston** Biochemistry)

'Having experienced a year in a working environment, I am more confident and more employable than students without this experience.' (**Aston** Business Studies)

'At Sanolfi in Toulouse, I learned to think on my feet – no two days were the same.' (**Aston** European Studies)

'I have seen how an organisation works at first-hand, learned how academic skills may be applied in a working environment, become proficient in the use of various software, acquired new skills in interpersonal relationships and communications and used my period away to realign my career perspectives.' (**Aston** European Studies)

'I was working alongside graduate employees and the firm offered me a job when I graduated.' (**Bath** Mathematics)

Employers, too, gain from having students ...

'We meet a lot of enthusiastic potential recruits who bring new ideas into the firm, and we can offer them commercially sponsored help for their final year project.'

'The quality of this student has remained high throughout the year. He will do well for his next employer, whoever that may be. However, I sincerely hope that it will be with us.'

University staff advise ...

'We refer to sandwich courses as professional placements, not "work experience" which is a phrase we reserve for short non-professional experiences, for example summer or pre-university jobs. The opportunity is available to all students but their success in gaining a good placement depends on academic ability.' (**Bath**)

'Where a placement year is optional, those who opt for it are more likely to be awarded a First or an Upper Second compared to those who don't, not because they are given more marks for doing it, but because they always seem to have added context and motivation for their final year.' (**Aston**)

When choosing your sandwich course, check with the university (a) that the institution will guarantee a list of employers, (b) whether placement experience counts towards the final degree result, (c) that placements are paid and (d) that placements are validated by professional bodies. Finally, once you start on the course, remember that your first-year academic performance will be taken into account by potential employers. Now read on!

WHAT DO EMPLOYERS REQUIRE WHEN CONSIDERING STUDENTS?

Aston (Biol) Successful second-year undergraduates; (Bus) Number of UCAS points, degree programme, any prior experience; (Eng) UCAS points scores and expected degree classification; (Mech Eng) Students interviewed and selected by the company according to student ability, what they are studying and specific needs of the job. **Bath** (Chem) 'Good students': Upper Second or above and non-international students (those without work visas); (Mech Elec Eng) Subject-based, eg electronics, aerospace, computing and electrical engineering; (Mech Eng) Good communication, IT and social skills; (Maths) Interest in positions of responsibility, teamwork, integrity, self-motivation, analytical ability, communication, recent work experience, knowledge of the company, desire to work for the company, predicted 2.1; (Phys) Many organisations have cut-offs regarding students' first-year performance (eg must be heading for a 2.1 although some require better than this), some need students to be particularly good in some areas (eg lab work, computer programming), many require UK nationality with minimum residency condition. **Brunel** Requirements not usually specified except for IT jobs since they need technical skills. **Cardiff Met** (Clsrm Asst) Disclosure and Barring Service (DBS) checks. **Kingston** (Bus Law) Theoretical knowledge and a stated interest in certain areas (eg finance, human resources, marketing, sales, IT), excellent communication skills, teamwork, ability to prioritise, time management and a professional attitude; (Sci) Grades are rarely mentioned: it's usually a specific module or course requirement undertaken by the students that they are looking for, as well as a good attitude, motivation, initiative: a good all-rounder. **Loughborough** (Civ Eng) Target specific courses.

WHAT ARE THE ADVANTAGES OF PLACEMENTS TO THE STUDENTS?

Aston (Biol) Many take jobs with their placement employers (eg NHS), gaining valuable research and clinical experience; (Bus) Graduate job offers, sponsorship through the final year of the course, gym membership, staff discounts; (Eng) Some students are fast-tracked into full-time employment and, in some cases, have been given higher starting salaries as a result of the placement with the company; (Mech Eng) Offers of full-time employment on graduation, bursaries for their final year of study, final year projects following placements, better class of degree. **Bath** (Chem) Sponsorships for final year project work, offers of full-time employment, PhD offers and work-to-study courses, industrial references, establishment of prizes; (Maths) Sponsorship in the second year, graduate employment, bonuses during placement, travel abroad during placement, sponsorship during final year; (Phys) Job offers on graduation, sponsored final year, improved study skills for final year, job market awareness, career decisions. **Bournemouth** All undergraduate full-time degrees offer students the opportunity to undertake work placements. The majority are paid and, in some cases, students may be eligible for financial support during their placement year. **Brunel** Higher percentage of students get Firsts, many students get a job offer from the placement provider, higher salaries often paid to sandwich course students, some students get exemptions from professional exams, eg ACCA, ACA and IMechE. **Cardiff Met** (Clsrm Asst) Good experience in team work, classroom experience, coaching, mentoring: decisions made whether or not to follow a teaching career. **Kingston** (Bus Law) Sponsorships fewer these days but students return with more confidence and maturity and better able to complete their final year; 70% receive job offers on completion of a successful placement; (Sci) Full-time employment on graduation and occasionally part-time work in the final year; many students are encouraged to write their final year dissertation while on placement and benefit from the company's support, subject matter and validation. **Liverpool** A year in industry can bring a number of benefits and positive impacts for students. There is strong evidence that placements are valuable in terms of enhancing academic skills, improving employment prospects and increasing an understanding of the world of work. It can also increase their social mobility and potential salary throughout their careers. **Loughborough** (Civ Eng) Most students are sponsored by their firms and perform better in their final examinations; (Prod Des) Final year bursary for some students, offer of employment by the sponsor and a final year design project for the sponsor.

DEGREE APPRENTICESHIP COURSES

An alternative route to studying for a degree is by way of a degree apprenticeship course. These courses are particularly suitable for those who have completed lower-level apprenticeships and wish to study further in order to advance their career; however, the qualifications are suitable for anyone. Degree apprenticeship courses combine a full degree with practical work. They are designed in partnership with employers – apprentices will be employed throughout and earning a wage, with part-time study taking place at a university. They can be completed to bachelor's or master's degree level and take between three and six years to complete, depending on the level of the course. Degree apprenticeships are only available in vocational subjects, with established subject requirements set for entry. Opportunities are currently available in sectors such as engineering, business management, financial services and within the construction and digital industries. Around 100 institutions currently offer higher and degree apprenticeships. For further information see www.prospects.ac.uk/jobs-and-work-experience/apprenticeships/degree-apprenticeships and www.ucas.com/apprenticeships.

MATURE APPLICANTS

There are a great many mature students following first degree courses in UK universities and colleges. The following is a list of key points a group of mature students found useful in exploring and deciding on a university course.

- Check with your nearest university or college to find out about the courses they can offer, for example degrees, diplomas, full-time, part-time.
- Some institutions will require examination passes in some subjects, others may not.
- If entry requirements are an obstacle, prospective students should approach their local colleges for information on Access or distance-learning courses such as those offered by the National Extension College. These courses are fast-growing in number and popularity, offering adults an alternative route into higher education other than A-levels. They are usually developed jointly by colleges of further education and the local higher education institution.
- Demands of the course – how much time will be required for study? What are the assignments and the deadlines to be met? How is your work assessed – unseen examinations, continuous assessment, practicals?
- The demands on finance – cost of the course – loan needed – loss of earnings – drop in income if changing to another career – travel requirements – accommodation – need to work part-time for income?
- The availability and suitability of the course – geographical location – competition for places – where it will lead – student support services, for example childcare, library.
- What benefits will you derive? Fulfilment, transferable skills, social contacts, sense of achievement, enjoyment, self-esteem, career enhancement?
- Why would employers want to recruit you? Ability to adapt to the work scene, realistic and balanced approach, mature attitude to work?
- Why would employers not want to recruit you? Salary expectations, inability to fit in with younger colleagues, limited mobility? However, some employers particularly welcome older graduates: civil service, local authorities, health service, religious, charitable and voluntary organisations, teaching, social/probation work, careers work, housing.

MODULAR COURSES AND CREDIT ACCUMULATION AND TRANSFER SCHEMES (CATS)

Courses can also differ considerably not only in their content but in how they are organised. Many universities and colleges of higher education have modularised their courses which means you can choose modules of different subjects, and 'build' your course within specified 'pathways' with the help and approval of your course tutor. It also means that you are likely to be assessed after completing each module, rather than in your last year for all your previous years' learning. In almost every course the options and modules offered include some that reflect the research interests of individual members of staff. In some courses subsidiary subjects are available as minor courses alongside a Single Honours course. In an increasing number of courses these additional subjects include a foreign language, and the importance of this cannot be over-emphasised, as language skills are increasingly in demand by employers, and studying a language may also open up opportunities for further study abroad. A popular option in the past was the Erasmus+ programme (replaced by the new Turing Scheme, see **Chapter 4**), which enabled university students to apply for courses in Europe for periods of up to a year, with some of the courses being taught in English. Many institutions have introduced Credit Accumulation and Transfer Schemes (CATS). These allow students to be awarded credits for modules or units of study they have successfully completed which are accumulated towards a certificate, diploma or degree. They can also put their completed modules towards higher education study in other universities or colleges. Students wanting to transfer their credits should talk to the admissions office of the university they want to enter as there may be additional special subjects or module requirements for the degree they want to study.

FOUNDATION DEGREES AND FOUNDATION COURSES

Foundation courses, not be confused with Foundation degrees, normally require two years' full-time study, or longer for part-time study. They are also often taught in local colleges and may be taken part-time to allow students to continue to work. In comparison a Foundation degree can lead into the second or final year of related Honours degree courses when offered by the university validating the Foundation degree. Two-year Higher National Diplomas will also qualify for entry into the second or final year of degree courses. These, too, are often offered at universities as well as colleges of further education and partnership colleges linked to universities.

Part-time degrees and lifelong learning or distance learning courses are also often available and details of these can be found on university websites and in prospectuses. Some universities publish separate prospectuses for part-time courses.

NEXT STEPS

When choosing your course remember that one course is not better than another – it is just different. The best course for you is the one which best suits you. To give some indication of the differences between courses, see **Chapter 3**. After provisionally choosing your courses, read the prospectuses again carefully to be sure that you understand what is included in the three, four or more years of study. Each institution differs in its course content even though the course titles may be the same and courses differ in other ways, for example:

- methods of assessment (eg unseen examinations, continuous assessment, project work, dissertations)
- contact time with tutors
- how they are taught (for example, frequency and size of lectures, seminars)
- practicals; field work requirements
- library, computing, laboratory and studio facilities
- amount of free study time available.

These are useful points of comparison between courses in different institutions when you are on an Open Day visit or making final course choices. Other important factors to consider when comparing courses include the availability of opportunities for studying and working abroad during your course, professional body accreditation of courses leading to certain professional careers (see **Appendix 3**), and the career destinations of previous graduates.

Once you have chosen your course subject(s) and the type of course you want to follow, the next step is to find out about the universities and colleges offering courses in your subject area, how much a higher education course will cost you and what financial help is available. The next chapter, **University Choice and Finance**, provides information to help you do this.

TAKING A GAP YEAR

Choosing your course is the first decision you need to make, the second is choosing your university and then, for an increasing number, the third is deciding whether or not to take a gap year. But there lies the problem. Because of the very large number of things to do and places to go, you'll find that you almost need a gap year to choose the right one!

Planning ahead is important but, in the end, bear in mind that you might be overtaken by events, not least in failing to get the grades you need for a place on the course or at the university you were counting on. This could mean repeating A-levels and re-applying, which in turn could mean waiting for interviews and offers and deferring the start of your 'gap'.

Once you have decided to go, however, it's a question of whether you will go under your own steam or through a gap year agency. Unless you are streetwise, or preferably 'world wise', then an agency offers several advantages. Some agencies may cover a broad field of opportunities while others will focus on a specific region and activity, such as the African Conservation Experience, offering animal and plant conservation work in game and nature reserves in southern Africa.

When making the choice, some students will always prefer a 'do-it-yourself' arrangement. However, there are many advantages to going through specialist agencies. Not only can they offer a choice of destinations and opportunities but also they can provide a lot of essential and helpful advice before your departure on issues such as health precautions and insurance. Support is also available in the case of accidents or illnesses when a link can be established between the agency and parents.

Finally, in order to enhance your next university or college application, applying for a job for the year could be an even better option than spending a year travelling. Not only will it provide you with some financial security but it will also introduce you to the world of work, which could be more challenging than the Inca Trail!

GRADUATE OUTCOMES

Graduate Outcomes is a survey produced by the Higher Education Statistics Agency (HESA). The survey replaced the Destinations of Leavers from Higher Education (DLHE) survey in 2020. Graduates are asked to take part in the survey 15 months after graduation, with the aim of helping current and future students gain an insight into career destinations and development. Results of the 2021/22 survey can be obtained from www.graduateoutcomes.ac.uk.

The table on pages 14–15 shows the destinations of graduates by the subject they studied. Details are given of the total number of graduates surveyed whose destinations have been recorded – not the total number who graduated in that subject. Employment figures relate to those in permanent paid employment after 15 months in a variety of occupations not necessarily related to their degree subject. 'Further study' includes research into a subject-related field, higher degrees, private study or, alternatively, career training involving work and further study.

GRADUATE OUTCOMES BY SUBJECT AREA OF DEGREE AND ACTIVITY

NB When viewing percentages in this table, please note that percentage calculations exclude unknown values.

Subject area of degree	Full-time employment	Part-time employment	Unknown pattern of employment	Voluntary or unpaid work
Agriculture, food & related subjects	58%	14%	0%	2%
Architecture, building & planning	71%	6%	0%	1%
Biological & sport sciences	51%	11%	0%	2%
Business & management	66%	8%	1%	1%
Computing	64%	9%	1%	1%
Design, creative & performing arts	46%	27%	1%	2%
Education & teaching	70%	10%	0%	1%
Engineering & technology	69%	5%	0%	0%
Geography, earth & environmental studies	63%	7%	0%	1%
Historical, philosophical & religious studies	48%	12%	0%	2%
Languages & area studies	49%	15%	0%	1%
Law	61%	6%	0%	1%
Mathematical sciences	60%	5%	0%	1%
Medicine & dentistry	69%	7%	0%	1%
Media, journalism & communications	62%	15%	1%	1%
Physical sciences	55%	6%	0%	1%
Psychology	53%	12%	0%	2%
Social sciences	60%	9%	0%	1%
Subjects allied to medicine	63%	12%	0%	1%
Veterinary science	79%	6%	0%	0%

Employment and further study	Full-time further study	Part-time further study	Other including travel, caring for someone or retired	Unemployed	Total with known outcomes
8%	5%	0%	7%	5%	100%
10%	2%	0%	4%	4%	100%
11%	12%	0%	5%	6%	100%
9%	3%	0%	6%	6%	100%
9%	4%	1%	4%	8%	100%
9%	3%	0%	6%	7%	100%
8%	2%	0%	5%	3%	100%
8%	6%	0%	5%	6%	100%
8%	10%	0%	5%	5%	100%
12%	11%	1%	9%	5%	100%
11%	8%	1%	8%	6%	100%
12%	7%	1%	6%	6%	100%
11%	12%	1%	5%	7%	100%
13%	6%	0%	3%	2%	100%
6%	3%	0%	5%	7%	100%
10%	15%	0%	6%	6%	100%
14%	6%	1%	7%	5%	100%
11%	6%	0%	6%	5%	100%
10%	4%	0%	7%	3%	100%
7%	2%	0%	4%	2%	100%

2 | UNIVERSITY CHOICE AND FINANCE

CHOOSING YOUR UNIVERSITY OR COLLEGE

The choice

You choose a holiday because of its location (noisy or quiet), the accommodation and the facilities. It's the same with universities or colleges – some are in or near a city, others are in quiet rural locations; some have good accommodation for students, some don't; some are easy to reach, others are at a distance. You may already know where some of the very popular universities are located, others you have no idea! Don't let that put you off. Find out where they are.

So once you have chosen your degree subject, find out as much as you can about the universities or colleges offering it; attend open days and talk to the students, particularly those taking your choice of degree – they will tell you the good and not so good points about the university and the course. Institutions always arrange open days, although you can also walk onto the campuses for a look around at any time without prior arrangement.

ACTION POINTS

Before deciding on your preferred universities and courses, check out the following points.

Teaching staff

How do the students react to their tutors? Do staff have a flair and enthusiasm for their subject? Are they approachable? Do they mark students' work regularly and give helpful feedback helpful, or are students left to get on with their own work with very little direction? What are the research interests of the staff?

Teaching styles

How will you be taught, for example, lectures, seminars, tutorials? Are lectures popular? If not, why not? How much online learning will you have? How much time will you be expected to work on your own? If there are field courses, how often are they arranged and are they compulsory? How much will they cost?

Facilities

Are the facilities of a high standard and easily available? Is the laboratory equipment 'state of the art' or just adequate? Are the libraries well-stocked with software packages, books and journals? What are the computing facilities? Is there plenty of space to study or do workspaces become overcrowded? Do students have to pay for any materials?

New students

Are there induction courses for new students? What student services and facilities are available? Is it possible to buy second-hand copies of set books?

Work placements

Are work placements an optional or compulsory part of the course? Who arranges them? Are the placements popular? Do they count towards your degree? Are work placements paid? How long are they?

Transferable skills

Transferable skills are now regarded as important by all future employers. Does the department provide training in communication skills, teamwork, time-management and information technology as part of the degree course?

Accommodation

How easy is it to find accommodation? Where are the halls of residence? Are they conveniently located for libraries and lecture theatres? Are they self-catering? Alternatively, what is the cost of meals in the university refectory? Which types of student accommodation are the most popular? What is the annual cost of accommodation? If there is more than one campus, is a shuttle-bus service provided?

Costs

Find out the costs of materials, accommodation and travel in addition to tuition fees (see below) and your own personal needs. What are the opportunities for earning money, on or off campus? Does the department or faculty have any rules about part-time employment?

Useful resources

www.theguardian.com/education/universityguide
www.timeshighereducation.com/world-university-rankings
www.thecompleteuniversityguide.co.uk
www.ucas.com
The Times & the Sunday Times Good University Guide
A Guide to Uni Life, Lucy Tobin (Trotman)

FINANCE: WHAT WILL IT COST AND WHAT HELP IS THERE?

Tuition fees and other costs

Tuition fees are charged for degree courses in England, Wales and Northern Ireland. Precise details of the level of the tuition fee to be charged will appear on each university and college website, since levels may vary. The maximum fee currently set for English and Welsh institutions is £9,535 per year (for accelerated degrees, universities in England can charge annual fees of £11,440); in Northern Ireland it is £4,855 for their home students, but £9,535 for students from elsewhere in the UK. Eligible students in Scotland pay £1,820 which is covered by the Student Awards Agency for Scotland (SAAS); other UK students pay the full fee of £9,535 in Scottish universities.

Tuition fee loans are available and are repaid once the student has graduated and is earning above a certain threshold; currently these are £25,000 for students from England, £27,295 for students from Wales, £31,395 for students from Scotland and £24,990 for students from Northern Ireland.

Students also face additional costs. University accommodation is usually the highest single cost in a typically weekly budget and varies between universities. On top of this, there are personal living costs, and possibly travel expenses. Certain courses will also require students to pay for special equipment, particularly for courses of a practical nature such as Art, Architecture and Music.

Means-tested maintenance loans are available for students to help with living costs. Details are available from local authorities and university websites. Disabled Students' Allowances (DSAs) (non-repayable) are also available to those who live in England, to cover some of the extra costs because of mental health problems, physical disabilities, long-term illness or learning difficulties, for example dyslexia or dyspraxia. These allowances come on top of any other student finance and do not depend on household income. (See www.gov.uk/disabled-students-allowance-dsa.)

University scholarships These are usually merit-based and are often competitive, although some universities offer valuable scholarships to new entrants who have achieved top grades at A-level. Scholarships vary considerably and are often subject-specific, offered through faculties or departments, so check the availability of any awards with the subject departmental head. Additionally, there are often music, choral and organ awards, and scholarships and bursaries for sporting achievement. Entry scholarships are offered by several universities which normally stipulate that the applicant must place the university as their first choice and achieve the specified high grades. Changes in bursaries and scholarships take place every year so it is important to check university and college websites. See also www.thecompleteuniversityguide.co.uk.

University bursaries These are usually paid in cases of financial need: all universities charging course fees are obliged to offer some bursaries to students from lower-income families. The term 'bursary' is usually used to denote an award to students requiring financial assistance or who are disadvantaged in various ways. Universities are committed to fair access to all students from lower income backgrounds, and individual universities and colleges have bursaries, trust funds and sponsorships for those students, although reports suggest that many such students fail to claim the money due to them. These non-repayable awards are linked to the student's family income and vary between universities. See also www.thecompleteuniversityguide.co.uk.

Useful websites

Students from England www.gov.uk/student-finance
Students from Scotland www.saas.gov.uk
Students from Wales www.studentfinancewales.co.uk
Students from Northern Ireland www.studentfinanceni.co.uk
www.thestudentroom.co.uk/student-finance

For comprehensive finance information see the useful websites above and other sources listed in **Appendix 4**.

INFORMATION SOURCES

Prospectuses, websites and open days are key sources of the information you need to help you decide where to study. **Chapter 9** provides a directory of institutions, with full contact details, for you to use in your research. Other sources of information include the books and websites listed in **Appendix 4**, the professional associations listed in **Appendix 3**, and the websites given in the subject tables in **Chapter 7**. It is important to take time to find out as much as you can about your preferred universities, colleges and courses, and to explore their similarities and differences. The following chapter, **Universities and Admissions**, gives you information about the types of courses offered by each university and how they are organised. This is important information that you need to know when choosing your university or college because those factors affect, for example, the amount of choice you have in what you study, and the opportunities you have for sandwich placements (see **Chapter 1**). You therefore need to read **Chapter 3** to give you an insight into universities so that you can find the one that is right for you.

3 UNIVERSITIES AND ADMISSIONS

UNIVERSITIES, COLLEGES AND THEIR COURSES

Choosing a degree subject is one step of the way to higher education (see **Chapter 1**), choosing a university or college is the next stage (see **Chapters 2** and **9**). However, in addition to such features as location, entry requirements, accommodation, students' facilities and the subjects offered, many universities differ in the way they organise and teach their courses. The course profiles which follow aim to identify the main course features of each of the institutions and to provide some brief notes about the types of courses they offer and how they differ.

Although universities and colleges have their own distinct identities and course characteristics, they have many similarities. Apart from full-time and sandwich courses, one-year Foundation courses are also offered in many subjects which can help the student to either convert or build on existing qualifications to enable them to start an Honours degree programme. All universities and colleges also offer one-year international Foundation courses for overseas students to provide a preliminary introduction to courses and often to provide English language tuition.

ADMISSIONS POLICIES

Although the UCAS application process is standard for all undergraduate Honours degree courses (see **Chapter 4**) the admissions policies adopted by individual departments in universities and colleges often differ, and will depend on the popularity of the course and the quality of applicants.

Mature students (defined as those aged over 21 on entry) are often interviewed. Normal published offers may not apply to mature students. In all institutions certain courses require Disclosure and Barring Service (DBS) checks or medical examinations; students should check these requirements before applying for courses.

The acceptance of deferred entry varies, depending on the chosen course, and many admissions tutors ask that the intention to take a Gap Year be included on the application if firm arrangements have been made.

Several universities and colleges advise that if a student fails to achieve the grades required for an offer, they may still be awarded a place; however, they may receive a changed offer for an alternative course. Applicants are strongly advised to be wary of such offers, unless the course is similar to the original course choice.

Applicants for places at popular universities or for popular courses cannot assume that they will receive an offer even if their predicted grades are the same or higher than a stated standard offer. Even though the government has removed the cap on the number of places that universities in England are able to offer, meaning that they can admit an unlimited number of home undergraduates for most courses, not every institution has adopted these reforms.

All institutions have a number of schemes in place to enable admissions tutors to identify and make offers to applicants who, for example, may have had their education affected by circumstances outside their control. A major initiative is Widening Participation in which various schemes can assist school and college students in getting into university. These programmes focus on specific groups of students and communities including:

- students from low participation areas
- low-performing schools and colleges or those without a strong history of progression to higher education
- students with disabilities
- people living in deprived geographical areas, including deprived rural areas

- students from black or ethnic minority backgrounds
- students from the lower socio-economic groups 4–8 including mature learners
- students requiring financial assistance or who are disadvantaged in various ways
- families with little or no experience of higher education
- students from homes with low household incomes
- students returning to study after a period of time spent away.

Applicants are strongly advised to check prospectuses and websites for up-to-date information on admissions and, in particular, on alternative qualifications to A-levels as well as any entrance test to be taken (see also **Chapter 5**). Applicants whose first language is not English should refer to **Chapter 8** for details of the English Language entry requirements.

The following information provides a selection of relevant aspects of admissions policies and practice for the institutions listed.

COURSE AND ADMISSIONS PROFILES

Aberdeen One of the oldest universities in the UK, based on two campuses in Old Aberdeen and Foresterhill, as well as a dedicated overseas campus in Qatar. Students applying for the MA degree in Arts and Social Sciences are admitted to a degree rather than a subject, selecting from a range of courses in the first year, leading up to the final choice of subject and Honours course in the fourth year. The BSc degree is also flexible but within the Science framework. Engineering students follow a common core course in Years 1 and 2, specialising in Year 3. There is less flexibility, however, in some vocational courses such as Primary Education, Law, Medicine and Dentistry. For some degree programmes, highly qualified applicants may be admitted to the second year of the course. Courses also include Divinity and Theology, Music, Life Sciences, Medical Sciences and Business.

In personal statements and the referees' reports, selectors look for evidence of subject knowledge and understanding, commitment, motivation and responsibility, and the ability to cope with a university education. Almost all degrees make unconditional offers, which, in the Scottish university tradition, admit students to study their specific subject within its broader subject area, for example Engineering. The University also makes contextual offers; information on these can be found on the 'Widening access criteria' page of the University's website.

Abertay A city centre university in Dundee. Courses have a strong vocational bias and are offered in the Schools of Applied Sciences; Business, Law and Social Sciences; and Design and Informatics (its undergraduate video games design courses are ranked inside the top twenty-five in the world by the Princeton Review 2024).

Only a small number of courses require applicants to be interviewed. Applicants for the Computer Arts degree are required to provide a portfolio of artworks. The University can make contextual offers to disadvantaged applicants. Most courses offer built-in placements providing valuable work experience opportunities. Make sure to check the website for the most up-to-date information before applying.

Aberystwyth The University has two campuses and multiple sites for research and agricultural activities, with the main Penglais Campus located on the north east side of the town. Single, Joint and major/minor Honours courses are offered on a modular basis. In Year 1 core topics related to the chosen subject are studied alongside optional subjects. This arrangement allows some flexibility for change when choosing final degree subjects in Years 2 and 3 provided appropriate pathways and module prerequisites are followed. Some students take a year in industry or commerce between Years 2 and 3.

All offers are made on the basis of academic criteria, and personal statements and references are important. Offers will be made predominantly on the basis of the application form but interviews are required for some subjects. Candidates will not normally be interviewed unless there are special reasons for doing so, e.g. the candidate has been away from study for a long time. All those receiving an offer will be invited to visit the University and their chosen academic department.

Anglia Ruskin The University has campuses in Cambridge, Chelmsford, Peterborough and Writtle. Courses are modular which enables students to choose from a range of topics in addition to the compulsory subject core modules. Courses are delivered by four Faculties: Arts, Humanities, Education and Social Sciences; Business and Law; Health, Medicine and Social Care; Science and Engineering. Many programmes have a strong vocational focus, with a focus on employability, and opportunities for placements and/or study abroad.

The University interviews all shortlisted applicants for Medicine, Midwifery, Nursing, Occupational Therapy, Operating Department Practice, Paramedic Science, Physician Associate, Physiotherapy and Social Work. For details of entry to the School of Medicine, see the University website.

Arden This private university offers a combination of careers-focused distance and blended learning degree courses, with nine campuses across London, Birmingham, Leeds, Manchester and overseas in Berlin. Blended learning degrees require students to spend two days a week at their chosen campus, as well as carrying out a minimum of 25 hours of self-guided study. Arden offers a wide range of undergraduate, postgraduate and degree apprenticeship courses in the Faculties of Business, Social Sciences and STEM.

There are several intake dates throughout the year. The University welcomes applicants who do not meet the academic requirements for their desired course but can evidence relevant work experience. Applicants with recognised prior learning from another institution may be considered for exemption from some modules.

Arts London University of the Arts London (UAL) is Europe's largest specialist art and design university, comprising six colleges: Camberwell College of Arts, Central Saint Martins, Chelsea College of Arts, London College of Communication, London College of Fashion and Wimbledon College of Arts. It is also home to the Creative Computing Institute; Decolonising Arts Institute; Fashion, Textiles and Technology Institute and the AKO Storytelling Institute. Together, these facilities offer a wealth of courses at pre-degree, undergraduate and postgraduate level in art, computing, design, fashion, media, communication and performing arts.

A wide range of qualifications are accepted, including A-Levels, T-Levels, BTEC Extended Diplomas, UAL Extended Diploma (or equivalent). Many students complete a pre-degree course to prepare for their first year of undergraduate study. The application process varies depending on the chosen course and whether the applicant is from the UK or overseas. Many courses require candidates to submit a portfolio of work and attend an interview as part of the selection process.

Aston A campus university in Birmingham city centre. The University offers modular courses in Single Honours degrees and Joint Honours (usually in related areas). Most degrees allow students to spend the third year on a one-year sandwich placement. Courses are taught in the Colleges of Business and Social Sciences, Engineering and Physical Sciences and Health and Life Sciences.

Offers are not normally made simply on the basis of UCAS points. Interviews are only used for medical school entry and in special cases, for example, mature students, or those with non-standard entry qualifications. BTEC awards are acceptable and a mix of BTEC and A-levels welcomed. High-achieving Level 3 Diploma students in relevant subjects will be considered. Key Skills will be taken into account but will not be included in offers; Access programmes are accepted.

Bangor A university situated in the small coastal city of Bangor, North Wales. The University's Colleges of Arts, Humanities and Social Sciences; Medicine and Health; and Science and Engineering offer a wide range of subjects. Students can choose to study Single or Joint Honours courses; some courses offer a four-year undergraduate degree e.g. MEnvSci, MSci, MArts, MEng. Almost all undergraduate degrees provide students with the opportunity to complete a work placement.

The University considers each application on its merit – assessing applicants' potential to succeed on and benefit from the course. It uses the UCAS Tariff when making offers in addition to programme-specific requirements. For a degree course, the points total should include at least two GCE A-levels or equivalent Level 3 qualifications (e.g. BTECs, Access, Irish Highers, International Baccalaureate, Welsh Baccalaureate, Scottish Advanced Highers and others). The University also welcomes applications from mature applicants, individuals with European qualifications and international applicants (subject to minimum English language requirements).

Bath The University is situated on a large campus on a hill above the city. It is well-known for its Sports Training Village (STV), which is equipped with Olympic-standard training facilities for swimming, athletics, shooting and bobsleigh. Courses in engineering, humanities, management, science and social science can be taken as Single and Combined Honours degrees composed of core units and optional units, allowing students some flexibility in shaping their courses. A central feature of all programmes is the opportunity to take a professional placement as part of the degree: this is usually taken as either one 12-month placement or two periods of six months.

Some departments interview promising applicants; those not receiving an offer can obtain feedback on the reasons for their rejection. Students are encouraged to take the Extended Project Qualification (EPQ), in addition to A-levels, and to provide details on their personal statement.

Bath Spa Bath Spa is comprised of three campuses located in and around the city: Newton Park, Locksbrook and Sion Hill. It offers a full complement of creative, cultural and humanities-based courses, alongside social sciences and sciences. Most courses – Single Honours awards, specialised awards and Combined Honours awards – are part of a flexible modular scheme with students taking up to six modules per year. The option to take a Professional Placement Year is available to undergraduate students of any discipline.

All eligible candidates for art and design and music and performing arts courses are invited to attend an interview or audition. Applicants with offers for subjects which do not require an audition or interview, and are not taught at a partner college, will be invited to an Applicant Visit Day. Gap years are acceptable for most courses.

Bedfordshire The campuses of Bedfordshire University are situated in Luton, Bedford, Milton Keynes, Putteridge Bury and at the internationally renowned Stoke Mandeville Hospital in Aylesbury. Degree courses place a strong focus on employability, and most courses provide students with the opportunity to undertake a year in industry.

The University offers advice and guidance to enquirers and applicants throughout the admissions process on its 'Help in Applying to the University' webpage. The University considers applicants with a wide range of Level 3 qualifications and will hold interviews and auditions for a number of courses.

Birmingham The University is situated on a large campus on the edge of the city centre, with an overseas campus located in Dubai. Single subject and Joint Honours courses are offered. In Joint Honours courses the two chosen subjects may have common ground or can be disparate, for example mathematics and a modern language. Some major/minor combinations are also possible. The modular system provides opportunities for students to study a subject outside their main degree. An International Foundation Year at the Birmingham International Academy is available for overseas students from 12-year secondary education systems.

Courses are academic and 75% of the personal statement should relate to why the applicant wants to study the subject for which they have applied. The Extended Project Qualification (EPQ) is accepted in addition to three A-levels with applicants being made an alternative offer of one grade lower plus the EPQ in addition to the standard offer. The University now has a standard overall IB points requirement of 32 points for every course (excluding liberal arts and natural sciences) and makes offers relating to the higher level subject scores. Gap years are acceptable and should be mentioned on the UCAS application or as soon as arrangements have been made.

Birmingham (UC) Situated in the heart of the UK's second largest city, University College Birmingham offers undergraduate, postgraduate and Higher Apprenticeship courses, many of which are awarded and accredited by the University of Warwick. The University College specialises in vocational courses, preparing students for industry by providing them with career-focused education and training. Courses include national and international placement opportunities, and international study-abroad programmes are available with partner universities in Australia, China, Malaysia, Thailand and the United States.

Interviews are required for nursing, midwifery, and healthcare courses. Students should complete a direct application if they wish to apply only to Birmingham UC; this will be submitted to UCAS on their behalf. The University College offers support workshops for applicants unfamiliar with the UCAS process; more information is available on its 'Undergraduate Application' webpage.

Birmingham City Courses are offered on two main campuses and additional sites throughout the city. Many courses have a vocational focus and include sandwich placements. Music and acting courses are offered through the Royal Birmingham Conservatoire. There is also an extensive International Exchange Programme, with many courses abroad being taught in English.

Some applicants will be called to interview and others invited to the department before an offer is made. If the required grades of an offer are not achieved it may still be possible to be accepted onto a course. Deferred entry can be arranged. Students with offers will have the opportunity to attend an Offer Holder Day.

Birmingham Newman The University is comprised of a small campus in a residential area eight miles from the city centre. A full range of full-time and part-time degree courses can be chosen with a focus on Initial Teacher Training qualifications. Small classes mean that students receive personalised attention and assistance from academic staff.

Applicants are advised to submit an accurate and well-presented application. Personal statements are applicants' chance to stand out, show their qualities and demonstrate what they can bring to the University. Entry requirements are based on the UCAS tariff.

Bishop Grosseteste A single-site university campus close to Lincoln city centre with consistently high rates of student satisfaction. It has a strong reputation in primary education courses but also offers a varied selection of subjects at Foundation and Single Honours degree as well as a very large number of joint degrees in subject areas such as psychology, sport and the creative arts. Employability is central to all courses with most incorporating work placements and live projects.

Candidates are advised to attend an Open Day prior to applying. Applicant days are held for students who have applied for a non-teaching course or a course that does not require an interview.

Bournemouth A university with two main campuses and several other sites located in and around the coastal town of Bournemouth. The University has a strong focus on employability and offers a range of undergraduate degrees leading to BA, BSc and LLB. Courses are designed with direct input from employers, every undergraduate student has the opportunity to do a placement (including opportunities to work and study abroad), and a number of courses are accredited by respected industry bodies. The university offers subjects in all aspects of management, media and communication, science and technology and health and social sciences.

Academic qualifications are an important part of the application, but this is not the only factor Bournemouth University may take into account when assessing applications. Each application is considered on an individual basis, with a range of contextual factors taken into account. Additional study may be valuable for breadth of study, and the university will look at a range of qualifications and subjects, including vocational qualifications.

Bournemouth Arts Based on a single campus in the town of Poole, Arts University Bournemouth specialises in arts, performance, design and media courses. The majority of courses offer industry placements and live briefs within the course. AUB courses are designed to prepare students for the creative industries.

The University interviews the majority of applicants who meet or potentially will meet entry requirements or invites them to a post-offer Applicant Day. All undergraduate courses (excluding BA Architecture) require a minimum range of 112–120 UCAS Tariff points. There is a selection process which is based on each applicant's UCAS application, qualifications and an electronic portfolio.

BPP A private university with study centres located in key business locations throughout England, BPP University was the UK's first publicly owned company to be awarded degree-awarding powers. In collaboration with businesses and industry bodies from their specialist areas, the University has developed a wide range of undergraduate and postgraduate degree courses, professional qualifications, specialised CPD courses and apprenticeships. Courses focus on business and the professions covering business, law, accountancy, psychology and health subjects. A variety of placement options are available to students.

A range of qualifications will be considered; some courses require applicants to attend an interview. Applicants must meet the minimum entry requirements to gain admission; applicants who can evidence prior learning may seek advanced admission with exemption from parts of the programme.

Bradford A city centre university with high-tech learning environments including its motion capture studio and Bloomberg Trading Room. Honours degree courses are offered, many of which are vocational, leading to professional accreditation, and include sandwich placements in industry and commerce. Subjects are taught in the Faculties of Engineering and Digital Technologies, Health Studies, Life Sciences and Management, Law and Social Sciences.

Offers will be based on UCAS points. Many courses require specific subjects to A-level standard or the equivalent, with particular grades. The University's typical offers are a guide; factors other than academic achievement will be taken into account, such as evidence of relevant experience, skills or ability. GCSE English at grade 4 or C and above – or the equivalent – is a standard requirement for all courses and GCSE Maths at grade 4 or C is required for many more. Some courses require an interview as part of the selection criteria.

Brighton Based over three campuses in Brighton on the south coast of England. Over 150 undergraduate degree courses are available in a variety of subject areas from medicine to engineering, psychology to illustration, sport science to English literature. Many courses give students the opportunity to undertake industrial placements or other professional work-based opportunities.

Brighton welcomes applications from students with qualifications and experience other than traditional A-levels. Access courses and BTEC are acceptable alternative qualifications. The University has a Widening Participation initiative across all its courses and makes contextual offers in consideration of applicants' backgrounds. Applicants to health and social care courses, as well as photography and teaching, will be required to attend an interview.

Brighton and Sussex (MS) Students at the Brighton and Sussex Medical School are members of both the University of Sussex and the University of Brighton and, as such, enjoy access to facilities on both campuses. Students spend their first two years on the Falmer campus in Brighton and then move on to associated teaching hospitals and community settings. Teaching is 'systems integrated' so students are exposed to the clinical environment from Year 1 with hands-on, fully interactive sessions and simulation rooms. Cadaver dissection is also part of the course from Year 1, so students get a real understanding of human anatomy, enhancing their learning experience. As the Medical School is small, so are class sizes, meaning that students have a strong relationship with academic and support staff.

Standard offers usually include three A grades at A-level with a minimum of an A grade in Biology and Chemistry. All applicants, to include graduates and Access applicants, are required to have a grade 6 (or B) or above in GCSE Maths and English Language or English Literature. UCAT test results are used to select applicants for interview who meet or are predicted to meet the entry requirements.

Bristol A leading research university offering Single or Joint Honours degrees. A number of courses include a year of industrial experience or the opportunity to study or work abroad. Most courses take three or four years to complete and are modular in structure. Dentistry, Medicine and Veterinary Science are longer in duration and take five or six years to complete. Most science and engineering courses offer a choice of four-year integrated master's (MEng, MSci) as well as the three-year bachelor's (BEng, BSc) courses.

Bristol is a popular university with a high level of competition for places on all courses. A* grades may be included in the offers for some applicants depending on the application and the course applied for; where it may be included, this is shown in the typical offers published in the online course finder. Students choosing to take the Extended Project may receive two offers, one of which includes the Extended Project, for example, AAA or AAB plus the Extended Project. The University does not generally use unit grade information when making a decision, but it may be used if applicants do not meet the terms of their offer. Most subjects will consider an application to defer entry, but applicants should indicate their intention to defer in the personal statement, giving information about their plans. In fairness to applicants applying in the next admissions cycle, the number of deferred places may be limited. Applicants for Law will be required to sit the LNAT **(see Chapter 5)**. The acceptability of resitting qualifications varies depending on the course, and is outlined in each course's admissions statement. The following courses always hold interviews before making an offer: Dentistry, Medicine and Veterinary Science.

Brunel A campus-based university in West London (Uxbridge). All courses are made up of self-contained modules enabling students, within their scheme of studies, to choose a broad range of topics or greater specialisation as they prefer. Some modern language modules may be taken, depending on the timetable of the chosen subjects. Almost all degree courses are available in a three-year full-time mode or in four-year thick or thin sandwich courses which combine academic work with industrial experience organised through a very successful on-campus placement centre. Some exchange schemes also operate in Europe, USA and other worldwide locations. Degree programmes are offered across three Colleges: College of Engineering, Design and Physical Sciences (including Computing and Mathematics), College of Business, Arts and Social Sciences (including Theatre, Education, Journalism, English and Law) and the College of Health, Medicine and Life Science (including Biomedical Science, Psychology, Physiotherapy, Occupational Therapy and Sport Science). Many courses are accredited by professional institutions recognised by employers.

All applicants are interviewed for design and medicine courses. The required grades for your course must normally come from at least three full A-level passes, although candidates offering a combination of AS and A-levels or BTEC and A-level courses may be considered. All applicants usually need a minimum of five GCSEs at grade C/4 or above, including English and Maths. Some courses may require a higher grade at GCSE in English and/or Maths, and some courses specify additional subjects – all GCSE requirements are listed on the website.

Buckingham The private University of Buckingham has around 3,300 students and its three campuses are within 15 minutes' walking distance. It specialises in subjects with excellent employment prospects. Its Law school puts a heavy emphasis on international and commercial subjects, while its Business school has developed a strong service management specialism, and is the first to establish an undergraduate Venture Creation Programme (Business Enterprise). The University's Computing courses offer career development opportunities with flexible modes of study. It is the first university to launch an independent medical school. The University offers a range of undergraduate programmes, with entry points in January and September and students can complete a traditional three-year Honours degree in just two years.

Candidates apply through UCAS or directly online via the University's website. Following the reforms of A-levels and GCSEs, and the changes to the UCAS Tariff, the University makes grade offers based on the best three A-levels taken.

Bucks New Buckinghamshire New University's campuses are located in four towns just outside of London, and students travel between its Uxbridge and High Wycombe campuses on its free shuttle bus service. Students choose from a wide range of subjects delivered by nine academic schools: Art, Design and Performance, Aviation and Security, Business and Law, Creative and Digital Industries, Engineering and the Built Environment, Health and Social Care Professions, Human and Social Sciences, Hotel and Hospitality and Nursing and Midwifery.

The University is happy to consider applicants on a case by case basis and mature students (aged 21+) with relevant experience/interest are encouraged to apply. It accepts a range of equivalent qualifications at Level 3 and requires Level 2 maths and English for the majority of its courses. Admissions tests will be used for entry to operating department practice and social work courses. The University offers an unconditional offer scheme for certain courses.

Cambridge The University has 29 undergraduate colleges located throughout the city: Christ's, Churchill, Clare, Corpus Christi, Downing, Emmanuel, Fitzwilliam, Girton, Gonville and Caius, Homerton, Hughes Hall (mature students only), Jesus, King's, Lucy Cavendish, Magdalene, Murray Edwards (female students only), Newnham (female students only), Pembroke, Peterhouse, Queens', Robinson, St Catharine's, St Edmund's (mature students only), St John's, Selwyn, Sidney Sussex, Trinity, Trinity Hall, and Wolfson (mature students only). Undergraduate courses are offered in Arts and Sciences. Three-year degree courses (Triposes) provide a broad introduction to the subject followed by options at a later stage, and are divided into Part 1 (one or two years) and Part 2. In some Science and Engineering courses there is a fourth year (Part 3). Students studying courses in Modern and Medieval Languages and Asian and Middle Eastern Studies participate in a year abroad. In college-based teaching sessions (supervisions), essays are set for discussion to support university lectures, seminars and practicals.

The typical A-level offer for arts subjects (excluding Economics) is A*AA. For science subjects and Economics it is A*A*A. Colleges modify offers to take account of individual circumstances. Self-discipline, motivation and commitment are required together with the ability to think critically and independently, plus passion or, at the very least, real enthusiasm for the chosen course. Applicants are encouraged to take the Extended Project (EPQ) although it will not be a requirement of any offer. Critical Thinking is not considered acceptable as a third A-level subject for any course at Cambridge. All undergraduate degree courses (excluding Anglo-Saxon, Norse, and Celtic, History of Art and Land Economy) require applicants to take an admission assessment. Applicants will take the assessments either pre-interview or at interview, depending on the course for which they apply. Some courses require applicants to register in advance for the admission assessment; please see the University's 'Admission tests and assessments' webpage for further information. Please also see **Chapter 5** for information you need to know before completing and submitting your application. Cambridge is strongly in favour of and will continue to use UMS scores at the end of Year 12 as long as they are available. Students are strongly encouraged to take at least three and possibly four subjects, reformed or not, at the end of Year 12. Information should appear in the UCAS reference in cases where school policy limits the student's opportunity to take AS subjects.

Canterbury Christ Church The University is made up of the main Canterbury Campus, the Medway Campus where a number of health and education programmes are taught, and the Salomons Institute of Applied Psychology, which is located in the centre of Royal Tunbridge Wells. The University offers a wide range of BA, BSc, LLB and BMus programmes as well as an extensive Combined Honours scheme. The University offers undergraduate initial teacher training (primary and secondary), a wide range of degrees that lead to professions within healthcare as well as subjects in arts and humanities, social and applied sciences, childhood and education sciences, and health studies.

Applications are considered individually and the University takes into account academic qualifications in addition to paying great attention to the personal statement and the reference(s) provided. All offers are tailored to individual applications. Some courses require applicants to achieve specific grades and for some applicants need to have studied a particular subject. The University offers a range of extended degrees where students can study a foundation year (Year 0) and then progress onto Year 1 (Level 4) of the degree programme. For details about the Kent and Medway Medical school, see the relevant entry in this book and the School's website. The University makes contextual offers to Medicine and Surgery applicants from disadvantaged backgrounds.

Cardiff A leading research university located in the centre of Wales' capital city. The University offers over 300 undergraduate degree programmes which are modular in structure, enabling students to tailor components of their degree to suit their interests. Up to 100 degree courses offer some or all of their modules through the medium of Welsh, allowing students the option to submit work and take exams in Welsh. Many degree schemes have a vocational and professional content with a period of attachment in industry, and there are well-established links with universities abroad.

Applicants are required to take three A-levels for degree courses. Deferred entry is acceptable. Key Skills should be mentioned in an application but will not form part of an offer. Applicants without formal qualifications but who have professional experience may be considered for some courses.

Cardiff Met Campuses are located at Llandaff and Cyncoed. Cardiff Metropolitan University specialises in courses that are career-orientated and have been designed in conjunction with business and industry. All of the courses are created with the working world in mind and include work placements, visiting lecturers, and options for sandwich courses.

Students from Foundation degree courses or with HNC/HND qualifications should contact the course director before applying. Applications are considered on an individual basis with all contextual information taken into account, so applicants with predicted grades that fall below the entry requirements will still be considered. Prior study, work experience and training can count as credit towards the applicant's course of study. Interviews are required for most art and design courses and professional courses such as Teacher Training and healthcare courses.

Central Lancashire The University is based on a single site campus in Preston city centre, with smaller campuses at Burnley, Westlakes, London and another campus in Cyprus. Its academic schools cover a wide range of subjects with over 350 employment-focused undergraduate programmes. Many subjects offer optional modules which gives extra choice within programmes. Foundation entry route is available for most Honours degree programmes. A number of integrated master's courses are offered, in addition to sandwich courses. Work experience is a key part of a large number of courses and many courses offer the opportunity to study abroad for a year.

Interviews are required for Dentistry, health courses, Medicine and performing arts courses. Some courses also require applicants to attend an audition or submit a portfolio. Successful applicants are invited to attend an Offer Holder Day.

Chester The University of Chester has a number of sites situated around the city, as well as three nearby University Centres offering practice-based courses. It offers an extensive range of Single and Combined Honours courses across its learning sites: from arts and media, science and engineering, social sciences, humanities, business and management, and specialist vocational pathways to nursing and education. Education, health and social care courses are offered at the University Centre Warrington, the University Centre Birkenhead is a dedicated health and nursing site, and the University Centre Reaseheath in Nantwich is a land-based site with a commitment to sustainability and conservation. Students in select courses can apply for paid sandwich placements in consultation with their faculty during their second year of study.

Entry requirements for combined honours degrees range from 96 to 112 points and 104 to 120 points for single honours degrees. The University accepts mixed combinations of qualifications, including A-level Critical Thinking. Chester conducts interviews for applicants to art and design, performing arts, education, health and social care courses. Deferred entry is acceptable on all courses apart from Children's Nursing and Midwifery.

Chichester The University of Chichester is comprised of Bishop Otter Campus in the city centre and Bognor Regis Campus in the coastal town of Bognor. It offers bachelor degree programmes in a range of subjects covering allied health, business, creative industries, engineering, humanities, psychology and social sciences, social work and social care, sport and physical education, teacher education, and the visual and performing arts.

Applicants for professional programmes, such as Nursing or Teacher Training, will be interviewed. Applicants for programmes in the creative arts, such as Acting, will be auditioned. Most other admissions decisions are made on the basis of the application form.

City St George's City, University of London and St George's, University of London merged on 1st August 2024 to form City St George's, University of London. It is now one of the largest higher education institutions in London, and is one of the city's most important suppliers of the health workforce. The merged institution combines St George's world-leading specialism in medical and biomedical allied health education with City's wide range of three-year and four-year programmes leading to degrees in the subject areas of business, management, finance and accounting, computing, engineering and mathematical sciences, English, health sciences (including Nursing, Radiography and Speech Therapy), history, law, music and social sciences. The result is a career-focused and interdisciplinary university.

Interviews are required for most health science courses and admissions tests are required for some courses. Applicants are expected to satisfy the minimum entry requirements for their specific course, but all applications are considered on an individual basis, taking into any account contextual information. In extenuating circumstances, the A-level offer may be reduced by one or two grades.

Coventry The University is situated in the city centre, with further institutes offering more vocationally based courses located in Coventry, London and Scarborough as part of the Coventry University Group. Coventry University courses are designed with employability in mind. Most courses offer the chance to spend a year working in industry or working or studying abroad. Individual programmes of study are usually made up of compulsory modules, core options from a prescribed list and free choice modules.

The University is committed to providing a professional, fair, equal and transparent service to all applicants. It therefore welcomes applications from those who have significant work or life experience and who may not necessarily meet the published academic requirements for their chosen course. Coventry University makes offers for full degree courses based on three A-levels (or equivalent). AS are not usually included in these offers, and there are no plans at present to make any changes to this approach; AS grades may still be considered but two AS will not be accepted in place of one A level.

Cranfield A postgraduate university, specialising in technology and management, located between Bedford and Milton Keynes. Cranfield University offers courses in aerospace, defence and security, design, energy and sustainability, environment and agrifood, manufacturing and materials, transport systems, water, and management. Defence education courses are offered through Cranfield Defence and Security, based in the Defence Academy of the UK in Shrivenham.

The minimum entry requirement to postgraduate study is a lower second-class (2.2) undergraduate degree with honours, or an equivalent international qualification, or relevant work experience combined with a degree classification below a second-class honours. Each application is considered on an individual basis, so applicants without the minimum requirement may still be accepted if able to demonstrate suitability. Some courses may have additional entry requirements and require applicants to attend an interview.

Creative Arts Specialist university with campuses at Canterbury, Epsom and Farnham, academic facilities at Maidstone TV Studios and an Institute for Creative Innovation in Xiamen, China. The University's architecture and design courses, together with fine art and visual communications, are based at its Canterbury campus, while the Epsom campus is home to its respected School of Fashion and Textiles and the UK's first Business School for the Creative Industries. Foundation and Honours degree courses are offered covering art and design, architecture, media and communications. Some courses allow for a short work placement.

Applicants must meet the specific course UCAS tariff offer to be considered. The University does welcome applications from mature applicants who may not have the required qualifications but who can evidence relevant experience. Portfolios are required for applications to most courses; the University does not expect this to be a near-professional piece of work but a showcase of applicants' early thoughts and ideas.

Cumbria The University of Cumbria has seven campuses across the north-west and London. It offers a wide range of courses, both taught and research-based, spanning arts, business, education, health, humanities, law, policing, social science, sport, STEM and the outdoors. The University has an extensive portfolio at both undergraduate level and postgraduate level and many courses have the option to undertake placements which gives students the much needed practical experience.

The University accepts a wide range of qualifications for course entry. Required Tariff points vary across all disciplines and some courses have specific GCSE requirements. All entry requirements and course codes can be found on its website, in its prospectus or on the UCAS website. Interviews are required for professional policing, teaching, health and social care and some art and design courses. The University also offers undergraduate courses with Foundation entry, an alternative route to accessing higher education and all the experiences you'd expect as a full-time student.

De Montfort A campus-based University situated in the centre of Leicester. De Montfort University Leicester (DMU) offers a wide range of over 200 undergraduate and postgraduate courses, both full-time and part-time, tailored to meet the needs of today's employers. The University uses a block teaching method, requiring students to study one module at a time and benefit from regular assessments rather than numerous end of year exams.

DMU welcomes applications from UK, European and international students with a wide range of qualifications and experience. Entry requirements differ between courses and can be found on the specific course page on the DMU website. Health and social care courses require interviews and portfolios are required for art and design courses.

Derby A university spread over campuses in Derby, Chesterfield, Buxton and Leek. Courses at the Derby campus are offered across four subject areas: arts, humanities and education; business, law and social sciences; science and engineering; and health, psychology and social care. There is also a comprehensive Joint Honours programme offering two subjects divided equally into three modules of each subject in the first year of study. Most courses then offer students the option to continue studying a joint pathway or choose a major/minor pathway.

The University uses UCAS tariff points as a guide. Selectors look for applicants who can demonstrate their enthusiasm and motivation, as well as their potential to benefit from coming to university. Applicants without formal qualifications may be able to gain entry to degree programmes by evidencing the required communication and learning skills, along with the necessary knowledge, experience and motivation. They may be required to take the Access course or Foundation course first.

Dundee The University of Dundee offers a wide range of undergraduate degrees. Many of its courses are vocational and offer professional accreditation. Its academic schools cover Art and Design; Business; Dentistry; Health Sciences; Humanities, Social Sciences and Law; Life Sciences; Medicine and Science and Engineering.

Some courses interview as part of the admissions process. Advanced entry is available for most courses. While the university desires applicants to earn their place by having achieved a strong set of grades, it recognises that formal qualifications are not the only measure of an applicant's potential. The University is fully supportive of the recognition of informal (experiential) learning. Each application is examined in detail, taking into account individual circumstances. Offers to applicants who are repeating their examinations will remain the same as any previous offer.

Durham The University consists of 16 colleges and one postgraduate-only college located across the city of Durham. Courses are based within four Faculties: Arts and Humanities, Durham University Business School, Science, Social Sciences and Health. The university offers named routes within Natural Sciences and courses in Liberal Arts and Combined Honours in Social Sciences for students to design their own degree by choosing two to three subjects from the wide range available. Many of the courses also offer placement and study-abroad opportunities. A Foundation Programme is designed for students from under-represented groups in higher education and supports students to develop the skills and subject knowledge required for successful study at degree level.

The Durham admissions policy states that the following factors are considered when an application is reviewed: A-level or equivalent grades; GCSE performance; the personal statement; the school/college reference; the development of study skills; motivation for the chosen degree programme; independence of thought and working; skills derived from non-academic activities, e.g. sport, the arts, and voluntary and community work; and contextual evidence of merit and potential. Students applying for more than one type of course or institution may submit a substitute personal statement. Admission decisions are made by admissions selectors. Successful applicants will be informed of the decision on their application before a college is allocated. Durham does not use interviews as a means of selection except in specific circumstances. These include applications to courses where external bodies determine that interviewing is compulsory (for example, applicants to Primary Education), applications to the Foundation Centre, applications where the candidate is without recent and/or relevant qualifications and applications where applicants have had a break in their study prior to application. The need for an interview will be determined by academic departments on an individual basis having considered all the information provided in the application.

Dyson The Dyson Institute of Engineering and Technology offers a four-year integrated MEng in Engineering. This employer-sponsored degree combines a rigorous academic programme with the practical application of this knowledge to real engineering problems at Dyson, all without tuition fees and while earning a salary. Students learn from specialist academics and Dyson engineers in the world-leading facilities on Dyson's technology campus in Malmesbury, Wiltshire, working three days a week and studying the other two.

Applicants should demonstrate strong academic performance and evidence their ability to cope with the professional demands that come with being a Dyson Engineer, alongside studying. If applicants do not have Physics at A Level (or equivalent) a condition of their offer will be to attend, complete and pass an assessment at Dyson's 10-day Physics Summer School.

East Anglia Located two miles from the centre of Norwich, the University of East Anglia's campus offers all the day-to-day facilities students are likely to need. UEA's world-leading research covers arts and humanities, medicine and health, science and social sciences. Work placements are embedded in UEA's degrees, enabling students to put their subject knowledge into practice.

Interviews are necessary for some courses. Deferred entry is welcome for most courses. Lower contextual offers are made to disadvantaged students for the majority of the University's courses. Where the Admissions Service wishes to make an offer to an applicant who does not meet the general entry requirements, the case will be referred to the relevant Associate Dean for Admissions or Head of School for consideration. Applicants with a gap in educational history may be asked to evidence academic study in the last five years.

East London The University, based on the Stratford, Docklands and University Square Stratford campuses in East London, offers Single Honours and Combined Honours programmes. A wide range of courses are offered by the five academic schools of Business and Law; Health, Sport and Bioscience; Childhood and Social Care; Arts and Creative Industries; Architecture, Computing and Engineering. Courses provide a flexibility of choice and are based on a modular structure with compulsory and optional course units. A very large number of extended degrees are also available for applicants who do not have the normal university entrance requirements.

UEL views applications holistically, considering non-academic factors when making decisions and offering a place. The Admissions team will also consider any relevant life or work experience. Some students may be called for interview and in some cases an essay or a portfolio may be required. The interviewers will be looking for evidence of a real interest in the chosen subject. Rejected applicants may receive an offer of a place on an extended degree or on another course.

Edge Hill The University in Ormskirk, Lancashire has three-year programmes including Business Management, English, Film, Geography, History, Law, Media, Midwifery, Nursing, Drama, social and psychological sciences, sports and teacher training courses. The University started training doctors in 2020. Some courses include short work placements, and students have the opportunity to undertake paid sandwich placements.

Some courses require applicants to attend an interview. Those applicants who receive offers are invited to visit the University. For details of entry to the Medicine course, see the University website. Applicants can expect to receive a decision from the University within 10 working days, in normal circumstances.

Edinburgh The University has numerous campuses around the city, as well as a Veterinary School campus in the town of Roslin. The ancient University of Edinburgh's degree programmes are designed to include four years of study giving a broad and flexible education. Most programmes in the arts, humanities, engineering, sciences or social sciences allow students to study a range of subjects in Years 1 and 2, before specialising in the next two. There is a considerable choice of subjects although there may be restrictions in the case of high-demand subjects such as English, Economics and Psychology. General or Ordinary degrees take three years and Honours degrees take four years. Joint Honours degrees are also offered.

Entry to Edinburgh is competitive. Admission decisions are made by the admissions offices of the University's three colleges: the College of Arts, Humanities and Social Science, the College of Science and Engineering and the College of Medicine and Veterinary Medicine. Decisions on the majority of applications will be made after the UCAS deadline, once all applications have been received. All offers will be expressed in grades, not Tariff points. Entry requirements are typically expressed in a range. Applicants will be entered into the selection process if they have met or are predicted to meet or exceed the lower grade level listed. Offers are made to the highest qualified applicants, so entry into the selection process does not guarantee an offer. Due to high levels of competition, applicants will usually be expected to achieve the upper grade level to receive an offer.

Edinburgh Napier Edinburgh Napier is located across three campuses. The University offers over 150 undergraduate courses with a focus on work-based learning, giving students the tools to build the foundations of their career. Students choose between Single and Joint Honours degrees.

Where the admissions selection process involves an interview, audition or portfolio review, the application will be sent to the academic department for consideration. Entry requirements are the minimum criteria for admission and attainment of these requirements does not guarantee an offer, especially in competitive subject areas. Decisions are made on an individual basis; applicants should provide as much information as possible to aid the admissions team in their decision-making. Feedback for unsuccessful applications is available upon request.

Essex The main University campus is located near Colchester. Undergraduate departments are grouped in schools of study covering faculties of study covering arts and humanities, science and health and social sciences. Degree schemes in health and business are also offered at the Southend campus and degree schemes in performing arts are offered at both Southend and Loughton campuses.

The wide range of qualifications the University considers include the following: A-levels, BTEC qualifications, International Baccalaureate Diploma and Certificates, QAA Approved Access to HE Diplomas, Open University courses and practising professional qualifications. The typical offer for most courses requires applicants to achieve specific grades in three A-levels (or equivalent), although the University considers additional qualifications. Selected UK based applicants are usually called for interview.

Exeter The University has three faculties: Environment, Science and Economy; Humanities, Arts and Social Sciences; Health and Life Sciences. Most courses include an optional study-abroad opportunity. Courses are taught across three main campuses, two in Exeter and one in Cornwall at Penryn near Falmouth. Subjects taught in Cornwall include biosciences, English, history, geological sciences, law and mining engineering.

The University welcomes applications from students from all backgrounds. Key indicators include predicted and achieved academic performance in Level 2 and 3 qualifications; candidates would normally be expected to take three A-levels (or the equivalent). Deferred applications are welcome.

Falmouth Falmouth University is located in the towns of Falmouth and Penryn, on Cornwall's south coast. This University offers creative-focused courses in a wide range of subjects from fine art to robotics, events management to marketing. Falmouth's industry connections, professional facilities and in-house agencies enable students to gain a head start in industry. Students have the option of undertaking paid opportunities and international placements. Flexible online courses are also offered alongside campus-based undergraduate and postgraduate degrees.

The University typically looks for applicants to have between 104 and 120 UCAS tariff points or equivalent. The majority of courses require applicants to attend an interview and present a portfolio. Falmouth advises applicants to value quality over quantity and use the portfolio to tell a story, showcasing a variety of techniques and processes.

Glasgow The University has two campuses in Glasgow and a third in the town of Dumfries. Applicants choose a degree from the Colleges of Arts and Humanities; Medical, Veterinary & Life Sciences; Science & Engineering; Social Sciences. The flexible degree structure in arts, sciences and social sciences allows students to build their own degree programme from the courses on offer. Honours degrees normally take four years, with the decision for Honours taken at the end of Year 2. Primary Education, Global Sustainable Development and Environmental Science and Sustainability can be studied at the Dumfries Campus, where the School of Social and Environmental Sustainability is located.

Offers are made until late March. The University does not interview applicants except for entry to Community Development, Dentistry, Medicine, Music, Nursing, Teaching and Veterinary Medicine and Surgery. Deferred entry is not guaranteed for all subjects so check with the University. See the University website for up-to-date information.

Glasgow Caledonian A predominately campus-based university, located in the centre of Glasgow with a second campus in London and a college for master's programmes in New York. The University offers a wide range of career-focused programmes at its Academic Schools: Glasgow School for Business and Society, School of Computing, Engineering and Built Environment, and School of Health and Life Sciences.

The University accepts a wide range of qualifications for entry, depending upon the programme. Applicants must achieve grades equal to or surpassing standard requirements to receive a place, unless personal circumstances qualify them as a widening access student.

Gloucestershire The University is located in Cheltenham and Gloucester with more than 80 courses all made up of individual study units (modules). Some are compulsory for the chosen course but other modules can be chosen from other subjects. All courses have strong employability focus with many opportunities to undertake placements and internships.

Students failing to meet the UCAS Tariff requirements may be eligible for entry based on life or work experience following an interview. Entry with BTEC, NVQ Level 3, International Baccalaureate Diplomas and Access to Higher Education qualifications is acceptable. Feedback for applications is available upon request.

Greater Manchester A small, tight-knit university community in Bolton, with an excellent reputation for student support. A range of courses are offered, designed with the workplace in mind, with many offering vocational or professional content and work experience elements. The University offers a number of two-year Foundation courses, including fashion, media production and cloud computing.

Academic offers are based on UCAS points from at least two A-levels (or equivalent) for most courses. Students should complete a direct application if they wish to apply only to Greater Manchester; this will be submitted to UCAS on their behalf. The University is committed to giving equal consideration to factors other than formal academic qualifications such as work experience and vocational qualifications – any relevant information should be listed in the application.

Greenwich Greenwich University has two campuses in south-east London and a third in Medway, Kent. The University's facilities include first-class advanced laboratories and three campus libraries. Over 200 undergraduate courses are on offer and degrees consist of a combination of compulsory and optional modules. Students can complete internships and placements while studying, and will also have the chance to undertake paid part-time work at the university.

Each application is considered on an individual basis. All information supplied is taken into account, as well as applicants' performance at interview or assessment event, research proposal or portfolio assessment. Interviews are required for art and design, performance arts, teaching, health and pharmacy courses. Mature applicants with previous qualifications and/or relevant experience may be exempt from certain modules of a degree or be allowed entry with lower requirements.

Harper Adams Based in Newport, Shropshire, with a second site in Telford, the University specialises in agricultural science, animal health and wellbeing, food production and technology. Twelve month industry placements are a compulsory part of all undergraduate degrees.

Interviews only take place for international students. Work experience is a prerequisite for admission to Veterinary Nursing and is strongly advised if you intend to study Veterinary Physiotherapy or Applied Zoology, as well as courses in agriculture, animal sciences, business, engineering, food sciences, land and property management and wildlife. The University accepts T level qualifications, and through its Access to Harper contextualised offer scheme aims to make study more accessible to students from a wide range of backgrounds.

Heriot-Watt This campus university near Edinburgh has five schools offering courses in Energy, Geoscience, Infrastructure and Society, Engineering and Physical Sciences, Social Sciences, Mathematical and Computer Sciences, and Textiles and Design which is based at the University's Scottish Borders campus. A third specialist campus, Heriot-Watt Orkney, is home to the International Centre for Island Technology (ICIT).

Admissions decisions are made through the Faculty 'Hubs'. The personal statement is regarded as highly important and students are advised to include all relevant interests and work experience. The University welcomes a wide range of entry qualifications.

Hertfordshire Full-time and sandwich courses are offered as well as Joint courses. All Hertfordshire students have a work exposure strand in their degrees and the close links with employers contribute to a consistently good work placement and graduate employment record. All students have the opportunity to develop self-employment skills through tailor-made packages in addition to their subject expertise and proficiency.

Applicants wanting to take a gap year should finalise their arrangements before asking for deferment and accepting a place. Once a place has been accepted for the following year it will not be possible to change their application for entry to the current year. They would need to withdraw their application and apply again through Clearing. Offers to applicants who are repeating examinations are the same.

HSU Established in 1965 as Europe's first chiropractic training provider, the Health Sciences University (previously AECC University College) has multiple campuses in Bournemouth and London. HSU specialises in chiropractic and other healthcare disciplines. The Garnet Campus in Bournemouth is home to the recently developed Integrated Rehabilitation Centre (IRC), offering sports and exercise rehabilitation services to the general public. Subject areas include chiropody, rehabilitation, sports and psychology, radiography and medical imaging and osteopathy. The University runs a number of patient clinics which gives students the opportunity to receive on-site clinical training.

HSU aims to process an initial assessment of applications within two working weeks. For some courses, applicants are required to attend an interview. Deferred applications are accepted, provided the applicant has met the conditions of their offer within the same academic cycle in which they applied.

Huddersfield The modular approach to study provides a flexible structure to all courses, which are offered as full-time or sandwich options. Most courses are vocational and all students have the opportunity to gain work experience, including placements and industry standard projects.

The University accepts a wide range of qualifications, including the EPQ and Core Maths. Huddersfield will consider applicants' qualifications and/or predicted grades equally, irrespective of any re-takes. Interviews are required for art and design courses, performing arts, teaching, health and social care and the Science Extended Degree leading to a BSc. Scholarships in the first year of study are available to students achieving 120 points or more whose family income is less than £25,000 per annum.

Hull All full-time courses are made up of core and optional modules and are taught on the Hull campus. The opportunity to learn a language is available for all students irrespective of their degree course subject.

All criteria for selection are set by the academic faculty. A mandatory interview process operates for shortlisted applicants for some courses, particularly those leading to professional qualifications. Applications are also welcomed from those who can demonstrate Level 3 work-based learning such as Advanced Apprenticeships and NVQ 3. Bridging study may be recommended by way of a Foundation year. Most courses welcome applications for deferred entry although this should be stated on the application. The University makes contextual (lower) offers to applicants on schemes including Pathways to STEM, Next Steps York and Realising Opportunities.

Hull York (MS) The Medical School is a partnership between the Universities of Hull and York with teaching and learning facilities on both campuses. Offer holders are allocated a campus at random. From year three onwards students will undertake placements in clinical sites across the region.

Hull York Medical School offers a Medicine with a Gateway Year programme, allowing locally based UK applicants who meet Widening Participation requirements to apply for Medicine with lower expected grades. See Medicine in **Chapter 7.**

Imperial London The University's main campus is located in South Kensington but it also has a number of other campuses around London and the south east. Medicine is mainly based at the South Kensington and Charing Cross Campuses, with community-based experiences at General Practices, along with clinical placements and attachments at a wide range of teaching hospitals. The College offers world-class programmes in Science, Medicine, Engineering and Management. Joint Honours courses and degree courses with a year abroad are also available. Science courses are offered primarily in one principal subject, but flexibility is provided by the possibility to transfer at the end of the first year and by the choice of optional subjects in the later years of the course. A Humanities programme is also open to all students with a wide range of options, while the Imperial College Business School offers Management courses which form an integral part of undergraduate degrees. Work experience and placements are a feature of all courses.

Applicants are normally required to have three A-levels, but applicants with other qualifications of equivalent standard and students with other competencies are also welcome. Most departments require applicants to attend an interview. Applicants for entry to Year 2 of some courses can also be considered if they have completed the first year of a comparable degree at another institution with a high level of achievement, but they need to contact the relevant department before applying. A College Admissions and Appeals and Complaints procedure is available to applicants dissatisfied with the way their application has been considered.

Keele Keele University's leafy campus in Staffordshire, which is among the largest in the UK, is readily accessible from Birmingham, Manchester and London. Flexibility is provided through either interdisciplinary Single Honours degrees, bringing together a number of topics in an integrated form, or Dual Honours degrees in which two principal subjects are studied to degree level to the same depth as a Single Honours course. Business School courses with sandwich placements are available.

Keele's conditional offers to candidates are usually made in terms of specified grades from the qualifications they are studying. Some of its degree courses require a specific subject background. It welcomes applications from candidates with non-traditional qualifications and will take into consideration prior learning, experience and alternative qualifications. Applicants are normally required to have completed studies in the last three years. Contextual offers for applicants from a disadvantaged background are made for all subjects apart from the clinical vocations (e.g. Pharmacy, Medicine, Nursing) and Social Work. Further information about its approach and entry requirements can be found on the 'Admissions FAQs' webpage. Interviews are required for Medicine, Midwifery, Nursing, Paramedic Science, Pharmacy, Physiotherapy, Radiography and Social Work.

Kent The University's main campuses are in Canterbury and Medway in the South East of England, with specialist centres in Europe where study and research are underpinned by the exceptional facilities and resources of locations in Brussels and Paris. Many courses have a year in industry, giving valuable practical experience ahead of your final year of study. The majority of programmes offer the opportunity to study or work abroad. Single Honours courses can include the option of taking up to 25% of the degree in another subject, or to change the focus of a degree at the end of the first year. Many social sciences and humanities subjects are available as Joint Honours programmes on a 50/50 basis or as major/minor Honours degrees. The University of Kent and Canterbury Christ Church University established a medical school (Kent and Medway) in 2020.

The University accepts a wide range of qualifications. Applicants returning to study after a long break are advised to contact the admissions staff before making a UCAS application. The University offers integrated Foundation year study in a number of degree subjects and an international Foundation year programme is available to non-UK students. Deferred entry is acceptable but should be mentioned on the UCAS application. The University will make contextual offers to applicants from disadvantaged backgrounds across all subjects. The University does not use the UCAS Tariff when making offers.

Kingston Kingston University is based in Kingston upon Thames, a busy riverside town in Surrey within an easy commuting distance from central London. It has four campuses, each with its own character, but all of which combine state-of-the-art facilities with a friendly study environment. Its courses have a modular structure, and several of them are available to study as Joint Honours which allows students to combine two different subjects. The two subjects can be studied equally (half-field), or one subject can be focused on more than the other (major-minor fields). All students have the opportunity to study abroad during their degree and can choose from 30 countries spanning five continents. They can also learn one of nine languages through the Kingston Language Scheme for free during their time at the University.

Once the University has received an application from UCAS, it looks carefully at each applicant's academic record, references and personal statement. Some courses at Kingston University have an interview as part of the selection process where one or two people will interview you to find out if you have the intellectual capability, knowledge and passion to benefit from your chosen course. If you don't have an interview, you'll be invited to an offer holder day instead where you will get to experience taster sessions of the course you have applied for.

Lancaster The University is situated on a large campus some distance from the city and consists of several colleges. Each college has its own social activities and events. The degree programme is split into Part 1 (Year 1) and Part 2 (Years 2 and 3). Students for many degrees will have the opportunity to take minor modules in other subject areas alongside their major. Whereas the following programmes will be made up entirely of compulsory and optional modules in the major subject area: Architecture, Law, Physics, Engineering, Medicine, Sports and Exercise Science, Biochemistry, Biology, Biomedicine and Biomedical Science. Single and Joint courses are offered in a wide range of subjects. There are study opportunities abroad in Europe, the USA and Canada, the Far East and Australasia. Many courses are offered with a placement year. The University has overseas campuses in China, Germany, Ghana, Indonesia and Malaysia.

The University accepts a wide range of qualifications and offers are based on the best three A-level (or equivalent) results. Some departments interview applicants prior to making an offer. All applicants are invited to an informal post-offer Applicant Visit Day which encourages discussions with admissions tutors and current students.

Leeds One of the largest city-based single-site campuses in the UK and a member of the Russell Group, the University of Leeds offers excellence in learning and teaching in a wide range of courses in most subject areas, including an extensive offering of Joint Honours degrees. Opportunities to study abroad and/or undertake industrial placements are offered as part of most courses.

The University welcomes students with a variety of qualifications. The University normally expects applicants to have completed three A-levels (or equivalent) in one sitting, and for the School of Law this is compulsory. Many courses do not accept General Studies and Critical Thinking. However, if applicants narrowly miss their offer then high grades in General Studies and Critical Thinking may be considered. Some courses, including Medicine, Midwifery and Social Work, require an interview.

Leeds Arts The only specialist arts university in the north of England. All higher education courses are taught in the Blenheim Walk building, located in central Leeds. BA courses are offered in Art and Design, Fashion and Textiles, Fine Art and Graphics and Photography. Students have the opportunity to undertake work experience, and professional modules enable students to research the creative industries and connect with companies.

The University accepts a wide range of qualifications and experience. In making a decision, the University assesses each applicant's academic performance and potential to succeed on the chosen course. Many courses require applicants to submit examples of work.

Leeds Beckett The University has two well-connected city campuses with state-of-the-art facilities. Many of the degrees are vocational with links to industry and commerce. Courses are modular with core studies and optional modules. Degree programmes are offered in 13 different schools including the School of Clinical and Applied Sciences, Carnegie School of Education and the Leeds Business School.

Most offers are made in UCAS Tariff points, and interviews are held for some courses. Deferred entry is acceptable, although applicants should be aware that some courses may change slightly each year. The University considers each application on its own merits; some courses require applicants to submit a portfolio.

Leeds Trinity An employability-focused university located in Horsforth, a town in the City of Leeds municipality, with a second campus in Leeds city centre. The University offers undergraduate, postgraduate and Foundation courses in a wide range of subject areas, including business; children, young people and families; computer science; criminology, sociology and policing; English; film and television production; health and social care; journalism; law; philosophy, ethics and religion; photography; primary and secondary education; psychology; sociology; sport and wellbeing; and theology and religious studies. Professional work placements are embedded into the University's undergraduate degrees, and most courses include the opportunity to study abroad. Leeds Trinity University has a Catholic foundation but is committed to providing maximum support to all students irrespective of their faith.

All applicants receiving an offer for non-interviewing courses will be invited to an Offer-holder Day. Some courses do require an interview – these courses are specified in the UCAS entry requirements. The

University makes Tariff-based offers. All entry requirements are listed in the course-specific entry requirements on the University's website and through UCAS. Any experience described on the applications is always taken into account, alongside students' academic profiles. A large range of qualifications is accepted, including T levels. To meet the minimum entry requirement, the University expects applicants to hold five qualifications, including two Level 3 qualifications (or equivalent).

Leicester The main campus is situated one mile south of Leicester city centre in the East Midlands. The University also has an overseas campus, the Leicester International Institute, Dalian University of Technology, in China. Single Honours courses are offered in all the main disciplines. The main subject of study may be supported by one or two optional modules. Joint Honours courses, which are split equally between the subjects, are also offered. Apart from Medicine, all programmes have a common modular structure with compulsory modules and a wide choice of optional modules.

Most courses do not interview applicants although invitations to visit the University will follow any offers made. Most typical offers are made on the basis of three A-levels. For some courses an offer will be made if an EPQ is being taken with three A-levels. Other qualifications are considered, including the Access to HE Diploma, BTEC Nationals. Applications from suitably qualified students are also considered for second year entry for some programmes. The University makes contextual offers in all subject areas, apart from Medicine, clinical sciences and some law courses. Contact the subject department for further information.

Lincoln The University's main Brayford Pool campus is located in the heart of Lincoln. Its Riseholme Campus, north of the city, is home to the Lincoln Institute for Agri-Food Technology (LIAT), and its Holbeath Campus, south of the county, is where the National Centre for Food Manufacturing is based. Subjects are split over two academic colleges: the College of Arts, Social Sciences and Humanities, and the College of Health and Science. Single and Joint subject degrees are offered on a modular basis, with some subjects offering the chance to study abroad. The degree at the University of Nottingham Lincoln Medical School is delivered by the University of Nottingham, with placements based in Lincoln.

On some courses, notably Art and Design and Architecture, an interview with a portfolio is sometimes required before an offer can be made. The University accepts a wide range of qualifications but students without the standard entry requirements may still be offered a place on the basis of prior experience and qualifications. For details of entry to the Medical School, see the University website.

Liverpool The University has a main campus in the city centre, as well as a nearby Veterinary Science campus in Leahurst, Wirral, and an overseas campus in Suzhou, China. It offers degrees in the Faculties of Humanities and Social Sciences, Science and Engineering and Health and Life Sciences. Apart from courses with a clinical component, programmes are modular. The University offers many degrees with an industrial placement year and there is the opportunity for students studying many subjects to spend a year of their degree in China. The Faculty of Humanities and Social Sciences offers the 'Honours Select' programme allowing students to combine subjects from across the Faculty as Joint (50:50) or major/minor (75:25) degrees. Paid work placements are the norm in Computer Science, Engineering, Accounting, Business, Communications and Media, Marketing, and Chemistry.

Decisions on offers for most schools/departments are made centrally. The exceptions are in the Schools of Medicine, Dentistry, Health Sciences and Veterinary Science. Most departments will invite applicants to visit the University before or after an offer is made. Some departments require interviews. Offers are normally based on three A-levels or equivalent (a wide range of qualifications are accepted). Entry requirements are reviewed annually. The University makes discounted offers of one grade lower on its Scholars Scheme.

Liverpool Hope The University has a main teaching campus, creative and performing arts campus and residential-only campus in Liverpool, as well as an outdoor education centre in Snowdonia, North Wales. With integrated Catholic and Anglican colleges, it is Europe's only university with an ecumenical foundation. Applicants from all backgrounds are welcomed. Liverpool Hope offers a wide range of Single and Combined Honours undergraduate degrees. The University offers small group teaching, which means students are taught by research-active lecturers and benefit from insights into their research.

Each application is assessed on its own merits. The policy is to select those candidates who demonstrate they have an academic ability and personal motivation to succeed in their chosen programme of study. The admissions decision will rest primarily on the qualifications and also on the aspirations of the applicant in relation to their chosen programme of study. Selectors will take into account the evidence provided on the application form against the criteria for that particular course.

Liverpool John Moores The University has over 30 buildings across two city campuses. Courses are offered in the Faculties of Arts, Professional & Social Studies, Business & Law, Health, Science and Engineering & Technology. The majority of courses provide the opportunity for work-based learning or for a year-long industrial placement. The majority of programmes in the Faculty of Science and Faculty of Engineering & Technology also offer a Foundation pathway.

Students are encouraged to include all relevant interests and work experience in their personal statement. The University welcomes a wide range of entry qualifications. Applicants are required to have a minimum of Grade C/4 or above in GCSE English and Maths or its equivalent, and a pass in two GCE A level subjects or equivalent (for some courses specific subjects). If an applicant fails to receive an offer for their chosen course then an offer for an alternative course may be made. The University will make adjusted offers to care leavers and students estranged from their families.

London (Birk) Part of the University of London, this leading research university is based in Bloomsbury. Over 100 undergraduate degree courses are offered by the Faculty of Business and Law, the Faculty of Humanities and Social Sciences and the Faculty of Science. The University offers evening study degrees and many subjects give students the option to complete their studies full-time over three years or part-time over four years. Some part-time degrees over six years are also offered.

The University welcomes applicants without traditional qualifications; decisions are made by assessing each applicant's qualifications, knowledge and previous work experience. In some cases, Birkbeck's judgement of an applicant's academic potential may result in waiving formal entry requirements. Part-time undergraduate, all certificate and short course and all postgraduate applications are made directly through its website. Full-time undergraduate applications are made through UCAS.

London (Court) The Courtauld Institute of Art is an internationally acclaimed teaching and research centre specialising in art history and conservation. This self-governing College of the University of London offers one undergraduate degree programme, the BA (Hons) History of Art. This seeks to attract students of the highest calibre, who are driven by an insatiable curiosity to learn about the visual arts and their histories.

The University welcomes applicants who can demonstrate interest in art history and enthusiasm for it. Entry is competitive, but the Courtauld is committed to admitting students with the best ability and potential regardless of their educational background or financial resources. You will not be required to have studied history of art previously, however, advanced study in the humanities is a significant advantage, as is the EPQ. No interviews required.

London (Gold) Goldsmiths specialises in the creative, cultural and social spheres and is situated in New Cross, south-east London. The University takes an innovative and interdisciplinary approach to its degree courses, which include art, design, drama, computing, media, the arts, education and social sciences. An undergraduate degree is made up of 360 credits from core and optional modules – 120 at each level. Some courses offer unpaid, credit-bearing work placement modules. Some degree programmes also include an industrial placement year.

Goldsmiths welcomes applications from students with A-levels or equivalent qualifications. While entry requirements are stipulated, candidates are assessed individually and may receive an offer that differs from the published grades. When an applicant does not meet the academic conditions of their offer, their application will be reconsidered as a whole and their offer may still be confirmed. Some applicants are interviewed, in particular those for art and design degrees for which examples of current art and design work are required before interview. Applicants requiring deferred entry (which may or may not be acceptable depending on the course) should contact the admissions tutor before applying.

London (Inst Paris) The Institute was established as part of London University in 1969, and specialises in the humanities and social sciences. It offers two undergraduate programmes taught over three years in Paris, leading to a London University BA. Courses are taught in French for those minoring or majoring in French Studies, and in English for those minoring or majoring in International Politics. More subjects are available as minor options. The University offers non-credit-bearing French courses to help students without prior French qualifications expand their language skills.

The University accepts a wide range of qualifications. If applicants do not have the entry requirements to be automatically eligible, the Admissions Panel will consider their application on an individual basis. In cases where applicants provide evidence of recognised and accredited prior learning, the number of courses required to complete the degree will be reduced.

London (Institute of Banking and Finance) A private university college offering six fully online, distance learning undergraduate degrees. Courses are designed by industry experts and focus on financial services and related professions. LIBF provides students with flexibility, giving them the ability to schedule their exams while equipping them with the skills and expertise sought by employers in the industry.

Applications are submitted through UCAS. Applicants are expected to have two subjects at A level or equivalent, as well as Maths and English at GCSE grade C/4, or equivalent. However, the University encourages applications from those who do not meet the academic requirements. All applications are viewed holistically and contextual offers are made on an individual basis.

London (Institute of Cancer Research) A postgraduate college of the University of London with laboratories and scientific facilities across two sites in Chelsea and Sutton. This world-class research institute has an excellent record of achievement, offering a MSc in Oncology as well as PhD studentships and short Radiotherapy and imaging training courses. Paid summer scholarships are available to undergraduate students wishing to gain hands-on cancer research experience.

Applications should be made directly to the Institute. The minimum entry requirements for MSc Oncology include a graduate medical degree, at least two years of postgraduate experience in clinical medicine and registration with the UK GMC. For more detailed information please visit the ICR website.

London (Interdisciplinary School) Located in Whitechapel, east London, the School was founded in 2017 and welcomed its first cohort of 100 students in 2021. It offers a Bachelor of Arts and Sciences in Interdisciplinary Problems and Methods. The degree has a vocational focus, and is designed to give students the knowledge and skills to enter the modern workplace. The course is taught by a diverse group of academics, entrepreneurs and educationalists, including philosophers, journalists, behavioural scientists and mathematicians.

Applicants can apply via UCAS or directly through the Interdisciplinary School's website. There is no minimum bar for grades. All eligible applicants will be invited to a Selection Day, consisting of two online interviews. Offers are made on the basis of your performance at interview and your academic grades in the context of your background.

London (King's) The College on the Strand offers more than 180 degree programmes in the Faculty of Arts and Humanities, Faculty of Dentistry, Oral and Craniofacial Sciences, Faculty of Life Sciences and Medicine, The Dickson Poon School of Law, Florence Nightingale Faculty of Nursing, Midwifery and Palliative Care, Faculty of Natural, Mathematical and Engineering Sciences, Institute of Psychiatry, Psychology and Neuroscience, Faculty of Social Science and Public Policy and King's Business School at the Guy's, Strand, Waterloo, Denmark Hill and St Thomas's campuses. The degree course structure varies with the subject chosen and consists of Single Honours, Joint Honours, Combined Honours and major/minor courses. Most courses enable students to take optional modules alongside core modules.

The majority of courses require three A-levels. Applicants to the Department of Mathematics are required to take Further Mathematics. A-level General Studies and Critical Thinking are not included in offers, though their contribution to a student's overall development is valued. Deferred entry is acceptable if the conditions of the offer have been met.

London (LSHTM) A postgraduate university, specialising in public and global health. The School offers intensive master's and research degrees as well as distance learning programmes, short courses and free online courses. Students will have the opportunity to learn from experts with current real-world research experience at one of the world's leading public health universities.

Applicants to intensive master's programmes will need to have either a second-class honours degree (or equivalent) in a relevant discipline, a degree in medicine recognised by the GMC or awarded by an overseas institution recognised by the UK ENIC or GMC, or have relevant professional training or experience equivalent to a second-class honours degree. For more information please visit the LSHTM website.

London (QM) Queen Mary University of London is a leading research-intensive university with its main integrated teaching, research and residential campus in Mile End. It has five additional campuses in London and also has a presence in China, Malta, Paris and Singapore. Many courses offer students the opportunity to undertake a year in industry.

For all full-time programmes, students should apply online through UCAS. Each application is considered on its individual merits; selectors look for academic merit as well as a demonstrated ability to succeed on the chosen course of study. It may be possible for students to join undergraduate degree programmes at the beginning of the second and sometimes the third year. Those wishing to transfer their degree studies from another UK higher education institution may be considered but should contact the subject department before applying.

London (RH) The University is situated in Egham, Surrey. It offers Single, Joint and major/minor undergraduate Honours degrees in a wide range of subjects across six schools: Business and Management; Engineering, Physical and Mathematical Sciences; Humanities; Law and Social Sciences; Life Sciences and the Environment and Performing and Digital Arts. All students have the opportunity to undertake a placement year either abroad or in the UK.

Royal Holloway is committed to operating a fair, transparent and professional admissions process. At minimum, the University requires three passes at A level (or equivalent). No undergraduate courses require an interview as part of the standard process. Deferred entries of one year are acceptable. The University may make contextual offers based on an applicant's socio-economic background.

London (RVC) Campuses in London and in Hertfordshire. Courses are offered in Veterinary Medicine, Biological Sciences and Bioveterinary Sciences (the latter two do not qualify graduates to practise as veterinary surgeons). There is also a Veterinary Gateway course and Veterinary Nursing programme.

Applications for deferred entry are considered but the offer conditions must be met in the same academic year as the application. Applicants holding offers from RVC who fall slightly below the grades required may be considered subject to available places on the course. Applicants who do not meet the minimum entry requirements are not normally considered.

London (SOAS) Single-subject degrees focusing on Asia, Africa and the Near East include compulsory and optional units, and open option modules which students can choose from different departments in SOAS or, in most degree programmes, from another college of the University of London. In addition, two-subject degrees give great flexibility in the choice of units, enabling students to personalise their degrees to match their interests.

Particular attention is paid to past and predicted academic performance and offers may be made without an interview. SOAS is happy to consider deferred entry, which should be stated on the UCAS application. SOAS judges applications holistically; while academic ability is prioritised SOAS looks for a personal statement which is authentic to the applicant and demonstrates their enthusiasm for the subject.

London (UCL) Subjects are organised in Faculties: Arts and Humanities, Brain Sciences, Built Environment (the Bartlett), Engineering Sciences, Laws, Life Sciences, Mathematical and Physical Sciences, Medical Sciences (including the UCL Medical School), Population Health Sciences, Social and Historical Sciences. In addition, there is the School of Slavonic and East European Studies and the UCL Institute of Education. UCL also offers a cross-disciplinary degree in Arts and Sciences (BASc), based on the US liberal arts model.

UCL welcomes applications from students proposing to spend a pre-university year engaged in constructive activity in the UK or abroad. Those wanting to enter the second year of a degree programme should make early contact with the relevant subject department to obtain approval. Applications are assessed on the basis of the personal statement, reference and the predicted academic performance, as well as additional assessment methods such as essays, questionnaires, aptitude tests and interviews. Decisions on admission are final and there is normally no right of appeal.

London LSE London School of Economics and Political Science is a leading social science specialist offering over 40 undergraduate degrees across a wide range of social science subjects. Degrees are three years long, except Philosophy, Politics and Economics (PPE), which is a four-year programme. All undergraduates study a compulsory course called 'LSE 100: Understanding the causes of things' which actively challenges them to analyse questions of current public concern and develops their critical skills.

A wide range of international qualifications are accepted for direct entry to the School. The standard entry requirements for the majority of the School's undergraduate programmes are based on three A-levels (or equivalent). Standard A-Level offers range from AAB to A*AA – applicants should check individual degree requirements. Intense competition for places means that high predicted grades on the application will not guarantee an offer. Each applicant is considered on their merit and in competition with the rest of the applicant cohort in a given admissions cycle. Each application is viewed holistically; assessing the merit, potential, motivation, skills and qualities of applicants by considering all the information presented on the application form. This includes, but is not limited to, academic achievements and qualifications. The personal statement, academic reference and additional social and educational contextual data also form an important part of the selection process. For applicants from the UK who are eligible for Home tuition fees, contextual information is used to gain a more complete picture of the educational and individual context of an applicant. This allows the School's admissions selectors to assess achievement and potential while recognising the challenges an applicant may have faced in their educational or individual circumstances. Eligible students may be considered for a contextual offer. More details are available on the LSE website. It is unlikely there will be any vacancies when A-level results are published. LSE does not typically participate in Clearing.

London Met A public research university spread across two city centre campuses offering a broad range of courses. Single and Joint Honours courses are made up of compulsory and optional modules allowing students some flexibility to follow their particular interests. Sandwich placement options are offered on a wide range of degree programmes, and shorter placements are also available on a number of courses.

The University considers each application comprehensively on its own merit, valuing applicants' potential as well as any prior achievements. The minimum academic entry requirement for all courses is 2–3 A-levels at grade C or above, or equivalent. Some courses require applicants to attend an audition or interview.

London Regent's Regent's private university offers undergraduate and postgraduate programmes delivered in an international learning environment. Programmes range from US-style Liberal Studies degrees to industry-led UK degree programmes in business, psychology, acting, film, media and fashion subject areas.

The University considers each application comprehensively on its own merit, valuing applicants' potential as well as any prior achievements. The minimum academic entry requirement for all courses is 2–3 A Levels at grade C or above, or equivalent. Some courses require applicants to attend an audition or interview.

London South Bank A University offering career-focused and industry-relevant degrees through its School of Applied Sciences, Arts and Creative Industries, Built Environment and Architecture, LSBU Business School, Engineering, Law and Social Sciences and the Institute of Health and Social Care. All courses have flexible modes of study and many vocational courses offer sandwich placements.

Applicants not achieving the grades required for their chosen course should contact the University, which may still be able to make an offer of a place. All applicants are interviewed for courses in the School of Arts and Creative Industries and the Institute of Health and Social Care. LSBU advises applicants that around 65% of the personal statement should focus on academic interest in the course and 35% on the applicant and their abilities.

Loughborough Loughborough is a single-site campus university that offers a range of courses across 22 different academic schools and departments. Degrees are structured using a combination of compulsory and optional modules so that study can be tailored to individual interest. All undergraduates have the option to incorporate a year of paid industry experience into study, where students can practise skills learned in a professional environment. As a result, Loughborough students have high graduate employment prospects and are often sought after by top national and international recruiters.

As well as academic qualifications, the University considers a wide range of criteria when reviewing applications. Selectors look for a proven ability to succeed on the course, as well as evidence of enthusiasm. The majority of programmes allow deferred entry; Loughborough typically allows students to defer their application twice before asking them to re-apply.

Manchester A research-driven university offering Single and Joint Honours courses which are divided into course units, some of which are compulsory, some optional, and some are taken from a choice of subjects offered by other schools and faculties. A comprehensive Combined Studies degree enables students to choose course units from Arts, Humanities, Social Sciences and Sciences, and this provides the flexibility for students to alter the emphasis of their studies from year to year.

Strong examination results are the main factor in the admission of students to courses, and the University accepts a wide range of qualifications. All decisions are made by the academic departments according to their individual requirements. For example, some programmes may require the applicant to have GCSE Maths at grade 4 (or C) or above for entry, others may require a compulsory subject at A-level. Other factors that are considered are prior and predicted grades, evidence of knowledge and commitment in the personal statement, and teacher references. Some courses may also take into account performance at interview, aptitude tests and portfolios. Where places are limited, they are offered to those eligible applicants who best meet the selection criteria and who, according to the admissions team, are most likely to benefit from their chosen course and to contribute to both their academic school and the wider university.

Manchester Met A large number of courses involve industrial and commercial placements. It is also possible to take Combined Honours degrees selecting a combination of two or three subjects. Many programmes have a modular structure with compulsory and optional core modules.

Admissions staff look for personal statements showing evidence of the applicants' motivation and commitment to their chosen courses, work or voluntary experience relevant to any chosen career, and extra-curricular activities, achievements and interests which are relevant to the chosen courses.

Marjon Plymouth Marjon University is based on an open, green campus, with easy access to Plymouth city centre and the beaches of Devon and Cornwall. The campus includes accommodation, a sports centre and pool. The University is student-centred, and regularly features in the top universities in the country for student satisfaction. Subject areas include health professions, including psychology and psychotherapies, sport and wellbeing, education and teacher training, journalism, business and creative arts. Teaching focuses on building students' confidence and transferable skills, alongside subject knowledge, using professional-standard facilities and equipment which prepare students for future careers.

The University welcomes applications from students with disabilities, who are well catered for on campus. Most teaching and health and social care courses require applicants to attend an interview. Selectors look for applicants who use the personal statement to illustrate the reasons behind their course choice, why their qualifications equip them for the course, and evidence of motivation to learn at a higher level. Applicants are also encouraged to provide information about relevant work experience, extracurricular activities and interests.

Medway Sch Pharm The School is part of a collaboration between the Universities of Greenwich and Kent. It offers one four-year undergraduate Pharmacy (MPharm) degree which helps students apply for pre-registration training, various postgraduate and research pharmaceutical degrees, and short courses for health professionals. Degrees are fully accredited by the General Pharmaceutical Council (GPhC).

See **Pharmacy and Pharmaceutical Sciences** in **Chapter 7**.

Middlesex A career-focused university with campuses in London and overseas in Dubai and Mauritius. Single and Joint Honours courses are offered on a modular basis by the University's Faculties of Arts and Creative Industries; Business and Law; Health, Social Care and Education; and Science and Technology. Most programmes have an optional work placement and sandwich placements are available in a variety of programmes.

A flexible approach is taken to the admissions process. If an applicant fails to meet the academic requirements of their offer, the University will seek to recognise their potential in a different way. Applicants will be required to attend an interview for courses in the arts and creative industries, as well as Nursing, Midwifery and Social Work courses. Some courses start in January.

Newcastle Single, Joint and Combined Honours programmes are offered. Some programmes provide students with the opportunity to defer their choice of final degree to the end of the first or second year. In Accountancy and Finance there is a 'Flying Start Programme' sandwich course which offers paid work experience. Several courses are offered with optional placements. The University has overseas campuses in Singapore and Malaysia.

The University accepts a wide range of qualifications and combinations of qualifications for entry to its degree programmes. Offers are made in terms of grades to be achieved (UCAS Tariff points are not used). The University makes contextual offers to applicants from disadvantaged backgrounds, particularly in psychology, law and computing courses. Generous scholarships are offered to new undergraduate students.

Northampton The University of Northampton offers Single Honours, Joint Honours, Foundation degrees, HNDs and top-up courses. The University also offers a Year 0 in some courses for those who do not meet its entry requirements. There are also placement opportunities in the third year for certain courses, particularly within the business school. A range of courses and learning options are available including full- and part-time, distance learning and two-year fast track degrees.

Entry requirements usually range from BCC to ABB for BA/BSc degrees depending on the course. If minimum entry requirements are not met, the University encourages applicants to contact the Admissions team and inform them of any relevant work, voluntary experience or independent study. Around 40% of courses require applicants to attend an interview or audition.

Northumbria Northumbria University is located in Newcastle upon Tyne and also has a campus in London. It offers a diverse range of degree programmes, with an emphasis on vocational studies. Single and Joint Honours programmes are available, and most programmes have the option of a study-abroad or placement year.

The University accepts a wide range of qualifications for entry onto its degree programmes, including combined qualifications. Standard entry criteria are based on UCAS tariff points, but other qualifications are considered. Interviews are compulsory for most courses in Health and Teaching and portfolios are required for creative courses. There are no admissions tests. Northumbria University is committed to raising aspirations through widening participation. Destination Northumbria is a supported entry scheme for prospective students with specific academic and background criteria. Further details can be found on the University's 'Destination Northumbria' webpage. A contextual scheme is in operation for prospective students with specific backgrounds.

Norwich Arts The University offers three and four-year undergraduate degrees designed to help students build their creative careers. Courses are practical and project-based, enabling students to grow their portfolios and interact with visiting industry professionals. An Integrated Foundation Year (Year 0) is available for students wishing to learn a new subject or develop their skills and confidence before undertaking a degree.

The University accepts a wide range of qualifications and uses UCAS tariff points. Most courses require applicants to submit a portfolio; applicants to BA Acting are required to attend an audition. Applications are mainly assessed through the portfolio, so the University encourages applications from those without formal qualifications or who do not meet the minimum entry requirements.

Nottingham The University boasts a number of campuses both in the UK and abroad, with overseas campuses located in China and Malaysia. Single and Joint Honours courses are available, with some industrial placements. Programmes are modular with compulsory and optional modules, the latter giving some flexibility in the selection of topics from outside the chosen subject field. Degree programmes are offered in the Faculties of Arts, Engineering, Medicine and Health Sciences, Science and Social Sciences. In addition, study-abroad opportunities are currently offered at over 200 institutions worldwide, through schemes such as Universitas 21 and Turing, which has replaced the Erasmus+ programme; almost all students can apply to complete a study and/or work placement abroad. Please check the university's website for further details. The University of Nottingham delivers a Medicine degree in collaboration with the University of Lincoln.

Due to high demand there is no guarantee that an offer will be made to applicants whose grade predictions match the requirements for their chosen course. Selectors look for applicants who can demonstrate motivation and provide a strong reason to study their chosen course, as well as evidence of relevant extracurricular activities. For details of entry to the Medical School, see the University website.

Nottingham Trent The University has sites with cutting-edge facilities in and around Nottingham, and in London. Degree programmes are offered in a range of subjects. Many courses are vocational with industrial and commercial placements and some students are also able to spend periods of time studying at a partner university around the world.

The UCAS personal statement is seen as a key part of the application process; the University website provides a guide on its possible content and preparation. Offers are based on the UCAS tariff. Both academic and vocational qualifications, including T Levels, are considered alongside any relevant experience. Nottingham Trent will always try to make an offer, even when the minimum academic requirements have not been met.

NU London Northeastern University London (formerly New College of the Humanities) offers undergraduate degrees in Business, Data Science, Economics, English, History, Law, Philosophy, Politics & International Relations, Psychology, as well as joint honours degrees in Computer Science & Business, Politics & Data Science, Philosophy & Computer Science. The degrees allow students to create their own academic pathway from a wide range of elective courses that are designed to complement and contextualise their main subject area. Students typically experience lectures of 20 students or fewer, small group seminars and tutorials. Scholarships and bursaries are offered.

Students may apply directly to the University, via UCAS or through Common App at any time. NU London will consider applications individually and on their merits. The University welcomes applications from students whose achieved or predicted grades are up to two grades below the typical offer requirements. An Admissions adviser will review the application and decide whether they would like to invite the applicant to interview. Decisions are quick – usually within two weeks of the interview. As well as personal details and academic records, applicants are required to supply a reference and a personal statement. NU London considers applications for deferred entry on an individual basis and cannot guarantee this being offered.

Open University Distance learning and part-time higher education courses. Degree and diploma courses are offered in the following subject areas: arts and humanities, business and management, computing and ICT, education, early years, engineering and technology, environmental development and international studies, health and social care, languages, law, mathematics and statistics, psychology, science and social sciences. Students study at home and are sent learning materials by the OU, maintaining contact with their tutors by email, post and telephone. See also **Chapter 1**.

There are no formal entry qualifications for admission to courses.

Oxford The University has 30 colleges and five private halls admitting undergraduates. Colleges: Balliol, Brasenose, Christ Church, Corpus Christi, Exeter, Harris Manchester (mature students only), Hertford, Jesus, Keble, Lady Margaret Hall, Lincoln, Magdalen, Mansfield, Merton, New, Oriel, Pembroke, St Anne's, St Catherine's, St Edmund Hall, St Hilda's, St Hugh's, St John's, St Peter's, Somerville, Queen's, Trinity, University, Wadham, Worcester. Permanent Private Halls: Blackfriars, Regent's Park College, St Benet's Hall, St Stephen's House, Wycliffe. Candidates apply to a college and for a Single or Joint Honours programme.

Courses are offered with a core element plus a variety of options. Weekly contact with a college tutor assists students to tailor their courses to suit personal interests. Arts students are examined twice, once in the first year (Preliminary or Honour Moderations examinations) and at the end of the course (Final Honours School). Science students are similarly examined although in some subjects examinations also take place in the second year.

Entrance requirements range from A*A*A to AAA depending on the course. There are specific subject requirements for some courses, particularly in the sciences. Once any subject requirements are met, any other subjects at A-level are acceptable for admission purposes with the exception of General Studies and Global Perspectives and Research (and both General Studies and Critical Thinking for Medicine and Biomedical Sciences). It is generally recommended that students take those subjects which they enjoy the most and those in which they are most likely to achieve top grades. However, as the selection criteria for the University of Oxford are entirely academic, it is also a good idea for students to consider how best they can demonstrate their academic abilities in their choice of subjects. Admissions tests and written work are often part of the application process. Other equivalent qualifications such as Scottish Advanced Highers, American APs/SAT/ACT and the International Baccalaureate are also very welcome. Oxford does not participate in UCAS Clearing or Extra. Please see the University website for more details.

Oxford Brookes Single Honours courses are offered with modules chosen from a field of study or, alternatively, Combined Honours courses in which two subjects are chosen. These subjects may be in related or unrelated subjects. Mandatory placement years are involved in courses in Applied Languages, Building Surveying, and Construction Project Management. Optional placement years are offered in Accounting, Biological Sciences, Business, Economics, Marketing and Motor Sport Engineering.

Conditional offers are now expressed in terms of UCAS Tariff points rather than in grades. Oxford Brookes welcomes applicants with a mixture of qualifications (e.g. 1 A-level plus BTEC National Diploma, or 2 A-levels plus 1 Cambridge Pre-U Certificate).

Plymouth A public research university comprised of two campuses with state-of-the-art teaching and research facilities. A broad portfolio of degree courses is available from the University's Faculty of Arts, Humanities and Business, Faculty of Science and Engineering and Faculty of Health. Single Honours courses are offered, with many vocational programmes offering work placements.

The University looks for evidence in the UCAS personal statement of your understanding of the course, good numeracy and literacy skills, motivation and commitment, work experience or placement or voluntary work, especially if it is relevant to your course, any sponsorships or placements you have applied for, and your possible plans for a gap year.

Plymouth (AU) With state-of-the-art facilities and professional workspaces spread across four city centre sites, AU Plymouth is the UK's newest specialist arts university. Business and professional practice is embedded in the structure of all undergraduate programmes, and all students have the opportunity to undertake a sandwich year placement.

All applicants are required to submit a portfolio. A portfolio guide is available to download on the University website. Candidates without formal qualifications are invited to apply if they can provide evidence of their creativity. Applications directly into the second and third year are also welcomed.

Portsmouth Around 75% of undergraduate students are studying professionally accredited courses, and many more study on courses that offer real-life learning. Simulated learning environments include a mock courtroom, a newsroom, a health simulation suite, a £1m model pharmacy and a forensic house, where criminologists work on staged crime scenes, and a new £57m sports centre. Most courses include work placements and there is also the opportunity for all students to learn a foreign language.

Applications are considered using a variety of methods and a range of the following are taken into account depending on the course applied for: actual and predicted grades, references, personal statements, interviews and tests. Different courses use different criteria and selection methods to reflect the nature and demands of the course. For all courses, academic achievement through prior learning or experience is important, as is the potential to succeed, as demonstrated through commitment to the subject. The University can make contextual offers to students from disadvantaged backgrounds.

Queen Margaret A single-site campus just outside Edinburgh with high-tech learning and research facilities. QMU offers a wide range of professionally relevant courses in the areas of healthcare; social sciences; creative arts; business, management and enterprise; and primary and secondary teaching. Many courses offer work placements and are accredited by professional bodies.

QMU has a general minimum entry requirement of at least two full A Levels (or equivalent) at grade D or above. The EPQ is welcomed but A level General Studies is not accepted for entry to any course. Alongside grades, selectors look for proof of motivation, suitability and skills. Applicants to courses which lead to eligibility for professional registration must illustrate an exploration of their chosen profession in the personal statement.

Queen's Belfast The academic year is divided into three semesters of 13 weeks each (two teaching semesters and one assessment period), with degree courses (pathways) normally taken over three years of full-time study. Six modules are taken each year (three in each semester) and, in theory, a degree can involve any combination of six Level 1 modules. Single, Joint and Combined Honours courses are offered and, in addition, major/minor combinations; some courses include sandwich placements. The University's overseas campus, China Queen's College, was jointly established by China Medical University and Queen's University Belfast in 2014 and is based in Shenyang, China.

Applications for admission to full-time undergraduate courses are made through UCAS. Interviews are essential for Medicine, Dentistry, Midwifery, Nursing and Social Work. Offers are made in terms of grades on the basis of three A-levels or equivalent, rather than UCAS points. Unsuccessful applicants may be considered for alternative courses. Applicants returning to study will need to demonstrate evidence of academic study within the last five years.

Ravensbourne Univ A small, industry-centred university in central London, Ravensbourne University hosts more than 100 creative businesses which its students can get involved in. The University has a strong focus on the vocational and the creative, offering a range of courses which include fashion, product design, architecture, music production, and broadcasting.

Many courses require applicants to be interviewed and/or submit a portfolio displaying relevant examples of creative work. The University offers workshops to help applicants prepare their portfolio. Entry to undergraduate courses is based on two A-levels or equivalent. Where a candidate has not met the minimum academic requirements, their demonstrated motivation and any relevant experience may be considered in evaluating their potential to succeed on the course and they may still be admitted.

Reading The University of Reading offers more than 250 undergraduate courses in arts, humanities, business, social science and science. The modular structure of its courses allows students to specialise in the areas that interest them most, while still developing core subject knowledge. If applicants are interested in studying two related subjects, it also has a wide range of combined degrees to choose from. Many courses include a mandatory placement year. The University also has an overseas campus in Malaysia.

Typical offers are presented in terms of A-level grades, but applications are welcomed from those presenting a wide range of qualifications. The University makes contextual offers across all subject areas, which are typically two grades lower than the top end of the published grade. In recognition of the preparation that the Extended Project Qualification provides to students, for several degree courses the University also makes offers of one grade lower provided the applicant obtains a B in the EPQ.

Richmond (Am Int Univ) This private University offers four-year undergraduate degree programmes blending the US and UK educational systems. All students graduate with a dual UK and US degree accredited by several professional bodies, broadening their career horizons. Every undergraduate student will take the Liberal Arts programme alongside their major subject.

Candidates can apply through UCAS, directly to the institution, or through the Common Application. Students are encouraged to visit before applying. All degree programmes require the same minimum entry requirement of qualifications equivalent to 96 UCAS tariff points.

Robert Gordon A professionally focused university based in Aberdeen. Courses are offered across a broad range of subject areas including computing, art and design; creative industries; engineering, business and law; the health professions and architecture and the built environment. Many courses offer work placements.

A wide range of qualifications are accepted, and students with work experience or non-standard qualifications are invited to apply. Interviews are required for courses in the Gray's School of Art, the School of Health Sciences, the School of Nursing, Midwifery and Paramedic Practice and the School of Pharmacy, Applied Sciences and Public Health. The University makes contextual offers to applicants from disadvantaged backgrounds.

Roehampton Roehampton has a 54-acre parkland campus in south-west London with historic buildings alongside modern, cutting edge facilities. The campus provides a close-knit community feel for students and is made up of four historic colleges and six academic departments. There are over 50 programmes offered at undergraduate level and Roehampton is also one of the principal providers of initial teacher training in the UK.

Tariffs for entry to undergraduate programmes vary depending on the programme; please check the website for full details. A wide range of qualifications are accepted, including BTECs, A-levels and T Levels. The University considers applications as a whole, taking into account applicants' achievements and future potential. There may be additional requirements so please check before applying.

Royal Agricultural Univ The RAU is located in Cirencester, Gloucestershire, and has been at the forefront of agricultural education for nearly 200 years. There are more than 1200 undergraduates and postgraduates studying subjects ranging from agriculture and rural land management to sustainable food systems, real estate, cultural heritage business and equine science.

Offers are usually made based on A-level grades between CCC and BCC, depending on the course. Some courses do not accept A-level General Studies or Critical Thinking. T-levels and vocational qualifications are accepted. RAU welcomes applications from those who do not meet the minimum entry requirements and will consider evidence of any relevant experience. Any undergraduate or postgraduate course applicant may be subject to an academic interview where applicants do not meet the standard entry criteria for the programmes as published.

Salford A public research university located across three campuses. A broad range of courses are offered by the School of Arts, Media and Creative Technology, the School of Science, Engineering and Environment, the School of Health and Society and Salford Business School. The University offers BA, BSc and BEng degrees with teaching methods depending on the degree. There is a wide range of professionally accredited programmes, many involving work placements. All undergraduates may study a foreign language.

Entry requirements vary between courses but typically range from 112 to 120 UCAS tariff points. A wide range of qualifications are accepted, from A/AS levels to BTEC awards. Interviews are currently required for applications to some courses in the School of Arts, Media and Creative Technology and the School of Health and Society.

Sheffield The teaching year consists of two semesters (two periods of 15 weeks). Courses are fully modular, with the exceptions of Dentistry and Medicine. Students register for a named degree course which has a number of core modules, some optional modules chosen from a prescribed range of topics, and some unrestricted modules chosen from across the University.

The University considers qualifications already achieved (including GCSEs), predicted grades and personal statements as the most important parts of an application. Interviews are not a prerequisite of admission, however some departments do interview to further assess the motivation and personal qualities of applicants. Departments that interview include Medicine, Dentistry, Orthoptics, Human Communication Science (for Speech Science) and Social Work. The Applicant Information Desk can help with any questions applicants have about the process of applying to Sheffield and the current status of their application.

Sheffield Hallam A large number of vocational courses are offered in addition to those in arts, humanities and social sciences. Most of the undergraduate courses offered by the University can be done as a sandwich course incorporating a work placement, usually between the second and third years. Most students are able to study an additional language from French, German, Italian, Spanish and Chinese, through the University Language Scheme.

The University's minimum entry requirement for an undergraduate degree is two A level passes and GCSE grades C or 4 in English Language and Maths, though individual programmes may make further specifications. Some courses require candidates to attend an interview and/or audition. The SHU Progress programme supports candidates with the application process who may be facing barriers to education due to personal circumstances.

Solent A public research university based in Southampton. Courses are offered in many vocational subjects. There are opportunities for students to gain work experience in the form of industrial placements alongside academic study.

Admissions staff look for applicants' reasons for their course choice, and for evidence of their abilities and ambitions. Most undergraduate courses require applicants to have at minimum two A levels or equivalent qualifications. BTECs are accepted; T Levels are accepted on their own for Foundation and year 1 entry. Scholarships specific to the year of entry are available and awarded as a tuition fee reduction.

South Wales The University has five campuses spread across three locations: Cardiff, Pontypridd in the South Wales Valleys (Glyntaff, Treforest and Sport Park campuses), and Newport. Many of the courses are vocational and can be studied as Single or Joint Honours courses or major/minor degrees.

Applicants for courses in art and design, teacher training and BSc Social Work are interviewed. USW seeks applicants with a proven capacity to participate in their chosen course, and the motivation to succeed. Applications are considered on an individual basis, taking into account relevant work/life experiences alongside qualifications. A small number of courses do not accept deferred applications, so all applicants wishing to defer their entry should first check their chosen course page or contact the Enquiries & Admissions Team.

Southampton A wide range of courses is offered in the Faculties of Arts and Humanities, Engineering and Physical Sciences, Environmental and Life Sciences, Medicine and Social Sciences. Programmes are generally for three years. All students have the chance to study a language as part of their degree and there are many opportunities for students to study abroad, including through the Turing Scheme (which has replaced the Erasmus+ programme) whether or not they are studying modern languages.

The University looks for a well-considered personal statement, focusing on your reasons for choosing a particular course, the skills you would bring to it, information about any relevant work experience, your career ideas, your personal interests related to the course, and your thoughts about 'what makes you stand out in a crowd'.

St Andrews A very wide range of subjects is offered across the Faculties of Arts, Divinity, Medicine and Science. A flexible programme is offered in the first two years when students take several subjects. The decision of which subject to complete your Honours degree in is made at the end of the second year when students choose between Single or Joint Honours degrees for the next two years. A broadly based General degree programme is also offered lasting three years. After two years of a General degree programme students may transfer onto a named Honours degree programme if they meet the requirements of the department(s). The University is reputed to be strong in sciences and in International Relations.

The University has introduced a tiered approach to its entry requirements with 'Standard' and 'Minimum' entry requirements for each subject. Entry is highly competitive and grades alone will not guarantee admission. All aspects of the application, including the personal statement, contextual information and any relevant experience, are considered. Alternative entry routes are available to applicants from underrepresented areas, those unable to attain the required grades, and those returning to education after a break.

St Mary's A Catholic university in Twickenham, London, offering flexible, modular degree options which allow a great deal of choice to both Joint and Single Honours students. Practical and theoretical studies are followed in the Acting course. Students of all faiths and backgrounds are welcomed.

Offers are made through UCAS. Interviews and/or preparatory work is required for applications to teaching, physiotherapy and acting programmes. Each application is considered on its individual merits, taking into account contextual information and experience. Access qualifications are considered. Most courses do not accept A-levels in General Studies or Critical Thinking and AS grades on the application are not considered.

St Mary's (UC) St Mary's University College Belfast is a Catholic higher education institution in Northern Ireland, affiliated to Queen's University Belfast. St Mary's delivers degree programmes in teacher education as well as a BA (Hons) degree in Liberal Arts which draws upon American and European liberal arts programmes.

Applications should be made directly to St Mary's UC. The general minimum entry requirement is passes in at least five subjects, including two A-level passes, or passes in at least four subjects, including three A-level passes. Two AS-levels are not accepted in place of one A-level. An interview is required for initial teacher education courses. Applications for deferred entry are considered on an individual basis.

Staffordshire The main campus at Stoke-on-Trent offers a diverse range of courses in art and design, business, computing, engineering, film, sound and vision, humanities, law, psychology, social sciences, science and sports science. The Centre of Health Innovation in Stafford offers simulation-based courses in Health Professions, while the new London Campus offers courses specialising in games, computing and technology. Courses can be taught full-time or part-time, while a selection of courses can be taught on a 'Fast Track' two-year basis.

The University provides various ways to support prospective students with their applications and personal statements. This includes advice over the phone, workshops on campus or at schools and colleges, online information and tailored advice at Open Days.

Stirling A flexible system operates in which students can delay their final degree choice until midway through the course. The University year is divided into two 15-week semesters, from September to December and January to May with a reading/study block and exams at the end of each semester. Innovative January entry is possible to some degree programmes. There are over 170 single and combined degrees with the opportunity to study a range of disciplines in the first two years. Subjects range across the arts, social sciences and sciences.

Admissions are administered through a central office. It is essential to include in the personal statement your reasons for choosing your specified course. The University also looks for evidence of your transferable skills, for example communication skills and teamwork, and how you acquired these, for example through work experience, voluntary work, academic studies, hobbies and general life experience. The University makes contextual offers across all disciplines.

Stranmillis (UC) This is a college of Queen's University Belfast, focusing on teacher training courses with European and international exchanges as part of the degrees. All undergraduate students complete an extensive programme of professional work placements.

Candidates for teacher training courses will be called for interview. Entry to the Primary BEd and Early Childhood Studies courses is highly competitive. In the interest of objectivity, when reviewing undergraduate applications academic grades are given priority and the applicant's previous academic background may also be considered. Applications for deferred entry are not accepted.

Strathclyde Based in the heart of Glasgow, Scotland's largest city, the University of Strathclyde is home to around 30,000 students from over 140 countries. A credit-based modular system operates with a good degree of flexibility in course choices. The University offers many vocational courses in the Faculties of Engineering, Humanities and Social Sciences, Science and in the Strathclyde Business School. There are also degree programmes in arts subjects, education and law.

Formal interviews are required for some vocational courses; informal interviews are held by some science and engineering courses. Candidates are considered on grades rather than UCAS tariff points. Admission is considered on a competitive basis and standard entry requirements for each course are normally the minimum. Applications for deferred entry are considered on an exceptional basis.

Suffolk The University of Suffolk is situated in central Ipswich and is based on the waterfront. A wide range of employability-focused degree courses are offered in the arts, business, social sciences, humanities, technology, health, and sciences.

Entry requirements are expressed in UCAS tariff points and differ between courses. Applicants for some courses, including arts, health, social work and courses with a work placement, are required to attend an interview or portfolio review. Applicants to professional health courses must attend a Selection Day. More information can be found on the University's 'Admissions' webpage.

Sunderland The University of Sunderland provides a range of courses across five Faculties: Arts and Creative Industries, Business, Law and Tourism, Education and Society, Health Sciences and Wellbeing and Technology. All courses are geared towards employability, with work placements and visiting lecturers from some of the biggest companies in the UK. Several courses can include an option to study abroad in various locations including Australia, USA, Germany, France and more.

The University holds informal interviews for certain courses, when applicants will be asked to present their portfolio, to give an audition, or to talk about themselves and why they want to study for that particular course. For details of entry to the School of Medicine, see the University website. The University accepts BTEC National Diplomas and Certificates provided 112 UCAS points have been achieved. A brief reason for rejection will be provided to unsuccessful applicants who applied through UCAS. Applicants who fail to meet the standard entry requirements may still be offered a place in their chosen course or an alternative course.

Surrey Located a short distance from Guildford, the University of Surrey is home to Stag Hill Campus and Manor Park Campus. It offers a wide variety of undergraduate degree programmes. The University works with over 2,300 partner organisations in the UK and overseas as it feels very strongly that professional training is an integral part of university life. A professional training year allows students to put their skills into practice and to experience a real professional environment.

Offers are expressed in grades, rather than UCAS tariff points. Applications from those who narrowly miss out on achieving the entry requirements will still be considered. The University is willing to consider deferring an application for one year, providing it considers that this will benefit the applicant's studies. Contact the admissions staff if you are considering deferred entry.

Sussex Teaching is structured around 10 schools of study and the Brighton and Sussex Medical School. Courses cover a wide range of subjects in humanities, life sciences, science and technology, social sciences and cultural studies. Students are registered in a school depending on the degree taken. In addition, students can customise their degree through a range of pathways, placements and study-abroad programmes.

If you are applying to do an undergraduate course in Social Work, Primary and Early Years Education (with Qualified Teacher Status) BA or Medicine, you will need to attend an interview. If you do not have formal academic qualifications, you may be asked to attend an interview. There are workshops within the admissions process for Drama Studies and portfolio reviews for Product Design. Workshops take place on Applicant Visit Days.

Swansea Courses are offered in a wide range of subject areas including social sciences, business, economics and law, engineering, languages, medicine and health sciences and science. Degree courses are modular with the opportunity to take some subjects outside the chosen degree course. Part-time degrees are available and study-abroad arrangements are possible in several subject areas.

All applicants applying for undergraduate degrees (with the exception of 'professional' programmes where an interview is an integral part of the selection process) who apply offering the requisite subjects (and grades at GCSE) can expect to receive a conditional offer of a place.

Teesside The Middlesbrough campus offers courses at undergraduate and postgraduate level, emphasising professionalism through work placements, volunteering, live projects, accredited courses and graduate internships. UK students obtaining a placement as part of their course normally receive a full fee waiver for their placement year. Optional placement years are available on courses in business, art and design, computing and engineering sciences. Popular courses include Dental Hygiene, Midwifery, Children's Nursing and Paramedic Practice.

Interviews are held for a number of courses, and successful applicants are given an individualised offer. Conditional offers are made in UCAS Tariff points. For some courses you may need to include points from certain subjects in your Tariff points score. New undergraduate students are provided with an iPad to access university resources and to use throughout their studies (eligibility criteria are available on the University's website).

Trinity Saint David The University has four main campuses in south-west Wales: in Swansea's city centre, in central Cardiff and in the rural towns of Lampeter and Carmarthen. Study at the Lampeter campus comprises Single and Joint Honours degrees in the humanities, and Carmarthen offers a range of courses, including business, sport and health, performing arts, and education studies. It also has campuses in London and Birmingham.

The University guarantees to give equal consideration to all applicants irrespective of when their applications are received. Applicants are advised to use the personal statement to present an authentic and well-rounded picture of themselves, demonstrating their compatibility with the course. Entry is based on individual merit.

UCO Now a school within the Health Sciences University, this is the largest and oldest osteopathic school in the UK, based in London. Its undergraduate four-year Master of Osteopathy (M.Ost) course involves a minimum of 1,000 hours of clinical training, and postgraduate courses are also offered.

Shortlisted applicants will be invited to attend an interview and evaluation day at the UCO. Selectors look for applicants who can demonstrate they have the motivation, commitment and skills necessary for successfully completing the course. If applicants fail to meet the selection criteria, they may be offered a place on an alternative course. Feedback for unsuccessful applications is available on request.

UHI The University of the Highlands and Islands offers over 300 courses across a wide range of subject areas at centres throughout Scotland including Argyll, Inverness, Moray, North Highland, Outer Hebrides, Perth, Orkney, Shetland and West Highland.

Entry requirements are expressed in grades which vary between courses. Prior learning is recognised and may be used in place of standard entry requirements provided the learning can be assessed. For any programme of study, applicants may be invited to one of the University's locations to learn more about the course and study experience at UHI; this is not part of the selection process. Deferred entry is acceptable to the majority of courses. Feedback for unsuccessful applications is available on request.

Ulster The University of Ulster is based on three sites spread across Northern Ireland: Jordanstown (Belfast), Coleraine and Magee (Derry), and it has branch campuses in Birmingham and London. The Faculties of Computing, Engineering and the Built Environment, Life and Health Sciences, Arts, Humanities and Social Sciences and Ulster University Business School offer a wide range of courses. There are various styles of learning supported by formal lectures and many courses include periods of work placement.

The general minimum entry requirement for all programmes is a minimum of passes in five subjects, including two A level (grades A–E) or equivalent and three GCSE (grades A–C/4–9) or equivalent. Ulster accepts different combinations of qualifications e.g. A-levels and BTECs. Applicants to healthcare and Social Work courses will be required to attend an interview.

Univ Law The private University of Law offers undergraduate Law degrees with a variety of full-time, part-time and online study options, all based on a traditional three-year full-time Qualifying Law Degree. There is a choice of where to study, with 17 campuses in locations across the UK, as well as international sites in Hong Kong and Berlin. Those seeking greater flexibility can choose to study entirely online. The courses combine academic rigour and practical skills, taught by qualified lawyers, often in small group workshops, with a strong emphasis on individual tutor contact and feedback. Employability is built into the course, through learning materials and teaching. It is also possible to continue postgraduate study with the University's LLM Legal Practice Course (SQE1&2) to practise as a solicitor or its Bar Professional Training Course (BPTC) to prepare students for life as a barrister. De Broc is the business school of the University of Law. It offers undergraduate business degrees with a focus on providing the training employers are looking for so that students are ready to do business from day one. If applicants are interested in a particular business specialism, the school offers pathways in finance, marketing and human resource management. The flexible course structure also allows students to switch to an alternative route should your aspirations change. It also offers undergraduate criminology, policing and psychology degrees.

Apply through UCAS for full-time courses, and for part-time courses apply direct to the University of Law.

UWE Bristol The University consists of several campuses in Bristol including Frenchay Campus (the largest), City Campus (Creative Industries), and Glenside Campus (Health and Applied Sciences). The University offers Single and Combined Honours courses organised on a modular basis which gives much flexibility in the choice of options. Many courses include optional sandwich placements and, in addition, students on many programmes have the opportunity to undertake a period of study in another country.

Offers may vary between applicants since selection is based on individual merit. The University's general minimum entry requirement is two A-levels or an equivalent qualification; T-levels and BTECs are accepted. Most offers will be made in terms of UCAS Tariff points with specific subjects required for some programmes.

Warwick Courses are offered by departments in the Faculties of Arts, Science, Engineering and Medicine and Social Sciences, which only accepts graduate applications. The University's undergraduate students can either choose single-subject degrees or combine two or more subjects in a Joint Honours degree. Options offered in each course provide some flexibility for you to tailor your course to your own areas of academic interest. Whatever course you choose, you can apply to study abroad, and many of the University's courses have inbuilt overseas experiences. Some of its degrees offer work placements and/or professional accreditation.

Before you decide to apply, you should check the entry requirements for your course. Selectors prefer applicants with a diverse range of subjects, therefore overlapping subjects, such as Accounting and Business Studies for Warwick Business School courses, should be avoided. Due to high levels of competition, Warwick cannot make offers to all applicants who meet, or even exceed, the standard entry requirements. Feedback can be provided if requested for candidates whose applications have been unsuccessful. The University welcomes applications for deferred entry.

West London The University's West London Campus comprises two locations in Ealing and Brentford. Subjects offered include Business and Accounting, Law and Criminology, Tourism, Aviation, Hospitality and Leisure, Computing and Engineering, Music and Performing Arts, Film, Media and Design, Education, Forensic Science and Psychology. In addition, a specialist education centre, the Berkshire Institute for Health, offers a range of courses in Nursing and Midwifery. Credit-rated Honours courses are offered, many with year-long work placements between Years 2 and 3. There is a large mature student intake.

The University accepts a wide range of qualifications for entry to all of its undergraduate courses. It is also possible to transfer credits achieved at another university to a course at this university. There is an overseas campus in the United Arab Emirates, and the University has partnerships with institutions in Europe and the Far East.

West Scotland UWS has campuses in Ayr, Dumfries, Lanarkshire, London and Paisley and provides a range of vocationally related courses, with a combination of links with employers, practical opportunities and professional recognition.

Applications are considered by the Admissions Office against previously agreed academic entry qualifications provided by the following Schools: Business and Creative Industries, Computing, Engineering and Physical Sciences, Education and Social Sciences and Health and Life Sciences. Within the four schools, applicants may be invited to attend an audition or interview prior to an offer being made.

Westminster Based in the heart of London with over a million businesses within a 20-mile radius, the University of Westminster offers a wide range of practice-based and career-focused courses that help students gain the skills and experience required to succeed in professional life. It also has an overseas campus, Westminster International University in Tashkent (WIUT), located in Uzbekistan.

Interviews are usually required for media, art and design courses. Applicants for creative courses should bring a portfolio of practical work to interviews. Applicants with non-standard qualifications or relevant work experience may be considered on an individual basis. Candidates who do not meet the minimum entry requirements for their chosen course are advised to contact the admissions team as they may still be considered.

Winchester The University offers undergraduate and postgraduate study in a range of subjects within the arts, humanities, social sciences, business, law, sport, education, and health and social care. Single Honours courses generally encompass core modules, complemented by a range of optional modules which enable students to tailor their degree towards their own interests.

Interviews are required for health and wellbeing courses, teaching courses and performing arts courses. A wide range of scholarships and bursaries are available. Entry requirements are expressed using UCAS Tariff points, with a typical range of between 104 and 120 points. A wide range of qualifications are considered, including the EPQ, Critical Thinking, General Studies and own-language A-levels.

Wolverhampton A large number of specialist and Joint Honours degrees are offered and many have work placements at home or abroad. Except for courses linked to specific professional requirements, programmes are modular providing flexibility of choice.

Admissions staff make decisions on the basis of the application, and may invite applicants for interview or audition. If an applicant cannot meet the entry requirements for the chosen course, the University may offer an alternative course, or give the applicant feedback about why it was unable to offer a place.

Worcester A wide range of undergraduate courses in education, health, sport, arts, humanities, sciences and business are on offer with Single and Joint Honours degrees available. The University is spread across four sites located in and around the West Midlands city: St John's campus, City campus, Severn campus and Lakeside campus.

The University accepts a wide range of qualifications including Access to HE Diplomas. The majority of offers are based on UCAS Tariff points but some courses have specific subject or GCSE requirements. Many courses require interviews before an offer is made, including Primary Education and Nursing courses. The personal statement is highly important and applicants are advised to reflect on interests, work experience, voluntary experience, extra-curricular activities and achievements relevant to their chosen course. If the applicant fails to receive an offer for their chosen course then an offer for an alternative course may be made.

Wrexham Formerly Glyndŵr University, the University is based in Wrexham in north-east Wales. It offers a wide range of courses covering areas such as art and design, business, computing, creative media technology, education, engineering, health, social science and sport. It also has a dedicated rural campus in nearby Northop for Animal and Environment based courses and a research centre for the opto-electronics technology industry at St Asaph Business Park. The University places a big emphasis on developing employability and linking courses with industry requirements. As well as traditional degree pathways, it has a range of four-year degree options that allow students to incorporate either a Foundation year or industrial placement into their degree.

Offers are usually based on UCAS Tariff point requirements. Most undergraduate courses require 112 UCAS Tariff points, and 48–72 Tariff points are required for courses including a Foundation year. UCAS points may be counted from a wide variety of qualifications but offers are usually made based on points from GCE A-levels or equivalent. An interview is always required for nursing courses. Other subject areas do not interview as standard, but may decide to interview applicants if deemed appropriate. Applications are welcomed from candidates who do not possess the standard qualifications but who can demonstrate their capacity to pursue the course successfully. Entrance can be based on past experience, skills, prior learning and the potential to succeed, particularly for entry onto a programme including a Foundation year.

Writtle (UC) Now a college within Anglia Ruskin University, Writtle College is situated in Chelmsford, Essex and is one of the largest land-based colleges in the UK. Higher and further education courses include agriculture and horticulture; sport performance, coaching and football academies; animal studies, equine and dog grooming; floristry and creative crafts.

Application details for the full range of courses offered are available on Anglia Ruskin University's 'Admissions' webpage.

York More than forty departments and centres cover a range of subjects in the arts and humanities, sciences, social sciences and medicine. The 'Languages for All' programme enables any student to take a course in any one of a number of languages, in addition to which there are several opportunities to build a period abroad into a degree course.

Applications are reviewed holistically and on an individual basis. Meeting the academic entry requirements does not guarantee the applicant an offer, especially on highly competitive courses. Any supporting information on the personal statement is valued. Interviews are required for medicine and social work, and candidates may be invited to interview for music, theatre and film and television courses. There are optional interviews for Maths. Hull York Medical School offers a Medicine with a Gateway Year programme, allowing locally based UK applicants who meet Widening Participation requirements to apply for Medicine with lower expected grades.

York St John A city centre university with five Schools: Arts; Education, Language and Psychology; Humanities; Science, Technology and Health; and York Business School. These offer a range of specialist degrees with Joint Honours courses offered in business, counselling, education, health studies, information technology, languages and linguistics, management, psychology and sport. The University also has a postgraduate campus in London.

Interviews are compulsory for Primary Education, health (such as Physiotherapy) and arts courses. Entry offers are expressed using UCAS Tariff points. The minimum entry requirement for all courses is two passes at A level and three GSCE subjects at Grade C or above, including English Language, or equivalent qualifications. Some courses include specific subject requirements. The University will endeavour to provide alternative routes of entry to those with non-standard qualifications. All successful applicants are invited to an offer holder.

4 | APPLICATIONS

ENTRY REQUIREMENTS

Before applying to universities and colleges, be sure that you have the required subjects and qualifications for entry to your chosen course. Details of entry requirements are available direct from the universities and colleges. You will need to check:

(i) the general entry requirements for courses

(ii) any specific subject requirements to enter a particular course, for example, study of specified A-levels and (where required) AS, Scottish Highers/Advanced Highers, Extended Project Qualification, GCSEs, Scottish Nationals, BTEC qualifications (for example, Diploma, Certificate) or T-levels. The course requirements are set out in prospectuses and on websites

(iii) any age, health, Disclosure and Barring Service (DBS) clearance or other requirements for entry to particular courses and universities and colleges. For entry to some specific courses, such as Medicine and Nursing, offers are made subject to health screening and immunisation requirements. Owing to government regulations, some universities will insist on a minimum age at entry of 18 years. Check university and college websites and prospectuses for these particular course requirements

(iv) admissions tests required by a number of universities for a range of subjects, including Dentistry, Law, Medicine and Veterinary Science/Medicine. Offers of places made by these universities are dependent on an applicant's performance in the relevant test. It is important to find out full details about universities' course requirements for possible admissions tests well before submitting the UCAS application and to make all the necessary arrangements for registering and taking any required admissions tests. See **Chapter 5** and check university/college and admissions tests websites for the latest information.

Potential applicants should ask the advice of teachers, careers advisers and university and college advisers before submitting their application.

APPLICATIONS FOR UNIVERSITY AND COLLEGE COURSES THROUGH UCAS

UCAS, the organisation responsible for managing applications to higher education courses in the UK, deals with applications for admission to full-time and sandwich first degrees, Foundation degrees, Diploma of Higher Education and Higher National Diploma courses and some full-time Higher National Certificate courses in nearly all universities (but not the Open University), university colleges, colleges and institutes of higher education, specialist colleges and some further education colleges. The UCAS Undergraduate scheme also is applicable for those applying for teacher training courses in Scotland and Wales.

The UCAS application process

Full details of application procedures and all course information can be found on the UCAS website (www.ucas.com).

Applications are made online through the UCAS Hub at www.ucas.com, which has been designed for all applicants whether they are applying through a UCAS-registered centre, such as a school or college, or applying independently from anywhere in the world.

Applications for 2026 entry can be started from 13 May 2025 but cannot be sent to UCAS until 2 September 2025. The first deadline is 15 October by 18.00 (UK time) for applications to the universities of Oxford or Cambridge and applications for most courses in Medicine, Dentistry and Veterinary Science/Medicine. The deadline to apply for all other courses is 14 January 2026 by 18.00 (UK time). You can still apply after this deadline up to 30 June, but institutions may not be able to consider you.

On the UCAS application, you have up to five course choices unless you are applying for Dentistry, Medicine or Veterinary Science/Medicine. For these courses only four choices are permitted, although you can add course choices that have the January deadline later.

Each university or college makes any offer through the UCAS system. UCAS does not make offers, or recruit on behalf of universities and colleges. It does not advise applicants on their choice of subject although it does publish material which applicants may find useful.

Applicants may receive an 'unconditional' offer in the case of those who already hold the required qualifications, or, for those awaiting examination results, a 'conditional' offer or a rejection. When all decisions have been received from universities or colleges, applicants may finally hold up to two offers: a firm choice (first) offer and an insurance offer.

Applicants who have made five choices and have no offers or have declined any offers received can use **Extra**. Applicants are told if they become eligible for **Extra** and can apply online for one further course at a time at www.ucas.com. **Extra** runs from 26 February until 4 July 2026. Courses available in **Extra** can be found in the search tool at www.ucas.com. Applicants not placed through this system will be eligible to contact institutions with vacancies in **Clearing** from 5 July. If you're holding a confirmed place and decide you no longer want it, from early July you can use online self-release into Clearing by using the 'decline my place' button in your application. You should only use this button if you no longer wish to take up your place at your firm choice and you have spoken to your university or college and/or an adviser at your school/centre.

If you already have your qualifications and are not waiting for any exam results, your place can be confirmed at any time after you send in your application. However, for thousands of applicants confirmation starts on the day when the A-level examination results are released. Clearing vacancies are listed in the search tool from early July to October. Applicants meeting the conditions of their offers for their firm choice will receive confirmation from their university or college and may still be accepted even if their results are slightly lower than those stipulated in the original offer. If rejected by their firm choice university/college, applicants will have their places confirmed by their insurance choice institution providing they have obtained the right grades. Applicants who are unsuccessful with both their institutions will be eligible to go into **Clearing**, in which they can select an appropriate course in the same or a different institution where places are available. In 2024 76,210 applicants obtained places through **Clearing**, and 4,600 applicants found a place though **Extra**.

UCAS TIMETABLE

2 September 2025	UCAS begins accepting applications.
15 October 2025	Deadline for UCAS to receive applications to Oxford University or the University of Cambridge, and applications to most courses in Medicine, Dentistry or Veterinary Medicine/Science.
14 January 2026	Deadline for UCAS to receive applications from UK and EU applicants for all other courses.
Until 30 June	Applications received by UCAS are forwarded to the institutions for consideration at their discretion. Applications received after 30 June are processed through **Clearing**.
26 February–4 July	Applicants who have made five choices and have no offers or who have declined any offers received can use **Extra** to apply for one further course at a time at www.ucas.com. Institutions will show which courses have vacancies in **Extra** on the UCAS website. Details of the **Extra** service can be found at www.ucas.com/extra.
6 May	Applicants receiving decisions from all their choices by 31 March must reply to their offers by this date (except applicants applying through **Extra**).
3 June	Applicants receiving decisions from all their choices by 13 May must reply to their offers by this date (except applicants applying through **Extra**).

30 June	Applications received after this date are entered directly into **Clearing**.
5 July	**Clearing** starts and **Clearing** vacancies are shown in the UCAS search tool. You can apply for a course using **Clearing** if you're not already holding an offer from a university or college or you've declined your firm place using the 'decline my place' button in your application.
August	Scottish SQA results published.
August	A-level and AS results published. (See **What To Do on Results Day ... and After** below.)

PLEASE NOTE

- You are not required to reply to any university/college offers until you have received your last decision.
- You cannot send a firm acceptance to more than one offer.
- If you decide not to go to university or college this year, you can withdraw your application. But don't forget, you will not be able to reapply until next year.
- Remember to tell the institutions and UCAS if you change your address, or change your examination board, subjects or arrangements.

Information on the special arrangements for applications for Law, Medicine and Dentistry can be found under separate headings in Chapter 5.

APPLICATIONS FOR MUSIC COURSES AT CONSERVATOIRES

UCAS Conservatoires handles applications for practice-based music, dance, drama and musical theatre courses. Applications can be made simultaneously to a maximum of six of the UCAS conservatoires listed below, and simultaneous applications can also be made through both UCAS Undergraduate and UCAS Conservatoires systems. Full details of UCAS Conservatoires are given on www.ucas.com/conservatoires. The conservatoires taking part in this online admissions system are:

- LAMDA (London Academy of Music and Dramatic Art) www.lamda.ac.uk
- Leeds Conservatoire www.leedsconservatoire.ac.uk
- Royal Academy of Music www.ram.ac.uk
- Royal Birmingham Conservatoire www.bcu.ac.uk/conservatoire
- Royal College of Music www.rcm.ac.uk
- Royal Conservatoire of Scotland www.rcs.ac.uk
- Royal Northern College of Music www.rncm.ac.uk
- Royal Welsh College of Music & Drama www.rwcmd.ac.uk
- Trinity Laban Conservatoire of Music and Dance www.trinitylaban.ac.uk

The Guildhall School of Music & Drama and the Royal Central School of Speech and Drama are not part of the UCAS Conservatoires scheme, so students wishing to apply will have to make their applications directly to those schools. There is an application fee, which varies depending on the conservatoire and course for which you apply; the fee includes the audition fee, which is charged by all conservatoires. For more details, see https://conservatoiresuk.ac.uk.

APPLICATIONS FOR TEACHER TRAINING COURSES

Applicants intending to start a course of initial teacher training in England leading to Qualified Teacher Status can find information on the Get Into Teaching website https://getintoteaching.education.gov.uk. See also www.ucas.com/teaching-in-the-uk for full details of applying for undergraduate (and postgraduate) training courses. Northern Irish, Scottish and Welsh students should apply through UCAS Undergraduate for teacher training courses.

APPLICATIONS FOR DEGREE APPRENTICESHIP COURSES

Applications for degree apprenticeship courses in England are handled by GOV.UK (www.gov.uk/apply-apprenticeship). It is likely that the employer and university will jointly recruit for their vacancies, to ensure that both are satisfied that the applicant can meet their respective requirements. You can also find lots of useful information on the UCAS website at www.ucas.com/apprenticeships or use UCAS' apprenticeship search (www.ucas.com/explore/search/apprenticeships) to search for apprenticeship vacancies. Deadlines for vacancies vary, so you'll need to keep an eye on these. Please also see page 11.

THE UCAS APPLICATION

In the choices section of your application, all your university/college choices (a maximum of five) are to be listed, but remember that you should not mix your subjects. For example, in popular subject areas such as English, History or Physiotherapy, it is safer to show total commitment by applying for all courses in the same subject and not to include second and/or third subject alternatives on the form. (See advice in separate tables in **Chapter 7** for **Medicine**, **Dentistry** and **Veterinary Science/Medicine**.)

A brief glance at the subject tables in **Chapter 7** will give you some idea of the popularity of various courses. In principle, institutions want the best applicants available so if there are large numbers of applicants the offers made will be higher. For Medicine and a number of other courses, offers in terms of A-level grades are now reaching AAA or A* grades, and sometimes with additional grades at AS, where school policy does not limit your opportunity to take AS subjects (in which case alternative A-level offers may be given). Conversely, for the less popular subjects, the offers can be much lower – down to CCC.

Similarly, some institutions are more popular (not necessarily better) than others. Again, this popularity can be judged easily in the tables in **Chapter 7**: the higher the offer, the more popular the institution. Popular universities often are located in attractive towns or cities such as Bristol, Exeter, Warwick, Bath or York. Because of the intense competition for places at the popular universities, applications to five of them could result in rejections from all of them! (If you are not good enough for one of them you won't be good enough for the other four!) Spread your choice of institutions.

When you have chosen your courses and your institutions, look again at the offers made and compare these with the grades projected by your teachers. It is most important to maximise your chances of a place by choosing institutions which might make you a range of offers. When all universities have considered your application you can hold only two offers (one firm and one insurance offer) and naturally it is preferable for one to be lower than the other in case you do not achieve the offer grades or equivalent points for your first choice of university or college.

You can see grade profiles of students previously accepted and offer rates for the course under the entry requirements in the UCAS search tool at www.ucas.com/search. This is historical data, so doesn't tell you what a university or college will accept this year – it's there to give an indication of the grade profiles they previously accepted. You can find out more at www.ucas.com/understanding-entry-grades-data.

The other section of the UCAS application that deserves careful thought is the personal statement. This seems simple enough but it is the only part of the application where you can put in a personal bid for a place! In short, you are asked to give relevant background information about yourself, your interests, your experience and your choice of course and career. Give yourself plenty of time to prepare your personal statement as this part of your application could make all the difference to getting an offer or not. You can find everything you need to know about writing your personal statement on the UCAS website at www.ucas.com/writing-your-personal-statement.

THE PERSONAL STATEMENT

The statement is your only opportunity to make a personal bid for your chosen courses. For students applying to start courses in 2026, the personal statement has changed from one long piece of text, to three separate sections in response to three specific questions. The character count will be 4,000 characters in total, and each section (question) requires a minimum character count of 350 characters. Below are the questions and some guidance on what you could include in each section. The questions are as follows:

1. Why do you want to study this course or subject?

This is your opportunity to showcase your passion for and knowledge of your chosen subject area, and to demonstrate to universities and colleges why they are a good fit for you and your future ambitions. Examples of what you might write about are:

- Your motivation for studying the course(s) – you can show this by describing what first interested you in the subject and why you are passionate about it.
- Your knowledge of this subject area and how it combines your interests and academic skills.
- Your career plans and how your chosen course ties into these.

2. How have your qualifications and studies helped you to prepare for this course or subject?
This is your chance to shout about the relevant or transferable skills you've gained from your formal education, and highlight your understanding of how they will help you succeed in this subject area. Examples of what you might write about here are:

- How your studies or training relate to your chosen course(s) or subject area.
- What relevant or transferable skills you have that make you a great candidate.
- Any relevant educational achievements.
- Any relevant supercurricular activities – how you have gone above and beyond the curriculum to demonstrate commitment to the subject.

Remember that your qualifications will be listed elsewhere in your application, so you don't need to repeat them here.

3. What else have you done to prepare outside of education, and why are these experiences useful?
This is your chance to talk about any other activities (ideally in the last three to four years) you've been involved in outside of your formal education, or personal experiences. Try to ensure these are relevant to the course, or that you can evidence relevant skills you've gained that will help you succeed at university. This section is likely to be highly personal to you. Examples of what you might write about here are:

- Work experience, employment, or volunteering, perhaps to evidence teamwork and/or any other essential skills.
- Personal life experiences or responsibilities (e.g. being a prefect, mentor or a member of a society or team).
- Hobbies and any extracurricular or outreach activities.
- Achievements outside of school or college.
- Post-education activities.

You can find lots more advice and helpful resources, including videos and personal statement guides on different subject areas, at www.ucas.com/new-ps.

Finally, plan your personal statement carefully. Although you are not required to write in continuous prose, it is advisable to do so as this is likely to make a better impression on admissions tutors. Your statement should be written in good, clear English, and it is essential that your spelling and grammar be accurate throughout. Keep a copy of your complete application for reference if you are called for interview.

Admissions tutors always stress the importance of the reference from your head teacher or form tutors. Most schools and colleges will make some effort to find out why you want to apply for a particular course, but if they do not ask, do not take it for granted that they will know! Consequently, although you have the opportunity to write about your interests on the form, it is still a good idea to tell your teachers about them. Also, if you have to work at home under difficult conditions or if you have any medical problems, your teachers must be told since these points should be mentioned on the reference.

Deferred entry

Although application is usually made in the autumn of the year preceding the proposed year of entry, admissions tutors may be prepared to consider an application made two years before entry, so that the applicant can, perhaps, gain work experience or spend a period abroad. Policies on deferred entry may differ from department to department, so you should check with admissions tutors before applying. Simply remember that there is no guarantee that you will get the grades you need or a place at the university of your first choice at the first attempt! If not, you may need to repeat A-levels and try again. It may be better not to apply for deferred entry until you are certain in August of your grades and your place.

APPLICATIONS TO OXBRIDGE

The universities of Oxford and Cambridge offer a wealth of resources and opportunities to students, including highly personalised teaching in tutorials (at Oxford) or supervisions (at Cambridge), where groups of two or three students meet to discuss their work with a tutor (Oxford) or supervisor (Cambridge). The college system is also a key advantage of an Oxbridge education, as students gain all the benefits of studying at a large and internationally acclaimed university, as well as the benefits of life in the smaller college community. *NB: You can only apply to either Oxford or Cambridge on your UCAS Application, and not both.*

University of Cambridge

Those applying to Cambridge need to complete their UCAS application listing Cambridge as one of their university choices and send it to UCAS by 15 October 2025, 18.00 (UK time). You can indicate your choice of college or make an Open application if you have no preference. Open applicants are allocated to colleges that have had fewer applicants per place for your chosen subject. For more information, see www.undergraduate.study.cam.ac.uk/apply/how/ucas-application.

Following the submission of your application to UCAS, you will receive an email from the University, confirming the arrival of your application and giving you the website address of their online My Cambridge Application (MCA), which you will then need to complete by 22 October 2025, 18.00 (UK time). For more information, see www.undergraduate.study.cam.ac.uk/apply/how/cambridge-application.

The Extenuating Circumstances Form (ECF) has been designed to ensure that the Cambridge colleges have the information they require in order to accurately assess any applicant who has experienced particular personal or educational disadvantage through health, personal problems, disability or difficulties with schooling. If necessary, the ECF should normally be completed and submitted by the applicant's school/college by 22 October. Further details can be obtained at www.undergraduate.study.cam.ac.uk/apply/how/disrupted-studies.

Interviews usually take place in Cambridge in December, and will generally be in-person if you live in the UK and online if you live outside of the UK. For more information, see www.undergraduate.study.cam.ac.uk/apply/after/cambridge-interviews.

Depending on your selected course, you may also need to register and prepare for an admissions assessment and/or submit examples of written work. Applicants will take the written assessments either pre-interview or at interview (or both for some courses). See www.undergraduate.study.cam.ac.uk/apply/how/admission-tests for the complete list of tests and registration requirements for each course, and www.undergraduate.study.cam.ac.uk/apply/after/written-work-portfolio for how to submit written work or a portfolio. See also **Chapter 5** for information you need to know before completing and submitting your application.

By the end of January, applicants receive either an offer conditional upon certain grades in examinations to be taken the following summer, or a rejection. Alternatively, you may be placed in a pool for further consideration. Decisions are made on the basis of academic record, reference, personal statement, submitted work/test results and interviews. The conditions set are grades to be obtained in examinations such as A-levels, Scottish Highers/Advanced Highers or the International Baccalaureate. See www.undergraduate.study.cam.ac.uk/apply/after/application-decisions for more information.

College policies

All colleges that admit undergraduates use the selection procedures described in **Chapter 5**. However, there will be some minor variations between the various colleges, within each college and also between subjects. Further information about the policies of any particular college can be found in the Cambridge Undergraduate Prospectus and may also be obtained from the admissions tutor of the college concerned. No college operates a quota system for any subject except Medicine and Veterinary Medicine, for which there are strict quotas for the University from which places are allocated to each college.

Full details of the admissions procedure are contained in the current Cambridge Undergraduate Prospectus, which is available online at www.undergraduate.study.cam.ac.uk, from where you can also order a hard copy if necessary.

To find out more

The University holds two Open Days a year; these are highly recommended as a great way to meet tutors and current students and find out more. In 2025, the Open Days are on 10 and 11 July (see www.undergraduate.study.cam.ac.uk/events/cambridge-open-days). You can also visit www.undergraduate.study.cam.ac.uk/find-out-more/widening-participation for further information about widening participation and outreach at Cambridge.

University of Oxford

Those applying to Oxford need to complete their UCAS application listing Oxford as one of their university choices and send it to UCAS by 15 October 2025, 18.00 (UK time). You can indicate your choice of college or make an Open application if you have no preference.

You can only apply to one undergraduate course at Oxford. You can also express a preference for a particular college if you wish, or you can make an open application. Open applicants are allocated to colleges that have had fewer applicants per place for your chosen subject. However, once an application has been allocated to a college, this is final. Therefore, if there are any colleges you do not want to go to, you should name a college preference rather than submitting an open application. For more advice on this, visit www.ox.ac.uk/admissions/undergraduate/colleges/do-you-choose-a-college.

The colleges all provide a high standard of academic teaching for all the courses they offer, and the facilities are generally similar. For more information on the college system, visit www.ox.ac.uk/admissions/undergraduate/colleges/what-are-oxford-colleges and if you have any particular requirements then you can read about the colleges in more detail at www.ox.ac.uk/admissions/undergraduate/colleges/a-z-of-colleges.

Many Oxford courses require candidates to sit a written test in the autumn as part of their application. All admissions tests are online and taken at a Pearson VUE test centre (located across the UK and overseas). Separate registration is required for tests, and deadlines strictly adhered to, so it is really important to check the details for your course in the summer before you apply. At the time of writing, it is unclear what these changes will be, so it is essential you check www.ox.ac.uk/admissions/undergraduate/applying-to-oxford/guide/admissions-tests for the latest information from August 2025 onward. Some courses also ask candidates to submit examples of their written work by 10 November; see www.ox.ac.uk/admissions/undergraduate/applying-to-oxford/guide/written-work for more information. See also **Chapter 5** for information you need to know before completing and submitting your application.

Shortlisted candidates will be invited for interviews held in December, and all interviews in 2025 for 2026 entry are to be held online. The interview is a crucial part of the selection process. Candidates will usually be interviewed by two tutors (occasionally more) at their college of preference (if they have specified one), or the college they have been allocated to (if they submitted an open application or their chosen college is oversubscribed), and they may also be interviewed by other colleges. The University works hard to ensure that the best candidates are successful, whichever college you have applied to. This means a lot of successful applicants receive an offer from a college they did not specify on their application. Visit www.ox.ac.uk/admissions/undergraduate/applying-to-oxford/guide/interviews for up-to-date and comprehensive information about the interview process.

When considering your application, tutors will take into account all the information that has been provided in order to assess your suitability and potential for your chosen course. This includes your performance at interview, academic record, personal statement, academic reference and predicted grades, alongside any admissions tests or any written work required. Each application is considered carefully on its individual merits, including contextual information about candidates' educational background (UK applicants only) where possible.

All candidates will be notified as to whether their application was successful or not about eight to ten weeks after the deadline. Successful applicants who have not completed their school-leaving examinations will be made conditional offers based on final grades. These will probably be between A*A*A and AAA at A-level, 38–40 points in the International Baccalaureate (including core points) with 6s and 7s in the Higher Level subjects, or other equivalent qualifications (see www.ox.ac.uk/admissions/undergraduate/courses/admission-requirements/uk-qualifications and www.ox.ac.uk/admissions/undergraduate/applying-to-oxford/for-international-students/international-qualifications).

Full details of the admissions procedure can be found on www.ox.ac.uk/admissions/undergraduate/applying-to-oxford and www.ox.ac.uk/admissions/undergraduate/applying-to-oxford/guide.

To find out more

The University holds three Open Days a year: two in late June or early July, and one in mid-September (see www.ox.ac.uk/admissions/undergraduate/open-days-and-visits). These are highly recommended as a great way to meet tutors and current students and find out more. In 2025, the Open Days are on 2 and 3 July and 19 September. You can also visit www.ox.ac.uk/admissions/undergraduate for further information about undergraduate admissions and outreach at Oxford.

APPLICATIONS TO THE RUSSELL GROUP

The 24 Russell Group (https://russellgroup.ac.uk) universities are research-intensive institutions whose aim is to have global reach socially, economically and culturally. The Russell Group is composed of the following universities:

- University of Birmingham
- University of Bristol
- University of Cambridge
- Cardiff University
- Durham University
- University of Edinburgh
- University of Exeter
- University of Glasgow
- Imperial College London
- King's College London
- University of Leeds
- University of Liverpool
- London School of Economics and Political Science (LSE)
- University of Manchester
- Newcastle University
- University of Nottingham
- University of Oxford
- Queen Mary University of London
- Queen's University Belfast
- University of Sheffield
- University of Southampton
- University College London
- University of Warwick
- University of York.

For those interested in studying at any of the above universities, the Russell Group has published information on what it terms 'Informed Choices', ie how subjects taken at sixth form or college can affect students' options at university and beyond, and which subject choices can open up various degrees. This information can be found at www.informedchoices.ac.uk. Additional information on studying at a Russell Group university can be found at https://russellgroup.ac.uk/for-students.

APPLICATIONS TO IRISH UNIVERSITIES

All applications to universities, colleges of education and institutes of technology, along with some specialist colleges, in the Republic of Ireland are made through the Central Applications Office. Both the CAO website (www.cao.ie) and www.educationinireland.com/en/How-Do-I-Apply-/Apply-for-a-Course/Undergraduate-Courses give details of all institutions and the application procedure. Applications are made by 1 February. Individual institutions publish details of their entry requirements for courses, but unlike applications through UCAS in the UK, no conditional offers are made. Applicants are judged purely on their academic ability; as such, offers are made in August following the release of Irish Leaving Certificate results, and successful students are required to quickly accept or decline the offer.

APPLICATIONS TO COMMONWEALTH UNIVERSITIES

Details of over 400 institutions in 40 commonwealth countries (all charge fees) are published on the website of the Association for Commonwealth Universities, www.acu.ac.uk. If you are specifically looking for institutions in Australia, then you can also look at www.idp.com/australia, or for institutions in Canada you can also look at www.studyincanada.com.

APPLICATIONS TO AMERICAN UNIVERSITIES

There is a very large number of universities and colleges offering degree course programmes in the USA; some institutions are independent and others state-controlled. Students applying to study in the USA can apply to up to 20 (out of more than 1,000) institutions through the Common Application, the central admissions system. However, unlike the UK, where UCAS controls nearly all university and college applications, it is still necessary to apply to American institutions directly and pay an individual application fee to each; a full list of participating Common Application colleges can be found at www.commonapp.org. Most American universities will expect applicants to have A-levels or IB qualifications, and may also require students to complete either the SAT or ACT admissions tests. As universities and colleges in the US set their own admissions policies, you will need to check the individual requirements of each of your chosen institutions. The SAT Reasoning Test covers mathematical and evidence-based reasoning abilities. In some cases, applicants may be required to complete a writing task as part of the reasoning test, as well as taking SAT II tests which are based on specific subjects. The ACT tests English, maths, comprehension and scientific reasoning. Some universities require applicants to take the ACT with writing, which includes an additional writing task. Both the SAT and the ACT can be taken at centres in the UK: see www.collegeboard.org and www.act.org respectively for details. Practice tests can be sourced from Kaplan at www.kaptest.com.

Unlike the usual specialised subject degrees at UK universities, in the USA you just apply as an undergraduate, rather than to a specific degree. 'Liberal Arts' programmes in the USA have considerable breadth and flexibility, although subjects requiring greater specialised knowledge, such as Medicine and Law, require further study at Medical or Law School.

While each institution has its own admissions requirements and timetable, in general early application deadlines are mid-November and regular application deadlines are between January and March.

Because of the complexities of an application to American universities, such as financial implications, visas, etc., students should make use of the wealth of information available from the US-UK Fulbright Commission (www.fulbright.org.uk/going-to-the-usa/undergraduate), an organisation that seeks to promote educational exchange between the US and the UK.

Another very useful webpage is www.prospects.ac.uk/postgraduate-study/study-abroad/study-in-the-usa#how-to-apply. And, as it is important to be able to identify the differences between and the quality of institutions, valuable guides can be sourced through www.petersons.com/graduate-schools.aspx.

THE TURING SCHEME

The Turing Scheme is a UK government study and work abroad programme, and applies to countries across the world. Funding helps participants cover travel expenses and costs of living, and helps with administrative funding for delivering the projects. The scheme helps organisations enhance their existing international ties and form new relationships around the world. During the 2023/24 academic year, the Turing Scheme supported over 41,000 students, of which 71% were from disadvantaged backgrounds, to study and work in over 160 destinations around the world. For more details on the Turing Scheme, see www.gov.uk/government/publications/turing-scheme-international-study-and-work-placements/overview-of-the-turing-scheme. Please note that students cannot apply directly for the Turing Scheme funding, but must do so through their education provider.

AND FINALLY ... BEFORE YOU SEND IN YOUR APPLICATION

- CHECK that you have passes at grade 4/C or higher in the GCSE (or equivalent) subjects required for the course at the institutions to which you are applying. FAILURE TO HAVE THE RIGHT GCSE SUBJECTS OR THE RIGHT NUMBER OF GRADE 4/C OR ABOVE PASSES IN GCSE WILL RESULT IN A REJECTION.

- CHECK that you are taking (or have taken) the A-level subjects required for the course at the institution to which you are applying. FAILURE TO BE TAKING OR HAVE TAKEN THE RIGHT A-LEVELS WILL ALSO RESULT IN A REJECTION.
- CHECK that the A-levels and any other qualifications you are taking will be accepted for the course for which you are applying. Some subjects and institutions do not stipulate any specific A-levels, only that you are required to offer two or three subjects at A-level. In the view of some admissions tutors NOT ALL A-LEVELS CARRY THE SAME WEIGHT (see **Chapter 1**).
- CHECK that you can meet the requirements for all relevant admissions/interview tests.
- CHECK that you have made all the necessary arrangements for sitting any required admissions tests.
- CHECK that you can meet any age, health and DBS requirements for entry to your listed courses.

WHAT TO DO ON RESULTS DAY ... AND AFTER

You can collect your results from your school or college, or you can arrange to receive them via email or post. It's a good idea to go into school or college to receive them in person, so that you can get support and advice from teachers and careers advisors about your options if you need it.

UCAS receives your exam results directly and will update UCAS Hub with the outcome of your university applications on results day. The system will be busy, so you might need to be patient to find out whether you've been successful.

When you do get your results one of four things will happen:

- You receive confirmation of your place from the university you selected as your firm choice, and accept it.
- You have not met the offer from your firm choice, but you receive confirmation from the university you selected as your insurance choice and accept it.
- You have met and exceeded the offer made by your firm choice and decide to try to swap courses by going through **Clearing** (see below).
- You have not met the requirements of any offers and need to go through **Clearing** (see below).

If you just miss your offers or have achieved the right grades but not in the right subjects, then telephone or email the universities and colleges to see if they can still offer you a place. Universities may revise their offer and admit you if they still have places, or if you missed the grade by only a few marks it may suggest that you try for a remark. ALWAYS HAVE YOUR UCAS PERSONAL ID AVAILABLE WHEN YOU CALL. Their decisions may take a few days. You should check the universities and colleges in your order of preference. Your first choice must not accept you before you contact your second choice.

IF YOU HAVE AN OFFER AND THE RIGHT GRADES BUT ARE NOT ACCEPTING THAT OR AN ALTERNATIVE PLACE, TELL THE UNIVERSITY OR COLLEGE. Someone else is waiting for your place!

Clearing

Clearing is the name given to the system in which all remaining course vacancies are advertised on the UCAS website. In **Clearing**, you contact the universities directly that have publicised course vacancies and give them your grades and UCAS ID number. If you think that you might need to use the **Clearing** system, it is best to be well prepared because the vacancies are filled very quickly. **Clearing** is open from 5 July to 19 October.

From 5 July you can use online self-release into **Clearing** by using the 'decline my place' button in your application. You should only use this button if you no longer wish to take up your place at your firm choice and you have spoken to your university or college and/or an adviser at your school/centre.

If you learn that you do not have a place because you have missed the grades in your offer you'll know you're in **Clearing** if your application status says 'You are in **Clearing**' or '**Clearing** has started', and your **Clearing** number will be displayed.

If you have not applied to any university or college earlier in the year then you can also apply through **Clearing**. Check the tables in **Chapter 7** to identify which institutions normally make offers matching your results, check **Clearing** vacancy listings, and then telephone or email the institution before completing your application.

Alongside their search tool, which includes over 30,000 course options, UCAS also offers **Clearing Plus**, a tool that 'matches' candidates to a list of courses in UCAS Hub. If you find yourself in **Clearing**, it is advisable to check the 'View matches' button; if you find a course you like, select the 'I'm interested' button. If the university or college still has available places, they will contact you to discuss further and possibly make you an offer.

If you have met and exceeded the conditional requirements of your firm choice, you could potentially swap your place for one on another course that you prefer. Since more than 70,000 students get a course through **Clearing**, it is highly recommended that you find the course of your preference as soon as possible, as this is a first come, first served system.

Once you have found an alternative course, you will need to phone the university yourself. Be prepared to answer questions about why you really want to study on that course. If they agree to accept you, and you in turn agree to accept them, this will happen during the phone call.

If you're given an offer you want to accept, and are not committed to a place at any other university or college, you can add a **Clearing** choice in your application. You can only add one choice at a time, but if the university or college doesn't, for some reason, confirm your place, you'll be able to add another.

REMEMBER – There are many thousands of students just like you. Admissions tutors have a mammoth task checking how many students will be taking up their places since not all students whose grades match their offers finally decide to do so! If you are applying for a place through **Clearing** it may be late September before you know you have a place, so BE PATIENT AND STAY **CALM**!

Good luck!

5 ADMISSIONS TESTS, SELECTION OF APPLICANTS AND INTERVIEWS

The selection of applicants by universities and colleges takes many forms. Competition for places is tough. Great importance is attached not only to applicants' predicted A-level grades and GCSE attainments, but also to other aspects of their applications, especially the school reference and the personal statement and, for some courses and some institutions, performance at interview, and performance in admissions tests.

ADMISSIONS TESTS

Admissions tests are now increasingly used for undergraduate entry to specific courses and specific institutions. These include national subject-based tests such as LNAT and UCAT (see below) which are used for selecting applicants for entry to specified courses at particular institutions in subjects such as Law, Medicine, Dentistry and Veterinary Sciences. Admissions tests are also set by individual universities and colleges (or commercial organisations on their behalf) for entry, again, to particular courses in the individual institutions. Examples include the subject-based admissions tests used by many universities and colleges for entry to particular courses in subjects such as Art, Dance, Construction, Design, Drama and other Performance-based courses, Education and Teacher Training, Economics, Engineering, Journalism, Languages, Music, Nursing and Social Work.

Admissions tests are usually taken before or at interview and, except for courses requiring auditions or portfolio inspections, they are generally timed, unseen, written, or online tests. They can be used on their own, or alongside other selection methods used by university and college admissions staff, including:

- questionnaires or tests to be completed by applicants prior to interview and/or offer
- examples of school work to be submitted prior to interview and/or offer
- written tests at interview
- mathematical tests at interview
- practical tests at interview
- a response to a passage at interview
- performance-based tests (for example, for Music, Dance, Drama).

With regard to tests, applicants should check prospectuses and subject websites as soon as possible since, in some cases, early registration is required. This is especially important for applicants to Oxford and Cambridge and for those applying for Law, Medicine, Dentistry and Veterinary Science who may be required to take the LNAT or UCAT.

Here is a list of commonly used admissions tests, and this is followed by degree subject lists showing subject-based and individual institutions' admissions tests.

Engineering and Science

Engineering and Science Admissions Test (ESAT)

The ESAT is a new admissions test that initially will be used by Cambridge for Engineering, Natural Sciences, Chemical Engineering and Biotechnology, and Veterinary Medicine, and by Imperial London for Physics and most Engineering courses. It is expected that other universities will use the ESAT in future.

Law

Law National Aptitude Test (LNAT)

The LNAT is an on-screen test for applicants to specified undergraduate Law programmes at Bristol, Cambridge, Durham, Glasgow, London (King's), London (LSE), London (SOAS), London (UCL) and Oxford universities. (See ***Law*** below, and **Law** in the subject tables in **Chapter 7**.) Applicants need to check universities' websites and the LNAT website (www.lnat.ac.uk) for the UCAS codes for courses requiring applicants to sit the LNAT. Details of LNAT (which includes multiple-choice and essay questions), practice papers, registration dates, test dates, test centres and fees are all available on the LNAT website.

Mathematics

Mathematics Admissions Test (MAT)

The MAT is required by the University of Oxford for Mathematics and Computer Science courses, and for joint honour courses including these subjects. See www.ox.ac.uk/admissions/undergraduate/applying-to-oxford/guide/admissions-tests/mat.

Sixth Term Examination Paper (STEP)

STEP is a mathematics examination with questions that are similar in style to undergraduate mathematics. It consists of two papers and candidates must sit either one or both, depending on the the requirements of the universities they have applied to. For details, see the individual universities' websites and STEP pages on the Oxford Cambridge and RSA (OCR) website (www.ocr.org.uk/students/step-mathematics).

Test of Mathematics for University Admission (TMUA)

The TMUA is a test that allows applicants to courses such as Mathematics, Economics or Computer Science to demonstrate their ability in mathematical reasoning and thinking, and can result in a reduced offer. It consists of two 75-minute, multiple-choice papers. For more details, see https://esat-tmua.ac.uk/about-the-tests/tmua-test/.

Medicine, Dentistry, Veterinary Science/Medicine, and related subjects

Most medical schools require applicants to sit the University Clinical Aptitude Test (UCAT) or, for graduate entry, the Graduate Australian Medical Schools Admissions Test (GAMSAT) for specified Medicine courses. Applicants are advised to check the websites of all universities and medical schools offering Medicine for their latest admissions requirements, including admissions and aptitude tests, and to check the UCAT website www.ucat.ac.uk (and for graduate entry www.gamsat.co.uk) for the latest information.

The University Clinical Aptitude Test (UCAT)

The UCAT is a clinical aptitude test used by the majority of medical and dental schools in the selection of applicants for Medicine and Dentistry, alongside their existing selection processes, for undergraduate entry. The tests are not curriculum-based and do not have a science component. No revision is necessary; there is no textbook and no course of instruction. In the first instance, the UCAT is a test of cognitive skills involving problem-solving and critical reasoning. With test centres located across the UK, it is an on-screen test (not paper-based), and is marked electronically. Some bursaries are available to help towards the cost of the test. Applicants who require extra time due to a disability or medical condition should register for the UCATSEN. Further details (including the most recent list of universities requiring applicants to sit the UCAT) are found on the website www.ucat.ac.uk. See also the **Dentistry** and **Medicine** subject tables in **Chapter 7**, the entries for ***Dentistry*** and ***Medicine*** below, and **Chapter 4** for application details. See www.ucat.ac.uk.

Modern and Medieval Languages

The Modern and Medieval Languages Written Assessment (MML)

This written test is used by the University of Cambridge for selecting applicants for entry to courses involving modern and medieval languages. See www.undergraduate.study.cam.ac.uk/courses/modern-and-medieval-languages.

General Admissions Tests

Thinking Skills Assessment (TSA)

The TSA is a computer-based test that tests applicants' critical thinking and problem-solving skills. The test is used by the University of Oxford for entry to several courses (see below). The TSA is made up of two parts: Section 1 consists of 50 multiple-choice questions, which applicants have 90 minutes to complete, and Section 2 is a 30-minute writing task. Candidates applying for Philosophy, Politics and Economics at the University of Oxford will be required to to take both sections of the TSA, whereas applicants to all other courses will only need to take Section 1.

LSE UG Admissions Assessment (UGAA)

The LSE UGAA is used by the London School of Economics and Political Science for some applicants with non-traditional educational backgrounds. The test is not subject or course specific and consists of English comprehension exercises, essay questions and mathematical problems.

Test of Academic Reasoning for Admissions (TARA)
For 2026 entry, University College London has introduced TARA, a new admissions test for applicants to various mathematical and social science courses. This computer-based test is run by UAT UK and Pearson VUE and is designed to test general skills, such as critical thinking, problem-solving and effective communication. It is possible that it will be adopted by other universities in future. See www.esat-tmua.ac.uk.

DEGREE SUBJECT EXAMPLES OF UNIVERSITIES AND COLLEGES USING TESTS AND ASSESSMENTS

Many universities and colleges set their own tests for specific subjects so it is important to check the websites for your preferred institutions and courses for the latest information about their applications and selection processes. The following list provides a guide to the subjects and some of the institutions requiring admissions tests and other forms of assessment. Due to the constant changes in admissions policies, this is not a complete list. However, applicants for these subjects should be guided as to the requirements of those universities requiring tests.

Acting
Marjon Audition.

African, Asian and Middle Eastern Studies
Cambridge Applicants wishing to study a European language will be required to take the relevant MML at-interview admissions assessment. Some colleges require an at-interview written assessment. Check college websites for submitted work requirements.
Oxford Two pieces written work required.

Anglo Saxon, Norse and Celtic
Cambridge No admission assessment. Check college websites for submitted work requirements.

Anthropology
Oxford See **Archaeology**.

Archaeology
Cambridge All applicants take the ARCHAA at interview. Check college websites for submitted work requirements.
Oxford (Arch Anth) Two recent marked essays are required, preferably in different subjects, plus a short essay of no more than 500 words in response to a set question – required before interview. No written test at interview. (Class Arch Anc Hist) Two pieces of written work required. No written test at interview.

Architecture
Cambridge ARCHITAA taken at interview. Portfolio of recent work required at interview. PDF of artwork must be submitted prior to interview.
Cardiff (Archit) Portfolio must be submitted.
Dundee Candidates applying for advanced entry will be required to submit a portfolio of prior work.
Falmouth Interview required.
Huddersfield Portfolio of work to be discussed at interview.
Liverpool Portfolio and selection workshop.
London Met Portfolio and interview required.
London South Bank Portfolio and usually an interview are required.
Manchester Met Portfolio of work required.
Nottingham Portfolio of work required.
Nottingham Trent Portfolio of work is required.
Plymouth Digital portfolio of work required.
Reading Interview and portfolio which shows evidence of creative ability and 3-dimensional understanding required.
Sheffield Portfolio required.
Westminster Interview required.
York Interview required.

Art and Design

Arts London Portfolio required.
Brunel (Prod Des Eng, Ind Des) All applicants are required to attend an interview including a portfolio review as part of the selection process.
Greater Manchester (Fash) You may be required to attend for interview and provide a portfolio of appropriate work.
Hertfordshire (Fash Des) Portfolio and interview required.
Huddersfield Portfolio and interview required.
Liverpool Hope Interview and portfolio.
Plymouth Portfolio presentation required.
Portsmouth Shortlisted applicants will need to attend an interview with a portfolio of work.
Reading Interview and portfolio of work required.
Robert Gordon Interview required.
South Wales Interview required.

Art and Design (Fine Art)

Cardiff Met Interview required.
Chester Interview required.
Chichester Interview and portfolio.
Cumbria Interview required.
Falmouth Interview required.
Greater Manchester Interview required.
Leeds Beckett Interview required.
Liverpool John Moores Interview required.
London (Gold) Interview required.
Newcastle Interview required.
Oxford Portfolio submitted digitally. Pre-interview submission of more recent work to be discussed at interview.
Plymouth Interview required.
UHI Interview required.
York St John Interview required.

Art and Design (Interior, Product and Industrial Design)

Bournemouth Interview and portfolio of work required.
Brunel All applicants are required to attend an interview including a portfolio review as part of the selection process.
Cardiff Met Interview required.
Chester Interview required.
Dundee Portfolio of up to 15 pages of work required. Interview may be required.
Falmouth Interview required.
Leeds Beckett Interview required.
Liverpool (LIPA) Interview required.
London (Royal Central Sch SpDr) Interview required.
London Regent's Interview required.
London South Bank Interview required.
Northampton Interview required.
Northumbria Interview required.
Nottingham Trent Interview required.
Ravensbourne Univ Interview and portfolio required.
South Wales Interview required.
Sussex Interview and portfolio review required.
York St John Interview required.

Biochemistry

Cambridge Interview required.
Oxford Interview required.

Biological Sciences
Cambridge Interview required.
Manchester Interview required.
Oxford Interview required.

Biology
Oxford Interview required.

Business
Liverpool (LIPA) Interview required.
UHI Interview required.

Business and Management Courses
Reading Interview required (Acc Bus).

Chemistry
Bristol Interview required.
Imperial London Interview required.
Oxford No written work or test required.

Classics (see also Archaeology)
Cambridge All applicants take the CAA at interview, with separate tests for the three- and four-year courses. Check college websites for submitted work requirements.
Oxford For all Classics courses, two essays or commentaries required, normally in areas related to Classics, and submitted in November. CAT also required.

Classics and Asian and Middle Eastern Studies
Oxford Two pieces written work required; at least one should be on a classical topic if already studying a classical subject. CAT also required.

Classics and English
Oxford Two pieces of written work required, one relevant to Classics and one to English. CAT also required.

Classics and Modern Languages
Oxford One Classics essay and two modern language essays required, one in the chosen language and one in English. CAT and MLAT also required.

Community Studies/Development
Marjon Interview.

Computer Games Development
Bournemouth Portfolio of work required.

Computer Science
Cambridge All applicants take the TMUA. Pre-interview assessment required. Some colleges require applicants to take the CSAT at interview. Check www.cam.ac.uk/assessment.
Oxford No written work required. MAT required. See also **Mathematics**.

Computer Science and Information Technology
Buckingham Interview required.
Falmouth Interview required.
Imperial London Interview required.

Costume Design and Construction
Queen Margaret Candidates will be required to submit an online portfolio of images. Candidates will also be asked to complete a design exercise and to take part in a phone interview.

Dance

Bucks New Interview required.
Chichester Audition and interview. Applicants are also required to submit an essay reviewing a live or recorded performance.
City St George's Interview required (Prof Dance Musl Thea).
Falmouth Interview required.
Northern (Sch Contemp Dance) Interview required.

Dental

Portsmouth Interview.

Dentistry

Aberdeen Entrants must sit UCAT.
Birmingham Interview required.
Bristol Interview required.
Cardiff Interview required.
Dundee Interview required.
Edinburgh Interview required.
Glasgow UCAT and interview.
Glasgow Caledonian Interview required.
Leeds Interview required; UCAT.
Liverpool Interview required; entrants require UCAT.
London (King's) UCAT. Shortlisted applicants will be invited to interview.
London (QM) Interview required.
Manchester UCAT and interview.
Newcastle Entrants must sit the UCAT. Shortlisted applicants will be invited to interview.
Plymouth (Dntl Srgy) UCAT or GAMSAT. Shortlisted applicants will be invited to interview (MMI). (Dntl Thera Hyg) Shortlisted applicants will be invited to interview (MMI).
Queen's Belfast Interview required.
Sheffield Interview required.
Teesside Interview required.
UHI Interview required.

Dietetics

Cardiff Met Interview required.
Chester Interview required.
Coventry Interview required.
Hertfordshire Interview.
Leeds Beckett Interview required.
London Met Interview required.
Plymouth Interview.
Surrey Interview required.
Ulster Interview.

Drama

Arts London Interview required.
Birmingham City Interview required.
Bournemouth Arts Interview required.
Chichester Interview required.
Colchester (UC) Interview required.
Exeter Optional workshop session.
Falmouth Interview required.
Guildhall (Sch Mus Dr) Interview required.
Huddersfield Applicants will be invited to a selection day, at which they will participate in a workshop by way of an audition. Some applicants may also be invited to interview.

Kent Interview required.
Liverpool (LIPA) Audition.
Liverpool Hope Applicants will be required to submit a video performing a 2-minute speech from a play.
Liverpool John Moores Interview required.
London (QM) Interview required.
London (Royal Central Sch SpDr) Three rounds of auditions.
London Met Interview required.
Manchester Interview required.
Plymouth Audition workshop required.
Portsmouth Interview and workshop or video submission (if applicants are unable to attend a workshop).
RConsvS Interview required.
Roehampton Interview required.
Rose Bruford (Coll) Interview required.
Royal Welsh (CMusDr) Interview required.
Warwick Interview required.
Winchester Applicants are required to attend an interview.

Economics

Buckingham Interview required.
Cambridge Most applicants are required to take the TMUA. Some colleges require applicants to take a college-set written assessment at interview. Check college websites for submitted work requirements.
Oxford (Econ Mgt) No written work required. TSA S1 required.

Education Studies (see also Teacher Training)

Cambridge Some colleges require applicants to take the EAA at interview. Check college websites for written work requirements.
Glasgow Interview required.
Oldham (Univ Campus) Interview required.
Stirling Interview required.

Engineering

Brunel Interview required.
Cambridge ESAT pre-interview. Some colleges require applicants to take a college-set written assessment at interview. See college websites for details.
Cardiff Met Interview required.
Dyson Interview required.
Imperial London Interview required.
Liverpool (LIPA) Interview required (Snd Tech).
Loughborough Interview required.
Manchester Interview required.
Oxford Interview required. No written work required. All candidates take the PAT.
Wolverhampton Interview required (Mech).
York Interview required (Electron Eng Mus Tech Sys; Mus Tech Sys).

English

Cambridge All colleges require applicants to take a college-set written assessment at interview. Check college websites for submitted work requirements.
Falmouth Interview required.
Greater Manchester Interview required.
Huddersfield Interview required.
London (Birk) Interview required.
London (UCL) Interview required.
Oxford (Engl Lang Lit) One recent marked essay. (Engl Modn Langs) MLAT. One English essay and two modern language essays required, one in the chosen language and one in English.
Portsmouth (Crea Writ) Applicants may be required to submit a portfolio of written work.

European Studies (see also Modern and Medieval Languages)
Cambridge Interview required.
Manchester Interview required (Russ Jap).
Oxford (Euro Mid E Langs) MLAT; no written work required.

Film, Radio and TV Studies
Bournemouth Arts (Flm Prod) Digital portfolio including a show reel or short film(s), and additional audiovisual or written material demonstrating wider interest in the arts.
Falmouth Interview required.
Gloucestershire Interview required.
London Met Interview required.
Portsmouth (Film Prod) Applicants without relevant qualifications may be asked to submit a digital portfolio.
Solent Interview required.
South Wales Portfolio required.
UWE Bristol Interview required.
Warwick Interview required.

Geography
Cambridge Some colleges require applicants to undertake a written assessment at interview. The assessment may vary by college. Check college websites for submitted work requirements.
Oxford Interview required.

Health Sciences/Studies
BCNO Group Interview required.
Bournemouth Interview required.
Brighton Interview required.
Canterbury Christ Church Interview required.
City St George's Interview required.
Dundee Interview required.
East Anglia Interview required.
Greater Manchester Interview required.
Liverpool Interview required.
London (St George's) Interview required.
Manchester Interview required.
Middlesex Interview required.
Plymouth Interview required.
Portsmouth Interview required.
Sheffield Interview required.
Southampton Interview required.
Strathclyde Interview required.
Surrey Interview required.
Trinity Saint David Interview required.
UHI Interview required.
UWE Bristol Interview required.

History
Cambridge Some colleges require applicants to take the HAA at interview. Check college websites for submitted work requirements.
Huddersfield Interview required.
Liverpool John Moores Mature students and non-standard applicants will be required to submit an essay and/or attend an interview.
London (Gold) Applicants may be asked to attend an interview.
Oxford An essay on a historical topic is required. (Hist Modn Langs) One essay on a historical topic and MLAT required.

History of Art

Cambridge All applicants take the HAA at interview. Check college websites for submitted work requirements.

Oxford Two pieces of work required: (a) a marked essay of up to 2,000 words from an A-level or equivalent course, and (b) no more than 750 words responding to an item of art, architecture or design to which the applicant has had first-hand access with a photograph or photocopy of the item provided if possible. No written test.

Human Sciences

Oxford Interview. No written work required. All candidates must take the TSA.

Human Sciences/Human Biosciences

Oxford Interview required.

Journalism

City St George's Interview required.
East Anglia Interview required.
Falmouth Interview required.
Gloucestershire Interview required.
London (Gold) Interview required.
Marjon Interview.
Portsmouth All applicants will be invited to attend a workshop and must bring a portfolio of work.
Sunderland Interview required.
Wolverhampton Interview required.

Journalism (see also Media Studies)

Kent Applicants will be invited to interview and sit a written test.

Land Economy

Cambridge Check college websites for individual requirements.

Law

Buckingham Interview required.
Cambridge LNAT pre-interview. Check college websites for submitted work requirements.
Durham LNAT.
Glasgow LNAT.
Leicester Interview required (Law Fr Mait).
London (King's) LNAT.
London (UCL) LNAT.
London LSE LNAT.
Nottingham LNAT.
Oxford No written work required. All applicants take the LNAT. (Law; Law St Euro) LNAT, plus an oral test in the relevant European language at interview for candidates applying for the French, German, Italian or Spanish law options.
Worcester Interview required.

Linguistics

Cambridge All applicants take the LAA at interview. Check college websites for submitted work requirements.

Materials Science/Metallurgy

Cambridge Interview required.
Imperial London Interview required.
Loughborough Interview required.
Manchester Interview required.
Oxford No written work required. All candidates must take the PAT.

Mathematics

Cambridge Some colleges may require applicants to take a written assessment at interview. Check college websites for details.
Imperial London TMUA.
London LSE TMUA is recommended but not mandatory.
Manchester Interview required (Math Phys).
Oxford Interview. MAT required. No written work required.

Media Studies

Coventry Applicants may be required to attend a portfolio showcase, activity session or audition, or submit a digital portfolio.
Falmouth Interview required.
Greater Manchester Interview required.
Plymouth (AU) Interview required.
York Interview required.

Medical Imaging

Exeter Interview (MMI).

Medicine

Aberdeen Interview required. Entrants must sit UCAT.
Aston UCAT and MMI.
Bangor Interview required.
Birmingham UCAT and interview.
Brighton UCAT and interview.
Brighton and Sussex (MS) UCAT and interview.
Bristol UCAT and interview.
Buckingham Applicants will attend a selection event, including MMI.
Cambridge UCAT and interview.
Cardiff Entrants must sit UCAT. Multiple Mini Interview (MMI).
City St George's Interview required. GAMSAT is required for the four-year Graduate Stream course. UCAT is required for the five-year course.
Dundee Entrants must sit UCAT and attend an interview.
East Anglia UCAT and interview.
Edinburgh UCAT and interview.
Exeter UCAT or GAMSAT required. MMI also required.
Glasgow UCAT and interview.
Hull UCAT and interview.
Hull York (MS) UCAT and interview.
Imperial London Interview and UCAT required.
Keele UCAT. MMI also required, including numeracy test.
Kent Medway Med Sch UCAT required. Shortlisted applicants will be invited to interview (MMI).
Lancaster UCAT and interview (MMI).
Leeds UCAT. Shortlisted candidates will be invited to interview.
Leicester Entrants must sit UCAT. High scoring applicants will be invited to interview.
Liverpool Interview required. Entrants require UCAT. Graduate entrants must complete GAMSAT.
London (King's) UCAT. Shortlisted applicants will be invited to interview.
London (QM) Interview required. Entrants must sit UCAT.
London (St George's) Interview required. GAMSAT is required for the four-year Graduate Stream course. UCAT is required for the five-year course.
London (UCL) Interview required. (Six-year course) UCAT.
Manchester UCAT and interview.
Newcastle Interview required. Entrants must sit the UCAT.
Nottingham UCAT and Multiple Mini Interviews (MMI).
Oxford Interview required. No written work required. UCAT required.

Plymouth UCAT or GAMSAT. Shortlisted applicants will be invited to interview (MMI).
Queen's Belfast UCAT and interview (MMI).
Sheffield Entrants must sit UCAT and attend an MMI.
Southampton Interview required. Entrants must sit UCAT.
St Andrews Interview required. Entrants must sit UCAT.

Midwifery

Bangor Interview required.
Birmingham City Interview required.
Bournemouth Interview required.
Bradford Interview.
Brighton Interview required.
Central Lancashire Interview required.
City St George's Interview required.
Coventry Interview required.
Cumbria Online assessment and interview.
De Montfort Interview required.
East Anglia Interview required.
Edge Hill Interview required.
Edinburgh Napier Interview required.
Greenwich Interview required.
Hertfordshire Interview including a group workshop and MMI.
Huddersfield Interview.
Hull Literacy and numeracy test during interview.
Keele Interview required.
Kingston Interview required.
Leeds Interview required.
Leicester Interview (MMI).
Liverpool John Moores Interview required.
London (King's) Interview required.
London South Bank Interview required.
Manchester Interview required.
Middlesex Interview required.
Northampton Interview required.
Northumbria Interview required.
Oxford Brookes Interview required.
Queen's Belfast Interview required.
Robert Gordon Interview required.
Sheffield Hallam Interview required.
South Wales Interview required.
Staffordshire Interview required.
Surrey Interview required.
Swansea Interview required.
Teesside Shortlisted applicants will be invited to interview.
UWE Bristol Interview required.
West London Interview required.
Winchester Interview.
Wolverhampton Interview required.
Worcester Interview required.

Modern and Medieval Languages (see also African, Asian and Middle Eastern Studies and Classics and Asian and Middle Eastern Studies)

Cambridge All applicants take the MMLAA. Check college websites for submitted work requirements.
Oxford (Euro Mid E Langs; Modn Langs; Modn Langs Ling) MLAT; no written work required

Music

Aberdeen Interview required.

Bath Spa (Commer Mus) Applicants must provide three original compositions. Applicants must perform music at interview.

Birmingham Interview required.

Birmingham City Portfolio required for some courses.

Brunel Interview required.

Cambridge Some colleges may require applicants to take a written test at interview. Check college websites for details.

Cardiff Applicants are required to attend an interview day, including an audition and short interview.

Chester Interview required.

Chichester Audition and interview.

City St George's Portfolio of recordings or an audition may be required for applicants with alternative or international qualifications. Interview required (Prof Dance Musl Thea).

Colchester (UC) Audition including instrumental or vocal performance. Applicants are advised to bring a portfolio.

Coventry Applicants may be required to attend a portfolio showcase, activity session or audition, or submit a digital portfolio.

Derby Applicants must submit a portfolio, including composition and arrangement work, and performance recordings.

Edinburgh Applicants without formal performance qualifications are required to submit an audition video.

Edinburgh Napier Portfolio.

Falmouth Interview required.

Glasgow Interview and audition, including two performance pieces.

Gloucestershire Interview required.

Guildhall (Sch Mus Dr) Audition or portfolio required. Overseas applicants may submit a recorded audition.

Huddersfield Audition.

Leeds Interview required.

Leeds Beckett Interview required.

Liverpool Interview or audition at an Applicant Interview and Music Experience Day.

Liverpool (LIPA) Interview required.

Liverpool Hope Interview and audition including performance of two pieces of music.

London (Gold) Interview required. Candidates will be invited to an applicant day, including a performance. Candidates who cannot attend the applicant day will be invited to submit a portfolio.

London (King's) Only borderline applicants or candidates with non-standard qualifications are interviewed.

London (RAcMus) (Mus) Applicants must submit a 30 minute long recorded audition with a minimum of two works. Shortlisted applicants will be invited to interview.

Manchester Interview required.

Newcastle Interview required.

Northampton Interview required.

Oxford No written test. Candidates are required to submit a video recording audition of up to 5 minutes. Candidates without keyboard skills to ABRSM Grade V may be asked to take a keyboard sight-reading test at interview. Two teacher-marked essays, plus one or two examples of marked harmony and counterpoint required. Examples of composition are optional.

RCMus Audition required. Applicants may submit a video audition if they are unable to travel to an audition.

RConsvS Audition.

Reading Interview required.

Royal Welsh (CMusDr) Principal Study audition including aural and sightreading tests. Interview and practical session, and online musicianship test also required.

South Wales Interview. Portfolio may be required.

Southampton Interview required.

Surrey Interview required.

Trinity Saint David Interview required.

UHI Interview required.
West London Applicants may be invited to an audition and interview; see www.uwl.ac.uk.
York Interview and audition.

Musical Theatre

Chichester Audition.
Liverpool Hope Audition including performance of two songs. Applicants will also be required to submit a video of their work in dance and/or drama to be discussed at audition.

Natural Sciences

Cambridge ESAT pre-interview. Some colleges require applicants to take a college-set written assessment at interview. Check college websites for details.

Nursing

Abertay Interview required.
Anglia Ruskin Interview required.
Bangor Interview required.
Birmingham Interview required.
Birmingham City Interview.
Birmingham Newman Interview required.
Bournemouth Interview.
Bradford Interview required.
Brighton Literacy and numeracy assessments during interview.
Brunel Interview required.
Bucks New Interview.
Canterbury Christ Church Interview required.
Central Lancashire Interview required.
Chichester Interview required.
City St George's Interview.
Coventry Applicants will be required to attend a selection event and interview.
Cumbria Interview.
De Montfort Interview required.
Derby Interview.
Dundee Interview required.
East Anglia Interview.
Edge Hill Interview required.
Edinburgh Interview required.
Edinburgh Napier Interview required.
Essex Interview.
Exeter Interview required.
Glasgow Caledonian Interview required.
Greenwich Interview required.
Hertfordshire Interview.
Huddersfield Interview.
Hull Interview required.
Keele Interview.
Kingston Interview required.
Leeds Interview required.
Leeds Beckett Interview required.
Leicester Interview (MMI).
Lincoln Interview required.
Liverpool Interview.
Liverpool John Moores Interview required.
London (King's) Interview required.
London South Bank Interview.
Manchester Interview required.

Manchester Met Interview required.
Marjon Interview required.
Middlesex Interview required.
Northampton Interview required.
Northumbria Interview required.
Nottingham Interview required.
Oxford Brookes Interview required.
Plymouth Interview.
Portsmouth Interview.
Queen's Belfast Interview required.
Sheffield Hallam Interview required.
Staffordshire Interview required.
Stirling Interview.
Suffolk Interview.
Surrey Interview required.
Swansea Interview required.
Teesside Interview (MMI).
UHI Interview required.
Ulster Interview required.
UWE Bristol Values-based interview.
West London Individual values-based interview.
West Scotland Interview required.
Winchester Interview including group activity/discussion, situation judgement activity and one-to-one interview.
Wolverhampton Interview including scenario-based questions.
Worcester Interview required.
Wrexham Interview including numeracy screening and literacy task.
York Interview required.

Nursing and Midwifery
Cardiff Multiple Mini Interview (MMI).

Nutrition
Chester Interview required (Nutr Diet).

Occupational Therapy
Bournemouth Interview required.
Brunel Interview required.
Canterbury Christ Church Interview required.
Coventry Interview required.
Cumbria Interview required.
Derby Interview.
East Anglia Interview required.
Huddersfield Interview.
Northumbria Interview required.
Oxford Brookes Interview required.
Plymouth Interview.
Queen Margaret Interview.
Teesside Interview required.
UWE Bristol Interview.
Wrexham Interview.

Operating Department Practice
Anglia Ruskin Interview required.
Birmingham City Interview required.
Bournemouth Interview required.
Bucks New Interview and online numeracy and literacy test required.

Canterbury Christ Church Interview.
Coventry Interview required.
East Anglia Interview required.
Edge Hill Interview required.
Greater Manchester Interview required.
Huddersfield Interview required.
Leicester Interview.
London South Bank Interview required.
Northumbria Interview required.
Portsmouth Interview required.
Sheffield Hallam Interview required.
Teesside Interview required.
West London Interview required.

Optometry (Ophthalmic Optics)
Manchester Interview required.
Sheffield Interview required.
UHI Interview required.

Paramedic Practitioner
Plymouth Interview.

Paramedic Science
Bournemouth Interview.
Hertfordshire Interview.
Portsmouth Interview.

Pharmacy
Brighton Online mathematics test and interview.
Keele Interview.
Leicester Interview required.
Portsmouth Shortlisted applicants must attend an interview, including an admissions test.

Pharmacy and Pharmaceutical Sciences
Bath Interview required.
Bradford Interview required.
Cardiff Interview required.
Central Lancashire Interview required.
De Montfort Interview required.
East Anglia Interview required.
Huddersfield Interview required.
Kingston Interview required.
Liverpool John Moores Interview required.
London (UCL) Interview required.
Loughborough Interview required.
Manchester Interview required.
Nottingham Interview required.
Reading Interview required.
Robert Gordon Interview required.
Strathclyde Interview required.
Wolverhampton Interview required.

Philosophy
Cambridge Check college websites for submitted work requirements.
Oxford (Phil Modn Langs) MLAT; no written work required. (Phil Theol) PhilAT and one piece of written work. (Phil Pol Econ (PPE)) TSA; no written work required. (Phil Psy Ling (PPL)) TSA; no written work required.

Photography

Arts London Interview required.
Bath Spa Interview required.
Bournemouth Arts Interview required.
Chester Interview required.
Cumbria Interview required.
Falmouth Interview required.
Gloucestershire Interview required.
Greater Manchester Interview required.
Huddersfield Portfolio required.
Norwich Arts Interview required.
Nottingham Trent Interview required.
Oxford Brookes Interview required.
Plymouth Portfolio.
Solent Interview required.
Staffordshire Interview required.
Sunderland Interview required.
UWE Bristol Interview required.
Westminster Interview required.

Physical Education

Chichester Interview including audit for mathematics and English.
Edinburgh Interview required.
RAc Dance Interview required.
Trinity Saint David Interview required.

Physics

Cambridge Interview required.
Imperial London Interview required.
Lancaster Interview required.
Manchester Interview required.
Oxford PAT; no written work required.

Physiotherapy

Birmingham Interview required.
Bournemouth Interview required.
Bradford Interview.
Brighton Interview.
Brunel Shortlisted applicants will be required to attend a selection day.
Brunel Interview required.
Canterbury Christ Church Interview required.
Cardiff Interview required.
Chichester Interview required.
City St George's Interview required.
Coventry Interview required.
Cumbria Interview required.
East Anglia Interview.
East London Interview required.
Essex Interview.
Huddersfield Interview.
Keele Interview.
Leeds Beckett Interview required.
Leicester Interview.
Liverpool Interview.
London (King's) Interview required.

London (St George's) Interview required.
Manchester Met Interview required.
Northumbria Interview required.
Nottingham Interview required.
Oxford Brookes Interview required.
Plymouth Interview.
Robert Gordon Selection event including interview.
Robert Gordon Interview required.
Sheffield Hallam Interview required.
Teesside Interview required.
Ulster Interview.
UWE Bristol Interview required.
Winchester Interview.
Worcester Interview required.
York St John Interview required.

Podiatry (Chiropody)

Cardiff Met Interview required.
Durham New (Coll) Interview required.
Huddersfield Interview. Individual students may be required to take a biology test.
Northampton Interview required.
Plymouth Interview.
Teesside Interview required.

Politics

Cambridge Interview required.
London (Inst Paris) Interview required.
Oxford See (Phil Pol Econ (PPE)) under **Philosophy**.

Psychology

Buckingham Interview required.
Cambridge Some colleges require applicants to undertake a written assessment at interview. The assessment may vary by college. Check college websites for submitted work requirements.
Exeter (App Psy Clin) Interview, including group and individual interviews.
Greater Manchester Interview required.
Oxford Interview required. TSA; no written work required.
Reading Interview required (App Psy).

Radiography

Bangor Interview required.
Birmingham City Interview required.
Bradford Interview required.
Canterbury Christ Church Interview required.
Cardiff Interview required.
City St George's Interview required (Radiog Onc, Diag Radiog).
Cumbria Interview required.
Derby Interview required.
Exeter Interview required.
Hertfordshire Interview required.
Keele Interview.
Leeds Interview required.
Leicester Interview required.
Liverpool Interview.
London (St George's) Interview required (Radiog Onc).
London South Bank Interview required.
Portsmouth Interview required.

Sheffield Hallam Interview required.
Teesside Interview required.
UWE Bristol Interview required.

Religious Studies

Cambridge No admission assessment. Check college websites for submitted work requirements.
Oxford (Theol Relgn) No test; one piece of marked written work or marked response to an unseen exam question. (Relgn As Mid E St) one piece of marked written work or marked response to an unseen exam question.

Social Work

Bath Interview required.
Bedfordshire Interview required.
Birmingham Shortlisted applicants may be required to complete a written test and attend an interview.
Birmingham City All applicants will be required to attend an interview. Applicants who do not meet standard entry requirements but have relevant work experience are required to submit a portfolio.
Bournemouth Interview.
Bradford Interview required.
Brighton Assessment at interview.
Bucks New Applicants will be invited to a selection day, including a written test, group activity and individual interview.
Canterbury Christ Church Interview required.
Cardiff Met Shortlisted applicants will be invited to interview.
Central Lancashire Interview required.
Chichester Interview required.
Coventry Interview required.
Cumbria Interview required.
Derby Interview.
East Anglia Interview including a group participation activity.
East London Interview required.
Edge Hill Interview required.
Essex Interview.
Gloucestershire Interview required.
Greenwich Interview required.
Hertfordshire Interview, written assessment and group discussion required.
Hull Interview and written test during a selection day.
Keele Interview.
Kent Applicants will complete a written test, followed by an interview and observed group discussion.
Kingston Interview required.
Lancaster Interview required.
Leeds Beckett Interview required.
Liverpool Hope Interview required.
London (Gold) Applicants will be invited to a selection day, including a written test, an individual interview, and a group discussion.
London Met Shortlisted applicants will be invited to an interview day, including a test, a group exercise and an individual interview.
London South Bank Interview required.
Manchester Met Interview required.
Middlesex Interview required.
Northumbria Interview required.
Nottingham Trent Interview required.
Oxford Brookes Interview required.
Plymouth Interview.
Portsmouth Shortlisted applicants are subject to a holistic and multidimensional assessment process,

including a group discussion, individual presentation and an interview.
Queen's Belfast Interview required.
Robert Gordon Interview. Numeracy tests for applicants without appropriate certificated level of mathematics.
Salford Interview required.
Sheffield Hallam Interview required.
Solent Interview required.
South Wales Interview required.
Stirling Scenario-based written assessment.
Strathclyde Interview required.
Sunderland Interview required.
Sussex Interview required.
Swansea Interview required.
Teesside Interview required.
UWE Bristol Interview.
West London Interview required.
Winchester Interview.
Wolverhampton Interview including a written test, group discussion and individual interview.
Worcester Interview required.
Wrexham Interview.

Speech Pathology/Sciences/Therapy
Birmingham City Interview required.
Cardiff Met Interview required.
City St George's Interview required.
East Anglia Interview required.
Essex Interview.
Huddersfield Interview required.
Leeds Beckett Interview required.
Marjon Interview required.
Middlesex Interview required.
Reading Interview.

Teacher Training
Bangor Interview required.
Birmingham Newman Interview required.
Brighton Interview.
Cambridge Interview required.
Canterbury Christ Church Interview.
Cardiff Met Interview including literacy, numeracy and digital competency tests.
Chester Applicants may be invited to interview.
Chichester Interview.
Durham Candidates will be invited to a selection day, including an individual interview, presentation, and tests to assess written English and other skills.
Edge Hill Interview required.
Edinburgh Interview required (P Educ Gael).
Glasgow Interview required.
Gloucestershire Interview required.
Greenwich Interview required.
Hertfordshire Admissions test at interview.
Huddersfield Interview required.
Kingston Interview required.
Leeds Beckett Interview required.
Leeds Trinity Interview required.
Liverpool John Moores Interview required.
Manchester Met Interview required.

Marjon Interview required.
Middlesex Interview required.
Northumbria Interview required.
Nottingham Trent Interview required.
Oxford Brookes Interview required.
Plymouth (BEd courses) Interview required.
Plymouth Interview required.
Portsmouth Interview required.
Reading Interview.
Roehampton Interview including a group task, mathematics and English tasks, and individual interview.
Sheffield Hallam Interview including a teaching task.
St Mary's Interview.
Stranmillis (UC) Interview required.
Sunderland Interview required.
UWE Bristol Interview including group interview, micro-teach session, and literacy and numeracy tasks.
West Scotland Interview required.
Winchester Interview. Applicants are expected to demonstrate competency in Fundamental skills in English and Mathematics during the selection process.
Wolverhampton Interview required.
Worcester Interview required.
York St John Interview required.

Veterinary Science/Medicine

Bristol Interview required.
Cambridge ESAT pre-interview.
Edinburgh Interview required.
Glasgow Interview. Some applicants may be asked to complete an online ethical reasoning test.
Harper Keele Vet Sch Interview required.
Liverpool Interview.
London (RVC) Interview required.
Middlesex Interview required.
Nottingham Interview required.
Nottingham Trent Interview required.
Surrey Interview required.
Wrexham Interview required.

SELECTION OF APPLICANTS

University and college departmental admissions tutors are responsible for selecting candidates, basing their decisions on the policies of acceptable qualifications established by each institution and, where required, applicants' performance in admissions tests. There is little doubt that academic achievement, aptitude and promise are the most important factors although other subsidiary factors may be taken into consideration. The outline which follows provides information on the way in which candidates are selected for degree and diploma courses.

- Grades obtained by the applicant in GCE A-level and equivalent examinations and the range of subjects studied may be considered.
- Applicant's performance in aptitude and admissions tests, as required by universities and colleges.
- Academic record of the applicant throughout his or her school career, especially up to A-level, Highers, Advanced Highers or other qualifications and the choice of subjects. If you are taking general studies at A-level confirm with the admissions tutor that this is acceptable.
- Time taken by the applicant to obtain good grades at GCSE/Scottish Nationals and A-level/Scottish Highers/Advanced Highers.
- Forecast or the examination results of the applicant at A-level (or equivalent) and headteacher's report.

- The applicant's intellectual development; evidence of ability and motivation to follow the chosen course.
- The applicant's range of interests, both in and out of school; aspects of character and personality.
- The vocational interests, knowledge and experience of the applicant particularly if they are choosing vocational courses.

INTERVIEWS

Fewer applicants are now interviewed than in the past but even if you are not called you should make an effort to visit your chosen universities and/or colleges before you accept any offer. Interviews may be in-person or online. Interviews may be arranged simply to give you a chance to see the institution and the department and to meet the staff and students. Alternatively, interviews may be an important part of the selection procedure for specific courses such as Law, Medicine and Teaching. If they are, you need to prepare yourself well. Most interviews last approximately 20–30 minutes and you may be interviewed by more than one person. For practical subjects such as Music and Drama almost certainly you will be asked to perform, and for artistic subjects, to take examples of your work. For some courses you may also have a written or other test at interview (see above).

How best can you prepare yourself?

- Prepare well – interviewers are never impressed by applicants who only sit there with no willingness to take part.
- Read up on the prospectus and course details. Know how their course differs from any others you have applied for and be able to say why you prefer theirs.
- Show enthusiasm and, for vocational courses, the ability to work with others.
- Take a moment to think before rushing your answers at interview.
- You will always be asked if you have any questions for the interviewers, so prepare some!

Questions which you could ask might focus on the ways in which work is assessed, the content of the course, field work, work experience, teaching methods, accommodation and, especially for vocational courses, contacts with industry, commerce or the professions. Examples include: How many students are admitted to the course each year? What are the job prospects for graduates? How easy is it to change from your chosen course to a related course? Don't ask questions that are already answered in the prospectus!

These are only a few suggestions and other questions may come to mind during the interview, which, above all, should be a two-way flow of information. It is also important to keep a copy of your UCAS application (especially your personal statement) for reference since your interview will probably start with a question about something you have written.

Usually interviewers will want to know why you have chosen the subject and why you have chosen their particular institution. They will want to see how motivated you are, how much care you have taken in choosing your subject, how much you know about your subject, what books you have read. If you have chosen a vocational course they will want to find out how much you know about the career it leads to, and whether you have visited any places of work or had any work experience. If your chosen subject is also an A-level subject you will be asked about your course and the aspects of the course you like the most.

Try to relax. For some people interviews can be an ordeal; most interviewers know this and will make allowances. The following extract from the University of Manchester's website will give you some idea of what admissions tutors look for.

- 'You should remember that receiving an interview invite means that the admissions tutors are impressed with your application so far and you are in the running for an offer of a place at that university. It is an opportunity for you to discuss a subject that you and the interviewer share an interest in.'
- 'Interviewers will be looking for you to demonstrate how you met the criteria advertised in the

prospectus and UCAS entry profiles, but will not always ask you about them directly. Some examples of criteria used by admissions tutors include: interest, motivation and commitment to the subject; the ability to study independently; the ability to work with others; the ability to manage time effectively; an interest in the university.'

In the tables in **Chapter 7** (**Selection interviews, Interview advice and questions** and **Reasons for rejection**) you will also find examples of questions which have been asked in recent years for which you might prepare, and non-academic reasons why applicants have been rejected! **Chapter 4, Applications**, provides a guide through the process of applying to your chosen universities and courses and highlights key points for your action.

Try to turn up looking smart (it may not matter, but it can't be wrong). A previous applicant was more specific: 'Dress smartly but sensibly so you are comfortable for travelling and walking round the campus.'

MULTIPLE MINI INTERVIEWS (MMIS)

MMIs involve the applicants participating in a number of small interviews and tasks. An example of the structure of an MMI could be eight seven-minute interviews (also called stations), with interviewees having a minute between stations. The format of each station will vary, but you will receive instructions explaining what you will be required to do, so ensure you listen carefully and read any written instructions to give you a good idea of what you will be facing.

MMIs are often used in the belief that they can provide the interviewers with a more accurate indication of an applicant's personality and character attributes than the traditional panel interview, which can be heavily coached for.

Some universities divulge very little about the exact detail of the MMI they offer, while others will provide some detail about what the interviewees will face. Students should be prepared to be tested on their ability to communicate and interact with others; to undertake basic observation and memory tasks; to undertake manual dexterity tasks, depending on the chosen course; to analyse different methods of data presentation, eg tables and graphs; to make a presentation.

6 HOW TO USE THE SUBJECT TABLES

The subject tables in the next chapter represent the core of the book, listing degree courses offered by all UK universities and colleges. These tables are designed to provide you with the information you need so that you can match your abilities and interests with your chosen degree subject, prepare your application and find out how applicants are selected for courses.

At the top of each table there is a brief overview of the subject area, together with a selection of websites for organisations that can provide relevant careers or course information. This is then followed by the subject tables themselves in which information is provided in sequence under the following headings.

Course offers information
- Subject requirements/preferences (GCSE/A-level/other requirements)
- Your target offers and examples of degree courses
- Alternative offers

Degree Apprenticeships

Examples of colleges offering courses in this subject field

Choosing your course
- Universities and colleges teaching quality
- Top research universities and colleges (REF 2021)
- Examples of sandwich degree courses

Admissions information
- Admissions tutors' advice
- Advice to applicants and planning the UCAS personal statement
- Selection interviews
- Interview advice and questions
- Reasons for rejection (non-academic)

Graduate destinations and employment
- Career note

Other degree subjects for consideration

When selecting a degree course it is important to try to judge the points score or grades that you are likely to achieve and compare them with the offers listed under **Your target offers and examples of degree courses**. However, even though you might be capable of achieving the indicated grades or UCAS Tariff points, it is important to note that these are likely to be the minimum grades or points required and that there is no guarantee that you will receive an offer: other factors in your application, such as the personal statement, references, and admissions test performance will be taken into consideration (see also **Chapters 3** and **5**).

University departments frequently adjust their offers, depending on the numbers of candidates applying, so you must not assume that the offers and policies published now will necessarily apply to courses starting in 2026 or thereafter. Even though offers may change during the 2025/26 application cycle, you can assume that the offers published in this book represent the typical academic levels at which you should aim.

Below are explanations of the information given under the headings in the subject tables. It is important that you read these carefully so that you understand how they can help you to choose and apply for courses that are right for you.

COURSE OFFERS INFORMATION

Subject requirements/preferences

Brief information is given on the GCSE and A-level requirements. Specific A-level subject requirements for individual institutions are listed separately. Other requirements are sometimes specified, where these are relevant to the course subject area, for example, medical requirements for health-related courses and Disclosure and Barring Service (DBS) clearance. Check prospectuses and websites of universities and colleges for course requirements.

YOUR TARGET OFFERS AND EXAMPLES OF DEGREE COURSES

Universities and colleges offering degree courses in the subject area are listed in descending order according to the number of UCAS Tariff points and/or A-level grades they are likely to require applicants to achieve. The UCAS Tariff points total is listed down the left-hand side of the page, and to the right appear all the institutions (in alphabetical order) likely to make offers in this Tariff point range. (Information on the UCAS Tariff is given in **Appendix 1** and guidance on how to calculate your offers is provided on every other page of the subject tables in this book. Please also read the information in the **Important Note** box on page 91.)

The courses included on the offers line are examples of the courses available in the subject field at that university or college. You will need to check prospectuses and websites for a complete list of the institution's Single, Joint, Combined or Major/Minor Honours degree courses available in the subject. For each institution listed, the following information may be given.

Name of institution

Note that the name of an institution's university college or campus may be given in brackets after the institution title, for example London (King's) or Kent (Medway Sch Pharm). Where the institution is not a university, further information about its status may also be given to indicate the type of college – for example (UC) to mean University College or (CAg) to mean College of Agriculture. This is to help readers to differentiate between the types of colleges and to help them identify any specialisation a college may have, for example art or agriculture. A full list of abbreviations used is given under the heading **INSTITUTION ABBREVIATIONS** later in this chapter.

Grades/points offer

After the institution's name, a line of offers information is given, showing a typical offer made by the institution for the courses indicated in brackets. The printed offers are standard offers only, but many universities are now publishing contextual offers that take into account students' personal circumstances (see also **Chapter 3**). Offers may be reduced after the publication of A-level results, particularly if a university or college is left with spare places. However, individual course offers listed in the tables in **Chapter 7** are abridged and should be used as a first source of reference and comparison only. It is not possible to publish all the variables relevant to each offer: applicants must check prospectuses and websites for full details of all offers and courses. All offers listed in the tables in **Chapter 7** refer to degree courses only. Applicants should note however that some courses in the same subject areas are also available at lower levels with lower offers, eg Foundation courses, Diplomas of Higher Education and Certificates; these are published on university and college websites.

Depending on the details given by institutions, the offers may provide information as follows.

- **Grades** The specific grades, or average grades, required at A-level or, if specified, EPQ for the listed courses. (NB Graded offers may require specific grades for specific subjects.) A-level grades are always presented in capital letters; EPQ grades are shown in lower case. The offer AAB+aEPQ would indicate two grade As and one grade B at A-level, plus an additional EPQ at grade a. Offers are usually shown in terms of three A-level grades although some institutions accept two grades with the same points total.

NB Unit grade and module information, now introduced into the admissions system, is most likely to be required by universities where a course is competitive, or where taking a specific unit is necessary or desirable for entry. Check with institutions' websites for their latest information.

- **The UCAS Tariff points system** A-levels, AS, International Baccalaureate (IB), Scottish Highers, the Progression Diploma and a range of other qualifications have a unit value in the UCAS Tariff system (see **UCAS 2026 Entry Tariff Points** tables in **Appendix 1**). Where a range of Tariff points is shown, for example 112–120 points, offers are usually made within this points range for these specified courses. Note that, in some cases, an institution may require a points score which is higher than the specified grade offer given. This can be for a number of reasons – for example, you may not be offering the standard subjects that would have been stipulated in a grades offer. In such cases additional points may be added by way of AS grades, Functional/Essential Skills, the Extended Project Qualification, etc.

Unit value of A-level grades in the UCAS Tariff points system:

A* = 56 pts; A = 48 pts; B = 40 pts; C = 32 pts; D = 24 pts; E = 16 pts

Some universities make offers for entry to each course by way of A-level grades, others make Tariff points offers while others will make offers in both A-level grades and in Tariff points. Applicants should be sure that the A-level subjects they are taking are acceptable for their chosen course and for A-level grades and points offers. A Tariff points offer will not usually discriminate between the final year exam subjects being taken by the applicant unless otherwise stated, although certain GCSE subjects may be stipulated eg English or mathematics.

Admission tutors have the unenviable task of trying to assess the number of applicants who will apply for their courses against the number of places available and so judging the offers to be made. However, since the government removed the cap on the number of places that universities in England are able to offer, English universities can admit an unlimited number of home undergraduates, though not every institution has adopted these reforms. Nevertheless, it is still important when reading the offers tables to be aware that variations occur each year. Lower offers or equivalents may be made to disadvantaged students, mature and international applicants.

See **Chapter 3** for information from universities about their admissions policies including, for example, information about their expected use of A*, unit grades, the Progression Diploma, the Extended Project Qualification and the Cambridge Pre-U in their offers for applicants. See **Appendix 1** for **UCAS 2026 Entry Tariff Points** tables.

- **Admissions tests for Law, Medicine and Veterinary Science/Medicine** Where admissions tests form part of a university's offer for any of these subjects, this is indicated on the offers line in the subject tables for the relevant university. This is shown by '+LNAT' (for Law), or '+UCAT' (for Medicine). For example, the offers lines could read as follows:

  Cardiff – AAA incl chem+biol+interview+UCAT (Med 5 yrs) (IB 36 pts HL 666 incl chem/biol+sci/maths)
  Durham – A*AA+LNAT (Law) (IB 38 pts)

Entry and admissions tests will be required for 2026 by a number of institutions for a wide range of subjects: see **Chapter 5** and the subject tables in **Chapter 7** for more information and check university websites and prospectuses.

Course title(s)

After the offer, an abbreviated form of the course title(s) to which the offers information refers is provided in brackets. Unless otherwise indicated, this course title represents all other courses in this subject offered by the institution, including joint courses. The abbreviations used (see **COURSE ABBREVIATIONS** at the end of this chapter) closely relate to the course titles shown in the institutions' prospectuses. When the course gives the opportunity to study abroad this can be indicated on the offers line by including 'St Abrd' after the abbreviated course title. For example:

Lancaster – AAB incl maths (Econ (St Abrd)) (IB 35 pts HL 6 maths)

When experience in industry is provided as part of the course (not necessarily a sandwich course) this can be indicated on the offers line by including 'Yr Ind' after the abbreviated course title. For example:

Liverpool – ABB (Bus Mgt (Yr Ind)) (IB 33 pts)

Sometimes the information in the offers line relates to more than one course (see **Worcester** below). In such cases, each course title is separated with a semicolon.

Worcester – 112 pts (PE Spo St; PE Dance)

When a number of joint courses exist in combination with a Major subject, they may be presented using a list separated by slashes – for example '(Int Bus Fr/Ger/Span)' indicates International Business with

French or German or Spanish. Some titles may be followed by the word 'courses' – for example, (Hist courses):

Bishop Grosseteste – 96–112 pts (Hist courses; Arch Hist)

This means that the information on the offers line refers not only to the Single Honours course in Archaeology History, but also to the range of History courses. For some institutions with extensive Combined or Joint Honours programmes, the information given on the offers line may specify (Comb Hons) or (Comb courses).

For Engineering courses, BSc is included as an abbreviation in the subject line if the course is also offered at the same institution as a BEng degree with different entry requirements. For example:

Anglia Ruskin – 96 pts (Civ Eng (BSc)) (IB 24 pts)

Sometimes, where relevant, the offers line shows integrated master's degree courses (four year courses which combine three years of undergraduate study with a fourth year of postgraduate level study). In such cases, an abbreviation showing the type of degree course appears at the end of the course offer. For example:

Bristol – ABB–AAA incl maths (Elec Electron Eng (MEng)) (IB 32–36 pts HL 6 maths)

Courses awaiting validation are usually publicised in prospectuses and on websites. However, these are not included in the tables in **Chapter 7** since there is no guarantee that they will run. You should check with the university that a non-validated course will be available.

To help you understand the information provided under the **YOUR TARGET OFFERS AND EXAMPLES OF DEGREE COURSES** heading, the box below provides a few examples with their meaning explained underneath.

OFFERS LINES EXPLAINED

136 pts [University/University College name] – AAB (Acc Fin)
For the Accounting Finance course the University requires grades of AAB (136 pts) at A-level.

152 pts [University/University College name] – A*AA incl chem+biol+UCAT (Med 6 yrs)
For the 6 year Medicine course the University requires one A and two A grades at A-level, with two of these subjects in Chemistry and Biology, plus the UCAT.*

104 pts [University/University College name] – 104–120 pts (Geog)
For Geography, the University usually requires 104 UCAS Tariff points, but offers may range up to 120 UCAS Tariff points.

ALTERNATIVE OFFERS

In each of the subject tables, offers are shown in A-level grades or equivalent UCAS Tariff points, and in some cases as points offers of the International Baccalaureate Diploma (see below). However, applicants taking Scottish Highers/Advanced Highers, the Advanced Welsh Baccalaureate – Skills Challenge Certificate, the International Baccalaureate Diploma, BTEC, the Extended Project, T-levels, Music examinations and Art and Design Foundation Studies should refer to **Appendix 1 – UCAS 2026 Entry Tariff Points**. For more information, see www.ucas.com/undergraduate/what-and-where-study/entry-requirements/ucas-tariff-points or contact the institution direct.

IB offers

A selection of IB points offers appears at the end of some university/subject entries, along with any requirements for points gained from specific Higher Level (HL) subjects. Where no specific subjects are named for HL, the HL points can be taken from any subject. For comparison of entry requirements, applicants with IB qualifications should check the A-level offers required for their course and then refer to **Appendix 1** which gives the revised IB UCAS Tariff points for 2026 entry. The figures under this subheading indicate the number or range of International Baccalaureate (IB) Diploma points likely to be requested in an offer. A range of points indicates variations between Single and Joint Honours courses.

Applicants offering the IB should check with prospectuses and websites and, if in doubt, contact admissions tutors for the latest information on IB offers.

Scottish offers

Scottish Honours degrees normally take four years. However, students with very good qualifications may be admitted into the second year of courses (Advanced entry, also known as Articulation). In some cases it may even be possible to enter the third year.

Please check individual university and college websites for details of Advanced entry.

Contextual offers

These offers are made by most universities to disadvantaged students wishing to be considered for university places. In most cases these are lower offers by one or two grades compared to the standard offers.

IMPORTANT NOTE ON THE COURSE OFFERS INFORMATION

The information provided in **Chapter 7** is presented as a first reference source as to the target levels required. Institutions may alter their standard offers in the light of the qualifications offered by applicants.

The offers they publish do not constitute a contract and are not binding on prospective students: changes may occur between the time of publication and the time of application in line with market and student demand.

The points levels shown on the left-hand side of the offers listings are for ease of reference for the reader: not all universities will be making offers using the UCAS Tariff points system and it cannot be assumed that they will accept a points equivalent to the grades they have stipulated. Check university and college prospectuses, and also their websites, for their latest information before submitting your application.

DEGREE APPRENTICESHIPS

Examples of degree apprenticeships offered by some universities, designed in partnerships with employers. To check degree apprenticeship vacancies and details, refer to GOV.UK (www.gov.uk/apply-apprenticeship) or UCAS (www.ucas.com/apprenticeships).

EXAMPLES OF COLLEGES OFFERING COURSES IN THIS SUBJECT FIELD

Examples of courses offered by some local colleges – but also check your local college. To check details of courses, refer to college websites and **Chapter 9** Sections 2 and 3.

CHOOSING YOUR COURSE

The information under this heading (to be read in conjunction with **Chapter 1**) covers factors that are important to consider in order to make an informed decision on which courses to apply for. The information is organised under the following subheadings.

Universities and colleges teaching quality

The Discover Uni website (https://discoveruni.gov.uk) provides official information where available for different subjects and universities and colleges in the UK to help prospective students and their advisers make comparisons between them and so make informed choices about what and where to study. Information is updated annually and is available for each subject taught at each university and college (and for some further education colleges). The Quality Assurance Agency (www.qaa.ac.uk) reviews the quality and standards of all universities and colleges and official reports of their reviews are available on their website but it is important to note their dates of publication.

Top research universities and colleges (REF 2021)

The Research Excellence Framework (REF) is the system for evaluating the standard of research in higher education institutions covering certain subject areas. The results of the 2021 Research Excellence Framework (REF) were published in May 2022. The leading universities in the relevant subject areas are listed in the order of achievement. It should be noted that not all subjects were assessed.

Examples of sandwich degree courses

This section lists examples of institutions that offer sandwich placements for some of their courses in the subject field shown. The institutions listed offer placements of one-year duration and do not include language courses or work experience or other short-term placements. Check with the institutions too, since new courses may be introduced and others withdrawn depending on industrial or commercial arrangements. Further information on sandwich courses with specific information on the placements of students appears in **Chapter 1**.

NB During a period of economic uncertainty, universities and colleges may have problems placing students on sandwich courses. Applicants applying for courses are therefore advised to check with admissions tutors that these courses will run, and that placements will be available.

ADMISSIONS INFORMATION

Under this heading, information gathered from the institutions has been provided. This will be useful when planning your application.

Admissions tutors' advice

This section appears occasionally and offers helpful guidance on what in particular admissions tutors are looking for in the UCAS application and/or interview. See also **Chapters 4** and **5**.

Advice to applicants and planning the UCAS personal statement

This section offers guidelines on information that could be included in the personal statement section of your UCAS application. In most cases, applicants will be required to indicate why they wish to follow a particular course and, if possible, to provide positive evidence of their interest. See also **Chapters 4** and **5**.

Selection interviews

A sample of institutions that normally use the interview as part of their selection procedure is listed here. Those institutions adopting the interview procedure will usually interview only a small proportion of applicants. It is important to use this section in conjunction with **Chapters 3** and **5**.

Interview advice and questions

This section includes information from institutions on what candidates might expect in an interview to cover, and examples of the types of interview questions posed in recent years. Also refer to **Chapters 3** and **5**: these chapters provide information on tests and assessments which are used in selecting students.

Reasons for rejection (non-academic)

Academic ability and potential to succeed on the course are the major factors in the selection (or rejection) of applicants. Under this subheading, admissions tutors give other reasons for rejecting applicants.

GRADUATE DESTINATIONS AND EMPLOYMENT

See **Graduate Outcomes** in **Chapter 1** for the results of the Graduate Outcomes 2021/22 survey; this survey monitors the career destinations of leavers from higher education 15 months after graduation.

Career note

Short descriptions of the career destinations of graduates in the subject area are provided.

OTHER DEGREE SUBJECTS FOR CONSIDERATION

This heading includes some suggested alternative courses that have similarities to the courses listed in the subject table.

ABBREVIATIONS USED IN THE SUBJECT TABLES IN CHAPTER 7

INSTITUTION ABBREVIATIONS

The following abbreviations are used to indicate specific institutions or types of institution:

Ac	Academy
AI	Arts Institute
AMD	Academy of Music and Drama
AUP	Arts University Plymouth
Birk	Birkbeck (London University)
BITE	British Institute of Technology, England
CA	College of Art(s)
CAD	College of Art and Design
CAFRE	College of Agriculture, Food and Rural Enterprise
CAg	College of Agriculture
CAgH	College of Agriculture and Horticulture
CAT	College of Advanced Technology or Arts and Technology
CComm	College of Communication
CDC	College of Design and Communication
CECOS	London College of IT and Management
CFash	College of Fashion
CHort	College of Horticulture
CmC	Community College
CMus	College of Music
CMusDr	College of Music and Drama
Coll	College/Collegiate
Consv	Conservatoire
Court	Courtauld Institute (London University)
CT	College of Technology
CTA	College of Technology and Arts
Educ	Education
FRA	Fashion Retail Academy (London)
Gold	Goldsmiths (London University)
GSA	Guildford School of Acting
HOW	Heart of Worcestershire College
IA	Institute of Art(s)
IFHE	Institute of Further and Higher Education
Inst	Institute
King's	King's College (London University)
LeSoCo	Lewisham Southwark College
LIBF	London Institute of Banking and Finance
LIPA	Liverpool Institute of Performing Arts
LIS	London Interdisciplinary School
LSE	London School of Economics and Political Science
LSST	London School of Science and Technology
Met	Metropolitan
MS	Medical School
NCC	New City College
NU London	Northeastern University London
QM	Queen Mary (London University)
RAc Dance	Royal Academy of Dance
RAcMus	Royal Academy of Music
RConsvS	Royal Conservatoire of Scotland

RCMus	Royal College of Music
Reg Coll	Regional College
Reg Fed	Regional Federation (Staffordshire)
RH	Royal Holloway (London University)
RNCM	Royal Northern College of Music
RVC	Royal Veterinary College (London University)
SA	School of Art
SAD	School of Art and Design
Sch	School
Sch SpDr	School of Speech and Drama
SMO	Sabhal Mòr Ostaig
SOAS	School of Oriental and African Studies (London University)
SRUC	Scotland's Rural College
UC	University College
UCEM	University College of Estate Management
UCFB	University College of Football Business
UCL	University College (London University)
UCO	University College of Osteopathy
UHI	University of the Highlands and Islands
Univ	University

COURSE ABBREVIATIONS

The following abbreviations are used to indicate course titles and admissions tests:

Ab	Abrahamic
Abrd	Abroad
Acc	Accountancy/Accounting
Accs	Accessories
Acdm	Academic
Acoust	Acoustics/Acoustical
Acq	Acquisition
Act	Actuarial
Actg	Acting
Actn	Action
Actr	Actor
Actv	Active
Actvsm	Activism
Actvt(s)	Activity/Activities
Acu	Acupuncture
Add	Additional
Adlscn	Adolescence
Adlt	Adult
Admin	Administration/Administrative
Adt	Audit
Adv	Advertising
Advc	Advice
Advnc	Advanced
Advntr	Adventure
Aero	Aeronautical/Aeronautics
Aerodyn	Aerodynamics
Aero-Mech	Aero-mechanical
Aerosp	Aerospace
Aeroth	Aerothermal
Af	Africa(n)
Affrs	Affairs
Age	Ageing
Agncy	Agency
Agribus	Agribusiness
Agric	Agriculture/Agricultural
Agri-Fd	Agri-Food
Agrofor	Agroforestry
Agron	Agronomy
Aid	Aided
Aircft	Aircraft
Airln	Airline
Airpt	Airport
Airvhcl	Airvehicle
Akkdn	Akkadian
ALN	Additional Learning Needs
Am	America(n)
Amen	Amenity
AMELAT	Asian and Middle Eastern Languages Admissions Test
AMESAA	Asian and Middle Eastern Studies Admissions Assessment
Analys	Analysis
Analyt	Analytical/Analytics
Anat	Anatomy/Anatomical
Anc	Ancient
Anim	Animal
Animat	Animation
Animatron	Animatronics
Anth	Anthropology
Antq	Antique(s)
App(s)	Applied/Applicable/Applications
Appar	Apparel
Appr	Appropriate
Apprsl	Appraisal

Aqua	Aquaculture/Aquatic
Ar	Area(s)
Arbc	Arabic
Arbor	Arboriculture
Arch	Archaeology/Archaeological
ARCHAA	Archaeology Admissions Assessment
Archit	Architecture/Architectural
ARCHITAA	Architecture Admissions Assessment
Archvl	Archival
Aroma	Aromatherapy
Arst	Artist
Artfcts	Artefacts
Artif	Artificial
As	Asia(n)
ASNCAA	Anglo-Saxon, Norse and Celtic Admissions Assessment
Ass	Assessment
Assoc	Associated
Assoct	Associate
Asst	Assistant
Assyr	Assyriology
Ast	Asset
Astnaut	Astronautics/Astronautical
Astrbiol	Astrobiology
Astro	Astrophysics
Astron	Astronomy
A-Sxn	Anglo-Saxon
Ated	Accelerated
Atel	Atelier
Atlan	Atlantic
Atmos	Atmospheric/Atmosphere
Attrctns	Attractions
Auc	Auctioneering
Aud	Audio
Audiol	Audiology
Audtech	Audiotechnology
Aus	Australia(n)
Austr	Australasia
Auth	Author/Authoring/Authorship
Auto	Automotive
Autom	Automated/Automation
Automat	Automatic
Autombl	Automobile
Autsm	Autism
AV	Audio Video
Avion	Avionic(s)
Avn	Aviation
Ay St	Ayurvedic Studies

Bank	Banking
Bch	Beach
Bd	Based
Bdwk	Bodywork
Bev	Beverage
BHS	British Horse Society
Bhv	Behaviour(al)
Bib	Biblical
Bio Ins	Bio Instrumentation
Bioarch	Bioarchaeology
Bioch	Biochemistry/Biochemical
Biocomp	Biocomputing
Biodiv	Biodiversity
Bioelectron	Bioelectronics
Bioeng	Bioengineering
Biogeog	Biogeography
Biogeosci	Biogeoscience
Bioinform	Bioinformatics
Biokin	Biokinetics
Biol	Biological/Biology
Biom	Biometry
Biomat	Biomaterials
Biomed	Biomedical/Biomedicine
Biomol	Biomolecular
Biophys	Biophysics
Bioproc	Bioprocess
Biorg	Bio-organic
Biosci	Bioscience(s)
Biotech	Biotechnology
Biovet	Bioveterinary
Bkbnd	Bookbinding
Bld	Build(ing)
Bldstck	Bloodstock
Blksmthg	Blacksmithing
Blt	Built
Bngli	Bengali
Braz	Brazilian
Brew	Brewing
Brit	British
Brnd	Brand(ing)
Broad	Broadcast(ing)
Bspk	Bespoke
Bty	Beauty
Bulg	Bulgarian
Burm	Burmese
Bus	Business
Buy	Buying
Byz	Byzantine

CAA	Classics Admissions Assessment
CAD	Computer Aided Design
Callig	Calligraphy
Can	Canada/Canadian
Canc	Cancer
Cap	Capital
Carb	Carbon
Cardio	Cardiology
Cardiov	Cardiovascular
Carib	Caribbean
Cart	Cartography
Cat	Catering

CAT	Classics Admissions Test
CATS	Credit Accumulation and Transfer Scheme
Cell	Cellular
Celt	Celtic
Cent	Century
Ceram	Ceramics
Cert	Certificate
Ch Mgt	Chain Management
Chart	Chartered
Chc	Choice
Chch	Church
Chem	Chemistry
Cheml	Chemical
Chin	Chinese
Chiro	Chiropractic
Chld	Child/Children/Childhood
Chlng	Challenge(s)
Chn	Chain
Chng	Change
Choreo	Choreography
Chr	Christian(ity)
Chrctr	Character
Chtls	Chattels
Cits	Cities
Civ	Civil(isation)
Class	Classical/Classics
Clim	Climate/Climatic
Clin	Clinical
Cllct	Collect(ing)
Clnl	Colonial
Cloth	Clothing
Clsrm	Classroom
Cmbt	Combat
Cmc	Comic
Cmdy	Comedy
Cmn	Common
Cmnd	Command
Cmplrs	Compilers
Cmpn	Companion
Cmpsn	Composition
Cmpste(s)	Composite(s)
Cmwlth	Commonwealth
Cncr	Cancer
Cnflct	Conflict
Cnma	Cinema/Cinematics/ Cinematography
Cnslg	Counselling
Cnsltncy	Consultancy
Cnt	Central
Cntnt	Content
Cntrms	Countermeasures
Cntry	Country(side)
Cntxt	Context
Cnty	Century
Coach	Coaching
Cog	Cognitive
Col	Colour
Coll	Collaborative
Comb	Combined
Combus	Combustion
Comm(s)	Communication(s)
Commer	Commerce/Commercial
Commun	Community
Comp	Computation/Computer(s)/ Computerised/Computing
Compar	Comparative
Complem	Complementary
Con	Context
Conc	Concept
Concur	Concurrent
Cond	Conductive
Condit	Conditioning
Cons	Conservation
Conslt	Consultant
Constb	Constable
Constr	Construction
Consum	Consumer
Cont	Contour
Contemp	Contemporary
Contnl	Continental
Contr	Control
Conv	Conveyancing
Cord	Cordwainers
Corn	Cornish
Corp	Corporate/Corporation
Cos	Cosmetic
Cosmo	Cosmology
Coun	Counter
Cr	Care
Crckt	Cricket
Crcs	Circus
Crdc	Cardiac
Crea	Creative/Creation
Crft(s)	Craft(s)/Craftsmanship
Crim	Criminal
Crimin	Criminological/Criminology
Crit	Criticism/Critical
Crm	Crime
Cro	Croatian
Crr	Career
Crsn	Corrosion
Crtn	Cartoon
Cru	Cruise
Crypt	Cryptography
CSAT	Computer Science Admissions Test
Cstl	Coastal
Cstm	Costume
Cstmd	Customised
Ctln	Catalan
Ctlys	Catalysis

Ctzn	Citizenship
Culn	Culinary
Cult	Culture(s)/Cultural
Cur	Curation/Curating
Cy	Cyber
Cyber	Cybernetics/Cyberspace
Cybercrim	Cybercrime
Cyberscrty	Cybersecurity
Cybertron	Cybertronics
Cym	Cymraeg
Cz	Czech
Dan	Danish
Decn	Decision
Decr	Decoration/Decorative
Def	Defence
Defer	Deferred Choice
Deg	Degree
Demcr	Democratic
Dept	Department
Des	Design(er)
Desr	Desirable
Dest	Destination(s)
Dev	Development(al)
Devsg	Devising
Df	Deaf
Diag	Diagnostic
Diet	Diet/Dietetics/Dietitian
Dif	Difficulties
Dig	Digital
Dip	Diploma
Dip Ing	Diplom Ingeneur
Dipl	Diplomacy
Dir	Direct/Direction/Director/Directing
Dis	Disease(s)
Disab	Disability
Disas	Disaster
Discip	Disciplinary
Diso	Disorders
Disp	Dispensing
Dist	Distributed/Distribution
Distil	Distillation/Distilling
Div	Divinity
d/l	distance learning
Dnstry	Dentistry
Dntl	Dental
Doc	Document(ary)
Dom	Domestic(ated)
Dr	Drama
Drg	Drawing
Dri	Drink
Drs	Dress
Dscrt	Discrete
Dscvry	Discovery
Dsply	Display
Dtbs	Databases
Dth	Death
Dvc	Device
Dvnc	Deviance
Dvsd	Devised
Dynmcs	Dynamics
E	East(ern)
EAA	Education Admissions Assessment
ECAA	Economics Admissions Assessment
Ecol	Ecology/Ecological
Ecomet	Econometrics
e-Commer	E-Commerce
Econ	Economic(s)
Econy	Economy/Economies
Ecosys	Ecosystem(s)
Ecotech	Ecotechnology
Ecotour	Ecotourism
Ecotox	Ecotoxicology
Edit	Editorial/Editing
Educ	Education(al)
Educr	Educare
Efcts	Effects
Effic	Efficiency
EFL	English as a Foreign Language
Egypt	Egyptian/Egyptology
Elec	Electric/Electrical
Elecacoust	Electroacoustics
Electromech	Electromechanical
Electron	Electronic(s)
ELAT	English Language Admissions Test
ELT	English Language Teaching
Ely	Early
Emb	Embryo(logy)
Embd	Embedded
Embr	Embroidery
Emer	Emergency
Emp	Employment
Ener	Energy
Eng	Engineer(ing)
Engl	English
Engmnt	Engagement
Engn	Engine
Enhncd	Enhanced
Ent	Enterprise
Enter	Entertainment
Entomol	Entomology
Entre	Entrepreneur(ship)
Env	Environment(s)/Environmental
EPQ	Extended Project Qualification
Eql	Equal
Eqn	Equine/Equestrian

Equip	Equipment
Equit	Equitation
Ergon	Ergonomics
ESAT	Engineering and Science Admissions Test
Est	Estate
Eth	Ethics
Ethl	Ethical
Eth-Leg	Ethico-Legal
Ethn	Ethnic
Ethnol	Ethnology
Ethnomus	Ethnomusicology
EU	European Union
Euro	Europe/European
Eval	Evaluation
Evnglstc	Evangelistic
Evnt(s)	Event(s)
Evol	Evolution(ary)
Ex	Executing
Excl	Excellence
Exer	Exercise
Exhib	Exhibition
Exmp	Exempt(ing)
Exp	Export
Explor	Exploration
Explsn	Explosion
Expltn	Exploitation
Expmtl	Experimental
Expnc	Experience
Expr	Expressive
Exprs	Express
Ext	Extended
Extr	Exterior
Extrm	Extreme
Fabs	Fabric(s)
Fac	Faculty
Fact	Factor(s)
Facil	Facilities
Fash	Fashion
Fbr	Fibre
Fctn	Fiction
Fd	Food
Fdn	Foundation
Fd Sc	Foundation degree in Science
Filmm	Filmmaking
Fin	Finance/Financial
Finn	Finnish
Fish	Fishery/Fisheries
Fit	Fitness
Fl	Fluid
Fld	Field
Flex	Flexible
Flm	Film
Flor	Floristry
Fmaths	Further Mathematics
Fmly	Family
Fn	Fine
Foot	Footwear
For	Foreign
Foren	Forensic
Foss	Fossil(s)
Fr	French
Frchd	Franchised
Frcst	Forecasting
Frm	Farm
Frmwk	Framework
Frnc	France
Frshwtr	Freshwater
Frst	Forest
Frstr	Forester
Frsty	Forestry
Frtlty	Fertility
Fst Trk	Fast Track
Fstvl	Festival(s)
Ftbl	Football
Ftre	Feature(s)
Ftwr	Footwear
Furn	Furniture
Fut	Futures
GAA	Geography Admissions Assessment
Gael	Gaelic
Gam	Gambling
GAMSAT	Graduate Australian Medical School Admission Test
Gdn	Garden
Gdnc	Guidance
Gem	Gemmology
Gen	General
Genet	Genetics
Geochem	Geochemistry
Geog	Geography/Geographical
Geoinform	Geoinformatics
Geol	Geology/Geological
Geophys	Geophysics
Geophysl	Geophysical
Geopol	Geopolitics
Geosci	Geoscience
Geosptl	Geospatial
Geotech	Geotechnics
Ger	German(y)
Gerc	Germanic
GIS	Geographical Information Systems
Gk	Greek
Glf	Golf
Gllry	Gallery/Galleries
Glob	Global(isation)
Gls	Glass
Gm(s)	Game(s)

Gmg	Gaming
Gmnt	Garment
Gmtc	Geomatic
Gndr	Gender
Gnm	Genome/Genomics
Gold	Goldsmithing
Gov	Government
Govn	Governance
Gr	Grade
Graph	Graphic(s)
Grgn	Georgian
Grn	Green
Guji	Gujerati
HAA	History Admissions Assessment
HAAA	History of Art Admissions Assessment
Hab	Habitat
Hack	Hacking
Hard	Hardware
HAT	History Aptitude Test
Haz	Hazard(s)
Heal	Healing
Heb	Hebrew
Herb	Herbal
Herit	Heritage
Herp	Herpetology
Hi	High
Hisp	Hispanic
Hist	History/Historical
HL	IB Higher level
Hlcst	Holocaust
Hlnds	Highlands
Hlth	Health
Hlthcr	Healthcare
Hm	Home
Hnd	Hindi
Hol	Holistic
Hom	Homeopathic
Homin	Hominid
Horol	Horology
Hort	Horticulture
Hosp	Hospital
Hous	Housing
HR	Human Resource(s)
Hrdrs	Hairdressing
Hrs	Horse
Hse	House
HSPSAA	Human, Social and Political Sciences Admissions Assessment
Hspty	Hospitality
Htl	Hotel
Hum	Human(ities)
Hung	Hungarian
Hydrog	Hydrography
Hydrol	Hydrology
Hyg	Hygiene
Iber	Iberian
Ice	Icelandic
ICT	Information and Communications Technology
Id	Idea(s)
Idnty	Identity
Illus	Illustration
Imag	Image/Imaging/Imaginative
Immer	Immersive
Immun	Immunology/Immunity
Impair	Impairment
Imprv	Improvement
Incl	Including
Incln	Inclusion
Inclsv	Inclusive
Ind	Industrial/Industry/Industries
Indep	Independent
Indiv	Individual(s)
Indsn	Indonesian
Inf	Information
Infec	Infectious/Infection
Infml	Informal
Inform	Informatics
Infra	Infrastructure
Inftq	Informatique
Injry	Injury
Innov	Innovation
Ins	Insurance
Inst	Institute/Institution(al)
Instln	Installation
Instr	Instrument(ation)
Int	International
Integ	Integrated/Integration
Intel	Intelligent/Intelligence
Inter	Interior(s)
Interact	Interaction/Interactive
Intercult	Intercultural
Interd	Interdisciplinary
Intermed	Intermedia
Interp	Interpretation/Interpreting
Intlctl	Intellectual
Intnet	Internet
Intr	Interest(s)
Intrmdl	Intermodal
Inv	Investment
Invstg	Investigating/Investigation(s)/Investigative
IPML	Integrated Professional Master in Language
Ir	Irish
Is	Issues
Isl	Islands
Islam	Islamic

Isrl	Israel/Israeli
IT	Information Technology
Ital	Italian
ITE	Initial Teacher Education
ITT	Initial Teacher Training
Jap	Japanese
Jew	Jewish
Jewel	Jewellery
Jrnl	Journalism
Jud	Judaism
Juris	Jurisprudence
Just	Justice
Knit	Knit(ted)
Kntwr	Knitwear
Knwl	Knowledge
Kor	Korean
KS	Key Stage
LAA	Linguistics Admissions Assessment
Lab	Laboratory
Lang(s)	Language(s)
Las	Laser
Lat	Latin
Lcl	Local
LD	Learning Disabilities
Ldr	Leader
Ldrshp	Leadership
Lea	Leather
Leg	Legal
Legis	Legislative
Leis	Leisure
Lf	Life
Lfstl	Lifestyle
Lgc	Logic
Lib	Library
Librl	Liberal
Libshp	Librarianship
Lic	Licensed
Lic de Geog	Licence de Geographie
Lic de Let	Licence de Lettres
Ling	Linguistics
Lit	Literature/Literary/Literate
Litcy	Literacy
LNAT	Law National Aptitude Test
Lnd	Land(scape)
Lndbd	Land-based
Lns	Lens
Log	Logistics
Lrn	Learn
Lrng	Learning
Ls	Loss
Lsr	Laser
Ltg	Lighting
Ltr	Later
Lv	Live
Lvstk	Livestock
Lw	Low
Mach	Machine(ry)
Mag	Magazine
Mait	Maitrise Internationale
Mak	Making/Maker
Mand	Mandarin
Manuf	Manufacture/Manufacturing
Map	Map(ping)
Mar	Marine
Marit	Maritime
Mark	Market(ing)
Masch	Maschinenbau
Mat	Material(s)
Mat	Mathematics Admissions Test
Mathem	Mathematical
Maths	Mathematics
Mbl	Mobile
Measur	Measurement
Mech	Mechanical
Mecha	Mechatronic(s)
Mechn	Mechanisation
Mechnsms	Mechanisms
Med	Medicine/Medical
Medcnl	Medicinal
Mediev	Medieval
Medit	Mediterranean
Ment	Mentoring
Metal	Metallurgy/Metallurgical
Meteor	Meteorology/Meteorological
Meth	Method(s)
Mgng	Managing
Mgr	Manager
Mgrl	Managerial
Mgt	Management
Microbiol	Microbiology/Microbiological
Microbl	Microbial
Microcomp	Microcomputer/ Microcomputing
Microelec	Microelectronics
Mid E	Middle Eastern
Midwif	Midwifery
Min	Mining
Miner	Minerals
Mix	Mixed
Mkup	Make-up
MLAT	Modern Languages Admissions Test
Mling	Multilingual
Mltry	Military
MMath	Master of Mathematics

MMLAA	Medieval and Modern Languages Admissions Assessment
Mnd	Mind
Mnrts	Minorities
Mnstry	Ministry
Mnswr	Menswear
Mntl Hlth	Mental Health
Mntn	Mountain
Mntnce	Maintenance
Mny	Money
Mod	Modular
Modl	Modelling/Modelmaking
Modn	Modern
Modnty	Modernity
Mol	Molecular
Monit	Monitoring
MORSE	Mathematics, Operational Research, Statistics and Economics
MOst	Master's in Osteopathy
Mov	Movement/Moving
Mrchnds	Merchandise/Merchandising
Mrchnt	Merchant
Mrl	Moral
Msg	Massage
Mslm	Muslim
Mtl	Metal(s)
Mtlsmth	Metalsmithing
Mtlwk	Metalwork(ing)
Mtn	Motion
Mtr	Motor
Mtrcycl	Motorcycle
Mtrg	Motoring
Mtrspo	Motorsport(s)
Multid	Multi-disciplinary
Multim	Multimedia
Mus	Music(ian)
Muscskel	Musculoskeletal
Musl	Musical
Musm	Museum(s)
Mushp	Musicianship
Myan	Myanmar
N	New
N Af	North Africa (n)
N Am	North America
Nanoelectron	Nanoelectronics
Nanosci	Nanoscience
Nanotech	Nanotechnology
Nat	Nature/Natural
Natpth	Naturopathy
Navig	Navigation
Nbrhd	Neighbourhood
Nds	Needs
Neg	Negotiated
Net	Networks/Networking
Neur	Neural
Neuro	Neuroscience
Neurophys	Neurophysiology
Neuropsy	Neuropsychology
News	Newspaper
NGO	Non-Governmental Organisation(s)
NI	Northern Ireland/Northern Irish
Nnl	National
Norw	Norwegian
Npli	Nepali
Nrs	Norse
Ns	News
NSAA	Natural Sciences Admissions Assessment
Ntv	Native
Nucl	Nuclear
Num	Numerate
Nurs	Nursing
Nursy	Nursery
Nutr	Nutrition(al)
Nvl	Naval
NZ	New Zealand
Obj(s)	Object(s)
Obs	Observational
Occ	Occupational
Ocean	Oceanography
Ocn	Ocean
Ocnc	Oceanic
Oeno	Oenology
Ofce	Office
Off	Offshore
Offrd	Off-road
Okl	Oklahoma
Onc	Oncology
Onln	Online
Op(s)	Operation(s)
Oph	Ophthalmic
Oprtg	Operating
Opt	Optical
Optim	Optimisation
Optn/s	Optional/Options
Optoel	Optoelectronics
Optom	Optometry
OR	Operational Research
Ord	Ordinary
Org	Organisation(s)/Organisational
Orgnc	Organic
Orgnsms	Organisms
Orn	Ornithology
Orth	Orthoptics
Orthot	Orthotics
Oseas	Overseas
Ost	Osteopathy

Out	Outdoor
Out Act	Outdoor Activity
Outsd	Outside
Ovrs	Overseas
P	Primary
PAA	Philosophy Admissions Assessment
P Cr	Primary Care
Pacif	Pacific
Pack	Packaging
PActv	Physical Activity
Pal	Palaeobiology
Palae	Palaeoecology/Palaeontology
Palaeoenv	Palaeoenvironments
Paramed	Paramedic(al)
Parasit	Parasitology
Parl	Parliamentary
Part	Participation
Pat	Patent
PAT	Physics Aptitude Test
Path	Pathology
Pathobiol	Pathobiological
Pathogen	Pathogenesis
Patt	Pattern
Pblc	Public
PBSAA	Psychological and Behavioural Sciences Admissions Assessment
Pce	Peace
PE	Physical Education
Ped	Pedagogy
Per	Person(al)/Personalised
Perf	Performance/Performed
Perfum	Perfumery
Pers	Personnel
Persn	Persian
Petrol	Petroleum
PGCE	Postgraduate Certificate in Education
Pharm	Pharmacy
Pharmacol	Pharmacology
Pharml	Pharmaceutical
Phil	Philosophy/Philosophies/ Philosophical
PhilAT	Philosophy Admissions Test
Philgy	Philology
Phn	Phone
Phon	Phonetics
Photo	Photography/Photographic
Photojrnl	Photojournalism
Photon	Photonic(s)
Phys	Physics
Physio	Physiotherapy
Physiol	Physiology/Physiological
Physl	Physical
Pks	Parks
Plan	Planning
Planet	Planetary
Plas	Plastics
Play	Playwork
Plcg	Police/Policing
Plcy	Policy
Plmt	Placement
Plnt	Plant
Plntsmn	Plantsmanship
Plt	Pilot
Pltry	Poultry
PMaths	Pure Mathematics
Pntg	Painting
Pod	Podiatry/Podiatric
Pol	Politics/Political
Polh	Polish
Pollut	Pollution
Poly	Polymer(ic)
Pop	Popular
Popn	Population
Port	Portuguese
Postcol	Postcolonial
PPE	Philosophy, Politics and Economics or Politics, Philosophy and Economics
PPI	Private Pilot Instruction
Ppl	People
Ppr	Paper
Pptry	Puppetry
PR	Public Relations
Prac	Practice(s)/Practical
Practnr	Practitioner
Prchsng	Purchasing
Prcrmt	Procurement
Prdcl	Periodical
Precsn	Precision
Pref	Preferable/Preferred
Prehist	Prehistory
Prelim	Preliminary
Prem	Premises
Proc	Process(ing)
Prod	Product(s)/Production/Produce
Prodg	Producing
Prof	Professional/Proffesiynol/ Professions
Prog	Programme/Programming
Proj	Project
Prom	Promotion
Prop	Property/ies
Pros	Prosthetics
Prot	Protection/Protected
Proto	Prototyping
Prplsn	Propulsion
Prscr	Prescribing
Prsts	Pursuits

Prt	Print
Prtcl	Particle
Prtd	Printed
Prtg	Printing/Printmaking
Prtshp	Partnership
Prvntn	Prevention
Pst	Post
Pstrl	Pastoral
Psy	Psychology/Psychological
Psychobiol	Psychobiology
Psyling	Psycholinguistics
Psysoc	Psychosocial
Psytrpy	Psychotherapy
Pt	Port
p/t	part-time
Ptcl	Particle
Pub	Publishing/Publication
Pvt	Private
Pwr	Power
Pwrcft	Powercraft
Qntm	Quantum
Qry	Quarry
Qtrnry	Quaternary
QTS	Qualified Teacher Status
Qual	Quality
Qualif	Qualification
Quant	Quantity/Quantitative
Rad	Radio
Radiog	Radiography
Radiothera	Radiotherapy
Rbr	Rubber
Rce	Race
Rcycl	Recycling
Rdtn	Radiation
Realsn	Realisation
Rec	Recording(s)
Reclam	Reclamation
Recr	Recreation
Reg	Regional
Regn	Regeneration
Rehab	Rehabilitation
Rel	Relations
Relgn	Religion(s)
Relig	Religious
Reltd	Related
Rem Sens	Remote Sensing
Ren	Renaissance
Renew	Renewable(s)
Rep	Representation
Repro	Reproductive
Reqd	Required
Res	Resource(s)
Resid	Residential
Resoln	Resolution
Resp	Response
Respir	Respiratory
Restor	Restoration
Rev	Revenue
Rflxgy	Reflexology
Rgby	Rugby
Rgstdn	Registered
Rgstrn	Registration
Rl	Real
Rlblty	Reliability
Rlwy	Railway
Rmnc	Romance
RN	Registered Nurse
Rnwl	Renewal
Robot	Robotic(s)
Rom	Roman
Romn	Romanian
Rsch	Research
Rspnsb	Responsibility
Rsrt	Resort
Rstrnt	Restaurant
Rtl	Retail(ing)
Rts	Rights
Rur	Rural
Russ	Russian
Rvr	River
S	Secondary
S As	South Asian
Sansk	Sanskrit
Sat	Satellite
Sbstnce	Substance
Scand	Scandinavian
Sch	School
Schlstc	Scholastic
Schm	Scheme
Sci	Science(s)/Scientific
Scn	Scene
Scnc	Scenic
Scngrph	Scenographic/Scenography
Scot	Scottish
Scr	Secure
Script	Scriptwriting
Scrn	Screen
Scrnwrit	Screenwriting
Scrts	Securities
Scrty	Security
Sctr	Sector
Sculp	Sculpture/Sculpting
Sdlry	Saddlery
SE	South East
Sec	Secretarial
Semicond	Semiconductor
SEN	Special Educational Needs
Serb Cro	Serbo-Croat

Serv	Services
Set	Settings
Sex	Sexual
Sfty	Safety
Sgnl	Signal
Ship	Shipping
Silver	Silversmithing
Simul	Simulation
Sit Lrng	Situated Learning
Sk	Skills
Slav	Slavonic
Slf	Self
Sln	Salon
Slovak	Slovakian
Slp	Sleep
Sls	Sales
Sml	Small
Smt	Smart
Smtc	Semitic
Snc	Sonic
Snd	Sound
Sndtrk	Soundtrack
Sndwch	Sandwich
Snr	Senior
Sng	Song
Spir	Spiritual
Soc	Social
Sociol	Sociology
SocioLeg	Socio-Legal
Socling	Sociolinguistics
Soft	Software
Sol	Solution(s)
Solic	Solicitors
Soty	Society
Sov	Soviet
Sp	Speech
Span	Spanish
Spat	Spatial
Spc	Space
Spcrft	Spacecraft
Spec	Special/Specialism(s)/ Specialist
Spec Efcts	Special Effects
Sply	Supply
Spn	Spain
Spo	Sport(s)
Spotrf	Sportsturf
Spowr	Sportswear
Sppt(d)	Support(ed)
Sprtng	Supporting
Sqntl	Sequential
Srf	Surf(ing)
Srgy	Surgery
SS	Solid-state
St	Studies/Study
St Reg	State Registration
Stans	Statistician
Stats	Statistics/Statistical
Std	Studio
STEM	Science, Technology, Engineering and Mathematics
STEP	Sixth Term Examination Papers
Stg	Stage
Stgs	Settings
Stnds	Standards
STQ	Scottish Teaching Qualification
Str	Stringed
Strat	Strategic/Strategy
Strf	Stratified
Strg	Strength
Strt	Street
Struct	Structural/Structures
Stry	Story
Stt	State
Stwdshp	Stewardship
Styl	Styling
Sub	Subject
Surf	Surface
Surv	Surveying
Sust	Sustainability/Sustainable
Swed	Swedish
Swli	Swahili
Sxlty	Sexuality
Sys	System(s)
Systmtc	Systematic
TAA	Theology Admissions Assessment
Tam	Tamil
Tap	Tapestry
TARA	Test of Academic Reasoning for Admissions
Tax	Taxation
Tax Rev	Taxation and Revenue
Tbtn	Tibetan
Tcnqs	Techniques
Teach	Teaching
Tech	Technology/Technologies/ Technician/Technical
Technol	Technological
TEFL	Teaching English as a Foreign Language
Telecomm	Telecommunication(s)
Ter	Terrestrial
Terr	Terror
TESOL	Teaching English to Speakers of Other Languages
Testmt	Testament
Tex	Textile(s)
Thbred	Thoroughbred
Thea	Theatre
Theol	Theology

Theor	Theory/Theoretical
Ther	Therapeutic
Thera	Therapy
Thngs	Things
Thpst	Therapist
Tht	Thought
Tiss	Tissue
Tlrg	Tailoring
Tm	Time
Tmbr	Timber
TMUA	Test of Mathematics for University Admission
Tnnl	Tunnel(ling)
Tns	Tennis
Topog	Topographical
Tour	Tourism
Tox	Toxicology
TQ	Teaching Qualification
Tr	Trade
Tr Stands	Trading Standards
Trad	Traditional
Trans	Transport(ation)
Transat	Transatlantic
Transl	Translation
Transnl Med Sci	Translational Medical Science
Trav	Travel
Trfgrs	Turfgrass
Trg	Training
Trnsf	Transformation
Trnrs	Trainers
Trpcl	Tropical
Trpl	Triple
TSA	Thinking Skills Assessment
Tstmnt	Testament
Ttl	Total
Turk	Turkish
TV	Television
Twn	Town
Typo	Typographical/Typography
UCAT	University Clinical Aptitude Test
Ukr	Ukrainian
Un	Union
Undwtr	Underwater
Unif	Unified
Up	Upland
Urb	Urban
USA	United States of America
Usr	User
Util	Utilities/Utilisation
Val	Valuation
Vasc	Vascular
Vcl	Vocal
Veh	Vehicle
Vert	Vertebrate
Vet	Veterinary
Vib	Vibration
Vict	Victorian
Vid	Video
Viet	Vietnamese
Virol	Virology
Vis	Visual(isation)
Vit	Viticulture
Vkg	Viking
Vl(s)	Value(s)
Vntr	Venture
Vnu	Venue
Voc	Vocational
Vol	Voluntary
Vrtl Rlty	Virtual Reality
Vsn	Vision
Vstr	Visitor
Wdlnd	Woodland
Welf	Welfare
Wk	Work
Wkg	Working
Wkplc	Workplace
Wkr	Worker
Wlbng	Well-being
Wldlf	Wildlife
Wls	Wales
Wmnswr	Womenswear
Wn	Wine
Wrbl	Wearable
Writ	Writing/Writer
Wrld	World
Wrlss	Wireless
Wst	Waste(s)
Wstn	Western
Wtr	Water
Wtrspo	Watersports
Wvn	Woven
www	World Wide Web
Ycht	Yacht
Ychtg	Yachting
Yng	Young
Yrs	Years
Yth	Youth
Zool	Zoology
3D	Three-dimensional

7 SUBJECT TABLES

ACCOUNTANCY/ACCOUNTING

(see also **Finance**)

Accountancy and Accounting degree courses include accounting, finance, economics, law, management, qualitative methods and information technology. Depending on your chosen course, other topics will include business law, business computing, a study of financial institutions and markets, management accountancy, statistics, taxation and auditing, while at some institutions an optional language might be offered. Many, but not all, Accountancy and Accounting degrees give exemptions from the examinations of some or all of the accountancy professional bodies. Single Honours courses are more likely to give full exemptions, while Joint Honours courses are more likely to lead to partial exemptions. Students should check with universities and colleges about which professional bodies offer exemptions for their courses before applying. Most courses are strongly vocational and many offer sandwich placements or opportunities to study Accountancy/Accounting with a second subject.

Useful websites www.accaglobal.com/uk; www.cimaglobal.com; www.cipfa.org; www.tax.org.uk; www.icaew.com; www.ifa.org.uk

NB The points totals shown to the left of the institutions are for ease of reference only. It must not be assumed that Tariff points are always used by institutions or that they can be substituted for an offer in grades. The level of an offer is not necessarily indicative of the quality of a course.

COURSE OFFERS INFORMATION

Subject requirements/preferences GCSE English and mathematics required: popular universities may require 7 or 8/9 (A or A*). **AL** Mathematics (A or B) or accounting (A or B) required or preferred for some courses. Some popular universities are now making lower offers for disadvantaged and other students.

Your target offers and examples of degree courses

152 pts **Edinburgh** – A*AA (Acc Fin) (IB 39 pts HL 666)

Warwick – A*AA incl maths (Acc Fin; Acc Fin (Yr Ind)) (IB 38 pts HL 5 maths)

144 pts **Bath** – AAA–A*AB/AAB+aEPQ incl maths (Acc Fin (Yr Ind)) (IB 36 pts HL 666/765 incl HL 6 maths); AAA–A*AB/AAB+aEPQ incl maths (Acc Fin) (IB 36 pts HL 666/765 incl HL 6 maths)

Birmingham – AAA (Acc Fin) (IB 32 pts HL 666)

Bristol – AAA–A*AB (Acc Mgt; Acc Mgt (Yr Abrd); Acc Mgt (Yr Ind)) (IB 36 pts HL 18 pts); AAA–A*AB incl maths (Acc Fin; Acc Fin (Yr Abrd); Acc Fin (Yr Ind)) (IB 36 pts HL 18 pts incl 6 maths)

City St George's – AAA (Acc Fin; Acc Fin (Yr Ind)) (IB 35 pts HL 4 maths)

Exeter – AAA (Acc Bus (Yr Abrd); Acc Bus (Yr Ind)) (IB 36 pts HL 666)

Leeds – AAA (Acc Fin) (IB 35 pts HL 17 pts incl 5 Engl/maths)

London (QM) – AAA (Acc Mgt) (IB 36 pts HL 666 incl 4 maths)

London LSE – AAA incl maths (Acc Fin) (IB 38 pts HL 766 incl 6 maths)

Manchester – AAA (Acc; Acc Fin) (IB 36 pts HL 666)

Nottingham – AAA (Acc; Fin Acc Mgt) (IB 36 pts)

Strathclyde – AAA incl maths (Acc; Acc Hspty Tour Mgt; Acc Mark) (IB 36 pts HL 5 maths); (Acc Fin) (IB 38 pts HL 6 maths)

136 pts **Durham** – AAB (Acc Fin) (IB 36 pts); (Acc Fin (Yr Abrd); Acc Fin (Yr Ind); Acc Mgt; Acc Mgt (Yr Abrd); Acc Mgt (Yr Ind)) (IB 36 pts HL 665 incl 5 maths)
Exeter – AAB (Acc Bus) (IB 34 pts HL 665)
Glasgow Caledonian – AAB (Acc)
Liverpool – AAB (Acc Fin) (IB 35 pts)
Loughborough – AAB (Acc Fin Mgt) (IB 35 pts HL 665)
Queen's Belfast – AAB (Acc; Acc Fr/Span)
Reading – AAB+interview (Acc Bus) (IB 34 pts HL 4 incl maths+Engl)
Sheffield – AAB (Acc Fin Mgt) (IB 34 pts)
Southampton – AAB/ABB+aEPQ (Acc Fin; Acc Fin (Yr Ind)) (IB 34 pts HL 17 pts)
York – AAB (Acc Bus Fin Mgt; Acc Bus Fin Mgt (Yr Ind)) (IB 35 pts)

128 pts **Cardiff** – ABB–AAB (Acc Fin) (IB 32–34 pts HL 665–666); ABB–AAB (Acc Fin (Yr Ind)) (IB 32–34 pts HL 665–666); (Acc; Acc (Yr Ind)) (IB 32–34 pts HL 665–666 pts)
East Anglia – ABB (Acc Fin) (IB 32 pts); ABB–BBB+aEPQ (Acc Fin (Yr Abrd); Acc Fin (Yr Ind)) (IB 32 pts)
Essex – ABB (Acc (Yr Abrd)) (IB 32 pts HL 655)
Glasgow – ABB–AAA incl maths (Acc Fin) (IB 36 pts HL 665 incl Engl/maths)
Kent – ABB (Acc Fin; Acc Fin (Yr Abrd); Acc Fin (Yr Ind))
Lancaster – ABB (Acc Fin; Acc Mgt) (IB 32 pts HL 16 pts)
Leicester – ABB–BBB+bEPQ (Acc Fin) (IB 30 pts)
London (RH) – ABB–AAB (Acc Fin) (IB 32 pts HL 655 incl maths)
Nottingham Trent – 128 pts (Acc Fin; Acc Fin (Yr Ind))
Reading – ABB (Acc Fin; Acc Fin (Yr Ind); Acc Mgt; Bus Mgt (Acc)) (IB 32 pts)
Surrey – ABB (Acc Fin) (IB 33 pts)

120 pts **BPP** – BBB (3 yr course) BBB (2 yr course) 120–128 pts (Acc Fin) (IB 30 pts HL 555)
Brunel – BBB 120 pts (Acc) (IB 30 pts)
Dundee – BBB (Acc) (IB 30 pts HL 555)
Glasgow – BBB–AAB incl maths (Acc Maths) (IB 34 pts HL 655 incl maths)
Greenwich – 120 pts (Acc Fin)
Kingston – 120–136 pts (Acc Fin)
Leeds Beckett – 120 pts (Acc Fin) (HL 554)
London South Bank – BBB 120 pts (Acc Fin; Acc Fin (Yr Ind))
Stirling – BBB (Acc) (IB 30 pts)
Sussex – BBB–ABB (Acc Fin; Acc Fin (Yr Ind)) (IB 30–32 pts)
Swansea – BBB–ABB (Acc; Acc Fin (Yr Ind)) (IB 32–33 pts); BBB–ABB (Acc (Yr Ind)) (IB 32–33 pts)
Ulster – BBB incl maths/econ/phys/acc (Acc Law) (IB 27 pts HL 13 pts)
Westminster – BBB–AAB 120–136 pts (Acc)

112 pts **Abertay** – BBC (Acc Fin) (IB 27 pts)
Bedfordshire – 112 pts (Acc)
Birmingham City – BBC 112 pts (Bus Fin) (IB 28 pts HL 14 pts)
Bradford – BBC 112 pts (Acc Fin; Acc Fin (Yr Ind))
Buckingham – BBC–BBB (Acc Fin) (IB 30–32 pts)
Canterbury Christ Church – BBC 112 pts (Acc) (IB 29 pts)
Cardiff Met – 112 pts (Acc) (HL 55)
Coventry – BBC (Acc Fin; Acc Fin (Yr Abrd); Acc Fin (Yr Ind)) (IB 24 pts)
De Montfort – 112 pts (Acc Fin) (IB 26 pts)
Derby – BBC–BBB 112–120 pts (Acc Fin)
East London – 112 pts (Acc Fin) (IB 24 pts HL 15 pts)
Edge Hill – BBC–BBB 112–120 pts (Acc)
Essex – BBC–BBB 112–120 pts (Acc; Acc (Yr Ind)) (IB 29–30 pts HL 554–555)
Heriot-Watt – BBC–ABB 112–128 pts (Acc Fin) (IB 29 pts)
Hertfordshire – BBC–BBB 112–120 pts (Acc; Acc (Yr Abrd); Acc (Yr Ind))
Huddersfield – BBC–BBB 112–120 pts (Acc Fin (Yr Ind)); BBC–BBB 112–120 pts (Acc Fin)
Hull – BBC 112 pts (Acc; Acc (Yr Abrd); Acc (Yr Ind)) (IB 28 pts)

Lincoln – 112 pts (Acc Fin)
Liverpool Hope – BBC (Acc Fin) (IB 28 pts)
Liverpool John Moores – BBC 112 pts (Acc Fin (Yr Ind)) (IB 28 pts); BBC–ABB 112–128 pts (Acc Fin)
Middlesex – BBC 112 pts (Acc Fin; Acc Fin (Yr Ind); Bus Acc)
Northampton – BBC (Acc Fin)
Northumbria – 112 pts (Acc; Acc (Yr Ind))
Plymouth – 112–128 pts (Acc Fin; Acc Fin (Yr Ind)) (IB 28–32 pts HL 4)
Portsmouth – BBC–BBB 112–120 pts (Acc Fin (Yr Ind)) (IB 29 pts); BBC–BBB 112–120 pts (Acc Fin) (IB 29 pts)
Roehampton – 112 pts (Acc)
Sheffield Hallam – BBC 112 pts (Acc Fin; Foren Acc)
Solent – 112–128 pts (Acc Fin)
South Wales – 112 pts (Acc Fin)
UWE Bristol – 112 pts (Acc Fin; Acc Fin (Yr Ind))
Ulster – BBC incl maths/econ/phys/acc (Acc) (IB 26 pts HL 13 pts)
Univ Law – BBC (Acc Fin)
West London – BBC 112–120 pts (Acc Fin); BBC 112–120 pts (Acc Fin (Yr Ind))
Worcester – 112 pts (Acc Fin)

104 pts **Bangor** – 104–136 pts (Acc Fin)
Bath Spa – BCC–BBB (Bus Mgt (Acc)) (IB 32 pts)
Bournemouth – 104–120 pts (Acc; Acc Fin; Acc Fin (Yr Ind)) (IB 28–31 pts)
Brighton – BCC–BBB 104–120 pts (Acc Fin; Acc Fin (Yr Ind)) (IB 26 pts)
Central Lancashire – 104–120 pts (Acc Fin)
Chester – BCC–BBC (Acc Fin) (IB 26 pts); BCC–BBC (Acc Fin (Yr Ind)) (IB 26 pts)
Chichester – BCC–BBB 104–120 pts (Acc Fin (Yr Ind)) (IB 28 pts); BCC–BBB 104–120 pts (Acc Fin) (IB 28 pts)
Edinburgh Napier – BCC (Acc) (IB 28 pts HL 654)
Gloucestershire – BCC 104 pts (Acc Fin; Acc Fin (Yr Ind))
Greater Manchester – 104 pts (Acc)
Manchester Met – BCC–BBC 104–112 pts (Acc Fin; Bank Fin) (IB 26 pts)
Oxford Brookes – BCC 104 pts (Acc Econ; Acc Fin; Acc Fin (Yr Ind)) (IB 29 pts)
Robert Gordon – BCC (Acc Data Sci; Acc Fin) (IB 28 pts)
Salford – BCC–BBC 104–112 pts (Acc Fin; Acc Fin (Yr Ind)) (IB 30 pts)
Winchester – BCC–BBB 104–120 pts (Acc Fin)
York St John – (Acc Fin)

96 pts **Aberystwyth** – CCC–BBB 96–120 pts (Acc Fin) (IB 26–30 pts)
Anglia Ruskin – 96 pts (Acc Fin; Acc Fin (Yr Ind)) (IB 24 pts)
Birmingham Newman – 96 pts (Acc Fin)
London (Birk) – CCC–ABB 96–128 pts (Acc)
London Met – CCC 96 pts (Acc Fin)
Richmond (Am Int Univ) – CCC 96 pts (Acc Fin) (IB 26 pts)
Wolverhampton – CCC (Acc Law)

88 pts **Bucks New** – 88–112 pts (Acc Fin)
Trinity Saint David – 88 pts+interview (Acc)

80 pts **Teesside** – 80–104 pts (Acc Fin)
Wrexham – 80–112 pts (Acc Fin Mgt)

48 pts **Greater Manchester** – 48 pts (Acc (Fdn Yr))
Solent – 48 pts (Acc Fin (Fdn Yr))
Wolverhampton – DD (Acc Fin)

24 pts **UHI** – D (Acc Fin)

Alternative offers See **Chapter 6** and **Appendix 1** for grades/UCAS Tariff points information for other examinations.

DEGREE APPRENTICESHIPS

Aston (Acc Fin Mgr); BPP (Acc/Tax Prof); Brighton (Prof Acc); Chichester (Acc Fin Mgr); Exeter (Acc Fin Mgr); Glasgow Caledonian (Acc); Robert Gordon (Acc); Ulster (Acc Fin).

EXAMPLES OF COLLEGES OFFERING COURSES IN THIS SUBJECT FIELD

Accrington and Rossendale (Coll); Barking and Dagenham (Coll); Bath (Coll); Blackburn (Coll); Blackpool and Fylde (Coll); Bournemouth and Poole (Coll); Bradford College (UC); Bridgwater and Taunton (Coll); Bury (Coll); Chesterfield (Coll); Cornwall (Coll); Craven (Coll); Derby (Coll); East Riding (Coll); East Sussex (Coll); Exeter (Coll); Farnborough (CT); Hartlepool (CFE); HOW (Coll); Leeds City (Coll); Lewisham (Coll); London City (Coll); London South East (Coll); Macclesfield (Coll); Manchester (Coll); Mont Rose (Coll); NCC Redbridge; Neath Port Talbot (Coll); Nescot; North Notts (Coll); North West London (Coll); Norwich City (Coll); Nottingham (Coll); Oldham (Univ Campus); Peterborough (UC); Plymouth City (Coll); Redcar and Cleveland (Coll); Richmond-upon-Thames (Coll); South City Birmingham (Coll); South Gloucestershire and Stroud (Coll); St Helens (Coll); Tameside (Coll); TEC Partnership; Telford (Coll); Weymouth (Coll); Yeovil (Coll).

CHOOSING YOUR COURSE (SEE ALSO CH.1)

Universities and colleges teaching quality See www.qaa.ac.uk; www.discoveruni.gov.uk.

Examples of sandwich degree courses Anglia Ruskin; Aston; Bath; Bedfordshire; Birmingham City; Bournemouth; Bradford; Brighton; Brunel; Canterbury Christ Church; Cardiff; Cardiff Met; Central Lancashire; Chester; Chichester; City St George's; Coventry; De Montfort; Derby; Durham; East Anglia; Essex; Exeter; Gloucestershire; Greenwich; Hertfordshire; Huddersfield; Hull; Kent; Lancaster; Leeds; Leeds Beckett; Liverpool John Moores; London South Bank; Loughborough; Manchester Met; Middlesex; Northumbria; Nottingham Trent; Oxford Brookes; Portsmouth; Reading; Salford; Sheffield; Sheffield Hallam; South Wales; Southampton; Surrey; Sussex; Teesside; Ulster; UWE Bristol; Warwick; West London; Westminster; Wolverhampton; Worcester; York.

ADMISSIONS INFORMATION

Advice to applicants and planning the UCAS personal statement Universities look for good numerical and communication skills, interest in the business and financial world, teamwork, problem-solving and computing experience. On the UCAS application you should be able to demonstrate your interest in and understanding of accountancy and to give details of any work experience or work shadowing undertaken. Try to arrange meetings with accountants, work shadowing or work experience in accountants' offices, commercial or industrial firms, town halls, banks or insurance companies and describe the work you have done. Obtain information from the main accountancy professional bodies (see Appendix 3). Refer to current affairs which have stimulated your interest from articles in the *Financial Times, The Economist* or the business and financial sections of the weekend press.

Selection interviews **Yes** Reading (Acc Bus), Trinity Saint David; **Some** Cardiff, Liverpool John Moores, Wolverhampton; **No** Birmingham, Bristol, East Anglia, London LSE.

Interview advice and questions Be prepared to answer questions about why you have chosen the course, the qualities needed to be an accountant, and why you think you have these qualities! You should also be able to discuss any work experience you have had and to describe the differences in the work of chartered, certified, public finance and management accountants. See also **Chapter 5**.

Reasons for rejection (non-academic) Poor English. Lack of interest in the subject because they realise they have chosen the wrong course! No clear motivation. Course details not researched.

GRADUATE DESTINATIONS AND EMPLOYMENT

(See **Chapter 1, Graduate Outcomes**.)

Career note Most Accountancy/Accounting graduates enter careers in finance.

OTHER DEGREE SUBJECTS FOR CONSIDERATION

Actuarial Studies; Banking; Business Studies; Economics; Financial Services; Insurance; International Securities and Investment Banking; Mathematics; Quantity Surveying; Statistics.

ACTUARIAL SCIENCE/STUDIES

Actuaries deal with the evaluation and management of financial risks, particularly those associated with insurance companies and pension funds. Studies focus on business economics, financial mathematics, probability and statistics, computer mathematics, statistics for insurance, and mathematics in finance and investment. Most courses include compulsory and optional subjects. Although Actuarial Science/Studies degrees are vocational and give full or partial exemptions from some of the examinations of the Institute and Faculty of Actuaries, students are not necessarily committed to a career as an actuary on graduation. However, many graduates go on to be actuary trainees, leading to one of the highest-paid careers.

Useful websites www.actuaries.org.uk; www.soa.org; www.beanactuary.org

NB The points totals shown to the left of the institutions are for ease of reference only. It must not be assumed that Tariff points are always used by institutions or that they can be substituted for an offer in grades. The level of an offer is not necessarily indicative of the quality of a course.

COURSE OFFERS INFORMATION

Subject requirements/preferences GCSE Most institutions require grades 7 or 5/6 (A or B) in English and mathematics. **AL** Mathematics at a specified grade required. Some popular universities are now making lower offers for disadvantaged and other students.

Your target offers and examples of degree courses

152 pts **London LSE** – A*AA incl A* maths (Act Sci; Act Sci (Yr Ind)) (IB 38 pts HL 766 incl maths)
Manchester – A*AA incl A* maths (Act Sci Maths) (IB 37 pts HL 766 pts incl 7 maths)
Queen's Belfast – A*AA incl maths (Act Sci Risk Mgt) (IB 36 pts HL 666 incl maths)

144 pts **City St George's** – AAA incl maths (Act Sci) (IB 35 pts HL 18 pts incl 6 maths)
Leeds – AAA/A*AB incl A maths+fmaths/AS maths (Act Maths) (HL 17 pts incl 6 maths)
London (QM) – AAA incl maths (Act Sci) (IB 36 pts 666 incl maths)
Southampton – AAA incl maths (Maths Act Sci) (IB 36 pts HL 18 pts incl 6 maths)
York – AAA incl maths (Act Sci) (IB 36 pts HL 6 maths)

136 pts **East Anglia** – AAB incl A maths (Act Sci; Act Sci (Yr Ind)) (IB 33 pts HL 6 maths)
Heriot-Watt – AAB incl maths (4 yr course) AAA incl maths (3 yr course) (Act Sci) (IB 28 pts (4 yr course) 30 pts (3 yr course) HL 6 maths (4 yr course) 7 maths (3 yr course)); AAB incl maths (5 yr course) AAA incl maths (4 yr course) (Act Sci Dip Ind Trg) (IB 28 pts (5 yr course) 30 pts (4 yr course) HL 6 maths (5 yr course) 7 maths (4 yr course))
Kent – AAB incl A maths (Act Sci (Yr Ind)) (IB 30 pts HL 15 pts incl 6 maths); (Act Sci) (IB 30 pts HL 15 pts incl 6 maths)
Liverpool – AAB incl A maths (Act Maths) (IB 35 pts HL 6 maths)

128 pts **Essex** – ABB incl maths/fmaths (Act Sci; Act Sci (Yr Ind)) (IB 32 pts HL 665 incl 5 maths)
Leicester – ABB–AAB/BBB–ABB+bEPQ incl maths (Maths Act Sci; Maths Act Sci (Yr Ind)) (IB 30 pts HL 5 maths)

120 pts **Swansea** – BBB–ABB (Act Sci) (IB 32 pts HL 6 maths)

Alternative offers See **Chapter 6** and **Appendix 1** for grades/UCAS Tariff points information for other examinations.

DEGREE APPRENTICESHIPS

BPP (Act).

CHOOSING YOUR COURSE (SEE ALSO CH.1)

Universities and colleges teaching quality See www.qaa.ac.uk; www.discoveruni.gov.uk.

Top research universities and colleges (REF 2021) See **Mathematics**.

Examples of sandwich degree courses City St George's; East Anglia; Essex; Heriot-Watt; Kent; Leeds; Leicester; London LSE; Queen's Belfast.

ADMISSIONS INFORMATION

Advice to applicants and planning the UCAS personal statement Demonstrate your knowledge of this career and its training, and mention any contacts you have made with an actuary. (See **Appendix 3** for contact details of professional associations for further information.) Any work experience or shadowing in insurance companies should be mentioned, together with what you have learned about the problems facing actuaries. It is important to show motivation and sheer determination for training as an actuary as it is long and tough (up to three or four years after graduation). Mathematical flair, an ability to communicate and an interest in business are paramount.

Selection interviews No East Anglia, London LSE.

Interview advice and questions In view of the demanding nature of the training, it is important to have spent some time discussing this career with an actuary in practice. Questions, therefore, may focus on the roles of the actuary and the qualities you need to succeed. You should also be ready to field questions about your AL mathematics course and the aspects of it you most enjoy. See also **Chapter 5**.

GRADUATE DESTINATIONS AND EMPLOYMENT

(See **Chapter 1, Graduate Outcomes.**)

Career note Graduates commonly enter careers in finance, many taking further examinations to qualify as actuaries.

OTHER DEGREE SUBJECTS FOR CONSIDERATION

Accountancy; Banking; Business Studies; Economics; Financial Risk Management; Financial Services; Insurance; Mathematics; Money, Banking and Finance; Statistics.

AFRICAN, ASIAN AND MIDDLE EASTERN STUDIES

(including **Arabic, Ancient Near Eastern Studies, East Asian Studies, South Asian Studies, Swahili, Thai, Vietnamese**; see also **Chinese, History (Ancient), Japanese, Religious Studies**)

These courses allow students to specialise in the language, history, religion and culture of one or two of a vast range of nations and people-groups. Arabic is one of the world's most widely used languages, spoken by more than 300 million people in over 20 countries in the Middle East and North Africa. Study of the language also includes Islamic and modern Middle Eastern history, while a course in Middle Eastern Studies will include an optional language such as Arabic, Persian or Turkish (Edinburgh, Exeter). Links between Britain and Arabic-speaking countries have increased considerably in recent years and most of the larger UK organisations with offices in the Middle East have only a relatively small pool of Arabic-speaking graduates from which to recruit future employees each year. African Studies courses also tend to be multi-disciplinary and cover several subject areas, including anthropology, history, geography, sociology and languages. Students may learn a language such as Yoruba (Nigeria), Amharic (Ethiopia) or Zulu (South Africa). Asian Studies courses offer the opportunity to study languages such as Korean, Japanese, Vietnamese and Thai. Both African and Asian studies are often studied as a Joint Honours with another subject.

Useful websites www.ciol.org.uk; www.languageadvantage.com; www.languagematters.co.uk; www.upi.com; www.merip.org; www.memri.org; www.mei.edu

NB The points totals shown to the left of the institutions are for ease of reference only. It must not be assumed that Tariff points are always used by institutions or that they can be substituted for an offer in grades. The level of an offer is not necessarily indicative of the quality of a course.

COURSE OFFERS INFORMATION

SUBJECT REQUIREMENTS/PREFERENCES GCSE English, mathematics and a foreign language usually required. A high grade in Arabic may be required. **AL** A modern language is usually required or preferred. Some popular universities are now making lower offers for disadvantaged and other students.

YOUR TARGET OFFERS AND EXAMPLES OF DEGREE COURSES

152 pts **Cambridge** – A*AA+interview+test (As Mid E St) (IB 41–42 pts HL 776)
Durham – A*AA (Comb Hons Soc Sci) (IB 38 pts HL 666)

144 pts **Oxford** – 144 pts (Class As Mid E St) (IB 39 pts HL 666); AAA+interview (As Mid E St incl Jap/Arab/Chin/Heb) (IB 39 pts HL 666); AAA+interview+CAT (Class As Mid E St) (IB 39 pts HL 666); AAA+interview+AMELAT (As Mid E St incl Jap/Arab/Chin) (IB 39 pts HL 666)
St Andrews – AAA incl hist (Art Hist Mid E St) (IB 38 pts HL 666)

136 pts **Leeds** – AAB (Mid E St Pol) (IB 35 pts HL 16 pts); AAB 136 pts (Chin Jap St) (IB 35 pts HL 16–17 pts)
Nottingham – AAB (Int Rel As St) (IB 32 pts HL 665)
St Andrews – AAB (Arbc Econ) (IB 36 pts HL 665); (Arbc Maths) (IB 36 pts HL 665 incl 6 maths); AAB incl hist (Arbc Mid E St) (IB 36 pts HL 665 incl hist)

128 pts **Edinburgh** – ABB (Arbc courses; Islam St; Mid E St; Persn Soc Anth; Persn St) (IB 34–36 pts HL 655–665)
Exeter – ABB (Arbc Islam St; Mid E St; Modn Langs Arbc) (IB 32 pts HL 655)
Leeds – ABB (Arbc Islam Mid E N Af St; As Pacif St Int Rel; Islam Mid E N Af St; Thai St) (IB 34 pts HL 16 pts)
London (SOAS) – ABB (Arbc Comb Hons; E As St; Kor) (IB 32 pts HL 655)
London (UCL) – ABB incl A Fr (Fr As Af Lang) (IB 34 pts HL 16 incl 6 Fr)
Manchester – ABB (Arbc St; Mid E St) (IB 34 pts HL 655)
Sheffield – ABB/BBB+bEPQ (Kor St) (IB 33 pts); ABB–BBB+bEPQ (E As St) (IB 33 pts)
Sussex – ABB (Anth Lang) (IB 34 pts)

120 pts **Birmingham** – BBB (Soc Anth Af St) (IB 32 pts HL 555)

104 pts **Westminster** – BCC 104 pts (Arbc Ling)

96 pts **Central Lancashire** – 96–112 pts (As Pacif St); 96–112 pts incl lang (Modn Langs (2 Langs) (Fr/Span/Jap/Russ/Chin/Kor))
Islamic (Coll) – CCC (Hawza St; Islam St)

ALTERNATIVE OFFERS See **Chapter 6** and **Appendix 1** for grades/UCAS Tariff points information for other examinations.

CHOOSING YOUR COURSE (SEE ALSO CH.1)

UNIVERSITIES AND COLLEGES TEACHING QUALITY See www.qaa.ac.uk; www.discoveruni.gov.uk.

ADMISSIONS INFORMATION

ADVICE TO APPLICANTS AND PLANNING THE UCAS PERSONAL STATEMENT Describe any visits to, or your experience of living in, Arabic-speaking countries. Develop a knowledge of Middle Eastern cultures, history and politics and mention these topics on the UCAS application. Provide evidence of language-learning skills and experience.

SELECTION INTERVIEWS Yes Cambridge, Oxford (As Mid E St) 83% (success rate 31%)

INTERVIEW ADVICE AND QUESTIONS For Arabic, the applicant will need to be able to justify their reasons for wanting to study Arabic or other languages and to discuss their interest in, and awareness of, cultural, social and political aspects of the Middle East. Applicants interviewing for a place on an African or Asian Studies course should describe any visits they have made to African or Asian countries and why they wish to study particular regions in more depth. It is expected that applicants will be up to date with political developments in relevant countries and willing to discuss any aspects which interest them.

GRADUATE DESTINATIONS AND EMPLOYMENT

(See **Chapter 1, Graduate Outcomes.**)

Career note Graduates of African and Asian studies work in a wide range of areas, including education, public relations, the third sector, journalism and consultancy. A significant number pursue further study. Arabic-language skills are currently sought after in areas such as cyber-security, national intelligence and security (GCHQ) and by the charity sector.

OTHER DEGREE SUBJECTS FOR CONSIDERATION

Anthropology; Archaeology; Classical Studies; Hebrew; History; Persian; Politics; Turkish.

AGRICULTURAL SCIENCES/AGRICULTURE

(including **Forestry**; see also **Animal Sciences, Food Science/Studies and Technology, Horticulture, Landscape Architecture, Surveying and Real Estate Management, Zoology**)

Courses in Agriculture recognise that modern farming practice requires sound technical and scientific knowledge, together with appropriate management skills, and most courses focus to a greater or lesser extent on all these requirements. Your choice of course depends on your particular interest and aims: some courses will give greater priority than others to practical application. Most graduates enter the agriculture industry while others move into manufacturing, wholesale and retail work. Agricultural courses specialise in crop and animal production and will also include agri-business and environmental issues. Forestry courses cover all aspects of the importance of forests from the biological, ecological, environmental, economic and sociological aspects with practical involvement in the establishment of forests and their control, growth, health and quality. Rural Estate and Land Management courses relate to the purchase and sale of country property, residential agency in towns, the management of commercial property portfolios, investment funds and the provision of valuation and technical services. Countryside management courses cover the uses of the countryside including tourism, land use, and ecosystems and environmental aspects.

Useful websites www.gov.uk/government/organisations/department-for-environment-food-rural-affairs; www.gov.uk/government/organisations/natural-england; www.lantra.co.uk; www.forestryengland.uk; www.nfuonline.com; www.nfyfc.org.uk; http://iagre.org; www.bbsrc.ac.uk; www.wwoof.org.uk

NB The points totals shown to the left of the institutions are for ease of reference only. It must not be assumed that Tariff points are always used by institutions or that they can be substituted for an offer in grades. The level of an offer is not necessarily indicative of the quality of a course.

COURSE OFFERS INFORMATION

Subject requirements/preferences GCSE English and mathematics usually required; chemistry sometimes required. Practical experience may be required. **AL** One or two maths/biological science subjects may be required or preferred. Geography may be accepted as a science subject. Similar requirements apply for Agricultural Business Management courses. (Crop Sci) Two science subjects may be required. (Cntry Mgt) Geography or biology may be preferred. Some popular universities are now making lower offers for disadvantaged and other students.

Your target offers and examples of degree courses

128 pts **Newcastle** – ABB incl sci (Agric) (IB 32 pts HL biol/chem)

120 pts **CAFRE** – BBB incl chem/biol (Agric Tech)

Nottingham – BBB incl sci (Agric) (IB 28 pts HL 555 incl sci)

Queen's Belfast – BBB–ABB incl biol/chem (Agric Tech)

Reading – BBB (Agric Bus Mgt; Agric Bus Mgt (Yr Ind)) (IB 30 pts); BBB incl sci (Agric; Agric (Yr Ind)) (IB 30 pts HL sci)

104 pts **Cumbria** – BBD–BBB 104–120 pts (Frst Mgt); BBD–BBB 104–120 pts (Frst Mgt (Yr Ind))

Royal Agricultural Univ – BCC (Agric; Agric (Yr Ind); Rur Lnd Mgt; Rur Lnd Mgt (Yr Ind)) (IB 26 pts)
SRUC – BCC incl sci/geog (Agric)
96 pts **Aberystwyth** – CCC–BBB 96–120 pts (Agric; Agric Anim Sci) (IB 26–30 pts); CCC–BBB 96–120 pts (Agric Anim Sci (Yr Ind)) (IB 26–30 pts); CCC–BBB 96–120 pts (Agric (Yr Ind)) (IB 26–30 pts)
Cumbria – CCC–BBC 96–112 pts (Wdlnd Ecol Cons); CCC–BBC 96–112 pts (Wdlnd Ecol Cons (Yr Ind))
Harper Adams – 96–112 pts (Agric courses) (IB 28 pts); 96–120 pts+interview (Agric Eng) (IB 28 pts HL 5 maths)
Hartpury (Coll) – CCC–BBC 96–112 pts (Agric)
Royal Agricultural Univ – 96 pts (Bldstck Perf Hrs Mgt; Bldstck Perf Hrs Mgt (Yr Ind)) (IB 26 pts)
Writtle (UC) – 96 pts (Agric) (IB 24 pts)
88 pts **Bangor** – 88–120 pts incl sci (Cons Frsty; Frsty) (HL 5 sci); 88–120 pts incl sci (Cons Frsty (Yr Ind); Frsty (Yr Ind)) (HL 5 sci)
Reading – CCD–BBB (Agric Fdn) (IB 24–30 pts)
80 pts **Warwickshire (Coll)** – 80 pts (Sust Hort Tech (Agritech))
72 pts **Aberystwyth** – DDD–CCC 72–96 pts (Agric Fdn) (IB 24–26 pts)
56 pts **Royal Agricultural Univ** – CD 56 pts (Agric Frm Mgt Fdn) (IB 24 pts)
48 pts **Myerscough (Coll)** – 48 pts incl C+interview (Arbor Tree Mgt) (IB 24 pts)

Harper Adams – 6 GCSE incl C maths+Engl+sci (Agric (Fdn))

Alternative offers See **Chapter 6** and **Appendix 1** for grades/UCAS Tariff points information for other examinations.

DEGREE APPRENTICESHIPS

Cumbria (Prof Frstr).

EXAMPLES OF COLLEGES OFFERING COURSES IN THIS SUBJECT FIELD

Askham Bryan (Coll); Bicton (Coll); Bishop Burton (Coll); Bridgend (Coll); Bridgwater and Taunton (Coll); Craven (Coll); Duchy Coll (UC); Easton (Coll); Hadlow (UC); Hartpury (Coll); Moulton (Coll); Myerscough (Coll); Northumberland (Coll); Plumpton (Coll); Reaseheath (UC); Sir Gâr (Coll); Sparsholt (Coll).

CHOOSING YOUR COURSE (SEE ALSO CH.1)

Universities and colleges teaching quality See www.qaa.ac.uk; www.discoveruni.gov.uk.

Top research universities and colleges (REF 2021) (Agriculture, Veterinary and Food Science) East Anglia; Queen's Belfast; Liverpool; Glasgow; Bristol; Cambridge; Plymouth; London (RVC); Stirling; Nottingham.

Examples of sandwich degree courses Aberystwyth; Bangor; CAFRE; Cumbria; Harper Adams; Newcastle; Nottingham; Queen's Belfast; Reading; Royal Agricultural Univ.

ADMISSIONS INFORMATION

Advice to applicants and planning the UCAS personal statement First-hand farming experience is essential for most courses and obviously important for all. Check prospectuses and websites. Describe the work done. Details of experience of work with agricultural or food farms (production and laboratory work), garden centres, even with landscape architects, could be appropriate. Keep up-to-date with European agricultural and fishing policies and mention any interests you have in these areas. Read farming magazines and discuss any articles which have interested you. You may even have had first-hand experience of the serious problems facing farmers. Discuss your interest or experience in practical conservation work. Ability to work both independently or as a member of a team is important. (See also **Appendix 3**.) **Forestry** Contact the Forestry Commission and the Woodland Trust and try to arrange visits to forestry centres, local community woodlands and forests and to the Woodland Trust's sites. Discuss the work with forest officers and learn about future plans for specific forest areas and describe any visits made. Mention any experience of forestry or wood processing industries (for example, visits to forests and mills, work experience in relevant organisations). (See also **Appendix 3**.)

Selection interviews Yes Myerscough (Coll); **No** Harper Adams.

Interview advice and questions You should be up-to-date with political and scientific issues concerning the farming community in general and how these problems might be resolved. You are likely to be questioned on your own farming background (if relevant) and your farming experience. Questions asked in the past have included: What special agricultural interests do you have? What types of farms have you worked on? What farming publications do you read and which agricultural shows have you visited? What is meant by the term 'sustainable development'? Are farmers custodians of the countryside? What are the potential sources of non-fossil-fuel electricity generation? See also **Chapter 5**. **Forestry** Work experience or field courses attended are likely to be discussed and questions asked such as: What is arboriculture? On a desert island how would you get food from wood? How do you see forestry developing in the next hundred years? What aspects of forestry are the most important? See also **Chapter 5**.

Reasons for rejection (non-academic) Insufficient motivation. Too immature. Unlikely to integrate well. Lack of practical experience with crops or animals.

GRADUATE DESTINATIONS AND EMPLOYMENT

(See **Chapter 1, Graduate Outcomes.**)

Career note The majority of graduates entered the agricultural industry while others moved into manufacturing, the wholesale and retail trades and property development. For Forestry, opportunities exist with the Forestry Commission as supervisors, managers and in some cases, scientists. Other employers include private landowners (especially in Scotland), co-operative forest societies, local authorities and commercial firms.

OTHER DEGREE SUBJECTS FOR CONSIDERATION

Agroforestry; Animal Sciences; Biochemistry; Biological Sciences; Biology; Biotechnology; Chemistry; Conservation Management; Ecology (Biological Sciences); Environmental Sciences; Estate Management (Surveying); Food Science and Technology; Forestry; Horticulture; Land Surveying; Landscape Architecture; Plant Sciences; Veterinary Science; Zoology.

AMERICAN STUDIES

Courses normally cover American history, politics and literature, although there are opportunities to study specialist fields such as drama, film studies, history of art, linguistics, politics or sociology. In some universities, a year, term or semester spent in the USA (or Canada) is compulsory or optional while at other institutions the course lasts three years without a placement abroad.

Useful websites www.historynet.com; www.theasa.net

NB The points totals shown to the left of the institutions are for ease of reference only. It must not be assumed that Tariff points are always used by institutions or that they can be substituted for an offer in grades. The level of an offer is not necessarily indicative of the quality of a course.

COURSE OFFERS INFORMATION

Subject requirements/preferences GCSE Specific grades in some subjects may be specified by some popular universities. **AL** English, a modern language, humanities or social science subjects preferred. Some popular universities are now making lower offers for disadvantaged and other students.

YOUR TARGET OFFERS AND EXAMPLES OF DEGREE COURSES

136 pts **East Anglia** – AAB incl Engl (Engl Am Lit) (IB 33 pts HL 5 Engl)
Manchester – AAB incl Engl/hist/pol (Am St) (IB 35 pts HL 665)

128 pts **East Anglia** – ABB 128 pts (Am St) (IB 32 pts)
Leicester – ABB-BBB+bEPQ incl Engl (Engl Am St) (IB 30 pts HL 6 Engl)
London (RH) – ABB–AAB (Engl Am Lit) (IB 32 pts HL 665)
Sussex – ABB (Am St courses) (IB 32 pts)

112 pts **Essex** – BBC–BBB 112–120 pts (Am (US) St Flm) (IB 29–30 pts HL 554–555); BBC–BBB 112–120 pts (Crimin Am St) (IB 29–30 pts HL 554–555)
Northumbria – 112 pts (Am St)
Swansea – BBC–ABB 112–128 pts (Am St) (IB 32 pts)

104 pts **Manchester Met** – 104–112 pts (Engl Am Lit) (IB 26 pts)
Portsmouth – BCC–BBC 104–112 pts (Hist Am St) (IB 25 pts)
York St John – 104 pts (Am St courses)

64 pts **Rose Bruford (Coll)** – 64 pts+audition/portfolio (Am Thea Arts)

ALTERNATIVE OFFERS See **Chapter 6** and **Appendix 1** for grades/UCAS Tariff points information for other examinations.

CHOOSING YOUR COURSE (SEE ALSO CH.1)

UNIVERSITIES AND COLLEGES TEACHING QUALITY See www.qaa.ac.uk; www.discoveruni.gov.uk.

EXAMPLES OF SANDWICH DEGREE COURSES East Anglia; Essex; Manchester; Nottingham; Sussex.

ADMISSIONS INFORMATION

ADVICE TO APPLICANTS AND PLANNING THE UCAS PERSONAL STATEMENT Visits to America should be described, and any knowledge or interests you have of the history, politics, economics and the culture of the USA should be included on the UCAS application. The US Embassy in London may be a useful source of information. American magazines and newspapers are good reference sources and also give a good insight to life in the USA. Applicants should demonstrate an intelligent interest in both North American literature and history in their personal statement. State why you are interested in the subject and dedicate at least half of your personal statement to how and why your interest has developed – for example through extra-curricular reading, projects, films and academic study.

SELECTION INTERVIEWS No East Anglia.

INTERVIEW ADVICE AND QUESTIONS Courses often focus on history and literature so expect some questions on any American literature you have read and also on aspects of American history, arts and culture. You may also be questioned on visits you have made to America (or Canada) and your impressions. Current political issues might also be raised, so keep up-to-date with the political scene. See also **Chapter 5**.

REASONS FOR REJECTION (NON-ACADEMIC) If personal reasons prevent year of study in America.

GRADUATE DESTINATIONS AND EMPLOYMENT

(See **Chapter 1, Graduate Outcomes.**)

CAREER NOTE All non-scientific careers are open to graduates. Start your career planning during your degree course and obtain work experience.

OTHER DEGREE SUBJECTS FOR CONSIDERATION

Business Studies; Cultural Studies; English Literature; Film Studies; Government; History; International History; International Relations; Latin-American Literature/Studies; Politics.

ANIMAL SCIENCES

(including **Equine Science**; see also **Agricultural Sciences/Agriculture, Biological Sciences, Biology, Physiology, Psychology, Veterinary Science/Medicine, Zoology**)

Animal Science is a broad-based subject including the study of farm and companion animals and wildlife conservation and management. The more specialised courses include a range of specialisms including animal biology, nutrition and health, behavioural studies and welfare. Equine Science involves specialised studies in areas such as breeding, equine business, horsemanship, performance, stud management, event management, veterinary techniques and injuries. Some scholarships are available.

USEFUL WEBSITES www.rspca.org.uk; www.bhs.org.uk; www.wwf.org.uk; www.bsas.org.uk

NB The points totals shown to the left of the institutions are for ease of reference only. It must not be assumed that Tariff points are always used by institutions or that they can be substituted for an offer in grades. The level of an offer is not necessarily indicative of the quality of a course.

COURSE OFFERS INFORMATION

SUBJECT REQUIREMENTS/PREFERENCES GCSE Mathematics/science subjects required. Also check any weight limits on equitation modules. **AL** One or two science subjects usually required for scientific courses; biology and chemistry preferred. Some popular universities are now making lower offers for disadvantaged and other students.

YOUR TARGET OFFERS AND EXAMPLES OF DEGREE COURSES

136 pts **Exeter** – AAB incl A sci (Anim Bhv (Yr Prof Prac) (Cornwall)) (IB 34 pts HL 665 incl 6 sci)

128 pts **Exeter** – ABB incl sci (Anim Bhv (Cornwall)) (IB 32 pts HL 655 incl 5 sci)

Newcastle – ABB incl biol+sci (Anim Sci) (IB 32 pts HL 6 biol)

Sussex – ABB incl sci (Zool) (IB 32 pts HL 5 biol/chem/phys)

120 pts **Kent** – BBB incl sci/maths (Ecol Cons; Ecol Cons (Yr Prof Prac)) (HL 665)

Nottingham – BBB incl biol (Anim Sci) (IB 28 pts HL 555 incl biol)

Reading – BBB incl biol+sci (Biovet Sci) (IB 30 pts incl HL 5 biol+sci)

SRUC – BBB incl biol/chem (App Anim Sci)

Stirling – BBB incl sci/maths (Anim Biol) (IB 30 pts incl sci/maths)

112 pts **Aberdeen** – BBC incl maths/sci (Anim Bhv) (IB 32 pts HL 555 incl maths/sci)

Anglia Ruskin – 112 pts incl biol/psy (Anim Bhv)

Bangor – 112–136 pts incl biol (Zool Anim Bhv) (HL 5 biol)

Canterbury Christ Church – BBC 112 pts incl sci (Anim Sci) (IB 29 pts)

Nottingham Trent – BBC incl biol 112 pts (Anim Biol); BBC incl sci 112 pts (Eqn Spo Sci; Wldlf Cons)

Oxford Brookes – BBC 112 pts (Eqn Sci) (IB 30 pts)

104 pts **Aberystwyth** – BCC–BBB incl B biol 104–120 pts (Anim Bhv; Anim Sci) (IB 28–30 pts HL 5 biol)

Bournemouth – 104–120 pts (Ecol Wldlf Cons) (IB 28–31 pts)

Chester – BCC–BBC incl biol/psy 104–112 pts (Anim Bhv; Anim Welf Sci) (IB 28 pts HL 5 biol/psy)

Cumbria – 104–120 pts (Ecol Wldlf Cons (Yr Ind)); 104–120 pts incl biol/geog/cons/env sci (Ecol Wldlf Cons); BCC–BBC 104–112 pts+interview+portfolio (Wldlf Media)

Edinburgh Napier – BCC incl sci (Anim Cons Biol) (IB 28 pts HL 654 incl 5 sci)

Gloucestershire – 104–120 pts (Wldlf Cons Biol)

Lincoln – BCC incl biol/psy (Anim Bhv Welf) (IB 28 pts HL 5 biol/psy)

Liverpool John Moores – BCC–BBC incl biol/geog/sci 104–112 pts (Wldlf Cons); BCC–BBC incl biol/sci 104–112 pts (Anim Bhv)

Manchester Met – BCC incl biol/hum biol 104–112 pts (Anim Bhv Cons) (IB 26 pts HL 5 biol)

Myerscough (Coll) – 104 pts+interview (Anim Sci Bhv) (IB 24 pts)

Oxford Brookes – BCC incl sci 104 pts (Biodiv Wldlf Cons) (IB 29 pts)
South Wales – BCC incl sci 104 pts (Nat Hist)
Winchester – BCC–BBB 104–120 pts (Anim Sci Cons)

96 pts **CAFRE** – 96 pts incl sci (Eqn Mgt)
Harper Adams – 96–104 pts (Anim Bhv Welf (Clin)) (IB 28 pts HL 5 pts); 96–120 pts (App Anim Sci) (IB 28 pts HL 5 pts)
Moulton (Coll) – 96 pts (Anim Bhv Sci Welf) (IB 24 pts)
Royal Agricultural Univ – 96 pts (Bldstck Perf Hrs Mgt; Bldstck Perf Hrs Mgt (Yr Ind)) (IB 26 pts); CCC 96 pts (Eqn Sci Bus; Eqn Sci Bus (Yr Ind)) (IB 26 pts)
South Wales – CCC incl biol+sci 96 pts (Int Wldlf Biol)
Teesside – 96–112 pts (Anim Sci Welf)
Wolverhampton – 96 pts incl biol/sci (Anim Bhv Wldlf Cons; Anim Bhv Wldlf Cons (Yr Ind))
Worcester – 96–104 pts incl biol+sci (Biol Sci (Zool))
Wrexham – 96–112 pts (Anim Bhv Welf Cons Sci)
Writtle (UC) – 96 pts (Eqn courses)

80 pts **Norwich City (Coll)** – 80 pts (Anim Sci)

64 pts **Sparsholt (Coll)** – CC incl sci (App Anim Sci) (IB 24 pts HL 4 biol)

ALTERNATIVE OFFERS See **Chapter 6** and **Appendix 1** for grades/UCAS Tariff points information for other examinations.

EXAMPLES OF COLLEGES OFFERING COURSES IN THIS SUBJECT FIELD

Barnsley (Coll); Bedford (Coll); Bicton (Coll); Bishop Burton (Coll); Calderdale (Coll); Canterbury (Coll); Central Bedfordshire (Coll); Cornwall (Coll); Craven (Coll); Derby (Coll); Duchy Coll (UC); Easton (Coll); Guildford (Coll); Hadlow (UC); Hartpury (Coll); Kingston Maurward (Coll); Kirklees (Coll); Lancaster and Morecambe (Coll); Moulton (Coll); Myerscough (Coll); Northumberland (Coll); Pembrokeshire (Coll); Petroc; Plumpton (Coll); Reaseheath (UC); Sir Gâr (Coll); SMB CG; South Devon (Coll); South Gloucestershire and Stroud (Coll); South Staffordshire (Coll); Sparsholt (Coll); Stamford (Coll); TEC Partnership; Warwickshire (Coll); West Anglia (Coll); Weston (Coll); Wiltshire (Coll); Wirral Met (Coll).

CHOOSING YOUR COURSE (SEE ALSO CH.1)

UNIVERSITIES AND COLLEGES TEACHING QUALITY See www.qaa.ac.uk; www.discoveruni.gov.uk.

TOP RESEARCH UNIVERSITIES AND COLLEGES (REF 2021) See **Agricultural Sciences/Agriculture** and **Biological Sciences**.

EXAMPLES OF SANDWICH DEGREE COURSES Aberystwyth; Anglia Ruskin; Bournemouth; Cumbria; Harper Adams; Liverpool John Moores; Manchester Met; Nottingham Trent; Oxford Brookes; Reading; Royal Agricultural Univ; Wolverhampton.

ADMISSIONS INFORMATION

ADVICE TO APPLICANTS AND PLANNING THE UCAS PERSONAL STATEMENT Describe any work you have done with animals which generated your interest in this subject. Work experience in veterinary practices, on farms or with agricultural firms would be useful. Read agricultural/scientific journals for updates on animal nutrition or breeding. For equine courses, details of practical experience with horses (eg BHS examinations, Pony Club tests) should be included.

SELECTION INTERVIEWS Yes Cumbria (Wldlf Media), Myerscough (Coll); **No** Anglia Ruskin, Harper Adams, Stirling.

INTERVIEW ADVICE AND QUESTIONS Questions are likely about your experience with animals and your reasons for wishing to follow this science-based subject. Other questions asked in recent years have included: What do your parents think about your choice of course? What are your views on battery hens and the rearing of veal calves? The causes of blue-tongue disease, foot and mouth disease and BSE may also feature. (Eqn courses) Students should check the level of riding ability expected (eg BHS Level 2 or PC B-test level). Check the amount of riding, jumping and competition work on the course. (See also **Chapter 5**.)

Reasons for rejection (non-academic) Uncertainty as to why applicants chose the course. Too immature. Unlikely to integrate well.

GRADUATE DESTINATIONS AND EMPLOYMENT

(See **Chapter 1, Graduate Outcomes.**)

Career note The majority of graduates obtained work with animals while others moved towards business and administration careers. This is a specialised subject area and undergraduates should start early to make contacts with organisations and gain work experience.

OTHER DEGREE SUBJECTS FOR CONSIDERATION

Agriculture; Biological Sciences; Biology; Food Science; Natural Sciences; Veterinary Science; Zoology.

ANTHROPOLOGY

(including **Social Anthropology**; see also **Archaeology, Sociology**)

Anthropology is the study of people's behaviour, beliefs and institutions and the diverse societies in which they live, and is concerned with the biological evolution of human beings. It also involves our relationships with other primates, the structure of communities and the effects of diet and disease on human groups. Alternatively, social or cultural anthropology covers aspects of social behaviour regarding family, kinship, marriage, gender, religion, political structures, law, psychology and language. Anthropology is also offered in combination with several other subjects such as Archaeology (London (UCL) and Southampton) and the study of forensics (Dundee and Bradford).

Useful websites www.britishmuseum.org; www.therai.org.uk; www.theasa.org

NB The points totals shown to the left of the institutions are for ease of reference only. It must not be assumed that Tariff points are always used by institutions or that they can be substituted for an offer in grades. The level of an offer is not necessarily indicative of the quality of a course.

COURSE OFFERS INFORMATION

Subject requirements/preferences GCSE English and mathematics usually required. A foreign language may be required. **AL** Biology and geography preferred for some biological anthropological courses. (Soc Anth) No specific subjects required. Some popular universities are now making lower offers for disadvantaged and other students.

Your target offers and examples of degree courses

152 pts **Cambridge** – A*AA+interview+HSPSAA (Hum Soc Pol Sci) (IB 41–42 pts HL 776)

144 pts **Oxford** – AAA (Arch Anth) (IB 38 pts HL 666)

136 pts **Bristol** – AAB (Anth) (IB 34 pts HL 17 pts)
Durham – AAB (Anth; Anth Arch; Anth Sociol) (IB 36 pts HL 665)
Edinburgh – AAB (Arch Soc Anth) (IB 36 pts HL 665)
Exeter – AAB (Anth; Arch Anth; Sociol Anth) (IB 34 pts HL 665)
London (UCL) – AAB (Arch Anth) (IB 36 pts HL 17 pts)
London LSE – AAB (Anth Law; Soc Anth) (IB 37 pts HL 666)
St Andrews – AAB 136–160 pts (Soc Anth courses) (IB 36 pts HL 665)
Sussex – AAB (Anth courses) (IB 34 pts)

128 pts **Birmingham** – ABB (Anth courses) (IB 32 pts HL 655)
Dundee – ABB incl biol (Foren Anth) (IB 32 pts HL 655 incl biol)
East Anglia – ABB (Arch Anth Art Hist (St Abrd)) (IB 32 pts)
Edinburgh – ABB–AAA (Soc Anth courses) (IB 34–37 pts HL 655–666)
London (SOAS) – ABB (Soc Anth) (IB 32 pts HL 655)
Manchester – ABB (Compar Relgn Anth; Soc Anth Crimin) (IB 34 pts HL 655)
Queen's Belfast – ABB (Anth courses) (IB 33 pts HL 655)
Sussex – ABB (Anth Lang) (IB 34 pts)

120 pts **Liverpool** – BBB–BBC+bEPQ (Evol Anth) (IB 30 pts)
London (Gold) – BBB (Anth courses) (IB 33 pts HL 655)
Southampton – BBB–ABB (Arch Anth) (IB 30–32 pts HL 15–16 pts)
112 pts **Aberdeen** – BBC (Anth; Anth Fr/Ger) (IB 32 pts HL 555)
Bradford – BBC incl sci 112 pts (Foren Anth) (HL 6 sci+HL 3 Engl+maths)
Brunel – BBC–ABB (Anth; Anth Sociol) (IB 29 pts)
Portsmouth – BBC–ABB incl sci 112–128 pts (Palae) (IB 25 pts)
104 pts **Bournemouth** – 104–120 pts (Anth; Arch Anth; Arch Anth Foren Sci; Sociol Soc Anth) (IB 28–31 pts)
Central Lancashire – 104–112 pts (Arch Anth)
Liverpool John Moores – 104–112 pts (Foren Anth)
Oxford Brookes – BCC 104 pts (Anth; Anth Sociol) (IB 29 pts)
Plymouth – 104–120 pts (Anth) (IB 26–28 pts)
Winchester – 104–120 pts (Anth)
96 pts **Trinity Saint David** – 96–112 pts (Anth courses)

ALTERNATIVE OFFERS See **Chapter 6** and **Appendix 1** for grades/UCAS Tariff points information for other examinations.

CHOOSING YOUR COURSE (SEE ALSO CH.1)

UNIVERSITIES AND COLLEGES TEACHING QUALITY See www.qaa.ac.uk; www.discoveruni.gov.uk.

TOP RESEARCH UNIVERSITIES AND COLLEGES (REF 2021) (Anthropology and Development Studies) London LSE (Anth); East Anglia; Manchester (Dev St); London (SOAS) (Anth); Oxford (Dev St); Bristol; Sussex; Manchester (Soc Anth); Reading; Birmingham.

EXAMPLES OF SANDWICH DEGREE COURSES Bournemouth; Bradford; Brunel; Essex; Kent; Liverpool John Moores.

ADMISSIONS INFORMATION

ADVICE TO APPLICANTS AND PLANNING THE UCAS PERSONAL STATEMENT Visits to museums should be discussed; for example, museums of anthropology (London, Oxford, Cambridge). Describe any aspect of the subject which interests you (including books you have read) and how you have pursued this interest. Give details of any overseas travel. Give reasons for choosing course: since this is not a school subject, you will need to convince the selectors of your knowledge and interest.

SELECTION INTERVIEWS Yes Cambridge, Oxford (Arch Anth) 58% (success rate 16%); **No** East Anglia, London LSE, Oxford Brookes.

INTERVIEW ADVICE AND QUESTIONS This is a broad subject and questions will tend to emerge as a result of your interests in aspects of anthropology or social anthropology and your comments on your personal statement. Past questions have included: What stresses are there among the nomads of the North African desert? What is a society? What is speech? If you dug up a stone axe, what could you learn from it? What are the values created by a capitalist society? Discuss the role of women since the beginning of this century.

REASONS FOR REJECTION (NON-ACADEMIC) Lack of commitment. Inability to deal with a more philosophical (less positivist) approach to knowledge.

GRADUATE DESTINATIONS AND EMPLOYMENT

(See **Chapter 1, Graduate Outcomes.**)

CAREER NOTE All non-scientific careers are open to graduates. However, career planning should start early and efforts made to contact employers and gain work experience.

OTHER DEGREE SUBJECTS FOR CONSIDERATION

Archaeology; Egyptology; Heritage Studies; History; Human Sciences; Political Science; Psychology; Religious Studies; Social Science; Sociology.

ARCHAEOLOGY

(see also **Anthropology, History (Ancient)**)

Courses in Archaeology differ between institutions but the majority focus on the archaeology of Europe, the Mediterranean and Middle Eastern countries and on the close examination of discoveries of prehistoric communities and ancient, medieval and post-medieval societies. Hands-on experience is involved in all courses as well as a close study of the history of the artefacts themselves. All courses will involve excavations in the UK or abroad. A number of universities combine Archaeology with History and Anthropology while Bournemouth combines it with Forensic Sciences. Southampton also has a Centre for Maritime Archaeology.

Useful websites http://new.archaeologyuk.org; www.english-heritage.org.uk; www.britishmuseum.org; www.archaeologists.net

NB The points totals shown to the left of the institutions are for ease of reference only. It must not be assumed that Tariff points are always used by institutions or that they can be substituted for an offer in grades. The level of an offer is not necessarily indicative of the quality of a course.

COURSE OFFERS INFORMATION

Subject requirements/preferences GCSE English and mathematics or science usually required for BSc courses. **AL** history, geography, English or a science subject may be preferred for some courses and two science subjects for Archaeological Science courses. Some popular universities are now making lower offers for disadvantaged and other students.

Your target offers and examples of degree courses

152 pts **Cambridge** – A*AA+interview+ARCHAA (Arch) (IB 40–42 pts HL 776)
144 pts **Oxford** – AAA (Arch Anth) (IB 38 pts HL 666); (Class Arch Anc Hist) (IB 39 pts HL 666)
St Andrews – AAA incl hist (Mediev Hist Arch) (IB 38 pts HL 666 incl hist)
136 pts **Bristol** – AAB (Arch Anth) (IB 34 pts HL 17 pts)
Durham – AAB (Anc Hist Arch; Anth Arch; Arch) (IB 36 pts HL 665)
Edinburgh – AAB (Arch; Arch Soc Anth) (IB 36 pts HL 665); AAB. (Arch Anc Hist) (IB 36 pts HL 665)
Exeter – AAB (Arch Anth) (IB 34 pts HL 665)
London (UCL) – AAB (Arch Anth) (IB 36 pts HL 17 pts)
Warwick – AAB (Anc Hist Class Arch) (IB 34 pts)
128 pts **Birmingham** – ABB (Arch courses) (IB 32 pts HL 655)
East Anglia – ABB (Arch Anth Art Hist (St Abrd)) (IB 32 pts)
Edinburgh – ABB (Archit Hist Arch; Celt Arch) (IB 34 pts HL 655)
Leicester – ABB–BBB+bEPQ (Anc Hist Arch) (IB 30 pts)
London (UCL) – ABB (Arch; Class Arch Class Civ) (IB 34 pts HL 16 pts)
Manchester – ABB (Arch; Arch Anth) (IB 34 pts HL 655)
Nottingham – ABB (Anc Hist Arch; Arch Geog) (IB 30 pts HL 655); ABB incl A hist (Arch Hist) (IB 30 pts HL 655 incl 6 hist)
York – ABB (Arch; Hist Arch) (IB 34 pts); ABB incl sci (Bioarch) (IB 34 pts incl HL sci/maths)
120 pts **Exeter** – BBB–ABB (Arch) (IB 30–32 pts HL 555–655)
Kent – BBB–ABB (Class Arch St) (HL 665)
Liverpool – BBB (Arch; Arch Anc Civ; Egypt) (IB 30 pts)
Newcastle – BBB incl sci (Arch) (IB 30 pts HL 555 incl sci)
Nottingham – BBB (Arch) (IB 28 pts HL 555)
Queen's Belfast – BBB (Arch; Arch Palae) (IB 32 pts HL 655)
Southampton – BBB–ABB (Arch) (IB 30 pts HL 15–16 pts)
112 pts **Aberdeen** – BBC incl maths/sci (Arch) (IB 32 pts HL 555 pts incl maths/sci)
Bradford – BBC 112 pts (Arch courses) (HL 3 Engl/maths)
Canterbury Christ Church – BBC (Arch courses) (IB 29 pts)

London (Birk) – 112 pts (Arch)
Portsmouth – BBC–ABB incl sci 112–128 pts (Palae) (IB 25 pts)
Swansea – BBC–ABB 112–128 pts (Egypt Anc Hist) (IB 32 pts)
104 pts **Bangor** – 104–128 pts (Hist Arch); 104–128 pts (Herit Arch Hist)
Bournemouth – 104–120 pts (Arch; Arch Anth; Arch Anth Foren Sci) (IB 28–31 pts)
Cardiff – BCC–BBB (Arch courses) (IB 29–31 pts HL 655–665)
Central Lancashire – 104–112 pts (Arch; Arch Anth)
Chester – BCC–BBC (Arch courses) (IB 28 pts)
Glasgow – BCC–AAB incl B sci (Arch) (IB 32–34 pts HL 555–655 incl sci)
Winchester – BCC–BBC 104–112 pts (Arch)
96 pts **Bishop Grosseteste** – 96–112 pts (Arch Hist)
Cardiff – CCC–BBC (Cons Objs Musm Arch) (IB 28–30 pts HL 555–655)
Trinity Saint David – 96 pts+interview (Arch)
Winchester – CCC–BBC 96–112 pts (Arch Prac)
72 pts **UHI** – BC (Arch; Arch Sci; Hist Arch)

ALTERNATIVE OFFERS See **Chapter 6** and **Appendix 1** for grades/UCAS Tariff points information for other examinations.

DEGREE APPRENTICESHIPS

Bishop Grosseteste (Arch Spec).

EXAMPLES OF COLLEGES OFFERING COURSES IN THIS SUBJECT FIELD

Truro and Penwith (Coll).

CHOOSING YOUR COURSE (SEE ALSO CH.1)

UNIVERSITIES AND COLLEGES TEACHING QUALITY See www.qaa.ac.uk; www.discoveruni.gov.uk.

TOP RESEARCH UNIVERSITIES AND COLLEGES (REF 2021) (Archaeology) Reading; Durham; Southampton; Cambridge; Leicester; York; Exeter; Oxford; Cardiff; London (UCL).

EXAMPLES OF SANDWICH DEGREE COURSES Bournemouth; Bradford; East Anglia; Reading; York.

ADMISSIONS INFORMATION

ADVICE TO APPLICANTS AND PLANNING THE UCAS PERSONAL STATEMENT First-hand experience of digs and other fieldwork should be described. The Council for British Archaeology (see **Appendix 3**) can provide information on where digs are taking place. Describe any interests in fossils and any museum visits as well as details of visits to current archaeological sites. Your local university archaeological department or central library can also provide information on contacts in your local area (each county council employs an archaeological officer). Since this is not a school subject, the selectors will be looking for good reasons for your choice of subject. Gain practical field experience and discuss this in the personal statement. Show your serious commitment to archaeology through your out-of-school activities (eg fieldwork, museum experience) (see **Chapter 5**). (See also **Anthropology**.)

SELECTION INTERVIEWS Yes Cambridge, Oxford (Arch Anth) 58% (success rate 16%), (Class Arch Anc Hist) 91% (success rate 18%), Trinity Saint David; **Some** Bristol; **No** Bradford, Cardiff, East Anglia, Leicester, Newcastle.

INTERVIEW ADVICE AND QUESTIONS Questions will be asked about any experience you have had in visiting archaeological sites or taking part in digs. Past questions have included: How would you interpret archaeological evidence, for example a pile of flints, coins? What is stratification? How would you date archaeological remains? What recent archaeological discoveries have been made? How did you become interested in archaeology? With which archaeological sites in the UK are you familiar? See also **Chapter 5**.

REASONS FOR REJECTION (NON-ACADEMIC) (Mature students) Inability to cope with essay-writing and exams.

GRADUATE DESTINATIONS AND EMPLOYMENT

(See **Chapter 1, Graduate Outcomes.**)

Career note Vocational opportunities closely linked to this subject are limited. However, some graduates aim for positions in local authorities, libraries and museums. A number of organisations covering water boards, forestry, civil engineering and surveying also employ field archaeologists.

OTHER DEGREE SUBJECTS FOR CONSIDERATION

Ancient History; Anthropology; Classical Studies; Classics; Geology; Heritage Studies; History; History of Art and Architecture; Land Economy; Medieval History.

ARCHITECTURE

(including **Architectural Technology and Architectural Engineering**; see also **Art and Design (Interior, Product and Industrial Design), Building and Construction, Landscape Architecture**)

Courses in Architecture provide a broad education consisting of technological subjects covering structures, construction, materials and environmental studies. Project-based design work is an integral part of all courses and in addition, history and social studies will also be incorporated into degree programmes. After completing the first three years leading to a BA (Hons), students aiming for full professional status take a further two-year course leading to, for example, a BArch, MArch or Diploma, and after a year in an architect's practice, the final professional examinations are taken. There is also a close link between architecture and civil engineering in the construction of large projects eg The Shard, Sydney Opera House and the construction of bridges and other major projects. Several architectural engineering courses are offered, for example Bath, Loughborough and Glasgow offer courses which, while focussing on civil engineering, also introduce creative design elements working on inventive and imaginative design solutions.

Useful websites www.ciat.org.uk; www.architecture.com; www.rias.org.uk; www.ciob.org; www.citb.co.uk

NB The points totals shown to the left of the institutions are for ease of reference only. It must not be assumed that Tariff points are always used by institutions or that they can be substituted for an offer in grades. The level of an offer is not necessarily indicative of the quality of a course.

COURSE OFFERS INFORMATION

Subject requirements/preferences GCSE English and mathematics, in some cases at certain grades, are required in all cases. A science subject may also be required. **AL** Mathematics and/or physics required or preferred for some courses. Art and design may be preferable to design and technology. Art is sometimes a requirement and many schools of architecture prefer it; a portfolio of art work is often requested and, in some cases, a drawing test will be set. MEng courses not listed below unless otherwise stated. Some popular universities are now making lower offers for disadvantaged and other students.

Your target offers and examples of degree courses

152 pts **Bath** – A*AA/AAA+aEPQ incl maths (Struct Archit Eng (MEng)) (IB 36 pts HL 766 incl maths); A*AA–AAA+aEPQ (Archit) (IB 36 pts HL 766)
Cambridge – A*AA+interview+ARCHITAA+portfolio (Archit) (IB 40–42 pts HL 776)
Edinburgh – A*AA (Archit) (IB 39 pts HL 666)
Southampton – A*AA/AAA+aEPQ incl A maths+sci (Civ Eng Archit (MEng)) (IB 38 pts HL 19 pts incl 6/7 maths)

144 pts **Leeds** – AAA incl maths (Archit Eng) (HL 18 pts incl 5 maths); (Archit) (HL 5 maths)
Liverpool – AAA/AAB+aEPQ+portfolio (Archit) (IB 36 pts)
Manchester – AAA (Archit) (IB 36 pts HL 666)
Manchester Met – AAA 144 pts+portfolio (Archit)

Newcastle – AAA+portfolio (Archit) (IB 36 pts)
Nottingham – AAA+portfolio (Archit) (IB 36 pts); AAA incl maths+phys/chem/art+portfolio (Archit Env Des (MEng)) (IB 36 pts HL 5 maths)
Queen's Belfast – AAA+portfolio (Archit) (IB 36 pts HL 666); AAA incl maths+sci/tech/geog (Struct Eng Archit (MEng)) (IB 36 pts HL 666 incl maths+sci/tech/geog)
Sheffield – AAA (Archit) (IB 36 pts); AAA–AAB+aEPQ incl maths (Archit Eng (MEng); Struct Eng Archit (MEng)) (IB 36 pts HL 6 maths)
UWE Bristol – 144 pts (Archit)

136 pts **Arts London** – AAB 136 pts+portfolio (Archit) (IB 35 pts)
Birmingham City – AAB 136 pts+portfolio (Archit) (IB 34 pts)
Cardiff – AAB–AAA+portfolio (Archit) (IB 34–36 pts HL 666)
Lancaster – AAB (Archit) (IB 35 pts HL 16 pts)
Liverpool – AAB/ABB+aEPQ incl maths (Archit Eng; Archit Eng (MEng)) (IB 35 pts HL 5 maths)
London (UCL) – AAB+interview+portfolio (Archit) (IB 36 pts HL 17 pts); AAB+portfolio (Archit Interd St) (IB 36 pts HL 17 pts)
Oxford Brookes – AAB+interview+portfolio (Archit) (IB 33 pts)
UWE Bristol – 136 pts (Archit Plan)
York – AAB+interview (Archit) (IB 35 pts)

128 pts **Bournemouth Arts** – ABB 128 pts+portfolio (Archit)
Central Lancashire – 128–136 pts+interview+portfolio (Archit)
Coventry – ABB (Archit) (IB 34 pts)
Creative Arts – 128 pts+portfolio (Archit) (IB 29–32 pts HL 16 pts)
Edinburgh – ABB (Archit Hist Arch; Archit Hist Herit) (IB 34 pts HL 655); ABB–AAA incl maths+ sci/comp/eng/des tech (Struct Eng Archit) (IB 32–37 pts HL 555–666 incl maths+sci/comp/eng/des tech)
Glasgow (SA) – ABB incl maths/phys+interview+portfolio (Archit) (IB 30 pts HL 18 pts incl Engl+maths/phys)
Greenwich – ABB 128 pts+interview+portfolio (Archit)
Kent – ABB–AAB+portfolio (Archit)
Kingston – 128–144 pts+portfolio (Archit)
Leeds Beckett – 128 pts+interview+portfolio (Archit) (HL 554)
Liverpool John Moores – ABB 128 pts+portfolio (Archit)
Loughborough – ABB incl maths (Archit Eng) (IB 34 pts HL 655 incl maths)
Newcastle – ABB+portfolio (Archit Urb Plan) (IB 32 pts HL 555)
Northumbria – 128 pts+portfolio (Archit)
Nottingham – ABB incl maths+sci/geog/geol/comp/econ (Archit Env Eng) (IB 32 pts HL 5 maths+sci/geog/geol)
Nottingham Trent – 120–128 pts+portfolio (Archit)
Reading – ABB+interview+portfolio (Archit) (IB 32 pts)
Salford – 128 pts+portfolio (Archit) (IB 32 pts)
Sheffield Hallam – ABB 128 pts+interview+portfolio (Archit) (IB 28 pts)
Trinity Saint David – 128 pts (Archit)
Wolverhampton – AAC+portfolio (Archit)

120 pts **Dundee** – BBB (Archit) (IB 30 pts HL 555 incl Engl)
East London – BBB 120 pts+interview+portfolio (Archit) (IB 24 pts HL 15 pts)
Glasgow – BBB–AAB incl maths+phys (Civ Eng Archit) (IB 34 pts HL 655 incl maths+phys)
Huddersfield – BBB–AAB 120–136 pts+interview+portfolio (Archit; Archit (Int))
Leeds Beckett – 120 pts+portfolio (Inter Archit)
London Met – BBB incl art/hum/soc sci 120 pts+interview+portfolio (Archit)
Norwich Arts – BBB+interview+portfolio (Archit) (IB 27 pts)
Strathclyde – BBB–ABB incl maths/phys 120 pts+portfolio (Archit St) (IB 32–34 pts HL 5 Engl+maths/phys)
UWE Bristol – 120 pts incl maths/phys (Archit Env Eng) (HL 5 maths)

Westminster – BBB 120 pts+portfolio+interview (Archit Env Des); BBB–AAB 120–136 pts+interview+portfolio (Archit)

112 pts **Anglia Ruskin** – 112 pts+portfolio (Archit) (IB 24 pts)
Birmingham City – BBC 112 pts (Archit Tech) (IB 28 pts)
Cardiff – BBC–ABB incl B maths (Archit Eng) (IB 30–32 pts HL 655–665 incl 6 maths)
Coventry – BBC (Archit Tech) (IB 29 pts)
De Montfort – 112–136 pts+interview+portfolio (Archit) (IB 32 pts)
Derby – BBC–BBB 112–120 pts (Archit Tech Prac)
East London – 112 pts (Archit Des Tech) (IB 24 pts HL 15 pts)
Leeds Beckett – 112 pts (Archit Tech)
Lincoln – BBC 112 pts+portfolio (Archit)
London South Bank – 112 pts (Archit Tech); BBC 112–128 pts+interview+portfolio (Archit)
Nottingham Trent – 112–120 pts (Archit Tech)
Portsmouth – BBC–BBB 112–120 pts+portfolio (Inter Archit Des) (IB 25 pts); BBC–BBB 112–120 pts+interview+portfolio (Archit) (IB 25 pts)
Solent – 112–128 pts (Archit Des Tech)
UWE Bristol – 112 pts (Archit Tech Des)
Ulster – BBC+portfolio (Archit) (IB 25 pts HL 12 pts); BBC incl sci/maths/tech/des (Archit Tech Mgt) (IB 25 pts HL 12 pts incl maths/sci)
West London – BBC–BBB 112–120 pts (Archit Des Tech)
Westminster – BBC–ABB 112–128 pts (Archit Tech)

104 pts **Bath Spa** – BCC–BBB (Archit) (IB 32 pts)
Brighton – BCC–AAB 104–136 pts+portfolio (Archit) (IB 27 pts)
Falmouth – 104–120 pts (Archit)
Heriot-Watt – BCC–BBB incl maths (Archit Eng) (IB 28 pts HL 5 maths)
Liverpool John Moores – BCC 104 pts (Archit Tech)
Northampton – BCC 104 pts (Archit Tech)
Plymouth – 104–136 pts+portfolio (Archit) (IB 26–34 pts)
Robert Gordon – BCC incl Engl/maths/sci+portfolio (Archit MArch) (IB 28 pts HL 5 Engl/maths/sci)

96 pts **Archit Assoc Sch London** – CCC 96 pts+portfolio (Archit)
Cardiff Met – CCC–BBB 96–120 pts (Archit Des Tech) (IB 24 pts)
Edinburgh Napier – CCC (Archit Tech) (IB 26 pts HL 555)
Robert Gordon – CCC incl Engl (Archit Tech) (IB 26 pts incl HL Engl)
Wolverhampton – CCC+portfolio (Archit Des Tech)

80 pts **Wrexham** – 80–112 pts (Archit Des Tech)

64 pts **Ravensbourne Univ** – CC+interview+portfolio (Archit) (IB 24 pts)

Alternative offers See **Chapter 6** and **Appendix 1** for grades/UCAS Tariff points information for other examinations.

DEGREE APPRENTICESHIPS

Birmingham City (Archit); Cambridge (Archit); Central Lancashire (Archit Tech); Kent (Archit); London Met (Archit); London South Bank (Archit Asst); Northumbria (Archit); Nottingham (Archit); Nottingham Trent (Archit); Portsmouth (Archit Asst, Archit); Oxford Brookes (Archit); Sheffield Hallam (Archit); UWE Bristol (Archit).

EXAMPLES OF COLLEGES OFFERING COURSES IN THIS SUBJECT FIELD

London South East (Coll); Weymouth (Coll).

CHOOSING YOUR COURSE (SEE ALSO CH.1)

Universities and colleges teaching quality See www.qaa.ac.uk; www.discoveruni.gov.uk.

Top research universities and colleges (REF 2021) (Architecture, Built Environment and Planning) Cambridge; Loughborough; Sheffield; Cardiff; Manchester; London (UCL); Kent; Edinburgh; Heriot-Watt; Glasgow.

Examples of sandwich degree courses Bath; Coventry; Derby; Edinburgh; Glasgow (SA); Liverpool John Moores; Loughborough; Northumbria; Nottingham Trent; Portsmouth; Robert Gordon; Sheffield; UWE Bristol.

ADMISSIONS INFORMATION

The following universities require a portfolio and evidence of art/design ability – Anglia Ruskin, Architectural Association School of Architecture, Arts London, Arts University Bournemouth, Birmingham City, Brighton, Cambridge, Cardiff, Central Lancashire, Central London, Creative Arts, De Montfort, East London, Glasgow (SA), Greenwich, Huddersfield, Kent, Kingston, Leeds Beckett, Lincoln, Liverpool, Liverpool John Moores, London Met, London South Bank, Manchester Met, Newcastle, Northumbria, Norwich Arts, Nottingham, Nottingham Trent, Oxford Brookes, Plymouth, Portsmouth, Queen's Belfast, Ravensbourne, Reading, Salford, Robert Gordon, Sheffield Hallam, Strathclyde, Ulster, Westminster, Wolverhampton. Check with other universities.

Bath Preference for applicants with high proportion of GCSEs at 8/9 (A*). A-level mathematics, physics and art or design technology highly desirable. **Cambridge** Art provides a better preparation than design technology. **Liverpool** A lower grade offer if portfolio impressive. **Manchester** Two art and/or design A-levels not advised. **UWE Bristol** Architecture and Environmental Engineering degree gives RIBA status.

Advice to applicants and planning the UCAS personal statement You should describe any visits to historical or modern architectural sites and give your opinions. Contact architects in your area and try to obtain work shadowing or work experience in their practices. Describe any such work you have done. Develop a portfolio of drawings and sketches of buildings and parts of buildings (you will probably need this for your interview). Show evidence of your reading on the history of architecture in Britain and modern architecture throughout the world. Discuss your preferences among the work of leading 20th and 21st century world architects (see **Chapter 4** and also **Appendix 3**).

Selection interviews Yes Cambridge, Cardiff Met, Falmouth, Huddersfield, London Met, Ravensbourne Univ, Reading, Sheffield Hallam, Westminster, York; **Some** Bath, Sheffield (mature students and applicants with non-standard qualifications); **No** Birmingham City, Cardiff, Derby, Dundee, Kingston, Manchester Met, Newcastle, West London.

Interview advice and questions Most Architecture departments will expect to see evidence of your ability to draw; portfolios are often requested at interview and, in some cases, drawing tests are set prior to the interview. You should have a real awareness of architecture with some knowledge of historical styles as well as examples of modern architecture. If you have gained some work experience then you will be asked to describe the work done in the architect's office and any site visits you have made. Questions in the past have included the following: What is the role of the architect in society? Is the London Eye an eyesore? Discuss one historic and one 21st century building you admire. Who is your favourite architect? What sort of buildings do you want to design? How would you make a place peaceful? How would you reduce crime through architecture? Do you like the University buildings? Do you read any architectural journals? Which? What is the role of an architectural technologist? See also **Chapter 5**.

Reasons for rejection (non-academic) Weak evidence of creative skills. Portfolio of artwork does not give sufficient evidence of design creativity. Insufficient evidence of interest in architecture. Unwillingness to try freehand sketching.

GRADUATE DESTINATIONS AND EMPLOYMENT

(See **Chapter 1, Graduate Outcomes.**)

Career note Further study is needed to enter architecture as a profession. Opportunities exist in local government or private practice – areas include planning, housing, environmental and conservation fields. Architectural technicians support the work of architects and may be involved in project management, design presentations and submissions to planning authorities.

OTHER DEGREE SUBJECTS FOR CONSIDERATION

Building; Building Surveying; Civil Engineering; Construction; Heritage Management; History of Art and Architecture; Housing; Interior Architecture; Interior Design; Landscape Architecture; Property Development; Quantity Surveying; Surveying; Town and Country Planning; Urban Studies.

ART AND DESIGN (GENERAL)

(including **Drawing and Painting**; see also **Art and Design (3D Design), Art and Design (Graphic Design), Combined and Liberal Arts Courses, Communication Studies/Communication, Drama, Media Studies, Photography**)

Art and Design and all specialisms remain one of the most popular subjects. Many of the courses listed here cover aspects of fine art, graphic or three-dimensional design, but to a less specialised extent than those listed in the other Art and Design tables. Travel and visits to art galleries and museums are strongly recommended by many universities and colleges. Note that for entry to many Art and Design courses it is often necessary to follow an Art and Design Foundation course first: check with your chosen institution.

Art and Design degree courses cover a wide range of subjects. These are grouped together in six tables: Art and Design (General), Art and Design (Fashion and Textiles), Art and Design (Fine Art), Art and Design (Graphic Design), Art and Design (Interior, Product and Industrial Design), Art and Design (3D Design). (History of Art and Photography are listed in separate tables.)

Useful websites www.artscouncil.org.uk; www.designcouncil.org.uk; www.theatredesign.org.uk; www.arts.ac.uk; www.dandad.org; www.csd.org.uk; www.creativefuture.org.uk

The points total shown to the left of the institutions are for ease of reference only. It must not be assumed that Tariff points are always used by institutions or that they can be substituted for an offer in grades. The level of an offer is not necessarily indicative of the quality of a course.

COURSE OFFERS INFORMATION

Subject requirements/preferences Entry requirements for Art and Design courses vary between institutions and courses (check prospectuses and websites). Most courses require an Art and Design Foundation course and a portfolio of work demonstrating potential and visual awareness. **GCSE** Five subjects at grades 7–4 (A–C), or a recognised equivalent. **AL** Grades or points may be required. (Des Tech) Design technology or a physical science may be required or preferred. (Crea Arts courses) Music/art/drama may be required. All institutions will require candidates to attend, usually with portfolios. Some popular universities are now making lower offers for disadvantaged and other students.

Your target offers and examples of degree courses

128 pts **Leeds** – ABB incl art/des (Art Des) (IB 34 pts HL 16 pts incl 5 vis arts)
120 pts **Reading** – BBB+portfolio (Art courses) (IB 30 pts); BBB incl Engl+portfolio (Art Crea Writ) (IB 30 pts HL 5 Engl)
112 pts **Birmingham City** – BBC 112 pts+portfolio (Art Des) (IB 28 pts)
Bournemouth Arts – BBC–BBB 112–120 pts+interview (Evnts Mgt)
Coventry – BBC+portfolio (Gms Art) (IB 28 pts)
De Montfort – B art des 112 pts+portfolio (Gm Art) (IB 26 pts HL 6 art des)
Portsmouth – BBC–BBB 112–120 pts (Comp Animat Vis Efcts) (IB 25 pts)
Staffordshire – BBC 112 pts+portfolio+interview (Gms Art)
104 pts **Derby** – BCC 104 pts+portfolio (Crea Expr Arts Hlth Wlbng (Dance/Dr/Mus/Art))
Falmouth – 104–120 pts+interview+portfolio (Drg)
Manchester Met – 104–112 pts+portfolio (Crfts) (IB 26 pts)
South Wales – BCC incl art/art des 104 pts+portfolio (Crea Ther Arts)
96 pts **Cardiff Met** – CCC–BBB 96–120 pts+interview+portfolio (Arst Des (Mak)) (IB 24 pts)

Hereford (CA) – 96–112 pts+interview+portfolio (Contemp Des Crfts); 96–112 pts+portfolio (Illus)
Westminster – CCC–BBB 96–120 pts+portfolio (Illus)
64 pts **Rose Bruford (Coll)** – CC 64 pts+interview+portfolio (Scnc Arts (Constr Props Pntg))

Alternative offers See **Chapter 6** and **Appendix 1** for grades/UCAS Tariff points information for other examinations.

DEGREE APPRENTICESHIPS

Teesside (Cur).

EXAMPLES OF COLLEGES OFFERING COURSES IN THIS SUBJECT FIELD

Banbury and Bicester (Coll); Barnet and Southgate (Coll); Barnsley (Coll); Blackburn (Coll); Blackpool and Fylde (Coll); Bradford College (UC); Brighton Met (Coll); Chelmsford (Coll); Chesterfield (Coll); Chichester (Coll); Cornwall (Coll); Doncaster (Coll); Ealing, Hammersmith and West London (Coll); East Coast (Coll); East Surrey (Coll); East Sussex (Coll); Exeter (Coll); Furness (Coll); Grŵp Llandrillo Menai; Hugh Baird (Coll); Hull (Coll); Kingston (Coll); Loughborough (Coll); Manchester (Coll); NCC Redbridge; North Warwickshire and South Leicestershire (Coll); Norwich City (Coll); Nottingham (Coll); Pembrokeshire (Coll); Peter Symonds (Coll); Portsmouth (Coll); Richmond-upon-Thames (Coll); Rotherham (CAT); South and West Cheshire (Coll); South Devon (Coll); South Essex (Coll); Southampton City (Coll); Southport (Coll); Stockport (Coll); Sunderland (Coll); TEC Partnership; Totton (Coll); Truro and Penwith (Coll); Tyne Coast (Coll); Wakefield (Coll); West Herts (Coll); Westminster City (Coll); Windsor Forest (Coll); Wirral Met (Coll); Yeovil (Coll).

CHOOSING YOUR COURSE (SEE ALSO CH.1)

Top research universities and colleges (REF 2021) (Art and Design: History, Practice and Theory) Oxford; St Andrews; London (UCL) (Art Hist); London (Birk); Westminster; York; London (SOAS); Sussex; Birmingham; Manchester.

Examples of sandwich degree courses Coventry; Huddersfield; Lincoln; Portsmouth.

ADMISSIONS INFORMATION

Advice to applicants and planning the UCAS personal statement Admissions tutors look for a wide interest in aspects of art and design. Discuss the type of work and the range of media you have explored through your studies to date. Refer to visits to art galleries and museums and give your opinions of the styles of paintings and sculpture, both historical and present day. Mention art-related hobbies. Good drawing skills and sketchbook work, creative and analytical thinking will be needed.

Selection interviews Yes Cardiff Met, Hereford (CA), Huddersfield, Robert Gordon, South Wales, Westminster; **No** Lincoln.

Interview advice and questions Admissions tutors will want to see both breadth and depth in the applicant's work and evidence of strong self-motivation. They will also be interested to see any sketchbooks or notebooks. However, they do not wish to see similar work over and over again! A logical, ordered presentation helps considerably. Large work, especially three-dimensional work, can be presented by way of photographs. Video or film work should be edited to a running time of no more than 15 minutes. Examples of written work may also be provided. Past questions have included: How often do you visit art galleries and exhibitions? Discuss the last exhibition you visited. What are the reactions of your parents to your choice of course and career? Do you think that modern art has anything to contribute to society compared with earlier art? Is a brick a work of art? Show signs of life – no apathy! Be eager and enthusiastic.

Reasons for rejection (non-academic) Lack of enthusiasm for design issues or to acquire design skills. Poorly presented practical work. Lack of interest or enthusiasm in contemporary visual arts. Lack of knowledge and experience of the art and design industry.

GRADUATE DESTINATIONS AND EMPLOYMENT

(See **Chapter 1, Graduate Outcomes.**)

Career note Many Art and Design courses are linked to specific career paths which are achieved through freelance consultancy work or studio work. Some graduates enter teaching and many find other areas such as retail and management fields. Opportunities for fashion and graphic design specialists exceed those of other areas of art and design. Opportunities in industrial and product design and three-dimensional design are likely to be limited and dependent on the contacts that students establish during their degree courses. Only a very limited number of students committed to painting and sculpture can expect to succeed without seeking alternative employment.

OTHER DEGREE SUBJECTS FOR CONSIDERATION

Animation; Architecture; Art Gallery Management; Communication Studies; Computer Studies; Education; Film Studies; History of Art; Media Studies; Photography; see other **Art and Design** tables.

ART AND DESIGN (FASHION AND TEXTILES)

(including **Printed Textiles and Surface Pattern Design**)

Fashion Design courses involve drawing and design, research, pattern cutting and garment construction for clothing for menswear and womenswear, with specialisation often offered later in the course. First year Textiles courses will involve the study of constructed textile technology techniques such as knitting and stitching, leading to specialisation later. Within digital textiles, the focus is on fashion for interiors and students will experiment with techniques such as laser knitting and digital fabric printing. Courses may also cover design for textiles, commercial production and marketing. Some institutions have particularly good contacts with industry and are able to arrange sponsorships for students.

Useful websites https://londonfashionweek.co.uk; www.textileinstitute.org; www.creativefuture.org.uk; www.britishfashioncouncil.co.uk; www.designcouncil.org.uk

NB The points totals shown to the left of the institutions are for ease of reference only. It must not be assumed that Tariff points are always used by institutions or that they can be substituted for an offer in grades. The level of an offer is not necessarily indicative of the quality of a course.

COURSE OFFERS INFORMATION

Subject requirements/preferences AL A textile-related subject may be required. Some popular universities are now making lower offers for disadvantaged and other students.

Your target offers and examples of degree courses

136 pts **Manchester** – AAB+interview (Fash Mgt) (IB 35 pts HL 665)

128 pts **Edinburgh** – ABB+portfolio (Fash; Jewel Silver; Perf Cstm; Tex) (IB 34 pts HL 655)

Glasgow (SA) – ABB+interview+portfolio (Fash Des) (IB 30 pts HL 18 pts incl Engl+maths)

Kingston – 128–144 pts incl art/des+portfolio (Fash)

Leeds – ABB incl art/des+portfolio (Fash Des Innov) (IB 34 pts HL 16 pts incl 5 vis arts+4 Engl)

120 pts **Loughborough** – BBB/ABC+portfolio (Tex Des) (IB 32 pts HL 555)

Southampton (Winchester SA) – BBB (Fash Mark Mgt) (IB 30 pts HL 15 pts); BBB+portfolio (Fash Des) (IB 30 pts HL 15 pts)

Trinity Saint David – 120 pts+interview+portfolio (Surf Patt Tex) (IB 32 pts)

112 pts **Arts London** – 112 pts+interview (Fash Jrnl Cntnt Crea; Fash PR Comm); 112 pts+interview+portfolio (Cstm Perf; Hair Mkup Pros Perf) (IB 25 pts); BBC+interview+portfolio (Cord Fash Bags Accs; Cord Ftwr; Crea Dir Fash; Fash Cont; Fash Des Dev; Fash Des Tech (Wmnswr); Fash Imag Illus; Fash Jewel; Fash Spowr; Fash Tex courses); BBC 112 pts (Fash Mgt) (IB 25 pts)

Birmingham City – BBC 112 pts (Fash Bus Prom) (IB 28 pts HL 14 pts); BBC 112 pts+portfolio (Fash Des courses) (IB 28 pts HL 14 pts)
Bournemouth Arts – BBC–BBB 112–120 pts (Des Cstm Perf); BBC–BBB 112–120 pts+portfolio (Fash; Tex Des); (Mkup Media Perf) (HL 555); BBC–BBB 112–120 pts+portfolio+interview (Fash Comm)
Chester – 112 pts (Fash Comm Mark (Soc Media)) (IB 28 pts)
Coventry – 112 pts+portfolio (Fash) (IB 29 pts)
Creative Arts – 112 pts+interview+portfolio (Fash Atel; Tex) (IB 27–30 pts HL 15 pts)
De Montfort – 112 pts (Fash Buy courses) (IB 26 pts); 112 pts+portfolio (Cont Fash; Fash Tex Des; Tex Des) (IB 26 pts)
East London – 112 pts+portfolio (Fash Des) (IB 24 pts HL 15 pts)
Hertfordshire – BBC–BBB incl art/des 112–120 pts+portfolio (Fash Fash Bus)
Leeds Beckett – 112 pts (Fash)
Liverpool John Moores – BBC 112 pts+portfolio (Fash Des Comm)
London Met – BBC 112 pts+interview+portfolio (Fash)
Middlesex – BBC 112 pts+portfolio (Fash; Fash Comm Styl)
Northampton – BBC (Fash Mark Prom)
Northern SA – 112 pts+interview+portfolio (Tex Surf Des)
Northumbria – 112 pts+portfolio (Fash; Fash Des Mark)
Nottingham Trent – 112 pts+portfolio (Fash Des; Fash Kntwr Des Knit Tex; Tex Des); BBC 112–120 pts (Fash Comm Prom; Fash Mark Brnd)
Portsmouth – BBC–BBB 112–120 pts (Fash Des) (IB 25 pts); BBC–BBB 112–120 pts (Fash Mark) (IB 29 pts)
Sheffield Hallam – BBC incl art/des/des tech/tex/graph 112 pts+portfolio (Fash Des)
Staffordshire – BBC 112–120 pts (Fash)
UWE Bristol – 112 pts+portfolio (Fash Comm)
West London – BBC 112 pts (Fash Ind Brnd Mark; Fash Prom Imag)

104 pts **Bath Spa** – BCC–BBB incl B tex/art/des 104–120 pts+interview+portfolio (Tex Des) (IB 32 pts HL 5 art); BCC–BBB incl B tex/art/des 104–120 pts+portfolio (Fash Des) (IB 28 pts HL 5 art)
Brighton – BCC–BBB 104–120 pts (Fash Des Hist) (IB 26 pts); BCC–BBB 104–120 pts+portfolio (Fash Des Bus St) (IB 30 pts)
Derby – BCC–BBC 104–112 pts+portfolio (Fash Des)
Falmouth – 104–120 pts+interview+portfolio (Fash Des; Fash Photo; Tex Des)
Greater Manchester – 104 pts+interview+portfolio (Spec Mkup FX Flm TV)
Heriot-Watt – BCC (Fash Brnd Prom) (IB 29 pts); BCC+portfolio (Fash) (IB 29 pts); BCC incl Engl+interview (Des Text) (IB 29 pts)
Huddersfield – BCC–BBB 104–120 pts+interview+portfolio (Cstm Tex); BCC–BBB 104 pts+interview+portfolio (Fash Mark)
Leeds Arts – 104–120 pts (Fash Mark); 104–120 pts+portfolio (Fash Des)
Manchester Met – BCC–BBC 104–112 pts (Fash Buy Mrchnds) (IB 26 pts); BCC–BBC 104–112 pts+portfolio (Fash; Fash Des Tech; Tex Prac) (IB 26 pts)
Northampton – BCC+interview+portfolio (Fash Text Ftwr Accs)
Norwich Arts – BCC+portfolio (Fash; Tex Des) (IB 26 pts)
Plymouth (AU) – 104–120 pts+portfolio (Fash Des; Fash Media Mark)
Queen Margaret – BCC+portfolio (Cstm Des Constr) (IB 28 pts)
Robert Gordon – BCC (Fash Mgt) (IB 27 pts)
Salford – 104–112 pts incl art des+interview+portfolio (Fash Des) (IB 31 pts incl art/des)
Solent – 104–120 pts (Fash Mgt Mark); 104–120 pts+portfolio (Fash Des; Fash Styl Crea Dir)
Sunderland – 104–120 pts+interview (Fash Jrnl)
Ulster – BCC–BBB 104–120 pts+portfolio (Tex Art Des Fash) (IB 24 pts HL 12 pts)
Westminster – BCC 104 pts (Fash Bus Mgt Prof Expnc)
Winchester – BCC–BBB 104–120 pts (Fash Bus Mark) (HL 44)

96 pts **Anglia Ruskin** – 96 pts incl art/des/media+portfolio (Fash Des) (IB 24 pts)
Bedfordshire – 96 pts+portfolio (Fash Des)

Cardiff Met – CCC–BBB 96–120 pts+interview+portfolio (Tex Des) (IB 24 pts)
Central Lancashire – 96 pts+portfolio (Fash Prom Mark)
Greater Manchester – 96 pts incl art/des+interview+portfolio (Commer Surf Des)
Hereford (CA) – 96–112 pts+portfolio (Jewel Des; Tex Des)
London Met – CCC 96 pts (Fash Mark Bus Mgt)
South Wales – BCC 96 pts (Fash Prom); CCC incl art/des 96 pts (Fash Des)
Sunderland – 96–112 pts+portfolio+interview (Fash Des Prom)
Teesside – 96–112 pts+portfolio (Fash)

88 pts **Bucks New** – 88–112 pts+interview+portfolio (Fash Des)

80 pts **Bradford College (UC)** – 80 pts+interview+portfolio (Fash)
West London – 80 pts+portfolio (Fash Des Accs)

64 pts **Arts London** – 64 pts+interview+portfolio (Fash Des (Mnswr)) (IB 24 pts)
London (Royal Central Sch SpDr) – 64–120 pts+interview+portfolio (Cstm Constr)
Ravensbourne Univ – CC+interview+portfolio (Fash; Fash Prom Comms) (IB 24 pts)
Robert Gordon – CC incl art/des+Engl+interview+portfolio (Fash Tex Des) (IB 24 pts HL vis arts+Engl)

ALTERNATIVE OFFERS See **Chapter 6** and **Appendix 1** for grades/UCAS Tariff points information for other examinations.

EXAMPLES OF COLLEGES OFFERING COURSES IN THIS SUBJECT FIELD

Barnet and Southgate (Coll); Barnfield (Coll); Basingstoke (CT); Bath (Coll); Blackburn (Coll); Blackpool and Fylde (Coll); Bournemouth and Poole (Coll); Bradford College (UC); Central Bedfordshire (Coll); Central Campus, Sandwell (Coll); Chelmsford (Coll); City and Islington (Coll); Doncaster (Coll); Dudley (Coll); East Coast (Coll); Gloucestershire (Coll); Havering (Coll); Hull (Coll); Leicester (Coll); Liverpool City (Coll); Newcastle (Coll); North Warwickshire and South Leicestershire (Coll); Rotherham (CAT); Sir Gâr (Coll); South City Birmingham (Coll); South Essex (Coll); South Gloucestershire and Stroud (Coll); South Thames (Coll); Southwark (Coll); Tresham (CFHE); Walsall (Coll); West Herts (Coll); Wigan and Leigh (Coll); York (Coll).

CHOOSING YOUR COURSE (SEE ALSO CH.1)

UNIVERSITIES AND COLLEGES TEACHING QUALITY See www.qaa.ac.uk; www.discoveruni.gov.uk.

TOP RESEARCH UNIVERSITIES AND COLLEGES (REF 2021) See **Art and Design (General)**.

EXAMPLES OF SANDWICH DEGREE COURSES Anglia Ruskin; Arts London; Bath Spa; Bedfordshire; Birmingham City; Brighton; Central Lancashire; Coventry; Creative Arts; De Montfort; East London; Hertfordshire; Huddersfield; Kingston; Leeds; Loughborough; Manchester Met; Northumbria; Nottingham Trent; Portsmouth; Robert Gordon; Solent; South Wales; Ulster; Westminster.

ADMISSIONS INFORMATION

ADVICE TO APPLICANTS AND PLANNING THE UCAS PERSONAL STATEMENT A well-written statement is sought, clearly stating an interest in fashion and how prior education and work experience relate to your application. You should describe any visits to exhibitions and, importantly, your views and opinions. Describe any work you have done ('making' and 'doing' skills, if any, for example, pattern cutting, sewing) or work observation in textile firms, fashion houses, even visits to costume departments in theatres can be useful. These contacts and visits should be described in detail, showing your knowledge of the types of fabrics and production processes. Give opinions on trends in haute couture, and show awareness of the work of others. Provide evidence of materials handling (see also **Appendix 3**). Show good knowledge of the contemporary fashion scene. See also **Art and Design (Graphic Design)**.

SELECTION INTERVIEWS Yes Arts London, Bath Spa (Text Des), Bradford College (UC), Falmouth, Greater Manchester, Huddersfield, Northampton, Northern SA, Ravensbourne Univ; **Some** Salford, UWE Bristol; **No** West London.

Interview advice and questions Questions mostly originate from student's portfolio. See also **Art and Design (General)** and **Chapter 5**.

Reasons for rejection (non-academic) Portfolio work not up to standard. Not enough research. Not articulate at interview. Lack of sense of humour, and inflexibility. Narrow perspective. Lack of resourcefulness, self-motivation and organisation. Complacency, lack of verbal, written and self-presentation skills. Not enough experience in designing or making clothes. See also **Art and Design (General)**.

GRADUATE DESTINATIONS AND EMPLOYMENT

(See **Chapter 1, Graduate Outcomes.**)

Career note See **Art and Design (General)**.

OTHER DEGREE SUBJECTS FOR CONSIDERATION

History of Art; Retail Management; Theatre Design.

ART AND DESIGN (FINE ART)

(including **Painting and Printmaking and Sculpture and Environmental Art**; see also **Art and Design (Graphic Design), Photography**)

Fine Art courses are essentially practice-based courses encouraging students to find their own direction through additional intellectual and theoretical studies. The work will involve a range of activities which cover painting, illustration and sculpture. Additional studies can also involve electronic media, film, video, photography and print, although course options will vary between institutions. A more specialised study in the field of Sculpture and Environmental Art is offered at Glasgow School of Art, taking sculpture outside art galleries and museums and into the public domain where students focus on drawing, wood and metal fabrication, photography, video, computers and sound. As in the case of most Art degrees, admission to courses usually requires a one-year Foundation Art course before applying.

Useful websites www.artcyclopedia.com; www.nationalgallery.org.uk; www.britisharts.co.uk; www.tate.org.uk; www.creativefuture.org.uk; www.a-n.co.uk/news; www.artscouncil.org.uk

NB The points totals shown to the left of the institutions are for ease of reference only. It must not be assumed that Tariff points are always used by institutions or that they can be substituted for an offer in grades. The level of an offer is not necessarily indicative of the quality of a course.

COURSE OFFERS INFORMATION

Subject requirements/preferences See **Art and Design (General)**. Some popular universities are now making lower offers for disadvantaged and other students.

Your target offers and examples of degree courses

144 pts **Oxford** – AAA+interview+portfolio (Fn Art) (IB 38 pts HL 666)

128 pts **Derby** – ABB 128 pts+portfolio (Fn Art)

Dundee – ABB incl art/des+interview+portfolio (Fn Art) (IB 32 pts HL 655 incl art/des)

Edinburgh – ABB+portfolio (Fn Art; Illus) (IB 34 pts HL 655)

Glasgow (SA) – ABB+portfolio (Fn Art Photo); (Pntg Prtg; Sculp Env Art) (IB 30 pts HL 18 pts incl Engl+maths)

Lancaster – ABB+portfolio (Fn Art) (IB 32 pts HL 16 pts)

Leeds – ABB–BBB+aEPQ+portfolio (Fn Art) (IB 34 pts HL 16 pts incl Engl)

London (UCL) – ABB+interview+portfolio (Fn Art) (IB 34 pts HL 16 pts)

Loughborough – ABB+interview+portfolio (Fn Art) (IB 34 pts HL 655)

120 pts **Kingston** – 120–136 pts+portfolio (Fn Art)

Newcastle – BBB–AAB+interview+portfolio (Fn Art) (IB 30–34 pts HL 555)

Reading – BBB+portfolio (Art courses; Fn Art) (IB 30 pts)
Southampton (Winchester SA) – BBB+portfolio (Fn Art) (IB 30 pts HL 15 pts)
Trinity Saint David – 120 pts+interview+portfolio (Fn Art (Std Site Con)) (IB 32 pts)

112 pts **Birmingham City** – BBC 112 pts+portfolio (Fn Art) (IB 28 pts)
Bournemouth Arts – BBC–BBB 112–120 pts+portfolio (Fn Art)
Coventry – BBC+portfolio (Fn Art) (IB 29 pts)
Creative Arts – 112 pts+portfolio (Fn Art courses) (IB 27–30 pts HL 15 pts)
De Montfort – 112 pts+portfolio (Fn Art) (IB 26 pts)
East London – BBC 112 pts+portfolio (Fn Art) (IB 24 pts HL 15 pts)
Leeds Beckett – 112 pts (Fn Art)
Liverpool John Moores – BBC 112 pts+interview+portfolio (Fn Art)
London Met – BBC 112 pts+interview+portfolio (Fn Art)
Middlesex – BBC 112 pts+portfolio (Fn Art)
Northumbria – 112 pts+portfolio (Fn Art)
Nottingham Trent – 112 pts+portfolio+interview (Fn Art)
Oxford Brookes – BBC+interview+portfolio (Fn Art) (IB 30 pts)
Sheffield Hallam – BBC 112 pts incl art/des+interview+portfolio (Fn Art)
Staffordshire – BBC–BBB 112–120 pts+portfolio (Fn Art)
UWE Bristol – 112 pts+portfolio+interview (Fn Art)
Worcester – BBC 112 pts+portfolio (Fn Art Psy)

104 pts **Aberystwyth** – BCC–BBB incl art 104–120 pts+portfolio (Fn Art; Fn Art Art Hist) (IB 28–30 pts)
Bath Spa – BCC–BBB incl art/des 104–120 pts+interview+portfolio (Fn Art) (IB 32 pts HL 5 art)
Brighton – BCC–BBB 104–120 pts+portfolio (Fn Art; Fn Art Pntg) (IB 30 pts)
Chester – BCC–BBC+interview+portfolio (Fn Art) (IB 28 pts)
Cumbria – BCC–BBC 104–112 pts+interview+portfolio (Fn Art)
Falmouth – 104–120 pts+interview+portfolio (Fn Art)
Huddersfield – 104–112 pts+portfolio (Fn Art)
Leeds Arts – 104–120 pts+portfolio (Fn Art)
Lincoln – 104 pts+interview+portfolio (Fn Art) (IB 28 pts)
Liverpool Hope – BCC 104 pts+portfolio (Fn Art) (IB 24 pts)
Manchester Met – BCC–BBC 104–112 pts+portfolio (Fn Art) (IB 26 pts)
Northampton – BCC incl art+interview+portfolio (Fn Art; Fn Art Pntg Drg)
Norwich Arts – BCC+portfolio (Fn Art) (IB 26 pts)
Plymouth (AU) – 104–112 pts+portfolio (Fn Art)
Salford – 104–112 pts+interview+portfolio (Fn Art) (IB 31 pts)
Solent – 104–120 pts+portfolio (Fn Art)
Worcester – BCC 104 pts+portfolio (Fn Art)
York St John – 104 pts+interview+portfolio (Fn Art)

96 pts **Anglia Ruskin** – 96 pts+portfolio (Fn Art)
Bedfordshire – 96 pts+portfolio (Art Des)
Cardiff Met – CCC–BBB 96–120 pts+interview+portfolio (Fn Art) (IB 24 pts)
Central Lancashire – 96 pts+portfolio (Fn Art)
Chichester – CCC–BBB incl art/photo/tex 96–120 pts+interview+portfolio (Fn Art courses) (IB 28 pts HL 5 vis arts)
Gloucestershire – CCC–BBB 96–120 pts+interview (Fn Art)
Hereford (CA) – 96–112 pts+portfolio (Fn Art)
Plymouth – 96–144 pts+portfolio (Fn Art) (IB 26 pts)
Sunderland – BBC 96–112 pts+portfolio+interview (Fn Art)
Teesside – 96–112 pts+portfolio (Fn Art)
Ulster – CCC+portfolio (Fn Art) (IB 24 pts HL 12 pts)
Westminster – CCC–BBB 96–120 pts+portfolio (Fn Art Mix Media)
Wolverhampton – CCC/BCD 96 pts+portfolio (Fn Art)
Wrexham – 96–112 pts+portfolio+interview (Fn Art)

64 pts **Arts London (Central St Martins)** – 64–80 pts+portfolio (Fn Art) (IB 24 pts)
Colchester (UC) – 64 pts+interview+portfolio (Fn Art)

Robert Gordon – CC incl art/des+portfolio+interview (Fn Art) (IB 24 pts)
UHI – CC+interview+portfolio (Fn Art)
40 pts **London (Gold)** – 40 pts+art fnd+interview+portfolio (Fn Art)

Alternative offers See **Chapter 6** and **Appendix 1** for grades/UCAS Tariff points information for other examinations.

EXAMPLES OF COLLEGES OFFERING COURSES IN THIS SUBJECT FIELD

Bath (Coll); Blackpool and Fylde (Coll); Bradford College (UC); Bury (Coll); City and Islington (Coll); City of Oxford (Coll); Cornwall (Coll); Craven (Coll); Doncaster (Coll); Exeter (Coll); Grŵp Llandrillo Menai; Harrogate (Coll); Havering (Coll); Leicester (Coll); Liverpool City (Coll); Newcastle (Coll); Sheffield (Coll); South Gloucestershire and Stroud (Coll); St Helens (Coll); Stamford (Coll); Sunderland (Coll); TEC Partnership; Tyne Coast (Coll); Weymouth (Coll).

CHOOSING YOUR COURSE (SEE ALSO CH.1)

Universities and colleges teaching quality See www.qaa.ac.uk; www.discoveruni.gov.uk.

Top research universities and colleges (REF 2021) See **Art and Design (General)**.

Examples of sandwich degree courses Anglia Ruskin; Bath Spa; Bedfordshire; Coventry; Creative Arts; Lancaster; Manchester Met; Northumbria; Oxford Brookes; Plymouth; Sheffield Hallam; Westminster.

ADMISSIONS INFORMATION

Advice to applicants and planning the UCAS personal statement Since this is a subject area that can be researched easily in art galleries, you should discuss not only your own style of work and your preferred subjects but also your opinions on various art forms, styles and periods. Keep up to date with public opinion on controversial issues. Give your reasons for wishing to pursue a course in Fine Art. Visits to galleries and related hobbies, for example reading, cinema, music, literature should be mentioned. Show the nature of your external involvement in art. (See also **Appendix 3**.)

Selection interviews Yes Bath Spa, Cardiff Met, Chester, Chichester, Cumbria, Falmouth, Greater Manchester, Lincoln, Liverpool John Moores, London (Gold), London (UCL), London Met, Loughborough, Newcastle, Oxford, Oxford Brookes, Plymouth, Robert Gordon, Salford, Sheffield Hallam, Sunderland, UHI, Wrexham, York St John; **Some** Brighton, Dundee, Nottingham Trent, UWE Bristol; **No** De Montfort, Kent.

Interview advice and questions Questions asked on portfolio of work. Be prepared to answer questions on your stated opinions on your UCAS application and on current art trends and controversial topics reported in the press. Discussion covering the applicant's engagement with contemporary fine art practice. Visits to exhibitions, galleries etc. Ambitions for their own work. How do you perceive the world in a visual sense? Who is your favourite living artist and why? See also **Art and Design (General)** and **Chapter 5**.

Reasons for rejection (non-academic) Lack of a fine art specialist portfolio. No intellectual grasp of the subject – only interested in techniques.

GRADUATE DESTINATIONS AND EMPLOYMENT

(See **Chapter 1, Graduate Outcomes.**)

Career note See **Art and Design (General)**.

OTHER DEGREE SUBJECTS FOR CONSIDERATION

Art Gallery Management; History of Art; see other **Art and Design** tables.

ART AND DESIGN (GRAPHIC DESIGN)

(including **Advertising, Animation, Design, Graphic Communication, Illustration and Visual Communication**; see also **Art and Design (Fine Art), Art and Design (General), Film, Radio and TV Studies**)

Graphic Design ranges from the design of websites, books, magazines and newspapers to packaging and advertisements. Visual communication uses symbols as teaching aids and also includes TV graphics. An Art Foundation course is usually taken before entry to degree courses. Graphic Design students are probably the most fortunate in terms of the range of career opportunities open to them on graduation. These include advertising, animation, book and magazine illustration, film, interactive media design, typography, packaging, photography and work in publishing and television. Courses cover the essential element of creative thinking alongside the normal industrial practices of scriptwriting, character design, storyboarding, animation, and sound design.

Useful websites www.graphic-design.com; www.creativefuture.org.uk; www.designcouncil.org.uk

NB The points totals shown to the left of the institutions are for ease of reference only. It must not be assumed that Tariff points are always used by institutions or that they can be substituted for an offer in grades. The level of an offer is not necessarily indicative of the quality of a course.

COURSE OFFERS INFORMATION

Subject requirements/preferences See **Art and Design (General)**. Some popular universities are now making lower offers for disadvantaged and other students.

Your target offers and examples of degree courses

136 pts **Dundee** – AAB+interview+portfolio (Graph Des) (IB 32 pts HL 655)

128 pts **Dundee** – ABB incl art des+interview+portfolio (Animat) (IB 32 pts HL 655)

Edinburgh – ABB+portfolio (Graph Des) (IB 34 pts HL 655)

Leeds – ABB incl art/des/media/portfolio (Graph Comm Des) (IB 34 pts HL 16 pts incl 5 vis arts+4 Engl)

Loughborough – ABB+portfolio (Graph Des) (IB 34 pts HL 655)

120 pts **Brunel** – BBB+portfolio (Vis Efcts Mtn Graph) (IB 30 pts)

Kingston – 120–136 pts incl art/des+portfolio (Graph Des)

Portsmouth – BBB–ABB (Vrtl Prod)

Reading – BBB+portfolio (Graph Comm) (IB 30 pts)

Southampton (Winchester SA) – BBB incl art/des+portfolio (Graph Comm) (IB 30 pts HL 15 pts incl art/des)

Trinity Saint David – BBB 120 pts+interview+portfolio (Animat Vis Efcts; Graph Des; Illus) (IB 32 pts)

112 pts **Birmingham City** – BBC+portfolio 112 pts (Graph Des) (IB 28 pts); BBC 112 pts+portfolio (Vis Efcts) (IB 28 pts)

Bournemouth Arts – BBB 112–120 pts+portfolio (Comm Des Strat); BBC–BBB 112–120 pts+portfolio (Animat Prod; Graph Des; Illus)

Canterbury Christ Church – BBC 112 pts+portfolio (Graph Des) (IB 29 pts)

Coventry – BBC+interview+portfolio (Graph Des) (IB 29 pts); BBC incl art/des+interview+ portfolio (Animat; Illus) (IB 29 pts HL vis arts/des tech)

Creative Arts – 112 pts+interview+portfolio (Animat; Graph Des) (IB 27–30 pts HL 15 pts)

Derby – BBC 112 pts+portfolio (Graph Des)

East London – 112 pts+interview+portfolio (Graph Des) (IB 24 pts HL 15 pts); 112 pts+portfolio (Animat) (IB 24 pts HL 15 pts)

Edge Hill – BBC–BBB 112–120 pts+portfolio+interview (Animat)

Greenwich – 112 pts+interview+portfolio (Graph Dig Des)

Hertfordshire – BBC–BBB 112–120 pts+interview+portfolio (Graph Des) (HL vis arts); BBC–BBB incl art/des 112–120 pts+interview (2D Dig Animat; 3D Animat Vis Efcts)

Hull – BBC 112 pts (Graph Des) (IB 28 pts)
Kent – BBC (Dig Des) (HL 655)
Leeds Arts – BBC incl art/des 112 pts+portfolio (Vis Comm)
Liverpool John Moores – BBC incl art/des 112 pts+interview+portfolio (Graph Des Illus)
London Met – BBC 112 pts+interview+portfolio (Graph Des)
Middlesex – BBC 112 pts+portfolio (Animat; Graph Des; Illus)
Northumbria – 112 pts+portfolio (Graph Des)
Nottingham Trent – BBC 112 pts+portfolio (Graph Des)
Oxford Brookes – BBC 112 pts+portfolio+interview (Graph Des) (IB 30 pts)
Portsmouth – BBC–BBB 112–120 pts+interview+portfolio (Illus) (IB 25 pts); BBC–BBB 112–120 pts+portfolio (Graph Des) (IB 25 pts); BBC–BBB 112–120 pts+portfolio (Animat) (IB 25 pts)
Sheffield Hallam – BBC 112 pts+portfolio (Animat); BBC 112 pts+portfolio (Graph Des)
Staffordshire – BBC 112 pts+portfolio (Crtn Cmc Arts; Graph Des; Illus)
Suffolk – BBC+portfolio (Graph Des); BBC 112 pts+portfolio (Graph Des (Graph Illus))
UWE Bristol – 112 pts+interview+portfolio (Animat; Graph Des)

104 pts **Bath Spa** – BCC–BBB incl art/des 104–120 pts+interview+portfolio (Graph Des) (IB 32 pts HL 5 art)
Brighton – BCC–BBB 104–120 pts+portfolio (Graph Des) (IB 30 pts)
Chester – BCC–BBC+interview+portfolio (Graph Des) (IB 28 pts HL 5 vis arts)
Chichester – BCC–BBC 104–112 pts+portfolio (3D Anim Vis Efcts) (IB 28 pts)
Cumbria – BCC–BBC 104–112 pts+interview+portfolio (Graph Des; Illus)
De Montfort – 104 pts incl art des+portfolio (Animat; Graph Des; Graph Des (Illus)) (IB 24 pts HL 5 art des)
Derby – BCC–BBC 104–112 pts+portfolio (Animat)
Falmouth – 104–120 pts+interview+portfolio (Animat; Graph Des; Illus)
Gloucestershire – BCC 104 pts (Mark (Adv Brnd))
Huddersfield – BCC–BBB 104–120 pts+interview+portfolio (Graph Des); BCC–BBC 104–112 pts+interview+portfolio (Illus); BCC–BBC 104–120 pts+interview+portfolio (Graph Des Animat)
Leeds Arts – 104–120 pts (Graph Des); 104–120 pts+portfolio (Animat)
Lincoln – 104 pts (Animat Vis Efcts; Graph Des; Illus) (IB 28 pts)
Liverpool Hope – BCC 104 pts+portfolio (Graph Des) (IB 24 pts)
Manchester Met – BCC–BBC 104–112 pts+portfolio (Graph Des; Illus Animat) (IB 26 pts)
Northampton – BCC 104 pts+interview+portfolio (Graph Comm Des; Illus)
Norwich Arts – BCC+interview+portfolio (Animat; Graph Comm; Graph Des; Illus) (IB 26 pts); BCC 104 pts+portfolio (Flm Mov Imag Prod) (IB 26 pts)
Plymouth (AU) – 104–120 pts+portfolio (Graph Des; Illus)
Solent – 104–120 pts+interview+portfolio (Graph Des); 104–120 pts incl art des+portfolio (Animat)
South Wales – BCC 104 pts (Adv)
Ulster – BCC 104 pts+portfolio (Animat) (IB 24 pts HL 12 pts)
Worcester – BCC 104 pts (Animat courses)
York St John – 104 pts+portfolio (Graph Des)

96 pts **Anglia Ruskin** – 96 pts incl art/des/media+portfolio (Animat Illus; Illus) (IB 24 pts)
Bedfordshire – 96 pts (Animat; Graph Des)
Cardiff Met – 96–120 pts+interview+portfolio (Graph Des Comm) (IB 24 pts)
Central Lancashire – 96 pts+portfolio (Animat; Graph Des)
Derby – CCC 96 pts+portfolio (Illus)
Edinburgh Napier – CCC incl art des/des tech+portfolio (Graph Des) (IB 27 pts HL 654 incl vis art/des tech)
Gloucestershire – CCC–BBB 96–120 pts+interview (Graph Des)
Greater Manchester – 96 pts incl art/des+interview+portfolio (Animat Illus)
Hereford (CA) – 96–112 pts+portfolio (Graph Media Des; Illus)
Plymouth – 96–120 pts+interview+portfolio (Graph Des) (IB 26–28 pts); 96–120 pts+portfolio (Gm Arts Des) (IB 28 pts)

Robert Gordon – CCC (Gms Des) (IB 26 pts)
South Wales – CCC incl art des 96 pts+interview+portfolio (Graph Comm)
Sunderland – 96–112 pts+interview+portfolio (Graph Des; Illus Des)
Teesside – 96–112 pts+portfolio (Animat; Gms Art; Graph Des)
Ulster – CCC+portfolio (Graph Des) (IB 24 pts HL 12 pts)
Westminster – CCC 96 pts+portfolio (Gms Art); CCC–BBB 96–120 pts+portfolio (Animat; Graph Des; Illus)
Wolverhampton – CCC/BCD 96 pts+portfolio (Graph Des)
Wrexham – 96–112 pts+interview+portfolio (Graph Des); 96–112 pts+interview/portfolio (Comics; Illus)

88 pts **Bucks New** – 88–112 pts (Animat); 88–112 pts+interview+portfolio (Crea Adv; Graph Des)
West Scotland – CDD incl art des/photo/graphs 88 pts+portfolio (Comp Animat Arts) (IB 24 pts incl art)

64 pts **Arts London (Camberwell CA)** – CC+portfolio (Graph Des) (IB 24 pts)
Ravensbourne Univ – CC+interview+portfolio (Adv Brnd Des; Animat; Graph Des; Mtn Graph) (IB 24 pts)

40 pts **Arden** – 40 pts+portfolio (Graph Des)

Alternative offers See **Chapter 6** and **Appendix 1** for grades/UCAS Tariff points information for other examinations.

DEGREE APPRENTICESHIPS

Manchester Met (Crea Dig Des); Middlesex (Dig Des); Sheffield Hallam (Crea Dig Des).

EXAMPLES OF COLLEGES OFFERING COURSES IN THIS SUBJECT FIELD

Banbury and Bicester (Coll); Barking and Dagenham (Coll); Barnet and Southgate (Coll); Birmingham Met (Coll); Blackburn (Coll); Bristol City (Coll); Bury (Coll); Canterbury (Coll); Cornwall (Coll); Craven (Coll); Doncaster (Coll); Durham New (Coll); Exeter (Coll); Farnborough (CT); Gloucestershire (Coll); Harlow (Coll); Havering (Coll); Hugh Baird (Coll); Kirklees (Coll); Leicester (Coll); Milton Keynes (Coll); NCC Redbridge; Newcastle (Coll); Northern SA; Nottingham (Coll); Oldham (Coll); Rotherham (CAT); Sheffield (Coll); South Cheshire (Coll); South Gloucestershire and Stroud (Coll); Southport (Coll); St Helens (Coll); Stamford (Coll); Stockport (Coll); Truro and Penwith (Coll); Tyne Coast (Coll); West Suffolk (Coll); Weston (Coll); Wigan and Leigh (Coll); York (Coll).

CHOOSING YOUR COURSE (SEE ALSO CH.1)

Universities and colleges teaching quality See www.qaa.ac.uk; www.discoveruni.gov.uk.

Top research universities and colleges (REF 2021) See **Art and Design (General)**.

Examples of sandwich degree courses Anglia Ruskin; Bath Spa; Brunel; Central Lancashire; Coventry; Edge Hill; Hertfordshire; Huddersfield; Loughborough; Northumbria; Portsmouth; Teesside; Ulster; Wolverhampton.

ADMISSIONS INFORMATION

Advice to applicants and planning the UCAS personal statement Discuss your special interest in this field and any commercial applications that have impressed you. Discuss the work you are enjoying at present and the range of media that you have explored. Show your interests in travel, architecture, the arts, literature, film, current affairs (see also **Appendix 3** for contact details of relevant professional associations). Have an awareness of the place of design in society.

Selection interviews Yes Bath Spa, Bucks New (Crea Adv; Graph Des), Cardiff Met, Chester, Coventry, Creative Arts, Cumbria, East London (Graph Des), Falmouth, Gloucestershire, Greater Manchester, Greenwich, Hertfordshire, Leeds Beckett, Liverpool John Moores, London Met, Northampton, Norwich Arts, Oxford Brookes, Plymouth (Graph Des), Ravensbourne Univ, Sunderland, Trinity Saint David, Wrexham; **Some** Dundee, Edge Hill, Huddersfield, Salford, Solent (Graph Des), UWE Bristol, York St John; **No** De Montfort, Kingston, Northumbria, Portsmouth, West London.

Interview advice and questions Questions may be asked on recent trends in graphic design from the points of view of methods and designers and, particularly, art and the computer. Questions are usually asked on applicant's portfolio of work. See also **Art and Design (General)** and **Chapter 5**.

Reasons for rejection (non-academic) Not enough work in portfolio. Inability to think imaginatively. Lack of interest in the arts in general. Lack of drive. Tutor's statement indicating problems. Poorly constructed personal statement. Inability to talk about your work. Lack of knowledge about the chosen course. See also **Art and Design (General)**.

GRADUATE DESTINATIONS AND EMPLOYMENT

(See **Chapter 1, Graduate Outcomes.**)

Career note See **Art and Design (General)**.

OTHER DEGREE SUBJECTS FOR CONSIDERATION

Art Gallery Management; Film and Video Production; History of Art; Multimedia Design, Photography and Digital Imaging. See also other **Art and Design** tables.

ART AND DESIGN (INTERIOR, PRODUCT AND INDUSTRIAL DESIGN)

(including **Footwear Design, Furniture Design, Interior Design, Product Design, Product Design Technology, Theatre Design and Transport Design**; see also **Architecture, Art and Design (3D Design)**)

The field of industrial design is extensive and degree studies are usually preceded by an Art Foundation course. Product Design is one of the most common courses in which technological studies (involving materials and methods of production) are integrated with creative design in the production of a range of household and industrial products. Other courses on offer include Furniture Design, Interior, Theatre, Automotive and Transport Design. It should be noted that some Product Design courses have an engineering bias. Interior Design courses involve architectural considerations and courses will include aspects of building practices, materials, products and finishes. Historical studies of period designs and styles will also be included: see Subject requirements/preferences below. These are stimulating courses but graduate opportunities in this field are very limited. Good courses will have good industrial contacts for sandwich courses or shorter work placements – check with course leaders (or students) before applying.

Useful websites www.ergonomics.org.uk; www.creativefuture.org.uk; www.productdesignforums.com; www.carbodydesign.com; www.bild.org.uk; www.csd.org.uk; www.designcouncil.org.uk; www.theatredesign.org.uk

NB The points totals shown to the left of the institutions are for ease of reference only. It must not be assumed that Tariff points are always used by institutions or that they can be substituted for an offer in grades. The level of an offer is not necessarily indicative of the quality of a course.

COURSE OFFERS INFORMATION

Subject requirements/preferences Interior Architecture Design courses require an art portfolio. **AL** Check Product Design, Industrial Design and Engineering Design course requirements since these will often require mathematics and/or physics. Some popular universities are now making lower offers for disadvantaged and other students.

Your target offers and examples of degree courses

144 pts **Glasgow** – AAA incl maths+phys (Prod Des Eng (MEng)) (IB 38 pts HL 666 incl maths+phys)
Leeds – AAA+interview+portfolio (Prod Des) (IB 35 pts HL 18 pts)

128 pts **Brunel** – ABB+interview+portfolio (Ind Des) (IB 31 pts HL 4 Engl+maths); ABB incl maths/phys+interview+portfolio (Prod Des Eng) (IB 31 pts HL 5 maths/phys)

Dundee – ABB+portfolio (Inter Env Des) (IB 32 pts HL 655); (Prod Des) (IB 32 pts HL 655)
Edinburgh – ABB+portfolio (Inter Des; Prod Des) (IB 34 pts HL 655)
Glasgow (SA) – ABB+portfolio (Inter Des; Prod Des)
Loughborough – ABB+portfolio (Ind Des) (IB 34 pts HL 655); ABB incl maths/phys+portfolio (Prod Des Tech) (IB 34 pts HL 655 incl 5 maths/phys)
Nottingham – ABB incl maths (Prod Des Manuf) (IB 30 pts HL 655 incl maths)
Oxford Brookes – ABB 128 pts+portfolio+interview (Inter Archit) (IB 32 pts)

120 pts **Birmingham City** – BBB 120 pts+portfolio (Inter Archit Des) (IB 30 pts)
Bournemouth Arts – BBB 120 pts (Crea Dir; Inter Archit Des; Inter Archit Des Hlth Wlbng); BBB 120 pts+portfolio (Dig Tech Des; Sust Des)
Glasgow – BBB–AAB incl maths+phys (Prod Des Eng) (IB 34 pts HL 655 incl maths+phys)
Leeds Beckett – 120 pts (Prod Des); 120 pts+portfolio (Inter Archit)
London South Bank – BBB incl art/des+portfolio+interview (Prod Des)
Northumbria – 120 pts+portfolio (Inter Archit)
Strathclyde – BBB–AAB (Prod Des Eng (MEng)) (IB 32–36 pts HL 5 maths+phys); BBB–ABB incl maths/phys/des tech (Prod Des Innov) (IB 32–34 pts HL 5 maths/phys)
Sussex – BBB–ABB incl art/des+portfolio (Prod Des) (IB 32 pts HL vis arts/des tech)
Trinity Saint David – 120 pts+interview+portfolio (Auto Trans Des; Prod Furn Des) (IB 32 pts)
Westminster – BBB–AAB 120–136 pts+portfolio+interview (Inter Archit)

112 pts **Aston** – BBC incl sci/tech (Prod Des Innov) (IB 29 pts HL 554 incl sci/tech)
Birmingham City – BBC 112 pts+portfolio (Prod Des) (IB 28 pts)
Canterbury Christ Church – BBC 112 pts (Prod Des Eng) (IB 29 pts)
Coventry – BBC+portfolio+interview (Inter Archit Des; Prod Des) (IB 29 pts)
De Montfort – 112 pts+portfolio (Ftwr Des; Inter Des; Prod Des) (IB 26 pts)
East London – 112 pts incl art/des+interview+portfolio (Prod Des) (IB 24 pts HL 15 pts); 112 pts incl art/des+portfolio (Inter Des) (IB 24 pts HL 15 pts)
Hertfordshire – BBC–BBB incl art/des 112–120 pts+portfolio (Inter Archit Des)
Kingston – 112–128 pts incl art/des+portfolio (Inter Des); incl art/des 112–128 pts incl art/des+portfolio (Prod Furn Des)
London Met – BBC 112 pts+interview+portfolio (Inter Archit Des; Prod Furn Des)
Middlesex – BBC–BBB 112–120 pts+interview+portfolio (Inter Des)
Northumbria – 112 pts+portfolio (Furn Prod Des; Prod Des)
Nottingham Trent – 112 pts+interview+portfolio (Furn Prod Des; Prod Des); 112–120 pts+portfolio (Inter Archit Des)
Portsmouth – BBC–BBB 112–120 pts+portfolio (Inter Archit Des) (IB 25 pts); BBC–BBB 112–120 pts+portfolio (Prod Des Innov) (IB 29 pts)
Sheffield Hallam – BBC incl art/des/graph 112 pts+portfolio (Prod Des); BBC incl art/des 112 pts+portfolio (Inter Archit Des) (IB 28 pts)
UWE Bristol – 112 pts+portfolio+interview (Inter Des); 112 pts incl art/des tech+portfolio (Prod Des) (HL des tech/vis arts); 112 pts incl art/sci/maths/des tech+portfolio (Prod Des Tech) (HL maths/des tech/vis arts)

104 pts **Bournemouth** – 104–120 pts+interview+portfolio (Prod Des) (IB 28–31 pts)
Brighton – BCC–BBB inch tech 104–120 pts+portfolio (Prod Des) (IB 27 pts)
Chester – BCC–BBC incl art des/fn art/prod des/media/photo+interview+portfolio (Prod Des) (IB 28 pts)
Falmouth – 104–120 pts+interview+portfolio (Inter Des)
Huddersfield – BCC–BBB 104–120 pts+interview+portfolio (Inter Des)
Lincoln – 104 pts (Inter Archit Des; Prod Des) (IB 28 pts)
Manchester Met – BCC–BBC 104–112 pts+portfolio (Inter Des; Prod Des) (IB 26 pts)
Northampton – BCC+interview+portfolio (Inter Archit Spat Des; Prod Des)
Solent – 104–120 pts+portfolio+interview (Inter Des Decr)
York St John – 104 pts+interview (Prod Des); 104 pts+portfolio (Inter Des)

96 pts **Anglia Ruskin** – 96 pts incl art/des/media+portfolio (Inter Des) (IB 24 pts incl art/des/media)

Bangor – 96–128 pts incl des tech/art/eng+interview+portfolio (Prod Des)
Bedfordshire – 96 pts (Inter Archit Des)
Cardiff Met – CCC–BBB 96–120 pts+interview+portfolio (Prod Des) (IB 24 pts)
Central Lancashire – 96 pts+portfolio (Inter Des)
Edinburgh Napier – CCC incl art/prod des/des/tech+portfolio (Inter Spat Des; Prod Des) (IB 27 pts HL 654 incl art/prod des/des/tech)
Ravensbourne Univ – CCC+interview+portfolio (Inter Des Env Archit) (IB 24 pts)
Salford – 96–112 pts (Inter Des) (IB 31 pts incl art des/des tech)
South Wales – CCC incl art des 96 pts+portfolio (Inter Des)
Teesside – 96–112 pts+portfolio (Inter Des)
Ulster – CCC incl art des/tech des+portfolio (Des (Prod Ceram Silver Jewel))

64 pts **Liverpool (LIPA)** – CC 64 pts+interview (Thea Perf Des; Thea Prod Tech)
London (Royal Central Sch SpDr) – 64–120 pts+interview+portfolio (Ltg Des; Prod Ltg; Prop Mak; Scnc Pntg Stg Scrn; Set Constr Stg Scrn)
London Regent's – CC+interview+portfolio (Inter Des)
Ravensbourne Univ – CC+interview+portfolio (Prod Des) (IB 24 pts)

Alternative offers See **Chapter 6** and **Appendix 1** for grades/UCAS Tariff points information for other examinations.

DEGREE APPRENTICESHIPS

Bournemouth and Poole Coll (Prod Des Dev).

EXAMPLES OF COLLEGES OFFERING COURSES IN THIS SUBJECT FIELD

Banbury and Bicester (Coll); Barking and Dagenham (Coll); Bradford College (UC); Bury (Coll); Chichester (Coll); Doncaster (Coll); East Riding (Coll); Gloucestershire (Coll); Havering (Coll); Manchester (Coll); Moulton (Coll); Newcastle (Coll); North Warwickshire and South Leicestershire (Coll); South Essex (Coll); Stockport (Coll); Truro and Penwith (Coll); West Suffolk (Coll).

CHOOSING YOUR COURSE (SEE ALSO CH.1)

Universities and colleges teaching quality See www.qaa.ac.uk; www.discoveruni.gov.uk.

Top research universities and colleges (REF 2021) See **Art and Design (General)**.

Examples of sandwich degree courses Anglia Ruskin; Aston; Bournemouth; Brighton; Brunel; Coventry; De Montfort; Hertfordshire; Huddersfield; London South Bank; Loughborough; Manchester Met; Middlesex; Northumbria; Nottingham Trent; Portsmouth; Sheffield Hallam; South Wales; Staffordshire; Sussex; Teesside; UWE Bristol.

ADMISSIONS INFORMATION

Advice to applicants and planning the UCAS personal statement Your knowledge of design in all fields should be described, including any special interests you may have, for example in domestic, rail and road aspects of design, and visits to exhibitions, motor shows. **School/college reference:** Tutors should make it clear that the applicant's knowledge, experience and attitude match the chosen course – not simply higher education in general. Admissions tutors look for knowledge of interior design and interior architecture, experience in three-dimensional design projects (which include problem-solving and sculptural demands), model-making experience in diverse materials, experience with two-dimensional illustration and colour work, and computer skills. Knowledge of computer-aided design (CAD) and photography is also helpful. See also **Art and Design (Graphic Design)**.

Selection interviews Yes Bangor, Bournemouth, Brunel, Cardiff Met, Chester, Falmouth, Huddersfield, Liverpool (LIPA), London (Royal Central Sch SpDr), London Met, London Regent's, Middlesex, Northampton, Nottingham Trent, Oxford Brookes, Ravensbourne Univ, Solent, Trinity Saint David, Westminster; **Some** Coventry, Dundee, London South Bank, Northumbria, Salford, South Wales, UWE Bristol; **No** De Montfort.

Interview advice and questions Applicants' portfolios of artwork form an important talking-point throughout the interview. Applicants should be able to discuss examples of current design and new developments in the field and answer questions on the aspects of industrial design which interest them. See also **Art and Design (General)** and **Chapter 5**.

Reasons for rejection (non-academic) Mature students without formal qualifications may not be able to demonstrate the necessary mathematical or engineering skills. Poor quality and organisation of portfolio. Lack of interest. Inappropriate dress. Lack of enthusiasm. Insufficient portfolio work (eg exercises instead of projects). Lack of historical knowledge of interior design. Weak oral communication. See also **Art and Design (General)**.

GRADUATE DESTINATIONS AND EMPLOYMENT

(See **Chapter 1, Graduate Outcomes.**)

Career note See **Art and Design (General)**.

OTHER DEGREE SUBJECTS FOR CONSIDERATION

Architectural Studies; Architecture; Art Gallery Management; Design (Manufacturing Systems); History of Art; Manufacturing Engineering; Multimedia and Communication Design and subjects in other **Art and Design** tables.

ART AND DESIGN (3D DESIGN)

(including **Ceramics, Design Crafts, Glass and Ceramics, Jewellery and Metalwork, Modelmaking and Silversmithing and Jewellery**; see also **Art and Design (General), Art and Design (Interior, Product And Industrial Design)**)

This field covers a range of specialisations which are involved in the manufacture of products in metal, ceramics, glass and wood, and also digital design. Some courses approach the study in a broad, comprehensive manner while other universities offer specialised courses in subjects such as Silversmithing and Jewellery (Glasgow School of Art and Sheffield Hallam), or Glass and Ceramics (University of Sunderland). The Birmingham City University course in Horology is the only course in the UK offering the study of time measurement and watches and clocks, both mechanical and electronic.

Useful websites www.ergonomics.org.uk; www.creativefuture.org.uk; www.glassassociation.org.uk; www.naj.co.uk; www.cpaceramics.com; www.ccskills.org.uk; www.dandad.org; www.designcouncil.org.uk

NB The points totals shown to the left of the institutions are for ease of reference only. It must not be assumed that Tariff points are always used by institutions or that they can be substituted for an offer in grades. The level of an offer is not necessarily indicative of the quality of a course.

COURSE OFFERS INFORMATION

Subject requirements/preferences See **Art and Design (General)**. Some popular universities are now making lower offers for disadvantaged and other students.

Your target offers and examples of degree courses

128 pts **Dundee** – ABB+portfolio (Jewel Metal Des) (IB 32 pts HL 655)
Edinburgh – ABB+portfolio (Jewel Silver) (IB 34 pts HL 655)
Glasgow (SA) – ABB+portfolio (Silver Jewel) (IB 30 pts HL 18 incl HL 5 Engl)

112 pts **Birmingham City** – BBC 112 pts+interview (Horol) (IB 28 pts); BBC 112 pts+portfolio (Jewel Objs) (IB 28 pts)
Bournemouth Arts – BBC–BBB 112–120 pts+portfolio (Modl) (HL 555)
Creative Arts – 112 pts+portfolio (Jewel Silver) (IB 27–30 pts HL 15 pts)
De Montfort – 112 pts+portfolio (Des Crfts) (IB 26 pts)

Hertfordshire – BBC–BBB incl art/des 112–120 pts+interview (3D Animat Vis Efcts)
Sunderland – BBC 112 pts+interview+portfolio (Arst Des Mak Gls Ceram)
104 pts **Greater Manchester** – 104 pts incl art/des+interview+portfolio (Spec Efcts Modl Flm TV)
96 pts **Cardiff Met** – CCC–BBB 96–120 pts+interview+portfolio (Ceram) (IB 24 pts)
Hereford (CA) – 96–112 pts+interview+portfolio (Arst Blksmthg); 96–112 pts+portfolio (Jewel Des)
Ulster – CCC incl art des/tech des+portfolio (Des (Prod Ceram Silver Jewel))
Wrexham – 96–112 pts+interview+portfolio (App Art)
64 pts **Robert Gordon** – CC incl art/des/des tech+Engl/hist+interview+portfolio (Prod Ceram Jewel) (IB 24 pts HL vis arts+Engl/hist)
Rose Bruford (Coll) – CC 64 pts+portfolio (Crea Ltg Contr)

Alternative offers See **Chapter 6** and **Appendix 1** for grades/UCAS Tariff points information for other examinations.

DEGREE APPRENTICESHIPS

Manchester Met (Crea Dig Des); Middlesex (Dig Des); Teesside (Crea Dig Des).

EXAMPLES OF COLLEGES OFFERING COURSES IN THIS SUBJECT FIELD

Barking and Dagenham (Coll); Bedford (Coll); Havering (Coll); Sir Gâr (Coll); York (Coll).

CHOOSING YOUR COURSE (SEE ALSO CH.1)

Universities and colleges teaching quality See www.qaa.ac.uk; www.discoveruni.gov.uk.

Top research universities and colleges (REF 2021) See **Art and Design (General)**.

Examples of sandwich degree courses Creative Arts; Hertfordshire.

ADMISSIONS INFORMATION

Advice to applicants and planning the UCAS personal statement Describe your art studies and your experience of different types of materials used. Discuss your special interest in your chosen field. Compare your work with that of professional artists and designers and describe your visits to museums, art galleries, exhibitions etc. Portfolios of recent work should demonstrate drawing skills, visual awareness, creativity and innovation, showing examples of three-dimensional work in photographic or model form. See also **Art and Design (Graphic Design)**.

Selection interviews Yes Birmingham City, Cardiff Met, De Montfort, Greater Manchester, Hereford (CA), Robert Gordon, Sunderland; **Some** Dundee.

Interview advice and questions Questions focus on the artwork presented in the student's portfolio. See also **Art and Design (General)** and **Chapter 5**.

Reasons for rejection (non-academic) Lack of pride in their work. No ideas. See also **Art and Design (General)**.

GRADUATE DESTINATIONS AND EMPLOYMENT

(See **Chapter 1, Graduate Outcomes.**)

Career note See **Art and Design (General)**.

OTHER DEGREE SUBJECTS FOR CONSIDERATION

Design Technology; see other **Art and Design** tables.

ASTRONOMY AND ASTROPHYSICS

(including **Planetary Science with Astronomy and Space Science and Robotics**; see also **Geology/Geological Sciences, Physics**)

All Astronomy-related degrees are built on a core of mathematics and physics which, in the first two years, is augmented by an introduction to the theory and practice of astronomy or astrophysics. Astronomy emphasises observational aspects of the science and includes a study of the planetary system while Astrophysics tends to pursue the subject from a more theoretical standpoint. Some universities have onsite observatories (Central Lancashire and Lancaster). Courses often combine Mathematics or Physics with Astronomy.

Useful websites www.ras.org.uk; www.scicentral.com; www.iop.org; www.britastro.org

NB The points totals shown to the left of the institutions are for ease of reference only. It must not be assumed that Tariff points are always used by institutions or that they can be substituted for an offer in grades. The level of an offer is not necessarily indicative of the quality of a course.

COURSE OFFERS INFORMATION

Subject requirements/preferences GCSE English and a foreign language may be required by some universities; specified grades may be stipulated for some subjects. **AL** Mathematics and physics usually required. Some popular universities are now making lower offers for disadvantaged and other students.

Your target offers and examples of degree courses

160 pts **Cambridge** – A*A*A incl sci/maths+interview+ESAT (Nat Sci (Astro)) (IB 41–42 pts HL 776 incl sci/maths)
Durham – A*A*A incl phys+maths (Phys Astron (MPhys)) (IB 38 pts HL 776 incl phys+maths)
Manchester – A*A*A incl A* maths+phys+interview (Phys Astro) (IB 38 pts HL 776 incl 7 maths+phys)

152 pts **Birmingham** – A*AA incl maths+phys (Phys Astro) (IB 32 pts HL 766 incl maths+phys)
Bristol – A*AA incl maths+phys (Phys Astro) (IB 38 pts HL 18 pts incl 76 maths+phys)
London (UCL) – A*AA incl maths+phys (Astro) (IB 39 pts HL 19 incl 76 maths+phys)

144 pts **Exeter** – AAA incl maths+sci (Nat Sci) (IB 36 pts HL 666 incl 6 maths+sci)
Lancaster – AAA incl maths+phys+interview (Phys Astro) (IB 36 pts HL 16 incl 6 maths+phys)
Leeds – AAA incl maths+phys (Phys Astro) (HL 18 pts incl 5 maths+phys)
Nottingham – AAA incl maths+phys (Phys Astron; Phys Theor Astro) (IB 34 pts HL 666 incl maths+phys)
St Andrews – AAA incl maths+phys (Astro) (IB 38 pts HL 666 incl maths+phys)
Sussex – AAA incl maths+phys (Astro) (IB 34 pts HL 6 maths+phys)

136 pts **London (QM)** – AAB incl A maths+phys (Astro (MSci)) (IB 34 pts HL 665 incl 6 maths+phys)
London (RH) – AAB–AAA incl maths+phys (Astro) (HL 666 incl maths+phys)
Manchester – AAB incl sci+interview (Earth Planet Sci) (IB 35 pts HL 665 incl sci)
Sheffield – AAB incl maths+phys (Phys Astro) (IB 34 pts HL 5/6 maths+phys)
Sussex – AAB incl maths (Phys Astro) (IB 30 pts HL 5 maths)
York – AAB incl A maths+phys (Phys Astro) (IB 35 pts HL 6 maths+phys)

128 pts **Edinburgh** – ABB–AAA incl A maths+B phys (Astro) (IB 32–37 pts HL 655–666)
Exeter – ABB–AAA incl maths+phys (Phys Astro (MPhys)) (IB 32–36 pts HL 655–666 incl maths+phys)
Keele – ABB incl B maths/phys (Astro (MSci)) (IB 32 pts HL 655 incl maths/phys)
Kent – ABB incl B maths (Astron Spc Sci Astro) (HL 665 incl maths); ABB incl maths (Phys Astro) (HL 665)
Leicester – ABB incl maths+phys (Phys Astro; Phys Spc Sci) (IB 30 pts HL 5 maths+phys)
Liverpool – ABB incl maths+phys (Phys Astron) (IB 33 pts HL 6 maths+phys)

Liverpool John Moores – ABB incl maths+phys 128 pts (Phys Astron)
London (QM) – ABB incl maths+phys (Phys (Astro)) (IB 32 pts HL 655 incl 6 maths/phys)
Queen's Belfast – ABB incl maths+phys (Phys Astro) (IB 33 pts HL 655 incl maths+phys)
Surrey – ABB incl maths+phys (Phys Astron; Phys Nucl Astro) (IB 33 pts HL 5 maths+phys)
Swansea – ABB–A*AB incl maths+phys (Phys Ptcl Phys Cosmo) (IB 32 pts HL 5 maths+phys)

120 pts **Cardiff** – BBB–AAB incl maths+phys (Astro; Phys Astron) (IB 31–34 pts HL 665–666 incl 6 maths+phys)
Central Lancashire – BBB incl phys+maths 120 pts (Astro) (HL 5 maths+phys)
Glasgow – BBB–AAB incl maths+phys (Astron courses; Phys Astro) (IB 34 pts HL 655 incl maths+phys)
Hertfordshire – BBB–ABB incl maths+phys 120–128 pts (Astro) (HL 4 maths+phys)
Hull – BBB incl maths+phys (Phys Astro) (IB 30 pts HL 6 maths+phys)
Nottingham Trent – C maths+phys 120 pts (Phys Astro)

112 pts **Aberystwyth** – BBC–BBB incl B maths+phys 112–120 pts (Spc Sci Robot) (IB 28–30 pts HL 5 maths+phys)

104 pts **London (Birk)** – BCC incl sci 104 pts (Planet Sci Astron Astrbiol)

96 pts **Surrey** – CCC incl maths+sci (Phys Astron Fdn)

ALTERNATIVE OFFERS See **Chapter 6** and **Appendix 1** for grades/UCAS Tariff points information for other examinations.

CHOOSING YOUR COURSE (SEE ALSO CH.1)

UNIVERSITIES AND COLLEGES TEACHING QUALITY See www.qaa.ac.uk; www.discoveruni.gov.uk.

TOP RESEARCH UNIVERSITIES AND COLLEGES (REF 2021) See **Physics**.

EXAMPLES OF SANDWICH DEGREE COURSES Hertfordshire; Keele; Kent; Surrey.

ADMISSIONS INFORMATION

ADVICE TO APPLICANTS AND PLANNING THE UCAS PERSONAL STATEMENT Books and magazines you have read on astronomy and astrophysics are an obvious source of information. Describe your interests and why you have chosen this subject. Visits to observatories would also be important. (See also **Appendix 3**.)

SELECTION INTERVIEWS Yes Cambridge, Lancaster, Manchester

INTERVIEW ADVICE AND QUESTIONS You will probably be questioned on your study of physics and the aspects of the subject you most enjoy. Questions in the past have included: Can you name a recent development in physics which will be important in the future? Describe a physics experiment, indicating any errors and exactly what it was intended to prove. Explain weightlessness. What is a black hole? What are the latest discoveries in space? See also **Chapter 5**.

GRADUATE DESTINATIONS AND EMPLOYMENT

(See **Chapter 1, Graduate Outcomes.**)

CAREER NOTE The number of posts for professional astronomers is limited although some technological posts are occasionally offered in observatories. However, degree courses include extensive mathematics and physics so many graduates can look towards related fields including telecommunications and electronics.

OTHER DEGREE SUBJECTS FOR CONSIDERATION

Aeronautical/Aerospace Engineering; Computer Science; Earth Sciences; Geology; Geophysics; Mathematics; Meteorology; Mineral Sciences; Oceanography; Physics.

BIOCHEMISTRY

(see also **Biological Sciences, Chemistry, Food Science/Studies and Technology, Pharmacy and Pharmaceutical Sciences**)

Biochemistry is the study of life at molecular level – how genes and proteins regulate cells, tissues and ultimately whole organisms – you! It's a subject which provides the key to understanding how diseases arise and how they can be treated; it is the core of many areas of biology and is responsible for a large number of breakthroughs in medicine and biotechnology. At Newcastle, Year 1 of the course consists of modules in cell biology, biochemistry, microbiology and immunology, genetics, pharmacology and physiology with transfers between degrees possible at the end of the year. This is a pattern reflected in many other university courses. Many courses also allow for a placement in industry in the UK or in Europe or North America.

Useful websites www.biochemistry.org; www.bioworld.com; www.annualreviews.org; www.ibms.org; www.acb.org.uk; see also **Biological Sciences** and **Biology**.

NB The points totals shown to the left of the institutions are for ease of reference only. It must not be assumed that Tariff points are always used by institutions or that they can be substituted for an offer in grades. The level of an offer is not necessarily indicative of the quality of a course.

COURSE OFFERS INFORMATION

Subject requirements/preferences GCSE English, mathematics and science usually required; leading universities often stipulate grades 7–5/6 (A–B). **AL** Chemistry required and biology usually preferred by most universities; one or two mathematics/science subjects usually required. Some popular universities are now making lower offers for disadvantaged and other students.

Your target offers and examples of degree courses

160 pts **Cambridge** – A*A*A incl sci/maths+interview ESAT (Nat Sci (Bioch)) (IB 41–42 pts HL 776 incl sci/maths)

152 pts **Oxford** – A*AA incl chem+maths/sci+interview (Bioch (Mol Cell)) (IB 39 pts HL 766 incl 7 chem)

144 pts **Bristol** – AAA incl chem+sci/maths (Bioch; Bioch Med Bioch) (IB 36 pts HL 18 pts incl 6 chem+ 6 sci/maths); (Bioch Mol Biol Biotech) (IB 36 pts HL 18 pts incl 6 chem+sci/maths)

Durham – AAA incl chem+maths (Bioch) (IB 37 pts HL 666 chem+maths)

Exeter – AAA–A*AA incl biol+chem (Bioch (Yr Ind)) (IB 36 pts HL 666 incl biol+chem)

Imperial London – AAA incl chem+sci/maths (Bioch; Bioch (Yr Ind/Rsch)) (IB 38 pts HL 6 chem+biol/maths); (Bioch courses) (IB 38 pts HL 6 chem+sci/maths)

London (King's) – AAA incl chem+biol (Bioch) (IB 35 pts HL 666 incl chem+biol)

London (UCL) – AAA incl chem+biol+maths (Bioch) (IB 38 pts HL 18 pts incl 5 chem+biol+maths)

136 pts **Bath** – AAB incl A chem+biol (Bioch) (IB 35 pts HL 665 incl 6 chem+biol)

Birmingham – AAB incl chem+sci (Bioch; Med Bioch) (IB 32 pts HL 665 incl chem+sci)

Dundee – AAB incl biol+chem (Bioch) (IB 32 pts HL 655 incl biol+chem)

Lancaster – AAB incl chem+sci/maths (Bioch) (IB 35 pts HL 16 pts incl 6 chem+sci/maths)

Leeds – AAB–AAA incl chem+sci (Bioch) (IB 34–35 pts HL 17–18 pts incl 6 chem+sci); (Med Bioch) (IB 34–35 pts HL 18 pts incl 6 chem+sci)

London (QM) – AAB incl chem (Bioch (Yr Ind)) (IB 35 pts HL 665 incl chem)

Newcastle – AAB incl biol/chem+maths/sci (Bioch) (IB 34 pts HL 5 biol/chem+maths/sci)

Nottingham – AAB incl chem+sci (Bioch; Bioch Mol Med) (IB 34 pts HL 5/6 chem+sci)

Sheffield – AAB incl chem+sci (Bioch; Bioch Comb Hons) (IB 34 pts HL 65 chem+sci)

Southampton – AAB incl chem+sci (Bioch) (IB 34 pts HL 17 pts incl 6 chem+sci)

St Andrews – AAB incl biol+chem (Bioch) (IB 36 pts HL 665 incl 6 chem+biol)

Warwick – AAB–AAA incl biol+chem 136–144 pts (Bioch) (IB 34–36 pts HL 5 biol+chem)

York – AAB incl chem+sci/maths (Bioch) (IB 35 pts HL 6 chem+sci); AAB–A*AA incl chem+sci/maths (Chem Biol Medcnl Chem) (IB 35–36 pts HL 6 chem+sci/maths)

128 pts **Aberdeen** – ABB 128 pts (Bioch Ind Plmt) (IB 36 pts)
Cardiff – ABB–AAB incl biol/chem (Bioch) (IB 32–34 pts HL 665–666 incl 6 biol/chem)
East Anglia – ABB incl chem (Bioch) (IB 32 pts HL 5 chem); (Bioch (Yr Ind)) (IB 32–33 pts HL 5 chem)
Edinburgh – ABB–AAA incl biol+chem (Biol Sci (Bioch)) (IB 32–37 pts HL 555–666 incl 5 biol+chem)
Exeter – ABB–AAB incl biol+chem (Bioch) (IB 32–34 pts HL 655–665 incl 5 biol+chem)
Keele – ABB incl chem+sci (Bioch) (IB 32 pts HL 655 chem+sci)
Leicester – ABB–AAB incl sci (Biol Sci (Bioch); Med Bioch) (IB 30 pts HL 65 sci)
Liverpool – ABB incl biol+chem (Bioch) (IB 33 pts HL 6/5 biol/chem)
London (QM) – ABB–AAB incl chem (Bioch) (IB 35 pts HL 655 incl chem)
Manchester – AAB–AAA incl chem+sci/maths+interview (Bioch) (IB 35–36 pts HL 655–666 incl chem+sci); ABB–A*AA incl chem+sci/maths+interview (Bioch (Yr Ind); Med Bioch) (IB 33–36 pts HL 655–666 incl chem+sci)

120 pts **Aberdeen** – BBB incl maths/sci (Bioch) (IB 32 pts HL 555 incl maths/sci)
Aston – BBB incl biol+chem (Bioch (Yr Ind)) (IB 31 pts HL 555 incl biol+chem)
Brunel – BBB–AAB incl sci 120–136 pts (Biomed Sci (Bioch)) (IB 30 pts HL 5 sci)
Glasgow – BBB–AAB incl biol/chem (Bioch) (IB 34 pts HL 655 incl HL chem)
Keele – ABC/BBB incl chem (Bioch Comb Hons) (IB 30 pts HL 5 chem)
Kent – BBB incl chem+biol 120 pts (Bioch) (HL 566 incl chem+biol)
London (RH) – BBB–ABB incl biol+sci (Med Bioch; Mol Biol Env Chng) (IB 32 pts HL 555 incl biol+sci)
Nottingham Trent – BBB incl biol 120 pts (Bioch)
Queen's Belfast – BBB incl chem+biol (Bioch) (IB 32 pts HL 655 incl chem+biol)
Strathclyde – BBB incl biol/chem+sci (Bioch courses) (IB 30 pts HL 55 biol/chem+sci)
Sussex – BBB incl chem (Bioch) (IB 30 pts HL 5 chem)
Swansea – BBB–AAB incl chem+sci 120–136 pts (Bioch) (IB 32–34 pts HL chem+sci)

112 pts **East London** – BBC 112 pts (Bioch Biotech) (IB 25 pts HL 15 pts)
Hertfordshire – BBC–BBB incl chem+sci 112–120 pts (Bioch (St Abrd)); (Bioch) (HL 4 chem+sci)
Huddersfield – BBC incl chem+sci 112 pts (Med Bioch)
Kingston – BBC incl chem+biol 112–128 pts (Bioch)
London (RH) – BBC–BBB incl biol+sci 112–120 pts (Bioch) (IB 32 pts HL 555 incl biol+sci)
London Met – BBC incl biol (Bioch)
Portsmouth – BBC–BBB incl biol+chem 112–120 pts (Bioch) (IB 25 pts HL 6 biol+chem)
Salford – 112 pts incl biol+chem (Bioch) (IB 30 pts HL 4 biol+chem)
Sheffield Hallam – BBC incl biol+chem 112 pts (Bioch)
Surrey – BBB incl biol/chem+sci/maths 112–128 pts (Bioch) (IB 32 pts HL 5 biol/chem+sci/maths)
Swansea – BBC–AAB incl biol+chem 112–136 pts (Bioch Genet) (IB 32–34 pts HL biol+chem)

104 pts **Aberystwyth** – BCC–BBB incl B chem 104–120 pts (Bioch; Genet Bioch) (IB 28–30 pts HL 5 chem)
Chester – BCC–BBC incl B chem (Bioch) (IB 28 pts HL 5 chem)
Essex – BCC–BBB incl chem+sci/maths 104–120 pts (Bioch) (IB 29–30 pts HL 544 chem+sci/maths)
Huddersfield – BCC–BBC incl chem+sci 104–112 pts (Bioch)
Lincoln – 104 pts incl biol/chem (Bioch) (IB 28 pts HL biol/chem)
Liverpool John Moores – BCC–BBB incl biol/chem 104–120 pts (Bioch)
Northampton – BCC incl chem (Bioch)

96 pts **Reading** – CCC incl biol+chem/BBB (Bioch Fdn) (IB 24–30 pts); CCC incl chem+sci 96–120 pts (Bioch) (IB 30 pts HL 5 chem)
Westminster – CCC incl sci 96–120 pts (Bioch) (HL 44 sci)
Wolverhampton – CCC incl biol/chem (Bioch)
Worcester – 96–104 pts incl biol+sci (Biol (Bioch))

Alternative offers See **Chapter 6** and **Appendix 1** for grades/UCAS Tariff points information for other examinations.

DEGREE APPRENTICESHIPS

Bradford (Lab Sci, Adv Clin Prac, Biomed Sci); Central Lancashire (App Biomed Sci); East Anglia (App Biomed Sci); Kent (Tech Sci, Clin Trls, Lab Sci); Manchester Met (Lab Sci); Portsmouth (App Biomed Sci); Salford (Biomed Path Lab Sci); West London (Bioinform Sci); Westminster (App Biomed Sci).

CHOOSING YOUR COURSE (SEE ALSO CH.1)

Universities and colleges teaching quality See www.qaa.ac.uk; www.discoveruni.gov.uk.

Top research universities and colleges (REF 2021) See **Biological Sciences**.

Examples of sandwich degree courses Aberystwyth; Aston; Bath; Bristol; Brunel; Cardiff; East Anglia; East London; Essex; Exeter; Hertfordshire; Huddersfield; Imperial London; Keele; Kent; Kingston; Leeds; Lincoln; Liverpool John Moores; London (RH); Manchester; Newcastle; Nottingham Trent; Portsmouth; Queen's Belfast; Reading; Salford; Sheffield; Sheffield Hallam; Surrey; Sussex; Warwick; Wolverhampton; York.

ADMISSIONS INFORMATION

Advice to applicants and planning the UCAS personal statement It is important to show by reading scientific journals that you have interests in chemistry and biology beyond the exam syllabus. Focus on one or two aspects of biochemistry that interest you. Attend scientific lectures (often arranged by universities on Open Days), find some work experience if possible, and use these to show your understanding of what biochemistry is. Give evidence of your communication skills and time management. (See **Appendix 3**.)

Selection interviews Yes Cambridge, Oxford (44% (success rate 13%)); **Some** Bath; **No** Cardiff, East London, Keele, Kingston, Leeds, Salford.

Interview advice and questions Questions will be asked on your study of chemistry and biology and any special interests. They will also probe your understanding of what a course in Biochemistry involves and the special features offered by the university. In the past questions have been asked covering Mendel, genetics, RNA and DNA. See also **Chapter 5**.

Reasons for rejection (non-academic) Borderline grades plus poor motivation. Failure to turn up for interviews or answer correspondence. Inability to discuss subject. Not compatible with A-level predictions or references.

GRADUATE DESTINATIONS AND EMPLOYMENT

(See **Chapter 1, Graduate Outcomes.**)

Career note Biochemistry courses involve several specialities which offer a range of job opportunities. These include the application of biochemistry in industrial, medical and clinical areas with additional openings in pharmaceuticals and agricultural work, environmental science and in toxicology.

OTHER DEGREE SUBJECTS FOR CONSIDERATION

Agricultural Sciences; Agriculture; Biological Sciences; Biology; Biotechnology; Botany; Brewing; Chemistry; Food Science; Genetics; Medical Sciences; Medicine; Microbiology; Neuroscience; Nursing; Nutrition; Pharmaceutical Sciences; Pharmacology; Pharmacy; Plant Science.

BIOLOGICAL SCIENCES

(including **Biomedical Materials Science, Biomedical Science, Brewing and Distilling, Forensic Science, Immunology, Medical Science and Virology and Immunology**; see also **Animal Sciences, Biochemistry, Biology, Biotechnology, Environmental Sciences, Genetics, Marine/Maritime Studies, Medicine, Microbiology, Natural Sciences, Neuroscience, Nursing and Midwifery, Pharmacology, Plant Sciences, Psychology, Zoology**)

Biological Science (in some universities referred to as Biosciences) is a fast-moving, rapidly expanding and wide subject area, ranging from, for example, conservation biology to molecular genetics. Boundaries between separate subjects are blurring and this is reflected in the content and variety of the courses offered. Many universities offer a common first year allowing final decisions to be made later in the course. Since most subjects are research-based, students undertake their own projects in the final year. It should be noted that some Medical Science courses provide a foundation for graduate entry to medical schools. Check with universities.

Useful websites www.ibms.org; www.bbsrc.ukri.org; www.csofs.org; www.immunology.org; see also **Biochemistry** and **Biology**.

NB The points totals shown to the left of the institutions are for ease of reference only. It must not be assumed that Tariff points are always used by institutions or that they can be substituted for an offer in grades. The level of an offer is not necessarily indicative of the quality of a course.

COURSE OFFERS INFORMATION

Subject requirements/preferences GCSE English, mathematics and science usually required. **AL** Chemistry usually required plus one or two other mathematics/science subjects, biology preferred. (Ecol) Biology and one other science subject may be required or preferred. (Neuro) Mathematics/science subjects with chemistry and/or biology required or preferred. Some popular universities are now making lower offers for disadvantaged and other students.

Your target offers and examples of degree courses

160 pts **Cambridge** – A*A*A incl sci/maths+interview+ESAT (Nat Sci (Biol Biomed Sci)) (IB 41–42 pts HL 776)

152 pts **Bath** – A*AA incl maths/sci (Nat Sci) (IB 36 pts HL 766 incl maths/sci)

Nottingham – A*AA incl sci/maths (Nat Sci) (IB 36 pts HL 766 incl sci/maths)

Oxford – A*AA incl biol+sci/maths+interview (Biol) (IB 39 pts HL 7 sci/maths); A*AA incl sci/maths+interview+BMSAT (Biomed Sci) (IB 39 pts HL 766 incl sci/maths)

144 pts **Bath** – AAA/A*AB–AAB+aEPQ incl A biol+chem (Biomed Sci) (IB 36 pts HL 666 incl 6 biol+chem)

Durham – AAA incl biol/chem+sci (Biol Sci) (IB 37 pts HL 666 incl biol/chem+sci)

Exeter – AAA incl biol+sci (Biol Sci (Yr Abrd); Biol Sci (Yr Ind)) (IB 36 pts HL 666 incl biol+sci)

Imperial London – AAA incl biol+sci/maths (Biol Sci; Med Biosci) (IB 38 pts HL 6 biol+sci/maths); (Biol Sci Span Sci) (IB 38 pts HL 66 incl biol+sci/maths)

Leeds – AAA incl biol/chem+sci (Biol Sci; Biol Sci (Biotech Ent)) (HL 665 incl biol/chem+sci)

London (King's) – AAA incl biol+chem (Biomed Sci) (IB 35 pts HL 666 incl biol+chem)

London (UCL) – AAA incl biol+chem (Bioproc N Med (Sci Eng)) (IB 38 pts HL 18 pts incl 5/6 biol+chem); AAA incl biol+chem+maths (Biomed Sci) (IB 38 pts HL 18 pts incl 6 biol+chem+maths); AAA incl biol+sci/maths (Biol Sci) (IB 38 pts HL 18 pts incl 6 biol 5 sci/maths); AAA incl sci (Bioproc N Med (Bus Mgt)) (IB 38 pts HL 18 pts incl 6 sci)

Newcastle – AAA incl biol (Psy Biol) (IB 36 pts HL 666 incl biol)

136 pts **Birmingham** – AAB/ABB+aEPQ incl biol/chem+sci (Biomed Mat Sci) (IB 32 pts HL 665 incl chem/biol); AAB incl biol+sci (Biol Sci) (IB 32 pts HL 665 incl biol+sci)

Bristol – AAB incl chem+sci/maths (Cell Mol Med) (IB 34 pts HL 17 incl 65 chem+sci/maths); (Canc Biol Immun; Virol Immun) (IB 34 pts HL 17 pts incl 65 chem+sci/maths)

Dundee – AAB incl biol+chem (Biol Sci) (IB 30 pts HL 555 incl biol+chem)

East Anglia – AAB+aEPQ incl biol (Biol Sci (Yr Ind)) (IB 33 pts HL 5 biol)
Edinburgh – AAB incl biol+chem (Med Sci) (IB 34 pts HL 655 incl biol+chem)
Lancaster – AAB incl biol+sci/maths (Biomed Sci) (IB 35 pts HL 16 pts incl 6 biol+sci/maths)
Leeds – AAB incl biol/chem+sci (Biomed Sci) (HL 665 incl biol/chem+sci)
Leicester – AAB incl biol/chem+sci (Clin Sci) (IB 32 pts HL 665 incl biol/chem+sci)
Liverpool – AAB incl A biol (Anat Hum Biol) (IB 34 pts HL 6 biol)
London (QM) – AAB incl biol+sci/maths (Biomed Sci) (IB 35 pts HL 665 biol+sci/maths)
London (UCL) – AAB incl biol+chem/phys/maths (App Med Sci) (IB 36 pts HL 17 pts incl biol+chem/phys/maths)
Loughborough – AAB incl biol (Biol Sci) (IB 35 pts HL 665 incl biol)
Manchester – AAB–AAA incl sci/maths+interview (Biomed Sci) (IB 35–36 pts HL 665–666 incl sci)
Newcastle – AAB incl biol/chem+sci/maths (Biomed Genet; Biomed Sci; Med Sci (Defer)) (IB 34 pts HL 5 biol/chem+sci/maths)
Sheffield – AAB incl sci (Biol Sci) (IB 34 pts HL 65 chem+sci); AAB–ABB+bEPQ incl sci (Biomed Sci) (IB 34 pts HL 65 sci)
Southampton – AAB incl biol/chem+sci (Biomed Sci) (IB 34 pts HL 17 pts incl 65 chem/biol+sci)
Warwick – AAB incl biol+sci/AAA incl biol (Biomed Sci) (IB 34–36 pts HL 5 biol+sci/maths)
York – AAB incl biol+chem/maths/phys/psy (Biomed Sci) (IB 35 pts HL 6 biol+chem/maths/phys/psy)

128 pts **Aberdeen** – ABB incl chem+sci/maths (Biomed Sci courses) (IB 34 pts HL 6 chem+sci/maths)
Bristol – ABB incl sci/maths (Palae Evol) (IB 32 pts HL 16 pts incl 55 sci/maths)
Cardiff – ABB–AAB incl biol/chem (Biomed Sci) (IB 32–34 pts HL 655–666 incl 6 biol/chem); (Biol Sci (Zool)) (IB 32–34 pts HL 665–666 incl 6 biol/chem)
Dundee – ABB incl biol (Foren Anth) (IB 32 pts HL 655 incl biol)
East Anglia – ABB–BBB+aEPQ incl biol (Biol Sci (Yr Abrd)) (IB 32 pts HL 5 biol); ABB–BBB+aEPQ incl biol+sci/maths (Biomed) (IB 32 pts HL 5 biol+sci/maths)
Edinburgh – ABB–AAA incl biol+chem (Biol Sci; Biol Sci (Immun)) (IB 32–37 pts HL 555–666 incl biol+chem); (Biol Sci (Zool)) (IB 32–37 pts HL 655–666 incl biol+chem); ABB–AAB incl biol+chem (Infec Dis) (IB 32–36 pts HL 655–665 incl biol+chem)
Exeter – ABB–AAB incl biol+sci (Hum Biosci) (IB 32–34 pts HL 655–665 incl 5 biol+sci); (Biol Sci) (IB 34 pts HL 55 incl biol+sci)
Leicester – ABB–AAB incl sci/maths (Biol Sci; Biol Sci (Genet)) (IB 30 pts HL 65 sci/maths)
Liverpool – ABB/BBB+aEPQ incl biol+chem (Biol Med Sci) (IB 33 pts HL 65 biol/chem); ABB/BBB+aEPQ incl biol+sci (Biol Sci) (IB 33 pts HL 65 incl 6 biol)
Manchester – ABB–A*AA incl sci/maths+interview (Biomed Sci (Yr Ind)) (IB 33–36 pts HL 655–666 incl sci)
Queen's Belfast – ABB–AAB incl biol+chem (Biomed Sci) (IB 33–34 pts HL 655 incl biol+chem)
Reading – ABB incl biol+sci (Med Sci) (IB 32 pts HL 5 biol+sci)
Warwick – ABB incl biol+sci/AAB incl biol (Biol Sci) (IB 34–36 pts HL 5 biol+sci/maths)

120 pts **Aberdeen** – BBB incl maths/sci (Immun) (IB 32 pts HL 555 incl maths/sci); BBB incl sci/maths (Biol Sci) (IB 32 pts HL 555 incl sci/maths)
Aston – BBB/BBC+bEPQ incl biol (Biol Sci; Biomed Sci) (IB 31 pts HL 555 incl biol)
Bournemouth – 120–128 pts (Med Sci) (IB 31–33 pts HL 55)
Bradford – BBB incl biol/chem 120 pts (Biomed Sci) (HL 6 biol/chem)
Brunel – BBB incl maths/sci (Lf Sci) (IB 30 pts HL 5 sci); BBB incl sci (Biomed Sci; Biomed Sci (Genet)) (IB 30 pts HL 5 sci)
Central Lancashire – BBB incl sci (Med Sci)
Coventry – BBB incl biol (Biomed Sci) (IB 30–32 pts HL 5 biol)
De Montfort – 120 pts incl biol/chem (Biomed Sci) (IB 28 pts HL 6 biol/chem); (Med Sci) (IB 28 pts HL 6 chem/biol)
East Anglia – BBB/ABC–BBC+aEPQ incl biol (Biol Sci) (IB 31 pts HL 5 biol)
Glasgow – BBB–AAB incl biol/chem (Immun) (IB 32–36 pts HL 655–665 incl biol/chem)
Keele – BBB incl B chem/biol (Foren Sci) (IB 30 pts HL 555 chem/biol)

Kent – BBB incl B biol (Biomed Sci) (HL 566); BBB incl chem/biol (Foren Sci) (IB 30 pts HL 14 pts incl 5 chem/biol)
Leeds Beckett – BBB incl B biol 120 pts (Biomed Sci) (IB 25 pts HL 6 biol)
Lincoln – BBB incl biol/chem (Biomed Sci) (IB 30 pts HL 5 biol/chem)
London (RH) – BBB–ABB incl biol+chem/maths/phys (Biomed Sci) (IB 32 pts HL 555 incl biol+chem/maths/phys); BBB–ABB incl biol+sci (Mol Biol Env Chng) (IB 32 pts HL 555 incl biol+sci)
London (RVC) – BBB–ABB incl biol/chem (Biol Sci) (HL 655)
Northumbria – BBB incl biol/chem/app sci 120 pts (Foren Sci)
Nottingham Trent – BBB incl biol 120 pts (Biomed Sci); BBB incl chem+sci/maths 120 pts (Foren Sci)
Queen's Belfast – BBB incl biol+sci/maths/geog (Biol Sci) (IB 32–33 pts HL 655 incl biol+sci/maths/geog)
Reading – BBB incl biol+sci (Biol Sci; Biol Sci (Yr Ind); Biomed Sci; Biomed Sci (Yr Ind)) (IB 30 pts HL 5 biol+sci)
Sheffield Hallam – BBB incl biol 120 pts (Biomed Sci)
Strathclyde – BBB incl biol/chem+sci (Biomed Sci; Immun Pharmacol) (IB 30 pts HL 5 biol/chem+sci)
Sunderland – 120 pts incl biol/chem (Biomed Sci)
Surrey – BBB incl biol/chem+sci/maths (Biomed Sci)
Sussex – BBB–ABB incl biol+sci/maths 120–128 pts (Biomed Sci) (IB 30–32 pts HL 5 biol+sci/maths)
Swansea – BBB–ABB incl biol (Biol Sci Defer) (IB 32 pts HL 5 biol)
UWE Bristol – BBB incl biol/chem+sci 120 pts (Biomed Sci) (HL 6 biol/chem); BBB incl biol/chem 120 pts (Foren Sci) (HL 6 biol/chem)
Ulster – BBB incl sci/maths (Biomed Sci; Per Med) (IB 26 pts HL 13 pts incl sci/maths)

112 pts **Anglia Ruskin** – 112 pts incl biol/chem/app sci (Foren Sci) (IB 26 pts HL biol/chem)
Bedfordshire – 112 pts (Biomed Sci)
Bradford – BBC incl B chem/biol 112 pts (Foren Med Sci) (HL 655 incl 6 chem/biol); BBC incl B chem 112 pts (Foren Sci) (HL 655 incl 6 chem); BBC incl biol+chem 112 pts (Clin Sci) (HL 56 biol+chem)
Canterbury Christ Church – BBC 112 pts incl sci (Foren Invstg; Hum Biol) (IB 29 pts)
Cardiff Met – BBC incl biol+sci 112 pts (Biomed Sci)
Chester – BBC incl biol/app sci (Biomed Sci) (IB 26 pts HL 5 biol)
City St George's – BBC incl biol+chem (Biomed Sci) (IB 32 pts HL 14 pts incl 5 biol+chem)
Coventry – BBC incl biol (Biol Foren Sci) (IB 30 pts HL 5 biol)
De Montfort – 112 pts incl sci (Foren Sci) (IB 26 pts HL 6 sci)
Derby – BBC–BBB incl biol/chem 112–120 pts (Foren Sci)
East London – BBC incl B biol/chem 112 pts (Biomed Sci) (IB 25 pts HL 15 pts incl biol+chem)
Essex – BBC incl biol (Biol Sci) (IB 29–30 pts HL 544 incl biol); BBC incl chem/biol+sci/maths (Biomed Sci) (IB 29–30 pts HL 555–554 incl chem/biol+sci/maths)
Glasgow Caledonian – BBC incl chem (Biomed Sci) (IB 28 pts HL chem)
Heriot-Watt – BBC–ABB incl sci/maths (Biol Sci) (IB 27 pts HL 5 sci)
Hertfordshire – BBC–BBB incl biol/chem+sci 112–120 pts (Biomed Sci) (IB 112–120 pts HL 4)
Huddersfield – BBC incl B sci 112 pts (Biomed Sci); BBC incl chem+sci 112 pts (Med Bioch); BBC incl chem 112 pts (Foren Analyt Sci)
Hull – BBC incl biol/app sci 112 pts (Biomed Sci) (IB 28 pts HL 5 biol)
Kingston – BBC incl biol+sci 112–128 pts (Biomed Sci); BBC incl biol/chem 112–128 pts (Foren Sci); BBC incl biol 112–128 pts (Biol Sci)
Liverpool John Moores – BBC incl biol/chem 112 pts (Foren Sci); BBC incl chem/biol 112 pts (Biomed Sci) (IB 26 pts)
London Met – BBC incl B biol 112 pts (Biomed Sci); BBC incl C biol 112 pts (Biol Sci; Foren Sci); BBC incl biol (Med Biosci)
London South Bank – 112 pts (Biomed Sci; Foren Sci)

Manchester Met – BBC incl biol/app sci 112–120 pts (Biomed Sci) (IB 28 pts HL 5 biol)
Middlesex – BBC–BBB incl sci 112–120 pts (Biomed Sci)
Northumbria – BBC incl biol 112 pts (Biomed Sci)
Nottingham Trent – BBC incl biol 112 pts (Biol Sci)
Plymouth – BBC incl B biol+sci 112–128 pts (Biomed Sci) (IB 26–30 pts HL 5 biol+sci)
Portsmouth – BBC–BBB incl biol+sci/maths 112–120 pts (Biomed Sci) (IB 29 pts)
Roehampton – 112 pts incl biol/chem (Biol Sci; Biomed Sci)
Staffordshire – BBC incl biol/chem 112 pts (Foren Sci) (IB 30 pts); BBC incl biol 112 pts (Biol Sci; Biomed Sci) (IB 28 pts)
Suffolk – BBC incl biol/sci (Biol Sci)
Sunderland – 112 pts incl chem (Cos Sci)
UWE Bristol – BBC incl sci 112 pts (Biol Sci) (HL 5 sci)
West London – BBC incl sci 112–120 pts (Biomed Sci)

104 pts **Bangor** – 104–128 pts incl biol+sci (Biomed Sci) (HL 5 biol+chem); 104–128 pts incl biol+sci/maths (Med Sci) (HL biol+chem)
Bournemouth – 104–120 pts (Biol Sci; Foren Sci) (IB 28–31 pts)
Brighton – BCC–BBB incl biol+chem 104–120 pts (Biomed Sci) (IB 26 pts HL biol+sci); BCC–BBB incl biol 104–120 pts (Biol Sci) (IB 26 pts HL biol+sci)
Central Lancashire – 104–112 pts incl biol/chem/app sci (Foren Sci) (HL biol/chem)
Chester – BCC–BBC incl biol/app sci (Foren Biol) (IB 26 pts HL 5 biol/chem)
Cumbria – BCC–BBC 104–112 pts (Crimin Foren Invstg)
Edinburgh Napier – BCC incl sci (Biol Sci; Biomed Sci) (IB 28 pts HL 654 incl 5 sci)
Glasgow Caledonian – BCC (Biol Sci)
Gloucestershire – 104–120 pts (Wldlf Cons Biol)
Greenwich – 104 pts incl biol+chem (App Biomed Sci) (HL 5 sci); (Biomed Sci) (IB 26 pts HL 5 sci); 104 pts incl sci (Foren Sci; Foren Sci Crimin) (IB 26 pts HL 5 sci)
Heriot-Watt – BCC–BBB incl maths+chem/biol (Brew Distil) (IB 29 pts HL 6 maths+5 sci)
Hertfordshire – BCC–BBC incl biol/chem+sci 104–112 pts (Biol Sci); (Biol Sci (St Abrd)) (HL 4)
Lincoln – BCC incl biol/chem/app sci (Foren Sci) (HL 4 biol/chem)
Liverpool John Moores – 104–112 pts (Foren Anth)
Northampton – BCC incl biol/chem/phys 104 pts (Biol Sci) (HL biol/chem/phys)
Oxford Brookes – 104 pts incl sci (Biol Sci) (IB 29 pts); BCC incl sci 104 pts (Biol Sci Hum Biosci; Biomed Sci; Med Sci) (IB 29 pts HL sci)
Plymouth – 104–128 pts (Biol Sci) (IB 28–32 pts HL 5 biol+sci)
Robert Gordon – BCC incl chem+sci/maths (Foren Analyt Sci) (IB 27 pts HL 4 chem+sci/maths)
Salford – 104–112 pts incl biol (Hum Biol Infec Dis) (IB 29 pts HL 4 biol)
West London – BCC 104–120 pts (Foren Sci)

96 pts **Abertay** – CCC incl biol (Biomed Sci) (IB 27 pts HL 4 biol); CCC incl sci (Foren Sci) (IB 27 pts HL 4 sci)
De Montfort – 96 pts incl chem+sci (Pharml Cos Sci) (IB 24 pts HL 6 chem+sci)
Glasgow Caledonian – CCC incl chem (Foren Invstg) (IB 26 pts HL chem)
Greenwich – CCC incl biol/phys/spo sci 96–104 pts (Biol (Ext)) (IB 26 pts HL 5 biol)
London (Birk) – CCC–BBB incl sci 96–120 pts (Biomed)
Reading – CCC incl biol+sci/BBB (Biol Sci Fdn; Biomed Sci Fdn) (IB 24–30 pts)
Teesside – 96–112 pts incl biol/app sci (Biol Sci); 96–112 pts incl biol/chem/app sci (Foren Sci)
West Scotland – CCC incl biol 96 pts (App Biosci Zool) (IB 24 pts HL 3 biol); CCC incl chem 96 pts (Foren Sci) (IB 24 pts HL chem)
Westminster – CCC–BBB incl sci 96–120 pts (Biol Sci; Biomed Sci) (HL 4 sci)
Wolverhampton – CCC/BCD incl biol/chem (Foren Sci); CCC/BCD incl sci (Biomed Sci)
Worcester – 96–104 pts incl biol (Foren App Biol); 96–104 pts incl biol/chem (Biomed Sci)

80 pts **Bedfordshire** – 80 pts (Biol Sci); 80 pts incl sci (Foren Sci)
Stirling – BB incl biol/chem (App Biol Sci) (IB 28 pts)
Wrexham – 80–112 pts incl sci (Foren Sci)

Alternative offers See **Chapter 6** and **Appendix 1** for grades/UCAS Tariff points information for other examinations.

DEGREE APPRENTICESHIPS

Bradford (Lab Sci, Adv Clin Prac, Biomed Sci); Hertfordshire (App Biomed Sci); Kent (App Biosci); Portsmouth (App Biomed Sci).

EXAMPLES OF COLLEGES OFFERING COURSES IN THIS SUBJECT FIELD

Birmingham Met (Coll); Bishop Burton (Coll); Brighton Met (Coll); Cornwall (Coll); Ealing, Hammersmith and West London (Coll); Haringey, Enfield and North East London (Coll); Hull (Coll); Liverpool City (Coll); Nescot; Peterborough (UC); Petroc; Plymouth City (Coll); South Devon (Coll); Sunderland (Coll); Weymouth (Coll).

CHOOSING YOUR COURSE (SEE ALSO CH.1)

Universities and colleges teaching quality See www.qaa.ac.uk; www.discoveruni.gov.uk.

Top research universities and colleges (REF 2021) (Biological Sciences) London (Institute of Cancer Research); Dundee; Cambridge; Sheffield; Oxford; Manchester; Edinburgh; Bristol; York, Imperial London.

Examples of sandwich degree courses Anglia Ruskin; Bournemouth; Bradford; Brighton; Brunel; Central Lancashire; Coventry; East Anglia; Essex; Exeter; Greenwich; Hertfordshire; Huddersfield; Imperial London; Kent; Kingston; Lincoln; London (RH); Manchester; Newcastle; Northampton; Northumbria; Nottingham; Nottingham Trent; Plymouth; Reading; Robert Gordon; Roehampton; Sheffield; Staffordshire; Stirling; Sunderland; Surrey; Ulster; UWE Bristol; West Scotland.

ADMISSIONS INFORMATION

Advice to applicants and planning the UCAS personal statement Read scientific journals and try to extend your knowledge beyond the A-level syllabus. Discuss your special interests, for example, ecology, microbiology, genetics or zoology (read up thoroughly on your interests since questions could be asked at interview). Mention any voluntary attendance on courses, work experience, voluntary work, or holiday jobs. Demonstrate good oral and written communication skills and be competent at handling numerical data. Interest in the law for Forensic Science courses. See **Appendix 3**.

Selection interviews Yes Cambridge, Manchester, Oxford (Bio) 48% (success rate 15%), (Biomed Sci) 24% (success rate 8%); **Some** Bristol (Mature students); **No** Anglia Ruskin, Birmingham, Cardiff Met, City St George's, Derby, Imperial London, London (RH), Newcastle, Swansea, UWE Bristol.

Interview advice and questions You are likely to be asked about your main interests in biology and your choice of specialisation in the field of biological sciences or, for example, about the role of the botanist, specialist microbiologist in industry, your understanding of biotechnology or genetic engineering. Questions likely to be asked on any field courses attended. If you have a field course workbook, take it to interview. See also **Chapter 5**.

GRADUATE DESTINATIONS AND EMPLOYMENT

(See **Chapter 1, Graduate Outcomes.**)

Career note Degrees in biological science subjects often lead graduates into medical, pharmaceutical, veterinary, food and environmental work, research and education, in both the public and private sectors (see also **Biology**). Sandwich courses are offered at a number of institutions enabling students to gain paid experience in industry and commerce, often resulting in permanent employment on graduation. In recent years there has been a considerable increase in the number of Biomedical Science courses designed for students interested in taking a hands-on approach to studying the biology of disease. However, students should be warned that the ever-popular Forensic Science courses may not always pave the way to jobs in this highly specialised field.

OTHER DEGREE SUBJECTS FOR CONSIDERATION

Biochemistry; Biology; Biotechnology; Botany; Chemistry; Consumer Sciences; Ecology; Environmental Health; Environmental Science; Genetics; Genomics; Immunology; Microbiology; Pharmaceutical Sciences; Pharmacology; Pharmacy; Physiology; Plant Sciences; Psychology; Sport and Exercise Science; Toxicology; Virology; Zoology.

BIOLOGY

(including **Marine Biology**; see also **Animal Sciences, Biological Sciences, Biotechnology, Environmental Sciences, Microbiology, Plant Sciences, Zoology**)

The science of biology is a broad and rapidly developing subject that increasingly affects our lives. Biologists address the challenges faced by human populations such as disease, conservation and food production, and the continuing advances in such areas as genetics and molecular biology that have applications in medicine and agriculture. (See also under **Biological Sciences**.)

USEFUL WEBSITES www.rsb.org.uk; www.mba.ac.uk; www.bbsrc.ukri.org; see also **Biochemistry**.

NB The points totals shown to the left of the institutions are for ease of reference only. It must not be assumed that Tariff points are always used by institutions or that they can be substituted for an offer in grades. The level of an offer is not necessarily indicative of the quality of a course.

COURSE OFFERS INFORMATION

SUBJECT REQUIREMENTS/PREFERENCES GCSE Mathematics and English stipulated in some cases. **AL** Biology and chemistry important, other science subjects may be accepted. Two and sometimes three mathematics/science subjects required including biology. Some popular universities are now making lower offers for disadvantaged and other students.

YOUR TARGET OFFERS AND EXAMPLES OF DEGREE COURSES)

152 pts **Durham** – A*AA incl biol/chem/maths (Nat Sci) (IB 38 pts HL 666–766 incl biol/chem/maths)
Oxford – A*AA incl biol+sci/maths+interview (Biol) (IB 39 pts HL 7 sci/maths)

144 pts **Bristol** – AAA incl sci/maths (Biol) (IB 36 pts HL 18 pts incl 66 sci/maths)
Imperial London – AAA incl biol+sci/maths (Biol Sci Ger Sci; Ecol Env Biol) (IB 38 pts HL 6 biol+sci/maths)
Lancaster – AAA incl sci (Biology (Yr Abrd)) (IB 36 pts HL 16 pts incl sci)
London (King's) – AAA incl chem+biol (Anat Dev Hum Biol) (IB 36 pts HL 18 pts incl 6 chem+biol)
Sheffield – AAA/AAB+bEPQ incl biol+sci (Biol (MBiolSci); Biol (Yr Abrd)) (IB 36 pts HL 6 biol+sci)

136 pts **Bath** – AAB/ABB+aEPQ incl biol+sci/maths (Biol) (IB 36 pts HL 665 incl 6 biol+sci/maths)
Birmingham – AAB incl biol+sci (Hum Biol) (IB 32 pts HL 665 incl biol+sci)
Bristol – AAB incl chem+sci/maths (Canc Biol Immun) (IB 34 pts HL 17 pts incl 65 chem+sci/maths)
Exeter – AAB incl sci 136 pts (Cons Biol Ecol (Yr Ind)) (IB 34 pts HL 665 incl sci)
Lancaster – AAB incl sci (Biol courses) (IB 35 pts HL 16 pts incl sci)
Leeds – AAB incl biol+sci (Biol) (HL 665 biol+sci)
Liverpool – AAB incl A biol (Anat Hum Biol) (IB 34 pts HL 6 biol)
Loughborough – AAB incl sci (Hum Biol) (IB 35 pts HL 665 incl 5 biol+sci)
Manchester – AAB–AAA incl sci (Biol Sci Soty) (IB 35–36 pts HL 665–666 incl sci); AAB–AAA incl sci+lang (Biol Modn Lang) (IB 35–36 pts HL 665–666 incl sci+lang); AAB–AAA incl sci/maths 136–144 pts (Biol) (IB 35–36 pts HL 665–666 incl sci/maths)
Nottingham – AAB incl biol+sci (Biol) (IB 34 pts HL 665 biol+sci)
Sheffield – AAB/ABB+bEPQ–AAA incl biol/sci (Biol) (IB 34 pts HL 65 biol+sci)
Southampton – AAB incl biol+sci (Biol) (IB 34 pts HL 17 pts incl 65 biol+sci)

St Andrews – AAB incl biol+sci/maths (Biol Arbc; Biol courses) (IB 36 pts HL 665 incl 6 biol+sci)
York – AAB incl biol+sci (Biol; Mol Cell Biol) (IB 35 pts HL 6 biol+sci)

128 pts **Edinburgh** – ABB–AAA incl biol+chem (Biol Sci (Evol Biol)) (IB 32–37 pts HL 555–666 incl biol+chem); ABB–AAB incl biol+chem (Repro Biol) (IB 34 pts HL 655 incl 65 biol+chem)
Exeter – ABB–AAB incl B sci (Cons Biol Ecol) (IB 32–34 pts HL 655–665 incl 5 sci); ABB–AAB incl sci (Evol Biol) (IB 32–34 pts HL 655–665 incl 5 sci)
Keele – ABB incl sci/maths (Biol) (IB 32 pts HL 655 sci/maths)
Leeds – ABB incl biol (Biol Hist Phil Sci) (IB 34 pts HL 16 pts incl 6 biol)
Liverpool – ABB/BBB+aEPQ incl biol+sci/maths/geog (Mar Biol) (IB 33 pts HL 6 biol 5 sci)
London (QM) – ABB incl biol (Biol) (IB 34 pts HL 655 incl biol)
Manchester – ABB–A*AA incl sci (Cell Biol (Yr Ind); Cell Biol Modn Lang; Dev Biol; Mol Biol) (IB 33–36 pts HL 655–666 incl sci); ABB–A*AA incl sci/maths (Biol (Yr Ind)) (IB 33–36 pts HL 655–666 incl sci/maths)
Newcastle – ABB incl biol+sci (Mar Biol) (IB 32 pts HL 6 biol); ABB–AAB incl biol+sci (Biol) (IB 32–34 pts HL 6 biol)
Nottingham – ABB incl biol (Env Biol) (IB 32 pts HL 5 biol)
Southampton – ABB incl biol+sci (Mar Biol; Mar Biol Ocean) (IB 32 pts HL 16 pts incl 5 biol+sci)

120 pts **Aberdeen** – BBB incl maths/sci (Biol; Cons Biol) (IB 32 pts HL 555 incl maths/sci)
Coventry – BBB incl biol (Hum Biosci) (IB 32 pts HL 5 biol)
Dundee – BBB incl B maths+biol/chem (Mathem Biol) (IB 30 pts HL 555 incl maths+chem+biol/phys)
Glasgow – BBB–AAB incl biol/chem (Mar Frshwtr Biol) (IB 34 pts HL 655 biol/chem)
Hull – BBB incl biol/app sci 120 pts (Biol) (IB 30 pts HL 5 biol)
Kent – BBB incl biol (Biol courses) (HL 665 incl biol)
London (RH) – BBB–ABB incl biol (Biol) (IB 32 pts HL 555 incl biol); BBB–ABB incl biol+sci (Mol Biol Env Chng) (IB 32 pts HL 555 incl biol+sci)
Portsmouth – BBB–ABB incl biol 120–128 pts (Biol) (IB 25 pts)
Queen's Belfast – BBB–ABB incl biol+chem/geog/maths/phys (Mar Biol) (IB 32–33 pts HL 655 incl biol+chem/geog/maths/phys)
Stirling – BBB incl sci/maths (Biol) (IB 30 pts)
Strathclyde – BBB incl chem+biol (Microbiol) (IB 30 pts HL 5 chem+biol)
Sussex – BBB–ABB incl sci (Biol) (IB 30–32 pts HL 5 sci)
Swansea – BBB–ABB incl biol (Biol) (IB 32 pts HL 5 biol)

112 pts **Aberdeen** – BBC incl maths/sci (Mar Biol) (IB 32 pts HL 555 incl maths/sci)
Bangor – 112–144 pts incl biol+sci (Mar Biol) (HL 5)
Canterbury Christ Church – BBC 112 pts incl sci (Hum Biol) (IB 29 pts)
Chester – BCC–BBC incl biol/app sci (Biol courses) (IB 26 pts HL 5 biol)
Derby – BBC–BBB incl biol 112–120 pts (Biol)
Edge Hill – BBC–BBB 112–120 pts (Biol)
Essex – 112–120 pts (Hum Biol) (IB 29–30 pts HL 544 incl biol)
Heriot-Watt – BBC–ABB incl sci/maths (Mar Biol) (IB 27 pts HL 5 sci)
Huddersfield – BBC incl sci 112 pts (Med Biol)
Liverpool John Moores – BBC incl sci (Biol)
Middlesex – BBC–BBB incl biol 112–120 pts (Biol)
Nottingham Trent – incl biol 112 pts (Zoo Biol)
Plymouth – 112–128 pts incl sci (Mar Biol)
Portsmouth – BBC–BBB incl biol 112–120 pts (Mar Biol) (IB 25 pts)
Sheffield Hallam – BBC incl C biol 112 pts (Biol; Hum Biol)

104 pts **Aberystwyth** – BCC–BBB incl B biol 104–120 pts (Biol; Mar Frshwtr Biol; Plnt Biol) (IB 28–30 pts HL 5 biol)
Bangor – 104–128 pts incl biol+sci (Biol) (HL 5 biol)
Bath Spa – BCC–BBB incl biol 104–120 pts (Biol) (IB 32 pts HL 5 incl biol)
Central Lancashire – 104–120 pts (Biol)

Chester – BCC–BBC incl biol/app sci (Foren Biol) (IB 26 pts HL 5 biol/chem)
Edinburgh Napier – BCC incl sci (Anim Cons Biol; Mar Frshwtr Biol) (IB 28 pts HL 654 incl 5 sci)
Gloucestershire – 104–120 pts (Biol)
Huddersfield – BCC incl sci 104 pts (Biol (Mol Cell))
Lincoln – BCC incl biol/chem (Biol) (HL 5 biol/chem)
Manchester Met – BCC–BBC incl biol/app sci 104–112 pts (Biol (Yr Abrd/Yr Ind)) (IB 26 pts HL 5 biol)
Salford – BCC incl biol 104–112 pts (Biol) (IB 30 pts HL 4 biol)
Ulster – BCC incl sci/maths (Biol) (IB 24 pts HL 12 pts incl 5 sci)

96 pts **Greater Manchester** – 96 pts incl biol+interview (Med Biol)
South Wales – CCC incl biol+sci 96 pts (Int Wldlf Biol); CCC incl biol 96 pts (Biol)
Worcester – 96–104 pts incl biol+sci (Biol)

ALTERNATIVE OFFERS See **Chapter 6** and **Appendix 1** for grades/UCAS Tariff points information for other examinations.

DEGREE APPRENTICESHIPS

Bradford (Lab Sci, Adv Clin Prac, Biomed Sci); Central Lancashire (App Biomed Sci); East Anglia (App Biomed Sci); Kent (Tech Sci, Clin Trls, Lab Sci); Manchester Met (Lab Sci); Portsmouth (App Biomed Sci); Salford (Biomed Path Lab Sci); West London (Bioinform Sci); Westminster (App Biomed Sci).

EXAMPLES OF COLLEGES OFFERING COURSES IN THIS SUBJECT FIELD

Bishop Burton (Coll); Blackpool and Fylde (Coll); Bournemouth and Poole (Coll); Brighton Met (Coll); Leeds City (Coll); Liverpool City (Coll); Manchester (Coll); North Hertfordshire (Coll); Solihull (Coll); South Devon (Coll); Sparsholt (Coll); SRUC; Truro and Penwith (Coll); Walsall (Coll).

CHOOSING YOUR COURSE (SEE ALSO CH.1)

UNIVERSITIES AND COLLEGES TEACHING QUALITY See www.qaa.ac.uk; www.discoveruni.gov.uk.

TOP RESEARCH UNIVERSITIES AND COLLEGES (REF 2021) See **Biological Sciences**.

EXAMPLES OF SANDWICH DEGREE COURSES Aberystwyth; Bangor; Bath; Birmingham; Coventry; Essex; Exeter; Gloucestershire; Huddersfield; Keele; Kent; Lancaster; Leeds; Lincoln; Liverpool John Moores; London (RH); Loughborough; Manchester; Manchester Met; Middlesex; Newcastle; Northumbria; Nottingham Trent; Sheffield Hallam; Swansea; Teesside; Ulster; York.

ADMISSIONS INFORMATION

ADVICE TO APPLICANTS AND PLANNING THE UCAS PERSONAL STATEMENT See **Biochemistry**, **Biological Sciences** and **Appendix 3**.

SELECTION INTERVIEWS Yes Oxford (Bio) 48% (success rate 15%); **Some** Bath, Manchester; **No** Anglia Ruskin, London (RH), Sheffield, Swansea, York.

INTERVIEW ADVICE AND QUESTIONS Questions are likely to focus on your studies in biology, on any work experience or any special interests you may have in biology outside school. In the past, questions have included: Is the computer like a brain and, if so, could it ever be taught to think? What do you think the role of the environmental biologist will be in the next 40–50 years? Have you any strong views on vivisection? You have a micro-organism in the blood: you want to make a culture. What conditions should be borne in mind? What is a pacemaker? What problems will a giraffe experience? How does water enter a flowering plant? Compare an egg and a potato. Discuss a family tree of human genotypes. Discuss fish farming in Britain today. What problems do fish face underwater? See also **Chapter 5**.

GRADUATE DESTINATIONS AND EMPLOYMENT

(See **Chapter 1, Graduate Outcomes.**)

Career note Some graduates go into research, but many will go into laboratory work in hospitals, food laboratories, agriculture, the environment and pharmaceuticals. Others go into teaching, management and other professional and technical areas.

OTHER DEGREE SUBJECTS FOR CONSIDERATION

Anatomy; Biochemistry; Biological Sciences; Biotechnology; Chemistry; Dentistry; Ecology; Environmental Health; Environmental Science/Studies; Food Science; Genomics; Health Studies; Medicine; Midwifery; Nursing; Nutrition; Optometry; Orthoptics; Pharmaceutical Sciences; Pharmacology; Pharmacy; Physiology; Physiotherapy; Plant Sciences; Radiography; Speech and Language Therapy; Zoology.

BIOTECHNOLOGY

(including **Prosthetics and Orthotics**; see also **Biological Sciences, Biology, Engineering (Medical), Microbiology**)

Biotechnology is essentially the application of biology to improve the quality of life. It is a multi-disciplinary subject which can involve a range of scientific disciplines covering chemistry, the biological sciences, microbiology and genetics. At Bangor, for example, the course involves medical and industrial applications, the environment, the food industry, and, because of its very favourable coastal location, marine biotechnology and fisheries genetics can be added to its programme. Medical engineering involves the design, installation, maintenance and provision of technical support for diagnostic, therapeutic and other clinical equipment used by doctors, nurses and other clinical healthcare workers.

Useful websites www.bbsrc.ukri.org; www.bioindustry.org

NB The points totals shown to the left of the institutions are for ease of reference only. It must not be assumed that Tariff points are always used by institutions or that they can be substituted for an offer in grades. The level of an offer is not necessarily indicative of the quality of a course.

COURSE OFFERS INFORMATION

Subject requirements/preferences GCSE Mathematics and science subjects required. **AL** Courses vary but one, two or three subjects from chemistry, biology, physics and mathematics may be required. Some popular universities are now making lower offers for disadvantaged and other students.

Your target offers and examples of degree courses

152 pts **Leeds** – A*AA incl maths+phys/chem/biol (Med Eng) (HL 18 pts incl 6 maths+phys/chem); (Med Eng (MEng)) (IB 36 pts HL 18 pts incl 6 maths+phys/chem)

144 pts **Bristol** – AAA incl chem+sci/maths (Bioch Mol Biol Biotech) (IB 36 pts HL 18 pts incl 6 chem+sci/maths)

Imperial London – AAA incl maths+phys/chem+interview (Biomat Tiss Eng (MEng)) (IB 38 pts HL 6 maths+phys/chem); AAA–A*AA incl chem+sci/maths (Biotech; Biotech (Yr Ind/Rsch)) (IB 38 pts HL 6 chem+biol/maths)

Leeds – AAA incl biol/chem+sci (Biol Sci (Biotech Ent)) (HL 665 incl biol/chem+sci)

136 pts **York** – AAB incl biol+sci (Biotech) (IB 35 pts HL 6 biol+sci)

128 pts **Edinburgh** – ABB–AAA incl biol+chem (Biol Sci (Biotech)) (IB 32–37 pts HL 555–666 incl biol+chem)

Manchester – ABB–A*AA incl sci/maths+interview (Biotech) (IB 35–36 pts HL 655–666 incl sci)

120 pts **Aberdeen** – BBB incl maths/sci (Biotech (App Mol Biol)) (IB 34 pts HL 655 incl maths/sci)

Glasgow – BBB–AAB incl biol/chem (Mol Cell Biol (Biotech)) (IB 34 pts HL 655 incl biol/chem)

Nottingham – BBB–ABB incl sci/maths (Biotech) (IB 30 pts HL 55 sci+maths)

Strathclyde – BBB–ABB incl maths+sci (Pros Orthot) (IB 32–34 pts HL 5 maths/phys)

104 pts **Bangor** – 104–128 pts incl biol+sci (Biol Biotech) (HL 5 biol)

Liverpool John Moores – BCC incl biol/chem 104 pts (Biotech)

Alternative offers See **Chapter 6** and **Appendix 1** for grades/UCAS Tariff points information for other examinations.

CHOOSING YOUR COURSE (SEE ALSO CH.1)

Universities and colleges teaching quality See www.qaa.ac.uk; www.discoveruni.gov.uk.

Examples of sandwich degree courses Imperial London; Leeds; Manchester; York.

ADMISSIONS INFORMATION

Advice to applicants and planning the UCAS personal statement See **Biological Sciences, Biochemistry** and **Appendix 3**.

Selection interviews No Imperial London, Leeds.

Interview advice and questions See **Biology**, **Biological Sciences** and **Chapter 5**.

GRADUATE DESTINATIONS AND EMPLOYMENT

(See **Chapter 1, Graduate Outcomes.**)

Career note Biotechnology, biomedical and biochemical engineering opportunities exist in medical, agricultural, food science and pharmaceutical laboratories. Some Bioengineering graduates apply for graduate medical courses and obtain both engineering and medical qualifications.

OTHER DEGREE SUBJECTS FOR CONSIDERATION

Agriculture; Biochemistry; Biological Sciences; Biomedicine; Chemistry; Food Technology; Genetics; Materials Science and Technology; Microbiology; Molecular Biology; Pharmacology.

BUILDING AND CONSTRUCTION

(including **Building Services Engineering and Construction and Project Management**; see also **Architecture, Engineering (Civil), Housing, Surveying and Real Estate Management**)

The building and construction industry covers a wide range of specialisms and is closely allied to civil, municipal and structural engineering (see under **Engineering (Civil)**). The specialisms include Construction Management involving accountancy, economics, law and estimating in addition to main studies in building materials and methods, construction techniques, and health and safety. Building Surveying which not only involves modules on building technology but also the study of the history of building techniques and styles, and enables the surveyor to diagnose and test all aspects of a building's performance and construction. Quantity Surveying is another specialism which relates to the financial planning of a building project covering costs (which can constantly change during the period of the project) as well as modifications which might be required to the original architect's plans. (See under **Surveying and Real Estate Management**.) Finally, Building Services Engineering is a career which involves specialised areas such as heating, lighting, acoustics, refrigeration and air conditioning. All university courses in these subjects will offer work placements.

Useful websites www.ciob.org; www.cibse.org; www.citb.co.uk; www.rics.org; www.cstt.org.uk; www.cbuilde.com

NB The points totals shown to the left of the institutions are for ease of reference only. It must not be assumed that Tariff points are always used by institutions or that they can be substituted for an offer in grades. The level of an offer is not necessarily indicative of the quality of a course.

COURSE OFFERS INFORMATION

Subject requirements/preferences GCSE English, mathematics and science usually required. **AL** Physics, mathematics or a technical subject may be required for some courses. Some popular universities are now making lower offers for disadvantaged and other students.

YOUR TARGET OFFERS AND EXAMPLES OF DEGREE COURSES

120 pts **London South Bank** – BBB 120–128 pts (Bld Surv)
Loughborough – BBB/ABC+interview (Constr Eng Mgt) (IB 32 pts HL 555)
Reading – BBB (Constr Mgt) (IB 30 pts)

112 pts **Birmingham City** – BBC 112 pts+interview (Constr Mgt) (IB 28 pts)
Central Lancashire – 112 pts incl maths (Bld Serv Sust Eng)
Coventry – BBC (Constr Proj Mgt)
Glasgow Caledonian – BBC incl maths+phys (Bld Serv Eng) (IB 30 pts HL maths/phys)
Greenwich – 112 pts (Constr Mgt); BBC 112 pts (Quant Surv)
Kingston – BBC–ABB 112–128 pts (Constr Eng Mgt)
Leeds Beckett – 112 pts (Constr Mgt) (HL 554)
London South Bank – BBC 112 pts (Commer Mgt (Quant Surv); Constr Mgt)
Northumbria – 112 pts (Constr Eng Mgt)
Nottingham Trent – 112 pts (Bld Surv; Quant Surv Commer Mgt); BBC 112 pts (Constr Mgt)
Oxford Brookes – BBC 112 pts+interview (Constr Proj Mgt) (IB 30 pts)
Portsmouth – BBC–ABB 112–128 pts (Constr Mgt)
Sheffield Hallam – BBC 112 pts (Constr Proj Mgt)
West London – BBC–BBB 112–120 pts (Constr Proj Mgt)

104 pts **Anglia Ruskin** – 104 pts (Constr Mgt) (IB 24 pts)
Brighton – BCC–BBB 104–120 pts (Constr Mgt) (IB 26 pts)
Central Lancashire – BCC 104 pts (Constr Proj Mgt)
Derby – BCC–BBC 104–112 pts (Constr Mgt)
Heriot-Watt – BCC–BBB (4 yr course) BBB (3 yr course) (Constr Proj Mgt) (IB 28 pts (4 yr course) 33 pts (3 yr course))
Salford – 104 pts (Constr Proj Mgt) (IB 29 pts)
Solent – 104–120 pts (Constr Mgt)
UWE Bristol – 104 pts (Constr Proj Mgt)
Ulster – BCC–BBC incl maths/sci 104–112 pts (Constr Eng Mgt) (IB 25 pts HL 12 pts incl 5 maths+sci)
Westminster – BCC–BBB 104–120 pts (Constr Mgt)

96 pts **Aston** – CCC–BBC (Constr Proj Mgt) (IB 28–29 pts HL 544–554)
Glasgow Caledonian – CCC (Constr Mgt)
Plymouth – CCC–BBC 96–112 pts (Constr Proj Mgt) (IB 26–28 pts)
Teesside – 96–112 pts (Constr Mgt)
Trinity Saint David – 96 pts+interview (Constr Mgt)
UCEM – 96 pts (Bld Surv)
Wolverhampton – CCC/BCD (Constr Mgt)

80 pts **Colchester (UC)** – 80 pts+interview (Constr Mgt (Quant Surv); Constr Mgt (Site Mgt))
Wrexham – 80–112 pts (Constr Mgt)

ALTERNATIVE OFFERS See **Chapter 6** and **Appendix 1** for grades/UCAS Tariff points information for other examinations.

DEGREE APPRENTICESHIPS

Birmingham City (Constr Site Mgt); Brighton (Chart Surv (Bld Surv)); Glasgow Caledonian (Constr Blt Env); Greater Manchester (Constr Proj Mgt); Greenwich (Constr Mgt); London South Bank (Commer Mgt (Quant Surv)); Northumbria (Chart Surv, Constr Quant Surv); Portsmouth (Bld Surv, Quant Surv, Constr Mgt); Robert Gordon (Constr Blt Env); Salford (Constr Proj Mgt); Teesside (Constr Site Mgt); UHI (Constr Blt Env); UWE Bristol (Constr Site Mgt); West London (Chart Surv (Bld Surv)); Westminster (Chart Surv (Bld Surv), Constr Quant Surv); Wrexham (Constr Mgt, Bld Surv, Quant Surv).

EXAMPLES OF COLLEGES OFFERING COURSES IN THIS SUBJECT FIELD

Accrington and Rossendale (Coll); Banbury and Bicester (Coll); Barnfield (Coll); Barnsley (Coll); Basingstoke (CT); Bath (Coll); Bedford (Coll); Birmingham Met (Coll); Blackpool and Fylde (Coll); Bournemouth and Poole (Coll); Bradford College (UC); Bury (Coll); Canterbury (Coll); Carshalton (Coll);

Chelmsford (Coll); Chesterfield (Coll); Croydon (UC); Darlington (Coll); Doncaster (Coll); Dudley (Coll); Durham New (Coll); Ealing, Hammersmith and West London (Coll); East Kent (Coll); East Riding (Coll); East Surrey (Coll); East Sussex (Coll); Eastleigh (Coll); Exeter (Coll); Furness (Coll); Gateshead (Coll); Gloucestershire (Coll); Gower Swansea (Coll); Hartlepool (CFE); Hull (Coll); Leicester (Coll); Lewisham (Coll); Lincoln (Coll); London UCK (Coll); MidKent (Coll); Nescot; North West London (Coll); Norwich City (Coll); Plymouth City (Coll); Redcar and Cleveland (Coll); Richmond-upon-Thames (Coll); South and West Cheshire (Coll); South Cheshire (Coll); South City Birmingham (Coll); South Essex (Coll); Southampton City (Coll); St Helens (Coll); Stamford (Coll); Stockport (Coll); Tameside (Coll); TEC Partnership; Trafford (Coll); Wakefield (Coll); Warrington and Vale Royal (Coll); West Suffolk (Coll); Westminster City (Coll); Wigan and Leigh (Coll); Windsor Forest (Coll); Wirral Met (Coll); York (Coll).

CHOOSING YOUR COURSE (SEE ALSO CH.1)

Universities and colleges teaching quality See www.qaa.ac.uk; www.discoveruni.gov.uk.

Top research universities and colleges (REF 2021) See **Architecture**.

Examples of sandwich degree courses Anglia Ruskin; Aston; Brighton; Central Lancashire; Coventry; Greenwich; Kingston; Leeds Beckett; Loughborough; Nottingham Trent; Portsmouth; Sheffield Hallam; Ulster; UWE Bristol; Wolverhampton.

ADMISSIONS INFORMATION

Advice to applicants and planning the UCAS personal statement Details of work experience with any levels of responsibility should be included. Make contact with any building organisation to arrange a meeting with staff to discuss careers in building. Give evidence of your ability to work in a team and give details of any personal achievements in technological areas and work experience. Building also covers civil engineering, surveying, quantity surveying etc and these areas should also be explored. See also **Appendix 3**.

Selection interviews **Some** Loughborough; **No** Derby, Northumbria.

Interview advice and questions Work experience in the building and civil engineering industries is important and you could be expected to describe any building project you have visited and any problems experienced in its construction. A knowledge of the range of activities to be found on a building site will be expected, for example the work of quantity and land surveyors and of the various building trades. See also **Chapter 5**.

Reasons for rejection (non-academic) Inability to communicate. Lack of motivation. Indecisiveness about reasons for choosing the course.

GRADUATE DESTINATIONS AND EMPLOYMENT

(See **Chapter 1, Graduate Outcomes.**)

Career note There is a wide range of opportunities within the building and construction industry for building technologists and managers. This subject area also overlaps into surveying, quantity surveying, civil engineering, architecture and planning and graduates from all these subjects commonly work together as members of construction teams.

OTHER DEGREE SUBJECTS FOR CONSIDERATION

Architectural Technology; Architecture; Civil Engineering; Property Planning and Development; Quantity Surveying; Surveying.

BUSINESS AND MANAGEMENT COURSES

(see also **Business and Management Courses (International and European), Business and Management Courses (Specialised), Economics, Hospitality and Event Management, Human Resource Management, Leisure and Recreation Management/Studies, Marketing, Retail Management, Tourism and Travel**)

Business degrees attract more applicants than any other degree subject, and students should try to assess the balance between theoretical studies and hands-on approaches offered by courses. Most universities offer a range of courses such as at Durham University, where in the first year of the Business and Management course, accounting, marketing and business management are covered. Transfers between business courses is a common feature at most institutions. As for the course content, financial studies form part of all courses with additional modules which may include marketing, business law and human resources. In the following section, there is also a section focusing on European and International Business courses for those with a language ability, and a further section on more specialised courses which cover advertising, airports, engineering, music, transport, travel and sport. Since this is a vocational subject, some work experience in the field is generally required prior to application.

Useful websites www.faststream.gov.uk; www.cgi.org.uk; www.adassoc.org.uk; www.cipr.co.uk; www.export.org.uk; www.ipsos.com; www.gov.uk/government/organisations/hm-revenue-customs; www.camfoundation.co.uk/about-us/; www.managers.org.uk; www.cipd.co.uk; www.instam.org

NB The points totals shown to the left of the institutions are for ease of reference only. It must not be assumed that Tariff points are always used by institutions or that they can be substituted for an offer in grades. The level of an offer is not necessarily indicative of the quality of a course.

COURSE OFFERS INFORMATION

Subject requirements/preferences GCSE Mathematics and English often at grade 7 or 5/6 (A or B) required. **AL** Mathematics required for some courses; in some cases grades A, B or C may be required. Some popular universities are now making lower offers for disadvantaged and other students.

Your target offers and examples of degree courses

152 pts **Durham** – A*AA incl maths (Econ Mgt) (IB 38 pts HL 666 incl maths)
London (King's) – A*AA incl hum/soc sci (Bus Mgt) (IB 35 pts HL 766 incl hum/soc sci)
London (UCL) – A*AA incl maths (Mgt Sci) (IB 39 pts HL 17 pts incl 7 maths)
London LSE – A*AA incl maths (Maths Stats Bus) (IB 38 pts HL 766 incl 7 maths)
Warwick – A*AA (Mgt) (IB 38 pts); A*AA incl maths+fmaths+phys (Phys Bus St) (IB 38 pts HL 6 maths+phys)

144 pts **Bath** – AAA/A*AB+interview (Mgt courses) (IB 36 pts HL 666/765)
Bristol – AAA–A*AB (Acc Mgt; Acc Mgt (Yr Abrd); Acc Mgt (Yr Ind)) (IB 36 pts HL 18 pts)
City St George's – AAA 144 pts (Bus Mgt) (IB 35 pts HL 18 pts incl 4 maths+Engl)
Exeter – AAA (Acc Bus (Yr Abrd); Acc Bus (Yr Ind)) (IB 36 pts HL 666)
Leeds – AAA (Bus Econ; Bus Mgt; Bus Mgt Mark) (IB 35 pts HL 17 pts)
London (QM) – AAA (Bus Mgt) (IB 36 pts HL 666)
London LSE – AAA incl maths (Mgt) (IB 38 pts HL 766 incl maths)
Manchester – AAA (Mgt courses) (IB 36 pts HL 666)
Nottingham – AAA (Mgt) (IB 36 pts)
St Andrews – AAA (Mgt courses) (IB 38 pts HL 666)

136 pts **Birmingham** – AAB (Bus Mgt courses) (IB 32 pts HL 665)
Durham – AAB (Bus Mgt) (IB 36 pts HL 665)
Exeter – AAB (Acc Bus; Bus Mgt) (IB 34 pts HL 665); AAB–AAA incl maths (Maths Mgt) (IB 34–36 pts HL 665–666 incl 6 maths)
Liverpool – AAB (Bus Mgt; Bus Mgt (Yr Ind)) (IB 35 pts)

Loughborough – AAB (Mgt courses) (IB 35 pts HL 665)
Newcastle – AAB (Bus Mgt) (IB 34 pts)
Reading – AAB+interview (Acc Bus) (IB 34 pts HL 4 incl maths+Engl)
Sheffield – AAB (Bus Mgt; Bus Mgt Comb Hons) (IB 34 pts)
Southampton – AAB/ABB+aEPQ (Bus Mgt) (IB 34 pts HL 17 pts); AAB/ABB+aEPQ incl maths/phys/stats (Econ Bus Mgt) (IB 34 pts HL 17 pts incl 5 maths/phys/stats)
Surrey – AAB (Bus Econ) (IB 34 pts)

128 pts **Aston** – ABB/BBB+bEPQ (Psy Bus) (IB 32 pts HL 655)
Cardiff – ABB–AAB (Bus Mgt) (IB 32–34 pts HL 665–666)
East Anglia – ABB/BBB+aEPQ (Bus Econ; Mark Mgt) (IB 32 pts)
Edinburgh – ABB–AAA incl maths (Bus courses) (IB 34–37 pts HL 655–666)
Lancaster – ABB (Acc Mgt; Bus Mgt; Mgt courses) (IB 32 pts HL 16 pts)
London (RH) – ABB–AAB (Econ Mgt; Econ Mgt (Yr Ind); Mgt Acc; Mgt Acc (Yr Ind)) (IB 32 pts HL 655)
Nottingham – ABB (Modn Langs Bus) (IB 30 pts HL 655)
Queen's Belfast – ABB (Bus Mgt (Yr Ind)) (IB 33 pts HL 655)
Reading – ABB (Bus Mgt; Bus Mgt (Entre Innov); Bus Mgt (HR Org Bhv); Int Bus Mgt) (IB 32 pts)
Surrey – ABB (Bus Mgt) (IB 33 pts)
Sussex – ABB (Mark Mgt) (IB 32 pts); ABB–AAB (Law Bus Mgt) (IB 32–34 pts)
York – ABB (Bus Crea Ind) (IB 34 pts)

120 pts **Aston** – BBB/BBC+bEPQ (Bus Mgt) (IB 31 pts HL 555)
Bournemouth Arts – BBB 120 pts (Crea Dir)
Brunel – BBB (Bus Mgt) (IB 30 pts)
Coventry – BBB (Glob Bus Mgt) (IB 27–30 pts)
Dundee – BBB (Bus Mgt) (IB 30 pts HL 555)
Essex – BBB (Bus Mgt) (IB 30 pts)
Glasgow – BBB–AAB incl hum (Bus Mgt Comb Hons) (IB 36 pts HL 665 incl Engl+hum)
Keele – BBB (Bus Mgt courses) (IB 30 pts HL 555)
Kent – BBB–AAB (Bus IT) (HL 4 maths)
Kingston – 120–136 pts (Bus Mgt)
Manchester Met – BBB 120–128 pts (Bus Mgt) (IB 30 pts)
Nottingham Trent – BBB 120 pts (Bus Mgt Comb Hons)
Southampton – BBB–ABB incl mus+gr 8 mus prac (Mus Bus Mgt) (IB 30–32 pts HL 15–16 incl 5 mus)
Stirling – BBB (Bus St) (IB 30 pts)
Strathclyde – BBB–ABB (Bus) (IB 30–32 pts)
Sussex – BBB–ABB (Bus Mgt St; Comp Bus Mgt; Econ Mgt St; Fin Bus) (IB 30–32 pts)
Swansea – BBB–ABB (Bus Mgt; Bus Mgt (Fin)) (IB 32–33 pts)

112 pts **Birmingham City** – BBC 112 pts (Bus courses; Fash Bus Prom) (IB 28 pts HL 14 pts)
Birmingham Newman – 112 pts (Bus Mgt)
Bournemouth Arts – BBB 112–120 pts+portfolio (Comm Des Strat)
Bradford – BBC 112 pts (Bus Mgt)
Buckingham – BBC–BBB+interview (Law Bus Mgt) (IB 31–32 pts)
Canterbury Christ Church – BBC 112 pts (Bus Mgt)
Cardiff Met – 112 pts (Bus Mgt (HR Mgt)) (HL 55); BBC 112 pts (Bus Mgt Law) (HL 55); BBC 112 pts+interview (Bus Mgt courses); (Bus Mgt Fin) (HL 55)
Chester – BBC (Bus Mgt) (IB 26 pts)
De Montfort – 112 pts (Bus Mgt courses; Bus courses) (IB 26 pts)
Derby – BBC–BBB 112–120 pts (Bus Mgt)
East London – 112 pts (Bus Mgt) (IB 24 pts HL 15 pts)
Greenwich – BBC 112 pts (Bus Entre Innov; Bus Mgt; Bus Prchsng Sply Chn Mgt)
Heriot-Watt – BBC–ABB (Mark) (IB 29 pts)
Huddersfield – BBC (Bus Mgt); BBC–BBB 112–120 pts (Bus Mgt Fin)
Hull – BBC 112 pts (Bus Mgt Fin Mgt; Bus courses) (IB 28 pts)

Leeds Beckett – 112 pts (Bus St); (Bus Mgt) (HL 55)
Leeds Trinity – BBC 112 pts (Acc Bus; Bus Mark; Bus Mgt)
Lincoln – BBC 112 pts (Bus Mgt) (IB 29 pts)
Liverpool Hope – BBC 112 pts (Bus Mgt) (IB 28 pts)
Liverpool John Moores – BBC (Bus Mgt) (IB 28 pts); BBC 112 pts (Bus Dig Mark; Bus Fin) (IB 28 pts)
London South Bank – 112 pts (Bus Mgt Comb Hons)
Middlesex – BBC 112 pts (Bus Mgt; Bus Mgt (Mark))
Northumbria – 112 pts (Bus Analyt; Bus HR Mgt; Bus Mark; Bus Mgt)
Nottingham Trent – 112 pts (Law Bus); BBC 112 pts (Bus)
Oxford Brookes – 112 pts (Bus Mgt) (IB 30 pts)
Plymouth – 112–128 pts (Bus Mgt) (IB 28–32 pts HL 4)
Portsmouth – BBC–BBB 112–120 pts (Bus Mgt; Law Bus) (IB 29 pts)
Robert Gordon – BBC (Bus Data Analyt; Bus Fin Econ; Mgt) (IB 29 pts)
Sheffield Hallam – BBC 112 pts (Bus Econ; Bus St; Bus courses)
Solent – BBC 112–128 pts (Bus Mgt)
Staffordshire – BBC 112 pts (Bus Mgt Sust) (IB 28 pts)
Suffolk – BBC+interview (Bus Mgt)
Sunderland – 112 pts (Bus Fin Mgt; Bus Mgt)
UWE Bristol – 112 pts (Bus Mgt courses; Bus courses)
Ulster – BBC (Bus St) (IB 25 pts)
Univ Law – BBC (Bus Mgt; Bus Mgt Mark)
West London – BBC 112 pts (Bus St)
Westminster – BBC 112 pts (Bus Mgt (Mark); Contemp Rtl); BBC–ABB 112–128 pts (Bus Mgt courses) (HL 4 Engl+maths)
Worcester – 112 pts (Bus Fin); BBC 112 pts (Bus courses)

104 pts **Bangor** – 104–136 pts (Bus Data Analyt; Bus Mgt)
Bath Spa – BCC–BBB 104–120 pts (Bus Mgt courses) (IB 32 pts); BCC–BBB (Bus Mgt (Acc)) (IB 32 pts)
Bournemouth – 104–120 pts (Acc; Bus Mgt) (IB 28–31 pts)
Brighton – BCC–BBB 104–120 pts (Bus Mgt Fin; Bus Mgt courses; Law Bus) (IB 26 pts); BCC–BBB 104–120 pts+portfolio (Fash Des Bus St) (IB 30 pts)
Buckingham – BCC–BBB+interview (Bus Mgt courses) (IB 30–32 pts)
Central Lancashire – 104–112 pts (Bus Mgt)
Chichester – BCC–BBB 104–120 pts (Bus Mgt) (IB 28 pts)
Cumbria – BCC–BBC 104–112 pts (Bus Mgt)
Edge Hill – BCC–BBC 104–112 pts (Bus Mgt)
Edinburgh Napier – BCC (Bus Mgt) (IB 28 pts HL 654); BCC 104 pts (Inform Bus) (IB 28 pts HL 654)
Glasgow Caledonian – BCC (Bus Mgt)
Gloucestershire – BCC 104 pts (Bus Mgt)
Greater Manchester – 104 pts (Bus Mgt)
Leeds Beckett – 104–120 pts (Int Tour Mgt) (HL 55)
Lincoln – 104 pts (Bus Mark); BCC 104 pts (Bus)
Manchester Met – BCC–BBC 104–112 pts (Bus HR Mgt) (IB 26 pts)
Northampton – BCC 104 pts (Bus Comp)
Queen Margaret – BCC (Bus Mgt) (IB 28 pts)
Robert Gordon – BCC (Bus Mgt) (IB 27 pts)
SRUC – BCC (Rur Bus Mgt)
Salford – BCC–BBC 104–112 pts (Bus Mgt) (IB 30 pts)
West Scotland – (Bus) (IB 24 pts)
Winchester – 104–120 pts (Bus Mgt courses) (HL 44)
York St John – BCC 104 pts (Bus Mgt)

96 pts **Abertay** – CCC (Mark Bus Mgt) (IB 27–28 pts)
Aberystwyth – CCC–BBB 96–120 pts (Bus Mgt) (IB 26–30 pts)

Anglia Ruskin – CCC 96 pts (Bus Mgt)
CAFRE – 96 pts incl bus/sci (Sust Agri-Fd Mgt)
London (Birk) – CCC–ABB 96–128 pts (Mgt)
London Met – CCC 96 pts (Bus Mgt)
London Regent's – CCC–AAA 96–144 pts (Bus courses)
Robert Gordon – CCC 96 pts (Bus Analyt) (IB 26 pts)
Roehampton – CCC 96 pts (Bus Mgt)
Royal Agricultural Univ – CCC (Bus Mgt) (IB 26 pts)
South Wales – CCC 96 pts (Bus Mgt)
St Mary's – 96–112 pts (Bus Law courses)
Sunderland – 96–112 pts (Bus HR Mgt; Bus Mark Mgt)
Wolverhampton – CCC/BCD 96 pts (Bus Mark); CCC 96 pts (Bus Mgt)
88 pts **Bucks New** – 88–112 pts (Bus Mgt)
Trinity Saint David – 88 pts (Bus Mgt)
80 pts **Teesside** – 80–104 pts (Bus Mgt; Law Bus Mgt)
Wrexham – 80–112 pts (Int Bus)
72 pts **St Mary's** – 72 pts (Bus Mgt)
64 pts **UHI** – CC (Bus Mgt)
Worcester – CC 64 pts (Bus St)

Open University – (Bus Mgt)

Alternative offers See **Chapter 6** and **Appendix 1** for grades/UCAS Tariff points information for other examinations.

DEGREE APPRENTICESHIPS

Aston (Chart Mgr); Bradford (Chart Mgr); Canterbury Christ Church (Snr Ldr); Central Lancashire (Bus Mgt); Chichester (Chart Mgr); East London (Chart Mgr); Exeter (Chart Mgr, Proj Mgt); Glasgow Caledonian (Bus Mgt); Gloucestershire (Chart Mgr, Facil Mgr, Snr Ldr); Greater Manchester (Rtl Bus Mgt (Chart Mgr)); Kent (Chart Mgr); Leeds Beckett (Bus Mgt Prac); London South Bank (Bus Mgt Bus Prac); Manchester Met (Chart Mgr); Northumbria (Chart Mgr, Proj Mgr); Portsmouth (Chart Mgr (Bus Ldrshp Mgt), Proj Mgt); Queen Margaret (Bus Mgt); Reading (App Mgt (Chart Mgr), Mgt Prac (Chart Mgr), Imprv Ldr (Mgng Bus Trnsf); Robert Gordon (Bus Mgt); Strathclyde (Chart Mgr, IT Mgt Bus, Bus Mgt); Teesside (Chart Mgr); UHI (Bus Mgt); West London (Bus Analyt, Chart Mgr, Exprs Del Mgr, Snr Ldr).

CHOOSING YOUR COURSE (SEE ALSO CH.1)

Universities and colleges teaching quality See www.qaa.ac.uk; https://discoveruni.gov.uk.

Top research universities and colleges (REF 2021) (Business and Management Studies) Cambridge; Imperial London; London Bus Sch; London LSE; Warwick; City St George's; Bath; Manchester; London (King's); Exeter.

Examples of sandwich degree courses Anglia Ruskin; Aston; Bangor; Bath; Bedfordshire; Birmingham City; Bournemouth; Bradford; Brighton; Brunel; Buckingham; Central Lancashire; Chester; Chichester; City St George's; Coventry; De Montfort; Derby; Exeter; Glasgow Caledonian; Gloucestershire; Greenwich; Harper Adams; Hertfordshire; Huddersfield; Hull; Keele; Kingston; Lancaster; Leeds; Liverpool; Liverpool John Moores; London (QM); London (RH); Loughborough; Manchester Met; Newcastle; Northumbria; Nottingham Trent; Oxford Brookes; Plymouth; Portsmouth; Queen's Belfast; Reading; Robert Gordon; Sheffield Hallam; South Wales; Staffordshire; Surrey; Sussex; Teesside; Ulster; Univ Law; UWE Bristol; Westminster; Wolverhampton.

ADMISSIONS INFORMATION

Admissions tutors' advice **Buckingham** Try to demonstrate that you have a genuine interest in business and explain why it fascinates you. Why have you decided to choose this particular course and how do you think it will add value to you in your pursuit of your career goals? **Leeds** Applicants taking the BTEC Extended Diploma may be required to take an additional Maths A-level paper.

Advice to applicants and planning the UCAS personal statement There are many different kinds of businesses and any work experience is almost essential for these courses. This should be described in detail: for example, size of firm, turnover, managerial problems, sales and marketing aspects, customers' attitudes. Any special interests in business management should also be included, for example, personnel work, purchasing, marketing. Give details of travel or work experience abroad and, for international courses, language expertise and examples of leadership and organising skills. Reference can be made to any particular business topics you have studied in the *Financial Times*, *The Economist* and the business sections in the weekend press. Applicants need to be sociable and ambitious team players. Say why you are interested in the course, identify your academic strengths, your personal strengths and interests. Check information on the websites of the Chartered Institute of Public Relations, the Chartered Institute of Marketing and the Chartered Institute of Personnel and Development. See **Appendix 3**; see also **Accountancy/Accounting**.

Selection interviews Yes Reading (Acc Bus), Winchester (Optional); **Some** Bath; **No** Anglia Ruskin, Bradford, Brighton, City St George's, Leeds, London Met, Plymouth, Portsmouth, Robert Gordon, Salford, Stirling, Swansea, Warwick, West London.

Interview advice and questions Any work experience you describe on the UCAS application will probably be the focus of questions which could include topics covering marketing, selling, store organisation and management and customer problems. Personal qualities are naturally important in a career in business, so be ready for such questions as: What qualities do you have which are suitable and important for this course? Describe your strengths and weaknesses. Why should we give you a place on this course? Is advertising fair? What qualities does a person in business require to be successful? What makes a good manager? What is a cash-flow system? What problems can it cause? How could supermarkets improve customer relations? See also **Chapter 5**.

Reasons for rejection (non-academic) Hadn't read the prospectus. Lack of communication skills. Limited commercial interest. Weak on numeracy and problem-solving. Lack of interview preparation (no questions). Lack of outside interests. Inability to cope with a year abroad. The candidate brought his parent who answered all the questions. See also **Marketing**.

GRADUATE DESTINATIONS AND EMPLOYMENT

(See **Chapter 1, Graduate Outcomes.**)

Career note The majority of graduates enter trainee management roles in business-related and administrative careers, many specialising in some of the areas listed in Other degree subjects for consideration below. The main graduate destinations are in finance, property development, wholesale, retail and manufacturing.

OTHER DEGREE SUBJECTS FOR CONSIDERATION

Accountancy; Banking; Business Information Technology; E-Business; Economics; Estate Management; Finance; Hospitality Management; Housing Management; Human Resource Management; Insurance; Leisure Management; Logistics; Marketing; Public Administration; Retail Management; Sports Management; Surveying.

BUSINESS AND MANAGEMENT COURSES (INTERNATIONAL AND EUROPEAN)

(including **Business Management with a European Language**; see also **Business and Management Courses, Business and Management Courses (Specialised), Hospitality and Event Management, Human Resource Management, Leisure and Recreation Management/Studies, Marketing, Retail Management, Tourism and Travel**)

Useful websites See **Business and Management Courses**.

NB The points totals shown to the left of the institutions are for ease of reference only. It must not be assumed that Tariff points are always used by institutions or that they can be substituted for an offer in grades. The level of an offer is not necessarily indicative of the quality of a course.

COURSE OFFERS INFORMATION

Subject requirements/preferences GCSE Mathematics and English often at grade 7 or 5/6 (A or B) required. A language will be stipulated for most courses in this subject area. In some cases grades 7, 5/6 or 4 (A, B or C) may be required. Some popular universities are now making lower offers for disadvantaged and other students.

Your target offers and examples of degree courses

152 pts **Edinburgh** – A*AA (Int Bus Fr/Ger/Span) (IB 39 pts HL 666)
Warwick – A*AA (Int Mgt) (IB 38 pts)

144 pts **Bath** – AAA/A*AB (Int Mgt) (IB 36 pts HL 765/666)
Exeter – AAA (Bus Mgt (Yr Ind)) (IB 36 pts HL 666)
Leeds – AAA (Int Bus; Int Bus Fin) (IB 35 pts HL 17 pts)
London (UCL) – AAA incl maths (Econ Bus E Euro St) (IB 38 pts HL 18 pts incl 6 maths)
Manchester – AAA (Int Mgt) (IB 36 pts HL 666)

136 pts **Bath** – AAB/ABB+aEPQ incl A Ger (Int Mgt Ger) (IB 36 pts HL 665 incl 6 Ger); AAB–ABB+aEPQ incl A Fr (Int Mgt Fr) (IB 36 pts HL 665 incl 6 Fr); AAB–ABB+aEPQ incl A Span (Int Mgt Span) (IB 36 pts HL 665 incl 6 Span)
Birmingham – AAB (Int Bus; Int Bus Lang) (IB 32 pts HL 665)
Brunel – AAB (Int Bus) (IB 30 pts)
Lancaster – AAB incl lang (Int Bus Mgt (Yr Abrd)) (IB 35 pts HL 16 pts)
Liverpool – AAB (Int Bus) (IB 35 pts)
London (King's) – AAB (Mgt Modn Langs (Yr Abrd)) (IB 35 pts HL 17 pts)
Loughborough – AAB (Int Bus) (IB 35 pts HL 665)
Newcastle – AAB (Int Bus Mgt) (IB 34 pts)
Sheffield – AAB (Int Bus Mgt (St Abrd)) (IB 34 pts)

128 pts **Cardiff** – ABB–AAB (Bus Mgt (Int Mgt)) (IB 32–34 pts HL 665–666); ABB–AAB incl lang (Bus Mgt Euro Lang) (IB 32–34 pts HL 665–666 incl 6 lang)
Edinburgh – ABB–AAA (Int Bus) (IB 34–37 pts HL 655–666)
Kent – ABB (Int Bus) (HL 566)
Lancaster – ABB 128 pts (Int Mgt) (IB 32 pts HL 16 pts)
London (QM) – ABB incl hum/soc sci (Russ Bus Mgt) (IB 32 pts HL 655)
London (RH) – ABB–AAB (Mgt Int Bus; Modn Langs Mgt) (IB 32 pts HL 655)
London (SOAS) – AAB (Mgt)
Queen's Belfast – ABB (Int Bus Fr/Ger/Mand) (IB 33 pts HL 655 incl lang)
Reading – ABB (Int Bus Mgt) (IB 32 pts)
Sheffield – ABB 128 pts (Bus Mgt Jap St) (IB 33 pts)
Surrey – ABB (Int Bus Mgt) (IB 32 pts)

120 pts **Dundee** – BBB 120 pts (Int Bus) (IB 30 pts HL 555)
Essex – BBB (Int Bus Entre) (IB 30 pts HL 555)
Gloucestershire – 120 pts (Int Bus Mgt)
Kingston – 120–136 pts (Int Bus)
Northumbria – 120 pts (Int Bus Mgt)
Nottingham Trent – 120 pts (Int Bus)
Portsmouth – BBB–ABB 120–128 pts (Int Bus) (IB 29–30 pts HL 664–665)
Stirling – BBB incl lang (Euro Langs Soty Int Mgt) (IB 28 pts)
Surrey – BBB incl Fr/Span (Bus Mgt Fr/Span) (IB 32 pts HL 5 lang)
Sussex – BBB–ABB (Int Bus) (IB 30–32 pts)

112 pts **Bradford** – BBC 112 pts (Int Bus Mgt)
Cardiff Met – BBC 112 pts (Int Bus Mgt) (HL 55)
Coventry – BBC (Int Bus Mgt) (IB 24 pts); BBC incl art/des (Int Fash Bus) (IB 29 pts incl vis arts/des tech)

De Montfort – 112 pts (Int Bus) (IB 26 pts)
Glasgow Caledonian – BBC (Int Bus)
Greenwich – BBC 112 pts (Int Bus)
Heriot-Watt – BBC–ABB (Int Bus Mgt) (IB 29 pts)
Hertfordshire – BBC–BBB 112–120 pts (Int Bus)
Huddersfield – BBC–BBB 112–120 pts (Int Bus)
Hull – BBC 112 pts (Int Bus) (IB 28 pts)
Keele – BBC (Int Bus Mgt) (IB 29 pts)
Leeds Beckett – 112 pts (Int Bus)
Liverpool John Moores – BBC 112 pts (Bus Int Bus Mgt)
Oxford Brookes – BBC 112 pts (Int Bus Mgt) (IB 30 pts)
Roehampton – 112 pts (Int Bus)
Sheffield Hallam – BBC incl Fr/Ger/Span 112 pts (Langs Int Bus (Fr/Ger/Span)); BBC–BBB 112–120 pts (Int Bus)
UWE Bristol – 112 pts (Int Bus)
Westminster – BBC–ABB 112–128 pts (Int Bus)

104 pts **Brighton** – BCC–BBB 104–120 pts (Int Bus Mgt) (IB 26 pts)
Central Lancashire – 104–112 pts (Int Bus)
Chester – BCC–BBC 104–112 pts (Int Bus Mgt) (IB 26 pts)
Edinburgh Napier – BCC (Int Bus Mgt) (IB 28 pts HL 654)
Lincoln – (Int Bus Mgt)
Manchester Met – BCC–BBC 104–112 pts (Int Bus Mgt) (IB 26 pts)
Middlesex – BCC–BBC 104–112 pts (Int Bus)
Robert Gordon – BCC (Int Bus Mgt) (IB 27 pts)
Salford – BCC–BBC 104–112 pts (Int Bus Mgt) (IB 30 pts)
Westminster – BCC–BBB 104–120 pts (Int Bus (Arbc/Chin/Fr/Span)) (HL 4 Engl)
York St John – 104 pts (Int Bus)

96 pts **Anglia Ruskin** – 96 pts (Int Bus Mgt) (IB 24 pts)
London Met – CCC 96 pts (Int Bus Mgt)
London Regent's – CCC–AAA 96–144 pts (Bus courses); CCC–AAA (Int Bus) (IB 24 pts)
Middlesex – CCC–BBC 96–112 pts (Int Tour Mgt (Span))
Wolverhampton – CCC 96 pts (Int Bus Mgt)

80 pts **Bedfordshire** – 80 pts (Int Bus)

ALTERNATIVE OFFERS See **Chapter 6** and **Appendix 1** for grades/UCAS Tariff points information for other examinations.

DEGREE APPRENTICESHIPS

See **Business and Management Courses**.

EXAMPLES OF COLLEGES OFFERING COURSES IN THIS SUBJECT FIELD

Blackburn (Coll); Bristol City (Coll); Cornwall (Coll); Doncaster (Coll); Durham New (Coll); Ealing, Hammersmith and West London (Coll); HOW (Coll); Newcastle (Coll); Nottingham (Coll); Riverside (Coll); South Essex (Coll).

CHOOSING YOUR COURSE (SEE ALSO CH.1)

UNIVERSITIES AND COLLEGES TEACHING QUALITY See www.qaa.ac.uk; www.discoveruni.gov.uk.

TOP RESEARCH UNIVERSITIES AND COLLEGES (REF 2021) See **Business and Management Courses**.

EXAMPLES OF SANDWICH DEGREE COURSES Anglia Ruskin; Bath; Bradford; Brighton; Brunel; De Montfort; Essex; Exeter; Greenwich; Hertfordshire; Huddersfield; Hull; Keele; Leeds Beckett; London (King's); Loughborough; Manchester Met; Middlesex; Newcastle; Northumbria; Nottingham Trent; Oxford Brookes; Portsmouth; Robert Gordon; Sheffield; Sheffield Hallam; Sussex.

ADMISSIONS INFORMATION

Advice to applicants and planning the UCAS personal statement See **Business and Management Courses**.

Selection interviews Some Bath, Loughborough; **No** Anglia Ruskin, Birmingham, Bradford, Brighton, De Montfort, Leeds, Robert Gordon, Stirling.

Interview advice and questions See **Business and Management Courses**.

Reasons for rejection (non-academic) See **Business and Management Courses**.

GRADUATE DESTINATIONS AND EMPLOYMENT

(See **Chapter 1, Graduate Outcomes.**)

Career note See **Business and Management Courses**.

OTHER DEGREE SUBJECTS FOR CONSIDERATION

Accountancy; Banking; Business Information Technology; E-Business; Economics; Estate Management; Finance; Hospitality Management; Housing Management; Human Resource Management; Insurance; Leisure Management; Logistics; Marketing; Public Administration; Retail Management; Sports Management; Surveying.

BUSINESS AND MANAGEMENT COURSES (SPECIALISED)

(including **Advertising, Agri-Business Management, Business, Marketing and Consumer Behaviour, Food Science with Business, Public Relations and Publishing**; see also **Business and Management Courses, Business and Management Courses (International and European), Hospitality and Event Management, Human Resource Management, Leisure and Recreation Management/Studies, Marketing, Retail Management, Tourism and Travel**)

Useful websites See **Business and Management Courses**.

NB The points totals shown to the left of the institutions are for ease of reference only. It must not be assumed that Tariff points are always used by institutions or that they can be substituted for an offer in grades. The level of an offer is not necessarily indicative of the quality of a course.

COURSE OFFERS INFORMATION

Subject requirements/preferences GCSE Mathematics and English often at grade 7 or 5/6 (A or B) required. **AL** Mathematics required for some courses. Some popular universities are now making lower offers for disadvantaged and other students.

Your target offers and examples of degree courses

144 pts **London (UCL)** – AAA incl chem+sci/maths (Chem Mgt St) (IB 38 pts HL 18 pts incl 6 chem+sci/maths)
Warwick – AAA incl maths+phys (Eng Bus Mgt) (IB 36 pts HL 6 maths+phys)

136 pts **Lancaster** – AAB (Adv Mark; Int Bus Mgt (Frnc)) (IB 35 pts HL 16 pts)
Loughborough – AAB (Geog Mgt) (IB 35 pts HL 665)
Ulster – AAB (Comm Adv Mark) (IB 28 pts HL 14 pts)

128 pts **Edinburgh** – ABB–AAA incl sci/maths (Ecol Env Sci Mgt) (IB 32–34 pts HL 555 incl sci/maths)
Leeds – ABB (Env Bus) (IB 34 pts HL 16 pts)
Newcastle – ABB (Agribus Mgt) (IB 32 pts)

120 pts **Cardiff** – BBB–AAB (Bus Mgt (Log Ops)) (IB 31–34 pts HL 665–666)
Derby – BBB 120 pts (Int Tour Mgt)
East Anglia – BBB/BBC+aEPQ (Glob Comm Bus Mgt) (IB 31 pts)
Reading – BBB (Agric Bus Mgt (Yr Ind)) (IB 30 pts)

Stirling – BBB (HR Mgt) (IB 30 pts)
West London – 120 pts (Air Trans Mgt (ATPL))

112 pts **Arts London** – 112 pts+interview (Fash PR Comm); BBC 112 pts (Fash Mgt) (IB 25 pts)
Coventry – BBC (Bus Mark) (IB 24 pts); BBC 112 pts (Disas Emer Mgt) (IB 29 pts); BBC incl art/des (Int Fash Bus) (IB 29 pts incl vis arts/des tech)
Creative Arts – 112 pts (Fash Bus Mgt) (IB 27–30 pts HL 15)
De Montfort – 112 pts (Adv Mark Comms) (IB 26 pts)
East London – 112 pts (HR Mgt) (IB 24 pts HL 15 pts); BBC 112 pts (Adv) (IB 25 pts HL 15 pts)
Essex – BBC–BBB 112–120 pts (Glob St Bus Mgt) (IB 29–30 pts HL 554–555)
Glasgow Caledonian – BBC (Risk Mgt)
Liverpool John Moores – BBC 112 pts (Evnts Mgt)
Middlesex – 112 pts (Adv PR Brnd) (IB 28 pts)
Nottingham Trent – 112 pts (Fash Mgt; Quant Surv Commer Mgt); BBC 112 pts (Constr Mgt)
Oxford Brookes – BBC 112 pts (Quant Surv Commer Mgt) (IB 30 pts)
Plymouth – 112–128 pts (Marit Bus) (IB 28–32 pts HL 4)
Sheffield Hallam – BBC 112 pts (IT Bus St)
Ulster – BBC incl sci/maths/tech (Eng Mgt) (IB 25 pts HL 12 pts incl 5 maths+sci)
West London – BBC 112 pts (Adv PR; Culn Arts Mgt)

104 pts **Arts London** – 104 pts (PR)
Bournemouth – 104–120 pts (Bus Mgt (Fin)) (IB 28–31 pts)
Buckingham – BCC–BBB (Bus Mgt App Comp) (IB 30–32 pts)
Central Lancashire – 104–112 pts (Int Tour Mgt)
Leeds Beckett – 104–120 pts (Spo Bus Mgt)
Manchester Met – BCC–BBC 104–112 pts (Adv Brnd Comm; Spo Bus Mgt) (IB 26 pts)
Robert Gordon – BCC (Fash Mgt) (IB 27 pts)
Royal Agricultural Univ – BCC (Rur Lnd Mgt; Rur Lnd Mgt (Yr Ind)) (IB 26 pts)
Solent – 104–120 pts (Fash Mgt Mark); 104–120 pts (Marit Bus)

96 pts **Harper Adams** – 96–112 pts+interview (Agric Frm Bus Mgt) (IB 28 pts)
Liverpool (LIPA) – CCC 96 pts+interview (Mgt (Mus Ind Mgt))
London Met – CCC 96 pts (Mus Bus)
South Wales – CCC 96 pts (Bus Mgt (Evnt Mgt))
UCEM – 96 pts (Rl Est Mgt)

88 pts **Bucks New** – 88–112 pts (Avn Mgt)
Trinity Saint David – 88 pts (Int Trav Tour Mgt)

80 pts **Birmingham (UC)** – CDD–CCC 80–96 pts (Bus Ent)
Colchester (UC) – 80 pts+interview (Constr Mgt (Site Mgt))
Sparsholt (Coll) – CCE incl sci (Aqua Fish Mgt) (IB 24 pts HL 4 sci)
Trinity Saint David – 80 pts (Spo Mgt)

64 pts **London (Royal Central Sch SpDr)** – 64–120 pts+interview+portfolio (Stg Mgt Tech Thea)
UHI – CC (Glf Mgt)

32 pts **Plymouth** – 32 pts (Marit Bus Fdn Yr) (IB 24–25 pts HL 4)

24 pts **UHI** – D+interview (Mus Bus)

ALTERNATIVE OFFERS See **Chapter 6** and **Appendix 1** for grades/UCAS Tariff points information for other examinations.

DEGREE APPRENTICESHIPS

See **Business and Management Courses**.

CHOOSING YOUR COURSE (SEE ALSO CH.1)

UNIVERSITIES AND COLLEGES TEACHING QUALITY See www.qaa.ac.uk; www.discoveruni.gov.uk.

TOP RESEARCH UNIVERSITIES AND COLLEGES (REF 2021) See **Business and Management Courses**.

EXAMPLES OF SANDWICH DEGREE COURSES Bournemouth; Central Lancashire; Coventry; De Montfort; Harper Adams; Leeds Beckett; Loughborough; Manchester Met; Newcastle; Nottingham Trent; Oxford Brookes; Reading; Sheffield Hallam; Solent; Ulster.

ADMISSIONS INFORMATION

Advice to applicants and planning the UCAS personal statement See **Business and Management Courses**.

Selection interviews **Yes** Liverpool (LIPA), UHI Perth; **Some** Arts London; **No** East Anglia, Harper Adams, Leeds, Robert Gordon, Sunderland, West London.

Interview advice and questions For Consumer Studies/Science, questions will stem from your special interests in this subject and in the past have included: What interests you in consumer behaviour? What are the advantages and disadvantages of measuring consumer behaviour? What is ergonomics? What do you understand by the term sustainable consumption? What world or national news has annoyed, pleased or upset you? What relevance do textiles and dress have to home economics? How would you react in a room full of fools?

GRADUATE DESTINATIONS AND EMPLOYMENT

(See **Chapter 1, Graduate Outcomes.**)

Career note See **Business and Management Courses**.

OTHER DEGREE SUBJECTS FOR CONSIDERATION

Accountancy; Banking; Business Information Technology; E-Business; Economics; Estate Management; Finance; Hospitality Management; Housing Management; Human Resource Management; Insurance; Leisure Management; Logistics; Marketing; Public Administration; Retail Management; Sports Management; Surveying.

CELTIC, IRISH, SCOTTISH AND WELSH STUDIES

(including **Celtic and Linguistics and Gaelic Studies**)

Strong evidence of Celtic civilisation and language exists in Ireland, Scotland, Wales, Cornwall, the Isle of Man and across the Celtic Sea in Brittany, although the Celts are believed to have inhabited much of Great Britain prior to the arrival of the Saxons and afterwards. In Great Britain, the Welsh language is spoken by 19% of the Welsh population, mainly in the border counties and Gwynedd, where it is reported that 70% of the population are fluent speakers. Scottish Gaelic is native to Scotland and bears strong similarities to the Irish language. The 'Scots' dialect of English is also spoken in the Lowlands and the Northern Isles. In Ireland, the native Irish language is taught in schools throughout the island. In the Gaeltacht areas of the Republic of Ireland, the language is used on an everyday basis. The content of courses in each of these languages, such as the Celtic option at Aberystwyth (the largest department of Welsh in the UK), will cover history, literature, and the language and its place in the modern world. Cambridge also offers a degree in Anglo Saxon, Norse and Celtic, unique in the UK for those fascinated by medieval history, literature, languages and archaeology. It is offered by all colleges and there are no specific subject requirements.

Useful websites http://gov.wales; www.bbc.co.uk/wales; www.daltai.com; www.eisteddfod.cymru; www.digitalmedievalist.com

NB The points totals shown to the left of the institutions are for ease of reference only. It must not be assumed that Tariff points are always used by institutions or that they can be substituted for an offer in grades. The level of an offer is not necessarily indicative of the quality of a course.

COURSE OFFERS INFORMATION

Subject requirements/preferences **GCSE** A foreign language or Welsh may be required. **AL** Welsh may be required for some courses. Some popular universities are now making lower offers for disadvantaged and other students.

YOUR TARGET OFFERS AND EXAMPLES OF DEGREE COURSES

152 pts **Cambridge** – A*AA+interview+ASNCAA (A-Sxn Nrs Celt) (IB 41–42 pts HL 776)
144 pts **St Andrews** – AAA incl hist (Scot Hist courses) (IB 38 pts HL 666 incl hist)
128 pts **Edinburgh** – ABB (Celt; Celt Arch; Celt Ling; Celt Scot Hist; Scot Ethnol; Scot St) (IB 34 pts HL 655); ABB+interview (P Educ Gael) (IB 34 pts HL 655); ABB incl Engl (Celt Engl Lit; Celt Scot Lit; Scot Lit) (IB 34 pts HL 655 incl 5 Engl); ABB–A*AA incl Engl (Engl Scot Lit) (IB 37–39 pts HL 655–666 incl 5 Engl)
Queen's Belfast – ABB incl Ir (Ir)
120 pts **Aberdeen** – BBB (Celt A-Sxn St; Celt A-Sxn St Comb Hons; Gael St) (IB 32 pts HL 555); BBC (Engl Scot Lit) (IB 32 pts HL 555)
Glasgow – BBB–AAB 120–136 pts (Gael Civ) (IB 38 pts); BBB–AAB incl hum (Celt Civ courses; Celt St courses) (IB 32–36 pts HL 655–665 incl Eng+hum); (Gael; Scot Lit) (IB 34 pts HL 655 incl Engl+hum)
Liverpool – BBB (Ir St Comb Hons) (IB 30 pts)
Stirling – BBB (Scot Hist) (IB 30 pts)
Swansea – BBB 120 pts (Welsh courses) (IB 32 pts)
104 pts **Aberystwyth** – BCC–BBB 104–120 pts (Welsh courses) (IB 28–30 pts); CCC–BBB 104–120 pts (Celt St) (IB 26–30 pts)
Cardiff – BCC–BBC incl Welsh (Welsh) (IB 29–30 pts HL 665)
96 pts **Aberystwyth** – CCC–BBB 96–120 pts (Hist Welsh Hist) (IB 26–30 pts)
Bangor – 96–128 pts (Prof Welsh (Cym Prof)) (HL 5 Welsh)
72 pts **UHI** – BC (Hist Arch); BC+interview (Gael Dev); BC+interview+audition (Gael Trad Mus)

ALTERNATIVE OFFERS See **Chapter 6** and **Appendix 1** for grades/UCAS Tariff points information for other examinations.

CHOOSING YOUR COURSE (SEE ALSO CH.1)

UNIVERSITIES AND COLLEGES TEACHING QUALITY See www.qaa.ac.uk; www.discoveruni.gov.uk.

ADMISSIONS INFORMATION

ADVICE TO APPLICANTS AND PLANNING THE UCAS PERSONAL STATEMENT Interests in this field largely develop through literature, museum visits or archaeology which should be fully described in the UCAS application.

SELECTION INTERVIEWS Yes Cambridge, Edinburgh (P Educ Gael), UHI (Gael Dev; Gael Trad Mus).

INTERVIEW ADVICE AND QUESTIONS Past questions have included: Why do you want to study this subject? What specific areas of Celtic culture interest you? What do you expect to gain by studying unusual subjects? See **Chapter 5**.

GRADUATE DESTINATIONS AND EMPLOYMENT

(See **Chapter 1, Graduate Outcomes.**)

CAREER NOTE See **Combined Courses** and **Languages**.

OTHER DEGREE SUBJECTS FOR CONSIDERATION

Anthropology; Archaeology; English; History; Linguistics.

CHEMISTRY

(see also **Biochemistry, Engineering (Chemical), Pharmacy and Pharmaceutical Sciences**)

There is a shortage of applicants for this subject despite the fact that it's the basis of many careers in the manufacturing industries, such areas as pharmaceuticals, medicine, veterinary science and health, agriculture, petroleum, cosmetics, plastics, the food industry, colour chemistry and aspects of the environment such as pollution and recycling. Most courses will offer a range of compulsory modules (possibly up to 75% of a course) and a series of optional modules. For example, at the University of York, compulsory modules will include organic, inorganic and physical chemistry. Optional modules on offer cover air quality and human health, analytical and forensic science, atmospheric chemistry and climate, biological chemistry, environmental chemistry, green chemistry, industrial management, materials chemistry and medical chemistry. These options at all universities enable students to begin to focus on special studies and lay a foundation for possible future careers.

Useful websites www.rsc.org; https://vrchemistry.chem.ox.ac.uk/

NB The points totals shown to the left of the institutions are for ease of reference only. It must not be assumed that Tariff points are always used by institutions or that they can be substituted for an offer in grades. The level of an offer is not necessarily indicative of the quality of a course.

COURSE OFFERS INFORMATION

Subject requirements/preferences GCSE English, mathematics/science subjects usually required. 7 or 5/6 (A/B) grades often stipulated by popular universities. **AL** Two science subjects including chemistry usually required. Some popular universities are now making lower offers for disadvantaged and other students.

Your target offers and examples of degree courses

160 pts **Cambridge** – A*A*A incl sci/maths+interview+ESAT (Nat Sci (Chem)) (IB 41–42 pts HL 776 incl sci/maths)

Oxford – A*A*A incl chem+maths+interview (Chem) (IB 40 pts HL 766 incl 7 chem+6 maths)

152 pts **Durham** – A*AA incl chem+maths (Chem) (IB 38 pts HL 666 incl chem+maths)

144 pts **Bristol** – AAA incl chem (Chem) (IB 36 pts HL 18 pts incl 6 chem)

Imperial London – AAA incl chem+maths+interview (Chem courses) (IB 38 pts HL 6 chem+maths); (Chem (Yr Ind/Rsch); Chem Medcnl Chem) (IB 38 pts HL 666 incl chem+maths); AAA incl chem+maths+phys+interview (Chem Mol Phys) (IB 38 pts HL 666 incl chem+maths)

London (King's) – AAA incl chem+sci/maths (Chem; Chem Biomed) (IB 35 pts HL 666 incl 6 chem+sci/maths)

London (UCL) – AAA incl chem+sci/maths (Chem; Chem Mgt St) (IB 38 pts HL 18 pts incl 6 chem+sci/maths); AAA incl maths+chem (Chem Maths) (IB 38 pts HL 18 pts incl 6 chem+maths)

Manchester – AAA incl chem+sci/maths+interview (Chem; Chem Medcnl Chem) (IB 36 pts HL 666 incl chem+sci/maths)

St Andrews – AAA incl chem (Chem) (IB 38 pts HL 666 incl chem+sci/maths/geog)

136 pts **Bath** – AAB–AAA incl chem+sci/maths (Chem courses) (IB 36 pts HL 665 incl 6 chem+5 sci/maths)

Leeds – AAB incl chem (Chem courses; Medcnl Chem) (IB 35 pts HL 16 pts incl 6 chem)

Loughborough – AAB incl chem+interview (Chem (MChem)) (IB 35 pts HL 665 incl chem)

Newcastle – AAB incl chem (Chem (MChem); Chem (Yr Ind)) (IB 33 pts HL 6 chem)

Nottingham – AAB–AAA incl A chem (Medcnl Biol Chem) (IB 32–34 pts HL 6 chem)

Sheffield – AAB incl chem (Chem) (IB 34 pts HL 5 chem)

Southampton – AAB incl chem (Chem) (IB 32–34 pts HL 16–17 pts incl 5 chem); AAB–AAA incl chem+sci/maths (Chem Medcnl Sci (MChem)) (IB 34–36 pts HL 17–18 pts incl 6 chem+sci/maths)

Warwick – AAB incl chem+sci/maths (Chem; Chem Medcnl Chem) (IB 34 pts HL 6 chem 5 maths/sci)

York – AAB–A*AA incl chem+sci/maths (Chem; Chem Atmos Env) (IB 35–36 pts HL 6 chem+sci/maths); AAB–A*AA incl chem+sci/maths (Chem Biol Medcnl Chem) (IB 35–36 pts HL 6 chem+sci/maths)

128 pts **Birmingham** – ABB–AAB incl chem (Chem; Chem Modn Lang) (IB 32 pts HL 655–665 incl chem)

Cardiff – ABB–AAB incl chem (Chem) (IB 32–34 pts HL 665–666 incl 6 chem)

Edinburgh – ABB–AAA incl chem+maths (Chem; Medcnl Biol Chem) (IB 32–37 pts HL 555–666 incl chem+maths)

Lancaster – ABB incl chem+sci/maths (Chem) (IB 32 pts HL 16 pts incl 6 chem+sci)
Leicester – ABB–AAB incl chem (Chem) (IB 30–32 pts HL 5 chem)
Liverpool – ABB/BBB+aEPQ incl chem+sci/maths (Chem) (IB 33 pts HL 6 chem 5 sci); ABB–AAB incl chem+sci (Chem (Yr Ind)) (IB 33 pts HL 6 chem 5 sci); ABB–ABB incl chem+sci (Medcnl Chem) (IB 33 pts HL 6 chem 5 sci)
London (QM) – ABB incl chem (Chem) (IB 34 pts HL 655 incl chem)
Loughborough – ABB incl chem+interview (Chem; Medcnl Pharml Chem) (IB 34 pts HL 655 incl chem)
Newcastle – ABB incl chem (Chem; Chem Medcnl Chem) (IB 32 pts HL 6 chem)
Nottingham – ABB–AAB incl A chem (Chem) (IB 32–34 pts HL 6 chem)
Nottingham Trent – ABB incl chem 128 pts (Chem (MChem))
Reading – ABB incl chem+interview (Chem (MChem)) (IB 32 pts)
Strathclyde – ABB incl chem+sci/maths (Chem Teach (MChem)) (IB 34 pts HL sci/maths); ABB incl sci/maths (Foren Analyt Chem (MChem)) (IB 34 pts HL sci/maths)

120 pts **Aberdeen** – BBB incl chem+sci/maths (Chem) (IB 32 pts HL 555 incl chem+sci/maths)
Aston – BBB/BBC+bEPQ incl chem (App Chem) (IB 31 pts HL 555 incl chem)
Dundee – BBB incl biol+chem (Biol Chem Drug Dscvry) (IB 30 pts HL 555 incl biol+chem)
East Anglia – BBB/ABC incl chem (Chem) (IB 31 pts HL 5 chem)
Glasgow – BBB–ABB incl chem+maths (Chem) (IB 32 pts HL 555 incl chem+maths)
Hull – BBB incl B chem (Chem) (IB 28 pts HL 6 chem)
Keele – BBB incl B chem (Chem) (IB 30 pts HL 555 incl chem)
Leicester – BBB–ABB incl chem (Medcnl Chem) (IB 28 pts HL 5 chem)
Nottingham Trent – BBB incl chem 120 pts (Medcnl Chem)
Queen's Belfast – BBB incl chem+sci (Chem; Medcnl Chem) (IB 32 pts HL 655 incl chem+sci)
Reading – BBB incl chem+interview (Chem; Chem Cos Sci) (IB 30 pts HL 5 chem)
Strathclyde – BBB incl chem+sci/maths (Chem (MChem)) (IB 30 pts HL chem+sci/maths)
Surrey – BBB incl chem+sci (Chem) (IB 32 pts HL 5 chem)
Sussex – BBB incl chem (Chem) (IB 30 pts HL 5 chem)
Swansea – BBB–AAB incl chem (Chem) (IB 32 pts HL 5 chem+maths)

112 pts **Aston** – BBC/BCC+bEPQ incl chem (Chem) (IB 29 pts HL 554 incl 5 chem)
Bradford – BBC incl chem 112 pts (Chem) (HL 655 incl 6 chem)
Chester – BBC incl chem 112 pts (Chem) (IB 26 pts HL 5 chem)
Huddersfield – BBC incl chem 112 pts (Chem) (HL 5 chem)
Kent – BBC incl chem/biol (Chem) (HL 5 sci)
Kingston – BBC incl chem+sci 112–128 pts (Chem)
London Met – BBC incl chem 112 pts (Chem)
Northumbria – 112 pts (Chem)
Nottingham Trent – (Chem)
Sheffield Hallam – BBC incl chem 112 pts (Chem)
Surrey – BBC incl chem+sci (Medcnl Chem) (IB 31 pts HL 5 chem+sci)
West Scotland – BBC incl chem (Chem) (IB 24 pts HL chem)

104 pts **Central Lancashire** – 104–112 pts incl chem (Chem) (HL 5 chem)
Greenwich – BCC incl chem 104 pts (Chem) (IB 26 pts HL 5 sci)
Heriot-Watt – BCC–BBB incl chem+maths/phys 104–120 pts (Chem courses) (IB 29 pts HL 5 chem+maths)
Lincoln – (Chem) (HL 5 chem)
Manchester Met – BCC incl chem 104–120 pts (Medcnl Pharml Chem (MChem)) (IB 26 pts HL 5 chem); BCC–BBC incl chem/app sci 104–112 pts (Chem) (IB 26 pts HL 5 chem)
Plymouth – BCC incl chem 104–112 pts incl chem (Chem) (IB 26–27 pts HL 4 chem)
South Wales – BCC incl chem+biol 104 pts (Foren Sci)

96 pts **Reading** – CCC–BBB (Chem Fdn) (IB 24–30 pts)
Teesside – CCC incl chem/app sci 96–112 pts (Chem)

Open University – (Nat Sci Chem)

Alternative offers See **Chapter 6** and **Appendix 1** for grades/UCAS Tariff points information for other examinations.

DEGREE APPRENTICESHIPS

Bradford (Chem); Greenwich (Chem); Kent (App Chem (Lab Sci)); Manchester Met (Chem Lab Sci).

EXAMPLES OF COLLEGES OFFERING COURSES IN THIS SUBJECT FIELD

Birmingham Met (Coll); Cornwall (Coll); Harrow (Coll); Leeds City (Coll); Liverpool City (Coll); Warrington and Vale Royal (Coll); Wirral Met (Coll).

CHOOSING YOUR COURSE (SEE ALSO CH.1)

Universities and colleges teaching quality See www.qaa.ac.uk; www.discoveruni.gov.uk.

Top research universities and colleges (REF 2021) (Chemistry) Bristol; Cambridge; London (UCL); Imperial London; London (King's); Oxford; Manchester; Liverpool; York; Edinburgh; St Andrews.

Examples of sandwich degree courses Bath; Cardiff; Dundee; East Anglia; Huddersfield; Imperial London; Kent; Kingston; Liverpool; Loughborough; Manchester Met; Newcastle; Northumbria; Nottingham Trent; Plymouth; Queen's Belfast; Reading; Sheffield Hallam; St Andrews; Surrey; Teesside; West Scotland; York.

ADMISSIONS INFORMATION

Advice to applicants and planning the UCAS personal statement Extend your knowledge beyond your exam studies by reading scientific journals and keeping abreast of scientific developments in the news. Discuss any visits to chemical firms and laboratories, for example, pharmaceutical, food science, rubber and plastic, paper, photographic, environmental health. See also **Appendix 3**.

Selection interviews Yes Bristol, Cambridge, Imperial London, Oxford (67% (success rate 19%)); **Some** Bath, East Anglia, London (QM), Loughborough, Teesside; **No** Huddersfield, Keele, London (UCL), Newcastle, Wolverhampton.

Interview advice and questions Be prepared for questions on your chemistry syllabus and aspects that you enjoy the most. In the past a variety of questions have been asked, for example: Why is carbon a special element? Discuss the nature of forces between atoms with varying intermolecular distances. Describe recent practicals. What is acid rain? What other types of pollution are caused by the human race? What is an enzyme? What are the general properties of benzene? Why might sciences be less popular among girls at school? What can a mass spectrometer be used for? What would you do if a river turned bright blue and you were asked how to test a sample? What would be the difference between metal and non-metal pollution? What is 'turning you on' in chemistry at the moment? See also **Chapter 5**.

Reasons for rejection (non-academic) Didn't attend interview. Rude and uncooperative. Arrived under influence of drink. Poor attitude and poor commitment to chemistry. Incomplete, inappropriate, illiterate personal statements.

GRADUATE DESTINATIONS AND EMPLOYMENT

(See **Chapter 1, Graduate Outcomes.**)

Career note A large number of Chemistry graduates choose to go on to further study as well as into scientific careers in research, analysis or development. Significant numbers also follow careers in a wide range of areas in management, teaching and retail work.

OTHER DEGREE SUBJECTS FOR CONSIDERATION

Agriculture; Biochemistry; Biological Sciences; Biomedical Science; Chemical Engineering; Environmental Science; Forensic Science; Genetics; Materials Science; Medicine; Microbiology; Oceanography; Pharmacology; Pharmacy.

CHINESE

(including **Korean**; see also **Languages**)

Assian languages are not necessarily difficult languages but they differ considerably in their writing systems which present their own problems for the new student. Even so, Chinese is not a language to be chosen for its novelty and students should have a strong interest in China and its people. In all courses, students should prepare for intensive language learning, the focus being on the written and spoken word supported by studies covering the history, politics and culture of China, and at the University of Leeds, additional studies of the Asia Pacific region. At Oxford (Asian and Middle Eastern Studies), it is possible to take an additional language from Japanese, Korean or Tibetan. The course in Chinese Studies at Durham also allows students to take modules in Japanese. It is customary in all universities to spend either the second or third year at a university in China. Several universities offer joint courses with Chinese universities.

Useful websites www.ciol.org.uk; www.bbc.co.uk/languages; www.china.org.cn; www.languageadvantage.com; www.languagematters.co.uk; www.thoughtco.com/asian-history-4133325

NB The points totals shown to the left of the institutions are for ease of reference only. It must not be assumed that Tariff points are always used by institutions or that they can be substituted for an offer in grades. The level of an offer is not necessarily indicative of the quality of a course.

COURSE OFFERS INFORMATION

Subject requirements/preferences GCSE A language is required. **AL** A modern language is usually required. Some popular universities are now making lower offers for disadvantaged and other students.

Your target offers and examples of degree courses

152 pts **Cambridge** – A*AA+interview+test (As Mid E St) (IB 41–42 pts HL 776)

144 pts **Oxford** – AAA+interview (As Mid E St incl Jap/Arab/Chin/Heb) (IB 39 pts HL 666); AAA+interview+AMELAT (As Mid E St incl Jap/Arab/Chin) (IB 39 pts HL 666)

136 pts **Durham** – AAB (Chin St (Yr Abrd)) (IB 36 pts HL 665 pts)

128 pts **Edinburgh** – ABB–AAB (Chin) (IB 34 pts HL 655)

Exeter – ABB incl Lat (Modn Langs Lat) (IB 32 pts HL 655 incl Lat)

Leeds – ABB (Chin (Modn); Chin courses) (IB 34 pts HL 16 pts)

London (SOAS) – ABB (Chin) (IB 35 pts HL 665)

Manchester – ABB+interview (Chin St) (IB 34 pts HL 655); ABB incl Chin (Chin Jap) (IB 34 pts HL 655); ABB incl Russ/Chin+interview (Russ Chin) (IB 34 pts HL 655 incl Russ/Chin); ABB incl lang+interview (Chin courses) (IB 34 pts HL 655)

Newcastle – ABB (Chin St; Ling Chin/Jap) (IB 32 pts)

Nottingham – ABB incl hist (Hist Contemp Chin St) (IB 32 pts HL 5 hist)

Sheffield – ABB/BBB+bEPQ (Chin St courses; Kor St) (IB 33 pts)

Southampton – ABB incl langs (Modn Langs) (IB 32 pts HL 16 pts incl 55 langs)

Sussex – ABB (Anth Lang) (IB 34 pts)

120 pts **Bangor** – 120–144 pts (Law Modn Langs)

London (Gold) – BBB (Int Rel Chin) (HL 655)

112 pts **Hertfordshire** – BBC–BBB 112–120 pts (Mand Comb Hons)

104 pts **Bangor** – 104–128 pts (Modn Langs Hist); 104–128 pts incl modn lang (Modn Langs) (HL 5 incl modn lang)

Chester – BCC–BBC (Chin Comb Hons) (IB 26 pts)

De Montfort – 104 pts (Educ St Mand)

Westminster – BCC–BBB 104–120 pts (Chin Engl Lang)

96 pts **Central Lancashire** – 96–112 pts incl lang (Modn Langs (2 Langs) (Fr/Span/Jap/Russ/Chin/Kor))

Trinity Saint David – 96 pts+interview (Chin St courses)

Alternative offers See **Chapter 6** and **Appendix 1** for grades/UCAS Tariff points information for other examinations.

CHOOSING YOUR COURSE (SEE ALSO CH.1)

Universities and colleges teaching quality See www.qaa.ac.uk; www.discoveruni.gov.uk.

Examples of sandwich degree courses Durham; Edinburgh; Manchester; Sheffield; Westminster.

ADMISSIONS INFORMATION

Advice to applicants and planning the UCAS personal statement It will be necessary to demonstrate a knowledge of China, its culture, political and economic background. Visits to the Far East should be mentioned, with reference to any features which have influenced your choice of degree course. See also **Appendix 3** under Languages.

Selection interviews Yes Cambridge, Oxford (83% (success rate 31%)); **No** Leeds.

Interview advice and questions You will be expected to convince the admissions tutor why you want to study the language. Your knowledge of Chinese culture, politics and society in general, and of Far Eastern problems, could also be tested. See also **Chapter 5**.

GRADUATE DESTINATIONS AND EMPLOYMENT

(See **Chapter 1, Graduate Outcomes.**)

Career note China is a country with a high economic growth rate and there are good opportunities for graduates, an increasing number being recruited by firms based in East Asia. Other opportunities exist in diplomacy, aid work and tourism throughout China, Taiwan and Mongolia as well as most non-scientific career areas in the UK. See also **Languages**.

OTHER DEGREE SUBJECTS FOR CONSIDERATION

Traditional Chinese Medicine; other Oriental languages.

CLASSICS AND CLASSICAL STUDIES/CIVILISATION

(see also **Archaeology, Greek, History (Ancient), Latin**)

Classics courses tend to focus on the study of Greek and Latin literature and language alongside topics such as the history, art, archaeology, drama and philosophy of Ancient Greece and Rome. Generally speaking, Classical Studies and Civilisation courses tend to focus more heavily on the wider life of the ancient world as revealed through these topics, whereas Classics courses seek to engage particularly with literature. Course entry requirements vary and Classics is by no means limited to those with prior knowledge of Greek and Latin.

At Oxford, home of the largest Classics department in the UK, two courses which do not require a previous knowledge of Latin or Greek are offered. Many Classical Studies degree courses offer these languages at beginner or advanced level, but applicants should check subject requirements carefully before applying.

Useful websites www.users.globalnet.co.uk/~loxias; www.classics.ox.ac.uk; www.cambridgescp.com; www.bbc.co.uk/history/ancient/greeks; www.bbc.co.uk/history/ancient/romans

NB The points totals shown to the left of the institutions are for ease of reference only. It must not be assumed that Tariff points are always used by institutions or that they can be substituted for an offer in grades. The level of an offer is not necessarily indicative of the quality of a course.

COURSE OFFERS INFORMATION

Subject requirements/preferences GCSE English and a foreign language usually required. Grades 8–9/7/5–6 (A*/A/B) may be stipulated. **AL** Check courses for Latin/Greek requirements. Some popular universities are now making lower offers for disadvantaged and other students.

YOUR TARGET OFFERS AND EXAMPLES OF DEGREE COURSES

152 pts **Cambridge** – A*AA incl Lat+interview+CAA (Class) (IB 41–42 pts HL 776 incl Lat)
Edinburgh – A*AA (Class Engl Lang; Class Ling; Class St) (IB 39 pts HL 666)

144 pts **Bristol** – AAA incl Engl (Engl Class St) (IB 36 pts HL 18 incl 6 Engl)
Durham – AAA (Class; Class Civ) (IB 37 pts HL 666)
Oxford – 144 pts (Class As Mid E St) (IB 39 pts HL 666); AAA+interview+CAT (Class; Class As Mid E St) (IB 39 pts HL 666); AAA+interview+CAT+MLAT (Class Modn Langs) (IB 39 pts HL 666); AAA incl Engl+interview+CAT (Class Engl) (IB 39 pts HL 666 incl Engl)
St Andrews – AAA (Art Hist Class St; Class St courses) (IB 36 pts HL 665); AAA incl for lang (Class) (IB 36 pts HL 665 incl 6 for lang)

136 pts **Bristol** – AAB (Class; Class St) (IB 34 pts HL 17 pts)
Edinburgh – AAB (Anc Medit Civ) (IB 36 pts HL 665)
Exeter – AAB–AAA incl Engl (Class St Engl courses) (IB 34–36 pts HL 665–666 incl 6 Engl); AAB–AAA incl Lat/class Gk (Class) (IB 34–36 pts HL 665–666 incl 5 Lat/class Gk); (Class (Emp Expnc)) (IB 34–36 pts HL 665–666 incl Lat/class Gk)
Leeds – AAB incl A Engl (Class Lit Engl) (IB 35 pts HL 16 pts incl 6 Engl)
London (King's) – AAB (Class St) (IB 35 pts HL 665); AAB incl A Lat/Gk (Class Anc Wrld) (IB 35 pts HL 665 incl 6 Lat/Gk); AAB incl Engl (Class St Engl) (IB 35 pts HL 665 incl 6 Engl)
London (UCL) – AAB incl A Gk/Lat 136 pts (Class Anc Wrld) (IB 36 pts)
Warwick – AAB (Class Civ) (IB 34 pts); AAB incl Lat/Anc Gk (Class) (IB 34 pts HL 6 Lat/Anc Gk)

128 pts **Birmingham** – ABB (Class Lit Civ) (IB 32 pts HL 655)
Edinburgh – ABB–AAB incl Lat/Gk (Class) (IB 34–36 pts HL 655–665 incl Lat/Gk)
Exeter – ABB (Class St Modn Langs) (IB 32 pts HL 655); ABB–AAA (Class St) (IB 32–36 pts)
Leeds – ABB–AAB (Class Civ) (IB 34–35 pts HL 16 pts)
London (UCL) – ABB (Class Arch Class Civ) (IB 34 pts HL 16 pts)
Manchester – ABB (Class; Class St) (IB 34 pts HL 655)
Newcastle – ABB (Class; Class St) (IB 32–35 pts HL 555)
Nottingham – ABB (Arch Class Civ; Class) (IB 32 pts); ABB–AAB (Class Civ) (IB 32–34 pts)

120 pts **Kent** – BBB–ABB (Class St); (Class Arch St) (HL 665)
Liverpool – BBB (Class; Class St) (IB 30 pts)
London (RH) – BBB–ABB (Class St) (IB 32 pts HL 555); BBB–ABB incl Lat/Gk (Class) (IB 32 pts HL 555 incl Lat/Gk)
Reading – BBB (Class St) (IB 30 pts)
Swansea – BBB 120 pts (Class St) (IB 32 pts)

96 pts **London (Birk)** – CCC–BBB incl Gk/Lat 96–120 pts (Class)
Trinity Saint David – 96 pts+interview (Class Civ)

88 pts **Reading** – CCD (Class Fdn) (IB 24 pts)

ALTERNATIVE OFFERS See **Chapter 6** and **Appendix 1** for grades/UCAS Tariff points information for other examinations.

CHOOSING YOUR COURSE (SEE ALSO CH.1)

UNIVERSITIES AND COLLEGES TEACHING QUALITY See www.qaa.ac.uk; www.discoveruni.gov.uk.

TOP RESEARCH UNIVERSITIES AND COLLEGES (REF 2021) (Classics) London (King's); Manchester; Warwick; Durham; Exeter; Kent; Oxford; Bristol; Edinburgh; Birmingham; Nottingham.

EXAMPLES OF SANDWICH DEGREE COURSES Exeter; Reading; Swansea.

ADMISSIONS INFORMATION

ADVICE TO APPLICANTS AND PLANNING THE UCAS PERSONAL STATEMENT Describe any visits made to classical sites or museums, or literature which you have read and enjoyed. Discuss any significant aspects which impressed you. Classics is an interdisciplinary subject and universities are looking for people who are versatile, imaginative and independently minded, so all types of extra-curricular activities (drama, music, philosophy, creative arts, politics, other languages and cultures) will be relevant.

Selection interviews Yes Cambridge, Oxford (Class) 95% interviewed (success rate 37%), (Class Engl) 85% (success rate 28%), (Class Modn Langs) 93% (success rate 42%); **Some** Bristol ((Engl Class St) Mature students and applicants with non-standard qualifications only), Manchester (Mature students only); **No** Swansea.

Interview advice and questions What do you think it means to study Classics? Do you think Classics is still a vital and central cultural discipline? What made you apply to study Classics at this university? There are often detailed questions on the texts which the students have read, to find out how reflective they are in their reading. See **Chapter 5**.

Reasons for rejection (non-academic) Did not demonstrate a clear sense of why they wanted to study Classics rather than anything else.

GRADUATE DESTINATIONS AND EMPLOYMENT

(See **Chapter 1, Graduate Outcomes.**)

Career note As with other non-vocational subjects, graduates enter a wide range of careers. In a small number of cases, this may be subject-related, such as work in museums and art galleries. However, much will depend on how the student's interests develop during the undergraduate years and career planning should be started at an early stage.

COMBINED AND LIBERAL ARTS COURSES

(see also **Art and Design (General), Social Sciences/Studies**)

Many different subjects are offered in Combined and Liberal Arts courses which are now becoming increasingly popular. These courses are particularly useful for those applicants who have difficulty in deciding on one specialist subject to follow, allowing students to mix and match according to their interests and often enabling them to embark on new subjects.

Useful websites www.artscouncil.org.uk; www.creativescotland.com; www.artsprofessional.co.uk

NB The points totals shown to the left of the institutions are for ease of reference only. It must not be assumed that Tariff points are always used by institutions or that they can be substituted for an offer in grades. The level of an offer is not necessarily indicative of the quality of a course.

COURSE OFFERS INFORMATION

Subject requirements/preferences The offers listed below are average offers. Specific offers will vary depending on the relative popularity of each subject. Check with the admissions tutor of your selected institution. **GCSE** English, mathematics or science and a foreign language may be required by some universities. **AL** Some joint courses may require a specified subject. Some popular universities are now making lower offers for disadvantaged and other students.

Your target offers and examples of degree courses

152 pts **Durham** – A*AA (Comb Hons Soc Sci) (IB 38 pts HL 666)
London (UCL) – A*AA (Arts Sci) (IB 39 pts HL 19 pts)

144 pts **Birmingham** – AAA–A*AA+admissions essay (Librl Arts Sci) (IB 32–34 pts)
Bristol – AAA incl arts+hum/lang (Librl Arts) (IB 36 pts HL 18 pts incl 6 arts+hum/lang)
Imperial London – AAA incl chem+sci/maths (Bioch courses) (IB 38 pts HL 6 chem+sci/maths)
Leeds – AAA (Librl Arts) (IB 35 pts HL 17 pts)
London (King's) – AAA (Librl Arts) (IB 35 pts HL 666)
Nottingham – AAA (Librl Arts) (IB 36 pts)
Warwick – AAA (Librl Arts) (IB 36 pts)
York – AAA (Librl Arts Span) (IB 36 pts)

136 pts **Exeter** – AAB (Librl Arts) (IB 34 pts HL 665); AAB–A*AA (Flex Comb Hons) (IB 34–38 pts HL 665–766)
Newcastle – AAB (Comb Hons) (IB 34 pts HL 66); AAB incl Engl (Engl Lit Comb Hons) (IB 34 pts HL 5 Engl)
Sheffield – AAB incl chem+sci (Bioch Comb Hons) (IB 34 pts HL 65 chem+sci)
128 pts **Cardiff** – ABB (Welsh Comb Hons) (IB 32 pts HL 665)
East Anglia – ABB (Int Rel Comb Hons) (IB 32 pts)
Liverpool – ABB (Flm St Comb Hons) (IB 33 pts)
London (RH) – ABB–AAB (Librl Arts) (IB 32 pts HL 555)
London (SOAS) – ABB (Glob Librl Arts)
Newcastle – ABB (Flm Prac) (IB 32 pts)
120 pts **Cardiff** – BBC–ABB (Anc Hist Comb Hons) (IB 30–32 pts HL 665–655)
Dundee – BBB (Librl Arts) (IB 30 pts HL 555)
Essex – BBB (Librl Arts) (IB 30 pts HL 555)
Kent – BBB (Cult St courses) (IB 30 pts HL 15 pts)
112 pts **Heriot-Watt** – BBC incl maths+sci (Comb St) (IB 31 pts HL 5 maths+sci)
104 pts **Bath Spa** – BCC–BBB 104–120 pts (Psy Comb Hons; Sociol Comb Hons) (IB 32 pts)
96 pts **Leeds Consv** – 96 pts+audition+gr 6–8 (Mus (Comb))

Open University – (Arts Hum (Engl/Fr/Ger/Span))

Alternative offers See **Chapter 6** and **Appendix 1** for grades/UCAS Tariff points information for other examinations.

CHOOSING YOUR COURSE (SEE ALSO CH.1)

Universities and colleges teaching quality See www.qaa.ac.uk; www.discoveruni.gov.uk.

Top research universities and colleges (REF 2021) See individual subject tables.

Examples of sandwich degree courses Leeds; Oxford Brookes; Roehampton.

ADMISSIONS INFORMATION

Advice to applicants and planning the UCAS personal statement Refer to tables for those subjects you've chosen.

Selection interviews Some Bristol (Mature students and applicants with non-standard qualifications only).

Interview advice and questions Questions will focus on your chosen subjects. See under individual subject tables. See also **Chapter 5**.

Reasons for rejection (non-academic) Lack of clarity of personal goals.

GRADUATE DESTINATIONS AND EMPLOYMENT

(See **Chapter 1, Graduate Outcomes.**)

Career note Graduates enter a wide range of careers covering business and administration, retail work, education, transport, finance, community and social services. Work experience during undergraduate years will help students to focus their interests.

OTHER DEGREE SUBJECTS FOR CONSIDERATION

See **Social Sciences/Studies**.

COMMUNICATION STUDIES/COMMUNICATION

(including **Communication and Media, Marketing Communication Management and Public Relations**; see also **Art and Design (General), Computer Science and Information Technology, Engineering (Communications), Film, Radio and TV Studies, Journalism, Media Studies, Speech Pathology/Sciences/Therapy**)

Communication Studies courses are often linked with Media Studies and as such attract large numbers of applicants; however the course content of your chosen course should be checked since there are several variations. Some courses are purely academic.

Useful websites www.camfoundation.co.uk/about-us/; www.aejmc.org

NB The points totals shown to the left of the institutions are for ease of reference only. It must not be assumed that Tariff points are always used by institutions or that they can be substituted for an offer in grades. The level of an offer is not necessarily indicative of the quality of a course.

COURSE OFFERS INFORMATION

Subject requirements/preferences GCSE English and mathematics grades 7–4 (A–C) may be required. **AL** No specific subjects required. Some popular universities are now making lower offers for disadvantaged and other students.

Your target offers and examples of degree courses

136 pts **Leeds** – AAB incl arts/hum/soc sci (Comm Media) (IB 35 pts HL 16 pts incl 5 Engl)
Newcastle – AAB (Media Comm Cult St) (IB 34 pts)
Ulster – AAB (Comm Adv Mark) (IB 28 pts HL 14 pts)

128 pts **East Anglia** – ABB 128 pts (Soty Cult Media) (IB 32 pts)
Exeter – ABB–AAB (Comms) (IB 32–34 pts HL 655–665)
Leeds – ABB incl art/des/media/portfolio (Graph Comm Des) (IB 34 pts HL 16 pts incl 5 vis arts+4 Engl)
Liverpool – ABB/BBB+aEPQ (Comm Media) (IB 33 pts)
Loughborough – ABB (Media Comm) (IB 34 pts HL 655)
Nottingham – ABB (Span Int Media Comms St) (IB 30 pts HL 655)

120 pts **East Anglia** – BBB/BBC+aEPQ (Glob Comm Bus Mgt) (IB 31 pts)
London (Gold) – BBB (Media Comms) (IB 33 pts HL 655)
Portsmouth – BBB–AAB (Glob Comm Media)
Sussex – BBB–ABB (Media Comms) (IB 30–32 pts)

112 pts **Birmingham City** – BBC 112 pts (Media Comm) (IB 28 pts HL 14 pts)
Brunel – BBC (Comm Media St) (IB 29 pts)
Coventry – BBC+portfolio (Media Comms) (IB 29 pts HL Engl)
Greenwich – BBC 112 pts (Media Comms)
Keele – BBC 112 pts (Media Comms) (IB 29 pts HL 554)
Leeds Beckett – BBC 112 pts (Media Comm Cult)
Northumbria – 112 pts+portfolio (Fash Comm)
Nottingham Trent – BBC 112 pts (Comm Soty courses)
Sheffield Hallam – BBC 112 pts (Mark Comms Adv)
UWE Bristol – BBC 112 pts (Media Comm)

104 pts **Bath Spa** – BCC–BBB 104–120 pts (Media Comms) (IB 32 pts)
Bournemouth – 104–120 pts (Comm Media; Mark Comm) (IB 28–31 pts)
Buckingham – BCC–BBB+interview (Dig Mark) (IB 30–32 pts)
De Montfort – 104 pts (Media Comm) (IB 24 pts)
Glasgow Caledonian – BCC (Media Comm)
Liverpool Hope – BCC 104 pts (Media Comm) (IB 24 pts)
Manchester Met – BCC 104–112 pts (Dig Media Comms) (IB 26 pts)
Oxford Brookes – BCC 104 pts (Comm Media Cult) (IB 29 pts)

96 pts **Aberystwyth** – CCC–BBB 96–120 pts (Media Comm St) (IB 26–30 pts)
Bedfordshire – 96 pts (Media Mark PR)
St Mary's – 96–112 pts (Comms Media Mark)
Sunderland – 96–112 pts (Media Cult Comm)

Alternative offers See **Chapter 6** and **Appendix 1** for grades/UCAS Tariff points information for other examinations.

CHOOSING YOUR COURSE (SEE ALSO CH.1)

Universities and colleges teaching quality See www.qaa.ac.uk; www.discoveruni.gov.uk.

Top research universities and colleges (REF 2021) (Communication, Cultural and Media studies, Library and Information Management) London LSE; Cardiff; Leicester (Musm St); London (Gold) (Media Comm Cult St); Loughborough; Glasgow; London (RH); Leicester (Media Comm); London (King's); Newcastle.

Examples of sandwich degree courses Bournemouth; Brunel; Liverpool; Loughborough.

ADMISSIONS INFORMATION

Advice to applicants and planning the UCAS personal statement Applicants should be able to give details of any work experience/work shadowing/discussions they have had in the media including, for example, in newspaper offices, advertising agencies, local radio stations or film companies (see also **Media Studies**).

Selection interviews Yes London (Gold).

Interview advice and questions Courses differ in this subject and, depending on your choice, the questions will focus on the type of course, either biased towards the media, or towards human communication by way of language, psychology, sociology or linguistics. See also separate subject tables and **Chapter 5**.

Reasons for rejection (non-academic) Unlikely to work well in groups. Poor writing. Misguided application, for example more practical work wanted. Poor motivation. Inability to give reasons for choosing the course. More practice needed in academic writing skills. Wrong course choice, wanted more practical work.

GRADUATE DESTINATIONS AND EMPLOYMENT

(See **Chapter 1, Graduate Outcomes.**)

Career note Graduates have developed a range of transferable skills in their courses which open up opportunities in several areas. There are obvious links with openings in the media, public relations and advertising.

OTHER DEGREE SUBJECTS FOR CONSIDERATION

Advertising; Art and Design; Cultural Studies; Digital Communications; English; Film, Radio and TV Studies; Information Studies; Journalism; Languages; Linguistics; Marketing; Media Studies; Psychology; Public Relations; Speech Sciences.

COMMUNITY STUDIES/DEVELOPMENT

(see also **Health Sciences/Studies, Nursing and Midwifery, Social and Public Policy and Administration, Social Work**)

These courses cover aspects of community social issues, for example housing, food, health, the elderly, welfare rights and counselling, and features of community development such as education, arts, sport and leisure. Many courses are vocational in nature and often linked with youth work. Courses are in Education, Housing, Social Sciences and Public Policy. Work experience always forms part of these courses and should also take place before you apply. Most courses will lead to professional qualifications.

USEFUL WEBSITES www.volunteeringmatters.org.uk; www.infed.org/mobi/developing-community

NB The points totals shown to the left of the institutions are for ease of reference only. It must not be assumed that Tariff points are always used by institutions or that they can be substituted for an offer in grades. The level of an offer is not necessarily indicative of the quality of a course.

COURSE OFFERS INFORMATION

SUBJECT REQUIREMENTS/PREFERENCES GCSE English and mathematics grade 7–4 (A–C) may be required at some institutions. **AL** No specific subjects required. Some popular universities are now making lower offers for disadvantaged and other students. **Other** Minimum age 19 plus youth work experience for some courses. Health and Disclosure and Barring Service (DBS) checks required for some courses.

YOUR TARGET OFFERS AND EXAMPLES OF DEGREE COURSES

120 pts **Sussex** – BBB (Chld Yth (Theor Prac)) (IB 30 pts)
112 pts **Birmingham Newman** – 112 pts (Wkg Chld Yng Ppl Fmly)
London Met – BBC 112 pts (Commun Ldrshp)
104 pts **Leeds Beckett** – 104 pts+interview (Yth Wk) (IB 24 pts)
West Scotland – BCC 104 pts (Commun Educ) (IB 24 pts)
Winchester – BCC–BBB 104–120 pts (Chld Yth St)
96 pts **Birmingham Newman** – 96 pts+interview (Yth Commun Wk)
Dundee – CCC/AB (Commun Edu) (IB 29 pts)
Glasgow – CCC–BBB 96–120 pts (Commun Dev) (IB 34 pts HL 655)
Sunderland – CCC–BBC 96–112 pts+interview (Commun Yth Wk St)
88 pts **Marjon** – CCD 88 pts+interview (Yth Commun Wk)
South Wales – CCD 88 pts+interview (Yth Commun Wk)
Winchester – CCD–BCC 88–104 pts (Hlth Soc Cr)
80 pts **Cardiff Met** – 80–104 pts+interview (Yth Commun Wk courses)
Trinity Saint David – CCE–CCC 80–96 pts (Yth Wk Soc Educ)
Ulster – CDD (Commun Yth Wk) (IB 24 pts HL 12 pts)
64 pts **London (Gold)** – CC+interview (Soc Sci Commun Dev Yth Wk)

ALTERNATIVE OFFERS See **Chapter 6** and **Appendix 1** for grades/UCAS Tariff points information for other examinations.

DEGREE APPRENTICESHIPS

Bishop Grosseteste (Yth Wkr); Chester (Soc Wk); Cumbria (Yth Wk); East London (Yth Wkr); Leeds Beckett (Yth Wk); Plymouth Marjon (Yth Wk); Sunderland (Commun & Yth Wk); Central Lancashire (Yth Wk & Commun Prac).

EXAMPLES OF COLLEGES OFFERING COURSES IN THIS SUBJECT FIELD

Blackburn (Coll); Bradford College (UC); Cornwall (Coll); East Kent (Coll); North Notts (Coll); Oldham (Coll); Oldham (Univ Campus); TEC Partnership; Truro and Penwith (Coll); Weston (Coll); York (Coll).

CHOOSING YOUR COURSE (SEE ALSO CH.1)

UNIVERSITIES AND COLLEGES TEACHING QUALITY See www.qaa.ac.uk; www.discoveruni.gov.uk.

EXAMPLES OF SANDWICH DEGREE COURSES Coventry; London Met; Sussex.

ADMISSIONS INFORMATION

ADVICE TO APPLICANTS AND PLANNING THE UCAS PERSONAL STATEMENT You should describe work you have done with people (elderly or young), particularly in a caring capacity, such as social work, or with the elderly or young children in schools, nursing, hospital work, youth work, community or charity work. You should also describe any problems arising and how staff dealt with them. See **Appendix 3**.

SELECTION INTERVIEWS Yes Cardiff Met, Marjon, South Wales, Sunderland.

Interview advice and questions This subject has a vocational emphasis and work experience, or even full-time work in the field, will be expected. Community work varies considerably, so, depending on your experiences, you could be asked about the extent of your work and how you would solve the problems which occur. See also **Chapter 5**.

Reasons for rejection (non-academic) Insufficient experience. Lack of understanding of community and youth work. Uncertain career aspirations. Incompatibility with values, methods and aims of the course. No work experience.

GRADUATE DESTINATIONS AND EMPLOYMENT

(See **Chapter 1, Graduate Outcomes.**)

Career note Social and welfare areas of employment provide openings for those wanting to specialise in their chosen field of social work. Other opportunities will also exist in educational administration, leisure and outdoor activities.

OTHER DEGREE SUBJECTS FOR CONSIDERATION

Communication Studies; Education; Health and Social Care; Nursing; Politics; Psychology; Social Policy and Administration; Social Work; Sociology; Youth Studies.

COMPUTER GAMES DEVELOPMENT

(including **Esports, Games Technology, Computer Science (Games), Games Design**; see also **Art and Design (3D Design), Computer Science and Information Technology**)

The UK gaming industry is the sixth largest in the world and the second largest in Europe, currently worth around £4.3 billion. There are now over 2,000 game companies based in the UK, which continue to create a wide range of internationally acclaimed titles. Game Design courses train students to plan, develop and test video games. Courses typically include programming, coding, 3D modelling, sound-editing and game mechanics. Computer Science courses with a focus on games tend to introduce general computer programming skills in Year 1, before building on this foundation by introducing modules specific to games development in Years 2 and 3. Many courses partner with gaming events, linking students with future employers and staying up to date with developments in the industry.

Useful websites www.ukie.org.uk/research; www.tiga.org/about-tiga-and-our-industry/about-uk-video-games-industry; www.thecreativeindustries.co.uk/industries/games

NB The points totals shown to the left of the institutions are for ease of reference only. It must not be assumed that Tariff points are always used by institutions or that they can be substituted for an offer in grades. The level of an offer is not necessarily indicative of the quality of a course.

COURSE OFFERS INFORMATION

Subject requirements/preferences GCSE Mathematics usually required. **AL** Mathematics, a science subject or computer science required for some courses. Some popular universities are now making lower offers for disadvantaged and other students.

Your target offers and examples of degree courses

128 pts **City St George's** – ABB 128 pts (Comp Sci Gms Tech) (IB 31 pts HL 5 maths)

120 pts **Bournemouth Arts** – BBB 120 pts+portfolio (Gms Art Des)
Brunel – BBB (Comp Sci (Dig Media Gms)) (IB 30 pts)
Huddersfield – BBB 120 pts (Comp Sci Gms Prog)
Manchester Met – BBB incl IT/comp sci/maths 120 pts (Comp Gms Dev) (IB 30 pts HL 5 IT)
Northumbria – 120 pts (Gms Comp)
Sussex – BBB–ABB 120–128 pts (Comp Dig Media Gms) (IB 30–32 pts)
Trinity Saint David – 120 pts+interview+portfolio (Comp Gms Des) (IB 32 pts)
UWE Bristol – 120 pts (Gms Tech)

112 pts **Bangor** – 112 pts (Comp Sci Gms Des)
Birmingham City – BBC incl sci/tech/maths/comp 112 pts (Comp Gms Tech) (IB 28 pts HL comp sci/chem/des tech/phys)
Bournemouth – BBC–ABB 112–128 pts+portfolio (Comp Animat Vis Efcts) (IB 30–32 pts)
Brunel – BBC (Gms Des) (IB 29 pts)
Derby – BBC–BBB 112–120 pts (Comp Gms Modl Animat; Comp Gms Prog)
East London – BBC 112 pts (Gm Des; Gm Prog) (IB 24 pts)
Hull – BBC 112 pts (Comp Sci Gms Prog) (IB 28 pts)
Leeds Beckett – 112 pts+interview+portfolio (Gms Des)
Middlesex – BBC–ABB 112–128 pts (Gms Des Dev)
Staffordshire – BBC 112 pts (Comp Gms Prog); BBC 112 pts+portfolio+interview (Gms Art)
Sunderland – BBC 112 pts+portfolio (Animat Gms Art)
Ulster – BBC 112 pts (Gms Des) (IB 25 pts HL 12 pts)
West London – BBC 112 pts (Gms Des Animat)
West Scotland – BBC 112 pts (Comp Gms Dev) (IB 24 pts)

104 pts **Abertay** – BCC incl maths (Comp Gms Tech) (IB 29 pts HL 4 maths)
Brighton – BCC–BBB 104–120 pts (Comp Sci Gms; Dig Gms Dev) (IB 26 pts)
Falmouth – 104–120 pts+interview (Comp Gms)
Lincoln – (Gms Comp)
Northampton – BCC 104 pts (Gms Des)
Norwich Arts – BCC (Gms Art Des) (IB 26 pts)
Trinity Saint David – BCC incl ICT/comp/maths/phys 104 pts (Comp Gms Dev)

96 pts **Aberystwyth** – CCC–BBB 96–120 pts (Comp Graph Vsn Gms) (IB 26–30 pts)
Anglia Ruskin – 96 pts (Comp Gms Tech) (IB 24 pts)
Central Lancashire – 96–112 pts (Comp Gms Dev)
Liverpool John Moores – CCC (Comp Gms Dev)
Robert Gordon – CCC (Gms Des) (IB 26 pts)
Sunderland – 96–112 pts (Gm Dev)
Teesside – 96–112 pts (Gms Des; Gms Prog); 96–112 pts+portfolio (Animat; Gms Art)
Westminster – CCC 96 pts+portfolio (Gms Art)

CHOOSING YOUR COURSE (SEE ALSO CH.1)

Examples of sandwich degree courses Anglia Ruskin; Central Lancashire; Hull; Liverpool John Moores.

ADMISSIONS INFORMATION

Advice to applicants and planning the UCAS personal statement See **Computer Science and Information Technology.**

Selection interviews Yes Falmouth.

Interview advice and questions
See **Computer Science and Information Technology.**

GRADUATE DESTINATIONS AND EMPLOYMENT

(See **Chapter 1, Graduate Outcomes.**)

COMPUTER SCIENCE AND INFORMATION TECHNOLOGY

(including **Artificial Intelligence, Business Information Systems, Computing, Computer Networks, Computer Science, Information Systems and Web Design and Development**; see also **Communication Studies/Communication, Information Management And Librarianship, Media Studies**)

Most universities and also colleges of further education offer Computer courses. The specialisms are many and varied, which can cause a problem when deciding which course to follow. For example, at Brunel University London, the Computer Science course has four specialisms with a choice from Artificial Intelligence, Digital Media and Games, Network Computing or Software Engineering, all with sandwich placements. At Plymouth University, there are over 17 computer courses including Computer and Information Security and Computer Science, while at Kingston, Liverpool John Moores and other institutions, Cyber Security and Computer Forensics courses are on offer. At all universities, there are considerable opportunities for financial support and future employment by choosing sandwich courses. Courses vary in content and in the specialisations offered, which may include software engineering, programming languages, artificial intelligence, data processing and graphics.

Useful websites www.bcs.org; www.techuk.org; www.iap.org.uk; www.tpdegrees.com/tech-partnership-legacy/

NB The points totals shown to the left of the institutions are for ease of reference only. It must not be assumed that Tariff points are always used by institutions or that they can be substituted for an offer in grades. The level of an offer is not necessarily indicative of the quality of a course.

COURSE OFFERS INFORMATION

Subject requirements/preferences GCSE Mathematics usually required. 8–9/7/5–6 (A*/A/B) grades may be stipulated for some subjects. **AL** Mathematics, a science subject or computer science required for some courses. Some popular universities are now making lower offers for disadvantaged and other students.

Your target offers and examples of degree courses

160 pts **Bristol** – A*A*A incl maths+fmaths (Maths Comp Sci) (IB 40 pts HL 18 pts incl 7 maths)

Cambridge – A*A*A incl maths+interview+TMUA+CSAT (Comp Sci) (IB 40–42 pts HL 776 incl maths)

Imperial London – A*A*A incl A* maths+interview (Comp (Artif Intel Mach Lrng) (MEng)) (IB 41 pts HL 7 maths); (Comp (Soft Eng) (MEng)) (IB 41–42 pts HL 7 maths); A*A*A incl maths+fmaths+interview (Maths Comp Sci) (IB 42 pts HL 7 maths); A*A*A incl maths+interview (Comp) (IB 42 pts HL 7 maths)

London (King's) – A*A*A* incl maths (Comp Sci) (IB 35 pts HL 776); A*A*A incl maths/fmaths (Comp Sci Mgt) (IB 35 pts HL 776 incl maths)

London (UCL) – A*A*A incl maths (Comp Sci; Mathem Comput (MEng)) (IB 40 pts HL 7 maths)

Warwick – A*A*A incl maths (Comp Sci) (IB 39 pts HL 766 incl maths)

152 pts **Bath** – A*AA incl maths (Comp Sci) (IB 36 pts HL 776 incl maths)

Birmingham – A*AA incl maths (Comp Sci; Comp Sci Soft Eng (MEng)) (IB 32 pts HL 766 incl 6 maths)

Bristol – A*AA incl A* maths (Comp Sci) (IB 38 pts HL 18 pts incl 7 maths)

Durham – A*AA incl maths (Comp Sci) (IB 38 pts HL 766 incl maths)

Oxford – A*AA incl maths/fmaths/comp+interview+MAT (Comp Sci) (IB 39 pts HL 766 incl 7 maths)

Southampton – A*AA incl maths (Comp Sci; Comp Sci Artif Intel (MEng); Comp Sci Cy Scrty (MEng)) (IB 38 pts HL 19 pts incl 6 maths); A*AA incl maths+phys/fmaths/comp sci/

electron (Electron Eng Comp Sys (MEng)) (IB 38 pts HL 19 pts incl 6 maths+phys/fmaths/comp sci)

144 pts **Leeds** – AAA incl maths/comp (Comp Sci; Comp Sci Artif Intel) (HL 18 pts incl 5 maths/comp)
Liverpool – AAA incl maths/comp sci (Comp Sci; Comp Sci (Yr Ind); Fin Comp) (IB 36 pts HL 5 maths/comp sci)
London (QM) – AAA (Comp Sci courses) (IB 36 pts HL 666)
Manchester – AAA (IT Mgt Bus; IT Mgt Bus (Yr Ind)) (IB 36 pts HL 666)
Nottingham – AAA incl comp (Comp Sci) (IB 38 pts HL 6 comp sci)
Queen's Belfast – AAA/A*AB incl maths (Maths Comp Sci (MSci)) (IB 36 pts HL 666 incl maths)
Sheffield – AAA incl maths (Comp Sci) (IB 38 pts HL 6 maths)
St Andrews – AAA incl maths (Comp Sci courses) (IB 38 pts HL 666 incl maths)
York – AAA incl maths (Comp Sci) (IB 36 pts HL 6 maths)

136 pts **Edinburgh** – AAB–A*A*A* incl A maths (Inform (MInf)) (IB 34–43 pts HL 655–766 incl 6 maths)
Exeter – AAB–AAA incl maths (Comp Sci) (IB 34–36 pts HL 665–666 incl 5 maths)
Lancaster – AAB (Comp Sci courses) (IB 35 pts HL 16 pts); AAB 136 pts (Cy Scrty) (IB 35 pts HL 16 pts); AAB incl A maths/fmaths 136 pts (Data Sci) (IB 35 pts HL 16 incl maths)
Loughborough – AAB (IT Mgt Bus) (IB 35 pts HL 665); AAB incl maths (Comp Sci; Comp Sci Artif Intel) (IB 35 pts HL 665 incl maths)
Newcastle – AAB (Comp Sci courses) (IB 34 pts)
Queen's Belfast – AAB–AAA incl comp/maths/soft sys dev (Comp Sci (MEng)) (IB 34–36 pts HL 665–666 incl comp/maths/soft sys dev)

128 pts **City St George's** – ABB 128 pts (Comp Sci) (IB 31 pts); (Comp Sci Gms Tech) (IB 31 pts HL 5 maths)
East Anglia – ABB incl maths/comp sci/phys/electron/econ (Comp Sci) (IB 32 pts HL 5 maths/comp sci/chem/phys/econ); ABB incl maths/comp sci/sci/econ/bus (Bus Inf Sys) (IB 32 pts HL 5 maths/comp sci/chem/phys/econ)
Edinburgh – ABB–A*A*A* incl maths (Artif Intel Comp Sci; Comp Sci courses) (IB 34–43 pts HL 655–766 incl 6 maths)
Glasgow – ABB–AAA incl maths (Comp Sci courses) (IB 38 pts HL 666 incl maths)
Leicester – ABB/BBB+bEPQ (Comp Sci) (IB 30 pts HL 4 maths)
London (RH) – ABB–AAB (Mgt Dig Innov) (IB 32 pts HL 655); ABB–AAB incl maths/phys/comp sci (Comp Sci) (IB 32 pts HL 655 incl maths/phys/comp sci)
London (UCL) – ABB 128 pts (Inf Soty) (IB 34 pts HL 16 pts)
Queen's Belfast – ABB (Bus IT) (IB 33 pts HL 655)
Reading – ABB (Comp Sci courses) (IB 32 pts)
Surrey – ABB incl maths (Comp Sci) (IB 33 pts HL 5 maths)

120 pts **Aberdeen** – BBB incl maths+sci (Comp Sci) (IB 32 pts HL 555 incl maths+sci)
Aston – BBB–BBC+bEPQ (Bus Comp IT; Comp Sci) (IB 31 pts HL 555)
Bangor – 120–128 pts (Comp Sci)
Brunel – BBB (Bus Comp; Comp Sci; Comp Sci (Artif Intel); Comp Sci (Net Comp)) (IB 30 pts)
Cardiff – BBB–ABB (Comp Sci; Comp Sci Scrty Foren) (IB 31–32 pts HL 665)
Coventry – BBB incl maths/phys/chem/tech/comp (Comp Sci) (IB 29 pts HL maths/phys/comp sci/stats)
Dundee – BBB incl maths+sci (Comp Sci) (IB 30 pts HL 555 incl maths+sci)
Hertfordshire – BBB–ABB 120–128 pts (Inf Tech) (HL 44 incl maths+phys)
Huddersfield – BBB 120 pts (Comp; Comp Sci; Web Prog)
Keele – BBB (Comp Sci) (IB 30 pts HL 555)
Kent – BBB–AAB (Bus IT; Comp Sci (Cy Scrty); Comp Sci courses) (HL 4 maths)
Leeds Beckett – 120 pts (Comp Sci) (HL 554)
London (Gold) – BBB (Comp Sci; Crea Comp) (IB 33 pts HL 655)
London South Bank – BBB 120 pts (Comp Sci)
Manchester Met – BBB incl IT/comp sci/maths/sci 120 pts (Comp Sci) (IB 30 pts HL 5 IT)

Northumbria – 120 pts (Net Cy Scrty)
Nottingham Trent – BBB incl IT/maths/sci 120 pts (Comp Sci courses)
Plymouth – 120–128 pts (Comp Sci) (IB 27–30 pts)
Portsmouth – BBB–ABB (Vrtl Prod)
Queen's Belfast – BBB–ABB incl comp/maths/soft sys dev (Comp Sci (Yr Ind)) (IB 32–33 pts HL 655 incl comp/maths/soft sys dev)
Stirling – BBB (Bus Comp; Comp Sci) (IB 30 pts)
Strathclyde – BBB (Comp Sci) (IB 30 pts HL 5 maths)
Sussex – BBB–ABB (Comp Sci; Comp Sci Artif Intel) (IB 30–32 pts)
Swansea – BBB–ABB (Comp Sci)
UWE Bristol – 120 pts (Comp Sci)

112 pts **Bangor** – 112 pts (Comp Sci Gms Des)
Birmingham City – BBC incl sci/tech/maths/comp 112 pts (Bus Inf Tech) (IB 28 pts HL 5 comp sci/chem/des tech/phys); (Comp Net Scrty; Comp Sci; Dig Foren) (IB 28 pts HL comp sci/chem/des tech/phys)
Bradford – BBC 112 pts (Comp Sci) (HL 3 maths)
Canterbury Christ Church – BBC 112 pts (Bus Inf Sys) (IB 29 pts); BBC incl maths/phys/comp sci (Comp Sci) (IB 29 pts)
De Montfort – 112 pts (App Comp; Bus Inf Sys; Comp Sci) (IB 26 pts)
Derby – BBC–BBB 112–120 pts (Comp Sci; Cy Scrty; IT)
East London – 112 pts (Comp Bus) (IB 24 pts HL 15 pts); (Comp Sci) (IB 24 pts HL 15 pts incl maths)
Greenwich – BBC 112 pts (Cy Scrty Dig Foren)
Heriot-Watt – BBC–ABB (Comp Sys courses) (IB 28 pts); BBC–ABB incl B maths (Comp Sci) (IB 28 pts HL 5 maths)
Hertfordshire – BBC–BBB 112–120 pts (Bus St Inf Sys)
Huddersfield – BBC–BBB 112–120 pts (IT)
Hull – BBC 112 pts (Comp Sci) (IB 28 pts)
Kingston – BBC 112–128 pts (Comp Sci; Cy Scrty Comp Foren)
Liverpool Hope – BBC 112 pts (Comp Sci) (IB 28 pts)
Liverpool John Moores – BBC 112 pts (Comp; Comp Foren)
Northumbria – 112 pts (Bus Analyt; Bus Comp; Comp IT Mgt; Comp Sci; Data Sci)
Oxford Brookes – BBC (Comp Sci; IT Bus) (IB 30 pts)
Plymouth – 112–120 pts (Comp Soft Dev) (IB 27–30 pts)
Portsmouth – BBC–BBB 112–120 pts (Comp; Comp Net Scrty; Comp Sci; Maths Mach Lrng) (IB 29 pts)
Salford – 112–120 pts incl maths/sci/comp (Comp Sci) (IB 30 pts HL 5 comp st)
Sheffield Hallam – BBC 112 pts (Comp Sci)
South Wales – BBC (Comp Sci)
Staffordshire – BBC 112 pts (Comp Sci)
Suffolk – BBC (Comp)
Sunderland – 112 pts (Comp Sci; Cyberscrty Dig Foren)
UWE Bristol – 112 pts (Bus Comp)
Ulster – BBC (Comp Sci) (IB 25 pts HL 12 pts)
West London – BBC 112 pts (Comp Sci; Cy Scrty); BBC–BBB 112–120 pts (IT Mgt Bus)

104 pts **Abertay** – BCC incl art/graph des/des tech+portfolio (Comp Arts) (IB 29 pts HL 4 vis art/fn art)
Anglia Ruskin – 104 pts (Comp Sci) (IB 24 pts)
Bangor – 104–128 pts (Comp Clim Sci)
Bath Spa – BCC (Crea Comp courses) (IB 32 pts)
Bournemouth – 104–120 pts (Bus Comp Analyt; Comp) (IB 28–31 pts)
Brighton – BCC–BBB 104–120 pts (Comp Sci; Comp Sci Artif Intel; Comp Sci Cy Scrty) (IB 26 pts)
Buckingham – BCC–BBB (Comp courses)
Cardiff Met – 104–112 pts (Bus Inf Sys; Comp Sci) (HL 55)

Chester – BCC–BBC 104–112 (Comp Sci) (IB 26 pts)
Chichester – BCC–BBB 104–120 pts (Comp Sci) (IB 30 pts HL 5 maths)
Edge Hill – BCC–BBC 104–112 pts (Comp courses)
Edinburgh Napier – BCC (Web Des Dev) (IB 27 pts HL 654); BCC incl maths/phys (Comp Sci) (IB 28 pts HL 654 incl 5 maths/phys)
Greater Manchester – 104 pts incl comp/tech (Comp Net Scrty)
Greenwich – BCC 104 pts (Maths Comp Sci)
Lincoln – (Comp Sci)
Liverpool Hope – BCC 104 pts (IT courses) (IB 24 pts)
Northampton – BCC 104 pts (Bus Comp)
Solent – 104–120 pts (Cy Scrty) (IB 28–32 pts)
South Wales – BCC 104 pts (Comp)
Trinity Saint David – 104 pts (Comp (Comp Net Cyberscrty); Comp (Data Inf Sys); Comp (Web Dev))
Winchester – 104–112 pts (Immer Tech)

96 pts **Aberystwyth** – CCC–BBB 96–120 pts (Bus IT; Comp Sci; Comp Sci Artif Intel; Web Dev) (IB 26–30 pts)
Bangor – 96 pts (Comp Inf Sys)
Central Lancashire – 96–112 pts (Comp)
Greater Manchester – CCC incl sci/tech/eng/maths 96 pts (Comp (Cy Scrty); Comp (Data Analys))
London Met – CCC (Comp Sci)
Robert Gordon – CCC (Comp Sci; Cy Scrty; Gms Des) (IB 26 pts); CCC 96 pts (Bus Analyt) (IB 26 pts)
Sunderland – CCC–BBC 96–112 pts (Net Cyberscrty)
Teesside – 96–112 pts (Artif Intel Comp Sci; Comp Sci; Data Sci; IT)
Ulster – CCC (Comp Sci (Soft Sys Dev)) (IB 24 pts HL 12 pts)
West Scotland – CCC 96 pts (Comp Net; Web Mbl Dev) (IB 24 pts); CCC incl maths/comp sci 96 pts (Comp Sci) (IB 24 pts)
Westminster – CCC–BBB 96–120 pts (Bus Inf Sys; Comp Net Scrty; Comp Sci)
Wolverhampton – CCC 96 pts (Comp IT; Comp Sci; Cyberscrty)
Worcester – CCC 96 pts (Comp)

88 pts **Bucks New** – 88–112 pts (Comp courses)

80 pts **Wrexham** – 80–112 pts (Cy Scrty)

24 pts **UHI** – D (Comp)

Open University – (Comp IT)

ALTERNATIVE OFFERS See **Chapter 6** and **Appendix 1** for grades/UCAS Tariff points information for other examinations.

DEGREE APPRENTICESHIPS

Aston (Dig Tech Sol); Bangor (App Data Sci, App Cyberscrty, App Soft Eng); Bath (Dig Tech Sol Spec); Birmingham (Comp Sci); Exeter (Dig Tech Sol Prof); Glasgow (Soft Eng); Glasgow Caledonian (Cyberscrty, Artif Intel Data Sci, Soft Dev); Gloucestershire (Cyberscrty Analyt, Cyberscrty, Data Analyt, Net Eng, Soft Eng); Greater Manchester (Dig Tech Sol Prof); Hertfordshire (Dig Tech Sol (Soft Eng)); Northumbria (Cyberscrty Tech Prof); Nottingham (Data Sci); Nottingham Trent (Dig Tech Sol Prof (Soft Eng)); Reading (Dig Tech Sol); Robert Gordon (Data Sci); Strathclyde (Cyberscrty, Dig Tech Sol, IT Soft Dev); Ulster (Comp Sci); West London (Cyberscrty Analyt, Data Analyt, IT Conslt, Soft Eng); Wrexham (Cyberscrty, Soft Eng).

CHOOSING YOUR COURSE (SEE ALSO CH.1)

UNIVERSITIES AND COLLEGES TEACHING QUALITY See www.qaa.ac.uk; www.discoveruni.gov.uk.

TOP RESEARCH UNIVERSITIES AND COLLEGES (REF 2021) (Computer Science and Informatics) Imperial London; Oxford; Birmingham; London (UCL); Warwick; Edinburgh; Bristol; London (QM); York; Leeds.

Examples of sandwich degree courses Aston; Bangor; Bath; Birmingham; Birmingham City; Bournemouth; Bradford; Brighton; Brunel; Cardiff; City St George's; Coventry; De Montfort; Derby; East Anglia; Edinburgh Napier; Gloucestershire; Greenwich; Huddersfield; Hull; Keele; Kent; Kingston; Leeds Beckett; Lincoln; Liverpool; Liverpool John Moores; London (QM); London (RH); Loughborough; Manchester; Manchester Met; Middlesex; Newcastle; Northumbria; Nottingham; Nottingham Trent; Oxford Brookes; Plymouth; Portsmouth; Queen's Belfast; Reading; Robert Gordon; Salford; Sheffield Hallam; Solent; Staffordshire; Stirling; Sunderland; Surrey; Sussex; Swansea; Teesside; Ulster; UWE Bristol; Westminster; Wolverhampton; York.

ADMISSIONS INFORMATION

Admission Tutors' advice Bournemouth It can be difficult for applicants to know when applying for courses what specialism they wish to follow. Our course offers a common first year with specialisms following in Years 2 and 3.

Advice to applicants and planning the UCAS personal statement Your computer and programming interests in and outside school or college should be described. It is also useful to give details of any visits, work experience and work shadowing relating to industrial or commercial organisations and their computer systems. (See **Appendix 3**.) Give details of your interests in, and knowledge of, computer hardware, software and multimedia packages. Contact the Chartered Institute for IT for information.

Selection interviews Yes Buckingham, Cambridge, Falmouth, Imperial London, Oxford (17% (success rate 5%)); **Some** Bath; **No** Anglia Ruskin, Bournemouth, Bradford, Brighton, East Anglia, Edinburgh, Keele, London Met, Loughborough, Manchester, Newcastle, Northampton, Nottingham Trent, Plymouth, Salford, UWE Bristol, West London.

Interview advice and questions While A-level computer studies is not usually required, you will be questioned on your use of computers and aspects of the subject which interest you. How do you organise your homework/social life? What are your strengths and weaknesses? Do you have any idea of the type of career you would like? See also **Chapter 5**.

Reasons for rejection (non-academic) Little practical interest in computers/electronics. Inability to work as part of a small team. Mismatch between referee's description and performance at interview. Unsatisfactory English. Can't communicate. Inability to convince interviewer of the candidate's worth. Incoherent, unmotivated, arrogant and without any evidence of good reason.

GRADUATE DESTINATIONS AND EMPLOYMENT

(See **Chapter 1, Graduate Outcomes.**)

Career note A high proportion of graduates go to work in the IT sector with some degrees leading towards particular fields (usually indicated by the course title). Significant areas include software design and engineering, web and internet-based fields, programming, systems analysis and administration.

OTHER DEGREE SUBJECTS FOR CONSIDERATION

Business Studies; Communications Engineering; Computer Engineering; Electrical and Electronic Engineering; Geographical Information Systems; Information Studies; Mathematics; Physics; Software Engineering.

DANCE/DANCE STUDIES

(see also **Drama**)

Dance courses abound, most offering a balance of theoretical and practical studies across a range of dance styles. The Royal Academy of Dance for example offers ballet, adult ballet, boys' ballet, creative and contemporary dance, West End jazz, street dance, and song and dance. Other institutions offer Dance combined with other subjects equally. Some universities offer Performance Arts with many courses covering the study of choreography, acting and directing, and acting and dance. While entry to Dance courses usually requires A-level grades, competitive entry to the most popular courses, such as the Contemporary Dance course at Trinity Laban, is by a demanding audition.

Useful websites www.cdmt.org.uk; www.onedanceuk.org; www.royalacademyofdance.org; www.royalballetschool.org.uk

NB The points totals shown to the left of the institutions are for ease of reference only. It must not be assumed that Tariff points are always used by institutions or that they can be substituted for an offer in grades. The level of an offer is not necessarily indicative of the quality of a course.

COURSE OFFERS INFORMATION

Subject requirements/preferences GCSE English usually required. **AL** No specific subjects required. Some popular universities are now making lower offers for disadvantaged and other students. **Other** Disclosure and Barring Service (DBS) checks required for some courses: check websites. Practical dance experience essential.

Your target offers and examples of degree courses

120 pts **West London** – BBB–ABB 120–128 pts (Musl Thea)
112 pts **Bedfordshire** – 112 pts+interview+audition (Dance Prof Prac)
Canterbury Christ Church – BBC 112 pts+interview+audition (Dance Educ) (IB 29 pts)
De Montfort – 112 pts+interview+audition (Dance) (IB 26 pts)
East London – 112 pts+interview+audition (Dance (Urb Prac)) (IB 24 pts HL 15 pts)
Edge Hill – BBC–BBB 112–120 pts+audition (Dance)
Kingston – BBC incl dance/perf arts 112–128 pts+portfolio (Dance)
Leeds Beckett – 112 pts+interview+audition (Dance)
Liverpool Hope – BBC 112 pts+audition (Dance courses) (IB 28 pts)
Middlesex – BBC–ABB 112–128 pts+audition (Dance Perf)
RAc Dance – BBC+RAD Intermediate+audition (Ballet Educ)
Roehampton – 112 pts+audition (Dance)
Salford – BBC 112 pts+audition (Dance) (IB 30 pts HL 6/5)
104 pts **Bath Spa** – BCC–BBB incl dance/perf arts 104–120 pts+audition (Dance) (IB 32 pts)
Chester – BCC–BBC+interview+audition (Dance) (IB 26 pts)
Derby – BCC 104 pts+portfolio (Crea Expr Arts Hlth Wlbng (Dance/Dr/Mus/Art))
Falmouth – 104–120 pts+audition+portfolio (Dance Choreo)
Lincoln – (Dance)
96 pts **Cardiff Met** – 96–112 pts (Spo Physl Educ Hlth (Dance)) (HL 6)
Central Lancashire – 96 pts+audition (Dance)
Chichester – CCC–BBB 96–120 pts+interview+audition (Dance) (IB 28 pts)
88 pts **Bucks New** – 88–112 pts+interview+audition (Dance)
64 pts **Greenwich** – 64 pts+audition (Prof Dance Musl Thea)
Liverpool (LIPA) – CC 64 pts+interview+audition (Dance)
32 pts **Trinity Laban Consv** – EE+interview+audition (Contemp Dance)
Northern (Sch Contemp Dance) – interview+audition (Dance (Contemp))
RConsvS – interview+audition (Modn Ballet)

Alternative offers See **Chapter 6** and **Appendix 1** for grades/UCAS Tariff points information for other examinations.

EXAMPLES OF COLLEGES OFFERING COURSES IN THIS SUBJECT FIELD

Bournemouth and Poole (Coll); City and Islington (Coll); Coventry (Coll); Doncaster (Coll); East Durham (Coll); Gateshead (Coll); Havering (Coll); Hull (Coll); Kingston (Coll); Leeds City (Coll); Leicester (Coll); Liverpool City (Coll); Manchester (Coll); Nottingham (Coll); Petroc; SMB CG; South Essex (Coll); South Gloucestershire and Stroud (Coll); Southwark (Coll); Stratford-upon-Avon (Coll); Sunderland (Coll); Wakefield (Coll); West Thames (Coll).

CHOOSING YOUR COURSE (SEE ALSO CH.1)

Universities and colleges teaching quality See www.qaa.ac.uk; www.discoveruni.gov.uk.

Top research universities and colleges (REF 2021) (Music, Drama, Dance, Performing Arts, Film and Screen Studies) London (QM) (Dr); London (RH); Manchester (Dr, Dance, Perf Arts, Flm Scrn St); London (Royal Central Sch Sp Dr); London (King's); London (SOAS); Cambridge; Roehampton (Dance); Kent; Huddersfield (Mus).

Examples of sandwich degree courses Bath Spa; Cardiff Met; Chichester; Falmouth; Kingston; RAc Dance.

ADMISSIONS INFORMATION

Advice to applicants and planning the UCAS personal statement Full details should be given of examinations taken and practical experience in contemporary dance or ballet. Refer to your visits to the theatre and your impressions. You should list the dance projects in which you have worked, productions in which you have performed and the roles. State any formal dance training you have had and the grades achieved. Applicants need to have dedication, versatility, inventiveness and individuality, practical experience of dance, theoretical ability and language competency.

Selection interviews Yes Bucks New, Chichester, Falmouth, Liverpool (LIPA), Northern (Sch Contemp Dance), Trinity Laban Consv.

Interview advice and questions Nearly all institutions will require auditions or interviews or attendance at a workshop. The following scheme required by **Liverpool (LIPA)** may act as a guide:

1 Write a short essay (500 words) on your own views and experience of dance. You should take into account the following.
  (i) Your history and how you have developed physically and intellectually in your run-up to applying to LIPA.
  (ii) Your main influences and what inspires you.
  (iii) What you want to gain from training as a dancer.
  (iv) Your ideas on health and nutrition as a dancer, taking into account gender and physicality.

2 All candidates must prepare **two** practical audition pieces.
  (i) Whatever you like, in whatever style you wish, as long as the piece does not exceed two minutes (please note: panel will stop anyone exceeding this time limit). There will be no pianist at this part of the session, so if you're using music please bring it with you. This devised piece should be created by you and this means that you should feel comfortable with it and that it expresses something personal about you. You should wear your regular practice clothes for your presentation.
  (ii) You are asked to sing a musical theatre solo as part of the audition and will be accompanied by a pianist. An accompanist is provided, but you must provide the sheet music for your song, fully written out for piano accompaniment and in the key you wish to sing (the accompanist will **not** transpose at sight). **Important** Do NOT choreograph your song. You should expect to sit on a high stool or stand when singing for the audition.

3 Additionally, all candidates will participate in a class given on the day of audition.
  (i) Please ensure that you are dressed appropriately for class with clothing you are comfortable in but allows your movement to be seen. In preparing the practical elements of the audition, please remember that audition panels are not looking for a polished performance. The panel will be looking for candidates' ability to make a genuine emotional and physical connection with the material that they are presenting which shows clear intent and focus.
  Remember that it is in your best interest to prepare thoroughly. Nerves inevitably play a part in any audition and can undermine even the best-prepared candidate. Your best defence is to feel confident in your preparation. See also **Chapter 5**.

Reasons for rejection (non-academic) Applicants more suitable for an acting or dance school course than a degree course. No experience of dance on the UCAS application. Limited dance skills.

GRADUATE DESTINATIONS AND EMPLOYMENT

(See **Chapter 1, Graduate Outcomes.**)

CAREER NOTE Teaching is the most popular career destination for the majority of graduates. Other opportunities exist as dance animators working in education or in the community to encourage activity and participation in dance. There is a limited number of openings for dance or movement therapists who work with the emotionally disturbed, the elderly or physically disadvantaged.

OTHER DEGREE SUBJECTS FOR CONSIDERATION

Arts Management; Drama; Education (Primary); Music; Performance Studies; Physical Education; Sport and Exercise Science.

DENTISTRY

(including **Dental Hygiene and Dental Therapy and Oral Health Science**)

Dentistry involves the treatment and prevention of a wide range of mouth diseases from tooth decay and gum disease to mouth cancer. Courses in Dentistry/Dental Surgery cover the basic medical sciences, human disease, clinical studies and clinical dentistry. The amount of patient contact will vary between institutions but will be considerable in all dental schools. Intercalated courses in other science subjects are offered on most courses. Courses in Oral Health Science and Dental Therapy and Hygiene lead to professional qualifications as therapists and hygienists providing advice and non-surgical treatment for children and adults to prevent tooth decay. Dental Technology courses similarly lead to a professional qualification to prepare crowns, bridges, partial and complete sets of dentures, and other orthodontic devices to replace and correct teeth.

USEFUL WEBSITES www.badn.org.uk; www.bsdht.org.uk; www.dla.org.uk

NB The points totals shown to the left of the institutions are for ease of reference only. It must not be assumed that Tariff points are always used by institutions or that they can be substituted for an offer in grades. The level of an offer is not necessarily indicative of the quality of a course.

COURSE OFFERS INFORMATION

SUBJECT REQUIREMENTS/PREFERENCES GCSE English, mathematics and science subjects required in most cases for Dentistry courses. 8–9/7/5–6 (A*/A/B) grades stipulated in certain subjects by many dental schools. AL Chemistry plus biology or another science subject usually required for Dentistry: see offers lines below. (Dntl Tech, Oral Hlth Sci) Science subject required or preferred. Some popular universities are now making lower offers for disadvantaged and other students. Many dental schools use admissions tests (eg UCAT: see **Chapter 5**). Evidence of non-infectivity or hepatitis B immunisation required and all new dental students screened for hepatitis C. Disclosure and Barring Service (DBS) check at enhanced level is also required. **London (King's) GCSE** English and maths grade 6 (B) if not offered at a higher level. **Manchester GCSE** Six subjects at grade 7 (A).

YOUR TARGET OFFERS AND EXAMPLES OF DEGREE COURSES

152 pts **London (King's)** – A*AA incl biol/chem+sci/maths+UCAT (Dnstry) (IB 35 pts HL 766 incl biol/chem+sci/maths)

London (QM) – A*AA incl chem/biol+sci/maths+UCAT+interview (Dnstry) (IB 38 pts HL 666 incl chem/biol+sci/maths)

144 pts **Birmingham** – AAA incl chem+biol+UCAT+interview (Dntl Srgy) (IB 32 pts HL 666 incl chem+biol)

Bristol – AAA incl chem+biol/phys/maths+UCAT+interview (Dnstry) (IB 36 pts HL 18 pts incl 6 chem+biol/phys/maths)

Cardiff – AAA incl chem+biol+UCAT (Dntl Srgy) (IB 36 pts HL 666 chem+biol)

Dundee – AAA incl chem+biol+UCAT+interview (Dnstry) (IB 37 pts HL 666 incl chem+biol)

Glasgow – AAA incl biol+chem+UCAT+interview (Dnstry) (IB 36 pts HL 666 incl chem+biol)

Leeds – AAA incl biol+chem+UCAT+interview (Dntl Srgy) (IB 35 pts HL 666 incl biol+chem)
Liverpool – AAA incl chem+biol+UCAT+interview (Dntl Srgy) (IB 36 pts HL 6 chem+biol)
Manchester – AAA incl chem+biol+UCAT+interview (Dnstry) (IB 36 pts HL 666 incl chem+biol)
Queen's Belfast – AAA incl biol+chem+UCAT+interview (Dntl Srgy) (IB 36 pts HL 666 incl biol+chem)
Sheffield – AAA incl chem+biol+UCAT+interview (Dntl Srgy) (IB 36 pts HL 6 chem+biol)

136 pts **Plymouth** – AAB–A*AA incl biol+sci/maths 136–152 pts+interview+UCAT (Dntl Srgy)

128 pts **Newcastle** – ABB incl biol+interview (Oral Dntl Hlth Sci) (IB 34 pts HL 5 biol); ABB incl chem+biol+UCAT+interview (Dntl Thera) (IB 32 pts HL 5 chem+biol)

120 pts **Birmingham** – BBB incl biol+interview (Dntl Hyg Thera) (IB 32 pts HL 555 incl biol)
Dundee – BBB incl biol+interview (Oral Hlth Sci) (IB 30 pts HL 555 incl biol)
Edinburgh – BBB incl biol+interview (Oral Hlth Sci) (IB 32 pts HL 555 incl biol)
Portsmouth – BBB–ABB incl B sci 120–128 pts+interview (Dntl Hyg Dntl Thera) (IB 29–30 pts); BBB–ABB incl sci 120–128 pts+interview (Dntl Hyg) (IB 29–30 pts)

112 pts **Cardiff** – BBC–BBB incl biol+interview (Dntl Thera Dntl Hyg) (IB 30–31 pts HL 655–665 incl 6 biol)
Glasgow Caledonian – BBC incl biol+interview (Oral Hlth Sci) (IB 28 pts HL biol)
Teesside – 112 pts+interview (Dntl Hyg)

104 pts **UHI** – BCC incl sci+interview (Oral Hlth Sci)

96 pts **Cardiff Met** – CCC incl sci/maths 96 pts (Dntl Tech) (HL 5 sci)

Alternative offers See **Chapter 6** and **Appendix 1** for grades/UCAS Tariff points information for other examinations.

EXAMPLES OF COLLEGES OFFERING COURSES IN THIS SUBJECT FIELD

Birmingham Met (Coll).

CHOOSING YOUR COURSE (SEE ALSO CH.1)

Universities and colleges teaching quality See www.qaa.ac.uk; www.discoveruni.gov.uk.

Top research universities and colleges (REF 2021) (Allied Health Professions, Dentistry, Nursing and Pharmacy) London (King's); Manchester; Southampton; Queen's Belfast; Nottingham; Swansea; Keele; Newcastle; Bath; Leeds.

ADMISSIONS INFORMATION

Advice to applicants and planning the UCAS personal statement UCAS applications listing four choices only should be submitted by 15 October. Applicants may add one alternative (non-Dentistry) course. On your UCAS application, show evidence of your manual dexterity, work experience and awareness of problems experienced by dentists. Details should be provided of discussions with dentists and work shadowing in dental surgeries. Employment (paid or voluntary) in any field, preferably dealing with people in an environment widely removed from your home or school, could be described. Discuss any specialised fields of dentistry in which you might be interested. See also **Appendix 3**.

Selection interviews Yes Aberdeen (Applicants are required to sit the UCAT test), Birmingham (Applicants are required to sit the UCAT test), Bristol (Applicants are required to sit the UCAT test), Cardiff, Dundee (Applicants are required to sit the UCAT test), Edinburgh (Applicants are required to sit the UCAT), Glasgow (Applicants are required to sit the UCAT test), Glasgow Caledonian (Applicants are required to sit the UCAT), Leeds (Applicants are required to sit the UCAT test), Liverpool (applicants are required to sit the UCAT test), London (King's) (Applicants are required to sit the UCAT test), London (QM) (Applicants are required to sit the UCAT test), Manchester (applicants are required to sit the UCAT test), Newcastle (Applicants are required to sit the UCAT test), Plymouth (Applicants are required to sit the UCAT), Portsmouth (Applicants are required to sit the UCAT), Queen's Belfast (applicants are required to sit the UCAT test), Sheffield (Applicants are required to sit the UCAT test), Teesside, UHI.

Interview advice and questions Dental work experience or work shadowing is essential (check with university websites) and, as a result, questions will be asked on your reactions to the work and your understanding of the different types of treatment that a dentist can offer. In the past, questions at interview have included: What is conservative dentistry? What does integrity mean? Do you think the first-year syllabus is a good one? What qualities are required by a dentist? What are prosthetics, periodontics, orthodontics? What causes tooth decay? Questions asked on the disadvantages of being a dentist, the future of dentistry and how you could show that you are manually dexterous. Other questions on personal attributes and spare time activities. What are the careers within the profession open to dentists? Questions on the future of dentistry (preventative and cosmetic dentistry), the problems facing dentists, the skills needed and the advantages and disadvantages of fluoride in water. How do you relax? How do you cope with stress? See also **Chapter 5**.

Reasons for rejection (non-academic) Lack of evidence of a firm commitment to dentistry. Lack of breadth of interests. Lack of motivation for a health care profession. Unprofessional attitude. Poor manual dexterity. Poor communication skills. Poor English. Lack of evidence of ability to work in groups. Not for the faint-hearted! More interested in running a business and making money than in caring for people.

GRADUATE DESTINATIONS AND EMPLOYMENT

(See **Chapter 1, Graduate Outcomes.**)

Career note The great majority of Dental Technology graduates gain employment in this career with job opportunities excellent. There are openings in the NHS, commercial dental laboratories and the armed services.

OTHER DEGREE SUBJECTS FOR CONSIDERATION

Anatomy; Biochemistry; Biological Sciences; Biomedical Materials Science; Chemistry; Medical Sciences; Medicine; Nursing; Optometry; Pharmacy; Physiology; Physiotherapy; Radiography; Speech Therapy/Sciences; Veterinary Medicine/Science.

DEVELOPMENT STUDIES

(see also **International Relations, Politics, Town and Urban Planning**)

Development Studies courses are multi-disciplinary and cover a range of subjects including economics, geography, sociology, social anthropology, politics, and natural resources, with special reference to countries overseas. Courses obviously overlap with International Relations degrees which should also be checked. The main focus of Development Studies is to identify and recognise problems arising overseas and how countries may be assisted in terms of poverty and health, as well as exploring wider issues concerning social and political perspectives. The unique degree course in this category is Charity Development at the University of Chichester with either Single Honours or Joint Honours. This course covers fund-raising practices, through events and campaigns, marketing and planning.

Useful websites www.devstud.org.uk; www.gov.uk/government/organisations/department-for-international-development; www.ids.ac.uk; see also **Politics**.

NB The points totals shown to the left of the institutions are for ease of reference only. It must not be assumed that Tariff points are always used by institutions or that they can be substituted for an offer in grades. The level of an offer is not necessarily indicative of the quality of a course.

COURSE OFFERS INFORMATION

Subject requirements/preferences GCSE Mathematics, English and a foreign language may be required. **AL** Science or social science subjects may be required or preferred for some courses. Some popular universities are now making lower offers for disadvantaged and other students.

Your target offers and examples of degree courses

152 pts	**Warwick** – A*AA (Glob Sust Dev Bus St) (IB 38 pts)
144 pts	**London (King's)** – AAA (Int Dev) (IB 36 pts HL 18 pts)
	Manchester – AAA (Dev St) (IB 36 pts HL 666)
136 pts	**Bath** – AAB/ABB+aEPQ (Int Dev Econ) (IB 36 pts HL 665)
	London (SOAS) – AAB (Glob Dev) (IB 34 pts HL 665)
	Sussex – AAB (Int Dev) (IB 34 pts)
	York – AAB (Glob Dev) (IB 35 pts)
128 pts	**East Anglia** – ABB (Glob Dev; Glob Dev Pol; Int Dev Anth) (IB 32 pts)
	Leeds – ABB (Int Dev) (IB 34 pts HL 655)
	Reading – ABB (Int Dev) (IB 32 pts)
	Sussex – ABB (Econ Int Dev; Int Rel Dev) (IB 32 pts)
120 pts	**Sussex** – BBB–ABB (Sociol Int Dev) (IB 30 pts)
112 pts	**East London** – BBC 112 pts (Sust Dev Soc Chng) (IB 24 pts HL 15 pts)
	Portsmouth – BBC–ABB 112–128 pts (Int Dev) (IB 25 pts)
104 pts	**Bath Spa** – BCC–BBB (Glob Dev Sust) (IB 32 pts)
	Westminster – BCC–BBB 104–120 pts (Int Rel Dev)
72 pts	**UHI** – BC (Sust Dev); BC+interview (Gael Dev)

Alternative offers See **Chapter 6** and **Appendix 1** for grades/UCAS Tariff points information for other examinations.

CHOOSING YOUR COURSE (SEE ALSO CH.1)

Universities and colleges teaching quality See www.qaa.ac.uk; www.discoveruni.gov.uk.

Top research universities and colleges (REF 2021) (Anthropology and Development Studies) London LSE (Anth); East Anglia; Manchester (Dev St); London (SOAS) (Anth); Oxford (Dev St); Bristol; Sussex; Manchester (Soc Anth); Reading; Birmingham.

Examples of sandwich degree courses Portsmouth; Reading.

ADMISSIONS INFORMATION

Admissions tutors' advice Discuss aspects of development studies which interest you, for example in relation to geography, economics, politics. Interests in Third World countries should be mentioned. Knowledge of current events.

Advice to applicants and planning the UCAS personal statement Some students think that Development Studies has something to do with property, with plants or with childhood. It is none of these and is about international processes of change, development, progress and crisis.

Interview advice and questions Since this is a multi-disciplinary subject, questions will vary considerably. Initially they will stem from your interests and the information given on your UCAS application and your reasons for choosing the course. In the past, questions at interview have included: Define a Third World country. What help does the United Nations provide in the Third World? Could it do too much? What problems does the United Nations face in its work throughout the world? Why Development Studies? What will you do in your gap year, and what do you want to achieve? See also **Chapter 5**.

GRADUATE DESTINATIONS AND EMPLOYMENT

(See **Chapter 1, Graduate Outcomes.**)

Career note The range of specialisms offered on these courses will encourage graduates to make contact with and seek opportunities in a wide range of organisations, not necessarily limited to non-governmental organisations and government agencies.

OTHER DEGREE SUBJECTS FOR CONSIDERATION

Economics; Environmental Science/Studies; Geography; Government; International Relations; Politics; Sociology; Sustainable Development.

DIETETICS

(see also **Food Science/Studies and Technology, Health Sciences/Studies, Nutrition**)

Courses are often linked with nutrition, and train students for a career as a dietitian. In addition to the scientific aspects of dietetics covering biochemistry, human physiology, food and clinical medicine, students are also introduced to health promotion, psychology, counselling and management skills. (See **Appendix 3**.)

Useful websites www.nutrition.org; www.bda.uk.com; www.dietetics.co.uk; www.skillsforhealth.org.uk

NB The points totals shown to the left of the institutions are for ease of reference only. It must not be assumed that Tariff points are always used by institutions or that they can be substituted for an offer in grades. The level of an offer is not necessarily indicative of the quality of a course.

COURSE OFFERS INFORMATION

Subject requirements/preferences GCSE English, mathematics and science usually required. **AL** Biology and/or chemistry may be required. Some popular universities are now making lower offers for disadvantaged and other students. **Other** Health and Disclosure and Barring Service (DBS) checks required and possible immunisation against hepatitis B for practice placements.

Your target offers and examples of degree courses

136 pts **Nottingham** – AAB incl biol/chem+sci+interview (Nutr Diet (MNutr)) (IB 32 pts HL 665)

128 pts **Coventry** – ABB incl biol+interview (Diet) (IB 32 pts HL 7 biol)

Hertfordshire – ABB–AAB incl biol+chem 128–136 pts+interview (Diet)

Leeds – ABB incl sci/maths (Fd Sci) (HL 16 pts incl sci/maths); (Fd Sci Nutr) (IB 34 pts HL 16 pts incl sci/maths)

Surrey – ABB incl biol+sci/maths+interview (Nutr Diet) (IB 33 pts HL 5 biol+sci/maths)

120 pts **London Met** – BBB incl biol+chem+interview (Diet Nutr)

Ulster – BBB incl sci/maths (Diet) (IB 26 pts HL 13 pts incl sci/maths)

Winchester – BBB–ABB 120–128 pts+interview (Nutr Diet) (HL 555 incl Engl+math+sci)

112 pts **Cardiff Met** – BC chem+biol 112–120 pts+interview (Hum Nutr Diet) (HL 6 biol+chem)

Chester – BBC–BBB incl biol+sci 112–120 pts+interview (Nutr Diet) (IB 28 pts HL 5 biol+chem)

Plymouth – BBC–ABB incl biol+sci/maths 112–128 pts+interview (Diet) (IB 28–30 pts HL 5 biol+sci/maths)

104 pts **Bath Spa** – BCC–BBB incl biol/PE (Hum Nutr) (IB 32 pts HL 5 biol)

Glasgow Caledonian – BCC incl chem (Hum Nutr Diet)

Robert Gordon – BCC incl chem+sci+interview (Nutr Diet) (IB 28 pts incl chem+sci)

88 pts **Queen Margaret** – AB incl chem/biol (Diet) (IB 28 pts)

Alternative offers See **Chapter 6** and **Appendix 1** for grades/UCAS Tariff points information for other examinations.

DEGREE APPRENTICESHIPS

Hertfordshire (Diet); Plymouth (Diet); Sheffield Hallam (Diet); Teesside (Diet).

CHOOSING YOUR COURSE (SEE ALSO CH.1)

Universities and colleges teaching quality See www.qaa.ac.uk; www.discoveruni.gov.uk.

Top research universities and colleges (REF 2021) See **Health Sciences/Studies**.

Examples of sandwich degree courses Surrey; Ulster.

ADMISSIONS INFORMATION

Advice to applicants and planning the UCAS personal statement Discuss the work with a hospital dietitian and describe fully work experience gained in hospital dietetics departments or with the schools meals services, and the problems of working in these fields. Admissions tutors expect applicants to have at least visited a dietetics department, and to be outgoing with good oral and written communication skills. Contact the British Dietetic Association (see **Appendix 3**).

Selection interviews Yes Cardiff Met, Chester, Coventry, Hertfordshire (Group interview), Leeds Beckett, London Met, Ulster.

Interview advice and questions Your knowledge of a career in dietetics will be fully explored and questions will be asked on your work experience and how you reacted to it. See also **Chapter 5**.

GRADUATE DESTINATIONS AND EMPLOYMENT

(See **Chapter 1, Graduate Outcomes.**)

Career note Dietitians are professionally trained to advise on diets and aspects of nutrition and many degree courses combine both subjects. They may work in the NHS as hospital dietitians collaborating with medical staff on the balance of foods for patients, or in local health authorities working with GPs, or in health centres or clinics dealing with infant welfare and antenatal problems. In addition, dietitians advise consumer groups in the food industry and government and may be involved in research. Courses can lead to professional registration: check with admissions tutors.

OTHER DEGREE SUBJECTS FOR CONSIDERATION

Biological Sciences; Biochemistry; Biology; Consumer Studies; Food Science; Health Studies; Hospitality Management; Human Nutrition; Nursing; Nutrition.

DRAMA

(including **Performing Arts/Studies, Theatre Arts, Theatre Studies and Theatre Design**; see also **Art and Design (General), Dance/Dance Studies**)

Drama courses are popular, with twice as many women as men applying each year. Lack of confidence in securing appropriate work at the end of the course, however, tends to encourage many applicants to bid for joint courses, although these are usually far more competitive since there are fewer places available. Most schools of acting and drama provide a strong vocational bias while university drama departments offer a broader field of studies combining theory and practice. For example, at London (Goldsmiths) the Drama and Theatre Arts degree offers a balance between acting and production.

Useful websites www.equity.org.uk; www.abtt.org.uk; www.thestage.co.uk; www.uktw.co.uk; www.stagecoach.co.uk; www.rada.ac.uk; www.artscouncil.org.uk

NB The points totals shown to the left of the institutions are for ease of reference only. It must not be assumed that Tariff points are always used by institutions or that they can be substituted for an offer in grades. The level of an offer is not necessarily indicative of the quality of a course.

COURSE OFFERS INFORMATION

Subject requirements/preferences GCSE English usually required. **AL** English, drama, theatre studies may be required or preferred. (Thea Arts) English, theatre studies or drama may be required for some courses. Some popular universities are now making lower offers for disadvantaged and other students. **Other** Disclosure and Barring Service (DBS) clearance required for some courses: check websites.

Your target offers and examples of degree courses

144 pts **Bristol** – AAA incl Engl (Thea Engl) (IB 36 pts HL 18 pts incl 6 Engl)

136 pts **Birmingham** – AAB (Dr courses) (IB 32 pts HL 665)

Bristol – AAB (Thea Perf St) (IB 34 pts HL 17 pts); AAB incl lang (Thea Modn Lang) (IB 34 pts HL 17 pts incl 5 lang)

Lancaster – AAB incl Engl (Thea Engl Lit) (IB 35 pts HL 16 pts incl 6 lit)

Manchester – AAB incl A Engl lit+interview (Dr Engl Lit) (IB 35 pts HL 665); AAB incl essay sub+interview (Dr) (IB 35 pts HL 665)
Warwick – AAB incl Engl+interview (Engl Thea St) (IB 34 pts HL 6 Engl)
York – AAB+interview (Thea Writ Dir Perf) (IB 35 pts)

128 pts **East Anglia** – ABB incl dr/thea st/Engl lit (Dr) (IB 32 pts HL 5 thea st/Engl)
Exeter – ABB–AAB+workshop (Dr) (IB 32 pts HL 655); ABB–AAB incl Engl lit (Engl Drama) (IB 34–36 pts HL 665–666 incl 5 Engl lit)
Lancaster – ABB (Dr Thea Perf; Thea Crea Writ) (IB 32 pts HL 16 pts)
Leeds – ABB incl arts/hum (Thea Perf) (IB 34 pts)
London (RH) – ABB–AAB incl Engl (Engl Dr) (IB 32 pts HL 655 incl Engl); ABB–AAB incl arts/hum (Dr Crea Writ) (IB 32 pts HL 655 incl 6 arts/hum)
Manchester – ABB incl essay sub (Dr Flm St) (IB 34 pts HL 655)
Reading – ABB (Thea Perf) (IB 32 pts)
Warwick – ABB+interview (Thea Perf St) (IB 32 pts)

120 pts **Glasgow** – BBB–AAB incl hum (Thea St) (IB 34 pts HL 655 incl Engl+hum)
Kent – BBB+workshop+interview (Dr Thea Perf Arts) (HL 665)
London (Gold) – BBB (Dr Thea Arts) (IB 33 pts HL 655)
London (QM) – BBB incl art/hum/soc sci (Dr) (IB 30 pts HL 555 incl art/hum/soc sci)
London (RH) – BBB incl mus (Mus Thea) (IB 32 pts HL 655 incl mus); BBB–ABB (Dr Act; Dr Phil; Dr Thea St; Perf Dig Arts) (IB 32 pts HL 655); BBB–ABB incl lang (Modn Lang Dr) (IB 32 pts HL 655)
Queen Margaret – BBB (Dr) (IB 30 pts)
Queen's Belfast – BBB (Dr) (IB 32 pts HL 655)
Reading – BBB incl Engl/thea st (Engl Lit Flm Thea) (IB 30 pts HL 5 Engl/thea st)
Sussex – BBB (Dr Flm St; Dr Thea Perf) (IB 30 pts)
West London – BBB–ABB 120–128 pts (Actg Stg Scrn; Musl Thea)

112 pts **Bournemouth Arts** – BBC–BBB 112–120 pts+interview+portfolio (Actg)
Brunel – BBC (Thea; Thea Crea Writ; Thea Engl) (IB 29 pts)
Canterbury Christ Church – BBC 112 pts (Perf Arts) (IB 29 pts)
De Montfort – 112 pts (Dr Thea) (IB 26 pts)
Derby – BBC 112 pts+portfolio (Thea Arts)
East London – 112 pts (Actg Stg Scrn) (IB 24 pts HL 15 pts)
Edge Hill – BBC–BBB 112–120 pts+audition (Dr)
Essex – ABB incl essay sub 112–120 pts+workshop (Dr) (IB 29–30 pts HL 554–555); BBC–BBB incl essay sub 112–120 pts (Dr Lit) (IB 29–30 pts HL 554–555)
Hull – BBC 112 pts (Dr) (IB 28 pts)
Kingston – 112–128 pts incl dr/perf arts/Engl lit+audition (Dr courses)
Leeds Beckett – 112 pts (Perf Arts)
London (Birk) – BBC 112 pts (Thea Perf)
London Met – 112 pts+interview+workshop (Thea Perf)
London South Bank – BBC (Actg Stg Scrn)
Middlesex – BBC 112 pts+portfolio (Thea)
Northampton – BBC+audition (Actg)
Sheffield Hallam – BBC 112 pts (Actg Perf)

104 pts **Bangor** – 104–128 pts (Engl Lit Dr) (HL 5 Engl)
Bath Spa – BCC–BBB incl dr/thea st/perf arts+audition (Dr) (IB 32 pts)
Chester – 104 pts+audition (Dr courses) (IB 28 pts); BCC–BBC incl dr/thea st 104–112 pts+interview+audition (Musl Thea Perf) (IB 26 pts HL 5 thea arts)
Chichester – BCC–BBB 104–120 pts+audition (Dr Thea Dir) (IB 28 pts)
Derby – BCC 104 pts+portfolio (Crea Expr Arts Hlth Wlbng (Dance/Dr/Mus/Art))
Falmouth – 104–120 pts+interview+audition (Actg)
Greenwich – BCC 104 pts+audition (Dr)
Huddersfield – BCC–BBB 104–120 pts (Mus Thea); BCC–BBB 104–120 pts+audition (Actg Perf; Actg Perf Engl Lang/Lit)
Lincoln – 104 pts+interview (Dr Thea Perf) (IB 28 pts)

Liverpool Hope – BCC 104 pts+audition (Dr Thea) (IB 24 pts)
Liverpool John Moores – BCC 104 pts+interview+audition (Perf Prod)
Manchester Met – BCC+audition (Actg) (IB 26 pts)
Plymouth – 104–112 pts+interview+audition workshop (Dr) (IB 26 pts)
Portsmouth – BCC–BBC 104–112 pts+interview (Thea) (IB 25 pts); BCC–BBB 104–120 pts+interview+workshop (Actg) (IB 25 pts)
Solent – 104–120 pts+audition (Actg Perf)
York St John – 104 pts (Dr Thea)

96 pts **Aberystwyth** – CCC–BBB 96–120 pts (Dr Thea) (IB 26–30 pts)
Anglia Ruskin – 96 pts (Dr Engl Lit) (IB 24 pts); 96 pts+audition (Dr) (IB 24 pts)
Birmingham City – CCC 96 pts incl dr+interview (App Thea (Commun Educ)) (IB 24 pts); CCC incl dr 96 pts+interview (Stg Mgt) (IB 24 pts)
Central Lancashire – 96 pts+audition (Actg; Mus Thea)
Chichester – CCC–BBC 96–112 pts+audition (Actg Flm) (IB 28 pts)
London (Royal Central Sch SpDr) – 96–120 pts+interview (Dr App Thea)
South Wales – CCC incl art/des 96 pts+portfolio (Perf Media); CCC incl art des sub 96 pts+interview+portfolio (Thea Dr)
St Mary's – CCC–BBC 96–112 pts+interview+audition (Actg)
Sunderland – 96–112 pts+audition+interview (Perf Arts)
Surrey (GSA) – CCC+interview+audition (Actg; Musl Thea) (IB 29 pts)
Winchester – CCC–BBC 96–112 pts+interview+audition (Musl Thea) (HL 44); CCC–BBC 96–112 pts+workshop+audition+interview (Actg) (HL 44)

80 pts **City St George's** – CDD 80 pts+interview (Prof Dance Musl Thea) (HL 5 incl Engl+maths)

72 pts **Liverpool (LIPA)** – BC 72–80 pts+interview+audition (App Thea Commun Dr)

64 pts **Arts London** – CC+audition (Actg Perf); CC+interview+portfolio (Thea Des) (IB 28 pts); CC+portfolio (Perf Des Prac)
Birmingham City – CC 64 pts+audition+interview (Actg) (IB 24 pts)
Liverpool (LIPA) – CC 64 pts+audition+interview (Actg); CC 64 pts+interview (Thea Perf Des; Thea Prod Tech)
London (Royal Central Sch SpDr) – 64 pts+audition (Actg); 64–120 pts+interview+portfolio (Perf Des; Snd Des Prod; Stg Mgt Tech Thea); CC+audition (Actg (Coll Dvsd Thea); Actg (Musl Thea))
London Regent's – CC+audition (Actg Stg Scrn)
Rose Bruford (Coll) – 64 pts+audition/portfolio (Am Thea Arts; Euro Thea Arts); CC 64 pts+audition (Actg; Actr Mushp); CC 64 pts+interview+portfolio (Cstm Prod; Stg Mgt)
Trinity Saint David – 64 pts+audition+interview (Actg)

32 pts **Arts Educ Sch** – EE+audition (Actg; Musl Thea)
Bristol Old Vic (Thea Sch) – EE+audition (Prof Actg)
Essex – EE 32 pts+audition+interview (Actg; Actg Contemp Thea)
Guildhall (Sch Mus Dr) – EE–AA+audition (Actg) (IB 24 pts); EE–AA 32 pts+interview (Prod Arts) (IB 24 pts)
RConsvS – EE+audition/interview (Actg; Contemp Perf Prac; Prod Arts Des) (IB 24 pts)
LAMDA – audition (Prof Actg)
London (RADA) – audition (Actg)
London Mountview (Ac Thea Arts) – audition (Perf (Actg); Perf (Musl Thea))
Royal Welsh (CMusDr) – audition (Actg); interview (Stg Mgt Tech Thea)

Alternative offers See **Chapter 6** and **Appendix 1** for grades/UCAS Tariff points information for other examinations.

EXAMPLES OF COLLEGES OFFERING COURSES IN THIS SUBJECT FIELD

Blackpool and Fylde (Coll); Bradford College (UC); Bury (Coll); Calderdale (Coll); Chichester (Coll); Coventry (Coll); Doncaster (Coll); East Durham (Coll); Exeter (Coll); Gateshead (Coll); Guildford (Coll); Havering (Coll); Hopwood Hall (Coll); Hull (Coll); Kingston (Coll); Leicester (Coll); Liverpool City (Coll);

Manchester (Coll); Middlesbrough (Coll); NCC Redbridge; Nottingham (Coll); Plymouth City (Coll); Richmond-upon-Thames (Coll); Sheffield (Coll); SMB CG; South Gloucestershire and Stroud (Coll); Southampton City (Coll); Stratford-upon-Avon (Coll); Sunderland (Coll); Tresham (CFHE); Wakefield (Coll); Warrington and Vale Royal (Coll); West Herts (Coll); West Thames (Coll); Westminster City (Coll).

CHOOSING YOUR COURSE (SEE ALSO CH.1)

UNIVERSITIES AND COLLEGES TEACHING QUALITY See www.qaa.ac.uk; www.discoveruni.gov.uk.

TOP RESEARCH UNIVERSITIES AND COLLEGES (REF 2021) (Music, Drama, Dance, Performing Arts, Film and Screen Studies) London (QM) (Dr); London (RH); Manchester (Dr, Dance, Perf Arts, Flm Scrn St); London (Royal Central Sch SpDr); London (King's); London (SOAS); Cambridge; Roehampton (Dance); Kent; Huddersfield (Mus).

ADMISSIONS INFORMATION

ADMISSIONS TUTORS' ADVICE Emphasis is placed on academic and practical abilities.

ADVICE TO APPLICANTS AND PLANNING THE UCAS PERSONAL STATEMENT List the plays in which you have performed and specify the characters played. Indicate any experience in other areas of theatre, especially directing or writing. Add any information on projects you have initiated or developed or worked on in theatre craft, such as set design, costume design, lighting design, prop-making, scene painting. List any community arts projects such as work with youth clubs, hospital radio, amateur dramatics, music/drama workshops and voluntary work within the arts. Show your strengths in dance and theatre, and your commitment to drama in all its aspects. See **Chapter 5** and also **Appendix 3**.

SELECTION INTERVIEWS Yes Arts London, Bath Spa, Birmingham City, Bournemouth Arts, Bucks New, Cambridge, Chichester, City St George's (Prof Dance Musl Thea), Essex, Falmouth, Greenwich, Kent, Lincoln, Liverpool (LIPA), Liverpool John Moores, London (Royal Central Sch SpDr), London Met, Manchester, Middlesex, Plymouth, Portsmouth, Royal Welsh (CMusDr) (Stg Mgt Tech Thea), St Mary's, Sunderland, Surrey (GSA), UWE Bristol, Warwick, Winchester, York; **Some** London Regent's, RConsvS, Rose Bruford (Coll); **No** Anglia Ruskin, Bishop Grosseteste, De Montfort, East Anglia, East London, Exeter.

INTERVIEW ADVICE AND QUESTIONS See also **Chapter 5**.

REASONS FOR REJECTION (NON-ACADEMIC) Poor ambition. Wrong expectations of the course. Several students clearly want drama school acting training rather than a degree course. Not enough background reading.

GRADUATE DESTINATIONS AND EMPLOYMENT

(See **Chapter 1, Graduate Outcomes.**)

CAREER NOTE Some graduates develop careers in performance, writing, directing and producing as well as wider roles within the theatre. Others go on to careers such as teaching, media management and retail where their creativity and communication skills are valued.

OTHER DEGREE SUBJECTS FOR CONSIDERATION

Art and Design (Costume Design, Stage Design); Arts Management; Dance; Education (Primary); English; Performance Studies.

ECONOMICS

(see also **Business and Management Courses, Mathematics, Philosophy, Politics and Economics (PPE), Statistics**)

Economics is about how society makes good use of the limited resources available. Degree courses cover all aspects of finance, taxation and monetary union between countries, aiming to equip the student to analyse economic problems in a systematic way and thus acquire an understanding of how economic systems work. Economics involves mathematics and statistics, and applicants without economics at AS or A-level should be prepared for this, although for BA courses, such as at the University of Leicester, mathematics is not required at A-level. All courses are quite flexible with specialisms coming later in the course, leading to a range of career choices. Many joint courses are often offered with combinations such as Politics, Management and Finance. The course at Cambridge in Land Economy focuses on the legal and economic aspects relative to the natural environment, covering business regulations and the financial aspects of real estate and development. The course is accredited by the Royal Institution of Chartered Surveyors and has a very high success rate of graduate employment. (See also the **Surveying and Real Estate Management** table.)

Useful websites www.iea.org.uk; www.res.org.uk; www.economist.com; www.neweconomics.org; see also **Finance**.

NB The points totals shown to the left of the institutions are for ease of reference only. It must not be assumed that Tariff points are always used by institutions or that they can be substituted for an offer in grades. The level of an offer is not necessarily indicative of the quality of a course.

COURSE OFFERS INFORMATION

Subject requirements/preferences GCSE English, mathematics and occasionally a foreign language required. 8–9/7/5–6 (A*/A/B) may be stipulated by some universities. **AL** Mathematics, economics or business studies may be required or preferred. Business studies may be preferred if economics is not offered. Applicants should note that many courses will accept students without economics (check prospectuses and websites). Some popular universities are now making lower offers for disadvantaged and other students.

Your target offers and examples of degree courses

160 pts **Cambridge** – A*A*A incl maths+interview+ECAA (Econ) (IB 40–42 pts HL 776 incl maths)
Warwick – A*A*A (Econ Pol Int St) (IB 39 pts HL 666); A*A*A incl maths (Econ; Econ Ind Org) (IB 39 pts HL 666 incl maths)

152 pts **Bath** – A*AA–AAA+aEPQ incl maths (Econ) (IB 36 pts HL 766 incl maths)
Bristol – A*AA incl maths (Econ courses) (IB 38 pts HL 18 pts incl 6 maths)
Cambridge – A*AA+interview (Lnd Econ) (IB 41–42 pts HL 776)
Durham – A*AA incl maths (Econ; Econ Mgt) (IB 38 pts HL 666 incl maths); A*AA incl maths+soc sci/hum (Econ Pol) (IB 38 pts HL 666 maths+soc sci/hum)
Edinburgh – A*AA (Econ Stats) (IB 39 pts HL 666); A*AA incl maths (Econ Fin) (IB 39 pts HL 666 incl maths)
London (UCL) – A*AA incl A* maths (Econ; Econ Stats; Geog Econ; Stats Econ Fin) (IB 39 pts HL 19 pts incl 7 maths)
London LSE – A*AA incl A* maths (Ecomet Mathem Econ; Econ; Maths Econ) (IB 38 pts HL 766 incl 7 maths)
Nottingham – A*AA (Econ Fr; Econ Ger; Econ Hisp St) (IB 36 pts HL 766); A*AA incl maths (Econ courses) (IB 38 pts)
Oxford – A*AA incl A maths+interview+TSA (Econ Mgt) (IB 39 pts HL 766 incl maths)

144 pts **Bath** – AAA/A*AB/AAB+aEPQ incl maths (Econ Pol) (IB 36 pts HL 666/765 incl maths)
Birmingham – AAA (Econ Pol) (IB 32 pts HL 666); AAA incl maths (Mathem Econ Stats) (IB 32 pts HL 666); AAA–A*AA (Econ Lang) (IB 32 pts HL 766); AAA–A*AA incl maths (Econ) (IB 32 pts HL 766)

Bristol – AAA incl maths (Phil Econ) (IB 36 pts HL 18 pts incl 6 maths); AAA–A*AB incl maths (Econ Acc) (IB 36 pts HL 18 pts incl 6 maths)
Edinburgh – AAA–A*AA incl maths (Econ courses) (IB 37–39 pts HL 665–666 incl maths)
Exeter – AAA–A*AA (Bus Econ; Bus Econ (Yr Ind); Econ; Econ Ecomet) (IB 36–38 pts HL 666–766); AAA–A*AA 144–152 pts (Econ Pol) (IB 36–38 pts HL 666–766)
Leeds – AAA (Bus Econ; Econ; Econ Fin) (IB 35 pts HL 17 pts)
London (QM) – AAA incl maths (Econ; Econ Comb Hons; Econ Fin Mgt) (IB 36 pts HL 666)
London (UCL) – AAA incl maths (Econ Bus E Euro St) (IB 38 pts HL 18 pts incl 6 maths)
London LSE – AAA incl A maths (Env Sust Dev Econ) (IB 38 pts HL 766 incl maths); AAA incl A maths+econ/hist (Econ Econ Hist) (IB 38 pts HL 766 incl maths+econ/hist); AAA incl maths (Pol Econ) (IB 38 pts HL 766 incl maths)
Loughborough – AAA (Bus Econ Fin; Econ) (IB 37 pts HL 666)
Manchester – AAA (Econ Pol; Econ Sociol) (IB 36 pts HL 666); AAA incl maths (Econ) (IB 36 pts HL 666 incl maths)
Newcastle – AAA (Econ; Econ Bus Mgt; Econ Fin) (IB 36 pts)
Nottingham – AAA (Ind Econ; Ind Econ Ins) (IB 36 pts)
Oxford – AAA+interview+HAT+TSA (Hist Econ) (IB 38 pts HL 666)
Sheffield – AAA incl maths (Econ Fin) (IB 36 pts HL 6 maths)
Southampton – AAA incl maths/fmaths (Econ Act Sci) (IB 36 pts HL 18 pts incl 6 maths); AAA–AAB+aEPQ incl A maths (Maths OR Stats Econ (MORSE)) (IB 36 pts HL 18 pts incl 6 maths)
St Andrews – AAA (Econ courses) (IB 38 pts HL 666)
York – AAA incl hist/class civ+maths (Hist Econ) (IB 36 pts HL 666 incl hist+maths); AAA incl maths (Econ Maths) (IB 36 pts HL 6 maths)

136 pts **Birmingham** – AAB (Pol Econ) (IB 32 pts HL 665)
Exeter – AAB–AAA incl maths (Maths Econ) (IB 34–36 pts HL 665–666 incl 6 maths)
Lancaster – AAB incl A maths/fmaths (Econ (St Abrd); Econ Comb Hons) (IB 35 pts HL 16 pts incl 6 maths); AAB incl maths (Econ; Econ (Yr Ind)) (IB 35 pts HL 16 pts incl 6 maths)
Liverpool – AAB (Bus Econ) (IB 35 pts); AAB incl maths (Econ) (IB 36 pts HL 6 maths)
London (SOAS) – AAB incl maths (Econ) (IB 35 pts HL 665)
London LSE – AAB incl A maths (Int Soc Pblc Plcy Econ) (IB 37 pts HL 666 incl maths)
Loughborough – AAB (Geog Econ) (IB 35 pts HL 665)
NU London – AAB (Econ courses) (IB 35 pts HL 665)
Newcastle – AAB (Pol Econ) (IB 34 pts)
Sheffield – AAB incl A maths (Econ Comb Hons) (IB 34 pts HL 6 maths)
Southampton – AAB/ABB+aEPQ incl maths/phys/stats (Econ Bus Mgt) (IB 34 pts HL 17 pts incl 5 maths/phys/stats); AAB incl maths (Econ Fin) (IB 34 pts HL 17 pts incl 5 maths); AAB–ABB+aEPQ incl maths/phys (Econ Acc) (IB 34 pts HL 17 pts incl 5 maths); ABB+aEPQ incl maths (Econ) (IB 34 pts HL 17 pts incl 5 maths)
Surrey – AAB (Bus Econ; Econ; Econ Fin) (IB 34 pts)
York – AAB incl maths (Econ; Econ Ecomet Fin; Econ Fin) (IB 35 pts HL 6 maths)

128 pts **Cardiff** – ABB–AAB (Bus Econ) (IB 32–34 pts HL 665–666); ABB–AAB incl Fr/Ger/Span (Bus Econ Euro Lang (Fr/Ger/Span)) (IB 32–34 pts incl 6 Fr/Ger/Span); ABB–AAB incl maths (Econ) (IB 32–34 pts HL 665–666 incl 6 maths)
East Anglia – ABB (Bus Fin Econ; Econ; Econ Acc) (IB 32 pts); ABB/BBB+aEPQ (Bus Econ) (IB 32 pts)
Hertfordshire – ABB–AAB 128–136 pts (Econ)
Lancaster – ABB incl maths (Econ Fin) (IB 32 pts HL 16 pts incl 6 maths)
Leicester – ABB (Econ Courses) (IB 30 pts)
London (RH) – ABB–AAB (Econ Mgt) (IB 32 pts HL 655)
Nottingham Trent – (Econ Int Fin Bank)
Queen's Belfast – ABB (Econ courses) (IB 33 pts HL 655)
Reading – ABB (Bus Econ) (IB 32 pts); ABB incl maths (Econ) (IB 32 pts)
Southampton – ABB (Econ Phil) (IB 32 pts HL 16 pts incl 5 maths); ABB incl maths (Pol Econ) (IB 32 pts HL 16 pts incl maths)
Sussex – ABB (Econ Int Dev) (IB 32 pts)

120 pts **Aberdeen** – BBB (Econ) (IB 32 pts HL 555)
Aston – BBB–BBC+bEPQ (Econ Mgt) (IB 31 pts HL 555)
Brunel – BBB (Econ Bus Fin) (IB 30 pts); BBB incl maths (Econ) (IB 30 pts HL 5 maths)
City St George's – BBB (Econ; Econ Acc) (IB 30 pts); BBB incl maths (Fin Econ) (IB 30 pts HL 5 maths)
Coventry – BBB (Econ courses) (IB 24 pts)
Dundee – BBB (Econ Span) (IB 30 pts HL 555); BBB incl sci/maths (Econ) (IB 30 pts HL 555 incl sci/maths)
Glasgow – BBB–AAB incl Engl/hum (Econ Comb Hons) (IB 36 pts HL 665 incl Engl/hum)
Greenwich – BBB 120 pts (Econ)
Huddersfield – BBB 120 pts (Econ)
Hull – BBB 120 pts (Bus Econ; Econ) (IB 30 pts)
Kingston – 120–136 pts (Bus Econ; Econ; Fin Econ)
London (Gold) – BBB (Econ) (IB 33 pts HL 655)
London (RH) – ABC–ABB incl A maths (Econ Maths) (IB 32 pts HL 654 incl 6 maths); BBB–ABB (Econ) (IB 32 pts HL 555 incl maths); (Econ Pol Int Rel; Fin Bus Econ) (IB 32 pts HL 655)
Nottingham Trent – 120–128 pts (Econ; Econ Bus)
Portsmouth – BBB 120–128 pts (Econ) (IB 29–30 pts)
Stirling – BBB (Econ) (IB 30 pts)
Strathclyde – BBB incl maths (Maths Stats Econ) (IB 30 pts HL 5 maths); BBB–ABB (Econ; Econ Psy; Soc Plcy Econ) (IB 30–32 pts)
Sussex – BBB–ABB (Econ; Econ Mgt St) (IB 30–32 pts)
Swansea – BBB–ABB (Econ courses) (IB 32–33 pts)

112 pts **Bradford** – BBC 112 pts (Econ; Fin Econ)
Buckingham – BBC–BBB (Econ) (IB 31–32 pts)
Cardiff Met – BBC 112 pts (Econ)
De Montfort – 112 pts (Econ) (IB 26 pts)
East London – BBC 112 pts (Econ) (IB 24 pts HL 15 pts)
Essex – BBC (Psy Econ) (IB 29 pts); (Bus Econ; Econ; Fin Econ; Int Econ; Mgt Econ) (IB 29 pts HL 554); BBC–BBB 112–120 pts (Econ Pol) (IB 29–30 pts HL 554–555)
Heriot-Watt – BBC–ABB (Econ) (IB 29 pts)
Hertfordshire – BBC–BBB 112–120 pts (Acc Econ; Bus Econ)
Keele – BBC (Econ Comb Hons) (IB 30 pts)
Kent – BBC–BBB (Econ)
Leeds Beckett – 112 pts (Bus Econ) (IB 25 pts)
Manchester Met – BBC–BBB 112–120 pts (Econ) (IB 26 pts)
Northumbria – 112 pts (Econ Fin)
Plymouth – 112–128 pts (Econ courses) (IB 28–32 pts)
Sheffield Hallam – BBC 112 pts (Bus Econ)
UWE Bristol – BBC incl maths 112 pts (Econ) (HL 5 maths)

104 pts **Bangor** – 104–136 pts (Econ)
Bournemouth – BCC–BBB 104–120 pts (Econ)
Chester – BCC–BBC (Econ Comb Hons) (IB 26 pts)
Coventry – BCC (Bus Econ) (IB 24 pts)
Northampton – BCC 104 pts (Econ)
Oxford Brookes – BCC 104 pts (Acc Econ) (IB 29 pts)
Salford – BCC–BBC 104–112 pts (Bus Mgt Econ) (IB 30 pts)
Winchester – BCC–BBB 104–120 pts (Econ Fin) (HL 44)

96 pts **Aberystwyth** – CCC–BBB 96–120 pts (Bus Econ; Econ) (IB 26–30 pts)
Anglia Ruskin – (Bus Econ)
London Met – CCC (Econ)

Open University – (Comb Soc Sci (Econ/Geog/Psy/Sociol); Econ Mathem Sci)

ALTERNATIVE OFFERS See **Chapter 6** and **Appendix 1** for grades/UCAS Tariff points information for other examinations.

DEGREE APPRENTICESHIPS

Kent (Prof Econ).

CHOOSING YOUR COURSE (SEE ALSO CH.1)

Universities and colleges teaching quality See www.qaa.ac.uk; www.discoveruni.gov.uk.

Top research universities and colleges (REF 2021) (Economics and Econometrics) London LSE; Warwick; London (UCL); Cambridge; Nottingham; Oxford; Bristol; Essex; London (QM); Surrey.

Examples of sandwich degree courses Anglia Ruskin; Aston; Bangor; Bath; Birmingham City; Bournemouth; Brighton; Brunel; Coventry; De Montfort; East Anglia; Essex; Exeter; Greenwich; Hertfordshire; Kent; Lancaster; Leeds Beckett; Liverpool; London (QM); Loughborough; Manchester Met; Newcastle; Nottingham Trent; Plymouth; Portsmouth; Reading; Salford; Sheffield Hallam; Surrey; UWE Bristol; Westminster.

ADMISSIONS INFORMATION

Advice to applicants and planning the UCAS personal statement Visits, work experience and work shadowing in banks, insurance companies, accountants' offices, etc should be described. Keep up-to-date with economic issues by reading *The Economist* and the *Financial Times* and find other sources of information. Describe any particular aspects of economics which interest you – and why. Make it clear on the statement that you know what economics is and why you want to study it. Give evidence of your interest in economics and your reasons for choosing the course and provide information about your sport/extracurricular activities and positions of responsibility.

Selection interviews Yes Buckingham, Cambridge, Oxford (Econ Mgt) 17% (success rate 5%); **Some** Essex, Loughborough; **No** Anglia Ruskin, Bristol, East Anglia, East London, Edinburgh, Keele, Leeds, London (RH), London (UCL), London LSE, London Met, Nottingham Trent, Swansea, UWE Bristol.

Interview advice and questions If you have studied economics at A-level or in other examinations, expect to be questioned on aspects of the subject. This is a subject which is constantly in the news, so keep abreast of developments and be prepared to be asked questions such as: What is happening to sterling at present? What is happening to the dollar? How relevant is economics today? What are your views on the government's economic policy? Do you think that the family is declining as an institution? Discuss Keynesian economics. Is the power of the Prime Minister increasing? What is a recession? How would you get the world out of recession? What causes a recession? See also **Chapter 5**.

Reasons for rejection (non-academic) Lack of knowledge about the course offered and the subject matter; lack of care in preparing personal statement; poor written English; the revelation on the statement that they want a course different from that for which they have applied!

GRADUATE DESTINATIONS AND EMPLOYMENT

(See **Chapter 1, Graduate Outcomes.**)

Career note Most graduates work within areas of business and finance, and in a range of jobs including management and administration posts across both public and private sectors.

OTHER DEGREE SUBJECTS FOR CONSIDERATION

Accountancy; Actuarial Studies; Administration; Banking; Business Studies; Development Studies; Estate Management; Financial Services; Government; Politics; Management Sciences/Studies; Property Development; Quantity Surveying; Social Sciences; Sociology; Statistics.

EDUCATION STUDIES

(see also **Physical Education, Social Sciences/Studies, Teacher Training**)

There are four types of degree courses in Education. Firstly, there are those universities providing an academic study of the subject at Single Honours level, covering the study of childhood and aspects of education such as psychology, sociology, philosophy and history (check with your chosen institution). Secondly, there are institutions offering degrees in Education with a professional practice qualification to teach, as in the degree course in Early Years Education at Edge Hill University. Thirdly, as in all degree subjects, there are many Joint Honours and combined degrees in which Education is taken with another academic subject, in which the two subjects may be taken equally or on a major/minor basis. Finally, there are specific degree courses in teacher training and professional practice leading directly to the classroom (see the **Teacher Training** table).

Useful websites www.gtcs.org.uk; www.ucas.com/teaching-in-the-uk; www.gov.uk/government/organisations/department-for-education; www.et-foundation.co.uk

NB The points totals shown to the left of the institutions are for ease of reference only. It must not be assumed that Tariff points are always used by institutions or that they can be substituted for an offer in grades. The level of an offer is not necessarily indicative of the quality of a course.

COURSE OFFERS INFORMATION

Subject requirements/preferences GCSE English and mathematics usually required. **AL** No subjects specified. Some popular universities are now making lower offers for disadvantaged and other students. **Plymouth** Maths, English and Science at **GCSE** grade 4 (C) or above. Plus interview, DBS checks (including overseas checks) and Fit2teach.

Your target offers and examples of degree courses

152 pts **Cambridge** – A*AA+interview+EAA (Educ) (IB 41–42 pts HL 776)
136 pts **Durham** – AAB+interview (Educ St) (IB 36 pts HL 665)
128 pts **Bath** – ABB/BBB+aEPQ (Educ Psy) (IB 35 pts HL 655)
Birmingham – ABB (Educ) (IB 32 pts HL 655)
London (UCL) – ABB (Educ Soty Cult) (IB 34 pts HL 655); ABB 128 pts (Ely Chld Educ) (IB 34 pts HL 555)
Sheffield – ABB (Educ Cult Chld) (IB 33 pts)
Southampton – ABB/BBB+aEPQ (Educ) (IB 32 pts HL 16 pts)
York – ABB (Sociol Educ) (IB 34 pts)
120 pts **East Anglia** – BBB–BBC+aEPQ (Educ) (IB 31 pts)
Glasgow – BBB–AAB incl sci/maths+interview (Des Tech Educ) (IB 34 pts HL 655 incl Engl+sci/maths)
Liverpool John Moores – BBB–ABB 120 pts+interview (P Educ QTS)
Manchester Met – BBB 120 pts+interview (P Educ) (IB 30 pts)
Newcastle – BBB (Educ) (IB 32 pts HL 555)
Reading – BBB (Educ St) (IB 30 pts); BBB+interview (P Educ QTS) (IB 30 pts)
Stirling – BBB (Educ P) (IB 30–32 pts)
York – BBB (Educ) (IB 31 pts)
115 pts **Trinity Saint David** – 115 pts (P Educ QTS)
112 pts **Brunel** – BBC–ABB (Educ) (IB 29 pts)
Canterbury Christ Church – BBC 112 pts (Educ St; Ely Chld St) (IB 29 pts)
Cardiff – BBC–BBB (Sociol Educ) (IB 29–31 pts HL 655–665)
Chester – 112 pts (Educ)
East London – BBC 112 pts (Spec Educ) (IB 24 pts HL 15 pts); BBC 112 pts incl soc sci/hum (Ely Chld St) (IB 24 pts HL 15 pts)
Essex – BBC (Chld St) (IB 29 pts HL 554)
Huddersfield – BBC 112 pts (Educ Ely Yrs)

Keele – BBC 112 pts (Educ) (IB 29 pts HL 554)
Leeds Beckett – 112 pts (Chld St)
London Met – BBC 112 pts (Educ)
Northumbria – 112 pts+interview (P Educ)
Nottingham Trent – 112 pts (Chld (Psy); Chld St; Educ; Ely Chld St)
Queen Margaret – BBC 112 pts (Educ St P) (IB 30 pts)
Roehampton – 112 pts (Educ Yth St)
Sheffield Hallam – BBC–BBB 112–120 pts (Chld Chld); BBC 112 pts (Educ Psy Cnslg)
Suffolk – BBC 112 pts (Chld)
West London – BBC 112 pts (Ely Chld St)

104 pts **Bath Spa** – BCC–BBB (P Educ QTS) (IB 32 pts); BCC–BBB (Educ) (IB 32 pts)
Bedfordshire – BCC 104 pts (Educ)
Brighton – BCC–BBB 104–120 pts (Educ) (IB 30 pts)
Cardiff – BCC–BBB (Educ) (IB 29–31 pts HL 655–665); BCC–BBB incl B Welsh (Welsh Educ) (IB 29–31 pts HL 655–665)
Cardiff Met – BCC+interview (P Educ QTS); BCC 104 pts (Educ Psy SEN; P Educ St)
Central Lancashire – 104–112 pts (Educ Comb Hons)
De Montfort – 104 pts (Educ St; Educ St Mand; Educ St Psy)
Derby – BCC–BBC 104–112 pts (Educ St; Ely Chld St)
Edge Hill – BCC–BBC 104–112 pts (Educ; Wkg Teach Ely Yrs)
Gloucestershire – BCC–BBC 104–112 pts (Physl Educ)
Hertfordshire – BCC–BBC 104–112 pts (Educ; Ely Chld Educ)
Hull – BCC 104 pts (Educ St courses; Ely Chld St) (IB 26 pts)
Liverpool Hope – BCC 104 pts (Educ; SEN courses) (IB 24 pts)
Liverpool John Moores – BCC–BBB (Educ P St); BCC 104 pts (Educ SEN)
Manchester Met – BCC–BBC 104–112 pts (Educ) (IB 25 pts)
Northampton – BCC (Educ St courses)
Oxford Brookes – BCC (Educ St) (IB 29 pts)
Portsmouth – BCC–BBC 104–112 pts (Chld Yth St; Ely Chld St) (IB 25 pts); BCC–BBC 104–112 pts+interview (P Educ QTS) (IB 28–29 pts)

96 pts **Aberystwyth** – CCC–BBB 96–120 pts (Educ Comb Hons) (IB 26–30 pts); CCC–BBC 96–112 pts (Chld St) (IB 26–30 pts)
Anglia Ruskin – 96 pts (P Educ St) (IB 24 pts)
Bangor – 96–128 pts (Chld Yth St)
Bedfordshire – 96 pts (Ely Chld Educ)
Birmingham Newman – 96 pts (Ely Chld St; St P Educ)
Bishop Grosseteste – 96–112 pts (Educ St courses)
Cardiff Met – 96–112 pts (Spo Physl Educ Hlth (Dance)) (HL 6)
Chester – CCC–BCC (Ely Chld P Educ) (IB 26 pts)
Chichester – 96–112 pts (Educ) (IB 26–28 pts); CCC–BBC 96–112 pts+interview (Out Advntr Educ)
Dundee – CCC+interview (Educ) (IB 28 pts HL 554 incl Engl)
East London – 96 pts (Educ St) (IB 24 pts HL 15 pts)
Gloucestershire – CCC 96 pts (Ely Chld St)
Leeds Trinity – 96–128 pts (Educ Mntl Hlth SEND)
Marjon – CCC (Out Advntr Educ)
Middlesex – CCC 96 pts (Educ St)
Northampton – CCC (Ely Chld St)
Oldham (Univ Campus) – 96 pts+interview (Educ Ely Yrs)
Plymouth – 96–112 pts (Ely Chld St) (IB 24–28 pts)
St Mary's – CCC–BCC 96–104 pts (Educ St) (IB 28 pts)
Staffordshire – CCC (Ely Chld St)
Sunderland – 96–112 pts (Educ St)

88 pts **Marjon** – CCD 88 pts (SEN Disab St)
Queen Margaret – CCD (Educ St) (IB 26 pts)

Trinity Saint David – 88 pts (Educ St); 88–104 pts (Ely Yrs Educ Cr)
Worcester – CCD 88 pts (Educ St courses)
80 pts **Bradford College (UC)** – CDD 80 pts (Educ St)
Cardiff Met – 80–104 pts+interview (Yth Commun Wk courses)
South Wales – CDD–BCC 80–104 pts (Ely Yrs Educ Prac) (IB 29 pts)
72 pts **Birmingham (UC)** – 72 pts (Ely Chld St)
Teesside – 72–96 pts (Chld Ely Chld; Educ St)
64 pts **Colchester (UC)** – 64 pts+interview (Ely Yrs P St)
South Essex (Coll) – 64 pts (Ely Yrs Educ Disab St)

ALTERNATIVE OFFERS See **Chapter 6** and **Appendix 1** for grades/UCAS Tariff points information for other examinations.

DEGREE APPRENTICESHIPS

Portsmouth (Educ Ldrship Mgt); Gloucestershire (Acdm Prof); UHI (Ely Lrn Chldcr).

EXAMPLES OF COLLEGES OFFERING COURSES IN THIS SUBJECT FIELD

Barnet and Southgate (Coll); Barnfield (Coll); Barnsley (Coll); Blackburn (Coll); Blackpool and Fylde (Coll); Bridgwater and Taunton (Coll); Bristol City (Coll); Buckinghamshire (Coll Group); Calderdale (Coll); Chesterfield (Coll); Cornwall (Coll); Craven (Coll); Derby (Coll); Duchy Coll (UC); East Riding (Coll); Exeter (Coll); Farnborough (CT); Grŵp Llandrillo Menai; Guildford (Coll); Harrogate (Coll); Havering (Coll); Hopwood Hall (Coll); Hull (Coll); Kirklees (Coll); Lakes (Coll); Lincoln (Coll); Liverpool City (Coll); Macclesfield (Coll); Nescot; Newcastle (Coll); Newham (CFE); Norland (Coll); North Lindsey (Coll); Norwich City (Coll); Nottingham (Coll); Peter Symonds (Coll); Peterborough (UC); Petroc; RAc Dance; Sheffield (Coll); South Cheshire (Coll); South City Birmingham (Coll); South Devon (Coll); Sunderland (Coll); TEC Partnership; Truro and Penwith (Coll); Wakefield (Coll); Warrington and Vale Royal (Coll); Warwickshire (Coll); West Anglia (Coll); Westminster City (Coll); Wirral Met (Coll); Yeovil (Coll).

CHOOSING YOUR COURSE (SEE ALSO CH.1)

UNIVERSITIES AND COLLEGES TEACHING QUALITY See www.qaa.ac.uk; www.discoveruni.gov.uk.

TOP RESEARCH UNIVERSITIES AND COLLEGES (REF 2021) (Education) Oxford; Durham; Birmingham; Cardiff; York; London (King's); London (UCL); Bristol; Manchester; Glasgow.

ADMISSIONS INFORMATION

SELECTION INTERVIEWS Yes Cambridge, Cardiff Met, Chichester, Colchester (UC), Dundee, Glasgow, Northumbria, Oldham (Coll), Oldham (Univ Campus), Portsmouth, Stirling; **No** Anglia Ruskin, Bishop Grosseteste, East Anglia.

REASONS FOR REJECTION (NON-ACADEMIC) Unable to meet the requirements of written standard English. Ungrammatical personal statements.

GRADUATE DESTINATIONS AND EMPLOYMENT

(See **Chapter 1, Graduate Outcomes.**)

CAREER NOTE Education Studies degrees prepare graduates for careers in educational administration although many will move into more general areas of business or into aspects of work with Social Services. Prospects are generally good. Courses in Childhood Studies could lead to work in health or childcare-related posts, in social work or administration.

OTHER DEGREE SUBJECTS FOR CONSIDERATION

Psychology; Social Policy; Social Sciences; Social Work.

ENGINEERING/ENGINEERING SCIENCES

(including **General Engineering, Integrated Engineering, Engineering Design and Product Design**; see also **Engineering (Manufacturing and Production), Transport Management and Planning**)

Mathematics and physics provide the basis of all Engineering courses, although several universities and colleges now provide one-year Foundation courses for applicants without science A-levels. Many of the Engineering courses listed below enable students to delay the decision of their final engineering specialism. Engineering courses at most universities offer a range of specialisms in which, after a common first or second year, the choice of specialism is made. The flexibility of these courses is considerable, for example, it is sometimes possible to transfer from the BEng degree to the MEng degree at the end of the first or second year. At some universities, eg Durham, the first two years of the course cover a broad engineering education for all students enabling them to decide on their specialism in Year 3 from Civil, Electronic or Mechanical Engineering. A similar scheme operates at Lancaster University, while at Bath, the Mechanical Engineering department offers a choice of five courses at the end of Year 2. Many institutions offer sandwich courses and firms also offer valuable sponsorships.

Engineering Council UK (ECUK) Statement
Recent developments in the engineering profession and the regulations that govern registration as a professional engineer (UK-SPEC) mean that MEng and bachelor's degrees are the typical academic routes to becoming registered.

Chartered Engineers (CEng) develop solutions to engineering problems, using new or existing technologies, through innovation, creativity and change. They might develop and apply new technologies, promote advanced designs and design methods, introduce new and more efficient production techniques, marketing and construction concepts, and pioneer new engineering services and management methods.

Incorporated Engineers (IEng) act as exponents of today's technology through creativity and innovation. They maintain and manage applications of current and developing technology, and may be involved in engineering design, development, manufacture, construction and operation. Both Chartered and Incorporated Engineers are variously engaged in technical and commercial leadership and possess effective interpersonal skills.

Most courses offer BEng and MEng degrees. MEng confers the minimum requirements to take the Initial Professional Development (IPD) training with an employer in order to obtain Chartered Engineer status, while the BEng does not. However, students taking a BEng may be able to switch onto an MEng course, as the first three years of an MEng are broadly similar to a BEng. Another route for BEng students is to subsequently undertake an MSc, which also allows access to IPD and Chartered Engineer status.

You should confirm with universities whether their courses are accredited for CEng or IEng by relevant professional engineering institutions. To become a Chartered or Incorporated Engineer, you will have to demonstrate competence and commitment appropriate to the registration category. On top of your academic knowledge, you will also need to demonstrate your professional development and experience. Most of this will come after you graduate but placements in industry during your degree course are also available. Both Chartered and Incorporated Engineers usually progress to become team leaders or to take other key management roles. For full information check www.engc.org.uk/ukspec.

Useful websites www.scicentral.com; www.engc.org.uk; https://epsrc.ukri.org; www.etrust.org.uk

NB The points totals shown to the left of the institutions are for ease of reference only. It must not be assumed that Tariff points are always used by institutions or that they can be substituted for an offer in grades. The level of an offer is not necessarily indicative of the quality of a course.

COURSE OFFERS INFORMATION

Subject requirements/preferences GCSE English, mathematics and a science subject required. **AL** Mathematics and/or physics, engineering or another science usually required. Design technology may be acceptable or in some cases required. Some popular universities are now making lower offers for disadvantaged and other students. Offers shown below refer to BEng or BSc courses unless otherwise stated; BSc only appears as an abbreviation if the course is offered at the same institution as a BEng with different requirements. **Cambridge** (Peterhouse, Trinity) STEP may be used as part of conditional offer. **Oxford AL** Mathematics and mechanics modules are recommended; further mathematics is helpful.

Your target offers and examples of degree courses

160 pts **Bath** – A*A*A/A*AA+aEPQ incl maths+phys (Mech Eng (MEng)) (IB 36 pts HL 766 incl maths+phys)
Cambridge – A*A*A incl maths+phys+interview+ESAT (Eng) (IB 41–42 pts HL 776 incl maths+phys)
Oxford – A*A*A incl maths+phys+interview+PAT (Eng Sci) (IB 40 pts HL 776 incl 7 maths+phys)

152 pts **Bristol** – A*AA incl maths+sci (Eng Des (MEng) (Yr Ind)) (IB 38 pts HL 18 pts incl 76 maths+sci)
Durham – A*AA incl maths+sci (Gen Eng) (IB 38 pts HL 666 incl maths+sci)

144 pts **Bristol** – AAA incl maths (Eng Maths) (IB 36 pts HL 18 pts incl 6 maths)
Exeter – AAA incl maths+sci (Eng (MEng); Eng Mgt (MEng); Eng Mgt (MEng) (Yr Ind)) (IB 36 pts HL 666 incl maths+sci)
Lancaster – AAA incl maths+physl sci (Eng (MEng) (St Abrd)) (IB 36 pts HL 16 pts incl 6 maths+physl sci)
London (QM) – AAA incl maths/phys (Des Innov Crea Eng (MEng)) (IB 36 pts HL 666 incl maths/phys+sci/des tech)
Nottingham – AAA incl maths+chem/phys (Cheml Eng Env Eng (Yr Ind); Env Eng) (IB 36 pts HL 6 maths+chem/phys)
Southampton – AAA incl maths+phys/chem/fmaths (Marit Eng (MEng)) (IB 36 pts HL 18 pts incl 6 maths+phys/chem)
Warwick – AAA incl maths+phys (Eng; Eng Bus Mgt) (IB 36 pts HL 6 maths+phys)
York – AAA incl maths (Eng (MEng)) (IB 36 pts HL 6 maths)

136 pts **Dyson** – AAB incl A maths+sci/tech/eng+interview (Eng) (IB 34 pts HL 17 pts incl 6 maths+sci/tech/eng)
Liverpool – AAB incl maths+sci (Eng (MEng)) (IB 35 pts HL 5 maths+phys); (Aero Eng Plt St; Eng) (IB 35 pts HL 5 maths+sci)
Southampton – AAB incl A maths+phys/chem/fmaths (Marit Eng) (IB 34 pts HL 17 pts incl 6 maths+phys/chem)

128 pts **Brunel** – ABB incl maths/phys+interview+portfolio (Prod Des Eng) (IB 31 pts HL 5 maths/phys)
Edinburgh – ABB–AAA incl maths+sci/des tech/eng (Eng) (IB 34–37 pts HL 655–666 incl maths+sci/des tech)
Exeter – ABB–AAB incl maths+sci (Eng; Eng Entre; Eng Mgt) (IB 32–34 pts HL 655–665 incl maths+sci)
Lancaster – ABB incl maths+physl sci (Eng) (IB 32 pts HL 16 pts incl 6 maths+physl sci)
Leicester – ABB incl maths+phys (Gen Eng) (IB 30 pts HL 5 maths+phys)
Loughborough – ABB incl maths+phys/des tech/eng+interview (Prod Des Eng) (IB 34 pts HL 655 incl maths+phys/des tech); ABB incl maths/phys+interview (Eng Mgt) (IB 34 pts HL 655 incl maths/phys); ABB incl maths/phys+portfolio (Prod Des Tech) (IB 34 pts HL 655 incl 5 maths/phys)

120 pts **Bangor** – C maths+phys 120–136 pts (Eng) (HL 5 maths+phys)
London South Bank – BBB 120 pts+portfolio (Eng Prod Des)
South Wales – BBB incl maths+num sub 120 pts (Auto Eng)
Strathclyde – BBB–ABB incl maths+phys (Prod Des Eng) (IB 32–34 pts HL 5 maths+phys)
UWE Bristol – 120 pts incl maths/phys (Archit Env Eng) (HL 5 maths)

112 pts **Aberdeen** – BBC incl maths+phys/des tech/eng (Eng) (IB 32 pts HL 6 maths+phys)
Aston – BBC incl maths+physl sci/tech (Des Eng) (IB 29 pts HL 554 incl 5 maths+phys)
Brighton – BBC–ABB 112–128 pts (Mech Eng (MEng)) (IB 28 pts HL 5 maths+phys)
East London – 112 pts incl art/des+interview+portfolio (Prod Des) (IB 24 pts HL 15 pts)
Portsmouth – BBC–BBB 112–120 pts+portfolio (Prod Des Innov) (IB 29 pts)
UWE Bristol – 112 pts incl art/sci/maths/des tech+portfolio (Prod Des Tech) (HL maths/des tech/vis arts)
Ulster – BBC incl sci/maths/tech (Eng Mgt) (IB 25 pts HL 12 pts incl 5 maths+sci)

104 pts **Bournemouth** – 104–120 pts+portfolio (Des Eng) (IB 28–31 pts)
Central Lancashire – BCC incl maths+phys/STEM 104 pts (Robot Eng) (HL 5 maths+phys)
Greenwich – 104 pts incl maths/physl sci (Eng Mgt) (IB 26 pts HL 5 maths+phys)
Heriot-Watt – BCC–BBB incl maths+sci (Eng) (IB 31 pts HL 5 maths+sci)
Manchester Met – BCC–BBC 104–112 pts+portfolio (Prod Des) (IB 26 pts)

96 pts **Cardiff Met** – CCC–BBB 96–120 pts+interview+portfolio (Prod Des) (IB 24 pts)

64 pts **Northampton** – DDE incl phys (Eng)

Open University – (Eng)

Alternative offers See **Chapter 6** and **Appendix 1** for grades/UCAS Tariff points information for other examinations.

DEGREE APPRENTICESHIPS

Cardiff (Eng); Central Lancashire (Bld Serv Sus Eng); Exeter (Min Mgt); Warwick (App Prof Eng), Wrexham (Lw Carb Ener Eff Sust).

EXAMPLES OF COLLEGES OFFERING COURSES IN THIS SUBJECT FIELD

Blackburn (Coll); Blackpool and Fylde (Coll); Bristol City (Coll); Bury (Coll); City and Islington (Coll); Cornwall (Coll); Coventry (Coll); East Kent (Coll); East Surrey (Coll); Grŵp Llandrillo Menai; Harlow (Coll); Lancaster and Morecambe (Coll); Loughborough (Coll); Manchester (Coll); Middlesbrough (Coll); Newcastle (Coll); North Kent (Coll); Northumberland (Coll); Redcar and Cleveland (Coll); Richmond-upon-Thames (Coll); Selby (Coll); South Devon (Coll); South Essex (Coll); St Helens (Coll); Stockport (Coll); Trafford (Coll); Tyne Coast (Coll); Warwickshire (Coll); West Nottinghamshire (Coll); West Suffolk (Coll); Westminster City (Coll); Windsor Forest (Coll).

CHOOSING YOUR COURSE (SEE ALSO CH.1)

Universities and colleges teaching quality See www.qaa.ac.uk; www.discoveruni.gov.uk.

Top research universities and colleges (REF 2021) (Engineering) Imperial London; Cambridge; Oxford; Southampton; London (UCL); Bristol; London (QM); Sheffield; Leeds; Birmingham.

Examples of sandwich degree courses Aston; Brunel; Cardiff; Central Lancashire; Leicester; London South Bank; Loughborough; Manchester Met; Nottingham; Portsmouth; Ulster.

ADMISSIONS INFORMATION

Admissions tutors' advice Leeds Applicants taking the BTEC Extended Diploma may be required to take an additional Maths A-level paper.

Advice to applicants and planning the UCAS personal statement Details of careers in the various engineering specialisms should be obtained from the relevant engineering institutions (see **Appendix 3**). This will enable you to describe your interests in various aspects of engineering. Contact engineers to discuss their work with them. Try to visit an engineering firm relevant to your choice of specialism.

Selection interviews Yes Brunel, Cambridge, Cardiff Met, Dyson, East London, Loughborough, Oxford (37% (success rate 16%)); **No** Strathclyde.

Interview advice and questions Since mathematics and physics are important subjects, it is probable that you will be questioned on the applications of these subjects too, for example, the transmission of electricity, nuclear power, aeronautics, mechanics, etc. Past questions have included:

Explain the theory of an arch; what is its function? What is the connection between distance and velocity and acceleration and velocity? How does a car ignition work? See also separate **Engineering** tables and **Chapter 5**.

Reasons for rejection (non-academic) Made no contribution whatsoever to the project discussions during the UCAS interview. Forged reference! Poor work ethic. Lack of motivation towards the subject area. Better suited to an alternative Engineering course. Failure to attend interview. Poor interview preparation.

GRADUATE DESTINATIONS AND EMPLOYMENT

(See **Chapter 1, Graduate Outcomes.**)

Career note A high proportion of Engineering graduates go into industry as engineers, technicians, IT specialists or managers, irrespective of their engineering speciality. However, the transferable skills gained during their courses are also valued by employers in other sectors.

OTHER DEGREE SUBJECTS FOR CONSIDERATION

Computer Science; Materials Science; Mathematics; Physics; Technology; all branches of Engineering (see also other **Engineering** tables).

ENGINEERING (ACOUSTICS AND SOUND)

(including **Audio Engineering and Sound Technology**; see also **Engineering (Electrical and Electronic), Film, Radio and TV Studies, Media Studies, Music**)

These courses, such as the one at the University of Southampton, focus on sound and vibration engineering, which covers many aspects of society, such as the motor industry, airlines, the environment, underwater communication, ultrasound, as used in medicine, and all communication systems. Courses also involve sound measurement, hearing, environmental health, and legal aspects of sound and vibration. Acoustics and sound are also extensively involved in the music industry, perhaps the most prestigious course being the Music and Sound Recording (Tonmeister) degree at the University of Surrey, which comprises music theory and practice, sound, acoustics, electronics and computer systems. The department has good links with and a high reputation in the music industry.

Most courses offer BEng and MEng degrees. MEng confers the minimum requirements to take the Initial Professional Development (IPD) training with an employer in order to obtain Chartered Engineer status, while the BEng does not. However, students taking a BEng may be able to switch onto an MEng course, as the first three years of an MEng are broadly similar to a BEng. Another route for BEng students is to subsequently undertake an MSc, which also allows access to IPD and Chartered Engineer status.

Engineering Council statement See **Engineering/Engineering Sciences**.

Useful websites www.ioa.org.uk; www.engc.org.uk

NB The points totals shown to the left of the institutions are for ease of reference only. It must not be assumed that Tariff points are always used by institutions or that they can be substituted for an offer in grades. The level of an offer is not necessarily indicative of the quality of a course.

COURSE OFFERS INFORMATION

Subject requirements/preferences AL Mathematics and physics usually required; music is also required for some courses. See also **Engineering/Engineering Sciences**. Offers shown below refer to BEng or BSc courses unless otherwise stated; BSc only appears as an abbreviation if the course is offered at the same institution as a BEng with different requirements. Some popular universities are now making lower offers for disadvantaged and other students.

YOUR TARGET OFFERS AND EXAMPLES OF DEGREE COURSES

144 pts **Glasgow** – AAA incl maths+phys (Electron Mus (MEng)) (IB 38 pts HL 666 incl maths+phys)
Southampton – AAA incl A maths+chem/phys/fmaths/electron (Acoust Eng) (IB 36 pts HL 18 pts incl 6 maths+phys/chem)
Surrey – AAA incl maths+mus+phys+interview (Mus Snd Rec (Tonmeister)) (IB 35 pts HL 6 maths)
York – AAA incl maths+interview (Electron Eng Mus Tech Sys (MEng); Mus Tech Sys (MEng)) (IB 36 pts HL 6 maths)

136 pts **Southampton** – AAB incl A maths+sci+B mus+audition (Acoust Mus) (IB 34 pts HL 17 pts incl 6 maths+phys+5 mus)

128 pts **York** – ABB incl maths+interview (Electron Eng Mus Tech Sys; Mus Tech Sys) (IB 34 pts HL 6 maths)

120 pts **Glasgow** – BBB–AAB incl maths+mus+phys (Electron Mus) (IB 34 pts HL 655 maths+phys)

112 pts **Birmingham City** – 112 pts incl sci/tech/maths/comp (Snd Eng Prod) (IB 28 pts HL phys/chem/des tech/comp sci)
Hertfordshire – BBC–BBB 112–120 pts (Aud Eng; Mus Prod Prom)
Liverpool (LIPA) – BBC 112 pts+interview (Snd Tech)
Liverpool John Moores – BBC 112 pts (Aud Mus Prod)
Salford – 112–120 pts incl maths/sci (Acoust Aud Eng) (IB 30 pts HL 5 maths/sci)
West London – BBC 112 pts (Snd Eng)

104 pts **Bournemouth** – 104–120 pts (Mus Snd Prod) (IB 28–31 pts)
Chichester – BCC–BBC 104–112 pts (Aud Prod Mus Tech) (IB 28 pts)
Huddersfield – BCC–BBB 104–120 pts (Snd Eng Mus Prod)
Lincoln – 104 pts (Snd Mus Prod) (IB 28 pts)
Solent – 104–120 pts (Pop Mus Prod)

96 pts **Arts London** – 96 pts (Snd Arts (Des))

64 pts **London (Royal Central Sch SpDr)** – 64–120 pts+interview+portfolio (Snd Des Prod)

24 pts **UHI** – D+interview (Aud Eng)

ALTERNATIVE OFFERS See **Chapter 6** and **Appendix 1** for grades/UCAS Tariff points information for other examinations.

CHOOSING YOUR COURSE (SEE ALSO CH.1)

UNIVERSITIES AND COLLEGES TEACHING QUALITY See www.qaa.ac.uk; www.discoveruni.gov.uk.

EXAMPLES OF SANDWICH DEGREE COURSES Birmingham City; Huddersfield; Salford; Surrey; York.

ADMISSIONS INFORMATION

ADVICE TO APPLICANTS AND PLANNING THE UCAS PERSONAL STATEMENT See **Engineering/Engineering Sciences**. See also **Appendix 3**.

SELECTION INTERVIEWS Yes Liverpool (LIPA), York.

INTERVIEW ADVICE AND QUESTIONS What interests you about acoustics engineering? What career do you have in mind on graduating? See also **Chapter 5**.

REASONS FOR REJECTION (NON-ACADEMIC) See **Engineering/Engineering Sciences**.

GRADUATE DESTINATIONS AND EMPLOYMENT

(See **Chapter 1, Graduate Outcomes.**)

CAREER NOTE Specialist topics on these courses will enable graduates to make decisions as to their future career destinations.

OTHER DEGREE SUBJECTS FOR CONSIDERATION

Audiology; Broadcast Engineering; Communications Engineering; Computer Engineering; Computer Science; Media Technology; Music; Radio and TV; Technology; Telecommunications Engineering and Electronic Engineering.

ENGINEERING (AERONAUTICAL AND AEROSPACE)

(see also **Engineering (Electrical and Electronic)**)

Courses cover the manufacture of military and civil aircraft, theories of mechanics, thermodynamics, electronics, computing and engine design. Avionics courses include flight and energy control systems, airborne computing, navigation, optical and TV displays, airborne communications, and radar systems for navigation and power. Aeronautical Engineering involves the design, construction and powering of aircraft, and similarly Aerospace Engineering covers aerodynamics, flight design and control propulsion, and communications. Pilot training, with an additional fee, is also included in some courses as at the universities of Brunel, Leeds, Kingston, Hertfordshire and Liverpool. Some courses also include spaceflight studies and the Electronic Engineering course at Bath can be combined with Space Science and Technology. (See also under **Business and Management Courses (Specialised)** and **Transport Management and Planning** for details of Aviation Management degrees.)

Most courses offer BEng and MEng degrees. MEng confers the minimum requirements to take the Initial Professional Development (IPD) training with an employer in order to obtain Chartered Engineer status, while the BEng does not. However, students taking a BEng may be able to switch onto an MEng course, as the first three years of an MEng are broadly similar to a BEng. Another route for BEng students is to subsequently undertake an MSc, which also allows access to IPD and Chartered Engineer status.

Engineering Council statement See **Engineering/Engineering Sciences**.

USEFUL WEBSITES www.aerosociety.com; www.engc.org.uk; www.theiet.org

NB The points totals shown to the left of the institutions are for ease of reference only. It must not be assumed that Tariff points are always used by institutions or that they can be substituted for an offer in grades. The level of an offer is not necessarily indicative of the quality of a course.

COURSE OFFERS INFORMATION

SUBJECT REQUIREMENTS/PREFERENCES See **Engineering/Engineering Sciences**. Offers shown below refer to BEng or BSc courses unless otherwise stated; BSc only appears as an abbreviation if the course is offered at the same institution as a BEng with different requirements.

YOUR TARGET OFFERS AND EXAMPLES OF DEGREE COURSES

160 pts **Bath** – A*A*A/A*AA+aEPQ incl maths+phys (Aerosp Eng) (IB 36 pts HL 766 incl maths+phys)

Cambridge – A*A*A incl maths+phys+interview+ESAT (Eng (Aerosp Aeroth Eng)) (IB 41–42 pts HL 776)

Imperial London – A*A*A incl maths+phys+interview+ESAT (Aero Eng (MEng); Aero Eng (Yr Abrd)) (IB 40 pts HL 7 maths+phys)

152 pts **Bristol** – A*AA incl maths+phys/chem/fmaths/comp sci (Aerosp Eng (MEng); Aerosp Eng (St Abrd) (MEng)) (IB 38 pts HL 18 pts incl 76 maths+phys/chem/fmaths/comp sci)

Durham – A*AA incl maths+sci (Aero Eng (MEng)) (IB 38 pts HL 666 incl maths+sci)

Leeds – A*AA incl maths+phys/chem (Aero Aerosp Eng) (IB 36 pts HL 18 pts incl 6 maths+phys/chem)

Manchester – A*AA incl maths+phys (Aerosp Eng (MEng); Aerosp Eng Mgt (MEng)) (IB 37 pts HL 766 incl maths+phys); (Aerosp Eng) (IB 37 pts HL 766 maths+phys)

Sheffield – A*AA/AAA+aEPQ incl maths+sci (Aerosp Eng (MEng); Aerosp Eng (PPI) (MEng)) (IB 38 pts HL 6 maths+sci)

Southampton – A*AA/A*AB+aEPQ incl A*A maths+phys (Aero Astnaut (Aerodyn) (MEng)) (IB 38 pts HL 19 pts 6 maths+phys); A*AA/A*AB+aEPQ incl maths+phys (Aero Astnaut (Spcrft Eng) (MEng)) (IB 38 pts HL 18 pts incl 6 maths+phys); (Aero Astnaut) (IB 38 pts HL 19 incl 6 maths+phys); (Aero Astnaut (Airvhcl Sys Des) (MEng); Mech Eng (Aerosp) (MEng)) (IB 38 pts HL 19 pts incl 6 maths+phys); A*AA incl A*A maths+phys (Aero Astnaut (MEng)) (IB 38 pts HL 19 pts incl 6 math+phys)

144 pts **Bath** – A*AB/AAA incl maths+sci/tech (Electron Eng Spc Sci Tech) (IB 36 pts HL 666/765 incl 6 maths+sci/tech)
Glasgow – AAA incl maths+phys (Aerosp Sys (MEng); Mech Eng Aero (MEng)) (IB 38 pts HL 666 incl maths+phys)
London (QM) – AAA incl maths+phys/chem (Aerosp Eng (MEng)) (IB 36 pts HL 666 incl maths+phys/chem)
Queen's Belfast – AAA incl maths+sci (Aerosp Eng (MEng)) (IB 36 pts HL 666 incl maths+sci)
Sheffield – AAA/AAB+aEPQ incl maths+sci (Aerosp Eng; Aerosp Eng (PPI)) (IB 36 pts HL 6 maths+sci)

136 pts **Brunel** – AAB incl A maths+B sci/geog/des tech (Aerosp Eng (MEng)) (IB 31 pts HL 6 maths+5 sci/geog/des tech)
Liverpool – AAB/ABB+aEPQ incl maths+sci (Aerosp Eng (MEng); Aerosp Eng Plt St (MEng)) (IB 35 pts HL 5 maths+phys); (Aerosp Eng) (IB 35 pts HL 5 maths+sci)
London (QM) – AAB incl maths+phys/chem (Aerosp Eng) (IB 34 pts HL 665 incl maths+phys/chem)
Loughborough – AAB incl maths+phys (Aero Eng) (IB 35 pts HL 665 incl maths+phys)
Nottingham – AAB incl AA maths+phys/fmaths (Aerosp Eng) (IB 34 pts HL 6 maths+phys)
Sheffield – AAB/ABB+bEPQ incl maths+sci (Aerosp Eng (Yr Ind)) (IB 34 pts HL 65 maths+sci)
Surrey – AAB incl maths+phys (Aerosp Eng (MEng)) (IB 34 pts)
Swansea – AAB incl maths (Aerosp Eng (MEng)) (IB 34 pts HL 5 maths)

128 pts **Hertfordshire** – ABB–AAB incl maths+phys/tech/eng 128–136 pts (Aerosp Eng (MEng)) (HL 5 phys+maths)
Kingston – incl maths+sci 128–144 pts (Aerosp Eng (MEng))
Leicester – ABB–BBB+bEPQ incl maths+phys (Aerosp Eng) (IB 30 pts HL 65 maths+phys)
Queen's Belfast – ABB incl maths+sci/fmaths/tech des (Aerosp Eng) (IB 33 pts HL 655 incl maths+sci)
Surrey – ABB incl maths+phys/fmaths (Aerosp Eng) (IB 33 pts)

120 pts **Brunel** – BBB–AAB incl maths+sci/geog/des tech (Aerosp Eng) (IB 30 pts HL 5 maths+sci/geog/des tech)
City St George's – BBB incl maths 120 pts (Aerosp Eng; Aerosp Eng (MEng)) (IB 30 pts HL 5 maths+sci)
Coventry – BBB incl maths+sci (Aerosp Sys Eng) (HL 15 pts incl maths)
Glasgow – BBB–AAB incl maths+phys (Aero Eng; Aerosp Sys) (IB 34 pts HL 655 incl maths+phys)
Hertfordshire – BBB–ABB incl maths+phys/tech/eng 120–128 pts (Aerosp Eng; Aerosp Eng Plt St) (HL 4 maths+phys)
Strathclyde – BBB–AAB incl maths+phys (Aero-Mech Eng (MEng)) (IB 32–36 pts HL 5 maths+phys); BBB–ABB incl maths+phys (Aero-Mech Eng) (IB 32–34 pts HL 5 maths+phys)
UWE Bristol – C maths 120 pts (Aerosp Eng (MEng)) (HL 6 maths)

112 pts **Brighton** – BBC–ABB incl maths+sci 112–128 pts (Aero Eng (MEng)) (IB 28 pts HL 5 maths+phys)
Coventry – BBC 112 pts (Avn Mgt)
Kingston – BBC incl maths+sci 112–128 pts (Aerosp Eng)
Sheffield Hallam – BBC incl maths+phys/chem/eng/comp sci 112 pts (Aerosp Eng)
Swansea – BCC–ABB incl B maths (Aerosp Eng) (IB 32 pts HL 5 maths)
UWE Bristol – C maths 112 pts (Aerosp Eng) (HL 5 maths)

104 pts **Brighton** – BCC–BBB incl maths+sci 104–120 pts (Aerosp Eng) (IB 26 pts HL 5 maths+phys)

96 pts **South Wales** – CCC incl maths+sci 96 pts (Aero Eng); CCC incl maths/num sub 96 pts (Aircft Mntnce Eng)
Teesside – CCC–BBC incl maths 96–112 pts (Aerosp Eng) (HL maths)
Wrexham – 96–112 pts incl maths/phys (Aero Eng)

Alternative offers See **Chapter 6** and **Appendix 1** for grades/UCAS Tariff points information for other examinations.

EXAMPLES OF COLLEGES OFFERING COURSES IN THIS SUBJECT FIELD

Blackpool and Fylde (Coll); Bristol City (Coll); Exeter (Coll); Newcastle (Coll); Solihull (Coll); Yeovil (Coll).

CHOOSING YOUR COURSE (SEE ALSO CH.1)

Universities and colleges teaching quality See www.qaa.ac.uk; www.discoveruni.gov.uk.

Examples of sandwich degree courses Bath; Brighton; Bristol; Brunel; City St George's; Coventry; Hertfordshire; Imperial London; Kingston; Leeds; London (QM); Loughborough; Queen's Belfast; Sheffield Hallam; South Wales; Surrey; Teesside; UWE Bristol.

ADMISSIONS INFORMATION

Advice to applicants and planning the UCAS personal statement Interest in engineering and aerospace. Work experience in engineering. Flying experience. Personal attainments. Relevant hobbies. Membership of Air Training Corps. See also **Engineering/Engineering Sciences**.

Selection interviews Yes Cambridge, Imperial London, Loughborough; **No** Bristol.

Interview advice and questions Why Aeronautical Engineering? Questions about different types of aircraft and flight principles of helicopters. Range of interests in engineering. See also **Chapter 5**.

Reasons for rejection (non-academic) See **Engineering/Engineering Sciences**.

GRADUATE DESTINATIONS AND EMPLOYMENT

(See **Chapter 1, Graduate Outcomes.**)

Career note Specialist areas of study on these courses will open up possible career directions. See also **Engineering/Engineering Sciences**.

OTHER DEGREE SUBJECTS FOR CONSIDERATION

Astronomy; Astrophysics; Computer Science; Electronics and Systems Engineering; Materials Science; Mathematics; Naval Architecture; Physics.

ENGINEERING (CHEMICAL)

(including **Fire Engineering, Nuclear Engineering and Petrol Engineering**; see also **Chemistry**)

Chemical engineers explore solutions to problems across the whole spectrum of industries involving oil and gas, petroleum, pharmaceuticals, cosmetics, food and drink, biotechnology, bioengineering and biomedical engineering, their role being concerned with the chemical properties of materials and also the safety aspects of projects. Petroleum engineers work in oil and gas projects which can include exploration, excavation and refining, and courses include the study of geology. Another branch is Fire Risk Engineering which invariably overlaps to some extent with Civil Engineering, as in the Fire and Leadership Studies course at the University of Central Lancashire. Finally, Nuclear Engineering focuses on the uses of nuclear energy, such as the provision of non-fossil fuels, and also covers power generation and the decommissioning of nuclear waste.

Most courses offer BEng and MEng degrees. MEng confers the minimum requirements to take the Initial Professional Development (IPD) training with an employer in order to obtain Chartered Engineer status, while the BEng does not. However, students taking a BEng may be able to switch onto an MEng course, as the first three years of an MEng are broadly similar to a BEng. Another route for BEng students is to subsequently undertake an MSc, which also allows access to IPD and Chartered Engineer status.

Engineering Council statement See **Engineering/Engineering Sciences**.

Useful websites www.icheme.org; www.engc.org.uk; www.bceca.org.uk

NB The points totals shown to the left of the institutions are for ease of reference only. It must not be assumed that Tariff points are always used by institutions or that they can be substituted for an offer in grades. The level of an offer is not necessarily indicative of the quality of a course.

COURSE OFFERS INFORMATION

SUBJECT REQUIREMENTS/PREFERENCES AL Mathematics and chemistry usually required. See also **Engineering/Engineering Sciences**. Offers shown below refer to BEng or BSc courses unless otherwise stated; BSc only appears as an abbreviation if the course is offered at the same institution as a BEng with different requirements. Some popular universities are now making lower offers for disadvantaged and other students.

YOUR TARGET OFFERS AND EXAMPLES OF DEGREE COURSES

160 pts **Cambridge** – A*A*A incl chem+maths+phys+interview+ESAT (Cheml Eng) (IB 41–42 pts HL 776 incl chem+maths+phys)

Imperial London – A*A*A incl maths+chem+sci+interview+ESAT (Cheml Eng (MEng)) (IB 40 pts HL 7 maths+chem 6 sci/econ)

Oxford – A*A*A incl maths+phys+interview+PAT (Eng Sci (Cheml Eng) (MEng)) (IB 40 pts HL 776 incl 7 maths+phys)

152 pts **Bath** – A*AA/AAA+aEPQ incl maths+chem (Cheml Eng; Cheml Eng (MEng)) (IB 36 pts HL 766 incl maths+chem)

Birmingham – A*AA/AAAA incl maths+chem/phys (Cheml Eng (MEng)) (IB 32 pts HL 766 incl 6 maths+chem/phys); A*AA incl chem+maths (Cheml Eng (MEng) (Yr Abrd)) (IB 32 pts HL 766 incl 6 chem+maths)

144 pts **Birmingham** – AAA incl chem/phys+maths (Cheml Eng) (IB 32 pts HL 666 incl 6 chem/phys+maths)

Lancaster – AAA incl maths+sci (Cheml Eng (MEng)) (IB 36 pts HL 16 pts incl 6 maths+sci)

Leeds – AAA incl maths+phys/chem (Cheml Eng courses) (HL 16 pts incl 6 maths+phys/chem)

London (UCL) – AAA incl chem+maths (Chem Eng) (IB 38 pts HL 18 incl 6 maths+chem); AAA incl maths+sci (Bioch Eng; Bioch Eng (MEng)) (IB 38 pts HL 18 pts incl 6 maths+sci)

Loughborough – AAA incl maths+chem/phys (Cheml Eng (MEng)) (IB 37 pts HL 666 incl maths+chem/phys)

Manchester – AAA incl maths+phys/chem+interview (Cheml Eng) (IB 36 pts HL 666 incl maths+phys/chem)

Nottingham – AAA incl maths+chem/phys (Cheml Eng; Cheml Eng (MEng); Cheml Eng Env Eng) (IB 34 pts HL 6 maths+chem/phys)

Sheffield – AAA incl maths+sci (Cheml Eng; Cheml Eng (MEng)) (IB 36 pts HL 6 maths+sci)

Southampton – AAA incl chem+maths (Cheml Eng) (IB 36 pts HL 18 pts)

136 pts **Brunel** – AAB incl A maths+B sci/geog/geol/des tech (Cheml Eng (MEng)) (IB 33 pts HL 6 maths+5 sci/geog/geol/des tech)

London (QM) – AAB incl maths+phys/chem (Cheml Eng) (IB 34 pts HL 665 incl maths)

128 pts **Aston** – ABB/BBB+bEPQ incl chem+maths (Cheml Eng (MEng)) (IB 32 pts HL 655 incl maths+chem)

Brunel – ABB incl maths+sci/geog/geol/env/des tech (Cheml Eng) (IB 31 pts HL 5 maths+sci/geog/geol/env/des tech)

Edinburgh – ABB–AAA incl maths+chem (Cheml Eng) (IB 32–37 pts HL 655–666 incl maths+chem)

Hull – ABB incl maths+chem 128 pts (Cheml Eng) (IB 32 pts HL 6 maths+chem)

Lancaster – ABB incl maths+sci (Cheml Eng; Nucl Eng) (IB 32 pts HL 16 pts incl 6 maths+sci)

Liverpool – ABB/BBB+aEPQ incl phys+maths (Phys Nucl Sci) (IB 33 pts HL 6 phys+maths)

Newcastle – ABB incl maths+chem (Cheml Eng) (IB 32 pts HL 6 maths+chem)

120 pts **Aberdeen** – BBB incl maths+chem+phys/des tech/eng (Petrol Eng) (IB 32 pts HL 5 maths+phys+chem)

Edinburgh – BBB–ABB incl maths+sci/eng/des tech (Struct Fire Sfty Eng) (IB 32–34 pts HL 555–655 incl maths+sci/des tech)

Nottingham Trent – 120 pts incl phys+maths (Phys Nucl Tech)
Queen's Belfast – BBB incl maths+sci/tech/geog (Ceml Eng) (IB 32 pts HL 655 incl maths+sci)
Strathclyde – BBB–ABB incl maths+chem/phys (Cheml Eng) (IB 32–36 pts HL 555 incl maths+chem+phys)
Surrey – BBB–ABB incl maths+chem (Cheml Eng) (IB 32–33 pts HL 5 maths+chem)

112 pts **Aberdeen** – BBC incl maths+phys/eng (Cheml Eng) (IB 32 pts HL 6 maths+phys)
Aston – BBC/BCC+bEPQ incl maths+STEM (Cheml Eng) (IB 31 pts HL 555 incl maths+chem)
Heriot-Watt – BBC–ABB incl maths+chem (Cheml Eng) (IB 29 pts HL maths+chem)
Huddersfield – BBC–BBB incl maths+phys/chem 112–120 pts (Cheml Eng Chem)
Sheffield Hallam – BBC–BBB 112–120 pts (Cheml Eng)
Teesside – 112–128 pts incl maths (Cheml Eng (MEng))

104 pts **Bradford** – BCC incl maths+sci 104 pts (Cheml Eng) (HL 5 maths+chem)
Central Lancashire – 104 pts incl maths+sci (Fire Eng)
Swansea – BCC–ABB incl B maths (Cheml Eng) (IB 32 pts)

96 pts **Teesside** – 96–112 pts incl maths (Cheml Eng)

West Scotland – HND 5 chem eng (Cheml Eng (Yr 3 Entry))

Alternative offers See **Chapter 6** and **Appendix 1** for grades/UCAS Tariff points information for other examinations.

DEGREE APPRENTICESHIPS

Greenwich (Sci Ind Proc Plnt Eng); Teesside (Sci Ind Proc Plnt Eng).

CHOOSING YOUR COURSE (SEE ALSO CH.1)

Universities and colleges teaching quality See www.qaa.ac.uk; www.discoveruni.gov.uk.

Top research universities and colleges (REF 2021) See **Engineering/Engineering Sciences**.

Examples of sandwich degree courses Aston; Bath; Bradford; Huddersfield; Hull; London (QM); Loughborough; Manchester; Queen's Belfast; Surrey; Teesside.

ADMISSIONS INFORMATION

Selection interviews Yes Cambridge, Imperial London, Loughborough, Manchester, Oxford (Eng Sci) 37% (success rate 16%); **Some** Bath; **No** London (UCL), Nottingham.

Interview advice and questions Past questions have included the following: How would you justify the processing of radioactive waste to people living in the neighbourhood? What is public health engineering? What is biochemical engineering? Discuss some industrial applications of chemistry. Regular incidents occur in which chemical spillage and other problems affect the environment – be prepared to discuss these social issues. See also **Chapter 5**.

Reasons for rejection (non-academic) See **Engineering/Engineering Sciences**.

GRADUATE DESTINATIONS AND EMPLOYMENT

(See **Chapter 1, Graduate Outcomes.**)

Career note Chemical engineering is involved in many aspects of industry and scientific development. In addition to the oil and chemical-based industries, graduates enter a wide range of careers including the design and construction of chemical process plants, food production, pollution control, environmental protection, energy conservation, waste recovery and recycling, medical science, health and safety, and alternative energy sources.

OTHER DEGREE SUBJECTS FOR CONSIDERATION

Biochemistry; Biotechnology; Chemistry; Cosmetic Science; Environmental Science; Food Science and Technology; Materials Science; Mathematics; Nuclear Engineering; Physics.

ENGINEERING (CIVIL)

(including **Architectural Engineering, Civil and Coastal Engineering, Civil and Environmental Engineering, Marine Technology with Offshore Engineering, Civil and Transportation Engineering**; see also **Building and Construction, Environmental Sciences**)

Civil engineers translate the work of architectural designs into reality, dealing with large scale projects such as high rise buildings, bridges, dock and harbour projects, roads, railways, dams, water supplies and reservoirs. In all major projects, civil engineers and architects work in close liaison as demonstrated at the University of Bath which has the only interdisciplinary Architecture and Civil Engineering department in the UK, in which students following either degree work together. The University of Leeds also offers a common first Engineering year for all students, who can switch courses with a choice of Architectural Engineering or Civil Engineering with specialisms in either Environmental Engineering, Project Management or Structural Engineering, which focuses on the materials used in construction.

Most courses offer BEng and MEng degrees. MEng confers the minimum requirements to take the Initial Professional Development (IPD) training with an employer in order to obtain Chartered Engineer status, while the BEng does not. However, students taking a BEng may be able to switch onto an MEng course, as the first three years of an MEng are broadly similar to a BEng. Another route for BEng students is to subsequently undertake an MSc, which also allows access to IPD and Chartered Engineer status.

Engineering Council statement See **Engineering/Engineering Sciences**.

USEFUL WEBSITES www.ice.org.uk; www.engc.org.uk; www.wisecampaign.org.uk; www.istructe.org

NB The points totals shown to the left of the institutions are for ease of reference only. It must not be assumed that Tariff points are always used by institutions or that they can be substituted for an offer in grades. The level of an offer is not necessarily indicative of the quality of a course.

COURSE OFFERS INFORMATION

SUBJECT REQUIREMENTS/PREFERENCES See **Engineering/Engineering Sciences**. Offers shown below refer to BEng or BSc courses unless otherwise stated; BSc only appears as an abbreviation if the course is offered at the same institution as a BEng with different requirements. Some popular universities are now making lower offers for disadvantaged and other students.

YOUR TARGET OFFERS AND EXAMPLES OF DEGREE COURSES

160 pts **Cambridge** – A*A*A incl maths+phys+interview+ESAT (Eng (Civ Struct Env Eng)) (IB 41–42 pts HL 776)

Imperial London – A*A*A incl maths+phys (Civ Eng (MEng)) (IB 40 pts HL 7 maths 6 phys)

Oxford – A*A*A incl maths+phys+interview+PAT (Eng Sci (Civ Eng) (MEng)) (IB 40 pts HL 776 incl 7 maths+phys)

152 pts **Bath** – A*AA/AAA+aEPQ incl maths (Civ Eng; Struct Archit Eng (MEng)) (IB 36 pts HL 766 incl maths)

Bristol – A*AA incl maths+sci (Civ Eng; Civ Eng (MEng)) (IB 38 pts HL 18 pts incl 76 maths+sci)

Durham – A*AA incl maths+sci (Civ Eng) (IB 38 pts HL 666 incl maths+sci)

London (UCL) – A*AA (Civ Eng) (IB 39 pts HL 19 pts)

Southampton – A*AA/A*AB+aEPQ incl maths+sci/geog (Civ Eng (MEng)) (IB 38 pts HL 19 pts incl 6 maths+sci); A*AA/AAA+aEPQ incl A maths+sci (Civ Eng Archit (MEng)) (IB 38 pts HL 19 pts incl 6/7 maths)

144 pts **Birmingham** – AAA incl maths (Civ Eng (MEng)) (IB 32 pts HL 666 incl maths)

Exeter – AAA incl maths+sci (Civ Eng (MEng); Civ Eng (MEng) (Yr Ind); Renew Ener Eng (MEng); Renew Ener Eng (MEng) (Yr Ind)) (IB 36 pts HL 666 incl 6 maths+sci)

Glasgow – AAA incl maths+phys (Civ Eng (MEng)) (IB 38 pts HL 666 incl maths+phys)

Leeds – AAA incl maths (Civ Env Eng) (IB 35 pts HL 18 pts incl 5 maths)
Manchester – AAA incl maths+phys (Civ Eng) (IB 36 pts HL 666 incl maths+phys)
Nottingham – AAA incl maths+sci/tech/geog/fmaths (Civ Eng (MEng)) (IB 34 pts HL 666 maths+sci)
Queen's Belfast – AAA incl maths+sci/tech/geog (Env Civ Eng (MEng); Struct Eng Archit (MEng)) (IB 36 pts HL 666 incl maths+sci/tech/geog)
Sheffield – AAA/AAB+aEPQ incl maths (Civ Eng; Civ Struct Eng (MEng)) (IB 36 pts HL 6 maths)
Southampton – AAA incl maths (Civ Eng) (IB 36 pts HL 18 pts incl 6 maths+sci)
Warwick – AAA incl maths+phys (Civ Eng) (IB 36 pts HL 6 maths+phys)

136 pts **Birmingham** – AAB incl maths (Civ Eng) (IB 32 pts HL 665 incl maths)
Brunel – AAB incl maths+sci/geog/env/des tech (Civ Eng) (IB 30 pts HL 5 maths+sci/geog/env/des tech)
Liverpool – AAB/ABB+aEPQ incl maths (Archit Eng (MEng); Civ Eng (MEng); Civ Struct Eng (MEng)) (IB 35 pts HL 5 maths); AAB incl maths (Civ Eng) (IB 35 pts HL 5 maths)
Newcastle – AAB incl maths+phys/chem/fmaths (Nvl Archit Mar Eng (MEng)) (IB 34 pts HL 6 maths+phys/chem); AAB incl maths+sci (Civ Eng (MEng) (Yr Ind)) (IB 32 pts HL 6 maths); (Civ Eng (MEng); Civ Struct Eng (MEng)) (IB 34 pts HL 6 maths)
Nottingham – AAB incl maths+sci/tech/geog/fmaths (Civ Eng) (IB 32 pts HL 665 maths+sci)
Queen's Belfast – AAB incl maths+sci/tech/geog (Civ Eng (MEng)) (IB 34 pts HL 665 incl maths+sci/tech/geog)

128 pts **Aberdeen** – ABB incl maths+phys/chem/des tech/eng (Civ Eng (MEng); Civ Env Eng (MEng); Civ Struct Eng (MEng)) (IB 34 pts HL 6 maths+phys)
Brunel – ABB–AAB incl A maths+B sci/geog/env/des tech (Civ Eng (MEng)) (IB 31 pts HL 5 maths+5 sci/geog/env/des tech)
Coventry – ABB incl maths (Civ Eng (MEng)) (IB 30 pts HL maths)
Dundee – ABB incl maths (Civ Struct Eng) (IB 32 pts HL 655 incl maths)
Edinburgh – ABB–AAA incl maths+ sci/comp/eng/des tech (Struct Eng Archit) (IB 32–37 pts HL 555–666 incl maths+sci/comp/eng/des tech); ABB–AAA incl maths+sci/eng/des tech (Civ Eng) (IB 32–34 pts HL 555 incl maths+sci/des tech)
Exeter – ABB–AAB incl maths+sci (Civ Eng; Renew Ener Eng) (IB 32–34 pts HL 655–665 incl 5 maths+sci)
Huddersfield – ABB–AAB incl maths+sci/tech 128–136 pts (Civ Eng (MEng))
Liverpool John Moores – ABB 128 pts (Civ Eng (MEng))
Loughborough – ABB incl maths (Civ Eng) (IB 34 pts HL 655 incl maths)
Newcastle – ABB incl maths+phys/chem/fmaths (Nvl Archit Mar Eng) (IB 32 pts HL 5 maths+phys/chem); ABB incl maths+sci (Civ Eng; Civ Eng (Yr Ind); Civ Struct Eng) (IB 32 pts HL 5 maths)

120 pts **Brunel** – BBB incl maths+sci/geog/env/des tech (Civ Eng (Env Eng)) (IB 30 pts HL 5 maths+sci/geog/env/des tech)
City St George's – BBB incl maths 120 pts (Civ Infra Eng) (IB 30 pts HL 5 maths); (Civ Infra Eng (MEng)) (IB 30 pts HL 6 maths)
Glasgow – BBB–AAB incl maths+phys (Civ Eng; Civ Eng Archit) (IB 34 pts HL 655 incl maths+phys)
Greenwich – 120 pts incl maths (Civ Eng) (IB 26 pts HL 5 maths+phys)
Hertfordshire – BBB–ABB incl maths 120–128 pts (Civ Eng (MEng)) (HL 555 incl maths+eng/tech/env)
Nottingham Trent – BBB 120 pts (Civ Eng)
Queen's Belfast – BBB incl maths+sci/tech/geog (Civ Eng) (IB 32 pts HL 655 incl maths+sci/tech/geog)
South Wales – BBB incl maths+sci 120 pts (Civ Eng)
Strathclyde – BBB–ABB incl maths+sci (Civ Eng) (IB 32–34 pts HL 5 maths+sci)
Surrey – BBB–ABB incl maths+sci/tech/fmaths (Civ Eng) (IB 32–33 pts)
Ulster – BBB incl maths+sci/tech (Civ Eng) (IB 26 pts HL 13 pts)

112 pts **Aston** – BBC–BBB incl maths+STEM (Civ Eng) (IB 29 pts HL 554 incl maths+STEM)

Cardiff – BBC–ABB incl B maths (Archit Eng; Civ Env Eng) (IB 30–32 pts HL 655–665 incl 6 maths); BBC–ABB incl maths (Civ Eng) (IB 30–32 pts HL 655–665 incl 6 maths)
Coventry – BBC incl maths (Civ Eng (BEng); Civ Env Eng (MEng)) (IB 27 pts HL maths); (Civ Env Eng) (IB 29 pts HL maths)
Derby – BBC–BBB incl maths/phys 112–120 pts (Civ Eng (BSc))
East London – 112 pts incl C maths (Civ Eng) (IB 24 pts HL 15 pts incl maths+phys)
Edinburgh Napier – BBC incl maths (Civ Eng (MEng); Civ Trans Eng (MEng)) (IB 29 pts HL 655 incl maths)
Heriot-Watt – BBC–ABB incl B maths (Civ Eng) (IB 30 pts HL 5 maths)
Hertfordshire – BBC–BBB incl maths 112–120 pts (Civ Eng) (HL 555 incl maths+eng/tech/env)
Huddersfield – BBC–BBB incl maths+sci/tech 112–120 pts (Civ Eng)
Kingston – 112–128 pts incl maths (Civ Eng)
Leeds Beckett – 112–128 pts incl maths+sci (Civ Eng)
Liverpool John Moores – BBC 112 pts (Civ Eng) (IB 24 pts)
London South Bank – BBC incl maths+phys 112–128 pts (Civ Eng)
Nottingham Trent – 112 pts (Civ Eng (BSc))
Plymouth – 112–128 pts incl C maths+sci/tech (Civ Cstl Eng) (IB 29–32 pts HL 4 maths); 112–128 pts incl maths+sci/tech (Civ Eng) (IB 29–32 pts HL 4 maths)
Portsmouth – BBC–BBB incl num sub 112–120 pts (Civ Eng) (IB 29 pts HL num sub)
Salford – incl maths+phys/chem/des tech 112 pts (Civ Eng) (IB 30 pts HL 5 maths+phys)
UWE Bristol – C maths 112 pts (Civ Eng) (HL 5 maths)
West London – BBC–BBB 112–120 pts (Civ Env Eng)

104 pts **Bradford** – BCC incl maths 104 pts (Civ Struct Eng) (HL 5 maths)
Brighton – BCC–BBB incl maths 104–120 pts (Civ Eng) (IB 26 pts HL 5 maths)
Edinburgh Napier – BCC incl maths (Civ Eng) (IB 28 pts HL 654)
Greater Manchester – 104 pts incl maths+sci (Civ Eng)
Swansea – BCC–ABB incl maths 104–128 pts (Civ Eng) (IB 30–32 pts HL 5 maths)

96 pts **Abertay** – CCC incl maths/sci (Civ Env Eng) (IB 27 pts)
Coventry – CCC incl maths 96 pts (Civ Eng (BSc)) (IB 29 pts HL maths)
Glasgow Caledonian – CCC incl maths/phys 96 pts (Env Civ Eng) (IB 26 pts HL 5 maths/phys)
Teesside – 96–112 pts incl maths (Civ Eng)
Trinity Saint David – 96 pts+interview (Civ Eng)
Wolverhampton – CCC/BCD incl maths 96 pts (Civ Eng)

88 pts **Anglia Ruskin** – 88 pts (Civ Eng) (IB 24 pts)
West Scotland – CCD incl maths+phys 88 pts (Civ Eng) (IB 24 pts incl maths+phys)

ALTERNATIVE OFFERS See **Chapter 6** and **Appendix 1** for grades/UCAS Tariff points information for other examinations.

DEGREE APPRENTICESHIPS

Exeter (Civ Eng); Glasgow Caledonian (Civ Eng); Greater Manchester (Civ Eng); Northumbria (Civ Eng); Portsmouth (Civ Eng); Queen's Uni Belfast (Civ Eng); Strathclyde (Civ Eng); Teesside (Civ Eng); West London (Civ Eng); UHI (Civ Eng); Wrexham (Civ Eng).

EXAMPLES OF COLLEGES OFFERING COURSES IN THIS SUBJECT FIELD

Birmingham Met (Coll); Blackburn (Coll); Bradford College (UC); Chelmsford (Coll); Chesterfield (Coll); Exeter (Coll); Guildford (Coll); Lakes (Coll); Leeds Building (Coll); Lincoln (Coll); London UCK (Coll); MidKent (Coll); Moulton (Coll); Norwich City (Coll); Plymouth City (Coll); Sheffield (Coll); South Devon (Coll); Wakefield (Coll); Wigan and Leigh (Coll).

CHOOSING YOUR COURSE (SEE ALSO CH.1)

UNIVERSITIES AND COLLEGES TEACHING QUALITY See www.qaa.ac.uk; www.discoveruni.gov.uk.

Examples of sandwich degree courses Bath; Bradford; Brighton; Cardiff; City St George's; Coventry; East London; Exeter; Kingston; Liverpool John Moores; London South Bank; Loughborough; Newcastle; Nottingham Trent; Plymouth; Portsmouth; Queen's Belfast; Salford; Surrey; Teesside; Ulster; UWE Bristol; West Scotland.

ADMISSIONS INFORMATION

Advice to applicants and planning the UCAS personal statement See **Engineering/Engineering Sciences**. Also read the magazine *New Civil Engineer* and discuss articles which interest you on your application. See also **Appendix 3**.

Selection interviews Yes Cambridge, Oxford (Eng Sci) 37% (success rate 16%); **Some** Bath, Loughborough; **No** Anglia Ruskin, Brighton, Bristol, London (UCL), Newcastle.

Interview advice and questions Past questions have included: Why have you chosen Civil Engineering? Have you contacted the Institution of Civil Engineers/Institution of Structural Engineers? How would you define the difference between the work of a civil engineer and the work of an architect? What would happen to a concrete beam if a load were applied? Where would it break and how could it be strengthened? The favourite question: Why do you want to be a civil engineer? What would you do if you were asked to build a concrete boat? Do you know any civil engineers? What problems were faced in building the Channel Tunnel? See also **Chapter 5**.

Reasons for rejection (non-academic) Lack of vitality. Lack of interest in buildings, the built environment or in civil engineering. Poor communication skills. See also **Engineering/Engineering Sciences**.

GRADUATE DESTINATIONS AND EMPLOYMENT

(See **Chapter 1, Graduate Outcomes.**)

Career note The many aspects of this subject will provide career directions for graduates with many openings with local authorities and commercial organisations.

OTHER DEGREE SUBJECTS FOR CONSIDERATION

Architecture; Building; Surveying; Town and Country Planning.

ENGINEERING (COMMUNICATIONS)

(including **Business Information Systems**; see also **Communication Studies/Communication, Engineering (Electrical and Electronic)**)

Communications engineering impacts on many aspects of the engineering and business world. Courses overlap considerably with Electronic, Computer, Digital, Media and Internet Engineering and provide graduates with expertise in such fields as telecommunications, mobile communications and microwave engineering, optoelectronics, radio engineering and internet technology. Sandwich courses and sponsorships are offered by several universities.

Most courses offer BEng and MEng degrees. MEng confers the minimum requirements to take the Initial Professional Development (IPD) training with an employer in order to obtain Chartered Engineer status, while the BEng does not. However, students taking a BEng may be able to switch onto an MEng course, as the first three years of an MEng are broadly similar to a BEng. Another route for BEng students is to subsequently undertake an MSc, which also allows access to IPD and Chartered Engineer status.

Engineering Council statement See **Engineering/Engineering Sciences**.

Useful websites See **Computer Science and Information Technology** and **Engineering (Electrical and Electronic)**.

NB The points totals shown to the left of the institutions are for ease of reference only. It must not be assumed that Tariff points are always used by institutions or that they can be substituted for an offer in grades. The level of an offer is not necessarily indicative of the quality of a course.

COURSE OFFERS INFORMATION

SUBJECT REQUIREMENTS/PREFERENCES See **Engineering/Engineering Sciences**. Offers shown below refer to BEng or BSc courses unless otherwise stated; BSc only appears as an abbreviation if the course is offered at the same institution as a BEng with different requirements. Some popular universities are now making lower offers for disadvantaged and other students.

YOUR TARGET OFFERS AND EXAMPLES OF DEGREE COURSES

152 pts **Southampton** – A*AA incl maths+phys/fmaths/electron/comp sci (Electron Eng Wrlss Comms (MEng)) (IB 38 pts HL 19 pts incl 6 maths+phys/comp sci)

144 pts **Bath** – A*AB/AAA/AAB+aEPQ incl maths+sci/tech (Comp Sys Eng (MEng)) (IB 36 pts HL 765/666 incl 6 maths+sci/tech); A*AB/AAA/ABB+aEPQ incl maths+sci/tech (Comp Sys Eng) (IB 36 pts HL 765/666 incl 6 maths+sci/tech)

120 pts **Aston** – BBB–BBC+bEPQ (Bus Comp IT) (IB 31 pts HL 555)

Brunel – BBB–ABB incl maths+sci/tech (Electron Elec Eng Comm Sys) (IB 30 pts HL 5 maths+sci/tech)

Kent – BBB incl maths+sci/tech (Electron Comms Eng) (IB 34 pts HL 15 pts incl 5 maths+sci)

112 pts **Birmingham City** – BBC incl sci/tech/maths/comp 112 pts (Bus Inf Tech) (IB 28 pts HL 5 comp sci/chem/des tech/phys)

Essex – BBC–BBB incl B maths/fmaths 112–120 pts (Comms Eng) (IB 29–30 pts HL 554–555 incl maths)

Huddersfield – BBC–BBB incl maths+sci/tech 112–120 pts (Electron Comm Eng)

104 pts **Liverpool Hope** – BCC 104 pts (IT courses) (IB 24 pts)

Northampton – BCC 104 pts (Comp Net Eng)

South Wales – BCC 104 pts (Comp)

88 pts **London Met** – CCD 88 pts (Electron Intnet Thngs)

ALTERNATIVE OFFERS See **Chapter 6** and **Appendix 1** for grades/UCAS Tariff points information for other examinations.

DEGREE APPRENTICESHIPS

Birmingham City (Broad Media Sys Eng).

CHOOSING YOUR COURSE (SEE ALSO CH.1)

UNIVERSITIES AND COLLEGES TEACHING QUALITY See www.qaa.ac.uk; www.discoveruni.gov.uk.

EXAMPLES OF SANDWICH DEGREE COURSES Aston; Brunel.

ADMISSIONS INFORMATION

ADVICE TO APPLICANTS AND PLANNING THE UCAS PERSONAL STATEMENT See **Engineering (Electrical and Electronic)** and **Appendix 3**.

SELECTION INTERVIEWS INTERVIEW ADVICE AND QUESTIONS See **Engineering (Electrical and Electronic)**.

REASONS FOR REJECTION (NON-ACADEMIC) See **Engineering (Electrical and Electronic)**.

GRADUATE DESTINATIONS AND EMPLOYMENT

(See **Chapter 1, Graduate Outcomes.**)

CAREER NOTE Many commercial organisations offer opportunities in the specialist areas described at the top of this table. Work placements and sandwich courses have, in the past, resulted in over 60% of graduates gaining employment with their firms.

OTHER DEGREE SUBJECTS FOR CONSIDERATION

Computer Science; Engineering (Computer, Control, Electrical, Electronic, Systems); Physics.

ENGINEERING (COMPUTER, CONTROL, SOFTWARE AND SYSTEMS)

The design and application of modern computer systems is fundamental to a wide range of disciplines which also include electronic, software and computer-aided engineering. Most courses give priority to reinforcing the essential transferable skills consisting of management techniques, leadership skills, literacy, presentation skills, business skills and time management. At many universities, Computer Engineering is offered as part of a range of Electronics degree programmes where the first and even the second year courses are common to all students, who then choose to specialise later. A year in industry is a common feature of many of these courses.

Most courses offer BEng and MEng degrees. MEng confers the minimum requirements to take the Initial Professional Development (IPD) training with an employer in order to obtain Chartered Engineer status, while the BEng does not. However, students taking a BEng may be able to switch onto an MEng course, as the first three years of an MEng are broadly similar to a BEng. Another route for BEng students is to subsequently undertake an MSc, which also allows access to IPD and Chartered Engineer status.

Engineering Council statement See **Engineering/Engineering Sciences**.

USEFUL WEBSITES See **Computer Science and Information Technology** and **Engineering/Engineering Sciences**.

NB The points totals shown to the left of the institutions are for ease of reference only. It must not be assumed that Tariff points are always used by institutions or that they can be substituted for an offer in grades. The level of an offer is not necessarily indicative of the quality of a course.

COURSE OFFERS INFORMATION

SUBJECT REQUIREMENTS/PREFERENCES See **Engineering/Engineering Sciences**. Offers shown below refer to BEng or BSc courses unless otherwise stated; BSc only appears as an abbreviation if the course is offered at the same institution as a BEng with different requirements. Some popular universities are now making lower offers for disadvantaged and other students.

YOUR TARGET OFFERS AND EXAMPLES OF DEGREE COURSES

160 pts **Cambridge** – A*A*A incl maths+phys+interview+ESAT (Eng (Inf Comp Eng)) (IB 41–42 pts HL 776)

Imperial London – A*A*A/A*AAA incl maths+phys+interview (Electron Inf Eng; Electron Inf Eng (MEng) (St Abrd)) (IB 40 pts HL 7 maths+phys); A*A*A incl A* maths+interview (Comp (Soft Eng) (MEng)) (IB 41–42 pts HL 7 maths)

Oxford – A*A*A incl maths+phys+interview+PAT (Eng Sci (Inf Eng)) (IB 40 pts HL 776 incl 7 maths+phys)

152 pts **Birmingham** – A*AA incl maths (Comp Sci Soft Eng (MEng)) (IB 32 pts HL 766 incl 6 maths)

Southampton – A*AA incl maths (Soft Eng) (IB 38 pts HL 19 pts incl 6 maths)

144 pts **Bath** – A*AB/AAA/AAB+aEPQ incl maths+sci/tech (Comp Sys Eng (MEng)) (IB 36 pts HL 765/666 incl 6 maths+sci/tech); A*AB/AAA/ABB+aEPQ incl maths+sci/tech (Comp Sys Eng) (IB 36 pts HL 765/666 incl 6 maths+sci/tech); AAA/A*AB/AAB+aEPQ incl maths+sci/tech (Elec Electron Eng (MEng)) (IB 36 pts HL 666/765 incl 6 maths+sci/tech)

Liverpool – AAA/AAB+aEPQ incl maths (Comp Sci Soft Dev) (IB 36 pts HL 5 maths/comp sci)

Loughborough – AAA incl maths+sci/tech/fmaths (Electron Comp Sys Eng (MEng)) (IB 37 pts HL 666 incl maths+sci)

Warwick – AAA incl maths (Comp Sys Eng) (IB 36 pts HL 6 maths)

136 pts **Dyson** – AAB incl A maths+sci/tech/eng+interview (Eng) (IB 34 pts HL 17 pts incl 6 maths+sci/tech/eng)

Lancaster – AAB 136 pts (Cy Scrty) (IB 35 pts HL 16 pts)

Queen's Belfast – AAB–AAA incl comp/maths/sci/tech (Soft Eng (MEng)) (IB 34–36 pts HL 665–666 incl comp/maths/sci/tech)
Sheffield – AAB/ABB+bEPQ incl maths+sci (Comp Sys Eng; Mecha Robot Eng) (IB 34 pts HL 65 maths+sci)

128 pts **Bangor** – C maths+phys/electron 128–144 pts (Comp Sys Eng (MEng)) (HL 5 maths+phys)
East Anglia – ABB incl maths/comp/electron/econ/phys (Comp Sys Eng (Yr Ind)) (IB 32 pts HL 5 maths/comp/econ/phys); ABB incl maths/comp/electron/econ/phys (Comp Sys Eng) (IB 32 pts HL 5 maths/comp/econ/phys)
Edinburgh – ABB–AAA incl A maths+B sci/comp/des tech/eng (Electron Comp Sci) (IB 34–37 pts HL 665–666 incl 6 maths+5 sci/des tech); ABB–AAA incl A maths+B sci/eng/des tech (Electron Comp Sci (MEng)) (IB 34–37 pts HL 665–666 incl 6 maths+5 sci/des tech)
Leicester – ABB (Soft Eng courses) (IB 30 pts)
Liverpool – ABB/BBB+aEPQ incl maths+sci/tech (Comp Sci Electron Eng; Comp Sci Electron Eng (MEng)) (IB 33 pts HL 5 maths+sci)
London (RH) – ABB–AAB incl comp sci/maths/phys (Comp Sci (Soft Eng)) (IB 32 pts HL 665 incl maths/comp sci/phys)
Loughborough – ABB incl maths+sci/tech/fmaths (Electron Comp Sys Eng) (IB 34 pts HL 655 incl maths+sci)
Newcastle – ABB incl maths/fmaths (Electron Comp Eng) (IB 32 pts HL 5 maths)

120 pts **Bangor** – C maths+phys 120–136 pts (Comp Sys Eng) (HL 5 maths+phys)
Brunel – BBB–AAB (Comp Sci (Soft Eng)) (IB 30 pts); BBB–AAB incl maths+sci/des tech (Comp Sys Eng) (IB 30 pts HL 5 maths+sci/des tech)
Glasgow – BBB–AAB incl maths+phys (Electron Soft Eng) (IB 34 pts HL 655 incl maths+phys)
Greenwich – 120 pts incl maths+sci/num sub (Comp Eng) (HL 55 maths+phys); BBB 120 pts (Soft Eng)
Hertfordshire – BBB–ABB 120–128 pts (Comp Sci (Soft Eng))
London South Bank – BBB incl math/physl sci 120 pts (Electron Comp Sys Eng)
Manchester Met – BBB incl IT/comp sci/maths/sci 120 pts (Soft Eng) (IB 30 pts HL 5 IT)
Nottingham Trent – incl IT/maths/sci 120 pts (Soft Eng)
Stirling – BBB (Soft Eng) (IB 28 pts)
Strathclyde – BBB incl maths (Soft Eng) (IB 30 pts HL 5 maths); BBB–AAB incl maths+phys (Comp Electron Sys (MEng)) (IB 32–36 pts HL 5 maths+phys); BBB–ABB incl maths+phys/eng sci (Comp Electron Sys) (IB 32–34 pts HL 5 maths+phys/eng sci)

112 pts **Aberdeen** – BBC incl maths+phys/chem/des tech/eng (Eng (Electron Soft)) (IB 32 pts HL 6 incl maths+phys)
Aberystwyth – BBC–BBB incl B maths+phys 112–120 pts (Spc Sci Robot) (IB 28–30 pts HL 5 maths+phys)
Bradford – BBC 112 pts (Soft Eng)
Cardiff – BBC–ABB (App Soft Eng) (IB 30–32 pts HL 655–665)
Coventry – BBC incl maths 112 pts (Comp Sys Eng) (IB 27 pts HL maths+phys/chem/des tech/IT)
De Montfort – 112 pts (Soft Eng) (IB 26 pts)
Essex – BBC–BBB 112–120 pts (Comp Electron; Comp Sys Eng) (IB 29–30 pts HL 554–555)
Huddersfield – BBC–BBB incl maths+sci/tech 112–120 pts (Electron Eng Comp Sys)
Hull – BBC 112 pts (Soft Eng) (IB 28 pts)
Liverpool John Moores – BBC 112 pts (Soft Eng)
Northumbria – 112 pts (Comp Net Cy Scrty)
Nottingham Trent – incl IT/maths/sci 112 pts (Cy Scrty)
Portsmouth – BBC–BBB 112–120 pts (Comp Net Scrty) (IB 29 pts)
Sheffield Hallam – BBC 112 pts (Soft Eng)
Staffordshire – BBC 112 pts (Comp Gms Prog)

104 pts **Bournemouth** – 104–120 pts (Soft Eng) (IB 28–31 pts)
Cardiff Met – 104–112 pts (Soft Eng) (HL 55)
Greater Manchester – 104 pts (Soft Eng); 104 pts incl maths/comp (Dig Tech Sol Net Eng)
Solent – 104–120 pts (Comp Sys Net Eng) (IB 28–32 pts)

Trinity Saint David – 104 pts incl IT/maths/phys+interview (Comp Soft Eng)
Winchester – BCC–BBB 104–120 pts (Soft Eng) (HL 44)
96 pts **Aberystwyth** – CCC–BBB 96–120 pts (Soft Eng (Yr Ind)) (IB 26–30 pts)
Bedfordshire – 96 pts (Comp Sci)
Edinburgh Napier – CCC (Comp Sys Net) (IB 27 pts HL 654)
London (RH) – CCC incl maths (Comp Sys Eng incl Fdn)
Sunderland – 96–112 pts (Gm Dev)
Teesside – 96–112 pts incl maths (Instr Contr Eng)
Wrexham – 96–112 pts incl maths/phys/comp (Soft Eng)
88 pts **Bucks New** – 88–112 pts (Soft Eng)
London Met – CCD 88 pts (Comp Sys Eng Robot)

Alternative offers See **Chapter 6** and **Appendix 1** for grades/UCAS Tariff points information for other examinations.

DEGREE APPRENTICESHIPS

Bangor (App Soft Eng); Central Lancashire (Soft Eng); Chester (Comp Sci Elec Eng); Chichester (Dig Tech Sol (Soft Eng)); Gloucestershire (Soft Eng); Greater Manchester (Dig Tech Sol (Soft Eng)); London QM (Dig Tech Sol (Soft Eng)); Nottingham Trent (Dig Tech Sol (Soft Eng)); Sheffield Hallam (Soft Eng); West London (Dig Tech Sol (Soft Eng)).

EXAMPLES OF COLLEGES OFFERING COURSES IN THIS SUBJECT FIELD

Accrington and Rossendale (Coll); Barking and Dagenham (Coll); Barnfield (Coll); Birmingham Met (Coll); Blackburn (Coll); Blackpool and Fylde (Coll); Bristol City (Coll); Cornwall (Coll); Doncaster (Coll); Farnborough (CT); Gateshead (Coll); Manchester (Coll); Newcastle (Coll); North Lindsey (Coll); Nottingham (Coll); Tyne Coast (Coll).

CHOOSING YOUR COURSE (SEE ALSO CH.1)

Universities and colleges teaching quality See www.qaa.ac.uk; www.discoveruni.gov.uk.

Top research universities and colleges (REF 2021) See **Computer Science and Information Technology**.

Examples of sandwich degree courses Aberystwyth; Bath; Bradford; Brunel; East Anglia; Greenwich; Huddersfield; London (RH); London South Bank; Loughborough; Manchester Met; Northumbria; Nottingham Trent; Sheffield Hallam; Stirling.

ADMISSIONS INFORMATION

Advice to applicants and planning the UCAS personal statement See **Computer Science and Information Technology**, **Engineering (Electrical and Electronic)** and **Appendix 3**.

Selection interviews Yes Cambridge, Dyson, Imperial London, Loughborough, Oxford (Eng Sci) 37% (success rate 16%), Trinity Saint David; **Some** Bath; **No** Bradford, East Anglia, Huddersfield.

Interview advice and questions See **Computer Science and Information Technology**, **Engineering (Electrical and Electronic)** and **Chapter 5**.

Reasons for rejection (non-academic) Lack of understanding that the course involves engineering. See also **Computer Science and Information Technology** and **Engineering (Electrical and Electronic)**.

GRADUATE DESTINATIONS AND EMPLOYMENT

(See **Chapter 1, Graduate Outcomes.**)

Career note Career opportunities extend right across the whole field of electronics, telecommunications, control and systems engineering.

OTHER DEGREE SUBJECTS FOR CONSIDERATION

Computer Science; Computing; Engineering (Aeronautical, Aerospace, Communications, Electrical and Electronic); Mathematics; Media (Systems/Engineering/Technology); Physics.

ENGINEERING (ELECTRICAL AND ELECTRONIC)

(see also **Engineering (Acoustics and Sound), Engineering (Aeronautical and Aerospace), Engineering (Communications)**)

Electrical and Electronic Engineering courses provide a sound foundation for those looking for a career in electricity generation and transmission, communications or control systems, including robotics. All courses cater to students wanting a general or more specialist engineering education and options should be considered when choosing degree courses. These could include optoelectronics and optical communication systems, microwave systems, radio frequency engineering and circuit technology. Many courses have common first years, allowing transfer in Year 2. Electronic Engineering courses also overlap closely with Information Technology and Information Systems Engineering, which involves electronic and digital information. This includes the internet and mobile phones. Most institutions have good industrial contacts and applicants should look closely at sandwich courses.

Most courses offer BEng and MEng degrees. MEng confers the minimum requirements to take the Initial Professional Development (IPD) training with an employer in order to obtain Chartered Engineer status, while the BEng does not. However, students taking a BEng may be able to switch onto an MEng course, as the first three years of an MEng are broadly similar to a BEng. Another route for BEng students is to subsequently undertake an MSc, which also allows access to IPD and Chartered Engineer status.

Engineering Council statement See **Engineering/Engineering Sciences**.

USEFUL WEBSITES www.theiet.org; www.engc.org.uk

NB The points totals shown to the left of the institutions are for ease of reference only. It must not be assumed that Tariff points are always used by institutions or that they can be substituted for an offer in grades. The level of an offer is not necessarily indicative of the quality of a course.

COURSE OFFERS INFORMATION

SUBJECT REQUIREMENTS/PREFERENCES See **Engineering/Engineering Sciences**. Offers shown below refer to BEng or BSc courses unless otherwise stated; BSc only appears as an abbreviation if the course is offered at the same institution as a BEng with different requirements. Some popular universities are now making lower offers for disadvantaged and other students.

YOUR TARGET OFFERS AND EXAMPLES OF DEGREE COURSES

160 pts **Cambridge** – A*A*A incl maths+phys+interview+ESAT (Eng (Elec Inf Sci/Elec Electron Eng)) (IB 41–42 pts HL 776)

Imperial London – A*A*A/A*AAA incl maths+phys+interview (Elec Electron Eng (MEng); Elec Electron Eng Mgt (MEng); Electron Inf Eng; Electron Inf Eng (MEng) (St Abrd)) (IB 40 pts HL 7 maths+phys)

Oxford – A*A*A incl maths+phys+interview+PAT (Eng Sci (Elec Eng) (MEng)) (IB 40 pts HL 776 incl 7 maths+phys)

152 pts **Durham** – A*AA incl maths+sci (Eng Elec; Eng Electron) (IB 38 pts HL 666 incl maths+STEM)

London (UCL) – A*AA incl maths (Electron Elec Eng) (IB 39 pts HL 19 pts incl 7 maths)

Southampton – A*AA incl maths+phys/fmaths/comp sci/electron (Electron Eng Comp Sys (MEng)) (IB 38 pts HL 19 pts incl 6 maths+phys/fmaths/comp sci); A*AA incl maths+phys/fmaths/electron/comp sci (Electron Eng Wrlss Comms (MEng)) (IB 38 pts HL 19 pts incl 6 maths+phys/comp sci); (Electron Eng Artif Intel (MEng); Electron Eng Mbl Scr Sys (MEng); Electron Eng Nanotech (MEng)) (IB 38 pts HL 19 pts incl 6 maths+phys/fmaths/comp sci)

144 pts **Bath** – A*AB/AAA incl maths+sci/tech (Electron Eng Spc Sci Tech) (IB 36 pts HL 666/765 incl 6 maths+sci/tech); AAA/A*AB/AAB+aEPQ incl maths+sci/tech (Elec Electron Eng; Elec Electron Eng (MEng)) (IB 36 pts HL 666/765 incl 6 maths+sci/tech)

Birmingham – AAA (Elec Electron Eng (MEng)) (IB 32 pts HL 666)

Bristol – AAA incl maths (Elec Electron Eng (MEng)) (IB 36 pts HL 18 pts incl 6 maths)
Exeter – AAA incl maths+sci (Electron Eng (MEng)) (IB 36 pts HL 666 incl maths+sci)
Glasgow – AAA incl maths+phys (Electron Elec Eng (MEng); Electron Mus (MEng)) (IB 38 pts HL 666 incl maths+phys)
Lancaster – AAA incl maths+physl sci (Electron Elec Eng (MEng)) (IB 36 pts HL 16 pts incl 6 maths+physl sci)
Leeds – AAA incl maths (Electron Elec Eng; Electron Elec Eng (MEng)) (IB 35 pts HL 18 pts incl 5 maths)
London (King's) – AAA incl maths/phys (Electron Eng) (IB 36 pts HL18 pts incl 6 maths/phys)
Loughborough – AAA incl maths+comp sci/fmaths/phys (Electron Elec Eng (MEng)) (IB 37 pts HL 666 incl maths+comp sci/phys); AAA incl maths+sci/tech/fmaths (Electron Comp Sys Eng (MEng)) (IB 37 pts HL 666 incl maths+sci)
Manchester – AAA incl maths+phys/electron/fmaths/chem (Elec Electron Eng) (IB 36 pts HL 666 maths+phys/chem)
Queen's Belfast – AAA incl maths+sci/tech/fmaths (Elec Electron Eng (MEng)) (IB 36 pts HL 666 incl maths+sci)
Sheffield – AAA–AAB+aEPQ incl maths+sci/electron (Elec Electron Eng (MEng)) (IB 36 pts HL 6 maths+sci/electron)
Southampton – AAA incl maths+phys/electron/fmaths (Elec Eng) (IB 36 pts HL 18 pts incl 6 maths+phys); AAA incl maths+phys/fmaths/electron/comp sci (Electron Eng) (IB 36 pts HL 18 pts incl 6 maths+phys/fmaths/comp sci)
Warwick – AAA incl maths+phys (Electron Eng) (IB 36 pts HL 6 maths+phys)
York – AAA incl maths (Electron Eng (MEng)) (IB 36 pts HL 6 maths)

136 pts **Birmingham** – AAB incl maths (Electron Elec Eng) (IB 32 pts HL 665 incl maths)
Dyson – AAB incl A maths+sci/tech/eng+interview (Eng) (IB 34 pts HL 17 pts incl 6 maths+sci/tech/eng)
Leeds – AAB–AAA incl maths+sci (Electron Comp Eng) (IB 35 pts HL 18 pts incl 5 maths)
Sheffield – AAB/AAB+aEPQ incl maths+sci/electron (Electron Comp Eng) (IB 34 pts HL 65 maths+sci/electron); AAB/ABB+bEPQ incl maths+sci/electron (Elec Eng) (IB 34 pts HL 6 maths 5 sci/electron); (Electron Eng) (IB 34 pts HL 65 maths+sci/electron)
Strathclyde – AAB incl maths+phys/chem/comp/tech/electron (Electron Dig Sys (MEng)) (IB 33 pts HL 5 maths+phys/chem/comp/tech/electron)
Surrey – AAB incl maths+phys/electron/comp/fmaths (Electron Eng (MEng)) (IB 34 pts); (Electron Eng Comp Sys (MEng)) (IB 34–35 pts HL 55 maths+comp/chem/phys)

128 pts **Aberdeen** – ABB incl maths+phys/chem/des tech/eng (Elec Electron Eng (MEng)) (IB 34 pts HL 6 maths+phys)
Bangor – C maths+phys/electron 128–144 pts incl maths+phys/electron (Electron Eng (MEng)) (HL 5 maths+phys)
Brunel – ABB–AAB incl A maths+B sci/geog/env/comp/des tech (Electron Elec Eng (MEng)) (IB 31 pts HL 5 maths+5 sci/geog/env/comp/des tech)
Edinburgh – ABB–AAA incl maths+sci/comp/eng (Elec Mech Eng; Electron Elec Eng) (IB 32–37 pts HL 655–666 incl maths+sci/comp/eng)
Exeter – ABB–AAB incl maths+sci (Electron Eng (Yr Ind)) (IB 32–34 pts HL 655–665 incl maths+sci)
Hull – ABB incl maths 128 pts (Elec Electron Eng) (IB 28 pts HL 5 maths); (Elec Electron Eng (MEng)) (IB 30 pts HL 5 maths)
Lancaster – ABB incl maths+physl sci (Electron Elec Eng) (IB 32 pts HL 16 pts incl 6 maths+physl sci)
Liverpool – ABB incl maths+sci (Elec Electron Eng; Elec Electron Eng (MEng)) (IB 33 pts HL 5 maths+sci)
London (QM) – ABB incl maths+sci (Elec Electron Eng) (IB 32 pts HL 655 incl maths+sci)
Loughborough – ABB incl maths+sci/tech/fmaths (Electron Comp Sys Eng) (IB 34 pts HL 655 incl maths+sci)

Newcastle – ABB incl maths/fmaths (Elec Electron Eng; Electron Comp Eng) (IB 32 pts HL 5 maths)
Nottingham – ABB incl maths+sci/electron (Elec Electron Eng; Electron Comp Eng; Electron Eng) (IB 30 pts HL 655 incl maths+sci); ABB–AAA incl maths+sci/electron (Elec Eng) (IB 30 pts HL 655 maths+sci)
Queen's Belfast – ABB incl maths+sci/tech/fmaths (Elec Electron Eng) (IB 33 pts HL 655 incl maths+sci)
Surrey – ABB incl maths+phys/electron/comp/fmaths (Electron Eng Comp Sys) (IB 33 pts HL 55 maths+comp/chem/phys); ABB incl maths+phys/electron/comp/fmaths/chem (Electron Eng) (IB 33 pts HL maths+comp/chem/phys)
Sussex – ABB incl maths (Elec Electron Eng) (IB 32 pts HL 5 maths)
York – ABB incl maths (Electron Eng) (IB 34 pts HL 6 maths)

120 pts **Brunel** – BBB–ABB incl maths+sci/tech (Electron Elec Eng Comm Sys) (IB 30 pts HL 5 maths+sci/tech)
Glasgow – BBB–AAB incl maths+mus+phys (Electron Mus) (IB 34 pts HL 655 maths+phys); BBB–AAB incl maths+phys (Electron Elec Eng) (IB 32–36 pts HL 655–665 incl maths+phys)
Greenwich – 120 pts incl maths+STEM (Elec Electron Eng) (IB 26 pts HL 5 maths+STEM)
Hertfordshire – BBB–ABB incl maths+phys/tech/eng 120–128 pts (Elec Electron Eng) (HL 5 maths+phys)
Kent – BBB incl maths+sci 120 pts (Elec Electron Eng) (HL 665 incl maths+sci)
London South Bank – BBB incl maths+physl sci 120–128 pts (Elec Electron Eng)
Plymouth – B maths+sci/tech 120–136 pts (Elec Electron Eng (MEng)) (IB 30–34 pts HL 5 maths+sci/tech)
Strathclyde – BBB–ABB incl maths+phys (Electron Elec Eng) (IB 32–34 pts HL 6 maths+phys)

112 pts **Aston** – BBC incl B maths+STEM (Elec Electron Eng) (IB 29 pts HL 554 incl maths+STEM); BBC incl maths+STEM (Elec Electron Eng (MEng); Electron Eng Comp Sci) (IB 29 pts HL 554 incl maths+STEM)
Bangor – 120–136 pts incl maths+phys/electron (Electron Eng) (HL 5 maths+phys)
Bedfordshire – 112 pts incl maths/phys/comp/electron/eng (Electron Eng)
Birmingham City – BBC incl maths 112 pts (Electron Eng) (IB 28 pts HL 5 maths)
Cardiff – BBC–ABB incl maths (Elec Electron Eng) (IB 30–32 pts HL 655–665 incl 6 maths)
Coventry – BBC incl maths (Elec Electron Eng) (IB 27 pts HL maths+phys/chem/des tech/IT)
De Montfort – 112 pts incl maths/phys (Elec Electron Eng) (IB 26 pts HL maths/phys)
Derby – BBC–BBB incl maths/phys 112–120 pts (Elec Electron Eng)
Essex – BBC–BBB 112–120 pts (Comp Electron) (IB 29–30 pts HL 554–555); BBC–BBB incl maths/fmaths 112–120 pts (Electron Eng) (IB 29–30 pts HL 554–555 incl maths+sci)
Heriot-Watt – BBC–ABB incl maths+phys/electron (Elec Electron Eng) (IB 29 pts HL 5 maths+phys)
Huddersfield – BBC–BBB incl maths+sci/tech 112–120 pts (Electron Comm Eng; Electron Eng)
Liverpool John Moores – BBC incl maths+sci/tech/eng/fmaths 112 pts (Elec Electron Eng) (HL 5 maths+phys)
Manchester Met – BBC incl maths/fmaths/stats 112–120 pts (Elec Electron Eng) (IB 28 pts HL maths)
Northumbria – 112 pts incl maths+sci/tech/comp sci (Elec Electron Eng)
Oxford Brookes – BBC 112 pts (Electromech Eng) (IB 30 pts)
Plymouth – C maths+sci/tech 112–128 pts (Elec Electron Eng) (IB 30 pts HL 4 maths+sci/tech)
Portsmouth – BBC–BBB incl maths/fmaths/stats/phys/electron 112–120 pts incl maths (Electron Eng) (IB 29 pts)
Sheffield Hallam – BBC 112 pts incl maths+sci (Elec Electron Eng)
South Wales – BBC incl maths+sci/geog 112 pts (Elec Electron Eng)
Staffordshire – BBC 112 pts (Elec Electron Eng)
UWE Bristol – 112 pts incl maths+sci/tech/eng (Electron Eng) (HL 5 maths+sci/tech)
Ulster – BBC (Electron Eng (Yr Ind)) (IB 25 pts HL 12 pts incl 5 maths+sci)

104 pts **Brighton** – BCC–BBB incl maths+physl sci 104–120 pts (Elec Electron Eng) (IB 26 pts)

Central Lancashire – C maths+phys/STEM 104–112 pts (Electron Eng) (HL 5 maths+phys)
Chichester – BCC–BBB incl maths 104–120 pts (Electron Elec Eng) (IB 30 pts HL 5 maths)
Edinburgh Napier – BCC incl maths+sci/tech (Elec Electron Eng) (IB 28 pts HL 654 incl sci/tech)
Robert Gordon – BCC incl B maths+phys/eng/des tech (Electron Elec Eng (MEng)) (IB 27 pts HL 55 maths+phys)
Solent – 104–120 pts pts incl maths/sci (Electron Eng)
Swansea – BCC–ABB incl maths (Electron Elec Eng) (IB 32 pts)

96 pts **Glasgow Caledonian** – CCC incl maths+sci/elec 96 pts (Elec Pwr Eng)
Robert Gordon – CCC incl maths+phys/eng/des tech (Electron Elec Eng) (IB 26 pts HL 55 maths+phys)
Sunderland – 96–112 pts incl maths/phys (Electron Elec Eng)
Teesside – 96–112 pts incl maths (Elec Electron Eng) (HL maths)
Wrexham – 96–112 pts incl maths/phys (Elec Electron Eng)

Alternative offers See **Chapter 6** and **Appendix 1** for grades/UCAS Tariff points information for other examinations.

DEGREE APPRENTICESHIPS

Bangor (App Elec Eng Sys); Central Lancashire (Prof Eng (Elec/Electron)); Chichester (Elec Tech Sppt Eng); Greater Manchester (Elec Eng); Hertfordshire (Eng (Electron)); London South Bank (Elec Electron Eng); Nottingham (Elec Mech Eng); Portsmouth (Elec Eng); South Wales (Elec Electron Eng); Teesside (Elec Tech Sppt Eng); Ulster (Elec Electron Eng); Wrexham (Ind Eng Des (Elec)).

EXAMPLES OF COLLEGES OFFERING COURSES IN THIS SUBJECT FIELD

Banbury and Bicester (Coll); Barking and Dagenham (Coll); Basingstoke (CT); Bedford (Coll); Birmingham Met (Coll); Blackburn (Coll); Blackpool and Fylde (Coll); Bournemouth and Poole (Coll); Bradford College (UC); Canterbury (Coll); Carshalton (Coll); Chesterfield (Coll); Darlington (Coll); Doncaster (Coll); Dudley (Coll); Ealing, Hammersmith and West London (Coll); East Surrey (Coll); East Sussex (Coll); Exeter (Coll); Farnborough (CT); Furness (Coll); Gateshead (Coll); Gloucestershire (Coll); Gower Swansea (Coll); Hartlepool (CFE); Havering (Coll); Hopwood Hall (Coll); Hull (Coll); Leeds City (Coll); Lincoln (Coll); Liverpool City (Coll); London City (Coll); London UCK (Coll); Loughborough (Coll); MidKent (Coll); Milton Keynes (Coll); Newcastle (Coll); North Lindsey (Coll); North Notts (Coll); North Warwickshire and South Leicestershire (Coll); Norwich City (Coll); Pembrokeshire (Coll); Plymouth City (Coll); Solihull (Coll); Southport (Coll); St Helens (Coll); Stockport (Coll); Stoke-on-Trent (Coll); Sunderland (Coll); Tameside (Coll); TEC Partnership; Tyne Coast (Coll); Uxbridge (Coll); Wakefield (Coll); Warrington and Vale Royal (Coll); Wigan and Leigh (Coll); York (Coll).

CHOOSING YOUR COURSE (SEE ALSO CH.1)

Universities and colleges teaching quality See www.qaa.ac.uk; www.discoveruni.gov.uk.

Examples of sandwich degree courses Aston; Bath; Birmingham City; Brighton; Brunel; Cardiff; Central Lancashire; City St George's; Coventry; Exeter; Glasgow Caledonian; Greenwich; Hertfordshire; Huddersfield; Imperial London; Liverpool; Liverpool John Moores; London (QM); Loughborough; Manchester Met; Northumbria; Plymouth; Portsmouth; Queen's Belfast; Sheffield Hallam; South Wales; Staffordshire; Sunderland; Surrey; Teesside; Ulster; UWE Bristol; York.

ADMISSIONS INFORMATION

Advice to applicants and planning the UCAS personal statement Applicants should show enthusiasm for the subject, for example, through career ambitions, hobbies, work experience, attendance at appropriate events, competitions, etc, and evidence of good ability in mathematics and a scientific mind. Applicants should also show that they can think creatively and have the motivation to succeed on a demanding course. See also **Engineering/Engineering Sciences** and **Appendix 3**.

Selection interviews Yes Cambridge, Dyson, Imperial London, Loughborough, Oxford (Eng Sci) 37% (success rate 16%); **Some** Bath; **No** Brighton, Bristol, Derby, Huddersfield, London (UCL), Nottingham, Plymouth, Sunderland, Surrey, UWE Bristol.

Interview advice and questions Past questions have included: How does a combustion engine work? How does a trumpet work? What type of position do you hope to reach in five to 10 years' time? Could you sack an employee? What was your last physics practical? What did you learn from it? What are the methods of transmitting information from a moving object to a stationary observer? Wire bending exercise – you are provided with an accurate diagram of a shape that could be produced by bending a length of wire in a particular way. You are supplied with a pair of pliers and the exact length of wire required and you are given 10 minutes to reproduce as accurately as possible the shape drawn. A three-minute talk has to be given on one of six subjects (topics given several weeks before the interview), such as 'The best is the enemy of the good'. Is there a lesson here for British industry? 'I was asked to take my physics file and discuss some of my conclusions in certain experiments.' Explain power transmission through the National Grid. How would you explain power transmission to a friend who hasn't done physics? See also **Chapter 5**.

Reasons for rejection (non-academic) Poor English. Inability to communicate. Frightened of technology or mathematics. Poor motivation and work ethic. Better suited to a less specialised engineering/science course. See also **Engineering/Engineering Sciences**.

GRADUATE DESTINATIONS AND EMPLOYMENT

(See **Chapter 1, Graduate Outcomes.**)

Career note Electrical and electronic engineering is divided into two main fields – heavy current (electrical machinery, distribution systems, generating stations) and light current (computers, control engineering, telecommunications). Opportunities exist with many commercial organisations.

OTHER DEGREE SUBJECTS FOR CONSIDERATION

Computer Science; Engineering (Aeronautical, Communications, Computer, Control); Mathematics; Physics.

ENGINEERING (MANUFACTURING AND PRODUCTION)

(see also **Engineering/Engineering Sciences**)

Manufacturing engineering is sometimes referred to as production engineering. It is a branch of the subject concerned with management aspects of engineering such as industrial organisation, purchasing, and the planning and control of operations. Manufacturing Engineering courses are therefore geared towards providing the student with a broad-based portfolio of knowledge in both the technical and business areas. Mechanical, product and design engineers develop systems and production processes relating to the overall progress and management of a product from its design to its final completion, including the materials used, the efficiency of the production line and development costs. For those students from an artistic background who wish to combine their design skills with the technical aspects of engineering, the BA Industrial Design and Technology course at Brunel University London is ideal. This course is taught by a cross-disciplinary team including mechanical and electrical engineers, practical designers and psychologists, and students are expected to discuss solutions to design problems. As in all Engineering courses, those offering industrial placements through sandwich courses provide many financial benefits (see **Chapter 1**).

Most courses offer BEng and MEng degrees. MEng confers the minimum requirements to take the Initial Professional Development (IPD) training with an employer in order to obtain Chartered Engineer status, while the BEng does not. However, students taking a BEng may be able to switch onto an MEng course, as the first three years of an MEng are broadly similar to a BEng. Another route for BEng students is to subsequently undertake an MSc, which also allows access to IPD and Chartered Engineer status.

Engineering Council statement See **Engineering/Engineering Sciences**.

Useful websites www.engc.org.uk; www.imeche.org; www.theiet.org

NB The points totals shown to the left of the institutions are for ease of reference only. It must not be assumed that Tariff points are always used by institutions or that they can be substituted for an offer in grades. The level of an offer is not necessarily indicative of the quality of a course.

COURSE OFFERS INFORMATION

Subject requirements/preferences See **Engineering/Engineering Sciences**. Offers shown below refer to BEng or BSc courses unless otherwise stated; BSc only appears as an abbreviation if the course is offered at the same institution as a BEng with different requirements. Some popular universities are now making lower offers for disadvantaged and other students.

Your target offers and examples of degree courses

152 pts **Bath** – A*AA/AAA+aEPQ incl maths+phys (Mech Eng Manuf Mgt (MEng)) (IB 36 pts HL 766 incl maths+phys)

144 pts **Glasgow** – AAA incl maths+phys (Prod Des Eng (MEng)) (IB 38 pts HL 666 incl maths+phys)
Manchester – AAA incl maths/phys/chem+interview (Mat Sci Eng (MEng)) (IB 36 pts HL 666 incl maths/phys/chem)
Warwick – AAA incl maths+phys (Manuf Mech Eng) (IB 36 pts HL 6 maths+phys)

136 pts **Nottingham** – AAB incl maths+phys (Manuf Eng) (IB 34 pts HL 6 maths)

128 pts **Brunel** – ABB+interview+portfolio (Ind Des) (IB 31 pts HL 4 Engl+maths)

120 pts **Strathclyde** – BBB–AAB (Prod Des Eng (MEng)) (IB 32–36 pts HL 5 maths+phys); BBB–ABB incl maths+phys (Prod Des Eng) (IB 32–34 pts HL 5 maths+phys)

112 pts **Aston** – BBC incl sci/tech (Prod Des Mgt) (IB 29 pts HL 554 incl sci/tech)
Liverpool John Moores – BBC 112 pts (Prod Des Eng)
Trinity Saint David – 112 pts (Mech Manuf Eng)

104 pts **Portsmouth** – 104–112 pts incl maths (Mech Manuf Eng) (IB 28–29 pts)

96 pts **Harper Adams** – 96–120 pts+interview (Agric Eng) (IB 28 pts HL 5 maths)

Alternative offers See **Chapter 6** and **Appendix 1** for grades/UCAS Tariff points information for other examinations.

DEGREE APPRENTICESHIPS

Aston (Prof Manuf Eng); Bournemouth (Manuf Eng, Prod Des Dev Eng); Buckinghamshire New (Manuf Eng); Canterbury Christ Church (Manuf Eng); Chichester (Manuf Eng); Newcastle (Prod Des Dev Eng); Portsmouth (Mech Manuf Eng); Robert Gordon (Eng Des Manuf, Eng Instr Measur Contr); Strathclyde (Eng Des Manuf); Teesside (Manuf Eng); Wrexham (Prod Eng).

EXAMPLES OF COLLEGES OFFERING COURSES IN THIS SUBJECT FIELD

Basingstoke (CT); Birmingham Met (Coll); Blackpool and Fylde (Coll); Bristol City (Coll); Central Bedfordshire (Coll); City and Islington (Coll); Darlington (Coll); Doncaster (Coll); Dudley (Coll); Exeter (Coll); Farnborough (CT); Hartlepool (CFE); Leeds City (Coll); Newcastle (Coll); North Warwickshire and South Leicestershire (Coll); Petroc; Solihull (Coll); Sunderland (Coll); Tyne Coast (Coll); Warwickshire (Coll); Weymouth (Coll); Wigan and Leigh (Coll).

CHOOSING YOUR COURSE (SEE ALSO CH.1)

Universities and colleges teaching quality See www.qaa.ac.uk; www.discoveruni.gov.uk.

Top research universities and colleges (REF 2021) See **Engineering/Engineering Sciences**.

Examples of sandwich degree courses Aston; Bath; Brunel.

ADMISSIONS INFORMATION

Advice to applicants and planning the UCAS personal statement Work experience or work shadowing in industry should be mentioned. See **Engineering/Engineering Sciences** and **Appendix 3**.

Selection interviews Yes Manchester.

Interview advice and questions Past questions include: What is the function of an engineer? Describe something interesting you have recently done in your A-levels. What do you know about careers in manufacturing engineering? Discuss the role of women engineers in industry. Why is a disc brake better than a drum brake? Would you be prepared to make people redundant to improve the efficiency of a production line? See also **Chapter 5**.

Reasons for rejection (non-academic) Mature students failing to attend interview are rejected. One applicant produced a forged reference and was immediately rejected. See also **Engineering/ Engineering Sciences**.

GRADUATE DESTINATIONS AND EMPLOYMENT

(See **Chapter 1, Graduate Outcomes.**)

Career note Graduates with experience in both technical and business skills have the flexibility to enter careers in technology or business management.

OTHER DEGREE SUBJECTS FOR CONSIDERATION

Business Studies; Computer Science; Engineering (Electrical, Mechanical); Physics; Technology.

ENGINEERING (MECHANICAL)

(including **Automotive Engineering, Mechatronics and Motorsport Engineering**)

Mechanical engineering is one of the most wide-ranging engineering disciplines. All courses involve the design, installation and maintenance of equipment used in industry. While Automotive Engineering deals with all forms of transport, specialisms are also offered in Motorsport Engineering at several universities, as well as Mining Engineering at the University of Exeter. Agricultural Engineering involves all aspects of off-road vehicle design and maintenance of other machinery used in agriculture. Several universities include a range of Engineering courses with a common first year allowing students to specialise from Year 2.

Most courses offer BEng and MEng degrees. MEng confers the minimum requirements to take the Initial Professional Development (IPD) training with an employer in order to obtain Chartered Engineer status, while the BEng does not. However, students taking a BEng may be able to switch onto an MEng course, as the first three years of an MEng are broadly similar to a BEng. Another route for BEng students is to subsequently undertake an MSc, which also allows access to IPD and Chartered Engineer status.

Engineering Council statement: See **Engineering/Engineering Sciences**.

Useful websites www.imeche.org; www.engc.org.uk; http://iagre.org

NB The points totals shown to the left of the institutions are for ease of reference only. It must not be assumed that Tariff points are always used by institutions or that they can be substituted for an offer in grades. The level of an offer is not necessarily indicative of the quality of a course.

COURSE OFFERS INFORMATION

Subject requirements/preferences See **Engineering/Engineering Sciences**. Offers shown below refer to BEng or BSc courses unless otherwise stated; BSc only appears as an abbreviation if the course is offered at the same institution as a BEng with different requirements. Some popular universities are now making lower offers for disadvantaged and other students.

YOUR TARGET OFFERS AND EXAMPLES OF DEGREE COURSES

160 pts **Bath** – A*A*A/A*AA+aEPQ incl maths+phys (Mech Eng (MEng)) (IB 36 pts HL 766 incl maths+phys)

Cambridge – A*A*A incl maths+phys+interview+ESAT (Eng (Mech Eng) (MEng)) (IB 41–42 pts HL 776)

Imperial London – A*A*A incl A* maths+phys+interview+online admissions test (Mech Eng (MEng)) (IB 40 pts HL 77 incl maths+phys)

Manchester – A*A*A incl maths+phys (Mech Eng; Mech Eng (MEng); Mech Eng Mgt) (IB 38 pts HL 776 incl maths+phys)

Oxford – A*A*A incl maths+phys+interview+PAT (Eng Sci (Mech Eng)) (IB 40 pts HL 776 incl maths+phys)

152 pts **Bath** – A*AA–AAA+aEPQ incl maths+phys (Mech Auto Eng (MEng)) (IB 36 pts HL 766 incl maths+phys)

Bristol – A*AA incl maths+phys (Mech Eng) (IB 38 pts HL 18 pts incl 76 maths+phys)

Durham – A*AA incl maths+phys (Mech Eng) (IB 38 pts HL 666 incl maths+phys)

Leeds – A*AA incl maths+phys (Auto Eng; Mech Eng) (HL 18 pts incl 6 maths+phys)

London (UCL) – A*AA incl maths+phys (Mech Eng (MEng); Mech Eng Bus Fin (MEng)) (IB 39 pts HL 19 pts incl 76 maths+phys)

Loughborough – A*AA incl maths+phys+interview (Mech Eng (MEng)) (IB 38 pts HL 766 incl maths+phys)

Nottingham – A*AA incl maths+phys/fmaths (Mech Eng (MEng)) (IB 38 pts HL 6 maths+phys)

Sheffield – A*AA incl maths+phys/chem (Mech Eng; Mech Eng (MEng)) (IB 38 pts HL 6 maths+phys/chem)

Southampton – A*AA/A*AB+aEPQ incl maths+phys (Mech Eng; Mech Eng (Aerosp) (MEng); Mech Eng (Auto) (MEng); Mech Eng (Biomed Eng) (MEng); Mech Eng (Eng Mgt) (MEng); Mech Eng (Mecha) (MEng); Mech Eng (Nvl Eng) (MEng); Mech Eng (Sust Ener Sys) (MEng)) (IB 38 pts HL 19 pts incl 6 maths+phys)

144 pts **Bath** – AAA–A*AB (Integ Mech Elec Eng (MEng)) (IB 36 pts HL 666/765 incl 6 maths+phys)

Birmingham – AAA incl maths (Mech Eng; Mech Eng (MEng)) (IB 32 pts HL 666 incl maths)

Exeter – AAA incl maths+sci (Mech Eng (MEng)) (IB 36 pts HL 6 maths+sci); (Mech Eng (MEng) (Yr Ind)) (IB 36 pts HL 666 incl maths+sci)

Lancaster – AAA incl maths+physl sci (Mech Eng (MEng)) (IB 36 pts HL 16 pts incl 6 maths+physl sci)

Leeds – AAA incl maths (Mecha Robot) (HL 18 pts incl 5 maths)

Liverpool – AAA incl maths+sci (Mech Eng (MEng)) (IB 35 pts HL 5 maths+phys)

London (QM) – AAA incl maths+phys/chem (Mech Eng (MEng)) (IB 36 pts HL 665 maths+phys/chem)

Manchester – AAA incl maths+phys/electron/fmaths+interview (Mecha Eng) (IB 36 pts HL 6 maths+phys)

Queen's Belfast – AAA incl maths+sci/fmaths (Mech Eng (MEng)) (IB 36 pts HL 666 incl maths+sci)

Warwick – AAA incl maths+phys (Auto Eng; Manuf Mech Eng; Mech Eng) (IB 36 pts HL 6 maths+phys)

York – AAA incl maths (Micro-mech Eng; Robot Eng) (IB 36 pts HL 6 maths)

136 pts **Birmingham** – AAB incl maths (Mech Eng (Auto)) (IB 32 pts HL 665 incl maths)

Dyson – AAB incl A maths+sci/tech/eng+interview (Eng) (IB 34 pts HL 17 pts incl 6 maths+sci/tech/eng)

Huddersfield – AAB incl maths+sci/tech 136 pts (Auto Mtrspo Eng (MEng); Mech Eng (MEng))

Liverpool – AAB incl maths+sci (Mech Eng) (IB 35 pts HL 5 maths+phys); AAB incl maths+sci/tech (Mecha Robot Sys (MEng)) (IB 35 pts HL 5 maths+sci)

London (QM) – AAB incl math+phys/chem (Mech Eng) (IB 34 pts HL 665)

Loughborough – AAB incl maths+phys (Mech Eng) (IB 35 pts HL 665 incl maths+phys)

Nottingham – AAB incl maths+phys/fmaths (Mech Eng) (IB 34 pts HL 6 maths+phys)

Swansea – AAB incl maths (Mech Eng (MEng)) (IB 34 pts HL 5 maths)

128 pts **Aberdeen** – ABB incl maths+phys/des tech/eng (Mech Eng Mgt (MEng)) (IB 34 pts HL 6 maths+phys)

Brunel – ABB incl maths+sci/geog/env/comp/des tech (Mech Eng) (IB 31 pts HL 5 maths+sci/geog/env/comp/des tech)

Cardiff – ABB–AAB incl maths (Mech Eng) (IB 32–34 pts HL 665–666 incl maths)

City St George's – ABB incl maths 128 pts (Mech Eng (MEng)) (IB 31 pts HL 6 maths+sci)

Edinburgh – ABB–AAA incl maths+phys/eng/des tech (Mech Eng) (IB 32–37 pts HL 555–666 incl maths+phys/des tech); ABB–AAA incl maths+sci/comp/eng (Elec Mech Eng) (IB 32–37 pts HL 655–666 incl maths+sci/comp/eng)

Exeter – ABB–AAB incl sci+maths (Mech Eng) (IB 32–34 pts HL 5 sci+maths)

Hull – ABB incl maths 128 pts (Mech Eng; Mech Med Eng) (IB 28 pts HL 5 maths); (Mech Eng (MEng); Mech Med Eng (MEng)) (IB 30 pts HL 5 maths)

Lancaster – ABB incl maths+physl sci (Mech Eng) (IB 32 pts HL16 pts incl 6 maths+physl sci)

Leicester – ABB incl maths+phys (Mech Eng; Mech Eng (MEng)) (IB 30 pts HL 5 maths)

Liverpool John Moores – ABB incl maths+phys/chem/comp/fmaths/eng 128 pts (Mech Eng (MEng)) (HL 6 maths+phys)

Newcastle – ABB incl maths+phys/chem/fmaths (Mech Eng) (IB 32 pts HL 5 maths+phys/chem)

Queen's Belfast – ABB incl maths+sci/tech/fmaths (Mech Eng) (IB 33 pts HL 655 incl maths+sci)

Salford – ABB incl maths+phys/chem/des tech/eng 128 pts (Mech Eng (MEng)) (IB 31 pts HL 6 maths+phys)

Sheffield Hallam – ABB incl maths+sci 128 pts (Mech Eng (MEng))

Ulster – ABB incl maths+sci/tech/eng (Mech Eng (MEng)) (IB 27 pts HL 13 pts incl 6 maths 5 sci)

120 pts **Aberdeen** – BBB incl maths+phys/des tech/eng (Eng (Mech)) (IB 32 pts HL 6 maths+phys)

Aston – BBB/BBC+bEPQ incl maths+physl sci/tech (Mech Eng (MEng)) (IB 31 pts HL 555 incl maths+phys)

Brunel – BBB–AAB incl maths+sci/geog/env/comp/des tech (Mech Eng (MEng)) (IB 30 pts HL 6 maths+5 sci/geog/env/comp/des tech)

City St George's – BBB incl maths 120 pts (Mech Des Eng) (IB 30 pts HL 5 maths+sci)

Coventry – BBB–ABB incl maths+sci/tech/eng (Mech Eng; Mtrspo Eng) (IB 15 pts HL 5 maths)

Dundee – BBB incl maths/phys+sci/eng (Mech Eng) (IB 30 pts HL 555 incl maths/phys+sci/eng)

Essex – BBB incl maths (Mecha Sys) (IB 30 pts HL 555 incl maths)

Glasgow – BBB–AAB incl maths+phys (Mech Des Eng; Mech Eng; Mech Eng Aero) (IB 34 pts HL 655 incl maths+phys)

Glasgow (SA) – BBB–AAB 120–136 pts (Prod Des Eng) (IB 34 pts HL 655)

Greenwich – BBC incl maths+physl sci 120 pts (Mech Eng) (IB 28 pts HL 5 maths+phys)

Hertfordshire – BBB–ABB incl maths+phys/tech/eng 120–128 pts (Mech Eng) (HL 4 maths+phys)

London South Bank – BBB incl maths/physl sci (Mech Eng)

Portsmouth – BBB–AAB incl maths 120–136 pts (Mech Eng (MEng)) (IB 29 pts)

South Wales – BBB incl maths+sci (Mech Eng)

Strathclyde – BBB–ABB incl maths+phys (Mech Eng) (IB 32 pts HL 5 maths+phys)

Surrey – BBB incl maths+phys (Mech Eng) (IB 32 pts)

Sussex – BBB–ABB incl maths (Mech Eng; Sust Auto Eng) (IB 30–32 pts HL 5 maths)

Swansea – BBB–ABB incl maths (Mech Eng) (IB 32 pts)

112 pts **Aston** – BBC/BCC+bEPQ incl maths+physl sci/tech (Mech Eng) (IB 29 pts HL 554 incl maths+phys)

Birmingham City – BBC incl maths 112 pts (Auto Eng; Mech Eng) (IB 28 pts HL 5 maths)

Bradford – BBC incl maths 112 pts (Mech Eng) (HL 5 maths)

Brighton – BBC–ABB 112–128 pts (Mech Eng (MEng)) (IB 28 pts HL 5 maths+phys); BBC–ABB incl maths+physl sci 112–128 pts (Auto Eng (MEng)) (IB 28 pts HL 5 maths+phys)
De Montfort – BBC incl maths/phys 112 pts (Mech Eng; Mecha) (IB 26 pts HL maths/phys)
Derby – BBC–BBB incl maths/phys 112–120 pts (Mech Eng; Mtrspo Eng)
Heriot-Watt – BBC–ABB incl maths+phys (Mech Eng) (IB 29 pts HL 5 maths+phys)
Hertfordshire – BBC–BBB incl maths+phys/tech/eng 112–120 pts (Auto Eng; Auto Eng Mtrspo) (HL 44 maths+phys)
Huddersfield – BBC–BBB incl maths+sci/tech 112–120 pts (Auto Mtrspo Eng; Mech Eng)
Kingston – BBC–ABB incl maths+phys/chem 112–128 pts (Mech Eng; Mech Eng (Auto))
Liverpool John Moores – BBC incl maths+phys/chem/comp/fmaths/eng 112 pts (Mech Eng) (HL 5 maths+phys)
Northumbria – 112 pts (Auto Eng; Mech Eng)
Oxford Brookes – BBC 112 pts (Electromech Eng) (IB 30 pts); BBC–BBB incl maths+sci 112–120 pts (Auto Eng Elec Veh; Mech Eng; Mech Eng (MEng); Mtrspo Eng) (IB 30–31 pts HL 5 maths+phys)
Plymouth – 112–128 pts incl maths+sci/tech (Mech Eng) (IB 26–30 pts HL 5 maths+sci/tech)
Portsmouth – BBC–BBB incl maths 112–120 pts (Mech Eng) (IB 29 pts HL 5 maths)
Sheffield Hallam – BBC incl maths+phys/eng/comp/chem 112 pts (Auto Eng); BBC incl maths+sci 112 pts (Mech Eng)
Solent – 112–128 pts incl maths/sci (Mech Eng)
Staffordshire – BBC 112 pts (Auto Mtrspo Eng; Mech Eng)
Sunderland – 112 pts (Mech Eng)
Trinity Saint David – 112 pts incl maths/phys (Auto Eng; Mech Eng; Mtrcycl Eng; Mtrspo Eng)
UWE Bristol – BBC incl maths+sci/tech/eng/comp 112 pts (Auto Eng; Mech Eng) (HL 5 maths+sci/tech/eng/comp)

104 pts **Brighton** – BCC–BBB incl maths+physl sci 104–120 pts (Auto Eng; Mech Eng) (IB 26 pts HL 5 maths+phys)
Central Lancashire – 104 pts incl maths+phys/STEM (Mtrspo Eng) (HL 5 maths+phys)
Chichester – BCC–BBB incl maths 104–120 pts (Mech Eng) (IB 30 pts HL 5 maths)
Greater Manchester – 104 pts incl maths+phys (Auto Perf Eng (Mtrspo))
Lincoln – 104 pts (Mech Eng) (HL 5 maths)
Manchester Met – BCC–BBC incl maths/fmaths 104–112 pts (Mech Eng) (IB 26 pts HL maths)
Portsmouth – 104–112 pts incl maths (Mech Manuf Eng) (IB 28–29 pts)
Robert Gordon – BCC incl maths+phys/eng/des tech (Mech Elec Eng (MEng)) (IB 27 pts HL 5 maths+phys); (Mech Eng (MEng)) (IB 27 pts HL 65 maths+phys)
Ulster – BCC–BBC incl maths+sci/tech/eng 104–112 pts (Mech Eng) (IB 25 pts HL 13 pts incl 5 maths+sci)
Wolverhampton – 104 pts+interview/portfolio review (Auto Eng); BCC incl maths+sci/tech 104 pts (Mech Eng)

96 pts **Edinburgh Napier** – CCC incl maths+sci/tech (Mech Eng) (IB 28 pts HL 654 incl sci/tech)
Greater Manchester – 96 pts incl maths+sci (Mech Eng; Mtrspo Tech)
Robert Gordon – CCC incl maths+phys/eng/des tech (Mech Eng) (IB 26 pt HL 5 maths+phys); (Mech Elec Eng; Mech Off Eng) (IB 26 pts HL 5 maths+phys)
Teesside – 96–112 pts incl maths (Mech Eng)
West Scotland – CCC incl maths+phys (Mech Eng) (IB 24 pts HL maths)
Wrexham – 96–112 pts incl maths/phys (Aero Eng)

80 pts **Anglia Ruskin** – 80 pts (Mech Eng) (IB 24 pts)

ALTERNATIVE OFFERS See **Chapter 6** and **Appendix 1** for grades/UCAS Tariff points information for other examinations.

DEGREE APPRENTICESHIPS

Bangor (App Mech Eng Sys); Greater Manchester (Mech Eng); Hertfordshire (Mech Eng); Portsmouth (Mech Manuf Eng); South Wales (Mech Eng); Ulster (Mech Manuf Eng); Wrexham (Mech Eng).

EXAMPLES OF COLLEGES OFFERING COURSES IN THIS SUBJECT FIELD

Banbury and Bicester (Coll); Barking and Dagenham (Coll); Barnet and Southgate (Coll); Basingstoke (CT); Bath (Coll); Bedford (Coll); Blackburn (Coll); Bradford College (UC); Bridgwater and Taunton (Coll); Canterbury (Coll); Chesterfield (Coll); Cornwall (Coll); Darlington (Coll); Doncaster (Coll); Dudley (Coll); East Surrey (Coll); East Sussex (Coll); Exeter (Coll); Farnborough (CT); Furness (Coll); Gateshead (Coll); Gloucestershire (Coll); Gower Swansea (Coll); Hartlepool (CFE); Lincoln (Coll); Loughborough (Coll); MidKent (Coll); Newcastle (Coll); North Lindsey (Coll); North Warwickshire and South Leicestershire (Coll); Norwich City (Coll); Pembrokeshire (Coll); Petroc; Plymouth City (Coll); South Devon (Coll); South Gloucestershire and Stroud (Coll); Southampton City (Coll); Southport (Coll); Tameside (Coll); TEC Partnership; Tyne Coast (Coll); Uxbridge (Coll); Wakefield (Coll); Wigan and Leigh (Coll); Wiltshire (Coll); Wirral Met (Coll); Yeovil (Coll).

CHOOSING YOUR COURSE (SEE ALSO CH.1)

Universities and colleges teaching quality See www.qaa.ac.uk; www.discoveruni.gov.uk.

Top research universities and colleges (REF 2021) See **Engineering/Engineering Sciences**.

Examples of sandwich degree courses Aston; Bath; Birmingham City; Bradford; Brighton; Cardiff; Central Lancashire; City St George's; Coventry; De Montfort; Glasgow Caledonian; Harper Adams; Hertfordshire; Huddersfield; Imperial London; Kingston; Leicester; Liverpool John Moores; London (QM); Loughborough; Manchester Met; Oxford Brookes; Plymouth; Portsmouth; Queen's Belfast; Salford; Sheffield Hallam; South Wales; Staffordshire; Sunderland; Surrey; Teesside; Ulster; UWE Bristol; West Scotland; Wolverhampton.

ADMISSIONS INFORMATION

Advice to applicants and planning the UCAS personal statement Work experience. Hands-on skills. An interest in solving mathematical problems related to physical concepts. Enjoyment in designing mechanical devices or components. Interest in engines, structures, dynamics or fluid flow and efficient use of materials or energy. Apply to the Year in Industry Scheme (www.etrust.org.uk) for placement. Scholarships are available to supplement the scheme. See **Engineering/Engineering Sciences** and **Appendix 3**.

Selection interviews Yes Cambridge, Dyson, Imperial London, Oxford (Eng Sci) 37% (success rate 16%), Wolverhampton; **Some** Greater Manchester, Leicester; **No** Bradford, Brighton, Bristol, Huddersfield, Newcastle, Sunderland.

Interview advice and questions Past questions include: What mechanical objects have you examined and/or tried to repair? How do you see yourself in five years' time? What do you imagine you would be doing (production, management or design engineering)? What engineering interests do you have? What qualities are required to become a successful mechanical engineer? Do you like sixth-form work? Describe the working of parts on an engineering drawing. How does a fridge work? What is design in the context of mechanical engineering? What has been your greatest achievement to date? What are your career plans? See also **Engineering/Engineering Sciences** and **Chapter 5**.

Reasons for rejection (non-academic) See **Engineering/Engineering Sciences**.

GRADUATE DESTINATIONS AND EMPLOYMENT

(See **Chapter 1, Graduate Outcomes.**)

Career note Mechanical Engineering graduates have a wide choice of career options. Apart from design and development of plant and machinery, they are also likely to be involved in production processes and working at various levels of management. Mechanical engineers share interests such as structures and stress analysis with civil and aeronautical engineers, and electronics and computing with electrical and software engineers.

OTHER DEGREE SUBJECTS FOR CONSIDERATION

Engineering (Aeronautical/Aerospace, Building, Computer (Control, Software and Systems), Electrical/Electronic, Manufacturing, Marine); Materials Science; Mathematics; Physics; Product Design; Technologies.

ENGINEERING (MEDICAL)

(including **Biomedical Engineering, Mechanical and Medical Engineering and Medical Physics**; see also **Biotechnology**)

Biomedical engineering lies at the interface between engineering, mathematics, physics, chemistry, biology and clinical practice. This makes it a branch of engineering that has the most direct effect on human health. It is a rapidly expanding interdisciplinary field that applies engineering principles and technology to medical and biological problems. Biomedical engineers work in fields as diverse as neurotechnology, fluid mechanics of the blood and respiratory systems, bone and joint biomechanics, biosensors, medical imaging, synthetic biology and biomaterials. These can lead to the creation of novel devices such as joint replacements and heart valves, new surgical instruments, rehabilitation protocols and even prosthetic limbs.

USEFUL WEBSITES www.assclinsci.org; www.ipem.ac.uk; www.healthcareers.nhs.uk

NB The points totals shown to the left of the institutions are for ease of reference only. It must not be assumed that Tariff points are always used by institutions or that they can be substituted for an offer in grades. The level of an offer is not necessarily indicative of the quality of a course.

COURSE OFFERS INFORMATION

SUBJECT REQUIREMENTS/PREFERENCES GCSE/AL Subjects taken from mathematics, physics, chemistry and biology. Some popular universities are now making lower offers for disadvantaged and other students. Offers shown below refer to BEng or BSc courses unless otherwise stated; BSc only appears as an abbreviation if the course is offered at the same institution as a BEng with different requirements.

YOUR TARGET OFFERS AND EXAMPLES OF DEGREE COURSES

152 pts **Imperial London** – A*AA incl maths+phys+interview (Biomed Eng (MEng)) (IB 39 pts HL 666 incl maths+phys)

Leeds – A*AA incl maths+phys/chem/biol (Med Eng) (HL 18 pts incl 6 maths+phys/chem); (Med Eng (MEng)) (IB 36 pts HL 18 pts incl 6 maths+phys/chem)

London (UCL) – A*AA incl maths+phys (Med Phys (MSci)) (IB 36 pts HL 17 pts incl 6 maths+phys)

144 pts **Glasgow** – AAA incl maths+phys (Biomed Eng (MEng)) (IB 38 pts HL 666 incl maths+phys)

London (QM) – AAA incl maths+phys/chem (Biomed Eng (MEng)) (IB 36 pts HL 665 incl maths+phys/chem)

Queen's Belfast – AAA/A*AB incl maths+phys (Phys Med Apps (MSci)) (IB 36 pts HL 666 incl maths+phys)

Sheffield – AAA incl maths+sci (Bioeng (MEng)) (IB 36 pts HL 6 maths+sci)

York – AAA incl maths (Med Eng) (IB 36 pts HL 6 maths)

136 pts **London (King's)** – AAB incl maths+phys (Biomed Eng) (IB 35 pts HL 665 incl maths+phys)

London (QM) – AAB incl maths+phys/chem (Biomed Eng) (IB 34 pts HL 665 incl maths+phys/chem)

Sheffield – AAB incl maths+sci (Bioeng) (IB 34 pts HL 6 maths 5 sci)

Surrey – AAB incl maths+phys (Biomed Eng (MEng)) (IB 34 pts HL 6 maths 5 phys)

128 pts **Cardiff** – ABB–AAB incl maths (Med Eng) (IB 32–34 pts HL 5 maths)

Hull – ABB incl maths 128 pts (Mech Med Eng) (IB 28 pts HL 5 maths); (Mech Med Eng (MEng)) (IB 30 pts HL 5 maths)

Queen's Belfast – ABB incl maths+phys (Phys Med Apps) (IB 33 pts HL 655 incl maths+phys)

Surrey – ABB incl maths+phys (Biomed Eng) (IB 33 pts HL 5 maths+phys)

120 pts **City St George's** – BBB incl maths 120 pts (Biomed Eng) (IB 30 pts HL 5 maths+phys)

Dundee – BBB incl maths+sci/eng (Biomed Eng) (IB 30 pts HL 555 incl maths+sci/eng)

Glasgow – BBB–AAB incl maths+phys (Biomed Eng) (IB 34 pts HL 655 incl maths+phys)

Kent – BBB–ABB incl maths+sci (Biomed Eng) (HL 55 incl maths+sci)
Reading – BBB incl maths+sci (Biomed Eng) (IB 30 pts HL 5 maths+sci)
Swansea – BBB–ABB incl maths (Biomed Eng) (IB 32 pts HL 5 maths)
112 pts **Bradford** – BBC incl maths 112 pts (Biomed Eng) (HL 5 maths)

Alternative offers See **Chapter 6** and **Appendix 1** for grades/UCAS Tariff points information for other examinations.

CHOOSING YOUR COURSE (SEE ALSO CH.1)

Universities and colleges teaching quality See www.qaa.ac.uk; www.discoveruni.gov.uk.

Examples of sandwich degree courses Cardiff; City St George's; Hull; Leeds; London (QM); Surrey.

ADMISSIONS INFORMATION

Selection interviews No Swansea.

GRADUATE DESTINATIONS AND EMPLOYMENT

(See **Chapter 1, Graduate Outcomes.**)

Career note High rate of graduate employment. *Money* magazine ranks Biomedical Engineering number 1 for job growth prospects for the next 10 years.

OTHER DEGREE SUBJECTS FOR CONSIDERATION

Biological Sciences; Prosthetics; Orthotics.

ENGLISH

(including **Creative Writing**; see also **Journalism, Languages, Linguistics, Literature**)

English courses continue to be extremely popular and competitive and include English Literature, English and English Language. Bear in mind that the content of courses can vary considerably. English Literature courses are popular because they are often an extension of A-level or equivalent studies and will offer a wide range of modules. At the University of Sheffield, the course covers the study of literature, poetry, fiction and drama from Old English to the 21st century along with modules such as American Literature, Gothic Literature and Renaissance Literature. However, English Language courses break the mould and offer a broader interpretation of English with studies in the use of language, grammar, the meaning of words, language in the workplace, in broadcasting and other aspects of society, Pidgin and Creole English, methods of communication and linguistics. Admissions tutors will expect students to have read widely outside their A-level syllabus.

Useful websites www.bl.uk; www.lrb.co.uk; www.3ammagazine.com/3am; www.bibliomania.com

NB The points totals shown to the left of the institutions are for ease of reference only. It must not be assumed that Tariff points are always used by institutions or that they can be substituted for an offer in grades. The level of an offer is not necessarily indicative of the quality of a course.

COURSE OFFERS INFORMATION

Subject requirements/preferences GCSE English language and English literature required and a foreign language may be preferred. Grades may be stipulated. **AL** English with specific grades usually stipulated. Modern languages required for joint courses with languages. Some popular universities are now making lower offers for disadvantaged and other students.

Your target offers and examples of degree courses

152 pts **Cambridge** – A*AA+interview+ASNCAA (A-Sxn Nrs Celt) (IB 41–42 pts HL 776); A*AA incl Engl+interview+ELAT (Engl) (IB 40–42 pts HL 776 incl Engl)
Durham – A*AA incl Engl (Engl Lit) (IB 38 pts HL 666 incl Engl)

Edinburgh – A*AA (Class Engl Lang) (IB 39 pts HL 666); A*AA incl Engl (Engl Lit) (IB 39 pts HL 666 incl Engl)

144 pts **Bristol** – AAA (Engl Ger) (IB 36 HL 18 pts incl 6 Engl); AAA incl Engl (Engl Class St) (IB 36 pts HL 18 incl 6 Engl); (Engl; Thea Engl) (IB 36 pts HL 18 pts incl 6 Engl)
East Anglia – AAA incl Engl+portfolio (Engl Lit Crea Writ) (IB 34 pts HL 6 Engl)
Exeter – AAA incl Engl lit (Engl (Emp Expnc); Engl (St Abrd)) (IB 36 pts HL 6 Engl)
London (UCL) – AAA incl Engl (Engl) (IB 38 pts HL 6 Engl)
Manchester – AAA incl Engl (Engl Lit courses) (IB 36 pts HL 666)
Nottingham – AAA incl Engl (Engl; Engl Crea Writ) (IB 36 pts HL 6 Engl)
Oxford – AAA incl Engl+interview (Engl Lang Lit) (IB 38 pts HL 666 incl Engl); AAA incl Engl+interview+MLAT (Engl Modn Langs) (IB 38 pts HL 666 incl Engl)
St Andrews – AAA incl Engl (Engl courses) (IB 38 pts HL 666 incl Engl)
Warwick – A*AB/AAA incl Engl (Engl Lit Crea Writ) (IB 36 pts HL 6 Engl); AAA/A*AB incl Engl (Engl Lit) (IB 38 pts HL 6 Engl)
York – AAA/A*AB incl Engl (Engl) (IB 36 pts HL 666 incl Engl); AAA incl Engl+hist (Engl Hist) (IB 36 pts HL 666 incl Engl+hist)

136 pts **Birmingham** – AAB incl Engl (Engl; Engl Crea Writ; Engl Lang Ling) (IB 32 pts HL 665 incl Engl)
East Anglia – AAB incl Engl (Engl Am Lit; Engl Lit; Engl Lit Comb Hons) (IB 33 pts HL 5 Engl)
Exeter – AAB incl Engl lit (Engl) (IB 34 pts HL 665 Engl); AAB–AAA incl Engl (Class St Engl courses) (IB 34–36 pts HL 665–666 incl 6 Engl)
Lancaster – AAB (Engl Lang) (IB 35 pts HL 16 pts); AAB incl Engl (Engl Lang Crea Writ; Engl Lang Lit; Engl Lit) (IB 35 pts HL 16 pts incl 6 lit)
Leeds – AAB incl Engl (Engl Lang Lit) (IB 35 pts HL 16 pts incl 6 Engl)
London (King's) – AAB incl Engl (Compar Lit) (IB 35 pts HL 17 pts incl 6 Engl); (Class St Engl) (IB 35 pts HL 665 incl 6 Engl); AAB incl Engl/lang/psy (Engl Lang Ling) (IB 35 pts HL 665 incl 6 Engl/lang/psy)
London (UCL) – AAB incl A Gk+Engl (Gk Eng) (IB 36 pts HL 17 pts incl 6 Gk+Engl)
Loughborough – AAB incl Engl (Engl; Engl Spo Sci) (IB 35 pts HL 665 incl Engl)
NU London – AAB+interview (Engl courses) (IB 35 pts HL 665)
Nottingham – AAB incl Engl (Engl Lang Lit) (IB 32 pts HL 665 Engl)
Sheffield – AAB incl art/hum (Engl Lang Lit) (IB 34 pts HL 5 art/hum); AAB–ABB+bEPQ (Engl Comb Hons; Engl Lang Ling) (IB 34 pts); AAB–ABB+bEPQ incl art/hum (Engl Lit) (IB 34 pts HL 5 art/hum)
Southampton – AAB/ABB+aEPQ incl Engl+Fr/Ger/Span (Engl Fr/Ger/Span) (IB 34 pts HL 17 pts incl 5 Engl+Fr/Ger/Span)
Warwick – AAB incl Engl lit+Fr (Engl Fr) (IB 34 pts HL 5 Engl lit+Fr)
York – AAB incl Engl (Engl Hist Art; Engl Ling; Engl Phil; Engl Pol) (IB 35 pts HL 6 Engl)

128 pts **East Anglia** – ABB incl Engl (Flm St Engl Lit) (IB 32 pts HL 5 Engl)
Edinburgh – ABB (Engl Lang) (IB 34 pts HL 655); ABB–A*AA incl Engl (Engl Scot Lit) (IB 37–39 pts HL 655–666 incl 5 Engl)
Exeter – ABB–AAB incl Engl (Engl Film TV St) (IB 32–34 pts HL 6 Engl); ABB–AAB incl Engl lit (Engl Drama) (IB 34–36 pts HL 665–666 incl 5 Engl lit)
Leicester – ABB/BBB+bEPQ incl Engl (Engl courses) (IB 30 pts HL 6 Engl)
Liverpool – ABB incl Engl (Engl) (IB 33 pts HL 6 Engl)
London (QM) – ABB (Engl Lang Ling) (IB 32 pts HL 655); ABB incl Engl lit/Engl lang lit (Engl; Engl Lit Ling) (IB 32 pts HL 655 incl 6 Engl)
London (RH) – ABB–AAB (Engl Am Lit) (IB 32 pts HL 665); ABB–AAB incl Engl (Engl; Engl Dr) (IB 32 pts HL 655 incl Engl); ABB–AAB incl arts/hum (Dr Crea Writ) (IB 32 pts HL 655 incl 6 arts/hum)
Newcastle – ABB (Engl Lang) (IB 32 pts); ABB incl Engl (Engl Lang Lit) (IB 32 pts HL 5 Engl)
Nottingham – ABB incl Engl (Engl Hisp St) (IB 32 pts HL 5 Engl)
Queen's Belfast – ABB incl Engl (Engl courses) (IB 33 pts HL 655 incl Engl)
Sheffield – ABB (Engl Phil) (IB 33 pts)

Southampton – ABB (Engl Hist) (IB 32 pts HL 16 pts); ABB/BBB+aEPQ incl Engl (Flm Engl; Phil Engl) (IB 32 pts HL 16 pts incl 5 Engl); ABB incl Engl (Engl) (IB 32 pts HL 16 pts incl 5 Engl)
Sussex – ABB (Engl Lang Lit) (IB 32 pts)

120 pts **Aberdeen** – BBB (Engl) (IB 32 pts HL 555); BBC (Engl Scot Lit) (IB 32 pts HL 555)
Cardiff – BBB–AAB incl Engl (Engl Lit) (IB 31–34 pts HL 665–666 incl 6 Engl)
Dundee – BBB (Engl Flm St) (IB 30 pts HL 555 incl Engl); BBB incl Engl lit (Engl) (IB 30 pts HL 555)
Essex – BBB (Crea Writ; Engl Lang courses) (IB 30 pts HL 555)
Glasgow – BBB–AAB (Engl Lang Ling; Engl Lit) (IB 34 pts HL 655 incl Engl+hum)
Hull – BBB 120 pts (Engl) (IB 30 pts)
Kent – BBB (Engl Lang Ling) (HL 665)
London (Gold) – BBB incl Engl (Engl; Engl Crea Writ) (IB 33 pts HL 655)
Reading – BBB (Engl Lang courses) (IB 30 pts); BBB incl Engl (Engl Lang Lit; Engl Lit Crea Writ) (IB 30 pts HL 5 Engl); BBB incl Engl/hist/sociol/phil/dr+interview (P Educ Engl Spec) (IB 30 pts HL 5 Engl/hist/sociol/phil/dr)
Stirling – BBB (Engl St) (IB 30 pts)
Strathclyde – BBB–ABB (Engl courses) (IB 30 pts)
Surrey – BBB–AAB incl Engl (Engl Lit) (IB 32–33 pts); BBB incl Engl (Engl Lit Crea Writ) (IB 32 pts)
Sussex – BBB–ABB (Engl; Engl Comb Hons) (IB 30–32 pts)
Swansea – BBB (Engl courses) (IB 32 pts)

112 pts **Aston** – BBC/BCC+bEPQ (Engl Lang) (IB 29 pts HL 554)
Birmingham City – BBC incl Engl 112 pts (Engl; Engl Crea Writ; Engl Lang Lit) (IB 28 pts HL 14 pts)
Bournemouth Arts – BBC–BBB 112–120 pts (Crea Writ) (HL 555)
Brunel – BBC (Engl; Engl Crea Writ; Thea Crea Writ; Thea Engl) (IB 29 pts)
Buckingham – BBC–BBB (Engl Lit) (IB 31–32 pts)
Canterbury Christ Church – BBC (Engl Lit) (IB 29 pts)
Cardiff – BBC–BBB (Engl Lang) (IB 31–32 pts HL 665)
Coventry – BBC (Engl Lit) (IB 29 pts)
De Montfort – 112 pts (Engl Lit) (IB 26 pts)
Derby – BBC–BBB incl Engl 112–120 pts (Crea Writ Pub; Engl)
East London – 112 pts incl Engl (Crea Writ Scrn) (IB 24 pts HL 15 pts)
Edge Hill – BBC–BBB 112–120 pts (Engl; Engl Lang; Engl Lit); BBC–BBB 112–120 pts+portfolio (Crea Writ)
Edinburgh Napier – BBC incl Engl (Engl; Engl Flm) (IB 29 pts HL 655 incl Engl)
Essex – BBC–BBB 112–120 pts (Engl Lang Lit; Engl Lit) (IB 29–30 pts HL 554–555)
Hertfordshire – BBC–BBB 112–120 pts (Engl Lit)
Keele – BBC 112 pts (Engl Lit) (IB 29 pts)
Kingston – 112 pts (Engl)
Leeds Beckett – 112 pts (Engl Lit) (HL 55)
Liverpool Hope – BBC 112 pts (Engl Lang) (IB 28 pts)
Liverpool John Moores – BBC 112 pts (Crea Writ Flm St)
London Met – BBC 112 pts (Crea Writ Engl Lit)
Northumbria – 112 pts (Engl Lang Lit; Engl Lit Crea Writ)
Nottingham Trent – 112 pts (Engl)
Portsmouth – 112–120 pts+portfolio (Crea Writ) (IB 25 pts)
Sheffield Hallam – BBC 112 pts (Crea Writ; Engl)
Staffordshire – BBC 112 pts (Engl Lit Crea Writ)
Sunderland – 112 pts (Engl Crea Prof Writ)
Swansea – BBC–ABB 112–128 pts (Engl Lang Engl Lit) (IB 32 pts)
UWE Bristol – 112 pts (Engl Lit; Engl Lit Writ)

104 pts **Aberystwyth** – BCC–BBB 104–120 pts (Engl Lit) (IB 28–30 pts)
Arts London – 104 pts (Mag Jrnl Pub) (IB 24 pts)
Bangor – 104–128 pts (Engl Lit Dr) (HL 5 Engl); 104–128 pts (Engl Lang Engl Lit) (HL 5 Engl)

Bath Spa – BCC–BBB incl Engl (Crea Writ; Engl Lit) (IB 32 pts HL 5 Engl)
Bedfordshire – 104 pts (Engl)
Bournemouth – 104–120 pts (Engl) (IB 28–31 pts)
Brighton – BCC–BBB incl Engl/sociol/psy 104–120 pts (Engl Lit) (IB 26 pts)
Cardiff Met – 104 pts (Engl Crea Writ; Media Comms)
Central Lancashire – 104–112 pts incl Engl (Engl Lang Crea Writ; Engl Lang Lit; Engl Lit) (HL Engl)
Chester – BCC–BBC incl Engl (Engl Lit) (IB 28 pts HL 5 Engl); BCC–BBC incl Engl 104–112 pts (Crea Writ courses; Engl Lang Lit courses; Engl Lang courses) (IB 26 pts HL 5 Engl)
Chichester – BCC–BBB 104–120 pts (Engl Lit) (IB 28 pts HL 4 Engl)
City St George's – BCC incl Engl (Engl) (IB 28 pts HL 55)
De Montfort – 104 pts (Crea Writ Comb Hons; Engl Lang Comb Hons) (IB 24 pts)
Falmouth – 104–120 pts+interview (Engl Crea Writ)
Greenwich – BCC 104 pts (Crea Writ; Engl Lang Lit)
Huddersfield – BCC–BBB 104–120 pts+interview (Engl Lang courses); BCC–BBB incl Engl 104–120 pts+interview (Engl Lit); BCC–BBB 104–120 pts+audition (Actg Perf Engl Lang/Lit)
Liverpool Hope – BCC 104 pts (Engl Lit) (IB 24 pts)
Liverpool John Moores – BCC 104 pts (Crea Writ); BCC incl Engl 104 pts (Hist Engl Lit); (Engl Lit) (HL Engl)
Manchester Met – 104–112 pts (Engl; Engl Am Lit; Engl Crea Writ) (IB 26 pts)
Northampton – BCC (Engl courses)
Portsmouth – 104–120 pts incl Engl (Engl Lang Ling) (IB 25 pts)
Roehampton – 104–120 pts (Engl Lit)
South Wales – BCC incl Engl 104 pts (Engl Crea Writ)
Westminster – BCC–BBB 104–120 pts (Chin Engl Lang); BCC–BBB incl hum/soc sci 104–120 pts (Engl Lang courses) (HL 5 Engl)
Winchester – 104–120 pts (Crea Writ) (HL 44); 104–120 pts incl Engl/art/hum/soc sci (Engl courses) (HL 44)
Worcester – 104 pts (Engl Lang courses); BCC Engl 104 pts (Engl Lit courses)
York St John – 104 pts (Crea Writ; Engl Lang Ling; Engl Lit)

96 pts **Anglia Ruskin** – 96 pts incl Engl (Writ Engl Lit) (IB 24 pts); C Engl 96 pts (Engl Lit) (IB 24 pts HL 4 Engl)
Bangor – 96–120 pts (Engl Lang courses); (Engl Lit courses) (HL 5 Engl)
Birmingham Newman – 96 pts incl hum/soc sci (Engl)
Bishop Grosseteste – 96–112 pts (Engl courses)
Chichester – 96–120 pts incl Engl/dr/crea writ (Crea Writ Engl) (IB 28 pts HL 4 Engl)
Gloucestershire – CCC (Crea Writ; Engl Crea Writ); CCC 96 pts (Engl Lit Crea Writ)
Greater Manchester – 96 pts incl Engl+interview/portfolio (Engl); 96 pts incl Engl lang+interview/portfolio (Crea Writ)
London (Birk) – CCC–ABB 96–128 pts+interview (Engl)
Marjon – 96–104 pts (Prof Engl); CCC incl Engl/hum 96 pts (Engl)
St Mary's – CCC–BBC 96–112 pts (Crea Prof Writ; Engl Lit)
Teesside – 96–112 pts (Engl Crea Writ; Engl St)
Wolverhampton – CCC/BCD 96 pts (Crea Prof Writ courses; Engl courses)

72 pts **UHI** – BC incl Engl (Lit)

Alternative offers See **Chapter 6** and **Appendix 1** for grades/UCAS Tariff points information for other examinations.

EXAMPLES OF COLLEGES OFFERING COURSES IN THIS SUBJECT FIELD

Accrington and Rossendale (Coll); Birmingham Met (Coll); Blackpool and Fylde (Coll); Bournemouth and Poole (Coll); Bradford College (UC); Craven (Coll); Doncaster (Coll); Farnborough (CT); Newham (CFE); South Devon (Coll); TEC Partnership; Truro and Penwith (Coll); West Suffolk (Coll); Yeovil (Coll).

CHOOSING YOUR COURSE (SEE ALSO CH.1)

Universities and colleges teaching quality See www.qaa.ac.uk; www.discoveruni.gov.uk.

Top research universities and colleges (REF 2021) (English Language and Literature) Newcastle; London (Birk); Bedfordshire; Leeds; Edinburgh; York; Oxford Brookes; Oxford; Southampton; Nottingham.

Examples of sandwich degree courses Aston; Coventry; Hertfordshire; Huddersfield; Loughborough; Surrey.

ADMISSIONS INFORMATION

Admissions tutors' advice Buckingham In a situation where everyone is trying to show off, it's amazing how powerful sincerity is. What poems, novels, or drama have really excited you? English Literature is a great subject, but why do you really want to read it?

Advice to applicants and planning the UCAS personal statement Applicants should read outside their subject. Details of any writing you have done (for example poetry, short stories) should be provided. Theatre visits and play readings are also important. Keep up-to-date by reading literary and theatre reviews in the national newspapers (keep a scrapbook of reviews for reference). Evidence is needed of a good writing style. Favourite authors, spare-time reading. Ability to write lucidly, accurately and succinctly. Evidence of literary enthusiasm. General interest in communications – verbal, visual, media.

Selection interviews Yes Cambridge, Falmouth, Greater Manchester, Huddersfield, London (Birk), London (UCL), Oxford (Engl Lang Lit) 66% (success rate 23%), (Engl Modn Langs) 83% (success rate 31%), Reading (P Educ Engl Spec); **Some** Bristol (mature students and applicants with non-standard qualifications); **No** Anglia Ruskin, Bishop Grosseteste, Canterbury Christ Church, Chichester, De Montfort, London (King's), London (RH), Middlesex, Newcastle.

Interview advice and questions Questions will almost certainly be asked on set A-level texts and any essays which have been submitted prior to the interview. You will also be expected to have read outside your A-level subjects and to answer questions about your favourite authors, poets, dramatists, etc. Questions in the past have included: Do you think that class discussion plays an important part in your English course? What is the value of studying a text in depth rather than just reading it for pleasure? What is the difference between satire and comedy? Are books written by women different from those written by men? Why would you go to see a production of *Hamlet*? What are your views on the choice of novels for this year's Booker Prize? What books are bad for you? If you could make up a word, what would it be? Short verbal tests and a précis may be set. See also **Chapter 5**.

Reasons for rejection (non-academic) Some are well-informed about English literature – others are not. Inability to respond to questions about their current studies. Lack of enthusiasm for the challenge of studying familiar subjects from a different perspective. Must be able to benefit from the course. Little interest in how people communicate with each other.

GRADUATE DESTINATIONS AND EMPLOYMENT

(See **Chapter 1, Graduate Outcomes.**)

Career note English graduates work in the media, publishing, management, public and social services, business, administration and IT, retail sales, the cultural industries and the teaching profession. Those who have undertaken courses in Creative Writing could aim for careers in advertising, public relations or journalism.

OTHER DEGREE SUBJECTS FOR CONSIDERATION

Communication Studies; Drama; Language courses; Linguistics; Literature; Media Studies.

ENVIRONMENTAL SCIENCES

(including **Climate Change, Ecology, Environmental Hazards, Environmental Health, Environmental Management and Meteorology and Climate Science**; see also **Biological Sciences, Biology, Engineering (Civil), Geography, Geology/Geological Sciences, Health Sciences/Studies, Marine/Maritime Studies, Town and Urban Planning**)

Environmental Sciences courses need to be researched carefully since the content offered by different institutions can vary considerably. The emphasis may be biological or geographical and courses can cover marine, legal, social and political issues. Some courses focus on ecological issues, either environmental or industrial, while others focus on environmental hazards and health, so expect some overlap in many courses. There are some vocational courses in this category with professional status which allow graduates to progress into certain professions. For example, they may choose to become an environmental health officer whose role is concerned with all aspects of public health, covering food safety, housing, health and safety, and environmental protection.

USEFUL WEBSITES www.cieh.org; www.endsreport.com; www.enn.com; http://iagre.org; www.gov.uk/government/organisations/department-for-environment-food-rural-affairs; http://socenv.org.uk; www.the-ies.org; www.noc.ac.uk; www.britishecologicalsociety.org; www.rmets.org

NB The points totals shown to the left of the institutions are for ease of reference only. It must not be assumed that Tariff points are always used by institutions or that they can be substituted for an offer in grades. The level of an offer is not necessarily indicative of the quality of a course.

COURSE OFFERS INFORMATION

SUBJECT REQUIREMENTS/PREFERENCES GCSE English, mathematics and a science (often chemistry or biology) usually required. **AL** One or two science subjects are usually stipulated; mathematics may be required. (Meteor) Mathematics, physics and another science may be required sometimes with specified grades, eg mathematics and physics grade B. Some popular universities are now making lower offers for disadvantaged and other students.

YOUR TARGET OFFERS AND EXAMPLES OF DEGREE COURSES

144 pts **Imperial London** – AAA incl biol+sci/maths (Ecol Env Biol) (IB 38 pts HL 6 biol+sci/maths)
Leeds – AAA incl sci/maths/geog/econ/sociol/hist/law/Engl (Sust Env Mgt (Int)) (IB 35 pts HL 17 pts)
London LSE – AAA incl A maths (Env Sust Dev Econ) (IB 38 pts HL 766 incl maths)

136 pts **Durham** – AAB incl sci/maths/geog/psy (Clim Sci) (IB 36 pts HL 665 incl sci)
Leeds – AAB–AAA incl biol (Ecol Cons Biol) (IB 34–35 pts HL 17–18 pts incl 6 biol+sci)
London (UCL) – AAB (Env Geosci) (IB 36 pts HL 17 pts)
St Andrews – AAB incl biol+sci/maths (Env Earth Sci) (IB 36 pts HL 665 incl maths/sci)
York – AAB incl biol+sci (Ecol) (IB 35 pts HL 6 biol+chem/maths); AAB–A*AA incl chem+sci/maths (Chem Atmos Env) (IB 35–36 pts HL 6 chem+sci/maths)

128 pts **Birmingham** – ABB incl sci/maths/geog/psy/comp (Env Sci) (IB 32 pts HL 655)
East Anglia – ABB incl maths (Mar Sci) (IB 32 pts HL 5 maths)
Edinburgh – ABB–AAA incl maths+phys (Geophys Meteor) (IB 32–34 pts HL 655 incl 6 maths +5 phys); (Phys Meteor) (IB 32–37 pts HL 655–666 incl 6 maths+5 phys); ABB–AAA incl sci/maths (Ecol Env Sci Mgt) (IB 32–34 pts HL 555 incl sci/maths); ABB–AAA incl sci/maths/geog (Ecol Env Sci) (IB 32–34 pts HL 555 incl sci/maths)
Exeter – ABB incl geol/sci/maths (Env Geosci) (IB 32 pts HL 655 incl geol/sci); ABB–AAB 128–136 pts (Env Hum) (IB 32–34 pts); ABB–AAB incl B sci (Cons Biol Ecol) (IB 32–34 pts HL 655–665 incl 5 sci); ABB–AAB incl sci/maths/geog/tech/psy/PE (Env Sci) (IB 32–34 pts HL 5 sci/maths/geog/tech/psy/PE)
Lancaster – ABB incl sci/maths (Ecol Cons; Env Sci) (IB 32 pts HL 16 pts incl 6 sci)
Leeds – ABB incl maths/sci/geog (Env Sci) (HL 16 pts incl 5 maths/sci); ABB incl sci/maths/geog/econ/sociol/hist/law/pol/Engl (Sust Env Mgt) (IB 34 pts HL 16 pts)

Liverpool – ABB incl sci/maths/geog (Env Sci) (IB 33 pts HL 4 sci)
London (QM) – ABB incl sci/maths/geog/geol/psy (Env Sci) (IB 32 pts HL 655 incl sci/maths/geog/geol/psy)
Manchester – ABB (Env Mgt) (IB 34 pts HL 655); ABB incl sci (Env Sci) (IB 34 pts HL 655 incl sci)
Newcastle – ABB incl maths/sci/geog/psy (Env Sci (Yr Ind)) (IB 32 pts HL 5 maths/sci/geo/psy); ABB incl sci/maths/geog/psy (Env Sci) (IB 32 pts HL 5 sci/maths/geog/psy)
Nottingham – ABB incl biol (Env Biol) (IB 32 pts HL 5 biol); ABB incl sci/maths (Env Sci) (IB 32 pts HL 5 sci)
Reading – ABB incl biol/geog/env sci/maths (Ecol Wldlf Cons) (IB 32 pts HL 5 biol/geog/env sci/maths); ABB incl maths (Meteor Clim) (IB 32 pts HL 5 maths)
Sheffield – ABB (Lnd Archit) (IB 33 pts); ABB incl geog/sci (Env Sci) (IB 33 pts HL 5 geog/sci)
Southampton – ABB incl sci/maths/geog/psy (Env Sci) (IB 32 pts HL 16 pts incl 5 sci)
York – ABB incl sci/maths/geog/psy (Env Sci) (IB 34 pts)

120 pts **Aberdeen** – BBB incl maths/sci (Ecol; Env Sci) (IB 32 pts HL 555 incl maths/sci)
Bournemouth Arts – BBB 120 pts+portfolio (Sust Des)
Brunel – BBB (Env Sci) (IB 30 pts)
Dundee – BBB (Env Sust) (IB 30 pts HL 555); BBB incl sci (Env Sci) (IB 30 pts HL 555 incl sci)
East Anglia – BBB/ABC incl geog/maths/econ/sci (Env Sci) (IB 32 pts HL 5 geog/maths/econ/sci)
Keele – BBB (Env Sci; Env Sust) (IB 30 pts HL 555)
Kent – BBB (Env Soc Sci (Yr Ind)) (IB 30 pts HL 15 pts); BBB incl sci/maths (Ecol Cons; Ecol Cons (Yr Prof Prac)) (HL 665)
Liverpool – BBB (Env Plan) (IB 31 pts)
London (RH) – BBB–ABB incl biol/geog/env sci+sci/maths (Ecol Cons) (IB 32 pts HL 555 incl biol/geog/env+sci); BBB–ABB incl sci (Earth Clim Env Chng) (IB 30 pts HL 554 incl sci)
Plymouth – 120–144 pts incl biol (Mar Biol Cstl Ecol) (IB 30–36 pts HL biol)
Portsmouth – BBB–ABB (Env Sci Mgt) (IB 25 pts)
Reading – BBB (Env Mgt Sust) (IB 30 pts); BBB incl sci (Env Sci) (IB 30 pts HL 5 sci)
Stirling – BBB incl sci/geog/geol/maths (Env Sci Out Educ) (IB 28 pts HL sci/geog/geol/maths); (Ecol Cons; Env Sci) (IB 30 pts HL sci/geog/geol/maths)
Sussex – BBB–ABB incl biol (Ecol Cons) (IB 30–32 pts HL 5 biol)
Ulster – BBB incl sci/maths/geog/hm econ/hlth soc cr (Env Hlth) (IB 26 pts HL 13 pts incl sci)

112 pts **Canterbury Christ Church** – BBC (Wldlf Ecol Cons Sci) (IB 29 pts)
Chester – BBC 112 pts (Geog Nat Haz Mgt) (IB 26 pts HL 5 geog)
Derby – BBC–BBB incl sci/geog 112–120 pts (Env Sust)
Greenwich – 112 pts incl sci/geog (Env Sci) (IB 28 pts HL 55 incl sci+geog)
Hertfordshire – BBC–BBB 112–120 pts (Env Mgt Ecol) (HL 44)
Leeds Beckett – 112 pts (Env Hlth) (HL 554)
Liverpool Hope – BBC 112 pts (Env Sci) (IB 28 pts)
Northumbria – 112 pts (Env Sci)
Nottingham Trent – BBC 112 pts (Ecol Cons); BBC incl sci 112 pts (Env Sci)
Portsmouth – BBC–ABB incl sci/maths/geog 112–128 pts (Mar Env Sci) (IB 25–26 pts HL 5 sci/maths/geog)
UWE Bristol – C sci 112 pts (Env Sci; Wldlf Ecol Cons Sci) (HL 5 sci)

104 pts **Aberystwyth** – BCC–BBB incl biol 104–120 pts (Ecol) (IB 28–30 pts HL 5 biol)
Bangor – 104–128 pts incl sci/maths/geog/econ (Env Cons; Env Sci) (HL 5 sci)
Bournemouth – 104–120 pts (Env Sci) (IB 28–31 pts)
Brighton – BCC–BBB 104–120 pts (Env Sci) (IB 26 pts); BCC–BBB incl sci 104–120 pts (Ecol Cons) (IB 26 pts HL 5 biol)
Gloucestershire – (Ecol Env Sci)
Manchester Met – BCC–BBC incl geog/sci/maths 104–112 pts (Env Sci (St Abrd)) (IB 26 pts HL 5 geog/sci)
Northampton – BCC (Env Sci)
Plymouth – 104–112 pts (Env Mgt Sust; Env Sci) (IB 26–27 pts)

Ulster – BCC incl STEM (Env Sci) (IB 24 pts HL 12 pts)
Westminster – BCC 104 pts (Glob Chlng)
Winchester – BCC–BBB 104–120 pts (Anim Sci Cons)

96 pts **Bath Spa** – BCC–BBB incl sci/geog (Env Sci) (IB 32 pts HL 5 sci/geog)
Black Mountains (Coll) – CCC–BBB pts 96–120 pts (Sust Fut Arts Ecol Sys Chng) (IB 24 pts)
Cardiff Met – 96–104 pts (Env Hlth) (HL 55)
Glasgow – CCC–BBB (Env Sci Sust) (IB 32 pts HL 555 incl sci)
Glasgow Caledonian – CCC incl maths+phys (Env Mgt)
Kingston – 96–120 pts (Env Sci)
Reading – CCC–BBB incl biol/geog/env sci/maths (Ecol Wldf Cons Fdn) (IB 24–30 pts HL biol/geog/env sci/maths)
Teesside – 96–112 pts (Env Sci)

80 pts **Sparsholt (Coll)** – CCE incl sci (Aqua Fish Mgt) (IB 24 pts HL 4 sci)

64 pts **UHI** – CC incl sci (Env Sci)

Open University – (Env St)

Alternative offers See **Chapter 6** and **Appendix 1** for grades/UCAS Tariff points information for other examinations.

DEGREE APPRENTICESHIPS

Anglia Ruskin (Env Practnr); Kingston (Env Sci); UWE Bristol (Env Practnr); Wrexham (Lw Carb Ener Sust).

EXAMPLES OF COLLEGES OFFERING COURSES IN THIS SUBJECT FIELD

Askham Bryan (Coll); Bedford (Coll); Birmingham Met (Coll); Bishop Burton (Coll); Cornwall (Coll); Duchy Coll (UC); Durham New (Coll); Easton (Coll); Hadlow (UC); Hartpury (Coll); Kingston Maurward (Coll); Leeds City (Coll); Moulton (Coll); Myerscough (Coll); Petroc; Plymouth City (Coll); Sparsholt (Coll); Truro and Penwith (Coll); Weston (Coll); York (Coll).

CHOOSING YOUR COURSE (SEE ALSO CH.1)

Universities and colleges teaching quality See www.qaa.ac.uk; www.discoveruni.gov.uk.

Top research universities and colleges (REF 2021) (Earth Systems and Environmental Sciences) Cambridge; Bristol; Birmingham; East Anglia; Southampton; Manchester; Oxford; Cardiff; Reading; Leeds.

Examples of sandwich degree courses Brighton; Glasgow Caledonian; Greenwich; Hertfordshire; Keele; Kingston; Leeds; Manchester Met; Newcastle; Nottingham Trent; Reading; Teesside; Ulster; UWE Bristol.

ADMISSIONS INFORMATION

Advice to applicants and planning the UCAS personal statement 'We want doers, not just thinkers' is one comment from an admissions tutor. Describe any field courses which you have attended; make an effort to visit one of the National Parks. Discuss these visits and identify any particular aspects which impressed you. Outline travel interests. Give details of work as a conservation volunteer and other outside-school activities. Strong communication skills, people-oriented work experience. Watch your spelling and grammar! What sparked your interest in environmental science? Discuss your field trips. (Env Hlth courses) A basic knowledge of environmental health as opposed to environmental sciences. Work experience in an environmental health department is looked upon very favourably. See also **Appendix 3**.

Selection interviews No Newcastle, Sheffield Hallam, UWE Bristol.

Interview advice and questions Environmental issues are constantly in the news, so keep abreast of developments. You could be asked to discuss particular environmental problems in the area in which you live and to justify your stance on any environmental issues on which you have strong opinions. See also **Chapter 5**.

Reasons for rejection (non-academic) Inability to be aware of the needs of others.

GRADUATE DESTINATIONS AND EMPLOYMENT

(See **Chapter 1, Graduate Outcomes.**)

Career note Some graduates find work with government departments, local authorities, statutory and voluntary bodies in areas like land management and pollution control. Others go into a range of non-scientific careers.

OTHER DEGREE SUBJECTS FOR CONSIDERATION

Biological Sciences; Biology; Chemistry; Earth Sciences; Environmental Engineering; Geography; Geology; Meteorology; Ocean Sciences/Oceanography; Town and Country Planning.

EUROPEAN STUDIES

(including **Russian and East European Studies**; see also **French, German, International Relations, Languages**)

European Studies courses provide the opportunity to study one or two main languages along with a broad study of economic, political, legal, social and cultural issues within the broad context of the European community. Other similar specific courses such as European History or European Politics allow the student to focus on an individual subject area.

Useful websites www.europa.eu; www.turing-scheme.org.uk; see also **Languages**.

NB The points totals shown to the left of the institutions are for ease of reference only. It must not be assumed that Tariff points are always used by institutions or that they can be substituted for an offer in grades. The level of an offer is not necessarily indicative of the quality of a course.

COURSE OFFERS INFORMATION

Subject requirements/preferences GCSE English and a foreign language for all courses and possibly mathematics. Grades may be stipulated. **AL** A modern language usually required. Some popular universities are now making lower offers for disadvantaged and other students.

Your target offers and examples of degree courses

152 pts **Cambridge** – A*AA incl lang+interview+MMLAA (Modn Mediev Langs) (IB 41–42 pts HL 776 incl lang)
Durham – A*AA incl lang (Comb Hons Soc Sci (Russ)) (IB 38 pts HL 6 lang)
London (UCL) – A*AA (Euro Soc Pol St) (IB 39 pts HL 19 pts)

144 pts **Durham** – AAA 144 pts (Modn Langs Cult (Yr Abrd) (Russ)) (IB 37 pts HL 666)
Oxford – AAA+interview+MLAT (Modn Langs (Russ+2nd Lang)) (IB 38 pts HL 666); AAA+interview+MLAT+OLAT (Euro Mid E Langs (Cz/Russ)) (IB 38 pts HL 666)

136 pts **Bath** – AAB–ABB+aEPQ incl lang (Int Pol Modn Langs (Fr/Span/Ger) (Yr Abrd)) (IB 35 pts HL 665 incl lang)
Birmingham – AAB incl hist (Modn Langs Hist) (IB 32 pts HL 665 incl 6 hist)
London (King's) – AAB (Euro St (Fr/Ger/Span) (Yr Abrd)) (IB 35 pts HL 17 pts)
London (UCL) – AAB (Pol Sociol E Euro St) (IB 36 pts HL 17 pts)
Warwick – AAB (Ling Russ) (IB 34 pts)

128 pts **Birmingham** – ABB incl lang (Modn Langs (Yr Abrd)) (IB 32 pts HL 655)
Bristol – ABB incl lang (Modn Langs) (IB 32 pts HL 16 pts incl 5 langs)
Exeter – ABB (Modn Langs Arbc) (IB 32 pts HL 655)
Leeds – ABB (Russ Comb Hons) (IB 34 pts HL 16 pts)
London (QM) – ABB incl hum/soc sci (Russ Bus Mgt) (IB 32 pts HL 655)
London (UCL) – ABB (Bulg/Czech/Finn/Hung/Polh/Romn/Slovak E Euro St; Lang Cult; Russ St) (IB 34 pts HL 16 pts); ABB incl hist (Russ Hist) (IB 34 pts HL 16 pts incl 5 hist)

Manchester – ABB incl Russ/Chin+interview (Russ Chin) (IB 34 pts HL 655 incl Russ/Chin); ABB incl Russ/Jap+interview (Russ Jap) (IB 34 pts HL 655 incl Russ/Jap)
Nottingham – ABB (Modn Euro St) (IB 30 pts HL 655); (Russ St) (IB 32 pts); ABB incl hist (Hist E Euro Cult St) (IB 32 pts HL 5 hist)
Sheffield – ABB/BBB+bEPQ incl lang (Modn Langs Cult (Yr Abrd)) (IB 33 pts HL 5 lang)
St Andrews – ABB (Russ courses) (IB 36 pts HL 655)
120 pts **Essex** – BBB (Euro St (Yr Abrd)) (IB 30 pts)
Glasgow – BBB–AAB incl Engl/hum (Cnt E Euro St) (IB 36 pts HL 665 incl Engl+hum); BBB–AAB incl hum (Russ) (IB 34 pts HL 655 incl Engl+hum)
112 pts **Essex** – BBC (Euro St Modn Langs) (IB 29 pts HL 554)
96 pts **Central Lancashire** – 96–112 pts incl lang (Modn Langs (2 Langs) (Fr/Span/Jap/Russ/Chin/Kor))

ALTERNATIVE OFFERS See **Chapter 6** and **Appendix 1** for grades/UCAS Tariff points information for other examinations.

CHOOSING YOUR COURSE (SEE ALSO CH.1)

UNIVERSITIES AND COLLEGES TEACHING QUALITY See www.qaa.ac.uk; www.discoveruni.gov.uk.

TOP RESEARCH UNIVERSITIES AND COLLEGES (REF 2021) See **Languages**.

EXAMPLES OF SANDWICH DEGREE COURSES Cambridge; Essex; London (King's); London (UCL); Manchester.

ADMISSIONS INFORMATION

ADVICE TO APPLICANTS AND PLANNING THE UCAS PERSONAL STATEMENT Try to identify an interest you have in the country relevant to your studies. Visits to that country should be described. Read the national newspapers and magazines and keep up-to-date with political and economic developments. Show your interest in the culture and civilisation of Europe as a whole, through, for example, European travel. Show your motivation for choosing the course and give details of your personal achievements and any future career plans, showing your international awareness and perspective.

SELECTION INTERVIEWS Yes Cambridge, Manchester (Russ Jap), Oxford (Modn Langs (Russ+2nd Lang)) 94% (success rate 44%); (Euro Mid E Langs) 91% (success rate 37%).

INTERVIEW ADVICE AND QUESTIONS While your interest in studying a language may be the main reason for applying for this subject, the politics, economics and culture of European countries are constantly in the news. You should keep up-to-date with any such topics concerning your chosen country and be prepared for questions. A language test may occupy part of the interview. See also **Chapter 5**.

REASONS FOR REJECTION (NON-ACADEMIC) Poor powers of expression. Lack of ideas on any issues. Lack of enthusiasm.

GRADUATE DESTINATIONS AND EMPLOYMENT

(See **Chapter 1, Graduate Outcomes.**)

CAREER NOTE See **Languages**.

OTHER DEGREE SUBJECTS FOR CONSIDERATION

Business and Management; History; International Relations; Politics; Language courses.

FILM, RADIO AND TV STUDIES

(see also **Art and Design (Graphic Design), Communication Studies/Communication, Engineering (Acoustics and Sound), Media Studies, Photography**)

Many course are offered in Film, Radio and TV Studies. The Film, Photography and Media course at the University of Leeds combines theory with practice, covering digital film and photography with options in TV production, film editing, and documentary production. By contrast, the Exeter course presents a broad chronological and geographical coverage from the silent film to the Hollywood classics. It's therefore important to choose courses with care, particularly the theoretical and practical content of courses. At Brunel University, practical studies occupy up to 40% of the Film and Television Studies course. It is often possible to study Film, Radio and TV Studies as part of a combined degree. For example, at the University of Chester, it is possible to study Radio Production with Business Management or Television Production.

Useful websites www.bfi.org.uk; www.mtv.com/news/movies; www.allmovie.com; www.societyinmotion.com; www.imdb.com; www.fwfr.com; www.bafta.org; www.movingimage.us; http://film.britishcouncil.org; www.filmsite.org; www.festival-cannes.com/en; www.bbc.co.uk/careers; www.rogerebert.com; www.bectu.org.uk

NB The points totals shown to the left of the institutions are for ease of reference only. It must not be assumed that Tariff points are always used by institutions or that they can be substituted for an offer in grades. The level of an offer is not necessarily indicative of the quality of a course.

COURSE OFFERS INFORMATION

Subject requirements/preferences GCSE English usually required. Courses vary, check prospectuses. **AL** English may be stipulated for some courses. Some popular universities are now making lower offers for disadvantaged and other students.

Your target offers and examples of degree courses

144 pts **St Andrews** – AAA (Flm St Int) (IB 38 pts HL 666)

136 pts **Bristol** – AAB (Flm TV) (IB 34 pts HL 17 pts)
Lancaster – AAB incl Engl (Flm Engl Lit) (IB 35 pts HL 16 pts incl 6 lit)
Leeds – AAB (Flm Photo Media) (IB 35 pts HL 16 pts)
London (King's) – AAB incl Engl (Compar Lit Flm St) (IB 35 pts HL 17 pts incl 6 Engl)
Manchester – AAB incl Engl/hist/pol (Flm St courses) (IB 35 pts HL 665 incl Engl/hist/pol)
Warwick – AAB+interview+portfolio (Flm St) (IB 34 pts HL 6 Engl/hist/pol)
York – AAB (Flm TV Prod) (IB 35 pts)

128 pts **East Anglia** – ABB (Flm TV St) (IB 32 pts); ABB incl Engl (Flm St Engl Lit) (IB 32 pts HL 5 Engl)
Edinburgh – ABB+portfolio (Flm TV) (IB 34 pts HL 655)
Exeter – ABB–AAB (Flm TV St) (IB 32–34 pts HL 655–665)
Lancaster – ABB (Flm Sociol; Flm St) (IB 32 pts HL 16 pts)
Leeds – ABB (Flm St) (IB 34 pts HL 16 pts)
Leeds Beckett – 128 pts+portfolio (Filmm) (HL 554)
Liverpool – ABB (Flm St Comb Hons) (IB 33 pts)
London (QM) – ABB incl hum/soc sci (Flm St) (IB 32 pts HL 655 incl hum/soc sci)
Manchester – ABB incl essay sub (Dr Flm St) (IB 34 pts HL 655)
Newcastle – ABB (Flm Media; Flm Prac) (IB 32 pts)
Nottingham – ABB (Flm TV St) (IB 32 pts)
Reading – ABB+interview (Flm TV; Flm Thea) (IB 32 pts)
Southampton – ABB/BBB+aEPQ incl Engl (Flm Engl) (IB 32 pts HL 16 pts incl 5 Engl); ABB incl essay sub (Flm St) (IB 32 pts HL 16 pts); ABB incl hist (Flm Hist) (IB 32 pts HL 16 pts incl 5 hist)
UWE Bristol – 128 pts+interview+portfolio (Filmm)
Warwick – ABB incl Engl+interview+portfolio (Flm Lit) (IB 34 pts HL 6 Engl)
Westminster – ABB–AAB 128–136 pts+interview+portfolio (Flm)

120 pts **Aberdeen** – BBB (Flm Vis Cult) (IB 32 pts HL 555)
Dundee – BBB (Engl Flm St) (IB 30 pts HL 555 incl Engl)
Essex – BBB (Flm St) (IB 30 pts HL 555)
Glasgow – BBB–AAB (Flm TV St Comb Hons) (IB 34 pts HL 655 incl Engl+hum)
Kent – BBB (Flm courses)
Leicester – BBB (Flm Media St) (IB 28 pts)
London (RH) – BBB–ABB (Flm St) (IB 32 pts HL 655)
Queen Margaret – BBB (Thea Flm) (IB 30 pts)
Queen's Belfast – BBB (Flm St courses) (IB 32 pts HL 655)

Reading – BBB+interview+portfolio (Art Flm/Thea) (IB 30 pts); BBB incl Engl/thea st (Engl Lit Flm Thea) (IB 30 pts HL 5 Engl/thea st)
Stirling – BBB (Flm Media) (IB 30 pts)
Sunderland – 120 pts (Flm Prod)
Surrey – BBB incl maths+interview (Flm Prod Broad Eng) (IB 32 pts)
Sussex – BBB (Dr Flm St) (IB 30 pts); BBB–ABB (Flm St) (IB 30–32 pts)

112 pts **Birmingham City** – BBC 112 pts (Dig Flm Prod) (IB 28 pts); BBC 112 pts+portfolio (Vis Efcts) (IB 28 pts)
Bournemouth Arts – BBC–BBB 112–120 pts+portfolio (Animat Prod); BBC–BBB 112–120 pts+portfolio+interview (Flm Prod)
Bradford – BBC 112 pts (Flm TV Prod)
Brunel – BBC (Flm Prod; Flm Prod Thea; Flm TV St; Flm TV St Engl) (IB 29 pts)
Canterbury Christ Church – BBC (Flm Prod) (IB 29 pts)
Creative Arts – 112 pts+interview+portfolio (Flm Prod) (IB 27–30 pts HL 15 pts)
East London – 112 pts (Flm) (IB 24 pts HL 15 pts)
Edge Hill – BBC–BBB 112–120 pts (Flm; Flm Broad Prod; Media)
Edinburgh Napier – BBC incl Engl (Engl Flm) (IB 29 pts HL 655 incl Engl)
Essex – BBC–BBB 112–120 pts (Flm St Lit) (IB 29–30 pts HL 554–555)
Greenwich – BBC 112 pts (Flm St; Flm TV Prod)
Hertfordshire – BBC–BBB 112–120 pts (Engl Lang Flm; Flm TV Prod)
Hull – BBC 112 pts (Flm St) (IB 28 pts)
Keele – BBC 112 pts (Flm St) (IB 29 pts)
Kingston – 112–128 pts+portfolio (Filmm)
Leeds Trinity – 112 pts (Flm; TV Prod)
Liverpool John Moores – BBC 112 pts (Crea Writ Flm St; Flm St)
London Met – BBC 112 pts (Jrnl Flm TV St); BBC 112 pts+interview+portfolio (Flm TV St)
London South Bank – +interview (Flm TV Prac)
Middlesex – 112 pts (Flm)
Northumbria – 112 pts (Flm)
Oxford Brookes – BBC 112 pts (Flm) (IB 30 pts)
Plymouth (AU) – 112 pts+portfolio+interview (Flm St)
Portsmouth – 112–120 pts (Flm St) (IB 25 pts)
Roehampton – 112 pts (Flm Prod)
Sheffield Hallam – BBC 112 pts (Flm TV Prod)
Solent – 112–128 pts+interview (Flm Prod; Flm TV)
Staffordshire – BBC 112 pts (Flm Prod)
Suffolk – BBC+interview+portfolio (Dig Flm Prod)
Sunderland – 112 pts (Flm Media); 112 pts+portfolio+interview (Photo Vid Dig Imag)
Winchester – 112–120 pts (Flm Prod) (HL 44)

104 pts **Arts London** – 104 pts+portfolio (Flm TV)
Bath Spa – BCC–BBB (Flm Scrn St courses) (IB 32 pts)
Bournemouth – 104–120 pts (TV Prod) (IB 28–32 pts)
Chester – (Flm Media St)
Chichester – BCC–BBC 104–112 pts (Dig Flm Prod Scrnwrit) (IB 28 pts)
Cumbria – BCC–BBB 104–120 pts+interview+portfolio (Flm TV)
De Montfort – 104 pts (Flm St Comb Hons) (IB 24 pts)
Derby – BCC–BBC 104–112 pts+portfolio (Flm Hi-End TV Prod)
Falmouth – 104–120 pts+interview (Flm)
Lincoln – (Flm TV St)
Manchester Met – 104–112 pts+interview+portfolio (Filmm) (IB 26 pts); BCC 104–112 pts (Flm Media St) (IB 26 pts)
Northampton – BCC (Flm Scrn St Comb Hons)
Norwich Arts – BCC 104 pts+portfolio (Flm Mov Imag Prod) (IB 26 pts)
Queen Margaret – BCC (Flm Media) (IB 28 pts)
Sheffield Hallam – BCC 104 pts (Flm St)

Solent – 104–120 pts+interview (TV Prod)
West Scotland – BCC (Broad Prod (TV Rad)) (IB 24 pts); BCC 104 pts (Filmm Scrnwrit) (IB 24 pts)
Worcester – 104 pts (Filmm; Media Flm St)
York St John – 104 pts (Flm St)

96 pts **Aberystwyth** – CCC–BBB 96–120 pts (Flm TV St) (IB 26–30 pts)
Anglia Ruskin – 96 pts (Flm) (IB 24 pts); 96 pts+portfolio (Flm TV Prod) (IB 24 pts)
Bangor – 96–120 pts (Flm St courses)
Central Lancashire – 96–112 pts (Flmm; Media TV Prod; Scrnwrit Flm TV Rad)
Gloucestershire – CCC–BBB 96–120 pts+interview (Flm Prod)
Plymouth – 96–144 pts (Filmm) (IB 28 pts)
South Wales – CCC–BBC incl art/des 96–112 pts+interview+portfolio (Flm)
Teesside – 96–112 pts (Flm TV Prod)
Winchester – 96–112 pts (Flm Media St); (Flm St) (HL 44)
Wolverhampton – CCC/BCD 96 pts (Media Flm TV St)

88 pts **Bucks New** – 88 pts (Flm TV Prod)

80 pts **Bedfordshire** – 80 pts (TV Prod)

64 pts **Ravensbourne Univ** – CC+portfolio (Dig Flm Prod) (IB 24 pts)

32 pts **RConsvS** – EE+interview+audition (Filmm) (IB 24 pts)

Alternative offers See **Chapter 6** and **Appendix 1** for grades/UCAS Tariff points information for other examinations.

EXAMPLES OF COLLEGES OFFERING COURSES IN THIS SUBJECT FIELD

Accrington and Rossendale (Coll); Barking and Dagenham (Coll); Barnsley (Coll); Birmingham Met (Coll); Bournemouth and Poole (Coll); Bradford College (UC); Buckinghamshire (Coll Group); Bury (Coll); Central Film Sch; Chesterfield (Coll); Chichester (Coll); Cornwall (Coll); Croydon (UC); Doncaster (Coll); East Surrey (Coll); Exeter (Coll); Farnborough (CT); Gloucestershire (Coll); Harrow (Coll); Hereford (CA); Hull (Coll); Manchester (Coll); Northern SA; Nottingham (Coll); Rotherham (CAT); SMB CG; South Devon (Coll); South Staffordshire (Coll); TEC Partnership; Truro and Penwith (Coll); Warwickshire (Coll); West Thames (Coll); Weston (Coll); Wiltshire (Coll).

CHOOSING YOUR COURSE (SEE ALSO CH.1)

Universities and colleges teaching quality See www.qaa.ac.uk; www.discoveruni.gov.uk.

Top research universities and colleges (REF 2021) (Music, Drama, Dance, Performing Arts, Film and Screen Studies) London (QM) (Dr); London (RH); Manchester (Dr, Dance, Perf Arts, Flm Scrn St); London (Royal Central Sch SpDr); London (King's); London (SOAS); Cambridge; Roehampton (Dance); Kent; Huddersfield (Mus).

Examples of sandwich degree courses Bangor; Birmingham City; Bournemouth Arts; Bradford; Greenwich; Hertfordshire; Huddersfield; Portsmouth; Surrey; Wolverhampton.

ADMISSIONS INFORMATION

Selection interviews Yes Bournemouth Arts, Falmouth, Gloucestershire, Huddersfield, London Met, Solent, UWE Bristol, Warwick; **Some** Bournemouth, Bristol, East Anglia, Liverpool John Moores, South Wales, Surrey, York; **No** Canterbury Christ Church, Chichester, Essex, Hertfordshire, Leeds Beckett, Middlesex, Nottingham, Wolverhampton.

Interview advice and questions Questions will focus on your chosen field. In the case of films, be prepared to answer questions not only on your favourite films but on the work of one or two directors you admire and early Hollywood examples. See also **Chapter 5**.

Reasons for rejection (non-academic) Not enough drive or ambition. No creative or original ideas. Preference for production work rather than practical work. Inability to articulate the thought process behind the work in the applicant's portfolio. Insufficient knowledge of media affairs. Lack of knowledge of film history. Wrong course choice, wanted more practical work.

GRADUATE DESTINATIONS AND EMPLOYMENT

(See **Chapter 1, Graduate Outcomes.**)

Career note Although this is a popular subject field, job opportunities in film, TV and radio are limited. Successful graduates frequently have gained work experience with companies during their undergraduate years. The transferable skills (verbal communication etc) will open up other career opportunities.

OTHER DEGREE SUBJECTS FOR CONSIDERATION

Animation; Communication Studies; Creative Writing; Media Studies; Photography.

FINANCE

(including **Finance and Investment Banking, Financial Services and Property, Finance and Investment**; see also **Accountancy/Accounting**)

Courses involving finance are wide ranging and can involve accountancy, actuarial work, banking, economics, financial services, insurance, international finance, marketing, quantity surveying, real estate management, and risk management. Some courses are theoretical, others, such as accountancy and real estate management, are vocational, providing accreditation to professional bodies. A large number of courses are offered with commercial and industrial placements over six months or a year (which includes paid employment) and many students have found that their connection with a firm has led to offers of full-time employment upon graduation.

Useful websites www.cii.co.uk; www.financialadvice.co.uk; www.fnlondon.com; www.worldbank.org; www.libf.ac.uk; www.ft.com

NB The points totals shown to the left of the institutions are for ease of reference only. It must not be assumed that Tariff points are always used by institutions or that they can be substituted for an offer in grades. The level of an offer is not necessarily indicative of the quality of a course.

COURSE OFFERS INFORMATION

Subject requirements/preferences GCSE Most institutions will require English and mathematics grade 4 (C) minimum. **AL** Mathematics may be required or preferred. Some popular universities are now making lower offers for disadvantaged and other students.

Your target offers and examples of degree courses

160 pts **Imperial London** – A*A*A incl A*A* maths+fmaths+TMUA/STEP (Maths Stats Fin) (IB 39 pts HL 76 incl maths)

152 pts **Edinburgh** – A*AA (Acc Fin) (IB 39 pts HL 666); A*AA incl maths (Econ Fin) (IB 39 pts HL 666 incl maths)

London (UCL) – A*AA incl A* maths (Stats Econ Fin) (IB 39 pts HL 19 pts incl 7 maths); A*AA incl maths+phys (Mech Eng Bus Fin (MEng)) (IB 39 pts HL 19 pts incl 76 maths+phys)

Manchester – A*AA incl A* maths+interview (Maths Fin) (IB 37 pts HL 766 incl 7 maths)

Warwick – A*AA incl maths (Acc Fin; Acc Fin (Yr Ind)) (IB 38 pts HL 5 maths)

144 pts **Bath** – AAA–A*AB/AAB+aEPQ incl maths (Acc Fin (Yr Ind)) (IB 36 pts HL 666/765 incl HL 6 maths); AAA–A*AB/AAB+aEPQ incl maths (Acc Fin) (IB 36 pts HL 666/765 incl HL 6 maths)

Birmingham – AAA (Acc Fin) (IB 32 pts HL 666)

Bristol – AAA–A*AB incl maths (Acc Fin; Acc Fin (Yr Abrd); Acc Fin (Yr Ind)) (IB 36 pts HL 18 pts incl 6 maths)

City St George's – AAA (Bank Int Fin; Inv Fin Risk Mgt) (IB 35 pts); (Acc Fin (Yr Ind)) (IB 35 pts HL 4 maths)

Exeter – AAA (Acc Fin (Yr Abrd)) (IB 36 pts HL 666); AAA–A*AA incl maths (Econ Fin; Econ Fin (Yr Ind)) (IB 36–38 pts HL 666–766 incl maths)

Lancaster – AAA incl maths/fmaths (Maths Fin) (IB 36 pts HL 16 pts incl 6 maths)

Leeds – AAA (Econ Fin; Int Bus Fin) (IB 35 pts HL 17 pts); (Acc Fin) (IB 35 pts HL 17 pts incl 5 Engl/maths); AAA/A*AB incl maths (Fin Maths) (HL 17 pts incl 6 maths)
Liverpool – AAA (Law Acc Fin) (IB 36 pts); AAA incl maths/comp sci (Fin Comp) (IB 36 pts HL 5 maths/comp sci)
London LSE – AAA incl maths (Acc Fin) (IB 38 pts HL 766 incl 6 maths)
Loughborough – AAA (Bus Econ Fin) (IB 37 pts HL 666)
Manchester – AAA (Acc Fin; Fin) (IB 36 pts HL 666)
Newcastle – AAA (Econ Fin) (IB 36 pts)
Nottingham – A*AB/AAA–A*AA incl maths (Fin Maths) (IB 36 pts HL 6 maths); AAA (Fin Acc Mgt; Ind Econ Ins) (IB 36 pts)
Queen's Belfast – AAA incl maths 144 pts (Fin Risk Mgt (Yr Ind)) (IB 36 pts HL 666 incl 6 maths)
Sheffield – AAA incl maths (Econ Fin) (IB 36 pts HL 6 maths)
Southampton – AAA incl maths (Maths Fin) (IB 36 pts HL 18 pts incl 6 maths)
St Andrews – AAA (Fin Econ) (IB 38 pts HL 666)
Strathclyde – AAA incl maths (Acc Fin) (IB 38 pts HL 6 maths)

136 pts **Durham** – AAB (Acc Fin) (IB 36 pts); (Acc Fin (Yr Abrd); Acc Fin (Yr Ind)) (IB 36 pts HL 665 incl 5 maths)
Exeter – AAB (Acc Fin; Acc Fin (Yr Ind)) (IB 34 pts HL 665)
Lancaster – AAB incl maths (Acc Fin Maths) (IB 35 pts HL 16 pts incl 6 maths)
Liverpool – AAB (Acc Fin; Acc Fin (Yr Ind)) (IB 35 pts); AAB incl maths (Maths Fin) (IB 35 pts HL 6 maths)
Loughborough – AAB (Fin Mgt) (IB 34–35 pts HL 665); (Acc Fin Mgt) (IB 35 pts HL 665)
Newcastle – AAB (Acc Fin; Acc Fin (Yr Ind)) (IB 34 pts); (Bus Acc Fin) (IB 34 pts HL 555 incl maths); AAB–A*BB incl maths (Maths Fin) (IB 34 pts HL 6 maths)
Reading – AAB 136 pts (Rl Est Fin) (IB 34 pts)
Sheffield – AAB (Acc Fin Mgt) (IB 34 pts); AAB incl maths (Fin Maths) (IB 34 pts HL 6 maths)
Southampton – AAB/ABB+aEPQ (Acc Fin; Acc Fin (Yr Ind)) (IB 34 pts HL 17 pts); AAB incl maths (Econ Fin) (IB 34 pts HL 17 pts incl 5 maths)
Surrey – AAB (Econ Fin) (IB 34 pts)
York – AAB (Acc Bus Fin Mgt; Acc Bus Fin Mgt (Yr Ind)) (IB 35 pts); AAB incl maths (Econ Ecomet Fin; Econ Fin) (IB 35 pts HL 6 maths)

128 pts **Cardiff** – ABB–AAB (Bank Fin) (IB 32–34 pts HL 655–665); (Acc Fin) (IB 32–34 pts HL 665–666); ABB–AAB (Acc Fin (Yr Ind)) (IB 32–34 pts HL 665–666)
East Anglia – ABB (Bus Fin Econ) (IB 32 pts)
Glasgow – ABB–AAA incl maths (Acc Fin) (IB 36 pts HL 665 incl Engl/maths)
Kent – ABB (Acc Fin; Acc Fin (Yr Abrd); Acc Fin (Yr Ind))
Lancaster – ABB (Acc Fin; Fin) (IB 32 pts HL 16 pts); ABB incl maths (Econ Fin) (IB 32 pts HL 16 pts incl 6 maths)
Leicester – ABB/BBB+bEPQ (Fin; Fin Econ Bank) (IB 30 pts); ABB–BBB+bEPQ (Acc Fin) (IB 30 pts)
London (Institute of Banking and Finance) – ABB–AAB (Fin Inv Risk) (IB 28–30 pts)
London (QM) – ABB incl maths (Maths Fin Acc) (IB 32 pts HL 655 incl maths)
London (RH) – ABB–AAB (Acc Fin) (IB 32 pts HL 655 incl maths)
Nottingham Trent – (Econ Int Fin Bank); 128 pts (Acc Fin; Acc Fin (Yr Ind))
Queen's Belfast – ABB incl maths (Fin (Yr Ind)) (IB 33 pts HL 655 incl maths)
Reading – ABB (Acc Fin; Acc Fin (Yr Ind)) (IB 32 pts); ABB incl maths (Fin Inv Bank) (IB 32 pts)
Surrey – ABB (Acc Fin) (IB 33 pts); ABB incl A maths (Fin Maths) (IB 33 pts HL 6 maths)

120 pts **Aberdeen** – BBB (Fin courses) (IB 32 pts HL 555)
Aston – BBB (Fin) (IB 31 pts HL 555)
Brunel – BBB (Econ Bus Fin) (IB 30 pts); BBB incl maths (Fin Acc) (IB 30 pts HL 5 maths)
City St George's – BBB incl maths (Fin Econ) (IB 30 pts HL 5 maths)
Dundee – BBB (Fin Econ; Int Fin) (IB 30 pts HL 555)
Glasgow – BBB–AAB incl maths (Fin Stats) (IB 34 pts HL 655 incl maths)

Greenwich – 120 pts (Acc Fin; Fin Inv Bank)
Hertfordshire – BBB–ABB 120–128 pts (Fin); BBB–ABB incl maths 120–128 pts (Fin Maths) (HL 4 maths)
Keele – BBB (Acc Fin) (IB 30 pts HL 555)
Kingston – 120–136 pts (Acc Fin)
Leeds Beckett – 120 pts (Acc Fin) (HL 554)
London (Institute of Banking and Finance) – BBB–ABB (Bank Fin)
London (RH) – BBB–ABB (Fin Bus Econ) (IB 32 pts HL 655)
London South Bank – BBB 120 pts (Acc Fin; Acc Fin (Yr Ind))
Nottingham Trent – (Prop Fin Inv)
Stirling – BBB (Fin) (IB 30 pts)
Strathclyde – BBB–ABB (Fin courses) (IB 30 pts)
Sunderland – 120 pts (Acc Fin)
Sussex – BBB–ABB (Acc Fin; Fin Bus) (IB 30–32 pts)
Swansea – BBB–ABB (Acc Fin; Acc Fin (Yr Ind); Bus Mgt (Fin)) (IB 32–33 pts)
Westminster – BBB–AAB 120–136 pts (Fin)

112 pts **Abertay** – BBC (Acc Fin) (IB 27 pts)
Birmingham City – BBC 112 pts (Acc Fin) (IB 28 pts); (Bus Fin) (IB 28 pts HL 14 pts)
Bradford – BBC 112 pts (Acc Fin; Acc Fin (Yr Ind))
Buckingham – BBC–BBB (Acc Fin) (IB 30–32 pts)
Cardiff Met – BBC 112 pts+interview (Bus Mgt Fin) (HL 55)
Chester – BBC 112 pts (Bus Fin) (IB 26 pts)
East London – 112 pts (Acc Fin) (IB 24 pts HL 15 pts)
Essex – BBC (Bank Fin; Fin; Fin Econ) (IB 29 pts HL 554)
Glasgow Caledonian – BBC (Fin Inv Risk)
Greenwich – 112 pts (Bus Fin)
Heriot-Watt – BBC–ABB 112–128 pts (Acc Fin) (IB 29 pts)
Huddersfield – BBC–BBB 112–120 pts (Acc Fin (Yr Ind)); BBC–BBB 112–120 pts (Acc Fin)
Hull – BBC 112 pts (Bus Mgt Fin Mgt; Fin Mgt) (IB 28 pts)
Lincoln – 112 pts (Acc Fin)
Liverpool Hope – BBC (Acc Fin) (IB 28 pts)
Liverpool John Moores – BBC 112 pts (Acc Fin (Yr Ind)) (IB 28 pts); BBC–ABB 112–128 pts (Acc Fin)
Middlesex – BBC (Bank Fin); BBC 112 pts (Acc Fin; Acc Fin (Yr Ind))
Northampton – BBC (Acc Fin)
Northumbria – 112 pts (Econ Fin; Fin Inv Mgt)
Plymouth – 112–128 pts (Acc Fin; Acc Fin (Yr Ind)) (IB 28–32 pts HL 4); 112–128 pts incl maths (Maths Fin) (IB 30 pts HL 5 maths)
Portsmouth – 112–128 pts incl maths (Maths Fin Mgt) (IB 29 pts); BBC–BBB 112–120 pts (Econ Fin Bank) (IB 29 pts); BBC–BBB 112–120 pts (Acc Fin (Yr Ind)) (IB 29 pts); BBC–BBB 112–120 pts (Acc Fin) (IB 29 pts)
Sheffield Hallam – BBC 112 pts (Acc Fin)
Solent – 112–128 pts (Acc Fin)
South Wales – 112 pts (Acc Fin)
Sunderland – 112 pts (Bus Fin Mgt)
UWE Bristol – 112 pts (Acc Fin; Acc Fin (Yr Ind); Bank Fin)
West London – BBC 112–120 pts (Acc Fin); BBC 112–120 pts (Acc Fin (Yr Ind))
Worcester – 112 pts (Bus Fin)

104 pts **Bangor** – 104–136 pts (Bank Fin); 104–136 pts (Acc Fin)
Bournemouth – 104–120 pts (Acc Fin; Acc Fin (Yr Ind); Bus Mgt (Fin)) (IB 28–31 pts)
Brighton – BCC–BBB 104–120 pts (Acc Fin; Acc Fin (Yr Ind); Fin Inv) (IB 26 pts)
Chichester – BCC–BBB 104–120 pts (Acc Fin (Yr Ind)) (IB 28 pts); BCC–BBB 104–120 pts (Acc Fin) (IB 28 pts)
Edinburgh Napier – BCC (Fin Serv) (IB 28 pts HL 654)
Gloucestershire – BCC 104 pts (Acc Fin; Acc Fin (Yr Ind))

Greenwich – BCC incl maths 104 pts (Fin Maths) (HL 5 maths)
Lincoln – 104 pts (Bus Fin)
Manchester Met – BCC–BBC 104–112 pts (Acc Fin; Bank Fin) (IB 26 pts)
Oxford Brookes – BCC 104 pts (Acc Fin; Acc Fin (Yr Ind); Econ Fin Int Bus) (IB 29 pts)
Robert Gordon – BCC (Acc Fin) (IB 28 pts)
Winchester – BCC–BBB 104–120 pts (Acc Fin); (Econ Fin) (HL 44)
York St John – (Acc Fin)

96 pts **Aberystwyth** – CCC–BBB 96–120 pts (Acc Fin; Bus Fin) (IB 26–30 pts)
Anglia Ruskin – 96 pts (Bank Fin) (IB 24 pts)
Bangor – 96–128 pts (Bank Fin Tech)
London Met – CCC 96 pts (Bank Fin)
London Regent's – CCC–AAA 96–144 pts (Bus courses)
Richmond (Am Int Univ) – CCC 96 pts (Acc Fin) (IB 26 pts)

88 pts **Bucks New** – 88–112 pts (Bus Fin)

80 pts **Teesside** – 80–104 pts (Acc Fin)

48 pts **Solent** – 48 pts (Acc Fin (Fdn Yr))
Wolverhampton – DD (Acc Fin)

ALTERNATIVE OFFERS See **Chapter 6** and **Appendix 1** for grades/UCAS Tariff points information for other examinations.

DEGREE APPRENTICESHIPS

Aston (Acc Fin Mgr); Chichester (Acc Fin Mgr); Exeter (Acc Fin Mgr, Fin Serv Prof); London QM (Fin Serv Prof); Northeastern (Acc Fin Mgr); Ulster (Acc Fin).

EXAMPLES OF COLLEGES OFFERING COURSES IN THIS SUBJECT FIELD

Barnet and Southgate (Coll); Blackburn (Coll); Manchester (Coll); Norwich City (Coll); Pearson (Coll).

CHOOSING YOUR COURSE (SEE ALSO CH.1)

UNIVERSITIES AND COLLEGES TEACHING QUALITY See www.qaa.ac.uk; www.discoveruni.gov.uk.

EXAMPLES OF SANDWICH DEGREE COURSES Aston; Bangor; Bath; Birmingham City; Bournemouth; Bradford; Brighton; Bristol; Brunel; Chichester; City St George's; Coventry; De Montfort; Durham; Exeter; Gloucestershire; Greenwich; Hertfordshire; Huddersfield; Kent; Kingston; Lancaster; Leeds Beckett; Liverpool; Liverpool John Moores; London South Bank; Loughborough; Manchester Met; Middlesex; Newcastle; Nottingham Trent; Oxford Brookes; Plymouth; Portsmouth; Queen's Belfast; Reading; Sheffield Hallam; Southampton; Surrey; Sussex; Swansea; Teesside; UWE Bristol; Warwick; West London; Westminster; Wolverhampton; York.

ADMISSIONS INFORMATION

ADVICE TO APPLICANTS AND PLANNING THE UCAS PERSONAL STATEMENT Visits to banks or insurance companies should be described, giving details of any work experience or work shadowing done in various departments. Discuss any particular aspects of finance etc which interest you. See also **Appendix 3**.

SELECTION INTERVIEWS **Yes** Buckingham; **No** Huddersfield, Stirling.

INTERVIEW ADVICE AND QUESTIONS Banking involves both high street and merchant banks, so a knowledge of banking activities in general will be expected. In the past mergers have been discussed and also the role of the Bank of England in the economy. The work of the accountant may be discussed. See also **Chapter 5**.

REASONS FOR REJECTION (NON-ACADEMIC) Lack of interest. Poor English. Lacking in motivation and determination to complete the course.

GRADUATE DESTINATIONS AND EMPLOYMENT

(See **Chapter 1, Graduate Outcomes.**)

Career note Most graduates enter financial careers. Further study is required to qualify as an accountant and to obtain other professional qualifications, eg Institute of Banking.

OTHER DEGREE SUBJECTS FOR CONSIDERATION

Accountancy; Actuarial Studies; Business Studies; Economics.

FOOD SCIENCE/STUDIES AND TECHNOLOGY

(see also **Agricultural Sciences/Agriculture, Biochemistry, Dietetics, Hospitality and Event Management, Nutrition**)

Food Science courses are purely scientific and technical in their approach with the study of food composition and storage in order to monitor food quality, safety and preparation. Scientific elements cover biochemistry, chemistry and microbiology, focussing on human nutrition and, in some courses, dietetics, food processing and management. However, these courses are not to be confused with Culinary Arts subjects which lead to careers in food preparation. There are also several business courses specialising in food, such as Food Product Management and Marketing options. The unique course in this category, however, is the Viticulture and Oenology course offered at Plumpton College in partnership with the University of Brighton, which involves the study of grape growing and wine-making.

Useful websites www.sofht.co.uk; www.ifst.org; www.gov.uk/government/organisations/department-for-environment-food-rural-affairs; http://iagre.org

NB The points totals shown to the left of the institutions are for ease of reference only. It must not be assumed that Tariff points are always used by institutions or that they can be substituted for an offer in grades. The level of an offer is not necessarily indicative of the quality of a course.

COURSE OFFERS INFORMATION

Subject requirements/preferences GCSE English, mathematics and a science. **AL** One or two mathematics/science subjects; chemistry may be required. Some popular universities are now making lower offers for disadvantaged and other students.

Your target offers and examples of degree courses

128 pts **Leeds** – ABB incl sci/maths (Fd Sci) (HL 16 pts incl sci/maths)
Newcastle – ABB (Fd Bus Mgt Mark) (IB 32 pts); ABB–AAB incl biol/chem+STEM (Hum Nutr) (IB 32 pts HL 5 biol/chem+STEM); ABB–AAB incl sci (Nutr Fd Mark) (IB 32 pts HL 5 biol/chem+STEM)
Nottingham – ABB incl sci/maths+fd tech/econ/geog (Fd Sci Nutr) (IB 30 pts HL 655); (Fd Sci) (IB 30 pts HL 655 incl sci)
Reading – ABB incl sci/maths (Fd Sci; Fd Tech Bioproc; Nutr Fd Sci) (IB 32 pts HL 5 sci/maths)

120 pts **Liverpool John Moores** – BBB–ABB incl sci (Nutr)
Surrey – BBB–ABB incl biol/chem+sci/maths (Fd Sci Nutr) (IB 32–33 pts HL 5 biol/chem+maths/sci)

112 pts **Coventry** – BBC incl biol/chem/fd tech (Fd Sci) (IB 30 pts HL 5 biol/chem)
Northumbria – B incl sci/fd tech/hm econ 112 pts (Fd Sci Nutr)
Sheffield Hallam – BBC–BBB 112–120 pts (Fd Nutr)

104 pts **Bath Spa** – BCC–BBB (Fd Nutr) (IB 32 pts)

96 pts **Abertay** – CCC (Fd Consum Sci; Fd Sci Nutr Wlbng; Fit Nutr Hlth) (IB 27 pts)
CAFRE – 96 pts incl bus/sci (Sust Agri-Fd Mgt); 96 pts incl sci/hm econ (Fd Innov Mgt)
Cardiff Met – CC incl sci/fd tech 96–104 pts (Fd Sci Nutr) (HL 5 sci)
Teesside – 96 pts (Nutr)
Ulster – CCC incl sci/maths/env tech/hm econ (Fd Nutr) (IB 24 pts HL 12 pts incl 5 sci/maths/hm econ)

88 pts **Harper Adams** – 88–104 pts (Fd Bus Mgt) (IB 28 pts)

Glasgow Caledonian – HND biol/biomed sci/app sci BB (Fd Sci (Yr 3 Entry))

Alternative offers See **Chapter 6** and **Appendix 1** for grades/UCAS Tariff points information for other examinations.

DEGREE APPRENTICESHIPS

Harper Adams (Fd Ind Tech Prof); Lincoln (Fd Ind Tech Prof); Nottingham Trent (Fd Ind Tech Prof); Sheffield Hallam (Fd Ind Tech Prof).

EXAMPLES OF COLLEGES OFFERING COURSES IN THIS SUBJECT FIELD

Bridgwater and Taunton (Coll); CAFRE; Cornwall (Coll); Plumpton (Coll).

CHOOSING YOUR COURSE (SEE ALSO CH.1)

Universities and colleges teaching quality See www.qaa.ac.uk; www.discoveruni.gov.uk.

Top research universities and colleges (REF 2021) See **Agricultural Sciences/Agriculture**.

Examples of sandwich degree courses Cardiff Met; Coventry; Northumbria; Reading; Sheffield Hallam.

ADMISSIONS INFORMATION

Advice to applicants and planning the UCAS personal statement Visits, work experience or work shadowing in any food manufacturing firm, or visits to laboratories, should be described on your UCAS application. Keep up-to-date with developments by reading journals relating to the industry.

Selection interviews No Harper Adams.

Interview advice and questions Food science and technology is a specialised field and admissions tutors will want to know your reasons for choosing the subject. You will be questioned on any experience you have had in the food industry. More general questions may cover the reasons for the trends in the popularity of certain types of food, the value of junk food and whether scientific interference with food is justifiable. See also **Chapter 5**.

Reasons for rejection (non-academic) Too immature. Unlikely to integrate well. Lack of vocational commitment.

GRADUATE DESTINATIONS AND EMPLOYMENT

(See **Chapter 1, Graduate Outcomes.**)

Career note Employment levels for food science/studies and technology graduates are high mainly in manufacturing and retailing and increasingly with large companies.

OTHER DEGREE SUBJECTS FOR CONSIDERATION

Biochemistry; Biological Sciences; Biology; Biotechnology; Chemistry; Consumer Studies; Crop Science; Dietetics; Health Studies; Hospitality Management; Nutrition; Plant Science.

FRENCH

(see also **European Studies, Languages**)

Applicants should select courses according to the emphasis which they prefer. Courses could focus on literature or language (or both), or on the written and spoken word, as in the case of interpreting and translating courses, or on the broader study of French culture, political and social aspects found on European Studies courses.

Useful websites http://europa.eu; www.languageadvantage.com; www.languagematters.co.uk; www.ciol.org.uk; www.lemonde.fr; www.institut-francais.org.uk; www.academie-francaise.fr; www.institut-de-france.fr; www.sfs.ac.uk; https://academic.oup.com/fs

NB The points totals shown to the left of the institutions are for ease of reference only. It must not be assumed that Tariff points are always used by institutions or that they can be substituted for an offer in grades. The level of an offer is not necessarily indicative of the quality of a course.

COURSE OFFERS INFORMATION

Subject requirements/preferences GCSE French, mathematics (for business courses), grade levels may be stipulated. **AL** French is usually required at a specific grade and in some cases a second language may be stipulated. Some popular universities are now making lower offers for disadvantaged and other students.

Your target offers and examples of degree courses

152 pts **Edinburgh** – A*AA (Int Bus Fr/Ger/Span) (IB 39 pts HL 666)
Nottingham – A*AA (Econ Fr) (IB 36 pts HL 766)

144 pts **Bristol** – AAA incl hist (Hist Fr) (IB 36 pts HL 16 pts)
Durham – AAA incl lang (Modn Langs Cult (Yr Abrd)) (IB 37 pts HL 666 incl lang)
Edinburgh – AAA incl lang (Fr) (IB 34–37 pts HL 655–666 incl 5 lang)
Oxford – AAA incl Fr+interview+MLAT (Modn Langs (Fr)) (IB 38 pts HL 666 incl Fr)

136 pts **Bath** – AAB–ABB+aEPQ incl A Fr (Int Mgt Fr) (IB 36 pts HL 665 incl 6 Fr); AAB–ABB+aEPQ incl lang (Int Pol Modn Langs (Fr/Span/Ger) (Yr Abrd)) (IB 35 pts HL 665 incl lang)
Birmingham – AAB incl hist (Modn Langs Hist) (IB 32 pts HL 665 incl 6 hist)
Bristol – AAB (Fr Comb Hons) (IB 34 pts HL 17 pts)
London (King's) – AAB (Euro St (Fr/Ger/Span) (Yr Abrd); Mgt Modn Langs (Yr Abrd); Phil Modn Lang (Yr Abrd)) (IB 35 pts HL 17 pts); AAB incl hist (Fr Hist (Yr Abrd)) (IB 35 pts HL 17 pts incl hist)
Southampton – AAB/ABB+aEPQ incl Engl+Fr/Ger/Span (Engl Fr/Ger/Span) (IB 34 pts HL 17 pts incl 5 Engl+Fr/Ger/Span)
St Andrews – AAB incl A Fr (Fr courses) (IB 36 pts HL 665 incl 6 Fr)
Warwick – AAB incl Fr (Fr Comb Hons) (IB 34 pts HL 5 Fr)
York – AAB incl Fr (Fr Ling (Yr Abrd)) (IB 35 pts); (Fr Ital Lang (Yr Abrd); Fr Span Lang (Yr Abrd)) (IB 35 pts HL 6 Fr); AAB incl Fr+hist/class civ (Hist Fr) (IB 35 pts HL 6 Fr+hist); AAB incl Fr/Ger (Fr Ger (Yr Abrd)) (IB 35 pts HL 6 Fr/Ger)

128 pts **Bristol** – ABB (Hist Art Fr) (IB 32 pts HL 16 pts); ABB incl lang (Modn Langs) (IB 32 pts HL 16 pts incl 5 langs)
Dundee – ABB incl AB Engl+lang (Law Langs) (IB 32 pts HL 655 incl Engl)
Exeter – ABB (Class St Modn Langs; Modn Langs Arbc) (IB 32 pts HL 655); ABB incl Lat (Modn Langs Lat) (IB 32 pts HL 655 incl Lat); ABB–AAB incl Fr (Fr Arbc) (IB 32–34 pts HL 5 Fr)
Lancaster – ABB incl Fr (Fr St) (IB 32 pts HL 6 Fr)
Leeds – ABB incl Fr (Fr) (IB 34 pts HL 16 pts incl 5 Fr)
London (Inst Paris) – ABB incl Fr+interview (Fr St) (IB 32 pts HL 6 Fr)
London (King's) – ABB incl Fr (Mod Langs (Fr) (Yr Abrd)) (IB 33 pts HL 16 pts)
London (RH) – ABB–AAB (Modn Langs Mgt) (IB 32 pts HL 655)
London (UCL) – ABB incl A Fr (Fr As Af Lang) (IB 34 pts HL 16 incl 6 Fr); (Fr) (IB 34 pts HL 16 pts incl 6 Fr)
Manchester – ABB (Fr St) (IB 34 pts HL 655)
Newcastle – ABB incl Fr (Ling Fr) (IB 32 pts HL 5 Fr)
Nottingham – ABB incl Fr (Fr Comb Hons) (IB 30 pts HL 5 Fr); (Fr St) (IB 30 pts HL 655 incl Fr)
Queen's Belfast – ABB incl Fr (Fr; Fr Comb Hons) (IB 33 pts HL 655 incl 6 Fr)
Sheffield – ABB/BBB+bEPQ incl lang (Modn Langs Cult (Yr Abrd)) (IB 33 pts HL 5 lang)
Southampton – ABB incl langs (Modn Langs) (IB 32 pts HL 16 pts incl 55 langs)
Sussex – ABB (Anth Lang) (IB 34 pts)
Warwick – ABB incl A Fr/Ger/Ital/Span (Modn Langs) (IB 32 pts HL 6 Fr/Ger/Ital/Span); ABB incl Fr (Fr St) (IB 32 pts HL 5 Fr)

120 pts **Bangor** – 120–144 pts (Law Modn Langs)
Glasgow – BBB–AAB incl hum (Fr) (IB 34 pts HL 655 incl Engl/hum)
Kent – BBB (Modn Langs) (HL 566)

Leicester – BBB/BBC+bEPQ (Modn Langs Comb Hons) (IB 28 pts HL 6 lang); BBB–BBC+aEPQ incl Ital/lang (Modn Langs) (IB 28 pts HL 6 Ital/lang)
Liverpool – BBB incl Fr (Fr) (IB 30 pts HL 6 Fr)
London (QM) – BBB incl hum/soc sci (Fr courses) (IB 30 pts HL 555 incl hum/soc sci)
London (RH) – BBB–ABB (Modn Langs Lat) (IB 32 pts HL 655); BBB–ABB+gr 7 (Modn Langs Mus) (IB 32 pts HL 655); BBB–ABB incl lang (Modn Lang Dr) (IB 32 pts HL 655)
Reading – BBB (Modn Langs (Fr)) (IB 30 pts)
Stirling – BBB incl lang (Fr) (IB 28 pts)
Strathclyde – BBB–ABB incl Fr (Fr courses) (IB 30–32 pts)
Surrey – BBB (Modn Lang (Fr Span)) (IB 32 pts)

112 pts **Aberdeen** – BBC (Anth Fr/Ger; Fr courses) (IB 32 pts HL 555)
Cardiff – BBC–ABB (Modn Langs (Chin/Fr/Ger/Ita/Jap/Port/Span)) (IB 30–32 pts HL 655–665)
Essex – BBC–BBB 112–120 pts (Fr St Modn Langs) (IB 29–30 pts HL 554–555)
Heriot-Watt – BBC incl B lang (App Modn Langs Transl (Fr/Span/Ger/Chin)) (IB 30 pts HL 5 lang)
London (RH) – BBC–BBB (Modn Langs) (IB 30 pts HL 555)
Swansea – BBC–ABB 112–128 pts (Modn Langs) (IB 32 pts)

104 pts **Aberystwyth** – BCC–BBB 104–120 pts (Fr Comb Hons) (IB 28–30 pts HL 5 Fr)
Bangor – 104–128 pts (Modn Langs Hist); 104–128 pts incl modn lang (Modn Langs) (HL 5 incl modn lang)
Chester – BCC–BBC (Fr Comb Hons) (IB 28 pts)
London (Birk) – BCC 104 pts (Modn Langs (Fr/Ger/Ital/Jap/Span) (Yr Abrd))
Westminster – BCC–BBB 104–120 pts (Fr courses)

96 pts **Central Lancashire** – 96–112 pts incl lang (Modn Langs (2 Langs) (Fr/Span/Jap/Russ/Chin/Kor))
Portsmouth – CCC–BCC 96–104 pts (Modn Langs) (IB 25 pts)

Alternative offers See **Chapter 6** and **Appendix 1** for grades/UCAS Tariff points information for other examinations.

CHOOSING YOUR COURSE (SEE ALSO CH.1)

Universities and colleges teaching quality See www.qaa.ac.uk; www.discoveruni.gov.uk.

Top research universities and colleges (REF 2021) See **Languages**.

Examples of sandwich degree courses Bangor; Durham; London (King's); York.

ADMISSIONS INFORMATION

Advice to applicants and planning the UCAS personal statement Visits to France (including exchange visits) should be described, with reference to any particular cultural or geographical features of the region visited. Providing information about your contacts with French friends and experience in speaking the language are also important. Express your willingness to work/live/travel abroad and show your interests in French life and culture. Read French newspapers and magazines and keep up-to-date with news stories etc. See also **Appendix 3**.

Selection interviews **Yes** London (Inst Paris), Oxford (Modn Langs) 94% (success rate 44%); **Some** London (UCL); **No** Warwick.

Interview advice and questions Questions will almost certainly be asked on your A-level texts, in addition to your reading outside the syllabus – books, magazines, newspapers etc. Part of the interview may be conducted in French and written tests may be involved. See also **Chapter 5**.

Reasons for rejection (non-academic) Candidate unenthusiastic, unmotivated, ill-informed about the nature of the course (had not read the prospectus). Not keen to spend a year abroad.

GRADUATE DESTINATIONS AND EMPLOYMENT

(See **Chapter 1, Graduate Outcomes.**)

Career note See **Languages**.

OTHER DEGREE SUBJECTS FOR CONSIDERATION

European Studies; International Business Studies; Literature; other language.

GENETICS

(see also **Biological Sciences, Microbiology**)

Genetics is at the cutting edge of modern biology, as demonstrated by the recent developments in genomics and biotechnology leading to considerable advances in the treatment of disease and genetic engineering. Studies can cover such fields as genetic counselling, population genetics, pharmaceuticals, pre-natal diagnoses, cancer biology, evolution, forensic genetics, plant biology and food quality. Possibly an ideal option for keen science students looking for a degree allied to medicine.

Useful websites www.academic.oup.com/genetics; www.nature.com/subjects/genetics; www.genetics.org.uk; see also **Biological Sciences**.

NB The points totals shown to the left of the institutions are for ease of reference only. It must not be assumed that Tariff points are always used by institutions or that they can be substituted for an offer in grades. The level of an offer is not necessarily indicative of the quality of a course.

COURSE OFFERS INFORMATION

Subject requirements/preferences GCSE English, mathematics and science subjects. **AL** Chemistry and/or biology are usually required or preferred. Some popular universities are now making lower offers for disadvantaged and other students.

Your target offers and examples of degree courses

160 pts **Cambridge** – A*A*A incl sci/maths+interview+ESAT (Nat Sci (Genet)) (IB 41–42 pts HL 776)

144 pts **London (King's)** – AAA incl biol+chem (Mol Genet) (IB 36 pts HL 18 pts incl biol+chem)

136 pts **Leeds** – AAB–AAA incl biol+sci (Genet) (IB 31 pts HL 665 incl biol+sci)

Manchester – AAB–AAA incl sci/maths (Genet) (IB 35–36 pts HL 665–666 incl sci); AAB–AAA incl sci/maths+interview (Genet (Yr Ind)) (IB 35–36 pts HL 665–666 incl chem+sci); AAB–AAA incl sci/maths+lang (Genet Modn Lang) (IB 35–36 pts HL 665–666 incl sci+lang)

Newcastle – AAB incl biol/chem+sci/maths (Biomed Genet) (IB 34 pts HL 5 biol/chem+sci/maths)

York – AAB incl biol+sci/maths (Genet) (IB 35 pts HL 6 biol+sci/maths)

128 pts **East Anglia** – ABB incl biol (Mol Biol Genet) (IB 32 pts HL 5 biol)

Edinburgh – ABB–AAA incl biol+chem (Biol Sci (Genet)) (IB 32–37 pts HL 655–666)

Leicester – ABB incl sci/maths (Med Genet) (IB 30 pts HL 65 sci/maths); ABB–AAB incl sci/maths (Biol Sci (Genet)) (IB 30 pts HL 65 sci/maths)

London (QM) – ABB incl biol (Med Genet) (IB 32 pts HL 655 incl biol)

Sussex – ABB incl sci (Genet) (IB 32 pts HL 5 sci)

120 pts **Brunel** – BBB incl sci (Biomed Sci (Genet)) (IB 30 pts HL 5 sci)

Glasgow – BBB–AAB incl biol/chem (Genet) (IB 34 pts HL 655–665 incl 6 biol/chem)

112 pts **Essex** – BBC–BBB incl biol 112–120 pts (Genet) (IB 29–30 pts HL 554–555 incl biol)

London (RH) – BBC–BBB incl biol+sci (Genet) (IB 30 pts HL 555 incl biol+sci)

Swansea – BBC–AAB incl biol+chem 112–136 pts (Bioch Genet) (IB 32–34 pts HL biol+chem)

104 pts **Aberystwyth** – BCC–BBB incl B chem 104–120 pts (Genet Bioch) (IB 28–30 pts HL 5 chem); BCC–BBB incl biol 104–120 pts (Genet) (IB 28–30 pts HL 5 biol)

Huddersfield – BCC incl sci 104 pts (Med Genet)

Oxford Brookes – BCC–BBB incl sci 104–120 pts (Biol Sci Genet Gnm) (IB 29 pts)

Swansea – BCC–AAB incl biol+sci 104–136 pts (Genet; Med Genet) (IB 32–34 pts HL biol+sci)

Alternative offers See **Chapter 6** and **Appendix 1** for grades/UCAS Tariff points information for other examinations.

DEGREE APPRENTICESHIPS

East Anglia (App Biomed Sci); Manchester Met (Lab Sci); Wolverhampton (App Biomed Sci).

CHOOSING YOUR COURSE (SEE ALSO CH.1)

Universities and colleges teaching quality See www.qaa.ac.uk; www.discoveruni.gov.uk.

Top research universities and colleges (REF 2021) See **Biological Sciences**.

Examples of sandwich degree courses Brunel; Essex; Huddersfield; Leeds; Manchester; York.

ADMISSIONS INFORMATION

Advice to applicants and planning the UCAS personal statement See **Biological Sciences**.

Selection interviews Yes Cambridge; **No** Swansea.

Interview advice and questions Likely questions will focus on your A-level science subjects, particularly biology, why you wish to study genetics, and on careers in genetics. See also **Chapter 5**.

GRADUATE DESTINATIONS AND EMPLOYMENT

(See **Chapter 1, Graduate Outcomes.**)

Career note See **Biological Sciences**.

OTHER DEGREE SUBJECTS FOR CONSIDERATION

Biochemistry; Biological Sciences; Biology; Biotechnology; Human Sciences; Immunology; Life Sciences; Medical Biochemistry; Medical Biology; Medicine; Microbiology; Molecular Biology; Natural Sciences; Physiology; Plant Sciences.

GEOGRAPHY

(see also **Environmental Sciences**)

The content and focus of Geography courses will vary between universities, although many similarities exist between BA and BSc courses apart from entry requirements. For example, at the University of Birmingham, the course is flexible offering topics from migration and urban and social changes, to natural hazards and global environmental changes, with decisions on the paths to take between human and physical geography being delayed. At Leeds, the BA course focuses on human geography and the BSc course on physical aspects. This is a subject deserving real research between the offerings of a wide range of institutions in view of the variety of topics on offer, for example, rural, historical, political or cultural geography at Exeter, environmental geography and climate change at East Anglia, and physical oceanography as part of the BSc course at Plymouth.

Useful websites www.metoffice.gov.uk; www.rgs.org; www.ordnancesurvey.co.uk; http://geographical.co.uk; www.nationalgeographic.com; www.cartography.org.uk; www.gov.uk/government/organisations/natural-england; www.geography.org.uk; www.publicprofiler.org; www.esri.com/en-us/what-is-gis/overview

NB The points totals shown to the left of the institutions are for ease of reference only. It must not be assumed that Tariff points are always used by institutions or that they can be substituted for an offer in grades. The level of an offer is not necessarily indicative of the quality of a course.

COURSE OFFERS INFORMATION

Subject requirements/preferences GCSE Geography usually required. Mathematics/sciences often required for BSc courses. **AL** Geography is usually required for most courses. Mathematics/science subjects required for BSc courses. Some popular universities are now making lower offers for disadvantaged and other students.

YOUR TARGET OFFERS AND EXAMPLES OF DEGREE COURSES

152 pts **Cambridge** – A*AA+interview+GAA (Geog) (IB 41–42 pts HL 776)
Durham – A*AA (Comb Hons Soc Sci) (IB 38 pts HL 666); A*AA incl geog/sci (Geog courses) (IB 38 pts HL 666 incl geog/sci)
London (UCL) – A*AA incl A* maths (Geog Econ) (IB 39 pts HL 19 pts incl 7 maths)
Oxford – A*AA+interview (Geog) (IB 39 pts HL 766)

144 pts **London (UCL)** – AAA (Geog) (IB 38 pts HL 18 pts)
London LSE – AAA (Geog) (IB 38 pts HL 766); AAA incl maths (Geog Econ) (IB 38 pts HL 766 incl maths)
St Andrews – AAA (Geog) (IB 38 pts HL 666)

136 pts **Birmingham** – AAB (Geog) (IB 32 pts HL 665)
Bristol – AAB–AAA (Geog) (IB 34–36 pts HL 16–17 pts)
Exeter – AAB–AAA incl B hum/soc sci (Geog) (IB 34–36 pts HL 665–666 incl hum/soc sci)
Leeds – AAB incl hum/soc sci (Geog Trans St) (IB 35 pts HL 16 pts incl 5 hum/soc sci); AAB incl soc sci/hum (Geog courses) (HL 17/16 pts incl 5 soc sci/hum)
London (King's) – AAB (Geog) (IB 35 pts HL 17 pts)
Loughborough – AAB (Geog; Geog Econ; Geog Mgt; Geog Spo Sci) (IB 35 pts HL 665)
Manchester – AAB (Geog) (IB 35 pts HL 665)
Nottingham – AAB (Geog Bus) (IB 32 pts HL 665)
Sheffield – AAB–ABB+bEPQ (Geog) (IB 34 pts)
Southampton – AAB/ABB+aEPQ incl geog (Geog) (IB 34 pts HL 17 pts)
York – AAB incl geog/geol+sci/maths/env st/psy (Physl Geog Env) (IB 35 pts HL 6 geog/geol+sci/maths/env st/psy)

128 pts **Birmingham** – ABB (Geog Urb Reg Plan Comb Hons) (IB 32 pts HL 655)
Dundee – ABB incl geog (Geog) (IB 32 pts HL 655 incl sci)
East Anglia – ABB (Geog) (IB 32 pts); ABB incl geog/maths/econ/sci (Geog (Yr Ind)) (IB 32 pts HL 5 geog/maths/econ/sci)
Lancaster – ABB incl geog (Geog; Physl Geog) (IB 32 pts HL 16 pts incl 6 geog)
Leicester – ABB–BBB incl sci (Physl Geog Geol) (IB 30 pts HL 55 sci); ABB/BBB+bEPQ (Geog; Hum Geog) (IB 30 pts)
Liverpool – ABB incl geog/sci (Geog) (IB 33 pts)
London (QM) – ABB (Geog; Hum Geog) (IB 32 pts HL 655)
Newcastle – ABB incl geog (Geog Urb Plan) (IB 32 pts HL 5); ABB incl maths/sci (Geog) (IB 32 pts HL 6 maths/sci)
Nottingham – ABB (Arch Geog) (IB 30 pts HL 655)
Southampton – ABB (Popn Sci) (IB 32 pts HL 16 pts)
Sussex – ABB (Geog Anth) (IB 32 pts); ABB incl geog/sci (Geog) (IB 32 pts HL 5 geog/sci)

120 pts **Cardiff** – BBB–ABB (Hum Geog) (IB 31–34 HL 665–666)
Edinburgh – BBB–ABB incl geog/maths/sci (Earth Sci Physl Geog) (IB 30–32 pts HL 555–655 incl geog/maths/sci)
Glasgow – BBB–ABB incl sci (Geog) (IB 32–36 pts HL 555–665 incl sci)
Hull – BBB 120 pts (Geog) (IB 30 pts)
Keele – BBB (Geog (Physl/Hum)) (IB 30 pts HL 555)
London (RH) – BBB–ABB (Geog; Hum Geog) (IB 32 pts HL 655); (Physl Geog) (IB 32 pts HL 655)
Queen's Belfast – BBB incl geog (Geog) (IB 32 pts HL 655 incl geog)
Reading – BBB incl geog (Geog (Hum Physl); Geog (Hum); Geog (Physl)) (IB 30 pts); (Geog Econ (Reg Sci)) (IB 30 pts HL 4 maths)
Stirling – BBB incl sci/maths/geog (Env Geog Out Educ) (IB 28 pts HL sci/maths/geog)

112 pts **Aberdeen** – BBC incl maths/sci (Geog) (IB 32 pts HL 555 incl maths/sci)
Bangor – CC geog/sci/maths 112–128 pts (Physl Geog Ocean)
Brunel – BBC–ABB 112 pts (Geog) (IB 29 pts)
Canterbury Christ Church – BBC 112 pts (Geog) (IB 29 pts)
Cardiff – BBC–ABB (Hum Geog Plan) (IB 30–32 pts HL 655–665)
Chester – 112 pts (Geog) (IB 28 pts)

Coventry – BBC 112 pts (Disas Emer Mgt; Geog) (IB 29 pts)
Edge Hill – BBC incl geog/env sci (Geog); BBC–BBB incl geog/geol/env sci (Geol Physl Geog)
Gloucestershire – 112–128 pts (Geog courses)
Heriot-Watt – BBC (Geog) (IB 29 pts)
Hertfordshire – BBC–BBB 112–120 pts (Geog) (HL 44)
Leeds Beckett – 112 pts (Hum Geog) (IB 25 pts)
London (Birk) – BBC 112 pts (Geog)
Northumbria – 112 pts (Geog)
Nottingham Trent – 112 pts incl geog/sci (Geog)
Plymouth – 112–120 pts incl sci/maths/geog/tech (Physl Geog Geol) (IB 28–30 pts)
Portsmouth – BBC–BBB 112–120 pts (Geog) (IB 25 pts)
Sheffield Hallam – BBC–BBB 112–120 pts (Geog)
Swansea – BBC–ABB incl geog (Env Sci Clim Emer; Geog) (IB 32 pts HL 5 geog)
UWE Bristol – 112 pts (Geog)
Worcester – BBC 112 pts (Geog)

104 pts **Bangor** – 104–136 pts incl geog (Geog) (HL 5 geog)
Bath Spa – BCC–BBB incl geog/sociol/econ/sci (Geog) (IB 32 pts HL 6 geog/sociol/econ/sci)
Bournemouth – 104–120 pts (Geog) (IB 28–31 pts)
Brighton – BCC–BBB 104–120 pts (Geog) (IB 26 pts)
Liverpool Hope – BCC 104 pts (Geog) (IB 24 pts)
Liverpool John Moores – BCC–BBC incl sci/geog 104–112 pts (Geog)
Manchester Met – BCC–BBC incl geog 104–112 pts (Geog (St Abrd); Hum Geog (St Abrd)) (IB 26 pts HL 5 geog)
Northampton – BCC (Geog)
Oxford Brookes – BCC 104 pts (Geog) (IB 29 pts)
Plymouth – 104–112 pts (Geog) (IB 26–27 pts)
Ulster – BCC incl geog (Geog) (IB 24 pts HL 12 pts incl geog)
Winchester – BCC–BBB 104–120 pts (Geog) (HL 44)

96 pts **Aberystwyth** – CCC–BBB 96–120 pts (Geog; Hum Geog; Physl Geog) (IB 26–30 pts)
Kingston – 96–120 pts (Geog Comb Hons)

Open University – (Comb Soc Sci (Econ/Geog/Psy/Sociol); Geog Env Sci)

Alternative offers See **Chapter 6** and **Appendix 1** for grades/UCAS Tariff points information for other examinations.

CHOOSING YOUR COURSE (SEE ALSO CH.1)

Universities and colleges teaching quality See www.qaa.ac.uk; www.discoveruni.gov.uk.

Top research universities and colleges (REF 2021) (Geography and Environmental Studies) Durham; Bristol; Southampton; Glasgow; Oxford; Leeds; London (RH); London LSE; Exeter; Cambridge; London (UCL).

Examples of sandwich degree courses Brighton; Cardiff; Coventry; East Anglia; Hertfordshire; Kingston; Loughborough; Manchester Met; Northumbria; Nottingham Trent; Plymouth; Reading; Sheffield Hallam; Ulster.

ADMISSIONS INFORMATION

Advice to applicants and planning the UCAS personal statement Visits to, and field courses in, any specific geographical region should be fully described. Study your own locality in detail and get in touch with the area planning office to learn about any future developments. Read geographical magazines and describe any special interests you have – and why. Be aware of world issues and have travel experience.

Selection interviews Yes Cambridge, Oxford (65% (success rate 20%)); **No** East Anglia, London (RH), London (UCL), Manchester, Newcastle, Worcester.

Interview advice and questions Geography is a very broad subject and applicants can expect to be questioned on their syllabus and those aspects which they find of special interest. Some questions in the past have included: What fieldwork have you done? What are your views on ecology? What changes in the landscape have you noticed on the way to the interview? Explain in simple meteorological terms today's weather. Why are earthquakes almost unknown in Britain? What do you enjoy about geography and why? Are there any articles of geographical importance in the news at present? Discuss the current economic situation in Britain and give your views. Questions on the Third World, on world ocean currents and drainage and economic factors worldwide. What do you think about those people who consider global warming nonsense? Expect to comment on local geography and on geographical photographs and diagrams. See also **Chapter 5**.

Reasons for rejection (non-academic) Lack of awareness of the content of the course. Failure to attend interview. Poor general knowledge. Lack of geographical awareness.

GRADUATE DESTINATIONS AND EMPLOYMENT

(See **Chapter 1, Graduate Outcomes.**)

Career note Geography graduates enter a wide range of occupations, many in business and administrative careers. Depending on specialisations, areas could include agriculture, forestry, hydrology, transport, market research and retail. Teaching is also a popular option.

OTHER DEGREE SUBJECTS FOR CONSIDERATION

Agriculture; Anthropology; Civil Engineering; Countryside Management; Development Studies; Environmental Engineering/Science/Studies; Forestry; Geology; Geomatic Engineering; Surveying; Town Planning; Urban Land Economics; Urban Studies.

GEOLOGY/GEOLOGICAL SCIENCES

(including **Earth Sciences, Geophysics and Geoscience**; see also **Astronomy and Astrophysics, Environmental Sciences**)

Topics in Geology courses include the physical and chemical constitution of the earth, exploration geophysics, oil and marine geology (oceanography) and seismic interpretation. Earth Sciences covers geology, environmental science, physical geography and can also include business studies and language modules. No previous knowledge of geology is required for most courses.

Useful websites www.geolsoc.org.uk; www.bgs.ac.uk; www.noc.ac.uk; www.scicentral.com; http://britgeophysics.org

NB The points totals shown to the left of the institutions are for ease of reference only. It must not be assumed that Tariff points are always used by institutions or that they can be substituted for an offer in grades. The level of an offer is not necessarily indicative of the quality of a course.

COURSE OFFERS INFORMATION

Subject requirements/preferences GCSE English, mathematics and a science required. **AL** One or two mathematics/science subjects usually required. Geography may be accepted as a science subject. Some popular universities are now making lower offers for disadvantaged and other students.

Your target offers and examples of degree courses

160 pts **Cambridge** – A*A*A incl sci/maths+interview+ESAT (Nat Sci (Earth Sci)) (IB 41–42 pts HL 776)

152 pts **Oxford** – A*AA/AAAA+interview (Earth Sci (Geol)) (IB 39 pts HL 766)

144 pts **Durham** – AAA incl sci (Earth Sci (MSci)) (IB 37 pts HL 666 incl sci)

Imperial London – AAA incl maths+phys+interview (Geophys) (IB 38 pts HL 6 maths+phys); AAA incl sci/maths/geog+interview (Geol) (IB 38 pts HL 6 sci/maths/geog)

136 pts **Durham** – AAB incl sci (Geol; Geosci) (IB 36 pts HL 665 incl sci); AAB incl sci+maths (Geophys) (IB 36 pts HL 665 incl sci)

Leeds – AAB incl maths (Geophys Atmos Sci) (HL 16 pts incl 5 maths)
Leicester – AAB incl sci/maths/geog (Geol (MGeol)) (IB 30 pts HL 5 sci)
London (UCL) – AAB (Env Geosci) (IB 36 pts HL 17 pts); AAB incl maths+phys (Geophys) (IB 36 pts HL 17 pts incl maths+phys); AAB incl sci (Earth Sci; Geol) (IB 36 pts HL 17 pts incl sci); AAB incl sci/maths (Earth Sci (Int) (MSci)) (IB 36 pts HL 17 pts incl 5 sci/maths)
Manchester – AAB incl sci+interview (Earth Planet Sci) (IB 35 pts HL 665 incl sci)
St Andrews – AAB incl biol+sci/maths (Env Earth Sci) (IB 36 pts HL 665 incl maths/sci); AAB incl sci/maths/geog (Geol) (IB 36 pts HL 665 incl sci/maths/geog)

128 pts **Birmingham** – ABB incl sci (Geol; Geol (MSci)) (IB 32 pts HL 655)
Bristol – ABB incl maths/sci (Env Geosci; Geol) (IB 32 pts HL 16 pts incl 55 maths/sci)
Edinburgh – ABB–AAA incl maths+phys (Geophys; Geophys Meteor) (IB 32–34 pts HL 655 incl 6 maths+5 phys); (Geophys Geol) (IB 32–34 pts HL 655 incl maths+phys)
Exeter – ABB–AAB incl sci/geol (Geol) (IB 32 pts HL 655 incl sci); (Res Explor Geol) (IB 32 pts HL 655 incl sci/geol)
Lancaster – ABB incl sci (Earth Env Sci) (IB 32 pts HL 16 pts incl 6 sci)
Leeds – ABB incl sci/maths/geog (Geol) (HL 16 pts incl 5 maths/sci); (Env Geosci) (HL 16 pts incl 5 sci)
Leicester – ABB–BBB incl sci (Physl Geog Geol) (IB 30 pts HL 55 sci); ABB incl sci/maths/geog (Env Geosci) (IB 33 pts)
Liverpool – ABB/BBB+aEPQ incl maths+phys (Geol Geophys (MESci)) (IB 33 pts HL 4 maths+phys); ABB/BBB+aEPQ incl sci (Earth Sci (MESci); Env Geosci; Geol; Geol Physl Geog) (IB 33 pts HL 4 sci)

120 pts **Edinburgh** – BBB–ABB incl geog/maths/sci (Earth Sci Physl Geog) (IB 30–32 pts HL 555–655 incl geog/maths/sci); BBB–ABB incl maths/sci/geog (Earth Sci) (IB 30–32 pts HL 555–655 incl maths/sci/geog)
Keele – BBB (Geol Comb Hons) (IB 30 pts HL 555)
London (RH) – BBB–ABB incl sci (Geosci (MSci)) (IB 32 pts HL 655 incl sci); BBB–ABB incl sci/maths (Geol; Geol (Yr Ind)) (IB 32 pts HL 655 incl sci)
Southampton – BBB–ABB incl sci/maths/geog (Geol) (IB 32 pts HL 16 pts incl 5 sci)

112 pts **Aberdeen** – BBC incl maths/sci (Geol) (IB 32 pts HL 555 incl maths/sci)
Cardiff – BBC–ABB incl sci (Explor Geol; Explor Geol (MSci); Geol; Geol (MSci)) (IB 30–32 pts HL 655–665 incl sci)
Edge Hill – BBC–BBB incl geog/geol/env sci (Geol Physl Geog)
Plymouth – 112–120 pts incl sci/maths/geog (Geol) (IB 28–30 pts); 112–120 pts incl sci/maths/geog/tech (Physl Geog Geol) (IB 28–30 pts)
Portsmouth – BBC–BBB incl sci/maths/geog 112–120 pts (Earth Sci) (IB 25 pts)

104 pts **Bangor** – BC sci/maths/geog 120–144 pts incl sci/maths/geog (Geol Ocean) (HL 65 sci)
Cardiff – BCC–ABB incl sci (Env Geosci; Env Geosci (MSci)) (IB 29–32 pts HL 655–665 incl sci)
Glasgow – BCC–BBB incl B sci (Env Geosci) (IB 32 pts HL 555 incl sci)
London (Birk) – BCC 104 pts (Geol)

96 pts **Aberystwyth** – CCC–BBB incl sci 96–120 pts (Env Earth Sci) (IB 26–30 pts HL 5 sci)

Open University – (Nat Sci (Earth Sci))

Alternative offers See **Chapter 6** and **Appendix 1** for grades/UCAS Tariff points information for other examinations.

DEGREE APPRENTICESHIPS

Keele (Geosci).

CHOOSING YOUR COURSE (SEE ALSO CH.1)

Universities and colleges teaching quality See www.qaa.ac.uk; www.discoveruni.gov.uk.

Top research universities and colleges (REF 2021) See **Environmental Sciences**.

Examples of sandwich degree courses Cardiff; Leeds; London (RH); Portsmouth.

ADMISSIONS INFORMATION

Advice to applicants and planning the UCAS personal statement Visits to any outstanding geological sites and field courses you have attended should be described in detail. Apart from geological formations, you should also be aware of how geology has affected humankind in specific areas in the architecture of the region and artefacts used. Evidence of social skills could be given. See also **Appendix 3**.

Selection interviews Yes Cambridge, Imperial London, Manchester, Oxford (90% (success rate 25%)); **Some** Bristol (mature students and applicants with non-standard qualifications); **No** Edinburgh, London (RH).

Interview advice and questions Some knowledge of the subject will be expected and applicants could be questioned on specimens of rocks and their origins. Past interviews have included questions on the field courses attended, and the geophysical methods of exploration in the detection of metals. How would you determine the age of this rock (sample shown)? Can you integrate a decay curve function and would it help you to determine the age of rocks? How many planes of crystallisation could this rock have? What causes a volcano? What is your local geology? See also **Chapter 5**.

GRADUATE DESTINATIONS AND EMPLOYMENT

(See **Chapter 1, Graduate Outcomes.**)

Career note Areas of employment include mining and quarrying, the oil and gas industry, prospecting and processing.

OTHER DEGREE SUBJECTS FOR CONSIDERATION

Archaeology; Civil and Mining Engineering; Environmental Science; Geography; Meteorology; Oceanography; Physics.

GERMAN

(see also **European Studies, Languages**)

There are fewer Single Honours German courses than formerly, although the subject is offered jointly with other subjects, particularly other languages and business and management studies, at many universities. German courses range from those which focus on language and literature (eg Edinburgh), those which emphasise fluency of language and communication (eg Hull) and those offering translation studies (eg Heriot-Watt).

Useful websites www.goethe.de; www.ciol.org.uk; www.languageadvantage.com; www.languagematters.co.uk; www.faz.net; www.sueddeutsche.de; http://europa.eu; www.gslg.org.uk; https://womeningermanstudies.wordpress.com

NB The points totals shown to the left of the institutions are for ease of reference only. It must not be assumed that Tariff points are always used by institutions or that they can be substituted for an offer in grades. The level of an offer is not necessarily indicative of the quality of a course.

COURSE OFFERS INFORMATION

Subject requirements/preferences GCSE English and German are required. **AL** German required usually at a specified grade. Some popular universities are now making lower offers for disadvantaged and other students.

Your target offers and examples of degree courses

152 pts **Bristol** – A*AA/A*A*B incl Ger+LNAT (Law Ger) (IB 38 pts HL 18 pts incl 5 Ger)
Cambridge – A*AA incl lang+interview+MMLAA (Modn Mediev Langs) (IB 41–42 pts HL 776 incl lang)

Edinburgh – A*AA (Int Bus Fr/Ger/Span) (IB 39 pts HL 666)
Nottingham – A*AA (Econ Ger) (IB 36 pts HL 766)

144 pts **Birmingham** – AAA incl Ger (Law Ger Law) (IB 32 pts HL 666 incl Ger)
Bristol – AAA (Engl Ger) (IB 36 HL 18 pts incl 6 Engl)
Imperial London – AAA incl biol+sci/maths (Biol Sci Ger Sci) (IB 38 pts HL 6 biol+sci/maths)
Oxford – AAA+interview+MLAT (Modn Langs (Ger)) (IB 38 pts HL 666)

136 pts **Bath** – AAB/ABB+aEPQ incl A Ger (Int Mgt Ger) (IB 36 pts HL 665 incl 6 Ger); AAB–ABB+aEPQ incl lang (Int Pol Modn Langs (Fr/Span/Ger) (Yr Abrd)) (IB 35 pts HL 665 incl lang)
Birmingham – AAB incl hist (Modn Langs Hist) (IB 32 pts HL 665 incl 6 hist)
Bristol – AAB (Ger courses) (IB 34 pts HL 17 pts)
London (King's) – AAB (Euro St (Fr/Ger/Span) (Yr Abrd)) (IB 35 pts HL 17 pts)
Southampton – AAB/ABB+aEPQ incl Engl+Fr/Ger/Span (Engl Fr/Ger/Span) (IB 34 pts HL 17 pts incl 5 Engl+Fr/Ger/Span)
St Andrews – AAB (Ger courses) (IB 36 pts HL 665)
Warwick – AAB incl Engl lit+lang (Engl Ger) (IB 34 pts HL 5 Engl lit+lang); AAB incl lang (Ger Comb Hons) (IB 34 pts HL 5 lang)
York – AAB (Ger courses) (IB 35 pts); AAB incl Fr/Ger (Fr Ger (Yr Abrd)) (IB 35 pts HL 6 Fr/Ger)

128 pts **Birmingham** – ABB incl lang (Modn Langs (Yr Abrd)) (IB 32 pts HL 655)
Bristol – ABB incl lang (Modn Langs) (IB 32 pts HL 16 pts incl 5 langs)
Dundee – ABB incl AB Engl+lang (Law Langs) (IB 32 pts HL 655 incl Engl)
Edinburgh – ABB (Ger) (IB 34 pts HL 655)
Exeter – ABB (Class St Modn Langs) (IB 32 pts HL 655); ABB incl Lat (Modn Langs Lat) (IB 32 pts HL 655 incl Lat)
Lancaster – ABB (Ger St courses) (IB 32 pts HL 16 pts)
Leeds – ABB incl Ger (Ger courses) (IB 34 pts HL 16 pts incl 5 Ger)
London (King's) – ABB incl Ger (Modn Langs (Ger)) (IB 33 pts HL 16 pts)
London (QM) – ABB (Ger courses) (IB 32 pts HL 655)
London (RH) – ABB–AAB (Modn Langs Mgt) (IB 32 pts HL 655)
Manchester – ABB (Ger St; Ger courses) (IB 34 pts HL 655)
Nottingham – ABB (Ger; Ger Comb Hons) (IB 30 pts HL 655)
Sheffield – ABB/BBB+bEPQ incl lang (Modn Langs Cult (Yr Abrd)) (IB 33 pts HL 5 lang)
Southampton – ABB incl langs (Modn Langs) (IB 32 pts HL 16 pts incl 55 langs)
Sussex – ABB (Anth Lang) (IB 34 pts)
Warwick – ABB incl A Fr/Ger/Ital/Span (Modn Langs) (IB 32 pts HL 6 Fr/Ger/Ital/Span)

120 pts **Bangor** – 120–144 pts (Law Modn Langs)
Glasgow – BBB–AAB (Ger Comb Hons) (IB 34 pts HL 655 incl Engl+hum)
Kent – BBB (Modn Langs) (HL 566)
Leicester – BBB/BBC+bEPQ (Modn Langs Comb Hons) (IB 28 pts HL 6 lang)
Liverpool – BBB (Ger courses) (IB 30 pts HL 6 lang)
London (QM) – BBB (Ger Ling) (IB 30 pts HL 555); BBB incl hum/soc sci (Ger Compar Lit) (IB 30 pts HL 555 incl hum/soc sci)
London (RH) – BBB–ABB (Modn Langs Lat) (IB 32 pts HL 655); BBB–ABB+gr 7 (Modn Langs Mus) (IB 32 pts HL 655); BBB–ABB incl lang (Modn Lang Dr) (IB 32 pts HL 655)
Reading – BBB (Mod Langs (Ger)) (IB 30 pts)

112 pts **Aberdeen** – BBC (Anth Fr/Ger; Ger courses) (IB 32 pts HL 555)
Cardiff – BBC–ABB (Modn Langs (Chin/Fr/Ger/Ita/Jap/Port/Span)) (IB 30–32 pts HL 655–665)
Heriot-Watt – BBC incl B lang (App Modn Langs Transl (Fr/Span/Ger/Chin)) (IB 30 pts HL 5 lang)
London (RH) – BBC–BBB (Modn Langs) (IB 30 pts HL 555)
Swansea – BBC–ABB 112–128 pts (Modn Langs) (IB 32 pts)

104 pts **Aberystwyth** – BCC–BBB incl B Ger 104–120 pts (Ger Comb Hons) (IB 28–30 pts HL 5 Ger)
Bangor – 104–128 pts (Modn Langs Hist); 104–128 pts incl modn lang (Modn Langs) (HL 5 incl modn lang)
London (Birk) – BCC 104 pts (Modn Langs (Fr/Ger/Ital/Jap/Span) (Yr Abrd))

96 pts **Central Lancashire** – 96–112 pts incl lang (Modn Langs (2 Langs) (Fr/Span/Jap/Russ/Chin/Kor))
London (Birk) – CCC–ABB incl Ger 96–128 pts (Ger)
Portsmouth – CCC–BCC 96–104 pts (Modn Langs) (IB 25 pts)

Alternative offers See **Chapter 6** and **Appendix 1** for grades/UCAS Tariff points information for other examinations.

CHOOSING YOUR COURSE (SEE ALSO CH.1)

Universities and colleges teaching quality See www.qaa.ac.uk; www.discoveruni.gov.uk.

Top research universities and colleges (REF 2021) See **Languages**.

Examples of sandwich degree courses Bangor; London (King's).

ADMISSIONS INFORMATION

Advice to applicants and planning the UCAS personal statement Describe visits to Germany or a German-speaking country and the particular cultural and geographical features of the region. Contacts with friends in Germany and language experience should also be mentioned, and if you are bilingual, say so. Read German newspapers and magazines and keep up-to-date with national news.

Selection interviews Yes Cambridge, Oxford (Modn Langs) 94% (success rate 44%); **No** London (UCL), Sheffield, Swansea.

Interview advice and questions Questions asked on A-level syllabus. Part of the interview may be in German. What foreign newspapers and/or magazines do you read? Questions on German current affairs, particularly politics and reunification problems, books read outside the course, etc. See also **Chapter 5**.

Reasons for rejection (non-academic) Unstable personality. Poor motivation. Insufficient commitment. Unrealistic expectations. Not interested in spending a year abroad.

GRADUATE DESTINATIONS AND EMPLOYMENT

(See **Chapter 1, Graduate Outcomes.**)

Career note See **Languages**.

OTHER DEGREE SUBJECTS FOR CONSIDERATION

East European Studies; European Studies; International Business Studies.

GREEK

(see also **Classics and Classical Studies/Civilisation, Languages, Latin**)

Courses are offered in Ancient and Modern Greek, covering the language and literature from ancient times to the present day. Some Classics and Classical Studies courses (see separate tables) also provide the opportunity to study Greek from scratch.

Useful websites www.greek-language.com; www.greek-gods.org; www.fhw.gr; www.greeklanguage.gr

NB The points totals shown to the left of the institutions are for ease of reference only. It must not be assumed that Tariff points are always used by institutions or that they can be substituted for an offer in grades. The level of an offer is not necessarily indicative of the quality of a course.

COURSE OFFERS INFORMATION

Subject requirements/preferences GCSE English and a foreign language required. Greek required by some universities. **AL** Latin, Greek or a foreign language may be specified by some universities. Some popular universities are now making lower offers for disadvantaged and other students.

YOUR TARGET OFFERS AND EXAMPLES OF DEGREE COURSES

152 pts **Cambridge** – A*AA+interview (Modn Mediev Langs (Class Gk)) (IB 41–42 pts HL 776); A*AA incl Lat+interview+CAA (Class) (IB 41–42 pts HL 776 incl Lat)

144 pts **Oxford** – AAA+interview+MLAT (Modn Langs (Modn Gk)) (IB 38 pts HL 666)
St Andrews – AAA incl lang (Gk courses) (IB 36 pts HL 665 incl 6 lang)

136 pts **Edinburgh** – AAB (Anc Hist Gk; Gk St) (IB 36 pts HL 665)
London (UCL) – AAB incl A Gk+Engl (Gk Eng) (IB 36 pts HL 17 pts incl 6 Gk+Engl)

120 pts **Glasgow** – BBB–AAB incl hum (Gk) (IB 34 pts HL 655 incl Engl/hum)
London (RH) – BBB–ABB (Gk) (IB 32 pts HL 555)

ALTERNATIVE OFFERS See **Chapter 6** and **Appendix 1** for grades/UCAS Tariff points information for other examinations.

CHOOSING YOUR COURSE (SEE ALSO CH.1)

UNIVERSITIES AND COLLEGES TEACHING QUALITY See www.qaa.ac.uk; www.discoveruni.gov.uk.

TOP RESEARCH UNIVERSITIES AND COLLEGES (REF 2021) See **Classics and Classical Studies/Civilisation**.

EXAMPLES OF SANDWICH DEGREE COURSES Edinburgh; Glasgow; London (RH); St Andrews; Warwick.

ADMISSIONS INFORMATION

ADVICE TO APPLICANTS AND PLANNING THE UCAS PERSONAL STATEMENT See **Classics and Classical Studies/Civilisation**.

SELECTION INTERVIEWS **Yes** Cambridge, Oxford (Modn Langs) 94% (success rate 44%); **No** London (RH).

INTERVIEW ADVICE AND QUESTIONS Questions asked on A-level syllabus. Why do you want to study Greek? What aspects of this course interest you? (Questions will develop from answers.) See also **Chapter 5**.

REASONS FOR REJECTION (NON-ACADEMIC) Poor language ability.

GRADUATE DESTINATIONS AND EMPLOYMENT

(See **Chapter 1, Graduate Outcomes.**)

CAREER NOTE See **Languages**.

OTHER DEGREE SUBJECTS FOR CONSIDERATION

Ancient History; Classical Studies; Classics; European Studies; Philosophy.

HEALTH SCIENCES/STUDIES

(including **Deaf Studies, Nutrition, Orthoptics, Osteopathy, Paramedic Science, Prosthetics and Orthotics and Public Health**; see also **Community Studies/Development, Dietetics, Environmental Sciences, Nursing and Midwifery, Nutrition, Pharmacology, Pharmacy and Pharmaceutical Sciences, Physiotherapy, Radiography, Social Sciences/Studies, Speech Pathology/Sciences/Therapy**)

Health Sciences/Studies is a broad subject field which includes courses covering both practical applications concerning health and well-being (some of which border on nursing) and also the administrative activities involved in the promotion of health in the community. Also included are some specialised courses which include chiropractic, involving the healing process by way of manipulation, mainly in the spinal region, and osteopathy in which joints and tissues are manipulated to correct abnormalities. See **Physiotherapy**. Audiology is concerned with the treatment and diagnosis of hearing and balance disorders while prosthetics involves the provision and fitting of artificial limbs and orthotics is concerned with making and fitting braces, splints and special footwear to ease pain and to assist movement.

Useful websites www.rsph.org.uk; www.bmj.com; www.aor.org.uk; www.baap.org.uk; https://chiropractic-uk.co.uk; www.osteopathy.org.uk; www.who.int; www.csp.org.uk; www.baaudiology.org; www.thebsa.org.uk; www.healthcareers.nhs.uk; www.gcc-uk.org; www.uco.ac.uk; www.osteopathy.org.uk; www.collegeofparamedics.co.uk

NB The points totals shown to the left of the institutions are for ease of reference only. It must not be assumed that Tariff points are always used by institutions or that they can be substituted for an offer in grades. The level of an offer is not necessarily indicative of the quality of a course.

COURSE OFFERS INFORMATION

Subject requirements/preferences GCSE English, mathematics and a science important or essential for some courses. **AL** Mathematics, chemistry or biology may be required for some courses. Some popular universities are now making lower offers for disadvantaged and other students. **Other** Health checks and Disclosure and Barring Service (DBS) clearance required for many courses. (Paramed Sci) Full clean manual UK driving licence with at least a provisional C1 category required by some universities.

Your target offers and examples of degree courses

136 pts **Durham** – AAB (Hlth Hum Sci) (IB 36 pts HL 665)

128 pts **Aston** – ABB incl biol/phys (Hlthcr Sci (Audiol)) (IB 32 pts HL 655 incl biol/phys)
Brighton – ABB incl sci/soc sci+interview (Paramed Sci) (IB 32 pts)
East Anglia – ABB incl biol/chem/PE+interview (Paramed Sci) (IB 32 pts HL 5 sci)
Huddersfield – ABB incl sci 128 pts+interview (Paramed Sci)
Leeds – ABB incl sci/maths+interview (Audiol) (IB 34 pts HL 555 incl sci/maths)
London (UCL) – ABB (Popn Hlth Sci) (IB 34 pts HL 16 pts)
Manchester – ABB incl sci/maths/psy+interview (Hlthcr Sci (Audiol)) (IB 34 pts HL 655 incl sci/maths/psy)
Southampton – ABB incl sci (Audiol) (IB 32 pts HL 16 pts incl 5 sci); (Crdc Physiol) (IB 32 pts HL 16 pts incl sci)
Surrey – ABB+interview (Paramed Sci) (IB 33 pts HL 555 incl sci)

120 pts **Bournemouth** – 120–128 pts (Med Sci) (IB 31–33 pts HL 55)
Brunel – BBB incl sci (Biomed Sci (Hum Hlth)) (IB 30 pts HL 5 sci)
City St George's – BBB incl biol+sci/maths+interview (Hlthcr Sci (Physiol Sci)) (IB 32 pts HL 15 pts incl 5 biol); BBB incl sci+interview (Paramed Sci) (IB 30 pts HL 14 pts incl 5 biol/chem)
Dundee – BBB incl biol+interview (Oral Hlth Sci) (IB 30 pts HL 555 incl biol)
HSU – BBB incl biol+sci (MChiro) (IB 34 pts HL 5 biol+sci)
Liverpool – BBB incl sci/maths+interview (Orth) (IB 30 pts HL 6 biol)
Middlesex – C sci 120 pts+interview (Hlthcr Sci (Audiol))
Portsmouth – BBB incl sci 120 pts+interview (Paramed Sci) (IB 25 pts)
Salford – BBB incl maths/phys/eng 120 pts (Pros Orthot) (IB 28 pts)
Sheffield – BBB incl sci+interview (Orth) (IB 32 pts HL 5 sci)
Strathclyde – BBB–ABB incl maths+sci (Pros Orthot) (IB 32–34 pts HL 5 maths/phys)
Swansea – BBB incl biol sci/physl educ+interview (Ost) (IB 32 pts); BBB incl sci/maths+interview (Hlthcr Sci (Audiol))
Worcester – BBB incl sci 120 pts+interview (Paramed Sci)

112 pts **BCNO Group** – BBC 112 pts incl sci+interview (Ost Med); BBC incl sci/PE/psy 112 pts incl sci+interview (Ost) (IB 32 pts HL 55 sci)
Bournemouth – 112–128 pts incl sci/physl educ+interview (Paramed Sci)
Bradford – BBC incl biol+chem 112 pts (Clin Sci) (HL 56 biol+chem)
Canterbury Christ Church – BBC 112 pts (Hlth Lfstl Sci; Mntl Hlth Wlbng; Pblc Hlth) (IB 29 pts); BBC 112 pts+interview (Paramed Sci) (IB 29 pts)
Cardiff Met – 112–120 pts (Biomed Sci Hlth Exer Nutr) (HL 56 incl biol+sci); BBC incl biol+sci 112 pts+interview (Hlthcr Sci) (HL 56 biol+sci)
East London – 112 pts (Publc Hlth) (IB 24 pts HL 15 pts)
Greenwich – 112 pts (Pblc Hlth)
HSU – BBC incl biol+sci (MOst)

Hertfordshire – BBC–BBB incl sci 112–120 pts (Paramed Sci)
Keele – BBC 112 pts (Hlth Soc Cr) (IB 29 pts HL 554)
Kingston – C sci/psy/PE 112–128 pts (Spo Exer Sci (Nutr))
Liverpool John Moores – BBC 112 pts (Hlth Soc Cr)
London Met – BBC 112 pts (Hlth Soc Cr)
Marjon – BBC incl biol 112 pts+interview (Ost Med (MOst))
Nottingham Trent – 112 pts incl sci/PE (Spo Sci Hlth Nutr)
Plymouth – BBC–ABB incl sci 112–128 pts+interview (Paramed Sci) (IB 28–32 pts HL 5 biol/chem)
Robert Gordon – BCC+interview (Paramed) (IB 28 pts)
South Wales – BBC incl B biol+sci/maths (MChiro)
Swansea – BBC–BBB (Hlth Soc Cr) (IB 30–32 pts)
UWE Bristol – 112 pts incl sci/soc sci+interview (Paramed Sci) (IB 25 pts HL 6 sci/soc sci)
Ulster – BBC (Hlth Soc Cr Plcy) (IB 25 pts HL 12 pts)
West London – BBC 112 pts (Pblc Hlth)

104 pts **Edge Hill** – BCC–BBC 104–112 pts (Hlth Soc Cr)
Glasgow Caledonian – BCC incl biol+interview (Paramed Sci); BCC incl sci (Orth)
Liverpool Hope – BCC 104 pts (Hlth Wlbng Comb Hons) (IB 24 pts)
Solent – 104–120 pts incl sci (Hlth Nutr Exer Sci)
UHI – BCC incl sci+interview (Oral Hlth Sci)
West Scotland – BCC incl biol 104 pts (Coll Hlth Soc Cr) (IB 24 pts HL biol)

96 pts **Bangor** – 96–112 pts (Hlth Soc Cr)
Cardiff Met – 96 pts (Hlth Soc Cr)
Derby – CCC 96 pts (Hlth Soc Cr)
Greater Manchester – 96 pts+interview (Hlth Soc Cr); 96 pts incl biol+interview (Med Biol)
Lincoln – 96 pts (Hlth Soc Cr) (IB 27 pts)
Nescot – 96 pts incl sci (Ost Med)
Nottingham Trent – 96 pts (Hlth Soc Cr)
Sunderland – 96–112 pts (Hlth Soc Cr)
Teesside – 96–112 pts incl sci (Hlth Sci)
Ulster – CCC incl sci/maths (Hlth Physiol)
Wolverhampton – CCC/BCD 96 pts (Df St courses; Hlth Soc Cr; Hlth Wlbng)

88 pts **Bucks New** – 88–112 pts (Hlth Soc Sci)
Trinity Saint David – 88 pts (Hlth Soc Cr)
Winchester – CCD–BCC 88–104 pts (Hlth Soc Cr)

80 pts **Anglia Ruskin** – 80 pts (Pblc Hlth)

64 pts **UHI** – CC (Hlth Soc St)

Open University – (Hlth Soc Cr)

Alternative offers See **Chapter 6** and **Appendix 1** for grades/UCAS Tariff points information for other examinations.

DEGREE APPRENTICESHIPS

Aston (Hlthcr Sci (Audiol)); Brighton (Advnc Clin Practnr, Asst Practnr); Chester (Advnc Clin Prac); Essex (Snr Ldr (Hlth Soc Cr), Asst Practnr, Advnc Clin Prac); Exeter (Snr Ldr Hlthcr); Gloucestershire (Hlthcr Sci (Vasc Sci)); Huddersfield (Advnc Clin Prac, Paramed Sci); Kent (Clin Trials Spec); Manchester Met (Hlthcr Sci Practnr); Sheffield Hallam (Hlthcr Sci Practnr, Oprtg Dep Practnr, Enhcd Clin Practnr (Paramed), Advnc Clin Practnr); UWE Bristol (Pblc Hlth Practnr); York (Advnc Clin Practnr).

EXAMPLES OF COLLEGES OFFERING COURSES IN THIS SUBJECT FIELD

Accrington and Rossendale (Coll); Bedford (Coll); Blackburn (Coll); Blackpool and Fylde (Coll); Bradford College (UC); Bridgwater and Taunton (Coll); Bristol City (Coll); Buckinghamshire (Coll Group); Chesterfield (Coll); City of Oxford (Coll); Cornwall (Coll); Doncaster (Coll); Duchy Coll (UC); Durham New (Coll); Exeter (Coll); Grŵp Llandrillo Menai; Hugh Baird (Coll); Hull (Coll); Leeds City (Coll); Lincoln (Coll); London South East (Coll); Manchester (Coll); Myerscough (Coll); Newcastle (Coll); Norwich City

(Coll); Petroc; Sir Gâr (Coll); South and West Cheshire (Coll); Sparsholt (Coll); St Helens (Coll); Stockport (Coll); TEC Partnership; Tresham (CFHE); Truro and Penwith (Coll); Wakefield (Coll); Warwickshire (Coll); Westminster City (Coll); Weston (Coll); Wigan and Leigh (Coll); York (Coll).

CHOOSING YOUR COURSE (SEE ALSO CH.1)

Universities and colleges teaching quality See www.qaa.ac.uk; www.discoveruni.gov.uk.

Top research universities and colleges (REF 2021) (Public Health, Health Services and Primary Care) Imperial London; Cambridge; Bristol; Oxford; Birmingham; London (UCL); Southampton; Aberdeen; York; Liverpool.

ADMISSIONS INFORMATION

You should describe any work with people you have done, particularly in a caring capacity, for example, working with the elderly, nursing, hospital work. Show why you wish to study this subject. You should give evidence of your ability to communicate and to work in a group. Evidence needed of applicants' understanding of the NHS and health care systems. Osteopathy applicants should provide clear evidence of why they want to work as an osteopath: work shadowing in an osteopath's practice is important and should be described. Give details of any work using your hands. **City St George's** Work experience required.

Selection interviews Yes BCNO Group, Bournemouth, Brighton, Canterbury Christ Church, Cardiff Met, City St George's, Dundee, East Anglia, Glasgow Caledonian, Greater Manchester, Huddersfield (Paramed Sc), Leeds, Liverpool, Manchester, Marjon, Middlesex, Plymouth, Portsmouth, Robert Gordon, Sheffield, Southampton, Surrey, Swansea, Trinity Saint David, UHI, UWE Bristol; **No** Anglia Ruskin.

Interview advice and questions Courses vary considerably and you are likely to be questioned on your reasons for choosing the course at that university or college. If you have studied biology, then questions on the A-level syllabus are possible and you could also be asked to discuss any work experience you have had. (Ost) What personal qualities would you need to be a good osteopath? What have you done that you feel demonstrates a sense of responsibility? What would you do if you were not able to secure a place on an Osteopathy course this year? See also **Chapter 5**.

Reasons for rejection (non-academic) Some students are mistakenly looking for a professional qualification in, for example, occupational therapy or nursing.

GRADUATE DESTINATIONS AND EMPLOYMENT

(See **Chapter 1, Graduate Outcomes.**)

Career note Graduates enter a very broad variety of careers depending on their specialism. Opportunities exist in the public sector, for example, management and administrative positions with health and local authorities and in health promotion.

OTHER DEGREE SUBJECTS FOR CONSIDERATION

Audiology; Biological Sciences; Biology; Community Studies; Consumer Studies; Dentistry; Dietetics; Medicine; Environmental Health; Nursing; Nutrition; Occupational Therapy; Optometry; Physiotherapy; Psychology; Podiatry; Radiography; Speech Therapy; Sport Science.

HISTORY

(including **Heritage Studies and Medieval Studies**; see also **History (Ancient), History (Economic and Social), History of Art**)

Degrees in History cover a very broad field with many courses focusing on British and European history. However, specialised History degrees are available which cover other regions of the world and all courses will offer a wide range of modules.

USEFUL WEBSITES www.english-heritage.org.uk; www.historytoday.com; www.archives.com; www.historynet.com; www.archives.org.uk; http://royalhistsoc.org; www.nationalarchives.gov.uk; www.history.ac.uk

NB The points totals shown to the left of the institutions are for ease of reference only. It must not be assumed that Tariff points are always used by institutions or that they can be substituted for an offer in grades. The level of an offer is not necessarily indicative of the quality of a course.

COURSE OFFERS INFORMATION

SUBJECT REQUIREMENTS/PREFERENCES GCSE English and a foreign language may be required or preferred. **AL** History usually required at a specified grade. (Mediev St) History or English Literature required for some courses. Some popular universities are now making lower offers for disadvantaged and other students.

YOUR TARGET OFFERS AND EXAMPLES OF DEGREE COURSES

152 pts **Cambridge** – A*AA+interview+HAA (Hist) (IB 40–42 pts HL 776)
Durham – A*AA incl hist (Hist) (IB 38 pts HL 666 incl hist)
Edinburgh – A*AA (Hist; Hist Pol) (IB 39 pts HL 666)

144 pts **Bristol** – AAA incl hist (Hist Fr) (IB 36 pts HL 16 pts); (Hist) (IB 36 pts HL 18 pts incl 6 hist)
Leeds – AAA incl hist (Hist) (IB 35 pts HL 17 pts incl 6 hist)
London (King's) – AAA incl hist (Hist) (IB 35 pts HL 666 incl hist); (War St Hist) (IB 38 pts HL 18 pts)
London (UCL) – AAA incl hist (Hist; Hist (Yr Abrd)) (IB 38 pts HL 18 pts incl 6 hist)
London LSE – AAA (Hist; Int Rel Hist; Pol Hist) (IB 38 pts HL 766)
Manchester – AAA incl hist (Hist) (IB 36 pts HL 666 incl hist); AAA incl hist/pol/gov (Pol Modn Hist) (IB 36 pts HL 666 incl hist/pol/gov)
Nottingham – AAA incl Engl+hist (Engl Hist) (IB 36–34 pts HL 6 Engl+hist)
Oxford – AAA (Class Arch Anc Hist) (IB 39 pts HL 666); AAA+interview+HAT (Anc Modn Hist; Hist; Hist Pol) (IB 38 pts HL 666); AAA+interview+HAT+MLAT (Hist Modn Langs) (IB 38 pts HL 666); AAA+interview+HAT+TSA (Hist Econ) (IB 38 pts HL 666)
St Andrews – AAA incl hist (Mediev Hist Arch; Mediev Hist courses; Modn Hist courses; Scot Hist courses) (IB 38 pts HL 666 incl hist)
Warwick – AAA incl hist (Hist) (IB 36 pts HL 6 hist)
York – AAA/A*AB incl hist (Hist) (IB 36 pts HL 6 hist); AAA incl Engl+hist (Engl Hist) (IB 36 pts HL 666 incl Engl+hist)

136 pts **Birmingham** – AAB incl hist (Hist Comb Hons) (IB 32 pts HL 665); (Modn Langs Hist) (IB 32 pts HL 665 incl 6 hist)
East Anglia – AAB (Hist) (IB 33 pts); (Modn Hist) (IB 33 pts HL 5 hist); AAB incl Engl/hist (Lit Hist) (IB 33 pts HL 5 Engl/hist)
Exeter – AAB (Hist; Hist (Emp Expnc)) (IB 34 pts HL 665)
Lancaster – AAB (Hist; Hist Int Rel; Hist Phil; Hist Pol; Mediev Ely Modn St) (IB 35 pts HL 16 pts)
Leeds – AAB incl hist (Hist Phil) (IB 35 pts HL 16 pts incl 6 hist)
London (King's) – AAB incl hist (Fr Hist (Yr Abrd)) (IB 35 pts HL 17 pts incl hist)
London (UCL) – AAB (Hist Phil Sci) (IB 36 pts HL 17 pts)
NU London – AAB+interview (Hist courses) (IB 35 pts HL 665)
Newcastle – AAB incl hist (Hist) (IB 34 pts HL 6 hist)
Nottingham – AAB incl A hist (Hist) (IB 34 pts HL 6 hist)
Sheffield – AAB incl hist/class civ (Hist Comb Hons) (IB 34 pts HL 5 hist); AAB–ABB+bEPQ incl hist/class civ (Hist; Hist Pol) (IB 34 pts HL 6 hist)
Southampton – AAB incl hist (Hist; Modn Hist Pol) (IB 34 pts HL 17 pts incl 5 hist)
York – AAB incl Fr+hist/class civ (Hist Fr) (IB 35 pts HL 6 Fr+hist)

128 pts **East Anglia** – ABB (Hist Pol) (IB 32 pts HL 5 hist); ABB/ABC–BBB+aEPQ incl hist (Am Hist) (IB 32 pts HL 5 hist)
Edinburgh – ABB (Archit Hist Herit; Celt Scot Hist) (IB 34 pts HL 655)
Exeter – ABB–AAB (Hist Int Rel; Hist Pol) (IB 32–34 pts HL 655–665)

Leeds – ABB incl biol (Biol Hist Phil Sci) (IB 34 pts HL 16 pts incl 6 biol)
Leicester – ABB–BBB+bEPQ (Anc Hist Hist) (IB 30 pts); (Hist; Hist Am St; Modn Contemp Hist) (IB 30 pts HL 6)
Liverpool – ABB (Hist) (IB 33 pts)
London (QM) – ABB incl hist (Hist; Hist Pol; Mediev Hist) (IB 32 pts HL 655 incl hist)
London (RH) – ABB–AAB (Hist) (IB 32 pts HL 655)
London (SOAS) – ABB (Hist) (IB 33 pts HL 555)
London (UCL) – ABB incl hist (Russ Hist) (IB 34 pts HL 16 pts incl 5 hist)
Loughborough – ABB (Hist; Hist Int Rel; Hist Pol) (IB 34 pts HL 655)
Manchester – ABB incl hist (Hist courses) (IB 34 pts HL 655 incl 6 hist)
Nottingham – ABB incl A hist (Anc Hist Hist) (IB 30 pts HL 655); ABB incl hist (Hist Contemp Chin St; Hist E Euro Cult St) (IB 32 pts HL 5 hist)
Queen's Belfast – ABB (Hist courses) (IB 33 pts HL 655)
Southampton – ABB (Engl Hist) (IB 32 pts HL 16 pts); ABB incl hist (Flm Hist; Phil Hist) (IB 32 pts HL 16 pts incl 5 hist)

120 pts **Aberdeen** – BBB (Hist) (IB 32 pts HL 555)
Cardiff – BBB–ABB (Hist) (HL 665 incl 6 hist); (Pol Modn Hist) (IB 31–32 pts HL 665)
Dundee – BBB (Hist; Scot Hist St) (IB 30 pts HL 555)
Glasgow – BBB–AAB (Hist; Scot Hist) (IB 34 pts HL 655 incl Engl+hum)
Hull – BBB (Hist) (IB 30 pts)
Kent – BBB incl hist/hum (Hist courses; Mltry Hist)
Leicester – BBB–BBC+bEPQ (Int Rel Hist) (IB 28 pts)
London (Gold) – BBB (Hist; Hist Pol) (IB 33 pts HL 655)
Reading – BBB incl hist (Hist; Modn Langs Hist) (IB 30 pts HL 5 hist)
Stirling – BBB (Hist; Scot Hist) (IB 30 pts)
Strathclyde – BBB–ABB (Hist) (IB 30 pts)
Sussex – BBB–ABB (Hist; Hist Comb Hons) (IB 30–32 pts)

112 pts **Brunel** – BBC–ABB (Mltry Int Hist) (IB 29 pts)
Buckingham – BBC–BBB (Hist Pol) (IB 31–32 pts)
Canterbury Christ Church – BBC 112 pts (Hist) (IB 29 pts)
Chichester – 112 pts (Hist)
City St George's – BBC (Hist) (IB 29 pts HL 555)
Coventry – BBC (Hist Pol) (IB 29–31 pts)
De Montfort – 112 pts incl hist (Hist) (IB 26 pts)
Derby – BBC–BBB incl hist/pol/class st 112–120 pts (Hist)
Edge Hill – BBC–BBB 112–120 pts (Hist; Hist Pol)
Essex – BBC (Hist; Modn Hist) (IB 29 pts HL 554)
Hertfordshire – BBC–BBB 112–120 pts (Hist)
Keele – BBC (Hist) (IB 29 pts)
Leeds Beckett – 112 pts (Hist)
Liverpool Hope – BBC 112 pts (Hist) (IB 28 pts)
Liverpool John Moores – BBC 112 pts (Hist)
London (Birk) – BBC 112 pts (Pol Phil Hist)
Northumbria – 112 pts (Hist; Hist Pol)
Nottingham Trent – 112 pts (Hist; Hist Pol)
Sheffield Hallam – BBC 112 pts (Hist)
Suffolk – BBC incl hist 112 pts (Hist)
Swansea – BBC 112–128 pts (Hist) (IB 32 pts)
UWE Bristol – 112 pts (Hist)

104 pts **Bangor** – 104–128 pts (Herit Arch Hist; Hist; Mediev Ely Modn Hist; Modn Contemp Hist)
Bath Spa – BCC–BBB incl hist (Hist) (IB 32 pts HL 5 hist)
Central Lancashire – 104–112 pts (Hist)
Chester – BCC–BBC incl hist/class civ/pol/sociol 104–112 pts (Hist) (IB 26 pts HL 5 hist)
Greenwich – BCC 104 pts (Hist)
Huddersfield – BCC–BBB incl hist 104–120 pts+interview (Hist)

Lincoln – (Engl Hist)
Manchester Met – 104–112 pts (Hist Comb Hons) (IB 26 pts); BCC–BBC 104–112 pts (Hist) (IB 26 pts)
Northampton – BCC incl hist (Hist courses)
Oxford Brookes – BCC 104 pts (Hist) (IB 29 pts)
Plymouth – 104–112 pts (Pol) (IB 26–28 pts); B hist/class civ/econ/law 104–112 pts (Hist courses) (IB 26–28 pts HL 5 hist/class civ/econ/law)
Portsmouth – 104–120 pts incl hist (Hist) (IB 25 pts); BCC–BBC 104–112 pts (Hist Am St) (IB 25 pts)
Roehampton – 104–120 pts (Hist)
South Wales – BCC 104 pts (Hist)
Westminster – BCC–BBB incl Engl/hum 104–120 pts (Engl Lit Hist)
Winchester – 104–120 pts (Hist; Mediev Hist) (HL 44)
Worcester – 104–112 pts (Hist courses)
York St John – 104 pts (Hist)

96 pts **Aberystwyth** – CCC–BBB 96–120 pts (Cult Herit St Lib Archv Musm) (IB 26–30 pts); CCC–BBB 96–120 pts (Hist; Hist Welsh Hist; Mediev Ely Modn Hist; Modn Contemp Hist) (IB 26–30 pts)
Anglia Ruskin – 96 pts (Hist) (IB 24 pts)
Birmingham Newman – 96 pts (Hist)
Bishop Grosseteste – 96–112 pts (Arch Hist; Hist courses)
Gloucestershire – CCC–BBC 96–112 pts (Hist)
London (Birk) – CCC–BBB 96–120 pts (Hist)
St Mary's – CCC–BBC 96–112 pts (Hist)
Teesside – 96–112 pts (Hist)
Wolverhampton – CCC/BCD 96 pts (Hist; Pol Hist)

72 pts **UHI** – BC (Hist Arch; Hist Pol)

Trinity Saint David – interview (Hist courses)

ALTERNATIVE OFFERS See **Chapter 6** and **Appendix 1** for grades/UCAS Tariff points information for other examinations.

EXAMPLES OF COLLEGES OFFERING COURSES IN THIS SUBJECT FIELD

North Lindsey (Coll); Peterborough (UC); South Devon (Coll); Truro and Penwith (Coll).

CHOOSING YOUR COURSE (SEE ALSO CH.1)

UNIVERSITIES AND COLLEGES TEACHING QUALITY See www.qaa.ac.uk; www.discoveruni.gov.uk.

EXAMPLES OF SANDWICH DEGREE COURSES Bangor; London (King's) (Hist Modn Lang); London (UCL); Plymouth.

ADMISSIONS INFORMATION

ADVICE TO APPLICANTS AND PLANNING THE UCAS PERSONAL STATEMENT Show your passion for the past! Visits to places of interest should be mentioned, together with any particular features which impressed you. Read historical books and magazines outside your A-level syllabus. Mention these and describe any special areas of study which interest you. (Check that these areas are covered in the courses for which you are applying!)

SELECTION INTERVIEWS **Yes** Cambridge, Huddersfield, London (Gold), Oxford (Hist) 71% (success rate 24%), (Hist Econ) 37% (success rate 10%), (Hist Modn Lang) 84% (success rate 26%), (Hist Pol) 37% (success rate 11%); **Some** Bristol (mature students and applicants with non-standard qualifications), Cardiff, Sheffield Hallam (mature students and applicants with non-standard qualifications); **No** Anglia Ruskin, Bishop Grosseteste, Canterbury Christ Church, Chichester, De Montfort, East Anglia, London (RH), London (UCL), Plymouth, Warwick, Winchester.

Interview advice and questions Questions are likely to be asked on those aspects of the history A-level syllabus which interest you. Examples of questions in previous years have included: Why did imperialism happen? If a Martian arrived on Earth what aspect of life would you show him/her to sum up today's society? Has the role of class been exaggerated by Marxist historians? What is the difference between power and authority and between patriotism and nationalism? Did Elizabeth I have a foreign policy? What is the relevance of history in modern society? Who are your favourite monarchs? How could you justify your study of history to the taxpayer? See also **Chapter 5**.

Reasons for rejection (non-academic) Personal statements which read like job applications, focusing extensively on personal skills and saying nothing about the applicant's passion for history. Poor use of personal statement combined with predicted grades. Little commitment and enthusiasm. No clear reason for choice of course. Little understanding of history. Absence or narrowness of intellectual pursuits. Deception or concealment on the UCAS application. Knowledge of 19th century history (chosen subject) did not have any depth. Unwillingness to learn. Narrow approach to subject. Failure to submit requested information.

GRADUATE DESTINATIONS AND EMPLOYMENT

(See **Chapter 1, Graduate Outcomes.**)

Career note Graduates enter a broad spectrum of careers. While a small number seek positions with museums and galleries, most will enter careers in management, public and social services and retail as well as the teaching profession.

OTHER DEGREE SUBJECTS FOR CONSIDERATION

Ancient History; Anthropology; Archaeology; Economic and Social History; Government; History of Art; International Relations; Medieval History; Politics.

HISTORY (ANCIENT)

(see also **African, Asian and Middle Eastern Studies, Archaeology, History**)

Ancient History covers the Greek and Roman world, the social, religious, political and economic changes taking place in the Byzantine period and the medieval era which followed.

Useful websites http://royalhistsoc.org; www.guardians.net; www.ancientworlds.net; www.bbc.co.uk/history/ancient

NB The points totals shown to the left of the institutions are for ease of reference only. It must not be assumed that Tariff points are always used by institutions or that they can be substituted for an offer in grades. The level of an offer is not necessarily indicative of the quality of a course.

COURSE OFFERS INFORMATION

Subject requirements/preferences GCSE A foreign language or classical language may be required. **AL** History or Classical Civilisation may be preferred subjects. Some popular universities are now making lower offers for disadvantaged and other students.

Your target offers and examples of degree courses

144 pts **Durham** – AAA (Anc Hist) (IB 37 pts)
London (UCL) – AAA incl hist/class civ (Anc Hist) (IB 38 pts HL 18 pts incl 6 hist)
Oxford – AAA+interview+HAT (Anc Modn Hist) (IB 38 pts HL 666)
St Andrews – AAA (Anc Hist Comb Hons) (IB 36 pts HL 665)

136 pts **Bristol** – AAB (Anc Hist) (IB 34 pts HL 17 pts)
Durham – AAB (Anc Hist Arch) (IB 36 pts HL 665)
Edinburgh – AAB (Anc Hist; Anc Hist Gk; Anc Medit Civ) (IB 36 pts HL 665); (Anc Hist Lat) (IB 36 pts HL 665); AAB. (Arch Anc Hist) (IB 36 pts HL 665)
Exeter – AAB–AAA (Anc Hist) (IB 34–36 pts HL 665–666)

London (King's) – AAB (Anc Hist) (IB 35 pts HL 17 pts)
Warwick – AAB (Anc Hist Class Arch) (IB 34 pts)
128 pts **Birmingham** – ABB (Anc Hist; Anc Mediev Hist; Arch Anc Hist) (IB 32 pts HL 655)
Leicester – ABB–BBB+bEPQ (Anc Hist Arch; Anc Hist Hist) (IB 30 pts)
Manchester – ABB (Anc Hist) (IB 34 pts HL 655)
Nottingham – ABB (Anc Hist; Anc Hist Arch) (IB 30 pts HL 655); ABB incl A hist (Anc Hist Hist) (IB 30 pts HL 655)
120 pts **Cardiff** – BBC–ABB (Anc Hist Comb Hons) (IB 30–32 pts HL 665–655)
Kent – BBB (Anc Hist) (IB 30 pts HL 665)
Liverpool – BBB (Anc Hist; Arch Anc Civ) (IB 30 pts)
London (RH) – BBB–ABB (Anc Hist; Anc Hist Phil) (IB 32 pts HL 655)
112 pts **Swansea** – BBC–ABB 112–128 pts (Anc Hist Hist; Egypt Anc Hist) (IB 32 pts); BBC–ABB 112–128 pts (Anc Mediev Hist) (IB 32 pts)
96 pts **Trinity Saint David** – 96–112 pts+interview (Anc Hist); 96–112 ptsinterview (Anc Civ)

Alternative offers See **Chapter 6** and **Appendix 1** for grades/UCAS Tariff points information for other examinations.

CHOOSING YOUR COURSE (SEE ALSO CH.1)

Universities and colleges teaching quality See www.qaa.ac.uk; www.discoveruni.gov.uk.

Top research universities and colleges (REF 2021) See **Classics and Classical Studies/Civilisation**.

ADMISSIONS INFORMATION

Advice to applicants and planning the UCAS personal statement Any information about experience of excavation or museum work should be given. Visits to Greece and Italy to study archaeological sites should be described. Show how your interest in, for example, Ancient Egypt developed through, for example, reading, television and the internet. Be aware of the work of the career archaeologist, for example, sites and measurement officers, field officers and field researchers (often specialists in pottery, glass, metalwork). See also **History**.

Selection interviews Yes Oxford (67% (success rate 24%)); **Some** Bristol (Mature applicants only); **No** London (RH).

Interview advice and questions See **History**.

GRADUATE DESTINATIONS AND EMPLOYMENT

(See **Chapter 1, Graduate Outcomes**.)

Career note See **History**.

OTHER DEGREE SUBJECTS FOR CONSIDERATION

Anthropology; Archaeology; Classical Studies; Classics; Greek; History of Art; Latin.

HISTORY (ECONOMIC AND SOCIAL)

(see also **History**)

Economic and Social History is a study of societies and economies and explores the changes that have taken place in the past, and the causes and consequences of those changes. The study can cover Britain, Europe and other major powers.

Useful websites http://royalhistsoc.org; www.ehs.org.uk; see also **Economics** and **History**.

NB The points totals shown to the left of the institutions are for ease of reference only. It must not be assumed that Tariff points are always used by institutions or that they can be substituted for an offer in grades. The level of an offer is not necessarily indicative of the quality of a course.

COURSE OFFERS INFORMATION

Subject requirements/preferences GCSE Mathematics usually required and a language may be preferred. **AL** History preferred. Some popular universities are now making lower offers for disadvantaged and other students.

Your target offers and examples of degree courses

152 pts **Edinburgh** – A*AA incl maths 152 pts (Hist Econ) (IB 39 pts HL 666 incl maths)

144 pts **London LSE** – AAA incl A maths+econ/hist (Econ Econ Hist) (IB 38 pts HL 766 incl maths+econ/hist)

York – AAA incl hist/class civ+maths (Hist Econ) (IB 36 pts HL 666 incl hist+maths)

128 pts **Manchester** – ABB incl A hist/sociol (Hist Sociol) (IB 34 pts HL 655 incl 6 hist/sociol)

120 pts **Glasgow** – BBB–AAB incl Engl/hum (Econ Soc Hist courses) (IB 36 pts HL 665 incl Engl/hum)

Alternative offers See **Chapter 6** and **Appendix 1** for grades/UCAS Tariff points information for other examinations.

CHOOSING YOUR COURSE (SEE ALSO CH.1)

Universities and colleges teaching quality See www.qaa.ac.uk; www.discoveruni.gov.uk.

Examples of sandwich degree courses Edinburgh; Manchester; York.

ADMISSIONS INFORMATION

Advice to applicants and planning the UCAS personal statement See **History**.

Selection interviews Interview advice and questions See **History**.

GRADUATE DESTINATIONS AND EMPLOYMENT

(See **Chapter 1, Graduate Outcomes.**)

Career note See **History**.

OTHER DEGREE SUBJECTS FOR CONSIDERATION

Economics; Government; History; Politics; Social Policy and Administration; Sociology.

HISTORY OF ART

(see also **History**)

History of Art (and Design) courses differ slightly between universities although most will focus on the history and appreciation of European art and architecture from the 14th to 20th centuries. Some courses also cover the Egyptian, Greek and Roman periods and at London (SOAS), Asian, African and European Art. The history of all aspects of design and film can also be studied in some courses.

Useful websites www.artchive.com; www.artcyclopedia.com; http://theartguide.com; www.galleries.co.uk; https://cryptoart.com; www.nationalgallery.org.uk; www.britisharts.org; www.tate.org.uk

NB The points totals shown to the left of the institutions are for ease of reference only. It must not be assumed that Tariff points are always used by institutions or that they can be substituted for an offer in grades. The level of an offer is not necessarily indicative of the quality of a course.

COURSE OFFERS INFORMATION

Subject requirements/preferences GCSE English required and a foreign language usually preferred. **AL** History is preferred for some courses. Some popular universities are now making lower offers for disadvantaged and other students.

Your target offers and examples of degree courses

152 pts **Cambridge** – A*AA+interview+HAA (Hist Art) (IB 41–42 pts HL 776)

Edinburgh – A*AA (Hist Art) (IB 39 pts HL 666)

144 pts **London (Court)** – AAA (Hist Art) (IB 35 pts)
Oxford – AAA+interview (Hist Art) (IB 38 pts HL 666)
St Andrews – AAA (Art Hist; Art Hist Class St; Art Hist Psy) (IB 36 pts HL 665); AAA incl hist (Art Hist Mid E St) (IB 38 pts HL 666)

136 pts **East Anglia** – AAB (Hist Art) (IB 33 pts)
Edinburgh – AAB (Hist Art Hist Mus) (IB 36 pts HL 665)
London (UCL) – AAB (Hist Art) (IB 36 pts HL 17 pts)
York – AAB (Hist Art) (IB 35 pts HL 6 hist); AAB incl Engl (Engl Hist Art) (IB 35 pts HL 6 Engl); AAB incl hist/class civ (Hist Hist Art) (IB 35 pts HL 6 hist)

128 pts **Birmingham** – ABB (Hist Art) (IB 32 pts HL 655); ABB incl lang (Modn Langs Hist Art) (IB 32 pts HL 655)
Bristol – ABB (Hist Art; Hist Art Fr) (IB 32 pts HL 16 pts); ABB incl lang (Hist Art Modn Lang (Yr Abrd)) (IB 32 pts HL 16 pts incl 5 lang)
East Anglia – ABB (Arch Anth Art Hist (St Abrd); Hist Art Gllry Musm St) (IB 32 pts)
Exeter – ABB–AAB (Art Hist Vis Cult; Art Hist courses) (IB 32–34 pts HL 655–665)
Leeds – ABB (Hist Art) (IB 34 pts HL 16 incl 4 Engl)
London (SOAS) – ABB (His Art Comb Hons; Hist Art) (IB 32 pts HL 655)
Manchester – ABB (Hist Art) (IB 34 pts HL 655)
Nottingham – ABB (Art Hist Vis Cult) (IB 30 pts HL 655); ABB incl Engl (Hist Art Engl) (IB 30 pts HL 655)
Sussex – ABB (Art Hist) (IB 32 pts)
Warwick – ABB (Hist Art) (IB 32 pts)

120 pts **Glasgow** – BBB–AAB incl arts/hum (Hist Art) (IB 34 pts HL 655 incl Engl+hum)

112 pts **Aberdeen** – BBC (Hist Art) (IB 32 pts HL 555)
Essex – BBC–BBB 112–120 pts (Art Hist) (IB 29–30 pts HL 554–555); (Lit Art Hist) (IB 29–30 pts HL 554–555)
Liverpool John Moores – BBC 112 pts (Hist Art Musm St)
London (Birk) – BBC 112 pts (Hist Art; Hist Art Cur)

104 pts **Aberystwyth** – BCC–BBB 104–120 pts (Art Hist) (IB 28–30 pts); BCC–BBB incl art 104–120 pts+portfolio (Fn Art Art Hist) (IB 28–30 pts)
Brighton – BCC–BBB 104–120 pts (Fash Des Hist) (IB 26 pts)
Manchester Met – BCC–BBC 104–112 pts (Art Hist Cur) (IB 26 pts)
Plymouth – 104–112 pts (Art Hist) (IB 26–28 pts)

ALTERNATIVE OFFERS See **Chapter 6** and **Appendix 1** for grades/UCAS Tariff points information for other examinations.

EXAMPLES OF COLLEGES OFFERING COURSES IN THIS SUBJECT FIELD

South Gloucestershire and Stroud (Coll).

CHOOSING YOUR COURSE (SEE ALSO CH.1)

UNIVERSITIES AND COLLEGES TEACHING QUALITY See www.qaa.ac.uk; www.discoveruni.gov.uk.

TOP RESEARCH UNIVERSITIES AND COLLEGES (REF 2021) See **Art and Design (General)**.

EXAMPLES OF SANDWICH DEGREE COURSES East Anglia; Exeter; Leeds; Manchester; Manchester Met; Plymouth; Sussex; York.

ADMISSIONS INFORMATION

ADVICE TO APPLICANTS AND PLANNING THE UCAS PERSONAL STATEMENT Applicants for History of Art courses should have made extensive visits to art galleries, particularly in London, and should be familiar with the main European schools of painting. Evidence of lively interest required. Discuss your preferences and say why you prefer certain types of work or particular artists. You should also describe any visits to museums and any special interests in furniture, pottery or other artefacts.

Selection interviews Yes Cambridge, Oxford (42% (success rate 13%)); **Some** Bristol (mature students and applicants with non-standard qualifications), Manchester (mature students only); **No** Brighton, East Anglia, London (UCL).

Interview advice and questions Some universities set slide tests on painting and sculpture. Those applicants who have not taken History of Art at A-level will be questioned on their reasons for choosing the subject, their visits to art galleries and museums and their reactions to the art work which has impressed them. See **Chapter 5**.

Reasons for rejection (non-academic) Poorly presented practical work. Students who do not express any interest or enthusiasm in contemporary visual arts are rejected.

GRADUATE DESTINATIONS AND EMPLOYMENT

(See **Chapter 1, Graduate Outcomes.**)

Career note Work in galleries, museums and collections will be the objective of many graduates, who should try to establish contacts by way of work placements and experience during their undergraduate years. The personal skills acquired during their studies, however, open up many opportunities in other careers.

OTHER DEGREE SUBJECTS FOR CONSIDERATION

Art; Archaeology; Architecture; Classical Studies; Photography.

HORTICULTURE

(including **Garden Design**; see also **Agricultural Sciences/Agriculture, Landscape Architecture, Plant Sciences**)

Horticulture is a broad subject area covering amenity or landscape horticulture, production horticulture and retail horticulture.

Useful websites http://iagre.org; www.rhs.org.uk; www.horticulture.org.uk; www.sgd.org.uk

NB The points totals shown to the left of the institutions are for ease of reference only. It must not be assumed that Tariff points are always used by institutions or that they can be substituted for an offer in grades. The level of an offer is not necessarily indicative of the quality of a course.

COURSE OFFERS INFORMATION

Subject requirements/preferences GCSE Mathematics sometimes required. **AL** A science subject may be required or preferred for some courses. Some popular universities are now making lower offers for disadvantaged and other students.

Your target offers and examples of degree courses

104 pts **SRUC** – BCC incl sci (Hort (Plnt Sci Tech); Hort Plntsmn)
96 pts **Writtle (UC)** – 96 pts (Hort) (IB 24 pts)
80 pts **Cornwall (Coll)** – 80 pts (Hort (Plnt Sci))
Warwickshire (Coll) – 80 pts (Sust Hort Tech (Agritech))
64 pts **Hadlow (UC)** – 64 pts incl sci (Hort (Commer))

Alternative offers See **Chapter 6** and **Appendix 1** for grades/UCAS Tariff points information for other examinations.

EXAMPLES OF COLLEGES OFFERING COURSES IN THIS SUBJECT FIELD

Askham Bryan (Coll); Bicton (Coll); Bishop Burton (Coll); Bridgend (Coll); Bridgwater and Taunton (Coll); CAFRE; Capel Manor (Coll); Craven (Coll); Myerscough (Coll); SMB CG; Warwickshire (Coll).

CHOOSING YOUR COURSE (SEE ALSO CH.1)

Universities and colleges teaching quality See www.qaa.ac.uk; www.discoveruni.gov.uk.

ADMISSIONS INFORMATION

Advice to applicants and planning the UCAS personal statement Practical experience is important and visits to botanical gardens (the Royal Botanic Gardens, Kew or Edinburgh and the Royal Horticultural Society gardens at Wisley) could be described. Contact your local authority offices for details of work in parks and gardens departments. See also **Appendix 3**.

Selection interviews Interview advice and questions Past questions have included: How did you become interested in horticulture? How do you think this course will benefit you? Could you work in all weathers? What career are you aiming for? Are you interested in gardening? Describe your garden. What plants do you grow? How do you prune rose trees and fruit trees? Topics relating to the importance of science and horticulture. See also **Chapter 5**.

GRADUATE DESTINATIONS AND EMPLOYMENT

(See **Chapter 1, Graduate Outcomes.**)

Career note Graduates seeking employment in horticulture will look towards commercial organisations for the majority of openings. These will include positions as growers and managers with fewer vacancies for scientists involved in research and development and advisory services.

OTHER DEGREE SUBJECTS FOR CONSIDERATION

Agriculture; Biology; Crop Science; Ecology; Forestry; Landscape Architecture; Plant Sciences.

HOSPITALITY AND EVENT MANAGEMENT

(see also **Business and Management Courses, Business and Management Courses (International and European), Business and Management Courses (Specialised), Food Science/Studies and Technology, Leisure and Recreation Management/Studies, Tourism and Travel**)

Courses cover the full range of skills required for those working in the industry. Specific studies include hotel management, food and beverage supplies, equipment design, public relations and marketing. Depending on the course, other topics may include events management, tourism and the international trade.

Useful websites www.thebapa.org.uk; www.cordonbleu.edu; www.instituteofhospitality.org; www.people1st.co.uk; www.abpco.org

NB The points totals shown to the left of the institutions are for ease of reference only. It must not be assumed that Tariff points are always used by institutions or that they can be substituted for an offer in grades. The level of an offer is not necessarily indicative of the quality of a course.

COURSE OFFERS INFORMATION

Subject requirements/preferences GCSE English and mathematics usually required together with a foreign language for International Management courses. **AL** No specified subjects. Some popular universities are now making lower offers for disadvantaged and other students.

Your target offers and examples of degree courses

144 pts **Strathclyde** – AAA incl maths (Acc Hspty Tour Mgt) (IB 36 pts HL 5 maths)

120 pts **Coventry** – BBB 120 pts (Int Hspty Tour Mgt) (IB 27 pts)
Strathclyde – BBB–ABB (Hspty Tour Mgt) (IB 30–32 pts)

112 pts **Birmingham (UC)** – BCC 112 pts (Evnts Mgt) (IB 28 pts)
Bournemouth Arts – BBC–BBB 112–120 pts+interview (Evnts Mgt)
Canterbury Christ Church – BBC (Int Tour Hspty Mgt) (IB 29 pts); BBC 112 pts (Evnts Mgt) (IB 29 pts)

Chester – 112 pts (Evnts Mgt) (IB 28 pts)
Coventry – BBC 112 pts (Evnt Mgt) (IB 24 pts)
De Montfort – 112 pts (Arts Fstvl Mgt) (IB 26 pts)
East London – 112 pts (Hspty Mgt) (IB 24 pts HL 15 pts)
Greenwich – 112 pts (Evnt Mgt Innov; Int Tour Hspty Mgt)
Liverpool John Moores – BBC 112 pts (Evnts Mgt)
Sheffield Hallam – BBC 112 pts (Int Hspty Bus Mgt)
West London – BBC 112 pts (Evnt Mgt; Int Hspty Mgt)
Westminster – BBC 112 pts (Int Evnt Mgt)

104 pts **Bournemouth** – 104–120 pts (Evnts Mgt) (IB 28–31 pts)
Central Lancashire – 104–112 pts (Int Hspty Mgt)
Derby – BCC–BBB 104–120 pts (Int Hspty Mgt); BCC–BBB 104–120 pts (Evnts Mgt)
Gloucestershire – BCC 104 pts (Int Hspty Tour Mgt)
Hertfordshire – BCC–BBC 104–112 pts (Evnt Mgt)
Leeds Beckett – 104–120 pts (Evnts Mgt)
Lincoln – 104 pts (Evnts Mgt) (IB 28 pts)
Liverpool Hope – BCC 104 pts (Tour Mgt) (IB 24 pts)
Manchester Met – BCC–BBC 104–112 pts (Evnts Mgt; Int Hspty Bus Mgt) (IB 26 pts)
Northampton – BCC (Hspty Mgt)
Oxford Brookes – BCC 104 pts (Int Hspty Tour Mgt) (IB 29 pts)
Plymouth – 104–120 pts (Evnts Mgt) (IB 26–30 pts HL 4)
Surrey – BCC (Int Hspty Mgt; Int Hspty Tour Mgt) (IB 26 pts)
Winchester – BCC–BBB 104–120 pts (Evnt Mgt) (HL 44)

96 pts **Cardiff Met** – 96–112 pts (Evnts Mgt); CCC 96–112 pts (Int Tour Mgt)
Edinburgh Napier – CCC (Int Fstvl Evnt Mgt) (IB 27 pts HL 654)
Essex – CCC 96 pts (Hspty Mgt); (Evnts Mgt Hspty) (IB 26 pts HL 444)
London Met – CCC/BC 96 pts (Evnts Mgt)
Robert Gordon – CCC (Evnts Mgt; Int Hspty Mgt) (IB 26 pts)
South Wales – CCC 96 pts (Bus Mgt (Evnt Mgt))
Ulster – CCC (Int Hspty Mgt) (IB 24 pts HL 12 pts)
West Scotland – CCC 96 pts (Evnts Mgt; Evnts Tour Mgt) (IB 24 pts)
Wolverhampton – CCC/BCD 96 pts (Int Hspty Mgt)

88 pts **Bucks New** – 88–112 pts (Evnts Mgt)
Sunderland – 88–104 pts (Int Tour Hspty Mgt)
Trinity Saint David – 88 pts+interview (Evnts Int Fstvl Mgt)

80 pts **Birmingham (UC)** – CDD–CCC 80–96 pts (Int Hspty Tour Mgt)

24 pts **UHI** – D (Hspty Mgt)

Alternative offers See **Chapter 6** and **Appendix 1** for grades/UCAS Tariff points information for other examinations.

DEGREE APPRENTICESHIPS

Glasgow Caledonian (Bus Mgt (Hspty Mgt)); Gloucestershire (Hspty Mgr); Ulster (Int Hspty Mgt).

EXAMPLES OF COLLEGES OFFERING COURSES IN THIS SUBJECT FIELD

Accrington and Rossendale (Coll); Barnsley (Coll); Bedford (Coll); Birmingham Met (Coll); Blackburn (Coll); Blackpool and Fylde (Coll); Bournemouth and Poole (Coll); Bradford College (UC); Brighton Met (Coll); Bury (Coll); Cornwall (Coll); Craven (Coll); Darlington (Coll); Derby (Coll); Doncaster (Coll); Durham New (Coll); Ealing, Hammersmith and West London (Coll); East Riding (Coll); Furness (Coll); Grŵp Llandrillo Menai; Guildford (Coll); Hartlepool (CFE); Hull (Coll); Leicester (Coll); Liverpool City (Coll); London City (Coll); London UCK (Coll); Loughborough (Coll); LSST; Macclesfield (Coll); Manchester (Coll); MidKent (Coll); NCC Redbridge; Neath Port Talbot (Coll); Nescot; Newcastle (Coll); North Notts (Coll); Northumberland (Coll); Norwich City (Coll); Petroc; Plymouth City (Coll); Reaseheath (UC); Richmond-upon-Thames (Coll); Sheffield (Coll); South and West Cheshire (Coll); South Cheshire (Coll); South Devon (Coll); South Essex (Coll); Stratford-upon-Avon (Coll); TEC Partnership; Walsall (Coll);

Warwickshire (Coll); West Herts (Coll); West Suffolk (Coll); Westminster Kingsway (Coll); Weymouth (Coll); Wirral Met (Coll).

CHOOSING YOUR COURSE (SEE ALSO CH.1)

Universities and colleges teaching quality See www.qaa.ac.uk; www.discoveruni.gov.uk.

Examples of sandwich degree courses Birmingham (UC); Bournemouth; Cardiff Met; Central Lancashire; Derby; Gloucestershire; Leeds Beckett; Manchester Met; Oxford Brookes; Sheffield Hallam; Sunderland; Surrey; Wolverhampton.

ADMISSIONS INFORMATION

Advice to applicants and planning the UCAS personal statement Experience in dealing with members of the public is an important element in this work which, coupled with work experience in cafés, restaurants or hotels, should be described fully. All applicants are strongly recommended to obtain practical experience in catering or hotel work. Admissions tutors are likely to look for experience in industry and for people who are ambitious, sociable and team players. See also **Appendix 3**.

Selection interviews Yes Bournemouth Arts, Trinity Saint David; **No** Robert Gordon.

Interview advice and questions Past questions have included: What books do you read? What do you know about hotel work and management? What work experience have you had? What kind of job do you have in mind when you have qualified? How did you become interested in this course? Do you eat in restaurants? What types of restaurants? Discuss examples of good and bad restaurant organisation. What qualities do you have which make you suitable for management? See also **Chapter 5**.

Reasons for rejection (non-academic) Lack of suitable work experience or practical training. Inability to communicate. Lack of awareness of workload, for example shift working, weekend work.

GRADUATE DESTINATIONS AND EMPLOYMENT

(See **Chapter 1, Graduate Outcomes.**)

Career note These business-focused hospitality programmes open up a wide range of employment and career opportunities in both hospitality and other business sectors.

OTHER DEGREE SUBJECTS FOR CONSIDERATION

Business; Consumer Studies; Dietetics; Food Science; Health Studies; Leisure and Recreation Management; Management; Tourism and Travel.

HOUSING

(see also **Building and Construction, Surveying and Real Estate Management, Town and Urban Planning**)

These courses prepare students for careers in housing management although topics covered will also be relevant to other careers in business and administration. Modules will be taken in housing, law, finance, planning policy, public administration and construction.

Useful websites www.gov.uk/housing-local-and-community/housing; www.rtpi.org.uk; www.freeindex.co.uk/categories/property/construction/Property_Development

NB The points totals shown to the left of the institutions are for ease of reference only. It must not be assumed that Tariff points are always used by institutions or that they can be substituted for an offer in grades. The level of an offer is not necessarily indicative of the quality of a course.

COURSE OFFERS INFORMATION

Subject requirements/preferences GCSE English and mathematics required. **AL** No specified subjects. Some popular universities are now making lower offers for disadvantaged and other students.

Your target offers and examples of degree courses

112 pts **Leeds Beckett** – 112 pts (Hous St)
80 pts **Cardiff Met** – 80 pts (Hous St)
64 pts **Central Lancashire** – 64 pts (App Commun Soc Cr)

Alternative offers See **Chapter 6** and **Appendix 1** for grades/UCAS Tariff points information for other examinations.

EXAMPLES OF COLLEGES OFFERING COURSES IN THIS SUBJECT FIELD

Blackburn (Coll).

CHOOSING YOUR COURSE (SEE ALSO CH.1)

Universities and colleges teaching quality See www.qaa.ac.uk; www.discoveruni.gov.uk.

Examples of sandwich degree courses Leeds Beckett.

ADMISSIONS INFORMATION

Advice to applicants and planning the UCAS personal statement An interest in people, housing problems, social affairs and the built environment is important. Contacts with local housing managers (through local authority offices or housing associations) are important. Describe these contacts and your knowledge of the housing types and needs in your area. The planning department in your local council office will be able to provide information on the various types of developments taking place in your locality and how housing needs have changed during the past 50 years. See also **Appendix 3**.

Selection interviews Yes Cardiff Met.

Interview advice and questions Since the subject is not studied at school, questions are likely to be asked on reasons for choosing this degree. Other past questions include: What is a housing association? Why were housing associations formed? In which parts of the country would you expect private housing to be expensive and, by comparison, cheap? What is the cause of this? Have estates of multi-storey flats fulfilled their original purpose? If not, why not? What causes a slum? What is an almshouse? See also **Chapter 5**.

Reasons for rejection (non-academic) Lack of awareness of current social policy issues.

GRADUATE DESTINATIONS AND EMPLOYMENT

(See **Chapter 1, Graduate Outcomes.**)

Career note Graduates aiming for openings in housing will be employed mainly as managers with local authorities; others will be employed by non-profit-making housing associations and trusts and also by property companies owning blocks of flats.

OTHER DEGREE SUBJECTS FOR CONSIDERATION

Architecture; Building; Business Studies; Community Studies; Environmental Planning; Estate Management; Property Development; Social Policy and Administration; Social Studies; Surveying; Town Planning; Urban Regeneration.

HUMAN RESOURCE MANAGEMENT

(see also **Business and Management Courses, Business and Management Courses (International and European), Business and Management Courses (Specialised)**)

This is one of the many branches of the world of business and has developed from the role of the personnel manager. HR managers may be involved with the induction and training of staff, disciplinary and grievance procedures, redundancies and equal opportunities issues. In large organisations, some HR staff may specialise in one or more of these areas. Work experience dealing with the public should be stressed in the UCAS personal statement.

Useful websites www.hrmguide.co.uk; www.cipd.co.uk

NB The points totals shown to the left of the institutions are for ease of reference only. It must not be assumed that Tariff points are always used by institutions or that they can be substituted for an offer in grades. The level of an offer is not necessarily indicative of the quality of a course.

COURSE OFFERS INFORMATION

Subject requirements/preferences GCSE English and mathematics at 4 (C) or above. **AL** No subjects specified. Some popular universities are now making lower offers for disadvantaged and other students.

Your target offers and examples of degree courses

144 pts **Manchester** – AAA (Mgt (HR)) (IB 36 pts HL 666)
136 pts **Leeds** – AAB (Bus Mgt HR) (IB 35 pts HL 16 pts)
128 pts **Lancaster** – ABB (Mgt HR) (IB 32 pts HL 16 pts)
Reading – ABB (Bus Mgt (HR Org Bhv)) (IB 32 pts)
120 pts **Aston** – BBB/BBC+bEPQ (HR Bus Mgt) (IB 31 pts HL 555)
Cardiff – BBB–AAB (Bus Mgt (HR Mgt)) (IB 31–34 pts HL 665–666)
London (RH) – BBB–AAB (Mgt HR) (IB 32 pts HL 655)
Stirling – BBB (HR Mgt) (IB 30 pts)
Swansea – BBB–ABB (Bus Mgt (HR Mgt)) (IB 32–33 pts)
112 pts **Birmingham City** – BBC 112 pts (HR Mgt) (IB 28 pts)
Canterbury Christ Church – BBC 112 pts (HR Mgt) (IB 29 pts)
Cardiff Met – 112 pts (Bus Mgt (HR Mgt)) (HL 55)
Coventry – BBC 112 pts (Bus HR Mgt) (IB 24 pts)
De Montfort – 112 pts (HR Mgt) (IB 26 pts)
East London – 112 pts (HR Mgt) (IB 24 pts HL 15 pts)
Greenwich – 112 pts (HR Mgt Dev)
Hertfordshire – BBC–BBB 112–120 pts (Bus HR Mgt)
Keele – BBC (Bus HR Mgt) (IB 29 pts HL 554)
Leeds Beckett – 112 pts (HR Mgt Bus) (IB 25 pts)
Middlesex – BBC 112 pts (Bus Mgt (HR Mgt))
Northumbria – 112 pts (Bus HR Mgt)
Nottingham Trent – 112 pts (Bus Mgt HR)
West London – BBC 112 pts (Hum Res Mgt)
Westminster – BBC 112 pts (Bus Mgt (HR Mgt))
104 pts **Bath Spa** – BCC–BBB (Bus Mgt (HR Mgt)) (IB 32 pts)
Brighton – BCC–BBB 104–120 pts (Bus Mgt HR Mgt) (IB 26 pts)
Liverpool John Moores – BCC–BBB 104–120 pts (HR Mgt)
Northampton – BCC (HR Mgt courses)
Robert Gordon – BCC 104 pts (Bus Hum Res Mgt) (IB 27 pts)
Ulster – BCC (HR Mgt) (IB 24 pts HL 12 pts)
96 pts **Anglia Ruskin** – 96 pts (Bus HR Mgt)
Bedfordshire – 96 pts (HR Mgt)
South Wales – CCC 96 pts (HR Mgt)
Sunderland – 96–112 pts (Bus HR Mgt)
Wolverhampton – CCC/BCD 96 pts (HR Mgt)
88 pts **Bucks New** – 88–112 pts (Bus HR Mgt)

Alternative offers See **Chapter 6** and **Appendix 1** for grades/UCAS Tariff points information for other examinations.

DEGREE APPRENTICESHIPS

Glasgow Caledonian (Bus Mgt (HR Mgt)).

EXAMPLES OF COLLEGES OFFERING COURSES IN THIS SUBJECT FIELD

Barking and Dagenham (Coll); Basingstoke (CT); Bath (Coll); Bournemouth and Poole (Coll); Croydon (UC); London City (Coll); Manchester (Coll); Newcastle (Coll); North Lindsey (Coll); Plymouth City (Coll); South Gloucestershire and Stroud (Coll); St Helens (Coll).

CHOOSING YOUR COURSE (SEE ALSO CH.1)

Universities and colleges teaching quality See www.qaa.ac.uk; www.discoveruni.gov.uk.

Examples of sandwich degree courses Aston; Bath Spa; Bedfordshire; Birmingham City; Brighton; Chichester; Coventry; De Montfort; Hertfordshire; Leeds; Leeds Beckett; Liverpool John Moores; Northampton; Northumbria; Westminster.

ADMISSIONS INFORMATION

Advice to applicants and planning the UCAS personal statement See **Business and Management Courses**.

Selection interviews No Anglia Ruskin, De Montfort.

Interview advice and questions See **Business and Management Courses**.

Reasons for rejection (non-academic) See **Business and Management Courses**.

GRADUATE DESTINATIONS AND EMPLOYMENT

(See **Chapter 1, Graduate Outcomes.**)

Career note See under **Business and Management Courses**.

OTHER DEGREE SUBJECTS FOR CONSIDERATION

Business Studies; Information Systems; Management Studies/Sciences; Marketing; Psychology; Retail Management; Sociology; Sports Management.

HUMAN SCIENCES/HUMAN BIOSCIENCES

(see also **Medicine, Neuroscience**)

Human Sciences is a multi-disciplinary study relating to biological and social sciences and focuses on social and cultural behaviour. Topics range from genetics and evolution to health, disease, social behaviour and industrial societies. A typical course may include anatomy, physiology, bio-mechanics, anthropology and psychology.

Useful websites https://bbsrc.ukri.org; www.becominghuman.org; see also **Biology** and **Geography**.

NB The points totals shown to the left of the institutions are for ease of reference only. It must not be assumed that Tariff points are always used by institutions or that they can be substituted for an offer in grades. The level of an offer is not necessarily indicative of the quality of a course.

COURSE OFFERS INFORMATION

Subject requirements/preferences GCSE Science essential and mathematics usually required. **AL** Chemistry/biology usually required or preferred for some courses. Some popular universities are now making lower offers for disadvantaged and other students.

Your target offers and examples of degree courses

144 pts **London (UCL)** – AAA incl sci (Hum Sci) (IB 38 pts HL 18 pts incl 6 sci)
Oxford – AAA+interview+TSA (Hum Sci) (IB 38 pts HL 666)
136 pts **Birmingham** – AAB incl sci (Hum Sci) (IB 32 pts HL 665)
Durham – AAB (Hlth Hum Sci) (IB 36 pts HL 665)
Sussex – AAB (Psy Neuro) (IB 34 pts)
128 pts **Aberdeen** – ABB 128 pts (Biomed Sci (Anat)) (IB 34 pts)

Exeter – ABB incl biol+sci (Biomed Sci) (IB 32 pts HL 655)
120 pts **Coventry** – BBB incl biol (Hum Biosci) (IB 32 pts HL 5 biol)
112 pts **Cardiff** – BBC–ABB (Hum Soc Sci) (IB 30–32 pts HL 655–665)
104 pts **Oxford Brookes** – BCC incl sci 104 pts (Biol Sci Hum Biosci) (IB 29 pts HL sci)
Plymouth – 104–120 pts incl biol+maths/sci (Hum Biosci) (IB 28 pts HL 5 biol+sci)
Swansea – BCC–AAB incl biol/chem+STEM (App Med Sci) (IB 34 pts HL 66 biol/chem+STEM)
West Scotland – BCC incl biol 104 pts (App Biomed Sci) (IB 24 pts HL 444 incl biol)

ALTERNATIVE OFFERS See **Chapter 6** and **Appendix 1** for grades/UCAS Tariff points information for other examinations.

DEGREE APPRENTICESHIPS

Bradford (Lab Sci, Adv Clin Prac, Biomed Sci); Central Lancashire (App Biomed Sci); Kent (Lab Sci); Manchester Met (Hlthcr Sci Practnr); Sheffield Hallam (Hlthcr Sci Practnr); Westminster (Hlthcr Sci Practnr); Wolverhampton (Hlthcr Sci Practnr).

EXAMPLES OF COLLEGES OFFERING COURSES IN THIS SUBJECT FIELD

Blackpool and Fylde (Coll).

CHOOSING YOUR COURSE (SEE ALSO CH.1)

UNIVERSITIES AND COLLEGES TEACHING QUALITY See www.qaa.ac.uk; www.discoveruni.gov.uk.

EXAMPLES OF SANDWICH DEGREE COURSES Cardiff; Coventry; Durham; Exeter; Oxford Brookes; Plymouth; Swansea; West Scotland.

ADMISSIONS INFORMATION

ADVICE TO APPLICANTS AND PLANNING THE UCAS PERSONAL STATEMENT See **Biology** and **Anthropology**.

SELECTION INTERVIEWS Yes Oxford (48% (success rate 14%)); **No** London (UCL).

INTERVIEW ADVICE AND QUESTIONS Past questions have included: What do you expect to get out of a degree in Human Sciences? Why are you interested in this subject? What problems do you think you will be able to tackle after completing the course? Why did you drop PE as an A-level given that it's relevant to Human Sciences? How do you explain altruism, given that we are surely programmed by our genes to be selfish? How far is human behaviour determined by genes? What do you think are the key differences between animals and human beings? See also **Chapter 5**.

GRADUATE DESTINATIONS AND EMPLOYMENT

(See **Chapter 1, Graduate Outcomes.**)

CAREER NOTE As a result of the multi-disciplinary nature of these courses, graduates could focus on openings linked to their special interests or look in general at the scientific and health sectors. Health administration, social services work and laboratory-based careers are some of the more common career destinations of graduates.

OTHER DEGREE SUBJECTS FOR CONSIDERATION

Anthropology; Biology; Community Studies; Environmental Sciences; Life Sciences; Psychology; Sociology.

INFORMATION MANAGEMENT AND LIBRARIANSHIP

(including **Informatics**; see also **Computer Science and Information Technology, Media Studies**)

Information Management and Librarianship covers the very wide field of information. Topics covered include retrieval, indexing, computer and media technology, classification and cataloguing.

Useful websites www.emerald.com/insight/publication/issn/2050-3806; www.cilip.org.uk; www.bl.uk

NB The points totals shown to the left of the institutions are for ease of reference only. It must not be assumed that Tariff points are always used by institutions or that they can be substituted for an offer in grades. The level of an offer is not necessarily indicative of the quality of a course.

COURSE OFFERS INFORMATION

Subject requirements/preferences GCSE English, mathematics and occasionally a foreign language. **AL** No specified subjects. Some popular universities are now making lower offers for disadvantaged and other students.

Your target offers and examples of degree courses

144 pts **London (UCL)** – AAA (Inf Mgt Bus) (IB 38 pts HL 18 pts)
Manchester – AAA (IT Mgt Bus; IT Mgt Bus (Yr Ind)) (IB 36 pts HL 666)
136 pts **Edinburgh** – AAB–A*A*A* incl A maths (Inform (MInf)) (IB 34–43 pts HL 655–766 incl 6 maths)
Lancaster – AAB (Mgt IT) (IB 32 pts HL 16 pts)
Loughborough – AAB (IT Mgt Bus) (IB 35 pts HL 665)
128 pts **East Anglia** – ABB (Hist Art Gllry Musm St) (IB 32 pts)
London (UCL) – ABB 128 pts (Inf Soty) (IB 34 pts HL 16 pts)
120 pts **London (Gold)** – BBB (Cur) (IB 33 pts HL 655)
Reading – BBB (Musm Class St) (IB 30 pts)
112 pts **Essex** – BBC–BBB 112–120 pts (Cur) (IB 29–30 pts HL 554–555)
Huddersfield – BBC–BBB 112–120 pts (IT)
Liverpool John Moores – BBC 112 pts (Hist Art Musm St)
London (Birk) – BBC 112 pts (Hist Art Cur)
Northumbria – 112 pts (Comp IT Mgt)
Oxford Brookes – BBC (IT Bus) (IB 30 pts)
104 pts **Edge Hill** – BCC–BBC 104–112 pts (IT Mgt Bus)
96 pts **Aberystwyth** – CCC–BBB 96–120 pts (Cult Herit St Lib Archv Musm) (IB 26–30 pts)
Cardiff – CCC–BBC (Cons Objs Musm Arch) (IB 28–30 pts HL 555–655)

Alternative offers See **Chapter 6** and **Appendix 1** for grades/UCAS Tariff points information for other examinations.

EXAMPLES OF COLLEGES OFFERING COURSES IN THIS SUBJECT FIELD

Birmingham Met (Coll); Grŵp Llandrillo Menai.

CHOOSING YOUR COURSE (SEE ALSO CH.1)

Universities and colleges teaching quality See www.qaa.ac.uk; www.discoveruni.gov.uk.

Top research universities and colleges (REF 2021) (Communication, Cultural and Media Studies, Library and Information Management) London LSE; Cardiff; Leicester (Musm St); London (Gold) (Media Comm Cult St); Loughborough; Glasgow; Leicester (Media Comm); London (RH); London (King's); Newcastle.

Examples of sandwich degree courses East Anglia; Huddersfield; Lancaster; Loughborough; Manchester.

ADMISSIONS INFORMATION

Advice to applicants and planning the UCAS personal statement Work experience or work shadowing in local libraries is important but remember that reference libraries provide a different field of work. Visit university libraries and major reference libraries and discuss the work with librarians. Describe your experiences in the personal statement. See also **Appendix 3**.

Selection interviews Some Loughborough; **No** London (UCL).

Interview advice and questions Past questions include: What is it about librarianship that interests you? Why do you think you are suited to be a librarian? What does the job entail? What is the role of the library in school? What is the role of the public library? What new developments are taking place in libraries? Which books do you read? How often do you use a library? What is the Dewey number for the history section in the library? (Applicant studying A-level history.) See also **Chapter 5**.

GRADUATE DESTINATIONS AND EMPLOYMENT

(See **Chapter 1, Graduate Outcomes.**)

Career note Graduates in this subject area and in communications enter a wide range of public and private sector jobs where the need to process information as well as to make it easily accessible and user-friendly is very high. Areas of work could include web content, design and internet management and library management.

OTHER DEGREE SUBJECTS FOR CONSIDERATION

Business Information Systems; Communication Studies; Computer Science; Geographic Information Systems; Media Studies.

INTERNATIONAL RELATIONS

(including **International Development, Peace Studies and International Relations and War Studies**; see also **Development Studies, Economics, European Studies, History (Economic and Social), Philosophy, Philosophy, Politics and Economics (PPE), Politics**)

International Relations (IR) is a well-established field of study which encompasses aspects of political science, philosophy, global history and economics. A strong interest in international affairs and a desire to think, write and persuade using a range of political theories are prerequisites. Courses will typically build on a foundation of IR theories introduced in the first year (eg Realist, Liberal and Constructivist schools of thought) which draw upon political thinking spanning from the Ancient Greeks (eg Thucydides) to the twentieth century (eg Morgenthau, Buzan). Most universities offer modules which focus on specific areas of the world, such as South and Central Asia, as well as global issues such as terrorism, civil conflict and nuclear weapons. In recent years, IR has begun to focus more on feminist voices and non-western scholarship, with the need for truly global perspectives now recognised widely in the field.

Useful websites www.sipri.org; www.un.org; www.un.int; https://militarist-monitor.org; see also **Politics**.

NB The points totals shown to the left of the institutions are for ease of reference only. It must not be assumed that Tariff points are always used by institutions or that they can be substituted for an offer in grades. The level of an offer is not necessarily indicative of the quality of a course.

COURSE OFFERS INFORMATION

Subject requirements/preferences GCSE English; a foreign language usually required. **AL** No specified subjects. (War St) History may be required. Some popular universities are now making lower offers for disadvantaged and other students.

Your target offers and examples of degree courses

160 pts **Warwick** – A*A*A (Econ Pol Int St) (IB 39 pts HL 666)

152 pts **Edinburgh** – A*AA (Int Rel) (IB 39 pts HL 666); (Law Int Rel) (IB 39 pts HL 666 incl Engl); A*AA incl Engl (Glob Law) (IB 39 pts HL 666 incl Engl)

144 pts **Bath** – AAA/A*AB/AAB+aEPQ (Pol Int Rel) (IB 36 pts HL 666/765)

Bristol – AAA (Pol Int Rel) (IB 36 pts HL 18 pts)

Durham – AAA incl soc sci/hum (Int Rel) (IB 37 pts HL 666 incl soc sci/hum)

Exeter – AAA (Pol Int Rel) (IB 36 pts HL 666)

London (King's) – AAA (War St) (IB 36 pts HL 18 pts); AAA incl hist (War St Hist) (IB 38 pts HL 18 pts)

London LSE – AAA (Int Rel; Int Rel Hist) (IB 38 pts HL 766)

Manchester – AAA (Pol Int Rel) (IB 36 pts HL 666)

St Andrews – AAA (Int Rel courses) (IB 38 pts HL 666)
136 pts **Birmingham** – AAB (Int Rel; Pol Int Rel) (IB 32 pts HL 665)
Lancaster – AAB (Hist Int Rel) (IB 35 pts HL 16 pts)
Leeds – AAB (Int Rel) (IB 35 pts HL 655)
Nottingham – AAB (Int Rel As St) (IB 32 pts HL 665)
Sheffield – AAB–ABB+bEPQ (Int Rel Pol) (IB 34 pts); AAB–ABB+bEPQ incl hist/class civ (Hist Pol) (IB 34 pts HL 6 hist)
Sussex – AAB (Law Int Rel) (IB 34 pts)
York – AAB (Int Rel; Pol Int Rel) (IB 35 pts)
128 pts **Dundee** – ABB (Int Rel Pol) (IB 32 pts HL 655)
East Anglia – ABB (Int Rel; Int Rel Comb Hons) (IB 32 pts)
Exeter – ABB–AAB (Hist Int Rel; Hist Int Rel (St Abrd)) (IB 32–34 pts HL 655–665); ABB–AAB incl lang (Int Rel Modn Langs) (IB 32–34 pts HL 655–665)
Lancaster – ABB (Pce St Int Rel; Pol Int Rel) (IB 32 pts HL 16 pts); ABB 128 pts (Glob Relgn Int Rel) (IB 32 pts HL 16 pts)
London (Inst Paris) – ABB+interview (Int Pol) (IB 32 pts HL 655)
London (QM) – ABB (Int Rel Bus Mgt); (Int Rel) (IB 32 pts HL 655)
Loughborough – ABB (Hist Int Rel; Int Rel) (IB 34 pts HL 655)
Queen's Belfast – ABB (Int Rel Pol) (IB 33 pts HL 655)
Reading – ABB (Int Dev) (IB 32 pts)
Southampton – ABB (Int Rel; Pol Int Rel) (IB 32 pts HL 16 pts)
Surrey – ABB (Law Int Rel) (IB 33 pts)
Sussex – ABB (Int Rel; Int Rel Dev) (IB 32 pts)
120 pts **Leicester** – BBB–BBC+bEPQ (Int Rel; Int Rel Hist) (IB 28 pts)
London (Gold) – BBB (Int Rel) (IB 33 pts HL 655)
London (RH) – BBB–ABB (Econ Pol Int Rel; Pol Int Rel) (IB 32 pts HL 655)
Nottingham Trent – 120 pts (Int Law)
Reading – BBB (Int Rel Modn Langs (Fr/Ger/Ital/Span); Pol courses; War Pce Int Rel) (IB 30 pts); BBB 120 pts (Pol Int Rel) (IB 30 pts)
Stirling – BBB (Int Pol) (IB 28 pts)
Surrey – BBB (Int Rel) (IB 32 pts)
Swansea – BBB 120 pts (Int Rel; Int Rel Am St) (IB 32 pts)
112 pts **Aberdeen** – BBC (Pol Int Rel) (IB 32 pts HL 555)
Aston – BBC (Bus Int Rel; Pol Int Rel) (IB 29 pts HL 554)
Bradford – BBC 112 pts (Int Rel Pol Scrty St)
Brunel – BBC–ABB (Int Pol; Mltry Int Hist) (IB 29 pts)
Buckingham – BBC–BBB (Int Rel) (IB 31–32 pts)
Canterbury Christ Church – 112 pts (Int Rel)
Chester – 112 pts (Glob Affrs Pol Int Rel Span) (IB 28 pts)
Coventry – BBC 112 pts (Int Rel) (IB 29 pts)
De Montfort – 112 pts (Int Rel Pol) (IB 26 pts)
Derby – BBB 112 pts (Glob Affrs Pol)
Essex – BBC–BBB (Glob St Lat Am St) (IB 29–30 pts HL 554–554); (Int Rel) (IB 29–30 pts HL 554–555); BBC–BBB 112–120 pts (Glob St Bus Mgt) (IB 29–30 pts HL 554–555); (Glob St Hum Rts) (IB 29–30 pts HL 554–555)
Greenwich – 112 pts (Pol Int Rel)
Hull – BBC 112 pts (Pol Int Rel) (IB 28 pts)
Keele – BBC 112 pts (Int Rel) (IB 29 pts HL 554)
Leeds Beckett – 112 pts (Int Rel courses)
London (Birk) – BBC 112 pts (Glob Pol Int Rel)
London Met – BBC 112 pts (Law (Int Rel))
Middlesex – BBC–BBB 112 pts (Law Int Rel)
Nottingham Trent – 112 pts (Pol Int Rel); BBC 112 pts (Int Rel Comb Hons)
104 pts **Brighton** – BCC–BBB 104–120 pts (Pol Int Rel) (IB 26 pts)
Greenwich – BCC 104 pts (Langs Int Rel)

Lincoln – 104 pts (Int Rel) (IB 28 pts)
Liverpool Hope – BCC 104 pts (Int Rel Comb Hons) (IB 24 pts)
Manchester Met – 104–112 pts (Int Rel) (IB 26 pts)
Oxford Brookes – BCC 104 pts (Int Rel) (IB 29 pts)
Plymouth – 104–112 pts (Pol Int Rel) (IB 26–28 pts HL 4); 104–112 pts (Int Rel) (IB 26–28 pts HL 4)
Portsmouth – BCC–BBC 104–112 pts (Int Rel) (IB 25 pts)
Westminster – BCC 104 pts (Int Rel)
Winchester – BCC–BBB 104–120 pts (Pol Int Rel) (HL 44)

96 pts **London Met** – CCC (Int Rel)
Teesside – 96–112 pts (Pol Int Rel)
Wolverhampton – CCC/BCD 96 pts (War St)

Open University – (Int St courses)

Alternative offers See **Chapter 6** and **Appendix 1** for grades/UCAS Tariff points information for other examinations.

CHOOSING YOUR COURSE (SEE ALSO CH.1)

Universities and colleges teaching quality See www.qaa.ac.uk; www.discoveruni.gov.uk.

Top research universities and colleges (REF 2021) See **Politics**.

Examples of sandwich degree courses Aston; Bath; Brunel; Coventry; Exeter; Nottingham Trent; Plymouth; Portsmouth.

ADMISSIONS INFORMATION

Advice to applicants and planning the UCAS personal statement Describe any special interests you have in the affairs of any particular country. Contact embassies for information on cultural, economic and political developments. Follow international events through newspapers and magazines. Give details of any voluntary work you have done.

Selection interviews Yes London (Inst Paris); **No** De Montfort, East Anglia.

Interview advice and questions Applicants are likely to be questioned on current international events and crises between countries. See also **Chapter 5**.

GRADUATE DESTINATIONS AND EMPLOYMENT

(See **Chapter 1, Graduate Outcomes.**)

Career note See **Politics**.

OTHER DEGREE SUBJECTS FOR CONSIDERATION

Development Studies; Economics; European Studies; Government; Politics.

ITALIAN

(see also **Languages**)

The language and literature of Italy will feature strongly on most Italian courses. The majority of applicants have no knowledge of Italian. They will need to give convincing reasons for their interest and to show that they have the ability to assimilate language quickly. See also **Appendix 3** under **Languages**.

Useful websites http://europa.eu; www.governo.it; www.languageadvantage.com; http://italianstudies.org.uk; www.languagematters.co.uk; see also **Languages**.

NB The points totals shown to the left of the institutions are for ease of reference only. It must not be assumed that Tariff points are always used by institutions or that they can be substituted for an offer in grades. The level of an offer is not necessarily indicative of the quality of a course.

COURSE OFFERS INFORMATION

SUBJECT REQUIREMENTS/PREFERENCES GCSE English and a foreign language required. **AL** Italian may be required for some courses. Some popular universities are now making lower offers for disadvantaged and other students.

YOUR TARGET OFFERS AND EXAMPLES OF DEGREE COURSES

152 pts **Cambridge** – A*AA incl lang+interview+MMLAA (Modn Mediev Langs) (IB 41–42 pts HL 776 incl lang)

144 pts **Durham** – AAA incl lang (Modn Langs Cult (Yr Abrd)) (IB 37 pts HL 666 incl lang)
Oxford – AAA+interview+MLAT (Modn Langs (Ital)) (IB 38 pts HL 666)

136 pts **St Andrews** – AAB (Ital courses) (IB 36 pts HL 665)
Warwick – AAB incl Engl lit+lang (Engl Ital) (IB 34 pts HL 5 Engl lit+lang)
York – AAB incl Fr (Fr Ital Lang (Yr Abrd)) (IB 35 pts HL 6 Fr)

128 pts **Bristol** – ABB incl lang (Modn Langs (Ital)) (IB 32 pts HL 16 pts incl 5 lang); (Modn Langs) (IB 32 pts HL 16 pts incl 5 langs)
Edinburgh – ABB (Ital; Ital Ling) (IB 34 pts HL 655)
Exeter – ABB incl Lat (Modn Langs Lat) (IB 32 pts HL 655 incl Lat)
Leeds – ABB (Ital) (IB 34 pts HL 16 pts)
London (RH) – ABB–AAB (Modn Langs Mgt) (IB 32 pts HL 655)
London (UCL) – ABB (Ital) (IB 34 pts HL 16 pts)
Manchester – ABB (Ital St; Ital courses) (IB 34 pts HL 655)
Sheffield – ABB/BBB+bEPQ incl lang (Modn Langs Cult (Yr Abrd)) (IB 33 pts HL 5 lang)
Sussex – ABB (Anth Lang) (IB 34 pts)
Warwick – ABB incl A Fr/Ger/Ital/Span (Modn Langs) (IB 32 pts HL 6 Fr/Ger/Ital/Span)

120 pts **Bangor** – 120–144 pts (Law Modn Langs)
Glasgow – BBB–AAB incl hum (Ital Comb Hons) (IB 34 pts HL 655 incl Engl+hum)
Kent – BBB 120 pts (Modn Langs (Ital)) (HL 665)
Leicester – BBB/BBC+bEPQ (Modn Langs Comb Hons) (IB 28 pts HL 6 lang); BBB–BBC+aEPQ incl Ital/lang (Modn Langs) (IB 28 pts HL 6 Ital/lang)
London (RH) – BBB–ABB+gr 7 (Modn Langs Mus) (IB 32 pts HL 655); BBB–ABB incl lang (Modn Lang Dr) (IB 32 pts HL 655)
Reading – BBB (Modn Langs (Ital)) (IB 30 pts)

112 pts **London (RH)** – BBC–BBB (Modn Langs) (IB 30 pts HL 555)
Swansea – BBC–ABB 112–128 pts (Modn Langs) (IB 32 pts)

104 pts **Bangor** – 104–128 pts (Modn Langs Hist); 104–128 pts incl modn lang (Modn Langs) (HL 5 incl modn lang)
London (Birk) – BCC 104 pts (Modn Langs (Fr/Ger/Ital/Jap/Span) (Yr Abrd))

96 pts **Portsmouth** – CCC–BCC 96–104 pts (Modn Langs) (IB 25 pts)

ALTERNATIVE OFFERS See **Chapter 6** and **Appendix 1** for grades/UCAS Tariff points information for other examinations.

CHOOSING YOUR COURSE (SEE ALSO CH.1)

UNIVERSITIES AND COLLEGES TEACHING QUALITY See www.qaa.ac.uk; www.discoveruni.gov.uk.

TOP RESEARCH UNIVERSITIES AND COLLEGES (REF 2021) See **Languages**.

EXAMPLES OF SANDWICH DEGREE COURSES Bangor; Bristol; Durham; Edinburgh; Kent; Leeds; Leicester; London (Birk); London (RH); London (UCL); Manchester; Portsmouth; Reading; St Andrews; Warwick; York.

ADMISSIONS INFORMATION

Advice to applicants and planning the UCAS personal statement Describe any visits to Italy and experience of speaking the language. Interests in Italian art, literature, culture, society and architecture could also be mentioned. Read Italian newspapers and magazines and give details if you have a bilingual background. Give evidence of your interest and your reasons for choosing the course. See also **Appendix 3** under **Languages**.

Selection interviews Yes Cambridge, Oxford (Modn Langs) 94% (success rate 44%).

Interview advice and questions Past questions include: Why do you want to learn Italian? What foreign newspapers or magazines do you read (particularly if the applicant has taken A-level Italian)? Have you visited Italy? What do you know of the Italian people, culture, art? See also **Chapter 5**.

GRADUATE DESTINATIONS AND EMPLOYMENT

(See **Chapter 1, Graduate Outcomes.**)

Career note See **Languages**.

OTHER DEGREE SUBJECTS FOR CONSIDERATION

European Studies; International Business Studies; other languages.

JAPANESE

(see also **Languages**)

A strong interest in Japan and its culture is expected of applicants. A number of four-year joint courses are now offered, all of which include a period of study in Japan. Potential employers are showing an interest in Japanese. Students report that 'it is not a soft option'. They are expected to be firmly committed to a Japanese degree (for example, by listing only Japanese on the UCAS application), to have an interest in using their degree in employment and to be prepared for a lot of hard work. See **Appendix 3** under **Languages**.

Useful websites www.ciol.org.uk; www.languageadvantage.com; www.languagematters.co.uk; www.japanese-online.com; http://thejapanesepage.com; www.japanesestudies.org.uk

NB The points totals shown to the left of the institutions are for ease of reference only. It must not be assumed that Tariff points are always used by institutions or that they can be substituted for an offer in grades. The level of an offer is not necessarily indicative of the quality of a course.

COURSE OFFERS INFORMATION

Subject requirements/preferences GCSE A foreign language usually required. **AL** Modern language required for some courses. Some popular universities are now making lower offers for disadvantaged and other students.

Your target offers and examples of degree courses

152 pts **Cambridge** – A*AA+interview+test (As Mid E St) (IB 41–42 pts HL 776)

144 pts **Oxford** – AAA+interview (As Mid E St incl Jap/Arab/Chin/Heb) (IB 39 pts HL 666); AAA+interview+CAT (Class As Mid E St) (IB 39 pts HL 666); AAA+interview+AMELAT (As Mid E St incl Jap/Arab/Chin) (IB 39 pts HL 666)

136 pts **Durham** – AAB (Jap St) (IB 36 pts HL 665)

Edinburgh – AAB (Jap) (IB 34–36 pts HL 655–665); (Jap Ling) (IB 36 pts HL 665)

Leeds – AAB 136 pts (Chin Jap St) (IB 35 pts HL 16–17 pts)

128 pts **Birmingham** – ABB incl lang (Modn Langs (Yr Abrd)) (IB 32 pts HL 655)

East Anglia – ABB (Modn Langs (Yr Abrd)) (IB 32 pts)

Manchester – ABB+interview (Jap St) (IB 34 pts HL 655); ABB incl Chin (Chin Jap) (IB 34 pts HL 655); ABB incl Russ/Jap+interview (Russ Jap) (IB 34 pts HL 655 incl Russ/Jap)

Newcastle – ABB (Jap St; Ling Chin/Jap) (IB 32 pts)
Sheffield – ABB 128 pts (Bus Mgt Jap St) (IB 33 pts); ABB–BBB+bEPQ (Jap St) (IB 33 pts)
Sussex – ABB (Anth Lang) (IB 34 pts)
112 pts **Cardiff** – BBC–ABB (Modn Langs (Chin/Fr/Ger/Ita/Jap/Port/Span)) (IB 30–32 pts HL 655–665)
104 pts **London (Birk)** – BCC 104 pts (Jap St; Modn Langs (Fr/Ger/Ital/Jap/Span) (Yr Abrd))
Manchester Met – BCC–BBC 104–112 pts (TESOL Jap) (IB 26 pts)
Oxford Brookes – BCC 104 pts (Jap St) (IB 29 pts)
96 pts **Central Lancashire** – 96–112 pts incl lang (Modn Langs (2 Langs) (Fr/Span/Jap/Russ/Chin/Kor))

Alternative offers See **Chapter 6** and **Appendix 1** for grades/UCAS Tariff points information for other examinations.

CHOOSING YOUR COURSE (SEE ALSO CH.1)

Universities and colleges teaching quality See www.qaa.ac.uk; www.discoveruni.gov.uk.

Examples of sandwich degree courses Cambridge; Cardiff; Oxford Brookes.

ADMISSIONS INFORMATION

Advice to applicants and planning the UCAS personal statement Discuss your interest in Japan and your reasons for wishing to study the language. Know Japan, its culture and background history. Discuss any visits you have made or contacts with Japanese nationals. See also **Appendix 3** under **Languages**.

Selection interviews Yes Cambridge, Manchester (Jap; Russ Jap), Oxford (As Mid E St) 83% (success rate 31%).

Interview advice and questions Japanese is an extremely demanding subject and applicants are most likely to be questioned on their reasons for choosing this degree. They will be expected also to have some knowledge of Japanese culture, history and current affairs. See also **Chapter 5**.

Reasons for rejection (non-academic) Insufficient evidence of genuine motivation.

GRADUATE DESTINATIONS AND EMPLOYMENT

(See **Chapter 1, Graduate Outcomes.**)

Career note See **Languages**.

OTHER DEGREE SUBJECTS FOR CONSIDERATION

Asia-Pacific Studies; International Business Studies; Oriental Languages; South East Asia Studies.

JOURNALISM

(see also **Communication Studies/Communication, English, Media Studies**)

A passion for writing, good spelling, grammar and punctuation, and the ability to work under pressure are some of the qualities which all journalists require. The opportunities within journalism range from covering day-to-day news stories in the local and national press to periodicals and magazines covering specialist subjects. Journalism is also the foundation for work in local radio.

Useful websites www.journalism.co.uk; www.bjtc.org.uk; www.nctj.com; www.nuj.org.uk

The points totals shown to the left of the institutions are for ease of reference only. It must not be assumed that Tariff points are always used by institutions or that they can be substituted for an offer in grades. The level of an offer is not necessarily indicative of the quality of a course.

COURSE OFFERS INFORMATION

Subject requirements/preferences GCSE English and maths often required. **AL** No specific subjects required. Some popular universities are now making lower offers for disadvantaged and other students.

YOUR TARGET OFFERS AND EXAMPLES OF DEGREE COURSES

136 pts **Leeds** – AAB incl arts/hum/soc sci (Jrnl) (IB 35 pts HL 16 pts incl 5 Engl)
Newcastle – AAB (Jrnl Media Cult) (IB 34 pts)

128 pts **City St George's** – ABB 128 pts (Jrnl Pol Hist) (IB 31 pts); ABB 128 pts+interview (Jrnl) (IB 31 pts HL 555)
Sheffield – ABB (Jrnl St) (IB 33 pts)
Sussex – ABB (Media Jrnl) (IB 32 pts)

120 pts **Cardiff** – BBB–ABB incl Engl (Jrnl Media Engl Lit) (IB 31–32 pts HL 665 incl 6 Engl)
East Anglia – BBB 120 pts+interview (Broad Multim Jrnl (Plmt Yr)) (IB 31 pts)
Leicester – BBB/BBC+bEPQ (Jrnl; Jrnl Media) (IB 28 pts)
London (Gold) – BBB+interview (Jrnl) (IB 33 pts HL 655)
Stirling – BBB (Jrnl St) (IB 28 pts)
Strathclyde – BBB–ABB (Jrnl Media Comm courses) (IB 30–32 pts)
Trinity Saint David – 120 pts (Doc Photo Vis Actvsm) (IB 32 pts)

112 pts **Bedfordshire** – 112 pts (Sports Jrnl)
Birmingham City – BBC 112 pts (Jrnl) (IB 28 pts)
Cardiff – BBC–ABB (Media Jrnl Cult) (IB 30–32 pts HL 655–665); BBC–ABB 112–128 pts (Jrnl Comms) (IB 30–32 pts HL 655–665)
Coventry – BBC+portfolio (Jrnl) (IB 29 pts HL Engl)
Derby – BBC 112 pts+portfolio (Jrnl; Spec Spo Jrnl)
East London – 112 pts (Spo Jrnl) (IB 24 pts HL 15 pts)
Edinburgh Napier – BBC incl Engl/psy/sociol/class (Jrnl) (IB 29 pts HL 655 incl 5 Engl)
Glasgow Caledonian – BBC (Multim Jrnl)
Hertfordshire – BBC–BBB 112–120 pts (Jrnl Comb Hons)
Leeds Beckett – 112 pts (Jrnl) (IB 25 pts)
Leeds Trinity – 112 pts (Broad Dig Jrnl; Spo Jrnl)
Liverpool John Moores – BBC 112 pts (Jrnl) (IB 27 pts)
London Met – BBC 112 pts (Fash Mark Jrnl; Jrnl Flm TV St); BBC 112 pts+interview (Jrnl)
Middlesex – BBC 112 pts (Dig Med Comm)
Nottingham Trent – 112 pts (Broad Jrnl; Jrnl)
Portsmouth – 112–120 pts (Jrnl) (IB 25 pts)
Roehampton – 112 pts incl hum (Jrnl)
Staffordshire – BBC 112 pts (Spo Jrnl)
West London – BBC 112 pts (Jrnl Cntnt Crea)

104 pts **Arts London** – 104 pts (Mag Jrnl Pub) (IB 24 pts)
Bournemouth – 104–120 pts (Multim Jrnl) (IB 28–31 pts)
Brighton – BCC–BBB 104–120 pts (Spo Jrnl) (IB 26–30 pts)
Chester – 104 pts (Spo Jrnl) (IB 26 pts); BCC–BBC 104–112 pts (Jrnl) (IB 26 pts)
De Montfort – 104 pts (Jrnl) (IB 24 pts)
Falmouth – 104–120 pts+interview (Jrnl Crea Writ)
Huddersfield – BCC–BBC 104–112 pts+interview (Spo Jrnl); BCC–BBC 104–112 pts+interview (Multim Jrnl)
Lincoln – BCC 104 pts (Jrnl) (IB 28 pts)
Northampton – BCC incl Engl/hum (Multim Jrnl)
Robert Gordon – BCC incl Engl (Jrnl) (IB 27 pts HL 5 Engl)
Solent – 104–120 pts (Spo Jrnl)
South Wales – BCC 104 pts (Jrnl)
Sunderland – 104–120 pts (Jrnl; Spo Jrnl); 104–120 pts+interview (Fash Jrnl)
Winchester – BCC–BBB 104–120 pts (Jrnl) (HL 44)
Worcester – 104 pts (Jrnl)

96 pts **Bangor** – 96–128 pts (Media Flm Jrnl)
Central Lancashire – 96–112 pts (Jrnl; Spo Jrnl)
Gloucestershire – CCC–BBB 96–120 pts+interview (Jrnl; Photojrnl Doc Photo)
Marjon – CCC (Spo Jrnl); CCC 96 pts+interview (Jrnl)
Teesside – 96–112 pts (Flm TV Prod; Jrnl)

Wolverhampton – CCC/BCD 96 pts+interview (Jrnl)

48 pts **Buckingham** – DD 48 pts (Cntnt Crea Dig Media Jrnl (Integ Fdn))

ALTERNATIVE OFFERS See **Chapter 6** and **Appendix 1** for grades/UCAS Tariff points information for other examinations.

DEGREE APPRENTICESHIPS

Kent (Snr Jrnl); Sunderland (Snr Jrnl).

EXAMPLES OF COLLEGES OFFERING COURSES IN THIS SUBJECT FIELD

Darlington (Coll); Exeter (Coll); Harlow (Coll); Peterborough (UC); South Essex (Coll).

CHOOSING YOUR COURSE (SEE ALSO CH.1)

UNIVERSITIES AND COLLEGES TEACHING QUALITY See www.qaa.ac.uk; www.discoveruni.gov.uk.

EXAMPLES OF SANDWICH DEGREE COURSES Bangor; City St George's; Coventry; East Anglia; Hertfordshire; Huddersfield; Leeds; Portsmouth; Robert Gordon.

ADMISSIONS INFORMATION

ADMISSIONS TUTORS' ADVICE **Buckingham** As far as journalism and media are concerned you can't be just a wannabe any more. Keeping a blog (on any theme) is great; so is producing video for YouTube. Writing for a school magazine or newspaper is also well regarded. Active knowledge of current affairs and a wide frame of reference is to be commended. Having an interest in people is absolutely key.

SELECTION INTERVIEWS **Yes** East Anglia, Falmouth, Gloucestershire, Huddersfield, London (Gold), London Met, Marjon, Sunderland, Wolverhampton; **Some** City St George's, Worcester; **No** Northumbria.

GRADUATE DESTINATIONS AND EMPLOYMENT

(See **Chapter 1, Graduate Outcomes.**)

CAREER NOTE Some graduates go on to work directly in journalism for local, regional and national newspapers, magazines, broadcasting corporations and creative digital media agencies as journalists, press editors and publishing copy-editors. Many enter other areas, including PR, advertising, marketing, management, charity work, education, law and politics.

OTHER DEGREE SUBJECTS FOR CONSIDERATION

Communication Studies; English; Media Studies

LANDSCAPE ARCHITECTURE

(including **Garden Design**; see also **Agricultural Sciences/Agriculture, Architecture, Horticulture**)

Landscape architects shape the world you live in. They are responsible for urban design, the integration of ecology and the quality of the built environment. Courses in Landscape Architecture include project-based design, landscape theory, management, planning and design, ecology, construction, plant design and design practice. After completing the first three years leading to a BSc (Hons) or BA (Hons), students aiming for full professional status take a further one year in practice and one year to achieve their Master of Landscape Architecture (MLA). Courses with a foundation year are available at some institutions.

USEFUL WEBSITES www.landscapeinstitute.org; www.chooselandscape.org; www.bali.org.uk

NB The points totals shown to the left of the institutions are for ease of reference only. It must not be assumed that Tariff points are always used by institutions or that they can be substituted for an offer in grades. The level of an offer is not necessarily indicative of the quality of a course.

COURSE OFFERS INFORMATION

Subject requirements/preferences GCSE English, geography, art and design, mathematics and at least one science usually required. **AL** Preferred subjects for some courses include biology, geography and environmental science. A portfolio may also be required. Some popular universities are now making lower offers for disadvantaged and other students.

Your target offers and examples of degree courses

144 pts **Sheffield** – AAA+portfolio (Archit Lnd) (IB 36 pts)
136 pts **London (UCL)** – AAB (Urb Plan Des Mgt) (IB 36 pts HL 17 pts)
128 pts **Edinburgh** – ABB (Lnd Archit) (IB 34 pts HL 655)
Sheffield – ABB (Lnd Archit) (IB 33 pts)
120 pts **Leeds Beckett** – 120 pts+portfolio (Lnd Archit Des) (IB 26 pts)
112 pts **Birmingham City** – BBC 112 pts+portfolio (Lnd Archit) (IB 28 pts)
Greenwich – BBC 112 pts+interview+portfolio (Lnd Archit)
Westminster – BBC 112 pts (Urb Plan Des)
96 pts **Gloucestershire** – CCC–BBB 96–120 pts+interview (Lnd Archit)
Reaseheath (UC) – 96 pts (Lnd Archit)
64 pts **Ravensbourne Univ** – CC (Urb Lnd Archit) (IB 24 pts)

Alternative offers See **Chapter 6** and **Appendix 1** for grades/UCAS Tariff points information for other examinations.

EXAMPLES OF COLLEGES OFFERING COURSES IN THIS SUBJECT FIELD

Craven (Coll); Duchy Coll (UC).

CHOOSING YOUR COURSE (SEE ALSO CH.1)

Universities and colleges teaching quality See www.qaa.ac.uk; www.discoveruni.gov.uk.

ADMISSIONS INFORMATION

Advice to applicants and planning the UCAS personal statement Knowledge of the work of landscape architects is important. Arrange a visit to a landscape architect's office and try to organise some work experience. Read up on historical landscape design and visit country house estates with examples of outstanding designs. Describe these visits in detail and your preferences. Membership of the National Trust could be useful. See also **Appendix 3**.

Selection interviews Yes Gloucestershire, Greenwich; **No** Sheffield.

Interview advice and questions Applicants will be expected to have had some work experience and are likely to be questioned on their knowledge of landscape architectural work and the subject. Historical examples of good landscaping could also be asked for. See also **Chapter 5**.

Reasons for rejection (non-academic) Lack of historical knowledge and awareness of current developments. Poor portfolio.

GRADUATE DESTINATIONS AND EMPLOYMENT

(See **Chapter 1, Graduate Outcomes.**)

Career note Opportunities at present in landscape architecture are good. Openings exist in local government or private practice and may cover planning, housing, and conservation.

OTHER DEGREE SUBJECTS FOR CONSIDERATION

Architecture; Art and Design; Environmental Planning; Forestry; Horticulture.

LANGUAGES

(including **British Sign Language, European Studies, Modern Languages and Translation Studies; see separate language tables**; see also **Chinese, English, European Studies, French, German, Greek, Italian, Japanese, Latin, Linguistics, Russian and East European Studies, Scandinavian Studies, Spanish, Portuguese and Latin American Studies**)

Modern language courses usually offer three main options: a single subject degree commonly based on literature and language, a European Studies course, or two-language subjects which can often include languages different from those available at school (such as Scandinavian Studies, Russian and the languages of Eastern Europe, the Middle and Far East).

Useful websites www.ciol.org.uk; www.iti.org.uk; http://europa.eu; www.languageadvantage.com; www.omniglot.com; www.languagematters.co.uk

NB The points totals shown to the left of the institutions are for ease of reference only. It must not be assumed that Tariff points are always used by institutions or that they can be substituted for an offer in grades. The level of an offer is not necessarily indicative of the quality of a course.

COURSE OFFERS INFORMATION

Subject requirements/preferences GCSE English and a modern language required. In some cases grades 7 and/or 5/6 (A and/or B) may be stipulated. **AL** A modern foreign language required usually with a specified grade. Some popular universities are now making lower offers for disadvantaged and other students.

Your target offers and examples of degree courses

152 pts **Cambridge** – A*AA+interview+test (As Mid E St) (IB 41–42 pts HL 776); A*AA incl lang+interview+MMLAA (Modn Mediev Langs) (IB 41–42 pts HL 776 incl lang)

144 pts **Birmingham** – AAA–A*AA (Econ Lang) (IB 32 pts HL 766)

Durham – AAA incl lang (Modn Langs Cult (Yr Abrd)) (IB 37 pts HL 666 incl lang); AAA incl lang+hist (Modn Euro Langs Hist (Yr Abrd)) (IB 37 pts HL 666)

Oxford – AAA+interview (As Mid E St incl Jap/Arab/Chin/Heb) (IB 39 pts HL 666); AAA+interview+CAT+MLAT (Class Modn Langs) (IB 39 pts HL 666); AAA+interview+HAT+MLAT (Hist Modn Langs) (IB 38 pts HL 666); AAA+interview+MLAT (Modn Langs (Russ+2nd Lang); Modn Langs Ling) (IB 38 pts HL 666); (Phil Modn Langs) (IB 39 pts HL 666); AAA+interview+MLAT+AMELAT (Euro Mid E Langs (Cz/Russ)) (IB 38 pts HL 666); AAA+interview+AMELAT (As Mid E St incl Jap/Arab/Chin) (IB 39 pts HL 666); AAA incl Engl+interview+MLAT (Engl Modn Langs) (IB 38 pts HL 666 incl Engl)

St Andrews – AAA (Heb courses) (IB 36 pts HL 665)

136 pts **Bath** – AAB–ABB+aEPQ incl lang (Int Pol Modn Langs (Fr/Span/Ger) (Yr Abrd)) (IB 35 pts HL 665 incl lang)

Bristol – AAB incl lang (Phil Modn Lang; Pol Modn Lang) (IB 34 pts HL 17 pts incl 5 lang); AAB incl mus+lang (Mus Modn Lang) (IB 34 pts HL 17 pts incl 5 mus+lang)

Edinburgh – AAB incl lang (Span Port) (IB 37 pts HL 666 incl lang)

Manchester – AAB–AAA incl sci+lang (Biol Modn Lang) (IB 35–36 pts HL 665–666 incl sci +lang); AAB–AAA incl sci/maths (Microbiol Modn Lang) (IB 35–36 pts HL 665–666 incl sci); AAB–AAA incl sci/maths+lang (Genet Modn Lang) (IB 35–36 pts HL 665–666 incl sci+lang)

Sussex – AAB (Int Dev Lang) (IB 34 pts)

128 pts **Birmingham** – ABB incl lang (Modn Langs (Yr Abrd)) (IB 32 pts HL 655)

Bristol – ABB incl lang (Hist Art Modn Lang (Yr Abrd)) (IB 32 pts HL 16 pts incl 5 lang); (Modn Langs) (IB 32 pts HL 16 pts incl 5 langs)

East Anglia – ABB (Modn Langs (Yr Abrd)) (IB 32 pts); ABB incl B Fr/Span/Jap (Transl Media Modn Langs) (IB 32 pts HL 5 Fr/Span/Jap)

Exeter – ABB (Modn Langs Arbc) (IB 32 pts HL 655); ABB incl Lat (Modn Langs Lat) (IB 32 pts HL 655 incl Lat); ABB–AAB incl lang (Int Rel Modn Langs) (IB 32–34 pts HL 655–665)
Lancaster – ABB incl lang (Modn Langs (Yr Abrd)) (IB 32 pts HL 16 pts incl lang)
Leeds – ABB (Modn Lang Ling) (IB 34 pts HL 16 pts); ABB incl Russ (Port Russ) (IB 34 pts HL 16 pts incl 5 Russ)
Liverpool – ABB incl lang (Modn Langs (Yr Abrd)) (IB 33 pts HL 6 lang); ABB incl maths (Maths Langs) (IB 33 pts HL 6 maths)
London (SOAS) – ABB (Kor) (IB 32 pts HL 655)
London (UCL) – ABB (Lang Cult) (IB 34 pts HL 16 pts)
Newcastle – ABB incl Fr (Ling Fr) (IB 32 pts HL 5 Fr); ABB incl Fr/Ger/Span (Mod Langs Transl Interp; Modn Langs; Modn Langs Ling) (IB 32 pts HL 6 Fr/Ger/Span)
Nottingham – ABB (Modn Euro St; Modn Langs; Modn Langs Bus) (IB 30 pts HL 655); ABB incl lang (Modn Lang St (Yr Abrd)) (IB 30 pts HL 655)
Sheffield – ABB/BBB+bEPQ incl lang (Modn Langs Cult (Yr Abrd)) (IB 33 pts HL 5 lang)
Southampton – ABB incl langs (Modn Langs) (IB 32 pts HL 16 pts incl 55 langs)

120 pts **Leicester** – BBB/BBC+bEPQ (Modn Langs Comb Hons) (IB 28 pts HL 6 lang); BBB–ABB incl Fr/Span/Ital (Modn Langs Transl) (IB 28 pts HL 6 Fr/Span/Ital)
London (RH) – BBB–ABB (Modn Langs Lat) (IB 32 pts HL 655)
Reading – BBB incl hist (Modn Langs Hist) (IB 30 pts HL 5 hist)
Stirling – BBB incl lang (Euro Langs Soty Int Mgt; Modn Langs) (IB 28 pts)
Surrey – BBB (Modn Lang (Fr Span)) (IB 32 pts)

112 pts **Aberdeen** – BBC (Lang Ling (Yr Abrd)) (IB 32 pts HL 555)
Cardiff – BBC–ABB (Modn Langs (Chin/Fr/Ger/Ita/Jap/Port/Span)) (IB 30–32 pts HL 655–665)
Essex – BBC (Euro St Modn Langs) (IB 29 pts HL 554); BBC–BBB (Span St Modn Langs) (IB 29–30 pts HL 554–555); BBC–BBB 112–120 pts (Fr St Modn Langs; Lang St Ling; Modn Langs) (IB 29–30 pts HL 554–555)
Heriot-Watt – BBC incl B lang (App Modn Langs Transl (Fr/Span/Ger/Chin)) (IB 30 pts HL 5 lang); BBC incl lang (Brit Sign Lang (Interp Transl App Lang St); Modn Langs (Interp Transl) (Fr/Ger)/(Ger/Span)) (IB 30 pts HL 5 lang)
London (RH) – BBC–BBB (Modn Langs) (IB 30 pts HL 555)
London Met – BBC 112 pts (Transl)
Swansea – BBC–ABB 112–128 pts (Modn Langs) (IB 32 pts); BBC–ABB 112–128 pts (Modn Langs Transl Inter) (IB 32 pts)

104 pts **Aberystwyth** – BCC–BBB incl B lang 104–120 pts (Modn Langs (Yr Abrd)) (IB 28–30 pts HL 5 lang)
Bangor – 104–128 pts (Ling Modn Lang)
Chester – BCC–BBC incl lang 104–112 pts (Modn Langs) (IB 28 pts)
Greenwich – BCC 104 pts (Langs Int Rel)
London (Birk) – BCC 104 pts (Ling Lang)
Westminster – 104–120 pts incl Span (Transl (Span)) (HL 4 Span); BCC–BBB incl Fr 104–120 pts (Langs Transl) (HL 4 Fr/Span)

96 pts **Central Lancashire** – 96–112 pts incl lang (Modn Langs (2 Langs) (Fr/Span/Jap/Russ/Chin/Kor))
Portsmouth – CCC–BCC 96–104 pts (Modn Langs) (IB 25 pts)
Wolverhampton – CCC 96 pts (Brit Sign Lang (Interp))

Open University – (Lang St)

Alternative offers See **Chapter 6** and **Appendix 1** for grades/UCAS Tariff points information for other examinations.

CHOOSING YOUR COURSE (SEE ALSO CH.1)

Universities and colleges teaching quality See www.qaa.ac.uk; www.discoveruni.gov.uk.

Top research universities and colleges (REF 2021) (Modern Languages and Linguistics) York; Lancaster; Essex; Bristol; London (RH); Nottingham; Newcastle; Manchester; Liverpool; London (SOAS).

EXAMPLES OF SANDWICH DEGREE COURSES Aberdeen; Bath; Birmingham; Bristol; Durham; East Anglia; Lancaster; Liverpool; London (Birk); Manchester; Nottingham; Sheffield; Westminster; Wolverhampton.

ADMISSIONS INFORMATION

ADVICE TO APPLICANTS AND PLANNING THE UCAS PERSONAL STATEMENT Discuss any literature studied outside your course work. Students applying for courses in which they have no previous knowledge (for example, Italian, Portuguese, Modern Greek, Czech, Russian) would be expected to have done a considerable amount of language work on their own in their chosen language before starting the course. See also **Appendix 3**.

SELECTION INTERVIEWS Yes Cambridge, Oxford (Modn Langs) 94% (success rate 44%), (Modn Langs Ling) 93% (success rate 40%); **No** London (RH), Swansea.

INTERVIEW ADVICE AND QUESTIONS See also **Chapter 5**.

REASONS FOR REJECTION (NON-ACADEMIC) Lack of commitment to spend a year abroad. Poor references. Poor standard of English. No reasons for why the course has been selected. Poor communication skills. Incomplete applications, for example missing qualifications and reference.

GRADUATE DESTINATIONS AND EMPLOYMENT

(See **Chapter 1, Graduate Outcomes.**)

CAREER NOTE The only career-related fields for language students are teaching, which attracts some graduates, and the demanding work of interpreting and translating, to which only a small number aspire. The majority will be attracted to work in management and administration, financial services and a host of other occupations which may include the social services, law and property development.

OTHER DEGREE SUBJECTS FOR CONSIDERATION

Communication Studies; Linguistics; Modern Languages Education/Teaching.

LATIN

(see also **Classics and Classical Studies/Civilisation, Greek, Languages**)

Latin courses provide a study of the language, art, religion and history of the Roman world. This table should be read in conjunction with the **Classics and Classical Studies/Civilisation** table.

USEFUL WEBSITES www.thelatinlibrary.com; www.arlt.co.uk; www.cambridgescp.com

NB The points totals shown to the left of the institutions are for ease of reference only. It must not be assumed that Tariff points are always used by institutions or that they can be substituted for an offer in grades. The level of an offer is not necessarily indicative of the quality of a course.

COURSE OFFERS INFORMATION

SUBJECT REQUIREMENTS/PREFERENCES GCSE English, a foreign language and Latin may be stipulated. **AL** Check courses for Latin requirement. Some popular universities are now making lower offers for disadvantaged and other students.

YOUR TARGET OFFERS AND EXAMPLES OF DEGREE COURSES

152 pts **Cambridge** – A*AA+interview+test (Modn Mediev Langs (Class Lat)) (IB 41–42 pts HL 776); A*AA incl Lat+interview+CAA (Class) (IB 41–42 pts HL 776 incl Lat)
Edinburgh – A*AA (Lat St) (IB 39 pts HL 666)

144 pts **Oxford** – AAA+interview+CAT (Class) (IB 39 pts HL 666)
St Andrews – AAA incl lang (Lat courses) (IB 36 pts HL 665 incl 6 lang)

136 pts **Edinburgh** – AAB (Anc Hist Lat) (IB 36 pts HL 665)
London (UCL) – AAB incl A Engl+Lat (Latin (Comb Hons)) (IB 36 pts HL 17 pts incl 6 Engl+Lat)

	Warwick – AAB incl A Lat (Class (Lat)) (IB 34 pts HL 6 Lat)
128 pts	**Exeter** – ABB incl Lat (Modn Langs Lat) (IB 32 pts HL 655 incl Lat)
	Manchester – ABB (Lat courses) (IB 34 pts HL 655)
120 pts	**Glasgow** – BBB–AAB incl hum (Lat Comb Hons) (IB 34 pts HL 655 incl Engl+hum)
	London (RH) – BBB–ABB (Lat; Modn Langs Lat) (IB 32 pts HL 655)

Alternative offers See **Chapter 6** and **Appendix 1** for grades/UCAS Tariff points information for other examinations.

CHOOSING YOUR COURSE (SEE ALSO CH.1)

Universities and colleges teaching quality See www.qaa.ac.uk; www.discoveruni.gov.uk.

Top research universities and colleges (REF 2021) See **Classics and Classical Studies/Civilisation**.

Examples of sandwich degree courses Edinburgh; Exeter; Glasgow; St Andrews.

ADMISSIONS INFORMATION

Advice to applicants and planning the UCAS personal statement See **Classics and Classical Studies/Civilisation**.

Selection interviews Yes Cambridge; **No** London (RH).

Interview advice and questions See **Classics and Classical Studies/Civilisation**.

GRADUATE DESTINATIONS AND EMPLOYMENT

(See **Chapter 1, Graduate Outcomes.**)

Career note Graduates enter a broad range of careers within management, the media, commerce and tourism as well as social and public services. Some graduates choose to work abroad and teaching is a popular option.

OTHER DEGREE SUBJECTS FOR CONSIDERATION

Ancient History; Archaeology; Classical Studies; Classics.

LAW

(including **Criminology**; see also **Social Sciences/Studies**)

Law courses are usually divided into two parts. Part I occupies the first year and introduces the student to criminal and constitutional law and the legal process. Thereafter, many different specialised topics can be studied in the second and third years. Consult the subsection Interview advice and questions in order to gain a flavour of the types of questions raised in studying this subject. The course content is very similar for most courses. Applicants are advised to check with universities for their current policies concerning their use of the National Admissions Test for Law (LNAT). See Subject requirements/preferences below and also **Chapter 5**.

Useful websites www.barcouncil.org.uk; www.cilex.org.uk; www.lawcareers.net; www.lawsociety.org.uk; www.cps.gov.uk; www.gov.uk/government/organisations/hm-courts-and-tribunals-service; www.lawscot.org.uk; www.lawsoc-ni.org; www.rollonfriday.com; www.lnat.ac.uk

NB The points totals shown to the left of the institutions are for ease of reference only. It must not be assumed that Tariff points are always used by institutions or that they can be substituted for an offer in grades. The level of an offer is not necessarily indicative of the quality of a course.

COURSE OFFERS INFORMATION

Subject requirements/preferences GCSE Many universities will expect high grades. **AL** Arts, humanities, social sciences and sciences plus languages for courses combined with a foreign language. Some popular universities are now making lower offers for disadvantaged and other students. **All universities** Applicants offering art and music A-levels should check whether these subjects are acceptable.

YOUR TARGET OFFERS AND EXAMPLES OF DEGREE COURSES

152 pts **Bristol** – A*AA/A*A*B+LNAT (Law) (IB 38 pts HL 18 pts); A*AA/A*A*B incl Fr+LNAT (Law Fr) (IB 38 pts HL 18 pts incl 5 Fr); A*AA/A*A*B incl Ger+LNAT (Law Ger) (IB 38 pts HL 18 pts incl 5 Ger)
Cambridge – A*AA+interview (Lnd Econ) (IB 41–42 pts HL 776); A*AA+interview+CLT (Law) (IB 40–42 pts HL 776)
Durham – A*AA+LNAT (Law) (IB 38 pts HL 666)
Edinburgh – A*AA incl Engl (Glob Law; Law Acc; Law courses) (IB 39 pts HL 666 incl Engl)
Leeds – A*AA (Law) (IB 36 pts HL 666)
London (King's) – A*AA+LNAT (Law) (IB 35 pts HL 766); (Pol Phil Law) (IB 38 pts HL 19 pts); A*AA incl Fr/Ger+LNAT (Engl Law Fr Law/Ger Law) (IB 35 pts HL 766 incl 6 Fr/Ger)
London (QM) – A*AA (Law; Law Pol) (IB 36 pts HL 666)
London (UCL) – A*AA+LNAT (Law) (IB 39 pts HL 19 pts); A*AA incl Fr/Ger/Span+LNAT (Law Fr Law/Ger Law/Hisp Law) (IB 39 pts HL 19 pts incl 6 Fr/Ger/Span)
London LSE – A*AA+LNAT (Law) (IB 38 pts HL 766)
Manchester – A*AA (Law; Law Crimin; Law Pol) (IB 37 pts HL 766)
Nottingham – A*AA+LNAT (Law) (IB 38 pts); A*AA incl Fr/Span+LNAT (Law Fr Fr Law/Span Span Law) (IB 38 pts HL 6 Fr/Span)
Warwick – A*AA (Law; Law (St Abrd)) (IB 38 pts)

144 pts **Birmingham** – AAA (Law; Law Bus St) (IB 32 pts HL 666); AAA incl Ger (Law Ger Law) (IB 32 pts HL 666 incl Ger)
East Anglia – AAA (Law Am Law)
Exeter – AAA (Law; Law (Euro St); Law (Yr Ind)) (IB 36 pts HL 666)
Glasgow – AAA incl Engl+LNAT (Cmn Law) (IB 38 pts HL 666 incl Engl)
Liverpool – AAA (Law; Law Acc Fin) (IB 36 pts)
London (SOAS) – AAA (Law) (IB 37 pts HL 666)
Newcastle – AAA (Law) (IB 34 pts)
Oxford – AAA+interview+LNAT (Law; Law Euro Law) (IB 38 pts HL 666)
Queen's Belfast – AAA (Law) (IB 36 pts HL 666)
Sheffield – AAA/AAB+aEPQ (Law; Law (Euro Int)) (IB 36 pts)
Southampton – AAA (Euro Leg St; Int Leg St; Law) (IB 36 pts HL 18 pts)
York – AAA/A*AB/A*A*C (Law) (IB 36 pts)

136 pts **Aberdeen** – AAB (Law) (IB 34 pts)
Cardiff – AAB–AAA (Law; Law Crimin) (IB 34–36 pts HL 666)
East Anglia – AAB (Law Euro Leg Sys) (IB 33 pts); AAB/ABB+aEPQ (Law) (IB 33 pts)
Kent – AAB (Int Legal St (Yr Abrd); Law Comb Hons); AAB 136 pts (Law Pol) (HL 666)
Lancaster – AAB (Law; Law (St Abrd); Law Crimin) (IB 35 pts HL 16 pts)
Leicester – AAB (Law) (IB 33 pts); AAB incl lang (Law Modn Lang (Fr/Span/Ital)) (IB 33 pts); AAB–AAA incl Fr+interview (Engl Fr Law (Mait)) (IB 34–36 pts HL 6 Fr)
London LSE – AAB (Anth Law) (IB 37 pts HL 666)
NU London – AAB (Law) (IB 35 pts HL 665)
Reading – AAB (Law) (IB 34 pts)
Sheffield – AAB/ABB+bEPQ (Law Crimin) (IB 34 pts)
Sussex – AAB (Law Int Rel; Law Pol) (IB 34 pts)
Warwick – AAB (Law Sociol) (IB 34 pts); AAB incl Fr/Ger (Law Fr Law/Ger Law) (IB 34 pts HL 6 Fr/Ger)

128 pts **City St George's** – ABB 128 pts (Law) (IB 31 pts)
Dundee – ABB (Law (Scot Engl); Law Scot) (IB 32 pts HL 655); ABB incl AB Engl+lang (Law Langs) (IB 32 pts HL 655 incl Engl)
Essex – ABB incl Fr (Engl Fr Law (Mait)) (IB 32 pts HL 655 incl 6 Fr)
Greenwich – 128 pts (Law)
Huddersfield – ABB 128 pts (Law)

Keele – ABB (Law courses) (IB 32 pts HL 655)
London (RH) – ABB–AAB (Law) (IB 32 pts HL 665)
Stirling – ABB (Law) (IB 36 pts)
Sunderland – 128 pts (Law)
Surrey – ABB (Law; Law Crimin; Law Int Rel) (IB 33 pts)
Sussex – ABB–AAB (Law; Law Am St; Law Bus Mgt; Law Lang (Yr Abrd)) (IB 32–34 pts)

120 pts **Aston** – BBB (Law) (IB 31 pts HL 555)
Brunel – BBB (Law) (IB 30 pts)
De Montfort – 120 pts (Law) (IB 28 pts)
Edinburgh Napier – BBB incl Engl (Law) (IB 30 pts HL 655 incl Engl)
Hertfordshire – BBB–ABB 120–128 pts (Law)
Hull – BBB (Law Pol) (IB 30 pts); BBB 120 pts (Law) (IB 30 pts)
Kingston – 120 pts (Law)
Leeds Beckett – 120 pts (Law) (HL 554)
Liverpool John Moores – BBB 120 pts (Law; Law Crim Just)
Manchester Met – BBB 120 pts (Law) (IB 30 pts)
Northumbria – 120 pts (Law)
Nottingham Trent – 120 pts (Law)
Oxford Brookes – BBB 120 pts (Law) (IB 31 pts)
Sheffield Hallam – BBB 120 pts (Law; Law Crimin)
Swansea – BBB–AAB (Bus Law)
Ulster – BBB (Law) (IB 26 pts HL 13 pts); BBB incl Ir (Law Ir) (IB 26 pts HL 13 pts)
Univ Law – BBB (Law; Law Bus) (IB 29 pts)
Worcester – BBB 120 pts+interview (Law; Law Crimin)

112 pts **Birmingham City** – BBC 112 pts (Law; Law Am Leg St; Law Crim Just; Sociol Crimin) (IB 28 pts HL 14 pts)
Bradford – 112 pts (Bus St Law; Law)
Buckingham – BBC–BBB+interview (Law; Law Bus Mgt) (IB 31–32 pts)
Canterbury Christ Church – BBC (Law) (IB 29 pts)
Cardiff Met – BBC 112 pts (Bus Mgt Law) (HL 55)
Chester – BBC–BBB 112–120 pts (Law; Law Comb Hons) (IB 28 pts); BBC–BBB 112–120 pts (Law Crimin) (IB 28 pts)
Coventry – BBC (Law) (IB 24 pts)
Cumbria – BBC 112–128 pts (Law)
Derby – BBC–BBB 112–120 pts (Law; Law Crimin)
East London – 112 pts (Law) (IB 24 pts HL 15 pts)
Edge Hill – BBC–BBB 112–120 pts (Law; Law Crimin)
Essex – BBC (Law; Law Crimin; Law Hum Rts; Phil Law) (IB 29 pts HL 554)
Liverpool Hope – BBC 112 pts (Law Comb Hons) (IB 28 pts)
London Met – BBC 112 pts (Law; Law (Int Rel))
London South Bank – (Law)
Middlesex – BBC–ABB 112–128 pts (Law); BBC–BBB 112 pts (Law Int Rel)
Northampton – BBC (Law courses)
Nottingham Trent – 112 pts (Law Bus; Law Crimin; Law Psy)
Plymouth – 112–128 pts (Law) (IB 28–32 pts)
Portsmouth – 112–120 pts (Law; Law Crimin) (IB 29 pts); BBC–BBB 112–120 pts (Law Bus) (IB 29 pts)
Solent – 112–128 pts (Law)
Staffordshire – BBC 112 pts (Law)
UWE Bristol – 112 pts (Law; Law Crimin)
West London – BBC 112–128 pts (Law)
West Scotland – BBC 112 pts (Law) (IB 24 pts)
Westminster – BBC–ABB 112–128 pts (Euro Leg St; Law); BBC–ABB incl Fr 112–128 pts (Law Fr Law) (HL 6 Fr)
Winchester – 112–120 pts (Law; Law Comb Hons) (HL 44)

104 pts **Aberystwyth** – BCC–ABB 104–128 pts (Crim Law; Euro Law; Law) (IB 28–30 pts)
Bangor – 104–136 pts (Law Crimin; Law courses)
Bournemouth – 104–120 pts (Law) (IB 28–31 pts)
Brighton – BCC–BBB 104–120 pts (Law Bus) (IB 26 pts)
Bucks New – 104–128 pts (Bus Law; Law)
Central Lancashire – 104–112 pts (Law; Law Crimin)
Gloucestershire – (Law)
Lincoln – (Law)
Robert Gordon – BCC incl Engl (Law) (IB 28 pts HL 5 Engl)
South Wales – BCC 104 pts (Law; Law Crimin Crim Just)

96 pts **Abertay** – CCC (Law) (IB 28 pts)
Anglia Ruskin – 96 pts (Law) (IB 24 pts)
Chichester – CCC–BBB 96–120 pts (Law) (IB 28 pts)
London (Birk) – CCC–BBB 96–120 pts (Law)
St Mary's – 96–112 pts (Bus Law courses; Law)
Wolverhampton – CCC/BCD (Law)

88 pts **Teesside** – 88–112 pts (Law)

80 pts **Bedfordshire** – 80 pts (Law)
Teesside – 80–104 pts (Law Bus Mgt)

Open University – (Law)

ALTERNATIVE OFFERS See **Chapter 6** and **Appendix 1** for grades/UCAS Tariff points information for other examinations.

DEGREE APPRENTICESHIPS

Central Lancashire (Leg Prac); Ulster (Law).

EXAMPLES OF COLLEGES OFFERING COURSES IN THIS SUBJECT FIELD

Barnsley (Coll); Birmingham Met (Coll); Blackburn (Coll); Bury (Coll); Croydon (UC); Nottingham (Coll); Petroc; South Devon (Coll); South Thames (Coll); Truro and Penwith (Coll).

CHOOSING YOUR COURSE (SEE ALSO CH.1)

UNIVERSITIES AND COLLEGES TEACHING QUALITY See www.qaa.ac.uk; www.discoveruni.gov.uk.

TOP RESEARCH UNIVERSITIES AND COLLEGES (REF 2021) (Law) London (UCL); Kent; Bristol; Leeds; Glasgow; London (SOAS); Edinburgh; Warwick; Queen's Belfast; Birmingham.

EXAMPLES OF SANDWICH DEGREE COURSES Aston; Bournemouth; Bradford; Brighton; Bristol; Brunel; Coventry; De Montfort; Essex; Exeter; Hertfordshire; Huddersfield; Kent; Lancaster; Leeds; London (RH); Nottingham Trent; Plymouth; Portsmouth; Surrey; Sussex; UWE Bristol; Warwick; Westminster.

ADMISSIONS INFORMATION

ADMISSIONS TUTORS' ADVICE **Buckingham** A personal statement should demonstrate (at least a potential for) some of the key skills for the study of law: a passion or desire to study the subject, interest in other people and the world around us, powers of synthesis and analysis. Above all a statement should be articulate and succinct and show the applicant has an aptitude for effective communication. **London LSE** LNAT required.

ADVICE TO APPLICANTS AND PLANNING THE UCAS PERSONAL STATEMENT Visit the law courts and take notes on cases heard. Follow leading legal arguments in the press. Read the law sections in *The Independent, The Times* and the *Guardian*. Discuss the career with lawyers and, if possible, obtain work shadowing in lawyers' offices. Describe these visits and experiences and indicate any special areas of law which interest you. (Read *Learning the Law* by Glanville Williams.) Commitment is essential to the study of law as an academic discipline, not necessarily with a view to taking it up as a career.

When writing to admissions tutors, especially by email, take care to present yourself well. You should use communication as an opportunity to demonstrate your skill in the use of English. Spelling mistakes, punctuation errors and bad grammar suggest that you will struggle to develop the expected writing ability and may lead to your application being rejected. When writing to an admissions tutor, do not demand an answer immediately or by return or urgently. If your query is reasonable, the tutor will respond without such urging. Adding these demands is bad manners and suggests that you are doing everything at the last minute and increases your chances of a rejection.

The criteria for admission are: motivation and capacity for sustained and intense work; the ability to analyse and solve problems using logical and critical approaches; the ability to draw fine distinctions, to separate the relevant from the irrelevant; the capacity for accurate and critical observation, for sustained and cogent argument; creativity and flexibility of thought and lateral thinking; competence in English; the ability to express ideas clearly and effectively; a willingness to listen and to be able to give considered responses. See also **Appendix 3**. **Deferred entry** Check with your university choices since deferred entry will not necessarily be accepted.

Selection interviews **Yes** Buckingham, Cambridge, Leicester (Engl Fr Law (Mait)), Oxford (Law) 34% (success rate 11%), Worcester; **Some** Bristol, Liverpool John Moores, London (UCL) (Law Euro Leg Sys); **No** East London, Huddersfield, Kent, Sunderland, Surrey, Teesside, UWE Bristol, Warwick, West London.

Interview advice and questions Law is a highly competitive subject and applicants will be expected to have a basic awareness of aspects of law and to have gained some work experience, on which they are likely to be questioned. It is almost certain that a legal question will be asked at interview and applicants will be tested on their responses. Questions in the past have included: What interests you in the study of law? What would you do to overcome the problem of prison overcrowding if you were (a) a judge, (b) a prosecutor, (c) the Prime Minister? What legal cases have you read about recently? What is jurisprudence? What are the causes of violence in society? Have you visited any law courts? What cases did you see? A person arrives in England unable to speak the language. He lights a cigarette in a restaurant where smoking is not allowed. Can he be charged and convicted? What, in your opinion, would be the two basic laws in Utopia? What would happen if there were no law? Should we legalise euthanasia? If you could change any law, what would it be? How would you implement the changes? Where does honesty fit into law? For joint courses: What academic skills are needed to succeed? Why have you applied for a joint degree? See also **Chapter 5**.

Reasons for rejection (non-academic) Poorly informed about the subject. Badly drafted application. Underestimated workload. Poor communication skills.

GRADUATE DESTINATIONS AND EMPLOYMENT

(See **Chapter 1, Graduate Outcomes.**)

Career note Training places for the bar and solicitors' examinations remain extremely competitive. There are, however, alternative legal careers such as legal journalism, patent law, legal publishing and teaching. The course also proves a good starting point for careers in industry, commerce and the public service, while the study of consumer protection can lead to qualification as a Trading Standards officer.

OTHER DEGREE SUBJECTS FOR CONSIDERATION

Criminology; Economics; Government; History; International Relations; Politics; Social Policy and Administration; Sociology.

LEISURE AND RECREATION MANAGEMENT/ STUDIES

(see also **Business and Management Courses, Business and Management Courses (International And European), Business and Management Courses (Specialised), Hospitality and Event Management, Sports Sciences/Studies, Tourism and Travel**)

The courses cover various aspects of leisure and recreation and in particular, a wide range of outdoor activities. Specialist options include Recreation Management, Tourism and Countryside Management, all of which are offered as individual degree courses in their own right. Look out for other 'outdoor' activities in sport such as the two-year Foundation course in Surf Science and Technology offered at Cornwall College in partnership with Plymouth University. There is also an obvious link with Sports Studies, Physical Education and Tourism and Travel courses. See also **Appendix 3**.

Useful websites www.cimspa.co.uk; www.leisuremanagement.co.uk; www.thebapa.org.uk; www.leisureopportunities.co.uk; www.recmanagement.com; www.uksport.gov.uk

NB The points totals shown to the left of the institutions are for ease of reference only. It must not be assumed that Tariff points are always used by institutions or that they can be substituted for an offer in grades. The level of an offer is not necessarily indicative of the quality of a course.

COURSE OFFERS INFORMATION

Subject requirements/preferences GCSE Normally English and mathematics grades 7–4 (A–C). **AL** No specified subjects. Some popular universities are now making lower offers for disadvantaged and other students. **Other** Disclosure and Barring Service (DBS) clearance and health checks required for some courses.

Your target offers and examples of degree courses

144 pts **Edinburgh** – AAA (Spo Mgt) (IB 36 pts HL 665)
120 pts **Northumbria** – 120 pts (Spo Mgt)
Stirling – BBB incl sci/geog/geol/maths (Env Sci Out Educ) (IB 28 pts HL sci/geog/geol/maths)
112 pts **Portsmouth** – BBC–BBB 112–120 pts (Spo Mgt) (IB 25 pts)
Worcester – BBC 112 pts (Crckt Coach Mgt)
104 pts **Brighton** – BCC–BBB 104–120 pts (Spo Mgt) (IB 30 pts)
Central Lancashire – 104–120 pts (Out Advntr Ldrshp)
Cumbria – 104–120 pts (Out Advntr Env St; Out Ldrshp)
Gloucestershire – BCC 104 pts (Spo Bus Mgt)
Stranmillis (UC) – BCC (Hlth Physl Actvt Spo)
Winchester – BCC–BBB 104–120 pts (Spo Mgt) (HL 44)
96 pts **Chichester** – CCC–BBC 96–112 pts+interview (Out Advntr Educ)
Marjon – CCC (Out Advntr Educ)
Trinity Saint David – 96 pts (Out Advntr Educ)
64 pts **UHI** – CC (Advntr Tour Mgt; Glf Mgt)

Alternative offers See **Chapter 6** and **Appendix 1** for grades/UCAS Tariff points information for other examinations.

DEGREE APPRENTICESHIPS

Hertfordshire (Spo Bus Mgt).

EXAMPLES OF COLLEGES OFFERING COURSES IN THIS SUBJECT FIELD

Bedford (Coll); Blackburn (Coll); Bradford College (UC); Brighton Met (Coll); Durham New (Coll); Exeter (Coll); Leicester (Coll); Loughborough (Coll); Manchester (Coll); MidKent (Coll); Myerscough (Coll); Newcastle (Coll); Norwich City (Coll); South Devon (Coll); SRUC; TEC Partnership; Totton (Coll); Wakefield (Coll); West Herts (Coll); Wirral Met (Coll).

CHOOSING YOUR COURSE (SEE ALSO CH.1)

Universities and colleges teaching quality See www.qaa.ac.uk; www.discoveruni.gov.uk.

Top research universities and colleges (REF 2021) See **Sports Sciences/Studies**.

Examples of sandwich degree courses Trinity Saint David.

ADMISSIONS INFORMATION

Advice to applicants and planning the UCAS personal statement Work experience, visits to leisure centres and national parks and any interests you have in particular aspects of leisure should be described, for example, art galleries, museums, countryside management, sport. An involvement in sports and leisure as a participant or employee is an advantage. See also **Appendix 3**.

Selection interviews Interview advice and questions In addition to sporting or other related interests, applicants will be expected to have had some work experience and can expect to be asked to discuss their interests. What do you hope to gain by going to university? See also **Chapter 5**.

Reasons for rejection (non-academic) Poor communication or presentation skills. Relatively poor sporting background or knowledge.

GRADUATE DESTINATIONS AND EMPLOYMENT

(See **Chapter 1, Graduate Outcomes.**)

Career note Career opportunities exist in public and private sectors within leisure facilities, health clubs, the arts, leisure promotion, marketing and events management. Some graduates work in sports development and outdoor activities.

OTHER DEGREE SUBJECTS FOR CONSIDERATION

Business Studies; Events Management; Hospitality Management; Sports Studies; Tourism.

LINGUISTICS

(see also **English, Languages**)

Hi/Hello/Good day/Good morning – Linguistics is the study of language, the way we speak to our friends, or at an interview, the expressions we use, how we express ideas or emotions. The way in which children speak, the types of language used in advertising, or in sports reporting. Courses will include morphology (the formation of words), phonetics (the study of sounds), and semantics (the study of meanings). OK?/Understand?/Cheers! Linguistics graduates are well-equipped to undertake a variety of careers involving communication and language, including teaching, speech therapy and publishing.

Useful websites www.ciol.org.uk; www.cal.org; https://academic.oup.com/applij; www.linguisticsociety.org; www.sil.org; www.baal.org.uk

NB The points totals shown to the left of the institutions are for ease of reference only. It must not be assumed that Tariff points are always used by institutions or that they can be substituted for an offer in grades. The level of an offer is not necessarily indicative of the quality of a course.

COURSE OFFERS INFORMATION

Subject requirements/preferences GCSE English required and a foreign language preferred. **AL** English may be required or preferred for some courses. Some popular universities are now making lower offers for disadvantaged and other students.

Your target offers and examples of degree courses

152 pts **Cambridge** – A*AA+interview+LAA (Ling) (IB 41–42 pts HL 776)
Edinburgh – A*AA (Class Ling) (IB 39 pts HL 666)

136 pts **Edinburgh** – AAB (Jap Ling; Ling) (IB 36 pts HL 665)

Lancaster – AAB (Ling; Ling (St Abrd); Ling Phil; Ling Psy) (IB 35 pts HL 16 pts)
Leeds – AAB (Engl Lang Ling; Ling Phil) (IB 35 pts HL 16 pts)
London (UCL) – AAB (Ling) (IB 36 pts HL 17 pts)
Sheffield – AAB–ABB+bEPQ (Engl Lang Ling) (IB 34 pts)
Warwick – AAB (Ling Russ) (IB 34 pts)
York – AAB (Ling; Phil Ling) (IB 35 pts); AAB incl Fr (Fr Ling (Yr Abrd)) (IB 35 pts)

128 pts **Edinburgh** – ABB (Ital Ling) (IB 34 pts HL 655); (Ling Engl Lang) (IB 34–36 pts HL 655–665)
Leeds – ABB (Modn Lang Ling) (IB 34 pts HL 16 pts)
London (QM) – ABB (Engl Lang Ling) (IB 32 pts HL 655); ABB incl Engl lit/Engl lang lit (Engl Lit Ling) (IB 32 pts HL 655 incl 6 Engl)
London (SOAS) – ABB (Ling Comb Hons) (IB 32 pts HL 555)
Manchester – ABB (Ling courses) (IB 34 pts HL 655)
Newcastle – ABB (Ling; Ling Chin/Jap) (IB 32 pts); ABB incl Fr (Ling Fr) (IB 32 pts HL 5 Fr); ABB incl Fr/Ger/Span (Modn Langs Ling) (IB 32 pts HL 6 Fr/Ger/Span)
Queen's Belfast – ABB incl Engl (Engl Ling) (IB 33 pts HL 655 incl Engl)
Reading – ABB (Psy Lang Sci) (IB 32 pts)
Sheffield – ABB (Ling Comb Hons) (IB 33 pts)

120 pts **Glasgow** – BBB–AAB (Engl Lang Ling) (IB 34 pts HL 655 incl Engl+hum)
Kent – BBB (Engl Lang Ling) (HL 665)
London (QM) – BBB (Ger Ling) (IB 30 pts HL 555)

112 pts **Aberdeen** – BBC (Lang Ling (Yr Abrd)) (IB 32 pts HL 555)
Essex – BBC–BBB 112–120 pts (Lang St Ling; Ling) (IB 29–30 pts HL 554–555)
Nottingham Trent – 112 pts (Ling Comb Hons)
UWE Bristol – 112 pts (Engl Lang Ling)

104 pts **Bangor** – 104–128 pts (Ling Modn Lang); (Ling Engl Lang) (HL 5 Engl)
Brighton – BCC–BBB incl Engl (Engl Lang Ling) (IB 26 pts)
Central Lancashire – 104–112 pts (Engl Lang Ling)
London (Birk) – BCC 104 pts (Ling Lang)
Ulster – BCC (Lang Ling) (IB 24 pts HL 12 pts)
Westminster – BCC 104 pts (Arbc Ling); BCC–BBB (Engl Lang Ling) (HL 5 Engl)

Alternative offers See **Chapter 6** and **Appendix 1** for grades/UCAS Tariff points information for other examinations.

CHOOSING YOUR COURSE (SEE ALSO CH.1)

Universities and colleges teaching quality See www.qaa.ac.uk; www.discoveruni.gov.uk.

Top research universities and colleges (REF 2021) (Modern Languages and Linguistics) York; Lancaster; Essex; Bristol; London (RH); Nottingham; Newcastle; Manchester; Liverpool; London (SOAS).

Examples of sandwich degree courses Bangor; Leeds; Nottingham Trent; Sheffield; York (Fr Ling).

ADMISSIONS INFORMATION

Advice to applicants and planning the UCAS personal statement Give details of your interests in language and how it works, and about your knowledge of languages and their similarities and differences.

Selection interviews Yes Cambridge; **No** Brighton, Newcastle.

Interview advice and questions Past questions include: Why do you want to study linguistics? What does the subject involve? What do you intend to do at the end of your degree course? What answer do you give to your parents or friends when they ask why you want to study the subject? How and why does language vary according to sex, age, social background and regional origins? See also **Chapter 5**.

Reasons for rejection (non-academic) Lack of knowledge of linguistics. Hesitation about the period to be spent abroad.

GRADUATE DESTINATIONS AND EMPLOYMENT

(See **Chapter 1, Graduate Outcomes.**)

Career note Students enter a wide range of careers, with information management and editorial work in publishing offering some interesting and useful outlets.

OTHER DEGREE SUBJECTS FOR CONSIDERATION

Cognitive Science; Communication Studies; Education Studies; English; Psychology; Speech Sciences.

LITERATURE

(see also **English**)

This is a very broad subject introducing many aspects of the study of literature and aesthetics. Courses will vary in content. Degree courses in English and foreign languages will also include a study of literature.

Useful websites www.lrb.co.uk; www.3ammagazine.com/3am; www.bibliomania.com; www.bl.uk; www.acla.org

NB The points totals shown to the left of the institutions are for ease of reference only. It must not be assumed that Tariff points are always used by institutions or that they can be substituted for an offer in grades. The level of an offer is not necessarily indicative of the quality of a course.

COURSE OFFERS INFORMATION

Subject requirements/preferences GCSE English and a foreign language usually required. **AL** English may be required or preferred for some courses. Some popular universities are now making lower offers for disadvantaged and other students.

Your target offers and examples of degree courses

152 pts **Durham** – A*AA incl Engl (Engl Lit; Engl Lit Phil) (IB 38 pts HL 666 incl Engl); A*AA incl Engl+hist (Engl Lit Hist) (IB 38 pts HL 666 incl Engl+hist)
Edinburgh – A*AA incl Engl (Engl Lit) (IB 39 pts HL 666 incl Engl)

144 pts **Manchester** – AAA incl Engl (Engl Lit courses) (IB 36 pts HL 666)
Oxford – AAA incl Engl+interview (Engl Lang Lit) (IB 38 pts HL 666 incl Engl)
Warwick – A*AB/AAA incl Engl (Engl Lit Crea Writ) (IB 36 pts HL 6 Engl); AAA/A*AB incl Engl (Engl Lit) (IB 38 pts HL 6 Engl)

136 pts **East Anglia** – AAB incl Engl (Engl Am Lit; Engl Lit; Engl Lit Comb Hons) (IB 33 pts HL 5 Engl); AAB incl Engl/hist (Lit Hist) (IB 33 pts HL 5 Engl/hist)
Lancaster – AAB incl Engl (Engl Lang Lit; Engl Lit; Flm Engl Lit; Thea Engl Lit) (IB 35 pts HL 16 pts incl 6 lit)
Leeds – AAB incl A Engl (Class Lit Engl) (IB 35 pts HL 16 pts incl 6 Engl); AAB incl Engl (Engl Lang Lit) (IB 35 pts HL 16 pts incl 6 Engl)
London (King's) – AAB incl Engl (Compar Lit; Compar Lit Flm St) (IB 35 pts HL 17 pts incl 6 Engl)
Newcastle – AAB (Engl Lit (Comb Hons)) (IB 34 pts); AAB incl Engl (Engl Lit Comb Hons) (IB 34 pts HL 5 Engl)
Nottingham – AAB incl Engl (Engl Lang Lit) (IB 32 pts HL 665 Engl)
Sheffield – AAB incl art/hum (Engl Lang Lit) (IB 34 pts HL 5 art/hum); AAB–ABB+bEPQ incl art/hum (Engl Lit) (IB 34 pts HL 5 art/hum)

128 pts **Edinburgh** – ABB incl Engl (Celt Scot Lit; Scot Lit) (IB 34 pts HL 655 incl 5 Engl)
London (QM) – ABB incl Engl lit/Engl lang lit (Engl Lit Ling) (IB 32 pts HL 655 incl 6 Engl)
London (RH) – ABB–AAB (Engl Am Lit) (IB 32 pts HL 665)
Newcastle – ABB incl Engl (Engl Lang Lit) (IB 32 pts HL 5 Engl)
Sussex – ABB (Engl Lang Lit) (IB 32 pts)

Warwick – ABB incl Engl+interview+portfolio (Flm Lit) (IB 34 pts HL 6 Engl)
120 pts **Aberdeen** – BBC (Engl Scot Lit) (IB 32 pts HL 555)
Cardiff – BBB–AAB incl Engl (Engl Lit) (IB 31–34 pts HL 665–666 incl 6 Engl); BBB–ABB incl Engl (Jrnl Media Engl Lit) (IB 31–32 pts HL 665 incl 6 Engl)
Glasgow – BBB–AAB (Compar Lit Comb Hons; Engl Lit) (IB 34 pts HL 655 incl Engl+hum); BBB–AAB incl hum (Scot Lit) (IB 34 pts HL 655 incl Engl+hum)
Kent – BBB (Engl Lit) (HL 665)
London (QM) – BBB incl hum/soc sci (Ger Compar Lit) (IB 30 pts HL 555 incl hum/soc sci)
Reading – BBB incl Engl (Engl Lang Lit) (IB 30 pts HL 5 Engl); BBB incl Engl/thea st (Engl Lit Flm Thea) (IB 30 pts HL 5 Engl/thea st)
Surrey – BBB–AAB incl Engl (Engl Lit) (IB 32–33 pts); BBB incl Engl (Engl Lit Crea Writ) (IB 32 pts)
112 pts **Birmingham City** – BBC incl Engl 112 pts (Engl Lit courses) (IB 28 pts HL 14 pts)
Buckingham – BBC–BBB (Engl Lit) (IB 31–32 pts)
De Montfort – 112 pts (Engl Lit) (IB 26 pts)
Edge Hill – BBC–BBB 112–120 pts (Engl Lit)
Essex – BBC–BBB 112–120 pts (Engl Lang Lit; Engl Lit; Flm St Lit; Lit Art Hist) (IB 29–30 pts HL 554–555); BBC–BBB incl essay sub 112–120 pts (Dr Lit) (IB 29–30 pts HL 554–555)
Greenwich – 112 pts (Engl Lit)
Hertfordshire – BBC–BBB 112–120 pts (Engl Lit)
Leeds Beckett – 112 pts (Engl Lit) (HL 55)
London (RH) – BBC–BBB (Compar Lit Cult) (IB 30 pts HL 555)
Northumbria – 112 pts (Engl Lang Lit; Engl Lit Crea Writ; Engl Lit Hist)
Swansea – BBC–ABB 112–128 pts (Engl Lang Engl Lit) (IB 32 pts)
104 pts **Aberystwyth** – BCC–BBB 104–120 pts (Engl Lit) (IB 28–30 pts); BCC–BBB incl Engl 104–120 pts (Engl Lit Crea Writ) (IB 28–30 pts HL 5 Engl)
Bangor – 104–128 pts (Engl Lang Engl Lit) (HL 5 Engl)
Bath Spa – BCC–BBB incl Engl (Engl Lit) (IB 32 pts HL 5 Engl)
Brighton – BCC–BBB incl Engl/sociol/psy 104–120 pts (Engl Lit) (IB 26 pts)
Central Lancashire – 104–112 pts incl Engl (Engl Lit) (HL Engl)
Huddersfield – BCC–BBB incl Engl 104–120 pts+interview (Engl Lit; Engl Lit Crea Writ)
Liverpool Hope – BCC 104 pts (Engl Lit) (IB 24 pts)
Manchester Met – 104–112 pts (Engl Am Lit) (IB 26 pts)
Portsmouth – BCC–BBC 104–112 pts incl Engl (Engl Lit) (IB 25 pts)
Roehampton – 104–120 pts (Engl Lit)
Westminster – BCC 104 pts (Crea Prof Writ); BCC–BBB incl Engl/hum 104–120 pts (Engl Lit Hist)
Worcester – BCC Engl 104 pts (Engl Lit courses)
York St John – 104 pts (Crea Writ; Engl Lit)
96 pts **Anglia Ruskin** – 96 pts (Dr Engl Lit; Phil Engl Lit) (IB 24 pts); 96 pts incl Engl (Writ Engl Lit) (IB 24 pts)
Bishop Grosseteste – 96–112 pts (Engl courses)
Gloucestershire – CCC 96 pts (Engl Lit Crea Writ)
72 pts **UHI** – BC incl Engl (Lit)

Alternative offers See **Chapter 6** and **Appendix 1** for grades/UCAS Tariff points information for other examinations.

CHOOSING YOUR COURSE (SEE ALSO CH.1)

Universities and colleges teaching quality See www.qaa.ac.uk; www.discoveruni.gov.uk.

Top research universities and colleges (REF 2021) See **English**.

Examples of sandwich degree courses Anglia Ruskin; Bangor; Bath Spa; Birmingham City; Cardiff; Durham (Engl Lit Hist); East Anglia.

ADMISSIONS INFORMATION

Advice to applicants and planning the UCAS personal statement See **English**.

Selection interviews Yes Oxford (66% (success rate 23%)), Warwick (Flm Lit)

Interview advice and questions See **English**. See also **Chapter 5**.

GRADUATE DESTINATIONS AND EMPLOYMENT

(See **Chapter 1, Graduate Outcomes.**)

Career note Students enter a wide range of careers, with information management and editorial work in publishing offering some interesting and useful outlets. See also **English**, **Linguistics** and **Celtic, Irish, Scottish and Welsh Studies**.

MARINE/MARITIME STUDIES

(including **Marine Biology, Naval Architecture, Marine Geography and Oceanography**; see also **Environmental Sciences**)

A wide range of courses come under this category. These include Marine Business; Marine Law (world shipping, transport of goods, shipbroking, salvage rights, piracy); Marine Technology (marine engineering/nautical design); Marine Technology Offshore Engineering (marine structures, oil rigs, offshore engineering); Navigation Marine Science (merchant navy, yachts, superyachts); Naval Architecture with High Performance Crafts (design, construction, operation, large and small vessels, hydrofoils, hovercrafts); Shipping Port Management (international shipping, shipbroking, ship agency work) and Yacht and Powercraft Design (powerboats, yachts, superyachts). Other scientific courses cover marine applications with biology, chemistry, freshwater biology and geography.

Useful websites www.ukchamberofshipping.com; http://uksa.org; www.rya.org.uk; www.royalnavy.mod.uk; www.sstg.org; www.noc.ac.uk; www.nautinst.org; www.mcsuk.org; www.nmm-stena.com; www.imo.org; www.gov.uk/government/organisations/maritime-and-coastguard-agency; www.gov.uk/government/organisations/centre-for-environment-fisheries-and-aquaculture-science; www.mba.ac.uk

NB The points totals shown to the left of the institutions are for ease of reference only. It must not be assumed that Tariff points are always used by institutions or that they can be substituted for an offer in grades. The level of an offer is not necessarily indicative of the quality of a course.

COURSE OFFERS INFORMATION

Subject requirements/preferences GCSE Mathematics and science are required for several courses. **AL** Science or mathematics will be required or preferred for some courses. Some popular universities are now making lower offers for disadvantaged and other students.

Your target offers and examples of degree courses

144 pts **Southampton** – AAA incl maths+phys/chem/fmaths (Marit Eng (MEng)) (IB 36 pts HL 18 pts incl 6 maths+phys/chem)

136 pts **East Anglia** – AAB incl sci (Mar Sci (Yr Abrd)) (IB 33 pts HL 5 incl geo/math/econ/biol/chem/phys)

Newcastle – AAB incl maths+phys/chem/fmaths (Nvl Archit Mar Eng (MEng)) (IB 34 pts HL 6 maths+phys/chem)

Southampton – AAB incl A maths+phys/chem/fmaths (Marit Eng) (IB 34 pts HL 17 pts incl 6 maths+phys/chem)

St Andrews – AAB incl biol+sci/maths (Mar Biol) (IB 36 pts HL 665 incl biol+sci/maths)

128 pts **East Anglia** – ABB incl maths (Mar Sci) (IB 32 pts HL 5 maths); (Mar Sci (MSci)) (IB 33 pts HL 5 maths)

Liverpool – ABB incl biol+sci/maths/geog (Mar Biol Ocean) (IB 33 pts HL 5 biol+sci); ABB incl maths/sci (Ocn Sci) (IB 33 pts HL 5 maths/sci)

Liverpool John Moores – ABB incl maths+sci/tech/eng 128 pts (Mar Mech Eng (MEng)) (HL 6 maths+phys)

Newcastle – ABB incl biol+sci (Mar Biol) (IB 32 pts HL 6 biol); ABB incl maths+phys/chem/fmaths (Nvl Archit Mar Eng) (IB 32 pts HL 5 maths+phys/chem)

Southampton – ABB incl biol+sci (Mar Biol; Mar Biol Ocean) (IB 32 pts HL 16 pts incl 5 biol+sci); ABB incl sci/maths/geog+interview (Ocean) (IB 32 pts HL 16 pts incl 5 sci)

120 pts **Bangor** – BC sci/maths/geog 120–144 pts incl sci/maths/geog (Geol Ocean) (HL 65 sci)
Glasgow – BBB–AAB incl biol/chem (Mar Frshwtr Biol) (IB 34 pts HL 655 biol/chem)
Hull – BBB incl biol/app sci 120 pts (Mar Biol) (IB 30 pts HL 5 biol)
Plymouth – 120–144 pts incl biol (Mar Biol Cstl Ecol) (IB 30–36 pts HL biol); 120–144 pts incl biol+sci (Mar Biol Ocean) (IB 30–36 pts)
Queen's Belfast – BBB–ABB incl biol+chem/geog/maths/phys (Mar Biol) (IB 32–33 pts HL 655 incl biol+chem/geog/maths/phys)
Stirling – BBB incl sci/maths (Mar Frshwtr Biol) (IB 28 pts)
Strathclyde – BBB–ABB incl maths+phys (Nvl Archit Hi Perf Mar Veh; Nvl Archit Mar Eng; Nvl Archit Ocn Eng) (IB 32 pts HL 5 maths+phys)

112 pts **Aberdeen** – BBC incl maths/sci (Mar Biol) (IB 32 pts HL 555 incl maths/sci)
Bangor – CC geog/sci/maths 112–128 pts (Physl Geog Ocean); C sci/maths/geog 112–128 pts (Ocn Sci) (HL 5 sci)
Cardiff – BBC–ABB incl sci (Mar Geog) (IB 30–32 pts HL 655–665 incl sci); (Mar Geog (MSci)) (IB 30–34 pts HL 655–665)
Heriot-Watt – BBC–ABB incl sci/maths (Mar Biol) (IB 27 pts HL 5 sci)
Liverpool John Moores – BBC incl maths+phys/eng/tech 112 pts (Mar Mech Eng) (IB 26 pts HL 5 maths+phys)
Plymouth – 112–128 pts incl sci (Mar Biol); 112–128 pts (Marit Bus) (IB 28–32 pts HL 4); 112–128 pts incl sci (Ocn Sci Mar Cons) (IB 28–30 pts); 112–128 pts incl sci/maths/geog/psy/des tech (Ocn Explor Surv) (IB 26–28 pts); C maths+sci/tech 112–128 pts (Mar Tech) (IB 26–30 pts HL 5 maths+sci/tech)
Portsmouth – BBC–ABB incl sci/maths/geog 112–128 pts (Mar Env Sci) (IB 25–26 pts HL 5 sci/maths/geog); BBC–BBB incl biol 112–120 pts (Mar Biol) (IB 25 pts)

104 pts **Aberystwyth** – BCC–BBB incl B biol 104–120 pts (Mar Frshwtr Biol) (IB 28–30 pts HL 5 biol)
Edinburgh Napier – BCC incl sci (Mar Frshwtr Biol) (IB 28 pts HL 654 incl 5 sci)
Falmouth – 104–120 pts+portfolio+interview (Mar Nat Hist Photo)
Solent – 104–120 pts (Marit Bus; Ycht Des Prod); 104–128 pts (Ship Pt Mgt)
UHI – BCC incl sci (Mar Sci)

80 pts **Bangor** – 80–120 pts (Mar Vert Cons)

32 pts **Plymouth** – 32 pts (Marit Bus Fdn Yr) (IB 24–25 pts HL 4)

Alternative offers See **Chapter 6** and **Appendix 1** for grades/UCAS Tariff points information for other examinations.

EXAMPLES OF COLLEGES OFFERING COURSES IN THIS SUBJECT FIELD

Blackpool and Fylde (Coll); Cornwall (Coll); Plymouth City (Coll); South Devon (Coll); Southampton City (Coll); Sparsholt (Coll).

CHOOSING YOUR COURSE (SEE ALSO CH.1)

Universities and colleges teaching quality See www.qaa.ac.uk; www.discoveruni.gov.uk.

Examples of sandwich degree courses Bangor; Cardiff; East Anglia; Liverpool John Moores; Portsmouth.

ADMISSIONS INFORMATION

Advice to applicants and planning the UCAS personal statement This is a specialised field and, in many cases, applicants will have experience of marine activities. Describe these experiences, for example, sailing, snorkelling, fishing. See also **Appendix 3**.

Selection interviews Yes Falmouth, Southampton (Ocean).

Interview advice and questions Most applicants will have been stimulated by their studies in science or will have strong interests or connections with marine activities. They are likely to be questioned on their reasons for choosing the course. See also **Chapter 5**.

GRADUATE DESTINATIONS AND EMPLOYMENT

(See **Chapter 1, Graduate Outcomes.**)

Career note This subject area covers a wide range of vocational courses, each offering graduates an equally wide choice of career openings in either purely scientific or very practical areas.

OTHER DEGREE SUBJECTS FOR CONSIDERATION

Biology; Civil Engineering; Environmental Studies/Sciences; Geography; Marine Engineering; Marine Transport; Naval Architecture; Oceanography.

MARKETING

(including **Public Relations**; see also **Business and Management Courses, Business and Management Courses (International and European), Business and Management Courses (Specialised), Retail Management**)

Marketing courses are very popular and applications should include evidence of work experience or work shadowing. While marketing is also a subject included in all Business Studies courses, specialist marketing courses are also available focusing on Advertising (also included in Marketing and Graphic Design courses), Agriculture, Consumer Behaviour, Design, Fashion, Food, Leisure, Retail and Sport.

Useful websites www.adassoc.org.uk; www.cim.co.uk; www.ipa.co.uk; www.marketingtoday.com

NB The points totals shown to the left of the institutions are for ease of reference only. It must not be assumed that Tariff points are always used by institutions or that they can be substituted for an offer in grades. The level of an offer is not necessarily indicative of the quality of a course.

COURSE OFFERS INFORMATION

Subject requirements/preferences GCSE English and mathematics. **AL** No specified subjects required. Some popular universities are now making lower offers for disadvantaged and other students.

Your target offers and examples of degree courses

144 pts **Durham** – AAA (Mark Mgt) (IB 37 pts HL 665)
Leeds – AAA (Bus Mgt Mark) (IB 35 pts HL 17 pts)
Manchester – AAA (Mgt (Mark)) (IB 36 pts HL 666)
Southampton – AAA (Mark (Yr Ind)) (IB 36 pts HL 18 pts)

136 pts **Exeter** – AAB (Mark Mgt) (IB 34 pts HL 665)
Lancaster – AAB (Adv Mark; Mark Des; Mark Mgt; Mark Mgt (St Abrd)) (IB 35 pts HL 16 pts)
Liverpool – AAB (Mark) (IB 35 pts)
Loughborough – AAB (Mark Mgt) (IB 35 pts HL 665); AAB 136 pts (Mark) (IB 35 HL 665)
Manchester – AAB+interview (Fash Mgt) (IB 35 pts HL 665)
Newcastle – AAB (Mark; Mark Mgt) (IB 34 pts)
Ulster – AAB (Comm Adv Mark) (IB 28 pts HL 14 pts)

128 pts **Kent** – ABB (Mark) (HL 665)
Lancaster – ABB (Mark) (IB 32 pts HL 16 pts)
Sussex – ABB (Mark Mgt) (IB 32 pts)

120 pts **Aston** – BBB (Mark) (IB 31 pts HL 555)
Cardiff – BBB–AAB (Bus Mgt (Mark)) (IB 31–34 pts HL 665–666)
Coventry – BBB–ABB (Adv Dig Mark) (IB 30–31 pts)
London (RH) – BBB–ABB (Mgt Mark) (IB 32 pts HL 655)
Manchester Met – BBB–ABB 120–128 pts (Mark) (IB 30 pts)
Northumbria – 120 pts (Mark)
Nottingham Trent – 120 pts (Mark)
Oxford Brookes – BBB 120 pts (Bus Mark Mgt) (IB 31 pts)
Reading – BBB (Consum Bhv Mark) (IB 30 pts)

Southampton (Winchester SA) – BBB (Fash Mark Mgt) (IB 30 pts HL 15 pts)
Stirling – BBB (Mark; Rtl Mark) (IB 28 pts)
Strathclyde – BBB–ABB (Mark courses) (IB 30–32 pts)
Swansea – BBB–ABB (Bus Mgt (Mark); Mark) (IB 32–33 pts)

112 pts **Birmingham City** – BBC 112 pts (Mark; Mark Adv PR) (IB 28 pts HL 14 pts)
Bournemouth Arts – BBB 112–120 pts+portfolio (Comm Des Strat); BBC–BBB 112–120 pts+portfolio+interview (Fash Comm)
Bradford – BBC 112 pts (Mark)
Canterbury Christ Church – BBC 112 pts (Bus Mgt Mark; Mark) (IB 29 pts)
Cardiff Met – 112 pts (Mark Mgt)
Creative Arts – 112 pts+portfolio (Dig Mark Soc Media) (IB 27–30 pts HL 15 pts)
De Montfort – 112 pts (Adv Mark Comms; Mark) (IB 26 pts)
Derby – BBC 112 pts (Mark courses); BBC–BBB 112–120 pts (Mark (PR Adv))
East London – 112 pts (Mark) (IB 24 pts HL 15 pts); 112 pts+portfolio (Fash Mark Comm) (IB 24 pts HL 15 pts)
Essex – BBC–BBB 112–120 pts (Mark; Mark Mgt) (IB 29–30 pts HL 554–555)
Greenwich – 112 pts (Dig Mark Adv; Mark Brnd Mgt)
Heriot-Watt – BBC–ABB (Mark) (IB 29 pts)
Hertfordshire – BBC–BBB 112–120 pts (Mark)
Huddersfield – BBC–BBB 112–120 pts (Mark)
Hull – BBC 112 pts (Mark) (IB 28 pts)
Keele – BBC (Mark Comb Hons) (IB 29 pts HL 554)
Leeds Beckett – 112 pts (Mark; Mark Adv Mgt; Mark Mgt)
Liverpool John Moores – BBC 112 pts (Mark) (IB 26 pts)
London Met – BBC 112 pts (Fash Mark Jrnl)
London South Bank – 112 pts (Bus Mgt Mark; Mark Dig)
Middlesex – 112 pts (Adv PR Brnd) (IB 28 pts)
Northampton – BBC (Adv Dig Mark; Fash Mark Prom; Mark Comb Hons)
Northumbria – 112 pts (Bus Mark); 112 pts+portfolio (Fash Des Mark)
Nottingham Trent – BBC 112–120 pts (Fash Comm Prom; Fash Mark Brnd)
Portsmouth – BBC–BBB 112–120 pts (Mark) (IB 29 pts); BBC–BBB 112–120 pts (Fash Mark) (IB 29 pts)
Roehampton – 112 pts (Mark)
Sheffield Hallam – BBC 112 pts (Bus Mgt Mark; Mark; Mark Comms Adv)
Ulster – BBC (Mark) (IB 25 pts HL 12 pts)
West London – BBC 112 pts (Fash Ind Brnd Mark)
Westminster – BBC 112 pts (Bus Mgt (Mark); Mark Comms AI Integ); BBC–ABB 112–128 pts (Mark Mgt) (IB 27 pts)
Winchester – BBC–BBB 112–120 pts (Mark) (HL 44)
Worcester – 112 pts (Mark Adv PR)

104 pts **Bath Spa** – BCC–BBB (Bus Mgt (Mark); Mark) (IB 32 pts)
Bournemouth – 104–120 pts (Mark; Mark Comm) (IB 28–31 pts)
Brighton – BCC–BBB 104–120 pts (Mark Mgt) (IB 26 pts)
Buckingham – BCC–BBB+interview (Dig Mark) (IB 30–32 pts)
Central Lancashire – 104–112 pts (Bus Mark)
Chester – BCC–BBC 104–112 pts (Mark) (IB 28 pts)
Chichester – BCC–BBB 104–120 pts (Mark) (IB 28 pts)
Edge Hill – BCC–BBC 104–112 pts (Bus Mark; Mark)
Falmouth – 104–120 pts+interview (Crea Adv)
Gloucestershire – BCC 104 pts (Mark (Adv Brnd))
Huddersfield – BCC–BBB 104 pts+interview+portfolio (Fash Mark)
Leeds Arts – 104–120 pts (Fash Mark); 104–120 pts (Mark Comms)
Lincoln – 104 pts (Mark Adv) (IB 28 pts)
Liverpool Hope – BCC 104 pts (Dig Mark) (IB 24 pts)
Manchester Met – BCC–BBC 104–112 pts (Spo Mark Mgt) (IB 26 pts)

	Plymouth - 104-120 pts (Mark) (IB 23-32 pts)
	Plymouth (AU) - 104-120 pts+portfolio (Fash Media Mark)
	Queen Margaret - BCC incl Engl/media (PR Mark Comms) (IB 28 pts)
	Robert Gordon - BCC (Bus Mark; Dig Mark) (IB 27 pts)
	South Wales - BCC 104 pts (Adv)
	Ulster - BCC (HR Mgt) (IB 24 pts HL 12 pts)
	Winchester - BCC-BBB 104-120 pts (Fash Bus Mark) (HL 44)
	York St John - 104 pts (Mark)
96 pts	**Abertay** - CCC (Mark Bus Mgt) (IB 28 pts)
	Aberystwyth - CCC-BBB 96-120 pts (Mark) (IB 26-30 pts)
	Anglia Ruskin - CCC 96 pts (Bus Mark) (IB 24 pts)
	Bedfordshire - 96 pts (Mark)
	Edinburgh Napier - CCC (Mark Dig Media; Mark Mgt) (IB 27 pts HL 654)
	London Met - CCC 96 pts (Adv Mark Comms PR; Fash Mark Bus Mgt)
	Middlesex - 96 pts (Mark)
	South Wales - BCC 96 pts (Fash Prom); CCC 96 pts (Mark)
	St Mary's - 96-112 pts (Comms Media Mark)
	Sunderland - 96-112 pts (Bus Mark Mgt); 96-112 pts+portfolio+interview (Fash Des Prom)
	Wolverhampton - CCC/BCD 96 pts (Bus Mark; Dig Mark)
88 pts	**Bucks New** - 88-112 pts (Mark)
	Harper Adams - 88-104 pts (Fd Bus Mgt) (IB 28 pts)
80 pts	**Birmingham (UC)** - CDD-CCC 80-96 pts (Mark Mgt)
	Teesside - 80-104 pts (Mark)
64 pts	**Ravensbourne Univ** - CC+interview+portfolio (Fash Prom Comms) (IB 24 pts)

ALTERNATIVE OFFERS See **Chapter 6** and **Appendix 1** for grades/UCAS Tariff points information for other examinations.

DEGREE APPRENTICESHIPS

Aston (Dig Mark); Bedfordshire (Dig Mark); Central Lancashire (Dig Mark); Chichester (Dig Mark); Leeds Beckett (Dig Mark); Leeds Trinity (Dig Mark); London South Bank (Dig Mark); Manchester Met (Dig Mark); Nottingham Trent (Dig Mark); Portsmouth (Dig Mark).

EXAMPLES OF COLLEGES OFFERING COURSES IN THIS SUBJECT FIELD

Arts London (CFash); Bath (Coll); Birmingham Met (Coll); Blackpool and Fylde (Coll); Croydon (UC); Doncaster (Coll); ESE; Leeds City (Coll); Loughborough (Coll); Manchester (Coll); Newcastle (Coll); Nottingham (Coll); Pearson (Coll); Plymouth City (Coll); South City Birmingham (Coll); South Essex (Coll); TEC Partnership; Yeovil (Coll).

CHOOSING YOUR COURSE (SEE ALSO CH.1)

UNIVERSITIES AND COLLEGES TEACHING QUALITY See www.qaa.ac.uk; www.discoveruni.gov.uk.

EXAMPLES OF SANDWICH DEGREE COURSES Aston; Bath Spa; Bedfordshire; Birmingham City; Bournemouth; Bradford; Cardiff Met; Central Lancashire; Chester; Chichester; Coventry; De Montfort; Derby; Durham; Greenwich; Harper Adams; Hertfordshire; Huddersfield; Lancaster; Leeds Beckett; Liverpool John Moores; London (RH); London South Bank; Loughborough; Manchester Met; Newcastle; Northumbria; Nottingham Trent; Oxford Brookes; Plymouth; Portsmouth; Reading; Sheffield Hallam; Solent; Southampton; Staffordshire; Sussex; Teesside; Ulster; UWE Bristol; Westminster; Wolverhampton; Worcester.

ADMISSIONS INFORMATION

ADVICE TO APPLICANTS AND PLANNING THE UCAS PERSONAL STATEMENT See **Business and Management Courses** and **Appendix 3**.

SELECTION INTERVIEWS Yes Buckingham, Falmouth, Huddersfield (Fash Mark), Ravensbourne Univ; **No** Anglia Ruskin, De Montfort, Harper Adams, Manchester Met.

Interview advice and questions Past questions include: What is marketing? Why do you want to take a Marketing degree? Is sales pressure justified? How would you feel if you had to market a product which you considered to be inferior? See also **Chapter 5**.

Reasons for rejection (non-academic) Little thought of reasons for deciding on a Marketing degree. Weak on numeracy and problem solving. Limited commercial awareness. Poor interpersonal skills. Lack of leadership potential. No interest in widening their horizons, either geographically or intellectually. Limited understanding of the career. No clear reasons for wishing to do the course.

GRADUATE DESTINATIONS AND EMPLOYMENT

(See **Chapter 1, Graduate Outcomes.**)

Career note See **Business and Management Courses**.

OTHER DEGREE SUBJECTS FOR CONSIDERATION

Advertising; Art and Design; Business courses; Communications; Graphic Design; Psychology; Public Relations.

MATERIALS SCIENCE/METALLURGY

Materials Science is a broad subject which covers physics, chemistry and engineering at one and the same time! From its origins in metallurgy, materials science has now moved into the processing, structure and properties of materials, including ceramics, polymers, composites and electrical materials. Materials science and metallurgy are perhaps the most misunderstood of all careers, and applications for degree courses are low with very reasonable offers. Valuable bursaries and scholarships are offered by the Institute of Materials, Minerals and Mining (check with Institute – see **Appendix 3**). Polymer science is a branch of materials science and is often studied in conjunction with chemistry. It covers such topics as polymer properties and processing relating to industrial applications with, for example, plastics, paints and adhesives. Other courses under this heading include Fashion and Leather Technology. See also **Appendix 3**.

Useful websites www.makeuk.org/uksteel; www.iom3.org; https://epsrc.ukri.org; www.imm.org; www.icme.org.uk

NB The points totals shown to the left of the institutions are for ease of reference only. It must not be assumed that Tariff points are always used by institutions or that they can be substituted for an offer in grades. The level of an offer is not necessarily indicative of the quality of a course.

COURSE OFFERS INFORMATION

Subject requirements/preferences GCSE (Eng/Sci courses) Science/mathematics subjects. **AL** Mathematics, physics and/or chemistry required for most courses. (Poly Sci) Mathematics and/or physics usually required; design technology encouraged. Some popular universities are now making lower offers for disadvantaged and other students.

Your target offers and examples of degree courses

160 pts **Cambridge** – A*A*A incl sci/maths+interview+ESAT (Nat Sci (Mat Sci)) (IB 41–42 pts HL 776)

152 pts **Oxford** – A*AA incl maths+phys+interview+PAT (Mat Sci) (IB 40 pts HL 766 incl 7 maths/phys/chem)

144 pts **Birmingham** – AAA incl maths+phys/chem/des tech (Mat Sci Eng (MEng)) (IB 32 pts HL 666 incl maths+phys/chem/des tech)

Imperial London – AAA incl maths+phys/chem+interview (Biomat Tiss Eng (MEng)) (IB 38 pts HL 6 maths+phys/chem); (Mat Nucl Eng (MEng); Mat Sci Eng; Mat Sci Eng (MEng)) (IB 38 pts HL 6 maths+phys/chem)

London (QM) – AAA incl maths/phys/chem (Mat Sci Eng (MEng) (Yr Ind)) (IB 36 pts HL 666 incl maths/phys/chem)

Loughborough – AAA incl maths+phys+interview (Auto Mat (MEng)) (IB 37 pts HL 666 incl maths+phys); AAA incl maths/phys/chem+interview (Mat Sci Eng (MEng)) (IB 37 pts HL 666 incl maths/phys/chem)
Sheffield – AAA incl maths/phys/chem (Mat Sci Eng (MEng)) (IB 36 pts HL 6 maths/phys/chem)
St Andrews – AAA incl chem (Mat Chem) (IB 38 pts HL 666 incl chem+maths/sci)

136 pts **Birmingham** – AAB incl maths+sci (Mat Sci Eng) (IB 32 pts HL 665 incl maths+phys)
Manchester – AAB incl maths/phys/chem+interview (Mat Sci Eng) (IB 35 pts HL 665 incl maths/phys/chem)
Sheffield – AAB incl maths/phys/chem (Mat Sci Eng) (IB 34 pts HL 6/5 maths/phys/chem)
Swansea – AAB incl sci/maths (Mat Sci Eng (MEng)) (IB 34 pts)

128 pts **London (QM)** – ABB incl maths/phys/chem (Mat Sci Eng) (IB 32 pts HL 655 incl maths/phys/chem)
Loughborough – ABB incl maths+sci+interview (Biomat Eng) (IB 34 pts HL 655 incl maths+sci); ABB incl maths/phys/chem+interview (Auto Mat; Mat Sci Eng) (IB 34 pts HL 655 incl maths/phys/chem)

120 pts **Swansea** – BBB–ABB incl sci/maths (Mat Sci Eng) (IB 32 pts)

ALTERNATIVE OFFERS See **Chapter 6** and **Appendix 1** for grades/UCAS Tariff points information for other examinations.

EXAMPLES OF COLLEGES OFFERING COURSES IN THIS SUBJECT FIELD

Hereford (CA).

CHOOSING YOUR COURSE (SEE ALSO CH.1)

UNIVERSITIES AND COLLEGES TEACHING QUALITY See www.qaa.ac.uk; www.discoveruni.gov.uk.

TOP RESEARCH UNIVERSITIES AND COLLEGES (REF 2021) See **Engineering/Engineering Sciences**.

EXAMPLES OF SANDWICH DEGREE COURSES London (QM); Loughborough.

ADMISSIONS INFORMATION

ADVICE TO APPLICANTS AND PLANNING THE UCAS PERSONAL STATEMENT Read scientific and engineering journals and describe any special interests you have. Try to visit chemical or technological installations (rubber, plastics, glass, etc) and describe your visits. See also **Appendix 3**.

SELECTION INTERVIEWS **Yes** Cambridge, Imperial London, Manchester, Oxford (70% (success rate 26%)); **Some** Loughborough.

INTERVIEW ADVICE AND QUESTIONS Questions are likely to be based on AS/A-level science subjects. Recent examples include: Why did you choose Materials Science? How would you make each part of this table lamp (on the interviewer's desk)? Identify this piece of material. How was it manufactured? How has it been treated? (Questions related to metal and polymer samples.) What would you consider the major growth area in materials science? See also **Chapter 5**.

GRADUATE DESTINATIONS AND EMPLOYMENT

(See **Chapter 1, Graduate Outcomes.**)

CAREER NOTE Materials scientists are involved in a wide range of specialisms in which openings are likely in a range of industries. These include manufacturing processes in which the work is closely linked with that of mechanical, chemical, production and design engineers.

OTHER DEGREE SUBJECTS FOR CONSIDERATION

Aerospace Engineering; Biotechnology; Chemistry; Dentistry; Engineering Sciences; Mathematics; Mechanical Engineering; Medical Engineering; Plastics Technology; Physics; Product Design and Materials; Prosthetics and Orthotics; Sports Technology.

MATHEMATICS

(including **Mathematical Sciences**; see also **Economics, Statistics**)

Mathematics at degree level is an extension of A-level mathematics, covering pure and applied mathematics, statistics, computing, mathematical analysis and mathematical applications. Mathematics is of increasing importance and is used in the simplest of design procedures and not only in applications in the physical sciences and engineering. It also plays a key role in management, economics, medicine and the social and behavioural sciences.

Useful websites www.ima.org.uk; www.theorsociety.com; www.m-a.org.uk; www.mathscareers.org.uk; www.imo-official.org; http://bmos.ukmt.org.uk; http://maths.org; www.ukmt.org.uk

NB The points totals shown to the left of the institutions are for ease of reference only. It must not be assumed that Tariff points are always used by institutions or that they can be substituted for an offer in grades. The level of an offer is not necessarily indicative of the quality of a course.

COURSE OFFERS INFORMATION

Subject requirements/preferences GCSE English often required and mathematics is obviously essential at a high grade for leading universities. **AL** Mathematics, in several cases with a specified grade, required for all courses. Some popular universities are now making lower offers for disadvantaged and other students. **Other** Mathematics AEA or TMUA/STEP papers may be required by some universities (eg Imperial, Warwick). See also **Chapter 4**. NB The level of an offer may depend on whether an applicant is taking AS/A-level further maths; check websites.

Your target offers and examples of degree courses

168 pts **Bristol** – A*AA–A*A*A incl A*A maths+fmaths/sci/comp/econ (Maths Stats) (IB 40 pts HL 18 pts incl 7 maths 6 sci/econ/comp)

Manchester – A*A*A* incl maths (Comp Sci Maths) (IB 39 pts HL 777 incl 7 maths)

Warwick – A*A*A* incl maths+fmaths (Maths; Maths (MMath)) (IB 39 pts HL 666–766 incl maths)

160 pts **Bristol** – A*A*A incl maths+fmaths (Maths Comp Sci) (IB 40 pts HL 18 pts incl 7 maths); A*A*A incl maths+fmaths/sci/econ/comp sci (Maths) (IB 40 pts HL 18 pts incl 7 maths 6 sci/econ/comp sci)

Cambridge – A*A*A incl maths+interview+STEP (Maths) (IB 40–42 pts HL 776 incl maths)

Imperial London – A*A*A incl A*A* maths+fmaths+TMUA/STEP (Maths Stats; Maths Stats Fin) (IB 39 pts HL 76 incl maths); A*A*A incl maths+fmaths+MAT/STEP (Maths; Maths Mathem Comp; PMaths) (IB 39 pts HL 76 incl maths); A*A*A incl maths+fmaths+interview (Maths Comp Sci) (IB 42 pts HL 7 maths)

London (UCL) – A*A*A incl maths (Mathem Comput (MEng)) (IB 40 pts HL 7 maths); A*A*A incl maths+fmaths+STEP (Maths) (IB 40 pts HL 20 pts incl 7 maths)

Manchester – A*A*A incl maths+phys+interview (Maths Phys) (IB 38 pts HL 776 incl maths+phys)

Oxford – A*A*A incl A* maths+interview+MAT (Maths Phil; Maths Stats) (IB 39 pts HL 766 incl 7 maths); A*A*A incl maths+interview+MAT (Maths) (IB 39 pts HL 766 incl 7 maths)

St Andrews – A*A*A incl maths (App Maths; Maths; Maths Span; PMaths (MMath)) (IB 38 pts HL 666 incl maths)

Warwick – A*A*A incl maths (Dscrt Maths) (IB 39 pts HL 766 incl maths); A*A*A incl maths+fmaths (Maths Stats) (IB 39 pts HL 7 maths)

152 pts **Bath** – A*AA incl maths+fmaths (Maths) (IB 36 pts HL 766/765 incl 7/6 maths); A*AA–AAA+aEPQ incl maths+phys (Maths Phys) (IB 36 pts HL 766 incl maths+phys)

Bristol – A*AA incl maths (Maths Phil) (IB 38 pts HL 18 pts incl 7 maths)

Durham – A*AA–A*A*A incl maths+fmaths+TMUA (Maths) (IB 38 pts HL 766–776)

London (King's) – A*AA incl maths+fmaths (Maths) (IB 35 pts HL 766 incl 7 maths)

London LSE – A*AA incl A* maths (Ecomet Mathem Econ; Maths Econ) (IB 38 pts HL 766 incl 7 maths); A*AA incl maths (Maths Data Sci) (IB 38 pts HL 766 incl maths)
Manchester – A*AA incl A* maths (Maths Phil) (IB 37 pts HL 766 incl 7 maths); (Act Sci Maths) (IB 37 pts HL 766 pts incl 7 maths); A*AA incl A* maths+interview (Maths Fin) (IB 37 pts HL 766 incl 7 maths); A*AA incl maths+interview (Maths) (IB 37 pts HL 766 incl maths)
Nottingham – A*AA incl maths+phys (Mathem Phys) (IB 38 pts HL 666 incl maths+phys)

144 pts **Birmingham** – AAA incl maths/fmaths (Maths; Maths Bus Mgt) (IB 32 pts HL 666 incl maths)
Bristol – AAA incl maths (Eng Maths) (IB 36 pts HL 18 pts incl 6 maths)
East Anglia – AAA incl maths (Maths (MMath)) (IB 34 pts HL 6 maths)
Edinburgh – A*AB–A*AA incl maths (App Maths; Maths; Maths (MA); Maths Bus) (IB 34–38 pts HL 655–766 incl maths); (Maths Stats) (IB 34–38 pts HL 765–766 incl maths); (Maths Mus) (IB 38 pts HL 766 incl maths)
Lancaster – AAA incl maths/fmaths (Maths OR Stats Econ (MORSE)) (IB 35 pts HL 16 pts incl 6 maths); (Maths; Maths Fin; Maths Phil; Maths Stats) (IB 36 pts HL 16 pts incl 6 maths); AAA incl phys+maths (Theor Phys Maths) (IB 36 pts HL 16 pts incl 6 maths+phys)
Leeds – AAA/A*AB incl A maths (Maths Stats) (IB 35 pts HL 17 pts incl 6 maths); AAA/A*AB incl A maths+fmaths/AS maths (Act Maths) (HL 17 pts incl 6 maths); AAA/A*AB incl maths (Fin Maths; Maths) (HL 17 pts incl 6 maths)
London (King's) – AAA incl maths+fmaths (Maths Phil) (IB 36 pts HL 18 pts incl 6 maths)
London (QM) – AAA incl maths (Econ Stats Maths) (IB 36 pts HL 666 incl maths)
London (UCL) – AAA incl maths+chem (Chem Maths) (IB 38 pts HL 18 pts incl 6 chem+maths)
Loughborough – AAA/A*AB incl A maths (Maths Stats) (IB 37 pts HL 666 incl maths/HL 765 incl 7 maths); AAA/A*AB incl maths (Maths) (IB 37 pts HL 666 incl maths)
Nottingham – A*AB/AAA–A*AA incl maths (Fin Maths; Maths) (IB 36 pts HL 6 maths); AAA incl comp (Comp Sci) (IB 38 pts HL 6 comp sci)
Queen's Belfast – AAA/A*AB incl maths (Maths Comp Sci (MSci); Maths Stats OR (MMath)) (IB 36 pts HL 666 incl maths); AAA/A*AB incl maths+phys (App Maths Phys (MSci)) (IB 36 pts HL 666 incl maths+phys)
Sheffield – AAA/AAB+aEPQ incl maths (Maths (MMath)) (IB 36 pts HL 6 maths)
Southampton – AAA incl maths (Maths; Maths (MMath); Maths Act Sci; Maths Comp Sci; Maths Fin) (IB 36 pts HL 18 pts incl 6 maths); AAA incl maths+phys (Mathem Phys (MMath)) (IB 36 pts HL 18 pts incl 6 maths+phys); AAA incl maths/fmaths+phys (Phys Maths (MPhys)) (IB 36 pts HL 18 pts incl 6 maths/fmaths+phys); AAA–AAB+aEPQ incl A maths (Maths OR Stats Econ (MORSE)) (IB 36 pts HL 18 pts incl 6 maths); AAA–AAB+aEPQ incl A maths (Maths Stats) (IB 36 pts HL 18 pts incl 6 maths)
Surrey – AAA incl maths (Maths (MMath)) (IB 35 pts HL 6 maths)
York – AAA incl maths (Econ Maths; Maths; Maths Fin; Maths Stats) (IB 36 pts HL 6 maths)

136 pts **City St George's** – AAB incl maths/fmaths 136 pts (Maths Fin) (IB 33 pts HL 6 maths)
East Anglia – AAB incl maths (Maths) (IB 33 pts HL 6 maths); AAB incl maths (Maths Stats) (IB 33 pts HL 6 maths)
Exeter – AAB–AAA incl maths (Maths; Maths (Yr Ind); Maths Acc; Maths Econ; Maths Fin; Maths Mgt) (IB 34–36 pts HL 665–666 incl 6 maths); AAB–AAA incl maths+phys (Maths Phys) (IB 34–36 pts HL 665–666 incl maths+phys)
Lancaster – AAB incl maths (Acc Fin Maths) (IB 35 pts HL 16 pts incl 6 maths)
Liverpool – AAB incl maths (Maths Fin) (IB 35 pts HL 6 maths); AAB incl maths+phys (Mathem Phys (MMath)) (IB 35 pts HL 6 maths+phys)
London (QM) – AAB incl maths (Maths) (IB 34 pts HL 665 incl maths)
Loughborough – AAB incl maths+phys (Phys Maths) (IB 35 pts HL 665 incl maths+phys)
Newcastle – AAB/A*BB incl maths (Maths) (IB 34 pts HL 6 maths); AAB incl maths (Maths (MMath); Maths Stats) (IB 34 pts HL 6 maths); AAB–A*BB incl maths (Maths Fin) (IB 34 pts HL 6 maths)

Queen's Belfast – AAB/A*BB incl maths (Maths (MSci)) (IB 34 pts); (Maths; Maths Stats OR) (IB 34 pts HL 665 incl maths); AAB/A*BB incl maths+phys (App Maths Phys) (IB 34 pts HL 665 incl maths+phys); AAB incl maths (Maths Comp Sci)
Sheffield – AAB/ABB+bEPQ incl maths (Maths; Maths Comb Hons) (IB 34 pts HL 6 maths); AAB incl maths (Fin Maths) (IB 34 pts HL 6 maths)
St Andrews – AAB (Arbc Maths) (IB 36 pts HL 665 incl 6 maths)
Sussex – AAB incl maths+fmaths (Maths (MMath)) (IB 34 pts HL 6 maths)
York – AAB incl maths+phys (Maths Phys) (IB 35 pts HL 6 maths+phys)

128 pts **Aston** – ABB incl maths (Maths) (IB 32 pts HL 655 incl maths)
Brunel – ABB incl maths/fmaths (Fin Maths (MMath)) (IB 30 pts HL 6 maths)
Cardiff – ABB–AAB incl maths (Maths) (IB 32–34 pts HL 6 maths)
City St George's – ABB incl maths/fmaths 128 pts (Maths) (IB 31 pts HL 6 maths)
Edinburgh – ABB–AAA incl maths+phys (Mathem Phys) (IB 32–37 pts HL 655–666 incl 6 maths+ 5 phys)
Kent – ABB incl maths (Maths) (HL 6 maths)
Leicester – ABB/AAB+bEPQ incl maths (Maths) (IB 30 pts HL 5 maths)
Liverpool – ABB/BBB+aEPQ incl maths (Maths; Maths Econ; Maths Stats) (IB 33 pts HL 6 maths); ABB incl maths (Maths Langs) (IB 33 pts HL 6 maths)
London (QM) – ABB incl maths (Maths (MSci); Maths Fin Acc; Maths Stats) (IB 32 pts HL 655 incl maths)
London (RH) – ABB–AAB incl maths (Maths) (IB 32 pts HL 655 incl 6 maths); ABB–ABC incl maths (Maths Stats) (IB 32 pts HL 654 incl 6 maths)
Surrey – ABB incl A maths (Fin Maths; Maths courses) (IB 33 pts HL 6 maths); ABB–AAB incl maths (Maths Data Sci) (IB 33–34 pts HL 6 maths)
Swansea – ABB–AAB incl maths (Maths (MMath)) (IB 32–34 pts HL 6 maths)

120 pts **Aberdeen** – BBB incl maths+sci (App Maths; Maths) (IB 32 pts HL 555 incl maths+sci)
Brunel – ABC incl maths/fmaths (Maths) (IB 30 pts HL 6 maths)
Cardiff – BBB–AAB incl maths (Maths OR Stats) (IB 31–34 pts HL 665–666 incl maths)
Central Lancashire – 120 pts incl maths (Maths) (HL 6 maths)
Coventry – BBB–ABB incl maths (Maths courses) (IB 31 pts HL 5 maths)
Dundee – BBB incl B maths+biol/chem (Mathem Biol) (IB 30 pts HL 555 incl maths+chem+biol/phys); BBB incl maths 120 pts (Maths) (IB 30 pts HL 555)
Essex – BBB incl maths (Maths) (IB 30 pts HL 555 incl maths)
Glasgow – BBB–AAB incl maths (Acc Maths; Maths) (IB 34 pts HL 655 incl maths)
Heriot-Watt – BBB incl maths (Maths; Maths Comb Hons; Maths Stats) (IB 28 pts HL 5 maths); BBB–ABB incl maths+Span (Maths Span) (IB 28 pts HL 5 maths+Span)
Hertfordshire – BBB–ABB incl maths 120–128 pts (Fin Maths; Maths) (HL 4 maths)
Huddersfield – BBB incl maths 120 pts (Maths)
Hull – BBB incl maths (Maths) (IB 30 pts HL 6 maths)
London (RH) – ABC–ABB incl A maths (Econ Maths) (IB 32 pts HL 654 incl 6 maths)
Nottingham Trent – 120 pts incl maths (Maths; Spo Sci Maths)
Reading – ABC incl A maths (Maths; Maths Stats Data Sci) (IB 30 pts HL 6 maths)
Stirling – BBB incl maths (App Maths) (IB 30 pts)
Strathclyde – BBB incl maths (Maths Stats Econ) (IB 30 pts HL 5 maths); BBB–ABB incl maths (Maths courses) (IB 32 pts HL 6 maths)
Sussex – ABC–ABB incl maths (Maths Econ; Maths courses) (IB 30–32 pts HL 5 maths)
Swansea – BBB–ABB incl maths (Maths) (IB 32 pts HL 6 maths)
UWE Bristol – B maths 120 pts (Maths) (HL 6 maths)
West London – BBB 120 pts (Maths Stats)

112 pts **Brunel** – BBC incl maths/fmaths (Maths Comp Sci) (IB 29 pts HL 5 maths)
Coventry – BBC incl maths 112 pts (Maths Stats) (IB 31 pts HL 5 maths)
De Montfort – 112 pts incl maths (Maths) (IB 26 pts HL 6 maths)
Keele – ACC incl A maths 112 pts (Maths) (IB 29 pts HL 5 maths)
Liverpool Hope – BBC 112 pts (Maths) (IB 28 pts)
Liverpool John Moores – BBC incl maths 112 pts (Maths; Maths Fin) (HL 5 maths)

London (Birk) – BBC incl B maths 112 pts (Maths Stats)
Manchester Met – BBC incl maths 112–120 pts (Maths) (IB 28 pts HL 5 maths)
Northumbria – B maths 112 pts (Maths)
Oxford Brookes – BBC 112 pts (Maths courses) (IB 30 pts HL 5 maths)
Plymouth – 112–128 pts incl maths (Maths Fin) (IB 30 pts HL 5 maths)
Portsmouth – 112–128 pts incl maths (Maths Fin Mgt) (IB 29 pts); BBC–ABB 112–128 pts incl maths (Maths); BBC–BBB 112–120 pts (Maths Mach Lrng) (IB 29 pts); BBC–BBB 112–120 pts incl maths (Maths Stats) (IB 29 pts)
Sheffield Hallam – BBC incl maths 112 pts (Maths)

104 pts **Aberystwyth** – BCC–BBB incl B maths 104–120 pts (App Maths PMaths; App Maths Stats; Maths) (IB 28–30 pts HL 5 maths)
Chester – BCC–BBC 104–112 pts (Maths) (IB 26 pts HL 5 maths)
Chichester – BCC–BBC 104–112 pts (Maths) (IB 26–28 pts)
Greenwich – BCC 104 pts (Maths; Maths Comp Sci); BCC incl maths 104 pts (Fin Maths) (HL 5 maths)

96 pts **Wolverhampton** – BCD incl B maths 96 pts (Maths)

80 pts **London Met** – CCE incl maths (Maths)

72 pts **London Met** – CDE/BC 72 pts (Mathem Sci)

Open University – (Maths)

Alternative offers See **Chapter 6** and **Appendix 1** for grades/UCAS Tariff points information for other examinations.

EXAMPLES OF COLLEGES OFFERING COURSES IN THIS SUBJECT FIELD

Bradford College (UC); Bury (Coll).

CHOOSING YOUR COURSE (SEE ALSO CH.1)

Universities and colleges teaching quality See www.qaa.ac.uk; www.discoveruni.gov.uk.

Top research universities and colleges (REF 2021) (Mathematical Sciences) Oxford; Cambridge; Imperial London; Bristol; Glasgow; Warwick; Lancaster; Manchester; Edinburgh; Heriot-Watt.

Examples of sandwich degree courses Aston; Bath; Brunel; Cardiff; Coventry; East Anglia; Exeter; Greenwich; Hertfordshire; Kent; Lancaster; Liverpool John Moores; London (QM); Loughborough; Northumbria; Nottingham; Nottingham Trent; Plymouth; Portsmouth; Reading; Surrey; UWE Bristol; Wolverhampton; York.

ADMISSIONS INFORMATION

Admissions tutors' advice **Leeds** Applicants taking the BTEC Extended Diploma may be required to take an additional Maths A-level paper.

Advice to applicants and planning the UCAS personal statement Any interests you have in careers requiring mathematical ability could be mentioned, for example, engineering, computers (hardware and software) and business applications. Show determination, love of mathematics and an appreciation of the rigour of the course. Give details of your skills, work experience, positions of responsibility. A variety of non-academic interests to complement the applicant's academic abilities preferred. For non-UK students, fluency in oral and written English required.

Selection interviews **Yes** Cambridge, Manchester (Maths Phys), Oxford (Maths) 30% (success rate 9%), (Maths Phil) 39% (success rate 12%), (Maths Stats) 30% (success rate 9%); **Some** Bath, East Anglia, Imperial London, Loughborough, York; **No** Bishop Grosseteste, Bristol, Liverpool John Moores, London (RH), London LSE, Newcastle, Nottingham, UWE Bristol, Warwick.

Interview advice and questions Questions are likely to be asked arising from the information you have given in your UCAS application and about your interests in the subject. Questions in recent years have included: How many ways are there of incorrectly setting up the back row of a chess board? A ladder on a rough floor leans against a smooth wall. Describe the forces acting on the ladder and give the maximum possible angle of inclination possible. There are three particles connected by a string; the middle one is made to move – describe the subsequent motion of the particles. What mathematics books have you read outside your syllabus? Why does a ball bounce? Discuss the work of any renowned mathematician. Balance a pencil on your index fingers and then try to move both towards the centre of the pencil. Explain what is happening in terms of forces and friction. See also **Chapter 5**.

Reasons for rejection (non-academic) Usually academic reasons only. Lack of motivation. Uneasiness about how much mathematics will be remembered after a gap year.

GRADUATE DESTINATIONS AND EMPLOYMENT

(See **Chapter 1, Graduate Outcomes.**)

Career note Graduates enter a range of careers. While business, finance and retail areas are popular options, mathematicians also have important roles in the manufacturing industries. Mathematics offers the pleasure of problem-solving, the satisfaction of a rigorous argument and the most widely employable non-vocational degree subject. A student's view: 'Maths trains you to work in the abstract, to think creatively and to come up with concrete conclusions.' These transferable skills are much sought-after by employers. Employment prospects are excellent, with high salaries.

OTHER DEGREE SUBJECTS FOR CONSIDERATION

Accountancy; Actuarial Studies; Astronomy; Astrophysics; Computer Science; Economics; Engineering Sciences; Operational Research; Physics; Statistics.

MEDIA STUDIES

(including **Broadcast Media Technologies**; see also **Art and Design (General), Communication Studies/Communication, Computer Science and Information Technology, Engineering (Acoustics and Sound), Film, Radio and TV Studies, Information Management and Librarianship, Journalism, Photography**)

Intending Media applicants need to check course details carefully since this subject area can involve graphic design, illustration and other art courses as well as the media in the fields of TV, radio and journalism.

Useful websites www.bbc.co.uk/careers; www.newsmediauk.org; www.ppa.co.uk; www.thomsonreuters.com/en/careers.html; www.nctj.com; https://ipa.co.uk

NB The points totals shown to the left of the institutions are for ease of reference only. It must not be assumed that Tariff points are always used by institutions or that they can be substituted for an offer in grades. The level of an offer is not necessarily indicative of the quality of a course.

COURSE OFFERS INFORMATION

Subject requirements/preferences GCSE English and mathematics often required. **AL** No specified subjects required. Some popular universities are now making lower offers for disadvantaged and other students.

Your target offers and examples of degree courses

136 pts **Leeds** – AAB incl arts/hum/soc sci (Comm Media) (IB 35 pts HL 16 pts incl 5 Engl)
Newcastle – AAB (Jrnl Media Cult; Media Comm Cult St) (IB 34 pts)
York – AAB+interview (Interact Media) (IB 34 pts)

128 pts **East Anglia** – ABB (Glob Dev Media; Media St) (IB 32 pts)
Lancaster – ABB (Media Cult St) (IB 32 pts HL 16 pts)
Leicester – ABB/BBB+bEPQ (Media Comm; Media Soty Cult) (IB 30 pts)
Liverpool – ABB/BBB+aEPQ (Comm Media) (IB 33 pts)
Loughborough – ABB (Media Comm) (IB 34 pts HL 655)

Nottingham – ABB (Int Media Comm St; Span Int Media Comms St) (IB 30 pts HL 655)

120 pts **Brunel** – BBB+portfolio (Vis Efcts Mtn Graph) (IB 30 pts)
Kent – BBB 120 pts (Media St) (HL 665)
Leicester – BBB (Flm Media St) (IB 28 pts)
London (Gold) – BBB (Media Comms) (IB 33 pts HL 655)
Oxford Brookes – BBB 120 pts (Media Jrnl Pub) (IB 31 pts)
Surrey – BBB (Media Comm) (IB 32 pts)

112 pts **Arts London** – 112 pts+interview (Fash Jrnl Cntnt Crea)
Birmingham City – BBC 112 pts (Jrnl) (IB 28 pts)
Brunel – BBC (Comm Media St; Sociol (Dig Media)) (IB 29 pts)
Canterbury Christ Church – BBC 112 pts (Media Prod) (IB 29 pts)
Cardiff – BBC–ABB (Media Jrnl Cult) (IB 30–32 pts HL 655–665)
Coventry – BBC+portfolio (Media Comms) (IB 29 pts HL Engl)
East London – 112 pts (Media Comm) (IB 24 pts HL 15 pts)
Greenwich – BBC 112 pts (Media Comms)
Hull – BBC 112 pts (Media St) (IB 28 pts)
Keele – BBC 112 pts (Media Comms) (IB 29 pts HL 554)
Kingston – 112–128 pts (Media Comm)
Leeds Beckett – 112 pts (Broad Media Tech; Crea Media Tech); BBC 112 pts (Media Comm Cult)
London Met – BBC 112 pts (Media Comms)
Northumbria – 112 pts (Media Commun)
Nottingham Trent – 112 pts (Media Comb Hons; Media Prod)
Portsmouth – BBC–BBB 112–120 pts (Media St) (IB 25 pts)
Sheffield Hallam – BBC 112 pts+portfolio (Dig Media Prod); BBC–BBB 112–120 pts (Media Comm)
Swansea – BBC 112–128 pts (Media courses) (IB 32 pts)
UWE Bristol – 112 pts (Cult Med Crea Ind; Media Prod); BBC 112 pts (Media Comm)
West London – BBC 112 pts (Mark Soc Media; Media Comms)

104 pts **Arts London** – 104 pts (Contemp Media Cult; Mag Jrnl Pub) (IB 24 pts)
Bangor – 104–128 pts (Media St courses)
Bath Spa – BCC–BBB 104–120 pts (Media Comms) (IB 32 pts)
Bournemouth – 104–120 pts (Comm Media; Media Prod) (IB 28–32 pts)
Brighton – BCC–BBB 104–120 pts (Media Prod; Media St) (IB 30 pts)
Cardiff Met – 104 pts (Media Comms)
Chichester – BCC–BBC 104–112 pts (Media Comms; Spo Media) (IB 28 pts)
Cumbria – BCC–BBC 104–112 pts+interview+portfolio (Wldlf Media)
De Montfort – 104 pts (Jrnl; Media Comm) (IB 24 pts)
Edinburgh Napier – BCC incl des/mus/media (Dig Media Interact Des Glob) (IB 28 pts HL 654 incl des/mus/mark)
Falmouth – 104–120 pts+interview (Jrnl Crea Writ)
Glasgow Caledonian – BCC (Media Comm)
Huddersfield – BCC–BBC 104–112 pts+interview (Media Flm St)
Lincoln – 104 pts (Media Prod)
Liverpool Hope – BCC 104 pts (Media Comm) (IB 24 pts)
Liverpool John Moores – BCC incl hum 104 pts (Media Cult Comm)
Manchester Met – BCC 104–112 pts (Dig Media Comms; Flm Media St) (IB 26 pts)
Northampton – BCC (Crea Flm TV Dig Media Prod)
Oxford Brookes – BCC 104 pts (Comm Media Cult) (IB 29 pts)
Plymouth (AU) – 104–120 pts+portfolio (Fash Media Mark)
Queen Margaret – BCC incl Engl/media (Media Comms) (IB 28 pts)
Robert Gordon – BCC incl Engl (Media) (IB 27 pts HL 5 Engl)
Winchester – 104–120 pts (Dig Media Des; Media Comm courses) (HL 44)
Worcester – 104 pts (Media Flm St)
York St John – 104 pts (Media courses)

96 pts **Aberystwyth** – CCC–BBB 96–120 pts (Media Comm St) (IB 26–30 pts)
Anglia Ruskin – 96 pts (Media courses) (IB 24 pts)
Bangor – 96–128 pts (Media Flm Jrnl); B mus 96–120 pts (Crea Arts) (HL 5 mus)
Bedfordshire – 96 pts (Media Mark PR; Media Prod courses)
Central Lancashire – 96–112 pts (Flmm; Media Prod)
Chester – CCC–BCC 96–104 pts (Media TV Prod) (IB 26 pts)
Greater Manchester – 96 pts+interview+portfolio (Flm TV Prod)
Plymouth – 96–112 pts (Crea Media) (IB 26–28 pts)
South Wales – CCC incl art/des 96 pts+portfolio (Media Prod; Perf Media)
St Mary's – 96–112 pts (Comms Media Mark)
Sunderland – 96–112 pts (Media Cult Comm)
Teesside – 96–112 pts (Flm TV Prod)

64 pts **Ravensbourne Univ** – CC+portfolio (Edit Pst Prod) (IB 24 pts)

ALTERNATIVE OFFERS See **Chapter 6** and **Appendix 1** for grades/UCAS Tariff points information for other examinations.

EXAMPLES OF COLLEGES OFFERING COURSES IN THIS SUBJECT FIELD

Accrington and Rossendale (Coll); Blackpool and Fylde (Coll); Bridgwater and Taunton (Coll); Central Film Sch; East Riding (Coll); Farnborough (CT); Gloucestershire (Coll); HOW (Coll); Hugh Baird (Coll); Kingston (Coll); Leeds City (Coll); Macclesfield (Coll); Newcastle (Coll); Peterborough (UC); SMB CG; Stratford-upon-Avon (Coll); TEC Partnership; Truro and Penwith (Coll); Westminster Kingsway (Coll); Weston (Coll); Yeovil (Coll).

CHOOSING YOUR COURSE (SEE ALSO CH.1)

UNIVERSITIES AND COLLEGES TEACHING QUALITY See www.qaa.ac.uk; www.discoveruni.gov.uk.

TOP RESEARCH UNIVERSITIES AND COLLEGES (REF 2021) (Communication, Cultural and Media Studies, Library and Information Management) London LSE; Cardiff; Leicester (Musm St); London (Gold) (Media Comm Cult St); Loughborough; Glasgow; Leicester (Media Comm); London (RH); London (King's); Newcastle.

EXAMPLES OF SANDWICH DEGREE COURSES Bangor; Bournemouth; Brunel; Coventry; De Montfort; Huddersfield; Leeds; Manchester Met; Nottingham Trent; Portsmouth; Sheffield Hallam; Surrey.

ADMISSIONS INFORMATION

ADVICE TO APPLICANTS AND PLANNING THE UCAS PERSONAL STATEMENT Work experience or work shadowing is important. Contact local newspaper offices to meet journalists and to discuss their work. Contact local radio stations and advertising agencies, read newspapers (all types) and be able to describe the different approaches of newspapers. Watch TV coverage of news stories and the way in which the interviewer deals with politicians or members of the public. Give your opinions on the various forms of media. School magazine and/or any published work should be mentioned. A balance of academic and practical skills preferred. Creativity, problem-solving, cultural awareness, communication skills and commitment required. (International students: Fluency in written and spoken English required.) See also **Communication Studies/Communication** and **Appendix 3**.

SELECTION INTERVIEWS Yes Cumbria, Falmouth, Greater Manchester, Huddersfield, Plymouth (AU), York; **No** Cardiff, Liverpool John Moores, Sunderland, West London.

INTERVIEW ADVICE AND QUESTIONS Past questions include: Which newspapers do you read? Discuss the main differences between the national daily newspapers. Which radio programmes do you listen to each day? Which television programmes do you watch? Should the BBC broadcast advertisements? What do you think are the reasons for the popularity of *EastEnders*? Film or video work, if required, should be edited to a running time of 15 minutes unless otherwise stated. See also **Chapter 5**.

REASONS FOR REJECTION (NON-ACADEMIC) No clear commitment (to Broadcast Journalism) plus no evidence of experience (now proving to be essential). Mistaken expectations of the nature of the course. Can't write and doesn't work well in groups. Too specific and narrow areas of media interest, for example, video or scriptwriting. Lack of knowledge of current affairs.

GRADUATE DESTINATIONS AND EMPLOYMENT

(See **Chapter 1, Graduate Outcomes.**)

Career note See **Film, Radio and TV Studies**.

OTHER DEGREE SUBJECTS FOR CONSIDERATION

Advertising; Communication; English; Film, Radio, Video and TV Studies; Journalism; Photography; Public Relations.

MEDICINE

(see also **Biological Sciences, Human Sciences/Human Biosciences**)

Medicine is a highly popular choice of degree subject and career. All courses listed below include the same areas of study and all lead to a qualification and career in medicine. Medical schools aim to produce doctors who are clinically competent, who are able to see patients as people and have a holistic and ethical approach (including the ability to understand and manage each patient's case in a family and social context as well as in hospital), who treat patients and colleagues with respect, dignity and sensitivity, are skilled at teamwork and are prepared for continual learning. In several ways, these aims reflect the qualities selectors seek when interviewing applicants. In all cases, close attention will be paid to the confidential report on the UCAS application to judge the applicant's personality, communication skills, academic potential and commitment to a medical career. Methods of teaching may vary slightly, depending on the medical school. To achieve these aims, some medical schools adopt the system of self-directed learning (SDL) in which objectives are set to assess students' progress, and problem-based learning (PBL) which helps students to develop critical thinking and clinical problem-solving skills.

While there is a core curriculum of knowledge, the first three years integrate scientific and clinical experience, and there are fewer formal lectures than before, with more group and individual work. For outstanding students without science A-levels, some pre-medical courses are available. Most medical schools also offer an extra year of study, usually in the middle of the medical degree, to enable students to research a scientific subject leading to an 'intercalated' BSc degree. Additionally, elective periods abroad in the final year can sometimes be taken.

Medical students' and doctors' advice to applicants

'I did not fully appreciate how diverse medicine is as a career. Everyone has their own particular reasons for wishing to pursue it, but these will change as you progress through your career. There are many different pathways you can take which makes it all the more exciting ... and daunting! Choose your university carefully; in most medical degrees, you will only be based at university for the first two years, and thereafter you will be in hospitals around the area so choose a city or an area you want to work and live in.'

'Medicine is a career which can open many doors – as a family or hospital doctor, working in Africa treating children with infectious diseases, in a war zone, in a laboratory, in sport, in journalism, and in law, going on to study law, to specialise in medical law, I have friends who have done all of these things.'

'Get to know what the real working lives of doctors are. The attributes needed to see sick and needy people. The fact that the NHS is a public and not a private organisation and what this means in the changing world of medical knowledge. Some of this is very difficult to learn in sixth form but periods of work experience will help. In addition to talking to medical students and family friends who are doctors, browse through medical journals and medical websites. Every doctor has had their own individual experiences, good and bad, but the majority would still apply to medicine again if they were 17!'

Useful websites www.scicentral.com; www.ipem.ac.uk; www.bmj.com; www.admissionstesting.org; www.gmc-uk.org; www.healthcareers.nhs.uk; www.bma.org.uk; www.rcgp.org.uk; www.rcpath.org

NB The points totals shown to the left of the institutions are for ease of reference only. It must not be assumed that Tariff points are always used by institutions or that they can be substituted for an offer in grades. The level of an offer is not necessarily indicative of the quality of a course.

COURSE OFFERS INFORMATION

Subject requirements/preferences Check the university's website. Many universities stipulate that applicants must hold certain GCSE grades. Some popular universities are now making lower offers for disadvantaged and other students.
Aberdeen GCSE Grade 6 (B) in English and mathematics. Biology and physics or dual award science recommended.
Aston Grade 6 (B) or above in English language, mathematics, chemistry, biology or double science (or overseas equivalent).
Birmingham Minimum of grade 6 (B) in **GCSE** English language, mathematics, biology and chemistry. Dual science award acceptable as an alternative to biology and chemistry.
Brighton Applicants should hold **GCSE** English language/English literature and maths at Grade 6 (B) or above.
Brighton and Sussex (MS) Mathematics and English at grade 6 (B), or above.
Bristol Mathematics grade 7 (A) and English grade 4 (C).
Brunel GCSE English grade 4 (C) and Maths grade 5 (B).
Buckingham Grade 4 (C) in English and mathematics.
Cambridge Mathematics and dual science award (or biology and physics).
Cardiff 6 (B) in eight subjects (minimum). English or Welsh at grade 6 (B), mathematics at grade 6 (B), grades 66 (BB) in dual science.
Central Lancashire GCSE or equivalent to include English language at grade 6 (B) or higher with a broad study of sciences and mathematics.
City St George's Typically five subjects at grade 6 (B) are required including English language, mathematics and science subjects. Contact the admissions team for a more detailed breakdown of grade requirements.
Dundee Grade 6 (B) (minimum) in biology, mathematics and English.
East Anglia All applicants must have a minimum of six GCSEs (or two EU/International equivalent) passes at grade 7 (A) or above, to include mathematics and either two science subjects or double science. Applicants must also hold at least grade 6 (B) in English language. GCSE short courses are not accepted. Repeat GCSEs are accepted.
Edge Hill Applicants require five GCSEs at grade 6 (B) or above, including biology, chemistry, English language and mathematics. Double science is also accepted instead of separate GCSEs in biology and chemistry.
Edinburgh English, mathematics, biology, chemistry or dual science award at grade 6 (B) or higher.
Exeter Minimum grade 4 (C) in English language. Higher grades may be specified for individual programmes of study. International students should view requirements on the website.
Glasgow Grade 6 (B) or above in English.
Hull York (MS) Six subjects at grades 9–4 (A*–C) including English language and mathematics at grade 6 (B) or higher.
Imperial London For advice on the requirements please contact the School of Medicine.
Keele Five at grade 7 (A) and maths, science and English at grade 6 (B) as a minimum requirement.
Kent Level 6 (B) or higher in five subjects including English, mathematics, and biology, chemistry, physics or double science.
Kent Medway Med Sch Normally 9–6 (A* to B) in English language, mathematics and biology, chemistry or physics/double award science.
Lancaster Minimum grade 6 (B) in biology, chemistry, physics or general science, English language and maths. See the university's website for further details.
Leeds Six subjects at grade 6 (B) minimum including English language, mathematics, chemistry and biology or dual science award.
Leicester You must have achieved at least a grade 6 (B) in English language (as a first language), mathematics, double science/chemistry and biology. A minimum number of A* or 8/9 grades at GCSE not specified, but GCSE performance taken into consideration when selecting applicants for interview.

Lincoln Six GCSEs at grade 7 (A) including chemistry and biology or double science. Minimum grade 6 (B) in mathematics and English language.
Liverpool Nine GCSEs by end of Year 11 including English language, maths, biology, chemistry and physics or general science at grade 6 (B). A minimum score of 15 points from the best nine GCSEs or equivalent (where 9/8/7 (A*/A) = 2 points and 6 (B) = 1 point).
London (King's) Grade 6 (B) (minimum) in English and mathematics.
London (QM) Six subjects at 7–6 (A–B) minimum grades including English, mathematics and science subjects.
London (UCL) English and mathematics at grade 6 (B) minimum.
Manchester Seven subjects at grades 7/8 (A/A*). English language, mathematics and at least two science subjects at grade 6 (B) minimum.
Newcastle GCSE results not considered.
Nottingham Minimum of six GCSEs at grade 7 (A) including chemistry and biology or dual science. Grade 6 (B) in English and mathematics. For the University of Nottingham Lincoln Medical School, check the university's website.
Oxford Mathematics, biology and physics or dual science award if not taken at A-level.
Queen's Belfast GCSE mathematics and physics (or dual science award) at grade 4 (C) (or 44) if not taken at AS-level or A-level.
Southampton A minimum of seven subjects at grade 7 (A) including English language, mathematics with biology and chemistry or equivalent. (Widening Access course BM6) Five at grade 4 (C) including English language, mathematics with biology and chemistry or equivalent. (Students join the five-year programme on completion of Year Zero.)
St Andrews If not studied at AS or A level, applicants must have GCSE grade 5 (B) in biology, mathematics and English (language or literature). We accept CCEA GCSE grade C* as equivalent to grade 5 in numerical grading. In addition, there is a minimum requirement of five GCSEs at grade 7 (A), to be taken at one sitting. A level holders may be considered with fewer grades than five at grade 7 (A).
Sunderland Five subjects at grade 7 (A) with a minimum of grade 6 (B) in maths, English language, biology, chemistry and physics.
Swansea Mathematics and English/Welsh at grade 4 (C) or above.
Warwick GCSE results not considered; this is a graduate entry course.

YOUR TARGET OFFERS AND EXAMPLES OF DEGREE COURSES

160 pts **Cambridge** – A*A*A incl chem+sci/maths+interview+UCAT (Med 6 yrs) (IB 41–42 pts HL 776 incl chem+sci/maths)

152 pts **Aston** – A*AA incl chem+biol+MMI+UCAT (Med 5 yrs) (IB 37 pts HL 766 incl chem+biol)
Birmingham – A*AA incl chem+biol+interview+UCAT (Med Srgy 5 yrs) (IB 32 pts HL 766 incl chem+biol)
Edinburgh – A*AA incl chem+maths/sci+UCAT+interview (Med 6 yrs) (IB 40 pts HL 766 incl 7 chem)
Exeter – A*AA incl biol+chem+MMI+UCAT (Med) (IB 38 pts HL 766 biol+chem)
Keele – A*AA/AAA+aEPQ incl chem+biol+sci+interview+UCAT (Med 5 yrs) (IB 37 pts HL 766 incl chem/biol+sci)
Leicester – A*AA incl chem/biol+sci+interview+UCAT (Med 5 yrs) (IB 34 pts HL 766 incl chem/biol+sci)
London (King's) – A*AA incl chem+biol+interview+UCAT (Med 6 yrs) (IB 38 pts HL 19 pts incl 6 chem/biol)
London (QM) – A*AA incl chem/biol+sci/maths+interview+UCAT (Med 5 yrs) (IB 37 pts HL 666 incl chem/biol+sci/maths)
London (UCL) – A*AA incl chem+biol+interview+UCAT (Med 6 yrs) (IB 39 pts HL 19 pts incl 6 biol/chem)
Oxford – A*AA incl chem+sci/maths+interview+UCAT (Med 6 yrs) (IB 39 pts HL 766 incl chem+sci/maths)
Queen's Belfast – A*AA/AAAa incl chem+sci/maths+interview+UCAT (Med 5 yrs)

144 pts **Aberdeen** – AAA incl chem+sci/maths+UCAT (Med 5 yrs) (IB 36 pts HL 666 incl chem+sci/maths)

Bangor – AAA incl biol+sci+interview (Med) (IB 36 pts HL 6 biol+chem)
Brighton and Sussex (MS) – AAA incl biol+chem+UCAT (Med 5 yrs) (IB 36 pts HL 6 biol+chem)
Bristol – AAA incl chem+sci/maths+interview+UCAT (Med 5 yrs) (IB 36 pts HL 18 pts incl 6 chem+sci/maths)
Cardiff – AAA incl chem+biol+MMI+UCAT (Med 5 yrs) (IB 36 pts HL 19 pts incl chem/biol+sci/maths)
City St George's – AAA incl chem+biol+interview+UCAT (Med 5 yrs) (IB 36 pts HL 18 pts incl 6 chem+biol)
Dundee – AAA incl chem/biol+sci/maths 144 pts+interview+UCAT (Med 5 yrs) (IB 37 pts HL 666 incl chem+sci/maths)
East Anglia – AAA incl biol/chem+MMI+UCAT (Med 5 yrs) (IB 34 pts HL 666 incl biol/chem)
Glasgow – AAA incl chem+sci/maths+interview+UCAT (Med 5 yrs) (IB 38 pts HL 666 incl chem+biol)
Imperial London – AAA incl biol+chem+MMI+UCAT (Med 6 yrs) (IB 38 pts HL 6 biol+chem)
Lancaster – AAA incl biol/chem/psy+MMI+UCAT (Med Srgy 5 yrs) (IB 36 pts HL 6 biol/chem/psy)
Leeds – AAA incl chem+biol+interview+UCAT (Med Srgy 5 yrs) (IB 35 pts HL 666 incl chem)
Liverpool – AAA incl chem+sci/maths+UCAT (Med Srgy 5 yrs) (IB 36 pts HL 666 incl biol+chem)
Manchester – AAA biol/chem+sci+interview+UCAT (Med 6 yrs) (IB 36 pts HL 666 incl biol/chem+sci); AAA incl chem/biol+sci/maths+interview+UCAT (Med 5 yrs) (IB 36 pts HL 666 incl chem/biol+sci/maths)
Newcastle – AAA+UCAT (Med Srgy 5 yrs) (IB 36 pts HL 5 all subjects)
Nottingham – AAA incl chem+biol+interview+UCAT (Med 5 yrs) (IB 34 pts HL 666 incl chem+biol)
Sheffield – AAA incl chem/biol+sci+UCAT+interview (Med 5 yrs) (IB 36 pts HL 666 incl chem/biol+sci)
Southampton – AAA incl biol+sci+interview+UCAT (Med 5 yrs) (IB 36 pts HL 18 pts incl 6 biol+sci)
St Andrews – AAA incl chem+sci/maths+interview+UCAT (Med 6 yrs) (IB 38 pts HL 666 incl chem+sci/maths)

136 pts **Brunel** – AAB incl chem/biol+sci+UCAT+MMI (Med (5 yrs)) (IB 36 pts)
Hull York (MS) – AAB incl chem+biol+interview+UCAT (Med 5 yrs) (IB 31 pts HL 555 incl chem+biol)
Kent Medway Med Sch – AAB incl chem/biol+UCAT+MMI (Med 5 yrs) (IB 34 pts HL 6 chem/biol)
Liverpool – AAB incl A biol (Anat Hum Biol) (IB 34 pts HL 6 biol)
Plymouth – AAB–AAA incl A biol+sci/maths+UCAT+interview (Med Srgy 5 yrs) (IB 36–38 pts HL 6 biol+sci/maths)

128 pts **Buckingham** – ABB incl chem/biol+MMI (Med) (IB 34 pts HL 6 chem+biol)

112 pts **Bristol** – BBC incl B biol/chem+UCAT (Med (Gateway)) (IB 29 pts HL 5 biol/chem)
Hull – BBC–ABB incl biol+chem+UCAT+interview (Med (Gateway)) (IB 29–34 pts HL 14 pts incl 5 biol+chem)

ALTERNATIVE OFFERS See **Chapter 6** and **Appendix 1** for grades/UCAS Tariff points information for other examinations.

DEGREE APPRENTICESHIPS

Canterbury Christ Church (Oprtg Practnr); Greater Manchester (Advnc Clin Practnr); Nottingham (Advnc Clin Practnr); Strathclyde (Med Stans).

CHOOSING YOUR COURSE (SEE ALSO CH.1)

UNIVERSITIES AND COLLEGES TEACHING QUALITY See www.qaa.ac.uk; www.discoveruni.gov.uk.

Top research universities and colleges (REF 2021) (Clinical Medicine) Cambridge; Leicester; London (UCL); Glasgow; Imperial London; Liverpool School of Tropical Medicine; Oxford; London (Institute of Cancer Research); London (King's); Edinburgh.

ADMISSIONS INFORMATION

Admissions tutors' advice Policies adopted by all medical schools are very similar, although some medical schools use the Multiple Mini-Interview (MMI) format in which candidates rotate around different question stations, each one devoted to one question. Each interview usually lasts ten minutes. However, a brief outline of the information provided by admissions tutors is given below. Further information should be obtained direct from institutions.

Aberdeen Applicants must take the UCAT in the year of application. A cut-off score is not used. Overseas applicants may be interviewed abroad or in Aberdeen. The University uses the MMI format and interviews last up to an hour. Most offers are made by end of March. Points equivalent results not accepted. Re-sits only accepted in exceptional circumstances. These must be submitted in good time to be considered. Feedback for unsuccessful applicants upon request. International students English language entry requirement (or equivalent): IELTS 7.0 and 7.0 in speaking.

Aston Deferred entry and gap years are accepted, however interviews, UCAT and academic qualifications must be obtained in the year of the application. General studies and critical thinking not accepted.

Birmingham UCAT required. Non-academic interests and extra-curricular activities noted in addition to academic factors. General studies and critical thinking not accepted. MMI format used. Approximately 1,200 called for interview. Approximately 10% take a year off which does not jeopardise the chances of an offer, but candidates must be available for interview. Re-sit candidates who failed by a small margin are only considered in exceptional circumstances. Transfers of undergraduates from other medical schools not considered. International applicants must show a good standard of written and spoken English. Second time applicants considered if not previously rejected at interview.

Brighton and Sussex (MS) UCAT used to assess each applicant. All applicants required to have grade 6 (B) in maths and English GCSE. Candidates are interviewed if they have passed the first two stages of assessment (academic and personal statement if international; academic and UCAT score if a Home applicant). Work experience necessary, but this does not need to be any given length and does not have to be in particular health sector. Interviews for Medicine are Multi Mini Interviews (MMI) and are currently held in January, February and March. Resit applicants are welcome to apply but only if they have dropped in one grade and one subject (eg AAB). Applicants with lower grades but resitting can apply to us once they have re-sat their subjects and obtained AAA. All Year 1 medical school students are guaranteed accommodation as long as they apply by the deadline (some students who live in the local area may not be able to apply for accommodation due to more applicants requiring housing than rooms available). Teaching is 'systems integrated' so students are exposed to the clinical environment from Year 1. Cadaver dissection is also part of the course from Year 1, so students get a real understanding of human anatomy, enhancing their learning experience. As the medical school is small, so are class sizes, meaning that students have a strong relationship with academic and support staff.

Bristol No places are offered without an interview. MMI interview format (see above). Second time applicants rarely considered. The top applicants are called for an interview lasting an hour; the remainder grouped into two categories: 'hold' and 'unsuccessful' – some from the first two categories will be interviewed. Full details of the interview process are offered on the Bristol website. Widening participation panel considers appropriate candidates. Criteria for selection: UCAT, realistic and academic interest in medicine, commitment to helping others, wide range of interests, contribution to school/college activities, personal achievements. Interview criteria: reasons for wanting to study Medicine, awareness of current developments, communication skills, self-confidence, enthusiasm and determination to study, ability to cope with stress, awareness of the content of the course and career. General studies and critical thinking not acceptable. Subject content overlap (eg biology/PE/ sports science) not allowed. Deferred entry welcomed (except for A101 (Graduate Entry)), but applicants must be available for interview. Points equivalent results not accepted. International students English language requirement (or equivalent): IELTS 7.5. Some candidates are still applying without the right subjects or grade predictions. Visit www.bristol.ac.uk/study/undergraduate for up-to-date course and entry information.

Brunel Up until 2023, the course was only open to international fee paying students. For 2024 entry, 50 places were available for Home students. Please check website for more information www.brunel.ac.uk/study/undergraduate/medicine-mbbs.

Cambridge Most applicants for Medicine at Cambridge have at least three science/mathematics A-levels and some colleges require this or ask for particular A-level subject(s). UCAT used to assess each applicant. The standard undergraduate course is offered at all colleges except Hughes Hall. Normally two interviews lasting 20 minutes each. Films of interviews can be found on www.undergraduate.study.cam.ac.uk/applying/interviews. Approximately 80% of applicants are interviewed. Applicants are not usually required to submit examples of written work. Gap year acceptable but for positive reasons. Clinical studies from Year 4 at the Cambridge Clinical School (Addenbrooke's Hospital).

Cardiff Admission is determined by a combination of academic performance, non-academic skills, knowledge and completion of the UCAT test. Applications can be made in the Welsh language. Approximately 1,500 of the 3,500 applicants are called for interview. Cardiff uses the MMI format for interviews. Applications are assessed and scored as follows: 1. Medical motivation and awareness of career. 2. Caring ethos. 3. Sense of responsibility. 4. Evidence of a balanced approach to life. 5. Evidence of self-directed learning. 6. Referee's report.

Central Lancashire Interview format is MMI with 10 activity stations. All applicants invited to interview must provide a satisfactory enhanced DBS check or international equivalent and proof of ID. All applicants successful at interview will need to undergo occupational health screening as part of the enrolment process.

Chester Graduate Entry Medicine offered. Entry via 2.i honours degree or overseas equivalent. English language and minimum threshold mark in UCAT (or UCATSEN) are required.

City St George's Applicants must be taking A-level chemistry and biology or human biology. You will be required to complete your A-levels within two years of study and the standard offer is AAA. Applicants must have an average grade of B (6) across their top five GCSEs including English language, maths and dual award or the three single sciences. Applicants are also required to take the UCAT test in the year of application. Applicants who meet our A-level and GCSE requirements and achieve our required overall and section scores in UCAT will be offered an interview. All offers are made post-interview. Applicants are expected to have relevant work experience which is assessed at interview. The value of work experience lies with reflection. What have you gained? How has the experience affected your journey to study Medicine? What skills do you need to work on as a result of carrying out this experience? The English language requirement for international students is IELTS 7.0 with 7.0 in writing and no section less than 6.5. Deferred entry welcome. Medicine (six years, including Foundation year) is for mature non-graduate students only. Medicine (four years, Graduate stream) is for graduates with a 2.1 Hons degree in any discipline. Graduates are not eligible for the five-year Medicine programme.

Dundee No minimum UCAT cut-off score used, although candidates receiving offers in recent years have typically achieved around 2,720 pts. A fully integrated hospital and medical school. Preference given to candidates who achieve the right grades at the first sitting. A system of 10 seven-minute mini-interviews has been introduced which gives students separate opportunities to sell themselves. Deferred entry acceptable. Clinical attachments in Year 4. World-wide experience in final year electives.

East Anglia Criteria include academic requirements and UCAT. MMI format (see above) are used for the interviews, candidates visit each station for one question with five minutes at each station. English entry requirement IELTS 7.5. Clinical experience from Year 1.

Edge Hill For entry requirements to the university's new access to medicine course, see the university's website.

Edinburgh 278 places for around 2,300 applicants. All examination grades must be achieved at the first sitting; only in extenuating circumstances will re-sits be considered. All UCAT scores considered. The situational judgement section of the UCAT test is also considered. Equal weighting given to academic and non-academic criteria. Non-academic criteria score based on personal qualities and skills, evidence of career exploration prior to application, breadth and level of non-academic achievements and interests. Work experience and work shadowing, particularly in a hospital, viewed positively but the admissions panel recognises that not all applicants have equal opportunities to gain such experience. School-leaving applicants are not normally interviewed so references are important. Shortlisted graduate and mature applicants will be interviewed; 190 UK fee rate places available, around one in eleven receive an offer. International applicants not normally called for interview. Some clinical experience from Year 1. The six-year programme includes an intercalated research Honours year in Year 3.

Exeter Selection procedures include the assessment of UCAT or GAMSAT. Mini interviews are used. Selection policy updated annually. Always check the website for the latest advice.

Glasgow The initial screening process considers the applicant's academic achievement, personal statement and reference. The UCAT is the final part of the screening process and is used for allocation of interview. The range of UCAT scores considered changes each year as the performance of each admissions cohort varies. Approximately 750 applicants are interviewed. The interview session will last around 30 minutes and candidates are made aware of what to expect on the day in the invite to interview. Normally applicants will be interviewed by two panels, with two interviewers on each panel. Candidates will be given the option to select one of two scenarios immediately prior to their interview and will be expected to discuss the issues around the scenario with their panel. Obtaining work experience in a medical setting is not necessary to study or obtain entry to Medicine at Glasgow, but it is expected that candidates will have a realistic understanding of what a career in medicine entails and be aware of current issues facing the medical profession. Given the competitive nature of entry to medicine, unsuccessful applicants are welcome to reapply to Glasgow in future admissions cycles, providing they meet minimum academic entry requirements within seven years of entry. All potential applicants should be encouraged to visit the Medical School prior to applying.

Hull York (MS) Students apply to HYMS, not to either the University of Hull or York. Students allocated places at Hull or York by ballot for Years 1 and 2. Transfers from other medical schools not accepted. Disabilities listed on UCAS application do not affect the assessment of the application. UCAT required; approximately 670 called for interview, 440 offered places. MMI system involving a group interview of 20 minutes and two semi-structured individual interviews of 10 minutes, plus a 'scenario station' used. During the interview process, applicants will be scored on their motivation for a medical career, critical thinking skills, awareness and understanding of healthcare issues, communication skills, empathy, tolerance and resilience. A-level resits not usually accepted. Clinical placements from Year 1. International applicants English language (or equivalent requirement) IELTS 7.5 with at least 7 in each component. Students with band 4 in the Situational Judgement test will be rejected. The Medicine with a Gateway Year course (which requires widening participation criteria) is for UK applicants only and gives priority to applicants from the area around the Medical School.

Imperial London Approximately 850 candidates interviewed. Fifteen-minute interviews with panel of four or five selectors. Not aimed at being an intimidating experience – an evaluation of motivation, capacity to deal with stress, evidence of commitment to the values of the NHS constitution, evidence of working as a leader and team member, ability to multitask, likely contribution to university life, communication skills and maturity. Admissions tutor's comment: 'We look for resourceful men and women with wide interests and accomplishments, a practical concern for others and for those who will make a contribution to the life of the school and hospital.' Results within two weeks. Re-sits are only considered for candidates with extenuating circumstances. Approximately 600 offers made. Clinical contact in Year 1.

Keele Please check our website for details of our application process: www.keele.ac.uk/medicine/undergraduate/howtoapply.

Kent For entry requirements for the new medical school, check the university's website.

Lancaster The University delivers the curriculum at the academic base at Lancaster University and clinical placements in Years 2–5 at acute hospitals and primary care settings in Lancashire and Cumbria. UCAT required. Interviews in the MMI format with 12–14 different stations.

Leeds UCAT required. No cut-off point when assessing the results. 219 home students plus 18 non-EU students. Admissions tutor's comment: 'We use the MMI format for interviews [see above]. Consider your motivation carefully – we do!' Good verbal, non-verbal and presentational skills required. Candidates should: (i) be able to report on some direct experience of what a career in medicine is about; (ii) show evidence of social activities on a regular basis (eg part-time employment, organised community experiences); (iii) show evidence of positions of responsibility and interests outside medical and school activities. Disabled students should indicate their disability status on the UCAS form. Candidates must be available for interview; approximately 1,000 applicants interviewed. Points-equivalent results not accepted. International students' English language requirement (or equivalent): IELTS 7.5 including 7.5 in spoken English. Re-applications accepted from students who have achieved the right grades. Resits only considered in exceptional circumstances and with good supporting evidence; offer AAA. Transfers from other medical schools not encouraged. Ward based attachments begin in Years 1 and 2; clinical practice from Year 3. Applicants should hold the required A-level grades or a high class science or medically related degree.

Leicester UCAT required. Interview is MMI format – 8 stations assessing verbal and written communication, listening skills, compassion and respect, emotional intelligence, problem solving skills, motivation and ethical judgement. Deferred entry considered. Resits rarely considered and only on prior agreement from the admissions tutors. Transfers from other medical schools not considered. Patient contact in first semester, full body dissection. Integrated course.

Lincoln For entry requirements for the University of Nottingham Lincoln Medical School, see the university website.

Liverpool UCAT is required for all non-graduate applicants applying to the A100 programme. Graduate applicants to the A100 programme must offer GAMSAT. 255 Home places are available on the A100 Liverpool medical programme. Evidence of healthcare insight and awareness, caring contribution to the community, excellent communication and values that embody and underpin good healthcare practice is necessary. Interview is via MMI. Applicants wishing to take a gap year may be considered, but applicants must be available for interview. The Liverpool A100 medical programme usually has 23 places available for international students. Under-qualified international students may be able to apply to Liverpool International College prior to placing an application for the Liverpool A100 medical programme. The selection process at Liverpool is a three stage process which is competitive at each stage. Applications are placed via UCAS. For international students, certain minimum language requirements for the course may exist (IELTS of no less than 7.0 in each component).

London (King's) UCAT required. Personal statement a significant factor in selection. Emphasis placed on appreciation of academic, physical and emotional demands of the course, commitment, evidence of working in a caring environment, communication skills and interaction with the general public. Approximately 400 out of 6,000 applications are successful. The University interviews around 1,300 applicants every year using the MMI format and makes offers to approximately a third of them. Clinical contact in Year 1.

London (UCL) All candidates are required to take the UCAT. Two or three selectors interview applicants, each interview lasting 15–20 minutes; approximately 30% of applicants interviewed. Qualities sought include motivation, awareness of scientific and medical issues, ability to express and defend opinions, maturity and individual strengths. Deferred entry for good reason is acceptable. Minimum age of entry 18 years. Transfers from other medical schools considered. International students may take the University Preparation Certificate for Science and Engineering (UPCSE) which is the minimum entry requirement for entry to Medicine. 24 places for international applicants. Patient contact starts in Year 1.

Manchester 397 places for around 3,400 applicants. UCAT scores important. Threshold not disclosed. Seven interviews based on the MMI format (see above). Mitigating circumstances regarding the health or disposition of the candidate should appear in the referee's report. Any applicant who feels unwell before the interview should inform the admissions team and the interview will be re-scheduled; pleas of infirmity cannot be accepted after the interview! Candidates should be aware of the advantages and disadvantages of enquiry-based learning and opinions may be asked. Ethical questions may be raised. Decisions will be made by the end of March. Resit offers only made to applicants with extenuating circumstances; having AAB at first attempt A-level. Clinical attachments from Year 3. Application details on www.bmh.manchester.ac.uk/study/undergraduate.

Newcastle 367 places. The University runs multiple mini interviews. It does not stipulate its UCAT threshold until after the recruitment cycle has ended, and it only accepts resits in extenuating circumstances. Decisions on resits are made on an individual basis by the Sub-Dean of Admissions. The University accepts deferred entry. Clinical placements start in Year 3. Check the website for the latest up-to-date information before applying. Unlike many universities, Newcastle does not consider GCSEs as part of its entry requirements for Medicine.

Nottingham Up to date information on the Medicine programmes at the University of Nottingham and the application process is provided on the University's website, including for the University of Lincoln Medical School.

Oxford Your chances of being shortlisted rest on a number of factors although we do rely heavily on UCAT scores and the GCSE performances (where available) during shortlisting. A slightly weaker performance may be compensated by a very good UCAT score and vice versa. On average, our applicants hold about 80% of GCSEs at grade 8.5 (A and A*) (the University treats the new grades 8 and 9 as equivalent to A*). Critical thinking and general studies are not acceptable. Approximately 30% of applicants called for interview on the basis of academic performance, test score and information on the application form. Ratio of interviewees to places approximately 2.5 to 1. No student admitted without an interview. All colleges use a common set of selection criteria: 11% success rate. Candidate's comment (Lincoln College): 'Two interviewers and two interviews. Questions covered my hobbies and social life, and scientific topics to test my logical train of thought. A great university, but it's not the be-all and end-all if you don't get in.' Clinical experience commences in Year 4.

Queen's Belfast Majority of applicants are school-leavers. When considering applicants' GCSE performance, the best nine subjects will be scored on the basis of 4 points for an A* and 3 points for an A. Points will also be given or deducted on each UCAT paper. Offers for re-sitting applicants will be restricted. These applicants will have been expected to have missed their offer by one grade. A proportion of candidates will be called for interview. Interviews based on the MMI format. A small number of places are allocated to international applicants. Number of places restricted for resit applicants who have narrowly missed an offer at Queen's. Clinical experience from Year 1.

Sheffield Applications processed between October and end of March. Candidates may send additional information concerning extenuating circumstances or health problems via the University's Disrupted Studies form, which can be found at: www.sheffield.ac.uk/study/policies/disrupted-studies. UCAT required. MMI format used. A-level resits are not accepted. Gap year acceptable; medicine-related work very helpful. Clinical experience from Year 1. For more information, please see: www.sheffield.ac.uk/medicine/undergraduate/medicine-admissions.

Southampton 202 places available for five-year course. Please refer to the website for further information: www.southampton.ac.uk/medicine.

St Andrews 179 places for around 1,300 applicants. Medicine students take a full three-year programme leading to BSc (Hons), followed by clinical medicine at one of its partner medical schools. UCAT required. MMI format (see above) with six or more mini interviews or stations. Special attention given to international students and those who achieve qualifications at more than one sitting. As far as possible, the interview panel will reflect the gender and ethnic distribution of candidates for interview.

Sunderland For entry requirements for the School of Medicine, see the university's website.

Swansea Graduate entry only.

Warwick Selection includes interview and group activities. UCAT, work experience and a reference required. You should have, or be predicted to gain, a minimum of a 2.1 degree or overseas equivalent in any subject. Candidates with a 2.2 degree should hold a master's or doctoral qualification to be considered for entry.

Advice to applicants and planning the UCAS personal statement (See also **Admissions tutors' advice**) Nearly all universities now require the UCAT entry test to be taken before applying for Medicine. Check website (www.ucat.ac.uk) for details of test dates and test centres and with universities for their requirements. It is essential that you check for the latest information before applying and that you give yourself plenty of time to make arrangements for sitting this test (see also **Chapter 5**).

Admissions tutors look for certain personal qualities (See **Admissions tutors' advice**) and these will emerge in your personal statement, at the interview and on your school or college reference. There should be evidence of scientific interest, commitment, enthusiasm, determination, stability, self-motivation, ability to organise your own work, interest in the welfare of others, communication skills, modesty (arrogance and over-confidence could lead to rejection!), breadth of interest, leadership skills, stamina, and good physical and mental health.

Some kind of first-hand experience in a medical setting is almost obligatory for those applying for Medicine (see also under Admissions tutors' advice). Depending on your personal contacts in the medical profession, this could include observing operations (for example, orthopaedic surgery), working in hospitals and discussing the career with your GP. Remember that your friends and relatives may have medical conditions that they would be willing to discuss with you – and all this will contribute to your knowledge and show that you are informed and interested. Read medical and scientific magazines and keep up-to-date with important current issues – COVID-19, vaccinations, ageing population, mental health. Community work, clubs, societies, school and social activities should be mentioned. Show that you have an understanding of the role of health professionals in society and the social factors that influence health and disease. And finally, a comment from one admissions tutor: 'Don't rush around doing things just for your CV. If you are a boring student, be an incredibly well-read boring student! You can play netball, rugby, hockey, make beautiful music and paint with your feet, but if you fail to get the grades you'll be rejected.'

Selection interviews Yes Aberdeen, Aston, Bangor, Birmingham, Brighton and Sussex (MS), Bristol, Brunel, Buckingham, Cambridge, Cardiff, City St George's, Dundee, East Anglia, Edinburgh, Exeter, Glasgow, Hull York (MS), Imperial London, Keele, Kent Medway Med Sch, Lancaster, Leeds, Leicester, Liverpool, London (King's), London (QM), London (UCL), Manchester, Newcastle, Nottingham, Oxford (23% (success rate 8%)), Queen's Belfast, Sheffield, Southampton, St Andrews, Sussex.

Interview advice and questions Questions will vary between applicants, depending on their UCAS statements and their A-level subjects. Questions are likely to relate to A-level specific subjects, general medicine topics and unconnected topics (see also **Admissions tutors' advice**). The following questions will provide a guide to the range of topics covered in past interviews. Outline the structure of DNA. What is meant by homeostasis? Is a virus a living organism? What has been the most important advance in biology in the last 50 years? What interests you about (i) science, (ii) biology, (iii) chemistry? Why did you choose the particular A-level subjects you are doing? Why do you want to study Medicine/become a doctor? Do you expect people to be grateful? Why do you want to study here? Why should we take you? What do you do to relax? What do you do when you have three or four things to do, and they are all equally urgent? How do you balance work and all the outside activities you do? Do you agree with the concept of 'foundation trusts'? What do you think about polyclinics? Do you think NHS doctors and staff should be able to take private patients? If you were in charge of finances for a large health authority, what would be your priorities for funding? If you had to decide between saving the life of a young child and that of an old person, what would you do? Would you treat lung cancer patients who refuse to give up smoking? What do you understand by 'gene therapy'? Can you give any examples? In your opinion, what is the most serious cause for concern for the health of the UK? What do you want to do with your medical degree? What do you think the human genome project can offer medicine? Should we pay for donor organs? Where do you see yourself in 15 years' time? Who made the most valuable contribution to the 20th century? Why do you think research is important? Why is teamwork important? What do you think about the NHS's problems? Do you think that sport is important? What did you gain from doing work experience in a nursing home? What were the standards like? How does the medical profession deal with social issues? How could you compare your hobby of rowing to medicine? In doing a medical course, what would you find the most emotionally challenging aspect? How would you cope with emotional strain? Who should have priority for receiving drugs in a flu epidemic/pandemic? How would you deal with the death of a patient? What are stem cells? Why are they controversial? How is cloning done? What constitutes a human being? How can you measure intelligence? How do we combat genetic diseases? How are genes actually implanted? What do you want to talk about? If you were a cardiothoracic surgeon, would you perform a heart by-pass operation on a smoker? What are the negative aspects of becoming a doctor? At some interviews, essays may be set, eg (i) 'A scientific education is a good basis for a medical degree: discuss'; (ii) 'Only drugs that are safe and effective should be prescribed to patients: discuss'. Should someone sell their kidney? How would you describe a human to a person from Mars? Should obese people have treatment on the NHS? Occasionally applicants at interview may be given scenarios to discuss (see **Glasgow** under **Admissions tutors' advice**). See also **Chapter 5**.

REASONS FOR REJECTION (NON-ACADEMIC) Insufficient vocation demonstrated. No steps taken to gain practical experience relevant to medicine. Doubts as to the ability to cope with the stress of a medical career. Not enough awareness about the career. Lack of knowledge about the course. Applicant appears dull and lacking in enthusiasm and motivation. Lacking a caring, committed attitude towards people. No evidence of broad social, cultural or sporting interests or of teamwork. Poor or lack of communication skills. Arrogance. Over-confident at interview. Unrealistic expectations about being a doctor.

AGE AT ENTRY Applicants must be 17 years old on 30 September of the year of entry. However, some medical schools stipulate 17 years and six months, and a small number stipulate 18 years. Those considering entry at 17 would probably be advised to take a gap year.

HEALTH REQUIREMENTS Medical schools require all students to have their immunity status for hepatitis B, tuberculosis and rubella checked on entry. Offers are usually made subject to satisfactory health screening for hepatitis B. In line with advice from the General Medical Council, students will not be admitted to courses who are found to be e-antigen positive when screened within the first week of the course. Candidates accepting offers should assure themselves of their immunity status.

MATURE STUDENTS Medical schools usually accept a small number of mature students each year. Some medical schools accept non-graduates although A-level passes at high grades are usually stipulated. The majority of applicants accepted are likely to be graduates with a first or 2.1 degree. **Birmingham** Applications from mature candidates are welcomed, but the length of training which has to be taken will be considered when assessing applications. **Leeds** There is no upper age limit for the course. Applicants should hold the required A-level grades or a high class science degree. **Southampton** Applicants with nursing qualifications should hold two grade A A-levels including chemistry and biology.

ADVICE TO GRADUATE APPLICANTS Graduate applicants are considered by all medical schools. At some medical schools the Graduate Australian Medical Schools Admission Test (GAMSAT) is now being used to assess the aptitude of prospective applicants. Applicants at some institutions are selected on the basis of three criteria: (i) an Honours degree at 2.2 or above; (ii) the GAMSAT score; (iii) performance at interview. **City St George's** Some students think that science graduates are the only ones to do well in GAMSAT: 40% of those on the course do not have a science degree or A-levels; however, work experience is essential.

GRADUATE DESTINATIONS AND EMPLOYMENT

(See **Chapter 1, Graduate Outcomes.**)

CAREER NOTE Applicants should also bear in mind that while most doctors do work in the NHS, either in hospital services or in general practice, many graduates choose to work in other fields such as public health, pharmacology, the environment, occupational medicine with industrial organisations, the armed services and opportunities abroad.

OTHER DEGREE SUBJECTS FOR CONSIDERATION

Biomedical/Medical Materials Science; Biology; Biotechnology; Clinical Sciences; Dentistry; Dietetics; Genetics; Health Sciences; Immunology; Medical Biochemistry; Medical Engineering; Medical Microbiology; Medical Physics; Medical Product Design; Medical Sciences; Medicinal Chemistry; Midwifery; Nursing; Nutrition; Occupational Therapy; Optometry; Osteopathy; Pharmacology; Pharmacy; Physiology; Physiotherapy; Psychology; Radiography; Speech Sciences; Sports Medicine; Veterinary Medicine; Virology – and Law! (The work of doctors and lawyers is similar: both are required to identify the relevant information – clinical symptoms or legal issues!)

MICROBIOLOGY

(see also **Biological Sciences, Biology, Biotechnology, Genetics**)

Microbiology is a branch of biological science specialising in the study of micro-organisms: bacteria, viruses and fungi. The subject covers the relationship between these organisms and disease, and industrial applications such as food and drug production, waste-water treatment and future biochemical uses.

Useful websites www.microbiologysociety.org; www.nature.com/subjects/microbiology; www.asm.org; www.microbiologynetwork.com; see also **Biochemistry**, **Biological Sciences** and **Biology**.

NB The points totals shown to the left of the institutions are for ease of reference only. It must not be assumed that Tariff points are always used by institutions or that they can be substituted for an offer in grades. The level of an offer is not necessarily indicative of the quality of a course.

COURSE OFFERS INFORMATION

Subject requirements/preferences GCSE English and mathematics and science subjects. **AL** One or two mathematics/science subjects including chemistry and/or biology required or preferred; grades sometimes specified. Some popular universities are now making lower offers for disadvantaged and other students.

Your target offers and examples of degree courses

144 pts **Imperial London** – AAA incl biol+sci/maths (Microbiol) (IB 38 pts HL 6 biol+sci/maths)

136 pts **Bristol** – AAB incl chem+sci/maths (Cell Mol Med) (IB 34 pts HL 17 incl 65 chem+sci/maths); (Med Microbiol) (IB 34 pts HL 17 pts incl 6/5 chem+sci)

Leeds – AAB incl chem/biol+sci (Microbiol) (IB 31 pts HL 665 incl 6 chem/biol+sci)

Manchester – AAB–AAA incl sci/maths (Microbiol Modn Lang) (IB 35–36 pts HL 665–666 incl sci); AAB–AAA incl sci/maths+interview (Microbiol (Yr Ind)) (IB 35–36 pts HL 665–666 incl sci)

128 pts **Dundee** – ABB incl biol+chem (Microbiol) (IB 32 pts HL 655 incl biol+chem)

Edinburgh – ABB–AAA incl biol+chem (Biol Sci (Dev Regn Stem Cells); Biol Sci (Mol Biol)) (IB 32–37 pts HL 555–666 incl biol+chem)

Leeds – ABB incl chem/biol+sci (Med Microbiol) (IB 33 pts HL 17 pts incl 6 chem/biol+sci)

Leicester – ABB–BBB+bEPQ incl sci/maths (Med Microbiol) (IB 30 pts HL 65 sci/maths)

Liverpool – ABB incl biol+sci (Microbiol Infec) (IB 33 pts HL 6 biol)

Nottingham – ABB–AAB incl sci/maths/geog (Microbiol) (IB 32–34 pts HL 5 sci)

Reading – ABB incl biol+sci (Microbiol) (IB 32 pts HL 5 biol+sci)

120 pts **Glasgow** – BBB–AAB incl biol/chem (Microbiol; Mol Cell Biol (Biotech); Mol Cell Biol (Plnt Sci)) (IB 34 pts HL 655 incl biol/chem)

Nottingham Trent – BBB incl biol 120 pts (Microbiol)

Queen's Belfast – BBB–ABB incl biol+sci/maths (Microbiol) (IB 34 pts HL 665)

Stirling – BBB incl sci/maths (Cell Biol) (IB 28 pts)

Strathclyde – BBB incl biol/chem+sci (Immun Microbiol) (IB 30 pts HL 5 biol/chem+sci); BBB incl chem+biol (Microbiol) (IB 30 pts HL 5 chem+biol)

Surrey – BBB incl biol+sci/maths (Microbiol) (IB 32 pts)

112 pts **Aberdeen** – BBC incl maths/sci (Mol Cell Biol) (IB 32 pts HL 555)
Heriot-Watt – BBC–ABB (Biol (Cell Mol Biol)) (IB 27 pts HL 5 sci)
104 pts **Aberystwyth** – BCC–BBB incl B biol 104–120 pts (Microbiol) (IB 28–30 pts HL 5 biol)
Edinburgh Napier – BCC incl sci (App Microbiol) (IB 28 pts HL 654 incl 5 sci)
Huddersfield – BCC incl sci 104 pts (Biol (Mol Cell))
Manchester Met – BCC–BBC incl biol 104–112 pts (Microbiol Mol Biol (St Abrd)) (IB 26 pts HL 5 biol)

Alternative offers See **Chapter 6** and **Appendix 1** for grades/UCAS Tariff points information for other examinations.

DEGREE APPRENTICESHIPS

East Anglia (App Biomed Sci); Kent (Lab Sci); Manchester Met (Lab Sci); Portsmouth (App Biomed Sci).

EXAMPLES OF COLLEGES OFFERING COURSES IN THIS SUBJECT FIELD

St Helens (Coll).

CHOOSING YOUR COURSE (SEE ALSO CH.1)

Universities and colleges teaching quality See www.qaa.ac.uk; www.discoveruni.gov.uk.

Top research universities and colleges (REF 2021) See **Biological Sciences**.

Examples of sandwich degree courses Leeds; Manchester; Nottingham Trent; Reading; Surrey.

ADMISSIONS INFORMATION

Advice to applicants and planning the UCAS personal statement Relevant experience, particularly for mature students. See **Biological Sciences** and also **Appendix 3**.

Selection interviews **Some** Leeds; **No** Bristol.

Interview advice and questions Examples of past questions include: How much does the country spend on research and on the armed forces? Discuss reproduction in bacteria. What do you particularly like about your study of biology? What would you like to do after your degree? Do you have any strong views on vivisection? Discuss the differences between the courses you have applied for. What important advances have been made in the biological field recently? How would you describe microbiology? Do you know anything about the diseases caused by micro-organisms? What symptoms would be caused by which particular organisms? See also **Chapter 5**.

GRADUATE DESTINATIONS AND EMPLOYMENT

(See **Chapter 1, Graduate Outcomes.**)

Career note See **Biology**.

OTHER DEGREE SUBJECTS FOR CONSIDERATION

Animal Sciences; Biochemistry; Biological Sciences; Biology; Biotechnology; Genetics; Medical Sciences; Medicine; Molecular Biology; Pharmacology; Physiology.

MUSIC

(including **Music Technology**; see also **Engineering (Acoustics and Sound)**)

Theory and practice are combined to a greater or lesser extent in most university Music courses, and about 50% or more of graduates will go on to non-music careers. However, courses are also offered by conservatoires and schools of music where the majority of applicants are aiming to become professional musicians. For these courses, the ability to perform on an instrument is more important than academic ability and offers are therefore likely to be lower. When choosing music courses, the applicant should also be aware of the specialisms offered, such as classical, jazz, new music, popular music and film music (Leeds College of Music) in addition to courses in music production and music business. Music Journalism is also an option on some courses. See also **Appendix 2**. Some applications are made through UCAS Conservatoires (formerly CUKAS): see **Chapter 4** for details.

Useful websites www.ism.org; www.roh.org.uk; www.nyo.org.uk; www.ucas.com/conservatoires; www.artscouncil.org.uk; www.soundandmusic.org; http://gb.abrsm.org/en

NB The points totals shown to the left of the institutions are for ease of reference only. It must not be assumed that Tariff points are always used by institutions or that they can be substituted for an offer in grades. The level of an offer is not necessarily indicative of the quality of a course.

COURSE OFFERS INFORMATION

Subject requirements/preferences GCSE A foreign language and mathematics may be required. A good range of grades 9–6 (A*–B) for popular universities. **AL** Music plus an instrumental grade usually required. Some popular universities are now making lower offers for disadvantaged and other students.

Your target offers and examples of degree courses

152 pts **Cambridge** – A*AA incl mus+interview (Mus) (IB 41–42 pts HL 776 incl mus)

144 pts **Edinburgh** – A*AB–A*AA incl maths (Maths Mus) (IB 38 pts HL 766 incl maths)

Oxford – AAA incl mus+interview (Mus) (IB 38 pts HL 666 incl mus)

Surrey – AAA incl maths+mus+phys+interview (Mus Snd Rec (Tonmeister)) (IB 35 pts HL 6 maths)

136 pts **Bristol** – AAB incl mus (Mus) (IB 34 pts HL 17 pts incl 5 mus)

Durham – AAB incl mus (Mus) (IB 36 pts HL 665 incl mus)

Edinburgh – AAB (Hist Art Hist Mus) (IB 36 pts HL 665)

Leeds – AAB+gr 8+interview (Mus) (IB 35 pts HL 6 mus); AAB+interview+audition+gr 8 (Mus (Perf)) (IB 35 pts HL 6 mus); AAB incl mus+gr 8+interview (Mus Comb Hons) (IB 35 pts HL 6 music)

London (King's) – AAB incl mus+gr 6 (Mus) (IB 35 pts HL 665 incl mus)

London (RH) – AAB–AAA incl maths+phys+gr 7 (Phys Mus) (IB 34 pts HL 666 incl maths+mus+phys)

Manchester – AAB incl A mus+gr 8 (Mus) (IB 35 pts HL 665); AAB incl A mus+interview+ gr 8 (Mus Dr) (IB 35 pts HL 665)

Southampton – AAB incl A maths+sci+B mus+audition (Acoust Mus) (IB 34 pts HL 17 pts incl 6 maths+phys+5 mus)

York – AAB incl A mus+audition+interview (Mus) (IB 35 pts HL 6 mus)

128 pts **Birmingham** – ABB (Mus) (IB 32 pts HL 665)

Edinburgh – ABB+audition (Mus) (IB 34 pts HL 655)

Liverpool – ABB/BBB+aEPQ+interview+audition (Mus Pop Mus) (IB 33 pts HL 6 mus)

London (SOAS) – ABB (Mus Comb Hons) (IB 32 pts HL 655)

Newcastle – ABB+interview (Mus) (IB 32 pts)

Nottingham – ABB incl mus (Mus Phil) (IB 30 pts HL 655 incl mus); ABB incl mus/mus tech (Mus) (IB 30 pts HL 655 incl mus)

Sheffield – ABB incl mus+gr 8 (Mus) (IB 34 pts HL 5 mus); ABB incl music+gr 8 (Mus Comb Hons) (IB 33 pts HL 5 mus)

120 pts **Aberdeen** – BBB incl mus (Mus) (IB 32 pts HL 6 mus)

Cardiff – BBB–AAB incl mus+gr 8+audition+interview (Mus courses) (IB 31–32 pts HL 6 music)

Glasgow – BBB–AAB incl mus+gr 5 (Mus) (IB 34 pts HL 655 incl Engl+hum); BBB–AAB incl mus+gr 8+audition/portfolio (BMus) (IB 34 pts HL 655)

London (Gold) – BBB+interview (Mus; Pop Mus) (IB 33 pts HL 655)

London (RH) – BBB incl mus (Mus Thea) (IB 32 pts HL 655 incl mus); BBB–ABB+gr 7 (Modn Langs Mus) (IB 32 pts HL 655); (Mus Phil) (IB 32 pts HL 655 incl 6 mus); BBB–ABB incl mus+gr 7 (Mus Pol St) (IB 32 pts HL 655 incl mus)

Newcastle – BBB–AAB incl mus+interview+audition (Folk Trad Mus) (IB 30–34 pts)

Queen's Belfast – BBB incl mus (Mus) (IB 32 pts HL 655 incl mus)
Reading – BBB incl mus+gr 8+interview (P Ed Mus Spec) (IB 30 pts HL 5 mus)
Southampton – BBB–AAB incl mus+gr 8+audition+interview (Mus) (IB 30–32 pts HL 16 pts incl 5 mus); BBB–ABB incl mus+gr 8 mus prac (Mus Bus Mgt) (IB 30–32 pts HL 15–16 incl 5 mus)
Surrey – BBB incl mus+interview (Crea Mus Tech; Mus) (IB 32 pts)
Sussex – BBB–ABB+gr 7 (Mus; Mus Tech) (IB 30–32 pts HL 5 mus)
Trinity Saint David – 120 pts+interview+portfolio (Crea Mus Tech) (IB 32 pts)
West London – BBB–ABB 120–128 pts (Musl Thea)

112 pts **Birmingham City** – BBC 112 pts (Mus Bus) (IB 28 pts)
Brunel – BBC 112 pts (Mus) (IB 29 pts)
Canterbury Christ Church – BBC 112 pts (Mus (Pop Mus); Mus Prod; Thea Perf) (IB 29 pts)
City St George's – BBC incl mus 112 pts+gr 7+audition/interview (Mus courses) (IB 30 pts)
East London – 112 pts incl mus (Mus Perf Prod) (IB 24 pts HL 15 pts)
Edge Hill – BBC–BBB 112–120 pts (Mus Prod)
Hertfordshire – BBC–BBB 112–120 pts (Mus Cmpsn Snd Flm Gms; Mus Prod Prom)
Hull – BBC incl mus/mus tech 112 pts+gr 6 (Mus) (IB 28 pts HL 5 mus)
Keele – BBC (Mus Comb Hons) (IB 29 pts)
Kingston – 112–128 pts incl mus/mus tech+portfolio (Mus Tech)
Leeds Beckett – 112 pts (Mus Prod; Mus Tech; Perf Arts)
Liverpool (LIPA) – BBC 112 pts+interview (Snd Tech)
Middlesex – BBC 112 pts+audition+interview (Mus)
Staffordshire – BBC 112 pts (Mus Prod)
UWE Bristol – 112 pts incl mus/mus tech (Crea Mus Tech) (HL 5 mus)
West London – BBC 112–128 pts+gr 6+audition+interview (Perf Mus Mgt); BBC 112–128 pts incl mus+interview+portfolio (Cmpsn)
West Scotland – BCC incl eng 112 pts (Commer Mus) (IB 24 pts)

104 pts **Bath Spa** – BCC–BBB incl mus/mus tech+interview+portfolio (Commer Mus) (IB 32 pts)
Bournemouth – 104–120 pts (Mus Snd Prod) (IB 28–31 pts)
Brighton – BCC–BBB 104–120 pts+portfolio (Electron Mus Snd Arts) (IB 30 pts)
Chester – 104 pts+gr 8+audition (Pop Mus Perf) (IB 26 pts); BCC–BBC incl dr/thea st 104–112 pts+interview+audition (Musl Thea Perf) (IB 26 pts HL 5 thea arts)
Chichester – BBC 104–120 pts+audition (Musl Thea (Trpl Threat)) (IB 28 pts); BCC–BBC 104–112 pts (Aud Prod Mus Tech) (IB 28 pts)
De Montfort – 104 pts (Mus Prod) (IB 24 pts); (Mus Tech) (IB 24 pts HL 5 mus)
Derby – BCC 104 pts+portfolio (Crea Expr Arts Hlth Wlbng (Dance/Dr/Mus/Art)); BCC–BBC 104–112 pts+gr 7+portfolio (Pop Mus); BCC–BBC incl C comp/maths/sci/tech 104–112 pts+portfolio (Mus Prod)
Edinburgh Napier – BCC incl mus+Engl+gr 5+portfolio (Mus) (IB 29 pts HL 654 incl mus+Engl)
Falmouth – 104–120 pts+interview+audition (Crea Mus Tech; Mus; Pop Mus)
Huddersfield – BCC–BBB 104–120 pts (Mus Thea)
Liverpool Hope – BCC 104 pts+gr 5+interview+audition (Mus) (IB 24 pts)
Northampton – BCC+interview (Pop Mus courses)
Plymouth – 104 pts incl mus/mus tech+gr 6 (Mus) (IB 26 pts HL 4 mus)
Solent – 104–120 pts (Pop Mus Prod); BCC 104–120 pts (Dig Mus)
Winchester – 104–120 pts (Mus Snd Prod) (HL 44)
York St John – 104 pts (Mus courses)

96 pts **Anglia Ruskin** – 96 pts (Aud Mus Tech) (IB 24 pts); 96 pts incl mus/mus tech+portfolio (Mus courses) (IB 24 pts)
Bangor – 96–128 pts (Mus Dr); B mus 96–120 pts (Crea Arts) (HL 5 mus)
Central Lancashire – 96 pts+audition (Mus Thea)
Chichester – CCC–BBC 96–112 pts+audition (Mus) (IB 26 pts)
Gloucestershire – 96–120 pts+interview (Mus Bus); CCC–BBB 96–120 pts+interview (Pop Mus)
Leeds Consv – 96 pts+audition+gr 6–8 (Mus (Comb)); 96 pts incl mus+audition+gr 8/6 (Mus (Class); Mus (Jazz); Mus (Pop Mus)); 96 pts incl mus+portfolio (Mus (Prod))

Liverpool (LIPA) – CCC 96 pts+interview (Mgt (Mus Ind Mgt)); CCC incl mus/mus tech 96 pts+gr 5+audition (Mus courses)
South Wales – CCC incl art/des 96 pts+interview (Pop Commer Mus)
Teesside – 96–112 pts (Mus Tech)
Winchester – CCC–BBC 96–112 pts+interview+audition (Musl Thea) (HL 44)
88 pts **Bucks New** – 88–112 pts (Aud Mus Prod)
West Scotland – CCD incl mus+maths 88 pts (Mus Tech) (IB 24 pts)
80 pts **City St George's** – CDD 80 pts+interview (Prof Dance Musl Thea) (HL 5 incl Engl+maths)
72 pts **UHI** – BC+interview+audition (Gael Trad Mus)
64 pts **Ravensbourne Univ** – CC+portfolio (Mus Snd Prod) (IB 24 pts)
Rose Bruford (Coll) – CC 64 pts+audition (Actr Mushp)
32 pts **London (RAcMus)** – EE incl mus+gr 8+audition+interview (BMus courses) (IB 24 pts)
RConsvS – EE+audition (BMus courses; Musl Thea) (IB 24 pts)
RNCM – EE+gr 5+audition (Pop Mus)
Royal Welsh (CMusDr) – EE incl mus+gr 8+interview+audition (BMus (Instr Vcl)) (IB 24 pts)
24 pts **UHI** – D+interview+audition (Pop Mus)
RCMus – audition/portfolio+interview (BMus)

Alternative offers See **Chapter 6** and **Appendix 1** for grades/UCAS Tariff points information for other examinations.

EXAMPLES OF COLLEGES OFFERING COURSES IN THIS SUBJECT FIELD

Barnfield (Coll); Barnsley (Coll); Bath (Coll); Bedford (Coll); Birmingham Met (Coll); Blackpool and Fylde (Coll); Bournemouth and Poole (Coll); Bradford College (UC); Brighton Met (Coll); Buckinghamshire (Coll Group); Calderdale (Coll); City and Islington (Coll); Cornwall (Coll); Coventry (Coll); Doncaster (Coll); Dudley (Coll); Ealing, Hammersmith and West London (Coll); East Kent (Coll); East Surrey (Coll); Exeter (Coll); Fareham (Coll); Gateshead (Coll); Gloucestershire (Coll); Havant and South Downs (Coll); Havering (Coll); Hertford (Reg Coll); HOW (Coll); Hull (Coll); Kingston (Coll); Leicester (Coll); Liverpool City (Coll); Manchester (Coll); MidKent (Coll); Neath Port Talbot (Coll); Nescot; Newcastle (Coll); Oaklands (Coll); Petroc; Rotherham (CAT); Sheffield (Coll); South Essex (Coll); South Gloucestershire and Stroud (Coll); South Thames (Coll); TEC Partnership; Telford (Coll); Tresham (CFHE); Truro and Penwith (Coll); Westminster City (Coll); Wigan and Leigh (Coll).

CHOOSING YOUR COURSE (SEE ALSO CH.1)

Universities and colleges teaching quality See www.qaa.ac.uk; www.discoveruni.gov.uk.

Top research universities and colleges (REF 2021) (Music, Drama, Dance, Performing Arts, Film and Screen Studies) London (QM) (Dr); London (RH); Manchester (Dr, Dance, Perf Arts, Flm Scrn St); London (Royal Central Sch SpDr); London (King's); London (SOAS); Cambridge; Roehampton (Dance); Kent; Huddersfield (Mus).

Examples of sandwich degree courses Anglia Ruskin; Birmingham City; Bournemouth; Hertfordshire; Huddersfield; Leeds; Leeds Beckett; Reading; Staffordshire; Surrey; UWE Bristol.

ADMISSIONS INFORMATION

Advice to applicants and planning the UCAS personal statement In addition to your ability and expertise with your chosen musical instrument(s), it is also important to know your composers and to take a critical interest in various kinds of music. Reference should be made to these, visits to concerts listed and any special interests indicated in types of musical activity, for example, opera, ballet. Work with orchestras, choirs and other musical groups should also be included and full details given of any competitions entered and awards obtained. See **Chapter 4** for details of applications for Music courses at conservatoires.

Selection interviews Yes Aberdeen, Bath Spa, Birmingham, Brunel, Cambridge, Cardiff, Chester, Chichester, City St George's (Prof Dance Musl Thea), Falmouth, Glasgow, Gloucestershire, Leeds, Leeds Beckett (Perf Arts), Liverpool, Liverpool (LIPA), Liverpool Hope, London (Gold), London (RAcMus), Newcastle, Northampton, Oxford (93% (success rate 47%), RCMus, Reading, Royal Welsh (CMusDr),

South Wales, Southampton, Surrey, Trinity Saint David, UHI, West London, Winchester (Musl Thea), York; **Some** Manchester (Mature applicants with non-standard qualifications); **No** Bristol, Edinburgh, Huddersfield.

Interview advice and questions See Chapter 4 under Applications for Music Courses at Conservatoires.

Reasons for rejection (non-academic) Usually academic (auditions, practical, aural/written test). Dull, unenthusiastic students, ignorant about their subject, showing lack of motivation and imagination.

GRADUATE DESTINATIONS AND EMPLOYMENT

(See **Chapter 1, Graduate Outcomes.**)

Career note Some graduates go into performance-based careers, many enter the teaching profession and others go into a wide range of careers requiring graduate skills.

OTHER DEGREE SUBJECTS FOR CONSIDERATION

Acoustics; Drama; Musical Theatre; Performance Arts.

NATURAL SCIENCES

(see also **Biological Sciences**)

These are flexible courses allowing the student to gain a broad view of the origins and potential of sciences in general and then to focus in Years 2 and 3 on a specialist area of scientific study.

Useful websites www.scicentral.com; www.nature.com; see also **Biology**, **Chemistry** and **Physics**.

NB The points totals shown to the left of the institutions are for ease of reference only. It must not be assumed that Tariff points are always used by institutions or that they can be substituted for an offer in grades. The level of an offer is not necessarily indicative of the quality of a course.

COURSE OFFERS INFORMATION

Subject requirements/preferences GCSE Strong results, particularly in the sciences. **AL** Science subjects required. Some popular universities are now making lower offers for disadvantaged and other students.

Your target offers and examples of degree courses

160 pts **Cambridge** – A*A*A incl sci+maths+interview+ESAT (Nat Sci (Zool)) (IB 41–42 pts HL 776); A*A*A incl sci/maths+interview+ESAT (Nat Sci (Biol Biomed Sci); Nat Sci (Earth Sci); Nat Sci (Genet); Nat Sci (Mat Sci); Nat Sci (Neuro); Nat Sci (Physiol)) (IB 41–42 pts HL 776); (Nat Sci (Astro); Nat Sci (Bioch); Nat Sci (Chem)) (IB 41–42 pts HL 776 incl sci/maths)

152 pts **Bath** – A*AA incl maths/sci (Nat Sci; Nat Sci (St Abrd)) (IB 36 pts HL 766 incl maths/sci)

Durham – A*AA incl biol/chem/maths (Nat Sci) (IB 38 pts HL 666–766 incl biol/chem/maths)

Leeds – A*AA incl sci (Nat Sci) (IB 36 pts)

London (UCL) – A*AA incl sci/maths (Nat Sci) (IB 39 pts HL 19 pts incl 6 sci/maths)

Nottingham – A*AA incl sci/maths (Nat Sci) (IB 36 pts HL 766 incl sci/maths)

144 pts **Exeter** – AAA incl maths+sci (Nat Sci) (IB 36 pts HL 666 incl 6 maths+sci)

Lancaster – AAA–A*AA incl sci (Nat Sci) (IB 36–38 pts HL 16 pts incl 6 sci)

Loughborough – AAA incl sci (Nat Sci) (IB 37 pts HL 666 incl sci)

Open University – (Nat Sci Chem)

Alternative offers See **Chapter 6** and **Appendix 1** for grades/UCAS Tariff points information for other examinations.

DEGREE APPRENTICESHIPS

Keele (Env Practnr); Kingston (Env Sci); Wrexham (Lw Carb Ener Effic Sust).

CHOOSING YOUR COURSE (SEE ALSO CH.1)

Universities and colleges teaching quality See www.qaa.ac.uk; www.discoveruni.gov.uk.

Top research universities and colleges (REF 2021) See separate science tables.

Examples of sandwich degree courses Bath; Leeds; Loughborough.

ADMISSIONS INFORMATION

Advice to applicants and planning the UCAS personal statement See **Biology**, **Chemistry**, **Physics** and **Appendix 3**.

Selection interviews Yes Cambridge; **Some** Bath, London (UCL)

Interview advice and questions See **Chapter 5**.

GRADUATE DESTINATIONS AND EMPLOYMENT

(See **Chapter 1, Graduate Outcomes.**)

Career note These courses offer a range of science and in some cases non-scientific subjects, providing students with the flexibility to develop particular interests as they progress through the course.

OTHER DEGREE SUBJECTS FOR CONSIDERATION

Anatomy; Anthropology; Archaeology; Astrophysics; Biochemistry; Biological Sciences; Biology; Chemistry; Earth Sciences; Ecology; Genetics; Geography; Geology; History and Philosophy of Science; Neuroscience; Pharmacology; Physics; Plant Sciences; Psychology; Zoology.

NEUROSCIENCE

(including **Anatomical Science**; see also **Biological Sciences, Human Sciences/Human Biosciences, Physiology, Psychology**)

Courses in Neuroscience include the study of biochemistry, cell and molecular biology, genetics and physiology and focus on the structure and functions of the brain. It also overlaps with neurobiology, neuroanatomy, neurophysiology, pharmacology and psychology which in turn can involve the study of behavioural problems and mental processes, both conscious and unconscious. It is a field of research contributing to the treatment of such medical conditions as Parkinson's disease, Alzheimer's, schizophrenia and epilepsy. Studies will cover anatomical structures such as skeletal, muscular, cardiovascular and nervous systems and components such as muscle cells.

Useful websites www.innerbody.com; www.instantanatomy.net

NB The points totals shown to the left of the institutions are for ease of reference only. It must not be assumed that Tariff points are always used by institutions or that they can be substituted for an offer in grades. The level of an offer is not necessarily indicative of the quality of a course.

COURSE OFFERS INFORMATION

Subject requirements/preferences GCSE Mathematics usually required. **AL** One or two mathematics/science subjects usually required; biology and chemistry preferred. Some popular universities are now making lower offers for disadvantaged and other students.

Your target offers and examples of degree courses

160 pts **Cambridge** – A*A*A incl sci/maths+interview+ESAT (Nat Sci (Neuro)) (IB 41–42 pts HL 776)

144 pts **Birmingham** – AAA incl biol/hum biol (Hum Neuro) (IB 32 pts HL 666 incl biol)

Bristol – AAA incl sci/maths (Neuro) (IB 36 pts HL 18 pts incl 66 sci/maths)

London (King's) – AAA incl chem+biol (Neuro) (IB 36 pts HL 18 pts incl 6 biol+chem); (Anat Dev Hum Biol) (IB 36 pts HL 18 pts incl 6 chem+biol)
London (UCL) – AAA incl biol/psy+sci/maths 144 pts (Hum Neuro) (IB 38 pts HL 18 incl 6 biol/psy+ 5 sci/maths); AAA incl chem+sci/maths (Neuro) (IB 38 pts HL 18 pts incl 5 chem+sci)
Nottingham – AAA incl sci (Psy Cog Neuro) (IB 34 pts HL 666)

136 pts **Edinburgh** – AAB (Neuro) (IB 34 pts HL 655)
Leeds – AAB–AAA incl biol/chem+sci (Neuro) (IB 31 pts HL 665 incl biol/chem+sci)
London (RH) – AAB–AAA (Psy Clin Cog Neuro) (IB 34 pts HL 666)
Manchester – AAB–AAA incl sci/maths (Cog Neuro Psy; Neuro) (IB 35–36 pts HL 665–666 incl sci)
Nottingham – AAB incl biol/chem+sci/maths (Neuro) (IB 32 pts HL 665)
Reading – AAB (Psy Neuro) (IB 34 pts)
St Andrews – AAB incl sci/maths (Neuro) (IB 36 pts HL 665 incl sci/maths)
Sussex – AAB (Psy Neuro) (IB 34 pts)

128 pts **Cardiff** – ABB–AAB incl biol/chem (Biomed Sci) (IB 32–34 pts HL 655–666 incl 6 biol/chem)
Dundee – ABB incl biol (Anat Sci) (IB 32 pts HL 655)
Keele – ABB incl sci/maths/stats (Neuro) (IB 32 pts HL 6 sci)
Sussex – ABB incl biol (Med Neuro) (IB 32 pts HL 5 biol); ABB incl sci (Neuro) (IB 32 pts HL 5 sci)

120 pts **Bangor** – 120–144 pts (Psy Neuropsy)
Glasgow – BBB–AAB incl biol/chem (Anat; Neuro) (IB 34 pts HL 655 incl biol/chem)
Leicester – BBB–ABB (Psy Cog Neuro) (IB 30 pts)
London (Gold) – BBB (Psy Cog Neuro) (IB 33 pts HL 655)

112 pts **Aberdeen** – BBC incl maths+sci (Neuro Psy) (IB 32 pts HL 555 incl maths+sci)
Essex – BBC 112–120 pts (Psy Cog Neuro) (IB 29 pts HL 554)
Middlesex – BBC–BBB incl C sci 112–120 pts (Neuro)

104 pts **Central Lancashire** – 104–120 pts (Neuropsy)

Alternative offers See **Chapter 6** and **Appendix 1** for grades/UCAS Tariff points information for other examinations.

DEGREE APPRENTICESHIPS

Middlesex (Hlthcr Sci (Neurophys)); Portsmouth (App Biomed Sci).

CHOOSING YOUR COURSE (SEE ALSO CH.1)

Universities and colleges teaching quality See www.qaa.ac.uk; www.discoveruni.gov.uk.

Top research universities and colleges (REF 2021) See **Biological Sciences**.

Examples of sandwich degree courses Bristol; Cardiff; Leeds; Manchester.

ADMISSIONS INFORMATION

Advice to applicants and planning the UCAS personal statement Give reasons for your interest in this subject (usually stemming from school work in biology). Discuss any articles in medical and other scientific journals which have attracted your attention and any new developments in medicine related to neuroscience.

Selection interviews Yes Cambridge.

Interview advice and questions Questions are likely on your particular interests in biology and anatomy, why you wish to study the subject and your future career intentions. See also **Chapter 5**.

GRADUATE DESTINATIONS AND EMPLOYMENT

(See **Chapter 1, Graduate Outcomes.**)

Career note The subject leads to a range of careers in various laboratories, in government establishments, the NHS, pharmaceutical and food industries. It can also lead to postgraduate studies in physiotherapy, nursing, osteopathy and, in exceptional cases, in medicine, dentistry and veterinary science.

OTHER DEGREE SUBJECTS FOR CONSIDERATION

Biological Sciences; Biology; Genetics; Microbiology; Osteopathy; Physiology; Physiotherapy.

NURSING AND MIDWIFERY

(see also **Biological Sciences, Community Studies/Development, Health Sciences/Studies**)

Nursing and Midwifery courses are designed to equip students with the scientific and caring skills demanded by medical science in the 21st century. Courses follow a similar pattern with an introductory programme of study covering clinical skills, nursing practice and the behavioural and social sciences. Thereafter, specialisation starts in adult, child or mental health nursing, or with patients with learning disabilities. Throughout the three-year course, students gain extensive clinical experience in hospital wards, clinics, accident and emergency and high-dependency settings. UCAS handles applications for Nursing degree courses. Nursing is an all-graduate profession.

Useful websites www.scicentral.com; www.healthcareers.nhs.uk; www.nursingtimes.net; www.nmc.org.uk; www.rcn.org.uk; www.rcm.org.uk; see also **Health Sciences/Studies** and **Medicine**.

NB The points totals shown to the left of the institutions are for ease of reference only. It must not be assumed that Tariff points are always used by institutions or that they can be substituted for an offer in grades. The level of an offer is not necessarily indicative of the quality of a course.

COURSE OFFERS INFORMATION

Subject requirements/preferences GCSE English and a science subject. Mathematics required at several universities. **AL** Science subjects required for some courses. Some popular universities are now making lower offers for disadvantaged and other students. All applicants holding firm offers will require an occupational health check and Disclosure and Barring Service (DBS) clearance and are required to provide documentary evidence that they have not been infected with hepatitis B.

Your target offers and examples of degree courses

128 pts **Birmingham City** – ABB incl sci 128 pts+interview (Midwif) (IB 32 pts)
Bournemouth – 128–144 pts incl sci+interview (Midwif) (IB 32–34 pts HL 5 sci)
Bradford – ABB 128 pts+interview (Midwif) (HL 665)
City St George's – ABB 128 pts+interview (Midwif) (IB 31 pts HL 5 maths+eng)
Coventry – ABB incl sci/soc sci (Midwif) (IB 30 pts HL 15 pts)
East Anglia – ABB+interview (Midwif) (IB 32 pts)
Edinburgh – ABB+interview (Nurs St) (IB 34 pts HL 655)
Huddersfield – ABB incl biol 128 pts+interview (Midwif St)
Keele – ABB incl biol/hlth soc cr/psy/sociol+interview (Midwif) (IB 32 pts)
Kingston – ABB 128 pts+interview (Midwif)
Leeds – ABB incl biol+interview (Midwif) (IB 34 pts HL 16 pts incl 5 biol)
Leicester – ABB incl sci+interview (Midwif Ldrshp) (IB 30 pts HL 6 biol)
Liverpool John Moores – ABB 128 pts+interview (Midwif)
London (King's) – ABB (Nurs C) (IB 33 pts HL 16 pts); ABB+interview (Midwif Reg) (IB 33 pts HL 16 pts)
Manchester – ABB–AAB incl sci+interview (Midwif) (IB 34 pts HL 655 biol/chem)
Sheffield Hallam – ABB incl biol/hum biol 128 pts+interview (Midwif)
Southampton – ABB–AAB incl sci (Midwif) (IB 34 pts HL 17 pts incl sci)
Staffordshire – 128 pts (Midwif)
York – ABB incl sci (Midwif) (IB 34 pts incl sci); ABB incl sociol/sci+interview (Nurs C) (IB 34 pts HL 6 sociol/sci)

120 pts **Anglia Ruskin** – 120 pts+interview (Midwif) (IB 26 pts)

Bangor – 120–128 pts+interview (Midwif)
Birmingham – BBB+interview (Nurs A/MH/C) (IB 32 pts HL 555)
Birmingham City – BBB incl sci 120 pts+interview (Nurs A/C/LD/MH) (IB 30 pts)
Bradford – BBB 120 pts (Nurs C)
Brighton – BBB incl sci/soc sci+interview (Midwif) (IB 30 pts)
Cardiff – BBB–ABB+MMI (Midwif) (IB 31–32 pts HL 655)
Central Lancashire – 120 pts+interview (Midwif)
Chester – BBB incl biol/app sci 120 pts (Midwif) (IB 28 pts HL 5 biol)
Cumbria – BBB–ABB incl biol/PE 120–128 pts+interview (Midwif)
De Montfort – 120 pts (Nurs C) (IB 28 pts); B sci/soc sci 120 pts+interview (Midwif) (IB 28 pts HL sci/psy)
Derby – BBB 120 pts (Nurs MH)
Dundee – BBB (Nurs C) (IB 30 pts HL 555)
East Anglia – BBB+interview (Nurs A/C/MH) (IB 31 pts)
Edge Hill – BBB–ABB incl sci 120–128 pts+interview (Midwif)
Exeter – BBB (Nurs A) (IB 30 pts HL 555)
Glasgow – BBB–ABB incl sci/maths+interview (Nurs) (IB 34 pts HL 655 incl sci)
Greenwich – 120 pts+interview (Midwif)
Hertfordshire – BBB–ABB incl biol sci/bhv sci 120–128 pts+interview (Midwif)
Hull – BBB 120 pts (Nurs C) (IB 28 pts); BBB 120 pts+interview+test (Midwif) (IB 30 pts)
Kingston – BBB 120–136 pts+interview (Nurs C/MH) (IB 26 pts)
Leeds – BBB incl sci/maths/soc sci+interview (Nurs C) (IB 34 pts)
Leeds Beckett – 120 pts+interview (Nurs A/MH) (IB 26 pts)
Leicester – BBB incl sci+interview (Nurs Ldrshp MH A/C) (IB 28 pts HL 6 sci)
London (King's) – BBB+interview (Nurs MH) (IB 32 pts HL 555)
London South Bank – BBB 120 pts+MMI (Midwif)
Manchester – BBB (Nurs C) (IB 32 pts HL 555)
Middlesex – BBB+interview (Midwif)
Northumbria – 120 pts incl sci/hlth+interview (Midwif St)
Nottingham – BBB incl sci+interview (Nurs A/C/MH) (IB 28 pts HL 555)
Oxford Brookes – BBB incl sci 120 pts+interview (Midwif) (IB 31 pts)
Sheffield Hallam – BBB 120 pts (Nurs C)
South Wales – BBB+interview (Midwif; Nurs A/C/LD/MH) (IB 32 pts HL 17 pts)
Southampton – BBB (Nurs A/C/MH) (IB 30 pts HL 15 pts)
Surrey – BBB+MMI (Midwif) (IB 32 pts HL 555)
Swansea – BBB+interview (Midwif) (IB 32 pts)
Teesside – 120 pts incl sci+interview (Midwif)
UWE Bristol – C sci/soc sci 120 pts+interview (Midwif) (HL 5 sci/soc sci)
West London – 120 pts+interview (Midwif)
Winchester – 120–128 pts incl sci+interview (Midwif)
Wolverhampton – BBB incl sci/soc sci 120 pts+interview (Midwif)
Worcester – BBB incl sci/PE/sociol/hlth 120 pts+interview (Midwif)
York – BBB+interview (Nurs A/C/MH) (IB 31 pts)

112 pts **Anglia Ruskin** – 112 pts+interview (Nurs A/C/MH)
Bedfordshire – 112 pts (Midwif; Nurs A/C/MH)
Birmingham Newman – BBC 112 pts+interview (Nurs A/MH)
Bournemouth – 112–128 pts (Nurs MH) (IB 30–32 pts); 112–128 pts+interview (Nurs C) (IB 30–32 pts)
Bradford – BBC 112 pts+interview (Nurs A/MH)
Brighton – BBC incl sci/soc sci 112 pts+interview (Nurs A/C/MH) (IB 28 pts)
Brunel – BBC–ABB+interview (Nurs A/C/MH) (IB 29 pts)
Bucks New – BBC 112–136 pts+interview (Nurs A/C/MH) (IB 30 pts)
Canterbury Christ Church – BBC 112 pts+interview (Nurs A/C/MH) (IB 29 pts)
Cardiff – BBC–BBB+interview (Nurs A/C/MH) (IB 30–31 pts HL 655–665)
City St George's – BBC 112 pts+interview (Nurs A/C/MH) (IB 29 pts)

Coventry – BBC 112 pts+interview (Nurs A) (IB 27 pts HL 14 pts)
De Montfort – 112 pts+interview (Nurs A/MH/LD) (IB 26 pts)
Derby – BBC-BBB 112–120 pts+interview (Nurs A)
Essex – BBC-BBB 112–120 pts+interview (Nurs MH) (IB 29–30 pts HL 554–555); BBC-BBB 112–120 pts+interview (Nurs A) (IB 29–30 pts HL 554–555)
Greenwich – 112 pts+interview (Nurs A/C/LD/MH)
Hertfordshire – BBC-BBB 112–120 pts+interview (Nurs (A/C/LD/MH))
Huddersfield – BBC-BBB 112–120 pts+interview (Nurs A/C/LD/MH)
Hull – BBC 112 pts+interview (Nurs A/MH/LD) (IB 28 pts)
Keele – BBC+interview (Nurs A/C/MH) (IB 29 pts HL 554)
Kingston – BBC 112–128 pts+interview (Nurs A/LD) (IB 26 pts)
Leeds – BBC incl sci/maths/soc sci+interview (Nurs A/MH) (IB 34 pts HL 644)
Liverpool – BBC incl biol/soc sci+interview (Nurs)
London (King's) – BBC (Nurs A) (IB 31 pts HL 14 pts)
London South Bank – BBC/A*A* (Nurs A/C/MH)
Manchester – BBC incl sci/psy/hlth/app sci+interview (Nurs A) (IB 30 pts HL 554 incl sci)
Manchester Met – BBC 112 pts (Nurs MH)
Middlesex – BBC 112 pts+interview (Nurs A/C/MH)
Northampton – BBC incl sci/psy/sociol (Midwif)
Northumbria – 112 pts+interview (Nurs St A/C/LD/MH)
Oxford Brookes – BBC 112 pts (Nurs C) (IB 30 pts)
Portsmouth – BBC-BBB 112–120 pts incl sci/soc sci+interview (Nurs A; Nurs MH) (IB 25 pts)
Salford – 112–128 pts+interview (Midwif)
Sheffield Hallam – BBC 112 pts+interview (Nurs A/MH/LD)
Staffordshire – BBC 112 pts+interview (Nurs Prac A/C/MH)
Suffolk – BBC 112 pts+interview (Nurs A/C/MH)
Swansea – BBC-BBB 112–120 pts (Nurs C)
Teesside – 112 pts+interview (Nurs St A/C/LD/MH)
UWE Bristol – 112 pts+interview (Nurs A/C/LD/MH)
Ulster – BBC+interview (Nurs A/MH) (IB 25 pts HL 12 pts)
West London – BBC 112 pts+interview (Nurs A/C/LD/MH)
Worcester – 112 pts+interview (Nurs (A/C/MH))

104 pts **Abertay** – BCC 104 pts (Nurs MH/LD) (IB 27 pts HL 14 pts)
Bangor – 104–120 pts+interview (Nurs A/C/LD/MH)
Bournemouth – 104–120 pts+interview (Nurs A) (IB 32–34 pts)
Central Lancashire – 104 pts+interview (Nurs A/MH)
Chester – BCC-BBC 104–112 pts (Nurs C/LD/MH) (IB 26 pts)
Chichester – BCC 104–120 pts+interview (Nurs A)
Cumbria – 104–120 pts+interview (Nurs A/C/LD/MH)
Edge Hill – BCC-BBC 104–112 pts+interview (Nurs A/C/LD/MH)
Edinburgh Napier – BCC incl lit/biol/app sci (Midwif)
Lincoln – 104 pts+interview (Nurs A/C/MH)
Liverpool John Moores – 104–112 pts+interview (Nurs A/MH); BCC-BBB 104–120 pts+interview (Nurs C)
Manchester – BCC (Nurs MH) (IB 30 pts HL 544)
Manchester Met – BCC 104 pts+interview (Nurs A)
Marjon – BCC-BBB 104–120 pts (Nurs)
Northampton – BCC+interview (Nurs A/C/MH/LD)
Oxford Brookes – BCC 104 pts+interview (Nurs A/MH) (IB 29 pts)
Plymouth – 104–120 pts+interview (Nurs A/C/MH) (IB 26–30 pts)
Queen Margaret – BCC incl sci (Nurs) (IB 30 pts)
Queen's Belfast – BCC-BBC incl sci+interview (Nurs A/C/LD/MH); BCC-BBC incl sci/maths+MMI (Midwif Sci)
Robert Gordon – BCC incl Engl+sci (Midwif) (IB 27 pts)
Swansea – BCC+interview (Nurs A/MH)

UHI – BCC 104 pts+interview (Nurs A/MH)
Winchester – 104–120 pts+interview (Nurs A/C/LD/MH) (HL 44)
Wolverhampton – BCC 104 pts+interview (Nurs A/C/MH/LD)

96 pts **Abertay** – CCC+interview (Nurs MH) (IB 27 pts)
Stirling – CCC (Nurs A/MH) (IB 28 pts)
Wrexham – 96–112 pts+interview (Nurs A)

80 pts **West Scotland** – CDD incl biol/hum biol 80 pts+interview (Nurs A/MH) (IB 24 pts)

72 pts **Chester** – 72 pts (Nurs A) (IB 24 pts)
Edinburgh Napier – BC incl sci+Engl+interview (Nurs A/C/LD/MH)
Glasgow Caledonian – BC+interview (Nurs St (A/C/LD/MH)) (IB 28 pts)

64 pts **Dundee** – CC+interview (Nurs A/MH) (IB 24 pts HL 44)
Robert Gordon – CC incl Engl+sci (Nurs A/C/MH) (IB 24 pts)

Open University – (Nurs A)

Alternative offers See **Chapter 6** and **Appendix 1** for grades/UCAS Tariff points information for other examinations.

DEGREE APPRENTICESHIPS

Anglia Ruskin (Midwif); Bedfordshire (RN (A/C/MH)); Birmingham (Midwif); Birmingham City (RN (A/C/LD/MH)); Bournemouth (RN); BPP (RN); Brighton (RN); Brunel (Nurs); Canterbury Christ Church (Advnc Clin Practnr, Nurs Assoct, Occ Thpst, RN); Central Lancashire (RN, Midwif); Chester (Nurs Assoct); Chichester (RN); Cumbria (Midwif); De Montfort (Nurs); Derby (RN); East Anglia (Nurs (A)); East London (RN, Midwif); Essex (Nurs Assoct, RN, Occ Thpst); Greater Manchester (Nurs); Greenwich (Nurs (A), Midwif); Hertfordshire (RN (A)); Huddersfield (RN (A/C), Midwif); Keele (RN); Kingston (Nurs (A)); Northumbria (RN (A/C)); Nottingham Trent (RN); Liverpool John Moores (RN (A)); London South Bank (Nurs); Plymouth (RN); Plymouth Marjon (Nurs Assoct); Staffordshire (RN, Midwif); Sunderland (RN); Teesside (Nurs St (A/C/LD/MH), Occ Thpst); West London (Nurs (A/C/LD/MH), Midwif, Advnc Clin Practnr); Winchester (Nurs (A/C/LD/MH), Midwif); Wolverhampton (RN, Midwif); Worcester (RN); York (RN (A/C/MH)).

EXAMPLES OF COLLEGES OFFERING COURSES IN THIS SUBJECT FIELD

Central Campus, Sandwell (Coll); East Kent (Coll); MidKent (Coll); Oaklands (Coll).

CHOOSING YOUR COURSE (SEE ALSO CH.1)

Universities and colleges teaching quality See www.qaa.ac.uk; www.discoveruni.gov.uk.

Top research universities and colleges (REF 2021) (Allied Health Professions, Dentistry, Nursing and Pharmacy) London (King's); Manchester; Southampton; Queen's Belfast; Nottingham; Swansea; Keele; Newcastle; Bath; Leeds.

Examples of sandwich degree courses Brunel.

ADMISSIONS INFORMATION

Advice to applicants and planning the UCAS personal statement Experience of care work – for example in hospitals, old people's homes, children's homes – is important. Describe what you have done and what you have learned. Read nursing journals in order to be aware of new developments in the treatment of illnesses. Note, in particular, the various needs of patients and the problems they experience. Try to compare different nursing approaches with, for example, children, people with learning disabilities, old people and terminally ill people. If you underperformed at GCSE, give reasons. If you have had work experience or a part-time job, describe how your skills have developed, for example responsibility, communication, team building, organisational skills. How do you spend your spare time? Explain how your interests help with stress and pressure. See also **Appendix 3**. Contact NHS Student Bursaries for information about financial support; tel 0300 330 1345.

Selection interviews Yes Abertay, Anglia Ruskin, Bangor, Birmingham, Birmingham City, Birmingham Newman, Bournemouth, Bradford, Brighton, Brunel (Nurs), Bucks New, Canterbury Christ Church (Nurs), Cardiff, Central Lancashire, Chichester, City St George's, Coventry (Nurs), Cumbria, De Montfort, Derby,

Dundee, East Anglia, Edge Hill, Edinburgh, Edinburgh Napier, Essex, Exeter (Nurs), Glasgow Caledonian, Greenwich, Hertfordshire, Huddersfield, Hull, Keele, Kingston, Leeds, Leeds Beckett, Leicester, Lincoln, Liverpool, Liverpool John Moores, London (King's), London South Bank, Manchester, Manchester Met, Middlesex, Northampton (Nurs), Northumbria, Nottingham, Oxford Brookes, Plymouth, Portsmouth, Queen's Belfast, Robert Gordon, Salford, Sheffield Hallam, South Wales, Southampton, Staffordshire (Nurs), Suffolk, Surrey, Swansea, Teesside, UHI, Ulster, UWE Bristol, West London, West Scotland, Winchester, Wolverhampton, Worcester, Wrexham, York (Nurs); **Some** Stirling.

Interview advice and questions Past questions have included: Why do you want to be a nurse? What experience have you had in nursing? What do you think of the nurses' pay situation? Should nurses go on strike? What are your views on abortion? What branch of nursing most interests you? How would you communicate with someone who can't speak English? What is the nurse's role in the community? How should a nurse react in an emergency? How would you cope with telling a patient's relative that the patient was dying? Admissions tutors look for communication skills, team interaction and the applicant's understanding of health/society-related subjects. See also **Chapter 5**.

Reasons for rejection (non-academic) Insufficient awareness of the roles and responsibilities of a midwife or nurse. Lack of motivation. Poor communication skills. Lack of awareness of nursing developments through the media. (Detailed knowledge of the NHS or nursing practice not usually required.) Failed medical. Unsatisfactory health record. Not fulfilling the hepatitis B requirements or police check requirements. Poor preparation for the interview. Too shy. Only wants nursing as a means to something else, for example commission in the armed forces. Too many choices on the UCAS application, for example Midwifery, Physiotherapy, Occupational Therapy. No care experience. Some applicants have difficulty with maths – multiplication and division – used in calculating dosage for medicines.

GRADUATE DESTINATIONS AND EMPLOYMENT

(See **Chapter 1, Graduate Outcomes.**)

Career note The majority of Nursing graduates aim to enter the nursing profession.

OTHER DEGREE SUBJECTS FOR CONSIDERATION

Audiology; Biological Sciences; Biology; Community Studies; Dietetics; Education; Health Studies; Medicine; Nutrition; Occupational Therapy; Optometry; Pharmacology; Pharmacy; Physiotherapy; Podiatry; Psychology; Radiography; Social Policy and Administration; Social Work; Sociology; Speech Therapy; Veterinary Nursing.

NUTRITION

(see also **Dietetics, Food Science/Studies and Technology, Health Sciences/Studies**)

Nutrition attracts a great deal of attention in society and while controversy, claim and counter-claim seem to focus daily on the merits and otherwise of food, it is, nevertheless, a scientific study in itself. Courses involve topics relating to diet, health, nutrition and food policy, and are designed to prepare students to enter careers as specialists in nutrition and dietetics.

Useful websites www.nutrition.org.uk; www.nutritionsociety.org; see also under **Dietetics**.

NB The points totals shown to the left of the institutions are for ease of reference only. It must not be assumed that Tariff points are always used by institutions or that they can be substituted for an offer in grades. The level of an offer is not necessarily indicative of the quality of a course.

COURSE OFFERS INFORMATION

Subject requirements/preferences GCSE Mathematics and science usually required. **AL** Science subjects required for most courses, biology and/or chemistry preferred. Some popular universities are now making lower offers for disadvantaged and other students.

YOUR TARGET OFFERS AND EXAMPLES OF DEGREE COURSES

136 pts **Leeds** – AAB incl sci/maths (Nutr) (IB 35 pts HL 16 pts incl sci)
Nottingham – AAB incl biol/chem+sci+interview (Nutr Diet (MNutr)) (IB 32 pts HL 665)

128 pts **Leeds** – ABB incl sci/maths (Fd Sci Nutr) (IB 34 pts HL 16 pts incl sci/maths)
London (King's) – ABB incl chem+biol (Nutr Sci) (IB 33 pts HL 16 pts)
Newcastle – ABB–AAB incl biol/chem+STEM (Hum Nutr) (IB 32 pts HL 5 biol/chem+STEM); ABB–AAB incl sci (Nutr Fd Mark) (IB 32 pts HL 5 biol/chem+STEM)
Nottingham – ABB incl sci (Nutr) (IB 30 pts HL 655); ABB incl sci/maths+fd tech/econ/geog (Fd Sci Nutr) (IB 30 pts HL 655)
Reading – ABB incl sci/maths (Fd Sci; Nutr; Nutr Fd Sci) (IB 32 pts HL 5 sci/maths)
Surrey – ABB incl biol+sci/maths+interview (Nutr Diet) (IB 33 pts HL 5 biol+sci/maths)

120 pts **Coventry** – BBB incl biol/chem/fd tech 120 pts (Nutr Hlth) (IB 32 pts HL 5 biol/chem)
Leeds Beckett – 120 pts (Nutr); BBB incl chem+sci+interview (Diet)
Liverpool John Moores – BBB–ABB incl sci (Nutr)
London Met – BBB incl biol+chem+interview (Diet Nutr)
Surrey – BBB–ABB incl biol/chem+sci/maths (Fd Sci Nutr) (IB 32–33 pts HL 5 biol/chem+maths/sci); BBB incl biol+sci (Nutr) (IB 32 pts HL 5 biol+sci)
Winchester – BBB–ABB 120–128 pts+interview (Nutr Diet) (HL 555 incl Engl+math+sci)

112 pts **Cardiff Met** – 112–120 pts (Biomed Sci Hlth Exer Nutr) (HL 56 incl biol+sci); BC chem+biol 112–120 pts+interview (Hum Nutr Diet) (HL 6 biol+chem)
Central Lancashire – CC chem/biol/psy/maths/phys 112–128 pts (Nutr)
Chester – BBC incl biol/chem 112 pts (Hum Nutr) (IB 26 pts HL 5 biol/chem); BBC–BBB incl biol+sci 112–120 pts+interview (Nutr Diet) (IB 28 pts HL 5 biol+chem)
Hull – BBC 112 pts (Spo Exer Nutr) (IB 28 pts)
Kingston – C sci/psy/PE 112–128 pts (Spo Exer Sci (Nutr))
Liverpool Hope – BBC 112 pts (Nutr) (IB 28 pts)
London Met – C biol 112 pts (Hum Nutr)
Northumbria – B incl sci/fd tech/hm econ 112 pts (Fd Sci Nutr)
Nottingham Trent – 112 pts incl sci/PE (Spo Sci Hlth Nutr)
Roehampton – 112 pts (Nutr Hlth)
Sheffield Hallam – BBC–BBB 112–120 pts (Fd Nutr); BBC 112 pts (Nutr Diet Wlbng)
West London – BBC 112 pts (Nutr Fd Mgt)

104 pts **Bath Spa** – BCC–BBB (Fd Nutr) (IB 32 pts); BCC–BBB incl biol/PE (Hum Nutr) (IB 32 pts HL 5 biol)
Bournemouth – 104–120 pts incl sci (Nutr) (IB 28–31 pts)
Edge Hill – BCC–BBC 104–112 pts (Nutr Hlth)
Glasgow Caledonian – BCC incl chem (Hum Nutr Diet)
Greenwich – 104 pts incl biol+chem (Hum Nutr)
Liverpool Hope – BCC 104 pts (Spo Exer Nutr) (IB 24 pts)
Manchester Met – BCC 104–112 pts (Spo Exer Nutr) (IB 26 pts)
Oxford Brookes – BCC incl sci 104 pts (Nutr) (IB 29 pts)
Plymouth – B biol 104–120 pts (Nutr Exer Hlth) (IB 26–29 pts HL 5 biol+sci)
Robert Gordon – BCC incl chem+sci+interview (Nutr Diet) (IB 28 pts incl chem+sci)
Ulster – BCC incl sci/maths/tech (Hum Nutr) (IB 24 pts HL 12 pts incl 65 sci/maths/tech)

96 pts **Abertay** – CCC (Fd Sci Nutr Wlbng; Fit Nutr Hlth) (IB 27 pts)
Bedfordshire – 96 pts (Fd Nutr Sci)
CAFRE – 96 pts incl sci/hm econ (Fd Innov Mgt)
Cardiff Met – CC incl sci/fd tech 96–104 pts (Fd Sci Nutr) (HL 5 sci)
St Mary's – CCC–BBC 96–112 pts (Nutr)
Teesside – 96 pts (Nutr)
Ulster – CCC incl sci/maths/env tech/hm econ (Fd Nutr) (IB 24 pts HL 12 pts incl 5 sci/maths/hm econ)
Westminster – CCC incl chem/biol+sci (Hum Nutr) (HL 44 sci)

88 pts **Trinity Saint David** – 88 pts (Hlth Soc Cr)

80 pts **Queen Margaret** – BB incl chem/biol 80 pts (Nutr) (IB 26 pts)

Alternative offers See **Chapter 6** and **Appendix 1** for grades/UCAS Tariff points information for other examinations.

DEGREE APPRENTICESHIPS

Hertfordshire (Diet); Plymouth (Diet); Sheffield Hallam (Diet); Teesside (Diet).

EXAMPLES OF COLLEGES OFFERING COURSES IN THIS SUBJECT FIELD

Bradford College (UC); Truro and Penwith (Coll).

CHOOSING YOUR COURSE (SEE ALSO CH.1)

Universities and colleges teaching quality See www.qaa.ac.uk; www.discoveruni.gov.uk.

Top research universities and colleges (REF 2021) See **Agricultural Sciences/Agriculture**.

Examples of sandwich degree courses Coventry; Kingston; Leeds; Leeds Beckett; Liverpool John Moores; Manchester Met; Newcastle; Northumbria; Reading; Sheffield Hallam; Surrey; Teesside; Ulster.

ADMISSIONS INFORMATION

Advice to applicants and planning the UCAS personal statement Information on relevant experience, reasons for wanting to do the degree and careers sought would be useful. See also **Dietetics** and **Appendix 3**.

Selection interviews Yes Cardiff Met (Hum Nutr Diet), Chester (Nutr Diet), Leeds Beckett (Diet), London Met, Nottingham, Robert Gordon, Surrey (Nutr Diet), Trinity Saint David.

Interview advice and questions Past questions have focused on scientific A-level subjects studied and aspects of subjects enjoyed by the applicants. Questions then arise from answers. Extensive knowledge expected of nutrition as a career and candidates should have talked to people involved in this type of work, for example dietitians. They will also be expected to discuss wider problems such as food supplies in developing countries and nutritional problems resulting from famine. See also **Chapter 5**.

GRADUATE DESTINATIONS AND EMPLOYMENT

(See **Chapter 1, Graduate Outcomes.**)

Career note Nutritionists work in retail, health promotion and sport; others specialise in dietetics.

OTHER DEGREE SUBJECTS FOR CONSIDERATION

Biological Sciences; Biology; Consumer Studies; Dietetics; Food Sciences; Health Studies/Sciences.

OCCUPATIONAL THERAPY

(see also **Health Sciences/Studies, Physiotherapy**)

Everyday life involves washing, dressing, eating, walking, driving, shopping and going to work, all aspects which we take for granted – until we have an injury or illness. If this happened to you then during the recovery period, you would realise the importance of the occupational therapist's role. They assist people of all ages, not only those being treated with physical injuries/illness but others with mental health issues, the work being to identify the special problems they face and the practical solutions that are required to help them recover and maintain their daily living and working skills. The focus of the OT is on meaningful and functional activity. This may be achieved by advising on physical modifications to the home environment and potentially introducing new equipment and devices to make various activities easier along with task analysis. In the case of mental health OTs, they assist clients to re-establish routines and skills to allow them to return to living fulfilling lives. To achieve these results, occupational therapists often work with physiotherapists, psychologists, speech therapists and social workers among others. Most courses therefore involve anatomy, physiology, psychology, sociology, mental health and ethics. OTs can work in a very wide range of settings, acute care, long term care, social services and mental health plus many more. There are opportunities to specialise in burns, hand therapy, oncology and surgery, forensic psychology and prison rehabilitation to name but a few. Selectors look for maturity, initiative, tact, sound judgement, team work and organising ability. Occupational therapy is often very poorly understood by the general public. The profession is actually very diverse with therapists working in hospitals, schools, prisons, charities, voluntary organisations and in private practice.

Useful websites www.rcot.co.uk

NB The points totals shown to the left of the institutions are for ease of reference only. It must not be assumed that Tariff points are always used by institutions or that they can be substituted for an offer in grades. The level of an offer is not necessarily indicative of the quality of a course.

COURSE OFFERS INFORMATION

Subject requirements/preferences GCSE English, mathematics and science grade 7–4 (A–C). **AL** A social science or science subjects required or preferred for most courses. Some popular universities are now making lower offers for disadvantaged and other students. **Other** All applicants need to pass an occupational health check and obtain Disclosure and Barring Service (DBS) clearance.

Your target offers and examples of degree courses

120 pts **Bournemouth** – 120–136 pts+interview (Occ Thera) (IB 31–33 pts)
Bradford – BBB 120 pts (Occ Thera)
Brunel – BBB incl biol/chem/psy/sociol 120 pts+interview (Occ Thera) (IB 30 pts HL 5 biol/chem/psy/sociol)
Cardiff – BBB–ABB (Occ Thera) (IB 31–32 pts HL 655)
City St George's – BBB+interview (Occ Thera) (IB 32 pts HL 15 pts)
East Anglia – BBB+interview (Occ Thera) (IB 31 pts)
Liverpool – BBB incl soc sci/biol/PE (Occ Thera) (IB 30 pts HL 444 incl biol)
London South Bank – BBB 120 pts (Occ Thera) (IB 26 pts)
Southampton – BBB incl sci/soc sci (Occ Thera) (IB 30 pts HL 15 pts incl sci/soc sci)
UWE Bristol – 120 pts+interview (Occ Thera)
Ulster – BBB (Occ Thera)
Worcester – BBB 120 pts (Occ Thera)
York St John – BBB 120 pts (Occ Thera)

112 pts **Canterbury Christ Church** – BBC 112 pts+interview (Occ Thera)
Coventry – BBC 112 pts+interview (Occ Thera) (IB 29 pts HL 16 pts)
Cumbria – 112–120 pts+interview (Occ Thera)
Derby – BBC–ABB 112–128 pts+interview (Occ Thera)
Essex – BBC–BBB 112–120 pts (Occ Thera) (IB 29–30 pts HL 554–555)
Huddersfield – BBC–BBB incl biol/psy 112–120 pts (Occ Thera)
Northampton – BBC (Occ Thera)
Northumbria – 112 pts+interview (Occ Thera)
Plymouth – 112–128 pts incl sci/soc sci+interview (Occ Thera) (IB 28–32 pts HL 5 sci/soc sci)
Teesside – 112–128 pts+interview (Occ Thera)

104 pts **Bedfordshire** – 104–112 pts (Occ Thera)
Glasgow Caledonian – BCC (Occ Thera)
Oxford Brookes – BCC 104 pts (Occ Thera) (IB 29 pts)
Queen Margaret – BCC+interview (Occ Thera) (IB 28 pts)
Robert Gordon – BCC incl Engl+sci/hum+interview (Occ Thera) (IB 27 pts)

Alternative offers See **Chapter 6** and **Appendix 1** for grades/UCAS Tariff points information for other examinations.

DEGREE APPRENTICESHIPS

Brighton (Occ Thera); Bucks New (Occ Thpst); Canterbury Christ Church (Occ Thera); Central Lancashire (Occ Thera); Essex (Occ Thpst); Hertfordshire (Occ Thpst); Huddersfield (Occ Thera); Keele (Occ Thpst); London South Bank (Occ Thera); Northampton (Occ Thera); Northumbria (Occ Thera); Plymouth (Occ Thera); Sheffield Hallam (Occ Thpst); Sunderland (Occ Thpst); Wolverhampton (Occ Thera).

CHOOSING YOUR COURSE (SEE ALSO CH.1)

Universities and colleges teaching quality See www.qaa.ac.uk; www.discoveruni.gov.uk.

Top research universities and colleges (REF 2021) See **Health Sciences/Studies**.

Examples of sandwich degree courses Bedfordshire; Bournemouth; Bradford; Brunel; Coventry; Cumbria; Derby; East Anglia; Essex; Liverpool; Plymouth; Robert Gordon; UWE Bristol; Worcester.

ADMISSIONS INFORMATION

Admissions tutors' advice City St George's Work experience required.

Advice to applicants and planning the UCAS personal statement Contact your local hospital and discuss this career with the occupational therapists. Try to obtain work shadowing experience and make notes of your observations. Describe any such visits in full (see also Reasons for rejection (non-academic)). Applicants are expected to have visited two occupational therapy departments, one in a physical or social services setting, one in the mental health field. Good interpersonal skills. Breadth and nature of health-related work experience is important. Also skills, interests (for example, sports, design). Applicants should have a high standard of communication skills and experience of working with people with disabilities. See also **Appendix 3**.

Selection interviews Yes Bournemouth, Brunel, Canterbury Christ Church, City St George's, Coventry, Cumbria, Derby, East Anglia, Huddersfield, Northumbria, Oxford Brookes, Plymouth, Queen Margaret, Robert Gordon, Teesside, UWE Bristol, Worcester, Wrexham; **Some** York St John.

Interview advice and questions Since this is a vocational course, work experience is nearly always essential and applicants are likely to be questioned on the types of work involved and the career. Some universities may use admissions tests: check websites and see **Chapter 5**.

Reasons for rejection (non-academic) Poor communication skills. Lack of knowledge of occupational therapy. Little evidence of working with people. Uncertain about their future career. Lack of maturity. Indecision regarding the profession.

GRADUATE DESTINATIONS AND EMPLOYMENT

(See **Chapter 1, Graduate Outcomes.**)

Career note Occupational therapists (who work mostly in hospital departments) are involved in the rehabilitation of those who have required medical treatment and work with the young, aged and, for example, people with learning difficulties.

OTHER DEGREE SUBJECTS FOR CONSIDERATION

Audiology; Community Studies; Dietetics; Education; Health Studies/Sciences; Nursing; Nutrition; Physiotherapy; Podiatry; Psychology; Radiography; Social Policy and Administration; Social Work; Sociology; Speech Sciences.

OPERATING DEPARTMENT PRACTICE

This career involves working in areas involved in anaesthetics, intensive care, A&E, transplants and the air ambulance. In operating theatres, high-quality care is essential for patients before, during and after surgery.

Useful websites www.healthcareers.nhs.uk

NB The points totals shown to the left of the institutions are for ease of reference only. It must not be assumed that Tariff points are always used by institutions or that they can be substituted for an offer in grades. The level of an offer is not necessarily indicative of the quality of a course.

COURSE OFFERS INFORMATION

Subject requirements/preferences GCSE English, mathematics and a science. **AL** At least one science subject. Some popular universities are now making lower offers for disadvantaged and other students.

Your target offers and examples of degree courses

112 pts **Birmingham City** – 112 pts+interview (Oprtg Dept Prac) (IB 28 pts)
Bucks New – BBC 112–136 pts+interview (Oprtg Dept Prac) (IB 30 pts)
Canterbury Christ Church – BBC 112 pts+interview (Oprtg Dept Prac)
Central Lancashire – 112 pts (Oprtg Dept Prac)
Coventry – BBC 112 pts+interview (Oprtg Dept Prac) (IB 29 pts HL 14 pts)
East Anglia – BBC+interview (Oprtg Dept Prac) (IB 30 pts)
Greater Manchester – 112 pts+interview (Oprtg Dept Prac)
Hull – BBC 112 pts+interview (Oprtg Dept Prac) (IB 28 pts)
Leicester – BBC 112 pts+interview (Oprtg Dept Prac)
London South Bank – BBC+interview (Oprtg Dept Prac)
Northumbria – 112 pts+interview (Oprtg Dept Prac)
Portsmouth – BBC 112 pts incl sci+interview (Oprtg Dept Prac) (IB 29 pts)
Sheffield Hallam – BBC 112 pts+interview (Oprtg Dept Prac)
Staffordshire – BBC 112 pts (Oprtg Dept Prac)

104 pts **Bournemouth** – 104–120 pts+interview (Oprtg Dept Prac) (IB 28–31 pts)
Edge Hill – BCC–BBC 104–112 pts+interview (Oprtg Dept Prac)
Huddersfield – BCC–BBC 104–112 pts+interview (Oprtg Dept Prac)
West London – BCC 104 pts+interview (Oprtg Dept Prac)

96 pts **Anglia Ruskin** – 96 pts+interview (Oprtg Dept Prac)
Bedfordshire – 96 pts (Oprtg Dept Prac)
Teesside – 96 pts+interview (Oprtg Dept Prac)

Alternative offers See **Chapter 6** and **Appendix 1** for grades/UCAS Tariff points information for other examinations.

DEGREE APPRENTICESHIPS

Anglia Ruskin (Oprtg Dept Practnr); Bedfordshire (Oprtg Dept Practnr); Birmingham City (Oprtg Dept Prac); Bournemouth (Oprtg Dept Prac); Bucks New (Oprtg Dept Practnr); Canterbury Christ Church (Oprtg Dept Practnr); Central Lancashire (Oprtg Dept Prac); Derby (Oprtg Dept Practnr); East Anglia (Oprtg Dept Practnr); Gloucestershire (Oprtg Dept Practnr); Greater Manchester (Oprtg Dept Prac); Greenwich (Oprtg Dept Practnr); Huddersfield (Oprtg Dept Prac); Hull (Oprtg Dept Prac); London South Bank (Oprtg Dept Prac); Northumbria (Oprtg Dept Prac); Portsmouth (Oprtg Dept Prac); Sheffield Hallam (Oprtg Dept Practnr); Staffordshire (Oprtg Dept Practnr); Teesside (Oprtg Dept Practnr); West London (Oprtg Dept Practnr).

CHOOSING YOUR COURSE (SEE ALSO CH.1)

Universities and colleges teaching quality See www.qaa.ac.uk; www.discoveruni.gov.uk.

ADMISSIONS INFORMATION

Advice to applicants and planning the UCAS personal statement Applicants should have a scientific background and exhibit evidence of attention to detail.

Selection interviews Yes Anglia Ruskin, Birmingham City, Bournemouth, Bucks New, Canterbury Christ Church, Coventry, East Anglia, Edge Hill, Greater Manchester, Huddersfield, Hull, Leicester, London South Bank, Northumbria, Portsmouth, Sheffield Hallam, Teesside, West London.

GRADUATE DESTINATIONS AND EMPLOYMENT

(See **Chapter 1, Graduate Outcomes.**)

OTHER DEGREE SUBJECTS FOR CONSIDERATION

Nursing and Midwifery; Occupational Therapy; Physiotherapy; Podiatry.

OPTOMETRY (OPHTHALMIC OPTICS)

(including **Ophthalmic Dispensing and Orthoptics**)

Optometry courses (which are becoming increasingly popular) lead to qualification as an optometrist (previously known as an ophthalmic optician). They provide training in detecting defects and diseases in the eye and in prescribing treatment with, for example, spectacles, contact lenses and other appliances to correct or improve vision. Orthoptics includes the study of general anatomy, physiology and normal child development and leads to a career as an orthoptist. This involves the investigation, diagnosis and treatment of defects of binocular vision and other eye conditions. The main components of degree courses include the study of the eye, the use of diagnostic and measuring equipment and the treatment of eye abnormalities. See also **Appendix 3**.

USEFUL WEBSITES www.optical.org; www.orthoptics.org.uk; www.abdo.org.uk; www.college-optometrists.org

NB The points totals shown to the left of the institutions are for ease of reference only. It must not be assumed that Tariff points are always used by institutions or that they can be substituted for an offer in grades. The level of an offer is not necessarily indicative of the quality of a course.

COURSE OFFERS INFORMATION

SUBJECT REQUIREMENTS/PREFERENCES GCSE Good grades in English and science subjects usually required. **AL** Science subjects required for all Optometry courses. Mathematics usually acceptable. Some popular universities are now making lower offers for disadvantaged and other students. **Plymouth** 5 GCSEs to include English, Maths and Science at 6 (B). Plus interview, DBS and Occupational Health, Overseas checks required.

YOUR TARGET OFFERS AND EXAMPLES OF DEGREE COURSES

144 pts **Aston** – AAA/AAB+aEPQ incl sci/maths (Optom) (IB 32 pts HL 666 incl sci/maths)
Glasgow Caledonian – AAA incl sci+maths 144 pts (Optom Indep Prscr)

136 pts **Anglia Ruskin** – AAB incl sci/maths (Optom)
Bradford – AAB incl sci/maths 136 pts (Optom) (HL 666 incl sci)
City St George's – AAB incl sci/maths 136 pts+interview (Optom) (IB 33 pts HL 6 sci)
Glasgow Caledonian – AAB incl sci/maths (Optom) (IB 30 pts HL 665 incl sci+maths)
Hertfordshire – AAB–AAA incl sci/maths 136–144 pts (Optom (MOptom))
Manchester – AAB–AAA incl sci/maths+interview (Optom) (IB 35 pts HL 665 incl sci/maths)
UWE Bristol – 136 pts incl maths/sci (Optom (MSci)) (HL 56 incl maths/sci)

128 pts **Cardiff** – ABB–AAA incl sci/maths (Optom) (IB 32–36 pts HL 665–666 incl sci/maths)
Huddersfield – ABB–AAB incl sci/maths (Optom)
Plymouth – ABB incl maths/sci 128–136 pts (Optom) (IB 32–34 pts HL 6 maths/sci)
Ulster – ABB incl sci/maths (Optom) (IB 28 pts HL 14 pts incl sci/maths)

120 pts **Liverpool** – BBB incl sci/maths+interview (Orth) (IB 30 pts HL 6 biol)
Sheffield – BBB incl sci+interview (Orth) (IB 32 pts HL 5 sci)
UHI – BBB incl sci 120 pts+interview (Optom (Indep Prscr))

104 pts **Glasgow Caledonian** – BCC incl sci (Orth)

64 pts **Bradford College (UC)** – CC 64 pts incl sci/maths (Oph Disp)

ALTERNATIVE OFFERS See **Chapter 6** and **Appendix 1** for grades/UCAS Tariff points information for other examinations.

EXAMPLES OF COLLEGES OFFERING COURSES IN THIS SUBJECT FIELD

Bradford College (UC); City and Islington (Coll).

CHOOSING YOUR COURSE (SEE ALSO CH.1)

UNIVERSITIES AND COLLEGES TEACHING QUALITY See www.qaa.ac.uk; www.discoveruni.gov.uk.

ADMISSIONS INFORMATION

Advice to applicants and planning the UCAS personal statement For Optometry courses, contact with optometrists is essential, either work shadowing or gaining some work experience. Make notes of your experiences and the work done and report fully on the UCAS application on why the career interests you. See also **Appendix 3**.

Selection interviews Yes City St George's, Liverpool, Manchester, Sheffield, UHI; **No** Anglia Ruskin, Bradford.

Interview advice and questions Optometry is a competitive subject requiring applicants to have had some work experience on which they will be questioned. See also **Chapter 5**.

GRADUATE DESTINATIONS AND EMPLOYMENT

(See **Chapter 1, Graduate Outcomes.**)

Career note The great majority of graduates enter private practice either in small businesses or in larger organisations (which have been on the increase in recent years). A small number work in eye hospitals. Orthoptists tend to work in public health and education dealing with children and the elderly.

OTHER DEGREE SUBJECTS FOR CONSIDERATION

Health Studies; Nursing; Occupational Therapy; Physics; Physiotherapy; Radiography; Speech Studies.

PHARMACOLOGY

(including **Physiology and Pharmacology**; see also **Biological Sciences, Health Sciences/Studies**)

Pharmacology is the study of drugs and medicines, and courses focus on physiology, biochemistry, toxicology, immunology, microbiology and chemotherapy. Pharmacologists are not qualified to work as pharmacists. Toxicology involves the study of the adverse effects of chemicals on living systems. See also **Appendix 3** under Pharmacology.

Useful websites www.thebts.org; www.bps.ac.uk

NB The points totals shown to the left of the institutions are for ease of reference only. It must not be assumed that Tariff points are always used by institutions or that they can be substituted for an offer in grades. The level of an offer is not necessarily indicative of the quality of a course.

COURSE OFFERS INFORMATION

Subject requirements/preferences GCSE English, science and mathematics. **AL** Chemistry and/or biology required for most courses. Some popular universities are now making lower offers for disadvantaged and other students.

Your target offers and examples of degree courses

160 pts **Cambridge** – A*A*A incl sci/maths+interview+ESAT (Nat Sci (Pharmacol)) (IB 41–42 pts HL 776)

144 pts **London (King's)** – AAA incl chem+biol (Pharmacol) (IB 36 pts HL 18 pts incl 6 biol+chem)

136 pts **Bath** – AAB–ABB+aEPQ incl chem+sci/maths (Pharmacol) (IB 36 pts HL 665 incl chem+sci/maths)

Bristol – AAB incl chem+sci/maths (Pharmacol) (IB 34 pts HL 17 pts incl 6/5 chem+sci/maths)

Edinburgh – AAB incl biol+chem (Pharmacol) (IB 34 pts HL 655 incl biol+chem)

Leeds – AAB–AAA incl biol/chem+sci (Pharmacol) (IB 31 pts HL 665 incl biol/chem+sci)

Liverpool – AAB incl chem+sci (Pharmacol) (IB 34 pts HL 6 chem)

London (UCL) – AAB incl chem+sci/maths (Pharmacol) (IB 36 pts HL 17 pts incl 5 chem+sci/maths)

Manchester – AAB–AAA incl sci/maths (Pharmacol) (IB 35–36 pts HL 665–666 incl sci)

Newcastle – AAB incl biol/chem+maths/sci (Pharmacol) (IB 34 pts HL 5 biol/chem+maths/sci)

Nottingham – AAB incl chem+biol (Pharmacol) (IB 32 pts HL 665 incl chem+biol)
Southampton – AAB incl chem+sci/maths (Pharmacol) (IB 34 pts HL 17 pts incl 5/6 chem+sci/maths)

128 pts **Dundee** – ABB incl biol+chem (Pharmacol) (IB 32 pts HL 655 incl biol+chem)
Leicester – ABB–AAB incl sci/maths (Biol Sci (Physiol Pharmacol)) (IB 30 pts HL 6/5 sci/maths)

120 pts **City St George's** – BBB incl chem/biol (Clin Pharmacol) (IB 32 pts HL 15 pts incl chem/biol)
Glasgow – BBB–AAB incl biol/chem (Pharmacol) (IB 34 pts HL 655 incl biol/chem)
Hertfordshire – BBB–ABB incl biol/chem+sci/maths/geog/psy 120–128 pts (Pharmacol)
Nottingham Trent – BBB incl biol 120 pts (Pharmacol)
Reading – BBB incl biol+chem (Pharmacol) (IB 30 pts HL 5 biol+chem)
Strathclyde – BBB–ABB incl chem+biol (Pharmacol) (IB 30–32 pts HL 5 chem+biol)

112 pts **Aberdeen** – BBC incl maths/sci (Pharmacol) (IB 32 pts HL 555 incl maths/sci)
East London – B biol/chem 112 pts (Pharmacol) (IB 25 pts HL 15 pts incl biol+chem)
Kingston – C biol/chem 112–128 pts (Pharmacol)
London Met – C chem 112 pts (Pharmacol)
Portsmouth – BBC–BBB incl biol/chem+sci/maths 112–120 pts (Pharmacol) (IB 29 pts)
West London – BBC incl sci 112–120 pts (Pharmacol)

104 pts **Central Lancashire** – C biol/chem 104–120 pts (Physiol Pharmacol)
Chester – BCC–BBC incl chem (Pharmacol) (IB 26 pts HL 5 chem)
Glasgow Caledonian – BCC incl chem (Pharmacol)
Swansea – BCC–AAB incl chem+sci (Med Pharmacol) (IB 33 pts HL 6 chem+sci)

96 pts **Westminster** – CCC incl sci/maths 96 pts (Pharmacol Physiol)
Wolverhampton – CCC/BCD incl chem/biol 96 pts (Pharmacol)

Alternative offers See **Chapter 6** and **Appendix 1** for grades/UCAS Tariff points information for other examinations.

DEGREE APPRENTICESHIPS

Greenwich (Pharml Sci); London (King's) (Clin Pharmacol).

CHOOSING YOUR COURSE (SEE ALSO CH.1)

Universities and colleges teaching quality See www.qaa.ac.uk; www.discoveruni.gov.uk.

Examples of sandwich degree courses Bristol; East London; Kingston; Leeds; Manchester; Nottingham Trent.

ADMISSIONS INFORMATION

Advice to applicants and planning the UCAS personal statement Contact with the pharmaceutical industry is important in order to be aware of the range of work undertaken. Read pharmaceutical journals (although note that Pharmacology and Pharmacy courses lead to different careers). See also **Pharmacy and Pharmaceutical Sciences**.

Selection interviews Yes Cambridge; **Some** Bath; **No** Newcastle.

Interview advice and questions Past questions include: Why do you want to do Pharmacology? Why not Pharmacy? Why not Chemistry? How are pharmacologists employed in industry? What are the issues raised by anti-vivisectionists on animal experimentation? Questions relating to the A-level syllabus in chemistry and biology. See also **Chapter 5**.

Reasons for rejection (non-academic) Confusion between pharmacology, pharmacy and pharmaceutical sciences. One university rejected two applicants because they had no motivation or understanding of the course (one had A-levels at AAB!). Insurance against rejection for Medicine. Lack of knowledge about pharmacology as a subject.

GRADUATE DESTINATIONS AND EMPLOYMENT

(See **Chapter 1, Graduate Outcomes.**)

Career note The majority of pharmacologists work with the large pharmaceutical companies involved in research and development. A small number are employed by the NHS in medical research and clinical trials. Some will eventually diversify and become involved in marketing, sales and advertising.

OTHER DEGREE SUBJECTS FOR CONSIDERATION

Biochemistry; Biological Sciences; Biology; Biotechnology; Chemistry; Life Sciences; Medical Biochemistry; Medicinal Chemistry; Microbiology; Natural Sciences; Pharmaceutical Sciences; Pharmacy; Physiology; Toxicology.

PHARMACY AND PHARMACEUTICAL SCIENCES

(including **Herbal Medicine**; see also **Biochemistry, Chemistry, Health Sciences/Studies**)

Pharmacy is the science of medicines, involving research into chemical structures and natural products of possible medicinal value, the development of dosage and the safety testing of products. This table also includes information on courses in Pharmaceutical Science (which should not be confused with Pharmacy) which is a multi-disciplinary subject covering chemistry, biochemistry, pharmacology and medical issues. Pharmaceutical scientists apply their knowledge of science and the biology of disease to the design and delivery of therapeutic agents. Note: All Pharmacy courses leading to MPharm are four years. Only Pharmacy degree courses accredited by the Royal Phamaceutical Society of Great Britain lead to a qualification as a pharmacist. Check prospectuses and websites.

Useful websites www.rpharms.com; www.chemistanddruggist.co.uk

NB The points totals shown to the left of the institutions are for ease of reference only. It must not be assumed that Tariff points are always used by institutions or that they can be substituted for an offer in grades. The level of an offer is not necessarily indicative of the quality of a course.

COURSE OFFERS INFORMATION

Subject requirements/preferences GCSE English, mathematics and science subjects. **AL** Chemistry and one or two other sciences required for most courses. Some popular universities are now making lower offers for disadvantaged and other students.

Your target offers and examples of degree courses

136 pts **Bath** – AAB/ABB+aEPQ incl chem+sci/maths+interview (MPharm) (IB 35 pts HL 665 incl chem+sci/maths)

Birmingham – AAB incl chem+sci/maths (MPharm) (IB 32 pts HL 665 incl chem+sci/maths)

East Anglia – AAB incl chem+sci/maths+interview (MPharm) (IB 33 pts HL 5 chem+sci/maths)

London (King's) – AAB incl chem+sci/maths (MPharm) (IB 35 pts HL 17 pts incl 65 chem+sci/maths)

London (UCL) – AAB incl chem+sci/maths+interview (MPharm) (IB 36 pts HL 17 pts incl chem+sci/maths)

Manchester – AAB incl chem+maths/biol+interview (MPharm) (IB 35 pts HL 6 chem 6/5 maths/biol)

Newcastle – AAB incl chem+sci/maths (MPharm) (IB 34 pts HL 5 chem+sci/maths)

Nottingham – AAB incl chem+sci/maths+interview (MPharm) (IB 34 pts HL 665 incl 6 chem 6/5 sci/maths)

Queen's Belfast – AAB incl chem+sci/maths (MPharm) (IB 34 pts HL 665 incl chem+sci/maths)

Strathclyde – AAB incl chem+biol+interview (Pharm) (IB 34 pts HL 6 chem 6 biol)

Ulster – AAB incl chem+sci/maths (MPharm) (IB 28 pts HL 14 pts incl 6 chem 7 sci/maths)

128 pts **Bradford** – ABB incl chem/biol+sci 128 pts+interview (MPharm) (HL 665 incl 6 chem/biol+sci)

Cardiff – ABB–AAB incl chem/biol+sci/maths+interview (MPharm) (IB 32–34 pts HL 665 incl 6 chem/biol 6 sci/maths)
Hertfordshire – ABB–AAB incl chem+sci/maths 128–136 pts (MPharm)
Keele – ABB incl biol/chem+interview (MPharm) (IB 32 pts HL 655 incl 6 biol/chem)
Leicester – ABB incl biol/chem+sci+interview (MPharm) (IB 30 pts HL 665 incl chem+biol)
London (QM) – ABB incl chem (Pharml Chem) (IB 34 pts HL 655 incl chem)
Loughborough – ABB incl chem+interview (Medcnl Pharml Chem) (IB 34 pts HL 655 incl chem)
Medway Sch Pharm – ABB incl chem+sci (MPharm) (IB 32 pts HL 15 pts incl 5 chem+sci)
Reading – ABB incl chem+sci/maths+interview (MPharm) (IB 32 pts HL 6 chem 5 sci)

120 pts **Aston** – BBB–ABB incl chem+sci/maths (MPharm) (IB 32 pts HL 655 incl chem+sci/maths)
Brighton – BBB–ABB incl chem+sci 120–128 pts+interview+test (MPharm) (IB 32 pts HL 5 chem+biol)
Central Lancashire – BBB incl chem/biol+sci+interview (MPharm)
De Montfort – 120 pts incl chem+sci/maths/psy+interview (MPharm) (IB 30 pts HL 6 chem+sci/maths/psy)
Huddersfield – BBB–ABB incl chem+sci/maths 120–136 pts+interview (MPharm)
Kingston – 120–136 pts incl chem+sci/maths+interview (MPharm)
Leicester – BBB–ABB incl chem (Medcnl Chem) (IB 28 pts HL 5 chem)
Liverpool John Moores – BBB incl chem/biol+sci/maths/psy 120–128 pts (MPharm)
Portsmouth – BBB–AAB incl chem+sci/maths+interview+test (MPharm) (IB 29–30 pts)
Reading – BBB incl chem (Pharml Chem) (IB 30 pts HL 5 chem)
Sunderland – B chem+sci 120 pts (MPharm)
Swansea – BBB–ABB incl chem+sci (MPharm)
Wolverhampton – BBB incl chem+sci 120 pts+interview (MPharm)

112 pts **East London** – B biol/chem 112 pts (Pharml Sci) (IB 25 pts HL 15 pts incl biol+chem)
Hertfordshire – BBC–BBB incl C biol/chem+sci (Pharml Sci)
Kingston – C chem+sci/maths 112–128 pts (Pharml Sci)
London Met – C chem 112 pts (Pharml Sci)
Robert Gordon – BBC incl chem+sci/maths (MPharm) (IB 29 pts HL 6 chem 5 Engl+sci/maths)

104 pts **Greenwich** – 104 pts incl chem (Pharml Sci)
Huddersfield – BCC–BBC incl biol/chem 104–112 pts (Pharml Chem)
Lincoln – 104 pts (Pharml Sci) (IB 28 pts HL 4 sci)
Manchester Met – BCC incl chem 104–120 pts (Medcnl Pharml Chem (MChem)) (IB 26 pts HL 5 chem)
South Wales – BCC incl chem+sci 104 pts (Pharml Sci)

96 pts **De Montfort** – 96 pts incl chem+sci (Pharml Cos Sci) (IB 24 pts HL 6 chem+sci)
Reading – CCC–BBB (Pharml Chem Fdn) (IB 24–30 pts)
Wolverhampton – CCC/BCD incl chem 96 pts (Pharml Sci)

Alternative offers See **Chapter 6** and **Appendix 1** for grades/UCAS Tariff points information for other examinations.

DEGREE APPRENTICESHIPS

Greenwich (Pharml Sci); Ulster (App Pharml Sci).

CHOOSING YOUR COURSE (SEE ALSO CH.1)

Universities and colleges teaching quality See www.qaa.ac.uk; www.discoveruni.gov.uk.

Top research universities and colleges (REF 2021) (Allied Health Professions, Dentistry, Nursing and Pharmacy) London (King's); Manchester; Southampton; Queen's Belfast; Nottingham; Swansea; Keele; Newcastle; Bath; Leeds.

Examples of sandwich degree courses Bradford; De Montfort; Greenwich; Hertfordshire; Reading.

ADMISSIONS INFORMATION

Advice to applicants and planning the UCAS personal statement Work experience and work shadowing with a retail and/or hospital pharmacist is important, and essential for Pharmacy applicants. Read pharmaceutical journals, extend your knowledge of well-known drugs and antibiotics. Read up on the history of drugs. Attend Open Days or careers conferences. See also **Appendix 3**.

Selection interviews Yes Bath, Bradford, Brighton, Cardiff, Central Lancashire, De Montfort, East Anglia, Huddersfield, Keele, Kingston (MPharm), Leicester, Liverpool John Moores, London (UCL), Manchester, Nottingham, Portsmouth, Reading (MPharm), Robert Gordon, Strathclyde, Wolverhampton; **Some** Loughborough.

Interview advice and questions As work experience is essential for Pharmacy applicants, questions are likely to focus on this and what they have discovered. Other relevant questions could include: Why do you want to study Pharmacy? What types of work do pharmacists do? What interests you about the Pharmacy course? What branch of pharmacy do you want to enter? Name a drug – what do you know about it (formula, use, etc)? Name a drug from a natural source and its use. Can you think of another way of extracting a drug? Why do fungi destroy bacteria? What is an antibiotic? Can you name one and say how it was discovered? What is insulin? What is its source and function? What is diabetes? What type of insulin is used in its treatment? What is a hormone? What drugs are available over the counter without prescription? What is the formula of aspirin? What is genetic engineering? See also **Chapter 5**.

Reasons for rejection (non-academic) Poor communication skills. Poor knowledge of pharmacy and the work of a pharmacist.

GRADUATE DESTINATIONS AND EMPLOYMENT

(See **Chapter 1, Graduate Outcomes.**)

Career note The majority of Pharmacy graduates proceed to work in the commercial and retail fields, although opportunities also exist with pharmaceutical companies and in hospital pharmacies. There are also opportunities in agricultural and veterinary pharmacy.

OTHER DEGREE SUBJECTS FOR CONSIDERATION

Biochemistry; Biological Sciences; Biology; Biotechnology; Chemistry; Drug Development; Life Sciences; Medicinal Chemistry; Microbiology; Natural Sciences; Pharmacology; Physiology.

PHILOSOPHY

(see also **Philosophy, Politics and Economics (PPE), Psychology**)

Philosophy is one of the oldest and most fundamental disciplines, which examines the nature of the universe and humanity's place in it. Philosophy seeks to discover the essence of the mind, language and physical reality and discusses the methods used to investigate these topics.

Useful websites www.iep.utm.edu; www.philosophypages.com; http://royalinstitutephilosophy.org; see also **Religious Studies**.

NB The points totals shown to the left of the institutions are for ease of reference only. It must not be assumed that Tariff points are always used by institutions or that they can be substituted for an offer in grades. The level of an offer is not necessarily indicative of the quality of a course.

COURSE OFFERS INFORMATION

Subject requirements/preferences GCSE English and mathematics. A foreign language may be required. **AL** No specific subjects except for joint courses. Some popular universities are now making lower offers for disadvantaged and other students.

YOUR TARGET OFFERS AND EXAMPLES OF DEGREE COURSES

160 pts **Oxford** – A*A*A incl A* maths+interview+MAT (Maths Phil) (IB 39 pts HL 766 incl 7 maths)

152 pts **Bristol** – A*AA incl maths (Maths Phil) (IB 38 pts HL 18 pts incl 7 maths); A*AA incl maths+phys (Phys Phil) (IB 38 pts HL 18 pts incl 76 maths+phys)
Cambridge – A*AA+interview+test (Phil) (IB 41–42 pts HL 776)
Durham – A*AA incl Engl (Engl Lit Phil) (IB 38 pts HL 666 incl Engl)
London (King's) – A*AA+LNAT (Pol Phil Law) (IB 38 pts HL 19 pts)
Manchester – A*AA incl A* maths (Maths Phil) (IB 37 pts HL 766 incl 7 maths)
Oxford – A*AA+interview+TSA (Psy Phil Ling) (IB 39 pts HL 766)

144 pts **Bristol** – AAA (Phil; Phil Theol) (IB 36 pts HL 18 pts); AAA incl maths (Phil Econ) (IB 36 pts HL 18 pts incl 6 maths)
Durham – AAA (Phil) (IB 37 pts HL 666); AAA incl soc sci/hum (Phil Pol) (IB 37 pts HL 666)
Edinburgh – AAA (Phil) (IB 37 pts HL 666)
Exeter – AAA (Phil; Phil Pol) (IB 36 pts HL 666)
Lancaster – AAA incl maths/fmaths (Maths Phil) (IB 36 pts HL 16 pts incl 6 maths)
London (King's) – AAA (Phil courses) (IB 36 pts HL 18 pts); AAA incl maths+fmaths (Maths Phil) (IB 36 pts HL 18 pts incl 6 maths)
London (UCL) – AAA (Phil) (IB 38 pts HL 18 pts)
London LSE – AAA (Phil Lgc Sci Meth; Pol Phil) (IB 38 pts HL 766); AAA incl maths (Phil Econ) (IB 38 pts HL 766 incl maths)
Oxford – AAA+interview+MLAT (Phil Modn Langs) (IB 39 pts HL 666); AAA+PhilAT (Phil Theol) (IB 39 pts HL 666)
Warwick – AAA (Phil) (IB 34–36 pts)

136 pts **Birmingham** – AAB (Phil) (IB 32 pts HL 665)
Bristol – AAB (Sociol Phil) (IB 34 pts HL 17 pts); AAB incl lang (Phil Modn Lang) (IB 34 pts HL 17 pts incl 5 lang)
Lancaster – AAB (Ling Phil) (IB 35 pts HL 16 pts)
Leeds – AAB (Ling Phil; Phil; Phil Comb Hons) (IB 35 pts HL 16 pts); AAB incl hist (Hist Phil) (IB 35 pts HL 16 pts incl 6 hist)
Liverpool – AAB/ABB+aEPQ (Phil) (IB 35 pts)
London (King's) – AAB (Relgn Phil Eth) (IB 35 pts); (Phil Modn Lang (Yr Abrd)) (IB 35 pts HL 17 pts)
London (UCL) – AAB (Hist Phil Sci) (IB 36 pts HL 17 pts)
NU London – AAB (Phil courses) (IB 35 pts HL 665)
Nottingham – AAB (Phil) (IB 32 pts HL 665); AAB/A*BB (Phil Psy) (IB 32 pts HL 665); AAB incl A Engl (Engl Phil) (IB 32 pts HL 665 incl 6 Engl)
Sheffield – AAB/ABB+bEPQ (Phil Comb Hons; Pol Phil) (IB 34 pts); AAB–ABB+bEPQ (Phil) (IB 34 pts)
St Andrews – AAB (Phil courses) (IB 36 pts HL 665)
Warwick – AAB (Phil Comb Hons) (IB 36 pts)
York – AAB (Phil; Phil Ling; Phil Pol) (IB 35 pts); AAB incl Engl (Engl Phil) (IB 35 pts HL 6 Engl); AAB incl maths+phys (Phys Phil) (IB 35 pts HL 6 maths+phys)

128 pts **Central Lancashire** – ABB (Phil) (IB 32 pts HL 16 pts)
East Anglia – ABB (Phil; Phil Pol) (IB 32 pts)
Lancaster – ABB (Phil) (IB 32 pts HL 16 pts); ABB 128 pts (Glob Relgn Phil) (IB 32 pts HL 16 pts)
Liverpool – ABB (Maths Phil) (IB 33 pts)
Manchester – ABB (Phil; Theol St Phil Eth) (IB 34 pts HL 655)
Newcastle – ABB–AAB (Phil Comb Hons) (IB 32–34 pts HL 555–556)
Nottingham – ABB (Class Civ Phil; Phil Theol; Relgn Phil Eth) (IB 30 pts HL 655)
Queen's Belfast – ABB (Phil courses) (IB 33 pts HL 655)
Sheffield – ABB (Engl Phil) (IB 33 pts)
Southampton – ABB (Phil; Phil Pol) (IB 32 pts HL 16 pts); (Econ Phil) (IB 32 pts HL 16 pts incl 5 maths); ABB/BBB+aEPQ incl Engl (Phil Engl) (IB 32 pts HL 16 pts incl 5 Engl); ABB incl hist (Phil Hist) (IB 32 pts HL 16 pts incl 5 hist)

Sussex – ABB (Phil) (IB 32 pts)

120 pts **Dundee** – BBB (Euro Phil; Phil) (IB 30 pts HL 555)

Glasgow – BBB–AAB (Phil) (IB 34 pts HL 655 incl Engl+hum)

Hull – BBB 120 pts (Phil) (IB 30 pts)

London (RH) – BBB–ABB (Pol Phil) (IB 32 pts HL 655); BBB–ABB (Phil) (IB 32 pts HL 555); BBB–ABB+gr 7 (Mus Phil) (IB 32 pts HL 655 incl 6 mus)

Reading – BBB (Phil courses) (IB 30 pts); BBB+portfolio (Art Phil) (IB 30 pts)

Stirling – BBB (Phil) (IB 28 pts)

112 pts **Aberdeen** – BBC (Phil Comb Hons) (IB 32 pts HL 555); BBC incl maths+phys (Nat Phil) (IB 32 pts HL 555 incl maths+phys)

Cardiff – BBC–ABB (Phil) (IB 30–32 pts HL 655–665)

Essex – BBC (Phil Law) (IB 29 pts HL 554); BBC 112–120 pts (Phil Hist) (IB 29–30 pts HL 554–555); BBC–BBB 112–120 pts (Phil) (IB 29–30 pts HL 554–555)

Hertfordshire – 112–120 pts (Phil)

Keele – BBC (Phil) (IB 29 pts HL 554)

London (Birk) – BBC (Phil); BBC 112 pts (Pol Phil Hist)

Nottingham Trent – 112 pts (Phil Comb Hons)

UWE Bristol – 112 pts (Phil)

104 pts **Bangor** – 104–128 pts (Phil Eth Relgn)

Bath Spa – BCC–BBB 104–120 pts (Phil Eth) (IB 32 pts)

Birmingham Newman – 104–136 pts (Theol Phil)

Brighton – BCC–BBB 104–120 pts (Phil Pol Eth) (IB 26 pts)

Leeds Trinity – 104–136 pts (Phil Eth Relgn)

Liverpool Hope – BCC 104 pts (Phil Eth Comb Hons; Phil Eth Relgn) (IB 24 pts)

Manchester Met – 104–112 pts (Phil; Pol Phil) (IB 26 pts)

Oxford Brookes – BCC 104 pts (Phil) (IB 29 pts)

Winchester – 104–120 pts (Phil)

York St John – 104 pts (Relgn Phil Eth)

96 pts **Anglia Ruskin** – 96 pts (Phil; Phil Engl Lit) (IB 24 pts)

Bishop Grosseteste – 96–112 pts (Theol Phil Eth)

Chichester – CCC–BBC 96–112 pts (Phil Eth) (IB 28 pts)

Gloucestershire – CCC–BBC 96–112 pts (Relgn Phil Eth)

Roehampton – 96–112 pts (Phil Relgn Eth)

Trinity Saint David – 96–112 pts (Phil; Phil Comb Hons)

Open University – (Phil Psy St)

ALTERNATIVE OFFERS See **Chapter 6** and **Appendix 1** for grades/UCAS Tariff points information for other examinations.

CHOOSING YOUR COURSE (SEE ALSO CH.1)

UNIVERSITIES AND COLLEGES TEACHING QUALITY See www.qaa.ac.uk; www.discoveruni.gov.uk.

TOP RESEARCH UNIVERSITIES AND COLLEGES (REF 2021) (Philosophy) Birmingham; York; London (UCL); London LSE; Kent; Southampton; Manchester; Warwick; Glasgow; Cambridge.

ADMISSIONS INFORMATION

ADVICE TO APPLICANTS AND PLANNING THE UCAS PERSONAL STATEMENT Read Bertrand Russell's *Problems of Philosophy*. Refer to any particular aspects of philosophy which interest you (check that these are offered on the courses for which you are applying). Selectors will expect applicants to have read around the subject. Explain what you know about the nature of studying philosophy. Say what you have read in philosophy and give an example of a philosophical issue that interests you. Universities do not expect applicants to have a wide knowledge of the subject, but evidence that you know what the subject is about is important.

SELECTION INTERVIEWS Yes Cambridge, Oxford (Phil Mod Lang) 84% (success rate 30%), (PPE) 35% (success rate 11%), (Phil Theol) 38% (success rate 18%); **Some** Bristol, Dundee, Durham (Mature applicants with non-standard qualifications), East Anglia; **No** London (UCL), London LSE, Newcastle, Warwick.

Interview advice and questions Philosophy is a very wide subject and initially applicants will be asked for their reasons for their choice and their special interests in the subject. Questions in recent years have included: Is there a difference between being tactless and being insensitive? Can you be tactless and thin-skinned? Define the difference between knowledge and belief. Was the vertical distortion of El Greco's paintings a product of a vision defect? What is the point of studying philosophy? What books on philosophy have you read? Discuss the work of a renowned philosopher. What is a philosophical novel? Who has the right to decide your future – yourself or another? What do you want to do with your life? What is a philosophical question? What is the difference between a man's entitlements, his deserts and his attributes? What are morals? A good understanding of philosophy is needed for entry to degree courses, and applicants are expected to demonstrate this if they are called to interview. As one admissions tutor stated, 'If you find Bertrand Russell's *Problems of Philosophy* unreadable – don't apply!' See also **Chapter 5**.

Reasons for rejection (non-academic) Lack of knowledge of philosophy.

GRADUATE DESTINATIONS AND EMPLOYMENT

(See **Chapter 1, Graduate Outcomes.**)

Career note Graduates have a wide range of transferable skills that can lead to employment in many areas, eg management, public administration, publishing, banking and social services.

OTHER DEGREE SUBJECTS FOR CONSIDERATION

Divinity; History and Philosophy of Science; History of Art; Human Sciences; Psychology; Religious Studies; Science; Theology.

PHILOSOPHY, POLITICS AND ECONOMICS (PPE)

(see also **Economics, Philosophy, Politics**)

Philosophy, Politics and Economics is an interdisciplinary study combination. Graduates of this prestigious trio of disciplines include five Prime Ministers of the United Kingdom, including Rishi Sunak, as well as leaders of Australia and Pakistan. These days, PPE attracts the interest of those interested in governance and a wide range of other careers, including business, media and human rights. Although originally pioneered by Oxford University, a broad range of British universities now offer PPE. Courses encourage reflection on how Philosophy, Politics and Economics interrelate and bear influence upon public and political life and enable students to approach issues critically from different angles.

NB The points totals shown to the left of the institutions are for ease of reference only. It must not be assumed that Tariff points are always used by institutions or that they can be substituted for an offer in grades. The level of an offer is not necessarily indicative of the quality of a course.

COURSE OFFERS INFORMATION

Subject requirements/preferences GCSE Specific grades in some subjects may be specified by some popular universities. **AL** English, a modern language, humanities or social science subjects preferred. Some popular universities are now making lower offers for disadvantaged and other students.

Your target offers and examples of degree courses

152 pts **Durham** – A*AA incl maths+art/hum (PPE) (IB 38 pts HL 666 incl maths+art/hum)
London (King's) – A*AA (PPE) (IB 38 pts HL 19 pts)
London (UCL) – A*AA incl A* maths (PPE) (IB 39 pts HL 19 pts incl 7 maths)
London LSE – A*AA incl A* maths (PPE) (IB 38 pts HL 766 incl 7 maths)
Nottingham – A*AA (PPE) (IB 36 pts HL 766)
Warwick – A*AA (PPE) (IB 38 pts HL 4 maths)

144 pts **Exeter** – AAA (PPE) (IB 36 pts HL 666)
Leeds – AAA (PPE) (IB 35 pts HL 17 pts incl 5 maths)
Manchester – AAA (PPE) (IB 36 pts HL 666)
Oxford – AAA+interview+TSA (PPE) (IB 39 pts HL 766)
Queen's Belfast – AAA (PPE) (IB 36 pts HL 666)
136 pts **Lancaster** – AAB (PPE) (IB 35 pts HL 16 pts)
Loughborough – AAB (PPE) (IB 36 pts HL 665)
Sussex – AAB (PPE) (IB 34 pts)
York – AAB incl maths (PPE) (IB 35 pts incl maths)
128 pts **East Anglia** – ABB (PPE) (IB 32 pts)
Reading – ABB (PPE) (IB 32 pts)
Southampton – ABB incl maths/phys/stats (PPE) (IB 32 pts HL 16 pts incl 5 maths)
120 pts **London (Gold)** – BBB (PPE) (IB 33 pts HL 655)
London (RH) – BBB–ABB (PPE) (IB 32 pts HL 655)
Stirling – BBB (PPE) (IB 28 pts)
112 pts **Essex** – BBC–BBB 112–120 pts (PPE) (IB 29–30 pts HL 554–555)
Hull – BBC (PPE) (IB 28 pts)
104 pts **Bath Spa** – BCC–BBB 104–120 pts (PPE) (IB 32 pts)
72 pts **UHI** – BC (PPE)

Open University – (PPE)

Alternative offers See **Chapter 6** and **Appendix 1** for grades/UCAS Tariff points information for other examinations.

CHOOSING YOUR COURSE (SEE ALSO CH.1)

Universities and colleges teaching quality See www.qaa.ac.uk; www.discoveruni.gov.uk.

Examples of sandwich degree courses Lancaster; Loughborough; York.

ADMISSIONS INFORMATION

Admissions tutors' advice Admissions tutors expect evidence of capacity for sustained study, motivation and interest as well as an independent and reflective approach to learning. Reasoning, as demonstrated by the ability to analyse and solve problems using logical and critical approaches and construct and critically assess arguments, is also sought after. Finally, prospective students should show willingness and ability to express ideas clearly and effectively on paper and orally, as well as an ability to listen.

Selection interviews Yes Oxford (35% (success rate 11%)).

GRADUATE DESTINATIONS AND EMPLOYMENT

(See **Chapter 1, Graduate Outcomes**.)

OTHER DEGREE SUBJECTS FOR CONSIDERATION

Economics; History; International Relations; Philosophy; Politics.

PHOTOGRAPHY

(see also **Art and Design (Fine Art), Art and Design (General), Film, Radio and TV Studies, Media Studies**)

Photography courses offer a range of specialised studies involving commercial, industrial and still photography, portraiture and film, digital and video work. Increasingly this subject is featuring in Media courses. See also **Appendix 3**.

Useful websites www.the-aop.org; https://rps.org; www.1854.photography; www.bipp.com

NB The points totals shown to the left of the institutions are for ease of reference only. It must not be assumed that Tariff points are always used by institutions or that they can be substituted for an offer in grades. The level of an offer is not necessarily indicative of the quality of a course.

COURSE OFFERS INFORMATION

SUBJECT REQUIREMENTS/PREFERENCES GCSE Art and/or a portfolio usually required. **AL** One or two subjects may be required, including an art/design or creative subject. Some popular universities are now making lower offers for disadvantaged and other students. Most institutions will make offers on the basis of a portfolio of work.

YOUR TARGET OFFERS AND EXAMPLES OF DEGREE COURSES

136 pts **Leeds** – AAB (Flm Photo Media) (IB 35 pts HL 16 pts)

128 pts **Glasgow (SA)** – ABB+portfolio (Fn Art Photo)

120 pts **Coventry** – BBB+portfolio (Photo) (IB 31 pts)

Trinity Saint David – 120 pts (Doc Photo Vis Actvsm; Photo Arts) (IB 32 pts)

112 pts **Arts London** – 112 pts+interview+portfolio (Fash Photo) (IB 25 pts)

Birmingham City – BBC 112 pts+portfolio (Photo) (IB 28 pts HL 14 pts)

Bournemouth Arts – BBC–BBB 112–120 pts+portfolio+interview (Commer Photo; Photo)

Canterbury Christ Church – BBC 112 pts+portfolio (Photo) (IB 29 pts)

Creative Arts – 112 pts+portfolio (Photo) (IB 27–30 pts HL 15 pts)

De Montfort – 112 pts+portfolio (Photo Vid) (IB 26 pts)

East London – 112 pts+portfolio (Photo) (IB 24 pts HL 15 pts)

Kingston – 112–128 pts incl art des (Photo)

Middlesex – 112–128 pts+portfolio (Photo)

Nottingham Trent – BBC 112 pts+portfolio+interview (Photo)

Oxford Brookes – BBC 112 pts+interview+portfolio (Photo) (IB 30 pts)

Portsmouth – 112–120 pts+portfolio (Photo) (IB 25 pts)

Sheffield Hallam – BBC 112 pts+portfolio (Photo)

Staffordshire – BBC 112 pts+interview+portfolio (Photo)

Sunderland – 112 pts+portfolio+interview (Photo Vid Dig Imag)

UWE Bristol – 112 pts+interview+portfolio (Photo)

West London – BBC 112 pts+portfolio (Photo)

104 pts **Arts London** – 104 pts+portfolio (Photo) (IB 24 pts)

Bath Spa – BCC incl photo+portfolio+interview (Photo) (IB 32 pts HL 5 photo/art)

Bournemouth – 104–120 pts (Photo)

Brighton – BCC–BBB 104–120 pts+portfolio (Photo) (IB 30 pts)

Chester – BCC–BBC incl art/des/photo 104–112 pts+interview (Photo) (IB 26 pts HL 5 vis arts)

Cumbria – 104–112 pts+interview (Photo)

Derby – 104–112 pts+portfolio (Photo)

Falmouth – 104–120 pts+interview+portfolio (Fash Photo); 104–120 pts+portfolio+interview (Doc Edit Photo; Mar Nat Hist Photo; Photo)

Huddersfield – BCC–BBB 104–120 pts+portfolio (Photo)

Leeds Arts – 104–120 pts+portfolio (Photo)

Lincoln – 104 pts (Photo) (IB 28 pts)

Manchester Met – 104–112 pts+portfolio (Photo) (IB 26 pts)

Northampton – BCC+portfolio (Photo)

Norwich Arts – BCC 104 pts+interview+portfolio (Photo) (IB 26 pts)

Plymouth (AU) – 104–120 pts+portfolio (Photo)

Solent – 104–120 pts+interview+portfolio (Photo)

South Wales – BCC incl art des 104 pts+interview+portfolio (Doc Photo)

96 pts **Anglia Ruskin** – 96 pts incl art/des/media+portfolio (Photo) (IB 24 pts)

Bedfordshire – 96 pts (Photo)

Central Lancashire – 96 pts+portfolio (Photo)

Gloucestershire – CCC–BBB 96–120 pts+interview (Photo); CCC–BBB 96–120 pts+interview (Photojrnl Doc Photo)

Greater Manchester – 96 pts incl art/des/photo+interview+portfolio (Photo)
Hereford (CA) – 96–112 pts (Photo)
Northern SA – 96–112 pts+portfolio (Photo)
Plymouth – 96–120 pts+portfolio (Photo) (IB 26–28 pts)
South Wales – CCC 96 pts+portfolio (Photo)
Teesside – 96–112 pts (Photo)
Ulster – CCC+portfolio (Photo Vid) (IB 24 pts HL 12 pts)
Westminster – CCC 96 pts+portfolio (Photo); CCC–BBB pts 96–120 pts (Fash Photo)
Wolverhampton – CCC/BCD 96 pts+portfolio (Photo)
64 pts **Ravensbourne Univ** – CC+portfolio (Dig Photo) (IB 24 pts)

Alternative offers See **Chapter 6** and **Appendix 1** for grades/UCAS Tariff points information for other examinations.

EXAMPLES OF COLLEGES OFFERING COURSES IN THIS SUBJECT FIELD

Barking and Dagenham (Coll); Bedford (Coll); Birmingham Met (Coll); Blackburn (Coll); Blackpool and Fylde (Coll); Brighton Met (Coll); Bristol City (Coll); Buckinghamshire (Coll Group); Canterbury (Coll); Central Campus, Sandwell (Coll); City and Islington (Coll); Coventry (Coll); Doncaster (Coll); East Coast (Coll); East Surrey (Coll); East Sussex (Coll); Exeter (Coll); Farnborough (CT); Gloucestershire (Coll); Grŵp Llandrillo Menai; Havering (Coll); Hugh Baird (Coll); Hull (Coll); Kirklees (Coll); Leeds City (Coll); Leicester (Coll); Lincoln (Coll); Manchester (Coll); Milton Keynes (Coll); Myerscough (Coll); Newcastle (Coll); North Warwickshire and South Leicestershire (Coll); Northumberland (Coll); Nottingham (Coll); Rotherham (CAT); Sheffield (Coll); Sir Gâr (Coll); Solihull (Coll); South Devon (Coll); South Essex (Coll); South Gloucestershire and Stroud (Coll); South Staffordshire (Coll); Southampton City (Coll); Southport (Coll); Southwark (Coll); St Helens (Coll); Stamford (Coll); Stockport (Coll); TEC Partnership; Tresham (CFHE); Truro and Penwith (Coll); Wakefield (Coll); Walsall (Coll); Westminster City (Coll); Weston (Coll); Weymouth (Coll); Wiltshire (Coll); Wirral Met (Coll); Yeovil (Coll).

CHOOSING YOUR COURSE (SEE ALSO CH.1)

Universities and colleges teaching quality See www.qaa.ac.uk; www.discoveruni.gov.uk.

Examples of sandwich degree courses Bournemouth Arts; Coventry; Leeds; Portsmouth; Wolverhampton.

ADMISSIONS INFORMATION

Advice to applicants and planning the UCAS personal statement Discuss your interest in photography and your knowledge of various aspects of the subject, for example, digital, video, landscape, medical, wildlife and portrait photography. Read photographic journals to keep up-to-date on developments, particularly in photographic technology. You will also need first-hand experience of photography and to be competent in basic skills. See also **Appendix 3**.

Selection interviews Yes Arts London, Bath Spa, Bournemouth Arts, Chester, Cumbria, Falmouth, Gloucestershire, Greater Manchester, Norwich Arts, Nottingham Trent, Oxford Brookes, Solent, Staffordshire, Sunderland; **Some** East London (Mature applicants and those with non-standard qualifications), UWE Bristol; **No** De Montfort, Huddersfield, Plymouth, West London.

Interview advice and questions Questions relate to the applicant's portfolio of work which, for these courses, is of prime importance. Who are your favourite photographers? What is the most recent exhibition you have attended? Have any leading photographers influenced your work? Questions regarding contemporary photography. Written work sometimes required. See **Chapter 5**.

Reasons for rejection (non-academic) Lack of passion for the subject. Lack of exploration and creativity in practical work. Poorly presented portfolio.

GRADUATE DESTINATIONS AND EMPLOYMENT

(See **Chapter 1, Graduate Outcomes.**)

Career note Opportunities for photographers exist in a range of specialisms, including advertising and editorial work, fashion, medical, industrial, scientific and technical photography. Some graduates also go into photojournalism and other aspects of the media.

OTHER DEGREE SUBJECTS FOR CONSIDERATION

Art and Design; Digital Animation; Film, Radio and TV Studies; Media Studies; Moving Image; Radiography.

PHYSICAL EDUCATION

(see also **Education Studies, Sports Sciences/Studies, Teacher Training**)

Physical Education courses are very popular and unfortunately restricted in number. Ability in gymnastics or an involvement in sport are obviously important factors.

Useful websites www.afpe.org.uk; www.uksport.gov.uk; see also **Education Studies** and **Teacher Training**.

NB The points totals shown to the left of the institutions are for ease of reference only. It must not be assumed that Tariff points are always used by institutions or that they can be substituted for an offer in grades. The level of an offer is not necessarily indicative of the quality of a course.

COURSE OFFERS INFORMATION

Subject requirements/preferences GCSE English, mathematics and a science. **AL** PE, sports studies and science are preferred subjects and for some courses one of these may be required. Some popular universities are now making lower offers for disadvantaged and other students. **Other** Disclosure and Barring Service (DBS) check before starting the course. Declaration of Health usually required.

Your target offers and examples of degree courses

128 pts **Birmingham** – ABB–AAB (Spo PE Coach Sci) (IB 32 pts HL 655–665)
East Anglia – ABB (PE) (IB 32 pts)
Edinburgh – ABB+interview (PE) (IB 34 pts HL 655 incl 5 Engl)

120 pts **Hartpury (Coll)** – BBB 120 pts (PE Sch Spo)

112 pts **Bangor** – 112–144 pts (Spo Sci PE Coach)
Bedfordshire – 112 pts (Spo PE)
Canterbury Christ Church – BBC 112 pts (PE Spo Exer Sci)
Chester – 112 pts (PE Spo Coach) (IB 28 pts)
East London – 112 pts incl PE/spo/sci (Spo PE Dev) (IB 24 pts HL 15 pts)
Greenwich – 112 pts (Spo Exer Sci)
Liverpool John Moores – BBC (PE)
RAc Dance – BBC+RAD Intermediate+audition (Ballet Educ)
Sheffield Hallam – BBC 112 pts (PE Sch Spo)
Staffordshire – BBC 112 pts (PE Yth Spo Coach)

104 pts **Anglia Ruskin** – 104 pts (Spo Coach PE) (IB 24 pts)
Brighton – BCC–BBB (PE (QTS)) (IB 30 pts)
Cardiff Met – 104–112 pts (Spo PE Hlth) (HL 6)
Cumbria – BCC–BBC 104–112 pts (Spo Coach PE)
Edge Hill – BCC–BBC 104–112 pts (PE Sch Spo)
Greenwich – 104 pts (PE Spo)
Leeds Beckett – 104–120 pts incl sci (PE Out Educ); 104–120 pts incl sci/PE (PE courses)
Leeds Trinity – 104 pts (PE Sch Spo)
Liverpool Hope – BCC 104 pts (Spo PE) (IB 24 pts)
Oxford Brookes – BCC 104 pts (Spo Coach PE) (IB 29 pts)
Solent – 104–120 pts (PE)
Worcester – 104 pts (PE Spo Coach)

York St John – 104 pts (PE Spo Coach)
96 pts **Bedfordshire** – 96 pts (Spo Coach Dev)
Cardiff Met – 96–112 pts (Spo Physl Educ Hlth (Dance)) (HL 6)
Chichester – CCC–BBC 96–112 pts+interview (PE Spo Coach)
Marjon – CCC 96 pts (PE; Spo Coach PE)
Trinity Saint David – 96 pts+interview (PE)

ALTERNATIVE OFFERS See **Chapter 6** and **Appendix 1** for grades/UCAS Tariff points information for other examinations.

EXAMPLES OF COLLEGES OFFERING COURSES IN THIS SUBJECT FIELD

City and Islington (Coll); Doncaster (Coll); Hartpury (Coll).

CHOOSING YOUR COURSE (SEE ALSO CH.1)

UNIVERSITIES AND COLLEGES TEACHING QUALITY See www.qaa.ac.uk; www.discoveruni.gov.uk.

TOP RESEARCH UNIVERSITIES AND COLLEGES (REF 2021) See **Sports Sciences/Studies**.

ADMISSIONS INFORMATION

ADVICE TO APPLICANTS AND PLANNING THE UCAS PERSONAL STATEMENT Ability in gymnastics, athletics and all sports and games is important. Full details of these activities should be given on the UCAS application – for example, teams, dates and awards achieved, assisting in extra-curricular activities. Involvement with local sports clubs, health clubs, summer camps, gap year. Relevant experience in coaching, teaching, community and youth work.

SELECTION INTERVIEWS Yes Chichester, Edinburgh, RAc Dance, Trinity Saint David.

INTERVIEW ADVICE AND QUESTIONS The applicant's interests in physical education will be discussed, with specific questions on, for example, sportsmanship, refereeing, umpiring and coaching. Questions in the past have also included: What qualities should a good netball goal defence possess? How could you encourage a group of children into believing that sport is fun? Do you think that physical education should be compulsory in schools? Why do you think you would make a good teacher? What is the name of the Education Minister?

REASONS FOR REJECTION (NON-ACADEMIC) Poor communication and presentational skills. Relatively poor sporting background or knowledge. Lack of knowledge about the teaching of physical education and the commitment required. Lack of ability in practicalities, for example, gymnastics, dance when relevant. Poor self-presentation. Poor writing skills.

GRADUATE DESTINATIONS AND EMPLOYMENT

(See **Chapter 1, Graduate Outcomes.**)

CAREER NOTE The majority of graduates go into teaching although, depending on any special interests, they may also go on into the sport and leisure industry.

OTHER DEGREE SUBJECTS FOR CONSIDERATION

Coach Education; Exercise and Fitness; Exercise Physiology; Human Biology; Leisure and Recreation; Physiotherapy; Sport and Exercise Science; Sport Health and Exercise; Sport Studies/Sciences; Sports Coaching; Sports Development; Sports Engineering; Sports Psychology; Sports Therapy.

PHYSICS

(see also **Astronomy and Astrophysics**)

Physics is an increasingly popular subject and a wide variety of courses are available which enables students to follow their own interests and specialisations. Some course options are nanotechnology, medical physics, cosmology, environmental physics and biophysics.

Useful websites www.iop.org; www.iop.org/explore-physics; www.scicentral.com; www.ipem.ac.uk; https://epsrc.ukri.org; http://jobs.newscientist.com; www.nature.com/subjects/physics

NB The points totals shown to the left of the institutions are for ease of reference only. It must not be assumed that Tariff points are always used by institutions or that they can be substituted for an offer in grades. The level of an offer is not necessarily indicative of the quality of a course.

COURSE OFFERS INFORMATION

Subject requirements/preferences GCSE English, mathematics and science. **AL** Physics and mathematics are required for most courses. Some popular universities are now making lower offers for disadvantaged and other students.

Your target offers and examples of degree courses

160 pts **Cambridge** – A*A*A incl sci/maths+interview+ESAT (Nat Sci (Phys/Astro)) (IB 41–42 pts HL 776 incl sci/maths)

Durham – A*A*A incl phys+maths (Phys; Phys Astron (MPhys); Theor Phys (MPhys)) (IB 38 pts HL 776 incl phys+maths)

Imperial London – A*A*A incl maths+phys+interview (Phys (Yr Abrd) (MSci)) (IB 40 pts HL 766 incl maths+phys); A*A*A incl maths+phys+test (Phys) (IB 40 pts HL 766 incl maths+phys)

Manchester – A*A*A incl A* maths+phys+interview (Phys Astro) (IB 38 pts HL 776 incl 7 maths+phys); (Phys) (IB 38 pts HL 776 incl maths+phys)

152 pts **Bath** – A*AA–AAA+aEPQ incl maths+phys (Maths Phys; Phys) (IB 36 pts HL 766 incl maths+phys)

Birmingham – A*AA incl maths+phys (Phys) (IB 32 pts HL 766 incl maths+phys)

Bristol – A*AA incl maths+phys (Phys; Phys Astro; Phys Phil) (IB 38 pts HL 18 pts incl 76 maths+phys)

Durham – A*AA incl biol/chem/maths (Nat Sci) (IB 38 pts HL 666–766 incl biol/chem/maths)

London (UCL) – A*AA incl maths+phys (Med Phys (MSci); Phys Med Phys) (IB 36 pts HL 17 pts incl 6 maths+phys); (Phys) (IB 39 pts HL 19 pts incl 6 maths+phys)

Nottingham – A*AA incl maths+phys (Mathem Phys) (IB 38 pts HL 666 incl maths+phys)

Oxford – A*AA incl maths+phys+interview+PAT (Phys) (IB 39 pts HL 766 incl maths+phys)

Warwick – A*AA incl maths+fmaths+phys (Phys Bus St) (IB 38 pts HL 6 maths+phys); A*AA incl maths/fmaths+phys (Phys) (IB 38 pts HL 6 maths+phys)

144 pts **Lancaster** – AAA incl maths+phys+interview (Phys Astro; Theor Phys) (IB 36 pts HL 16 incl 6 maths+phys); (Phys (MPhys)) (IB 36 pts HL 16 pts incl 6 maths+phys); AAA incl phys+maths (Theor Phys Maths) (IB 36 pts HL 16 pts incl 6 maths+phys); AAA incl phys+maths+interview (Phys) (IB 36 pts HL 16 pts incl 6 maths+phys)

Leeds – AAA incl maths+phys (Phys Astro) (HL 18 pts incl 5 maths+phys); AAA incl phys+maths (Phys) (HL 18 pts incl 5 phys+maths); (Theor Phys) (HL 18 pts incl 6 phys+maths)

London (King's) – AAA incl maths+phys (Phys; Phys Phil; Phys Theor Phys) (IB 36 pts HL 18 pts)

Nottingham – AAA incl maths+phys (Phys) (IB 34 pts HL 66 incl maths+phys); (Phys Astron; Phys Med Phys; Phys Theor Astro; Phys Theor Phys) (IB 34 pts HL 666 incl maths+phys)

Queen's Belfast – AAA/A*AB incl maths+phys (Phys (MSci); Phys Med Apps (MSci)) (IB 36 pts HL 666 incl maths+phys)

Sheffield – AAA/AAB+aEPQ incl maths+phys (Theor Phys) (IB 36 pts HL 5/6 maths+phys); AAA incl maths+phys (Phys (MPhys)) (IB 36 pts HL 6 maths+phys)

Southampton – AAA–A*AA incl maths/fmaths+phys (Phys Nanotech (MPhys); Phys Qntm Sci Tech; Phys Spc Sci (MPhys)) (IB 36–38 pts HL 18–19 pts incl 6 maths/fmaths+phys); AAA incl maths+phys (Mathem Phys (MMath)) (IB 36 pts HL 18 pts incl 6 maths+phys); AAA incl maths/fmaths+phys (Phys Maths (MPhys)) (IB 36 pts HL 18 pts incl 6 maths/fmaths+phys)

St Andrews – AAA incl maths+phys (Phys) (IB 38 pts HL 666 incl maths+phys)

York – AAA incl maths+phys+interview (Phys (MPhys)) (IB 36 pts HL 6 maths+phys)

136 pts **East Anglia** – AAB incl maths+phys (Phys (MPhys)) (IB 33 pts HL 6/5 maths+phys)

Exeter – AAB–AAA incl maths+phys (Maths Phys) (IB 34–36 pts HL 665–666 incl maths+phys)

Liverpool – AAB incl maths+phys (Mathem Phys (MMath); Phys (MPhys); Theor Phys (MPhys)) (IB 35 pts HL 6 maths+phys)

Liverpool John Moores – AAB incl maths+phys 136 pts (Astro (MPhys))

London (QM) – AAB incl A maths+phys (Astro (MSci)) (IB 34 pts HL 665 incl 6 maths+phys); AAB incl maths+phys (Phys (MSci)) (IB 34 pts HL 665 incl 6 maths+phys)

London (RH) – AAB–AAA incl maths+phys (Phys; Phys Ptcl Phys; Theor Phys) (IB 34 pts HL 666 incl maths+phys); AAB–AAA incl maths+phys+gr 7 (Phys Mus) (IB 34 pts HL 666 incl maths+mus+phys)

Loughborough – AAB incl maths+phys (Phys) (IB 34 pts HL 665 incl maths+phys); (Eng Phys; Phys Maths) (IB 35 pts HL 665 incl maths+phys)

Newcastle – AAB incl maths+phys (Phys (MPhys); Theor Phys) (IB 34 pts HL 6 maths+phys)

Queen's Belfast – AAB incl maths+phys (Theor Phys) (IB 34 pts HL 665 incl maths+phys)

Sheffield – AAB/ABB+aEPQ incl maths+phys (Phys; Phys Comb Hons) (IB 34 pts HL 5/6 maths+phys); AAB incl maths+phys (Phys Astro) (IB 34 pts HL 5/6 maths+phys)

Southampton – AAB–AAA incl maths/fmaths+phys (Phys) (IB 34–36 pts HL 17–18 pts incl 6 maths/fmaths+phys)

Sussex – AAB incl maths (Phys; Phys Astro) (IB 30 pts HL 5 maths); AAB incl maths+phys (Theor Phys) (IB 30 pts HL 5 maths+phys)

Swansea – AAB–A*AB incl maths+phys (Phys (MPhys)) (IB 34 pts HL 6 maths+phys)

York – AAB incl A maths+phys (Phys Astro) (IB 35 pts HL 6 maths+phys); AAB incl maths+phys (Maths Phys; Phys Phil) (IB 35 pts HL 6 maths+phys); AAB incl maths+phys+interview (Phys; Theor Phys) (IB 35 pts HL 6 maths+phys)

128 pts **Cardiff** – ABB–AAA incl phys+maths (Phys (MPhys)) (IB 32–36 pts HL 665–666 incl phys+maths)

East Anglia – ABB incl maths+phys (Phys) (IB 32 pts HL 5 maths+phys)

Edinburgh – ABB–AAA incl maths+phys (Geophys; Geophys Meteor) (IB 32–34 pts HL 655 incl 6 maths+5 phys); (Comput Phys; Mathem Phys; Phys; Phys Meteor; Theor Phys) (IB 32–37 pts HL 655–666 incl 6 maths+5 phys)

Exeter – ABB–AAA incl maths+phys (Phys) (IB 32–36 pts HL 655–666 incl maths+phys); ABB–AAA incl maths+phys (Phys Astro (MPhys)) (IB 32–36 pts HL 655–666 incl maths+phys)

Keele – ABB incl B phys/maths (Phys Astro) (IB 32 pts HL 655 incl maths/phys); ABB incl phys+maths (Phys Comb Hons) (IB 32 pts HL 655)

Kent – ABB incl maths (Phys Astro) (HL 665); ABB incl maths/phys (Phys) (IB 30 pts HL 665)

Leicester – ABB incl maths+phys (Phys; Phys Astro; Phys Spc Sci) (IB 30 pts HL 5 maths+phys)

Liverpool – ABB/BBB+aEPQ incl phys+maths (Phys; Phys Med Apps; Phys Nucl Sci) (IB 33 pts HL 6 phys+maths)

Liverpool John Moores – ABB incl maths+phys 128 pts (Phys Astron)

London (QM) – ABB incl maths+phys (Phys (Astro)) (IB 32 pts HL 655 incl 6 maths/phys)

Queen's Belfast – ABB incl maths+phys (Phys; Phys Astro; Phys Med Apps) (IB 33 pts HL 655 incl maths+phys)

Surrey – ABB incl maths+phys (Phys; Phys Qntm Tech) (IB 33 pts); (Phys Astron; Phys Nucl Astro) (IB 33 pts HL 5 maths+phys)

Swansea – ABB–A*AB incl maths+phys (Phys Ptcl Phys Cosmo) (IB 32 pts HL 5 maths+phys); ABB incl A maths (Theor Phys) (IB 32 pts HL 5 maths+phys)

120 pts **Cardiff** – BBB–AAB incl maths+phys (Phys Astron) (IB 31–34 pts HL 665–666 incl 6 maths+phys); BBB–AAB incl phys+maths (Phys; Phys Med Phys) (IB 31–34 pts HL 6 phys+maths)

Central Lancashire – B maths+phys 120 pts (Phys) (HL 5 maths+phys)

Dundee – BBB incl maths+phys/eng (Phys) (IB 30 pts HL 555 incl maths+phys/eng)

Glasgow – BBB–AAB incl maths+phys (Phys) (IB 34 pts HL 655 incl maths+phys); (Phys Astro) (IB 34 pts HL 655 incl maths+phys)

Hertfordshire – BBB–ABB incl maths+phys (Phys) (HL 4 maths+phys)
Hull – BBB incl maths+phys (Phys; Phys Astro) (IB 30 pts HL 6 maths+phys)
Nottingham Trent – 120 pts incl phys+maths (Phys Nucl Tech); B maths+phys 120 pts (Phys Maths); C maths+phys 120 pts (Phys; Phys Astro)
Strathclyde – BBB incl phys+maths (Phys) (IB 30 pts HL 5 phys+maths)

112 pts **Aberdeen** – BBC incl maths+phys (Nat Phil; Phys) (IB 32 pts HL 555 incl maths+phys)
Aberystwyth – BBC–BBB incl B maths+phys 112–120 pts (Spc Sci Robot) (IB 28–30 pts HL 5 maths+phys); BBC–BBB incl maths+phys 112–120 pts (Phys courses) (IB 28–30 pts HL 5 maths+phys)
Portsmouth – BBC–BBB 112–120 pts incl maths+phys (Phys (MPhys)) (IB 29 pts)
Swansea – BBC–AAB incl B maths (Phys) (IB 32 pts HL 5 maths+phys)

104 pts **Heriot-Watt** – BCC–BBB incl maths+phys (Phys courses) (IB 29 pts)
Lincoln – 104 pts incl maths+phys (Phys) (IB 28 pts HL 5 maths+phys)
Salford – 104–112 pts incl maths+phys (Phys) (IB 30 pts HL 5 maths+phys)

88 pts **West Scotland** – CCD incl maths+phys 88 pts (Phys) (IB 24 pts incl maths+phys)

Open University – (Nat Sci (Phys))

Alternative offers See **Chapter 6** and **Appendix 1** for grades/UCAS Tariff points information for other examinations.

CHOOSING YOUR COURSE (SEE ALSO CH.1)

Universities and colleges teaching quality See www.qaa.ac.uk; www.discoveruni.gov.uk.

Top research universities and colleges (REF 2021) (Physics) Sheffield; Manchester; Cambridge; Birmingham; Bristol; Portsmouth; Nottingham; St Andrews; Oxford; Leeds.

Examples of sandwich degree courses Bath; Cardiff; East Anglia; Hertfordshire; Imperial London; Kent; Loughborough; Nottingham Trent; Portsmouth; Surrey; Sussex; West Scotland.

ADMISSIONS INFORMATION

Advice to applicants and planning the UCAS personal statement Admissions tutors look for potential, enthusiasm and interest in the subject so interests relating to maths and physics must be mentioned. An awareness of the range of careers in which physics is involved should also be mentioned on the UCAS application together with a demonstration of any particular interests, such as details on a physics or maths book you have read recently (not science fiction!). Make sure to mention if you have attended any courses, summer schools or day conferences on physics and engineering. See also **Appendix 3**.

Selection interviews Yes Cambridge, Imperial London, Lancaster, Manchester, Oxford (Phys) 29% (success rate 11%), York; **Some** Bath, Dundee, East Anglia, Loughborough; **No** Bristol, London (RH), St Andrews, Swansea, Warwick.

Interview advice and questions Questions will almost certainly focus on those aspects of the physics A-level course that the student enjoys. See also **Chapter 5**.

GRADUATE DESTINATIONS AND EMPLOYMENT

(See **Chapter 1, Graduate Outcomes.**)

Career note Many graduates go into scientific and technical work in the manufacturing industries. However, in recent years, financial work, management and marketing have also attracted many seeking alternative careers.

OTHER DEGREE SUBJECTS FOR CONSIDERATION

Astronomy; Astrophysics; Computer Science; Earth Sciences; Engineering subjects; Geophysics; Materials Science and Metallurgy; Mathematics; Meteorology; Natural Sciences; Oceanography; Optometry; Radiography.

PHYSIOLOGY

(see also **Animal Sciences, Neuroscience, Psychology**)

Physiology is the study of body function. Courses in this wide-ranging subject will cover the central nervous system, special senses and neuro-muscular mechanisms, and body-regulating systems such as exercise, stress and temperature regulation. The Bristol course is available for intercalation in which it is possible to follow a one-year stand-alone degree in any of the following subjects: Heart in Health and Disease/Sensational Neuroscience, Neuroscience of Pain/Future of Molecular Medicine, Cardiovascular Systems in Health and Disease/Brain Behaviour, Pharmacology of ion cells and synaptic transmission, Receptor signalling and non-drug therapies, Pharmacology of the Nervous System, Synaptic Plasticity, Synaptic Cell Biology, or Neurological and Psychiatric disorders.

USEFUL WEBSITES www.physoc.org; www.physiology.org; www.bases.org.uk; see also **Biological Sciences**.

NB The points totals shown to the left of the institutions are for ease of reference only. It must not be assumed that Tariff points are always used by institutions or that they can be substituted for an offer in grades. The level of an offer is not necessarily indicative of the quality of a course.

COURSE OFFERS INFORMATION

SUBJECT REQUIREMENTS/PREFERENCES GCSE Science and mathematics at grade 7 (A). Two science subjects are usually required; chemistry and biology are the preferred subjects. Some popular universities are now making lower offers for disadvantaged and other students.

YOUR TARGET OFFERS AND EXAMPLES OF DEGREE COURSES

160 pts **Cambridge** – A*A*A incl sci/maths+interview+ESAT (Nat Sci (Physiol)) (IB 41–42 pts HL 776)

144 pts **London (King's)** – AAA incl chem+biol (Med Physiol) (IB 36 pts HL 18 pts incl biol+chem)

136 pts **Bristol** – AAB incl sci/maths (Physiol Sci) (IB 34 pts HL 17 pts incl 6/5 maths/sci)
Leeds – AAB–AAA (Hum Physiol Physl Actvt Hlth) (IB 31 pts HL 665)
Manchester – AAB–AAA incl sci/maths (Med Physiol) (IB 35–36 pts HL 665–666 incl sci)
Newcastle – AAB incl biol/chem+maths/sci (Physiol Sci) (IB 34 pts HL 5 biol/chem+maths/sci)

128 pts **Edinburgh** – ABB–AAB incl biol+chem (Physiol) (IB 32–36 pts HL 65 biol+chem)
Leeds – ABB incl sci (Spo Sci Physiol) (IB 34 pts HL 17 pts incl 6 sci); ABB incl sci+MMI (Hlthcr Sci (Crdc Physiol)) (IB 34 pts HL 555 incl sci)
Leicester – ABB–BBB+bEPQ incl sci/maths (Med Physiol) (IB 30 pts HL 65 sci/maths)

120 pts **Sunderland** – 120 pts incl biol/chem (Physiol Sci)

112 pts **Aberdeen** – BBC incl maths/sci (Physiol (Yr Ind)) (IB 32 pts HL 555); (Physiol) (IB 32 pts HL 555 incl maths/sci)
East London – B biol/chem 112 pts (Med Physiol) (IB 25 pts HL 15 pts incl biol+chem)
Manchester Met – C biol 112–120 pts (Hum Physiol) (IB 28 pts HL 5 biol)

104 pts **Central Lancashire** – C biol/chem 104–120 pts (Physiol Pharmacol)
Plymouth – B biol+sci 104–120 pts (Clin Physiol) (IB 28 pts HL 5 biol+sci)

96 pts **Ulster** – CCC incl sci/maths (Hlth Physiol)
Westminster – CCC incl sci/maths 96 pts (Pharmacol Physiol)

ALTERNATIVE OFFERS See **Chapter 6** and **Appendix 1** for grades/UCAS Tariff points information for other examinations.

DEGREE APPRENTICESHIPS

Manchester Met (Hlthcr Sci Practnr); Middlesex (Hlthcr Sci (Cardiac Physiol); UWE Bristol (Hlthcr Sci Practnr (Physiol Sci)); Wolverhampton (Hlthcr Sci Practnr).

CHOOSING YOUR COURSE (SEE ALSO CH.1)

UNIVERSITIES AND COLLEGES TEACHING QUALITY See www.qaa.ac.uk; www.discoveruni.gov.uk.

Top research universities and colleges (REF 2021) See **Biological Sciences**.

Examples of sandwich degree courses Aberdeen; Leeds; Manchester Met.

ADMISSIONS INFORMATION

Advice to applicants and planning the UCAS personal statement See **Neuroscience** and **Biological Sciences**.

Selection interviews Yes Cambridge; **Some** Manchester; **No** Bristol, Newcastle.

Interview advice and questions Past questions include: What made you decide to do a Physiology degree? What experimental work have you done connected with physiology? What future career do you have in mind? What is physiology? Why not choose Medicine instead? What practicals do you do at school? See also **Chapter 5**.

GRADUATE DESTINATIONS AND EMPLOYMENT

(See **Chapter 1, Graduate Outcomes.**)

Career note See **Biology**.

OTHER DEGREE SUBJECTS FOR CONSIDERATION

Anatomy; Biochemistry; Biological Sciences; Biotechnology; Dentistry; Genetics; Health Studies; Medicine; Microbiology; Neuroscience; Nursing; Optometry; Pharmacology; Radiography; Sports Science.

PHYSIOTHERAPY

(including **Chiropractic, Sports Therapy and Veterinary Physiotherapy**; see also **Health Sciences/Studies**)

Physiotherapists work as part of a multi-disciplinary team with other health professionals and are involved in the treatment and rehabilitation of patients of all ages and with a wide variety of medical problems. Degree courses include periods of clinical practice. On successful completion of the three-year course, graduates are eligible for State Registration and Membership of the Chartered Society of Physiotherapy. Courses are very competitive. A-levels in biology or human biology and PE are usually specified with high grades. Check websites. Eligible students can benefit from a £5,000 annual maintenance grant, with up to £3,000 additional funding paid by the NHS Bursary Scheme in England (and similar support is available in the rest of the UK, but arrangements differ so it is important to consult the relevant authority). Bursaries are available based on individual circumstances. All courses expect applicants to have gained some work experience which can include caring and voluntary work.

Useful websites www.csp.org.uk; www.local-physio.co.uk; www.healthcareers.nhs.uk; www.physio-pedia.com

NB The points totals shown to the left of the institutions are for ease of reference only. It must not be assumed that Tariff points are always used by institutions or that they can be substituted for an offer in grades. The level of an offer is not necessarily indicative of the quality of a course.

COURSE OFFERS INFORMATION

Subject requirements/preferences GCSE English, mathematics and science subjects. Many universities stipulate 7/5–6 (A/B) grades in specific subjects. **AL** One or two science subjects are required. Some popular universities are now making lower offers for disadvantaged and other students. **Other** Occupational health check and Disclosure and Barring Service (DBS) clearance.

Your target offers and examples of degree courses

144 pts **Glasgow Caledonian** – AAA incl sci+MMI (Physio)

136 pts **Birmingham** – AAB incl biol/PE+interview (Physio) (IB 32 pts HL 665)

Bradford – AAB 136 pts+interview (Physio) (HL 765 incl 6 biol)

East Anglia – AAB incl biol/PE+interview (Physio) (IB 33 pts HL 6 biol)
Leeds Beckett – 136 pts incl sci+interview (Physio) (HL 554)
Liverpool – AAB incl biol/PE+interview (Physio) (IB 32 pts HL 665 incl 6 biol)
London (King's) – AAB incl sci/maths/soc sci+interview (Physio) (IB 35 pts HL 665 incl sci/maths/soc sci)
Nottingham – AAB incl biol/PE+interview (Physio) (IB 34 pts HL 6 biol)
Queen Margaret – AAB incl sci/maths (Physio) (IB 32 pts)
Southampton – AAB incl sci (Physio) (IB 34 pts HL 17 pts incl sci)

128 pts **Bournemouth** – 128–144 pts incl biol/PE+interview (Physio) (IB 32–34 pts HL 5 biol/PE)
Brighton – ABB incl biol/PE+interview (Physio) (IB 32 pts)
Brunel – ABB–AAB incl sci/maths+interview (Physio) (IB 31 pts HL 5 sci/maths)
Canterbury Christ Church – ABB incl sci+interview (Physio) (IB 32 pts)
Cardiff – ABB–AAB incl biol+interview (Physio) (IB 32–34 pts HL 665 incl biol)
Central Lancashire – ABB incl biol/psy/PE (Physio)
Chichester – ABB incl biol/sci 128–136 pts+interview (Physio) (IB 32 pts)
City St George's – ABB+interview (Physio) (IB 34 pts HL 16 pts)
Coventry – ABB inc biol (Physio) (IB 34 pts HL 6 biol)
Essex – ABB incl sci+interview (Physio) (IB 32 pts HL 655 incl sci)
Hertfordshire – ABB–AAB incl sci (Physio) (IB 33 pts HL 665)
Huddersfield – ABB incl biol/PE+interview (Physio)
Keele – ABB/A*BC/AAC incl biol/PE+interview (Physio) (IB 32 pts HL 655 incl sci)
Leicester – ABB incl biol/PE+interview (Physio) (IB 30 pts HL 6 biol)
Manchester Met – ABB incl biol/spo+interview (Physio) (IB 29 pts)
Oxford Brookes – ABB incl biol 128 pts+interview (Physio) (IB 32 pts)
Robert Gordon – ABB incl sci/maths+interview (Physio) (IB 32 pts HL 5 Engl+sci/maths)
Salford – incl sci (Physio) (IB 32 pts)
Sheffield Hallam – ABB 128 pts incl biol/PE+interview (Physio)
Teesside – 128 pts incl sci/soc sci+interview (Physio)
UWE Bristol – B biol 128 pts+interview (Physio) (HL 6 biol)
York St John – ABB incl biol/PE (Physio) (IB 34 pts)

120 pts **Cumbria** – 120–136 pts incl biol/PE+interview (Physio)
East London – BBB incl biol/chem 120 pts+interview+test (Physio) (IB 28 pts HL 15 pts incl biol+chem)
HSU – BBB incl biol+sci (MChiro) (IB 34 pts HL 5 biol+sci)
Harper Adams – B biol (Vet Physio) (IB 30 pts HL 6 biol)
Northumbria – C sci/hlth 120 pts+interview (Physio)
Plymouth – 120–136 pts+interview (Physio) (IB 33 pts HL 6 biol)
Ulster – BBB incl sci/maths+interview (Physio)
Winchester – 120–128 pts incl sci+interview (Physio) (HL 55)
Worcester – BBB incl biol/PE 120 pts+interview (Physio) (HL 6 biol)

112 pts **Chichester** – BBC–BBB incl biol/PE 112–120 pts (Spo Thera)

96 pts **St Mary's** – 96–128 pts (Physio)

Alternative offers See **Chapter 6** and **Appendix 1** for grades/UCAS Tariff points information for other examinations.

DEGREE APPRENTICESHIPS

Brighton (Physio); Central Lancashire (Physio); Essex (Physio); Greenwich (Physio); Huddersfield (Physio); Salford (Physio); Teesside (Physio).

EXAMPLES OF COLLEGES OFFERING COURSES IN THIS SUBJECT FIELD

Warwickshire (Coll).

CHOOSING YOUR COURSE (SEE ALSO CH.1)

Universities and colleges teaching quality See www.qaa.ac.uk; www.discoveruni.gov.uk.

Top research universities and colleges (REF 2021) See **Health Sciences/Studies**.

ADMISSIONS INFORMATION

Admissions tutors' advice City St George's Work experience required.

Advice to applicants and planning the UCAS personal statement Visits to, and work experience in, hospital physiotherapy departments are important, although many universities publicly state that this is not necessary. However, with the level of competition for this subject this is doubtful (see Reasons for rejection). Applicants must demonstrate a clear understanding of the nature of the profession. Give details of voluntary work activities. Take notes of the work done and the different aspects of physiotherapy. Explain your experience fully on the UCAS application. Outside interests and teamwork are considered important. Good communication skills are required. Observation placement within a physiotherapy department. See also **Appendix 3**.

Selection interviews Yes Birmingham, Bournemouth, Bradford, Brighton, Brunel, Canterbury Christ Church, Cardiff, Chichester, City St George's, Coventry, Cumbria, East Anglia, East London, Essex, Huddersfield, Keele, Leeds Beckett, Leicester, Liverpool, London (King's), Manchester Met, Northumbria, Nottingham, Oxford Brookes, Plymouth, Robert Gordon, Sheffield Hallam, Teesside, Ulster, UWE Bristol, Winchester, Worcester, York St John.

Interview advice and questions Physiotherapy is one of the most popular courses at present and work experience is very important, if not essential. A sound knowledge of the career, types of treatment used in physiotherapy and some understanding of the possible problems experienced by patients will be expected. Past interview questions include: How does physiotherapy fit into the overall health care system? If one patient was a heavy smoker and the other not, would you treat them the same? What was the most emotionally challenging thing you have ever done? Give an example of teamwork in which you have been involved. Why should we make you an offer? What is chiropractic? What is osteopathy? See also **Chapter 5**.

Reasons for rejection (non-academic) Lack of knowledge of the profession. Failure to convince the interviewers of a reasoned basis for following the profession. Failure to have visited a hospital physiotherapy unit. Lack of awareness of the demands of the course.

GRADUATE DESTINATIONS AND EMPLOYMENT

(See **Chapter 1, Graduate Outcomes.**)

Career note The professional qualifications gained on graduation enable physiotherapists to seek posts in the NHS where the majority are employed. A small number work in the community health service, particularly in rural areas, while others work in residential homes. In addition to private practice, there are also some opportunities in professional sports clubs.

OTHER DEGREE SUBJECTS FOR CONSIDERATION

Anatomy; Audiology; Biological Sciences; Health Studies; Leisure and Recreation; Nursing; Occupational Therapy; Osteopathy; Physical Education; Psychology; Sport Science/Studies.

PLANT SCIENCES

(see also **Biological Sciences, Biology, Horticulture**)

Plant Sciences cover such areas as plant biochemistry, plant genetics, plant conservation and plant geography. Botany encompasses all aspects of plant science and also other subject areas including agriculture, forestry and horticulture. Botany is basic to these subjects and others including pharmacology and water management. As with other biological sciences, some universities introduce Plant Sciences by way of a common first year with other subjects. Plant sciences has applications in the agricultural, biotechnological, horticultural and food industries.

USEFUL WEBSITES www.kew.org; www.anbg.gov.au; http://bsbi.org; www.theplantlist.org; https://cms.botany.org

NB The points totals shown to the left of the institutions are for ease of reference only. It must not be assumed that Tariff points are always used by institutions or that they can be substituted for an offer in grades. The level of an offer is not necessarily indicative of the quality of a course.

COURSE OFFERS INFORMATION

SUBJECT REQUIREMENTS/PREFERENCES GCSE Mathematics if not offered at A-level. **AL** One or two science subjects are usually required. Some popular universities are now making lower offers for disadvantaged and other students.

YOUR TARGET OFFERS AND EXAMPLES OF DEGREE COURSES

160 pts **Cambridge** – A*A*A incl sci/maths+interview+ESAT (Nat Sci (Plnt Sci)) (IB 41–42 pts HL 776)
144 pts **Bristol** – AAA incl biol+sci (Plnt Sci) (IB 36 pts HL 18 pts incl 66 biol+sci)
128 pts **Edinburgh** – ABB–AAA incl biol+chem (Biol Sci (Plnt Sci)) (IB 32–37 pts HL 655–666)
Nottingham – ABB incl biol (Plnt Biol) (IB 30 pts HL 655 incl biol)
120 pts **Glasgow** – BBB–AAB incl biol/chem (Mol Cell Biol (Plnt Sci)) (IB 34 pts HL 655 incl biol/chem)
112 pts **Aberdeen** – BBC incl maths+sci (Plnt Soil Sci) (IB 32 pts HL 555 incl maths+sci)
Canterbury Christ Church – BBC 112 pts incl sci (Plnt Sci) (IB 29 pts)
Edge Hill – BBC–BBB 112–120 pts (Plnt Sci)
104 pts **Aberystwyth** – BCC–BBB incl B biol 104–120 pts (Plnt Biol) (IB 28–30 pts HL 5 biol)
80 pts **Cornwall (Coll)** – 80 pts (Hort (Plnt Sci))

ALTERNATIVE OFFERS See **Chapter 6** and **Appendix 1** for grades/UCAS Tariff points information for other examinations.

CHOOSING YOUR COURSE (SEE ALSO CH.1)

UNIVERSITIES AND COLLEGES TEACHING QUALITY See www.qaa.ac.uk; www.discoveruni.gov.uk.

TOP RESEARCH UNIVERSITIES AND COLLEGES (REF 2021) See **Biological Sciences**.

ADMISSIONS INFORMATION

ADVICE TO APPLICANTS AND PLANNING THE UCAS PERSONAL STATEMENT Visit botanical gardens. See also **Biological Sciences** and **Appendix 4**.

SELECTION INTERVIEWS Yes Cambridge.

INTERVIEW ADVICE AND QUESTIONS You are likely to be questioned on your biology studies, your reasons for wishing to study Plant Sciences and your ideas about a possible future career. In the past, questions have been asked about Darwin's theory of evolution, photosynthesis and DNA and the value of gardening programmes on TV! See also **Chapter 5**.

GRADUATE DESTINATIONS AND EMPLOYMENT

(See **Chapter 1, Graduate Outcomes.**)

CAREER NOTE See **Biology** and **Horticulture**.

OTHER DEGREE SUBJECTS FOR CONSIDERATION

Agriculture; Biochemistry; Biological Sciences; Biology; Crop Science (Agronomy); Ecology; Food Science; Forestry; Herbal Medicine; Horticulture; Landscape Architecture.

PODIATRY (CHIROPODY)

A podiatrist's primary aim is to improve the mobility, independence and quality of life for their patients. They are autonomous healthcare professionals who deliver preventative, palliative, biomechanical, pharmacological and surgical interventions for lower limb problems. They work alone or are part of a multidisciplinary team. Courses lead to the eligibility for registration with the Health and Care Professions Council and some work shadowing prior to application is preferred by admissions tutors.

Useful websites https://rcpod.org.uk; www.healthcareers.nhs.uk; www.podiatrynetwork.com; www.podiatrytoday.com

NB The points totals shown to the left of the institutions are for ease of reference only. It must not be assumed that Tariff points are always used by institutions or that they can be substituted for an offer in grades. The level of an offer is not necessarily indicative of the quality of a course.

COURSE OFFERS INFORMATION

Subject requirements/preferences GCSE Mathematics and science subjects. **AL** Biology usually required or preferred. Some popular universities are now making lower offers for disadvantaged and other students. **Other** Hepatitis B, tuberculosis and tetanus immunisation; Disclosure and Barring Service (DBS) clearance (a pre-existing record could prevent a student from participating in the placement component of the course and prevent the student from gaining state registration).

Your target offers and examples of degree courses

120 pts **East London** – 120 pts incl sci/PE (Pod) (IB 28 pts HL 15 pts incl biol+chem)
Salford – 120 pts+interview (Pod) (IB 27 pts)
112 pts **Brighton** – BBC (Pod) (IB 28 pts)
Huddersfield – BBC–BBB 112–120 pts+interview (Pod)
Northampton – BBC (Pod)
Wolverhampton – BBC incl sci/soc sci (Pod)
104 pts **Glasgow Caledonian** – BCC incl sci (Pod)
Plymouth – C sci 104–120 pts (Pod) (IB 26–30 pts HL 5 sci)
Teesside – 104 pts+interview (Chiro)
96 pts **Cardiff Met** – 96–104 pts incl biol+interview (Pod)
Queen Margaret – CCC (Pod) (IB 28 pts)
64 pts **Durham New (Coll)** – 64 pts+interview (Pod)

Alternative offers See **Chapter 6** and **Appendix 1** for grades/UCAS Tariff points information for other examinations.

DEGREE APPRENTICESHIPS

East London (Pod); Huddersfield (Pod); Plymouth (Pod); Salford (Pod); Sunderland (Pod).

EXAMPLES OF COLLEGES OFFERING COURSES IN THIS SUBJECT FIELD

Durham New (Coll).

CHOOSING YOUR COURSE (SEE ALSO CH.1)

Universities and colleges teaching quality See www.qaa.ac.uk; www.discoveruni.gov.uk.

Examples of sandwich degree courses Teesside.

ADMISSIONS INFORMATION

Advice to applicants and planning the UCAS personal statement Visit a podiatrist's clinic to gain work experience/work shadowing experience. Applicants need the ability to communicate with all age ranges, to work independently, to be resourceful and to possess a focused approach to academic work. Admissions tutors look for evidence of an understanding of podiatry, some work experience, good people skills, and effective communication. Mature applicants must include an academic reference (not an employer reference). See also **Appendix 3**.

Selection interviews Yes Cardiff Met, Durham New (Coll), Huddersfield, Northampton, Plymouth, Teesside; **No** Southampton.

Interview advice and questions Past questions include: Have you visited a podiatrist's surgery? What do your friends think about your choice of career? Do you think that being a podiatrist could cause you any physical problems? With which groups of people do podiatrists come into contact? What are your perceptions of the scope of practice of podiatry? What transferable skills do you think you will need? See also **Chapter 5**.

Reasons for rejection (non-academic) Unconvincing attitude; poor communication and interpersonal skills; lack of motivation; medical condition or physical disabilities which are incompatible with professional practice; no knowledge of chosen profession; lack of work experience.

GRADUATE DESTINATIONS AND EMPLOYMENT

(See **Chapter 1, Graduate Outcomes.**)

Career note Many state-registered podiatrists are employed by the NHS while others work in private practice or commercially run clinics.

OTHER DEGREE SUBJECTS FOR CONSIDERATION

Audiology; Biological Sciences; Health Studies; Nursing; Occupational Therapy; Osteopathy; Physiotherapy.

POLITICS

(including **Government and European Politics**; see also **Development Studies, International Relations, Philosophy, Politics and Economics (PPE), Social Sciences/Studies**)

Politics is often described as the study of 'who gets what, where, when and how'. Courses have become increasingly popular in recent years and usually cover the politics and government of the major powers. Because of the variety of degree courses on offer, it is possible to study the politics of almost any country in the world.

Useful websites http://europa.eu; www.gov.uk/government/organisations/foreign-commonwealth-development-office; www.psa.ac.uk; www.parliament.uk; www.whitehouse.gov; www.amnesty.org; www.gov.uk; www.un.org; www.un.int

NB The points totals shown to the left of the institutions are for ease of reference only. It must not be assumed that Tariff points are always used by institutions or that they can be substituted for an offer in grades. The level of an offer is not necessarily indicative of the quality of a course.

COURSE OFFERS INFORMATION

Subject requirements/preferences GCSE English, mathematics and a foreign language may be required. **AL** No subjects specified; history useful but an arts or social science subject also an advantage. Some popular universities are now making lower offers for disadvantaged and other students.

Your target offers and examples of degree courses

160 pts **Warwick** – A*A*A (Econ Pol Int St) (IB 39 pts HL 666)

152 pts **Durham** – A*AA incl maths+soc sci/hum (Econ Pol) (IB 38 pts HL 666 maths+soc sci/hum)
Edinburgh – A*AA (Hist Pol; Pol) (IB 39 pts HL 666)
London (King's) – A*AA+LNAT (Pol Phil Law) (IB 38 pts HL 19 pts)
London (QM) – A*AA (Law Pol) (IB 36 pts HL 666)

144 pts **Bath** – AAA/A*AB/AAB+aEPQ (Pol Int Rel) (IB 36 pts HL 666/765); AAA/A*AB/AAB+aEPQ incl maths (Econ Pol) (IB 36 pts HL 666/765 incl maths)
Birmingham – AAA (Econ Pol) (IB 32 pts HL 666)
Bristol – AAA (Pol Int Rel) (IB 36 pts HL 18 pts)
Durham – AAA incl soc sci/hum (Phil Pol) (IB 37 pts HL 666); (Pol) (IB 37 pts HL 666 incl soc sci/hum)
Exeter – AAA (Pol; Pol Int Rel) (IB 36 pts HL 666); AAA–A*AA 144–152 pts (Econ Pol) (IB 36–38 pts HL 666–766)
London (King's) – AAA (Euro Pol; War St) (IB 36 pts HL 18 pts)
London LSE – AAA (Int Rel; Pol; Pol Hist; Pol Phil) (IB 38 pts HL 766); AAA incl maths (Pol Econ) (IB 38 pts HL 766 incl maths)
Oxford – AAA+interview+HAT (Hist Pol) (IB 38 pts HL 666)
Queen's Belfast – AAA (Law Pol) (IB 36 pts HL 666)
Warwick – AAA (Pol courses) (IB 34–36 pts)

136 pts **Birmingham** – AAB (Pol; Pol Econ; Pol Int Rel; Pol Soc Plcy) (IB 32 pts HL 665)
Bristol – AAB (Pol Sociol; Soc Plcy Pol) (IB 34 pts HL 17 pts); AAB incl lang (Pol Modn Lang) (IB 34 pts HL 17 pts incl 5 lang)
Kent – AAB 136 pts (Law Pol) (HL 666)
Lancaster – AAB (Hist Pol) (IB 35 pts HL 16 pts)
Leeds – AAB (Pol) (IB 35 pts HL 655)
Liverpool – AAB (Pol) (IB 35 pts)
London (SOAS) – AAB (Pol) (IB 34 pts HL 665)
London (UCL) – AAB (Pol Sociol E Euro St) (IB 36 pts HL 17 pts)
London LSE – AAB (Int Soc Pblc Plcy Pol) (IB 37 pts HL 666)
NU London – AAB (Pol Int Rel Comb Hons) (IB 35 pts HL 665)
Newcastle – AAB (Pol Econ) (IB 34 pts); (Pol) (IB 34 pts HL 555)
Nottingham – AAB (Int Rel As St) (IB 32 pts HL 665); (Pol Int Rel) (IB 32 pts HL 665)
Sheffield – AAB/ABB+bEPQ (Pol Phil) (IB 34 pts); AAB–ABB+bEPQ (Int Rel Pol; Pol) (IB 34 pts); AAB–ABB+bEPQ incl hist/class civ (Hist Pol) (IB 34 pts HL 6 hist)
Southampton – AAB incl hist (Modn Hist Pol) (IB 34 pts HL 17 pts incl 5 hist)
Sussex – AAB (Law Pol; Pol courses) (IB 34 pts)
Warwick – AAB (Pol Sociol) (IB 34 pts)
York – AAB (Phil Pol; Pol; Pol Int Rel; Soc Pol Sci) (IB 35 pts); AAB incl Engl (Engl Pol) (IB 35 pts HL 6 Engl)

128 pts **East Anglia** – ABB (Pol) (IB 32 pts); (Hist Pol) (IB 32 pts HL 5 hist)
Lancaster – ABB (Pol; Pol (St Abrd); Pol Int Rel; Pol Sociol) (IB 32 pts HL 16 pts); ABB 128 pts (Glob Relgn Pol) (IB 32 pts HL 16 pts)
London (Inst Paris) – ABB+interview (Int Pol) (IB 32 pts HL 655)
London (QM) – ABB (Pol) (IB 32 pts HL 655); ABB incl hist (Hist Pol) (IB 32 pts HL 655 incl hist)
Loughborough – ABB (Hist Pol; Pol) (IB 34 pts HL 655)
Manchester – ABB (Pol Soc Anth; Pol Sociol) (IB 34 pts HL 655)
Newcastle – ABB (Pol Sociol) (IB 32 pts)
Queen's Belfast – ABB (Int Rel Pol; Pol) (IB 33 pts HL 655)
Sheffield – ABB–BBB+bEPQ (Pol Sociol) (IB 33 pts)
Southampton – ABB (Phil Pol; Pol; Pol Int Rel) (IB 32 pts HL 16 pts); ABB incl Fr/Ger/Span (Modn Lang Pol (Fr/Ger/Span)) (IB 32 pts HL 16 pts incl 5 Fr/Ger/Span); ABB incl maths (Pol Econ) (IB 32 pts HL 16 pts incl maths)

120 pts **City St George's** – BBB (Pol) (IB 30 pts HL 555); BBB 120 pts (Int Pol) (IB 30 pts HL 555)
Dundee – BBB (Geopol; Pol) (IB 30 pts HL 555)
Glasgow – BBB–AAB incl Engl/hum (Pol) (IB 36 pts HL 665 incl Engl/hum)
Hull – BBB (Law Pol) (IB 30 pts)
Kent – BBB (Econ Pol) (HL 665); BBB 120 pts (Pol Int Rel) (HL 655)
Leicester – BBB–ABB (Pol; Pol Econ) (IB 28 pts)
London (Gold) – BBB (Int Rel; Pol) (IB 33 pts HL 655)

London (RH) – BBB–ABB (Pol; Pol Phil) (IB 32 pts HL 655); BBB–ABB (Econ Pol Int Rel; Pol Int Rel) (IB 32 pts HL 655); BBB–ABB incl mus+gr 7 (Mus Pol St) (IB 32 pts HL 655 incl mus)
Reading – BBB (Pol courses; War Pce Int Rel) (IB 30 pts); BBB 120 pts (Pol Int Rel) (IB 30 pts)
Stirling – BBB (Int Pol; Pol) (IB 28 pts)
Strathclyde – BBB–ABB (Pol courses) (IB 30–32 pts)
Surrey – BBB–ABB (Pol) (IB 32–33 pts)
Swansea – BBB 120 pts (Pol; Pol Soc Plcy) (IB 32 pts)

112 pts **Aberdeen** – BBC (Pol courses) (IB 32 pts HL 555)
Aston – BBC (Pol Int Rel; Pol Sociol) (IB 29 pts HL 554)
Brunel – BBC–ABB (Int Pol; Pol) (IB 29 pts)
Buckingham – BBC–BBB (Hist Pol) (IB 31–32 pts)
Canterbury Christ Church – BBC 112 pts (Pol; Pol Int Rel) (IB 29 pts)
Cardiff – BBC–ABB (Int Rel Pol; Pol) (IB 30–32 pts HL 655–665)
Coventry – BBC (Hist Pol; Pol) (IB 29 pts)
De Montfort – 112 pts (Int Rel Pol) (IB 26–28 pts)
Edge Hill – BBC–BBB 112–120 pts (Hist Pol)
Essex – BBC–BBB 112–120 pts (Econ Pol; Pol) (IB 29–30 pts HL 554–555)
Greenwich – 112 pts (Pol Int Rel)
Keele – BBC (Pol) (IB 29 pts HL 554)
Leeds Beckett – 112 pts (Pol) (IB 24 pts)
London (Birk) – BBC 112 pts (Pol Phil Hist)
London South Bank – 112 pts (Pol Int Rel)
Northumbria – 112 pts (Hist Pol)
Nottingham Trent – 112 pts (Hist Pol; Pol Int Rel); BBC 112 pts (Pol)
Sheffield Hallam – BBC–BBB 112–120 pts (Pol Int Rel)

104 pts **Brighton** – BCC–BBB 104–120 pts (Phil Pol Eth; Pol Int Rel) (IB 26 pts)
Chester – BCC–BBC 104–112 pts (Glob Affrs Pol Int Rrl) (IB 26 pts)
Chichester – BCC–BBB 104–120 pts (Pol Contemp Hist) (IB 28 pts)
Lincoln – 104 pts (Pol) (IB 28 pts)
Liverpool Hope – BCC 104 pts (Pol courses) (IB 24 pts)
Manchester Met – 104–112 pts (Pol; Pol Phil) (IB 26 pts)
Northampton – BCC (Int Rel Pol)
Oxford Brookes – BCC 104 pts (Econ Pol Int Rel; Int Rel Pol; Pol) (IB 29 pts)
Plymouth – 104–112 pts (Pol) (IB 26–28 pts); (Pol Int Rel) (IB 26–28 pts HL 4)
Portsmouth – 104–120 pts (Pol) (IB 25 pts)
Ulster – BCC (Pol Int St; Sociol Pol Int St) (IB 24 pts HL 12 pts)
West London – BCC 104–120 pts (Pol Int Rel)
Westminster – BCC–BBB 104–120 pts (Pol; Pol Int Rel)
Winchester – BCC–BBB 104–120 pts (Pol Int Rel) (HL 44)
Worcester – 104–120 pts (Pol Comb Hons)

96 pts **Aberystwyth** – CCC–BBB 96–120 pts (Pol) (IB 28–30 pts)
London Met – CCC (Pol Int Rel)
Teesside – 96–112 pts (Pol Int Rel)
Wolverhampton – CCC/BCD 96 pts (Pol Hist; Pol Soc Plcy)

72 pts **UHI** – BC (Hist Pol; Sociol Pol)

Alternative offers See **Chapter 6** and **Appendix 1** for grades/UCAS Tariff points information for other examinations.

DEGREE APPRENTICESHIPS

Kent (Plcy St).

EXAMPLES OF COLLEGES OFFERING COURSES IN THIS SUBJECT FIELD

Blackburn (Coll).

CHOOSING YOUR COURSE (SEE ALSO CH.1)

Universities and colleges teaching quality See www.qaa.ac.uk; www.discoveruni.gov.uk.

Top research universities and colleges (REF 2021) (Politics and International Studies) Strathclyde; London (RH); London LSE; Edinburgh; London (UCL); Essex; London (QM); Manchester; Warwick; Sheffield.

Examples of sandwich degree courses Aston; Bath; Brunel; Coventry; Essex; Lancaster; Leeds; Loughborough; Middlesex; Surrey.

ADMISSIONS INFORMATION

Advice to applicants and planning the UCAS personal statement Study the workings of government in the UK, Europe and other areas of the world, such as the Middle East, the Far East, America and Russia. Describe visits to the Houses of Commons and Lords and the debates taking place. Attend council meetings – county, town, district, village halls. Describe these visits and agendas. Read current affairs avidly. Be aware of political developments in the major countries and regions of the world including the Middle East, South America, the UK, Europe, USA, China, Korea and Russia. Keep abreast of developments in theatres of war. Explain your interests in detail.

Selection interviews Yes Cambridge, London (Inst Paris), Oxford (37% (success rate 11%)); **Some** Bath, Loughborough; **No** De Montfort, London LSE, London Met, Swansea, Warwick.

Interview advice and questions Questions may stem from A-level studies but applicants will also be expected to be up-to-date in their knowledge and opinions of current events. Questions in recent years have included: What constitutes a 'great power'? What is happening at present in the Labour Party? Define capitalism. What is a political decision? How do opinion polls detract from democracy? Is the European Union a good idea? Why? What is a 'spin doctor'? Are politicians hypocrites? See also **Chapter 5**.

GRADUATE DESTINATIONS AND EMPLOYMENT

(See **Chapter 1, Graduate Outcomes.**)

Career note The transferable skills gained in this degree open up a wide range of career opportunities. Graduates seek positions in management, public services and administration and in some cases in political activities.

OTHER DEGREE SUBJECTS FOR CONSIDERATION

Development Studies; Economics; Government; History; International Relations; Public Policy and Administration; Social Policy and Administration; Sociology.

PROFESSIONAL POLICING

(including **Police Studies**)

It is now a requirement for new police officers to be educated to degree level. The new Pre-join degree in Professional Policing is an academic knowledge-based degree covering the essential skills required to enter the police force. Graduates of the new degree course will still be required to undertake further work-based training on entering the force.

Useful websites www.college.police.uk

NB The points totals shown to the left of the institutions are for ease of reference only. It must not be assumed that Tariff points are always used by institutions or that they can be substituted for an offer in grades. The level of an offer is not necessarily indicative of the quality of a course.

COURSE OFFERS INFORMATION

Subject requirements/preferences GCSE English and mathematics at grade 4 (C) or above. **AL** No subjects specified. Some popular universities are now making lower offers for disadvantaged and other students.

Your target offers and examples of degree courses

112 pts **Birmingham City** – BBC (Prof Plcg) (IB 28 pts)
Canterbury Christ Church – BBC 112 pts (Prof Plcg) (IB 29 pts)
Derby – BBC–BBB (Prof Plcg)
Edge Hill – BBC–BBB 112–120 pts (Prof Plcg)
Northumbria – 112 pts (Prof Plcg)
Sheffield Hallam – BBC–BBB 112–120 pts (Prof Plcg)
Staffordshire – BBC (Prof Plcg)
Univ Law – BBC (Prof Plcg)
Winchester – BBC–BBB 112–120 pts (Prof Plcg) (HL 44)

104 pts **Central Lancashire** – 104–112 pts (Prof Plcg)
Chester – 104 pts (Prof Plcg) (IB 26 pts)
Cumbria – BCC–BBC 104–112 pts (Prof Plcg)
Gloucestershire – 104–120 pts (Prof Plcg)
Liverpool John Moores – BCC (Prof Plcg)
Northampton – BCC (Prof Plcg)
Nottingham Trent – (Prof Plcg)
South Wales – BCC 104 pts (Prof Plcg)
York St John – 104 pts (Prof Plcg)

96 pts **Bangor** – 96–112 pts (Prof Plcg)
De Montfort – 96 pts (Prof Plcg) (IB 24 pts)
Trinity Saint David – 96 pts (Prof Plcg)
Wolverhampton – CCC 96 pts (Prof Plcg)
Wrexham – 96–112 pts (Prof Plcg)

88 pts **Bucks New** – 88–112 pts (Plcg St Crim Invstg)

80 pts **Teesside** – 80–104 pts (Prof Plcg)

Alternative offers See **Chapter 6** and **Appendix 1** for grades/UCAS Tariff points information for other examinations.

DEGREE APPRENTICESHIPS

Anglia Ruskin (Prof Plcg Prac); Brunel (Plcg Constb); Buckinghamshire New University (Plcg Constb); Central Lancashire (Prof Plcg Prac); De Montfort (Plcg Constbl); Leeds Trinity (Plcg Constbl); Liverpool John Moores (Prof Plcg Prac); Northampton (Plcg Constb); Northumbria (Plcg Constb); Portsmouth (Plcg Constb); Salford (Prof Plcg Prac); Sheffield Hallam (Plcg Constb); Staffordshire (Prof Plcg Prac); Teesside (Prof Plcg Prac); UWE Bristol (Plcg Constb); West London (Plcg Constb).

CHOOSING YOUR COURSE (SEE ALSO CH.1)

Universities and colleges teaching quality See www.qaa.ac.uk; www.discoveruni.gov.uk.

GRADUATE DESTINATIONS AND EMPLOYMENT

(See **Chapter 1, Graduate Outcomes.**)

OTHER DEGREE SUBJECTS FOR CONSIDERATION

Criminal Justice; Criminology.

PSYCHOLOGY

(including **Autism Studies, Cognitive Science, Counselling Psychology and Forensic Psychology**; see also **Animal Sciences, Biological Sciences, Neuroscience, Philosophy, Physiology, Social Sciences/Studies**)

Psychology is a very popular subject, with the number of applications rising by 40,000 in the last 10 years. The study attracts three times more women than men. It covers studies in development, behaviour, perception, memory, language, learning and personality as well as social relationships and abnormal psychology. Psychology is a science and you will be involved in experimentation and statistical analysis. The degree is usually offered as a BSc or a BA course and there are many similarities between them; the differences are in the elective subjects which can be taken in the second and third years. Contrary to popular belief, psychology is not a study to enable you to psycho-analyse your friends – psychology is not the same as psychiatry!

To qualify as a chartered psychologist (for which a postgraduate qualification is required), it is necessary to obtain a first degree (or equivalent) qualification which gives eligibility for both Graduate Membership (GM) and the Graduate Basis for Chartered Membership (GBC) of the British Psychological Society (BPS). A full list of courses accredited by the British Psychological Society is available on the Society's website www.bps.org.uk. Specialisms in the subject include Educational, Clinical, Occupational and Forensic Psychology (see **Appendix 3**).

Behavioural Science covers the study of animal and human behaviour and offers an overlap between Zoology, Sociology, Psychology and Biological Sciences. Psychology, however, also crosses over into Education, Management Sciences, Human Resource Management, Counselling, Public Relations, Advertising, Artificial Intelligence, Marketing, Retail and Social Studies.

USEFUL WEBSITES www.psychology.org; www.bps.org.uk; www.socialpsychology.org; https://psychcentral.com

NB The points totals shown to the left of the institutions are for ease of reference only. It must not be assumed that Tariff points are always used by institutions or that they can be substituted for an offer in grades. The level of an offer is not necessarily indicative of the quality of a course.

COURSE OFFERS INFORMATION

SUBJECT REQUIREMENTS/PREFERENCES GCSE English, mathematics and a science. **AL** A science subject is usually required. Psychology may be accepted as a science subject. Some popular universities are now making lower offers for disadvantaged and other students.

YOUR TARGET OFFERS AND EXAMPLES OF DEGREE COURSES

160 pts **Cambridge** – A*A*A+interview+PBSAA (Psy Bhv Sci) (IB 40–42 pts HL 776); A*A*A incl sci/maths+interview+ESAT (Nat Sci (Psy)) (IB 41–42 pts HL 776 incl sci/maths)

152 pts **Bath** – A*AA–AAA+aEPQ (Psy) (IB 36 pts HL 766)
Bristol – A*AA incl sci/psy/geog (Psy) (IB 38 pts HL 18 pts incl 6 sci)
Edinburgh – A*AA incl sci/maths (Psy) (IB 39 pts HL 666 incl sci/maths)
Exeter – A*AA (Psy (Yr Ind); Psy Spo Exer Sci (Yr Ind)); A*AA incl sci (Psy (Yr Abrd)) (IB 38 pts HL 766 incl sci)
London (UCL) – A*AA incl sci/maths/psy (Psy) (IB 39 pts HL 19 pts incl 6 sci/maths/psy)
Oxford – A*AA+interview+TSA (Psy (Expmtl); Psy Phil Ling) (IB 39 pts HL 766)

144 pts **Birmingham** – AAA incl sci (Psy) (IB 32 pts HL 666)
Durham – AAA (Psy) (IB 37 pts)
Edinburgh – AAA incl sci/maths (Cog Sci (Hum)) (IB 37 pts HL 666 incl sci/maths)
Exeter – AAA incl sci (Psy) (IB 36 pts HL 666 incl sci); AAA incl sci+interview (App Psy (Clin) (MSci)) (IB 36 pts HL 6 sci)
Leeds – AAA incl sci/maths (Psy) (IB 35 pts HL 6 sci/maths)
Liverpool – AAA/AAB+aEPQ incl sci/maths (Psy (MPsycholSci)) (IB 36 pts HL 6 sci)

London (QM) – AAA incl sci/maths (Psy) (IB 36 pts HL 666 incl sci/maths)
Manchester – AAA incl sci/maths (Psy) (IB 36 pts HL 666 incl sci/maths)
Newcastle – AAA incl biol (Psy Biol) (IB 36 pts HL 666 incl biol); AAA incl sci (Psy) (IB 36 pts HL 666); AAA incl sci/maths (Psy Nutr) (IB 36 pts HL 666)
Nottingham – AAA incl sci (Psy Cog Neuro) (IB 34 pts HL 666); (Psy) (IB 36 pts HL 665)
Reading – AAA+interview (App Psy (Clin)) (IB 35 pts)
St Andrews – AAA (Art Hist Psy) (IB 36 pts HL 665)
Warwick – AAA (Psy) (IB 36 pts HL 5 maths)
York – AAA incl sci/maths (Psy) (IB 36 pts)

136 pts **Cardiff** – AAB–A*AA (Psy) (IB 34–37 pts HL 666–766)
City St George's – AAB 136 pts (Psy) (IB 33 pts HL 555)
Lancaster – AAB (Ling Psy; Psy) (IB 35 pts HL 16 pts)
Liverpool – AAB incl sci/maths (Psy) (IB 35 pts HL 6 sci/maths)
London (RH) – AAB–AAA (Psy) (IB 32 pts HL 665); (Psy Clin Cog Neuro) (IB 34 pts HL 666)
Loughborough – AAB (Psy; Spo Exer Psy) (IB 35 pts HL 665)
Manchester – AAB–AAA incl sci/maths (Cog Neuro Psy) (IB 35–36 pts HL 665–666 incl sci)
NU London – AAB (Psy) (IB 35 pts HL 665)
Nottingham – AAB/A*BB (Phil Psy) (IB 32 pts HL 665)
Reading – AAB (Psy; Psy Neuro) (IB 34 pts)
Sheffield – AAB incl sci/maths (Psy) (IB 34 pts HL 5 sci/maths)
Southampton – AAB (Educ Psy) (IB 34 pts HL 17 pts); AAB–AAA incl psy/sci/maths (Psy) (IB 34–36 pts HL 665–666 incl psy/sci/maths)
St Andrews – AAB (Psy) (IB 36 pts HL 665)
Sussex – AAB (Psy Neuro) (IB 34 pts)

128 pts **Aston** – ABB (Psy Sociol) (IB 32 pts HL 655)
East Anglia – ABB/BBB+aEPQ (Psy) (IB 32 pts)
Essex – ABB (Psy) (IB 32 pts HL 655)
Glasgow – ABB–AAA incl sci/maths (Psy) (IB 36 pts HL 665 incl sci/maths)
Hertfordshire – ABB–AAB (Psy) (HL 44)
Kent – ABB–AAB (Psy; Psy Clin Psy)
Leeds Beckett – 128 pts incl sci/maths (Psy courses) (HL 554 incl sci)
Liverpool John Moores – ABB 128 pts (Foren Psy Crim Just)
Manchester Met – ABB 128 pts (Psy) (IB 32 pts)
Queen's Belfast – ABB (Psy) (IB 33 pts HL 655)
Reading – ABB (Psy Lang Sci) (IB 32 pts); ABB+portfolio (Art Psy) (IB 32 pts)
Sunderland – 128 pts (Psy; Psy Cnslg)
Surrey – ABB (Psy) (IB 33 pts)
Sussex – ABB incl sci (Neuro) (IB 32 pts HL 5 sci); ABB–AAB (Psy) (IB 32–34 pts)
UWE Bristol – 128 pts (Psy courses)
York – ABB (Sociol Soc Psy) (IB 34 pts)

120 pts **Aberdeen** – BBB (Psy) (IB 32 pts HL 555)
Aston – BBB (Psy) (IB 31 pts HL 555)
Bangor – 120–144 pts (Psy; Psy Clin Hlth Psy; Psy Neuropsy)
Brunel – BBB (Psy; Psy (Spo Hlth Exer)) (IB 30 pts)
Coventry – BBB (Psy) (IB 30 pts HL 15 pts); BBB 120 pts (Spo Exer Psy) (IB 30 pts HL 15 pts)
Derby – BBB–ABB (Psy)
Dundee – BBB incl psy (Psy) (IB 30 pts HL 555)
Edge Hill – BBB–ABB 120–128 pts (Psy)
Greenwich – 120 pts (Psy)
HSU – BBB 120 pts (Cnslg Mntl Hlth) (IB 32 pts)
Huddersfield – BBB 120 pts (Psy; Psy Cnslg; Psy Crimin)
Hull – BBB–ABB (Psy) (IB 30 pts)
Keele – ABC/BBB (Psy) (IB 30 pts HL 555)
Kingston – 120–136 pts (Foren Psy; Psy courses)
Leicester – BBB–ABB (Psy; Psy Cog Neuro) (IB 30 pts)

Liverpool John Moores – BBB (Psy); BBB incl spo/sci/soc sci (Spo Psy)
London (Gold) – BBB (Psy; Psy Cog Neuro) (IB 33 pts HL 655)
London South Bank – BBB (Psy (Clin Psy))
Northumbria – 120 pts (Psy)
Nottingham Trent – BBB 120 pts (Psy)
Portsmouth – 120–128 pts (Foren Psy) (IB 29–30 pts); BBB–ABB 120–128 pts (Psy Sci (Dual)) (IB 29–30 pts)
Sheffield Hallam – BBB 120 pts (Psy)
Stirling – BBB (Psy) (IB 30 pts)
Strathclyde – BBB–ABB (Econ Psy) (IB 30–32 pts)
Swansea – BBB–AAB incl sci/maths 120–136 pts (Psy) (IB 33–34 pts)
UWE Bristol – 120 pts (Crimin Psy)
York St John – 120 pts (Psy)

112 pts **Aberdeen** – BBC incl maths+sci (Neuro Psy) (IB 32 pts HL 555 incl maths+sci)
Bangor – 112–136 pts (Spo Exer Psy)
Bedfordshire – 112 pts (Psy)
Birmingham City – BBC 112 pts (Psy) (IB 28 pts)
Bournemouth – 112–128 pts (Psy) (IB 30–32 pts)
Bradford – 112 pts (Psy)
Buckingham – BBC–ABB+interview (Psy) (IB 31–32 pts)
Canterbury Christ Church – 112 pts (Psy) (IB 29 pts)
Chester – 112 pts (Psy Span) (IB 28 pts); BBC–BBB 112–120 pts (Psy courses) (IB 28 pts)
Chichester – BBC–BBB 112–120 pts (Spo Exer Psy) (IB 28 pts)
De Montfort – 112 pts (Psy) (IB 30 pts)
East London – 112 pts (Foren Psy; Psy; Psycsoc St) (IB 24 pts HL 15 pts)
Essex – BBC (Psy Econ) (IB 29 pts); (Neur Eng Psy) (IB 29 pts HL 554); BBC 112–120 pts (Psy Cog Neuro) (IB 29 pts HL 554)
Greenwich – 112 pts (Crimin Crim Psy)
Greater Manchester – 112 pts+interview (Psy; Psy Psytrpy Cnslg)
Heriot-Watt – BBC–ABB (Psy courses) (IB 29 pts)
Hull – BBC (Psy Crimin) (IB 30 pts)
Leeds Beckett – 112 pts (Crimin Psy) (HL 554)
Leeds Trinity – 112 pts (Cnslg Psy; Foren Psy; Psy)
Lincoln – (Psy; Psy Mntl Hlth)
Liverpool Hope – BBC 112 pts (Psy) (IB 28 pts)
Liverpool John Moores – BBC 112 pts (Crimin Psy)
London South Bank – (Psy; Psy (Chld Dev))
Middlesex – BBC–BBB (Psy)
Northampton – BBC (Psy courses)
Northumbria – 112 pts (Gdnc Cnslg)
Nottingham Trent – 112 pts (Chld (Psy); Law Psy)
Oxford Brookes – BBC 112 pts (Psy) (IB 30 pts)
Plymouth – 112–120 pts (Psy) (IB 26–30 pts); 112–128 pts (Psy Sociol) (IB 28–32 pts)
Portsmouth – BBC–BBB 112–120 pts (Psy) (IB 29 pts)
Queen Margaret – BBC (Psy) (IB 30 pts)
Roehampton – 112 pts (Psy; Psy Cnslg)
Salford – 112 pts (Psy) (IB 31 pts)
Sheffield Hallam – BBC 112 pts (Crimin Psy; Educ Psy Cnslg)
Solent – 112–128 pts (Psy)
Staffordshire – BBC 112 pts (Psy)
Suffolk – BBC 112 pts (Psy Sociol)
Trinity Saint David – 112 pts (Psy)
Ulster – BBC (Psy courses) (IB 25 pts HL 12 pts)
Univ Law – BBC 112 pts (Psy)
West London – BBC 112–120 pts (Psy; Psy Crimin/Cnslg Theor)

Wolverhampton – BBC 112 pts (Psy Cnslg)
Worcester – 112 pts (Psy); BBC 112 pts+portfolio (Fn Art Psy)

104 pts **Anglia Ruskin** – 104 pts (Psy; Psy Crimin) (IB 24 pts)
Bath Spa – BCC (Psy) (IB 32 pts); BCC–BBB 104–120 pts (Psy Comb Hons) (IB 32 pts)
Birmingham Newman – 104 pts (Psy)
Brighton – BCC–BBB 104–120 pts (Psy Crimin; Psy Sociol) (IB 30 pts)
Bucks New – 104–128 pts (Psy; Psy Crimin)
Central Lancashire – 104–120 pts (Foren Psy; Neuropsy; Psy)
Chester – BCC 104 pts (Cnslg Sk Psy) (IB 26 pts)
Chichester – BCC–BBB 104–120 pts (Cnslg Psy) (IB 26–28 pts HL 5 sci); BCC–BBB incl psy/sci 104–120 pts (Psy) (IB 26 pts HL 4 sci); BCC–BBB incl sci/psy 104–120 pts (Educ Psy) (IB 26–28 pts HL 4 sci)
Cumbria – 104–128 pts (App Psy)
De Montfort – 104 pts (Educ St Psy)
Edinburgh Napier – BCC incl Engl (Psy Sociol) (IB 27 pts HL 654 incl 5 Engl); (Psy) (IB 29 pts HL 655 incl 5 Engl)
HSU – BCC–BBB 104–120 pts (Spo Exer Psy) (IB 28–32 pts)
London Met – BCC 104 pts (Psy)
Queen Margaret – BCC (Psy Sociol) (IB 28 pts)
Robert Gordon – BCC (App Psy) (IB 27 pts)
St Mary's – BCC–BBB 104–120 pts (Psy)
West Scotland – BCC 104 pts (Psy) (IB 27 pts)
Westminster – 104–120 pts (Psy; Psy Cnslg)

96 pts **Abertay** – CCC (Psy; Psy Cnslg; Psy Foren Invstg Psy) (IB 28 pts)
Aberystwyth – CCC–BBB 96–120 pts (Psy; Psy Crimin) (IB 26–30 pts)
Bishop Grosseteste – 96–112 pts (Psy Comb Hons)
Cardiff Met – 96–112 pts (Psy) (HL 55)
London (Birk) – CCC–BBB (Psy)
Portsmouth – CCC–BCC 96–112 pts (Sociol Psy) (IB 25 pts)
South Wales – CCC 96 pts (Psy; Psy Cnslg; Psy Dev Diso)
Wolverhampton – 96 pts (Psy)
Wrexham – 96–112 pts (Psy)

88 pts **Teesside** – 88–112 pts (Foren Psy; Psy; Psy Cnslg)
Trinity Saint David – 88 pts (Psy Cnslg)

80 pts **Teesside** – 80–104 pts (Psy Crimin)

72 pts **UHI** – BC (Psy)

48 pts **Univ Law** – 48 pts (Psy Fdn)

Open University – (Comb Soc Sci (Econ/Geog/Psy/Sociol); Psy)

Alternative offers See **Chapter 6** and **Appendix 1** for grades/UCAS Tariff points information for other examinations.

EXAMPLES OF COLLEGES OFFERING COURSES IN THIS SUBJECT FIELD

Bedford (Coll); Blackburn (Coll); Bradford College (UC); Colchester (UC); Croydon (UC); Doncaster (Coll); East Coast (Coll); Farnborough (CT); Guildford (Coll); Metanoia (Inst); Newham (CFE); Norwich City (Coll); Oldham (Univ Campus); Peterborough (UC); Petroc; South Devon (Coll); West Anglia (Coll); Wirral Met (Coll).

CHOOSING YOUR COURSE (SEE ALSO CH.1)

Universities and colleges teaching quality See www.qaa.ac.uk; www.discoveruni.gov.uk.

Top research universities and colleges (REF 2021) (Psychology, Psychiatry and Neuroscience) Imperial London; Edinburgh; Oxford; London (RH); Cambridge; London (UCL); Cardiff; York; London (Birk); Glasgow.

Examples of sandwich degree courses Aston; Bath; Bedfordshire; Bournemouth; Brunel; Cardiff; Coventry; Exeter; Hertfordshire; Kent; Leeds; Loughborough; Nottingham Trent; Plymouth; Portsmouth; Reading; Surrey; Ulster; UWE Bristol; Westminster.

ADMISSIONS INFORMATION

Advice to applicants and planning the UCAS personal statement Psychology is heavily over-subscribed so prepare well in advance by choosing suitable A-level subjects. Contact the Education and Social Services departments in your local authority office to arrange meetings with psychologists to gain a knowledge of the work. Make notes during those meetings and of any work experience gained and describe these fully on the UCAS application. Reference to introductory reading in psychology is important (many students have a distorted image of it). Demonstrate your interest in psychology through, for example, voluntary or other work experience. See also **Appendix 3**.

Selection interviews Yes Cambridge, Exeter (App Psy Clin), Greater Manchester, Oxford (Psy (Expmtl)) 35% (success rate 12%), (Psy Phil Ling) 35% (success rate 13%), Reading (App Psy); **Some** Buckingham, UHI (applicants with non-standard qualifications), Worcester (Fn Art Psy); **No** Bangor, Bishop Grosseteste, Bristol, Chichester, Essex, Huddersfield, London (UCL), Middlesex, Newcastle, Plymouth, Sunderland, Swansea.

Interview advice and questions Although some applicants will have studied the subject at A-level and will have a broad understanding of its coverage, it is still essential to have gained some work experience or to have discussed the career with a professional psychologist. Questions will focus on this and in previous years they have included: What have you read about psychology? What do you expect to gain by studying psychology? What are your parents' and teachers' views on your choice of subject? Are you interested in any particular branch of the subject? Is psychology an art or a science? Do you think you are well suited to this course? Why? Do you think it is possible that if we learn enough about the functioning of the brain we can create a computer that is functionally the same? What is counselling? Is it necessary? Know the differences between the various branches of psychology and discuss any specific interests, for example, in clinical, occupational, educational, criminal psychology and cognitive, neuro-, social or physiological psychology. What influences young children's food choices? What stereotypes do we have of people with mental illness? See also **Chapter 5**.

Reasons for rejection (non-academic) Lack of background reading and lack of awareness of psychology; poor communication skills; misunderstanding of what is involved in a degree course. Poor personal statement. Poor grades, especially in GCSE maths.

GRADUATE DESTINATIONS AND EMPLOYMENT

(See **Chapter 1, Graduate Outcomes.**)

Career note Clinical, educational and occupational psychology are the three main specialist careers for graduate psychologists, all involving further study. Ergonomics, human/computer interaction, marketing, public relations, human resource management, advertising, the social services, the prison and rehabilitation services also provide alternative career routes.

OTHER DEGREE SUBJECTS FOR CONSIDERATION

Anthropology; Behavioural Science; Cognitive Sciences; Education; Health Studies; Neuroscience; Sociology.

RADIOGRAPHY

(including **Medical Imaging and Radiotherapy**; see also **Health Sciences/Studies**)

Many institutions offer both Diagnostic and Therapeutic Radiography but applicants should check this, and course entry requirements, before applying. Information on courses is also available from the Society of Radiographers (see **Appendix 3**). Diagnostic Radiography is the demonstration on film (or other imaging materials) of the position and structure of the body's organs using radiation or other imaging media. Therapeutic Radiography is the planning and administration of treatment for patients suffering from malignant and non-malignant disease using different forms of radiation. Courses lead to state registration.

Useful websites www.sor.org; http://radiographycareers.co.uk; www.healthcareers.nhs.uk

NB The points totals shown to the left of the institutions are for ease of reference only. It must not be assumed that Tariff points are always used by institutions or that they can be substituted for an offer in grades. The level of an offer is not necessarily indicative of the quality of a course.

COURSE OFFERS INFORMATION

Subject requirements/preferences GCSE Five subjects including English, mathematics and a science subject (usually at one sitting). **AL** One or two sciences required; mathematics may be acceptable. (Radiothera) One science subject required for some courses. Psychology may not be considered a science subject at some institutions. Some popular universities are now making lower offers for disadvantaged and other students. **Other** Applicants required to have an occupational health check and a Disclosure and Barring Service (DBS) clearance. Visit to, or work experience in, a hospital imaging department often required/expected.

Your target offers and examples of degree courses

128 pts **Bradford** – ABB incl maths/sci/tech 128 pts+interview (Diag Radiog)
De Montfort – A sci 128 pts (Diag Radiog) (IB 28 pts HL 6 sci)
Derby – ABB incl sci 128 pts+interview (Diag Radiog)
Leeds – ABB incl sci (Diag Radiog) (IB 34 pts HL 555 incl sci)
Sheffield Hallam – ABB incl sci/maths+interview (Diag Radiog)

120 pts **Bangor** – BBC incl B biol/phys 120 pts+interview (Diag Radiog) (HL 6 biol/phys)
Birmingham City – BBB incl sci 120 pts+interview (Diag Radiog; Ther Radiog) (IB 30 pts)
City St George's – BBB incl sci+interview (Diag Radiog) (IB 30 pts HL 14 pts)
Exeter – BBB incl sci/maths/geog+interview (Med Imag (Diag Radiog)) (IB 30 pts HL 555 incl sci)
Gloucestershire – BBB incl sci (Diag Radiog)
Hertfordshire – BBB incl sci+interview (Diag Radiog Imag)
Keele – BBB incl sci+interview (Radiog (Diag Imag)) (IB 30 pts HL 5 sci)
Leicester – BBB+interview (Diag Radiog) (IB 28 pts)
Liverpool – BBB incl sci+interview (Ther Radiog Onc) (IB 30 pts HL 5 maths+biol/phys); (Diag Radiog) (IB 30 pts HL 555 incl biol)
London South Bank – BBB+interview (Thera Radiog); BBB incl sci (Diag Radiog)
Salford – 120 pts (Diag Radiog) (IB 32 pts)
Sheffield Hallam – BBB incl sci 120 pts+interview (Radiothera Onc)
UWE Bristol – C sci 120 pts incl sci+interview (Diag Radiog) (HL 5 sci)
Ulster – BBB incl sci/maths+HPAT (Diag Radiog Imag; Radiothera Onc)

112 pts **Canterbury Christ Church** – BBC 112 pts+interview (Diag Radiog)
Cardiff – BBC–BBB incl sci+interview (Diag Radiog Imag; Radiothera Onc) (IB 30–31 pts HL 655 incl sci)
City St George's – BBC incl maths/sci 112 pts (Thera Radiog Onc) (IB 29 pts); BBC incl sci+interview (Radiothera Onc) (IB 30 pts)
Cumbria – BBC–BBB 112–120 pts incl sci/maths+interview (Diag Radiog)

HSU – BBC–BBB incl sci (Radiog Diag Imag) (IB 30–32 pts)
Hertfordshire – BBC incl maths/sci 112 pts+interview (Ther Radiog)
Plymouth – BBC (Diag Radiog) (IB 28–30 pts HL 5 sci)
Portsmouth – BBC–BBB 112–120 pts incl sci/maths+interview (Diag Radiog Med Imag) (IB 29 pts)
Suffolk – BBC (Diag Radiog; Radiog Onc)
Teesside – 112 pts incl sci+interview (Diag Radiog)
104 pts Glasgow Caledonian – BCC incl sci (Diag Imag; Radiothera Onc) (IB 28 pts)
Robert Gordon – BCC incl sci/maths (Diag Radiog) (IB 27 pts HL 5 Engl)

Alternative offers See **Chapter 6** and **Appendix 1** for grades/UCAS Tariff points information for other examinations.

DEGREE APPRENTICESHIPS

Birmingham City (Diag Radiog); Bristol UWE (Diag Radiog); Bucks New (Diag Radiog); Canterbury Christ Church (Diag Radiog); Cumbria (Diag Radiog); Derby (Diag Radiog); Exeter (Diag Radiog); Hertfordshire (Diag Radiog); Keele (Diag Radiog); London South Bank (Diag Radiog); Sheffield Hallam (Diag Radiog); Teesside (Diag Radiog).

CHOOSING YOUR COURSE (SEE ALSO CH.1)

Universities and colleges teaching quality See www.qaa.ac.uk; www.discoveruni.gov.uk.

Top research universities and colleges (REF 2021) See **Health Sciences/Studies**.

ADMISSIONS INFORMATION

Admissions tutors' advice City St George's Work experience required.

Advice to applicants and planning the UCAS personal statement Contacts with radiographers and visits to the radiography departments of hospitals should be discussed in full on the UCAS application. See also **Appendix 3**.

Selection interviews Yes Bangor, Birmingham City, Bradford, Canterbury Christ Church, Cardiff, City St George's (Radiothera Onc, Diag Radiog), Cumbria, Derby, Exeter, Hertfordshire, Keele, Leeds, Leicester, Liverpool, London South Bank (Thera Radiog), Portsmouth, Robert Gordon, Sheffield Hallam, Teesside, UWE Bristol.

Interview advice and questions All applicants should have discussed this career with a radiographer and visited a hospital radiography department. Questions follow from these contacts. Where does radiography fit into the overall healthcare system? See also **Chapter 5**.

Reasons for rejection (non-academic) Lack of interest in people. Poor communication skills. Occasionally students may be unsuitable for the clinical environment, for example, they express a fear of blood and needles; poor grasp of radiography as a career. Unable to meet criteria for employment in the NHS, for example, health factors, criminal convictions, severe disabilities.

GRADUATE DESTINATIONS AND EMPLOYMENT

(See **Chapter 1, Graduate Outcomes.**)

Career note Most radiographers work in the NHS in hospital radiography departments undertaking diagnostic or therapeutic treatment. Others work in private healthcare.

OTHER DEGREE SUBJECTS FOR CONSIDERATION

Audiology; Forensic Engineering; Health Studies; Medical Physics; Nursing; Occupational Therapy; Physics; Podiatry; Speech Sciences.

RELIGIOUS STUDIES

(including **Biblical Studies, Divinity, Hebrew, Islamic Studies and Theology**; see also **African, Asian and Middle Eastern Studies**)

The subject content of these courses varies and students should check prospectuses carefully. They are not intended as training courses for ministry; an adherence to a particular religious denomination is not a necessary qualification for entry. Courses offer the study of the major religions – Christianity, Judaism, Islam, Buddhism and Hinduism. The comprehensive Lancaster course offers optional modules covering theological, sociological, anthropological, psychological and philosophical perspectives.

Useful websites www.theguardian.com/world/religion; www.jewfaq.org; https://virtualreligion.net; https://academic.oup.com/jis; www.sikhs.org; www.buddhanet.net; www.christianity.com

NB The points totals shown to the left of the institutions are for ease of reference only. It must not be assumed that Tariff points are always used by institutions or that they can be substituted for an offer in grades. The level of an offer is not necessarily indicative of the quality of a course.

COURSE OFFERS INFORMATION

Subject requirements/preferences GCSE English and mathematics. For teacher training, English, mathematics and science. **AL** Religious studies or theology may be required or preferred for some courses. Some popular universities are now making lower offers for disadvantaged and other students.

Your target offers and examples of degree courses

152 pts **Cambridge** – A*AA+interview+TAA (Theol Relgn Phil Relgn) (IB 41–42 pts HL 776)

144 pts **Durham** – AAA (Phil Theol) (IB 37 pts HL 666)

Oxford – AAA+interview (Relgn As Mid E St; Theol Relgn) (IB 38 pts HL 666); AAA+interview +test (Phil Theol) (IB 39 pts HL 666)

St Andrews – AAA (Bib St; Heb courses; Theol; Theol St) (IB 36 pts HL 665)

136 pts **Birmingham** – AAB (Pol Relgn Phil) (IB 32 pts HL 665)

Durham – AAB incl soc sci/hum (Theol courses) (IB 36 pts HL 665)

Exeter – AAB (Theol Relgn) (IB 34 pts HL 665)

London (King's) – AAB (Relgn Phil Eth) (IB 35 pts); (Sociol Pol Relgn) (IB 35 pts HL 665)

128 pts **Birmingham** – ABB (Theol Relgn) (IB 32 pts HL 655)

Bristol – ABB (Relgn Theol) (IB 32 pts HL 16 pts)

Edinburgh – ABB (Div Class; Relig St) (IB 34 pts HL 655); (Islam St) (IB 34–36 pts HL 655–665)

Lancaster – ABB 128 pts (Glob Relgn Int Rel; Glob Relgn Phil; Glob Relgn Pol) (IB 32 pts HL 16 pts)

Leeds – ABB (Islam St; Relig Theol Soty) (IB 34 pts HL 16 pts)

London (UCL) – ABB (Heb Jew St) (IB 34 pts HL 16 pts)

Manchester – ABB (Relgns Theol Eth) (IB 34 pts HL 655)

Nottingham – ABB (Relgn Cult Eth; Relgn Phil Eth) (IB 30 pts HL 655)

Sheffield – ABB (Phil Relgn Eth) (IB 33 pts)

120 pts **Glasgow** – BBB–AAB incl hum (Theol Relig St) (IB 34 pts HL 655 incl Engl+hum)

Stirling – BBB (Relgn courses) (IB 28 pts)

112 pts **Aberdeen** – BBC (Div; Theol Relgn) (IB 32 pts HL 555)

Canterbury Christ Church – BBC 112 pts (Theol) (IB 29 pts)

Cardiff – BCC–BBB (Relgn Theol) (IB 29–31 pts HL 655–665)

Essex – BBC–BBB 112–120 pts (Phil Relgn Eth) (IB 29–30 pts HL 554–555)

104 pts **Bangor** – 104–128 pts (Phil Eth Relgn)

Birmingham Newman – 104–136 pts (Theol Phil)

Chester – BCC–BBC 104–112 pts (Theol Relig St) (IB 26 pts)

Edge Hill – BCC–BBC 104–112 pts (Educ Relgn)

Leeds Trinity – 104–136 pts (Phil Eth Relgn)
Liverpool Hope – BCC 104 pts (Phil Eth Relgn; Theol Relig Spir) (IB 24 pts)
Manchester Met – 104–112 pts (Eth Relgn Phil) (IB 26 pts)
Winchester – BCC–BBB 104–120 pts (Phil Relgn Eth) (HL 44)
York St John – 104 pts (Relgn Phil Eth; Relgn Theol)

96 pts **Bishop Grosseteste** – 96–112 pts (Theol Phil Eth)
Gloucestershire – CCC–BBC 96–112 pts (Relgn Phil Eth)
Islamic (Coll) – CCC (Hawza St; Islam St)
Roehampton – 96–112 pts (Phil Relgn Eth)
St Mary's – 96–112 pts (Theol Relgn Eth)
Trinity Saint David – 96–112 pts (Relig St Comb Hons)

64 pts **UHI** – CC (Theol St)

12 pts **Aberdeen** – BBC (Theol) (IB 32 pts HL 555)

Trinity Saint David – interview (Theol Comb Hons)

Alternative offers See **Chapter 6** and **Appendix 1** for grades/UCAS Tariff points information for other examinations.

EXAMPLES OF COLLEGES OFFERING COURSES IN THIS SUBJECT FIELD

York St John.

CHOOSING YOUR COURSE (SEE ALSO CH.1)

Universities and colleges teaching quality See www.qaa.ac.uk; www.discoveruni.gov.uk.

Top research universities and colleges (REF 2021) (Theology and Religious Studies) Aberdeen; Exeter; London (King's); Birmingham; Kent; Cambridge; London (SOAS); Durham; Leeds; Nottingham.

ADMISSIONS INFORMATION

Advice to applicants and planning the UCAS personal statement An awareness of the differences between the main religions is important as is any special research you have done to help you decide on your preferred courses. Interests in the religious art and architecture of various periods and styles should be noted. Applicants should have an open-minded approach to studying a diverse range of religious traditions.

Selection interviews Yes Cambridge, Oxford (Relgn As Mid E St) 59% (success rate 18%), (Theol Relgn) 71% (success rate 40%); **Some** Durham, Manchester; **No** Bishop Grosseteste, Chester, Winchester.

Interview advice and questions Past questions have included: Why do you want to study Theology/Biblical Studies/Religious Studies? What do you hope to do after obtaining your degree? Questions relating to the A-level syllabus. Questions on current theological topics. Do you have any strong religious convictions? Do you think that your religious beliefs will be changed at the end of the course? Why did you choose Religious Studies rather than Biblical Studies? How would you explain the miracles to a 10-year-old? (BEd course.) Do you agree with the National Lottery? How do you think you can apply theology to your career? See also **Chapter 5**.

Reasons for rejection (non-academic) Students not attending Open Days may be rejected. Too religiously conservative. Failure to interact. Lack of motivation to study a subject which goes beyond A-level.

GRADUATE DESTINATIONS AND EMPLOYMENT

(See **Chapter 1, Graduate Outcomes.**)

Career note Although a small number of graduates may regard these courses as a preparation for entry to religious orders, the great majority enter other careers, with teaching particularly popular.

OTHER DEGREE SUBJECTS FOR CONSIDERATION

Community Studies; Education; History; Philosophy; Psychology; Social Policy and Administration; Social Work.

RETAIL MANAGEMENT

(see also **Business and Management Courses, Business and Management Courses (International and European), Business and Management Courses (Specialised), Marketing**)

This subject attracts a large number of applicants each year and it is necessary to have work experience before applying. The work itself varies depending on the type of retail outlet. After completing their courses graduates in a large department store will be involved in different aspects of the business, for example supervising shop assistants, warehouse and packing staff. They could also receive special training in the sales of particular goods, for example food and drink, clothing, furniture. Subsequently there may be opportunities to become buyers. In more specialised shops, for example shoes, fashion and food, graduates are likely to work only with these products, with opportunities to reach senior management.

USEFUL WEBSITES http://brc.org.uk; www.retail-week.com; www.theretailbulletin.com; www.retailchoice.com; https://nrf.com

NB The points totals shown to the left of the institutions are for ease of reference only. It must not be assumed that Tariff points are always used by institutions or that they can be substituted for an offer in grades. The level of an offer is not necessarily indicative of the quality of a course.

COURSE OFFERS INFORMATION

SUBJECT REQUIREMENTS/PREFERENCES GCSE English and mathematics at grade 4 (C) or above. **AL** No subjects specified. Some popular universities are now making lower offers for disadvantaged and other students.

YOUR TARGET OFFERS AND EXAMPLES OF DEGREE COURSES

120 pts **Stirling** – BBB (Rtl Mark) (IB 28 pts)

112 pts **Arts London** – BBC 112 pts (Fash Mgt) (IB 25 pts)
Birmingham City – BBC 112 pts (Fash Bus Prom) (IB 28 pts HL 14 pts)
Cardiff Met – 112 pts (Mark Mgt)
De Montfort – 112 pts (Fash Buy courses) (IB 26 pts)
Nottingham Trent – 112 pts (Fash Mgt)
Westminster – BBC 112 pts (Contemp Rtl)

104 pts **Bath Spa** – BCC–BBB (Bus Mgt Fash) (IB 32 pts)
FRA – 104–120 pts (Data Analyt Rtl); 104–112 pts (Usr Expnc Des Rtl); 104–120 pts (Buy Mrchnds)
Heriot-Watt – BCC (Fash Brnd Prom) (IB 29 pts)

Greater Manchester – (Bus Mgt (Rtl))

ALTERNATIVE OFFERS See **Chapter 6** and **Appendix 1** for grades/UCAS Tariff points information for other examinations.

DEGREE APPRENTICESHIPS

Greater Manchester (Rtl Bus Mgt).

EXAMPLES OF COLLEGES OFFERING COURSES IN THIS SUBJECT FIELD

Blackburn (Coll); Blackpool and Fylde (Coll); Durham New (Coll); Grŵp Llandrillo Menai; Hugh Baird (Coll); Hull (Coll); Leeds City (Coll); Newcastle (Coll).

CHOOSING YOUR COURSE (SEE ALSO CH.1)

UNIVERSITIES AND COLLEGES TEACHING QUALITY See www.qaa.ac.uk; www.discoveruni.gov.uk.

EXAMPLES OF SANDWICH DEGREE COURSES Arts London; Birmingham City.

ADMISSIONS INFORMATION

ADVICE TO APPLICANTS AND PLANNING THE UCAS PERSONAL STATEMENT See **Business and Management Courses**.

INTERVIEW ADVICE AND QUESTIONS See **Business and Management Courses**.

REASONS FOR REJECTION (NON-ACADEMIC) See **Business and Management Courses**.

GRADUATE DESTINATIONS AND EMPLOYMENT

(See **Chapter 1, Graduate Outcomes.**)

CAREER NOTE Majority of graduates work in business involved in marketing and retail work. Employment options include brand design, product management, advertising, PR, sales and account management.

OTHER DEGREE SUBJECTS FOR CONSIDERATION

Business Studies; Consumer Sciences/Studies; E-Commerce; Human Resource Management; Psychology; Supply Chain Management.

SCANDINAVIAN STUDIES

(see also **Languages**)

Scandinavian Studies provides students who enjoy languages with the opportunity to extend their language expertise to learn a modern Scandinavian language – Danish, Norwegian or Swedish – from beginner's level to Honours level in four years, including a year in Scandinavia. The three languages are very similar to each other and a knowledge of one makes it possible to access easily the literature and cultures of the other two. Viking Studies includes Old Norse, runology and archaeology.

USEFUL WEBSITES www.ciol.org.uk; www.languageadvantage.com; www.languagematters.co.uk; www.scandinaviahouse.org; https://scandinavianstudy.org

NB The points totals shown to the left of the institutions are for ease of reference only. It must not be assumed that Tariff points are always used by institutions or that they can be substituted for an offer in grades. The level of an offer is not necessarily indicative of the quality of a course.

COURSE OFFERS INFORMATION

SUBJECT REQUIREMENTS/PREFERENCES GCSE Foreign language preferred for all courses. **AL** A modern language may be required. Some popular universities are now making lower offers for disadvantaged and other students.

YOUR TARGET OFFERS AND EXAMPLES OF DEGREE COURSES

152 pts **Cambridge** – A*AA+interview+ASNCAA (A-Sxn Nrs Celt) (IB 41–42 pts HL 776)

128 pts **Edinburgh** – ABB (Celt; Scand St (Dan); Scand St (Norw); Scand St (Swed)) (IB 34 pts HL 655)

London (UCL) – ABB (Ice; Scand St; Vkg Old Nrs St) (IB 34 pts HL 16 pts)

ALTERNATIVE OFFERS See **Chapter 6** and **Appendix 1** for grades/UCAS Tariff points information for other examinations.

CHOOSING YOUR COURSE (SEE ALSO CH.1)

UNIVERSITIES AND COLLEGES TEACHING QUALITY See www.qaa.ac.uk; www.discoveruni.gov.uk.

ADMISSIONS INFORMATION

ADVICE TO APPLICANTS AND PLANNING THE UCAS PERSONAL STATEMENT Visits to Scandinavian countries could be the source of an interest in studying these languages. You should also be aware of cultural, political, geographical and economic aspects of Scandinavian countries. Knowledge of these should be shown in your statement.

SELECTION INTERVIEWS Yes Cambridge; **Some** London (UCL).

INTERVIEW ADVICE AND QUESTIONS Applicants in the past have been questioned on why they have chosen this subject area, on their visits to Scandinavia and on their knowledge of the country/countries and their people. Future career plans are likely to be discussed. See also **Chapter 5**.

REASONS FOR REJECTION (NON-ACADEMIC) One applicant didn't know the difference between a noun and a verb.

GRADUATE DESTINATIONS AND EMPLOYMENT

(See **Chapter 1, Graduate Outcomes.**)

CAREER NOTE See **Languages**.

OTHER DEGREE SUBJECTS FOR CONSIDERATION

Archaeology; European History/Studies; History; other modern languages, including, for example, Russian and East European languages.

SOCIAL AND PUBLIC POLICY AND ADMINISTRATION

(see also **Community Studies/Development, Social Work, Sociology**)

Social Policy is a multi-disciplinary degree that combines elements from sociology, political science, social and economic history, economics, cultural studies and philosophy. It is a study of the needs of society and how best to provide such services as education, housing, health and welfare services.

USEFUL WEBSITES www.local.gov.uk

NB The points totals shown to the left of the institutions are for ease of reference only. It must not be assumed that Tariff points are always used by institutions or that they can be substituted for an offer in grades. The level of an offer is not necessarily indicative of the quality of a course.

COURSE OFFERS INFORMATION

SUBJECT REQUIREMENTS/PREFERENCES GCSE English and mathematics normally required. **AL** No subjects specified. Some popular universities are now making lower offers for disadvantaged and other students.

YOUR TARGET OFFERS AND EXAMPLES OF DEGREE COURSES

152 pts **Cambridge** – A*AA+interview+HSPSAA (Hum Soc Pol Sci) (IB 41–42 pts HL 776)
Durham – A*AA (Comb Hons Soc Sci) (IB 38 pts HL 666)

144 pts **Edinburgh** – AAA (Soc Plcy courses) (IB 37 pts HL 666)

136 pts **Bath** – AAB–ABB+aEPQ (Soc Plcy) (IB 35 pts HL 665)
Birmingham – AAB (Pol Soc Plcy) (IB 32 pts HL 665)
Bristol – AAB (Soc Plcy; Soc Plcy Pol; Soc Plcy Sociol) (IB 34 pts HL 17 pts)
London LSE – AAB (Int Soc Pblc Plcy; Int Soc Pblc Plcy Pol) (IB 37 pts HL 666); AAB incl A maths (Int Soc Pblc Plcy Econ) (IB 37 pts HL 666 incl maths)

128 pts **Birmingham** – ABB (Soc Plcy) (IB 32 pts HL 655 incl Engl)
Leeds – ABB (Soc Plcy courses; Soc Pol Sociol Crim) (IB 34 pts HL 655)
Loughborough – ABB (Crimin Sociol) (IB 34 pts HL 655)
Queen's Belfast – ABB (Crimin Soc Plcy) (IB 33 pts HL 655)
Sheffield – ABB (Sociol Soc Plcy) (IB 33 pts)
Southampton – ABB (Sociol Crimin) (IB 32 pts HL 16 pts)

120 pts **Glasgow** – BBB–AAB incl Engl/hum (Soc Pblc Plcy) (IB 36 pts HL 665 incl Engl/hum)
Liverpool – BBB (Sociol Soc Plcy) (IB 30 pts)
Queen's Belfast – BBB (Soc Plcy Sociol) (IB 32 pts HL 655)

Stirling – BBB (Sociol Soc Plcy) (IB 28 pts)
Strathclyde – BBB–ABB (Soc Plcy Econ) (IB 30–32 pts)
Swansea – BBB–ABB (Crimin Soc Plcy) (IB 32–33 pts)
York – BBB (Soc Pblc Plcy) (IB 31 pts)

112 pts **Cardiff** – BBC–ABB (Crimin Soc Plcy) (IB 30–32 pts HL 655–665)

104 pts **Bangor** – 104–128 pts (Soc Plcy Comb Hons; Sociol Soc Pol)
Cardiff – BCC–BBB (Sociol Soc Plcy) (IB 29–31 pts HL 655–665)
Ulster – BCC (Soc Plcy Sociol) (IB 24–25 pts HL 12 pts)

96 pts **Lincoln** – 96 pts (Crimin Soc Plcy; Soc Plcy)
Wolverhampton – CCC/BCD 96 pts (Pol Soc Plcy; Soc Plcy courses; Sociol Soc Pol)

Alternative offers See **Chapter 6** and **Appendix 1** for grades/UCAS Tariff points information for other examinations.

DEGREE APPRENTICESHIPS

Birmingham City (Pblc Mgt Ldrshp); Portsmouth (Pblc Admin).

EXAMPLES OF COLLEGES OFFERING COURSES IN THIS SUBJECT FIELD

Barnfield (Coll); Blackburn (Coll); Canterbury (Coll); Central Bedfordshire (Coll); Chesterfield (Coll); Craven (Coll); Dearne Valley (Coll); Derby (Coll); Dudley (Coll); Durham New (Coll); East Surrey (Coll); Exeter (Coll); Grŵp Llandrillo Menai; Hull (Coll); Macclesfield (Coll); Manchester (Coll); Milton Keynes (Coll); Norwich City (Coll); Plymouth City (Coll); South Gloucestershire and Stroud (Coll); St Helens (Coll); Walsall (Coll); Weston (Coll).

CHOOSING YOUR COURSE (SEE ALSO CH.1)

Universities and colleges teaching quality See www.qaa.ac.uk; www.discoveruni.gov.uk.

Top research universities and colleges (REF 2021) See **Social Work**.

Examples of sandwich degree courses Bath; Leeds.

ADMISSIONS INFORMATION

Advice to applicants and planning the UCAS personal statement Careers in public and social administration are covered by this subject; consequently a good knowledge of these occupations and contacts with the social services should be discussed fully on your UCAS application. Gain work experience if possible. (See **Appendix 3** for contact details of some relevant organisations.)

Selection interviews Yes Cambridge; **Some** Loughborough; **No** London LSE, Swansea.

Interview advice and questions Past questions have included: What relevance has history to social administration? What do you understand by 'public policy'? What advantage do you think studying social science gives when working in policy fields? How could the image of public management of services be improved? Applicants should be fully aware of the content and the differences between all the courses on offer, why they want to study Social Policy and their career objectives. See also **Chapter 5**.

Reasons for rejection (non-academic) Some universities require attendance when they invite applicants to Open Days (check). Lack of awareness of current social issues. See also **Social Work**.

GRADUATE DESTINATIONS AND EMPLOYMENT

(See **Chapter 1, Graduate Outcomes.**)

Career note See **Social Sciences/Studies**.

OTHER DEGREE SUBJECTS FOR CONSIDERATION

Behavioural Science; Community Studies; Criminology; Economic and Social History; Economics; Education; Government; Health Studies; Human Resource Management; Law; Politics; Psychology; Social Work; Sociology; Women's Studies.

SOCIAL SCIENCES/STUDIES

(including **Combined Social Sciences, Criminal Justice, Criminology, Human Rights, Counter Terrorism and Cybercrime**; see also **Combined and Liberal Arts Courses, Education Studies, Health Sciences/Studies, Law, Politics, Psychology, Teacher Training**)

Most Social Sciences/Studies courses take a broad view of aspects of society, for example, economics, politics, history, social psychology and urban studies. Applied Social Studies usually focuses on practical and theoretical preparation for a career in social work. These courses are particularly popular with mature students and some universities and colleges offer shortened degree courses for those with relevant work experience.

Useful websites http://volunteeringmatters.org.uk

NB The points totals shown to the left of the institutions are for ease of reference only. It must not be assumed that Tariff points are always used by institutions or that they can be substituted for an offer in grades. The level of an offer is not necessarily indicative of the quality of a course.

COURSE OFFERS INFORMATION

Subject requirements/preferences GCSE Usually English and mathematics; a science may be required. **AL** No subjects specified. Some popular universities are now making lower offers for disadvantaged and other students. **Other** A Disclosure and Barring Service (DBS) check and relevant work experience required for some courses.

Your target offers and examples of degree courses

152 pts **Cambridge** – A*AA+interview+HSPSAA (Hum Soc Pol Sci) (IB 41–42 pts HL 776)
Durham – A*AA (Comb Hons Soc Sci) (IB 38 pts HL 666)
Manchester – A*AA (Law Crimin) (IB 37 pts HL 766)

144 pts **London (UCL)** – AAA (Soc Sci; Soc Sci Data Sci) (IB 38 pts HL 18 pts)

136 pts **Durham** – AAB (Crimin) (IB 36 pts HL 665)
Exeter – AAB (Crimin) (IB 34 pts HL 665)
Lancaster – AAB (Crimin Psy; Law Crimin) (IB 35 pts HL 16 pts)
London (King's) – AAB (Soc Sci) (IB 35 pts HL 17 pts)
Manchester – AAB (Crimin) (IB 35 pts HL 665); AAB–AAA incl sci (Biol Sci Soty) (IB 35–36 pts HL 665–666 incl sci)
York – AAB (Soc Pol Sci) (IB 35–36 pts)

128 pts **Bath** – ABB–BBB+aEPQ (Soc Sci) (IB 35 pts HL 655)
Bristol – ABB (Chld St) (IB 32 pts HL 16 pts)
East Anglia – ABB (Crimin) (IB 32 pts)
Glasgow Caledonian – ABB (Soc Sci)
Lancaster – ABB (Crimin) (IB 32 pts HL 16 pts)
Leeds – ABB (Chld St; Soc Plcy Crm) (IB 34 pts HL 655)
Leicester – ABB (Crimin Foren Psy) (IB 30 pts); ABB–BBB+bEPQ (Crimin) (IB 30 pts)
Liverpool John Moores – ABB 128 pts (Foren Psy Crim Just)
London (UCL) – ABB (Popn Hlth Sci) (IB 34 pts HL 16 pts); (Educ Soty Cult) (IB 34 pts HL 655)
Loughborough – ABB (Crimin Sociol) (IB 34 pts HL 655)
Manchester – ABB (Soc Anth Crimin) (IB 34 pts HL 655)
Queen's Belfast – ABB (Crimin) (IB 33 pts HL 655)
Surrey – ABB (Law Crimin) (IB 33 pts)

120 pts **Cardiff** – BBB–ABB (Crimin) (IB 31–34 pts HL 665–666); BBC–ABB (Crimin Sociol) (IB 30–32 pts HL 655–665)
City St George's – BBB 120 pts (Crimin Sociol)
Huddersfield – BBB 120 pts (Psy Crimin)
Leeds Beckett – 120 pts (Law Crimin) (HL 55)
Liverpool – BBB (Crimin) (IB 30 pts)

Liverpool John Moores – BBB 120 pts (Law Crim Just)
Portsmouth – BBB–AAB 120–136 pts (Coun Terr Intel Cybercrim) (IB 29–31 pts)
Stirling – BBB (Crimin Sociol) (IB 28 pts)
Stranmillis (UC) – BBB+interview (Ely Chld St)
Sunderland – 120 pts (Crimin)
Surrey – BBB (Crimin Sociol) (IB 32 pts)
Swansea – BBB–ABB (Soc Plcy)
UWE Bristol – 120 pts (Crimin Psy); BBB 120 pts (Crimin)
Ulster – BBB (Crimin Crim Just) (IB 24 pts HL 12 pts)

112 pts **Aberdeen** – BBC–BBB (Crimin Sociol) (IB 32 pts HL 555)
Birmingham City – BBC 112 pts (Crimin Plcg Invstg; Crimin courses) (IB 28 pts HL 14 pts)
Canterbury Christ Church – BBC 112 pts (App Crimin) (IB 29 pts)
Cardiff – BBC–ABB (Crimin Soc Plcy) (IB 30–32 pts HL 655–665)
Chester – BBC–BBB 112–120 pts (Law Crimin) (IB 28 pts); BCC–BBC 112 pts (Crimin) (IB 26 pts)
Coventry – BBC 112 pts (Crimin) (IB 27–29 pts)
De Montfort – 112 pts (Crimin) (IB 24 pts)
Derby – BBC–BBB 112–120 pts (Crimin)
East London – 112 pts (Crimin Crim Just) (IB 24 pts HL 15 pts)
Edge Hill – BBC–BBB 112–120 pts (Crimin)
Essex – BBC (Law Crimin; Law Hum Rts) (IB 29 pts HL 554); BBC–BBB 112–120 pts (Crimin; Crimin Am St; Sociol Crimin) (IB 29–30 pts HL 554–555)
Greater Manchester – 112 pts+interview (Crm Crim Just)
Greenwich – 112 pts (Crimin Crim Psy); BBC 112 pts (Crimin courses)
Hull – BBC (Psy Crimin) (IB 30 pts); BBC 112 pts (Crimin) (IB 28 pts)
Keele – BBC 112 pts (Crimin; Crimin Comb Hons) (IB 29 pts HL 554)
Kent – BBC (Crim Just Crimin) (HL 556); (Crimin) (IB 30 pts HL 15 pts)
Kingston – 112 pts (Crimin courses)
Leeds Beckett – 112 pts (Crimin Psy) (HL 554)
Liverpool John Moores – BBC 112 pts (Crim Just; Crimin; Crimin Psy)
London (Birk) – BBC 112 pts (Crimin Crim Just; Soc Pol Sci)
London (RH) – BBC–BBB (Soc Sci) (IB 30 pts HL 555); (Crimin Sociol) (IB 32 pts HL 655)
London Met – BBC 112 pts (Crimin courses)
London South Bank – 112 pts (Crimin)
Northumbria – 112 pts (Crimin; Crimin Foren Sci; Integ Hlth Soc Cr)
Nottingham Trent – 112 pts (Crimin; Law Crimin); BBC 112 pts (Comm Soty courses)
Portsmouth – BBC–BBB 112–120 pts (Crimin Crim Just; Crimin Cybercrim) (IB 29 pts)
Roehampton – 112 pts (Crimin Crim Just)
Sheffield Hallam – BBC 112 pts (Crimin; Crimin Psy; Crimin Sociol)
Solent – 112–128 pts (Crimin)
Staffordshire – BBC 112 pts (Crimin; Plcg Crim Invstg)
UWE Bristol – 112 pts (Law Crimin)
West London – BBC 112–120 pts (Crimin; Psy Crimin/Cnslg Theor)
Winchester – BBC–BBB 112–120 pts (Crimin) (HL 44)
Worcester – 112 pts (Crimin Plcg)

104 pts **Abertay** – BCC (Crimin Plcg/Sociol)
Aberystwyth – BCC–ABB 104–128 pts (Hum Rts) (IB 28–30 pts)
Bangor – 104–128 pts (Crimin Crim Just)
Brighton – BCC–BBB 104–120 pts (Psy Crimin; Soc Sci) (IB 26–30 pts)
Cardiff – BCC–BBB (Soc Sci) (IB 29–31 pts HL 655–665)
Central Lancashire – 104–112 pts (Crimin courses; Plcg Crim Invstg)
Chichester – BCC–BBB incl sci/psy 104–120 pts (Crimin Foren Psy) (IB 28 pts HL 4 sci)
Cumbria – BCC–BBC 104–112 pts (Crimin; Crimin Foren Invstg)
Edinburgh Napier – BCC incl Engl (Plcg Crimin; Soc Sci) (IB 28 pts HL 654 incl 5 Engl); (Crimin) (IB 28 pts HL 654 incl Engl)
Gloucestershire – BCC–BBB 104–120 pts (Crimin)

Greenwich – 104 pts incl sci (Foren Sci Crimin) (IB 26 pts HL 5 sci)
Huddersfield – BCC–BBC 104–112 pts (Crimin)
Leeds Trinity – 104 pts (Crimin Sociol)
Lincoln – 104 pts (Crimin)
Liverpool Hope – BCC 104 pts (Crimin) (IB 24 pts)
Liverpool John Moores – BCC 104 pts (Crimin Sociol)
Manchester Met – 104–120 pts (Crimin) (IB 26 pts)
Middlesex – BCC 104 pts (Crimin (Plcg Invstg); Crimin courses)
Northampton – BCC (Crimin)
Plymouth – 104–120 pts (Crimin) (IB 26–30 pts)
Robert Gordon – BCC (App Soc Sci) (IB 27 pts)
Solent – 104–120 pts (Crim Invstg Foren Psy)
West London – BCC 104 pts+interview (Soc Sci)
Westminster – BCC–BBB 104–120 pts (Crimin)

96 pts **Abertay** – CCC (Crimin) (IB 28 pts)
Aberystwyth – CCC–BBB 96–120 pts (Crimin) (IB 26–30 pts)
Anglia Ruskin – 96 pts (Crimin courses) (IB 24 pts)
Bedfordshire – 96 pts (Crimin)
Bishop Grosseteste – 96–112 pts (Ely Chld St courses)
Lincoln – 96 pts (Crimin Soc Plcy)
South Wales – CCC 96 pts (Crimin Yth Just)
Teesside – 96–112 pts (Crm Scn Sci)
West Scotland – CCC 96 pts (Crim Just) (IB 27 pts)
Wolverhampton – CCC/BCD 96 pts (Crimin Crim Just; Plcg Intel); CCC/BCD incl chem/biol 96 pts (Foren Sci Plcg)
Wrexham – 96–112 pts (Crimin Crim Just)

88 pts **Bucks New** – 88–112 pts (Crimin; Hlth Soc Sci)

80 pts **Teesside** – 80–104 pts (Crimin courses; Crm Invstg; Psy Crimin)

72 pts **Farnborough (CT)** – 72 pts (Psy Crimin)
UHI – BC (Soc Sci)

64 pts **London (Gold)** – CC+interview (Soc Sci Commun Dev Yth Wk)

Open University – (Comb Soc Sci (Econ/Geog/Psy/Sociol); Crimin Psy)

Alternative offers See **Chapter 6** and **Appendix 1** for grades/UCAS Tariff points information for other examinations.

EXAMPLES OF COLLEGES OFFERING COURSES IN THIS SUBJECT FIELD

Accrington and Rossendale (Coll); Blackburn (Coll); Blackpool and Fylde (Coll); Cornwall (Coll); Coventry (Coll); Derby (Coll); Doncaster (Coll); Ealing, Hammersmith and West London (Coll); Exeter (Coll); Gloucestershire (Coll); Grŵp Llandrillo Menai; Lincoln (Coll); Middlesbrough (Coll); MidKent (Coll); North Lindsey (Coll); Norwich City (Coll); Peterborough (UC); Richmond-upon-Thames (Coll); Sir Gâr (Coll); South Essex (Coll); Stamford (Coll); Truro and Penwith (Coll); Warwickshire (Coll); West Anglia (Coll); Wirral Met (Coll); York (Coll).

CHOOSING YOUR COURSE (SEE ALSO CH.1)

Universities and colleges teaching quality See www.qaa.ac.uk; www.discoveruni.gov.uk.

Top research universities and colleges (REF 2021) See individual social science subjects.

Examples of sandwich degree courses Bangor; Bath; Coventry; Middlesex; Portsmouth; Surrey.

ADMISSIONS INFORMATION

Advice to applicants and planning the UCAS personal statement The Social Sciences/Studies subject area covers several topics. Focus on these (or some of these) and state your main areas of interest, outlining your work experience, personal goals and motivation to follow the course. Show your interest in current affairs and especially in social issues and government policies.

Selection interviews Yes Cambridge, Greater Manchester, London (Gold), Stranmillis (UC); **Some** Bath; **No** Kingston, Sunderland, West London, Winchester.

Interview advice and questions Past questions have included: Define democracy. What is the role of the Church in nationalistic aspirations? Does today's government listen to its people? Questions on current affairs. How would you change the running of your school? What are the faults of the Labour Party/Conservative Party? Do you agree with the National Lottery? Is money from the National Lottery well spent? Give examples of how the social services have failed. What is your understanding of the social origins of problems? See also **Chapter 5**.

Reasons for rejection (non-academic) Stated preference for other institutions. Incompetence in answering questions.

GRADUATE DESTINATIONS AND EMPLOYMENT

(See **Chapter 1, Graduate Outcomes.**)

Career note Graduates find careers in all aspects of social provision, for example health services, welfare agencies such as housing departments, the probation service, police forces, the prison service, personnel work and residential care and other careers not necessarily linked with their degree subjects.

OTHER DEGREE SUBJECTS FOR CONSIDERATION

Business Studies; Community Studies; Economics; Education; Geography; Government; Health Studies; Law; Politics; Psychology; Public Administration; Social Policy; Social Work; Sociology; Urban Studies.

SOCIAL WORK

(see also **Community Studies/Development, Social and Public Policy and Administration**)

Social Work courses (which lead to careers in social work) have similarities to those in Applied Social Studies, Social Policy and Administration, Community Studies and Health Studies. If you are offered a place on a Social Work course which leads to registration as a social worker, you must undergo the Disclosure and Barring Service (DBS) check. You will also have to provide health information and certification. Check for full details of training and careers in social work with the Health and Care Council (see **Appendix 3**). Students from England may be eligible for student bursaries from the NHS Business Services Authority.

Useful websites www.ageuk.org.uk; www.samaritans.org; https://socialcare.wales; www.sssc.uk.com; https://niscc.info; www.basw.co.uk

NB The points totals shown to the left of the institutions are for ease of reference only. It must not be assumed that Tariff points are always used by institutions or that they can be substituted for an offer in grades. The level of an offer is not necessarily indicative of the quality of a course.

COURSE OFFERS INFORMATION

Subject requirements/preferences GCSE English and mathematics usually required. **AL** No subjects specified. Some popular universities are now making lower offers for disadvantaged and other students. **Other** Disclosure and Barring Service (DBS) check and an occupational health check required. Check also with universities for applicant minimum age requirements.

Your target offers and examples of degree courses

128 pts **Birmingham** – ABB+interview+test (Soc Wk) (IB 32 pts HL 655)
Edinburgh – ABB (Soc Wk) (IB 34 pts HL 655)
Leeds – ABB+interview+test (Soc Wk) (IB 34 pts HL 16 pts)
Nottingham – ABB+interview+test (Soc Wk) (IB 30 pts HL 655)
Queen's Belfast – ABB+interview (Soc Wk)

120 pts **Bath** – 120 pts (Soc Wk App Soc St)
Birmingham City – BBB 120 pts+interview+test (Soc Wk) (IB 30 pts)

Bradford – BBB 120 pts+interview (Soc Wk)
Central Lancashire – 120 pts+interview+test (Soc Wk)
Chester – BBB 120 pts (Soc Wk) (IB 28 pts)
Coventry – BBB 120 pts+interview (Soc Wk) (IB 30 pts HL 15 pts)
East Anglia – BBB+interview (Soc Wk) (IB 31 pts)
Edge Hill – BBB 120 pts+interview+test (Soc Wk)
Greenwich – 120 pts+interview (Soc Wk)
Hertfordshire – BBB–ABB 120–128 pts+interview (Soc Wk)
Hull – BBB 120 pts+interview+test (Soc Wk) (IB 30 pts)
Kent – BBB+interview (Soc Wk) (IB 30 pts HL 15 pts)
Kingston – BBB 120–136 pts+interview+test (Soc Wk)
Lancaster – BBB+interview+test (Soc Wk) (IB 30 pts HL 15 pts)
Leeds Beckett – 120 pts+interview (Soc Wk) (IB 26 pts)
Liverpool Hope – BBB 120 pts+interview (Soc Wk) (IB 28 pts)
London Met – BBB 120 pts+interview+test (Soc Wk)
London South Bank – BBB+interview (Soc Wk)
Manchester Met – BBB 120 pts+interview (Soc Wk) (IB 30 pts)
Northumbria – 120 pts+interview (Soc Wk)
Nottingham Trent – BBB 120 pts+interview (Soc Wk)
Salford – 120 pts+interview+test (Soc Wk)
Sheffield Hallam – BBB 120 pts+interview (Soc Wk)
Stirling – BBB+assessments (Soc Wk) (IB 28 pts)
Strathclyde – BBB–ABB+interview (Soc Wk)
Suffolk – BBB 120 pts (Soc Wk)
Sunderland – 120 pts (Soc Wk)
Wolverhampton – BBB 120 pts+interview (Soc Wk)
Worcester – 120 pts+interview (Soc Wk)
York – BBB+interview (Soc Wk) (IB 31 pts)

112 pts **Anglia Ruskin** – 112 pts+interview (Soc Wk) (IB 26 pts)
Bedfordshire – 112 pts+interview (Soc Wk)
Bournemouth – 112–128 pts+interview (Soc Wk) (IB 30–32 pts)
Brighton – BBC–ABB 112–128 pts+interview (Soc Wk) (IB 28–32 pts)
Canterbury Christ Church – BBC+interview (Soc Wk)
Derby – BBC–BBB 112–120 pts+interview (App Soc Wk)
East London – 112 pts+interview+test (Soc Wk) (IB 24 pts HL 15 pts)
Essex – BBC 112–120 pts+interview (Soc Wk) (IB 29–30 pts HL 554–555)
Glasgow Caledonian – BBC (Soc Wk)
Keele – BBC+interview+test (Soc Wk) (IB 29 pts)
Middlesex – 112 pts+interview+test (Soc Wk)
Northampton – BBC (Soc Wk)
Portsmouth – BBC–BBB 112–120 pts+interview (Soc Wk) (IB 25 pts)
Staffordshire – BBC 112 pts (Soc Wk)
Sussex – BBC–BBB+interview (Soc Wk) (IB 30 pts)
Teesside – 112–128 pts+interview (Soc Wk)
UWE Bristol – 112 pts+interview (Soc Wk)
West Scotland – BBC 112 pts (Soc Wk) (IB 27 pts)

104 pts **Bucks New** – 104–128 pts+interview+test (Soc Wk)
Cumbria – 104–120 pts+interview+test (Soc Wk)
Gloucestershire – BCC 104 pts (Soc Wk)
Oxford Brookes – BCC 104 pts+interview+test (Soc Wk) (IB 29 pts)
Plymouth – 104–120 pts (Soc Wk) (IB 26–30 pts)
Solent – 104–120 pts+interview (Soc Wk)
Swansea – BCC (Soc Wk) (IB 33–34 pts)

96 pts **Bedfordshire** – 96 pts (Hlth Soc Cr)
Cardiff Met – 96 pts (Hlth Soc Cr); 96 pts+interview+test (Soc Wk)

Chichester – CCC–BBC 96–112 pts+interview (Soc Wk) (IB 26–28 pts)
Greater Manchester – 96 pts+interview (Hlth Soc Cr)
London (Gold) – CCC+interview+test (Soc Wk) (IB 27 pts HL 555)
Northampton – CCC (Hlth Soc Cr Prac)
Robert Gordon – CCC (Soc Wk) (IB 26 pts)
South Wales – CCC+interview+test (Soc Wk) (IB 29 pts)
Winchester – 96–112 pts+interview (Soc Wk)

88 pts **Dundee** – AB–CCC (Soc Wk) (IB 29 pts HL 554)
Winchester – CCD–BCC 88–104 pts (Hlth Soc Cr)

80 pts **Birmingham (UC)** – CDD–CCC 80–96 pts (Hlth Soc Cr)
Wrexham – 80–112 pts+interview (Soc Wk)

64 pts **London (Gold)** – CC+interview (Soc Sci Commun Dev Yth Wk)

Open University – (Soc Wk)

Alternative offers See **Chapter 6** and **Appendix 1** for grades/UCAS Tariff points information for other examinations.

DEGREE APPRENTICESHIPS

Anglia Ruskin (Soc Wkr); Bradford (Soc Wkr); Brighton (Soc Wk); Bucks New (Soc Wk); Chester (Soc Wk); Central Lancashire (Soc Wk); Chichester (Soc Wk); Derby (Soc Wkr); East Anglia (Soc Wk); Gloucestershire (Soc Wk); Greater Manchester (Soc Wkr); Hertfordshire (Soc Wk); Hull (Soc Wk); Kent (Soc Wk); Kingston (Soc Wk); Leeds Beckett (Soc Wk); Lincoln (Soc Wk); Liverpool John Moores (Soc Wk); London South Bank (Soc Wkr); Manchester Met (Soc Wkr); Middlesex (Soc Wkr); Northumbria (Soc Wkr); Nottingham Trent (Soc Wkr); Open (Soc Wkr); Sheffield Hallam (Soc Wkr); Southampton (Soc Wkr); Staffordshire (Soc Wkr); Suffolk (Soc Wk); Sunderland (Soc Wk); Warwick (Soc Wk); Winchester (Soc Wk); Wolverhampton (Soc Wk).

EXAMPLES OF COLLEGES OFFERING COURSES IN THIS SUBJECT FIELD

Barnfield (Coll); Birmingham Met (Coll); Blackburn (Coll); Bradford College (UC); Cornwall (Coll); Durham New (Coll); East Coast (Coll); Exeter (Coll); Furness (Coll); Gateshead (Coll); Grŵp Llandrillo Menai; Harrogate (Coll); Hartlepool (CFE); HOW (Coll); Hull (Coll); Leeds City (Coll); Liverpool City (Coll); MidKent (Coll); Newcastle (Coll); North Lindsey (Coll); Norwich City (Coll); Nottingham (Coll); Sir Gâr (Coll); South Cheshire (Coll); South City Birmingham (Coll); South Gloucestershire and Stroud (Coll); South Thames (Coll); Southport (Coll); Stockport (Coll); TEC Partnership; Truro and Penwith (Coll); Warrington and Vale Royal (Coll); Warwickshire (Coll); Wiltshire (Coll); Wirral Met (Coll).

CHOOSING YOUR COURSE (SEE ALSO CH.1)

Universities and colleges teaching quality See www.qaa.ac.uk; www.discoveruni.gov.uk.

Top research universities and colleges (REF 2021) (Social Work and Social Policy) London LSE; Bristol; Kent; Southampton; East Anglia; Oxford; Glasgow; Birmingham; Bath; London (UCL).

ADMISSIONS INFORMATION

Advice to applicants and planning the UCAS personal statement The statement should show motivation for social work, relevant work experience, awareness of the demands of social work and give relevant personal information, for example disabilities. Awareness of the origins of personal and family difficulties, commitment to anti-discriminatory practice. Most applicants for these courses will have significant experience of a statutory care agency or voluntary/private organisation providing a social work or social care service. See also **Social and Public Policy and Administration** and **Appendix 4**.

Selection interviews Yes Anglia Ruskin, Bath, Bedfordshire (Soc Wk), Birmingham, Birmingham City, Bournemouth, Bradford, Brighton, Bucks New, Canterbury Christ Church, Cardiff Met, Central Lancashire, Chester, Chichester, Coventry, Cumbria, Derby, East Anglia, East London, Edge Hill, Essex, Gloucestershire, Greater Manchester, Greenwich, Hertfordshire, Hull, Keele, Kent, Kingston, Lancaster, Leeds, Leeds Beckett, Liverpool Hope, London (Gold), London Met, London South Bank, Manchester

Met, Middlesex, Northumbria, Nottingham, Nottingham Trent, Oxford Brookes, Plymouth, Portsmouth, Queen's Belfast, Robert Gordon, Salford, Sheffield Hallam, Solent, South Wales, Strathclyde, Sunderland, Sussex, Swansea, Teesside, UWE Bristol, Winchester (Soc Wk), Wolverhampton, Worcester, Wrexham, York; **No** Edinburgh, West Scotland.

Interview advice and questions What qualities are needed to be a social worker? What use do you think you will be to society as a social worker? Why should money be spent on prison offenders? Your younger brother is playing truant and mixing with bad company. Your parents don't know. What would you do? See also **Social and Public Policy and Administration** and **Chapter 5**.

Reasons for rejection (non-academic) Criminal convictions.

GRADUATE DESTINATIONS AND EMPLOYMENT

(See **Chapter 1, Graduate Outcomes.**)

Career note See **Social Sciences/Studies**.

OTHER DEGREE SUBJECTS FOR CONSIDERATION

Community Studies; Conductive Education; Criminology; Economics; Education; Health Studies; Law; Psychology; Public Sector Management and Administration; Social Policy; Sociology; Youth Studies.

SOCIOLOGY

(see also **Anthropology, Social and Public Policy and Administration**)

Sociology is the study of social organisation, social structures, systems, institutions and practices. Courses are likely to include the meaning and structure of, for example, race, ethnicity and gender, industrial behaviour, crime and deviance, health and illness. **NB** Sociology is not a training course for social workers, although some graduates take additional qualifications to qualify in social work.

Useful websites www.britsoc.co.uk; www.asanet.org; www.sociology.org.uk; www.sociology.org

NB The points totals shown to the left of the institutions are for ease of reference only. It must not be assumed that Tariff points are always used by institutions or that they can be substituted for an offer in grades. The level of an offer is not necessarily indicative of the quality of a course.

COURSE OFFERS INFORMATION

Subject requirements/preferences GCSE English and mathematics usually required. **AL** No subjects specified. Some popular universities are now making lower offers for disadvantaged and other students.

Your target offers and examples of degree courses

152 pts **Cambridge** – A*AA+interview+HSPSAA (Hum Soc Pol Sci) (IB 41–42 pts HL 776)
Edinburgh – A*AA (Sociol) (IB 39 pts HL 666)
144 pts **Manchester** – AAA (Econ Sociol) (IB 36 pts HL 666)
136 pts **Bath** – AAB–ABB+aEPQ (Sociol) (IB 35 pts HL 665)
Bristol – AAB (Pol Sociol; Soc Plcy Sociol; Sociol; Sociol Phil) (IB 34 pts HL 17 pts)
Durham – AAB (Anth Sociol; Sociol) (IB 36 pts HL 665)
Exeter – AAB (Sociol) (IB 34 pts HL 665)
London LSE – AAB (Sociol) (IB 37 pts HL 666)
Warwick – AAB (Law Sociol) (IB 34 pts)
128 pts **Aston** – ABB (Psy Sociol) (IB 32 pts HL 655)
Bath – ABB–BBB+aEPQ (Soc Sci) (IB 35 pts HL 655)
Birmingham – ABB (Educ Sociol) (IB 32 pts HL 655)
East Anglia – ABB 128 pts (Soty Cult Media) (IB 32 pts)
Lancaster – ABB (Crimin Sociol; Flm Sociol; Pol Sociol; Sociol) (IB 32 pts HL 16 pts)
Leeds – ABB (Soc Pol Sociol Crim; Sociol) (IB 34 pts HL 655)

Loughborough – ABB (Crimin Sociol; Sociol) (IB 34 pts HL 655)
Manchester – ABB (Pol Sociol; Sociol) (IB 34 pts HL 655)
Newcastle – ABB (Sociol) (IB 32 pts)
Nottingham – ABB (Crimin Sociol; Sociol) (IB 30 pts HL 655)
Sheffield – ABB (Sociol Soc Plcy) (IB 33 pts); ABB–BBB+bEPQ (Pol Sociol) (IB 33 pts)
Southampton – ABB (Sociol; Sociol Crimin) (IB 32 pts HL 16 pts)
Warwick – ABB (Sociol) (IB 32 pts)
York – ABB (Sociol; Sociol Educ; Sociol Soc Psy) (IB 34 pts)

120 pts **City St George's** – BBB 120 pts (Sociol Psy) (IB 30 pts); (Sociol) (IB 30 pts HL 555)
Glasgow – BBB–AAB incl Eng/hum (Sociol) (IB 36 pts)
Kent – BBB 120 pts (Crimin Sociol; Sociol)
Leicester – BBB–BBC+bEPQ (Sociol) (IB 28 pts)
Liverpool – BBB (Sociol) (IB 30 pts)
London (Gold) – BBB (Sociol) (IB 33 pts HL 655)
Queen's Belfast – BBB (Sociol courses) (IB 32 pts HL 655)
Stirling – BBB (Sociol Soc Plcy) (IB 28 pts)
Surrey – BBB (Sociol) (IB 32 pts)
Sussex – BBB–ABB (Sociol) (IB 30–32 pts)

112 pts **Aberdeen** – BBC (Sociol) (IB 32 pts HL 555)
Aston – BBC (Pol Sociol; Sociol courses) (IB 29 pts HL 554)
Birmingham City – BBC 112 pts (Sociol; Sociol Crimin) (IB 28 pts HL 14 pts)
Brunel – BBC (Sociol; Sociol (Dig Media)) (IB 29 pts); BBC–ABB (Anth Sociol) (IB 29 pts)
Canterbury Christ Church – BBC 112 pts (Sociol) (IB 29 pts)
Cardiff – BBC–ABB (Media Jrnl Cult) (IB 30–32 pts HL 655–665); BBC–ABB (Sociol) (IB 30–32 pts HL 665–665); BBC–BBB (Sociol Educ) (IB 29–31 pts HL 655–665)
Coventry – BBC 112 pts (Sociol; Sociol Crimin) (IB 29 pts)
Derby – 112 pts (Sociol Comb Hons); BBC–BBB 112–120 pts (Sociol)
East London – 112 pts (Psycsoc St) (IB 24 pts HL 15 pts)
Essex – BBC–BBB 112–120 pts (Glob St Hum Rts; Sociol; Sociol Crimin) (IB 29–30 pts HL 554–555)
Greenwich – 112 pts (Sociol)
Hull – BBC 112 pts (Crimin Sociol) (IB 28 pts)
Keele – BBC (Sociol)
Kingston – 112–128 pts (Sociol)
Leeds Beckett – 112 pts (Sociol)
London Met – BBC 112 pts (Sociol)
London South Bank – 112 pts (Sociol)
Middlesex – BBC 112 pts (Sociol Crimin)
Northumbria – 112 pts (Sociol)
Nottingham Trent – BBC 112 pts (Sociol)
Plymouth – 112–128 pts (Psy Sociol) (IB 28–32 pts)
Roehampton – 112 pts (Sociol)
Salford – 112 pts (Sociol) (IB 30–31 pts)
Sheffield Hallam – BBC–BBB 112–120 pts (Sociol)
Suffolk – BBC 112 pts (Psy Sociol)
UWE Bristol – 112 pts (Sociol)
West London – BBC–BBB 112–120 pts (Sociol)

104 pts **Bangor** – 104–128 pts (Sociol; Sociol (Comb Hons); Sociol Soc Pol)
Bath Spa – BCC–BBB 104–120 pts (Sociol Comb Hons) (IB 32 pts)
Bournemouth – 104–120 pts (Sociol) (IB 28–31 pts)
Brighton – BCC–BBB 104–120 pts (Psy Sociol; Sociol courses) (IB 26–30 pts)
Central Lancashire – 104–112 pts (Sociol)
Chester – BCC–BBC 104–112 pts (Sociol) (IB 26 pts)
Edge Hill – BCC–BBC 104–112 pts (Sociol)
Edinburgh Napier – BCC incl Engl (Psy Sociol) (IB 27 pts HL 654 incl 5 Engl)
Gloucestershire – BCC–BBB 104–120 pts (Sociol)

Liverpool John Moores – BCC 104 pts (Crimin Sociol); BCC–BBB 104–120 pts (Sociol) (IB 24 pts)
Manchester Met – BCC 104–112 pts (Crimin Sociol; Sociol) (IB 26 pts)
Northampton – BCC (Sociol)
Oxford Brookes – BCC 104 pts (Anth Sociol; Sociol) (IB 29 pts)
Plymouth – 104–120 pts (Sociol) (IB 26–28 pts HL 4)
Portsmouth – BCC–BBC 104–112 pts (Sociol) (IB 25 pts)
Queen Margaret – BCC (Psy Sociol; Sociol) (IB 28 pts)
Robert Gordon – BCC (App Sociol) (IB 27 pts)
Ulster – BCC (Sociol; Sociol Pol Int St) (IB 24 pts HL 12 pts)
West London – BCC 104 pts+interview (Soc Sci)
Westminster – BCC–BBB 104–120 pts (Sociol)
Worcester – 104 pts (Sociol)

96 pts **Aberystwyth** – CCC–BBB incl hum 96–120 pts (Sociol) (IB 26–30 pts)
Anglia Ruskin – 96 pts (Sociol) (IB 24 pts)
Bedfordshire – 96 pts (Crimin Sociol)
Bishop Grosseteste – 96–112 pts (Sociol)
Bradford – CCC 96 pts (Sociol)
Portsmouth – CCC–BCC 96–112 pts (Sociol Psy) (IB 25 pts)
Winchester – CCC–BBC 96–112 pts (Sociol) (HL 44)
Wolverhampton – CCC/BCD 96 pts (Sociol; Sociol Soc Pol)

88 pts **Peterborough (UC)** – 88 pts (Sociol)

80 pts **South Wales** – CDD 80–104 pts (Sociol) (IB 29 pts)

72 pts **Teesside** – 72–96 pts (Sociol)

Alternative offers See **Chapter 6** and **Appendix 1** for grades/UCAS Tariff points information for other examinations.

EXAMPLES OF COLLEGES OFFERING COURSES IN THIS SUBJECT FIELD

Blackburn (Coll); Bury (Coll); Cornwall (Coll); Farnborough (CT); Lincoln (Coll); Milton Keynes (Coll); Newham (CFE); Norwich City (Coll); Peterborough (UC); Petroc; Richmond-upon-Thames (Coll); South Devon (Coll); Totton (Coll); West Anglia (Coll).

CHOOSING YOUR COURSE (SEE ALSO CH.1)

Universities and colleges teaching quality See www.qaa.ac.uk; www.discoveruni.gov.uk.

Top research universities and colleges (REF 2021) (Sociology) Oxford; Cambridge; Manchester; York; City St George's; Lancaster; Essex; London LSE, London (King's); Cardiff.

Examples of sandwich degree courses Aston; Bath; Brunel; Coventry; Middlesex; Plymouth; Surrey.

ADMISSIONS INFORMATION

Advice to applicants and planning the UCAS personal statement Show your ability to communicate and work as part of a group and your curiosity about issues such as social conflict and social change between social groups. Discuss your interests in sociology on the personal statement. Demonstrate an intellectual curiosity about sociology and social problems. See also **Social Sciences/Studies**.

Selection interviews **Yes** Cambridge; **Some** Bath, London (Gold), Loughborough; **No** East London, Newcastle, St Mary's, Surrey, Warwick.

Interview advice and questions Past questions have included: Why do you want to study Sociology? What books have you read on the subject? How do you see the role of women changing in the next 20 years? See also **Chapter 5**.

Reasons for rejection (non-academic) Evidence of difficulty with written work. Non-attendance at Open Days (find out from your universities if your attendance will affect their offers). 'In the middle of an interview for Sociology, a student asked us if we could interview him for Sports Studies instead!' See also **Social and Public Policy and Administration**.

GRADUATE DESTINATIONS AND EMPLOYMENT

(See **Chapter 1, Graduate Outcomes.**)

Career note See **Social Sciences/Studies**.

OTHER DEGREE SUBJECTS FOR CONSIDERATION

Anthropology; Economic and Social History; Economics; Education; Geography; Government; Health Studies; History; Law; Politics; Psychology; Social Policy; Social Work.

SPANISH, PORTUGUESE AND LATIN AMERICAN STUDIES

(including **Hispanic Studies and Portuguese**; see also **Languages**)

Spanish, the world's second most spoken native language, can be studied with a vast array of other subjects. For those aspiring to gain an expertise in the Spanish-speaking world as well as the language, Latin American studies courses offer the opportunity to study the histories, ideologies, economics and politics of South and Central American states. Several courses offer the opportunity to study Portuguese.

Useful websites www.donquijote.co.uk; http://europa.eu; www.ciol.org.uk; www.languageadvantage.com; www.languagematters.co.uk; http://studyspanish.com; www.spanishlanguageguide.com.

NB The points totals shown to the left of the institutions are for ease of reference only. It must not be assumed that Tariff points are always used by institutions or that they can be substituted for an offer in grades. The level of an offer is not necessarily indicative of the quality of a course.

COURSE OFFERS INFORMATION

Subject requirements/preferences GCSE English, mathematics or science and a foreign language. **AL** Spanish required for most courses. Some popular universities are now making lower offers for disadvantaged and other students.

Your target offers and examples of degree courses

160 pts **St Andrews** – A*A*A incl maths (Maths Span) (IB 38 pts HL 666 incl maths)

152 pts **Cambridge** – A*AA incl lang+interview+MMLAA (Modn Mediev Langs) (IB 41–42 pts HL 776 incl lang)

Edinburgh – A*AA (Int Bus Fr/Ger/Span) (IB 39 pts HL 666)

Nottingham – A*AA (Econ Hisp St) (IB 36 pts HL 766)

144 pts **Edinburgh** – AAA incl lang (Span courses) (IB 34–37 pts HL 655–666 incl 5 lang)

Imperial London – AAA incl biol+sci/maths (Biol Sci Span Sci) (IB 38 pts HL 66 incl biol+sci/maths)

Oxford – AAA+interview+MLAT (Port courses) (IB 38 pts HL 666); AAA incl Span+interview+MLAT (Modn Langs Span) (IB 38 pts HL 666 incl Span)

York – AAA (Librl Arts Span) (IB 36 pts)

136 pts **Bath** – AAB–ABB+aEPQ incl A Span (Int Mgt Span) (IB 36 pts HL 665 incl 6 Span); AAB–ABB+aEPQ incl lang (Int Pol Modn Langs (Fr/Span/Ger) (Yr Abrd)) (IB 35 pts HL 665 incl lang)

Birmingham – AAB incl hist (Modn Langs Hist) (IB 32 pts HL 665 incl 6 hist)

London (King's) – AAB (Euro St (Fr/Ger/Span) (Yr Abrd)) (IB 35 pts HL 17 pts)

Southampton – AAB/ABB+aEPQ incl Engl+Fr/Ger/Span (Engl Fr/Ger/Span) (IB 34 pts HL 17 pts incl 5 Engl+Fr/Ger/Span)

St Andrews – AAB (Span courses) (IB 36 pts HL 665)

York – AAB (Span courses) (IB 35 pts); AAB incl Fr (Fr Span Lang (Yr Abrd)) (IB 35 pts HL 6 Fr)

128 pts **Birmingham** – ABB incl lang (Modn Langs Hist Art) (IB 32 pts HL 655)
Bristol – ABB incl lang (Modn Langs) (IB 32 pts HL 16 pts incl 5 langs)
Dundee – ABB incl AB Engl+lang (Law Langs) (IB 32 pts HL 655 incl Engl)
Exeter – ABB incl Lat (Modn Langs Lat) (IB 32 pts HL 655 incl Lat); ABB–AAB incl Span (Span Arbc) (IB 32–34 pts HL 655–665)
Lancaster – ABB (Span St) (IB 32 pts HL 16 pts); (Span St Geog) (IB 32 pts HL 16 pts incl 6 geog)
Leeds – ABB incl Span (Span; Span Port Lat Am St) (IB 34 pts HL 16 pts incl 6 Span)
London (QM) – ABB (Hisp St Pol/Bus Mgt) (IB 32 pts HL 655)
London (UCL) – ABB incl Span (Span Lat Am St) (IB 34 pts HL 16 pts incl 6 Span)
Manchester – ABB incl Span (Span Port Lat Am St) (IB 34 pts HL 655 incl Span); ABB incl Span/Port (Span Port) (IB 34 pts HL 655 incl Span/Port); ABB incl lang (Span courses) (IB 34 pts HL 655 incl lang)
Newcastle – ABB incl Span (Span Port Lat Am St) (IB 32 pts HL 6 Span)
Nottingham – ABB (Span Int Media Comms St) (IB 30 pts HL 655); ABB incl Èngl (Engl Hisp St) (IB 32 pts HL 5 Engl); ABB incl Span (Hisp St (Span)) (IB 32 pts); ABB incl hist (Hisp St Hist) (IB 32 pts HL 5 hist)
Queen's Belfast – ABB (Span; Span Port St) (IB 33 pts HL 655 incl Span)
Sheffield – ABB/BBB+bEPQ incl lang (Modn Langs Cult (Yr Abrd)) (IB 33 pts HL 5 lang)
Southampton – ABB incl langs (Modn Langs) (IB 32 pts HL 16 pts incl 55 langs)
Sussex – ABB (Anth Lang) (IB 34 pts)
Warwick – ABB incl A Fr/Ger/Ital/Span (Modn Langs) (IB 32 pts HL 6 Fr/Ger/Ital/Span); ABB incl lang (Hisp St courses) (IB 32 pts HL 5 lang)

120 pts **Bangor** – 120–144 pts (Law Modn Langs)
Dundee – BBB (Econ Span; Span courses) (IB 30 pts HL 555)
Glasgow – BBB–AAB (Span) (IB 34 pts HL 655 incl Engl/hum)
Heriot-Watt – BBB–ABB incl maths+Span (Maths Span) (IB 28 pts HL 5 maths+Span)
Kent – BBB (Modn Langs) (HL 566)
Leicester – BBB/BBC+bEPQ (Modn Langs Comb Hons) (IB 28 pts HL 6 lang); BBB–BBC+aEPQ incl Ital/lang (Modn Langs) (IB 28 pts HL 6 Ital/lang)
Liverpool – BBB (Hisp St) (IB 30 pts)
London (QM) – BBB (Hisp St Compar Lit/Flm/Ling) (IB 30 pts HL 555)
London (RH) – BBB–ABB (Modn Langs Lat) (IB 32 pts HL 655); BBB–ABB+gr 7 (Modn Langs Mus) (IB 32 pts HL 655); BBB–ABB incl lang (Modn Lang Dr) (IB 32 pts HL 655)
Northumbria – 120 pts (Int Bus Mgt Span)
Reading – BBB (Modn Langs (Span)) (IB 30 pts); BBB incl hist (Modn Langs Hist) (IB 30 pts HL 5 hist)
Stirling – BBB (Span Lat Am St) (IB 30 pts)
Strathclyde – BBB–ABB (Span courses) (IB 30–32 pts)
Surrey – BBB (Modn Lang (Fr Span)) (IB 32 pts)

112 pts **Aberdeen** – BBC (Span Lat Am St courses) (IB 32 pts HL 555)
Cardiff – BBC–ABB (Modn Langs (Chin/Fr/Ger/Ita/Jap/Port/Span)) (IB 30–32 pts HL 655–665)
Chester – 112 pts (Glob Affrs Pol Int Rel Span; Hist Span) (IB 26–28 pts)
Essex – BBC–BBB (Lat Am St courses; Span St Modn Langs) (IB 29–30 pts HL 554–555); (Glob St Lat Am St) (IB 29–30 pts HL 554–554)
Heriot-Watt – BBC incl B lang (App Modn Langs Transl (Fr/Span/Ger/Chin)) (IB 30 pts HL 5 lang)
London (RH) – BBC–BBB (Modn Langs) (IB 30 pts HL 555)
Swansea – BBC–ABB 112–128 pts (Modn Langs) (IB 32 pts); BBC–ABB 112–128 pts (Span courses) (IB 32 pts)

104 pts **Aberystwyth** – BCC–BBB incl B Span 104–120 pts (Span Comb Hons; Span Lat Am St) (IB 28–30 pts HL 5 Span)
Bangor – 104–128 pts (Modn Langs Hist); 104–128 pts incl modn lang (Modn Langs) (HL 5 incl modn lang)

London (Birk) – BCC 104 pts (Modn Langs (Fr/Ger/Ital/Jap/Span) (Yr Abrd))
Manchester Met – BCC incl B Span 104–112 pts (Span courses) (IB 26 pts)
Westminster – 104–120 pts incl Span (Transl (Span)) (HL 4 Span)
96 pts **Central Lancashire** – 96–112 pts incl lang (Modn Langs (2 Langs) (Fr/Span/Jap/Russ/Chin/Kor))
Portsmouth – CCC–BCC 96–104 pts (Modn Langs) (IB 25 pts)

ALTERNATIVE OFFERS See **Chapter 6** and **Appendix 1** for grades/UCAS Tariff points information for other examinations.

EXAMPLES OF COLLEGES OFFERING COURSES IN THIS SUBJECT FIELD

Richmond-upon-Thames (Coll).

CHOOSING YOUR COURSE (SEE ALSO CH.1)

UNIVERSITIES AND COLLEGES TEACHING QUALITY See www.qaa.ac.uk; www.discoveruni.gov.uk.

TOP RESEARCH UNIVERSITIES AND COLLEGES (REF 2021) See **Languages**.

EXAMPLES OF SANDWICH DEGREE COURSES Bangor; London (King's); York.

ADMISSIONS INFORMATION

ADVICE TO APPLICANTS AND PLANNING THE UCAS PERSONAL STATEMENT Visits to Spanish-speaking countries should be discussed. Study the geography, culture, literature and politics of Spain, Portugal and/or Latin American nations and discuss your interests in full. Further information could be obtained from embassies in London. See also **Appendix 3** under **Languages**.

SELECTION INTERVIEWS Yes Cambridge, Oxford (Modn Langs) 94% (success rate 44%); **Some** London (QM), London (UCL), Manchester; **No** Swansea.

INTERVIEW ADVICE AND QUESTIONS Candidates offering A-level Spanish are likely to be questioned on their A-level work, their reasons for wanting to take the subject and on their knowledge of Spain and Latin America and their peoples. Interest in these areas is important for all applicants. Student comment: 'Mostly questions about the literature I had read and I was given a poem and asked questions on it.' Questions were asked in the target language. 'There were two interviewers for the Spanish interview; they did their best to trip me up and to make me think under pressure by asking aggressive questions.' See **Chapter 5**.

GRADUATE DESTINATIONS AND EMPLOYMENT

(See **Chapter 1, Graduate Outcomes.**)

CAREER NOTE See **Languages**.

OTHER DEGREE SUBJECTS FOR CONSIDERATION

International Business Studies; Latin American Studies; Linguistics; see other language tables.

SPEECH PATHOLOGY/SCIENCES/THERAPY

(including **Healthcare Science**; see also **Communication Studies/Communication, Health Sciences/Studies**)

Speech Pathology/Sciences/Therapy is the study of speech and language problems. These can include failure to develop communication at the usual age, voice disorders, physical and learning disabilities and stammering. Courses lead to qualification as a speech therapist. This is one of many medical courses. See also **Medicine** and **Appendix 3**.

USEFUL WEBSITES www.rcslt.org; www.speechteach.co.uk; www.asha.org

NB The points totals shown to the left of the institutions are for ease of reference only. It must not be assumed that Tariff points are always used by institutions or that they can be substituted for an offer in grades. The level of an offer is not necessarily indicative of the quality of a course.

COURSE OFFERS INFORMATION

Subject requirements/preferences GCSE English language, a modern foreign language and biology/dual award science at grade 5/6 (B) or above. **AL** At least one science subject; biology may be stipulated, psychology and English language may be preferred. Some popular universities are now making lower offers for disadvantaged and other students. **Other** Disclosure and Barring Service (DBS) and occupational health checks essential for Speech Sciences/Speech Therapy applicants.

Your target offers and examples of degree courses

136 pts **Manchester** – AAB+interview (Sp Lang Thera) (IB 35 pts HL 665)
Newcastle – AAB incl sci (Sp Lang Thera) (IB 34 pts HL 555 incl sci)
Queen Margaret – AAB incl sci/maths/eng (Sp Lang Thera) (IB 32 pts)
Reading – AAB+interview (Sp Lang Thera) (IB 34 pts)
Sheffield – AAB/ABB+bEPQ (Sp Lang Thera) (IB 34 pts)

128 pts **Cardiff Met** – ABB+interview (Sp Lang Thera)
De Montfort – ABB 128 pts (Sp Lang Thera) (IB 30 pts)
East Anglia – ABB+interview (Sp Lang Thera) (IB 32 pts)
Huddersfield – ABB 128 pts+interview (Sp Lang Thera)
Leeds Beckett – ABB incl sci/psy/sociol/lang 128 pts+interview (Sp Lang Thera)
Reading – ABB (Psy Lang Sci) (IB 32 pts)
Strathclyde – ABB–AAB (Sp Lang Path) (IB 32 pts HL 6 Engl)

120 pts **Birmingham City** – BBB 120 pts+interview (Sp Lang Thera) (IB 30 pts)
Essex – BBC–BBB (Sp Lang Thera) (IB 29–30 pts HL 554–555)
Marjon – BBB 120 pts+interview (Sp Lang Thera) (IB 30–28 pts)
Middlesex – C sci 120 pts+interview (Hlthcr Sci (Audiol))

112 pts **City St George's** – BBC+interview (Sp Lang Thera) (IB 29 pts)
Greenwich – 112 pts (Sp Lang Thera)

Alternative offers See **Chapter 6** and **Appendix 1** for grades/UCAS Tariff points information for other examinations.

DEGREE APPRENTICESHIPS

Birmingham City (Sp Lang Thera); Chichester (Sp Lang Thera); Greenwich (Sp Lang Thera); Hertfordshire (Sp Lang Thera); Sheffield (Sp Lang Thera).

CHOOSING YOUR COURSE (SEE ALSO CH.1)

Universities and colleges teaching quality See www.qaa.ac.uk; www.discoveruni.gov.uk.

Examples of sandwich degree courses Birmingham City; Cardiff Met; De Montfort; East Anglia; Essex; Huddersfield; Leeds Beckett; Manchester; Manchester Met; Marjon; Middlesex; Reading; Sheffield.

ADMISSIONS INFORMATION

Advice to applicants and planning the UCAS personal statement Contact with speech therapists and visits to their clinics are an essential part of the preparation for this career. Discuss your contacts in full, giving details of any work experience or work shadowing you have done and your interest in helping people to communicate, showing evidence of good 'people skills'. See also **Appendix 3** and **Chapter 5**.

Selection interviews Yes Birmingham City, Cardiff Met, City St George's, East Anglia, Essex, Huddersfield, Leeds Beckett, Manchester Met, Marjon, Middlesex, Reading (Sp Lang Thera); **No** De Montfort.

Interview advice and questions Have you visited a speech and language therapy clinic? What did you see there? What made you want to become a speech therapist? What type of speech problems are there? What type of person would make a good speech therapist? Interviews often include an ear test (test of listening ability). See also **Chapter 5**.

Reasons for rejection (non-academic) Insufficient knowledge of speech and language therapy. Lack of maturity. Poor communication skills. Written language problems.

GRADUATE DESTINATIONS AND EMPLOYMENT

(See **Chapter 1, Graduate Outcomes.**)

Career note Speech therapists work mainly in NHS clinics, some work in hospitals and others in special schools or units for the mentally or physically handicapped. The demand for speech therapists is high.

OTHER DEGREE SUBJECTS FOR CONSIDERATION

Audiology; Communication Studies; Deaf Studies; Education; Health Studies; Linguistics; Psychology.

SPORTS SCIENCES/STUDIES

(see also **Leisure and Recreation Management/Studies, Physical Education**)

In addition to the theory and practice of many different sporting activities, Sports Sciences/Studies courses also cover the psychological aspects of sports and sports business administration. The geography, economics and sociology of recreation may also be included. The University Centres of Cricketing Excellence exist as part of a scheme introduced and funded by the England and Wales Cricket Board.

Useful websites www.uksport.gov.uk; www.laureus.com; www.wsff.org.uk; www.sta.co.uk; www.olympic.org; http://sportscotland.org.uk; www.thebapa.org.uk; www.bases.org.uk

NB The points totals shown to the left of the institutions are for ease of reference only. It must not be assumed that Tariff points are always used by institutions or that they can be substituted for an offer in grades. The level of an offer is not necessarily indicative of the quality of a course.

COURSE OFFERS INFORMATION

Subject requirements/preferences GCSE English, mathematics and, often, a science subject. **AL** Science required for Sport Science courses. PE required for some Sport Studies courses. Some popular universities are now making lower offers for disadvantaged and other students. **Other** Disclosure and Barring Service (DBS) disclosure required for many courses. Evidence of commitment to sport.

Your target offers and examples of degree courses

144 pts **Bath** – AAA–AAB+aEPQ incl maths/sci (Spo Exer Sci) (IB 36 pts HL 666/765 incl 6 maths/sci)
Edinburgh – AAA (Spo Mgt) (IB 36 pts HL 665)
Loughborough – AAA–A*AA incl sci/maths (Spo Exer Sci) (IB 37–38 pts HL 666–766 incl sci/maths)

136 pts **Bath** – AAB/A*AC/A*BB (Hlth Exer Sci) (IB 36 pts HL 665)
Durham – AAB (Spo Exer Physl Actvt) (IB 36 pts HL 665)
Edinburgh – AAB incl sci (App Spo Sci) (IB 34 pts HL 655 incl sci)
Leeds – AAB incl sci (Spo Exer Sci) (IB 34 pts); AAB–AAA (Hum Physiol Physl Actvt Hlth) (IB 31 pts HL 665)
Loughborough – AAB (Geog Spo Sci; Spo Mgt) (IB 35 pts HL 665); AAB incl Engl (Engl Spo Sci) (IB 35 pts HL 665 incl Engl)
Ulster – AAB incl hum/soc sci/spo (Spo St); AAB incl sci/maths/spo (Spo Exer Sci)

128 pts **Birmingham** – ABB (App Glf Mgt St) (IB 32 pts HL 655); ABB–AAA incl sci/maths (Spo Exer Hlth Sci) (IB 32 pts HL 655–666 incl sci/maths)
East Anglia – ABB (PE Spo Hlth) (IB 32 pts)
Edge Hill – ABB 128 pts (Spo Thera)

Essex – ABB incl sci/maths (Spo Exer Sci) (IB 32 pts HL 655)
Exeter – ABB–AAB incl sci (Exer Spo Sci) (IB 32–34 pts HL 655–665 incl sci)
Leeds – ABB incl sci (Spo Sci Physiol) (IB 34 pts HL 17 pts incl 6 sci)
London (King's) – ABB incl sci/maths/PE (Spo Exer Med Sci) (IB 33 pts HL 55 incl sci/maths)
Newcastle – ABB–AAB incl sci/maths (Spo Exer Sci) (IB 32–34 pts HL 5 sci)

120 pts **Bournemouth** – 120–136 pts incl biol/PE (Spo Thera) (IB 31–33 pts HL 5 biol/PE)
Brunel – BBB (Psy (Spo Hlth Exer)) (IB 30 pts); BBB–AAB incl sci/maths/PE (Spo Hlth Exer Sci; Spo Hlth Exer Sci (Coach)) (IB 30 pts HL 5 sci/maths/PE)
Cardiff Met – 120–128 pts (Spo Exer Sci) (HL 65 incl sci); 120–128 pts incl sci/maths/PE (Spo Condit Rehab Msg) (HL 56 incl sci)
Coventry – BBB 120 pts (Spo Exer Psy) (IB 30 pts HL 15 pts)
Derby – BBB–ABB incl sci/PE 120–128 pts (Spo Exer Sci); BBB–ABB 120–128 pts (Spo Thera Rehab)
Glasgow – BBB–AAB incl biol/chem (Spo Exer Sci) (IB 34 pts HL 655 incl biol/chem)
Gloucestershire – BBB 120 pts (Spo Thera)
HSU – BBB incl biol/PE (Spo Rehab) (IB 32 pts)
Liverpool John Moores – BBB 120 pts (Spo Exer Sci) (IB 26 pts)
Northumbria – 120 pts (Spo Exer Sci; Spo Mgt)
Nottingham Trent – 120 pts incl maths (Spo Sci Maths); 120 pts incl sci/PE (Spo Exer Sci; Spo Sci Mgt)
Stirling – BBB (Spo St) (IB 30 pts); BBB incl sci/maths (Spo Exer Sci) (IB 30 pts)
Strathclyde – BBB–ABB (Spo Physl Actvt) (IB 30–32 pts)
Surrey – BBB–ABB incl sci/PE (Spo Exer Sci) (IB 32–33 pts)
Swansea – BBB–ABB (Spo Exer Sci) (IB 32 pts)
UWE Bristol – C biol/PE 120 pts (Spo Rehab) (HL 5 biol/PE)

112 pts **Aberdeen** – BBC incl maths/sci (Spo Exer Sci) (IB 32 pts HL 555 incl maths/sci)
Bangor – 112–144 pts (Spo Sci PE Coach); 112–136 pts (Advntr Spo Sci; Spo Exer Psy; Spo Sci Exer)
Bedfordshire – 112 pts (Spo Exer Sci)
Birmingham City – BBC incl sci/maths/PE 112 pts (Spo Exer Sci) (IB 28 pts HL 4)
Birmingham Newman – 112 pts (Spo Exer Sci)
Bournemouth – 112–128 pts (Spo Exer Sci) (IB 30–32 pts)
Canterbury Christ Church – BBC 112 pts (Spo Exer Sci courses) (IB 29 pts)
Chester – 112 pts (Spo Exer Sci) (IB 28 pts)
Chichester – BBC–BBB 112–120 pts (Spo Exer Psy; Spo Exer Sci) (IB 28 pts)
Coventry – BBC 112 pts (Spo Mgt) (IB 24 pts)
Derby – BBC–BBB 112–120 pts (Spo Educ); BBC 112 pts (Spo Coach Dev)
East London – 112 pts (Spo Jrnl) (IB 24 pts HL 15 pts); 112 pts incl PE/spo/sci (Spo Exer Sci) (IB 24 pts HL 15 pts)
Greater Manchester – 112 pts incl spo/PE/sci+interview (Spo Rehab)
Greenwich – 112 pts (Spo Exer Sci)
Hertfordshire – BBC–BBB incl sci 112–120 pts (Spo Exer Sci)
Hull – BBC 112 pts (Spo Coach Perf Sci; Spo Exer Nutr; Spo Rehab) (IB 28 pts)
Kent – BBC 112 (Spo Thera Rehab) (HL 556); (Spo Exer Sci) (IB 30 pts HL 556)
Kingston – 112–128 pts (Spo Exer Sci; Spo Exer Sci (Coach Physl Educ))
Leeds Beckett – 112 pts incl sci/PE (Hlth Exer Sci) (HL 333 incl sci)
Leeds Trinity – 112 pts (Spo Jrnl; Spo Psy)
Liverpool John Moores – BBC 112 pts (Sci Ftbl; Spo Coach) (IB 27 pts)
London Met – 112 pts incl biol/hum biol (Spo Thera)
London South Bank – BBC 112 pts (Spo Exer Sci)
Manchester Met – BBC incl sci/PE 112–120 pts (Spo Exer Sci) (IB 28 pts HL 5 sci/PE)
Marjon – BBC 112 pts (Spo Exer Sci; Spo Thera)
Middlesex – 112 pts incl sci (Spo Exer Rehab)
Northampton – BBC (Spo St courses)
Nottingham Trent – 112 pts (Spo Sci Coach)

Portsmouth – BBC–BBB 112–120 pts (Spo Mgt) (IB 25 pts); BBC–BBB incl sci/PE 112–120 pts incl sci/PE (Spo Exer Sci) (IB 25 pts)
Roehampton – 112 pts incl sci/PE (Spo Exer Sci)
Sheffield Hallam – BBC 112 pts (Spo Bus Mgt; Spo Dev Coach); BBC incl PE/soc sci/sci 112 pts (Spo Exer Sci); BBC incl PE/spo sci/sci 112 pts (Physl Actvt Spo Hlth; Spo Coach)
Solent – 112–128 pts (Spo Exer Sci)
South Wales – BBC incl sci/PE 112 pts (Ftbl Coach Perf; Spo Coach Dev; Spo Exer Sci); BBC incl sci/maths/PE 112 pts (Rgby Coach Perf)
Staffordshire – BBC 112 pts (PE Spo Coach; Spo Exer Sci)
Sunderland – 112 pts (Spo Coach PE; Spo Exer Sci)

104 pts **Anglia Ruskin** – 104 pts incl sci/PE (Spo Exer Sci) (IB 24 pts)
Bournemouth – 104–120 pts (Spo Mgt) (IB 28–31 pts)
Brighton – BCC–BBB 104–120 pts (Spo Coach; Spo Exer Sci; Spo Mgt) (IB 26–30 pts)
Cardiff Met – 104–112 pts (Spo Coach; Spo PE Hlth) (HL 6)
Central Lancashire – 104–112 pts (Spo Exer Sci); 104–112 pts incl biol/PE/spo sci (Spo Thera); 104–120 pts (Out Advntr Ldrshp)
Chester – 104 pts (Spo Jrnl) (IB 26 pts)
Cumbria – 104–112 pts (Spo Rehab)
Edge Hill – BCC–BBC 104–112 pts (Spo Exer Sci)
Edinburgh Napier – BCC incl sci/PE (Spo Exer Sci) (IB 28 pts HL 654 incl 5 sci)
Gloucestershire – BCC 104 pts (Spo Bus Mgt); BCC 104–120 pts (Spo Exer Sci); BCC–BBC 104–112 pts (Physl Educ)
Greenwich – 104 pts (PE Spo)
HSU – BCC–BBB 104–120 pts (Spo Exer Psy) (IB 28–32 pts)
Hertfordshire – BCC–BBC 104–112 pts (Spo St)
Huddersfield – BCC–BBC 104–112 pts+interview (Spo Jrnl); BCC–BBC incl sci/PE 104–112 pts (Spo Exer Sci)
Leeds Trinity – 104 pts (Spo Exer Sci; Spo Thera Rehab)
Lincoln – 104 pts (Spo Exer Sci) (IB 28 pts)
Liverpool Hope – BCC 104 pts (Spo Exer Nutr; Spo Exer Sci; Spo Psy) (IB 24 pts)
London Met – 104 pts (Spo Exer Sci)
Manchester Met – BCC–BBC 104–112 pts (Spo Bus Mgt; Spo Mark Mgt) (IB 26 pts)
Oxford Brookes – BCC incl sci/maths/PE 104 pts (Spo Exer Sci) (IB 29 pts)
Robert Gordon – BCC incl Engl+sci+interview (App Spo Exer Sci) (IB 28 pts HL 555 incl Engl+sci)
Winchester – BCC–BBB 104–120 pts (Spo Coach PE; Spo Mgt) (HL 44)
Worcester – BBC 104 pts+interview (Spo Thera); BCC 104 pts (Spo Bus Mgt)
York St John – 104 pts (PE Spo Coach; Spo Exer Thera)

96 pts **Abertay** – CCC incl sci/maths/PE (Spo Exer) (IB 27 pts)
Aberystwyth – CCC–BBB 96–120 pts (Spo Exer Sci) (IB 26–30 pts)
Bedfordshire – 96 pts (Ftbl St; Spo Coach Dev)
Birmingham (UC) – CCC–BCC (Spo Thera)
Birmingham Newman – 96 pts (Spo Coach)
Bishop Grosseteste – 96–112 pts (Psy Spo)
Cardiff Met – 96–112 pts (Spo Physl Educ Hlth (Dance)) (HL 6)
Central Lancashire – 96–112 pts (Spo Jrnl)
Marjon – CCC 96 pts (Spo Dev)
Middlesex – 96 pts incl sci (Spo Exer Sci)
St Mary's – 96–112 pts incl sci (Spo Rehab; Strg Condit Sci); 96–112 pts incl sci (Spo Coach Sci; Spo Exer Sci)
Teesside – 96 pts (Spo Exer Sci)
Ulster – CCC incl sci/maths/spo (Spo Physl Actvt Hlth) (IB 24 pts HL 12 pts)
Wolverhampton – CCC 96 pts (Spo Exer Sci)

88 pts **Bucks New** – 88–112 pts (Spo Exer Sci)
Teesside – 88–112 pts incl spo/sci/PE (Spo Thera Rehab)

80 pts **Norwich City (Coll)** – 80 pts (Spo Hlth Exer Sci)
Trinity Saint David – 80 pts (Spo Mgt)
Wrexham – 80–112 pts (Spo Exer Hlth Sci)
72 pts **Coventry** – 72 pts (Spo Exer Thera)
West Scotland – DDD incl sci/PE 72 pts (Spo Exer Sci courses) (IB 24 pts HL 444 incl sci)
48 pts **Greater Manchester** – 48 pts+interview+portfolio (Spo Rehab Fdn Yr)

Alternative offers See **Chapter 6** and **Appendix 1** for grades/UCAS Tariff points information for other examinations.

DEGREE APPRENTICESHIPS

Hertfordshire (Spo Bus Mgt).

EXAMPLES OF COLLEGES OFFERING COURSES IN THIS SUBJECT FIELD

Accrington and Rossendale (Coll); Askham Bryan (Coll); Bishop Burton (Coll); Blackpool and Fylde (Coll); Bradford College (UC); Colchester (UC); Easton (Coll); Hartpury (Coll); Lakes (Coll); Leeds City (Coll); Manchester (Coll); Myerscough (Coll); NCC Hackney; Newcastle (Coll); North Kent (Coll); North Lindsey (Coll); Peterborough (UC); Plumpton (Coll); Reaseheath (UC); Sir Gâr (Coll); South Devon (Coll); South Essex (Coll); Stamford (Coll); Tameside (Coll); Warwickshire (Coll); Westminster City (Coll); Weston (Coll); York (Coll).

CHOOSING YOUR COURSE (SEE ALSO CH.1)

Universities and colleges teaching quality See www.qaa.ac.uk; www.discoveruni.gov.uk.

Top research universities and colleges (REF 2021) (Sports and Exercise Science, Leisure and Tourism) Exeter; Leicester; Bristol; London (King's); Bangor; Birmingham; Bath; Loughborough; Leeds; Nottingham.

Examples of sandwich degree courses Bath; Bedfordshire; Bournemouth; Brighton; Brunel; Coventry; Essex; Hertfordshire; Kingston; Leeds; Loughborough; Manchester Met; Nottingham Trent; Portsmouth; Robert Gordon; Ulster.

ADMISSIONS INFORMATION

Advice to applicants and planning the UCAS personal statement See also **Physical Education** and **Appendix 3**.

Selection interviews Yes Greater Manchester, Huddersfield (Spo Jrnl), Robert Gordon (App Spo Exer Sci), Worcester; **Some** Bath; **No** Anglia Ruskin, Edinburgh, St Mary's, West Scotland.

Interview advice and questions Applicants' interests in sport and their sporting activities are likely to be discussed at length. Past questions include: How do you strike a balance between sport and academic work? How many, and which, sports do you coach? For how long? Have you devised your own coaching programme? What age range do you coach? Do you coach unsupervised? See also **Chapter 5**.

Reasons for rejection (non-academic) Not genuinely interested in outdoor activities. Poor sporting background or knowledge. Inability to apply their science to their specialist sport. Illiteracy. Using the course as a second option to Physiotherapy. Arrogance. Expectation that they will be playing sport all day. When the course is explained to them, some applicants realise that a more arts-based course would be more appropriate.

GRADUATE DESTINATIONS AND EMPLOYMENT

(See **Chapter 1, Graduate Outcomes.**)

Career note Career options include sport development, coaching, teaching, outdoor centres, sports equipment development, sales, recreation management and professional sport.

OTHER DEGREE SUBJECTS FOR CONSIDERATION

Anatomy; Biology; Human Movement Studies; Leisure and Recreation Management; Nutrition; Physical Education; Physiology; Physiotherapy; Sports Equipment Product Design.

STATISTICS

(see also **Economics, Mathematics**)

Statistics has mathematical underpinnings but is primarily concerned with the collection, interpretation and analysis of data. Statistics are used to analyse and solve problems in a wide range of areas, particularly in the scientific, business, government and public services.

USEFUL WEBSITES www.rss.org.uk; www.gov.uk/government/statistics/announcements; https://www.ons.gov.uk

NB The points totals shown to the left of the institutions are for ease of reference only. It must not be assumed that Tariff points are always used by institutions or that they can be substituted for an offer in grades. The level of an offer is not necessarily indicative of the quality of a course.

COURSE OFFERS INFORMATION

SUBJECT REQUIREMENTS/PREFERENCES GCSE English and mathematics. **AL** Mathematics required for all courses. Some popular universities are now making lower offers for disadvantaged and other students.

YOUR TARGET OFFERS AND EXAMPLES OF DEGREE COURSES

160 pts **Bath** – A*A*A incl maths+fmaths (Maths Stats) (IB 36 pts HL 776 incl 6 maths; 766–775 incl 7 maths)
Bristol – A*AA–A*A*A incl A*A maths+fmaths/sci/comp/econ (Maths Stats) (IB 40 pts HL 18 pts incl 7 maths 6 sci/econ/comp)
Durham – A*A*A incl A*A* maths+fmaths+TMUA (Maths Stats) (IB 38 pts HL 766–776 incl 7 maths)
Imperial London – A*A*A incl A*A* maths+fmaths+TMUA/STEP (Maths Stats; Maths Stats Fin) (IB 39 pts HL 76 incl maths)
Oxford – A*A*A incl A* maths+interview+MAT (Maths Stats) (IB 39 pts HL 766 incl 7 maths)
St Andrews – A*A*A incl A* maths (Stats) (IB 38 pts HL 666 incl maths)
Warwick – A*A*A incl maths+fmaths (Maths Stats) (IB 39 pts HL 7 maths)

152 pts **London (King's)** – A*AA incl maths+fmaths (Maths Stats) (IB 38 pts HL 766 incl 7 maths)
London (UCL) – A*AA incl A* maths (Stats; Stats Econ Fin; Stats Mgt Bus; Stats Sci (Int)) (IB 39 pts HL 19 pts incl 7 maths)
London LSE – A*AA incl maths (Fin Maths Stats; Maths Stats Bus) (IB 38 pts HL 766 incl 7 maths)
Manchester – A*AA incl maths (Maths Stats) (IB 37 pts HL 766 incl maths)

144 pts **Birmingham** – AAA incl maths (Mathem Econ Stats) (IB 32 pts HL 666)
Edinburgh – A*AB–A*AA incl maths (Maths Stats) (IB 34–38 pts HL 765–766 incl maths)
Lancaster – AAA incl maths/fmaths (Maths Stats) (IB 36 pts HL 16 pts incl 6 maths)
Leeds – AAA/A*AB incl A maths (Maths Stats) (IB 35 pts HL 17 pts incl 6 maths)
Loughborough – AAA/A*AB incl A maths (Maths Stats) (IB 37 pts HL 666 incl maths/HL 765 incl 7 maths)
Nottingham – AAA/A*AB incl A maths (Stats) (IB 34 pts HL 666 incl maths)
Queen's Belfast – AAA/A*AB incl maths (Maths Stats OR (MMath)) (IB 36 pts HL 666 incl maths)
Southampton – AAA–AAB+aEPQ incl A maths (Maths OR Stats Econ (MORSE)) (IB 36 pts HL 18 pts incl 6 maths); AAA–AAB+aEPQ incl A maths (Maths Stats) (IB 36 pts HL 18 pts incl 6 maths)
York – AAA incl maths (Maths Stats) (IB 36 pts HL 6 maths)

136 pts **East Anglia** – AAB incl maths (Maths Stats) (IB 33 pts HL 6 maths)
Heriot-Watt – AAB incl maths (Stats Data Sci) (IB 28 pts HL 6 maths)
Newcastle – AAB incl maths (Data Sci; Maths Stats) (IB 34 pts HL 6 maths)
Queen's Belfast – AAB/A*BB incl maths (Maths Stats OR) (IB 34 pts HL 665 incl maths)

Sheffield – AAB incl maths (Maths Stats) (IB 34 pts HL 6 maths)
128 pts **London (QM)** – ABB incl maths (Maths Stats) (IB 32 pts HL 655 incl maths)
London (RH) – ABB–ABC incl maths (Maths Stats) (IB 32 pts HL 654 incl 6 maths)
Surrey – ABB–AAB incl maths (Maths Data Sci) (IB 33–34 pts HL 6 maths)
120 pts **Cardiff** – BBB–AAB incl maths (Maths OR Stats) (IB 31–34 pts HL 665–666 incl maths)
Glasgow – BBB–AAB incl maths (Fin Stats; Stats) (IB 34 pts HL 655 incl maths)
Heriot-Watt – BBB incl maths (Maths Stats) (IB 28 pts HL 5 maths)
Reading – ABC incl A maths (Maths Stats Data Sci) (IB 30 pts HL 6 maths)
Strathclyde – BBB incl maths (Maths Stats Econ) (IB 30 pts HL 5 maths)
West London – BBB 120 pts (Maths Stats)
112 pts **Coventry** – BBC incl maths 112 pts (Maths Stats) (IB 31 pts HL 5 maths)
Essex – BBC–BBB incl maths 112–120 pts (Stats) (IB 29–30 pts HL 554–555 incl 5 maths)
London (Birk) – BBC incl B maths 112 pts (Maths Stats)
Plymouth – 112–128 pts incl maths (Maths Stats) (IB 30 pts HL 5 maths)
Portsmouth – BBC–BBB 112–120 pts incl maths (Maths Stats) (IB 29 pts)
104 pts **Aberystwyth** – BCC–BBB incl B maths (PMaths Stats) (IB 28–30 pts HL 5 maths)
Chichester – BCC–BBC incl maths 104–112 pts (Maths Stats) (IB 26–28 pts HL 5 maths)
FRA – 104–120 pts (Data Analyt Rtl)
Greenwich – BCC incl maths 104 pts (Stats Data Analyt)

ALTERNATIVE OFFERS See **Chapter 6** and **Appendix 1** for grades/UCAS Tariff points information for other examinations.

DEGREE APPRENTICESHIPS

Bangor (App Data Sci); Cardiff Met (App Data Sci); Chichester (Data Sci); Hertfordshire (Data Sci); Keele (Data Sci); Newcastle (Dig Tech Sol (Data Analyt Spec)); Nottingham (Data Sci); Robert Gordon (Data Sci); Stirling (Data Sci); Sussex (Data Analyt Dig Sol Bus); York St John (Data Sci).

CHOOSING YOUR COURSE (SEE ALSO CH.1)

UNIVERSITIES AND COLLEGES TEACHING QUALITY See www.qaa.ac.uk; www.discoveruni.gov.uk.

TOP RESEARCH UNIVERSITIES AND COLLEGES (REF 2021) See **Mathematics**.

EXAMPLES OF SANDWICH DEGREE COURSES Bath; Cardiff; Coventry; Greenwich; Plymouth; Portsmouth; Reading; Surrey.

ADMISSIONS INFORMATION

ADVICE TO APPLICANTS AND PLANNING THE UCAS PERSONAL STATEMENT Admissions tutors like to see applicants demonstrate a real passion for mathematics and desire to learn. If there are any branches of mathematics that particularly interest you, these should be mentioned on the statement. See also **Mathematics** and **Appendix 3**.

SELECTION INTERVIEWS Yes Oxford (30% (success rate 9%)); **Some** Bath, East Anglia; **No** London (UCL), Newcastle.

INTERVIEW ADVICE AND QUESTIONS Questions could be asked on your A-level syllabus (particularly in mathematics). Applicants' knowledge of statistics and their interest in the subject are likely to be tested, together with their awareness of the application of statistics in commerce and industry. See also **Chapter 5**.

GRADUATE DESTINATIONS AND EMPLOYMENT

(See **Chapter 1, Graduate Outcomes.**)

CAREER NOTE See **Mathematics**.

OTHER DEGREE SUBJECTS FOR CONSIDERATION

Accountancy; Actuarial Sciences; Business Information Technology; Business Studies; Computer Science; Economics; Financial Services; Mathematical Studies; Mathematics.

SURVEYING AND REAL ESTATE MANAGEMENT

(including **Building Surveying, Quantity Surveying, Property Development and Rural Property Management.** For Property, Finance and Investment see under **Finance**; see also **Agricultural Sciences/Agriculture, Building and Construction, Housing, Town and Urban Planning**)

Surveying covers a very diverse range of careers and courses and following a Royal Institution of Chartered Surveyors (RICS) accredited course is the accepted way to become a Chartered Surveyor. There are three main specialisms – the Built Environment (Building Surveying, Project Management and Quantity Surveying); Land Surveying (Rural, Planning, Environmental, Minerals and Waste Management); and Property Surveying (Commercial and Residential Property and Valuation, Facilities Management, Art and Antiques). Student membership of the RICS is possible. Not all the courses listed below receive RICS accreditation; check with the university or college prior to applying.

Useful websites www.rics.org/eu/surveying-profession/what-is-surveying/rics-students; www.cstt.org.uk

NB The points totals shown to the left of the institutions are for ease of reference only. It must not be assumed that Tariff points are always used by institutions or that they can be substituted for an offer in grades. The level of an offer is not necessarily indicative of the quality of a course.

COURSE OFFERS INFORMATION

Subject requirements/preferences GCSE English and mathematics grade 7–4 (A–C). **AL** No subjects specified; mathematics useful. Some popular universities are now making lower offers for disadvantaged and other students.

Your target offers and examples of degree courses

152 pts **Cambridge** – A*AA+interview (Lnd Econ) (IB 41–42 pts HL 776)

136 pts **London (UCL)** – AAB (Urb Plan Rl Est) (IB 36 pts HL 17 pts)

128 pts **Manchester** – ABB (Plan Rl Est) (IB 34 pts HL 655)
Newcastle – ABB (Sust Lnd Bus Mgt) (IB 32 pts)
Ulster – ABB incl maths/phys/chem/biol/eng/constr (Quant Surv Commer Mgt) (IB 27 pts HL 13 pts incl maths+sci)

120 pts **Kingston** – 120–136 pts (Rl Est Mgt)
Leeds Beckett – 120 pts (Bld Surv; Quant Surv) (IB 30 pts HL 55)
London South Bank – BBB 120 pts (Quant Surv)
Loughborough – ABC/BBB 120 pts+interview (Commer Mgt Quant Surv) (IB 32 pts HL 555)
Oxford Brookes – BBB 120 pts+interview (Rl Est) (IB 31 pts)
Reading – BBB (Bld Surv; Quant Surv) (IB 30 pts)
UWE Bristol – 120 pts (Rl Est)

112 pts **Aberdeen** – BBC (Rl Est) (IB 32 pts HL 555)
Anglia Ruskin – 112 pts (Bld Surv; Quant Surv)
Birmingham City – BBC 112 pts (Quant Surv; Rl Est) (IB 28 pts HL 14 pts)
Coventry – BBC 112 pts (Bld Surv; Quant Surv Commer Mgt) (IB 29 pts)
East London – 112 pts (Surv Map Sci) (IB 24 pts HL 15 pts)
Greenwich – BBC 112 pts (Quant Surv)
Kingston – 112–128 pts (Bld Surv)
Liverpool John Moores – BBC–ABB 112–128 pts (Bld Surv; Quant Surv; Rl Est)
London South Bank – BBC 112 pts (Commer Mgt (Quant Surv))
Northumbria – 112 pts (Bld Surv; Quant Surv; Rl Est)
Nottingham Trent – 112 pts (Bld Surv; Quant Surv Commer Mgt; Rl Est)
Oxford Brookes – BBC 112 pts (Quant Surv Commer Mgt) (IB 30 pts)
Portsmouth – BBC–BBB 112–120 pts (Quant Surv) (IB 29 pts); BBC–BBB 112–120 pts (Prop Dev) (IB 29 pts)
Sheffield Hallam – BBC 112 pts (Bld Surv; Quant Surv)

UWE Bristol – 112 pts (Bld Surv; Quant Surv Commer Mgt)
Ulster – BBC (Rl Est) (IB 25 pts HL 12 pts)

104 pts **Brighton** – BCC–BBB 104–120 pts (Bld Surv) (IB 26 pts)
Central Lancashire – 104 pts (Quant Surv)
Derby – BCC–BBC 104–112 pts (Constr Mgt)
Harper Adams – 104 pts (Rl Est; Rur Ent Lnd Mgt; Rur Prop Rl Est) (IB 28 pts)
Oxford Brookes – BCC 104 pts (Prop Dev Plan) (IB 29 pts)
Royal Agricultural Univ – BCC 104 pts (Rl Est) (IB 26 pts)
Salford – 104 pts (Rl Est Dev Mgt) (IB 29 pts)
South Wales – BCC (Quant Surv Commer Mgt) (IB 29 pts)
Westminster – BCC–BBB 104–120 pts (Quant Surv Commer Mgt; Rl Est)

96 pts **Glasgow Caledonian** – CCC 96 pts (Bld Surv; Quant Surv) (IB 26 pts)
Plymouth – 96–112 pts (Bld Surv; Quant Surv) (IB 26–28 pts)
Robert Gordon – CCC (Quant Surv Commer Mgt) (IB 26 pts)
South Wales – CCC (Bld Surv)
Trinity Saint David – 96 pts (Quant Surv)
UCEM – 96 pts (Bld Surv; Quant Surv; Rl Est Mgt)
Wolverhampton – CCC/BCD 96 pts (Bld Surv; Quant Surv)

ALTERNATIVE OFFERS See **Chapter 6** and **Appendix 1** for grades/UCAS Tariff points information for other examinations.

DEGREE APPRENTICESHIPS

Anglia Ruskin (Quant Surv, Bld Surv); Birmingham City (Chart Surv); Brighton (Chart Surv (Bld Surv)); Central Lancashire (Chart Surv (Bld Surv)); Edinburgh Napier (Constr Blt Env); London South Bank (Chart Surv); Northumbria (Chart Surv); Nottingham Trent (Chart Surv); Portsmouth (Chart Surv (Bld Surv)); Salford (Rl Est Dev Mgt); Westminster (Quant Surv Commer Mgt, Constr Mgt).

EXAMPLES OF COLLEGES OFFERING COURSES IN THIS SUBJECT FIELD

Blackburn (Coll); South Cheshire (Coll); UCEM.

CHOOSING YOUR COURSE (SEE ALSO CH.1)

UNIVERSITIES AND COLLEGES TEACHING QUALITY See www.qaa.ac.uk; www.discoveruni.gov.uk. Check on RICS accreditation.

EXAMPLES OF SANDWICH DEGREE COURSES Anglia Ruskin; Birmingham City; Central Lancashire; Coventry; Glasgow Caledonian; Kingston; Leeds Beckett; Liverpool John Moores; London South Bank; Loughborough; Northumbria; Nottingham Trent; Oxford Brookes; Sheffield Hallam; UWE Bristol; Wolverhampton.

ADMISSIONS INFORMATION

ADMISSIONS TUTORS' ADVICE **Nottingham Trent** Candidates should demonstrate that they have researched the employment opportunities in the property and construction sectors.

ADVICE TO APPLICANTS AND PLANNING THE UCAS PERSONAL STATEMENT Surveyors work with architects and builders as well as in their own consultancies dealing with commercial and residential property. Work experience with various firms is strongly recommended depending on the type of surveying speciality preferred. Read surveying magazines.

SELECTION INTERVIEWS **Yes** Cambridge, Oxford Brookes (Rl Est); **Some** Loughborough; **No** Anglia Ruskin, Harper Adams, Kingston, Robert Gordon.

INTERVIEW ADVICE AND QUESTIONS What types of work are undertaken by surveyors? How do you qualify? What did you learn on your work experience? See also **Chapter 5**.

REASONS FOR REJECTION (NON-ACADEMIC) Inability to communicate. Lack of motivation. Indecisiveness about reasons for choosing the course.

GRADUATE DESTINATIONS AND EMPLOYMENT

(See **Chapter 1, Graduate Outcomes.**)

Career note See **Building and Construction**.

OTHER DEGREE SUBJECTS FOR CONSIDERATION

Architecture; Building and Construction; Civil Engineering; Estate Management; Town Planning; Urban Studies.

TEACHER TRAINING

(see also **Education Studies, Physical Education, Social Sciences/Studies**)

Abbreviations used in this table: ITE – Initial Teacher Education; ITT – Initial Teacher Training; P – Primary Teaching; QTS – Qualified Teacher Status; S – Secondary Teaching; STQ – Scottish Teaching Qualification.

Teacher training courses are offered in subject areas such as Art and Design (P); Biology (P S); Chemistry (S); Childhood (P); Computer Education (P); Creative and Performing Arts (P); Dance (P); Design and Technology (P S); Drama (P); English (P S); Environmental Science (P S); Environmental Studies (P); French (S); General Primary; Geography (P S); History (P S); Maths (P S); Music (P S); Physical Education/Movement Studies (P S); Religious Studies (P); Science (P S); Sociology (S); Textile Design (S); Welsh (S). For further information on teaching as a career see websites below and **Appendix 3** for contact details. Over 50 taster courses are offered each year to those considering teaching as a career. Applicants aiming to quickly become qualified primary teachers in the United Kingdom should take care to apply for undergraduate courses which confer Qualified Teacher Status (QTS). Note that many institutions listed below also offer one-year Postgraduate Certificate in Education (PGCE) courses which qualify graduates to teach at primary and secondary level across a range of subjects. For UK secondary teachers, an undergraduate degree in a traditional academic subject followed by a PGCE is still the most common route to the classroom, although this is beginning to change with the growing popularity of new vocational routes. All institutions will require candidates to attend for interview, often with literacy and numeracy tests.

Useful websites www.gtcs.org.uk; www.ucas.com/teaching-in-the-uk; www.gov.uk/government/organisations/department-for-education

NB The points totals shown to the left of the institutions are for ease of reference only. It must not be assumed that Tariff points are always used by institutions or that they can be substituted for an offer in grades. The level of an offer is not necessarily indicative of the quality of a course.

COURSE OFFERS INFORMATION

Subject requirements/preferences See **Education Studies**. Some popular universities are now making lower offers for disadvantaged and other students.

Your target offers and examples of degree courses

152 pts **Cambridge** – A*AA+interview+EAA (Educ) (IB 41–42 pts HL 776)
136 pts **Durham** – AAB+interview (Educ St) (IB 36 pts HL 665)
Stranmillis (UC) – AAB+interview (P Educ QTS)
128 pts **Durham** – ABB 128 pts+interview (P Educ) (IB 34 pts HL 665)
Edinburgh – ABB+interview (P Educ Gael) (IB 34 pts HL 655)
Strathclyde – ABB incl chem+sci/maths (Chem Teach (MChem)) (IB 34 pts HL sci/maths)
120 pts **Birmingham City** – BBB 120 pts+interview (P Educ QTS) (IB 30 pts)
Brighton – BBB (P Educ) (IB 30 pts)
Chester – 120 pts+interview (P Educ QTS) (IB 28 pts)
Glasgow – BBB–AAB incl Engl+interview (Educ P QTS) (IB 34 pts HL 655 incl Engl)
Leeds Beckett – 120 pts+interview (P Educ (QTS)) (IB 26 pts)

Liverpool Hope – BBB 120 pts (P Educ QTS) (IB 24 pts)
Liverpool John Moores – BBB–ABB 120 pts+interview (P Educ QTS)
Manchester Met – BBB 120 pts+interview (P Educ) (IB 30 pts)
Nottingham Trent – BBB 120 pts+interview+test (P Educ QTS)
Reading – BBB+interview (P Educ QTS) (IB 30 pts); BBB incl Engl/hist/sociol/phil/dr+interview (P Educ Engl Spec) (IB 30 pts HL 5 Engl/hist/sociol/phil/dr); BBB incl art+interview (P Educ Art Spec) (IB 30 pts HL 5 art); BBB incl mus+gr 8+interview (P Ed Mus Spec) (IB 30 pts HL 5 mus)
Sheffield Hallam – BBB–ABB 120–128 pts+interview (P Educ QTS)
Stirling – BBB (Educ P) (IB 30–32 pts)
Strathclyde – BBB–ABB (P Educ) (IB 30–32 pts)
Sunderland – BBB 120 pts+interview (P Educ)
West Scotland – BBB incl Engl 120 pts+interview (Educ) (IB 32 pts HL 444 incl Engl)
York St John – 120 pts+interview (P Educ)

115 pts **Trinity Saint David** – 115 pts (P Educ QTS)

112 pts **Bedfordshire** – 112 pts (P Educ QTS)
Birmingham Newman – BBC 112 pts+interview (P Educ QTS)
Bishop Grosseteste – 112 pts (P Educ QTS)
Canterbury Christ Church – BBC 112 pts+interview (P Educ QTS) (IB 29 pts)
Cumbria – BBC–ABB 112–128 pts+interview (P Educ QTS)
Edge Hill – BBC–BBB 112–120 pts+interview (P Educ QTS)
Gloucestershire – 112 pts+interview (P Educ QTS)
Greenwich – 112 pts+interview (P Educ QTS)
Hertfordshire – BBB–ABB 112–120 pts+interview (P Educ QTS)
Huddersfield – BBC 112 pts (Ely Yrs)
Hull – BBC 112 pts (P Teach St) (IB 28 pts)
Kingston – BBC–ABB 112–128 pts+interview+test (P Educ QTS) (IB 26 pts)
Leeds Beckett – 112 pts (P Educ 2 Yr) (IB 24 pts)
Leeds Trinity – 112–144 pts+interview (P Educ courses (QTS))
Marjon – BBC 112 pts+interview (P Educ QTS; PE (S Educ QTS))
Middlesex – 112 pts+interview (P Educ QTS)
Northumbria – 112 pts+interview (P Educ)
Nottingham Trent – 112 pts (Educ SEND Incln)
Plymouth – BBC 112 pts (P Educ) (IB 28 pts)
Roehampton – 112 pts+interview (P Educ QTS)
St Mary's – 112 pts+interview (P Educ QTS)
UWE Bristol – 112 pts+interview (P Educ QTS)
Winchester – BBC–BBB 112–120 pts+interview (P Educ QTS) (HL 44)
Worcester – BBC 112 pts+interview (P Educ QTS)

104 pts **Bangor** – 104–128 pts+interview (P Educ QTS)
Bath Spa – BCC–BBB (Ely Chld St; P Educ QTS) (IB 32 pts)
Bedfordshire – BCC 104 pts (Educ)
Cardiff Met – BCC+interview (P Educ QTS); BCC 104 pts (P Educ St)
Chichester – BCC–BBB 104–120 pts+interview (P Teach Ely Yrs QTS) (IB 26–28 pts)
Edge Hill – BCC–BBC 104–112 pts (Wkg Teach Ely Yrs); BCC–BBC 104–112 pts+interview (S Educ QTS courses)
Hull – BCC 104 pts (Ely Chld St) (IB 26 pts)
Liverpool John Moores – BCC–BBB (Educ P St)
Northampton – BCC (P Educ QTS)
Oxford Brookes – BCC 104 pts+interview (P Teach Educ) (IB 29 pts)
Portsmouth – BCC–BBC 104–112 pts+interview (P Educ QTS) (IB 28–29 pts)

96 pts **Bedfordshire** – 96 pts (Ely Chld Educ)
Birmingham City – 96 pts (Cond Educ) (IB 24 pts)
Gloucestershire – CCC 96 pts (Educ)
Winchester – CCC–BBC 96–112 pts (Educ; Ely Yrs Educ) (HL 44)

Wolverhampton – CCC/BCD 96 pts+interview+test (P Educ)
80 pts **South Wales** – CDD–BCC 80–104 pts (Ely Yrs Educ Prac) (IB 29 pts)

Alternative offers See **Chapter 6** and **Appendix 1** for grades/UCAS Tariff points information for other examinations.

DEGREE APPRENTICESHIPS

Brighton (Teach); London Met (Teach); Sunderland (Teach).

EXAMPLES OF COLLEGES OFFERING COURSES IN THIS SUBJECT FIELD

Bedford (Coll); Bishop Burton (Coll); Bradford College (UC); Carshalton (Coll); Cornwall (Coll); Grŵp Llandrillo Menai; Kensington Bus (Coll); Leeds City (Coll); Loughborough (Coll); Myerscough (Coll); Nottingham (Coll); Sir Gâr (Coll); South Cheshire (Coll); South Devon (Coll); South Essex (Coll); Wakefield (Coll); Warwickshire (Coll); Wigan and Leigh (Coll); Wiltshire (Coll); Yeovil (Coll).

CHOOSING YOUR COURSE (SEE ALSO CH.1)

Universities and colleges teaching quality See www.qaa.ac.uk; www.discoveruni.gov.uk.

Top research universities and colleges (REF 2021) See **Education Studies**.

ADMISSIONS INFORMATION

Admissions tutors' advice **Winchester** Functional Skills Level 2 English is not accepted for Teaching courses.

Advice to applicants and planning the UCAS personal statement Too many candidates are applying without the required GCSE qualifications in place or pending (maths, English, science). Any application for teacher training courses requires candidates to have experience of observation in schools and with children relevant to the choice of age range. Describe what you have learned from this. Any work with young people should be described in detail, indicating any problems which you may have seen which children create for the teacher. Applicants are strongly advised to have had some teaching practice prior to interview and should give evidence of time spent in a primary or secondary school and an analysis of activity undertaken with children. Give details of music qualifications, if any. Admissions tutors look for precise, succinct, well-reasoned, well-written statements (no mistakes!). See also **Chapter 5**.

Selection interviews **Yes** Bangor (P Educ QTS), Birmingham City (P Educ QTS), Birmingham Newman, Brighton, Cambridge, Canterbury Christ Church, Cardiff Met, Chester, Chichester, Cumbria, Durham, Edge Hill, Edinburgh (P Educ Gael), Glasgow, Gloucestershire (P Educ QTS), Greenwich, Hertfordshire, Huddersfield, Kingston, Leeds Beckett, Leeds Trinity, Liverpool John Moores (P Educ QTS), Manchester Met, Marjon, Middlesex, Northumbria, Nottingham Trent, Oxford Brookes, Portsmouth, Reading, Roehampton, Sheffield Hallam, St Mary's, Stranmillis (UC), Sunderland, UWE Bristol, West Scotland, Winchester (P Educ QTS), Wolverhampton, Worcester, York St John.

Interview advice and questions Questions invariably focus on why you want to teach and your experiences in the classroom. In some cases, you may be asked to write an essay on these topics. Questions in the past have included: What do you think are important issues in education at present? Discussion of coursework will take place for Art applicants.

Reasons for rejection (non-academic) Unable to meet the requirements of written standard English. Ungrammatical personal statements. Lack of research about teaching at primary or secondary levels. Lack of experience in schools. Insufficient experience of working with people.

GRADUATE DESTINATIONS AND EMPLOYMENT

(See **Chapter 1, Graduate Outcomes.**)

Career note See **Education Studies**.

OTHER DEGREE SUBJECTS FOR CONSIDERATION

Education Studies; Psychology; Social Policy; Social Sciences; Social Work.

TOURISM AND TRAVEL

(see also **Business and Management Courses, Business and Management Courses (International and European), Business and Management Courses (Specialised), Hospitality and Event Management, Leisure and Recreation Management/Studies**)

Tourism and Travel courses are popular; some are combined with Hospitality Management which thus provides students with two possible career paths. Courses involve business studies and a detailed study of tourism and travel. Industrial placements are frequently involved and language options are often included. See also **Appendix 3**.

USEFUL WEBSITES www.wttc.org; www.abta.com; www.thebapa.org.uk; www.itt.co.uk; www.tmi.org.uk

NB The points totals shown to the left of the institutions are for ease of reference only. It must not be assumed that Tariff points are always used by institutions or that they can be substituted for an offer in grades. The level of an offer is not necessarily indicative of the quality of a course.

COURSE OFFERS INFORMATION

SUBJECT REQUIREMENTS/PREFERENCES GCSE English and mathematics required. **AL** No subjects specified. Some popular universities are now making lower offers for disadvantaged and other students.

YOUR TARGET OFFERS AND EXAMPLES OF DEGREE COURSES

144 pts **Strathclyde** – AAA incl maths (Acc Hspty Tour Mgt) (IB 36 pts HL 5 maths)

120 pts **Derby** – BBB 120 pts (Int Tour Mgt)
Strathclyde – BBB–ABB (Hspty Tour Mgt) (IB 30–32 pts)

112 pts **Canterbury Christ Church** – BBC (Int Tour Hspty Mgt; Int Tour Mgt) (IB 29 pts)
Chester – 112 pts (Int Tour Mgt) (IB 28 pts)
East London – 112 pts (Tour Mgt) (IB 24 pts HL 15 pts)
Greenwich – 112 pts (Int Tour Hspty Mgt; Tour Mgt)
Hertfordshire – BBC–BBB 112–210 pts (Int Tour Mgt)
Northumbria – 112 pts (Tour Evnts Mgt)
West London – BBC 112 pts (Int Tour Mgt)
Westminster – BBC 112 pts (Tour Mgt)

104 pts **Bath Spa** – BCC–BBC (Bus Mgt (Tour Mgt)) (IB 32 pts)
Bournemouth – 104–120 pts (Tour Mgt) (IB 28–31 pts)
Brighton – BCC–BBB 104–120 pts (Bus Mgt Tour) (IB 26 pts)
Central Lancashire – 104–112 pts (Int Tour Mgt)
Coventry – 104 pts (Tour Hspty Mgt)
Gloucestershire – BCC 104 pts (Int Hspty Tour Mgt)
Hertfordshire – BCC–BBC 104–112 pts (Evnt Mgt Tour)
Leeds Beckett – 104–120 pts (Int Tour Mgt) (HL 55)
Lincoln – 104 pts (Int Tour Mgt) (IB 28 pts)
Liverpool Hope – BCC 104 pts (Tour Comb Hons; Tour Mgt) (IB 24 pts)
Manchester Met – BCC–BBC 104–112 pts (Int Tour Mgt) (IB 26 pts)
Northampton – BCC (Int Tour Mgt)
Plymouth – 104–120 pts (Int Tour Mgt) (IB 26–30 pts HL 4)
Surrey – BCC (Int Hspty Tour Mgt) (IB 26 pts)
York St John – 104 pts (Int Tour Hspty Mgt)

96 pts **Anglia Ruskin** – CCC 96 pts (Bus Tour Mgt) (IB 24 pts)
Bedfordshire – 96 pts (Int Tour Mgt; Trav Avn Tour Mgt)
Cardiff Met – CCC 96–112 pts (Int Tour Mgt)
Edinburgh Napier – CCC (Int Tour Airln Mgt; Int Tour Mgt) (IB 27 pts HL 654)
London Met – CCC 96 pts (Tour Trav Mgt)
Middlesex – 96–112 pts (Int Tour Mgt)
Robert Gordon – CCC (Int Tour Mgt) (IB 26 pts)

Ulster - CCC (Int Tour Mgt) (IB 24 pts HL 12 pts)
West Scotland - CCC 96 pts (Evnts Tour Mgt) (IB 24 pts)
Wolverhampton - CCC/BCD 96 pts (Tour Mgt)
88 pts **Bucks New** - 88-112 pts (Int Tour Mgt Air Trav)
Sunderland - 88-104 pts (Int Tour Hspty Mgt; Tour Avn Mgt)
Trinity Saint David - 88 pts (Int Trav Tour Mgt)
80 pts **Birmingham (UC)** - CDD 80 pts (Int Tour Mgt)
64 pts **UHI** - CC (Advntr Tour Mgt)

ALTERNATIVE OFFERS See **Chapter 6** and **Appendix 1** for grades/UCAS Tariff points information for other examinations.

DEGREE APPRENTICESHIPS

Cumbria (Vstr Econy); Gloucestershire (Hspty Mgt); Ulster (Int Hspty Mgt).

EXAMPLES OF COLLEGES OFFERING COURSES IN THIS SUBJECT FIELD

Barnet and Southgate (Coll); Barnsley (Coll); Basingstoke (CT); Bedford (Coll); Birmingham Met (Coll); Bishop Burton (Coll); Blackburn (Coll); Blackpool and Fylde (Coll); Bournemouth and Poole (Coll); Bradford College (UC); Brighton Met (Coll); Bury (Coll); Central Bedfordshire (Coll); Chelmsford (Coll); Cornwall (Coll); Craven (Coll); Dearne Valley (Coll); Derby (Coll); Dudley (Coll); Durham New (Coll); East Surrey (Coll); Grŵp Llandrillo Menai; Guildford (Coll); Hugh Baird (Coll); Hull (Coll); Kingston (Coll); Lancaster and Morecambe (Coll); Leeds City (Coll); Leicester (Coll); Liverpool City (Coll); London City (Coll); London UCK (Coll); Loughborough (Coll); Manchester (Coll); MidKent (Coll); Neath Port Talbot (Coll); Nescot; Newcastle (Coll); North Kent (Coll); North Notts (Coll); North Warwickshire and South Leicestershire (Coll); Northumberland (Coll); Norwich City (Coll); Nottingham (Coll); Redcar and Cleveland (Coll); South and West Cheshire (Coll); South Cheshire (Coll); South Devon (Coll); Sunderland (Coll); TEC Partnership; Uxbridge (Coll); West Herts (Coll); West Nottinghamshire (Coll); West Thames (Coll); Westminster City (Coll); Westminster Kingsway (Coll); Weston (Coll); Windsor Forest (Coll); Wirral Met (Coll).

CHOOSING YOUR COURSE (SEE ALSO CH.1)

UNIVERSITIES AND COLLEGES TEACHING QUALITY See www.qaa.ac.uk; www.discoveruni.gov.uk.

EXAMPLES OF SANDWICH DEGREE COURSES Birmingham (UC); Bournemouth; Brighton; Chester; Gloucestershire; Greenwich; Hertfordshire; Leeds Beckett; Lincoln; Manchester Met; Middlesex; Northumbria; Plymouth; Portsmouth; Sunderland; Surrey; Trinity Saint David; Wolverhampton.

ADMISSIONS INFORMATION

ADVICE TO APPLICANTS AND PLANNING THE UCAS PERSONAL STATEMENT Work experience in the travel and tourism industry is important - in agencies, in the airline industry or hotels. This work should be described in detail. Any experience with people in sales work, dealing with the public - their problems and complaints - should also be included. Travel should be outlined, detailing places visited. Genuine interest in travel, diverse cultures and people. Good communication skills required. See also **Appendix 3**.

SELECTION INTERVIEWS No Anglia Ruskin, Brighton, Sunderland, Surrey.

INTERVIEW ADVICE AND QUESTIONS Past questions have included: What problems have you experienced when travelling? Questions on places visited. Experiences of air, rail and sea travel. What is marketing? What special qualities do you have that will be of use in the travel industry? See also **Chapter 5**.

GRADUATE DESTINATIONS AND EMPLOYMENT

(See **Chapter 1, Graduate Outcomes.**)

CAREER NOTE See **Business and Management Courses**.

OTHER DEGREE SUBJECTS FOR CONSIDERATION

Airline and Airport Management; Business Studies; Events Management; Heritage Management; Hospitality Management; Leisure and Recreation Management; Travel Management.

TOWN AND URBAN PLANNING

(see also **Development Studies, Environmental Sciences, Housing, Surveying and Real Estate Management, Transport Management and Planning**)

Town and Urban Planning courses are very similar and some lead to qualification or part of a qualification as a member of the Royal Town Planning Institute (RTPI). Further information from the RTPI (see **Appendix 3**).

Useful websites www.rtpi.org.uk

NB The points totals shown to the left of the institutions are for ease of reference only. It must not be assumed that Tariff points are always used by institutions or that they can be substituted for an offer in grades. The level of an offer is not necessarily indicative of the quality of a course.

COURSE OFFERS INFORMATION

Subject requirements/preferences GCSE English and mathematics required. **AL** Geography may be specified. Note that a number of universities in the table below do not accept the UCAS Tariff. Some popular universities are now making lower offers for disadvantaged and other students.

Your target offers and examples of degree courses

152 pts **Cambridge** – A*AA+interview (Lnd Econ) (IB 41–42 pts HL 776)
144 pts **London LSE** – AAA (Env Sust Dev) (IB 38 pts HL 766)
136 pts **London (UCL)** – AAB (Urb Plan Des Mgt; Urb Plan Rl Est) (IB 36 pts HL 17 pts); AAB incl hum/soc sci (Urb St) (IB 36 pts HL 17 pts)
128 pts **Birmingham** – ABB (Geog Urb Reg Plan Comb Hons) (IB 32 pts HL 655)
Liverpool – ABB (Twn Reg Plan) (IB 33 pts)
Loughborough – ABB (Urb Plan) (IB 34 pts HL 655)
Manchester – ABB (Env Mgt) (IB 34 pts HL 655)
Newcastle – ABB 128 pts (Urb Plan) (IB 32 pts)
Sheffield – ABB (Geog Plan; Urb St) (IB 33 pts); ABB/BBB+bEPQ (Urb St Plan) (IB 33 pts)
120 pts **Dundee** – BBB (Urb Plan) (IB 30 pts HL 555)
Liverpool – BBB (Env Plan; Urb Plan) (IB 31 pts)
Queen's Belfast – BBB (Plan Env Dev) (IB 32 pts HL 655)
112 pts **Cardiff** – BBC–ABB (Urb Plan Dev) (IB 30–32 pts HL 655–665); (Hum Geog Plan) (IB 30–32 pts HL 655–665)
Leeds Beckett – 112 pts (Hum Geog Plan)
London South Bank – 112 pts (Urb Env Plan)
Nottingham Trent – 112 pts (Prop Dev Plan)
Ulster – BBC (Plan Regn Dev) (IB 25 pts)
Westminster – BBC 112 pts (Urb Plan Des)
104 pts **Oxford Brookes** – BCC 104 pts (Prop Dev Plan; Urb Des Plan Dev) (IB 29 pts)
UWE Bristol – 104 pts (Urb Plan)

Alternative offers See **Chapter 6** and **Appendix 1** for grades/UCAS Tariff points information for other examinations.

DEGREE APPRENTICESHIPS

Anglia Ruskin (Chart Twn Plan); Birmingham (Chart Twn Plan); Brighton (Chart Twn Plan); London South Bank (Chart Twn Plan); Oxford Brookes (Chart Twn Plan); Plymouth (Chart Twn Plan); Sheffield Hallam (Chart Twn Plan); UCL (Spat Twn Plan); UWE (Chart Twn Plan); Westminster (Chart Twn Plan).

CHOOSING YOUR COURSE (SEE ALSO CH.1)

Universities and colleges teaching quality See www.qaa.ac.uk; www.discoveruni.gov.uk.

Top research universities and colleges (REF 2021) See **Architecture**.

Examples of sandwich degree courses Cardiff; Nottingham Trent.

ADMISSIONS INFORMATION

Advice to applicants and planning the UCAS personal statement Visit your local planning office and discuss the career with planners. Know plans and proposed developments in your area and any objections to them. Study the history of town planning worldwide and the development of new towns in the UK during the 20th century, for example Bournville, Milton Keynes, Port Sunlight, Welwyn Garden City, Cumbernauld, and the advantages and disadvantages which became apparent. See also **Appendix 3**.

Selection interviews Yes Cambridge; **No** London (UCL), Newcastle.

Interview advice and questions Since Town and Urban Planning courses are vocational, work experience in a planning office is relevant and questions are likely to be asked on the type of work done and the problems faced by planners. Questions in recent years have included: If you were re-planning your home county for the future, what points would you consider? How are statistics used in urban planning? How do you think the problem of inner cities can be solved? Have you visited your local planning office? See also **Chapter 5**.

Reasons for rejection (non-academic) Lack of commitment to study for a professional qualification in Town Planning.

GRADUATE DESTINATIONS AND EMPLOYMENT

(See **Chapter 1, Graduate Outcomes.**)

Career note Town Planning graduates have a choice of career options within local authority planning offices. In addition to working on individual projects on urban development, they will also be involved in advising, co-ordinating and adjudicating in disputes and appeals. Planners also work closely with economists, surveyors and sociologists and their skills open up a wide range of other careers.

OTHER DEGREE SUBJECTS FOR CONSIDERATION

Architecture; Countryside Management; Environmental Studies; Geography; Heritage Management; Housing; Land Economy; Property; Public Administration; Real Estate; Sociology; Surveying; Transport Management.

TRANSPORT MANAGEMENT AND PLANNING

(including **Aviation Management, Cruise Management and Transport Design**; see also **Engineering/Engineering Sciences, Town and Urban Planning**)

Transport Management and Planning is a specialised branch of business studies with many applications on land, sea and air. It is not as popular as the less specialised Business Studies courses but is just as relevant and will provide the student with an excellent introduction to management and its problems.

Useful websites www.nats.aero; www.ciltuk.org.uk

NB The points totals shown to the left of the institutions are for ease of reference only. It must not be assumed that Tariff points are always used by institutions or that they can be substituted for an offer in grades. The level of an offer is not necessarily indicative of the quality of a course.

COURSE OFFERS INFORMATION

Subject requirements/preferences GCSE English and mathematics required. **AL** No subjects specified. Some popular universities are now making lower offers for disadvantaged and other students.

Your target offers and examples of degree courses

136 pts **Leeds** – AAB incl hum/soc sci (Geog Trans St) (IB 35 pts HL 16 pts incl 5 hum/soc sci)
120 pts **Cardiff** – BBB-AAB (Bus Mgt (Log Ops)) (IB 31–34 pts HL 665–666)
West London – 120 pts (Air Trans Mgt (ATPL))
112 pts **Coventry** – BBC 112 pts (Avn Mgt); BBC incl art/des 112 pts+portfolio (Auto Trans Des) (IB 27 pts)
Greenwich – 112 pts (Bus Log Sply Chn Mgt)
Northumbria – 112 pts (Bus Sply Chn Mgt)
Sheffield Hallam – BBC–BBB 112–120 pts (Airln Airpt Mgt)
Surrey – BBC (Int Airln Airpt Mgt) (IB 31 pts)
West London – BBC 112 pts (Air Trans Mgt)
104 pts **Bucks New** – 104–128 pts (Air Trans Commer Plt Trg)
96 pts **Edinburgh Napier** – CCC (Int Tour Airln Mgt) (IB 27 pts HL 654)
London Met – CCC 96 pts (Airln Airpt Avn Mgt)
88 pts **Bucks New** – 88–112 pts (Avn Mgt)
80 pts **Birmingham (UC)** – CDD 80 pts (Avn Airpt Mgt)
64 pts **Craven (Coll)** – 64 pts (Avn Mgt Ops)
Newcastle (Coll) – 64 pts (Airln Airpt Mgt)
48 pts **Middlesbrough (Coll)** – 48 pts (Airpt Airln Mgt)
32 pts **Plymouth** – 32 pts (Marit Bus Fdn Yr) (IB 24–25 pts HL 4)

Alternative offers See **Chapter 6** and **Appendix 1** for grades/UCAS Tariff points information for other examinations.

DEGREE APPRENTICESHIPS

Aston (Trans Plan); Wolverhampton (Civ Trans Eng).

EXAMPLES OF COLLEGES OFFERING COURSES IN THIS SUBJECT FIELD

Blackburn (Coll); Craven (Coll); MidKent (Coll); Newcastle (Coll); TEC Partnership; Wirral Met (Coll).

CHOOSING YOUR COURSE (SEE ALSO CH.1)

Universities and colleges teaching quality See www.qaa.ac.uk; www.discoveruni.gov.uk.

Examples of sandwich degree courses Cardiff; Coventry; Greenwich; Leeds; Plymouth; Sheffield Hallam.

ADMISSIONS INFORMATION

Advice to applicants and planning the UCAS personal statement Air, sea, road and rail transport are the main specialist areas. Contacts with those involved and work experience or work shadowing should be described in full. See also **Appendix 3**.

Selection interviews Some Middlesbrough (Coll) (Non-standard applicants).

Interview advice and questions Some knowledge of the transport industry (land, sea and air) is likely to be important at interview. Reading around the subject is also important, as are any contacts with management staff in the industries. Past questions have included: What developments are taking place to reduce the number of cars on the roads? What transport problems are there in your own locality? How did you travel to your interview? What problems did you encounter? How could they have been overcome? See also **Chapter 5**.

GRADUATE DESTINATIONS AND EMPLOYMENT

(See **Chapter 1, Graduate Outcomes.**)

Career note Many graduates will aim for openings linked with specialisms in their degree courses. These could cover air, rail, sea, bus or freight transport in which they will be involved in the management and control of operations as well as marketing and financial operations.

OTHER DEGREE SUBJECTS FOR CONSIDERATION

Air Transport Engineering; Civil Engineering; Environmental Studies; Logistics; Marine Transport; Town and Country Planning; Urban Studies.

VETERINARY SCIENCE/MEDICINE

(including **Bioveterinary Sciences and Veterinary Nursing**; see also **Animal Sciences**)

Veterinary Medicine/Science degrees enable students to acquire the professional skills and experience to qualify as veterinary surgeons. Courses follow the same pattern, combining scientific training with practical experience. The demand for these courses is considerable (see below) and work experience is essential prior to application. For those with good degrees in specified subjects, graduate entry programmes can lead to veterinary qualification. See also **Appendix 3**. Veterinary Nursing Honours degree courses combine both the academic learning and the nursing training required by the Royal College of Veterinary Surgeons, and can also include practice management. Foundation degrees in Veterinary Nursing are more widely available. Bioveterinary Sciences are usually three-year full-time BSc degree courses focusing on animal biology, management and disease, but do not qualify graduates to work as vets. For places in Veterinary Science/Medicine, applicants may select only four universities. Applicants to the University of Cambridge Veterinary School are required to sit the Natural Sciences Admissions Assessment (see **Chapter 5**).

Useful websites www.rcvs.org.uk; www.admissionstesting.org; www.bvna.org.uk; http://spvs.org.uk; www.bva.co.uk

NB The points totals shown to the left of the institutions are for ease of reference only. It must not be assumed that Tariff points are always used by institutions or that they can be substituted for an offer in grades. The level of an offer is not necessarily indicative of the quality of a course.

COURSE OFFERS INFORMATION

Subject requirements/preferences GCSE (Vet Sci/Med) Grade 5/6 (B) English, mathematics, physics, dual science if not at A-level. **AL** (Vet Sci/Med) See offers below. (Vet Nurs) Biology and another science may be required. Some popular universities are now making lower offers for disadvantaged and other students. **Other** Work experience essential for Veterinary Science/Medicine and Veterinary Nursing courses and preferred for other courses: check requirements. Health checks may be required. **Bristol** (Vet Sci) GCSE Grade 7 (A) in five subjects. Grade 7 (A) in mathematics if neither mathematics nor physics is offered at grade A at AS/A-level. **Glasgow** (Vet Med) GCSE Grade 6 (B) in English. **Liverpool** (Vet Sci) Minimum of seven GCSEs at grades 7776666 (7/A and 6/B) or above, including English, mathematics and physics (either as a separate subject or as dual award science) are required. **London (RVC)** (Vet Med) GCSE Grade 7 (A) in five subjects. **Nottingham** (Vet Med) GCSE Grade 7 (A) in five subjects.

Your target offers and examples of degree courses

152 pts **Cambridge** – A*AA incl chem+sci/maths+interview+ESAT (Vet Med) (IB 40–42 pts HL 776 incl chem+sci/maths)

144 pts **Aberystwyth** – AAA incl biol+chem (Vet Sci) (HL 666 incl biol+chem)

Bristol – AAA/A*AB incl chem+sci/maths (Vet Sci) (IB 36 pts HL 18 pts incl 6 chem+sci/maths)

Edinburgh – AAA incl chem+biol+interview (Vet Med) (IB 38 pts HL 666 incl chem+biol)

Glasgow – AAA incl chem+biol+interview (Vet Med Srgy) (IB 38 pts HL 666 incl chem+biol)

Harper Keele Vet Sch – AAA incl biol/chem+sci+interview (Vet Med Srgy) (IB 36 pts HL 666 incl biol/chem+sci)

Liverpool – AAA incl biol+chem (Vet Sci) (IB 36 pts HL 666 incl biol+chem)

London (RVC) – AAA incl chem+biol+interview (Vet Med) (HL 666 incl chem+biol)

Surrey – AAA incl chem+biol+interview (Vet Med Sci) (IB 35 pts HL 66)

136 pts **Nottingham** – AAB+interview (Vet Med Srgy Prelim Yr) (IB 34 pts HL 665); AAB incl chem+biol+interview (Vet Med Srgy) (IB 34 pts HL 665 incl biol+chem)

128 pts **Liverpool** – ABB incl biol+sci (Biovet Sci) (IB 33 pts HL 65 incl biol)
120 pts **Glasgow** – BBB–AAB incl chem+biol (Vet Biosci) (IB 32–36 pts HL 655–665)
Harper Adams – B biol (Vet Physio) (IB 30 pts HL 6 biol)
London (RVC) – BBB–ABB incl chem/biol+sci/maths (Biovet Sci) (HL 555–655 incl chem/biol+sci/maths)
Surrey – BBB incl biol+sci/maths (Vet Biosci) (IB 32 pts)
112 pts **Bristol** – BBC incl biol/chem+interview (Gateway Vet Sci) (IB 29 pts HL 5 biol/chem)
Chester – BBC incl biol (Biovet Sci) (IB 26 pts HL 5 biol)
Hartpury (Coll) – BBC incl biol (Biovet Sci) (HL 33 incl biol)
Middlesex – BBC–ABB incl biol 112–128 pts+interview (Vet Nurs)
Nottingham – BBC incl biol+chem+interview (Vet Med Gateway Yr) (IB 28 pts HL 554 incl 5 biol+chem)
104 pts **Aberystwyth** – BCC–ABB incl biol 104–128 pts (Eqn Vet Biosci; Vet Biosci) (IB 28–30 pts HL 5 biol)
Bishop Burton (Coll) – 104 pts (Biovet Sci)
Harper Adams – 104–120 pts (Vet Biosci (Yr Ind)) (IB 28 pts HL 5)
Lincoln – 104 pts (Biovet Sci)
London (RVC) – BCC incl biol+interview (Vet Nurs) (HL 544 incl 5 biol)
96 pts **Harper Adams** – C biol 96–112 pts (Vet Nurs courses) (IB 28 pts HL 5 biol)
London (RVC) – CCC incl chem+biol+interview (Vet Gateway) (HL 444 incl biol+chem)
80 pts **Sparsholt (Coll)** – CCE incl lf sci (Vet Nurs (FdSc)) (IB 25 pts HL 4 biol)
64 pts **Nottingham Trent** – C sci 64 pts+interview (Vet Nurs)
48 pts **Wrexham** – 48–72 pts+interview (Vet Nurs)

Alternative offers See **Chapter 6** and **Appendix 1** for grades/UCAS Tariff points information for other examinations.

EXAMPLES OF COLLEGES OFFERING COURSES IN THIS SUBJECT FIELD

Askham Bryan (Coll); Bishop Burton (Coll); Canterbury (Coll); Chichester (Coll); Cornwall (Coll); Derby (Coll); Duchy Coll (UC); Easton (Coll); Hartpury (Coll); Kingston Maurward (Coll); Leeds City (Coll); Myerscough (Coll); Northumberland (Coll); Plumpton (Coll); Sheffield (Coll); Sir Gâr (Coll); Sparsholt (Coll); Warwickshire (Coll); West Anglia (Coll).

CHOOSING YOUR COURSE (SEE ALSO CH.1)

Universities and colleges teaching quality See www.qaa.ac.uk; www.discoveruni.gov.uk.

Top research universities and colleges (REF 2021) (Agriculture, Food and Veterinary Sciences) Cambridge; Loughborough; Sheffield; Cardiff; Manchester; London (UCL); Kent; Edinburgh; Heriot-Watt; Glasgow.

Examples of sandwich degree courses Glasgow; Harper Adams; Harper Keele Vet Sch; Lincoln; London (RVC); Nottingham; Surrey; Wrexham.

ADMISSIONS INFORMATION

Advice to applicants and planning the UCAS personal statement Applicants for Veterinary Science must limit their choices to four universities and submit their applications by 15 October. They may add one alternative course. Work experience is almost always essential so discuss this in full, giving information about the size and type of practice and the type of work in which you were involved. As described below, there are several alternative options for work experience. These include work at a veterinary practice involving domestic animals, city and rural farms with dairy, beef cattle, sheep, pigs or poultry, kennels, catteries, laboratories, pet shops, wildlife parks, abattoirs and zoos. See also **Appendix 3**.

Selection interviews Yes Bristol (Gateway Vet Sci), Cambridge, Edinburgh, Glasgow (Vet Med Srgy), Harper Keele Vet Sch, Liverpool, London (RVC) (Vet med, Vet Gateway), Middlesex, Nottingham, Plymouth, Surrey (Vet Med Sci), Wrexham.

INTERVIEW ADVICE AND QUESTIONS Past questions have included: Why do you want to be a vet? Have you visited a veterinary practice? What did you see? Do you think there should be a Vet National Health Service? What are your views on vivisection? What are your views on intensive factory farming? How can you justify thousands of pounds of taxpayers' money being spent on training you to be a vet when it could be used to train a civil engineer? When would you feel it your responsibility to tell battery hen farmers that they were being cruel to their livestock? What are your views on vegetarians? How does aspirin stop pain? Why does it only work for a certain length of time? Do you eat beef? Outline the bovine TB problem. Questions on A-level science syllabus. See also **Chapter 5**.

REASONS FOR REJECTION (NON-ACADEMIC) Failure to demonstrate motivation. Lack of basic knowledge or understanding of ethical and animal issues.

GRADUATE DESTINATIONS AND EMPLOYMENT

(See **Chapter 1, Graduate Outcomes.**)

CAREER NOTE Most veterinary surgeons work in private practice with the remainder involved in research in universities, government-financed research departments and in firms linked with farming, foodstuff manufacturers and pharmaceutical companies.

OTHER DEGREE SUBJECTS FOR CONSIDERATION

Agricultural Science; Agriculture; Animal Sciences; Biological Sciences; Biology; Dentistry; Equine Dental Science; Equine Management; Equine Studies; Medicine; Zoology.

ZOOLOGY

(including **Animal Biology**; see also **Agricultural Sciences/Agriculture, Animal Sciences, Biological Sciences, Biology**)

Zoology courses have a biological science foundation and could cover animal ecology, marine and fisheries biology, animal population, development and behaviour and, on some courses, wildlife management and fisheries.

USEFUL WEBSITES www.biaza.org.uk; www.zsl.org; www.abwak.org

NB The points totals shown to the left of the institutions are for ease of reference only. It must not be assumed that Tariff points are always used by institutions or that they can be substituted for an offer in grades. The level of an offer is not necessarily indicative of the quality of a course.

COURSE OFFERS INFORMATION

SUBJECT REQUIREMENTS/PREFERENCES GCSE English and science/mathematics required or preferred. **AL** One or two sciences will be required. Some popular universities are now making lower offers for disadvantaged and other students.

YOUR TARGET OFFERS AND EXAMPLES OF DEGREE COURSES

160 pts **Cambridge** – A*A*A incl sci+maths+interview+ESAT (Nat Sci (Zool)) (IB 41–42 pts HL 776)

144 pts **Bristol** – AAA incl sci/maths (Zool) (IB 36 pts HL 18 pts incl 6/6 sci/maths)

Sheffield – AAA incl biol+sci (Zool (MBiolSci)) (IB 36 pts HL 6 biol+sci)

Southampton – AAB incl biol+sci/maths (Zool) (IB 34 pts HL 17 pts incl 5/6 biol+sci/maths)

136 pts **Birmingham** – AAB incl biol/hum biol+sci (Biol Sci (Zool)) (IB 32 pts HL 665 incl biol+sci)

Leeds – AAB incl biol+sci (Zool) (IB 34–35 pts HL 665 incl biol+sci)

Manchester – AAB–AAA incl sci/maths (Zool) (IB 35–36 pts HL 665–666 incl sci); AAB–AAA incl sci/maths+interview (Zool (Yr Ind)) (IB 35–36 pts HL 665–666 incl sci)

Newcastle – ABB incl biol/hum biol+sci (Mar Zool) (IB 32 pts HL 6 biol)

Nottingham – AAB incl biol+sci (Zool) (IB 32 pts HL 6/5 biol+sci)

Sheffield – AAB incl biol+sci (Zool) (IB 34 pts HL 6,5 biol+sci)

St Andrews – AAB incl biol+sci/maths (Zool) (IB 36 pts HL 665 incl 6 biol+sci/maths)

128 pts **Cardiff** – ABB–AAB incl biol/chem (Biol Sci (Zool)) (IB 32–34 pts HL 665–666 incl 6 biol/chem)
Edinburgh – ABB–AAA incl biol+chem (Biol Sci (Zool)) (IB 32–37 pts HL 655–666 incl biol+chem)
Exeter – ABB incl sci/maths 128–144 pts (Zool (Cornwall)) (IB 32–34 pts HL 655–665 incl sci/maths)
Lancaster – ABB incl sci/maths (Zool) (IB 32 pts HL 16 pts incl 6 sci)
Leicester – ABB–AAB incl sci/maths (Biol Sci (Zool)) (IB 30 pts HL 6/5 sci/maths)
Liverpool – ABB incl biol+sci (Zool) (IB 33 pts HL 6 biol)
London (QM) – ABB incl biol (Zool) (IB 32 pts HL 655 incl biol)
Newcastle – ABB–AAB incl biol+sci 128–136 pts (Zool) (IB 32–34 pts HL 6 biol)
Sussex – ABB incl sci (Zool) (IB 32 pts HL 5 biol/chem/phys)

120 pts **Glasgow** – BBB–AAB incl biol/chem (Zool) (IB 34 pts HL 655 incl biol/chem)
Hull – BBB incl biol 120 pts (Zool) (IB 30 pts HL 5 biol)
Queen's Belfast – BBB–ABB incl biol+sci/maths/geog (Zool) (IB 32 pts HL 655 incl sci/maths/geog)
Reading – BBB–ABB incl biol+sci/maths (Zool) (IB 30–32 pts HL 5 biol+sci)
Stirling – BBB incl sci/maths (Anim Biol) (IB 30 pts incl sci/maths)
Swansea – BBB–ABB incl biol/hum biol (Zool) (IB 32 pts HL 5 biol)

112 pts **Aberdeen** – BBC incl maths/sci (Zool) (IB 32 pts HL 555 incl maths/sci)
Anglia Ruskin – 112 pts incl biol (Zool) (IB 24 pts)
Bangor – 112–128 pts incl sci (Mar Vert Cons); 112–136 pts incl biol (Zool; Zool Cons; Zool Herp; Zool Mar Zool) (HL 5 biol)
Chester – 112 pts incl biol/chem (Zool) (IB 26 pts HL 5 biol); BCC–BBC incl biol 112 pts (Anim Bhv Biol/Psy) (IB 26 pts HL 5 biol)
Derby – BBC–BBB 112–120 pts (Zool)
Hartpury (Coll) – BBC incl biol 112 pts (Zool)
Liverpool John Moores – BBC–ABB incl biol 112–128 pts (Zool)
London (RH) – BBC–BBB incl biol (Zool) (IB 30 pts HL 555 incl biol)
Nottingham Trent – incl biol 112 pts (Zoo Biol)
Roehampton – 112 pts incl biol/sci (Zool)

104 pts **Aberystwyth** – BCC–BBB incl B biol 104–120 pts (Anim Bhv) (IB 28–30 pts HL 5 biol); BCC–BBB incl biol 104–120 pts (Zool) (IB 28–30 pts HL 5 biol)
Cumbria – BCC–BBC 104–112 pts+interview+portfolio (Wldlf Media)
Gloucestershire – 104–120 pts (Wldlf Cons Biol)
Harper Adams – 104–120 pts (App Zool; Zool Entomol; Zool Env Mgt) (IB 28 pts)
Lincoln – incl biol 104 pts (Zool) (IB 28 pts HL 5 biol)
Manchester Met – BCC incl biol/hum biol 104–112 pts (Anim Bhv Cons; Zool) (IB 26 pts HL 5 biol)
Myerscough (Coll) – 104 pts+interview (Zool) (IB 24 pts)
Oxford Brookes – BCC incl sci 104 pts (Biodiv Wldlf Cons) (IB 29 pts); BCC–BBB incl sci 104–120 pts (Biol Sci (Zool)) (IB 29 pts)
Plymouth – B biol+sci 104–128 pts (Zool) (IB 28–32 pts)
Salford – 104–112 pts incl biol (Zool) (IB 30 pts HL 4 biol)
South Wales – BCC incl sci 104 pts (Nat Hist)

96 pts **Reading** – CCC–BBB (Zool Fdn) (IB 24–30 pts)
South Wales – CCC incl biol+sci 96 pts (Int Wldlf Biol)
West Scotland – CCC incl biol 96 pts (App Biosci Zool) (IB 24 pts HL 3 biol)
Worcester – 96–104 pts incl biol+sci (Biol Sci (Zool))

80 pts **Cornwall (Coll)** – 80 pts (App Mar Zool)

64 pts **Reaseheath (UC)** – 64 pts (Zoo Mgt) (IB 24 pts HL 4 biol)
Royal Agricultural Univ – 64 pts (Anim Mgt Zool)

ALTERNATIVE OFFERS See **Chapter 6** and **Appendix 1** for grades/UCAS Tariff points information for other examinations.

EXAMPLES OF COLLEGES OFFERING COURSES IN THIS SUBJECT FIELD

Bishop Burton (Coll); Cornwall (Coll); Craven (Coll); Dudley (Coll); Easton (Coll); Guildford (Coll); Norwich City (Coll); South Gloucestershire and Stroud (Coll); Sparsholt (Coll).

CHOOSING YOUR COURSE (SEE ALSO CH.1)

Universities and colleges teaching quality See www.qaa.ac.uk; www.discoveruni.gov.uk.

Examples of sandwich degree courses Cardiff; Leeds; Liverpool John Moores; Manchester; Nottingham Trent; Reading.

ADMISSIONS INFORMATION

Advice to applicants and planning the UCAS personal statement Interests in animals should be described, together with any first-hand experience gained. Visits to zoos, farms, fish farms, etc and field courses attended should be described, together with any special points of interest you noted.

Selection interviews Yes Cambridge, Cumbria, Myerscough (Coll); **No** Derby, London (RH), Newcastle, Swansea.

Interview advice and questions Past questions have included: Why do you want to study Zoology? What career do you hope to follow on graduation? Specimens may be given to identify. Questions usually asked on A-level subjects. See also **Chapter 5**.

GRADUATE DESTINATIONS AND EMPLOYMENT

(See **Chapter 1, Graduate Outcomes.**)

Career note See **Biology**.

OTHER DEGREE SUBJECTS FOR CONSIDERATION

Animal Ecology; Animal Sciences; Aquaculture; Biological Sciences; Biology; Ecology; Fisheries Management; Marine Biology; Parasitology; Veterinary Science; Wildlife Management.

8 INFORMATION FOR INTERNATIONAL STUDENTS

The choice of a subject to study (from over 50,000 degree courses) and of a university or college (from more than 150 institutions) is a major task for students living in the UK. For overseas applicants it is even greater, and the decisions that have to be made need much careful planning, preferably beginning two years before the start of the course. **NB** Beware that there are some private institutions offering bogus degrees: check www.ucas.com to ensure your university and college choices are legitimate.

APPLICATIONS AND THE POINTS-BASED IMMIGRATION SYSTEM

In addition to submitting your application through UCAS (see **Chapter 4**) a Points-based Immigration System is in operation for overseas students. The main features of this system include:

- **Confirmation of Acceptance for Studies (CAS) number** When you accept an offer the institution will send you a CAS number which you will need to include on your visa application.
- **Maintenance** Students will need to show that they are able to pay for the first year's tuition fees, plus £1,334 per month for accommodation and living expenses if you are studying in London (which includes the University of London, institutions fully or partially in London, or in parts of Surrey, Hertfordshire and Essex), and £1,023 per month if you are studying in the rest of the UK. Additional funds and regulations apply for those bringing dependants into the UK.
- **Proof of qualifications** Your visa letter will list all the qualifications that you submitted to obtain your university place and original proof will be required of these qualifications when submitting your visa application. These documents will be checked by the Home Office. Any fraudulent documents will result in your visa application being rejected and a possible ban from entering the UK for 10 years.
- **Attendance** Once you have started your course, your attendance will be monitored. Non-attending students will be reported to the UK Border Agency.

Full details can be obtained from www.ukcisa.org.uk.

SELECTION, ADMISSION AND FINANCE

The first reason for making early contact with your preferred institution is to check their requirements for your chosen subject and their selection policies for overseas applicants. For example, for most Art and some Architecture courses you will have to present a portfolio of work or slides. For Music courses your application often will have to be accompanied by a recording you have made of your playing or singing and, in many cases, a personal audition will be necessary. For some universities and for some courses, the interview may take place either online or with a university or college representative in your own country.

The ability to speak and write good English is essential and many institutions require evidence of competence, for example scores from the International English Language Testing System (IELTS) or from the Trinity College London test (see www.ielts.org and www.trinitycollege.com/qualifications/SELT/UKVI). For some institutions, you may have to send examples of your written work. Each institution provides information about its English language entry requirements and a summary of this is given for each university listed below. International students should note that the recommended threshold for minimum English language requirements is CEFR level B2 (IELTS 5.5). This is a requirement for the visa application. Recent research indicates that students with a lower score may have difficulty in dealing with their course.

In the next chapter you will find a directory of universities and colleges in the UK, together with their contact details. Most universities and colleges in the UK have an overseas student adviser who can advise you on these and other points you need to consider, such as passports, visas, entry certificates, evidence of financial support, medical certificates, medical insurance, and the numbers of overseas students in the university from your own country. All these details are very important and need to be considered at the same time as choosing your course and institution.

The subject tables in **Chapter 7** provide a comprehensive picture of courses on offer and of comparative entry levels. However, before making an application, other factors should be considered, such as English language entry requirements (see above), the availability of English language teaching, living costs, tuition fees and any scholarships or other awards which might be offered. Detailed information about these can be obtained from the international offices in each university or college, British higher education fairs throughout the world and also the British Council (www.britishcouncil.org) offices abroad.

Below is a brief summary of the arrangements made by each university in the UK for international students aiming to take a full-time degree programme. The information is presented as follows:

- Institution.
- International student numbers.
- English language entry requirements for degree programmes, shown in IELTS scores. These vary between universities and courses, and can range from 7.5 to 5.5 and lower in some cases. See www.ielts.org. For full details, contact the university or college.
- Arrangements for English tuition courses.
- International Foundation courses.
- Annual tuition fees (approximate) for full-time undergraduate degree courses. Tuition fees also usually include fees for examinations and graduation. These figures are approximate and are subject to change each year. Following the UK's withdrawal from the EU on 31 January 2020, EU students no longer pay 'Home student' fees for the duration of their course.
- Annual living costs. These are approximate and based on regional average monthly costs reported by Save the Student's National Student Money Survey 2024, including rent, food, bills, course materials, clothes and transport in the UK, but not travel to or from the UK. For more details, see www.savethestudent.org/money/surveys/student-money-survey-2024-results.html. Band A: up to £950; Band B: £951–£999; Band C: £1,000–£1,099; Band D: £1,100–£1,199; and Band E: £1,200 and over. (Costs are likely to rise year by year in line with the rate of inflation in the UK.) Overseas students are normally permitted to take part-time work for a period of up to 20 hours per week if they are studying at degree level in the UK.
- Scholarships and awards for overseas students.

UNIVERSITY INFORMATION AND FEES FOR INTERNATIONAL UNDERGRADUATES

Applicants should check university websites before applying. **The fees published below (unless otherwise stated) are those to be charged to students in 2025/26 (check websites for 2026/27 fees).**

Aberdeen International students from over 130 countries. *English language entry requirement (or equivalent):* IELTS 6.0; Medicine 7.0. Pre-sessional English courses available on campus or online. *Fees:* £20,800–£24,800; Medicine £50,100. *Living costs:* Band C. International Student Scholarships available.

Abertay International students make up around 23% of the University's student body, with over 50 nationalities represented across the University. *English language entry requirement (or equivalent):* IELTS 6.0 (no band less than 5.5); BSc Mental Health Nursing and MSc Counselling 7.0. Pre-sessional English course available, language support provided throughout degree. *Fees:* £15,00–£15,500. *Living costs:* Band C.

Aberystwyth International students make up approximately a fifth of the University's student body. *English language entry requirement (or equivalent):* IELTS 6.5 (no band less than 5.5); BSc Computer Science and Business courses 6.0. International Foundation Certificate and pre-sessional English courses available. *Fees:* Arts and Social Science subjects £18,170; Science subjects £20,715. *Living costs:* Band D. Fee levels for international students are frozen at the level of entry for subsequent study years. International scholarships available.

Anglia Ruskin Students from 185 countries. *English language entry requirement (or equivalent):* IELTS 6.0, with minimum of 5.5 in each element. A one-year International Foundation programme is available. *Fees:* From £15,000. *Living costs:* Band D. Scholarships available.

Arden Provides distance or blended learning to students from over 140 countries. *English language entry requirement (or equivalent):* IELTS 6.0, with minimum of 5.5 in each element. *Fees:* Prices per course available on website. *Living costs:* Band E. Scholarships available.

Arts London A large number of international students from over 130 countries. *English language entry requirement (or equivalent):* IELTS 5.0–7.5. Pre-sessional English courses available on campus and online. *Fees:* £28,570. *Living costs:* Band E. Scholarships and bursaries available.

Aston International students from over 120 countries. *English language entry requirement (or equivalent):* IELTS 5.5–7.0. International Foundation programme offered as a bridge to the degree courses. Pre-sessional English classes also available for four, six, 12, 18 and 30 weeks. *Fees:* Humanities and Social Science courses £18,250; Engineering and Applied Science courses £21,500; Life and Health Sciences £21,500; Business School £18,250; Medicine £46,350. *Living costs:* Band D. Scholarships offered, including bursaries for Engineering and Science subjects.

Bangor Nearly 2,000 international students from 126 countries. *English language entry requirement (or equivalent):* IELTS 6.0–7.0, with minimum of 5.5. Pre-sessional English courses available. *Fees:* Arts, Humanities, Education and Law £17,000; Sciences £18,000–£20,000. *Living costs:* Band D. Nursing cost includes placement fee. International entrance scholarships available.

Bath 61% of students are international, representing over 162 nationalities. *English language entry requirement (or equivalent):* IELTS 6.5–7.0. Pre-sessional programmes available. *Fees:* Humanities and Social Sciences £22,800; Economics and Management £25,700; Science and Engineering £28,800; MArch Yr 1 £18,400, Yr 2 £28,800. *Living costs:* Band D. Scholarships, bursaries and awards available.

Bath Spa Staff and students from over 80 countries. *English language entry requirement (or equivalent):* IELTS 6.0 (minimum of 5.5 in all bands). Pre-sessional English courses for five or six weeks and 11 or 12 weeks. *Fees:* Classroom-based courses £15,750; laboratory/studio-based courses £16,905; School of Art & Design £17,585. *Living costs:* Band D.

Bedfordshire Students from around 115 countries. *English language entry requirement (or equivalent):* IELTS 6.0, with minimum of 5.5 in each band. Pre-sessional English course are available for two, four, eight, 12, and 16 weeks. *Fees:* £15,500 *Living costs:* Band D Scholarships available.

Birmingham Over 10,000 international students from approximately 150 countries. *English language entry requirement (or equivalent):* IELTS 6.0–7.0, depending on programme of study. Pre-sessional English language programmes last between six and 32 weeks depending on language proficiency (IELTS 4.0–7.0). *Fees:* Non-laboratory subjects £22,080–£25,860; Laboratory subjects £27,180–£30,000; Clinical courses £48,660. *Living costs:* Band D. Scholarships are offered by some subject departments including all Engineering subjects, Computer Science, Law, and Pharmacy.

Birmingham (UC) Over 3,100 international students from more than 70 countries. Specific entry requirements for each country are found on the College website. *English language entry requirement (or equivalent):* IELTS 6.0, with minimum of 5.5 in each band. Pre-sessional English programme for six, eight or 12 weeks depending on language ability. *Fees:* £14,000. *Living costs:* Band D.

Birmingham City Large number of international students from around 100 countries. *English language entry requirement (or equivalent):* IELTS 6.0, with minimum of 5.5 in each band. Pre-sessional language courses of two, six, 10 and 16 weeks. *Fees:* All undergraduate courses £16,085–£17,690; Conservatoire/Acting courses £19,970–£26,195. *Living costs:* Band D.

Birmingham Newman *English language entry requirement (or equivalent):* English language entry requirements (or equivalent): IELTS 6.5, with no component below 6.0. *Fees:* £16,000. *Living costs:* Band D.

Bishop Grosseteste *English language entry requirement (or equivalent):* IELTS 6.0, with minimum of 5.5 in each component. *Fees:* £13,600. *Living costs:* Band B.

Bournemouth A large number of international students. *English language entry requirement (or equivalent):* IELTS 6.0, with a minimum of 5.5 in each component. Pre-sessional English programmes from three to 39 weeks. *Fees:* £17,800–£18,800. *Living costs:* Band D. Some subject awards available.

Bournemouth Arts Students and staff from over 60 countries. *English language entry requirement (or equivalent):* IELTS: 6.0 overall, with a minimum of 5.5 in each band. English pre-sessional course available for six, eight, 12 or 16 weeks depending on language ability. *Fees:* Most courses £18,950 for Year 1 and 2; BA Animation, Costume, Film, Modelmaking £19,950 for Year 1 and 2; £17,950 for Year 3. *Living costs:* Band D.

BPP A private university dedicated to business and the professions with several study centres spread across England. Contact the University for information. *Fees:* Contact the University. *Living costs:* Band E.

Bradford International students make up 30% of the student body, representing over 120 countries. *English language entry requirement (or equivalent):* IELTS 6.0, with minimum of 5.0 in each element. Pre-sessional English language courses for six, 10, and 20 weeks. *Fees:* Lab-based courses £23,290; Classroom-based courses £19,560; Health Studies courses £19,560–£24,130. *Living costs:* Band C. Tuition fees will differ depending on individual fee status assessment. Scholarships available.

Brighton Over 3,000 international students from more than 150 countries. *English language entry requirement (or equivalent):* IELTS 6.0, with no less than 5.5 for each component. Pre-sessional English courses for six or 12 weeks. *Fees:* Classroom-based courses £15,900; Laboratory and workshop-based courses £15,900–£16,900; placement year £2,280. *Living costs:* Band D. Scholarships available.

Brighton and Sussex (MS) *English language entry requirement (or equivalent):* IELTS 7.0, with no less than 7.0 in each section. *Fees:* £44,500. *Living costs:* Band D. Fees will rise by 7% per year. Scholarships based on merit and financial need available.

Bristol International students from over 150 countries make up over 28% of the student population. *English language entry requirement (or equivalent):* IELTS 6.0–7.5 depending on programme of study. Pre-sessional language courses lasting six and 10 weeks and a year-long International Foundation programme. *Fees:* Arts and Social Sciences courses £23,900–£26,400 (excluding Film, Theatre, Innovation and Liberal Arts, for which the Science course fees apply); Science and Engineering courses £29,300–£31,300; Clinical courses £39,200–£46,500. *Living costs:* Band D. Scholarships and bursaries available.

Brunel Students represent over 150 countries. *English language entry requirement (or equivalent):* IELTS 6.0–7.0. Pre-sessional English language courses available. *Fees:* £19,430–£23,615; Medicine £49,395. *Living costs:* Band E. International, academic excellence and country-specific scholarships available.

Buckingham Students from over 100 different countries. *English language entry requirement (or equivalent):* IELTS 6.5, with a minimum of 6.0 in each component. Foundation English courses offered. *Fees:* Two-year degrees £44,000 (£22,000 x 2 years); three-year degrees £48,000 (£16,000 x 3 years); Medicine £202,500 (£45,000 x 4.5 years). *Living costs:* Band D. International high achiever scholarship and some bursaries available.

Bucks New International students from over 50 countries. *English language entry requirement (or equivalent):* IELTS 6.0, with a minimum of 5.5 in each element. *Fees:* From £15,150–£15,500. *Living costs:* Band D. Academic achievement scholarships available.

Cambridge International students make up 41% of the student body, representing around 140 countries. *English language entry requirement (or equivalent):* IELTS 7.5 overall, with minimum of 7.0 in each element. Pre- and in-sessional English support is available. *Fees:* Tuition fees range between £25,734 and £67,194, depending on the course studied. College fees vary between £9,275 and £12,950 per year, depending on the college. *Living costs:* Band D. Financial awards are offered to international students through the University of Cambridge and by some colleges. Scholarships for students from Hong Kong are also available.

Canterbury Christ Church International students from over 80 countries. *English language entry requirement (or equivalent):* IELTS 6.0, with a minimum of 5.5 in each section. Professional health undergraduate programmes require IELTS 7.0 overall with a minimum of 6.5 in each section. *Fees:* £15,500. *Living costs:* Band D. EEA National Transition Scholarships automatically awarded to those who meet all eligibility criteria. Skills based scholarships also available.

Cardiff Over 7,530 international students from more than 138 countries. *English language entry requirement (or equivalent):* IELTS 6.5–7.0. Pre-sessional language courses from eight to 20 weeks. In-sessional support is available. Induction course for all students. International Foundation courses for Business and Engineering. *Fees:* Arts-based courses £22,700; Business School courses £22,700; Science-based courses £28,200; Medicine £43,700; Dentistry £28,200 year 1, £43,700 years 2–5. *Living costs:* Band D. Scholarships available. Some healthcare science courses may be unavailable to international students.

Cardiff Met The University has over 1,200 international students enrolled from more than 143 countries. *English language entry requirement (or equivalent):* IELTS 6.0, with a minimum of 5.5 in each section. International Foundation course and pre-sessional English courses available. *Fees:* £16,000. *Living costs:* Band D. Scholarships available.

Central Lancashire International students from over 100 countries. *English language entry requirement (or equivalent):* IELTS 6.0; MBBS 7.0. *Fees:* All undergraduate courses £17,325; MBBS £49,000; BVMS £39,000; BSc Bioveterinary Sciences £26,250. *Living costs:* Band C. Scholarships and bursaries available for international students.

Chester Over 15,000 students from over 130 countries. *English language entry requirement (or equivalent):* IELTS 6.0, with a minimum of 5.5. International Foundation programmes available in Business, Law and Social Sciences, Engineering and Computing, Life Sciences and Creative Arts. *Fees:* £13,950. *Living costs:* Band C. International students are automatically considered for the University of Chester International Scholarships upon application.

Chichester International students from several countries. *English language entry requirement (or equivalent):* IELTS 6.0 or 5.5 if taking a joint degree with International English Studies. No component may be less than 5.5. Pre-sessional programme for five and 10 weeks available. *Fees:* All undergraduate courses £16,344; Adult Nursing and Physiotherapy £17,724. *Living costs:* Band D.

City St George's There are a variety of courses that international students can apply to. Full details on entry requirements for each individual course are available on the University website. *English language entry requirement (or equivalent):* IELTS 6.0 (6.5 for Music; 7.0–7.5 for English, Law, Journalism and health sciences). Pre-sessional English language courses are available as four-, eight- and 12-week programmes. *Fees:* Fees vary depending on the course (e.g. English £19,600; Music £17,850; Mathematics £19,370; Adult Nursing £30,700; Physiotherapy £27,750; Biomedical Science £27,750; Diagnostic Radiography £21,700; Medicine £46,250). *Living costs:* Band E. Academic scholarships available.

Coventry About 13,000 international students from over 150 countries. *English language entry requirement (or equivalent):* IELTS 5.0. International Foundation and pre-sessional English programmes available. *Fees:* Fees vary depending on the course; most courses cost approximately £16,800–£20,050 per year. *Living costs:* Band D. Scholarships available.

Cranfield International students from over 100 countries. *English language entry requirement (or equivalent):* IELTS 6.5, with at least 5.5 in each component. Pre-sessional English language courses available for five and ten weeks. *Fees:* £21,040–£40,255 depending on course; exclusively postgraduate. *Living costs:* Band D. International scholarships available.

Creative Arts *English language entry requirement (or equivalent):* IELTS 6.0 (no band less than 5.5). *Fees:* £17,500. *Living costs:* Band D. International scholarships available.

Cumbria *English language entry requirement (or equivalent):* IELTS 6.0, with at least 5.5 in each component; BSc Nursing, Midwifery, Occupational Therapy and Social Work 7.0; BSc Physiotherapy and Diagnostic Radiography 7.0, with no component less than 6.5. Online pre-sessional English courses are available for six and 12 weeks. *Fees:* £13,575; BA Social Work and pre-registration Health programmes £16,400. *Living costs:* Band C. International scholarships available.

De Montfort Thousands of international students from more than 130 countries. *English language entry requirement (or equivalent):* IELTS 5.5, with a minimum of 5.5 in each component. Pre-sessional English language courses and one-year International Foundation Certificate available. *Fees:* Art, Design and Humanities, and Business and Law £15,750; Engineering, Computing and Media £15,750-£16,250; Health and Life Sciences £15,750–£16,250. *Living costs:* Band B. DMU International Scholarship available.

Derby More than 2,000 international students from over 100 countries. *English language entry requirement (or equivalent):* IELTS 6.0–7.0. Courses offered to those needing tuition in English language. International Foundation Programme and pre-sessional English courses available. *Fees:* £14,900. *Living costs:* Band D. International scholarships available.

Dundee Around 12,000 full-time undergraduate international students. *English language entry requirement (or equivalent):* IELTS 6.0; MBChB Medicine 7.0. Foundation programme pathways in Art and Design, Business, Physical Science and Engineering, Life and Biomedical Sciences, and Social Sciences available. Pre- and in-sessional English courses available. *Fees:* Non-laboratory courses £22,500; laboratory courses £25,000–£27,400; Medicine and Dentistry £53,370. *Living costs:* Band C. International scholarships available.

Durham Over 4,500 international students from 156 countries. *English language entry requirement (or equivalent):* IELTS 6.5–7.0. Pre- and in-sessional English language programmes available. *Fees:* Arts £25,500–£25,750; Sciences £27,000–£32,500. *Living costs:* Band D. International scholarships available for students from Bangladesh, India, Malaysia, Nigeria, Pakistan and Vietnam. Undergraduate scholarships also available.

Dyson Check the website for details: www.dysoninstitute.com/applying/.

East Anglia Over 3,500 international students from 100 countries. *English language entry requirement (or equivalent):* IELTS 6.0 (higher for some courses). International Foundation and pre-sessional programmes available. *Fees:* Classroom-based subjects £19,250; laboratory-based subjects £24,400; Medicine £39,550. *Living costs:* Band D. International scholarships available.

East London International students from more than 135 countries. *English language entry requirement (or equivalent):* IELTS 5.5–6.0. Pre-sessional English courses of five weeks. *Fees:* £14,820; School of Architecture, Computing and Engineering £14,580. *Living costs:* Band E. Range of international scholarships available.

Edge Hill There is a small number of international students. *English language entry requirement (or equivalent):* IELTS 6.0, with a minimum of 5.5 in each element. Pre-sessional English language course and International Foundation Programme available. *Fees:* £16,500. *Living costs:* Band C. International students will automatically be considered for a scholarship upon application.

Edinburgh International students make up over 44% of the student population. *English language entry requirement (or equivalent):* IELTS 6.5–7.5. English language courses offered throughout the year. *Fees:* £28,000–£36,800; Medicine £49,900–£51,961; Veterinary Medicine £39,700. *Living costs:* Band C. Scholarships available for admission to certain schools.

Edinburgh Napier Students from over 180 countries. *English language entry requirement (or equivalent):* IELTS 6.0 overall with no component below 5.5. Pre- and in-sessional language support. *Fees:* Classroom-based and journalism courses £16,680; Laboratory-based courses £19,340. *Living costs:* Band C. International scholarships for students from a range of countries are available.

Essex International students from over 140 countries. *English language entry requirement (or equivalent):* IELTS 6.0. Pre-sessional English language programmes from five to 20 weeks and academic English classes provided during the year. *Fees:* Computer Science and Electronic Engineering £23,850; Laboratory-based courses in Life Sciences and Psychology £23,200; Law, Economics, Government and Mathematical Sciences £21,525; History, Sociology, Language and Linguistics £20,475; Oral Health Science £30,275. *Living costs:* Band D. A comprehensive package of scholarships and bursaries is available.

Exeter Around 7,500 international students from 150 countries. *English language entry requirement (or equivalent):* IELTS 6.5–7.5. International Foundation and Diploma programmes available as well as pre-sessional English language programmes of eight and 12 weeks. *Fees:* Arts, Humanities and Social Sciences (including Law) £23,700; Accounting and Finance, Business and Management and Economics £23,700; Biosciences, Mathematics, Geography, Psychology and Sports Sciences £29,700; Physics, Geology, Mining and Engineering £29,700; Combined Honours programmes that combine a science and a non-science subject £24,500; Medicine £29,700. *Living costs:* Band D. A range of scholarships and awards are available. Further information is available at www.exeter.ac.uk/study/funding/undergraduate/scholarships.

Falmouth International students from over 50 countries. *English language entry requirement (or equivalent):* IELTS 6.0, with a minimum of 5.5 in each component. Discipline-specific academic English courses available throughout the year. *Fees:* £17,950. *Living costs:* Band D. International scholarships available.

Glasgow International students from over 140 countries. *English language entry requirement (or equivalent):* IELTS 6.5 (higher for some courses). Pre- and in-sessional English language courses available. *Fees:* Arts and Social Sciences programmes £26,580; Engineering, Science, College of Medical, Veterinary and Life Sciences programmes £31,800; Clinical courses £58,890; Veterinary Medicine and Surgery £36,230. *Living costs:* Band C. Undergraduate Excellence Scholarships for international students are available.

Glasgow Caledonian Students from more than 130 countries. *English language entry requirement (or equivalent):* IELTS 6.0, with minimum 5.5 in each element. English language programmes available. *Fees:* £15,200. *Living costs:* Band C. Merit-based scholarships available.

Gloucestershire Welcomes international students from around the world. *English language entry requirement (or equivalent):* IELTS 6.0 (7.0 for paramedic science, physiotherapy, social work, nursing and journalism courses). *Fees:* £16,600. *Living costs:* Band D. International scholarships and bursaries available.

Greater Manchester International students of around 120 nationalities on campus. *English language entry requirement (or equivalent):* IELTS 6.0 (no band less than 5.5). English pre-sessional programmes for five, ten and 15 weeks. Subject-specific Foundation programmes also available. *Fees:* Most fees start at £15,950. *Living costs:* Band C. International scholarships available.

Greenwich More than 22,000 international students from over 100 countries. *English language entry requirement (or equivalent):* IELTS 6.0, with a minimum of 5.5 in each component. Pre-sessional English courses and International Foundation programmes available. *Fees:* £17,000–£18,150. *Living costs:* Band E. International scholarships available.

Harper Adams Students from around 30 different countries. *English language entry requirement (or equivalent):* IELTS 6.0, with a minimum of 5.5 in each component. *Fees:* £16,500. *Living costs:* Band D. Scholarships available.

Heriot-Watt One third of the student population are from outside of the UK, representing over 150 countries. *English language entry requirement (or equivalent):* IELTS 6.0 (6.5 for Actuarial Mathematics, Statistics, and Interpreting and Translating Languages programmes). Several English language courses are offered; these range in length depending on students' English level and the language demands of the degree they plan to study. *Fees:* Laboratory-based Science and Engineering courses £24,048; Non-laboratory-based courses £18,704. *Living costs:* Band C. Some international scholarships are available.

Hertfordshire International students from 140 countries. *English language entry requirement (or equivalent):* IELTS 6.0–7.0. English language tuition is offered in the one-year International Foundation course and in a pre-sessional intensive English course held during the summer months. *Fees:* £15,500. *Living costs:* Band D. International scholarships available.

HSU Roughly 30% of students are international. *English language entry requirement (or equivalent):* IELTS 6.0 (no band less than 5.5). *Fees:* £13,300–£16,560.

Huddersfield International students from over 100 countries. *English language entry requirement (or equivalent):* IELTS 6.0, with a minimum of 5.5 in each element. English language courses available and one-year International Foundation course in English language with options in Business, Computing and Engineering. *Fees:* Tuition fees range between £16,500 and £18,700; Nursing £19,800 (includes NHS placement fee). *Living costs:* Band B. International students are automatically considered for a scholarship of up to £4,000 per year upon application.

Hull International students from more than 100 countries. *English language entry requirement (or equivalent):* IELTS 6.0, with at least 5.5 in all components. Pre-sessional English language programmes available. *Fees:* Non-science programmes £16,500; Science programmes £19,500. *Living costs:* Band C. International scholarships available depending on the chosen subject and the student's country of origin.

Hull York (MS) The University offers up to 11 places for international students. *English language entry requirement (or equivalent):* IELTS 7.5, with a minimum of 7.0 in each component. *Fees:* £43,950. *Living costs:* Band C.

Imperial London International students from over 140 countries. *English language entry requirement (or equivalent):* IELTS 6.5–7.0. Pre-sessional English courses available for three weeks and six weeks. *Fees:* Engineering £40,940; Medicine £53,700; Medical Biosciences £37,900; Chemistry £41,650; Mathematics £39,100; Physics £41,650; Life Sciences ££41,650. *Living costs:* Band E. Scholarships available.

Keele Large number of overseas students. *English language entry requirement (or equivalent):* IELTS 6.0–7.0. Pre-sessional English language programmes for six and 11 weeks. International Foundation year degree programmes also available (entry IELTS 5.0). *Fees:* £16,600–£28,900; Medicine £45,100. *Living costs:* Band D. General, course-specific and country-specific scholarships available for international students. Bursaries also available.

Kent Over 100 different nationalities represented at the University. *English language entry requirement (or equivalent):* English language requirement (or equivalent): IELTS 6.0–7.0. Pre-sessional courses for four, six, ten and 16 weeks available. *Fees:* £19,300–£23,500; Medicine £49,700. *Living costs:* Band D. International scholarships available.

Kingston International students from 140 countries. *English language entry requirement (or equivalent):* IELTS 6.0–7.0. Pre-sessional English language and subject-specific Foundation-level courses available. Free English support during degree studies. *Fees:* Classroom-based courses £16,800; Art and Design courses £19,200; Pharmacy £18,800; Studio-based courses £18,500; Laboratory-based courses £18,500. *Living costs:* Band E. Fees are subject to annual increase. International scholarship worth £5,000 per year of study.

Lancaster International students from 142 countries. *English language entry requirement (or equivalent):* IELTS 6.5–7.0. Pre-sessional and in-session English language courses cover reading, writing, listening and speaking skills. *Fees:* £23,750–£28,675; Medicine £45,315. *Living costs:* Band C. Lancaster Global Scholarship of £2,000 in each year of study is available (subject to entry criteria).

Leeds More than 14,000 students from over 137 countries. *English language entry requirement (or equivalent):* IELTS 6.0–7.5, with a minimum of 5.5–6.5 in each component. *Fees:* £26,000–£32,250; Medicine £47,000. *Living costs:* Band C. International subject-specific scholarships available.

Leeds Arts The University has students of over 60 different nationalities. *English language entry requirement (or equivalent):* IELTS 5.5. *Fees:* BA degree courses £17,500; BMus £18,600. *Living costs:* Band C.

Leeds Beckett Students from over 140 countries and territories. *English language entry requirement (or equivalent):* IELTS 6.0 (IELTS 4.5 for the International Foundation programme, starting September, November or January). Also general English courses. *Fees:* £16,350 (most courses). *Living costs:* Band C. Scholarships available.

Leeds Trinity *English language entry requirement (or equivalent):* IELTS 6.0–7.0. Pre-sessional English course available. *Fees:* £12,000; BSc Nursing £14,500. *Living costs:* Band C. Scholarships based on academic and professional merit.

Leicester The University welcomes staff and students from over 150 countries. *English language entry requirement (or equivalent):* IELTS 6.5–7.5. Pre-sessional English language programmes from two to 40 weeks and on-going in-sessional programmes. *Fees:* £19,700—£24,500; Medicine £29,000. *Living costs:* Band B. International scholarships available.

Lincoln Staff and students from more than 100 countries. *English language entry requirement (or equivalent):* IELTS 6.0–7.0; 7.5 for Medicine. Pre- and in-sessional English language courses available. *Fees:* Humanities £16,600; Laboratory-based sciences £17,900; Medicine £36,400. *Living costs:* Band B. Scholarships for high-achieving international students. Engineering bursaries also available.

Liverpool 8,800 international students from 135 countries. *English language entry requirement (or equivalent):* IELTS 6.0–7.0. Pre-sessional English courses available from six to 40 weeks. *Fees:* £22,400–£27,950; Dentistry £44,550; Medicine and Veterinary Science £42,700. *Living costs:* Band C. Scholarships available, including special awards for students from Hong Kong. Tuition fees will not increase each year.

Liverpool Hope Approximately 600 international students (2021/22). *English language entry requirement (or equivalent):* IELTS 6.0. Language courses available. *Fees:* £13,000. *Living costs:* Band C. International Excellence bursary and international Electrical Engineering scholarship available.

Liverpool John Moores A large number of overseas students. *English language entry requirement (or equivalent):* IELTS 6.0. Pre-sessional and in-session English tuition available. *Fees:* Laboratory-based courses £18,250; Classroom-based courses £17,750. *Living costs:* Band C International Achievement and sports scholarships available.

London (Birk) International students from over 120 countries. *English language entry requirement (or equivalent):* IELTS 6.5 with 6.0 in each sub-test. Pre-sessional English courses and free online study skills materials available. *Fees:* £18,060; Archaeology £22,000. *Living costs:* Band E. Scholarships available.

London (Court) Students from around the world. *English language entry requirement (or equivalent):* IELTS 7.0, with no less than 6.5 in the Reading and Writing components. *Fees:* £25,700. *Living costs:* Band E. Scholarships available.

London (Gold) International students make up 20% of the student body, representing 135 countries. *English language entry requirement (or equivalent):* IELTS 5.5–7.5, depending on course. Pre-sessional programmes available. *Fees:* Art, Humanities and Social Sciences £19,640–£20,160; Psychology £20,840. *Living costs:* Band E. Scholarships available.

London (Inst Paris) *English language entry requirement (or equivalent):* IELTS 7.0, with 6.5 in Writing and no less than 5.5 in other components. *Fees:* £12,800.

London (Institute of Banking and Finance) The Institute offers a range of finance courses leading to professional qualifications. See the website for details: www.libf.ac.uk. *English language entry requirement (or equivalent):* IELTS 6.0, with no element below 5.5. *Fees:* £20,805 total cost for three years of study. *Living costs:* Band E. First year international scholarships available.

London (Institute of Cancer Research) Student population made up of individuals from all continents and backgrounds. The institute offers postgraduate and PhD courses. See the website for details: www.icr.ac.uk. *English language entry requirement (or equivalent):* IELTS 7.0, with a minimum of 6 in any one component. *Fees:* Research degrees £28,500; MSc in Oncology £12,170 (Part A/B); £3,505 (Part C).

London (Interdisciplinary School) Information about this institution is still being confirmed. Please visit www.lis.ac.uk for details. *English language entry requirement (or equivalent):* IELTS 7.0 overall, with a minimum of 6.5 in each component. *Fees:* £15,000. *Living costs:* Band E. International scholarships available.

London (King's) International students from 160 countries. *English language entry requirement (or equivalent):* IELTS 6.5–7.5. Pre-sessional summer courses and a one-year Foundation course available. *Fees:* Classroom-based £27,100; Laboratory-based £35,800; Pharmacy £31,600; Medicine £53,000. *Living costs:* Band E. Awards available.

London (LSHTM) *English language entry requirement (or equivalent):* IELTS 6.5–7.5. *Fees:* £27,540–£37,368. *Living costs:* Band E.

London (QM) Staff and alumni from over 170 countries. *English language entry requirement (or equivalent):* IELTS 6.0–7.0. Pre-sessional English Language courses available. International Foundation courses available. *Fees:* £25,000–£29,950; Medicine £49,950; Dentistry £48,700. *Living costs:* Band E. Subject-specific bursaries and scholarships available.

London (RH) Almost a third of students come from outside the UK. *English language entry requirement (or equivalent):* IELTS 6.5–7.0; Mathematics 6.0. Pre-sessional English course available. Foundation course with studies in English language and introduction to specialist studies in a range of degree subjects. *Fees:* £25,900–£28,900. *Living costs:* Band E. Bursaries and scholarships available.

London (RVC) Many international students from countries all over the world. *English language entry requirement (or equivalent):* IELTS 6.5–7.0. *Fees:* £17,150–£44,610. *Living costs:* Band E. International scholarships available.

London (SOAS) International students from 135 countries. *English language entry requirement (or equivalent):* IELTS 6.5. A 10-month Foundation programme and English language courses available with an entry requirement of IELTS 5.5–6.0 depending on the length. *Fees:* £21,990. *Living costs:* Band E. Scholarships and bursaries available.

London (UCL) Around 18,000 of students come from outside the UK. *English language entry requirement (or equivalent):* IELTS 6.5–7.5. *Fees:* £29,800–£43,500; Medicine £53,400. *Living costs:* Band E. Scholarships available.

London LSE International students from over 140 countries. *English language entry requirement (or equivalent):* IELTS 7.0 overall and 7.0 in each component. Academic English language courses available. *Fees:* £27,500–£34,000. *Living costs:* Band E. LSE Undergraduate Support Scheme and other scholarships are available.

London Met Students from 143 countries (2020/21). *English language entry requirement (or equivalent):* IELTS 6.0; Law, Biomedical Science, Nutrition and Translation 6.5. One-year International Foundation programme. Pre-sessional English language course for five or 10 weeks. *Fees:* £19,500. *Living costs:* Band E. EU Transition and International Excellence scholarships available to international students.

London Regent's Students from over 140 countries around the world. *English language entry requirement (or equivalent):* IELTS 6.0. English language courses available. *Fees:* £23,000–£26,000. *Living costs:* Band E. Scholarships available.

London South Bank Over 2,000 international students from over 130 countries. *English language entry requirement (or equivalent):* IELTS 6.0. Pre-study English courses and a University Foundation course for overseas students. *Fees:* From £14,900 *Living costs:* Band E. Range of international scholarships available.

Loughborough International students from over 130 countries. *English language entry requirement (or equivalent):* IELTS 6.5 with a minimum of 6.0 in all sub-tests. Pre-sessional courses available. *Fees:* £23,000–£28,600. *Living costs:* Band B. Self-funded international students are automatically considered for an international scholarship upon application.

Manchester A high proportion of international students from 170 countries. *English language entry requirement (or equivalent):* IELTS 5.5–7.0 depending on course. Foundation Year programme available as well as pre- and in-sessional English language courses. *Fees:* £25,000–£32,500; Medicine £38,000 (years 1 and 2), clinical tuition fees (years 3–5) are charged at the future rate which is applicable upon entering year 3; Dentistry £36,500 (year 1), clinical tuition fees (years 2–5) are charged at the future rate which is applicable upon entering year 2. *Living costs:* Band C. Some scholarships and bursaries are available. Check website for up to date information on clinical tuition fees.

Manchester Met International students from more than 100 countries. *English language entry requirement (or equivalent):* IELTS 6.0; Law, Physiotherapy and Architecture 6.5; Speech and Language Therapy 8.0 with no component below 7.5. General, academic and pre-sessional English language courses available. *Fees:* Normally between £17,000–£18,500. *Living costs:* Band C. Variety of international scholarships and awards available.

Marjon International students from over 60 countries. *English language entry requirement (or equivalent):* IELTS 6.0, with a minimum of 6.0 in each category. English Preparation Programme available. *Fees:* £14,600. *Living costs:* Band D.

Medway Sch Pharm Many students come from the EU and other parts of the world, including China, Canada, India, Iran and the USA. The Medway Students Association hosts numerous international societies for international students to socialise. *English language entry requirement (or equivalent):* IELTS 7.0, with a minimum of 7.0 in each component. *Fees:* £22,700. *Living costs:* Band D.

Middlesex International students from 122 nationalities. *English language entry requirement (or equivalent):* IELTS 6.0, with a minimum of 5.5 in each component; Nursing, Midwifery and Healthcare Science courses 7.0. Pre-sessional English course available. *Fees:* £16,600. *Living costs:* Band E. International bursaries and merit awards.

Newcastle Thousands of international students from around 145 countries. *English language entry requirement (or equivalent):* IELTS 6.5. Pre-sessional and Academic English courses available. *Fees:* Arts £23,800–£25,000; Sciences £24,400–£30,600; Dental Surgery £46,000; Medicine and Surgery £44,500. *Living costs:* Band D. International scholarships available.

Northampton Over 1,000 international students from over 100 countries. *English language entry requirement (or equivalent):* IELTS 6.0, with a minimum of 5.5 in each component. Pre-sessional English language courses available for four–11 weeks. *Fees:* £15,200; BSc Nursing £17,700; BSc Occupational Therapy and BSc Podiatry £16,200. *Living costs:* Band B. International Scholarship Scheme offers a 30% reduction in tuition fees based on academic achievement. Government scholarship schemes are also available.

Northumbria International students from 138 countries. *English language entry requirement (or equivalent):* IELTS 6.0–7.0; Engineering programmes 5.5. English language and Foundation courses available. *Fees:* £18,250–£19,750. *Living costs:* Band D. International scholarships available.

Norwich Arts Students from over 40 countries. *English language entry requirement (or equivalent):* IELTS 6.0, with a minimum of 5.5 in each section. *Fees:* £18,000. *Living costs:* Band D. Global and country-specific scholarships available.

Nottingham Students and staff from over 150 countries. *English language entry requirement (or equivalent):* IELTS 6.0–7.0 (7.5 for Medicine). Pre- and in-sessional English language courses available. *Fees:* £23,000–£30,750; Nursing Studies £13,450; Medicine £36,400; Veterinary Medicine and Surgery £38,400. *Living costs:* Band B. International scholarships available.

Nottingham Trent Large number of overseas students. *English language entry requirement (or equivalent):* IELTS 6.0–7.0. Pre-sessional English language courses for six, 10, or 15 weeks available. *Fees:* £17,150; School of Art & Design and Business School £17,900; courses based at the Confetti London campus £17,400. *Living costs:* Band B. International scholarships available.

NU London Around 30% of the student population is made up of international students. *English language entry requirement (or equivalent):* IELTS 6.5, with a minimum of 6.0 in each component. *Fees:* £22,250–£26,500. *Living costs:* Band E. All applicants are automatically considered for a scholarship award.

Open University International students in 157 countries. *English language entry requirement (or equivalent):* No formal qualification required but the applicant is asked to confirm that they are a competent user of English. The University recommends an IELTS score of 5.5–6.5. Activity to check English language competency available at www.open.ac.uk/courses/do-it/english-skills. *Fees:* Honours degrees £3,736 per year, £22,416 total cost.

Oxford 21% of undergraduate students are international citizens and come from over 140 countries. *English language entry requirement (or equivalent):* IELTS 7.5, with a minimum of 7.0 per component. English language courses available. *Fees:* £35,260–£59,260; Medicine £46,600 for pre-clinical years 1 to 3, £61,560 for years 4 to 6. *Living costs:* Band D. Limited scholarships for overseas students.

Oxford Brookes Over 2,700 international students from around 140 countries. *English language entry requirement (or equivalent):* IELTS 6.0; Law, Architecture, English Literature, Health and Social Care, and Nutrition 6.5. International Foundation Diploma and course-specific Foundation courses available. Pre-sessional English language courses also available. *Fees:* £15,950–£18,050. *Living costs:* Band D. £2,000 International Student Scholarships as well as other scholarships available.

Plymouth Around 2,000 international students from over 100 countries. *English language entry requirement (or equivalent):* IELTS 6.0. Pre-sessional English courses available. *Fees:* £17,600–£18,650; Medicine and Dentistry £40,700. *Living costs:* Band D. Undergraduate International Student Scholarship, as well as International Academic Excellence Scholarships available.

Plymouth (AU) The University welcomes a growing number of international students. *English language entry requirement (or equivalent):* IELTS 6.0, with a minimum score of 5.5 in each component. Pre-sessional English language courses available for five or 10 weeks. *Fees:* £16,500. *Living costs:* Band D. International scholarships available.

Portsmouth Over 5,700 international students from 150 different countries. *English language entry requirement (or equivalent):* IELTS 6.0. Pre-sessional English language courses from four to 15 weeks available. *Fees:* £16,200–£19,200. *Living costs:* Band D. International scholarships available.

Queen Margaret Around 5,000 students from over 80 countries. *English language entry requirement (or equivalent):* IELTS 6.0, with a minimum of 5.5 in each language skill. English language support available. *Fees:* £9,250–£17,325. *Living costs:* Band C. £3,000 QMU International Scholarships available.

Queen's Belfast International students from over 85 countries. *English language entry requirement (or equivalent):* IELTS 6.0–7.5. Pre-sessional English language courses for four to 10 weeks available, as well as English language preparation course and pathway programmes by INTO Queen's. *Fees:* Classroom-based courses £20,800; Laboratory component courses £25,300; Pre-clinical courses £36,900; Dentistry £37,600. *Living costs:* Band A. International scholarships available.

Ravensbourne Univ There are over 100 nationalities represented at Ravensbourne. *English language entry requirement (or equivalent):* IELTS 5.5. *Fees:* £17,000. *Living costs:* Band E. A range of scholarships and bursaries available for Student route visa holders.

Reading More than 4,500 students from over 160 countries. *English language entry requirement (or equivalent):* IELTS 6.5–7.0; Speech and Language Therapy 8.0. International Foundation programme offering English language tuition and a choice of 15 specialist pathways. Other pre-sessional English courses offered. *Fees:* Non-laboratory courses £25,250; Laboratory courses £29,950. *Living costs:* Band D. Vice Chancellor Global Scholarship Award, as well as course-specific scholarships available.

Richmond (Am Int Univ) *English language entry requirement (or equivalent):* IELTS 6.0, with no element lower than 5.5. English Language Level Test Preparation Course and online pre-sessional courses available. *Fees:* £17,500. *Living costs:* Band E. International scholarships available.

Robert Gordon 152 student nationalities are represented. *English language entry requirement (or equivalent):* IELTS 6.0. Pre-sessional English programme available for 10 and 13 weeks. *Fees:* £16,110–£17,720. Healthcare Practice £30,40. *Living costs:* Band C. Merit scholarships for specific subjects available.

Roehampton Students from more than 140 countries. *English language entry requirement (or equivalent):* IELTS 6.0, with a minimum of 5.5 in each component. International Foundation programme and pre-sessional English courses available. *Fees:* £14,750–£15,000; Adult Nursing £18,000. *Living costs:* Band E. International Excellence Scholarships of up to £4,000 per year available. Country-specific and talent-based scholarships also available.

Royal Agricultural Univ International students from 46 different countries. *English language entry requirement (or equivalent):* IELTS 6.0. *Fees:* £15,300. *Living costs:* Band D. International scholarships available.

Salford 4,500 international students. *English language entry requirement (or equivalent):* IELTS 6.0. English study programmes and a very comprehensive International Foundation year. *Fees:* £13,750–£20,340; International Foundation Year £13,750. *Living costs:* Band C. Scholarships and bursaries available.

Sheffield Over 10,000 international students from more than 150 countries. *English language entry requirement (or equivalent):* IELTS 6.0, with a minimum of 5.5 in each component. Preparatory English courses and an international summer school with English classes available. *Fees:* Arts, humanities, languages, law, management £22,680; Architecture, Science and Engineering £29,110; Medicine £43,150; Dentistry £46,190. *Living costs:* Band C. Faculty scholarships and international merit scholarships available.

Sheffield Hallam Around 18% of students are international. *English language entry requirement (or equivalent):* IELTS 6.0–7.0. International Foundation Programme and pre-sessional English language courses available. *Fees:* £16,655. *Living costs:* Band C. International scholarships available as well as country-specific scholarships.

Solent International students from over 100 countries. *English language entry requirement (or equivalent):* IELTS 6.0. Induction programme and language tuition available. *Fees:* £16,125. *Living costs:* Band D.

South Wales Over 2,500 international students from 180 countries. *English language entry requirement (or equivalent):* IELTS from 6.0. Pre-sessional course offered in English with course lengths of between five and 15 weeks depending on the applicant's proficiency. An International Foundation Programme is also offered. *Fees:* Business and Creative Industries £14,950; Computing, Engineering, Sciences and Education £15,260. *Living costs:* Band D. International students automatically considered for a scholarship upon application.

Southampton Over 10,000 international students from 130 countries. *English language entry requirement (or equivalent):* IELTS 6.0–7.0. Pre-sessional English courses offered and also an International Foundation programmes for Business, Humanities and Social Sciences, and Art and Design. *Fees:* £23,400–£30,500; Medicine £30,300, clinical years £59,400. *Living costs:* Band D. International Merit scholarship available, as well as country-specific scholarships.

St Andrews 41% of the student body is international. *English language entry requirement (or equivalent):* IELTS 7.0; Science 6.5; School of English 8.0. International Foundation programme available as well as pre- and in-sessional English language courses. *Fees:* £30,160; Medicine £36,990. *Living costs:* Band C. Scholarships available.

St Mary's International students from over 100 countries outside the UK, representing approximately 10% of the student population. Qualifications from any country will be considered and measured against British equivalents. *English language entry requirement (or equivalent):* IELTS 6.0 (minimum 5.5 in each component); Nutrition BSc and Physiotherapy BSc 6.5 (minimum 6.0 in each component). In-sessional English language programme available. *Fees:* £16,320–£16,890. *Living costs:* Band E.

St Mary's (UC) This small university has a close-knit community of students from a host of different places. *English language entry requirement (or equivalent):* A full list of acceptable English language qualifications and appropriate scores is available on request. It is recommended that prospective applicants consult the UKVI website at www.gov.uk/visas-immigration. *Fees:* £20,800. *Living costs:* Band A. St Mary's applicants may be eligible for international scholarships offered through Queen's University Belfast.

Staffordshire Students from over 75 countries. *English language entry requirement (or equivalent):* IELTS 6.0, with a minimum of 5.5 in each component. Some courses have higher entry criteria. English tuition available. *Fees:* £16,750; Nursing, Paramedic Science, Operating Department Practice, and Midwifery £19,000. *Living costs:* Band E. International scholarships available.

Stirling More than 30% of students are international. *English language entry requirement (or equivalent):* IELTS 6.0–7.0. Pre-sessional English courses available as well as an International Foundation in Business, Finance, Economics and Marketing. *Fees:* £18,400–£22,400. *Living costs:* Band C. Some scholarships are available. Please see www.stir.ac.uk/scholarships.

Stranmillis (UC) *English language entry requirement (or equivalent):* Requires a minimum of B2 level of English, equivalent to an IELTS overall mark of 6.5 with no individual band score less than 5.5. Students from non-English-speaking countries will be required to provide a recent copy of their IELTS certificate. In-sessional English language courses available. *Fees:* £20,800. *Living costs:* Band A. Stranmillis applicants may be eligible for international scholarships offered through Queen's University Belfast.

Strathclyde Students from over 140 countries. *English language entry requirement (or equivalent):* IELTS 6.5. Pre- and in-sessional English language courses available. *Fees:* £18,050–£27,750. *Living costs:* Band C. International scholarships available.

Suffolk International students from over 90 countries. *English language entry requirement (or equivalent):* IELTS 6.0, with minimum of 5.5 in each band; Professional Health degrees 7.0. *Fees:* £15,090–£18,380 *Living costs:* Band D. International scholarships available.

Sunderland International students make up over 40% of the student population, and come from over 100 countries. *English language entry requirement (or equivalent):* IELTS 6.0, with a minimum of 5.5 in each component. English language tuition available. *Fees:* £16,000. *Living costs:* Band D. International students are automatically considered for a £1,400 scholarship upon application.

Surrey Students from over 140 different countries. *English language entry requirement (or equivalent):* IELTS 6.5–7.5. Pre-sessional English language courses available for five, eight, or 11 weeks. *Fees:* £22,000–£26,000; Veterinary Medicine and Science £41,500; Medicine £46,300. *Living costs:* Band D. Scholarships and bursaries offered.

Sussex International students from over 150 countries. *English language entry requirement (or equivalent):* IELTS 6.0–7.0. The University offers a pre-sessional English and study skills course, intensive English course, and summer courses. International Foundation courses are also offered, covering English language tuition and a choice of Humanities or Law. *Fees:* £22,575–£26,250; Medicine £44,500. *Living costs:* Band D. International scholarships available.

Swansea Students from over 130 countries. *English language entry requirement (or equivalent):* IELTS 6.0–7.0. Pre-sessional English language courses available as well as support during degree courses. *Fees:* £17,500–£41,750. *Living costs:* Band D. International Excellence and course-specific scholarships.

Teesside 1,800 international students. *English language entry requirement (or equivalent):* IELTS 5.5–7.0. Pre-sessional English language courses available for six or 12 weeks. In-sessional tuition also available. *Fees:* £17,000. *Living costs:* Band D. Scholarships available for self-funded students.

Trinity Saint David International students are well represented at the University. *English language entry requirement (or equivalent):* IELTS 6.0, with a minimum of 5.5 in each component. International Foundation programme available. Pre-sessional English language courses offered for six or 10 weeks. *Fees:* £13,500. *Living costs:* Band D. International scholarships available.

UCO Students from across the world including Australia, Brazil and Europe. *English language entry requirement (or equivalent):* IELTS 6.5 or above. *Fees:* £13,300.

UHI *English language entry requirement (or equivalent):* IELTS 6.0, with a minimum of 5.5 in all four components; Nursing and Optometry 7.0, with a minimum of 6.5 in writing and 7.0 in all other components. *Fees:* Art, Humanities, Social Science and Business degrees £14,988; Science and Technology degrees £15,996. *Living costs:* Band C. International scholarships and bursaries available.

Ulster Students from over 70 countries. *English language entry requirement (or equivalent):* IELTS 6.0, with no band score under 5.5. Pre- and in-sessional English language courses available. *Fees:* £16,320. *Living costs:* Band E. International scholarships available.

Univ Law International students from over 120 countries. *English language entry requirement (or equivalent):* IELTS 6.0–7.0. Pre-sessional English language courses available. *Fees:* Non-London campus based £16,700; London campus based £17,550. *Living costs:* Band E. International scholarships available.

UWE Bristol More than 9,000 international students. *English language entry requirement (or equivalent):* IELTS 6.0, with a minimum of 5.5 in each component. Pre-sessional English language courses for five, 10, 15 and 25 weeks offered. *Fees:* £15,850. *Living costs:* Band D. Scholarships based on academic, sports and entrepreneurial excellence available as well as country- and programme-specific scholarships.

Warwick Over 9,500 international students from 147 countries. *English language entry requirement (or equivalent):* IELTS 6.0–7.0. Pre-sessional English language programmes and short courses available. *Fees:* £24,800–£31,620. *Living costs:* Band D. More than 20 country-specific international scholarships available.

West London A large number of international students. *English language entry requirement (or equivalent):* IELTS 6.0, with a minimum of 5.5 in each component. International Foundation programme and English language support available. *Fees:* £16,250. *Living costs:* Band E. International scholarships available.

West Scotland Over 3,000 international students from countries which represent a third of the globe. *English language entry requirement (or equivalent):* IELTS 6.0. Pre- and in-sessional English language courses available. English language Foundation course also offered. *Fees:* £15,250; Science courses (including Mathematics and Engineering) £18,000. *Living costs:* Band C. International scholarships available.

Westminster 48% of the student population is international, with more than 6,800 international students from 156 countries. *English language entry requirement (or equivalent):* IELTS 6.0. Pre- and in-sessional English courses available. *Fees:* £17,000. *Living costs:* Band E. International scholarships available.

Winchester 600 international students from over 60 countries. *English language entry requirement (or equivalent):* IELTS 5.5; Physiotherapy, Social Work, Journalism and Nursing 7.0. English language courses available. *Fees:* £16,700. *Living costs:* Band D. International scholarships available.

Wolverhampton International students from over 130 countries. *English language entry requirement (or equivalent):* IELTS 6.0–7.0. An English course and international student programme is available. *Fees:* Non-laboratory based courses £14,950; laboratory based courses £15,450. *Living costs:* Band D. Scholarships and bursaries available.

Worcester Over 1,300 international students. *English language entry requirement (or equivalent):* IELTS 6.0. Pre-sessional English language courses available for six or 10 weeks. *Fees:* £16,200. *Living costs:* Band D. International scholarships of up to £3,000 available.

Wrexham The University welcomes students from Europe and worldwide. *English language entry requirement (or equivalent):* IELTS 6.0, with a minimum of 5.5 in each element. Pre-sessional and intensive English language courses available. *Fees:* £11,750. *Living costs:* Band D. Scholarships available.

Writtle (UC) *Fees:* £15,900. *Living costs:* Band D. International scholarships available.

York 22,000 international students from over 150 countries. *English language entry requirement (or equivalent):* IELTS 6.0–7.0 (7.5 for Medicine). Pre-sessional English language courses available. *Fees:* Classroom-based courses £25,800; Laboratory-based courses (including Computer Science) £31,100; Medicine £43,950. *Living costs:* Band C. Several scholarships for overseas students.

York St John International students from over 100 countries. *English language entry requirement (or equivalent):* IELTS 6.0; BA Media Production: Journalism 7.5. Pre-sessional courses and International Foundation Programme available. *Fees:* £11,500–£14,000. *Living costs:* Band C. International scholarships available.

BRITISH OVERSEAS TERRITORIES STUDENTS

Students from British Overseas Territories are treated as home students for fee purposes at universities and other institutions of higher education in England, Wales and Northern Ireland, provided they meet residency requirements. The territories to which this policy applies are: Anguilla, Bermuda, British Antarctic Territory, British Indian Ocean Territory, British Virgin Islands, Cayman Islands, Falkland Islands, Gibraltar, Montserrat, Pitcairn, Henderson, Ducie and Oeno Islands, South Georgia and the South Sandwich Islands, St Helena and Dependencies (Ascension Island and Tristan de Cunha), Turks and Caicos Islands.

9 DIRECTORY OF UNIVERSITIES AND OTHER INSTITUTIONS OFFERING HIGHER EDUCATION COURSES

SECTION 1: UNIVERSITIES AND UNIVERSITY COLLEGES

Listed below are universities and university colleges in the United Kingdom that offer degree and diploma courses at higher education level. Applications to these institutions are submitted through UCAS except for part-time courses, private universities and colleges, and further education courses. For current information refer to the websites shown and also to www.ucas.com for a comprehensive list of degree and diploma courses (see Appendix 4).

Abbreviations used below A = Art and Design; **C** = Communication.

Aberdeen Tel 01224 272000; www.abdn.ac.uk
Abertay (Dundee) Tel 01382 308000; www.abertay.ac.uk
Aberystwyth Tel 01970 622900; www.aber.ac.uk
Anglia Ruskin (Cambridge) Tel 01245 686868; www.aru.ac.uk
Arden (Coventry) Tel 0800 268 7737; www.arden.ac.uk
Arts London Tel 020 7514 6000; www.arts.ac.uk
Aston (Birmingham) Tel 0121 204 3000; www.aston.ac.uk
Bangor Tel 01248 383717; www.bangor.ac.uk
Bath Tel 01225 383019; www.bath.ac.uk
Bath Spa Tel 01225 876180; www.bathspa.ac.uk
Bedfordshire (Luton) Tel 01582 743500; www.beds.ac.uk
Birmingham Tel 0121 414 3344; www.birmingham.ac.uk
Birmingham (UC) Tel 0121 604 1040; www.ucb.ac.uk
Birmingham City Tel 0121 331 6295; www.bcu.ac.uk
Birmingham Newman Tel 0121 476 1181; www.newman.ac.uk
Bishop Grosseteste (Lincoln) Tel 01522 527347; www.bgu.ac.uk
Bournemouth (Poole) Tel 01202 961916; www.bournemouth.ac.uk
Bournemouth Arts (Poole) Tel 01202 363228; www.aub.ac.uk
BPP (London) Tel 03300 603100; www.bpp.com
Bradford Tel 01274 232323; www.bradford.ac.uk
Brighton Tel 01273 644644; www.brighton.ac.uk
Brighton and Sussex (MS) Tel 01273 643528; www.bsms.ac.uk
Bristol Tel 0117 394 1649; www.bristol.ac.uk
Brunel (Uxbridge) Tel 01895 265599; www.brunel.ac.uk
Buckingham Tel 01280 820227; www.buckingham.ac.uk
Bucks New (High Wycombe) Tel 01494 605060; www.bucks.ac.uk
Cambridge Tel 01223 337733; www.cam.ac.uk
Canterbury Christ Church Tel 01227 928000; www.canterbury.ac.uk
Cardiff Tel 029 2087 9999; www.cardiff.ac.uk
Cardiff Met Tel 029 2041 6010; www.cardiffmet.ac.uk
Central Lancashire (Preston) Tel 01772 892444; www.uclan.ac.uk
Chester Tel 01244 511000; www1.chester.ac.uk
Chichester Tel 01243 816000; www.chi.ac.uk
City St George's (London) Tel 020 7040 5060; www.citystgeorges.ac.uk
Coventry Tel 024 7765 7688; www.coventry.ac.uk

Cranfield Tel 01234 750111; www.cranfield.ac.uk
Creative Arts (Farnham) Tel 01252 918291; www.uca.ac.uk
Cumbria Tel 01228 588 588; www.cumbria.ac.uk
De Montfort (Leicester) Tel 0116 250 6070; www.dmu.ac.uk
Derby Tel 01332 591167; www.derby.ac.uk
Dundee Tel 01382 383838; www.dundee.ac.uk
Durham Tel 0191 334 2000; www.durham.ac.uk
Dyson (Malmesbury) Tel 01666 334949; www.dysoninstitute.ac.uk
East Anglia (Norwich) Tel 01603 591515; www.uea.ac.uk
East London Tel 020 8223 3333; www.uel.ac.uk
Edge Hill (Ormskirk) Tel 01695 657000; www.edgehill.ac.uk
Edinburgh Tel 0131 650 1000; www.ed.ac.uk
Edinburgh Napier Tel 0333 900 6040; www.napier.ac.uk
Essex (Colchester) Tel 01206 873666; www.essex.ac.uk
Exeter Tel 0300 555 6060; www.exeter.ac.uk
Falmouth Tel 01326 254350; www.falmouth.ac.uk
Glasgow Tel 0141 330 2000; www.gla.ac.uk
Glasgow Caledonian Tel 0141 331 8630; www.gcu.ac.uk
Gloucestershire (Cheltenham) Tel 0333 014 1414; www.glos.ac.uk
Greater Manchester Tel 01204 900600; www.bolton.ac.uk
Greenwich (London) Tel 020 8331 8000; www.gre.ac.uk
Harper Adams (Newport) Tel 01952 815000; www.harper-adams.ac.uk
Heriot-Watt (Edinburgh) Tel 0131 449 5111; www.hw.ac.uk
Hertfordshire (Hatfield) Tel 01707 284800; www.herts.ac.uk
HSU (Bournemouth) Tel 01202 436200; www.hsu.ac.uk
Huddersfield Tel 01484 472625; www.hud.ac.uk
Hull Tel 01482 346311; www.hull.ac.uk
Hull York (MS) Tel 01904 321690; www.hyms.ac.uk
Imperial London Tel 020 7589 5111; www.imperial.ac.uk
Keele Tel 01782 734010; www.keele.ac.uk
Kent (Canterbury) Tel 01227 827272; www.kent.ac.uk
Kingston (Kingston upon Thames) Tel 020 3510 0106; www.kingston.ac.uk
Lancaster Tel 01524 65201; www.lancaster.ac.uk
Leeds Tel 0113 243 1751; www.leeds.ac.uk
Leeds Arts Tel 0113 202 8000; www.leeds-art.ac.uk
Leeds Beckett Tel 0113 812 3113; www.leedsbeckett.ac.uk
Leeds Trinity Tel 0113 283 7123; www.leedstrinity.ac.uk
Leicester Tel 0116 252 5281; www.le.ac.uk
Lincoln Tel 01522 886644; www.lincoln.ac.uk
Liverpool Tel 0151 794 5927; www.liverpool.ac.uk
Liverpool Hope Tel 0151 291 3000; www.hope.ac.uk
Liverpool John Moores Tel 0151 231 5090; www.ljmu.ac.uk
London (Birk) Tel 020 3907 0700; www.bbk.ac.uk
London (Court) Tel 020 3947 7777; www.courtauld.ac.uk
London (Gold) Tel 020 7078 5300; www.gold.ac.uk
London (Inst Paris) Tel 01 44 11 73 83; www.london.ac.uk/institute-in-paris
London (Institute of Banking and Finance) Tel 01227 818609; www.libf.ac.uk
London (Institute of Cancer Research) Tel 020 7352 8133; www.icr.ac.uk
London (Interdisciplinary School) Tel 020 3409 1912; www.lis.ac.uk

London (King's) Tel 020 7836 5454; www.kcl.ac.uk
London (LSHTM) Tel 020 7636 8636; www.lshtm.ac.uk
London (QM) Tel 020 3727 0940; www.qmul.ac.uk
London (RH) (Egham) Tel 01784 414944; www.royalholloway.ac.uk
London (RVC) Tel 020 7468 5147; www.rvc.ac.uk
London (SOAS) Tel 020 3510 6974; www.soas.ac.uk
London (UCL) Tel 020 8059 0939; www.ucl.ac.uk
London LSE Tel 020 7955 6613; www.lse.ac.uk
London Met Tel 020 7133 4200; www.londonmet.ac.uk
London Regent's Tel 020 7487 7625; www.regents.ac.uk
London South Bank Tel 020 7815 6161; www.lsbu.ac.uk
Loughborough Tel 01509 274403; www.lboro.ac.uk
Manchester Tel 0161 306 6000; www.manchester.ac.uk
Manchester Met Tel 0161 247 6969; www.mmu.ac.uk
Marjon (Plymouth) Tel 01752 636890; www.marjon.ac.uk
Medway Sch Pharm (Chatham) Tel 01634 202935; www.msp.ac.uk
Middlesex (London) Tel 020 8411 5555; www.mdx.ac.uk
Newcastle (Newcastle-upon-Tyne) Tel 0191 208 6000; www.ncl.ac.uk
Northampton Tel 0300 303 2772; www.northampton.ac.uk
Northumbria (Newcastle-upon-Tyne) Tel 0191 406 0901; www.northumbria.ac.uk
Norwich Arts Tel 01603 610561; www.norwichuni.ac.uk
Nottingham Tel 0115 951 5151; www.nottingham.ac.uk
Nottingham Trent Tel 0115 848 2999; www.ntu.ac.uk
NU London Tel 020 7637 4550; www.nulondon.ac.uk
Open University (Milton Keynes) Tel 0300 303 5303; www.open.ac.uk
Oxford Tel 01865 270000; www.ox.ac.uk
Oxford Brookes Tel 01865 741111; www.brookes.ac.uk
Plymouth Tel 01752 585858; www.plymouth.ac.uk
Plymouth (AU) Tel 01752 203434; www.aup.ac.uk [**A**]
Portsmouth Tel 023 9284 5566; www.port.ac.uk
Queen Margaret (Edinburgh) Tel 0131 474 4080; www.qmu.ac.uk
Queen's Belfast Tel 028 9097 3838; www.qub.ac.uk
Ravensbourne Univ (London) Tel 020 3040 3500; www.ravensbourne.ac.uk [**C**]
Reading Tel 0118 378 8372; www.reading.ac.uk
Richmond (Am Int Univ) (Richmond-upon-Thames) Tel 020 8332 8200; www.richmond.ac.uk
Robert Gordon (Aberdeen) Tel 01224 262728; www.rgu.ac.uk
Roehampton (London) Tel 020 8392 3232; www.roehampton.ac.uk
Royal Agricultural Univ (Cirencester) Tel 01285 889912; www.rau.ac.uk
Salford Tel 0161 295 4545; www.salford.ac.uk
Sheffield Tel 0114 222 8030; www.sheffield.ac.uk
Sheffield Hallam Tel 0114 225 5555; www.shu.ac.uk
Solent (Southampton) Tel 023 8201 5066; www.solent.ac.uk
South Wales (Pontypridd) Tel 0345 576 7778; www.southwales.ac.uk
Southampton Tel 023 8059 5000; www.southampton.ac.uk
St Andrews Tel 01334 462150; www.st-andrews.ac.uk
St Mary's (Twickenham) Tel 020 8240 2314; www.stmarys.ac.uk
St Mary's (UC) (Belfast) Tel 028 9032 7678; www.stmarys-belfast.ac.uk
Staffordshire (Stoke-on-Trent) Tel 01782 294400; www.staffs.ac.uk
Stirling Tel 01786 467046; www.stir.ac.uk

Stranmillis (UC) (Belfast) Tel 028 9038 1271; www.stran.ac.uk
Strathclyde (Glasgow) Tel 0141 552 4400; www.strath.ac.uk
Suffolk (Ipswich) Tel 01473 338833; www.uos.ac.uk
Sunderland Tel 0191 515 3000; www.sunderland.ac.uk
Surrey (Guildford) Tel 01483 682222; www.surrey.ac.uk
Sussex (Brighton) Tel 01273 606755; www.sussex.ac.uk
Swansea Tel 01792 205678; www.swansea.ac.uk
Teesside (Middlesbrough) Tel 01642 218121; www.tees.ac.uk
Trinity Saint David (Lampeter) Tel 01570 422351; www.uwtsd.ac.uk
UCO (London) Tel 020 7089 5316; www.uco.ac.uk
UHI (Inverness) Tel 01463 279190; www.uhi.ac.uk
Ulster (Belfast) Tel 028 9536 7890; www.ulster.ac.uk
Univ Law (London) Tel 0800 289 997; www.law.ac.uk
UWE Bristol Tel 0117 328 3333; www.uwe.ac.uk
Warwick (Coventry) Tel 024 7652 3523; www.warwick.ac.uk
West London Tel 0800 036 8888; www.uwl.ac.uk
West Scotland (Paisley) Tel 0800 027 1000; www.uws.ac.uk
Westminster (London) Tel 020 7911 5000; www.westminster.ac.uk
Winchester Tel 01962 841515; www.winchester.ac.uk
Wolverhampton Tel 0800 953 3222; www.wlv.ac.uk
Worcester Tel 01905 855111; www.worc.ac.uk
Wrexham Tel 01978 290666; www.wrexham.ac.uk
Writtle (UC) (Chelmsford) Tel 01245 424200; www.aru.ac.uk/student-life/life-on-campus/writtle-campus
York Tel 01904 320000; www.york.ac.uk
York St John Tel 01904 624624; www.yorksj.ac.uk

SECTION 2: SPECIALIST COLLEGES OF AGRICULTURE AND HORTICULTURE, ART, DANCE, DRAMA, FASHION, MUSIC AND HEALTH SCIENCES

Many colleges and institutes provide undergraduate and postgraduate courses in a wide range of subjects. While many universities and university colleges offer courses in art, design, music, drama, agriculture, horticulture and courses connected to the land-based industries, the specialist colleges listed below provide courses at many levels, often part-time, in these separate fields.

It is important that you read prospectuses and check websites carefully and go to Open Days to find out as much as you can about these colleges and about their courses which interest you. Applications for full-time courses at the institutions listed below are through UCAS.

Abbreviations used below A = Art and Design; **Ag** = Agriculture, Animals and Land-related courses; **C** = Communication; **D** = Drama, Performing and Theatre Arts; **Da** = Dance; **F** = Fashion; **HS** = Health Sciences; **H** = Horticulture and Landscape-related courses; **M** = Music; **T** = Technology and Engineering.
Academy of Live Technology (South Kirkby) Tel 01977 659880; www.academyoflivetechnology.co.uk [**D**]
Architectural Association School of Architecture Tel 020 7887 4000; www.aaschool.ac.uk
Arts Educational Schools London (London) Tel 020 8987 6666; www.artsed.co.uk [**A**]
Askham Bryan College (York) Tel 01904 772277; www.askham-bryan.ac.uk [**Ag**]
Banbury and Bicester College Tel 0808 612 6008; https://banbury.activatelearning.ac.uk
Belfast Metropolitan College Tel 028 9026 5265; www.belfastmet.ac.uk
Berkshire College of Agriculture (Maidenhead) Tel 01628 824444; www.bca.ac.uk [**Ag**]
Bicton College (Budleigh Salterton) Tel 0330 123 4782; www.bicton.ac.uk [**Ag**]
Bishop Burton College Tel 01964 553000; www.bishopburton.ac.uk [**Ag**]
Black Mountains College (Brecon) Tel 01874 711888; www.blackmountainscollege.uk
Bristol Old Vic Theatre School Tel 0117 973 3535; www.oldvic.ac.uk [**D**]

British and Irish Modern Music Institute (BIMM) (East Sussex) Tel 0344 2 646 666; www.bimm.ac.uk [**M**]

British College of Osteopathic Medicine and European School of Osteopathy (London) Tel 020 7435 6464; 01622 685989; bcnogroup.ac.uk

British Institute of Technology, England (London) Tel 020 8552 3071; www.bite.ac.uk

Camberwell College of Arts, University of the Arts London Tel 020 7514 6302; www.arts.ac.uk/colleges/camberwell-college-of-arts [**A**]

Capel Manor College (Enfield) Tel 0303 003 1234; www.capel.ac.uk [**H**]

Central Saint Martins College, University of the Arts London Tel 020 7514 7444; www.arts.ac.uk/colleges/central-saint-martins [**A**]

Chelsea College of Arts, University of the Arts London Tel 020 7514 7751; www.arts.ac.uk/colleges/chelsea-college-of-arts [**A**]

City and Guilds of London Art School Tel 020 7735 2306; www.cityandguildsartschool.ac.uk [**A**]

College of Agriculture, Food & Rural Enterprise (CAFRE) (Antrim) Tel 028 9442 6601; www.cafre.ac.uk [**Ag**]

College of Integrated Chinese Medicine (Reading) Tel 0118 950 8889; www.acupuncturecollege.org.uk

College of Osteopaths (Borehamwood) Tel 020 8905 1937; www.collegeofosteopaths.ac.uk

Dartington Arts School (Totnes) Tel 01803 847101; https://campus.dartington.org/arts-school/ [**A**]

Duchy College University Centre (Callington) Tel 0330 123 4784; www.duchy.ac.uk [**Ag**]

East 15 Acting School (Loughton) Tel 020 8508 5983; www.east15.ac.uk [**D**]

Easton College (Norwich) Tel 01603 731200; www.easton.ac.uk [**Ag**]

Fairfield School of Business (Croydon) Tel 020 8681 8305; https://fsb.ac.uk

Fashion Retail Academy (London) Tel 020 7307 2345; www.fashionretailacademy.ac.uk [**F**]

Futureworks School of Film, Television & Media (Manchester) Tel 0161 214 4600; www.futureworks.ac.uk/study/school-of-film-television-and-media/

Glasgow Clyde College Tel 0141 272 9000; www.glasgowclyde.ac.uk

Glasgow School of Art Tel 0141 353 4500; www.gsa.ac.uk [**A**]

Gray's School of Art, Robert Gordon University (Aberdeen) Tel 01224 262728; www.rgu.ac.uk/study/academic-schools/gray-s-school-of-art [**A**]

Guildford School of Acting, University of Surrey (Guildford) Tel 01483 682222; www.gsauk.org [**D**]

Guildhall School of Music and Drama (London) Tel 020 7628 2571; www.gsmd.ac.uk [**M**]

Hadlow University Centre (Tonbridge) Tel 01732 850551; www.hadlow.ac.uk [**Ag**]

Harper and Keele Veterinary School Tel Harper Adams 01952 820280; Keele 01782 732000; www.harperkeelevetschool.ac.uk

Hartpury College (Gloucester) Tel 01452 702244; www.hartpury.ac.uk [**Ag**]

Heatherley School of Fine Art (London) Tel 020 7351 4190; www.heatherleys.org [**A**]

Hereford College of Arts Tel 01432 273359; www.hca.ac.uk [**A**]

Inchbald School of Design (London) Tel 020 7730 5508; www.inchbald.co.uk [**A**]

Institute of Contemporary Music Performance (ICMP) (London) Tel 020 7328 0222; www.icmp.ac.uk [**M**]

Istituto Marangoni (London) Tel 020 3608 2401; www.istitutomarangoni.com [**F**]

Kent and Medway Medical School https://kmms.ac.uk

Kingston Maurward College (Dorchester) Tel 01305 215034; www.kmc.ac.uk [**Ag**]

Leeds Conservatoire Tel 0113 222 3400; www.leedsconservatoire.ac.uk [**M**]

Liverpool Institute for Performing Arts Tel 0151 330 3084; www.lipa.ac.uk [**D**]

Liverpool School of Tropical Medicine (Liverpool) Tel 0151 705 3100; www.lstmed.ac.uk

London Academy of Music and Dramatic Art (London) Tel 020 8834 0500; www.lamda.ac.uk [**M**]

London College of Communication, University of the Arts London Tel 020 7514 6500; www.arts.ac.uk/colleges/london-college-of-communication [**C**]

London College of Creative Music (LCCM) (London) Tel 020 3535 1080; www.lccm.org.uk

London College of Fashion, University of the Arts London Tel 020 7514 7400; www.arts.ac.uk/colleges/london-college-of-fashion [**F**]

London Studio Centre (North Finchley) Tel 020 7837 7741; www.londonstudiocentre.org [**D**]
Matrix College of Counselling and Psychotherapy (Wymondham) Tel 01953 797160; https://matrix.ac.uk
Metanoia Institute (London) Tel 020 8579 2505; www.metanoia.ac.uk
MetFilm School (London) Tel 020 8280 9119; www.metfilmschool.ac.uk
Mont Rose College (London) Tel 020 8556 5009; www.mrcollege.ac.uk
Mountview Academy of Theatre Arts Tel 020 3146 0204; www.mountview.org.uk [**D**]
Myerscough College (Preston) Tel 01995 642222; www.myerscough.ac.uk [**Ag**]
Northern School of Contemporary Dance (Leeds) Tel 0113 219 3000; www.nscd.ac.uk [**Da**]
Plumpton College Tel 01273 890454; www.plumpton.ac.uk [**Ag**]
Point Blank Music School (London) Tel 020 7729 4884; www.pointblankmusicschool.com [**M**]
Rose Bruford College (Sidcup) Tel 020 8308 2600; www.bruford.ac.uk [**D**]
Royal Academy of Dance (London) Tel 020 7326 8000; www.royalacademyofdance.org [**Da**]
Royal Academy of Dramatic Art (RADA) Tel 020 7636 7076; www.rada.ac.uk [**D**]
Royal Academy of Music, University of London Tel 020 7873 7373; www.ram.ac.uk [**M**]
Royal Central School of Speech and Drama, University of London Tel 020 7722 8183; www.cssd.ac.uk [**D**]
Royal College of Art Tel 020 7590 4444; www.rca.ac.uk [**A**]
Royal College of Music (London) Tel 020 7591 4300; www.rcm.ac.uk [**M**]
Royal Conservatoire of Scotland (Glasgow) Tel 0141 332 4101; www.rcs.ac.uk [**M**]
Royal Northern College of Music (Manchester) Tel 0161 907 5200; www.rncm.ac.uk [**M**]
Royal School of Needlework (Molesey) Tel 020 3166 6932; https://royal-needlework.org.uk/ [**A**]
Royal Welsh College of Music and Drama (Cardiff) Tel 029 2039 1361; www.rwcmd.ac.uk [**M**]
Ruskin School of Art, University of Oxford (Oxford) Tel 01865 276940; www.rsa.ox.ac.uk [**A**]
SAE Creative Media Institute (London) Tel 0333 011 2315; www.sae.edu
Scotland's Rural College (Edinburgh) Tel 0800 269 453; www.sruc.ac.uk [**Ag**]
Slade School of Fine Art, University College London Tel 020 7679 2313; www.ucl.ac.uk/slade [**A**]
SMB College Group (Melton Mowbray) Tel 01664 850850; www.smbcollegegroup.ac.uk [**Ag**]
South and City College Birmingham (Digbeth) Tel 0121 694 5000; www.sccb.ac.uk
Sparsholt College Hampshire (Winchester) Tel 01962 776441; www.sparsholt.ac.uk [**H**]
TEDI-London https://tedi-london.ac.uk
The Academy of Contemporary Music (ACM), Guildford Tel 01483 500800; www.acm.ac.uk [**M**]
The London School of Architecture Tel 020 7206 2585; www.the-lsa.org
The National Film and Television School (Beaconsfield) Tel 01494 671234; www.nfts.co.uk
The Northern School of Art (Middlesbrough) Tel 01642 288888; www.northernart.ac.uk [**A**]
Trinity Laban Conservatoire of Music and Dance (London) Tel 020 8305 4444; www.trinitylaban.ac.uk [**M**]
UK College of Business and Computing (UKCBC) (London) Tel 020 8518 4994; www.ukcbc.ac.uk
University Centre Reaseheath (Nantwich) Tel 01270 613284; www.reaseheath.ac.uk [**Ag**]
University College of Estate Management (Reading) Tel 0800 019 9697; www.ucem.ac.uk
West Dean College of Arts and Conservation (Chichester) Tel 01243 818318; www.westdean.org.uk [**A**]
Wimbledon College of Arts, University of the Arts London Tel 020 7514 9641; www.arts.ac.uk/colleges/wimbledon-college-of-arts [**A**]
Winchester School of Art, University of Southampton Tel 023 8059 6900; www.southampton.ac.uk/about/faculties-schools-departments/winchester-school-of-art [**A**]

SECTION 3: FURTHER EDUCATION AND OTHER COLLEGES OFFERING HIGHER EDUCATION COURSES

Changes are taking place fast in this sector, with the merger of colleges and the introduction of University Centres. These are linked to further education colleges and to one or more universities, and provide Foundation and Honours degree courses (often part-time) and sometimes postgraduate qualifications.

The following institutions appear under various subject headings in the tables in **Chapter 7** and are in UCAS for some of their courses. See prospectuses and websites for application details.

Abingdon and Witney College Tel 01235 555585; www.abingdon-witney.ac.uk
Accrington and Rossendale College Tel 01254 389933; www.accross.ac.uk
ANCC College (Hertfordshire) Tel 01920 443500; www.allnations.ac.uk
Andover College Tel 01264 360018; www.andover.ac.uk
Ayrshire College Tel 0300 303 0303; www1.ayrshire.ac.uk
Barking and Dagenham College (Romford) Tel 020 8090 3020; www.barkingdagenhamcollege.ac.uk
Barnet and Southgate College Tel 020 8266 4000; www.barnetsouthgate.ac.uk
Barnfield College (Luton) Tel 01582 569569; www.barnfield.ac.uk
Barnsley College Tel 01226 216123; www.barnsley.ac.uk
Basingstoke College of Technology Tel 01256 354141; www.bcot.ac.uk
Bath College Tel 01225 312191; www.bathcollege.ac.uk
Bedford College Tel 0345 658 8990; www.bedford.ac.uk
Bexhill College (Bexhill-on-Sea) Tel 01424 214545; www.bexhillcollege.ac.uk
Birmingham Metropolitan College Tel 0121 446 4545; www.bmet.ac.uk
Bishop Auckland College Tel 01388 443000; www.bacoll.ac.uk
Blackburn College Tel 01254 292929; www.blackburn.ac.uk
Blackpool and The Fylde College Tel 01253 504343; www.blackpool.ac.uk
Bolton College Tel 01204 482000; www.boltoncollege.ac.uk
Boston College Tel 01205 365701; www.boston.ac.uk
Bournemouth and Poole College Tel 01202 205205; www.thecollege.co.uk
Bracknell and Wokingham College Tel 0800 612 6008; https://bracknell.activatelearning.ac.uk/
Bradford College University Centre Tel 01274 088088; www.bradfordcollege.ac.uk
Bridgend College Tel 01656 302302; www.bridgend.ac.uk
Bridgwater and Taunton College Tel 01278 455464; www.btc.ac.uk/
Brighton Metropolitan College Tel 01273 667788; www.brightonmet.ac.uk
Bristol Baptist College Tel 0117 946 7050; www.bristol-baptist.ac.uk/
Brit College (London) Tel 020 7265 8497; www.britcollege.ac.uk
Brockenhurst College Tel 01590 625555; www.brock.ac.uk
Brooklands College (Weybridge) Tel 01932 797700; www.brooklands.ac.uk
Buckinghamshire College Group (Amersham; Aylesbury; High Wycombe) Tel 01296 588599; www.buckscollegegroup.ac.uk
Burnley College Tel 01282 733373; www.burnley.ac.uk
Burton and South Derbyshire College (Burton-on-Trent) Tel 01283 494400; www.bsdc.ac.uk
Bury College Tel 0161 280 8200; www.burycollege.ac.uk
Buxton and Leek College Tel 0800 074 0099; www.blc.ac.uk
Calderdale College (Halifax) Tel 01422 399316; www.calderdale.ac.uk
Cambridge Regional College (Cambridge; Huntingdon) Tel 01223 418200; 01480 379100; www.camre.ac.uk
Cambridge Theological Federation Tel 01223 767787; www.theofed.cam.ac.uk
Canterbury College Tel 01227 811111; www.canterburycollege.ac.uk
Carlisle College Tel 01228 822700; www.carlisle.ac.uk
Carmel College (St Helens) Tel 01744 452200; www.carmel.ac.uk
Carshalton College Tel 020 8544 4501; https://stcg.ac.uk/carshalton-college
CECOS London College Tel 020 7359 3316; www.cecos.ac.uk
Central Bedfordshire College (Dunstable) Tel 01582 477776; www.bedfordcollegegroup.ac.uk/central-bedfordshire-college/
Central Campus, Sandwell College (West Bromwich) Tel 0800 622 006; www.sandwell.ac.uk
Central Film School London (London) Tel 020 7377 6060; www.centralfilmschool.com

Chelmsford College Tel 01245 293170; www.chelmsford.ac.uk
Cheshire College – South and West (Ellesmere Port) Tel 01244 656555; www.ccsw.ac.uk
Cheshire College South and West (Crewe) Tel 01270 654654; www.ccsw.ac.uk
Chesterfield College Tel 01246 500500; www.chesterfield.ac.uk
Chichester College Tel 01243 786321; www.chichester.ac.uk
City and Islington College Tel 020 7832 5000; www.capitalccg.ac.uk/candi
City College Norwich Tel 01603 773311; www.ccn.ac.uk
City College Plymouth Tel 01752 305300; www.cityplym.ac.uk
City of Bristol College Tel 0117 312 5000; www.cityofbristol.ac.uk
City of Liverpool College Tel 0151 252 3000; www.liv-coll.ac.uk
City of London College Tel 020 7247 2177; www.clc-london.ac.uk
City of Oxford College Tel 0800 612 6008; https://oxford.activatelearning.ac.uk/
City of Portsmouth College Tel 023 9238 3131; www.city-of-portsmouth-college.ac.uk
City of Westminster College (London) Tel 020 7723 8826; www.cwc.ac.uk
City of Wolverhampton College Tel 01902 836000; www.wolvcoll.ac.uk
Cliff College (Sheffield) Tel 01246 584229; www.cliffcollege.ac.uk
Coleg Sir Gâr (Pwll) Tel 01554 748179; www.colegsirgar.ac.uk
Coleg y Cymoedd (Aberdare) Tel 01685 887500; www.cymoedd.ac.uk
College of Haringey, Enfield and North East London Tel 020 7832 5000; www.conel.ac.uk
College of North West London Tel 020 8208 5000; www.cnwl.ac.uk
College of West Anglia (Norfolk) Tel 01553 761144; www.cwa.ac.uk
Cornwall College (Redruth) Tel 0330 123 2523; www.cornwall.ac.uk
Coventry College Tel 024 7693 2932; www.coventrycollege.ac.uk
Craven College (Skipton) Tel 01756 791411; www.craven-college.ac.uk
Darlington College Tel 01325 503030; www.darlington.ac.uk
David Game Higher Education Centre (DGHE) (London) Tel 020 3220 0347; www.dghe.ac.uk
Dearne Valley College (Rotherham) Tel 01709 513355; www.dearne-coll.ac.uk
Derby College Tel 01332 387400; www.derby-college.ac.uk
Derwentside College (Consett) Tel 01207 585900; www.derwentside.ac.uk
Doncaster College Tel 0800 358 7575; www.don.ac.uk
Dudley College Tel 01384 363000; www.dudleycol.ac.uk
Ealing, Hammersmith and West London College Tel 020 7565 1200; www.wlc.ac.uk
East Coast College (Great Yarmouth; Lowestoft) Tel 0800 854 695; www.eastcoast.ac.uk
East Durham College (Peterlee) Tel 0191 518 2000; www.eastdurham.ac.uk
East Kent College (Broadstairs) Tel 01843 605040; www.broadstairscollege.ac.uk
East Riding College (Beverley) Tel 0345 120 0044; www.eastridingcollege.ac.uk
East Surrey College (Redhill) Tel 01737 772611; www.esc.ac.uk
East Sussex College (Hastings) Tel 030 300 39699; www.escg.ac.uk
Eastleigh College Tel 023 8091 1000; www.eastleigh.ac.uk
Edinburgh College Tel 0131 297 8300; www.edinburghcollege.ac.uk
Escape Studios (London) Tel 0203 4411 303; www.escapestudios.ac.uk
European School of Economics (London) Tel 020 3778 0303; www.ese.ac.uk
Exeter College Tel 01392 400500; www.exe-coll.ac.uk
Fareham College Tel 01329 815200; www.fareham.ac.uk
Farnborough College of Technology Tel 01252 405555; www.farn-ct.ac.uk
Forth Valley College (Falkirk) Tel 01324 403000; www.forthvalley.ac.uk
Furness College (Barrow-in-Furness) Tel 01229 825017; www.furness.ac.uk
Gateshead College Tel 0191 490 0300; www.gateshead.ac.uk
Global Banking School (London) Tel 020 8092 9440; https://globalbanking.ac.uk/

Gloucestershire College Tel 0345 155 2020; www.gloscol.ac.uk

Gower College Swansea Tel 01792 284000; www.gcs.ac.uk

Grantham College Tel 01476 400200; www.grantham.ac.uk

Grimsby Institute of Further and Higher Education Tel 0800 315 002; https://grimsby.ac.uk

Grŵp Llandrillo Menai (Colwyn Bay) Tel 01492 542338 Coleg Llandrillo; 01248 370125; Coleg Menai; 01341 422827 Coleg Meirion-Dwyfor; www.gllm.ac.uk

Guildford College Tel 0800 612 6008; https://guildford.activatelearning.ac.uk/

Halesowen College Tel 0121 602 7777; www.halesowen.ac.uk

Harlow College Tel 01279 868100; www.harlow-college.ac.uk

Harrogate College Tel 01423 879466; www.harrogate-college.ac.uk/

Harrow College Tel 020 8909 6000; www.harrow.ac.uk

Hartlepool College of Further Education Tel 01429 295000; www.hartlepoolfe.ac.uk

Havant and South Downs College (Waterlooville; Havant) Tel 023 9387 9999; www.hsdc.ac.uk

Havering College (Hornchurch) Tel 0330 135 9000; www.ncclondon.ac.uk/havering-campuses

Heart of Worcestershire College (Redditch) Tel 01527 572522; www.howcollege.ac.uk

Herefordshire and Ludlow College Tel 0800 032 1986; www.hlcollege.ac.uk

Hertford Regional College (Ware) Tel 01992 411400; www.hrc.ac.uk

Highland Theological College, University of the Highlands and Islands (Dingwall) Tel 01349 780000; www.htc.uhi.ac.uk

Holy Cross College (Bury) Tel 0161 762 4510; www.holycross.ac.uk

Hopwood Hall College (Rochdale) Tel 01706 345346; www.hopwood.ac.uk

Hugh Baird College (Bootle) Tel 0151 353 4444; www.hughbaird.ac.uk

Hull College Tel 01482 329943; www.hull-college.ac.uk

Hult International Business School (London) Tel 0207 341 8555; www.hult.edu

ICON College of Technology and Management (London) Tel 020 7377 2800; www.iconcollege.ac.uk

Isle of Wight College Tel 01983 526631; www.iwcollege.ac.uk

Kendal College Tel 01539 814700; www.kendal.ac.uk

Kensington College of Business (London) Tel 020 7404 6330; www.kcb.ac.uk/

Kidderminster College Tel 01562 820811; www.kidderminster.ac.uk

Kingston College (Kingston upon Thames) Tel 020 8546 2151; https://stcg.ac.uk/kingston-college

Kirklees College (Huddersfield) Tel 01484 437000; www.kirkleescollege.ac.uk

Knowsley Community College (Huyton) Tel 0151 477 5850; www.knowsleycollege.ac.uk

Lakes College, West Cumbria (Workington) Tel 01946 839300; www.lcwc.ac.uk

Lancaster and Morecambe College Tel 01524 66215; 0800 306 306; www.lmc.ac.uk

Leeds City College Tel 0113 386 1997; www.leedscitycollege.ac.uk

Leeds College of Building Tel 0113 222 6000; www.lcb.ac.uk

Leicester College Tel 0116 224 2240; www.leicestercollege.ac.uk

Leo Baeck College (London) Tel 020 8349 5600; www.lbc.ac.uk

Lewisham College (London) Tel 020 3757 3000; www.lewisham.ac.uk

Lincoln College Tel General Enquiries 01522 876000; Course Enquiries 030 030 32435.; www.lincolncollege.ac.uk

London Business School Tel 020 7000 7000; www.london.edu

London School of Commerce Tel 020 7357 0077; www.lsclondon.co.uk

London School of Management Education (Gants Hill) Tel 020 8594 8462; https://lsme.ac.uk/

London School of Science and Technology (Wembley) Tel 020 8795 3863; www.lsst.ac

London School of Theology (Northwood) Tel 01923 456000; https://lst.ac.uk

London South East Colleges (Bromley; Erith; Greenwich) Tel 020 3954 4000; www.lsec.ac.uk

Loughborough College Tel 01509 215831; www.loucoll.ac.uk

Luther King Centre (LKC) (Manchester) Tel 0161 249 2504; www.lutherking.ac.uk

Macclesfield College of Further and Higher Education Tel 01625 410000; www.macclesfield.ac.uk
Middlesbrough College Tel 01642 333333; www.mbro.ac.uk
MidKent College (Gillingham) Tel 01634 402020; www.midkent.ac.uk
Milton Keynes College Tel 01908 684444; www.mkcollege.ac.uk
Moorlands College (Christchurch) Tel 01425 674500; www.moorlands.ac.uk
Morley College (London) Tel 020 7450 1889; www.morleycollege.ac.uk
Moulton College Tel 01604 491131; www.moulton.ac.uk
Nazarene Theological College (Manchester) Tel 0161 445 3063; www.nazarene.ac.uk
Neath Port Talbot College Tel 03308 188100; www.nptcgroup.ac.uk
Nelson and Colne College Tel 01282 440200; www.nelson.ac.uk
Nelson College London (28-42 Clements Road Ilford) Tel 020 8514 0033; https://nelsoncollege.ac.uk
Nescot, North East Surrey College of Technology (Epsom) Tel 020 8394 3038; www.nescot.ac.uk
New City College Hackney (London) Tel 0330 135 9000; www.ncclondon.ac.uk/hackney-campus
New City College Redbridge (Romford) Tel 0330 135 9000; www.ncclondon.ac.uk/redbridge-campus
New City College Tower Hamlets (London) Tel 020 7510 7510; www.ncclondon.ac.uk/tower-hamlets-campus
New College Durham Tel 0191 375 4000; www.newcollegedurham.ac.uk
New College Swindon Tel 01793 611470; www.newcollege.ac.uk
Newbold College (Bracknell) Tel 01344 407407; www.newbold.ac.uk
Newbury College Tel 01635 845000; www.newbury-college.ac.uk
Newcastle College (Newcastle-upon-Tyne) Tel 0191 200 4000; www.ncl-coll.ac.uk
Newham College (London) Tel 020 8257 4000; www.newham.ac.uk
Norland College (Bath) Tel 01225 904040; www.norland.ac.uk
North East Scotland College (Aberdeen) Tel 01224 612330; www.nescol.ac.uk
North East Surrey College of Technology (NESCOT) (Epsom) Tel 020 8394 1731; www.nescot.ac.uk
North Hertfordshire College (Stevenage) Tel 01462 424242; www.nhc.ac.uk
North Kent College (Dartford) Tel 01322 629400; www.northkent.ac.uk
North Lindsey College (Scunthorpe) Tel 01724 281111; www.northlindsey.ac.uk
North Notts College (Worksop) Tel 01909 504500; www.nnc.ac.uk
North Shropshire College (Oswestry) Tel 0800 440 2281; www.nsc.ac.uk
North Warwickshire and South Leicestershire College (Nuneaton) Tel 0330 058 3000; www.nwslc.ac.uk
North West Regional College (Londonderry/Derry) Tel 028 7127 6000; www.nwrc.ac.uk
Northampton College Tel 0300 123 2344; www.northamptoncollege.ac.uk
Northern Regional College (Ballymena) Tel 0333 034 8197; www.nrc.ac.uk
Northumberland College (Ashington) Tel 0300 770 6000; www.northumberland.ac.uk
Nottingham College Tel 0115 910 0100; www.nottinghamcollege.ac.uk
NSCG Newcastle College (Newcastle-under-Lyme) Tel 01782 715111; https://nscg.ac.uk/newcastle-campus
NSCG Stafford College Tel 01785 223800; https://nscg.ac.uk/stafford-campus
Oak Hill College (London) Tel 020 8449 0467; www.oakhill.ac.uk
Oaklands College (St Albans) Tel 01727 737000; www.oaklands.ac.uk
Oldham College Tel 0161 785 4000; www.oldham.ac.uk
Oxford Business College Tel 0333 242 0000; www.oxfordbusinesscollege.ac.uk
Pembrokeshire College (Haverfordwest) Tel 01437 753000; www.pembrokeshire.ac.uk
Peter Symonds College (Winchester) Tel 01962 857500; www.psc.ac.uk
Peterborough Regional College Tel 0345 872 8722; https://peterborough.ac.uk
Petroc (Barnstaple) Tel 01271 345291; www.petroc.ac.uk
Preston College Tel 01772 225000; www.preston.ac.uk
Redcar and Cleveland College Tel 01642 473132; www.cleveland.ac.uk
Regent College (London) Tel 020 3870 6666; www.rcl.ac.uk

Regents Theological College (West Malvern) Tel 01684 588979; www.regents-tc.ac.uk
Richmond and Hillcroft Adult Community College (RHACC) (Surbiton) Tel 020 8891 5907; www.rhacc.ac.uk
Richmond-upon-Thames College (Twickenham) Tel 020 8607 8000; www.rutc.ac.uk
Riverside College (Widnes) Tel 0151 257 2800; www.riversidecollege.ac.uk
Rotherham College of Arts and Technology Tel 01709 362111; www.rotherham.ac.uk
Royal National College for the Blind (Hereford) Tel 01432 265 725; www.rnc.ac.uk
Runshaw College (Leyland) Tel 01772 642040; www.runshaw.ac.uk
Ruskin College Tel 01865 759600; www.ruskin.ac.uk
Sabhal Mòr Ostaig, University of the Highlands and Islands (Sleat) Tel 01471 888304; www.smo.uhi.ac.uk
Salford City College Tel 0161 631 5000; www.salfordcc.ac.uk
School of Advanced Study, University of London (London) Tel 020 7862 8653; www.sas.ac.uk
Scottish Association for Marine Science, University of the Highlands and Islands (Argyll) Tel 01631 559000; www.sams.ac.uk
Selby College Tel 01757 211000; www.selby.ac.uk
Sheffield College Tel 0114 260 2600; www.sheffcol.ac.uk
Shrewsbury College Tel 01743 653111; www.scg.ac.uk
Solihull College Tel 0121 678 7000; www.solihull.ac.uk
South Bank Colleges (London) Tel 020 7501 5000; www.southbankcolleges.ac.uk
South Cheshire College (Crewe) Tel 01270 654654; www.ccsw.ac.uk
South Devon College (Paignton) Tel 08000 380 123; www.southdevon.ac.uk
South Eastern Regional College (Bangor) Tel 0345 600 7555; www.serc.ac.uk
South Essex College Tel 0345 521 2345; www.southessex.ac.uk
South Gloucestershire and Stroud College Tel 0800 0567 253; www.sgscol.ac.uk
South Lanarkshire College (East Kilbride) Tel 01355 807780; www.south-lanarkshire-college.ac.uk
South Staffordshire College (Cannock) Tel 0300 456 2424; www.southstaffs.ac.uk
South Thames College (London) Tel 020 8918 7777; https://stcg.ac.uk/south-thames-college
South West College (Enniskillen) Tel 028 8225 0109; www.swc.ac.uk
Southampton City College Tel 023 8048 4848; www.southampton-city.ac.uk
Southern Regional College (Portadown) Tel 0300 123 1223; www.src.ac.uk
Southport College Tel 01704 392704; www.southport.ac.uk
Southwark College (London) Tel 020 3757 4000; www.southwark.ac.uk
Spurgeon's College (London) Tel 020 8683 8462; www.spurgeons.ac.uk
St Helens College Tel 0800 996 699; www.sthelens.ac.uk
St Mellitus College (London) Tel 020 7052 0573; https://stmellitus.ac.uk/
St Patrick's College (London) Tel 020 7287 6664; www.st-patricks.ac.uk
Stamford College Tel 01780 484300; www.stamford.ac.uk
Stockport College Tel 0161 296 5000; www.stockport.ac.uk
Stockton Riverside College (Stockton-on-Tees) Tel 01642 865400; www.stockton.ac.uk
Stoke-on-Trent College Tel 01782 208208; www.stokecoll.ac.uk
Stratford-upon-Avon College Tel 01789 266245; www.stratford.ac.uk
Strode College (Street) Tel 01458 844400; www.strode-college.ac.uk
Sunderland College Tel 0300 770 8000; www.sunderlandcollege.ac.uk
Tameside College (Ashton-under-Lyne) Tel 0161 908 6789; www.tameside.ac.uk
TEC Partnership (Grimsby) Tel 0800 315 002; https://tecpartnership.com/
Telford College Tel 01952 642200; www.telfordcollege.ac.uk
The Islamic College (London) Tel 020 8451 9993; www.islamic-college.ac.uk
The London College UCK Tel 020 7243 4000; www.lcuck.ac.uk
The Manchester College Tel 0333 322 2444; www.tmc.ac.uk
The Markfield Institute of Higher Education Tel 01530 244922; www.mihe.ac.uk

The Windsor Forest Colleges Group (Langley) Tel 01753 793000; www.windsor-forest.ac.uk
Tottenham Hotspur Foundation (London) Tel 020 8365 5138; www.tottenhamhotspur.com/the-club/foundation/
Totton College (Southampton) Tel 023 8087 4874; www.totton.ac.uk
Trafford College (Altrincham) Tel 0161 886 7070; www.trafford.ac.uk
Tresham College of Further and Higher Education (Kettering) Tel 01536 413123; https://bedfordcollegegroup.ac.uk/colleges-and-campuses/tresham-college/
Trinity College Bristol (Bristol) Tel 0117 968 2803; www.trinitycollegebristol.ac.uk
Truro and Penwith College Tel 01872 305000 Truro; 01736 809440 Penwith; www.truro-penwith.ac.uk
Tyne Coast College (South Shields) Tel 0191 427 3500; www.tynecoast.ac.uk
University Academy 92 Limited (Manchester) Tel 0161 507 1992; https://ua92.ac.uk
University Campus Oldham Tel 0161 344 8800; www.uco.oldham.ac.uk
University Centre Colchester Tel 01206 712000; www.colchester.ac.uk
University Centre Croydon Tel 020 8760 5934; www.croydonuniversitycentre.ac.uk
University Centre Peterborough Tel 01733 214466; www.ucp.ac.uk
University of the Highlands and Islands, Argyll (Dunoon) Tel 01631 559750; www.argyll.uhi.ac.uk
University of the Highlands and Islands, Inverness Tel 01463 273000; www.inverness.uhi.ac.uk
University of the Highlands and Islands, Moray (Elgin) Tel 01343 576000; www.moray.uhi.ac.uk
University of the Highlands and Islands, North, West and Hebrides Tel 01847 889000; www.nwh.uhi.ac.uk/en/
University of the Highlands and Islands, Orkney (Kirkwall) Tel 01856 569000; www.orkney.uhi.ac.uk
University of the Highlands and Islands, Perth Tel 01738 877000; www.perth.uhi.ac.uk
University of the Highlands and Islands, Shetland (Lerwick) Tel 01595 771000; www.shetland.uhi.ac.uk
USP College (Benfleet) Tel 01268 756111; www.uspcollege.ac.uk
Uxbridge College Tel 01895 853333; www.uxbridgecollege.ac.uk
Wakefield College Tel 01924 789111; www.wakefield.ac.uk
Walsall College Tel 01922 657000; www.walsallcollege.ac.uk
Waltham Forest College (London) Tel 020 8501 8501; www.waltham.ac.uk
Warrington and Vale Royal College Tel 01925 494494; https://wvr.ac.uk/
Warwickshire College (Roya Leamington Spa) Tel 0300 456 0047; www.wcg.ac.uk
Waverley Abbey College (Farnham) Tel 01252 784731; www.waverleyabbeycollege.ac.uk
West Herts College (Watford) Tel 01923 812345; www.westherts.ac.uk
West Nottinghamshire College (Mansfield) Tel 0808 100 3626; www.wnc.ac.uk
West Suffolk College (Bury St Edmunds) Tel 01284 701301; www.wsc.ac.uk
West Thames College (Isleworth) Tel 020 8326 2000; www.west-thames.ac.uk
Westminster Kingsway College (London) Tel 020 7832 5000; www.capitalccg.ac.uk/westking
Weston College (Weston-super-Mare) Tel 01934 411411; www.weston.ac.uk
Weymouth College Tel 01305 761100; www.weymouth.ac.uk
Wigan and Leigh College Tel 01942 761600; www.wigan-leigh.ac.uk
Wiltshire College (Chippenham) Tel 01225 350035; www.wiltshire.ac.uk
Wirral Metropolitan College (Birkenhead) Tel 0151 551 7777; www.wmc.ac.uk
Yeovil College Tel 01935 423921; www.yeovil.ac.uk
Yeovil College University Centre Tel 01935 845454; www.yeovil.ac.uk/university-centre/
York College Tel 01904 770100; www.yorkcollege.ac.uk

APPENDIX 1 UCAS 2026 ENTRY TARIFF POINTS TABLES

A-LEVELS AND AS • T-LEVELS• SCOTTISH HIGHERS/ADVANCED HIGHERS • ADVANCED SKILLS BACCALAUREATE WALES • IB INTERNATIONAL BACCALAUREATE DIPLOMA (IB CERTIFICATE IN HIGHER LEVEL; IB CERTIFICATE IN STANDARD LEVEL; IB CERTIFICATE IN EXTENDED ESSAY; IB CERTIFICATE IN THEORY OF KNOWLEDGE) • BTEC LEVEL 3 NATIONAL EXTENDED DIPLOMA • EXTENDED PROJECT • MUSIC EXAMINATIONS • APPRENTICESHIPS • ART AND DESIGN FOUNDATION STUDIES

A-levels and AS

Grade				Tariff points
A-level & Advanced VCE Double Award	A-level with additional AS	AS Double Award	AS & AS VCE	
A*A*				112
A*A				104
AA				96
AB				88
BB				80
	A*A			76
BC				72
	AA			68
CC	AB			64
CD	BB			56
	BC			52
DD				48
	CC			44
	CD			42
DE		AA		40
		AB		36
	DD			34
EE		BB		32
	DE			30
		BC		28
		CC		24
	EE	CD		22
		DD	A	20
		DE	B	16
		EE	C	12
			D	10
			E	6

T-levels

Please note that the Tariff score for T-levels has been allocated to the overall award:

Grade	Tariff points
D*	168
D	144
M	120
P (C or above on the core)	96
P (D or E on the core)	72

Scottish Highers/Advanced Highers

Grade	Higher Tariff points	Advanced Higher Tariff points
A	33	56
B	27	48
C	21	40
D	15	32

WJEC Level 3 Advanced Skills Baccalaureate Wales

Grade	Tariff points
A*	56
A	48
B	40
C	32
D	24
E	16

IBO International Baccalaureate Diploma

While the IB Diploma does not attract UCAS Tariff points, the constituent qualifications of the IB Diploma do, so the total Tariff points for an IB Diploma can be calculated by adding together each of the following four components:

IBO Certificate in Higher Level

Grade	Tariff points
H7	56
H6	48
H5	32
H4	24
H3	12
H2	0
H1	0

IBO Certificate in Standard Level

Grade	Tariff points
S7	28
S6	24
S5	16
S4	12
S3	6
S2	0
S1	0

IBO Certificate in Extended Essay

Grade	Tariff points
A	12
B	10
C	8
D	6
E	4

IBO Certificate in Theory of Knowledge

Grade	Tariff points
A	12
B	10
C	8
D	6
E	4

Certificates in Extended Essay and Theory of Knowledge are awarded Tariff points when the certificates have been taken individually.

BTEC Level 3 National Extended Diploma

Grade	Tariff points
D*D*D*	168
D*D*D	160
D*DD	152
DDD	144
DDM	128
DMM	112
MMM	96
MMP	80
MPP	64
PPP	48

Level 3/SQCF Level 6 apprenticeships

Duration	Tariff points
36 months	112
24 months	96
18 months	64
12 months	48

Extended Project

Grade	Tariff points
A*	28
A	24
B	20
C	16
D	12
E	8

Music examinations

Performance			Theory			Tariff points
Grade 8	Grade 7	Grade 6	Grade 8	Grade 7	Grade 6	
D						30
M						27
P						24
	D					16
	M					14
	P	D				12
		M	D			10
			M			9
		P	P	D		8
				M		7
				P	D	6
					M	5
					P	4

Additional points will be awarded for music examinations from the Associated Board of the Royal Schools of Music (ABRSM), University of West London, Rockschool and Trinity Guildhall/Trinity College London (music examinations at grades 6, 7, 8 (D=Distinction; M=Merit; P=Pass)).

Art and Design Foundation Studies

Grade	Tariff points
D	112
M	96
P	80

NB Full acknowledgement is made to UCAS for this information. For further details of all qualifications awarded UCAS Tariff points see www.ucas.com/ucas/tariff-calculator. Note that the Tariff is constantly updated and new qualifications are introduced each year.

APPENDIX 2 INTERNATIONAL QUALIFICATIONS

Universities in the UK accept a range of international qualifications and those which normally satisfy general entrance requirements are listed below. However, the specific levels of achievement or grades required for entry to degree courses with international qualifications will vary, depending on the popularity of the university or college and the chosen degree programme. The subject tables in **Chapter 7** provide a guide to the levels of entry to courses, although direct comparisons between A-level grades and international qualifications are not always possible. Most university websites give their own comparisons between A level grades and international grades. Students not holding the required qualifications should consider taking an International Foundation course.

International students whose mother tongue is not English and/or who have not studied for their secondary education in English will be required to pass a secure English language test (SELT) such as IELTS (International English Language Testing System) or the Trinity College London tests. Entry requirements vary between universities and courses. For the IELTS, scores can range from bands 1–9, but most universities' requirements range from 5.5 to 7.5.

Albania *Dëftesë Pjekurie* (Secondary School Leaving Certificate)/*Diplomë e Maturës Shtetërore* (Diploma of State Matura) plus International Foundation year

Algeria *Baccalauréat*

Argentina *Título de Bachiller* plus International Foundation year

Australia High School Certificate plus ATAR score of at least 80 or an Overall Position of 10 (Queensland)

Austria *Reifeprüfung/Matura* from *Allgemeinbildende Höhere Schulen* or *Reife und Diplomprüfung/Matura* from *Berufsbildende Höhere Schulen* (BHS)

Bahrain Secondary School Leaving Certificate plus International Foundation year or equivalent

Bangladesh Higher Secondary Certificate (HSC)/Intermediate Certificate plus International Foundation year or equivalent

Belarus Certificate of General Secondary Education plus International Foundation year or equivalent

Belgium *Diploma van Secundair Onderwijs/Diploma van de Hogere Secundaire Technische School* or *Abschlusszeugnis der Oberstufe des Sekundarunterrichts* or *Diplôme d'Aptitude à Accéder à l'Enseignement Supérieur/Certificat d'Enseignement Secondaire Superieur*

Bermuda Associate Degree of Arts, Science or Applied Science

Bosnia-Herzegovina *Matura/Svjedodžba o Završenoj Srednjoj Skoli* (Secondary School Leaving Certificate)

Botswana Botswana General Certificate of Secondary Education Examination (BGCSE) plus International Foundation year

Brazil *Certificado de Conclusão de Ensino Médio/Certificado de Ensino Médio* or *Título de Técnico/Diploma de Tecnico de Nivel Medio* plus International Foundation year

Brunei Brunei GCE A-level

Bulgaria *Diploma za Zavarsheno Sredno (Spetsialno) Obrazovanie* (Diploma of Completed Secondary (Specialised) Education)

Burma Basic Education Standard X Examination/Matriculation Examination plus International Foundation year or equivalent

Cameroon General Certificate of Education Advanced Level plus International Foundation year or equivalent

Canada Ontario Secondary School Diploma with a minimum of 65–70% in six grade 12 U or M courses or Alberta/British Columbia/Nova Scotia High/Secondary School Graduation Diploma/Certificate with a minimum of 65–70% in at least five grade 12 courses or Manitoba High School Diploma with a minimum of 65–70% in at least five 300-level Grade 12 subjects

Chile Completion of two years of *Título de Bachiller/Bachillerato* or *Licencia de Educación Media* with International Foundation year

China National College Entrance Examination (NCEE/*Gaokao)* with a minimum score of 75% overall and 75% in any required subjects or Huikao (Senior Secondary School Certificate) with International Foundation year

Colombia *Bachillerato* plus International Foundation year

Croatia *Svjedodžba o Maturi* (Certificate of Maturity)

Cyprus *Apolytirion* or *Devlet Lise Diplomasi* (State High School Diploma) with International Foundation year

Czech Republic *Vysvedceni o Maturitni Zkousce/Maturita*

Denmark *Studentereksamen* or *Højere Forberedelseseksamen* (HF) or *Højere Handelseksamen* (HHX) or *Højere Teknisk Eksamen* (HTX)

Egypt Certificate of General Secondary Education plus International Foundation year

Estonia *Gümnaasiumi lõputunnistus* (Secondary School Certificate) at grade 12 together with an appropriate overall grade earned on the *Riigieksamid* (Upper Secondary School National Examination) or *Diplom* (from a *Kutsekõrgharidus*)

Finland *Ylioppilastutkinto/Studentexamen* (Matriculation certificate)

France *Baccalauréat* or *Option Internationale du Baccalauréat* (OIB)

Germany *Zeugnis der Allgemeinen Hochschulreife/Abitur* or *Fachgebundene Hochschulreife/ Fachhochschulreife*

Greece *Apolytirio* of *Lykeio/Apolytirion* (minimum score 15) or appropriate scores in nationally examined Panhellenic Exams or appropriate scores in Network Foundation exams

Guyana Caribbean Advanced Proficiency Examination (CAPE) in three subjects

Hong Kong Hong Kong Diploma of Secondary Education (HKDSE) up to form 6 with score of 444

Hungary *Érettségi/Matura*

Iceland *Studentsprof*

India Higher Secondary School Certificate/Standard XII with an overall average of 60–65%

Indonesia *Ijazah-Sekolah Menengah Atas/Madrasah Aliyah* (SMA-MA) or *Surat Tanda Tamat Belajar Sekolah Menengah Umum Tingkat Atas* (STTB-SMA) (Certificate of Completion of Academic Secondary School) plus International Foundation year or equivalent

Iran *Peeshdaneshgahe* (pre-university certificate)

Iraq Certificate of Preparatory Education/Sixth Form Baccalauréat plus International Foundation year or equivalent

Ireland Irish Leaving Certificate Higher Level

Israel *Te'udat Bagrut/Bagrut* (Matriculation Certificate) with at least three subjects at levels 4 or 5

Italy *Esame di Stato* with good grades

Jamaica Caribbean Advanced Proficiency Examination (CAPE) in three subjects

Japan *Kotogakko Sotsugyo Shomeisho* (Upper Secondary School Leaving Certificate) plus International Foundation year or equivalent

Jordan *Tawjihi* (Secondary School Leaving Certificate) plus International Foundation year or equivalent

Kazakhstan Diploma of Completed Secondary Education plus International Foundation year or equivalent

Kenya Kenya Certificate of Secondary Education (KCSE) plus International Foundation year or equivalent

Kosovo *Diploma o Završenoj Srednjoj Skoli/Diplomë për Kryerjen e Shkollës së Mesme të Lartë/Matura* (High School Diploma)

Kuwait General Secondary Education Certificate plus International Foundation year or equivalent or Diploma/Certificate from PAAET Institute with an overall grade of Good (C or 2.0/4.0) or above

Latvia *Atestats par visparejo videjo izglitibu* (Attestation of General Secondary Education)

Lebanon *Baccalauréat General* or *Baccalauréat Technique* plus International Foundation year or equivalent

Libya Secondary Education Certificate plus International Foundation year or equivalent

Liechtenstein *Matura* (Type B or Type E)

Lithuania *Brandos Atestatas* (Certificate of Maturity)

Luxembourg *Diplôme de Fin d'Etudes Secondaires*

Macedonia Secondary School Leaving Diploma or Matura

Malawi Cambridge Overseas Higher School Certificate (COHSC) or a Malawi School Certificate of Education plus International Foundation year or equivalent

Malaysia *Sijil Tinggi Persekolahan Malaysia* (STPM, Malaysia Higher School Certificate) or Unified Examination Certificate (UEC) (Senior Middle Level) or *Sijil Pelajaran Malaysia* (SPM, Malaysia Certificate of Education) with grades of 1–6 plus International Foundation year or equivalent

Malta Advanced Matriculation (AM) or Matriculation Certificate Examination (University of Malta)

Mexico *Bachillerato* plus International Foundation year or equivalent

Moldova *Diploma de Bacalauréat* (Baccalaureate Diploma)

Montenegro *Maturski ispit/Diploma o završenoj srednjoj školi* (Secondary School Leaving Diploma)

Morocco *Diplôme du Baccalauréat* plus International Foundation year or equivalent

Netherlands *Diploma Voorbereidend Wetenschappelijk Onderwijs* (VWO)

Namibia Cambridge Overseas Higher School Certificate (COHSC)/GCE A level or a Namibia Senior Secondary Certificate (higher level) plus International Foundation year or equivalent

Nepal Higher Secondary Education Certificate plus International Foundation year or equivalent

Netherlands *Voorbereidend Wetenschappelijk Onderwijs* (VWO) with a grade of between 5.5–6.5

New Zealand University Entrance Certificate with National Certificates in Educational Achievement (NCEA) Level 3

Nigeria Senior Secondary School Certificate Education (SSCE)/West African Senior School Certificate (WASSC) plus International Foundation year or equivalent

Norway *Vitnemål for Videregående Opplæring* achieving *studiekompetanse* with a minimum grade of 3.5 overall

Oman General Secondary Education Certificate plus International Foundation year or equivalent

Pakistan Higher Secondary School Certificate plus International Foundation year or equivalent

Palestinian National Authority General Secondary Education Certificate plus International Foundation year or equivalent

Philippines High School Diploma plus International Foundation year or equivalent

Poland *Swiadectwo Dojrzałości/Matura*

Portugal *Certificado de fim de Estudos Secundários* or *Diploma Nível Secundário de Educação/Certificado Nível Secundário de Educação*

Qatar *Shahadat Al-Thanawaya Al-Aama* (General Secondary Education Certificate) or Qatar Senior School Certificate plus International Foundation year or equivalent

Russian Federation *Attestat o Srednem Obrzovanii* (Certificate of Secondary Education) plus International Foundation year or equivalent

Saudi Arabia *Thanawiya* (General Secondary Education Certificate) plus International Foundation year or equivalent

Serbia *Diploma o položenom završnom ispitu* (Diploma of Completed Final Examination) or *Diploma o položenom maturskom ispitu* (Secondary School Leaving Diploma) or *Diploma o stecenom srednem obrazovanju* (Diploma of Completed Secondary Education)

Sierra Leone West African Senior School Certificate (WASSC) plus International Foundation year or equivalent

Singapore Singapore/Cambridge GCE A-level

Slovakia *Maturitná skúška/Maturita* or *Vysvedcenie o Maturitnej Skúške* (School Leaving Certificate with Maturita from a SOU or SOŠ)

Slovenia *Matura*/Secondary School-Leaving Diploma/technical *Matura*

South Africa Senior Certificate (with matriculation endorsement) with minimum grades BBBCC or a National Senior Certificate with minimum grades of 66655

South Korea Korean High School Diploma plus International Foundation year or equivalent

Spain *Título de Bachillerato* or *Curso de Orientación Universitaria* (COU) (Pre-University course)

Sri Lanka Sri Lankan General Certificate of Education (Advanced level) qualifications

Sweden *Avgångsbetyg/Slutbetyg från Gymnasieskola*

Switzerland Federal Secondary School Leaving Certificate

Syria *Shahâda al-Thânawiyya al-camma* (Baccalauréat/General Secondary Certificate) plus International Foundation year or equivalent

Taiwan Senior High School Leaving Certificate plus International Foundation year or equivalent

Tanzania National Form VI Examination/Advanced Certificate of Secondary Education (ACSE) or Cambridge Overseas Higher School Certificate (COHSC)/East African Advanced Certificate of Education (EAACE)

Thailand Maw 6 (M6) with a score of 50% or above plus International Foundation year or equivalent

Tunisia *Baccalauréat* plus International Foundation year or equivalent

Turkey *Devlet Lise Diplomasi* (State High School Diploma) or *Lise Bitirme Diplomasi* (Private High School Diploma) plus International Foundation year or equivalent

Uganda Uganda Advanced Certificate of Education (UACE) or East African Advanced Certificate of Education or Cambridge Overseas Higher School Certificate (COHSC)

Ukraine Certificate of Complete General Secondary Education plus International Foundation year or equivalent

United Arab Emirates *Tawijihiyya* (Secondary Education Certificate) plus International Foundation year or equivalent

USA High School Graduation Diploma with a GPA of 3.0 overall plus good grades in SAT and/or APT/ACT

Uzbekistan *O'rta Ma'lumot To'g'risida Shahodatnoma* (Certificate of Completed Secondary Education) plus International Foundation year or equivalent

Venezuela *Título de Bachiller* plus International Foundation year or equivalent

Vietnam Upper Secondary School Graduation Diploma/National University Entrance Examination with a score of 5.0 or above plus International Foundation year or equivalent

Yemen *Shahadat Al-Thanawaya Al-Aama* (General Secondary Education Certificate) plus International Foundation year or equivalent

Zambia Zambia School Certificate plus International Foundation year or equivalent

Zimbabwe Cambridge Higher School Certificate or General Certificate of Education Advanced Level

APPENDIX 3
PROFESSIONAL ASSOCIATIONS

Professional associations vary in size and function and many offer examinations to provide members with vocational qualifications. However, many of the larger bodies do not conduct examinations but accept evidence provided by the satisfactory completion of appropriate degree and diploma courses. When applying for courses in vocational subjects, therefore, it is important to check whether your chosen course is accredited by a professional association, since membership of such bodies is usually necessary for progression in your chosen career after graduation.

Information about careers, which you can use as background information for your UCAS application, can be obtained from the organisations below listed under the subject table headings used in **Chapter 7**. Full details of professional associations, their examinations and the degree courses accredited by them are published in *British Qualifications* (see **Appendix 4**).

Some additional organisations that can provide useful careers-related information are listed below under the subject table headings and other sources of relevant information are indicated in the subject tables of **Chapter 7** and in **Appendix 4**.

Accountancy/Accounting
Accounting Technicians Ireland www.accountingtechniciansireland.ie
Association of Accounting Technicians www.aat.org.uk
Association of Chartered Certified Accountants www.accaglobal.com
Association of International Accountants www.aiaworldwide.com
Chartered Accountants Ireland www.charteredaccountants.ie
Chartered Institute of Internal Auditors www.iia.org.uk
Chartered Institute of Management Accountants www.cimaglobal.com
Chartered Institute of Public Finance and Accountancy www.cipfa.org
Chartered Institute of Taxation www.tax.org.uk
Institute of Chartered Accountants in England and Wales www.icaew.com
Institute of Chartered Accountants of Scotland www.icas.com
Institute of Financial Accountants www.ifa.org.uk

Actuarial Science/Studies
Institute and Faculty of Actuaries www.actuaries.org.uk

Agricultural Sciences/Agriculture
Innovation for Agriculture www.innovationforagriculture.org.uk
Institute of Chartered Foresters www.charteredforesters.org
Royal Forestry Society www.rfs.org.uk
Wood Technology Group www.iom3.org/group/wood-technology-group.html

Animal Sciences
British Horse Society www.bhs.org.uk
British Society of Animal Science www.bsas.org.uk

Anthropology
Association of Social Anthropologists of the UK and Commonwealth www.theasa.org
Royal Anthropological Institute www.therai.org.uk

Archaeology
Chartered Institute for Archaeologists www.archaeologists.net
Council for British Archaeology www.archaeologyuk.org

Architecture
Chartered Institute of Architectural Technologists www.architecturaltechnology.com
Royal Incorporation of Architects in Scotland www.rias.org.uk
Royal Institute of British Architects www.architecture.com

Art and Design
Arts Council England www.artscouncil.org.uk
Association of Illustrators www.theaoi.com
Association of Photographers www.the-aop.org
British Association of Art Therapists www.baat.org
British Association of Paintings Conservator-Restorers www.bapcr.org.uk
British Institute of Professional Photography www.bipp.com
Chartered Society of Designers www.csd.org.uk
Crafts Council www.craftscouncil.org.uk
Creative Scotland www.creativescotland.com
Design Council www.designcouncil.org.uk
Institute of Conservation www.icon.org.uk
Institute of Professional Goldsmiths www.ipgoldsmiths.com
National Society for Education in Art and Design www.nsead.org
Royal Society of Sculptors www.sculptors.org.uk
Textile Institute www.textileinstitute.org

Astronomy/Astrophysics
Royal Astronomical Society www.ras.ac.uk

Biochemistry (*see also* *Chemistry*)
Association for Clinical Biochemistry and Laboratory Medicine www.acb.org.uk
Biochemical Society www.biochemistry.org
British Society for Immunology www.immunology.org

Biological Sciences/Biology
British Society for Genetic Medicine www.bsgm.org.uk
Genetics Society www.genetics.org.uk
Institute of Biomedical Science www.Ibms.org
Royal Society of Biology www.rsb.org.uk

Building and Construction
Chartered Institute of Building www.ciob.org
Chartered Institution of Building Services Engineers www.cibse.org
Construction Industry Training Board www.citb.co.uk

Business and Management Courses
Chartered Governance Institute UK and Ireland www.cgi.org.uk
Chartered Institute of Personnel and Development www.cipd.co.uk
Chartered Institute of Public Relations www.cipr.co.uk
Chartered Management Institute www.managers.org.uk
Communications Advertising and Marketing Education Foundation www.camfoundation.co.uk
Department for Business, Energy and Industrial Strategy www.gov.uk/government/organisations/department-for-business-energy-and-industrial-strategy
Institute of Administrative Management www.instam.org
Institute of Export & International Trade www.export.org.uk
Institute of Practitioners in Advertising www.ipa.co.uk
Instructus Skills www.instructus-skills.org

Chemistry
National Nanotechnology Initiative www.nano.gov
Royal Society of Chemistry www.rsc.org

Computer Science and Information Technology
BCS The Chartered Institute for IT www.bcs.org
Institution of Analysts and Programmers www.iap.org.uk
Learning and Performance Institute www.thelpi.org

Dance
Council for Dance, Drama and Musical Theatre www.cdmt.org.uk

Dentistry
British Association of Dental Nurses www.badn.org.uk
British Association of Dental Therapists www.badt.org.uk
British Dental Association www.bda.org
British Society of Dental Hygiene and Therapy www.bsdht.org.uk
Dental Laboratories Association www.dla.org.uk
Dental Technologists Association www.dta-uk.org
General Dental Council www.gdc-uk.org

Dietetics
British Dietetic Association www.bda.uk.com

Drama
Equity www.equity.org.uk
Society of British Theatre Designers www.theatredesign.org.uk

Economics
Royal Economic Society www.res.org.uk

Education and Teacher Training
Department for Education www.gov.uk/government/organisations/department-for-education
Education Workforce Council www.ewc.wales
General Teaching Council for Northern Ireland www.gtcni.org.uk
General Teaching Council for Scotland www.gtcs.org.uk

Engineering/Engineering Sciences
Energy Institute www.energyinst.org
Engineering Council UK www.engc.org.uk
Institute for Manufacturing www.ifm.eng.cam.ac.uk
Institute of Acoustics www.ioa.org.uk
Institute of Marine Engineering, Science and Technology www.imarest.org
Institution of Agricultural Engineers www.iagre.org
Institution of Civil Engineers www.ice.org.uk
Institution of Engineering Designers www.ied.org.uk
Institution of Engineering and Technology www.theiet.org
Institution of Mechanical Engineers www.imeche.org
Nuclear Institute www.nuclearinst.com
Royal Aeronautical Society www.aerosociety.com

Environmental Science/Studies
Chartered Institute of Ecology and Environmental Management www.cieem.net
Chartered Institute of Environmental Health www.cieh.org
Chartered Institution of Wastes Management www.ciwm.co.uk
Chartered Institution of Water and Environmental Management www.ciwem.org

Environment Agency www.gov.uk/government/organisations/environment-agency
Institution of Environmental Sciences www.the-ies.org
Institution of Occupational Safety and Health www.iosh.com
Royal Environmental Health Institute of Scotland www.rehis.com
Society for the Environment www.socenv.org.uk

Film, Radio and TV Studies
British Film Institute www.bfi.org.uk
Screen Skills www.screenskills.com

Finance (including Banking and Insurance)
Chartered Banker Institute www.charteredbanker.com
Chartered Institute of Loss Adjusters www.cila.co.uk
Chartered Institute for Securities and Investment www.cisi.org
Chartered Insurance Institute www.cii.co.uk
London Institute of Banking and Finance www.libf.ac.uk
Personal Finance Society www.thepfs.org

Food Science/Studies and Technology
Institute of Food Science and Technology www.ifst.org
Society of Food Hygiene and Technology www.sofht.co.uk

Forensic Science
Chartered Society of Forensic Sciences www.csofs.org

Geography
British Cartographic Society www.cartography.org.uk
Royal Geographical Society with IBG www.rgs.org
Royal Meteorological Society www.rmets.org

Geology/Geological Sciences
Geological Society www.geolsoc.org.uk

Health Sciences/Studies
British Academy of Audiology www.baaudiology.org
British and Irish Orthoptic Society www.orthoptics.org.uk
British Association of Prosthetists and Orthotists www.bapo.com
British Chiropractic Association https://chiropractic-uk.co.uk
British Occupational Hygiene Society www.bohs.org
General Osteopathic Council www.osteopathy.org.uk
Institution of Occupational Safety and Health www.iosh.com
Institute of Osteopathy www.osteopathy.org
Society of Homeopaths www.homeopathy-soh.org

History
Royal Historical Society www.royalhistsoc.org

Horticulture
Chartered Institute of Horticulture www.horticulture.org.uk

Hospitality and Event Management
Institute of Hospitality www.instituteofhospitality.org
People 1st www.people1st.co.uk

Housing
Chartered Institute of Housing www.cih.org

Human Resource Management
Chartered Institute of Personnel and Development www.cipd.co.uk

Information Management and Librarianship
Chartered Institute of Library and Information Professionals www.cilip.org.uk

Landscape Architecture
Landscape Institute www.landscapeinstitute.org

Languages
Chartered Institute of Linguists www.ciol.org.uk
Institute of Translation and Interpreting www.iti.org.uk

Law
Bar Council www.barcouncil.org.uk
Chartered Institute of Legal Executives www.cilex.org.uk
Faculty of Advocates www.advocates.org.uk
Law Society of England and Wales www.lawsociety.org.uk
Law Society of Northern Ireland www.lawsoc-ni.org
Law Society of Scotland www.lawscot.org.uk

Leisure and Recreation Management/Studies
Chartered Institute for the Management of Sport and Physical Activity www.cimspa.co.uk

Linguistics
British Association for Applied Linguistics www.baal.org.uk
Royal College of Speech and Language Therapists www.rcslt.org

Marine/Maritime Studies
Nautical Institute www.nautinst.org

Marketing (including Public Relations)
Chartered Institute of Marketing www.cim.co.uk
Chartered Institute of Public Relations www.cipr.co.uk

Materials Science/Metallurgy
Institute of Materials, Minerals and Mining www.iom3.org

Mathematics
Council for the Mathematical Sciences www.cms.ac.uk
Institute of Mathematics and its Applications www.ima.org.uk
London Mathematical Society www.lms.ac.uk
Mathematical Association www.m-a.org.uk

Media Studies
British Broadcasting Corporation www.bbc.co.uk/careers
Chartered Institute of Editing and Proofreading www.ciep.uk
National Council for the Training of Journalists www.nctj.com
ScreenSkills www.screenskills.com
Society of Authors www.societyofauthors.org

Medicine
British Medical Association www.bma.org.uk
General Medical Council www.gmc-uk.org

Microbiology** (see also **Biological Sciences/Biology)
Microbiology Society www.microbiologysociety.org

Music
Independent Society of Musicians www.ism.org
Institute of Musical Instrument Technology www.imit.org.uk

Naval Architecture
Royal Institution of Naval Architects www.rina.org.uk

Neuroscience
InnerBody www.innerbody.com
Instant Anatomy www.instantanatomy.net

Nursing and Midwifery
Community Practitioners' and Health Visitors' Association www.unitetheunion.org
Health and Social Care in Northern Ireland www.hscni.net
Nursing and Midwifery Council www.nmc.org.uk
Royal College of Midwives www.rcm.org.uk
Royal College of Nursing www.rcn.org.uk

*Nutrition (see **Dietetics**)*

Occupational Therapy
Royal College of Occupational Therapists www.rcot.co.uk

Optometry
Association of British Dispensing Opticians www.abdo.org.uk
British and Irish Orthoptic Society www.orthoptics.org.uk
College of Optometrists www.college-optometrists.org
General Optical Council www.optical.org

Pharmacology
British Toxicology Society www.thebts.org

Pharmacy and Pharmaceutical Sciences
Royal Pharmaceutical Society of Great Britain www.rpharms.com

Photography
Association of Photographers www.the-aop.org
British Institute of Professional Photography www.bipp.com
Royal Photographic Society www.rps.org

*Physical Education (see **Education and Teacher Training** and **Sports Sciences/Studies**)*

Physics
Institute of Physics www.iop.org
Institute of Physics and Engineering in Medicine www.ipem.ac.uk

Physiotherapy
Association of Chartered Physiotherapists in Animal Therapy www.acpat.org
Chartered Society of Physiotherapy www.csp.org.uk

*Plant Sciences (see **Biological Sciences/Biology**)*

Podiatry (Chiropody)
Royal College of Podiatry www.rcpod.org

Psychology
British Psychological Society www.bps.org.uk

Radiography
Society and College of Radiographers www.sor.org

Social Work
Health and Care Professions Council www.hcpc-uk.org
Northern Ireland Social Care Council www.niscc.info
Scottish Social Services Council www.sssc.uk.com
Social Care Wales www.socialcare.wales

Sociology
British Sociological Association www.britsoc.co.uk

Speech Pathology/Sciences/Therapy
Royal College of Speech and Language Therapists www.rcslt.org

Sports Sciences/Studies
British Association of Sport and Exercise Sciences www.bases.org.uk
Chartered Institute for the Management of Sport and Physical Activity www.cimspa.co.uk
English Institute of Sport www.eis2win.co.uk
Society of Sports Therapists www.thesst.org
Sport England www.sportengland.org
Sportscotland www.sportscotland.org.uk
Sport Wales www.sport.wales
Sports Institute Northern Ireland www.sportni.net/performance/sports-institute-northern-ireland
UK Sport www.uksport.gov.uk

Statistics
Royal Statistical Society www.rss.org.uk

Surveying and Real Estate Management
Chartered Institute of Building www.ciob.org
Chartered Surveyors Training Trust www.cstt.org.uk
Propertymark www.propertymark.co.uk
Royal Institution of Chartered Surveyors www.rics.org

Tourism and Travel
Institute of Travel and Tourism www.itt.co.uk

Town and Urban Planning
Royal Town Planning Institute www.rtpi.org.uk

Transport Management and Planning
Chartered Institute of Logistics and Transport www.ciltuk.org.uk

Veterinary Science/Medicine/Nursing
Association of Chartered Physiotherapists in Animal Therapy www.acpat.org
British Veterinary Nursing Association www.bvna.org.uk
Royal College of Veterinary Surgeons www.rcvs.org.uk
Royal Veterinary College www.rvc.ac.uk

Zoology
Royal Entomological Society www.royensoc.co.uk
Zoological Society of London www.zsl.org

APPENDIX 4
BOOKLIST AND USEFUL WEBSITES

Unless otherwise stated, the publications in this list are all available from Trotman Publishing.

STANDARD REFERENCE BOOKS

British Qualifications 2020, 50th edition, Kogan Page
British Vocational Qualifications, 12th edition, Kogan Page

OTHER BOOKS AND RESOURCES

A Guide to Uni Life, Lucy Tobin
An Educator's Guide to University Applications, Wendy Heydorn & Laurence Goodwin
Getting into course guides: Art & Design Courses, Business & Economics Courses, Dental School, Engineering Courses, Law, Medical School, Oxford & Cambridge, Pharmacy and Pharmacology Courses, Physiotherapy Courses, Psychology Courses, Veterinary School
How to Complete Your UCAS Application: 2026 Entry, Ryan Moran & UCAS
Studying and Learning at University, Alan Pritchard, SAGE Study Skills Series
The Times Good University Guide 2026, Zoe Thomas, Times Books

USEFUL WEBSITES

Education, course and applications information

www.disabilityrightsuk.org
www.discoveruni.gov.uk (official information from UK universities and colleges for comparing courses)
www.gov.uk/browse/education
www.hesa.ac.uk (Higher Education Statistics Agency)
www.opendays.com (information on university and college Open Days)
www.turing-scheme.org.uk
www.ucas.com

Careers information

www.army.mod.uk
www.careerconnect.org.uk
www.healthcareers.nhs.uk
www.insidecareers.co.uk
www.milkround.com
www.prospects.ac.uk
www.trotman.co.uk

Gap years

www.etrust.org.uk/the-year-in-industry
www.prospects.ac.uk/jobs-and-work-experience/gap-year
www.yearoutgroup.org

Study overseas

www.acu.ac.uk (Association of Commonwealth Universities)
www.allaboutcollege.com
www.fulbright.org.uk (Fulbright Commission)
www.globalgrads.com

COURSE INDEX

A

Accountancy/Accounting 106
Actuarial Science/Studies 110
Advertising 136, 169
African, Asian and Middle-Eastern Studies 111
Agri-Business Management 169
Agricultural Sciences/Agriculture 113
American Studies 115
Anatomical Science 343
Ancient Near Eastern Studies 111
Animal Biology 427
Animal Sciences 117
Animation 136
Anthropology 119
Arabic 111
Archaeology 121
Architectural Engineering 123, 219
Architectural Technology 123
Architecture 123
Art and Design (3D Design) 142
Art and Design (Fashion and Textiles) 130
Art and Design (Fine Art) 133
Art and Design (General) 127
Art and Design (Graphic Design) 136
Art and Design (Interior, Product and Industrial Design) 139
Artificial Intelligence 186
Astronomy and Astrophysics 144
Audio Engineering 212
Autism Studies 383
Automotive Engineering 233
Aviation Management 423

B

Biblical Studies 390
Biochemistry 146
Biological Sciences 149
Biology 154
Biomedical Engineering 238
Biomedical Materials Science 149
Biomedical Science 149
Biotechnology 157
Bioveterinary Sciences 425
Brewing and Distilling 149
British Sign Language 298
Broadcast Media Technologies 322
Building and Construction 158
Building Services Engineering 158
Building Surveying 415
Business 169
Business and Management Courses 161
Business and Management Courses (International and European) 166
Business and Management Courses (Specialised) 169
Business Information System 186
Business Information Systems 222
Business Management with a European Language 166

C

Celtic and Linguistics 171
Celtic, Irish, Scottish and Welsh Studies 171
Ceramics 142
Chemistry 172
Chinese 176
Civil and Coastal Engineering 219
Civil and Environmental Engineering 219
Civil and Transportation Engineering 219
Classics and Classical Studies/Civilisation 177
Climate Change 244
Climate Science 244
Cognitive Science 383
Combined and Liberal Arts Courses 179
Combined Social Sciences 396
Communication and Media 181
Communication Studies/Communication 181
Community Studies/Development 182
Computer Games Development 184
Computer Networks 186
Computer Science 186

Computer Science and Information Technology 186
Computer Science (Games) 184
Computing 186
Construction and Project Management 158
Counselling Psychology 383
Counter Terrorism 396
Creative Writing 239
Criminal Justice 396
Criminology 301, 396
Cruise Management 423
Cybercrime 396

D

Dance/Dance Studies 190
Deaf Studies 269
Dental Hygiene 193
Dental Therapy 193
Dentistry 193
Design 136
Design Crafts 142
Development Studies 195
Dietetics 197
Divinity 390
Drama 198
Drawing and Painting 127

E

Earth Sciences 264
East Asian Studies 111
East European Studies 247
Ecology 244
Economics 202
Education Studies 206
Engineering (Acoustics and Sound) 212
Engineering (Aeronautical and Aerospace) 214
Engineering (Chemical) 216
Engineering (Civil) 219
Engineering (Communications) 222
Engineering (Computer, Control, Software and Systems) 224
Engineering Design 209
Engineering (Electrical and Electronic) 227
Engineering/Engineering Sciences 209
Engineering (Manufacturing and Production) 231
Engineering (Mechanical) 233
Engineering (Medical) 238
English 239
Environmental Hazards 244
Environmental Health 244
Environmental Management 244
Environmental Sciences 244
Equine Science 117
Esports 184
European Studies 298
European Studies 247

F

Film, Radio and TV Studies 248
Finance 252
Finance and Investment 252
Finance and Investment Banking 252
Financial Services and Property 252
Fire Engineering 216
Food Science/Studies and Technology 256
Food Science with Business 169
Footwear Design 139
Forensic Psychology 383
Forensic Science 149
Forestry 113
French 257
Furniture Design 139

G

Gaelic Studies 171
Games Design 184
Games Technology 184
Garden Design 280, 296
General Engineering 209
Genetics 260
Geography 261
Geology/Geological Sciences 264
Geophysics and Geoscience 264
German 266
Glass and Ceramics 142
Government and European Politics 378
Graphic Communication 136
Greek 268

H

Healthcare Science 407
Health Sciences/Studies 269
Hebrew 390
Herbal Medicine 358
Heritage Studies 272
Hispanic Studies and Portuguese 405
History 272
History (Ancient) 276
History (Economic and Social) 277
History Of Art 278

Horticulture 280
Hospitality and Event Management 281
Housing 283
Human Resource Management 284
Human Rights 396
Human Sciences/Human Biosciences 286

I

Illustration 136
Immunology 149
Informatics 287
Information Management and Librarianship 287
Information Systems 186
Integrated Engineering 209
Interior Design 139
International Development 289
International Relations 289
Islamic Studies 390
Italian 291

J

Japanese 293
Jewellery and Metalwork 142
Journalism 294

K

Korean 176

L

Landscape Architecture 296
Languages 298
Latin 300
Law 301
Leisure and Recreation Management/ Studies 306
Linguistics 307
Literature 309

M

Marine Biology 154, 311
Marine Geography 311
Marine/Maritime Studies 311
Marine Technology with Offshore Engineering 219
Marketing 313
Marketing and Consumer Behaviour 169
Marketing Communication Management 181
Materials Science/Metallurgy 316
Mathematical Sciences 318
Mathematics 318
Mechanical and Medical Engineering 238
Mechatronics 233
Media Studies 322
Medical Imaging 388
Medical Physics 238
Medical Science 149
Medicine 325
Medieval Studies 272
Meteorology 244
Microbiology 337
Modelmaking 142
Modern Languages 298
Motorsport Engineering 233
Music 338
Music Technology 338

N

Natural Sciences 342
Naval Architecture 311
Neuroscience 343
Nuclear Engineering 216
Nursing and Midwifery 345
Nutrition 269
Nutrition 349

O

Occupational Therapy 351
Oceanography 311
Operating Department Practice 353
Ophthalmic Dispensing 355
Optometry (Ophthalmic Optics) 355
Oral Health Science 193
Orthoptics 269, 355
Osteopathy 269

P

Painting and Printmaking 133
Paramedic Science 269
Peace Studies and International Relations 289
Performing Arts/Studies 198
Petrol Engineering 216
Pharmacology 356
Pharmacy and Pharmaceutical Sciences 358
Philosophy 360
Philosophy, Politics and Economics (Ppe) 363
Photography 364
Physical Education 367
Physics 368
Physiology 372

Physiology and Pharmacology 356
Planetary Science with Astronomy 144
Plant Sciences 375
Police Studies 381
Politics 378
Printed Textiles 130
Product Design 139, 209
Product Design Technology 139
Professional Policing 381
Property Development 415
Prosthetics and Orthotics 157, 269
Psychology 383
Public Health 269
Public Relations 169, 181, 313
Publishing 169

Q

Quantity Surveying 415

R

Radiography 388
Radiotherapy 388
Religious Studies 390
Retail Management 392
Rural Property Management 415
Russian 247

S

Scandinavian Studies 393
Sculpture and Environmental Art 133
Silversmithing and Jewellery 142
Social and Public Policy and Administration 394
Social Anthropology 119
Social Sciences/Studies 396
Social Work 399
Sociology 402
Sound Technology 212
South Asian Studies 111
Space Science 144
Space Science and Robotics 144
Spanish, Portuguese and Latin American Studies 405
Speech Pathology/Sciences/Therapy 407
Sports Sciences/Studies 409
Statistics 413
Surface Pattern Design 130
Surveying and Real Estate Management 415
Swahili 111

T

TEACHER TRAINING 417
Thai 111
Theatre Arts 198
Theatre Design 139, 198
Theatre Studies 198
Theology 390
Tourism and Travel 420
Town and Urban Planning 422
Translation Studies 298
Transport Design 139, 423
Transport Management and Planning 423

V

Veterinary Nursing 425
Veterinary Science/Medicine 425
Vietnamese 111
Virology and Immunology 149
Visual Communication 136

W

War Studies 289
Web Design and Development 186

Z

Zoology 427

NOTES

Notes